W9-CFR-645

CHASE'S ANNUAL EVENTS

Twenty-Ninth Year of Publication

J.LUYTS
PHIL.PROFES.
Inftitutio
ASTRONOMICA.

Special Days, Weeks & Months in **1986**

An Almanac and Survey of the Year:

A Calendar of Holidays, Holy Days, National and Ethnic Days, Seasons, Astronomical Phenomena, Festivals and Fairs, Anniversaries, Birthdays, Special Events and Traditional Observances of all kinds, the World over.

Compiled by
William D. and Helen M. Chase

**CONTEMPORARY
BOOKS, INC.**
CHICAGO

1986 ★ ★ *Chase's Annual Events* ★ ★ 1986

COPYRIGHT © 1985 BY WILLIAM D. CHASE and HELEN M. CHASE

NO PART OF THIS WORK MAY BE REPRODUCED OR COPIED IN ANY FORM OR BY ANY MEANS—INCLUDING GRAPHIC, ELECTRONIC, MECHANICAL, PHOTOCOPYING, OR INFORMATION STORAGE AND RETRIEVAL SYSTEMS—WITHOUT WRITTEN PERMISSION OF THE PUBLISHER. ANY SUCH REPRODUCTION OR COPYING WILL BE PROSECUTED TO THE FULL EXTENT OF THE LAW.

FOR PERMISSION TO REPRODUCE OR COPY ANY PORTION OF THE WORK, CONTACT THE PUBLISHER:

CONTEMPORARY BOOKS, INC.
180 NORTH MICHIGAN AVENUE
CHICAGO, ILLINOIS 60601

Composition by: Chas. P. Young Chicago, Inc.
Printed in U.S.A. by Webcrafters

A NOTE ABOUT OUR FRONT COVER ILLUSTRATION

Our front cover illustration is adapted from the frontispiece of the 1692 edition of *Astronomica Institutio*, a book by Dutch scholar Jan Luyts. It shows, left to right: Galilei Galileo, Rene Descartes, Jan Luyts, Tycho Brahe, Nicolaus Copernicus, and Claudius Ptolemaeus (Ptolemy). Luyts is seated at a table looked on and listened to by the astronomical sages of sixteen centuries. Around them is an array of telescopes, globes, celestial spheres and measuring instruments used by astronomers of their times. The illustration is reproduced here courtesy of the Adler Planetarium, 1300 South Lake Shore Drive, Chicago, IL 60605.

OTHER ILLUSTRATIONS

Back cover illustration: Honoré Daumier's "Ah! Comets . . . they always foretell some terrible events! . . ." Lithograph, 1858, from *Actualites*. Woodcuts at the beginning of each month are from *The Shepheards Calendar*, by Edmund Spenser, London, 1579. Other engravings used in this book have been selected to represent almanac illustration of the 15th-19th centuries. The "Peanuts" and "Garfield" illustrations are used with the permission of United Feature Syndicate, Inc.

Chase, William DeRoy, and Chase, Helen Elizabeth

Chase's annual events: special days, weeks and months in 1986, Chicago, Contemporary Books, Inc.   (c. 1985).

256 p., ill.,
Includes index and tables.
Published annually since 1958.
Previous title (1958-1983): Chases' Calendar of Annual Events.

1. Calendars, 2. Almanacs, 3. Holidays, 4. Festivals, 5. Chronology, 6. Anniversaries, 7. Manners and customs, 8. Year-books. I. Title, II. Subtitle: Special days, weeks and months.

D11.5C48   ISBN: 0-8092-5142-6
LC 57-14540   529.3 (calendars)
ISSN: 0740-5286   394.26 (holidays)

Suggested cataloging information

— NOTICE —

Events listed herein are not necessarily endorsed by the editors or publisher. Every effort has been made to assure the correctness of all entries, but neither the authors nor the publisher can warrant their accuracy. It is imperative, if financial plans are to be made in connection with dates or events listed herein, that principals be consulted for final information.

1986 ★ ★ *Chase's Annual Events* ★ ★ 1986

COPYRIGHT © 1985 BY WILLIAM D. CHASE and HELEN M. CHASE

Symbols Used In Text

☆ Indicates Presidential Proclamations

STATE & TERRITORY ABBREVIATIONS

Alabama	AL	Kansas	KS	Ohio	OH
Alaska	AK	Kentucky	KY	Oklahoma	OK
Arizona	AZ	Louisiana	LA	Oregon	OR
Arkansas	AR	Maine	ME	Pennsylvania	PA
American Samoa	AS	Maryland	MD	Puerto Rico	PR
California	CA	Massachusetts	MA	Rhode Island	RI
Canal Zone	CZ	Michigan	MI	South Carolina	SC
Colorado	CO	Minnesota	MN	South Dakota	SD
Connecticut	CT	Mississippi	MS	Tennessee	TN
Delaware	DE	Missouri	MO	Trust Territories	TT
District of Columbia	DC	Montana	MT	Texas	TX
Florida	FL	Nebraska	NE	Utah	UT
Georgia	GA	Nevada	NV	Vermont	VT
Guam	GU	New Hampshire	NH	Virginia	VA
Hawaii	HI	New Jersey	NJ	Virgin Islands	VI
Idaho	ID	New Mexico	NM	Washington	WA
Illinois	IL	New York	NY	West Virginia	WV
Indiana	IN	North Carolina	NC	Wisconsin	WI
Iowa	IA	North Dakota	ND	Wyoming	WY

COPYRIGHT © 1985 BY WILLIAM D. CHASE and HELEN M. CHASE

FOREWORD

For the 29th consecutive year we look at the manuscript of the forthcoming Chase's Annual Events and marvel at the abundance of celebrations and the richness of the observances. This edition contains more than 5,500 event listings—far exceeding all its predecessors.

We are especially pleased by a reader's comment: "You have given us in a most original way a conspectus of civilization in the United States. . ." That observation is valued because throughout our nearly three decades of compilation our first goal has been to provide an authoritative and well-documented guide to the happenings of the coming year. But we have attempted something else as well—to present an authentic cross-section of the year's celebration, from the humble happenings to the grand events, from rural and suburban communities to the great metropolises and world capitals.

We list the internationally sanctioned World's Fairs and Expositions, the presidential and royal proclamations, observances of the world's religions, traditional observances and major promotions of organizations and businesses. But we take equal pleasure in providing a generous sampling of local and regional events, and even catchy or whimsical celebrations.

In addition to the observance of national days, holy days, historic and birth anniversaries, there are gopher counts, town crier contests, rattlesnake round-ups, jumping frog and duck races, "world's largest" garage sales, historical re-enactments, arts and crafts shows, music festivals, rodeos, parades, homecomings, harvest fairs, festivals, religious pageants and an astonishing variety of other events.

In the 1986 edition the editors have elected to throw more light on the individual people who run our nation, who spend billions of our tax dollars and who determine our state and national priorities. We feel that public office holders ought to be as worthy of our attention as movie, television and sports figures. Accordingly, we have expanded our scope to include members of Congress, the Supreme Court, the President's Cabinet, and the Governor of every state. In this election year it seems especially appropriate to increase our awareness of the people who are responsible for the wise government of our nation.

A copy of *Chase's* in the hands of an archeologist or historian of some future century would, we hope, provide useful insight into our lives and times as well as a view of the vast variety of events and activities that vied for our attention.

The entries contained herein represent the editors' selection of the most important and most entertaining events known or scheduled for the coming year. For the most part they represent the following kinds of information:

PRESIDENTIAL PROCLAMATIONS: In addition to the complete list of proclamations issued, January 1, 1984-August 31, 1985, special observance proclamations for which there is continuing authority and a clear formula for dates of observance, are listed in the Chronology. This data has been supplied by The White House and the Federal Register.

NATIONAL DAYS AND STATE DAYS: National Days and public holidays of other nations are gleaned from U.S. Department of State documents and from information supplied by embassies or other agencies of the individual countries. State Days and statutory observances are furnished by the Governors' offices, or from designated official state agencies.

SPONSORED EVENTS: Events for which there is individual or organizational sponsorship are listed with the name of the event, inclusive dates of observance, place of observance (if local or regional), purpose, and the name and address of the sponsor. This information is reported from data supplied by the sponsors.

ASTRONOMICAL PHENOMENA: Information about eclipses, equinoxes and solstices, moon phases, and other astronomically related information is derived largely from data prepared by the U.S. Naval Observatory's Nautical Almanac Office.

Photo by Robert Chase

HISTORIC ANNIVERSARIES, FOLKLORIC EVENTS AND BIRTHDAYS: Compiled from a wide variety of materials dating from the Fifteenth Century to the present, and coming from virtually every part of the world, these entries are supported whenever possible by two or more independent sources. They represent the editors' choice of those having greatest interest and pertinence today.

RELIGIOUS OBSERVANCES: Principal observances of Christian, Jewish and Muslim faiths are presented with available background information from their respective calendars. Where known, the special observances of the Orient, religious and secular, including traditional Chinese and Hindu events also are listed.

The omission of an important event usually means that the dates of observance were set too late for inclusion. The editors welcome the submission of information for coming years from event sponsors and organizers. Final selection and format of information included in *Chase's Annual Events* must, of course, be the decision of the editors.

The editors express their gratitude to the thousands of readers, sponsoring agencies and organizations for information submitted. Special thanks are due The White House, State Governors, North American Aerospace Defense Command, U.S. Naval Observatory's Nautical Almanac Office, National Oceanic and Atmospheric Administration, United Nations Department of Public Information, Adler Planetarium and the British Tourist Authority.

Many librarians have assisted, but especially those of the Library of Congress, the British Library, University of Michigan Libraries, the Flint Public Library and the Ann Arbor Public Library. Individuals whose valued assistance is gratefully acknowledged include: The Hon. Dale E. Kildee, M.C., Computer Specialist Nan Collier, University of Michigan Professors Emeritus Carlton F. Wells (English) and Freeman D. Miller (Astronomy), Dan Marks, Dr. Leroy Doggett and the Secretary General of the International Bureau of Exhibitions.

Finally, our thanks to our three children and their families for their patience and untiring labors which have become more helpful with each year.

And now we urge our readers to join with us in the celebration of 1986.

Ann Arbor, Michigan   William D. Chase
10 August 1985   Helen M. Chase

COPYRIGHT © 1985 BY WILLIAM D. CHASE and HELEN M. CHASE

NATIONAL DAYS OF THE WORLD FOR 1986

*(Compiled from publications of the U.S. Department of State,
the United Nations and from information received from the countries listed.)*

Most nations set aside one or more days each year as National Public Holidays, often recognizing the anniversary of the attainment of independence, or the birthday of the country's ruler. Below the National Days are listed alphabetically. It should be noted that in some countries the Gregorian Calendar date of observance varies from year to year. See the Index and the main chronology for further details of observance, and for numerous holidays in addition to the National Days observed by the various countries.

Afghanistan	Apr 27
Albania	Nov 29
Algeria	Nov 1
Angola	Nov 11
Antigua and Barbuda	Nov 1
Argentina	May 25
Australia	Jan 26
Austria	Oct 26
Bahamas	July 10
Bahrain	Dec 16
Bangladesh	Mar 26
Barbados	Nov 30
Belgium	July 21
Belize	Sept 21
Benin	Nov 30
Bhutan	Dec 17
Bolivia	Aug 6
Botswana	Sept 30
Bourkina Fasso	Aug 4
Brazil	Sept 7
Brunei	Feb 23
Bulgaria	Sept 9
Burma	Jan 4
Burundi	July 1
Cameroon	May 20
Canada	July 1
Cape Verde	July 5
Central African Republic	Dec 1
Chad	June 7
Chile	Sept 18
Colombia	July 20
Comoros	July 6
Congo	Aug 15
Costa Rica	Sept 15
Cuba	Jan 1
Cyprus	Oct 1
Czechoslovakia	May 9
Denmark	Apr 16
Djibouti	June 27
Dominica	Nov 3
Dominican Republic	Feb 27
Ecuador	Aug 10
Egypt	July 23
El Salvador	Sept 15
Equatorial Guinea	Oct 12
Estonia	Feb 24
Ethiopia	Sept 12
Fiji	Oct 10
Finland	Dec 6
France	July 14
Gabon	Mar 12
Gambia	Feb 18
German Democratic Republic	Oct 7
Ghana	Mar 6
Great Britain	June 14
Greece	Mar 25
Grenada	Feb 7
Grenadines	Oct 27
Guatemala	Sept 15
Guinea	Oct 2
Guinea-Bissau	Sept 24
Guyana	Feb 23
Haiti	Jan 1
Holy See	Oct 22
Honduras	Sept 15
Hungary	Apr 4
Iceland	June 17
India	Jan 26
Indonesia	Aug 17
Iran	Feb 11
Iraq	July 17
Ireland	Mar 17
Israel	May 14
Italy	June 2
Ivory Coast	Dec 7
Jamaica	Aug 4
Japan	Apr 29
Jordan	May 25
Kampuchea	Apr 17
Kenya	Dec 12
Kiribati	July 12
Korea, Democratic People's Republic of	Sept 9
Korea, Republic of	Aug 15
Kuwait	Feb 25
Laos	Dec 2
Latvia	Nov 18
Lebanon	Nov 22
Lesotho	Oct 4
Liberia	July 26
Libyan Arab Jamahiriya	Sept 1
Lithuania	Feb 16
Luxembourg	June 23
Madagascar	June 26
Malawi	July 6
Malaysia	Aug 31
Maldives	July 26
Mali	Sept 22
Malta	Mar 31
Mauritania	Nov 28
Mauritius	Mar 12
Mexico	Sept 16
Monaco	Nov 19
Mongolia	July 11
Morocco	Mar 3
Mozambique	June 25
Nauru	Jan 31
Nepal	Dec 28
Netherlands	Apr 30
New Zealand	Feb 6
Nicaragua	Sept 15
Niger	Dec 18
Nigeria	Oct 1
Norway	May 17
Oman	Nov 18
Pakistan	Mar 23
Panama	Nov 3
Papua New Guinea	Sept 16
Paraguay	May 14
People's Republic of China	Oct 1
Peru	July 28
Philippines	June 12
Poland	July 22
Portugal	June 10
Qatar	Sept 3
Romania	Aug 23
Rwanda	July 1
Saint Christopher (St Kitts) and Nevis	Sept 19
Saint Lucia	Feb 22
Saint Vincent and the Grenadines	Oct 27
Sao Tome and Principe	July 12
Saudi Arabia	Sept 23
Senegal	Apr 4
Seychelles	June 5
Sierra Leone	Apr 19
Singapore	Aug 9
Solomon Islands	July 7
Somalia	Oct 21
South Africa	May 31
Spain	Oct 12
Sri Lanka	Feb 4
Sudan	Jan 1
Suriname	Nov 25
Swaziland	Sept 6
Sweden	June 6
Switzerland	Aug 1
Syria	Apr 17
Tanzania	Apr 26
Thailand	Dec 5
Togo	Apr 27
Tonga	June 4
Trinidad and Tobago	Aug 31
Tunisia	June 1
Turkey	Oct 29
Tuvalu	Oct 1
Uganda	Oct 9
Union of Soviet Socialist Republics	Nov 7 and 8
United Arab Emirates	Dec 2
United States of America	July 4
Uruguay	Aug 25
Vanuatu	July 30
Venezuela	July 5
Viet Nam	Sept 2
Western Samoa	June 1
Yemen	Sept 26
Yugoslavia	Nov 29
Zaire	Nov 24
Zambia	Oct 24
Zimbabwe	Apr 18

COPYRIGHT © 1985 BY WILLIAM D. CHASE and HELEN M. CHASE

HOW TO USE THIS BOOK
A KEY TO THE CHRONOLOGICAL ENTRIES

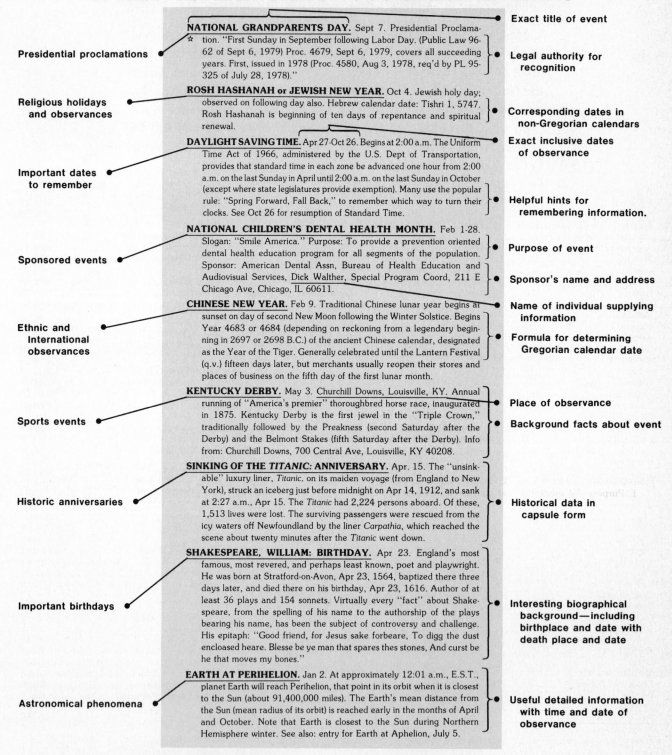

Presidential proclamations → **Exact title of event**

☆ **NATIONAL GRANDPARENTS DAY.** Sept 7. Presidential Proclamation. "First Sunday in September following Labor Day. (Public Law 96-62 of Sept 6, 1979) Proc. 4679, Sept 6, 1979, covers all succeeding years. First, issued in 1978 (Proc. 4580, Aug 3, 1978, req'd by PL 95-325 of July 28, 1978)." → **Legal authority for recognition**

Religious holidays and observances →

ROSH HASHANAH or JEWISH NEW YEAR. Oct 4. Jewish holy day; observed on following day also. Hebrew calendar date: Tishri 1, 5747. Rosh Hashanah is beginning of ten days of repentance and spiritual renewal. → **Corresponding dates in non-Gregorian calendars**

Important dates to remember → **Exact inclusive dates of observance**

DAYLIGHT SAVING TIME. Apr 27-Oct 26. Begins at 2:00 a.m. The Uniform Time Act of 1966, administered by the U.S. Dept of Transportation, provides that standard time in each zone be advanced one hour from 2:00 a.m. on the last Sunday in April until 2:00 a.m. on the last Sunday in October (except where state legislatures provide exemption). Many use the popular rule: "Spring Forward, Fall Back," to remember which way to turn their clocks. See Oct 26 for resumption of Standard Time. → **Helpful hints for remembering information.**

Sponsored events →

NATIONAL CHILDREN'S DENTAL HEALTH MONTH. Feb 1-28. Slogan: "Smile America." Purpose: To provide a prevention oriented dental health education program for all segments of the population. → **Purpose of event**

Sponsor: American Dental Assn, Bureau of Health Education and Audiovisual Services, Dick Walther, Special Program Coord, 211 E Chicago Ave, Chicago, IL 60611. → **Sponsor's name and address**

Ethnic and International observances → **Name of individual supplying information**

CHINESE NEW YEAR. Feb 9. Traditional Chinese lunar year begins at sunset on day of second New Moon following the Winter Solstice. Begins Year 4683 or 4684 (depending on reckoning from a legendary beginning in 2697 or 2698 B.C.) of the ancient Chinese calendar, designated as the Year of the Tiger. Generally celebrated until the Lantern Festival (q.v.) fifteen days later, but merchants usually reopen their stores and places of business on the fifth day of the first lunar month. → **Formula for determining Gregorian calendar date**

Sports events →

KENTUCKY DERBY. May 3. Churchill Downs, Louisville, KY. Annual running of "America's premier" thoroughbred horse race, inaugurated in 1875. Kentucky Derby is the first jewel in the "Triple Crown," traditionally followed by the Preakness (second Saturday after the Derby) and the Belmont Stakes (fifth Saturday after the Derby). Info from: Churchill Downs, 700 Central Ave, Louisville, KY 40208. → **Place of observance** / **Background facts about event**

Historic anniversaries →

SINKING OF THE *TITANIC*: ANNIVERSARY. Apr. 15. The "unsinkable" luxury liner, *Titanic*, on its maiden voyage (from England to New York), struck an iceberg just before midnight on Apr 14, 1912, and sank at 2:27 a.m., Apr 15. The *Titanic* had 2,224 persons aboard. Of these, 1,513 lives were lost. The surviving passengers were rescued from the icy waters off Newfoundland by the liner *Carpathia*, which reached the scene about twenty minutes after the *Titanic* went down. → **Historical data in capsule form**

Important birthdays →

SHAKESPEARE, WILLIAM: BIRTHDAY. Apr 23. England's most famous, most revered, and perhaps least known, poet and playwright. He was born at Stratford-on-Avon, Apr 23, 1564, baptized there three days later, and died there on his birthday, Apr 23, 1616. Author of at least 36 plays and 154 sonnets. Virtually every "fact" about Shakespeare, from the spelling of his name to the authorship of the plays bearing his name, has been the subject of controversy and challenge. His epitaph: "Good friend, for Jesus sake forbeare, To digg the dust encloased heare. Blesse be ye man that spares thes stones, And curst be he that moves my bones." → **Interesting biographical background—including birthplace and date with death place and date**

Astronomical phenomena →

EARTH AT PERIHELION. Jan 2. At approximately 12:01 a.m., E.S.T., planet Earth will reach Perihelion, that point in its orbit when it is closest to the Sun (about 91,400,000 miles). The Earth's mean distance from the Sun (mean radius of its orbit) is reached early in the months of April and October. Note that Earth is closest to the Sun during Northern Hemisphere winter. See also: entry for Earth at Aphelion, July 5. → **Useful detailed information with time and date of observance**

Chase's Annual Events consists of: 1) a chronology of the entire year within which each day's events are arranged alphabetically; 2) an alphabetical index which provides cross references to the chronological listings; 3) a complete list of presidential proclamations issued January 1, 1984-August 31, 1985; 4) National Days of the World, alphabetically arranged; 5) Astronomical Phenomena for the year; and 6) numerous appendices and special sections to augment the above.

COPYRIGHT © 1985 BY WILLIAM D. CHASE and HELEN M. CHASE

Januarye.

JANUARY 1 — WEDNESDAY

1st Day — Remaining, 364

WEDNESDAY, JANUARY ONE, 1986. First day of the first month of the Gregorian calendar year, Anno Domini 1986, being second after Leap Year, and (until July 4th) 210th year of American independence. 1986 will be the 6,699th year of the Julian Period, a time frame consisting of 7,980 years, which began at noon, Universal Time, Jan 1, 4713 B.C. Astronomers will note that Julian Day number 2,446,432 begins at noon, Universal Time, Jan 1, 1986 (representing the number of days since Julian calendar date Jan 1, 4713 B.C.). New Year's Day is a public holiday in the U.S. and in most other countries. Traditionally it is a time for personal stocktaking, for making resolutions for the coming year, and sometimes for recovering from the festivities of New Year's Eve. Financial accounting begins anew for businesses and individuals whose fiscal year is the calendar year. January 1 has been observed as the beginning of the year in most English-speaking countries since the British Calendar Act of 1751, prior to which the New Year began on March 25 (approximating the Vernal Equinox). Earth begins another orbit of the sun, during which it, and we, will travel some 583,416,000 miles, in 365.2422 days. New Year's Day has been called "Everyman's Birthday," and in some countries a year is added to everyone's age on January 1 rather than on the anniversary of one's birth.

ANNOUNCEMENT OF TEN BEST PUNS OF THE YEAR. Jan 1. Purpose: To salute the best punsters of the year and thus encourage word-play and combat illiteracy. Annually, January first. Sponsor: Internatl Save The Pun Foundation, John S. Crosbie, Box 5040, Station A, Toronto, Canada M5W 1N4.

ARKANSAS SESQUICENTENNIAL CELEBRATION. Jan 1-Dec 31. The state of Arkansas celebrates 150 years of statehood the whole year, with special activities geared toward June 13-15, 1986 "Chimes and Cheers: Salute to Statehood" at Little Rock, AR. Info from: Sesquicentennial Celebration Committee, 1111 S University, Suite 900, Little Rock, AR 72204.

ATLANTIC VISIONS DE L'ATLANTIQUE. Jan 1-June 30. Crafts from Canada's four Atlantic provinces. A major Canadian touring exhibition patronized by the Atlantic Premiers. Opened Confederation Centre, Charlottetown, PEI, touring Canada and the United States and finishing in 1986 at Muttart Gallery, Calgary. Info from: George Fry, NB Craft School, Box 6000, Fredericton, NB, Canada E3B 5H1.

BIRTH DEFECTS PREVENTION MONTH. Jan 1-31. Purpose: To enlist support of all Americans in the March of Dimes fight against birth defects. Sponsor: March of Dimes Birth Defects Foundation, 1275 Mamaroneck Ave, White Plains, NY 10605.

BLACK NAZARENE FIESTA. Jan 1-9. Manila, Philippine Islands. A traditional nine-day fiesta honors Quiapo district's patron saint, to whom many miracles are attributed by the faithful of this district of Manila. Cultural events, fireworks and parades culminate in a procession with the life-size statue of the Black Nazarene, starting at the historic Quiapo church, which dates from the 16th century.

CARTER CAVES CRAWLATHON. Jan 1-Feb 2. Purpose: For the stout of heart who like spelunking. A weekend of non-stop cave tours through the "roughest, dirtiest caves that can be found." Info from: KY Dept of Parks, John Tierney, Carter Caves State Resort Park, Olive Hill, KY 41164.

CIRCUMCISION OF CHRIST. Jan 1. Holy day in many Christian churches, celebrates Jesus' submission to Jewish law, on the octave day of Christmas. See also: Jan 1 entry for "Solemnity of Mary, Mother of God" for Roman Catholic observance since 1969 calendar reorganization.

COLUMBIA, SOUTH CAROLINA: 200TH ANNIVERSARY. Jan 1-Dec 31. Columbia, the capital of South Carolina will be celebrating its 200th anniversary during 1986. Info from: Columbia Bicentennial, Tootsie D. Brantley, Box 2826, Columbia, SC 29202.

COPYRIGHT REVISION LAW: ANNIVERSARY. Jan 1. The first major revision since 1909 of laws governing intellectual property in the U.S. was signed by President Ford on Oct 19, 1976, and took effect Jan 1, 1978. The act (Public Law 94-553) contains substantial revisions of the principles governing acquisition and duration of copyright, and deals with issues which have been raised in recent years concerning photocopying and the use of copyrighted works by public broadcasting and cable television systems.

COTTON BOWL CLASSIC. Jan 1. Dallas, TX. Info from: Cotton Bowl Athletic Assn, Box 47420, Dallas, TX 75247.

CUBA: LIBERATION DAY. Jan 1. A national holiday which celebrates the end of Spanish rule, Jan 1, 1899. Cuba, largest island of the West Indies, was a Spanish possession from its discovery by Columbus (Oct 27, 1492) until 1899. Under U.S. military control, 1899-1902 and 1906-1909, a republican government took over on Jan 28, 1909 and controlled the island until it was overthrown Jan 1, 1959 by Fidel Castro's revolutionary movement (which had started on July 26, 1953).

DEFENSE DEPOT TRACY: ANNIVERSARY. Jan 1. Purpose: Commemorates the establishment of Defense Depot Tracy, CA, as the first depot in the Defense Logistics Agency distribution system. Sponsor: Public Affairs Office, Defense Depot Tracy, Tracy, CA 95376.

EMANCIPATION PROCLAMATION ANNIVERSARY. Jan 1. Two of the most important presidential proclamations of American history are those of Sept 22, 1862, and of Jan 1, 1863, in which Abraham Lincoln, by executive proclamation freed the slaves in the rebelling states. "That on . . . (Jan 1, 1863) . . . all persons held as slaves within any state or designated part of a state, the people whereof shall then be in rebellion against the United States, shall be then, thenceforward, and forever, free . . ." See: "Thirteenth Amendment Anniversary" (Dec 18) for abolition of slavery in all states.

EMERSON, WILLIAM (BILL): BIRTHDAY. Jan 1. U.S. Representative of Missouri's 8th district, Republican, of Cape Girardeau, MO, was born in St. Louis, MO, Jan 1, 1938.

FIESTA BOWL FOOTBALL CLASSIC. Jan 1. Sun Devil Stadium, Tempe, AZ. Complementing Fiesta Bowl Football Classic are 40 events that comprise an entire festival, including the Fiesta Bowl Parade and National Pageant of Bands. Info from: Fiesta Bowl Office, 5144 E Camelback, Phoenix, AZ 85018.

FORSTER, E M: BIRTHDAY. Jan 1. Edward Morgan Forster, English author born at London, Jan 1, 1879. Especially remembered for his six novels: *Where Angels Fear to Tread* (1905), *The Longest Journey* (1907), *A Room with a View* (1908), *Howard's End* (1910), *A Passage to India* (1924) and the posthumously published *Maurice* (1971) which Forster had written about 1913-1914. He also achieved eminence for his short stories and essays and he collaborated on the libretto for one opera, Benjamin Britten's *Billy Budd* (1951). Forster died at Coventry, June 7, 1970.

COPYRIGHT © 1985 BY WILLIAM D. CHASE and HELEN M. CHASE

FROST, MARTIN: BIRTHDAY. Jan 1. U.S. Representative of Texas' 24th district, Democrat, of Dallas, TX, born at Glendale, CA, on Jan 1, 1942.

GOLDWATER, BARRY M: BIRTHDAY. Jan 1. U.S. Senator from Arizona, Republican, of Scottsdale, AZ, was born in Phoenix, AZ, on Jan 1, 1909.

HAITI: INDEPENDENCE DAY. Jan 1. A national holiday commemorating the proclamation of independence on Jan 1, 1804. Haiti, occupying the western third of the island Hispaniola (second largest of the West Indies), was a Spanish colony from the time of its discovery by Columbus in 1492 until 1697; then a French colony until the proclamation of independence in 1804.

HOLLINGS, ERNEST F: BIRTHDAY. Jan 1. U.S. Senator from South Carolina, Democrat, of Charleston, SC, born in Charleston on Jan 1, 1922.

HUGUENOT HERITAGE TERCENTENARY COMMEMORATION. Jan 1-Apr 30. England. Continues 1985 observance marking the 300th anniversary of the revocation of the Edict of Nantes. Many Huguenots found refuge in Britain, and events will take place in London and in many other areas where the Huguenots settled. Planned events include exhibitions, lecture tours and festivals. An International Week will be held Sept 26-Oct 2, and a Huguenot Heritage Trail is intended to link planned events.

INTERNATIONAL YEAR OF PEACE. Jan 1-Dec 31. In a resolution adopted Nov 16, 1982 the United Nations General Assembly accepted a recommendation to link International Year of Peace with the 40th anniversary of the UN and to proclaim 1986 to be International Year of Peace on Oct 24, 1985. The Assembly noted that "peace continues to be a goal instead of an achievement, in spite of the resolute efforts of the United Nations" and there is a need to "devote a specific time to concentrate the efforts of the UN and its Member States to promote the ideals of peace and give evidence of their commitment to peace in all viable ways."

IOWA HOMECOMING '86. Jan 1-Aug 24. Purpose: To encourage Iowans living outside the state to reunite with family and friends during the summer of 1986. Special activities at local festivals, county fairs and the state fair to draw former Iowans home. Info from: Iowa Development Commission, 600 E Court Ave, Des Moines, IA 50309.

JAPANESE ERA NEW YEAR. Jan 1. Beginning of the Year 2646, of the Japanese era.

JOY FROM THE WORLD. Jan 1-5. Purpose: To better understand the holiday traditions of others, Joy From The World shares art, music, dance, crafts and food. Sponsor: Science Museum of Virginia, Mary Randolph Spencer, 2500 W Broad St, Richmond, VA 23220.

KANSAS CITY, KANSAS: CENTENNIAL. Jan 1-Dec 31. Year long celebration. Info from: Convention and Visitors Bureau, Inc, Box 1576, Kansas City, KS 66117.

LAKESIDE, CALIFORNIA: CENTENNIAL. Jan 1-Dec 31. Year long celebration of Lakeside, California's 100th Birthday. Info from: Lakeside Historical Society, Shirley Anderson, Box 1886, Lakeside, CA 92040.

LYNCHBURG, VIRGINIA: BICENTENNIAL. Jan 1-Dec 31. Celebration of the 200th birthday of Lynchburg, Virginia. Year-long festivals and activities honoring Lynchburg, the city along the historic James River and Blue Ridge Mountains. Info from: Bicentennial Commission of Lynchburg, Brock L. Field, Exec Dir, Box 1132, Lynchburg, VA 24505.

January 1986

S	M	T	W	T	F	S
			1	2	3	4
5	6	7	8	9	10	11
12	13	14	15	16	17	18
19	20	21	22	23	24	25
26	27	28	29	30	31	

MUMMERS NEW YEAR'S DAY PARADE. Jan 1. Philadelphia, PA. World famous New Year's Day parade of spectacularly costumed Mummers string bands, clowns, marchers doing the traditional Mummers strut up Broad St. Info from: Philadelphia Conv & Visitors Bureau, Three Penn Ctr Plaza, Suite 2020, Philadelphia, PA 19102.

NATIONAL ENVIRONMENTAL POLICY ACT: ANNIVERSARY. Jan 1. The National Environmental Policy Act of 1969, establishing the Council on Environmental Quality, and making it federal government policy to protect the environment, took effect Jan 1, 1970.

NATIONAL HOBBY MONTH. Jan 1-31. Purpose: To promote the fun and creativity of models, crafts and collectibles. Sponsor: Hobby Industries of America, Susan Brandt, Dir of Communications, 319 E 54th St, Elmwood Park, NJ 07407.

NATIONAL SOUP MONTH. Jan 1-31. Purpose: To acknowledge and celebrate the nutritious, economical and versatile contribution of soup to the American diet of today and tomorrow. Sponsor: Campbell Soup Co, Communications Ctr, Campbell Place, Camden, NJ 08101.

NATIONAL VOLUNTEER BLOOD DONOR MONTH. Jan 1-31. Purpose: To honor volunteer blood donors and encourage public to donate to prevent annual January shortages. Sponsor: American Assn of Blood Banks, Lorry Rose, Dir of Communication, 1117 N 19th St, Suite 600, Arlington, VA 22209.

NEW YEAR'S DAY. Jan 1. Legal holiday in all states and territories of the U.S., and in most other countries.

NEW YEAR'S DISHONOR LIST. Jan 1. America's dishonor list of words banished from Queen's English. Overworked words and phrases (e.g. uniquely unique, first time ever, yuh know) annually banished by Unicorn Hunters of Lake Superior State College. Annually, January first. Info from: Bill Rabe, Lake Superior State College, Sault Ste. Marie, MI 49783.

NIAGARA FALLS FESTIVAL OF LIGHTS. Jan 1-5. (Observance continuing from November 23, 1984). The Festival of Lights features a combination of lighting displays and events "encompassed in the splendour of Niagara Falls in the winter." Info from: Niagara Falls Conv & Visitors Bureau, Box 786, Falls St Station, Niagara Falls, NY 14303.

ORANGE BOWL FOOTBALL CLASSIC. Jan 1. The champion of the Big-8 conference meets a nationally ranked opponent in the Orange Bowl Stadium. Info from: Ed Goss, Orange Bowl Committee, Box 350748, Miami, FL 33135.

PEACE CORPS: 25TH ANNIVERSARY. Jan 1-Dec 31. Purpose: National observance throughout 1986 of 25th anniversary of official establishment of the Peace Corps by Pres John F. Kennedy. Mar 1 was date of official establishment by signing of executive order. Since 1961, Peace Corps has sent more than 104,000 volunteers to over 90 developing countries to help their people help themselves. The volunteers have been assisting these people in projects such as health, education, water sanitation, agriculture, nutrition and forestry. Sponsor: Peace Corps, Hugh L. O'Neill, Dir of Public Affairs, 806 Connecticut Ave NW, Washington, DC 20526.

PRICE, CHARLES MELVIN: BIRTHDAY. Jan 1. U.S. Representative of Illinois' 21st district, Democrat, of East St. Louis, IL, born there on Jan 1, 1905.

PRUNE BREAKFAST MONTH. Jan 1-31. Purpose: To encourage Americans to start each day with a nutritious breakfast, to communicate the many benefits of prunes: their good taste, high nutrition and versatility, and to dispel misconceptions about prunes. Sponsor: California Prune Board. Info from: Ketchum Public Relations, Susan Mesick, 55 Union St, San Francisco, CA 94111.

REVERE, PAUL: BIRTHDAY. Jan 1. American patriot, silversmith and engraver, maker of false teeth, eye-glasses, picture frames and surgical instruments, is best remembered for his famous ride on Apr 18, 1775, celebrated in Longfellow's poem, "The Midnight Ride of Paul Revere." He was born at Boston on Jan 1, 1735, and died there on May 10, 1818. (See also: entry for Apr 18.)

COPYRIGHT © 1985 BY WILLIAM D. CHASE and HELEN M. CHASE

RHODE ISLAND: 350TH ANNIVERSARY. Jan 1-Dec 31. Year long celebration with special events throughout the state. Info from: Rhode Island Dept of Economic Development, State Tourism Div, 7 Jackson Walkway, Providence, RI 02903.

ROSE BOWL FOOTBALL GAME. Jan 1. Pasadena, California. Football conference champions from Big Ten and Pacific Ten meet. Tournament of Roses has been annual New Year's Day event since 1890; Rose Bowl football game since 1902. Sponsor: Pasadena Tournament of Roses Assn, 391 S Orange Grove Blvd, Pasadena, CA 91184.

ROSS, BETSY: BIRTHDAY. Jan 1. According to legend based largely on her grandson's revelations in 1870, needleworker Betsy Ross created the first stars-and-stripes flag in 1775, under instructions from George Washington. Her sewing, and her making of flags, were well known, but there is little corroborative evidence of her role in making the first stars-and-stripes. The account is generally accepted however in the absence of any documented claims to the contrary. She was born Elizabeth Griscom, at Philadelphia on Jan 1, 1752, and died there on Jan 30, 1836.

ROSS, BETSY: BIRTHDAY OBSERVANCE. Jan 1. Special noon-time ceremonies at Betsy Ross' tomb in Atwater Kent Gardens of Betsy Ross House in Philadelphia, PA. Info from: Abe S. Rosen, Rosen-Coren Agency, Inc, 4138 Benjamin Fox Pavilion, Foxcroft Sq, Jenkintown, PA 19046.

ST. BASIL'S DAY. Jan 1. St. Basil's or St. Vasily's feast day observed on Jan 1, by Eastern Orthodox churches. Special traditions for the day, such as St. Basil cakes, each containing a coin. Feast day observed on Jan 14 by those churches using Julian calendar.

SEWER BOWL. Jan 1. Mahone Bay, Nova Scotia. An annual offbeat football game held after a street parade with fun and frivolity between the Plungers and the Flushers. Info from: Dept of Tourism, Box 456, Halifax, NS B3J 2R5.

SHANGHAI PARADE. Jan 1. Lewisburg, WV. Purpose: A bit of Americana. Originally, a spontaneous promenade that included everyone who happened by. Sponsor: City of Lewisburg, P.L. Gainer, Mayor, Box 548, Lewisburg, WV 24901.

SILENT RECORD WEEK. Jan 1-7. Purpose: Commemorating the invention of Silent Record. A period of silence when most needed. Annually, first week in January. Sponsor: Hush Records, (Lake Superior State College Unicorn Hunters), W.T. Rabe, Sault Ste. Marie, MI 49783.

SOLEMNITY OF MARY, MOTHER OF GOD. Jan 1. Holy day of obligation in Roman Catholic church since calendar reorganization of 1969, replacing the Feast of the Circumcision which had been recognized for more than fourteen centuries. See also Jan 1 entry for Circumcision of Christ.

SUDAN: INDEPENDENCE DAY. Jan 1. National holiday. The Sudan was proclaimed a sovereign independent republic on Jan 1, 1956, ending its status as an Anglo-Egyptian condominium (since 1899).

SUGAR BOWL FOOTBALL CLASSIC. Jan 1. Louisiana Superdome, New Orleans, LA. Sponsor: Sugar Bowl, Louisiana Superdome, Mezzanine Level, 1500 Sugar Bowl Dr, New Orleans, LA 70112.

TEXAS SESQUICENTENNIAL. Jan 1-Dec 31. Texas. Purpose: Celebrations and special activities throughout the state by cities and towns as well as organizations in honor of Texas' 150th birthday. Info from: Texas 1986 Sesquicentennial Commission, Box 1986, Austin, TX 78767.

TOURNAMENT OF ROSES PARADE. Jan 1. Pasadena, CA. Theme: "A Celebration of Laughter." Annual rose parade starting at 8:20 a.m. P.S.T. will include floats, bands and equestrians. Sponsor: Pasadena Tournament of Roses Assn, 391 S Orange Grove Blvd, Pasadena, CA 91184.

UNITED NATIONS: AFRICAN TRANSPORT AND COMMUNICATIONS DECADE (1978-1988): YEAR NINE. Jan 1-Dec 31. Aim: To give active support to preparation and implementation of global strategy for solving Africa's transport and communications problems and mobilizing technical and financial resources required. Proclaimed by UN General Assembly in 1977. Info from: United Nations, Dept of Public Information, United Nations, NY 10017.

UNITED NATIONS: DECADE OF DISABLED PERSONS: YEAR FOUR. Jan 1-Dec 31. On Dec 3, 1982, the UN General Assembly proclaimed 1983-1992 United Nations Decade of Disabled Persons as a long-term plan of action. It followed the UN International Year of Disabled Persons (1981) "which had contributed to the acceptance by the community of the right of disabled persons to participate fully in the social life and development of their societies and enjoy living conditions equal to that of their fellow citizens." Info from: United Nations Dept of Public Information, United Nations, NY 10017.

UNITED NATIONS: INDUSTRIAL DEVELOPMENT DECADE FOR AFRICA (1980s): YEAR SEVEN. Jan 1-Dec 31. Purpose: To mobilize greater political commitment and financial and technical support for the industrialization of Africa. Proclaimed by United Nations General Assembly. Dec 1980. Info from: United Nations, Dept of Public Information, United Nations, NY 10017.

UNITED NATIONS: INTERNATIONAL DRINKING WATER SUPPLY AND SANITATION DECADE (1981-1990) YEAR SIX. Jan 1-Dec 31. Adequate drinking water and sanitation facilities for all peoples of the world by 1990 is objective of this Decade, recommended by the UN Water Conference held at Mar del Plata, Argentina, March 1977. Info from United Nations, Dept of Public Information, United Nations, NY 10017.

UNITED NATIONS: SECOND DISARMAMENT DECADE: YEAR SIX. Jan 1-Dec 31. United Nations General Assembly, in 1969, proclaimed the 1970's as a Disarmament Decade. Governments are urged to intensify efforts for: cessation of nuclear arms race, nuclear disarmament and elimination of other weapons of mass destruction, and for a treaty on general and complete disarmament under strict and effective international control. Info from: United Nations, Dept of Public Information, United Nations, NY 10017.

UNITED NATIONS: THIRD UNITED NATIONS DEVELOPMENT DECADE (YEAR SIX). Jan 1-Dec 31. Major United Nations program to promote world efforts to bridge enormous gap between advanced and developing countries, where two-thirds of world's people live. (1981-1990). Info from: United Nations, Dept of Public Information, United Nations, NY 10017.

UNIVERSITY OF VIRGINIA SCHOOL OF ENGINEERING AND APPLIED SCIENCE: 150TH ANNIVERSARY. Jan 1. Info from: University of Virginia, Thornton Hall, Charlottesville, VA 22901.

U.S.S.R.: NEW YEAR'S DAY OBSERVANCE. Jan 1. National holiday. Modern tradition calls for setting up New Year Trees in homes, halls, clubs, palaces of culture and in the hall of the Kremlin Palace. Children's parties with Grand-dad Frost and his granddaughter, Snow Girl. Games, songs, dancing, special foods, family gatherings and exchange of gifts and New Year's cards.

VANCOUVER, BRITISH COLUMBIA: CENTENNIAL. Jan 1-Dec 31. 1986 marks the 100th birthday of the incorporation of the City of Vancouver. Year-long series of celebrations. Info from: Vancouver Centennial Commission, Box 49386, Bentall 4, 1055 Dunsmuir St, Vancouver, BC V7X 1L5.

COPYRIGHT © 1985 BY WILLIAM D. CHASE and HELEN M. CHASE

'WEEKS' WEEK. Jan 1-7. Purpose: To call attention to all the weeks of importance in the forthcoming year and inform the public how they can participate, enjoy and aid each week that they consider worthy. Annually, first week in January. Sponsor: Richard R. Falk Associates, 147 W 42nd St, New York, NY 10036.

WESTERN PACIFIC HURRICANE SEASON. Jan 1-Dec 31. Season lasts all year, though most hurricanes occur June through Oct 1. (Western Pacific: West of International Dateline.) Info from: U.S. Dept of Commerce, Natl Oceanic and Atmospheric Administration, Rockville, MD 20852.

WHALE WATCHING. Jan 1-Mar 31. (Also Dec 1-31.) Purpose: To view the migration of the gray whales along the coast of California. Info from: California Office of Tourism, 1121 L St, Suite 103, Sacramento, CA 95814.

JANUARY 2 — THURSDAY
2nd Day — Remaining, 363

BACON, NATHANIEL: BIRTHDAY. Jan 2. Leader of "Bacon's Rebellion" in 1676 (Virginia). Born, Suffolk, England, Jan 2, 1647. Died, Gloucester County, VA, Oct 1676 (Exact date unknown).

EARTH AT PERIHELION. Jan 2. At approximately 12:01 a.m., E.S.T, planet Earth will reach Perihelion, that point in its orbit when it is closest to the sun (about 91,400,000 miles). The Earth's mean distance from the sun (mean radius of its orbit) is reached early in the months of April and October. Note that Earth is closest to the sun during Northern Hemisphere winter. See also: entry for Earth at Aphelion, July 5.

ENGLAND: INTERNATIONAL BOAT SHOW. Jan 2-12. Earls Court, London. Largest international boat show in Europe, displaying over 600 craft. Info from: Natl Boat Shows Ltd, Boating Industry House, Vale Rd, Oatlands Park, Weybridge, Surrey, England.

GEORGIA: RATIFICATION DAY. Jan 2. Fourth state to ratify constitution, on this day in 1788.

HAITI: ANCESTORS DAY. Jan 2. Commemoration of the Ancestors. Also known as Hero's Day. Public holiday.

JAPAN: KAKIZOME. Jan 2. Traditional Japanese festival gets underway when the first strokes of the year are made on paper with the traditional brushes.

NEW YEAR'S BLUEGRASS FESTIVAL. Jan 2-4. Convention Ctr, Jekyll Island, GA. Family Bluegrass Festival. Info from: Norman Adams, Box 98, Dahlonega, GA 30533.

RECREATIONAL VEHICLE, BOAT AND MOBILE HOME SHOW. Jan 2-5. Tucson Civic Plaza, Tucson, AZ. Info from: Dixie Green Promotions, Inc, 3141 W Christy Dr, Phoenix, AZ 85029.

RILEY, RICHARD W: BIRTHDAY. Jan 2. Richard W. Riley, Governor of South Carolina, Democrat, was born at Greenville, SC, on Jan 2, 1932.

ROSTENKOWSKI, DAN: BIRTHDAY. Jan 2. U.S. Representative of Illinois' 8th district, Democrat, of Chicago, IL, born there on Jan 2, 1928.

SPACE MILESTONE: LUNA 1 (USSR). Jan 2. First moon shot missed and became first spacecraft from Earth to orbit sun. Jan 2, 1959.

TAFT, HELEN HERRON: BIRTHDAY. Jan 2. Wife of William Howard Taft, 27th President of the U.S., born at Cincinnati, OH, Jan 2, 1861. Died May 22, 1943.

January 1986

S	M	T	W	T	F	S
			1	2	3	4
5	6	7	8	9	10	11
12	13	14	15	16	17	18
19	20	21	22	23	24	25
26	27	28	29	30	31	

WOLFE, JAMES: BIRTHDAY. Jan 2. English general who commanded the British army's victory over Montcalm's French forces on the Plains of Abraham in 1759. As a result, France surrendered Canada to England. Wolfe was born on Jan 2, 1727 (New Style) at Westerham, Kent. He died at the Plains of Abraham of battle wounds on Sept 13, 1759.

JANUARY 3 — FRIDAY
3rd Day — Remaining, 362

ALASKA: ADMISSION DAY. Jan 3. Became 49th State on this day in 1959.

ATTLEE, CLEMENT RICHARD: BIRTHDAY. Jan 3. English leader of the Labour Party, and Prime Minister (July 1945-Oct 1951) was born at London, Jan 3, 1883. Died there, Oct 8, 1967.

CHARLOTTE OBSERVER MARATHON AND RUNNER'S EXPO. Jan 3-4. Purpose: 26.2 mile marathon run plus 10K and 1 mile races. Finish of races and Runner's Expo at Charlotte Convention Ctr. Sponsor: The Charlotte Observer, Box 30294, Charlotte, NC 28230.

CONGRESS ASSEMBLES. Jan 3. The Constitution provides that "the Congress shall assemble at least once in every Year . . . " and the 20th Amendment specifies "and such meeting shall begin at noon on the 3rd day of January, unless they shall by law appoint a different day."

COOLIDGE, GRACE ANNA GOODHUE: BIRTHDAY. Jan 3. Wife of Calvin Coolidge, 30th President of the U.S., born at Burlington, VT, Jan 3, 1879. Died July 8, 1957.

ENGLAND: MODEL ENGINEER EXHIBITION. Jan 3-11. Wembley Conference Centre, Wembley, London. Exhibition of working models, static displays and demonstrations of model making.

GREAT AMERICAN MOTORCYCLE SHOW. Jan 3-5. Info from: Tarrant County Conv Ctr. 1111 Houston St, Fort Worth, TX 76102.

INTERNATIONAL SINGING COMPETITION PRETORIA 1986. Jan 3-11. Info from: Professor Hennie Joubexrt, University of South Africa, Box 392, Pretoria, South Africa.

LAKE PLACID OUTDOOR SPEED SKATING CHAMPION-SHIPS. Jan 3-5. Olympic Speed Skating Oval, Lake Placid, NY. Info from: Chamber of Commerce, Olympic Arena, Lake Placid, NY 12946.

LLOYD, MARILYN: BIRTHDAY. Jan 3. U.S. Representative of Tennessee's 3rd district, Democrat, of Chattanooga, TN was born in Fort Smith, AR, Jan 3, 1929.

MOON PHASE: LAST QUARTER. Jan 3. Moon enters Last Quarter phase at 2:47 p.m., E.S.T.

MOTT, LUCRETIA (COFFIN): BIRTHDAY. Jan 3. American teacher, minister, anti-slavery leader, and (with Elizabeth Cady Stanton), one of the founders of the women's rights movement in the U.S. Born at Nantucket, MA, Jan 3, 1793. Died near Philadelphia, Nov 11, 1880.

SHERLOCK HOLMES BIRTHDAY BREAKFAST. Jan 3. Algonquin Hotel, New York City. In honor of Mrs. Hudson, Holmes's landlady. No invitations, no reservations, no program but open to "Sherlockian Scholars" of all ilks. Sponsor: Old Soldiers of Baker Street, Lake Superior State College Unicorn Hunters, W.T. Rabe, Chief Medical Officer (Ret.), Lake Superior State College, Sault Ste Marie, MI 49783.

WHITLEY, CHARLES O: BIRTHDAY. Jan 3. U.S. Representative of North Carolina's 3rd district, Democrat, of Mount Olive, NC, born in Siler City, NC, Jan 3, 1927.

JANUARY 4 — SATURDAY
4th Day — Remaining, 361

BANGERTER, NORMAN H: BIRTHDAY. Jan 4. Norman H. Bangerter, Governor of Utah, Republican, was born at Granger, UT, on Jan 4, 1933.

COPYRIGHT © 1985 BY WILLIAM D. CHASE and HELEN M. CHASE

BRAILLE, LOUIS: BIRTHDAY. Jan 4. The inventor of a widely used touch system of reading and writing for the blind, was born at Coupvray, France, Jan 4, 1809. Permanently blinded at the age of three (by a leatherworking awl in his father's saddlemaking shop), Braille, ironically, developed a system of writing which used an awl-like stylus to punch marks in paper which could be felt by the blind. The system was largely ignored until after Braille's death, in poverty, and suffering from tuberculosis, on Mar 28, 1852.

BURMA: NATIONAL HOLIDAY. Jan 4. Independence Day. Became independent nation on this day in 1948 by virtue of treaty with Great Britain.

CHAMPIONSHIP CAT SHOW. Jan 4-5. Indianapolis, IN. Purpose: Exhibition and judging of longhair and shorthair purebred cats and kittens and mixed breed household pets. Sponsor: American Cat Fanciers Assn, Circle City Cat Club. Info from: Maribeth Echard, 8507 N Illinois St, Indianapolis, IN 46260.

GENERAL TOM THUMB'S BIRTHDAY. Jan 4. Charles Sherwood Stratton, perhaps the most famous dwarf in history, was born at Bridgeport, CT, on Jan 4, 1838. His growth almost stopped during his first year, but he eventually reached a height of 3 feet, 4 inches, and a weight of 70 pounds. "Discovered" by P.T. Barnum in 1842, Stratton, as "Gen. Tom Thumb" became an internationally known entertainer and on tour performed before Queen Victoria and other heads of state. On Feb 10, 1863, he married another dwarf, Lavinia Warren, before an overflow crowd at Grace Episcopal Church in New York City, an event recorded in popular lithograph by Currier and Ives. Stratton died at Middleborough, MA, on July 15, 1883.

GRIMM, JACOB: BIRTH ANNIVERSARY. Jan 4. German librarian, mythologist and philologist, born at Hanau, Jan 4, 1785. Best remembered for *Grimm's Fairy Tales* (in collaboration with his brother Wilhelm). Died at Berlin, Sept 20, 1863.

HOUSTON INTERNATIONAL BOAT, SPORT & TRAVEL SHOW. Jan 4-12. Astrohall, Houston, TX. Sponsor: Boating Trade Association of Metropolitan Houston, Info from: Houston Internatl Boat, Sport & Travel Show, Inc, 2600 Southwest Hwy, Suite 305, Houston, TX 77098.

JENKINS, EDGAR LANIER: BIRTHDAY. Jan 4. U.S. Representative of Georgia's 9th district, Democrat, of Jasper, GA, was born in Young Harris, GA, on Jan 4, 1933.

MOONLIGHT MADNESS SKI TOURS. Jan 4. (Also Feb 4, Mar 4 and Dec 4.) "The ultimate in night skiing. Enjoy the West Virginia mountains bathed in the light of the full moon." Info from: Elk River X-C Touring Ctr, Slatyfork, WV 26291.

SETON, ELIZABETH ANN BAYLEY: FEAST DAY. Jan 4. First American-born saint (beatified Mar 17, 1963, canonized Sept 14, 1975), born in New York City, Aug 28, 1774. She was founder of American Sisters of Charity, the first American order of Roman Catholic Nuns. Died, Baltimore, MD, Jan 4, 1821.

TRIVIA DAY. Jan 4. Purpose: In celebration of those who know all sorts of facts and/or have doctorates in uselessology. Annually, January fourth. Sponsor: Puns Corps, Robert L. Birch, Box 2364, Falls Church, VA 22042.

UTAH: ADMISSION DAY. Jan 4. Became 45th State on this day in 1896.

WYMAN, JANE: BIRTHDAY. Jan 4. Award-winning American actress, first wife of Ronald Wilson Reagan, 40th President of the U.S. She was born at St. Joseph, MO, Jan 4, 1914, married Reagan Jan 24, 1940. They were divorced in 1948.

JANUARY 5 — SUNDAY
5th Day — Remaining, 360

DECATUR, STEPHEN: BIRTHDAY. Jan 5. American naval officer (whose father and grandfather, both named Stephen Decatur, were also seafaring men) born at Sinepuxent, MD, Jan 5, 1779. In a toast at a dinner in Norfolk, in 1815, Decatur spoke his most famous words: "Our country! In her intercourse with foreign nations may she always be in the right; but our

country, right or wrong." He was mortally wounded in a duel with Commodore James Barron, at Bladensburg, MD, on the morning of Mar 22, 1820. Carried to his home in Washington, he died a few hours later.

DeWINE, MICHAEL: BIRTHDAY. Jan 5. U.S. Representative of Ohio's 7th district, Republican, of Cedarville, OH, was born in Springfield, OH, on Jan 5, 1947.

ITALY: EPIPHANY FAIR. Jan 5. Piazza Navona, Rome, Italy. On the eve of Epiphany a fair of toys, sweets and presents takes place among the beautiful Bernini Fountains.

JOHNSON, NANCY LEE: BIRTHDAY. Jan 5. U.S. Representative of Connecticut's 6th district, Republican, of New Britain, CT, born in Chicago, IL, on Jan 5, 1935.

MONDALE, WALTER FREDERICK: BIRTHDAY. Jan 5. Walter Frederick "Fritz" Mondale, 42nd Vice President of the U.S. and nominated Democratic Party candidate for President in 1984, was born Jan 5, 1928, in Ceylon, MN.

NATIONAL BOWLING WEEK. Jan 5-11. Purpose: To celebrate America's oldest and most popular indoor participation sport. Annually, first full week in January. Sponsor: Natl Bowling Council, Deborah Davidson, 1919 Pennsylvania Ave NW, Washington, DC 20006.

OLD CHRISTMAS. Jan 5. Jenny Wiley State Resort Park, Prestonsburg, KY. A celebration of Christmas as our forefathers celebrated in the mountains of Eastern Kentucky. Info from: Kentucky Dept of Parks, Capitol Plaza Tower, Frankfort, KY 40601.

PICCARD, JEANNETTE RIDLON: BIRTHDAY. Jan 5. First American woman to qualify as free balloon pilot (1934), one of first women to be ordained as Episcopal priest (1976). Pilot for record-setting balloon ascent into stratosphere (from Dearborn, MI, Oct 23, 1934) (57,579 ft) with her husband, Jean Felix Piccard (q.v.). Identical twin married to identical twin. Born at Chicago, IL, Jan 5, 1895. Died at Minneapolis, MN, May 17, 1981.

THREE KINGS PARADE. Jan 5. Miami, FL. Traditional day of celebration by Hispanic community. Info from: Al Wolfe Associates, Inc, 5225 NW 87th Ave, Miami, FL 33166.

TWELFTH NIGHT. Jan 5. Evening Before Epiphany. Twelfth Night marks the end of medieval Christmas festivities and the end of Twelfthtide (the 12-day season after Christmas and ending with Epiphany). Also called Twelfth Day Eve.

JANUARY 6 — MONDAY
6th Day — Remaining, 359

ARMENIAN CHRISTMAS. Jan 6. Christmas is observed on this day in the Armenian Church, "the oldest Christian national church."

CARNIVAL SEASON. Jan 6-Feb 11. A secular festival preceding Lent (q.v.). A time of merry-making and feasting before the austere days of Lenten fasting and penitence (40 weekdays between Ash Wednesday and Easter Sunday). The word "carnival" probably is derived from the Latin *carnem levare*, meaning "to remove meat." Depending on local custom, the carnival season may start any time between Nov 11 and Shrove Tuesday. Conclusion of the season is much less variable, being the close of Shrove Tuesday in most places. Observance varies considerably but the festival often includes many theatrical aspects (masks, costume and song), and has given its name (in

COPYRIGHT © 1985 BY WILLIAM D. CHASE and HELEN M. CHASE

the U.S.) to traveling amusement shows which may be seen throughout the year. Observed traditionally in Roman Catholic countries from Epiphany through Shrove Tuesday.

EDWARDS, DON: BIRTHDAY. Jan 6. U.S. Representative of California's 10th district, Democrat, of San Jose, CA, was born in San Jose, on Jan 6, 1915.

GREEK CROSS DAY. Jan 6. Tarpon Springs, FL. Epiphany services begin early in morning at St. Nicholas Cathedral and end at noon. Religious procession from church to Spring Bayou where young men of Orthodox faith await traditional blessings of the waters by chief celebrant Archbishop Iakovos who casts the cross into the waters. The lucky youth who retrieves it receives blessing, and tradition says good luck will follow him for the year. Festivities with Greek food, music, and dancing follow. Formal Epiphany Ball ends observance in evening. Info from: St. Nicholas Greek Orthodox Cathedral, Box 248, Tarpon Springs, FL 33589.

HAYM SALOMON DAY. Jan 6. American Revolutionary War patriot and financier was born at Lissa, Poland in 1740 (Exact date unknown). Salomon died at Philadelphia, Jan 6, 1785.

ITALY: LA BEFANA. Jan 6. A major Epiphany festival in which the "Befana," a kindly witch, bestows gifts on children—toys and candy for those who have been good, but a lump of coal or a pebble for those who have been naughty. The festival begins on the night of Jan 5th, with much noise and merrymaking (when the Befana is supposed to come down the chimneys on her broom, leaving gifts in children's stocking) and continues with joyous fairs, parades and other activities throughout Jan 6th.

MAROON FESTIVAL. Jan 6. Jamaica. Commemorates the 18th century Treaty of Cudjoe. While a Spanish colony, Jamaica's native inhabitants (Arawaks) were exterminated. The Spanish then imported African slaves to work their plantations. When the Spanish were driven out (1655) the Black slaves fled to the mountains. The "Maroons" (fugitive slaves) were permitted to settle in the north of the island in 1738. The 244th annual Maroon Festival (1983) at Accompong, St. Elizabeth, still sought "proper documentation for the 1,500 acres of land which became legally theirs in 1758."

MIX, TOM: BIRTHDAY. Jan 6. American motion picture actor, especially remembered for western cowboy films, born at Driftwood, PA, Jan 6, 1880. Died near Florence, AZ, Oct 12, 1940.

NEW MEXICO: ADMISSION DAY. Jan 6. Became 47th State on this day in 1912.

SANDBURG, CARL: BIRTHDAY. Jan 6. American author: poet, biographer, historian and folklorist, born Jan 6, 1878, at Galesburg, IL. Died, July 22, 1967, Flat Rock, NC.

THREE KINGS DAY. Jan 6. Major festival of Christian Church (esp. Eastern Orthodox) observed in many parts of the world with gifts, feasting, last lighting of Christmas lights, and burning of Christmas greens. Twelfth and last day of Feast of the Nativity. Commemorates visit of the Three Wise Men (Kings) to Bethlehem.

TWELFTH DAY or EPIPHANY. Jan 6. Known also as Old Christmas Day and Twelfth-tide. This, the twelfth day after Christmas celebrates the visit of the Magi, the first Gentile recognition of Christ. The Epiphany of Our Lord, one of the oldest Christian feasts, is observed in Roman Catholic churches in the U.S. on a Sunday between Jan 2 and 8. Theophany, of the Orthodox Church in America, is observed on this day in churches using the Gregorian calendar, and on Jan 19 in those churches using the Julian calendar.

January 1986

S	M	T	W	T	F	S
			1	2	3	4
5	6	7	8	9	10	11
12	13	14	15	16	17	18
19	20	21	22	23	24	25
26	27	28	29	30	31	

WISE, ROBERT ELLSWORTH, JR: BIRTHDAY. Jan 6. U.S. Representative of West Virginia's 3rd district, Democrat, of Clendenin, WV, born in Washington, DC, on Jan 6, 1948.

ZSCHAU, ED: BIRTHDAY. Jan 6. U.S. Representative of California's 12th district, Republican, of Los Altos, CA, born in Omaha, NE, on Jan 6, 1940.

JANUARY 7 — TUESDAY
7th Day — Remaining, 358

BULLFINCH EXCHANGE FESTIVAL (USOKAE). Jan 7. Dazaifu, Fukuoka Prefecture, Japan. "Good Luck" gilded wood bullfinches, mixed among many plain ones, are sought after by the throngs as priests of the Dazaifu Shrine pass them out in the dim light of a small bonfire.

ENGLAND: WCT WORLD DOUBLES TENNIS CHAMPIONSHIP. Jan 7-12. Royal Albert Hall, London. Top-class tennis from some of the best doubles players in the world. Organizer: World Championship Tennis.

FILLMORE, MILLARD: BIRTHDAY. Jan 7. Thirteenth President of the U.S. (July 10, 1850-Mar 3, 1853). Fillmore succeeded to the presidency upon the death of Zachary Taylor, but was unsuccessful in getting hoped-for nomination from his party in 1852. He ran for president in 1856 as candidate of the "Know-Nothing Party," whose platform demanded, among other things, that every government employee (federal, state and local), should be a native born citizen. Fillmore was born at Summerhill, NY, Jan 7, 1800, and died at Buffalo, NY, Mar 8, 1874. Now his birthday is often occasion for parties for which there is no other reason.

FIRST BALLOON FLIGHT ACROSS ENGLISH CHANNEL: ANNIVERSARY. Jan 7. Dr. John Jeffries, a Boston physician, and Jean-Pierre Blanchard, French aeronaut, on Jan 7, 1785, crossed the English Channel from Dover to Calais, landing in a forest after being forced to throw overboard all ballast, equipment and even most of their clothing to avoid forced landing in the icy waters of the English Channel. Blanchard's trousers are said to have been the last article thrown overboard.

GERMANY: MUNICH FASCHING CARNIVAL. Jan 7-Feb 11. From Jan 7 until Shrove Tuesday is Munich's famous carnival season. Costume balls popular throughout carnival. "High points on Fasching Sunday and Shrove Tuesday with great carnival doings outside at the Viktualienmarkt and on the Pedestrian Mall."

INTERLOCHEN ARTS ACADEMY. Jan 7-May 31. Concerts, art exhibitions, dance and drama productions and readings featuring students from each of the academy's fine arts divisions. Faculty concerts and well-known performers. Info from: Interlochen Arts Academy, Bruce W. Galbraith, Dir, Interlochen, MI 49643.

JAPAN: NANAKUSA. Jan 7. Festival dates back to the seventh century and recalls the seven plants served to the Emperor which are believed to have great medicinal value (shepherd's purse, chickweed, parsley, cottonweed, radish, hotoke-no-za and aona).

MATTINGLY, MACK: BIRTHDAY. Jan 7. U.S. Senator from Georgia, Republican, of St. Simons Island, GA, born in Anderson, IN, Jan 7, 1931.

MONTGOLFIER, JACQUES ETIENNE: BIRTHDAY. Jan 7. French merchant and inventor. With his older brother, Joseph Michel (q.v.), in Nov 1782, conducted experiments with paper and fabric bags filled with smoke and hot air, which led to invention of the hot air balloon and man's first flight. Died at Serrieres, Aug 2, 1799. See also entries for June 5 and Nov 1.

COPYRIGHT © 1985 BY WILLIAM D. CHASE and HELEN M. CHASE

JANUARY 8 — WEDNESDAY

8th Day — Remaining, 357

BATTLE OF NEW ORLEANS: ANNIVERSARY. Jan 8. British forces suffered crushing losses (over 2,000 casualties) in attack on New Orleans, Jan 8, 1815. Defending U.S. troops were led by General Andrew Jackson who became popular hero as result of victory. Tragically, neither side knew that the war had ended two weeks earlier, on Dec 24, 1814, with the signing of the Treaty of Ghent. Battle of New Orleans Day is observed in Louisiana and Massachusetts.

BIDDLE, NICHOLAS: BICENTENNIAL BIRTH ANNIVERSARY. Jan 8. American lawyer, diplomat, statesman, financier and scholar (completed his university studies at age 13) was born at Philadelphia, PA, on Jan 8, 1786, and died there on Feb 27, 1844.

COLLINS, WILLIAM WILKIE: BIRTHDAY. Jan 8. English novelist, author of *The Moonstone*, *The Woman in White*, and *The Dead Secret*, born at London, Jan 8, 1824. Died there, Sept 23, 1889.

GORTON, SLADE: BIRTHDAY. Jan 8. U.S. Senator from Washington, Republican, of Olympia, WA, born in Chicago, IL, on Jan 8, 1928.

MIDWIFE'S DAY. Jan 8. Greece. On St. Dominique's Day (Jan 8) in the villages of Eastern Macedonia and Thrace, Midwife's Day is celebrated to honor the midwife (Babo) of each village. On this day men must stay indoors while wives celebrate with food and wine. Gifts for the midwife, many interesting customs and songs. Men caught outside "will be stripped...and drenched with cold water." Info from: Greek Natl Tourist Organization, 168 N Michigan Ave, Chicago, IL 60601.

NATIONAL JOYGERM DAY. Jan 8. Purpose: "A day when Joygerms unfurled all over the world, hug, grin, smile and win over at least one gruff and grumpy grouch to the Joygerm Generation. The no dues-just do club devoted to spreading joy and cheer." Info from: Joygerm Joan E. White, Joygerms Unltd, Box 219, Eastwood Sta, Syracuse, NY 13206.

NATIONAL WESTERN STOCK SHOW. Jan 8-19. Denver Coliseum, Denver, CO. Purpose: "World's largest livestock show." Auctions, 4-H and FFA events, commercial exhibits and 23 rodeos. Sponsor: Western Stock Show Assn, 1325 E 46th Ave, Denver, CO 80216.

PEOPLE'S REPUBLIC OF CHINA: ANNIVERSARY OF DEATH OF CHOU. Jan 8. Anniversary of the death in 1976 of Chou En-Lai, Premier of the State Council of the People's Republic of China. Info from: Shanghai Travel & Tourism Administration, 14 Zhongshan Road (E.1), Shanghai.

PRESLEY: ELVIS (ARON): BIRTHDAY. Jan 8. Popular American rock singer, born Tupelo, MS, Jan 8, 1935. Died, Memphis, TN, Aug 16, 1977.

ST. GUDULA'S FEAST DAY. Jan 8. Virgin, patron saint of the City of Brussels, died Jan 8, probably in the year 712. Her relics were transferred finally to the church of St. Michael, in Brussels.

SPACE MILESTONE: LUNA 21 (USSR). Jan 8. Unmanned vehicle, launched Jan 8, 1973, landed on moon Jan 16, carrying Lunakhod, radio-controlled vehicle which explored 37-km distance over 4-month period. Jan 8, 1973.

JANUARY 9 — THURSDAY

9th Day — Remaining, 356

AVIATION IN AMERICA: BIRTHDAY. Jan 9. A Frenchman, Jean Pierre Blanchard, made the first manned free-balloon flight in America's history on Jan 9, 1793, at Philadelphia. The event was watched by President George Washington and many other high government officials. The hydrogen-filled balloon rose to a height of about 5,800 feet, travelled some 15 miles and landed 46 minutes later. Reportedly Blanchard had a passenger on the flight—a little black dog.

CATT, CARRIE LANE CHAPMAN: BIRTHDAY. Jan 9. American women's rights leader, founder (in 1919) of National League of Women Voters, born at Ripon, WI, Jan 9, 1859. Died at New Rochelle, NY, Mar 9, 1947.

CONNECTICUT: RATIFICATION DAY. Jan 9. Fifth State to ratify constitution, on this day in 1788.

GARCIA, ROBERT: BIRTHDAY. Jan 9. U.S. Representative of New York's 18th district, Democrat, of Bronx, NY, born in New York, Jan 9, 1933.

NEW YORK NATIONAL BOAT SHOW. Jan 9-19. New York Coliseum, New York, NY. Info from: Natl Marine Mfr, 353 Lexington Ave, New York, NY 10016.

NIXON, RICHARD MILHOUS: BIRTHDAY. Jan 9. Richard Nixon served as 36th Vice President of the U.S. (under President Dwight D. Eisenhower) Jan 20, 1953 to Jan 20, 1961. He was the 37th President of the U.S., serving Jan 20, 1969 to Aug 9, 1974 when he resigned the presidency while under threat of impeachment. Born at Yorba Linda, CA, Jan 9, 1913. First U.S. President to resign that office.

PANAMA: MARTYRS' DAY. Jan 9. Public holiday in Panama.

PHILIPPINES: FEAST OF THE BLACK NAZARENE. Jan 9. Culmination of a nine day fiesta, Manila's largest procession takes place in the afternoon of Jan 9, in honor of the Black Nazarene, whose shrine is at the Quiapo Church.

ST. GERMAIN, FERNAND JOSEPH: BIRTHDAY. Jan 9. U.S. Representative of Rhode Island's 1st district, Democrat, of Woonsocket, RI, born at Blackstone, MA, on Jan 9, 1928.

WORLDWIDE KIWANIS WEEK. Jan 9-25. Purpose: To encourage the creation of permanent relationships between Kiwanis clubs in different parts of the world. Sponsor: Program Development Dept, Kiwanis Internatl, 3636 Woodview Trace, Indianapolis, IN 46268.

JANUARY 10 — FRIDAY

10th Day — Remaining, 355

ALLEN, ETHAN: BIRTHDAY. Jan 10. Revolutionary War hero and leader of the Vermont "Green Mountain Boys," born at Litchfield, CT, Jan 10, 1738. Died at Burlington, VT, Feb 12, 1789.

ART DECO FESTIVAL. Jan 10-12. Miami Beach, FL. Walking and tram tours of Miami Beach's Art Deco District. Deco-oriented arts and crafts. Info from: Publicity Dept, City Hall, 1700 Convention Ctr Dr, Miami Beach, FL 33139.

HUMAN RELATIONS DAY. Jan 10. Purpose: To focus attention on human relations and acquisition of skills enabling achievement of the dreams of Dr Martin Luther King, Jr, for social justice for all mankind. Celebrated in the public schools of Flint, MI, as a tribute to Dr Martin Luther King, Jr, on the Friday nearest his birthday (Jan 15). Info from: Flint Community Schools, Len Blewett, Public Affairs Div, 923 E Kearsley St, Flint, MI 48502.

JEFFERS, ROBINSON: BIRTHDAY. Jan 10. American poet and playwright, born at Pittsburgh, PA, Jan 10, 1887. Died at Carmel, CA, Jan 20, 1962.

LEAGUE OF NATIONS: ANNIVERSARY. Jan 10. Through the Treaty of Versailles, the League of Nations came into existence on Jan 10, 1920, the effective date of the Treaty. Fifty nations entered into a Covenant designed to avoid war. The United States never joined the League of Nations which was dissolved on Apr 18, 1946.

COPYRIGHT © 1985 BY WILLIAM D. CHASE and HELEN M. CHASE

MOON PHASE: NEW MOON. Jan 10. Moon enters New Moon phase at 7:22 a.m., E.S.T.

SARATOGA ICE FISHING DERBY. Jan 10-12. Saratoga, WY. Prizes for fishermen who catch tagged fish in Saratoga Lake. Info from: Chamber of Commerce, Box 1095, Saratoga, WY 82331.

SPACE MILESTONE: SOYUZ 17 (USSR). Jan 10. Launched Jan 10, 1975, Cosmonauts A. Gubarev and G. Grechko completed 30-day space flight, landing Feb 9. Cosmonauts spent 28 days aboard Salyut 4, orbiting Space Station.

SPACE MILESTONE: SOYUZ 27 (USSR). Jan 10. Launched Jan 10, 1978, Cosmonauts Vladimir Dzhanibekov and Oleg Makarov linked with Salyut 6 space station which was already occupied by crew of Soyuz 26. Returned to Earth Jan 16 in Soyuz 26.

UNITED NATIONS GENERAL ASSEMBLY: ANNIVERSARY. Jan 10. On the 26th anniversary of the establishment of the unsuccessful League of Nations, delegates from 51 nations met in London, England, Jan 10, 1946, for the first meeting of the United Nations General Assembly.

JANUARY 11 — SATURDAY
11th Day — Remaining, 354

DE HOSTOS' BIRTHDAY. Jan 11. Puerto Rico. Celebrates birth on this day of Puerto Rican patriot and scholar, Eugenio Maria de Hostos (1839-1903).

FERRARY'S BIRTHDAY. Jan 11. Purpose: To observe the birthday of the internationally famous philatelist Philipp la Renotiere von Ferrary (1850-1917), who devoted his life to the study of stamps. Sponsor: The Philatelic Journalist, 154 Laguna Ct, St. Augustine Shores, FL 32086.

HALL, SAM BLAKELEY, JR: BIRTHDAY. Jan 11. U.S. Representative of Texas' 1st district, Democrat, of Marshall, TX, born in Marshall on Jan 11, 1924.

HAMILTON, ALEXANDER: BIRTHDAY. Jan 11. American statesman born, British West Indies, Jan 11, 1755 or 1757. Engaged in a duel with Aaron Burr early in the morning of July 11, 1804, at Weehawken, NJ. Mortally wounded there and died July 12, 1804.

HULA BOWL GAME. Jan 11. Aloha Stadium, Honolulu, Oahu, HI. College all-star football classic. Info from: Hawaii Visitors Bureau, Honolulu, HI 96815.

ICE FISHING CLINIC. Jan 11. Struble Lake, Honey Brook, PA. Participants learn basic techniques of ice fishing—when ice is safe, how to cut holes and what kind of lures and bait to use. Second Saturday in Jan. Info from: Chester County Parks & Recreation, 235 W Market St, West Chester, PA 19382.

JAMES, WILLIAM: BIRTHDAY. Jan 11. American psychologist and philosopher of distinguished family which included (his brother) novelist Henry James, was born at New York City on Jan 11, 1842. "There is no worse lie," he wrote in *Varieties of Religious Experience* (1902), "than a truth misunderstood by those who hear it." He died at Chocorua, NH, on Aug 26, 1910.

MACDONALD, JOHN A: BIRTHDAY. Jan 11. Canadian statesman, Sir John Alexander MacDonald, first prime minister of Canada, was born at Glasgow, Scotland, Jan 11, 1815. He died June 6, 1891. His birth anniversary is observed in Canada.

NEPAL: NATIONAL UNITY DAY. Jan 11. Kingdom-wide celebration paying homage to King Prithvinarayan Shah (1723-1775), founder of present house of rulers of Nepal and creator of the unified Nepal of today.

January *1986*	S	M	T	W	T	F	S
				1	2	3	4
	5	6	7	8	9	10	11
	12	13	14	15	16	17	18
	19	20	21	22	23	24	25
	26	27	28	29	30	31	

ORANGE BOWL MARATHON. Jan 11. Miami, FL. Starts in Miami Beach and ends in Coconut Grove. 26 miles, 385 yards beginning at 7 a.m. Runners from 42 states and 13 countries. Info from: Runners Internatl, 12306 SW 117 Court, Miami, FL 33186.

PAUL, ALICE: BIRTHDAY. Jan 11. Anniversary of the birth of Alice Paul, women's rights leader and founder of the National Woman's Party, in 1913, advocate of an equal rights amendment to the U.S. Constitution. Born at Moorestown, NJ, Jan 11, 1885. Died there, July 10, 1977.

PAUL BUNYAN SLED DOG RACES. Jan 11-12. Lake Bemidji, Bemidji, MN. Sponsor: Bemidji Chamber of Commerce and Tuffy's Dog Food. Info from: Todd Jansen, Box 850, Bemidji, MN 56601.

QUILLEN, JAMES H: BIRTHDAY. Jan 11. U.S. Representative of Tennessee's 1st district, Republican, of Kingsport, TN, born near Gate City, Scott County, VA, Jan 11, 1916.

JANUARY 12 — SUNDAY
12th Day — Remaining, 353

ANNUNZIO, FRANK: BIRTHDAY. Jan 12. U.S. Representative of Illinois' 11th district, Democrat, of Chicago, IL, born there Jan 12, 1915.

BURKE, EDMUND: BIRTHDAY. Jan 12. British orator, politician, and philosopher, born Dublin, Ireland, Jan 12, 1729. "Superstition is the religion of feeble minds," he wrote in 1790, but best remembered is "The only thing necessary for the triumph of evil is for good men to do nothing," not found in his writings but almost universally attributed to Burke. Died Beaconsfield, England, July 9, 1797.

FUSTER, JAIME B: BIRTHDAY. Jan 12. Commonwealth of Puerto Rico Resident Commissioner, 99th Congress, Democrat, (Popular Democratic Party) of Santurce, PR, born in Guayama, PR, on Jan 12, 1941.

LONDON, JACK: BIRTHDAY. Jan 12. American author of more than fifty books: short stories, novels, travel, stories of the sea and of the far north, many marked by brutal realism. He was born at San Francisco, CA, on Jan 12, 1876, and died near Santa Rosa, CA, Nov 22, 1916.

McEWEN, BOB: BIRTHDAY. Jan 12. U.S. Representative of Ohio's 6th district, Republican, of Hillsboro, OH, born there Jan 12, 1950.

MAN WATCHERS WEEK. Jan 12-18. Purpose: A week of appreciation for men who are well worth watching. Announcement of the ten most watchable men in the world. Sponsor: Suzy Mallery's Man Watchers, Inc. Suzy Mallery, 8033 Sunset, #363, Los Angeles, CA 90046.

MISSION SANTA CLARA DE ASIS ANNIVERSARY. Jan 12. California mission to the Indians founded Jan 12, 1777.

NATIONAL RETAIL MERCHANTS ASSOCIATION 75TH CONVENTION AND EXPOSITION. Jan 12-15. New York, NY. Info from: Michelle Bradlyn, NRMA, 100 W 31st St, New York, NY 10001.

PRINTING WEEK. Jan 12-18. Sponsor: Intl Assn of Printing House Craftsmen, 7599 Kenwood Rd, Cincinnati, OH 45236.

SWITZERLAND: MEITLISUNNTIG. Jan 12. On Meitlisunntig, the second Sunday in January, the girls of Meisterschwanden and Fahrwangen, in the Seetal district of Aargau, Switzerland, stage a procession in historical uniforms and a military parade before a feminine General Staff. According to tradition, the custom dates from the Villmergen War of 1712, when the women of both communes gave vital help that led to victory. Popular festival follows the processions.

TANZANIA: ZANZIBAR REVOLUTION DAY. Jan 12. National Day. Zanzibar became independent in Dec 1963, under a Sultan.

COPYRIGHT © 1985 BY WILLIAM D. CHASE and HELEN M. CHASE

JANUARY 13 — MONDAY

13th Day — Remaining, 352

ALGER, HORATIO, JR: BIRTHDAY. Jan. 13. American clergyman and author of more than 100 popular books for boys (some 20 million copies sold). Born at Revere, MA, Jan 13, 1834. Died at Natick, MA, July 18, 1899. Honesty, frugality and hard work assured that the heroes of his books would find success, wealth and fame.

CHASE, SALMON PORTLAND: BIRTHDAY. Jan. 13. American statesman, born at Cornish, NH, Jan 13, 1808. U.S. Senator, Secretary of the Treasury and Chief Justice of the Supreme Court. Salmon P. Chase, much of whose life was devoted to fighting slavery (popularly known as "attorney general for runaway Negroes") one of the founders of the Republican Party, whose hopes for becoming candidate (1856 and 1860) for President of the U.S. were dashed because his unconcealed anti-slavery views made him unacceptable, died at New York City, May 7, 1873. His portrait may be seen on U.S. currency (the $10,000 bill).

CUCKOO DANCING WEEK. Jan. 13-19. Purpose: To honor the memory of Laurel & Hardy whose theme, "The Dancing Cuckoos," shall be heard throughout the land as their movies are seen and their antics greeted by laughter in preparation for annual Sons of Desert Banquet in June in NYC. Sponsor: New Original Dancing Cuckoos of Lake Superior State College Unicorn Hunters, W.T. Rabe or Laurel and Hardy biographer John C. McCabe, Lake Superior State College, Sault Ste. Marie, MI 49783.

INTERNATIONAL PIANOFORTE COMPETITION PRETORIA 1986. Jan. 13-23. Info from: Professor Hennie Joubexrt, University of South Africa, Box 392, Pretoria, South Africa.

MADIGAN, EDWARD R: BIRTHDAY. Jan. 13. U.S. Representative of Illinois' 15th district, Republican, of Lincoln, IL, born there on Jan 13, 1936.

PLOUGH MONDAY. Jan. 13. England. Always the Monday after Twelfth Day . . . a time when work on the farm is resumed after the festivities of the twelve days of Christmas. On preceding Sunday ploughs may be blessed in churches. Celebrated with dances and plays.

STEPHEN FOSTER MEMORIAL DAY. Jan. 13. Presidential ☆ Proclamation 2957, Dec 13, 1951 (designating Jan 13, 1952), covers all succeeding years. (PL82-225 of Oct 27, 1951). Observed on the anniversary of Foster's death at New York City, in 1864. See also Foster's birth anniversary: July 4.

TEXAS CITRUS FIESTA. Jan. 13-Feb 2. Purpose: To celebrate the citrus harvest. Product costume shows and Parade of Oranges. Info from: Texas Citrus Fiesta, Box 407, Mission, TX 78572.

JANUARY 14 — TUESDAY

14th Day — Remaining, 351

ARNOLD, BENEDICT: BIRTHDAY. Jan. 14. American officer who deserted to the British during the Revolutionary War and whose name has since become synonymous with treachery. Born on Jan 14, 1741, Norwich, CT. Died June 14, 1801.

BULGARIA: VINEGROWER'S DAY. Jan. 14. Ancient holiday rite called Trifon Zarezan is inherited from the Thracians. Early in morning vines are pruned. Vinegrowers then sprinkle the pruned vine shoots with wine from a decorated wooden vessel, with wishes for fertility. Vine king chosen, followed by a feast in the meadow, with music, dancing and horse racing.

FORT WORTH BOAT SHOW. Jan. 14-19. Fort Worth. Info from: Tarrant County Conv Ctr, 1111 Houston St, Fort Worth, TX 76102.

JULIAN CALENDAR NEW YEAR'S DAY. Jan. 14. Begins year 6699 of the Julian Period.

NATIONAL PRINTING INK DAY. Jan. 14. Purpose: To highlight the essential contribution of printing inks to the dissemination of knowledge, culture, education and entertainment through service to the graphic arts and communications industries. Sponsor: Natl Assn of Printing Ink Mfrs, 550 Mamaroneck Ave, Harrison, NY 10528.

RATIFICATION DAY. Jan. 14. Anniversary of the act which officially ended the American Revolution and established the United States as a sovereign power. On Jan 14, 1784, the Continental Congress, meeting at Annapolis, Maryland, ratified the Treaty of Paris, thus fulfilling the Declaration of Independence of July 4, 1776.

SCHWEITZER, ALBERT: BIRTHDAY. Jan. 14. Alsatian philosopher, musician, physician, and winner of the 1952 Nobel Peace Prize, born Kayserberg, Upper Alsace, Jan 14, 1875. Died, Lambarene, Gabon, Sept 4, 1965.

SPACE MILESTONE: SOYUZ 4 (USSR). Jan. 14. First docking of two manned spacecraft (with Soyuz 5) and first interchange of spaceship personnel in orbit. Launch date was Jan 14, 1969.

WHIPPLE, WILLIAM: BIRTHDAY. Jan. 14. American patriot and signer of the Declaration of Independence. Born at Kittery, ME, on Jan 14, 1730. He died at Portsmouth, NH, on Nov 10, 1785.

JANUARY 15 — WEDNESDAY

15th Day — Remaining, 350

ACE, GOODMAN: BIRTHDAY. Jan. 15. Radio and TV writer, actor, columnist and humorist, Goodman Ace was born at Kansas City, MO, Jan 15, 1899. With his wife, Jane, created and acted the popular series of radio programs (1928-1945), "Easy Aces." Called "America's greatest wit," by Fred Allen, Goodman Ace died at New York City, Mar 25, 1982, soon after asking that his tombstone be inscribed "No flowers, please, I'm allergic."

ADULTS DAY. Jan. 15. Japan. National holiday. Day is set apart for youth of the country who have reached adulthood.

BRITISH MUSEUM ANNIVERSARY. Jan. 15. On Jan 15, 1759, the British Museum opened its doors at Montague House in London. Incorporated by Act of Parliament in 1753, following the death of British medical doctor and naturalist, Sir Hans Sloane, who had bequeathed his personal collection of books, manuscripts, coins, medals and antiquities to Britain. As the national museum and the national library of the United Kingdom the British Museum houses many of the world's most prized treasures.

GOLF: BOB HOPE CLASSIC. Jan. 15-19. Info from: Cliff Brown Public Relations, 39000 Bob Hope Dr, Rancho Mirage, CA 92270.

KING, MARTIN LUTHER, JR: BIRTH ANNIVERSARY. Jan. 15. Black civil rights leader, minister and recipient of the Nobel Peace Prize (1964), Martin Luther King, Jr, was born at Atlanta, GA, on Jan 15, 1929. He was assassinated at Memphis, TN, Apr 4, 1968. After his death many states and territories observed his birthday as a holiday. In 1983 the

COPYRIGHT © 1985 BY WILLIAM D. CHASE and HELEN M. CHASE

Congress approved HR 3706, "A bill to amend title 5, United States Code, to make the birthday of Martin Luther King, Jr, a legal public holiday." Signed by the president on Nov 2, 1983, it became Public Law 98-144. The law, effective "on the first January 1 that occurs after the two-year period following the date of the enactment of this Act," (1986) sets "the third Monday in January" for observance of King's birthday. First observance: Jan 20, 1986.

LIVINGSTON, PHILIP: BIRTHDAY. Jan 15. Merchant and signer of the Declaration of Independence, born, Albany, NY, Jan 15, 1716. Died, York, PA, June 12, 1778.

MOLIERE DAY. Jan 15. Most celebrated of French authors and dramatists, Jean Baptiste Poquelin, baptized at Paris, Jan 15, 1622, took the stage name, Moliere, when he was about 22 years old. While playing in a performance of his last play, *Le Malade Imaginaire* (about a hypochondriac afraid of death), Moliere became ill, and died within a few hours, Paris, Feb 17, 1673.

QUARTERLY ESTIMATED FEDERAL INCOME TAX PAYERS' DUE DATE. Jan 15. For those individuals whose fiscal year is the calendar year and who make quarterly estimated federal income tax payments, today is one of the due dates. (Jan 15, Apr 15, June 16, and Sept 15, 1986.)

JANUARY 16 — THURSDAY
16th Day — Remaining, 349

ALEXANDER, WILLIAM VOLLIE (BILL) JR: BIRTHDAY. Jan 16. U.S. Representative of Arkansas' 1st district, Democrat, of Osceola, AR, was born at Memphis, TN, Jan 16, 1934.

AUSTIN BOAT, SPORT & MOTORCYCLE SHOW. Jan 16-19. Palmer Auditorium, Austin, TX. Purpose: To highlight travel, water recreation, resorts and allied boating and recreational equipment. Info from: Highland Lakes Tourist Assn, Carol Stuewe, Dir, Box 1967, Austin, TX 78767.

DEAN, DIZZY: BIRTHDAY. Jan 16. Jay Hanna "Dizzy" Dean, major league pitcher (St. Louis Cardinals) and Baseball Hall of Fame member, was born at Lucas, AR, on Jan 16, 1911. Following his baseball playing career, Dean established himself as a radio and TV sports announcer and commentator, becoming famous for his innovative delivery. "He slud into third," reported Dizzy, who on another occasion explained that "Me and Paul (baseball player brother Paul "Daffy" Dean) . . . didn't get much education." Dean died at Reno, NV, July 17, 1974.

HALL, TONY P: BIRTHDAY. Jan 16. U.S. Representative of Ohio's 3rd district, Democrat, of Dayton, OH, born in Dayton on Jan 16, 1942.

INTERNATIONAL FINALS RODEO. Jan 16-19. Tulsa Assembly Ctr, Tulsa, OK. Top cowboys and cowgirls in national and regional standings compete for world championships in seven contests. Sponsor: Internatl Professional Rodeo Assn, Sandy Fulmer, Media Dept, Box 615, Pauls Valley, OK 73075.

JAPAN: HARU-NO-YABUIRI. Jan 16. Employees and servants who have been working over the holidays are given a day off.

MERMAN, ETHEL: BIRTHDAY. Jan 16. Musical-comedy star famous for her belting voice and brassy style. Born Ethel Agnes Zimmerman on Jan 16, 1908, 1909 or 1912 (the date changed the older she got) at Queens, New York. Died Feb 15, 1984, in New York City.

MICHELIN, ANDRE: BIRTHDAY. Jan 16. French industrialist who along with his brother Edouard started the Michelin Tire Company in 1888, manufacturing bicycle tires. They were the first to use demountable pneumatic tires on cars. He was born on Jan 16, 1853, at Paris and died there on Apr 4, 1931.

NATIONAL NOTHING DAY ANNIVERSARY. Jan 16. Anniversary of National Nothing Day, an event created by newspaperman Harold Pullman Coffin, and first observed in 1973 "to provide Americans with one national day when they can just sit without celebrating, observing or honoring anything." Since 1975, though many other events have been listed on that day, light-hearted traditional observance of Coffin's idea has continued. Coffin, a native of Reno, NV, died at Capitola, CA, Sept 12, 1981, at age 76.

PROHIBITION AMENDMENT ANNIVERSARY. Jan 16. Nebraska became 36th state to ratify prohibition amendment on Jan 16, 1919, and the 18th Amendment became part of the U.S. Constitution. One year later, Jan 16, 1920, the 18th Amendment took effect and the sale of alcoholic beverages became illegal in the U.S., with the Volstead Act providing for enforcement. The 21st Amendment, repealing the 18th, went into effect Dec 5, 1933.

SERVICE, ROBERT WILLIAM: BIRTHDAY. Jan 16. Canadian poet, born at Preston, England, Jan 16, 1874. Lived in the Canadian northwest for many years and perhaps best remembered for such ballads as: "The Shooting of Dan McGrew," and "The Cremation of Sam McGee," and for such books as *Songs of a Sourdough, Rhymes of a Rolling Stone* and *The Spell of the Yukon*. Died in France, Sept 11, 1958.

JANUARY 17 — FRIDAY
17th Day — Remaining, 348

BLESSING OF THE ANIMALS AT THE CATHEDRAL. Jan 17. Mexico. Church of San Antonio in Mexico City or Xochimilco provide best sights of chickens, cows and household pets gaily decorated with flowers. (Saint's day for San Antonio Abad, patron saint of domestic animals.)

CONGRESS OF TEN OUTSTANDING YOUNG AMERICANS. Jan 17-18. Tulsa, OK. Purpose: To honor ten young men and women whose achievements or contributions in their profession, community, state or nation have been outstanding. Info from: U.S. Jaycees, PR Dept, Box 7, Tulsa, OK 74121.

FRANKLIN, BENJAMIN: BIRTHDAY. Jan 17. "Elder statesman of the American Revolution," oldest signer of both the Declaration of Independence and the Constitution, scientist, diplomat, author, printer, publisher, philosopher, philanthropist, and self-made, self-educated man. Author of *Poor Richard's Almanack*, 1733-1758. Born at Boston, Jan 17, 1706. Died at Philadelphia, Apr 17, 1790. Franklin's birthday is commemorated each year by the Poor Richard Club of Philadelphia, with graveside observance.

In 1728 Franklin wrote a premature epitaph for himself. It first appeared in print in Ames's 1771 almanac:

The Body of BENJAMIN FRANKLIN

Printer

Like the Covering of an old Book
Its contents torn out
And stript of its Lettering and Gilding,
Lies here, Food for Worms;
But the Work shall not be lost,
It will (as he believ'd) appear once more
In a New and more beautiful Edition
Corrected and amended
By the Author.
He was born January 6th 1706 and
died _____ 17___

January 1986

S	M	T	W	T	F	S
			1	2	3	4
5	6	7	8	9	10	11
12	13	14	15	16	17	18
19	20	21	22	23	24	25
26	27	28	29	30	31	

COPYRIGHT © 1985 BY WILLIAM D. CHASE and HELEN M. CHASE

HAT DAY. Jan 17. Purpose: To celebrate the multitude of head coverings that people wear around the world. "Put on your favorite hat today!" (Traditionally the third Friday in January.) Sponsor: Hat Day Education Committee, Peter Rawitsch, Chairperson, Glenmont Elementary School, Route 9W, Glenmont, NY 12077.

HUTCHINS, ROBERT MAYNARD: BIRTHDAY. Jan 17. American educator, foundation executive and civil liberties activist, was born at Brooklyn, NY, on Jan 17, 1899. He was president and later chancellor of the University of Chicago where he introduced many educational concepts including the Great Books program. Hutchins died at Santa Barbara, CA, on May 14, 1977.

MOON PHASE: FIRST QUARTER. Jan 17. Moon enters First Quarter phase at 5:13 p.m., E.S.T.

PHILIPPINES: CONSTITUTION DAY. Jan 17. National. Simple rites to commemorate the 1935 ratification of the amended Philippine constitution.

POLAND: LIBERATION DAY. Jan 17. Celebration of liberation from Nazi oppression on Jan 17, 1945, of the City of Warsaw, by Soviet troops. Special ceremonies at the Monument to the Unknown Soldier, in Warsaw's Victory Square (which had been called Adolf Hitler Platz during the German occupation).

ST. ANTHONY'S DAY. Jan 17. Feast day honoring Egyptian hermit who became first Christian monk and who established communities of hermits; patron saint of domestic animals and patriarch of all monks. Lived about A.D. 251-354.

SEATTLE BOAT SHOW. Jan 17-26. The Kingdome, Seattle, WA. Info from: NW Marine Trade Assn, Mariner's Sq, Suite 233, 1900 N Northlake Way, Seattle, WA 98103.

THOMAS CRAPPER DAY. Jan 17. Possibly apochryphal stories claim this date as the anniversary of the death of Thomas Crapper, born at Thorpe, Yorkshire, England, in 1837 (exact date unknown). Died, Jan 17, 1910. Said to be prime developer of flush toilet mechanism as it is known today. Founder, London, 1861, of Thomas Crapper & Co, later patentees and manufacturers of sanitary appliances; Engineers by appointment to His majesty the King, and H.R.H., The Prince of Wales.

WALT DISNEY WORLD VILLAGE WINE FESTIVAL. Jan 17-19. Purpose: 60 wineries presented by vintners and winemakers presenting fine wines and wine related activities. Sponsor: Walt Disney World Village Wine Society, Carol Wilson, Chrmn, Box 35, Lake Buena Vista, FL 32830.

JANUARY 18 —SATURDAY

18th Day — Remaining, 347

CARROT FESTIVAL. Jan 18-26. Purpose: Carrot cooking contest, parade, tractor pull and art show, during carrot harvesting time. Sponsor: Holtville Chamber of Commerce, Box 185, Holtville, CA 92250.

CENTRAL FLORIDA ANTIQUE MARKET SHOW AND SALE. Jan 18-19. Volusia County Fairgrounds, DeLand, FL. Info from: Chamber of Commerce, Box 629, DeLand, FL 32721.

EVANS, JOHN V: BIRTHDAY. Jan 18. John V. Evans, Governor of Idaho, Democrat, was born at Malad, ID, on Jan 18, 1925.

INTERNATIONAL SIDE-SADDLE AWARDS BANQUET AND SEMINAR. Jan 18. Purpose: To certify new side-saddle riding judges and instructors, and recognize national champions in side-saddle riding. Sponsor: The Internatl Side-Saddle Organization, RD 2 Box 2055, Mt Holly, NJ 08060.

PHILADELPHIA SPORTS AND RECREATIONAL VEHICLE SHOW. Jan 18-26. Philadelphia Civic Ctr. Displays, exhibits and entertainment. Info from: Conv & Visitors Bureau, Three Penn Ctr Plaza, Suite 2020, Philadelphia, PA 19102.

PHILIPPINES: ATI-ATIHAN FESTIVAL. Jan 18-19. The Ati-Atihan Festival, held at Kalibo, Aklan province annually on the third weekend in January is one of the most colorful celebrations in the Philippines. It commemorates the peace pact between the Ati of Panay (pygmies) and the Malays who were early migrants in the islands. The townspeople blacken their bodies with soot, don colorful and bizarre costumes, and sing and dance in the streets. The festival also celebrates the Feast Day of Santo Nino (the infant Jesus).

POOH DAY. Jan 18. Anniversary of the birth of A(lan) A(lexander) Milne, English author, especially remembered for his children's stories, classics of their kind, about *Winnie the Pooh*, and *The House at Pooh Corner*. Also the author of *Mr. Pim Passes By*, *When We Were Very Young* and *Now We Are Six*, he was born at London, Jan 18, 1882, and died at Hartfield, England, Jan 31, 1956.

ROGET, PETER MARK: BIRTHDAY. Jan 18. English physician, best known as author of Roget's *Thesaurus of English Words and Phrases*, first published in 1852, but he was also the inventor of the "log-log" slide rule. Born at London, Jan 18, 1779. Died at West Malvern, Worcestershire, Sept 12, 1869.

TIP-UP TOWN USA ICE FESTIVAL. Jan 18-19. (Also Jan 25-26.) Houghton Lake, MI. Activities on ice. Torchlight parade, ice sculpturing, fishing, games and contests. Info from: Chamber of Commerce, Houghton Lake, MI 48629.

TUNISIA: NATIONAL HOLIDAY. Jan 18. Public holiday for Tunisian Revolution Day.

VERSAILLES PEACE CONFERENCE: ANNIVERSARY. Jan 18. French president Raymond Poincare formally opened the (World War I) Peace Conference at Versailles, France, Jan 18, 1919. It proceeded under the chairmanship of Georges Clemenceau. In May the Conference disposed of Germany's colonies and delivered a treaty to the German delegates on May 7, 1919, fourth anniversary of the sinking of the *Lusitania*. Final treaty signing ceremonies were completed at the palace in Versailles, on June 28, 1919.

WEBSTER, DANIEL: BIRTHDAY. Jan 18. American statesman and orator who said, on Apr 6, 1830, "The people's government, made for the people, made by the people, and answerable to the people." Born at Salisbury, NH, Jan 1782. Died at Marshfield, MA, Oct 24, 1852.

YUMA FIDDLER'S CONTEST. Jan 18-19. Info from: Yuma Jaycees, Box 2797, Yuma, AZ 85364.

JANUARY 19 — SUNDAY

19th Day — Remaining, 346

CONFEDERATE HEROES DAY. Jan 19. Texas. Observed on Robert E. Lee's birthday.

JAYCEE WEEK. Jan 19-25. Purpose: A nation-wide observance of the founding of the Jaycee movement. Info from: U.S. Jaycees, PR Dept, Box 7, Tulsa, OK 74121.

LEE, ROBERT EDWARD: BIRTHDAY. Jan 19. Greatest military leader of the Confederacy, he was the son of Revolutionary War General Henry (Light Horse Harry) Lee. His surrender, Apr 9, 1865, to Union General Ulysses S. Grant brought an end to the Civil War. Lee was born in Westmoreland County, VA, Jan 19, 1807. Died at Lexington, VA, Oct 12, 1870. His birthday is observed on this day in Arkansas, Georgia, Louisiana, South Carolina and Texas. Observed on third Monday in Jan in Alabama and Mississippi.

PACKARD, RON: BIRTHDAY. Jan 19. U.S. Representative of California's 43rd district, Republican, of Carlsbad, CA, born in Meridian, ID, on Jan 19, 1931.

POE, EDGAR ALLAN: BIRTHDAY. Jan 19. American poet and story writer, called "America's most famous man of letters," was born at Boston, MA, Jan 19, 1809. He was orphaned, in dire poverty, in 1811, and was raised by Virginia merchant John Allan. In 1836, he married his 13-year-old cousin, Virginia Clemm. A magazine editor of note, he is best remembered for his poetry (especially "The Raven") and for his tales of suspense. Alcohol addiction, a problem throughout his life, was the immediate cause of his death, at Baltimore, MD, Oct 7, 1849.

SMITH, DENNY: BIRTHDAY. Jan 19. U.S. Representative of Oregon's 5th District, Republican, of Salem, OR, Born in Ontario, OR, on Jan 19, 1938.

THOMAS, ISAIAH: BIRTHDAY. Jan 19. American printer, editor, almanac-publisher, and historian. Born Jan 19, 1749, Boston, MA. Died, Apr 4, 1831, Worcester, MA.

WAR CRIMES TRIAL (JAPAN): ANNIVERSARY. Jan 19. An international tribunal for the trial of far eastern war criminals was appointed by General Douglas MacArthur on Jan 19, 1946. The trial began at Tokyo on May 3, 1946, and ended more than two years later when the judgments were read, Nov 4-12, 1948. Of the 28 defendants 25 were brought to trial. Seven were sentenced to death by hanging (see entry for Dec 23), 16 were sentenced to life imprisonment, and two were given lesser prison terms.

WATT, JAMES: BIRTH ANNIVERSARY. Jan 19. Scottish engineer and inventor born in Greenock, Scotland on Jan 19, 1736. The modern steam engine grew out of his efficiency-improving inventions. He died at Heathfield, England, on Aug 19, 1819.

WORLD RELIGION DAY. Jan 19. Purpose: To proclaim the oneness of religion and the belief that religion will cause the unity of the world's peoples. Always the third Sunday in January. Info from: Baha'i Office of Public Affairs, Baha'i Natl Center, Wilmette, IL 60091.

JANUARY 20 — MONDAY
20th Day — Remaining, 345

AQUARIUS, THE WATER CARRIER. Jan 20-Feb 19. In the astronomical/astrological Zodiac, which divides the Sun's apparent orbit into twelve segments, the period Jan 20-Feb 18 is identified, traditionally, as the Sun-sign of Aquarius, the Water Carrier. The ruling planet is Uranus or Saturn.

BRAZIL: NOSSO SENHOR DO BONFIM FESTIVAL. Jan 20-30. Salvador, Bahia, Brazil. "Our Lady of the Happy Ending" Festival is one of Salvador's most colorful religious feasts. Climax comes with people carrying water to pour over church stairs and sidewalks to cleanse them of impurities.

BULGARIA: BABIN DEN. Jan 20. Celebrated throughout Bulgaria as Grandmother's Day. Traditional festivities.

GIBBONS, SAM M: BIRTHDAY. Jan 20. U.S. Representative of Florida's 7th district, Democrat, of Tampa, FL, born there Jan 20, 1920.

GUINEA-BISSAU: NATIONAL HEROES DAY. Jan 20. National holiday in the Republic of Guinea-Bissau.

January 1986

S	M	T	W	T	F	S
			1	2	3	4
5	6	7	8	9	10	11
12	13	14	15	16	17	18
19	20	21	22	23	24	25
26	27	28	29	30	31	

KING, MARTIN LUTHER, JR: BIRTHDAY OBSERVED. Jan 20. Public Law 98-144 provides for the observance as a legal public holiday of the birthday of Martin Luther King, Jr on the third Monday in January, beginning in 1986. See also his birth anniversary, Jan 15.

LEE-JACKSON DAY. Jan 20. Virginia. (Third Monday in January).

NATIONAL CLEAN-OFF-YOUR-DESK DAY. Jan 20. Purpose: To provide one day early each year for every desk worker to see the top of the desk and prepare for the following year's paper work. Observed on the third Monday in January. Sponsor: A.C. Moeller, Box 71, Clio, MI 48420.

SAN SEBASTIAN'S DAY. Jan 20. Patron of Rio de Janeiro, Brazil.

U.S. REVOLUTIONARY WAR: CESSATION OF HOSTILITIES. Jan 20. On Jan 20, 1783, The British and U.S. Commissioners signed a preliminary "Cessation of Hostilities," which was ratified by England's King George III on Feb 14, and which led to the Treaties of Paris and Versailles, Sept 3, 1783, ending the war.

JANUARY 21 — TUESDAY
21st Day — Remaining, 344

ANNIVERSARY OF NIKOLAI LENIN'S DEATH. Jan 21. U.S.S.R. (April 9, 1870-Jan 21, 1924).

BALDWIN, ROGER NASH: BIRTHDAY. Jan 21. Founder of the American Civil Liberties Union, called the "country's unofficial agitator for, and defender of, its civil liberties," Roger Baldwin was born Jan 21, 1884, at Wellesley, MA. He died Aug 26, 1981, at Ridgewood, NJ.

BRECKINRIDGE, JOHN CABELL: BIRTHDAY. Jan 21. Fourteenth Vice President of the U.S. (1857-1861) born, Lexington, KY, Jan 21, 1821. Died there May 17, 1875.

CLARK, BARNEY: BIRTHDAY. Jan 21. Dr Barney Bailey Clark, a Des Moines, WA, dentist, the first person to receive a permanent artificial heart, was born at Provo, UT, on Jan 21, 1921. The artificial heart (made of polyurethane plastic and aluminum) was implanted Dec 2, 1982, at the University of Utah Medical Center, Salt Lake City, UT. Clark lived almost 112 days after implantation of the artificial heart, dying Mar 23, 1983.

FITCH, JOHN: BIRTHDAY. Jan 21. American inventor, clockmaker, gunsmith, surveyor and steamboat developer, born at East Windsor, CT, Jan 21, 1743. He died at Bardstown, KY, July 2, 1798.

JACKSON, THOMAS JONATHAN (STONEWALL): BIRTHDAY. Jan 21. Confederate General and one of the most famous soldiers of the American Civil War, best known as "Stonewall" Jackson, born at Clarksburg, WV, Jan 21, 1824. Died of wounds received in battle near Chancellorsville, VA, May 10, 1863.

KIWANIS INTERNATIONAL: ANNIVERSARY. Jan 21. First Kiwanis Club was chartered on Jan 21, 1915 at Detroit, MI.

NATIONAL HUGGING DAY. Jan 21. Purpose: Since hugging is something everyone can do and since it is a healthful form of touching, this day should be spent hugging anyone accepting the hug, especially family and friends. Sponsor: Kevin C. Zaborney, 10434 Ataberry Dr, Clio, MI 48420.

JANUARY 22 — WEDNESDAY
22nd Day — Remaining, 343

AMPERE, ANDRE: BIRTHDAY. Jan 22. French physicist noted for his work in the field of electromagnetism. The electrical unit "ampere" is named for him. Born Jan 22, 1775, at Poleymieux, Ampere died at Marseille on June 10, 1836.

BACON, FRANCIS: BIRTHDAY. Jan 22. English statesman and essayist, born London, Jan 22, 1561. One may guess that Bacon was of short stature as he wrote (*Apothegms*) "Wise

COPYRIGHT © 1985 BY WILLIAM D. CHASE and HELEN M. CHASE

nature did never put her precious jewels into a garret four stories hight: and therefore . . . exceeding tall men had ever very empty heads." Died London, Apr 9, 1626.

BYRON, GEORGE GORDON: BIRTHDAY. Jan 22. English poet, born, London, Jan 22, 1788. Died of fever, at Missolonghi, Greece, Apr 19, 1824.

GRIFFITH, DAVID (LEWELYN) WARK: BIRTHDAY. Jan 22. D.W. Griffith, pioneer producer-director in the American motion picture industry, best remembered for his film, *The Birth of a Nation* (1915), was born at LaGrange, KY, Jan 22, 1875. Died at Hollywood, CA, July 23, 1948.

ST. PAUL WINTER CARNIVAL. Jan 22-Feb 9. St. Paul, MN. 100th Anniversary of carnival. Highlights for the anniversary include a 15 story Ice Palace, artistry in snow and ice, fine arts entertainment and spectator and participative sporting events. Sponsor: The St. Paul Winter Carnival Assn, 339 Bremer Bldg, St. Paul, MN 55101.

ST. VINCENT: FEAST DAY. Jan 22. Spanish deacon and martyr who died A.D. 304. Patron saint of wine growers. Old weather lore says if there is sun on this day good wine crops may be expected in the ensuing season.

SAXTON, H. JAMES: BIRTHDAY. Jan 22. U.S. Representative of New Jersey's 13th district, Republican, of Vincentown, NJ, born at Nicholson, PA, Jan 22, 1943.

STRINDBERG, AUGUST: BIRTHDAY. Jan 22. Swedish novelist and dramatist often called Sweden's greatest playwright. Born on Jan 22, 1849, at Stockholm, he died there of cancer on May 14, 1912.

UPJOHN, RICHARD: BIRTHDAY. Jan 22. American architect and founder of the American Institute of Architects in 1857. A Gothic revivalist, he designed many churches. Among his works were Trinity Chapel, New York; Corn Exchange Bank Building, New York; Central Congregational Church, Boston. Born on Jan 22, 1802, at Shaftesbury, England. He died on Aug 17, 1878, at Garrison, NY.

JANUARY 23 — THURSDAY
23rd Day — Remaining, 342

CARPER, THOMAS RICHARD: BIRTHDAY. Jan 23. U.S. Representative at large from Delaware, Democrat, of New Castle, DE, born in Beckley, WV, Jan 23, 1947.

CLASH DAY. Jan 23. Rockford, OH. Purpose: All employes wear their most colorful mis-matched outfit to beat the midwinter doldrums and to bring a smile to our residents' faces. Sponsor: Dorothy Trisel, Activities Dir, Shane Hill Nursing Home, 10731 SR 118, Rockford, OH 45882.

HANCOCK, JOHN: BIRTH ANNIVERSARY. Jan 23. American patriot and statesman, first signer of the Declaration of Independence, born Jan 23, 1737 (Jan 12, 1736/7 Old Style) at Braintree, MA. Died, Quincy, MA, Oct 8, 1793. His name has become part of the American language, referring to any handwritten signature. "Put your John Hancock on that!"

HEWES, JOSEPH: BIRTHDAY. Jan 23. Signer of the Declaration of Independence, born Kingston, NJ, Jan 23, 1730. Died Nov 10, 1779.

LAUTENBERG, FRANK R: BIRTHDAY. Jan 23. U.S. Senator from New Jersey, Democrat, of Montclair, NJ, born in Paterson, NJ on Jan 23, 1924.

NATIONAL HANDWRITING DAY. Jan 23. Popularly observed on birthday of John Hancock to encourage more legible handwriting.

NATIONAL PIE DAY. Jan 23. Purpose: To focus attention on pie as an art form, gastronomical delight and the joy it has brought to millions. Sponsor: Charlie Papazian, Box 1825, Boulder, CO 80306.

ONE-TOOTH RHEE LANDING DAY. Jan 23. Purpose: Observed in vicinity of all government offices to celebrate beginning of "confusionist" branch of American "burrocracy." One-Tooth Rhee, mythical Korean inventor of custom of having each official wear four hats, so that contradictory sets of

instructions can be given over each job title. Sponsor: Puns Corps, Robert L. Birch, Coordinator, 3108 Dashiell Rd, Falls Church, VA 22042.

RECREATIONAL VEHICLE, BOAT AND MOBILE HOME SHOW. Jan 23-26. Yuma Civic and Convention Ctr, Yuma AZ. Info from: Dixie Green Promotions, Inc, 3141 W Christy Dr, Phoenix, AZ 85029.

RUSSO, MARTY: BIRTHDAY. Jan 23. U.S. Representative of Illinois' 3rd district, Democrat, of South Holland, IL, was born in Chicago, IL Jan 23, 1944.

SHUSTER, BUD: BIRTHDAY. Jan 23. U.S. Representative of Pennsylvania's 9th district, Republican, of Everett, PA, born in Glassport, PA, on Jan 23, 1932.

STENDHAL: BIRTHDAY. Jan 23. The French author, Marie Henri Beyle, whose best known pseudonym was Stendhal, was born at Grenoble, Jan 23, 1783. Best remembered are his novels, *The Red and the Black* (1831) and *The Charterhouse of Parma* (1839). He died at Paris, Mar 23, 1842.

STEWART, POTTER: BIRTHDAY. Jan 23. Associate Justice of the Supreme Court of the United States (ret.), nominated by Pres. Eisenhower on Jan 17, 1959. (Oath of Office, May 15, 1959.) Justice Stewart was born at Jackson, MI, on Jan 23, 1915. He retired in July 1981.

JANUARY 24 — FRIDAY
24th Day — Remaining, 341

ACHELIS, ELISABETH: BIRTHDAY. Jan 24. Calendar reform advocate, editor, author born Brooklyn, NY, Jan 24, 1880. Authored "The World Calendar." Proposed calendar made every year the same, with equal quarters, each year beginning on Sunday, Jan 1, and each date falling on same day of week every year. Died New York City, Feb 11, 1973.

ALPO INTERNATIONAL SLED DOG CHAMPIONSHIPS. Jan 24-26. Last Friday, Saturday and Sunday in January. Sponsor: Alpo Petfoods, Inc. Info from: Chamber of Commerce, 30 Main St, Saranac Lake, NY 12983.

BOLIVIA: ALACITIS FAIR. Jan 24-26. La Paz. Traditional annual celebration by Aymara Indians on this date with prayers and offerings to god of prosperity.

CALIFORNIA GOLD DISCOVERY ANNIVERSARY. Jan 24. James W. Marshal, an employee of John Sutter, accidentally discovered gold while building a sawmill near Coloma, on Jan 24, 1848. Efforts to keep the discovery secret failed, and the gold rush was quickly under way.

COLONIAL WEEKEND. Jan 24-26. Colonial Williamsburg, Williamsburg, VA. Tours with theme "Architecture: Williamsburg Before and After." Info from: Colonial Williamsburg, Box C, Williamsburg, VA 23187.

DWYER, BERNARD J: BIRTHDAY. Jan 24. U.S. Representative of New Jersey's 6th district, Democrat, of Edison, NJ, born in Perth Amboy, NJ, on Jan 24, 1921.

GORDON, BARTON JENNINGS: BIRTHDAY. Jan 24. U.S. Representative of Tennessee's 6th district, Democrat, of Murfreesboro, TN, born there on Jan 24, 1949.

HAWKINS, PAULA: BIRTHDAY. Jan 24. U.S. Senator from Florida, Republican, of Winter Park, FL, born in Salt Lake City, UT, on Jan 24, 1927.

COPYRIGHT © 1985 BY WILLIAM D. CHASE and HELEN M. CHASE

KASTENMEIER, ROBERT WILLIAM: BIRTHDAY. Jan 24. U.S. Representative of Wisconsin's 2nd district, Democrat, of Sun Prairie, WI, was born at Beaver Dam, WI, on Jan 24, 1924.

NATIONAL ACTIVITY PROFESSIONALS DAY. Jan 24. Purpose: To honor all persons working with or within activity departments of nursing homes, day care centers or retirement homes. Annually, fourth Friday of January. Sponsor: Natl Assn Activity Professionals, Box 274, Park Ridge, IL 60068.

SNO-FEST '86. Jan 24-25. Keene, NH. Purpose: To raise money for charities. Snow sculptures, hay rides, ski races and ice skating. Sponsor: Keene Parks & Recreation Dept and WKBK. Info from: WKBK, Debbie McDougle, Box 564, Keene, NH 03431.

SPACE MILESTONE: COSMOS 954 (USSR). Jan 24. Nuclear equipped reconnaissance satellite launched Sept 18, 1977, fell into Earth's atmosphere and burned over northern Canada. Some radioactive debris reached ground on Jan 24, 1978.

SPACE MILESTONE: DISCOVERY (US). Jan 24. Space shuttle *Discovery* launched from and returned to Kennedy Space Center, FL, (Jan 24-27) deploying eavesdropping satellite in secret, all military mission, Jan 24-27, 1985.

SPEEDO SWIMMING MEET. Jan 24-26. Amersfoort, Holland. Info from: Federation Internationale De Natation Amateur, 208-3540 W 41st Ave, Vancouver, BC, Canada V6N 3E6.

SPOUSE'S DAY. Jan 24. Purpose: A holiday in celebration of the spouse. Husbands and wives are encouraged to share jobs, roles and responsibilities so that they may better appreciate each other. Sponsor: WCUZ AM/FM Radio, Attn: Kevin B. Reynolds, PR Dir, One McKay Tower, Grand Rapids, MI 49503.

TOGO: ECONOMIC LIBERATION DAY. Jan 24. National holiday.

U.S. TELEVISION AND RADIO COMMERCIALS FESTIVAL. Jan 24. Chicago, IL. Selection and recognition of the world's most outstanding television and radio commercials. Info from: U.S. Television & Radio Commercials Festival, J.W. Anderson, Chmn, 841 N Addison Ave, Elmhurst, IL 60126.

WHARTON, EDITH: BIRTHDAY. Jan 24. American author and Pulitzer Prize winner, born at New York City on Jan 24, 1862. Died Aug 11, 1937.

WORLDWIDE ANTIQUES SHOW. Jan 24-26. Tarrant County Conv Ctr, 1111 Houston St, Fort Worth, TX 76102.

JANUARY 25 — SATURDAY

25th Day — Remaining, 340

AVALANCHE CROSS COUNTRY SKI CLASSIC. Jan 25. Five- and 10-kilometer events. Info from: Chamber of Commerce, 28 S Lake St, Boyne City, MI 49712.

BIG ORANGE MUSIC FESTIVAL. Jan 25-Feb 9. Miami, FL. Indoor and outdoor concerts, heritage fair, food and crafts. Info from: Pace Concerts, Jack Firestone, Exec Dir, 2121 SW 27th Ave, Miami, FL 33145.

BOYLE, ROBERT; BIRTHDAY. Jan 25. Irish physicist, chemist and author, who formulated Boyle's Law in 1662, was born at Lismore, Ireland, Jan 25, 1627, and died at London, Dec 30, 1691.

BURNS, ROBERT: BIRTHDAY. Jan 25. Beloved Scottish poet ("Oh wad some power the giftie gie us To see oursels as others see us!"), born at Ayrshire, Scotland, Jan 25, 1759. Died at Dumfries, July 21, 1796. His birthday is widely celebrated, especially in Scotland, England and Newfoundland.

January 1986

S	M	T	W	T	F	S
			1	2	3	4
5	6	7	8	9	10	11
12	13	14	15	16	17	18
19	20	21	22	23	24	25
26	27	28	29	30	31	

CURTIS, CHARLES: BIRTHDAY. Jan 25. Thirty-first Vice President of the U.S. (1929-1933) born Topeka, KS, Jan 25, 1860. Died, Washington, DC, Feb 8, 1936.

FOND DU LAC WINTER CELEBRATION. Jan 25-26. Lake Winnebago. Sled dog weight pulls, snowmobile radar runs, motorcycle races, ice bowling and chili cook-off. Last weekend in January. Info from: Conv & Visitors Bureau, 207 N Main, Fond du Lac, WI 54935.

GREATER NEW YORK INTERNATIONAL AUTO SHOW. Jan 25-Feb 2. NY Coliseum, New York, NY. Info from: NY Conv & Visitors Bureau, Inc, 2 Columbus Circle, New York, NY 10019.

HAWAII: VOLCANO WILDERNESS MARATHON AND RIM RUN. Jan 25. Hawaii Volcanoes National Park, Hawaii. Info from: Hawaii Visitors Bureau, Honolulu, HI 96815.

JEWISH MUSIC SEASON. Jan 25-May 14. Info from: Jewish Music Council, 15 E 26th St, New York, NY 10010.

MAUGHAM, W SOMERSET: BIRTHDAY. Jan 25. English short story writer, novelist and playwright born at Paris, Jan 25, 1874. Among his best remembered books: *Of Human Bondage*, *Cakes and Ale* and *The Razor's Edge*. Maugham died at Cape Ferrat, France, Dec 16, 1965.

MOON PHASE: FULL MOON. Jan 25. Moon enters Full Moon phase at 7:31 p.m., E.S.T.

RATTLESNAKE ROUND-UP. Jan 25. Whigham, GA. Snake hunt, snake handling and cooking demonstrations and prizes for the most snakes and largest snake. Annually, last Saturday in January. Sponsor: Whigham Community Club, Myron R. Prevatte, Box 499, Whigham, GA 31797.

SCHAEFER, DANIEL: BIRTHDAY. Jan 25. U.S. Representative of Colorado's 6th district, Republican, of Lakewood, CO, born at Guttenberg, IA, on Jan 25, 1936.

SILVER CREEK CHALLENGE CROSS COUNTRY SKI RACE. Jan 25. Citizen's cross-country ski race through wooded, gently rolling terrain. Info from: Tawas Area Chamber of Commerce, 402 Lake St, Tawas City, MI 48763.

TU BI-SHEVAT. Jan 25. Hebrew calendar date: Shevat 15, 5746. The fifteenth day of the month of Shevat in the Hebrew calendar year is set aside as Hamishah Asar (New Year of the Trees or Jewish Arbor Day), a time to show respect and appreciation for trees and plants.

WOOLF, VIRGINIA: BIRTHDAY. Jan 25. English writer, critic and novelist. Author of *Jacob's Room* and *To the Lighthouse*. Women's rights activist. She was born at London on Jan 25, 1882, and died, of drowning, at Sussex, Mar 28, 1941.

JANUARY 26 — SUNDAY

26th Day — Remaining, 339

AUSTRALIA: AUSTRALIA DAY. Jan 26. Anniversary of first British settlement, at Sydney Cove, Jan 26, 1788. Formerly known as Foundation Day, or Anniversary Day, it has been observed since about 1817, and a public holiday since 1838. Observed on Jan 26 if a Monday, otherwise on the first Monday thereafter.

CRAFT, MODEL AND COLLECTIBLES CONVENTION AND TRADE SHOW. Jan 26-29. McCormick Pl Conv Ctr, Chicago, IL. Purpose: To show hobby products (dollhouse miniatures, crafts, models, adventure gaming, radio control) to wholesalers and retailers. Info from: Hobby Industries of America, 319 E 54th St, Elmwood Park, NJ 07407.

GRANT, JULIA DENT: BIRTHDAY. Jan 26. Wife of Ulysses Simpson Grant, 18th President of the U.S., born at St. Louis, MO, Jan 26, 1826. Died Dec 14, 1902.

HELICOPTER ASSOCIATION INTERNATIONAL: ANNUAL MEETING. Jan 26-28. Purpose: To promote helicopter operations worldwide, as a safe, efficient mode of transportation. Info from: HAI, Susan L. Danker, 1619 Duke St, Alexandria, VA 22314.

COPYRIGHT © 1985 BY WILLIAM D. CHASE and HELEN M. CHASE

HONG KONG: ARTS FESTIVAL. Jan 26-Feb 23. International Festival of the performing arts. Info from: Hong Kong Arts Festival, 18 Fenwick St, 9/F, Wanchai, Hong Kong.

INDIA: NATIONAL HOLIDAY. Jan 26. Republic Day, Anniversary of Proclamation of the Republic. Basant Panchmi. On Jan 26, 1929, Indian National Congress resolved to work for establishment of a sovereign republic. "India's greatest national festival" continues on two succeeding days.

INTERNATIONAL FORGIVENESS WEEK. Jan 26-Feb 1. Purpose: To forgive self, family, friends and associates, to forgive across economic lines within our nation, across cultural lines, across political lines and to finish by forgiving other nations. Observed week of full moon in Aquarius. Sponsor: San Francisco Miracles Foundation, Jo-Anne M. Hahn, Coord, 1040 Masonic Ave #2, San Francisco, CA 94117.

MacARTHUR, DOUGLAS: BIRTHDAY. Jan 26. American general, war hero, commander of Allied forces in Southwest Pacific Theatre during World War II, born at Little Rock, AR, Jan 26, 1880. Relieved of Far Eastern command by President Truman in April 1951. Died at Washington, DC, Apr 5, 1964.

MICHIGAN: ADMISSION DAY. Jan 26. Became 26th State on this day in 1837.

NATIONAL MEAT WEEK. Jan 26-Feb 1. Purpose: To improve consumer awareness of meat as a healthy part of a balanced and varied diet. A public relations/consumer education program sponsored by industry for consumers. Info from: American Meat Institute, Sara Lilygren, PR Mgr, Box 3556, Washington, DC 20007.

SNYDER, GENE: BIRTHDAY. Jan 26. U.S. Representative of Kentucky's 4th district, Republican, of Jefferson County, KY, born in Louisville, KY, Jan 26, 1928.

SUPER BOWL XX. Jan 26. Info from: The National Football League, PR Dept, 410 Park Ave, New York, NY 10022.

JANUARY 27 — MONDAY

27th Day — Remaining, 338

APOLLO I SPACECRAFT FIRE ANNIVERSARY. Jan 27. Three American astronauts, Virgil I. Grissom, Edward H. White and Roger B. Chaffee, died when fire suddenly broke out at 6:31 p.m., in *Apollo I* during a launching simulation test, as it stood on the ground at Cape Kennedy, FL, Jan 27, 1967. First launching in the Apollo program had been scheduled for Feb 27, 1967.

AUSTRALIA DAY (OBSERVED). Jan 27. Australia. Public holiday. Commemorates beginning of settlement, when Gov Phillip landed at Sydney Cove on Jan 26, 1788. When the date falls other than on a Monday, the holiday is held on the Monday following Jan 26, in order to give a long weekend. First proclaimed a public holiday in 1838.

EBEL U.S. PRO INDOOR TENNIS CHAMPIONSHIPS. Jan 27-Feb 2. The Spectrum, Philadelphia, PA. "One of the top indoor men's professional tennis tournaments featuring 48 players in singles and 24 teams in doubles." Info from: Philadelphia Indoor Tennis Corp, Suellen F. Foley, PR Dir, 536 Moredon Rd, Huntingdon Valley, PA 19006.

GOMPERS, SAMUEL: BIRTHDAY. Jan 27. Labor leader, first president of the American Federation of Labor, born at London, England, Jan 27, 1850. Died, Dec 13, 1924, at San Antonio, TX.

GUNPOWDER PLOT TRIAL ANNIVERSARY. Jan 27. The surviving conspirators in the "Gunpowder Treason," a plot to blow up parliament and the King on Nov 5, 1605, were brought to trial and convicted at London, Jan 27, 1606. Four days later they were executed "at the west end of St. Paul's Churchyard," accompanied by the usual barbarities. Though accounts vary considerably as to the facts and dates, an inscription on a contemporary engraving states: "The heads of Percy and Catesby after they were dead, were cut off and set upon the ends of Parliament House. Friday the last of January, 1606,

were executed in Parliament Yard: T. Winter, Rokenvood, Keys and Guido Fawkes, their quarters were placed over London gates and their heads upon London Bridge." See also entry for Guy Fawkes Day, Nov 5.

KERN, JEROME: BIRTHDAY. Jan 27. American composer born at New York City, Jan 27, 1885. Died there Nov 11, 1945.

MOZART, WOLFGANG AMADEUS: BIRTHDAY. Jan 27. "One of the world's greatest music-makers," born at Salzburg, Austria, Jan 27, 1756. A member of a gifted musical family, he began playing at age of three and started composing at age of five. He died at Vienna, Dec 5, 1791. While his birthplace is a shrine, his burial place is unknown.

TORRES, ESTEBAN EDWARD: BIRTHDAY. Jan 27. U.S. Representative of California's 34th district, Democrat, of La Puente, CA, born in Miami, AZ, on Jan 27, 1930.

VIETNAM WAR CEASE-FIRE. Jan 27. U.S. and North Vietnam, along with South Vietnam and the Viet Cong, signed an "Agreement on ending the war and restoring peace in Vietnam." Signed at Paris, Jan 27, 1973, effective at 8 a.m. Jan 28 Saigon time, thus ending U.S. combat role in a war which had involved American personnel stationed in Vietnam since defeated French forces had departed under terms of the Geneva Accords in 1954. Longest war in U.S. history. More than one million combat deaths (U.S. 46,079).

JANUARY 28 — TUESDAY

28th Day — Remaining, 337

BIRMINGHAM SPORT, BOAT AND TRAVEL SHOW. Jan 28-Feb 2. Birmingham/Jefferson Civic Ctr, Birmingham, AL. Info from: Double C Productions, Inc, Box 1678, Huntsville, TX 77340.

BLILEY, THOMAS JEROME JR.: BIRTHDAY. Jan 28. U.S. Representative of Virginia's 3rd district, Republican, of Richmond, VA, was born in Chesterfield County on Jan 28, 1932.

DOWNEY, THOMAS J: BIRTHDAY. Jan 28. U.S. Representative of New York's 2nd district, Democrat, of Amityville, NY, was born in Ozone Park, NY, Jan 28, 1949.

GOLF: SOUTHWEST SENIOR CHAMPIONSHIP. Jan 28-31. Yuma Golf and Country Club, 36 hole medal play tournament, limited to 100 players, 50 years of age and older. Sponsor: Caballeros de Yuma, Inc, Box 230, Yuma, AZ 85364.

GREAT SEAL OF THE UNITED STATES: ANNIVERSARY. Jan 28. Congress, on Jan 28, 1782, resolved that the Secretary of the Congress should "keep the public seal, and cause the same to be affixed to every act, ordinance or paper, which Congress shall direct . . ." Although the Great Seal did not exist yet, the Congress recognized the need for it. See also: entries for June 20, July 4 and Sept 16.

MacKENZIE, ALEXANDER: BIRTHDAY. Jan 28. Canadian statesman and prime minister (1873-1878), born at Perthshire, Scotland, Jan 28, 1822. Died at Toronto, Ontario, Apr 17, 1892.

MARTI, JOSE JULIAN: BIRTHDAY. Jan 28. Cuban author and political activist, born at Havana, Jan 28, 1853, exiled to Spain where he studied law before coming to the U.S., in 1890. Killed in battle at Dos Rios, Cuba. May 19, 1895.

COPYRIGHT © 1985 BY WILLIAM D. CHASE and HELEN M. CHASE

PICCARD, AUGUSTE: BIRTHDAY. Jan 28. Scientist, explorer born at Basel, Switzerland, Jan 28, 1884. Record-setting balloon ascents into stratosphere and ocean depth descents and explorations. Twin brother of Jean Felix Piccard, (q.v.). Died at Lausanne, Switzerland, Mar 24, 1962.

PICCARD, JEAN FELIX: BIRTHDAY. Jan 28. Scientist, engineer, explorer born at Basel, Switzerland Jan 28, 1884. Noted for cosmic-ray research and record-setting balloon ascensions into stratosphere. Reached 57,579 ft in sealed gondola piloted by his wife, Jeannette (q.v.) in 1934. Twin brother of Auguste Piccard (q.v.). Died at Minneapolis, MN on 79th birthday, Jan 28, 1963.

RWANDA: FEAST OF DEMOCRACY. Jan 28. Info from: Ambassade De La Republique Rwandaise, 1714 New Hampshire Ave, Washington, DC 20009.

STANLEY, HENRY MORTON: BIRTHDAY. Jan 28. Explorer, born in Wales, Jan 28, 1841. Leader of African expedition to find the missing missionary-explorer David Livingstone, who had not been heard from for more than two years. He started his search on Mar 21, 1871. Stanley found him at Ujiji, near Lake Tanganyika, on Nov 10, 1871, and his first words are said to have been the now-famous phrase: "Dr. Livingstone, I presume?" Stanley died at London, May 10, 1904.

UP HELLY AA: Jan 28. Lerwick, Shetland, Scotland. Norse galley burned in impressive ceremony symbolizing sacrifice to sun. Old Viking custom. Last Tuesday in January.

JANUARY 29 — WEDNESDAY
29th Day — Remaining, 336

CHEKHOV, ANTON PAVLOVICH: BIRTHDAY. Jan 29. Russian playwright and short story writer, especially remembered for *The Sea Gull, The Three Sisters* and *The Cherry Orchard*. Born at Taganrog on Jan 29, 1860 (New Style), he died on July 15, 1904, at the Black Forest spa at Badenweiler.

GREATER PORTLAND AUTO SHOW. Jan 29-31. Memorial Coliseum, Portland, OR. Info from: Convention & Visitors Assn, Inc, 26 SW Salmon, Portland, OR 97204.

KANSAS: ADMISSION DAY. Jan 29. Became 34th state on this day in 1861.

McKINLEY, WILLIAM: BIRTHDAY. Jan 29. 25th President of the U.S. Born at Niles, OH, Jan 29, 1843. Died in office, at Buffalo, NY, Sept 14, 1901, as result of gunshot wound by an anarchist assassin on Sept 6, 1901, while he was attending Pan American Exposition.

MARDI GRAS. Jan 29-Feb 11. Mobile, Alabama. Info from: Alabama Tourism and Travel, 532 S Perry St, Montgomery, AL 36130.

PAINE, THOMAS: BIRTH ANNIVERSARY. Jan 29. American Revolutionary leader, a corset-maker by trade, author of *Common Sense, The Age of Reason* and many other influential works, born at Thetford, England, Jan 29, 1737. Paine died at New York City, June 8, 1809, and his remains were moved to England by William Cobbett for re-burial there in 1819. Reburial was refused and the location of Paine's bones, said to have been distributed, is unknown. "These are the times that try men's souls" are opening words of his inspirational tract, *The Crisis.*

SPACE MILESTONE: SATURN SA-5 (US). Jan 29. Orbits record 19 tons. Launched on Jan 29, 1964.

SWAP-A-BROWN-BAG-LUNCH-DAY. Jan 29. Purpose: To relieve the doldrums of winter and of knowing exactly what your brown bag contains, swap a lunch with a friend. Annually, last Wednesday in January. Sponsor: Elk Ridge Brown Baggers, Box 24154, Elk Ridge, MD 21227.

JANUARY 30 — THURSDAY
30th Day — Remaining, 335

CHENEY, DICK: BIRTHDAY. Jan 30. U.S. Representative at large from Wyoming, Republican, of Casper, WY, born in Lincoln, NE, on Jan 30, 1941.

COWBOY POETRY GATHERING. Jan 30-Feb 1. Elko Convention Ctr, Elko, NV. Purpose: The event is dedicated to the men and women in the world of ranching who are continuing a century-old tradition of composing and reciting poetry about their world. Info from: Cowboy Poetry Gathering, Tara McCarty, Box 888, Elko, NV 89801.

FRANKLIN D. ROOSEVELT BIRTHDAY CELEBRATION. Jan 30. St Augustine, FL. Purpose: To commemorate birthday of F.D.R. (1882-1945). Only president elected to four terms. Ardent philatelist. Sponsor: Franklin D. Roosevelt Philatelic Society, Gustav Detjen, Jr, Pres, 154 Laguna Ct, St Augustine Shores, FL 32086.

KING CHARLES I EXECUTION ANNIVERSARY. Jan 30. English king beheaded by order of parliament under Oliver Cromwell Jan 30, 1649; considered a martyr by some. Observance by *Cavalier Comments,* Mark and Jennie Gist, Editors, 530 E Weber Rd, Columbus, OH 43202.

McKINNEY, STEWART B: BIRTHDAY. Jan 30. U.S. Representative of Connecticut's 4th district, Republican, of Green Farms, CT, was born at Pittsburgh, PA, on Jan 30, 1931.

MAHATMA GANDHI ASSASSINATION ANNIVERSARY. Jan 30. Religious and political leader of millions in India, Mohandas K. Gandhi, was assassinated at New Delhi, Jan 30, 1948. The assassin was a Hindu extremist, Ram Naturam. See also: Gandhi's birthday, Oct 2.

PARADA DEL SOL RODEO AND PARADE. Jan 30-Feb 2. Scottsdale, AZ. Street dance, rodeo and the "longest horse-drawn parade in the world." Info from: Chamber of Commerce, Box 129, Scottsdale, AZ 85252.

RECREATIONAL VEHICLE SHOW. Jan 30-Feb 2. Tarrant County Conv Ctr, 1111 Houston St, Fort Worth, TX 76102.

ROOSEVELT, FRANKLIN DELANO: BIRTHDAY. Jan 30. 32nd President of the U.S. (Mar 4, 1933-Apr 12, 1945). The only president to serve more than two terms, Roosevelt was elected to four consecutive terms. Born at Hyde Park, NY, Jan 30, 1882, he died in office, at Warm Springs, GA, Apr 12, 1945.

SPEED WEEKS. Jan 30-Feb 16. Daytona International Speedway, Daytona Beach, FL. Info from: Daytona Internatl Speedway, PR Dept, Daytona Beach, FL 32015.

STROH WINTER CARNIVAL FUN FAIR. Jan 30-Feb 2. St. Paul Civic Ctr, St. Paul, MN. Fashion and sporting exhibitions, comedy, live music, lifestyle booths, zoo demonstrations and tantalizing food and beverages. Sponsor: The St. Paul Winter Carnival Assn, 339 Bremer Bldg, St. Paul, MN 55101.

TUCHMAN, BARBARA W: BIRTHDAY. Jan 30. American journalist, historian and Pulitzer Prize winning author, born at New York City on Jan 30, 1912. Author of *The Guns of August* (1963), *Practising History* (1981), *The March of Folly* (1984) and many other books.

WOLF, FRANK R: BIRTHDAY. Jan 30. U.S. Representative of Virginia's 10th district, Republican, of Vienna, VA, born at Philadelphia, PA, Jan 30, 1939.

January 1986

S	M	T	W	T	F	S
			1	2	3	4
5	6	7	8	9	10	11
12	13	14	15	16	17	18
19	20	21	22	23	24	25
26	27	28	29	30	31	

COPYRIGHT © 1985 BY WILLIAM D. CHASE and HELEN M. CHASE

JANUARY 31 — FRIDAY

31st Day — Remaining, 334

CANADA'S COLDEST RECORDED TEMPERATURE ANNIVERSARY. Jan 31. At Whitehorse, in Canada's Yukon Territory, a temperature of 62 degrees below zero (Fahrenheit) was recorded on Jan 31, 1947, a record low for all of Canada's provinces and territories. Next lowest temperature was −60°F at Yellowknife, in the Northwest Territories, recorded also on Jan 31, 1947.

EARLY, JOSEPH D: BIRTHDAY. Jan 31. U.S. Representative of Massachusetts' 3rd district, Democrat, of Worcester, MA, born there Jan 31, 1933.

FRANCE: NICE CARNIVAL. Jan 31-Feb 11. The carnival at Nice dates from the 14th century and is celebrated each year during the twelve days ending with Shrove Tuesday. Derived from ancient rites of spring, carnival offers parades, floats, battles of flowers and of confetti, a fireworks display lighting up the entire Baie des Anges. King Carnival is burnt on his pyre at end of event.

GEPHARDT, RICHARD A: BIRTHDAY. Jan 31. U.S. Representative of Missouri's 3rd district, Democrat, of St. Louis, MO, born there on Jan 31, 1941.

GREY, ZANE: BIRTHDAY. Jan 31. American dentist who turned to writing. Author of numerous stories of the American western frontier. Translated into many languages and selling more than 10 million copies. *Riders of the Purple Sage* is one of his best remembered. Zane Grey was born at Zanesville, OH, on Jan 31, 1875, and died at Altadena, CA, Oct 23, 1939.

INTERNATIONAL CARL MARIA von WEBER COMPETITION FOR CHAMBER OPERA. Jan 31. Closing date for entries in the International Carl Maria von Weber Competition for Chamber Operas in 1986. The Competition is directed by the Dresden State Opera and the Dresden Musical Festival. Info from: Musikdramaturgie der Staatsoper, Dresden, DDR—8012 Dresden, Postfach 8.

NATIONAL SPORTING GOODS ASSOCIATION SPRING SHOW. Jan 31-Feb 2. Infomart & Market Hall, Dallas, TX. Info from: NSGA, Paul M. Prince, Senior Mgr, Trade Shows, 1699 Wall St, Mt Prospect, IL 60056.

NAURU: NATIONAL HOLIDAY. Jan 31. Republic of Nauru.

ROBINSON, JACKIE: BIRTHDAY. Jan 31. Jack Roosevelt Robinson, athlete and business executive, first Negro to enter professional baseball, was born at Cairo, GA, Jan 31, 1919. Played with Brooklyn Dodgers, 1947-1956. Voted National League's Most Valuable Player in 1949 and elected to the Baseball Hall of Fame in 1962. Died at Stamford, CT, Oct 24,

1972. A special commemorative Jackie Robinson postage stamp, in the Black Heritage USA Series, was issued in April, 1982.

SCHUBERT, FRANZ: BIRTHDAY. Jan 31. Austrian composer, born at Vienna on Jan 31, 1797, and died there, of typhus, on Nov 19, 1828. He was buried, at his request, near the grave of Beethoven. Schubert finished *his* work on his "Unfinished Symphony" (No 8) in 1822. On the hundredth anniversary of his death, 1928, a $10,000 prize was offered to "finish" the work. The protests were so great that the offer was withdrawn.

SLOVIK, EDDIE D: EXECUTION ANNIVERSARY. Jan 31. Anniversary of execution by firing squad of 24-year-old, Polish, Catholic Private Eddie D. Slovik, 36896415, born at Detroit, MI, Feb 18, 1920, member of Company G, 109th Infantry, 28th Division, U.S. Army. Pvt Slovik "was shot to death by a firing squad at 1005 hours, 31 Jan 1945, at St. Marie Aux Mines, France." His death sentence, first for desertion since Civil War, has been subject of controversy since.

SPACE MILESTONE: APOLLO 14 (US). Jan 31. Launched Jan 31, 1971, Astronauts Alan B. Shepard, Jr., and Edgar D. Mitchell landed on moon (Lunar Module "Antares") Feb 5. Command Module "Kitty Hawk" piloted by Stuart A. Roosa. Pacific splashdown on Feb 9.

SPACE MILESTONE: LUNA 9 (USSR). Jan 31. First soft landing on Moon, Feb 3. Transmitted photos. Launched Jan 31, 1966.

SPACE MILESTONE: PROJECT MERCURY TEST (US). Jan 31. First US recovery of large animal from space; Ham, the chimpanzee, successfully transmitted signals. Launched Jan 31, 1961.

SPACE MILESTONE: UNITED STATES SPACE EXPLORATION ANNIVERSARY. Jan 31. *Explorer I*, the first successful U.S. satellite was launched Jan 31, 1958. Weighing 31 lbs, *Explorer I* transmitted radio signals until May 23, 1958, and discovered the Van Allen Belt. Decayed Mar 31, 1970.

HALLEY'S COMET IN 1985 AND 1986

The most famous of all comets—Comet Halley—will make its next visit to the inner part of the Solar System in 1985 and 1986. The comet can sometimes be very spectacular to Earthbound viewers, as it was the last time it was around in late 1909 and much of 1910. This time, however, conditions will not be so favorable. Indeed, at the time when the comet is closest to the Sun (Feb. 9, 1986), it will be on the opposite side of the Sun from the Earth, making it impossible for us to see it. The comet should be visible but inconspicuous in the western sky after sunset in December, 1985, and January, 1986. After passing behind the Sun in February, 1986, it will be in the morning sky in March and April of that year. Although somewhat brighter than during the winter, it will be very far South and therefore quite difficult to observe in the United States. All in all, this will be one of the least impressive visits by the comet, although scientists all over the world are already preparing for the most exhaustive study of a comet in the history of astronomy.

Nautical Almanac Office, United States Naval Observatory

COPYRIGHT © 1985 BY WILLIAM D. CHASE and HELEN M. CHASE

Februarie.

FEBRUARY 1 — SATURDAY

32nd Day — Remaining, 333

AMERICAN HEART MONTH. Feb 1-28. Presidential Proclamation. "Always issued each year for February since 1964." (PL88-254 of Dec 30, 1963)

AMERICAN HEART MONTH. Feb 1-28. Purpose: Volunteers across the country spend one to four weeks canvassing neighborhoods and providing educational information about cardiovascular disease and stroke. Sponsor: American Heart Assn, Caroline Punches, Dir, Residential and Memorial Campaigns, 7320 Greenville Ave, Dallas, TX 75231.

AMERICAN HISTORY MONTH. Feb 1-28. Massachusetts.

AMERICAN MUSIC MONTH. Feb 1-28. Purpose: To support U.S. composers, provide extensive hearings for their works, and encourage their use by performing artists and students. Sponsor: Natl Federation of Music Clubs, 1336 N Delaware St, Indianapolis, IN 46202.

BLACK HISTORY MONTH. Feb 1-28. Traditionally the month containing Abraham Lincoln's birthday (Feb 12) and Frederick Douglass's presumed birthday (Feb 14). Observance of a special period to recognize achievements and contributions by Afro-Americans dates from Feb 1926, when it was launched by Dr. Carter G. Woodson and others. Variously designated for Negro History, Black History, Afro-American History, Black Heritage and Black Expressions, the observance period was initially for a week, but since 1976 for the entire month of February. Sponsor: Assn for the Study of Afro-American Life and History, Inc, W. Leanna Miles, Mng Dir, 1401 Fourteenth St, NW, Washington, DC 20005.

BLUE ANGEL GOLF TOURNAMENT. Feb 1-2. Barbara Worth Country Club. Info from: Chamber of Commerce. Box 3006, El Centro, CA 92244.

BLUE RIDGE COUNCIL "SKI-A-REE". Feb 1-2. Canaan Valley Ski Area, Davis, WV. Sponsor: Canaan Valley Resorts, John Lutz, Rt 1, Box 330, Davis, WV 26260.

DARTMOUTH WINTER CARNIVAL. Feb 1-10. Dartmouth, Nova Scotia. Winter activities for all ages. Info from: Dept of Tourism, Box 456, Halifax, NS B3J 2R5, Canada.

FREEDOM DAY. Feb 1. Anniversary of President Abraham Lincoln's approval, Feb 1, 1865, of the Thirteenth Amendment to the U.S. Constitution (abolishing slavery). "1. Neither slavery nor involuntary servitude, except as a punishment for crime whereof the party shall have been duly convicted, shall exist within the United States or any place subject to their jurisdiction. 2. Congress shall have power to enforce this article by appropriate legislation." The amendment had been proposed by the Congress on Jan 31, 1865; ratification was completed Dec 18, 1865.

GREAT AMERICAN SUMMER CAMP CELEBRATION. Feb 1-Sept 30. Purpose: To celebrate 125 years of organized camping in the U.S. and to honor the founding of the summer camp movement which today has some nine million youth and adults in day/resident camp programs year-round. Sponsor: American Camping Assn, Jim LeMonn, Media Relations, 200 W 20th St, New York, NY 10011.

GREENSBORO SIT-IN ANNIVERSARY. Feb 1. Commercial discrimination against Blacks and other minorities provoked a non-violent protest, Feb 1, 1960, which swept across the nation bringing dramatic changes. On that day, in Greensboro, NC, four students, Ezell Blair, Jr., Franklin McCain, Joseph McNeill and David Richmond, from the Agricultural and Technical College at Greensboro, sat down at a Woolworth store lunch counter and ordered coffee. Refused service, they remained all day. The following days similar sit-ins took place at the Woolworth lunch counter. Before the week was over they were joined by a few white students. The protest spread rapidly, especially in southern states, and more than 1,600 persons were reportedly arrested before the year was over for participating in them. The cause of civil rights for all became a cause for thousands of students and activists across the nation. In response equal accommodation irrespective of race reached lunch counters, hotels, and business establishments in thousands of places where it had been unknown before.

INTERNATIONAL FRIENDSHIP MONTH. Feb 1-28. Purpose: To encourage an exchange of letters among peoples of the world and create a better understanding for the purpose of promoting international peace. Sponsor: The Franklin D. Roosevelt Philatelic Society, 154 Laguna Ct, St. Augustine Shores, FL 32086.

INTERNATIONAL WINTER BALL. Feb 1. Civic Centre, Prince George, British Columbia. Purpose: Annual Mardi Gras celebration with international dinner and dance. Sponsor: Prince George Folkfest-Multicultural Heritage Society, Box 2469, Prince George, BC, Canada V2N 2S6.

LANTOS, THOMAS PETER: BIRTHDAY. Feb 1. U.S. Representative of California's 11th district, Democrat, of San Mateo, CA, born in Budapest, Hungary, on Feb 1, 1928.

LONGWOOD GARDENS WELCOME SPRING. Feb 1-Apr 30. Indoor conservatory display features thousands of colorful, fragrant spring bulbs, green lawns, palm trees, orchids and roses. Info from: Longwood Gardens, Kennett Square, PA 19348.

MOON PHASE: LAST QUARTER. Feb 1. Moon enters Last Quarter phase at 11:41 p.m., E.S.T.

NATIONAL CHERRY MONTH. Feb 1-28. Purpose: To publicize the fine eating qualities of the colorful red tart cherry. Info from: Berkel & Company, Rob Tietsma, 320 Federal Sq Bldg, Grand Rapids, MI 49503.

NATIONAL CHILDREN'S DENTAL HEALTH MONTH. Feb 1-28. Slogan: "Smile America." Purpose: To provide a prevention oriented dental health education program for all segments of the population. Sponsor: American Dental Assn, Bureau of Health Education and Audiovisual Services, Dick Walther, Special Program Coord, 211 E Chicago Ave, Chicago, IL 60611.

NATIONAL FREEDOM DAY. Feb 1. Presidential Proclamation 2824, Jan 25, 1949, covers all succeeding years (PL80-842 of June 30, 1948).

ORANGE BOWL: 10-K. Feb 1. Miami, FL. Length is 6.2 miles and open to anyone wishing to run. Info from: Runners Internatl, #207, 10585 SW 109 Court, Miami, FL 33176.

	S	M	T	W	T	F	S
February 1986							1
	2	3	4	5	6	7	8
	9	10	11	12	13	14	15
	16	17	18	19	20	21	22
	23	24	25	26	27	28	

COPYRIGHT © 1985 BY WILLIAM D. CHASE and HELEN M. CHASE

POTATO LOVER'S MONTH. Feb 1-28. Purpose: To recognize the potato as America's favorite vegetable and celebrate its contribution as an economical and nutritious food. Sponsor: The Potato Board. Info from: Rhonda Purwin, Ketchum Public Relations, 55 Union St, San Francisco, CA 94111.

ROBINSON CRUSOE DAY. Feb 1. Anniversary of the rescue, Feb 1, 1709, of Alexander Selkirk, Scottish sailor who had been put ashore (in Sept 1704) on the uninhabited island, Juan Fernandez, at his own request after a quarrel with his captain. His adventures formed the basis for Daniel Defoe's book, *Robinson Crusoe*. A day to be adventurous and self reliant.

SHAPE UP WITH PICKLES TIME. Feb 1-28. Purpose: To properly position the succulent pickle as a delicious and appropriate accompaniment to any low-calorie snack or meal. Sponsor: Pickle Packers Internatl. Info from: Burson-Marsteller, 1 E Wacker Dr, Chicago, IL 60601.

SUNBANK 24 AT DAYTONA. Feb 1-2. Daytona International Speedway, Daytona Beach, FL. Info from: Daytona Internatl Speedway, Larry Balewski, PR, Daytona Beach, FL 32015.

WINTERFEST. Feb 1-8. Grand Haven, MI. Purpose: To provide a family-orientated festival of the fine, visual and performing arts. Outdoor winter events and contests. Info from: Winterfest, Inc, Valerie Whiting, Box 330, Grand Haven, MI 49417.

WINTERFEST. Feb 1-9. Ski Beech Resort, Beech Mountain, NC. Purpose: Celebration of winter includes races for serious and not-so-serious skiers. Contests and festivals. Info from: Chamber of Commerce, Box 876, Beech Mountain, Banner Elk, NC 28604.

WINTERSKOL. Feb 1-9. Ski Incline, Incline Village, NV. Info from: Nevada Commission on Tourism, Capitol Complex, Carson City, NV 89710.

FEBRUARY 2 — SUNDAY
33rd Day — Remaining, 332

BENET, WILLIAM ROSE: CENTENNIAL BIRTH ANNIVERSARY. Feb 2. American poet and critic, born at Fort Hamilton, NY, on Feb 2, 1886. Benet died at New York, NY, on May 4, 1950.

BOY SCOUTS OF AMERICA SCOUT SUNDAY AND SABBATH. Feb 2 and Feb 8. Purpose: To emphasize through religious services that "A Scout is reverent" and to recognize religious institutions that use the scouting program. Info from: Boy Scouts of America, 1325 Walnut Hill Ln, Irving, TX 75038.

CANDLEMAS DAY or PRESENTATION OF THE LORD. Feb 2. Observed in Roman Catholic Church. Commemorates presentation of Jesus in the Temple and the purification of Mary 40 days after his birth. Candles blessed on this day since eleventh century. Formerly called the Feast of Purification of the Blessed Virgin Mary. Old Scottish couplet proclaims: "If Candlemas is fair and clear, There'll be two winters in the year."

GROUNDHOG DAY. Feb 2. Old belief that if the sun shines on Candlemas Day, or if the groundhog sees his shadow when he emerges on this day six weeks of winter will ensue.

GROUNDHOG DAY IN PUNXSUTAWNEY, PENNSYLVANIA. Feb 2. Widely observed traditional annual Candlemas Day event at which "Punxsutawney Phil, King of the weather prophets," is object of a search. Tradition is said to have been established by early German settlers. The official trek (which began in 1887) is followed by a weather prediction for the next six weeks.

HOMSTROM. Feb 2. Scuol, Switzerland. Burning of straw men on poles as symbol of winter's imminent departure. First Sunday in February.

INTERNATIONAL CLERGY APPRECIATION WEEK. Feb 2-8. Purpose: To commemorate the heroic death of four armed service chaplains who died aboard the *S.S. Dorchester* in 1943, and honor all clergy of all faiths. Sponsor: Civitan Internatl, Wendell Andrews, Exec Admn, Box 2102, Birmingham, AL 35201.

JOYCE, JAMES: BIRTHDAY. Feb 2. Irish novelist and poet born at Dublin, Feb 2, 1882. Died, Zurich, Switzerland, Jan 13, 1941.

LUXEMBOURG: CANDLEMAS. Feb 2. Traditional custom of Candlemas. At night, children sing a customary song wishing health and prosperity to their neighborhood and receive sweets in return. They carry special candles called "Lichtebengel" symbolizing the coming of spring.

MEXICO: DIA de la CANDELARIA. Feb 2. Mexico. All Mexico celebrates. Dances, processions, bullfights.

MID-SOUTH GROUNDHOG JAMBOREE. Feb 2. Purpose: Annual luncheon in honor of Groundhog's Day, featuring stories, articles and groundhog lore. Sponsor: Greater Memphis Groundhog Consortium, Memphis State University, Brister Library, Memphis, TN 38152.

MUFFIN MANIA WEEK. Feb 2-8. Purpose: To promote the widespread enjoyment of muffins throughout the United States. Sponsor: Liberty Publishing Company, Lynn McKain, 50 Scott Adam Rd, Cockeysville, MD 21030.

NATIONAL CORK BOARD WEEK. Feb 2-8. Purpose: To encourage communication and creativity in the work environment and to celebrate the creative use of the cork board as the unsung hero in the pursuit of office creativity, functionality and congeniality. Sponsor: Quartet Manufacturing Company. Info from: Jasculca/Terman & Associates, Gail Cowan, 730 N Franklin St, Suite 510, Chicago, IL 60610.

NFL PRO BOWL '86. Feb 2. Aloha Stadium, Honolulu, HI. All-star football game involving the National and American Conferences of National Football League. Info from: Hawaii Visitors Bureau, Honolulu, HI 96815.

"OFFICIAL" GROUNDHOG DAY IN SUN PRAIRIE, WI. Feb 2. Purpose: To predict the weather for the balance of winter. Inspection, at 7:15 a.m., C.S.T., to see if Jimmy the Groundhog has seen his shadow. Persons born on this date eligible for "official" groundhog birth certificate and groundhog club. Info from: Chamber of Commerce, 133 W Main St, Sun Prairie, WI 53590.

PERRY'S "BRR" (BIKE RIDE TO RIPPEY). Feb 2. Winter bike riding. Twenty-two miles of frigid fun. Sponsor: Chamber of Commerce, Kathy Hoskinson, Willis at First, Perry, IA 50220.

RAY, RICHARD BELMONT: BIRTHDAY. Feb 2. U.S. Representative of Georgia's 3rd district, Democrat, of Perry, GA, born in Crawford County, GA, on Feb 2, 1927.

WALTON, GEORGE: DEATH ANNIVERSARY. Feb 2. Signer of the Declaration of Independence, born Prince Edward County, VA 1741 (exact date unknown). Died Feb 2, 1804.

FEBRUARY 3 — MONDAY
34th Day — Remaining, 331

BEAN-THROWING FESTIVAL (SETSUBUN). Feb 3-4. Japan. Setsubun marks last day of winter according to lunar calendar. Throngs at temple grounds throw beans to drive away imaginary devils.

BLACKWELL, ELIZABETH: BIRTHDAY. Feb 3. The first woman physician. Elizabeth Blackwell, was born near Bristol, England, Feb 3, 1821. She and several other members of her family were active abolitionists, woman's suffrage advocates and pioneers in women's medicine. Her family moved to New York state in 1832, and she received a medical doctor's degree at Geneva, NY, in 1849, thereby becoming the first woman physician. She established a hospital in New York City with an all-woman staff, where she recruited and trained nurses for service in the Civil War. Returning to England in 1869, she

COPYRIGHT © 1985 BY WILLIAM D. CHASE and HELEN M. CHASE

continued to teach and practice medicine, until her death at Hastings, May 31, 1910. A United States postage stamp was issued in her honor in 1981.

CHAPPELL, WILLIAM V JR: BIRTHDAY. Feb 3. U.S. Representative of Florida's 4th district, Democrat, of Ocala, FL, was born at Kendrick, FL, Feb 3, 1922.

FIELDS, JACK M: BIRTHDAY. Feb 3. U.S. Representative of Texas' 8th district, Republican, of Humble, TX, born there on Feb 3, 1952.

FOUR CHAPLAINS MEMORIAL DAY. Feb 3. Commemorates four (George Fox, Alexander Goode, Clark Poling, John Washington) who sacrificed lifebelts and lives in torpedoing of *S.S. Dorchester* off Greenland, this day, 1943.

GOLF: SUNRISE SENIOR CLASSIC. Feb 3-9. Tournament Players Club, Ft Pierce, FL. Senior PGA Tour golf tournament. Info from: Sunrise Senior Classic, 4001 Patti Rizzo Plaza, Suite 103, Ft. Pierce, FL 33451.

HALFWAY POINT OF WINTER. Feb 3. In the Northern Hemisphere the midpoint of the winter season occurs on Feb 3 at 7:58 a.m., E.S.T. Winter, the shortest season of this year (lasting 88 days, 23 hours and 57 minutes), is half over!

LINCOLN, ABRAHAM: BIRTHDAY OBSERVANCE. Feb 3. Observed on this day (first Monday in February) in Delaware and Oregon. See also entry for Feb 12.

NATIONAL PAY YOUR BILLS WEEK. Feb 3-7. Purpose: A public service program designed to help consumers learn to use credit cautiously, manage money wisely and pay bills promptly. Observed annually, during first full week in February. Sponsor: American Collectors Assn Inc, 4040 W 70th St, Minneapolis, MN 55435.

ROCKWELL, NORMAN: BIRTHDAY. Feb 3. American artist and illustrator especially noted for his realistic and homey magazine cover art. Born at New York City, Feb 3, 1894. Died at Stockbridge, MA, Nov 8, 1978.

ROWLAND, JAMES ROY JR: BIRTHDAY. Feb 3. U.S. Representative of Georgia's 8th district, Democrat, of Dublin, GA, born in Wrightsville, GA on Feb 3, 1926.

SARBANES, PAUL S: BIRTHDAY. Feb 3. U.S. Senator from Maryland, Democrat, of Baltimore, MD, born in Salisbury, MD, on Feb 3, 1933.

SPACE MILESTONE: STS-10 (US). Feb 3. Shuttle Challenger launched Feb 3, 1984 from Kennedy Space Center, FL, with crew of five (Vance Brand, Robert Gibson, Ronald McNair, Bruce McCandless and Robert Stewart). On Feb 7, two astronauts became first to fly freely (propelled by their backpack jets) in space, untethered to any craft. Landed at Cape Canaveral, FL, on Feb 11.

STEIN, GERTRUDE: BIRTHDAY. Feb 3. Avant garde expatriate American writer, perhaps best remembered for her poetic declaration (in 1913): "Rose is a rose is a rose is a rose." Born at Allegheny, PA, Feb 3, 1874. Died at Paris, France, July 29, 1946.

FEBRUARY 4 — TUESDAY
35th Day — Remaining, 330

HOPKINS, MARK: BIRTHDAY. Feb 4. American educator, author and college president (Williams College), born at Stockbridge, MA, Feb 4, 1802. Died at Williamstown, MA, June 17, 1887.

February *1986*	S	M	T	W	T	F	S
							1
	2	3	4	5	6	7	8
	9	10	11	12	13	14	15
	16	17	18	19	20	21	22
	23	24	25	26	27	28	

LINDBERGH, CHARLES AUGUSTUS: BIRTHDAY. Feb 4. American aviator flew Atlantic Ocean, New York to Paris, nonstop, solo, May 20-21, 1927. Born Detroit, MI, Feb 4, 1902. Died Kipahula, Maui, HI, Aug 27, 1974. See also entry for May 20.

LUNDINE, STANLEY N: BIRTHDAY. Feb 4. U.S. Representative of New York's 34th district, Democrat, of Jamestown, NY, born there on Feb 4, 1939.

MICA, DANIEL ANDREW: BIRTHDAY. Feb 4. U.S. Representative of Florida's 14th district, Democrat, of Lake Worth, FL, was born at Binghamton, NY, Feb 4, 1944.

QUAYLE, DAN: BIRTHDAY. Feb 4. U.S. Senator from Indiana, Republican, of Huntington, IN, born at Indianapolis, IN, Feb 4, 1947.

RIEGLE, DONALD W JR: BIRTHDAY. Feb 4. U.S. Senator from Michigan, Democrat, of Flint, MI, born there on Feb 4, 1938.

SAN ANTONIO SPORT, BOAT AND RV SHOW. Feb 4-9. Convention Center Complex, San Antonio, TX. Info from: Double C Productions, Inc., Box 1678, Huntsville, TX 77340.

SRI LANKA: NATIONAL HOLIDAY. Feb 4. Democratic Socialist Republic of Sri Lanka observes Independence and National Day.

TORTURE ABOLITION DAY. Feb 4. On Feb 4, 1985, twenty countries signed a United Nations document entitled "Convention Against Torture and Other Cruel, Inhuman or Degrading Treatment or Punishment." Adopted Dec 10, 1984 by the UN General Assembly, it defined torture as any act "by which severe pain or suffering, whether physical or mental, is intentionally inflicted" to obtain information or a confession. Signatory countries were: Afghanistan, Argentina, Belgium, Bolivia, Costa Rica, Denmark, Dominican Republic, Finland, France, Greece, Iceland, Italy, Netherlands, Norway, Portugal, Senegal, Spain, Sweden, Switzerland and Uruguay.

USO BIRTHDAY. Feb 4. Purpose: To honor the civilian agency founded in 1941 that provides support worldwide for U.S. service people and their families. The United Service Organizations (USO) centers have served as a home away from home for hundreds of thousands of Americans.

FEBRUARY 5 — WEDNESDAY
36th Day — Remaining, 329

EDISON PAGEANT OF LIGHT. Feb 5-15. Commemorates the birthday of Thomas Alva Edison. Info from: Edison Pageant of Light, Inc, Mrs. Margie B. Willis, Box 1311, Ft Myers, FL 33902.

LONGEST WAR IN HISTORY: ENDING ANNIVERSARY. Feb 5. The Third Punic War, between Rome and Carthage, started in the year 149 B.C. It culminated in the year 146 B.C. when Roman soldiers led by Scipio razed Carthage to the ground. The desolated site was cursed and rebuilding forbidden. On Feb 5, 1985, 2,131 years after the war began, Ugo Vetere, mayor of Rome, and Chedli Klibi, mayor of Carthage, met at Tunis to sign a treaty of friendship officially ending the Third Punic War.

MEXICO: ANNIVERSARY OF THE CONSTITUTION. Feb 5. Mexico. Present constitution, embracing major social reforms, adopted on this day, 1917.

MONTANA STATE EXPO. Feb 5-10. Fairgrounds, Missoula, Montana. A blue ribbon fair featuring winners of local and regional contests. Info from: Travel Montana, 1424 9th Ave, Helena, MT 59620.

PEEL, ROBERT: BIRTHDAY. Feb 5. Sir Robert Peel, English statesman, established the Irish constabulary (known as the "Peelers"). Later, as England's Home Secretary he reorganized the London police, who thereafter were known as "Bobbies" after Sir Robert. Born at Lancashire, England, Feb 5, 1788, he died at London, July 2, 1850, from injuries received in a fall from his horse, while riding in Hyde Park.

COPYRIGHT © 1985 BY WILLIAM D. CHASE and HELEN M. CHASE

SARANAC LAKE WINTER CARNIVAL. Feb 5-9. Annually, the Wednesday before second weekend in February. Info from: Chamber of Commerce, 30 Main St, Saranac Lake, NY 12983.

SOCIETY OF ILLUSTRATORS ANNUAL EXHIBITION. Feb 5. (Also Mar 5, Mar 19 and Apr 16.) Purpose: A juried exhibition for the best in contemporary American illustration in four categories: Book, Editorial, Advertising and Institutional. Sponsor: Society of Illustrators, Terry Brown, Dir, 128 E 63rd St, New York, NY 10021.

STEVENSON, ADLAI EWING: BIRTHDAY. Feb 5. American statesman, Governor of Illinois, Democratic candidate for president in 1952 and 1956, U.S. representative to the United Nations, 1961-1965, was born at Los Angeles, CA, Feb 5, 1900. Died at London, England, July 14, 1965. (Not to be confused with his grandfather, Vice President Adlai Ewing Stevenson, born Oct 23, 1835. q.v.)

TANZANIA: CCM DAY. Feb 5. Chama cha Mapinduzi (CCM), Tanzania's sole political party was born through the merger of Tanganyika African National Union (TANU) and Afro-Shirazi Party (ASP) of Zanzibar, Feb 5, 1977. Feb 5 is also anniversary of the Feb 5, 1967, Arusha Declaration, defining Tanzania's policy of socialism and self-reliance.

WEATHERMAN'S DAY. Feb 5. Commemorates the birth of one of America's first weathermen, John Jeffries, a Boston physician who kept detailed records of weather conditions, 1774-1816 (with an interruption, Mar 4, 1776-May 27, 1790, when Loyalist Dr. Jeffries was obliged to leave Boston with the British Army. He returned to Boston after establishing a new career in England as a balloonist, crossing the English Channel Jan 7, 1785, and dining, in Paris, with Benjamin Franklin (Jan 11), American Ambassador to France and a fellow student of weather). Feb 5, 1744/5 Old Style—Sept 16, 1819. See also entry for Jan 7.

WITHERSPOON, JOHN: BIRTHDAY. Feb 5. Clergyman, signer of the Declaration of Independence, and reputed coiner of the word "Americanism" (in 1781), born near Edinburgh, Scotland, Feb 5, 1723. Died Nov 15, 1794.

FEBRUARY 6 — THURSDAY

37th Day — Remaining, 328

AARON BURR DAY. Feb 6. Annual observance on anniversary of Aaron Burr's birth. Although there is no national meeting, members are urged to hold informal dinner meetings to observe and celebrate the birthday of Col. Burr. Sponsor: Aaron Burr Association, Dr. Samuel Engle Burr, Jr, Pres Gen, RD#1, Route 33, Box 429, Hightstown, NJ 08520.

AMERICAN PHYSICAL THERAPY ASSOCIATION: COMBINED SECTIONS MEETING. Feb 6-9. Anaheim Marriott, Anaheim, CA. Purpose: Members from 17 physical therapy specialty groups meet to discuss current issues and new technologies. Info from: APTA, 1111 N Fairfax, Alexandria, VA 22314.

BURR, AARON: BIRTHDAY. Feb 6. Third Vice President of the U.S. (Mar 4, 1801-Mar 3, 1805). While vice president, Burr challenged Alexander Hamilton to a duel and mortally wounded him on July 11, 1804, at Weehawken, NJ. Indicted for the challenge and for murder he fled but later returned to Washington to complete his term of office (during which he presided over the impeachment trial of Supreme Court Justice Samuel Chase). In 1807, Burr was arrested, tried for treason (in an alleged scheme to invade Mexico), and acquitted. Born at Newark, NJ, Feb 6, 1756. Died, Staten Island, NY, on the day a final decree of divorce was issued to his second wife, Sept 14, 1836.

CORDOVA ICEWORM FESTIVAL. Feb 6-9. Purpose: A festival to perpetuate the iceworm, a character in Robert Service's poems. The celebration enables Cordovans to get out after a long winter and encourages visitors to visit Cordova. Everyone is welcome. Info from: Barbara A. Beedle, Chairman, Box 819, Cordova, AK 99574.

DIXIE NATIONAL RODEO. Feb 6-12. Coliseum, Jackson, Mississippi. Contestants from all over the U.S.A. Info from: Dept of Economic Dev, Box 849, Jackson, MS 39205.

FAUNTROY, WALTER EDWARD: BIRTHDAY. Feb 6. District of Columbia Delegate to 99th Congress, Democrat, of Washington, DC, born there on Feb 6, 1933.

MASSACHUSETTS: RATIFICATION DAY. Feb 6. Sixth State to ratify constitution, on this day in 1788.

MID-WINTER'S DAY. Feb 6. Purpose: Create euphoria by fiat in celebration that winter is half over. Sponsor: Richard Ankli, Broadway Fun Spot, 639 Fifth St, Ann Arbor, MI 48103.

NEW ZEALAND: WAITANGI DAY. Feb 6. Commemorates signing of treaty, 1840, between Maori and European peoples for development of New Zealand under British Crown.

REAGAN, RONALD WILSON: BIRTHDAY. Feb 6. Fortieth President of the U.S. Former sportscaster, motion picture actor, rancher, businessman, author (a 1965 autobiography titled "Where's the Rest of Me?" in collaboration with Richard G. Hubler), Governor of California (1967-1974), he was the oldest and the first divorced person to become president. Born Feb 6, 1911, at Tampico, IL. Married (1) Jane Wyman, Jan 25, 1940 (they were divorced in 1948); (2) Nancy Davis, Mar 4, 1952.

RUTH, "BABE:" BIRTH ANNIVERSARY. Feb 6. One of baseball's greatest heroes, George Herman "Babe" Ruth, was born at Baltimore, MD, on Feb 6, 1895. The left-handed pitcher, "Sultan of Swat" hit 714 home runs in 22 major league seasons of play, and played in 10 World Series. Ruth died at New York, NY, on Aug 16, 1948.

SCHEUER, JAMES H: BIRTHDAY. Feb 6. U.S. Representative of New York's 8th district, Democrat-Liberal, of Douglaston, NY, born in New York City, Feb 6, 1920.

FEBRUARY 7 — FRIDAY

38th Day — Remaining, 327

ANDREWS, MICHAEL ALLEN: BIRTHDAY. Feb 7. U.S. Representative of Texas' 25th district, Democrat, of Houston TX, born there on Feb 7, 1944.

ARBOR DAY (ARIZONA). Feb 7. In the counties of Apache, Navajo, Coconino, Mohave and Yavapai, the Friday following Apr 1, and in all other counties the Friday following Feb 1, in each year, shall be known as Arbor Day. See also entry for Apr 4.

BLAKE, EUBIE: BIRTHDAY. Feb 7. James Hubert "Eubie" Blake, American composer and pianist, writer of nearly 1,000 songs (including "I'm Just Wild About Harry," and "Memories of You"), was born at Baltimore, MD, on Feb 7, 1883. Recipient, at the White House, in 1981, of the Presidential Medal of Freedom. His last professional performance was in January, 1982. Blake died in Brooklyn, five days after his 100th birthday, on Feb 12, 1983.

CRUFTS DOG SHOW. Feb 7-9. Earls Court, London. Over 10,500 dogs from over 125 breeds compete for coveted best dog of show title. Info from: Crufts Dog Show, The Kennel Club, 1 Clarges St, London W1Y 8AB, England.

DICKENS, CHARLES: BIRTHDAY. Feb 7. English social critic and novelist, born at Portsmouth on Feb 7, 1812. Among his most successful books: *Oliver Twist, The Posthumous Papers of*

COPYRIGHT © 1985 BY WILLIAM D. CHASE and HELEN M. CHASE

the *Pickwick Club*, *David Copperfield* and *A Christmas Carol*. Dickens died at Gad's Hill, June 9, 1870, and was buried at Westminster Abbey.

GOLD RUSH DAYS. Feb 7-9. Purpose: Community-wide celebration of the Old West, rodeo, parade, carnival, gold panning. Sponsor: Chamber of Commerce, PO Drawer CC, Wickenburg, AZ 85358.

HOMESTEAD CHAMPIONSHIP RODEO. Feb 7-9. Purpose: A fundraiser with proceeds going to Homestead youth athletic and recreational projects. Sponsor: Homestead Rodeo Assn, Box 994, Homestead, FL 33030.

LEWIS, SINCLAIR: BIRTH ANNIVERSARY. Feb. 7. American novelist and social critic. Recipient of Nobel Prize for Literature (1930). Among his novels: *Main Street*, *Babbitt* and *It Can't Happen Here*. Born Harry Sinclair Lewis at Sauk Center, MN, on Feb 7, 1885, Lewis died at Rome, Italy Jan 10, 1951.

LONG, CATHY (MRS. GILLIS): BIRTHDAY. Feb 7. U.S. Representative of Louisiana's 8th district, Democrat, of Alexandria, LA, born at Dayton, OH, on Feb 7, 1924.

MARDI GRAS SNOW DAZE. Feb 7-17. A festival of winter fun and frolic. With emphasis on costumes, Mardi Gras features a parade, world championship snowgolf, over-the-line snowball, beard growing contest, Yukon gold digger races and other zany events. Info from: Mardi Gras of Winter, Box 383, Sta A, Prince George, BC, Canada V2L 4S2.

MIAMI HOME SHOW. Feb 7-12. Coconut Grove Exhibition Ctr, Miami, FL. Info from Perl Exposition Corp, 6915 Red Rd, Suite 228, Coral Gables, FL 33143.

MORE, SIR THOMAS: BIRTHDAY. Feb 7. Anniversary of birth of lawyer, scholar, author, Lord Chancellor of England, martyr and Saint, at London on Feb 7, 1478. Refusing to recognize Henry VIII's divorce from Queen Catherine, the "Man for all Seasons" was found guilty of treason and imprisoned in the Tower of London, Apr 17, 1534. He was beheaded at Tower Hill on July 6, 1535, and his head displayed from Tower Bridge. Canonized in 1935. Memorial observed on June 22.

PERCHVILLE USA. Feb 7-9. Tawas Bay, MI. Coronation of Perchville King and Queen, parade, fishing contests, ice sculptures and perch dinners. Info from: Chamber of Commerce, Box 608, Tawas City, MI 48763.

SAN ANTONIO LIVESTOCK EXPOSITION. Feb 7-16. San Antonio, TX. Livestock show and rodeo. Sponsor: San Antonio Livestock Expo, Inc, Box 20228, San Antonio, TX 78220.

SILVER SPUR RODEO. Feb 7-9. Yuma County Fairgrounds. Info from: Yuma Jaycees, 1798 Arizona Ave, Yuma, AZ 85364.

SPACE MILESTONE: SOYUZ 24 (USSR). Feb 7. Two cosmonauts dock at Salyut 5 space lab. Returned to Earth Feb 25. Launched on Feb 7, 1977.

THOMPSON KINSMEN WINTER CARNIVAL. Feb 7-9. Thompson, Manitoba, Canada. Features the King Okimow and Little Okimow of the North contests, sled dog races, snowshoe races and family activities. Info from: Travel Manitoba, Dept 5058, Winnipeg, Manitoba, Canada R3C 3H8.

FEBRUARY 8 — SATURDAY
39th Day — Remaining, 326

A ZOO AFFAIR. Feb 8-16. Purpose: Valentine's celebration. Sponsor: North Carolina Zoological Park, Rt 4, Box 83, Asheboro, NC 27203.

February 1986

S	M	T	W	T	F	S
						1
2	3	4	5	6	7	8
9	10	11	12	13	14	15
16	17	18	19	20	21	22
23	24	25	26	27	28	

AMERICAN BOWLING CONGRESS NATIONAL CHAMPIONSHIPS TOURNAMENT. Feb 8- June 7. Cashman Field Ctr, Las Vegas, NV. Approximately 9,000 five-man teams compete for $2 million in prize funds. Info from: American Bowling Congress, 5301 S 76th St, Greendale, WI 53129.

BOY SCOUTS OF AMERICA BIRTHDAY ANNIVERSARY. Feb 8. Purpose: Celebrates founding of youth organization incorporated in Washington, DC, in 1910 and chartered by Congress in 1916. Info from: Communications Div, Boy Scouts of America, 1325 Walnut Hill Ln, Irving, TX 75038.

BRAZIL: CARNIVAL IN BRAZIL. Feb 8-11. Especially in Rio de Janeiro, this carnival is said to be one of the great folk festivals left on earth, and the big annual event in the life of Brazilians. Starts on Saturday night before Ash Wednesday and continues through Shrove Tuesday.

CHINESE NEW YEAR CELEBRATION. Feb 8-16. Chinatown, Los Angeles, CA. Info from: Chinese Chamber of Commerce, Bill Hong, VP, 425 Ginling Way, Los Angeles, CA 90012.

DEAN, JAMES; BIRTHDAY. Feb 8. American stage, film and television actor who achieved immense popularity during a brief career, was born Feb 8, 1931 at Fairmont, IN. Best remembered for his role in *Rebel Without a Cause*. Dean died in an automobile accident on Sept 30, 1955, at age 24.

INTERNATIONAL 500 SNOWMOBILE RACE. Feb 8. Sault Ste Marie, MI. A 500 mile snowmobile race on enclosed one mile oval track, limited to pro enduro snowmobiles and drivers. Info from: Internatl 500 Committee, Box 500, Sault Ste Marie, MI 49783.

MIAMI BEACH FESTIVAL OF THE ARTS. Feb 8-9. Miami Beach Convention Center Grounds, Miami Beach, FL. Info from: Fine Arts Board, City Hall, 1700 Convention Ctr Dr, Miami Beach, FL 33139.

MID ATLANTIC SPORTS AND BOAT SHOW. Feb 8-16. Pavilion, Virginia Beach, VA. Info from: City of Virginia Beach, Office of Public Info, Municipal Ctr, Virginia Beach, VA 23456.

MOON PHASE: NEW MOON. Feb 8. Moon enters New Moon phase at 7:55 p.m., E.S.T.

MYERS, JOHN T: BIRTHDAY. Feb 8. U.S. Representative of Indiana's 7th district, Republican, of Covington, IN, was born on Feb 8, 1927.

NATIONAL INVENTORS DAY. Feb 8-9. Purpose: Demonstrations of patented inventions and the induction of inventors into the National Inventors Hall of Fame. Info from: Oscar Mastin, Assistant Dir of Info, Patent and Trademark Office, Washington, DC 20231.

NORTH AMERICAN OUTDOOR SPEED SKATING CHAMPIONSHIPS. Feb 8-9. Olympic Speed Skating Oval, Lake Placid, NY. Info from: Chamber of Commerce, Olympic Arena, Lake Placid, NY 12946.

SHERMAN, WILLIAM TECUMSEH: BIRTHDAY: Feb 8. American soldier, born at Lancaster, OH, Feb 8, 1820. General Sherman is especially remembered for his devastating march through Georgia and his statement, "War is Hell." Died at New York City, Feb 14, 1891.

SILVER SPUR RODEO PARADE. Feb 8. Yuma AZ. Info from: Yuma Jaycees, Box 2797, Yuma, AZ 85364.

SOUTHEAST FLORIDA SCOTTISH FESTIVAL. Feb 8. Purpose: To promote Scottish heritage, and support scholarships for the teaching of bagpiping, drumming and Scottish highland and country dancing. Sponsor: Scottish American Society of South Florida, Inc, Box 633, Miami Shores, FL 33153.

SPACE MILESTONE: ARABSAT-1. Feb 8. League of Arab States communications satellite launched into geosynchronous orbit from Kourou, French Guiana, by ESA Feb 8, 1985.

SPACE MILESTONE: BRASILSAT-1 (Brazil). Feb 8. Brazilian communications satellite launched into geosynchronous orbit from Kourou, French Guiana, by ESA Feb 8, 1985.

STANGELAND, ARLAN: BIRTHDAY. Feb 8. U.S. Representative of Minnesota's 7th district, Republican, of Barnesville, MN, born in Fargo, ND, Feb 8, 1930.

COPYRIGHT © 1985 BY WILLIAM D. CHASE and HELEN M. CHASE

STURGEON FISHING SEASON. Feb 8-Mar 1. Fond du Lac, WI. "Sturgeon Capitol of the World." Annually, second Saturday in February through Mar 1. Info from: Conv & Visitors Bureau, 207 N Main St, Fond du Lac, WI 54935.

VERNE, JULES: BIRTHDAY. Feb 8. French writer, sometimes called "father of science fiction," born at Nantes, Feb 8, 1828. Author of such works as: *Around the World in Eighty Days* and *Twenty Thousand Leagues Under the Sea.* Died at Amiens, France, Mar 24, 1905.

FEBRUARY 9 — SUNDAY
40th Day — Remaining, 325

ADE, GEORGE: BIRTHDAY. Feb 9. American newspaperman, playwright and humorist, born Feb 9, 1866, at Kentland, IN. Remembered especially for his *Fables in Slang,* published in 1900. He died at Brook, IN, May 16, 1944.

ARCA 200 LATE MODEL STOCK CAR RACE. Feb 9. Daytona International Speedway, Daytona Beach, FL. Info from: Daytona Internatl Speedway, Larry Balewski, PR, Daytona Beach, FL 32015.

BUSCH CLASH OF '86. Feb 9. Daytona International Speedway, Info from: Daytona Internatl Speedway, Larry Balewski, PR, Daytona Beach, FL 32015.

CHINESE NEW YEAR. Feb 9. Traditional Chinese lunar year begins at sunset on day of second New Moon following the Winter Solstice. Begins Year 4683 or 4684 (depending on reckoning from a legendary beginning in 2697 or 2698 B.C.) of the ancient Chinese calendar, designated as the Year of the Tiger. Generally celebrated until the Lantern Festival (q.v.) fifteen days later, but merchants usually reopen their stores and places of business on the fifth day of the first lunar month.

CIRCLE K INTERNATIONAL WEEK. Feb 9-15. Purpose: To highlight the work and activities of Circle K for the general public. Sponsor: Circle K Dept, Kiwanis Internatl, 3636 Woodview Trace, Indianapolis, IN 46268.

FASCHING SUNDAY. Feb 9. Germany and Austria. The last Sunday before Lent.

FUTURE BUSINESS LEADERS OF AMERICA-PHI BETA LAMBDA WEEK. Feb 9-15. Purpose: To observe the founding of Future Business Leaders of America chapters in high schools and Phi Beta Lambda chapters in post-secondary schools. Info from: Future Business Leaders of America, Phi Beta Lambda, Inc, Yvonne Easter, 1908 Association Dr, Reston, VA 22091.

HALLEY'S COMET: PERIHELION 1986. Feb 9. Halley's Comet will reach perihelion (point nearest the sun) on Feb 9, 1986. This is the 46th calculated perihelion of the comet since the earliest probable reference to its appearance—Oct 15, 1404 B.C. The comet's periodicity was first predicted and described by England's Astronomer Royal, Edmund Halley (q.v.) in the 18th Century. Note: Halley's Comet will be nearest Earth on Apr 11, 1986, at which time its distance from Earth will be about 39,060,000 miles.

HARRISON, WILLIAM HENRY: BIRTHDAY. Feb 9. Ninth President of the U.S. (Mar 4-Apr 4, 1841). His term of office was the shortest in our nation's history (32 days). He was the first president to die in office (of pneumonia contracted during inaugural ceremonies). Born at Berkeley, VA, Feb 9, 1773. Died at Washington, DC, Apr 4, 1841.

LOWELL, AMY: BIRTHDAY. Feb 9. American poet born at Brookline, MA, Feb 9, 1874. Died there May 12, 1925.

NATIONAL BASKETBALL ASSOCIATION: ALL-STAR GAME. Feb 9. Reunion Arena, Dallas, TX. Info from: Brian McIntyre, PR Dir, Natl Basketball Assn, Olympic Tower, 645 Fifth Ave, New York, NY 10022.

NATIONAL CARDIOPULMONARY WEEK. Feb 9-15. Purpose: In recognition of the allied health professionals who work in the fields of cardiovascular and pulmonary medicine. Sponsor: Natl Society for Cardiopulmonary Technology, 1133 Fifteenth St, NW, Suite 620, Washington, DC 20005.

NATIONAL CRIME PREVENTION WEEK. Feb 9-15. Purpose: To alert America to growing menace and cost of crime, and stimulate public interest in year-around crime prevention activities. Sponsor: The Natl Exchange Club, James A. Schnoering, Exec VP, 3050 Central Ave, Toledo, OH 43606.

NATIONAL FUTURE HOMEMAKERS OF AMERICA/ HERO WEEK: Feb 9-15. Purpose: To call the nation's attention to the activities and goals of our organization and home economics education. Sponsor: Future Homemakers of America, 1910 Association Dr, Reston, VA 22091.

NATIONAL PEACH COUNCIL CONVENTION. Feb 9-12. Asheville, NC. Purpose: To talk about industry needs and provide opportunity to see new products and equipment. Sponsor: Natl Peach Council, Box 1085, Martinsburg, WV 25401.

NATIONAL SALUTE TO HOSPITALIZED VETERANS. Feb 9-15. Purpose: To show disabled and hospitalized veterans that their sacrifices in behalf of the nation and our freedom are remembered and appreciated. Sponsor: Veterans Administration Central Office, Voluntary Service (135), Edward F. Rose, Dir, 810 Vermont Ave, NW, Washington, DC 20420.

SHROVETIDE. Feb 9-11. The three days before Ash Wednesday: Shrove Sunday, Monday and Tuesday, a time for confession and for festivity before the beginning of Lent.

SINGAPORE: CHINGAY PROCESSION. Feb 9. Spectacular parade with dances, dragons, pugilistic displays and stilt walkers. Singapore's alternative to New Year's firecrackers. Public holiday.

FEBRUARY 10 — MONDAY
41st Day — Remaining, 324

BUN DAY. Feb 10. Iceland. Children invade homes in the morning with colorful sticks and receive gifts of whipped cream buns (on the Monday before Shrove Tuesday).

CARNIVAL. Feb 10-11. Period of festivities, feasts, foolishness and gaiety immediately before Lent begins on Ash Wednesday. Ordinarily carnival includes the period of Fasching (the Feast of Fools), being the Monday and Tuesday immediately preceding Ash Wednesday. The period of carnival may also be extended to include the five days, Friday through Shrove Tuesday, or even longer periods in some areas.

DENMARK: STREET URCHINS' CARNIVAL. Feb 10. Observed on Shrove Monday.

FASCHING. Feb 10-11. Germany and Austria. Fasching, also called Fasnacht, Fasnet or Feast of Fools, is a Shrovetide festival with processions of masked figures, both beautiful and grotesque. Always the two days (Rose Monday and Shrove Tuesday) between Fasching Sunday and Ash Wednesday.

FEAST OF ST. PAUL'S SHIPWRECK. Feb 10. Valletta, Malta. Holy day of obligation. Commemorates shipwreck of St. Paul on the north coast of Malta in A.D. 60.

COPYRIGHT © 1985 BY WILLIAM D. CHASE and HELEN M. CHASE

GASPARILLA PIRATE INVASION AND PARADE. Feb 10. Tampa, FL. Local businessmen costumed as pirates sail into Tampa Bay in authentic pirate ship and capture the City of Tampa to lead a colorful victory parade. Sponsor: Ye Mystic Krewe of Gasparilla, PO Box 1514, Tampa, FL 33601.

HAWAIIAN OPEN GOLF TOURNAMENT. Feb 10-16. Waialae Country Club Golf Course, Honolulu, HI. PGA Golf Tournament featuring top professional golfers. Info from: Hawaii Visitors Bureau, Honolulu, HI 96815.

LAMB, CHARLES: BIRTHDAY. Feb 10. English literary critic, poet and essayist, born at London on Feb 10, 1775. Lamb died at Edmonton, England, Dec 27, 1834.

NATIONAL CARDIOVASCULAR TECHNOLOGISTS RECOGNITION WEEK. Feb 10-14. Purpose: To enhance public awareness of cardiovascular medicine and recognize the services of the cardiovascular technologists as part of the health care team. Sponsor: American Cardiology Technologists Assn, 1980 Isaac Newton Sq South, Reston, VA 22090.

PASTERNAK, BORIS LEONIDOVICH: BIRTHDAY. Feb 10. Russian poet and novelist, born at Moscow, Feb 10, 1890. Best known work: *Doctor Zhivago*. Died at Moscow, May 30, 1960.

PLIMSOLL DAY. Feb 10. A day to remember Samuel Plimsoll, "The Sailors' Friend." A coal merchant turned reformer and politician was elected to Parliament in 1868. He attacked the practice of overloading heavily insured ships, calling them "coffin ships." His persistence brought about amendment of Britain's Merchant Shipping Act. The Plimsoll Line, named for him, is a line on the side of ships marking maximum load allowed by law. Samuel Plimsoll was born at Bristol, Feb 10, 1824, and died at Folkestone, June 3, 1898.

ROSE MONDAY. Feb. 10. Germany and Austria. The Monday before Shrove Tuesday.

ROYBAL, EDWARD R: BIRTHDAY. Feb 10. U.S. Representative of California's 25th district, Democrat, of Los Angeles, CA, born in Albuquerque, NM, on Feb 10, 1916.

SHROVE MONDAY. Feb 10. The Monday before Shrove Tuesday.

TAYLOR, GENE: BIRTHDAY. Feb 10. U.S. Representative of Missouri's 7th district, Republican, of Sarcoxie, MO, born near Sarcoxie on Feb 10, 1928.

WHITE, WILLIAM ALLEN: BIRTHDAY. Feb 10. American newspaperman, owner and editor of the *Emporia Gazette*. He coined the phrase "tinhorn politician," and in one obituary, wrote of the deceased that he had "the talent of a meat-packer, the morals of a moneychanger and the manners of an undertaker." White was born at Emporia, KS, Feb 10, 1868, and died there Jan 29, 1944.

FEBRUARY 11 — TUESDAY
42nd Day — Remaining, 323

BELGIUM: BINCHE CARNIVAL. Feb 11. Mardi Gras. Carnival with the world-famous "Gilles." Binche, Belgium.

BENTSEN, LLOYD: BIRTHDAY. Feb 11. U.S. Senator from Texas, Democrat, of Houston, TX, born in Mission, TX, on Feb 11, 1921.

BURSTING DAY. Feb 11. Iceland. Feasting on salted mutton and thick pea soup. (Shrove Tuesday.)

CAMEROON: YOUTH DAY. Feb 11. Youth Day is observed as public holiday in Cameroon.

EDISON, THOMAS ALVA: BIRTHDAY. Feb 11. American inventive genius and holder of more than 1,200 patents (including the incandescent electric lamp, phonograph, electric dynamo and key parts of many now familiar devices such as the movie camera, telephone transmitter, etc.). Edison said "Genius is one percent inspiration and ninety-nine percent perspiration." His birthday is now widely observed as Inventors' Day. Born at Milan, OH, Feb 11, 1847. Died at Menlo Park, NJ, Oct 18, 1931.

FULLER, MELVILLE WESTON: BIRTHDAY. Feb 11. Eighth Chief Justice of the U.S. Supreme Court, born at Augusta, ME, Feb 11, 1833. Died at Sorrento, ME, July 4, 1910.

IRAN: NATIONAL DAY. Feb 11. National holiday observed in Iran.

JAPAN: EMPIRE DAY, FOUNDING OF NATION. Feb 11. National holiday, 660 BC is traditional date of founding of Japan by 1st emperor, Jimmu Tenno.

MARDI GRAS. Feb 11. Celebrated especially in New Orleans, LA, Mobile, AL, and certain Mississippi and Florida cities. Last feast before Lent. Although *Mardi Gras* (Fat Tuesday, literally) is properly limited to Shrove Tuesday, it has come to be popularly applied to the preceding two weeks of intensive celebration. Observed in many localities.

OXLEY, MICHAEL, GARVEN: BIRTHDAY. Feb 11. U.S. Representative of Ohio's 4th district, Republican, of Findlay, OH, born there on Feb 11, 1944.

PACZKI DAY IN HAMTRAMCK. Feb 11. Shrove Tuesday, the day before Lenten fasting begins, is the occasion for baking and selling the delicious pastry known as Paczki (pronounced "panchkey") which is described as a "distant cousin of the jelly doughnut." Especially observed among the Polish citizens of Hamtramck, MI, where a single bakery produced more than 20,000 of the delicacies for Paczki Day in 1982.

SHROVE TUESDAY. Feb 11. Always the day before Ash Wednesday. Sometimes called Pancake Tuesday. Public holiday in Florida.

SHROVETIDE PANCAKE RACE. Feb 11. Olney, Buckinghamshire, England, and Liberal, Kansas. The pancake race at Olney has been run since 1445. Competitors must be women over 16 years of age, wearing traditional housewife's costume including apron and headcovering. With a toss and a flip of the pancake on the griddle which each must carry, the ladies dash from market place to the parish church where the winner receives a kiss from the ringer of the Pancake Bell. Shriving service follows. Starting time for the race is usually 11:45 a.m. Always on Shrove Tuesday.

SPACE MILESTONE: OSUMI (Japan). Feb 11. First Japanese satellite and Japan becomes fourth nation to send satellite into space. Feb 11, 1970.

VATICAN CITY: INDEPENDENCE ANNIVERSARY. Feb 11. The Lateran Treaty, signed by Pietro Cardinal Gasparri and Benito Mussolini on Feb 11, 1929, guaranteed the independence of the State of Vatican City and recognized the sovereignty of the Holy See over it. Area is about 109 acres.

WHITE SHIRT DAY. Feb 11. Anniversary of UAW-GM agreement following 44-day sit-down strike at General Motors' Flint, MI, factories in 1937. "Blue-collar" workers traditionally wear white shirts to work on this day, symbolic of workingman's dignity won. Has been observed by proclamation in Flint, MI.

FEBRUARY 12 — WEDNESDAY
43rd Day — Remaining, 322

ADAMS, LOUISA CATHERINE JOHNSON: BIRTHDAY. Feb 12. Wife of John Quincy Adams, 6th President of the U.S., born at London, England, Feb 12, 1775. Died May 14, 1852.

ASH WEDNESDAY. Feb 12. Lent begins. Forty days to Easter Sunday not including Sundays. Named for use of ashes in ceremonial penance.

BROWN, HANK: BIRTHDAY. Feb 12. U.S. Represenative of Colorado's 4th district, Republican, of Greeley, CO, born in Denver, CO, on Feb 12, 1940.

	S	M	T	W	T	F	S
February 1986							1
	2	3	4	5	6	7	8
	9	10	11	12	13	14	15
	16	17	18	19	20	21	22
	23	24	25	26	27	28	

COPYRIGHT © 1985 BY WILLIAM D. CHASE and HELEN M. CHASE

DARWIN, CHARLES ROBERT: BIRTHDAY. Feb 12. Author and naturalist, born at Shrewsbury, England, Feb 12, 1809. Best remembered for his books: *On the Origin of Species by Means of Natural Selection, or the Preservation of Favoured Races in the Struggle for Life*, and *The Descent of Man and Selection in Relation to Sex*. Darwin died at Down, Kent, Apr 19, 1882.

HOUSTON LIVESTOCK SHOW AND RODEO. Feb 12-Mar 2. Astrodome, Houston, TX. Stock show with 29,000 entries. "Wild rodeo action" and top name musical entertainment. Info from: Houston Livestock Show and Rodeo Assn, Box 20070, Houston, TX 77225.

KOSCIUSKO, THADDEUS: BIRTHDAY. Feb 12. Polish patriot born in Lithuania, Feb 12, 1746. Died at Solothurn, Switzerland, Oct 15, 1817.

LENT BEGINS. Feb 12-Mar 29. Christian churches observe period of fasting and penitence (40 days, not including Sundays) beginning on Ash Wednesday and ending on the Saturday before Easter.

LEWIS, JOHN LLEWELLYN: BIRTHDAY. Feb 12. American labor leader born near Lucas, IA, Feb 12, 1880. His parents came to the U.S. from Welsh mining towns, and Lewis left school in the seventh grade to become a miner himself. Became leader of United Mine Workers of America and champion of all miners' causes. Died at Washington, DC, June 11, 1969.

LINCOLN, ABRAHAM: ANNIVERSARY OF BIRTH. Feb 12. Observance of the birth will be marked by the laying of a wreath at the door of the Birthplace Cabin at Abraham Lincoln Birthplace National Historic Site. Info from: U.S. Dept of the Interior, Natl Park Service, Rt 1, Hodgenville, KY 42748.

LINCOLN, ABRAHAM: BIRTHDAY. Feb 12. Sixteenth President of the U.S. (Mar 4, 1861-Apr 15, 1865), and the first to be assassinated (On Good Friday, Apr 14, 1865, while watching a performance of *Our American Cousin*, at Ford's Theatre in Washington). His presidency encompassed the tragic Civil War. Especially remembered are his Emancipation Proclamation (Jan 1, 1863), his Gettysburg Address (Nov 19, 1863) and his proclamation establishing the last Thursday of November as Thanksgiving Day. Lincoln's birthday is observed on this day in most states, but on the first Monday in February in Delaware and Oregon. Lincoln was born in Hardin County, KY, Feb 12, 1809, and died at Washington, DC, Apr 15, 1865.

NATIONAL FARM MACHINERY SHOW AND CHAMPIONSHIP TRACTOR PULL. Feb 12-15. Kentucky Fair and Expo Ctr. Agricultural machinery exhibits. Info from: NFMS, KY Fair & Expo Ctr, Box 37130, Louisville, KY 40233.

OGLETHORPE DAY. Feb 12. General James Edward Oglethorpe (born at London, England, Dec 22, 1696), with some 100 other Englishmen, landed at what is now Savannah, GA, on Feb 12, 1733. Naming the new colony Georgia for England's King George II, Oglethorpe was organizer and first governor of the colony, and founder of the city of Savannah. Oglethorpe Day and Georgia Day observed on this date, particularly in the state of Georgia.

SPACE MILESTONE: VENERA 1 (USSR). Feb 12. Spacecraft launched from space platform in experiment projecting satellite into interplanetary space. Feb 12, 1961.

SPECTER, ARLEN: BIRTHDAY. Feb 12. U.S. Senator from Pennsylvania, Republican, of Philadelphia, PA, born in Wichita, KS, Feb 12, 1930.

FEBRUARY 13 — THURSDAY

44th Day — Remaining, 321

ABDNOR, JAMES: BIRTHDAY. Feb 13. U.S. Senator from South Dakota, Republican, of Kennebec, SD, was born in Kennebec on Feb 13, 1923.

CHICOUTIMI CARNAVAL SOUVENIR "1886". Feb 13-23. Info from: Carnaval-Souvenir de Chicoutimi, Inc, 67, rue Jacques-Cartier ouest, Chicoutimi, Quebec, Canada G7J 1E9.

CHURCHILL, RANDOLPH HENRY SPENCER: BIRTHDAY. Feb 13. English politician and the father of Winston Churchill. Born at Blenheim, Woodstock, Oxfordshire, on Feb 13, 1849. He died at London on Jan 24, 1895.

FIRST MAGAZINE PUBLISHED IN AMERICA: ANNIVERSARY. Feb 13. Andrew Bradford published *The American Magazine*, Feb 13, 1741, just three days ahead of Benjamin Franklin's *General Magazine*.

FIRST PUBLIC SCHOOL IN AMERICA: ANNIVERSARY. Feb 13. The Boston Latin School opened on Feb 13, 1635 and is America's oldest public school.

FLORIDA CITRUS FESTIVAL AND POLK COUNTY FAIR. Feb 13-22. Winter Haven, FL. Info from: Florida Citrus Showcase, Box 9229, Winter Haven, FL 33880.

FORT WORTH HOME AND GARDEN SHOW. Feb 13-16. Tarrant County Convention Center, Fort Worth, TX 76102.

INDIAN NATIONAL FINALS RODEO AND POW WOW. Feb 13-16. State Fairgrounds, Albuquerque, NM. World championship all Indian rodeo, ceremonial Indian dances, trade fair and Miss Indian rodeo pageant. Info from: Indian Natl Finals Rodeo, Inc, Box 214996, Sacramento, CA 95821.

NATIONAL KRAUT AND FRANKFURTER WEEK. Feb 13-22. Purpose: To promote the century-old alliance of kraut and frankfurters. Sponsor: Natl Kraut Packers Assn, 108½ E Main St, St Charles, IL 60174. Info from: Burson-Marsteller, 1 E Wacker Dr, Chicago, IL 60601.

OUTSTANDING YOUNG FARMERS AWARDS CONGRESS. Feb 13-16. Jackson, MS. Purpose: To honor and recognize the achievements of "nation's finest" 18-35-year-old farmers. Sponsor: Deere & Co. Info from: U.S. Jaycees, Box 7, Tulsa, OK 74121.

PIAZZETTA, GIOVANNI BATTISTA: BIRTHDAY. Feb 13. Prominent 18th century Venetian painter. Notable among his works are the *Ecstasy of St. Francis* and *Fortune Teller*. Born on Feb 13, 1682 at Venice and died there Apr 28, 1754.

7-ELEVEN TWIN 125 MILE QUALIFYING RACES (FOR DAYTONA 500). Feb 13. Daytona International Speedway, Daytona Beach, FL. Info from: Daytona Internatl Speedway, Larry Balewski, PR, Daytona Beach, FL 32015.

TRUMAN, BESS (ELIZABETH) VIRGINIA WALLACE: BIRTHDAY. Feb 13. Wife of Harry S. Truman, 33rd President of the U.S., born at Independence, MO, Feb 13, 1885. She died there on Oct 18, 1982.

WOOD, GRANT: BIRTH ANNIVERSARY. Feb 13. American artist especially noted for his powerful realism and satirical paintings of the American scene. Born near Anamosa, Iowa, on Feb 13, 1892. Wood studied art in France. He was a printer, sculptor, wood worker, and a high school and college teacher. Among his best remembered works are: "American Gothic," "Fall Plowing" and "Stone City." Wood died at Iowa City, Feb 12, 1942, and is buried at the Riverside Cemetery, Anamosa, Iowa. See also: the Grant Wood Art Festival, held annually at Stone City/Anamosa, Iowa, on the second Sunday in June.

COPYRIGHT © 1985 BY WILLIAM D. CHASE and HELEN M. CHASE

FEBRUARY 14 — FRIDAY
45th Day — Remaining, 320

ALLAIN, WILLIAM A: BIRTHDAY. Feb 14. William A. Allain, Governor of Mississippi, Democrat, was born at Washington, MS, on Feb 14, 1928.

ANCHORAGE FUR RENDEZVOUS. Feb 14-23. "Alaska's largest celebration." Features three world championships: Sled dog races, dog weight pulling contest, snow machine race, "the most northerly Grand Prix race in the world." Carnival, native dances, blanket toss, snowshoe ball games, races and exhibits. Info from: Anchorage Fur Rendezvous, Public Info Officer, Box 100773, Anchorage, AK 99510.

ARIZONA: ADMISSION DAY. Feb 14. Became 48th State on this day in 1912.

BLAZ, BEN: BIRTHDAY. Feb 14. Guam Delegate to 99th Congress, Republican, of Ordot, GU, born in Agana, GU, on Feb 14, 1928.

BONER, WILLIAM HILL: BIRTHDAY. Feb 14. U.S. Representative of Tennessee's 5th district, Democrat, of Nashville, TN, born in Nashville on Feb 14, 1945.

BUDWEISER INTERNATIONAL RACE OF CHAMPIONS. Feb 14. Daytona International Speedway, Daytona Beach, FL. Info from: Daytona Internatl Speedway, Larry Balewski, PR, Daytona Beach, FL 32015.

CLOVERDALE CITRUS FAIR. Feb 14-17. Exhibits, art show, wine tasting, carnival, parade and family fun. Info from: Cloverdale Citrus Fair Assn, Box 445, Cloverdale, CA 95425.

FERRIS WHEEL DAY. Feb 14. Anniversary of the birth of George Washington Gale Ferris, American engineer and inventor, at Galesburg, IL on Feb 14, 1859. Among his many accomplishments as a civil engineer Ferris is best remembered as the inventor of the Ferris Wheel which he developed for the World's Columbian Exposition at Chicago in 1893. Built on the Midway Plaisance, the 250-feet-in-diameter Ferris Wheel (with 36 coaches, each capable of carrying 40 passengers), proved one of the greatest attractions of the fair. It was America's answer to the Eiffel Tower of the Paris International Exposition of 1889. Ferris died at Pittsburgh, PA, on Nov 22, 1896.

GERMANY: INTERNATIONAL FILMFEST BERLIN. Feb 14-25. Info from: Berliner Festspiele, Budapester Strasse 50, 1 Berlin 30.

GREAT AMERICAN CHOCOLATE FESTIVAL. Feb 14-17. Hotel Hershey & Country Club, Hershey, PA. Purpose: To provide an arena where chocolate lovers can sample till their hearts content in an elegant surrounding. Sponsor: Hotel Hershey, Sharon L. Hassinger, Assistant Gen Mgr, Sales Marketing, Box BB, Hershey, PA 17033.

GREGG, JUDD: BIRTHDAY. Feb 14. U.S. Representative of New Hampshire's 2nd district, Republican, of Greenfield, NH, born in Nashua, NH, Feb 14, 1947.

KOMFORT KOACH FLORIDA 200. (NASCAR Daytona Dash Series Race) Feb 14. Info from: Daytona Intl Speedway, Larry Balewski, PR, Daytona Beach, FL 32015.

LOVE, EDMUND GEORGE: BIRTHDAY. Feb 14. American teacher, historian, newspaper columnist and author Edmund Love was born at Flushing, MI, Feb 14, 1912. Said to be the only Love born on Valentine's Day. Among his books: *Subways Are for Sleeping*, *War Is a Private Affair*, *Arsenic and Red Tape* and *Hanging On*.

MARTINEZ, MATTHEW GILBERT, JR: BIRTHDAY. Feb 14. U.S. Representative of California's 30th district, Democrat, of Montebello, CA, was born at Walsenburg, CO, Feb 14, 1929.

February 1986

S	M	T	W	T	F	S
						1
2	3	4	5	6	7	8
9	10	11	12	13	14	15
16	17	18	19	20	21	22
23	24	25	26	27	28	

OREGON: ADMISSION DAY. Feb 14. Became 33rd State on this day in 1859.

PRESIDENT'S COMMITTEE ON EMPLOYMENT OF THE HANDICAPPED: NATIONAL POSTER CONTEST DEADLINE. Feb 14. Purpose: To sensitize young people to the problems and abilities of disabled people through the use of graphics. Sponsor: The President's Committee on Employment of the Handicapped, 1111 20th St, NW, Washington, DC 20036.

RACE RELATIONS DAY. Feb 14. A day designated by some churches to recognize the importance of interracial relations. Formerly was observed on Abraham Lincoln's birthday or on the Sunday preceding it. Since 1970, observance has generally been on Feb 14.

RIVERSIDE COUNTY'S NATIONAL DATE FESTIVAL. Feb 14-23. Official Riverside County Fair. Arabian Nights pageant, musical fantasy, camel and ostrich races and date exhibits. Info from: Riverside County's Natl Date Festival, PO Drawer NNNN, Indio, CA 92202.

ST. VALENTINE'S DAY. Feb 14. Celebrates the festival of two saints of this name martyred by the Roman Emperor Claudius on the same day. Now a festival of lovers and an occasion for exchange of affectionate or humorous greetings.

SNOWSATION 1986. Feb 14-16. Features chariot racing and other winter activities. Info from: Chamber of Commerce, Box 1095, Saratoga, WY 82331.

SPACE MILESTONE: LUNA 20 (USSR). Feb 14. Launched Feb 14, 1972. Unmanned lunar probe soft-landed on Moon, Feb 21, collected samples, and returned to Earth, Feb 25.

SPACE MILESTONE: SMM (US). Feb 14. Unmanned Delta rocket, a "Solar Maximum Mission Observatory," launched. Intended to study solar flares. Feb 14, 1980.

VALENTINE'S DAY MASSACRE. Feb 14. Anniversary of Chicago gangland executions in 1929, when gunmen posing as police shot seven members of the George "Bugs" Moran gang.

VITICULTURISTS' DAY (TRIFON ZAREZAN). Feb. 14. Bulgaria. Celebrated since Thracian times, festivities are based on cult of Dionysus, god of merriment and wine.

WALLET, SKEEZIX: "BIRTHDAY." Feb 14. Comic strip character in "Gasoline Alley," by Frank King, and the first cartoon character to grow and age with the days, weeks and years of publication. Foundling child of Walt and Phyllis Wallet, discovered on doorstep Feb 14, 1921, Skeezix grew through childhood, marriage, military service in World War II, returning home to parenthood and business after the war. Comic strip started in *Chicago Tribune*, Aug 23, 1919.

WHISKEY FLAT DAYS. Feb 14-17. Celebration in observance of the gold discovery in Whiskey Flats in 1884. Sponsor: Kernville Chamber of Commerce, Box 397, Kernville, CA 93238.

FEBRUARY 15 — SATURDAY
46th Day — Remaining, 319

ANTHONY, SUSAN BROWNELL: BIRTHDAY. Feb 15. American reformer and militant advocate of woman suffrage. She was arrested and fined in 1872 for voting — a criminal act if done by a woman! First American woman to have her likeness on coinage (1979, Susan B. Anthony dollar). Born at Adams, MA, Feb 15, 1820. Died at Rochester, NY, Mar 13, 1906.

BARRYMORE, JOHN: BIRTHDAY. Feb 15. American actor of famous acting family, born John Blythe at Philadelphia, PA, Feb 15, 1882. Died at Los Angeles, CA, May 29, 1942. U.S. Postal Service stamp was issued in June 1982 featuring Ethel, John and Lionel Barrymore.

BLOCK, JOHN R: BIRTHDAY. Feb 15. John R. Block, U.S. Secretary of Agriculture (sworn in on Jan 23, 1981), was born at Gilson, IL, on Feb 15, 1935.

COPYRIGHT © 1985 BY WILLIAM D. CHASE and HELEN M. CHASE

CERMAK, ANTON J: ASSASSINATION ANNIVERSARY. Feb 15. At Bay Front Park, Miami, FL, on Feb 15, 1933, an assassin aiming at President-elect Franklin D. Roosevelt had his aim deflected by a spectator. Cermak, mayor of Chicago, was struck and killed instead. Giuseppe (Joe) Zangara, the 32-year-old assassin, who had emigrated from Italy in 1923, was electrocuted at the Raiford, Florida State Prison, on Mar 20, 1933.

CLARK, ABRAHAM: BIRTHDAY. Feb 15. Signer of the Declaration of Independence, farmer and lawyer, born Feb 15, 1726. Died Sept 15, 1794.

CLARK AIR BASE: DR. MARTIN LUTHER KING, JR. TRACK AND FIELD MEET. Feb 15-16. Clark Air Base, Republic of the Philippines. Teams of men and women from all over the Pacific, Philippines and the U.S. compete. Info from: Chief, MWR Div, 3 CSG/SS, APO SF 96274.

EAGLE AWARENESS. Feb 15-16. Purpose: Entertaining and educational slide lecture about eagles, promoting public awareness of need for protection of all birds of prey. Live birds introduced to viewers. Sponsor: Pinnacle Mountain State Park, Rt 1, Box 34, Roland, AR 72135.

GOODY'S 300 (NASCAR Busch Late Model Sportsman stock car race). Feb 15. Daytona International Speedway, Daytona Beach, FL. Info from: Daytona Internatl Speedway, Larry Balewski, PR, Daytona Beach, FL 32015.

GRANT SEAFOOD FESTIVAL. Feb 15-16. Purpose: Promotion and conservation of the Indian River and its shelfish industry. Info from: Grant Community Club, Box 44, Grant, FL 32949.

HAWAII: GREAT WAIKOLOA HORSE RACES AND RODEO. Feb 15-16. Waikoloa Stables, Waikoloa, HI. Rodeo events with matched horse races on flat track. Info from: Hawaii Visitors Bureau, Honolulu, HI 96815.

IMPERIAL VALLEY LETTUCE CHARITY BALL. Feb 15. Purpose: To focus attention on the $89,161,000 lettuce industry we have here, in the Imperial Valley. Sponsor: Los Vigilantes, Box 3006, El Centro, CA 92243.

LUPERCALIA. Feb 15. Anniversary of ancient Roman fertility festival. Thought by some to have been established by Romulus and Remus who, legend says, were suckled by a she-wolf at Lupercal (a cave in Palestine). Goats and dogs were sacrificed. Lupercalia celebration persisted until the 5th century of the Christian era. Possibly a forerunner of Valentine's Day customs.

MENENDEZ de AVILES, PEDRO: BIRTHDAY. Feb 15. Spanish explorer and naval adventurer, born Feb 15, 1519. Explored Florida coastal regions for king of Spain and established a fort at St. Augustine in Sept 1565. He died Sept 17, 1574, at Santander, Spain.

NATIONAL FFA WEEK. Feb 15-22. Purpose: To promote the FFA organization and vocational argriculture education nationwide. Sponsor: Natl FFA Organization, Natl FFA Center, Information Dir, Box 15160, Alexandria, VA 22309.

REMEMBER THE MAINE DAY. Feb 15. American battleship, *Maine*, was blown up while at anchor in Havana harbor, at 9:40 p.m., on this day in 1898. The ship, under the command of Capt Charles G. Sigsbee, sank quickly and 260 members of its crew were lost. Inflamed public opinion in the U.S. ignored the lack of evidence to establish responsibility for the explosion. "Remember the Maine" became the war cry and a declaration of war against Spain followed in April 1898.

ROARING CAMP RAIL ENTHUSIAST FESTIVAL. Feb 15-17. Antique railroad demonstrations. Info from: Roaring Camp & Big Trees Narrow-gauge Railroad, Felton, Santa Cruz County, CA 95018.

SPANISH WAR MEMORIAL DAY AND MAINE MEMORIAL DAY. Feb 15. Massachusetts.

TIFFANY, CHARLES LEWIS: BIRTHDAY. Feb 15. American jeweler whose name became synonymous with high standards of quality, was born at Killingly, CT, Feb 15, 1812, and died at New York City on Feb 18, 1902. He was the father of artist, Louis Comfort Tiffany (q.v.).

WASHINGTON BIRTHDAY FESTIVAL. Feb 15-23. Eustis, FL. A festival in honor of our nation's first president. Info from: Chamber of Commerce, Box 1210, Eustis, FL 32726.

FEBRUARY 16 — SUNDAY
47th Day — Remaining, 318

BEAUSEJOUR WINTER FAREWELL. Feb 16-23. Beausejour, Manitoba, Canada. Canadian Power Toboggan Championship races. Info from: Travel Manitoba, Dept 5058, Winnipeg, Manitoba, Canada R3C 3H8.

BERGEN, EDGAR: BIRTHDAY. Feb 16. Actor, radio entertainer and ventriloquist, voice of Charlie McCarthy, Mortimer Snerd and Effie Klinker, born at Chicago, IL, Feb 16, 1903. Died at Las Vegas, NV, Sept 30, 1978.

BIG BROTHERS/BIG SISTERS APPRECIATION WEEK. Feb 16-22. Purpose: To focus community awareness on the unique service provided by the organization. Sponsor: Big Brothers/Big Sisters of America, 230 N 13th St, Philadelphia, PA 19107.

BROTHERHOOD/SISTERHOOD WEEK. Feb 16-22. Purpose: A kick-off period for programs emphasizing the need for year-round commitment to brotherhood/sisterhood. Sponsor: Natl Conference of Christians and Jews, Harry Robinson, PR Dir, 71 5th Ave, New York, NY 10003.

DAYTONA 500 NASCAR-FIA (Winston Cup Grand National stock car classic). Feb 16. Daytona International Speedway, Daytona Beach, FL. Info from: Daytona Internatl Speedway, Larry Balewski, PR, Daytona Beach, FL 32015.

FESTIVAL DU VOYAGEUR. Feb 16-23. Winnipeg, Manitoba, Canada. Music, food and "Joie de vivre" of the fur trade era. Shell Canada Sled Dog Classic, snowmobile and snowshoe races. Info from: Travel Manitoba, Dept 5058, Winnipeg, Manitoba, Canada R3C 3H8.

FLAHERTY, ROBERT JOSEPH: BIRTHDAY. Feb 16. American film maker, explorer and author, called "father of the documentary film," born at Iron Mountain, MI, Feb 16, 1884. Died at Dunnerston, VT, July 23, 1951. Films included: *Nanook of the North, Moana* and *Man of Aran*.

Le GATINEAU 55. Feb 16. Hull, Quebec, Canada. Canada's World Loppet Race, 55 km long, heads off and finishes at Gatineau Park. Info from: Box 69, Station A, Ottawa, Ont, K1N 8V3 Canada.

HARRIS, JOE FRANK: BIRTHDAY. Feb 16. Joe Frank Harris, Governor of Georgia, Democrat, was born at Atco, GA, on Feb 16, 1936.

HEALTH EDUCATION WEEK. Feb 16-22. New York State. Purpose: To promote healthful behavior and healthy lifestyles. Third full week in February. Sponsor: NY State Health Dept, Health Education Promotion Services Group, Corning Tower Bldg, Rm 1084, Empire State Plaza, Albany, NY 12237.

COPYRIGHT © 1985 BY WILLIAM D. CHASE and HELEN M. CHASE

INTERNATIONAL FRIENDSHIP WEEK. Feb 16-22. Purpose: Promotion of international friendship and the international language of Esperanto. Sponsor: Internatl Society of Friendship & Good Will, Dr. Stanley Drake, Pres, Box 756, Shelby, NC 28151.

KING, WAYNE: BIRTH ANNIVERSARY. Feb 16. American saxophonist and band leader, widely known as "the Waltz King," was born at Savannah, IL, on Feb 16, 1901. His own composition, "The Waltz You Save for Me," was his theme song. King died at age 84 at Paradise Valley, AZ, on July 16, 1985.

MOON PHASE: FIRST QUARTER. Feb 16. Moon enters First Quarter phase at 2:55 p.m., E.S.T.

POMQUET ACADIAN WINTER CARNIVAL. Feb 16-23. Pomquet, Nova Scotia. Winter carnival with parade, exhibits, dances and an Acadian supper and mass. Info from: Dept of Tourism, Box 456, Halifax, NS B3J 2R5 Canada.

RICHARDS, IVOR ARMSTRONG: BIRTHDAY. Feb 16. Author of many books on literary criticism, himself a "critic's critic," born at Sandbach, Cheshire, England, Feb 16, 1893. Died at Cambridge, England, Sept 7, 1979.

WILSON, HENRY: BIRTHDAY. Feb 16. Eighteenth Vice President of the U.S. (1873-1875), born, Farmington, NH, Feb 16, 1812. Died, Washington, DC, Nov 22, 1875.

WORLD CHAMPIONSHIP CRAB RACES. Feb 16. Crab races, crab dinners and entertainment. Info from: Chamber of Commerce, Box 246, Crescent City, CA 95531.

FEBRUARY 17 — MONDAY
48th Day — Remaining, 317

ANDERSON, MARIAN: BIRTHDAY. Feb 17. Foremost American contralto and one-time U.S. delegate to the United Nations. Marian Anderson was born in Philadelphia, PA, Feb 17, 1902. See also entry for Apr 9.

GEORGE WASHINGTON BIRTHDAY PARADE. Feb 17. Colonial regiments, military bands, fife and drum corps, bagpipe bands and floats. "Nation's largest parade honoring our first President." Info from: Alexandria Tourist Council, 221 King St, Alexandria, VA 22314.

GERONIMO: DEATH ANNIVERSARY. Feb 17. American Indian of the Chiricahua (Apache) tribe, was born about 1829 in Arizona. He was the leader of a small band of warriors whose devastating raids in Arizona, New Mexico and Mexico, caused the U.S. Army to send 5,000 men to recapture him after his first escape. He was confined at Fort Sill, OK, where he died on Feb 17, 1909, after dictating, for publication, the story of his life.

GREEN MONDAY. Feb 17. Cyprus. Green, or Clean, Monday is the first Monday of Lent. Lunch in the fields, with bread, olives and uncooked vegetables and no meat or dairy products.

HAYES, CHARLES ARTHUR: BIRTHDAY. Feb 17. U.S. Representative of Illinois' 1st district, Democrat, of Chicago, IL, born in Cairo, IL, on Feb 17, 1918.

JAMES E. SULLIVAN MEMORIAL AWARD BANQUET. Feb 17. Award dinner and ceremony for announcement of America's finest amateur athlete. Info from: Indiana Sports Corp, Susan Polakoff, PR Dir, 251 N Illinois, Suite 910, Indianapolis, IN 46204.

LAENNEC, RENE THEOPHILE HYACINTHE: BIRTHDAY. Feb 17. Famed French physician, author and inventor of the stethoscope, called "father of chest medicine." He wrote extensively about respiratory and heart ailments. Born at Quimper, France, on Feb 17, 1781. He died near there, Aug 13, 1826.

McCLURE, SAMUEL SIDNEY: BIRTHDAY. Feb 17. Irish-American newspaper editor and publisher, founder of newspaper syndicate, born in County Antrim, Ireland, Feb 17, 1857. Died at New York City, Mar 21, 1949.

NATIONAL FIELD TRIAL CHAMPIONSHIP. Feb 17-25. Ames Plantation, Grand Junction, TN. Purpose: To select the national champion all-age bird dog. Sponsor: Natl Field Trial Champion Assn, Box 389, Grand Junction, TN 38039.

PEALE, RAPHAEL: BIRTHDAY. Feb 17. American painter, member of famous family of early American painters, born at Annapolis, MD, Feb 17, 1774. Died Mar 4, 1825.

PRESIDENT'S DAY. Feb 17. Hawaii. Third Monday in February.

WASHINGTON, GEORGE: BIRTHDAY OBSERVANCE (LEGAL HOLIDAY). Feb 17. Legal public holiday (Public Law 90-363 sets Washington's Birthday observance on the third Monday in February each year—applicable to federal employees and to the District of Columbia). Observed on this day in all states. See also: entry for Feb 22.

FEBRUARY 18 — TUESDAY
49th Day — Remaining, 316

GAMBIA: NATIONAL HOLIDAY. Feb 18. Independence Day. Independence from Britain granted Feb 18, 1965. Referendum in April 1970 established The Gambia as a republic within the Commonwealth.

OREGON SHAKESPEAREAN FESTIVAL. Feb 18-Oct 26. Eleven plays in repertory in the indoor Angus Bowmer and Black Swan Theatres, and outdoor Elizabethan Stage (June 3-Sept 28). Info from: Oregon Shakespearean Festival Assn, Box 158, Ashland, OR 97520.

PEABODY, GEORGE: BIRTHDAY. Feb 18. American merchant and philanthropist, born Feb 18, 1795. Died Nov 4, 1869.

RABINOWITZ, SOLOMON: BIRTHDAY. Feb 18. Russian born author and humorist better known by his pen name, Sholem Aleichem, Rabinowitz was born in the Ukraine, Feb 18, 1859. Affectionately known in the U.S. as the "Jewish Mark Twain." He died at New York City, May 13, 1916.

TIFFANY, LOUIS COMFORT: BIRTHDAY. Feb 18. American artist, son of famed jeweler, Charles L. Tiffany (q.v.). Best remembered for his remarkable work with decorative iridescent "favrile" glass. Born at New York City on Feb 18, 1848, and died there Jan 17, 1933.

UNITED NATIONS CONFERENCE. Feb 18-Mar 21. Vienna. United Nations Conference on the Law of Treaties between States and International Organizations or between International Organizations.

WARNER, JOHN WILLIAM: BIRTHDAY. Feb 18. U.S. Senator from Virginia, Republican, born Feb 18, 1927.

WILLKIE, WENDELL LEWIS: BIRTHDAY. Feb 18. American lawyer, author, public utility executive and politician, born at Elwood, IN, Feb 18, 1892. Presidential nominee of the Republican Party in 1940. Remembered too for his book, *One World*, published in 1943. Willkie died at New York City, Oct 8, 1944.

YOUNG DIPLOMATS OF DALLAS: ANNIVERSARY. Feb 18. Purpose: To celebrate the anniversary of The Young Diplomats of Dallas, an organization formed "for the purpose of teaching international etiquette and good manners to our young people who will be our leaders of the future." Info from: Mary F. Seagraves, 6019 Hollis Ave, Dallas, TX 75227.

February *1986*	S	M	T	W	T	F	S
							1
	2	3	4	5	6	7	8
	9	10	11	12	13	14	15
	16	17	18	19	20	21	22
	23	24	25	26	27	28	

COPYRIGHT © 1985 BY WILLIAM D. CHASE and HELEN M. CHASE

FEBRUARY 19 — WEDNESDAY
50th Day — Remaining, 315

ANTIQUE AUTOMOBILE CLUB OF AMERICA: WINTER MEET. Feb 19-23. Fort Lauderdale, FL. Info from: Box 417, Hershey, PA 17033.

COPERNICUS, NICOLAUS: BIRTHDAY. Feb 19. Polish astronomer who revolutionized scientific thought with his Copernican theory which put the sun at the center of our planetary system. Born at Torun, Poland, Feb 19, 1473, he died in E Prussia on May 24, 1543.

DISNEY WORLD ON ICE. Feb 19-23. Memorial Coliseum, Portland, OR. Info from: Convention & Visitors Assn, Inc, 26 SW Salmon, Portland, OR 97204.

GARRICK, DAVID: BIRTHDAY. Feb 19. English actor and playwright born Feb 19, 1717. Died Jan 20, 1779.

HEDIN, SVEN: BIRTH ANNIVERSARY. Feb 19. Swedish explorer and scientist, Sven Anders Hedin, was born at Stockholm on Feb 19, 1865, and died there on Nov 26, 1952. His Tibetan explorations provided the first substantial knowledge of that region to the rest of the world.

KNIGHTS OF PYTHIAS: FOUNDING ANNIVERSARY. Feb 19. The social and fraternal order, the Knights of Pythias, was founded at Washington, DC, Feb 19, 1864.

KRAMER, KENNETH BENTLEY: BIRTHDAY. Feb 19. U.S. Representative of Colorado's 5th district, Republican, of Colorado Springs, CO, born in Chicago, IL, Feb 19, 1942.

MARDI GRAS CELEBRATION. Feb 19. Costumed merchants parade down Olvera Street for evening of music and fun before the beginning of Lent. Info from: El Pueblo de Los Angeles State Historic Park, 845 N Alameda St, Los Angeles, CA 90012.

FEBRUARY 20 — THURSDAY
51st Day — Remaining, 314

ATIYEH, VICTOR G: BIRTHDAY. Feb 20. Victor G. Atiyeh, Governor of Oregon, Republican, was born at Portland, OR, on Feb 20, 1923.

DOUGLASS, FREDERICK: DAY. Feb 20. American journalist, orator and antislavery leader, born, Tuckahoe, MD, probably in Feb 1817. Died, Anacostia Heights, DC, Feb 20, 1895. Original name before his escape from slavery, Frederick Augustus Washington Bailey.

ESCAPE '86 CONFERENCE. Feb 20-23. Pipestem State Park, Pipestem, WV. Purpose: To enhance the training of emergency service personnel and allow the exchange of new and innovative techniques. Sponsor: Pipestem State Park & Regional Educational Services, Pipestem, WV 25979.

FORT WORTH AUTO SHOW. Feb 20-23. Info from: Tarrant County Conv Ctr, 1111 Houston St, Ft Worth, TX 76102.

GREAT SOUTHWEST ROUNDUP OF DIRECT MARKETING FACTS AND STRATEGIES. Feb 20-21. Purpose: To provide a forum for the exchange of direct marketing expertise information, facts and strategies. Sponsor: Direct Marketing Assn of North Texas, J. Johnson, Box 1204, Arlington, TX 76004.

McCONNELL, MITCH: BIRTHDAY. Feb 20. U.S. Senator from Kentucky, Republican, of Louisville, KY, born in Colbert County, AL, Feb 20, 1942.

METHODIST COLLEGE FINE ARTS FESTIVAL. Feb 20-28. Purpose: To associate the fine arts with people of the area and this time. Sponsor: Methodist College, Dr. Jack Peyrouse, 5400 Ramsey St, Fayetteville, NC 28301.

PISCES, THE FISH. Feb 20-Mar 20. In the astronomical/astrological Zodiac, which divides the sun's apparent orbit into twelve segments, the period Feb 19-Mar 21 is identified, traditionally, as the sun-sign of Pisces, the Fish. The ruling planet is Neptune.

PRESCOTT, WILLIAM: BIRTHDAY. Feb 20. American revolutionary soldier, born, Groton, MA, Feb 20, 1726. Died Pepperell, MA, Oct 13, 1795. Credited with the order; "Don't fire until you see the whites of their eyes," at the Battle of Bunker Hill, June 17, 1775.

SPACE MILESTONE: FIRST AMERICAN IN SPACE ANNIVERSARY. Feb 20. John Herschel Glenn became the first American, and the third man, to orbit Earth, on Feb 20, 1962. Spacecraft Mercury-Atlas 6, made three orbits of Earth.

TAIWAN: TOURISM WEEK. Feb 20-26. Tourism Week embraces Tourism Day and the three days preceding and succeeding it. See Tourism Day (Lantern Festival) Mar 6.

FEBRUARY 21 — FRIDAY
52nd Day — Remaining, 313

ANDERSON, GLENN M: BIRTHDAY. Feb 21. U.S. Representative of California's 32nd district, Democrat, of San Pedro, CA, born in Hawthorne, CA, on Feb 21, 1913.

ANTHONY, BERYL FRANKLIN, JR: BIRTHDAY. Feb 21. U.S. Representative of Arkansas' 4th district, Democrat, of El Dorado, AR, born in El Dorado on Feb 21, 1938.

AUDEN, WYSTAN HUGH: BIRTHDAY. Feb 21. Pulitzer Prize winning American poet born at York, England, Feb 21, 1907. Died Sept 27, 1973.

BANGLADESH: MARTYRS DAY. Feb 21. National mourning day in memory of martyrs of the Bengali Language Movement in 1952. Mourners gather at the Azimpur graveyard and proceed to Shaheed Minar.

EAGLES WEEKEND. Feb 21-22. Lake Barkley State Resort Park, Cadiz, KY. A tribute to the great American Eagle. Field trips, guest speakers and presentations on the Eagle. Info from: Kentucky Dept of Parks, Capital Plaza Tower, Frankfort, KY 40601.

HELSINKI, FINLAND: SNOW RALLY. Feb 21-23. European Championships. Info from: Helsingin Urheiluautoilijat, Suoninkatu 1 C 00530, Helsinki, Finland.

LA BELLE SWAMP CABBAGE FESTIVAL. Feb 21-23. La Belle, FL. Celebration pays tribute to Florida's state tree, the cabbage palm and its tender growth bud. The edible heart of the palm is chopped crossways and prepared much like regular garden variety cabbage. Country music and crafts. Info from: Swamp Cabbage Festival, Box 176, La Belle, FL 33935.

MALCOLM X: ASSASSINATION ANNIVERSARY. Feb 21. Malcolm X, a Black leader who renounced the Black Muslim sect to form the Organization of Afro-American Unity, was shot and killed as he spoke to a rally at the Audubon Ballroom in New York City, on Feb 21, 1965. Three men were convicted of the murder in 1966 and sentenced to life in prison.

MIAMI INTERNATIONAL BOAT SHOW. Feb 21-26. Miami Beach Conv Ctr, Miami Beach, FL. Info from: Bruce Rubin Associates, 2655 Le Jeune Rd, Coral Gables, FL 33134.

"NEW YORKER" MAGAZINE: BIRTHDAY. Feb 21. First issue published on Feb 21, 1925.

COPYRIGHT © 1985 BY WILLIAM D. CHASE and HELEN M. CHASE

NOWAK, HENRY J: BIRTHDAY. Feb 21. U.S. Representative of New York's 33rd district, Democrat-Liberal, of Buffalo, NY, born in Buffalo, Feb 21, 1935.

PRESIDENT NIXON'S TRIP TO CHINA: ANNIVERSARY. Feb 21-28. Richard Nixon became the first U.S. president to visit any country not diplomatically recognized by the U.S. when he went to the People's Republic of China for meetings with Chairman Mao Tse-tung and Premier Chou En-Lai. Nixon arrived at Peking on Feb 21, 1972, and departed China on Feb 28. The "Shanghai Communique" (q.v) was issued Feb 27.

SANDINO, CESAR AUGUSTO: ASSASSINATION ANNIVERSARY. Feb 21. Nicaraguan guerilla leader after whom the Sandinistas of the present day are named. Sandino, born in 1893 (exact date unknown), was murdered (along with his brother and several aides) at Managua on Feb 21, 1934. He and his followers had eluded the occupying force of U.S. Marines as well as the Nicaraguan National Guard from 1927 until 1933. Regarded by the U.S. as an outlaw and a bandit, he is revered as a martyred patriot hero by many Nicaraguans. His successful resistance and the resulting widespread anti-U.S. feeling were largely responsible for inauguration of a U.S. counter action—the "Good Neighbor Policy" toward Latin American nations during the administration of Pres. Franklin D. Roosevelt.

SNOWE, OLYMPIA J: BIRTHDAY. Feb 21. U.S. Representative of Maine's 2nd district, Republican, of Auburn, ME, born in Augusta, ME, Feb 21, 1947.

SQUARE DANCE WEEKEND. Feb 21-22. Lake Cumberland State Resort Park, Jamestown, KY. Info from: Kentucky Dept of Parks, Capital Plaza Tower, Frankfort, KY 40601.

TRACK AND FIELD (INDOOR): NAIA MEN'S DIVISION CHAMPIONSHIP. Feb 21-22. Kansas City, MO. Info from: Natl Assn of Intercollegiate Athletics, 1221 Baltimore, Kansas City, MO 64105.

TRACK AND FIELD (INDOOR): NAIA WOMEN'S DIVISION CHAMPIONSHIP. Feb 21-22. Kansas City, MO. Info from: Natl Assn of Intercollegiate Athletics, 1221 Baltimore, Kansas City, MO 64105.

WASHINGTON MONUMENT ANNIVERSARY. Feb 21. Monument to first president was dedicated on Feb 21, 1885. Washington, DC.

FEBRUARY 22 — SATURDAY
53rd Day — Remaining, 312

AMERICAN BIRKEBEINER. Feb 22. America's largest cross country ski race with 10,000 competitors from nearly 40 states and a dozen foreign countries. A 55 kilometer race from Hayward to Telemark, WI, with shorter race for novice skiers. Info from: American Birkebeiner, Box 31, Hayward, WI 54843.

BADEN-POWELL, ROBERT: BIRTHDAY. Feb 22. British army officer who was founder of the Boy Scouts and Girl Guides, was born at London, Feb 22, 1857. He died in Kenya, Africa, Jan 8, 1941.

BRYANT, JOHN WILEY: BIRTHDAY. Feb 22. U.S. Representative of Texas' 5th district, Democrat, of Dallas, TX, born at Lake Jackson, TX, on Feb 22, 1947.

CLARK AIR BASE: SOUL FOOD EXTRAVAGANZA. Feb 22. Clark Air Base, Republic of the Philippines. Purpose: Soul food cookoff with categories in meat, fish and fowl, casseroles, rice and pasta dishes, salads, breads and desserts. Continuous live entertainment and competitive events. Info from: Mary C. Rike, Silver Wing Recreation Center, 3CSG/SSRR, APO SF 96274.

FESTIVAL OF WHALES. Feb 22-Mar 16. Dana Point Harbor, CA. A celebration of the annual migration of grey whales along the California coast. Music, exhibitions, lectures and films about whales. Info from: Dana Point Harbor Assn, Harry Helling, Educ Dir, 34675 Golden Lantern, Dana Point, CA 92629.

HATSUME FAIR. Feb 22-23. Purpose: Celebrates coming of spring with demonstrations and performances of Japanese arts. Bonsai, folk drumming, music and martial arts. Last weekend in February. Sponsor: The Morikami Museum, Larry Rosensweig, Dir, 4000 Morikami Park Rd, Delray Beach, FL 33446.

HOME WITH HEART EVENT. Feb 22. Purpose: Nursing home residents exercise (walk, rock in rocking chairs or roll in wheel chairs) for the American Heart Assn. Info from: Shane Hill Nursing Home, Dorothy Trisel, Activities Dir, 10731 SR118, Rockford, OH 45882.

INVITATIONAL CLAM CHOWDER FESTIVAL. Feb 22. Santa Cruz Beach Boardwalk, Santa Cruz, CA. Purpose: To dig up the answer to "who makes the world's greatest clam chowder?" Separate categories for restaurants and individuals. Boston, Manhattan and "New Jersey" style chowder. Info from: Glenn LaFrank, Santa Cruz Beach Boardwalk, 400 Beach St, Santa Cruz, CA 95060.

KENNEDY, EDWARD MOORE: BIRTHDAY. Feb. 22. U.S. Senator from Massachusetts, Democrat, of Boston, MA, born there Feb 22, 1932.

LOWELL, JAMES RUSSELL: BIRTHDAY. Feb 22. American essayist, poet and diplomat, born at Cambridge, MA, on Feb 22, 1819. He died there on Aug 12, 1891.

MAPLE SUGAR FESTIVAL. Feb. 22. The Tyler Arboretum, Lima, PA. Visitors learn about tree identification, sugaring methods and techniques necessary for the production of maple syrup. Sponsor: The Tyler Arboretum, 515 Painter Rd, Lima, PA 19037.

PARKE COUNTY MAPLE FAIR. Feb 22-23. (Also Mar 1-2). Purpose: to demonstrate the making of maple syrup in Parke County. Annually, last weekend in February, first weekend in March. Sponsor: Parke County Inc, Box 165, Rockville, IN 47872.

PEALE, REMBRANDT: BIRTHDAY. Feb 22. American portrait and historical painter, born in Bucks County, PA, on Feb 22, 1778. Died at Philadelphia on Oct 3, 1860.

POCONO WINTER CARNIVAL. Feb 22-Mar 2. Purpose: To bring people back to the Poconos and show them there is plenty of snow. Info from: Pocono Mountains Vacation Bureau, 1004 Main St, Box K, Stroudsburg, PA 18360.

SAINT LUCIA: NATIONAL HOLIDAY. Feb 22. Independence Day.

SCHOPENHAUER, ARTHUR: BIRTHDAY. Feb 22. German philosopher and author, born at Danzig, Feb 22, 1788. Died at Frankfurt am Main, Sept 21, 1860.

STAGGERS, HARLEY ORRIN, JR: BIRTHDAY. Feb 22. U.S. Representative of West Virginia's 2nd district, Democrat, of Keyser, WV, born on Feb 22, 1951.

WASHINGTON, GEORGE: BIRTHDAY ANNIVERSARY. Feb 22. First President of the United States ("First in war, first in peace, and first in the hearts of his countrymen" in the words of Henry "Light-Horse Harry" Lee), born in Westmoreland County, VA, on Feb 22 (New Style), Feb 11 (Old Style), 1732. Washington died at Mt Vernon, VA, Dec 14, 1799. See also: Legal birthday observance (established by Public Law 90-363) throughout the U.S. on the third Monday of February each year.

February 1986

S	M	T	W	T	F	S
						1
2	3	4	5	6	7	8
9	10	11	12	13	14	15
16	17	18	19	20	21	22
23	24	25	26	27	28	

COPYRIGHT © 1985 BY WILLIAM D. CHASE and HELEN M. CHASE

FEBRUARY 23 — SUNDAY

54th Day — Remaining, 311

BOULTER, ELDON BEAU: BIRTHDAY. Feb 23. U.S. Representative of Texas' 13th district, Republican, of Amarillo, TX, born at El Paso, TX, Feb 23, 1942.

BRUNEI: NATIONAL DAY. Feb 23. National holiday observed in Brunei.

DUBOIS, W.E.B.: BIRTHDAY. Feb 23. William Edward Burghardt Dubois, American educator and leader of movement for Black equality, was born at Great Barrington, MA, Feb 23, 1868. Died at Accra, Ghana, Aug 27, 1963.

GREAT AMERICAN YOUTH HOSTEL INTERNATIONAL BICYCLE TOUR. Feb 23. Purpose: To promote bicycle riding and international relations. Tour starts and ends in Chula Vista, CA. Fourth Sunday in February. Sponsor: San Diego Council American Youth Hostels, Inc, 1031 India St, San Diego, CA 92101.

GUYANA: NATIONAL HOLIDAY. Feb 23. Guyana became a republic Feb 23, 1970.

HANDEL, GEORGE FREDERICK: BIRTH ANNIVERSARY. Feb 23. Handel, born at Halle, Saxony, on Feb 23, 1685, and Johann Sebastian Bach (q.v.) born the same year, were perhaps the greatest masters of baroque music. Handel's most frequently performed work is the oratorio, *Messiah*, which was first heard in 1742. Handel died at London on Apr 14, 1759.

JENSEN BEACH FESTIVAL OF THE ARTS. Feb 23-Mar 2. Jensen Beach, FL. Info from: Chamber of Commerce, 1910 NE Commercial St, Jensen Beach, FL 33457.

LANTERN FESTIVAL. Feb 23. Traditional Chinese festival falls on 15th day of first month of Chinese lunar calendar year. Lantern processions mark end of the Chinese New Year holiday season. See also: entry for Chinese New Year, Feb 9.

PEPYS, SAMUEL: BIRTHDAY. Feb 23. English diarist, born at London, Feb 23, 1633. Wrote Pepys in his diary (Mar 10, 1666): "The truth is, I do indulge myself a little the more in pleasure, knowing that this is the proper age of my life to do it; and, out of my observation that most men that do thrive in the world do forget to take pleasure during the time that they are getting their estate, but reserve that till they have got one, and then it is too late for them to enjoy it." Pepys, whose diary, covering the period Jan 1, 1660-May 31, 1669, was originally written in shorthand, died at London, May 26, 1703.

STOKES, LOUIS: BIRTHDAY. Feb 23. U.S. Representative of Ohio's 21st district, Democrat, of Warrensville Heights, OH, was born in Cleveland, OH, on Feb 23, 1925.

SUGARIN' DAYS. Feb 23-Mar 2. Brukner Nature Center, Troy, OH. Tours of the sugar bush and demonstration of syrup making. Info from: Brukner Nature Center, 5995 Horseshoe Bend Rd, Troy, OH 45373.

TAIWAN: LANTERN FESTIVAL AND TOURISM DAY. Feb 23. Fifteenth day of the First Moon of the Lunar calendar, marks end of New Year holiday season. Lantern processions and contests.

TAYLOR, GEORGE: DEATH ANNIVERSARY. Feb 23. Signer of the Declaration of Independence, born 1716 (exact place and date unknown). Died, Feb 23, 1781.

WORLD MASTERS CROSS-COUNTRY SKI CHAMPIONSHIPS. Feb 23-28. Mt Van Hoevenberg, Lake Placid, NY. Info from: Chamber of Commerce, Olympic Arena, Lake Placid, NY 12946.

FEBRUARY 24 — MONDAY

55th Day — Remaining, 310

AMERICAN CAMPING ASSN: NATIONAL CONVENTION. Feb 24-28. Kansas City, MO. Purpose: To provide an educational experience for camp directors and staff of organized camps. Sponsor: American Camping Assn, Bradford Woods, Martinsville, IN 46151.

ESTONIA: INDEPENDENCE DAY. Feb 24. National holiday.

GREGORIAN CALENDAR DAY. Feb 24. Pope Gregory XIII, enlisting the expertise of distinguished astronomers and mathematicians, issued a Bull, Feb 24, 1582, correcting the Julian Calendar which was then ten days in error. The new calendar, named for him, the Gregorian Calendar, became effective on Oct 4, 1582, in most Catholic countries, in 1752 in Britain and the American colonies, in 1917 in the Soviet Union and at various other dates in other countries. It is the most widely used calendar in the world today. See also entries for Sept 2 and Oct 4.

GRIMM, WILHELM CARL: BIRTHDAY. Feb 24. German mythologist and author, born at Hanau, Feb 24, 1786. Best remembered for *Grimm's Fairy Tales*, in collaboration with his brother, Jacob. Died at Berlin, Dec 16, 1859.

HOMER, WINSLOW: BIRTHDAY. Feb 24. American artist born at Boston, MA, Feb 24, 1836. Noted for the realism of his work, from the Civil War reportage to the highly regarded rugged outdoor scenes of hunting and fishing, he died at his home at Prout's Neck, ME, Sept 29, 1910.

JACOBS, ANDREW, JR: BIRTHDAY. Feb 24. U.S. Representative of Indiana's 10th district, Democrat, of Indianapolis, IN, born there Feb 24, 1932.

MOON PHASE: FULL MOON. Feb 24. Moon enters Full Moon phase at 10:02 a.m., E.S.T.

WAGNER, HONUS: BIRTHDAY. Feb 24. American baseball great, born Feb 24, 1874. Died Dec 6, 1955.

FEBRUARY 25 — TUESDAY

56th Day — Remaining, 309

BIG "I" SHOW '86. Feb 25-27. Chicago, IL. Certified trade fair of automobiles, automotive parts and service equipment. Info from: Oleg Jerschkowsky, Trade Development, Room 3832, Internatl Trade Administration, U.S. Dept of Commerce, Washington, DC 20230.

CARUSO, ENRICO: BIRTHDAY. Feb 25. Italian operatic tenor of legendary voice and fame, was born at Naples, Feb 25, 1873, and died there Aug 2, 1921.

DAVIS, ADELLE: BIRTHDAY. Feb. 25. American nutritionist and author, born at Lizton, IN on Feb 25, 1905. Her message "you are what you eat" found an eager readership for her books, including *Let's Cook It Right* (1947) and *Let's Eat Right to Keep Fit* (1954). Davis died at age 70, of bone cancer, at Palo Verdes Estates, CA on May 31, 1974.

FREER, CHARLES LANG: BIRTH ANNIVERSARY. American art collector who endowed the Freer Gallery; presented to the Smithsonian Institution in 1906. Born at Kingston, NY on Feb 25, 1856, Freer died at New York City on Sept 25, 1919.

KUWAIT: NATIONAL HOLIDAY. Feb 25.

RENOIR, PIERRE AUGUSTE: BIRTHDAY. Feb 25. French impressionist painter, born at Limoges, Feb 25, 1841. Died at Cagnes, Provence, Dec 17, 1919.

SPACE MILESTONE: SOYUZ 32 (USSR). Feb 25. Launched on Feb 25, 1979, from Baikonur space center in Soviet Central Asia. Cosmonauts Vladimir Lyakhov and Valery Ryumin aboard, docked at Salyut 6 space station on Feb 26. Returned to Earth in Soyuz 34 after record 175 days in space on Aug 19, 1979.

COPYRIGHT © 1985 BY WILLIAM D. CHASE and HELEN M. CHASE

SURINAME: REVOLUTION DAY. Feb 25. Info from: Embassy of The Republic of Suriname, 2600 Virginia Ave NW, Washington, DC 20037.

FEBRUARY 26 — WEDNESDAY
57th Day — Remaining, 308

ACC CRAFTFAIR AT BALTIMORE. Feb 26-Mar 2. Baltimore Conv Ctr, Baltimore, MD. Info from: American Craft Enterprises, Inc, Box 10, New Paltz, NY 12561.

CODY, WILLIAM FREDERIC (BUFFALO BILL): BIRTHDAY. Feb 26. American frontiersman who claimed to have killed more than 4,000 buffaloes, was born at Scott County, IA, on Feb 26, 1846. Subject of many heroic wild west yarns, Cody became successful as a showman and exhibitionist, taking his acts across the U.S. and to Europe. He died on Jan 10, 1917, at Denver, CO.

DAUMIER, HONORÉ; BIRTHDAY. Feb 26. French painter and caricaturist famous for his satirical and comic lithographs. Once spent six months in prison for a caricature of Louis Philippe shown as *Gargantua* consuming the heavy taxes of the citizens. Born on Feb 26, 1808 at Marseille, France. He died on Feb 11, 1879 at Valmondois, France.

GLEASON, JACKIE: BIRTHDAY. Feb 26. American comedy actor especially famous for his long-running television series "The Honeymooners." Born at Brooklyn on Feb 26, 1916.

GRAND CANYON NATIONAL PARK: ANNIVERSARY. Feb 26. By Act of Congress, Grand Canyon National Park, Arizona, was established, Feb 26, 1919.

HUGO, VICTOR: BIRTHDAY. Feb 26. French author, born Feb 26, 1802. Died Paris, May 22, 1885.

NICOLAY, JOHN GEORGE: BIRTHDAY. Feb 26. Private secretary to Abraham Lincoln who along with John Hay produced the ten-volume biography *Abraham Lincoln: A History*. Born on Feb 26, 1832 at the village of Essington by Landau, Bavaria. He died on Sept 26, 1901 at Washington, DC

PORTLAND PROPERTY MANAGEMENT EXPO. Feb 26-27. Memorial Coliseum, Portland, OR. Info from: Convention & Visitors Assn, Inc, 26 SW Salmon, Portland, OR 97204.

PRINTING AND GRAPHICS ART CATALOG SHOW. Feb 26-Mar 6. Surabaya, Indonesia, Bangkok, Thailand, Kuala Lumpur, Malaysia. Info from: William Crawford, Trade Development, Room 3832, Internatl Trade Admin, U.S. Dept of Commerce, Washington, DC 20230.

FEBRUARY 27 — THURSDAY
58th Day — Remaining, 307

CHARRO DAYS. Feb 27-Mar 2. Brownsville, TX. Purpose: To combine the charm and culture of this two nation area. Many colorful events. Four days beginning last Thursday of February. Info from: Charro Days, Inc, Box 1904, Brownsville, TX 78520.

DOMINICAN REPUBLIC: NATIONAL HOLIDAY. Feb 27. Independence Day. Independence gained in 1844 at withdrawal of Haitians who had controlled the area for the past 22 years.

FARRELL, JAMES THOMAS: BIRTHDAY. Feb 27. American author, novelist and short-story writer, best known for his Studs Lonigan trilogy, born at Chicago, Feb 27, 1904. Died at New York City, Aug 22, 1979.

	S	M	T	W	T	F	S
February							1
1986	2	3	4	5	6	7	8
	9	10	11	12	13	14	15
	16	17	18	19	20	21	22
	23	24	25	26	27	28	

FONNER PARK THOROUGHBRED HORSE RACING. Feb 27-Apr 26. "Nebraska's finest 5/8 mile track." Enclosed heated grandstand and concourse. Info from: Hugh Miner, Mgr, Fonner Park, Box 490, Grand Island, NE 68802.

LA FIESTA DE LOS VAQUEROS. Feb 27-Mar 2. Tucson, AZ. Tucson celebrates its Old West heritage with parade, PRCA rodeo and other related rodeo events. Info from: Rodeo Committee, Chamber of Commerce, Box 991, Tucson, AZ 85702.

LONGFELLOW, HENRY WADSWORTH: BIRTHDAY. Feb 27. American poet, born Portland, ME, Feb 27, 1807. Died, Cambridge, MA, Mar 24, 1882.

NADER, RALPH: BIRTHDAY. Feb 27. American attorney, consumer advocate and author, born at Winsted, CT, Feb 27, 1934.

1986 WRITERS' WEEK (AUSTRALIA). Feb 27-Mar 8. Adelaide Festival Centre, Adelaide, South Australia. Info from: Writers' Week Comm, Adelaide Festival, King William Rd, Adlaide, South Australia 5000.

ST. GABRIEL POSSENTI: FEAST DAY. Feb 27. St. Gabriel of the Sorrowful Mother (Francis Possenti), Italian patron saint of young seminarians (1838-1862).

"SHANGHAI COMMUNIQUE" ANNIVERSARY. Feb 27. Pres. Richard Nixon and Chinese Premier Chou En-Lai issued a joint communique on Feb 27, 1972, describing their historic discussions and defining areas of difference and agreement. Nixon was the first U.S. president to visit any country not diplomatically recognized by the U.S.

TAMPA BAY SPORT AND RECREATIONAL VEHICLE SHOW. Feb 27-Mar 2. Expo Park Bldg, Florida State Fairgrounds, Tampa, FL. Info from: Double C Productions, Inc, Box 1678, Huntsville, TX 77340.

WALLOP, MALCOLM: BIRTHDAY. Feb 27. U.S. Senator from Wyoming, Republican, of Big Horn, WY, was born in New York, NY, Feb 27, 1933.

FEBRUARY 28 — FRIDAY
59th Day — Remaining, 306

ACTION LINE DAY. Feb 28. Purpose: To honor editors and the staffs of Action Line-type columns who work throughout the year to help and entertain their readers. Info from: The Times, Judy C. Brown, Action Line Ed, Box 847, Trenton, NJ 08605.

BLONDIN, CHARLES: BIRTHDAY. Feb 28. Daring French acrobat and aerialist (whose real name was Jean Francois Gravelet), was born at St. Omer, France, Feb 28, 1824. Especially remembered for his conquest of Niagara Falls (q.v., June 30). Blondin died at London, Feb 19, 1897.

DALLAS BOAT SHOW. Feb 28-Mar 9. Market Hall, Dallas, TX. Sponsor: Marine Assn of Dallas, 11511 Katy Fwy, Suite 335, Houston, TX 77079.

MONTAIGNE, MICHEL, DE: BIRTH ANNIVERSARY. Feb 28. French essayist and philosopher born Feb 28, 1533. Died Sept 13, 1592.

MYSTERY WEEKEND. Feb 28-Mar 2. Cumberland Falls State Resort Park, Corbin, KY. Your own mystery to solve . . . live out your fantasies of being the "Super Sleuth" as you investigate and gather clues to solve the mystery. Info from: Kentucky Dept of Parks, Capital Plaza Tower, Frankfort, KY 40601.

OLIN, JAMES R: BIRTHDAY. Feb 28. U.S. Representative of Virginia's 6th district, Democrat, of Roanoke, VA, born in Chicago, IL, Feb 28, 1920.

ROE, ROBERT A: BIRTHDAY. Feb 28. U.S. Representative of New Jersey's 8th district, Democrat, of Wayne, NJ, born there Feb 28, 1924.

SABO, MARTIN O: BIRTHDAY. Feb 28. U.S. Representative of Minnesota's 5th district, Democratic-Farmer-Labor, of Minneapolis, MN, born in Crosby, ND, Feb 28, 1938.

ST. LUCIE COUNTY FAIR. Feb 28-Mar 8. Ft Pierce, FL. Info from: Ron Cochran, Pres, Route 5, Box 170, Ft. Pierce, FL 33450.

COPYRIGHT © 1985 BY WILLIAM D. CHASE and HELEN M. CHASE

SALON NAUTIQUE '86. Feb 28-Mar 9. Place Bonaventure, Montreal, Quebec, Canada. Sailboats, cruisers, windsurfing, canoes, marine motors, accessories and equipment. Info from: P.R. Charette, Inc, 5890 Monkland, Suite 206, Montreal, Quebec, Canada H4A 1G2.

TENNIEL, JOHN: BIRTHDAY. Feb 28. English illustrator and cartoonist, Sir John Tenniel, was born at London on Feb 28, 1820. Best remembered for his illustrations for Lewis Carroll's *Alice's Adventures in Wonderland*, Tenniel died at London, Feb 25, 1914.

U.S.S. *PRINCETON* EXPLOSION ANNIVERSARY. Feb 28. On Feb 28, 1844, the newly built "war steamer," U.S.S. *Princeton*, cruising on the Potomac River with top government officials as its passengers, fired one of its guns (known, ironically, as the "Peacemaker") to demonstrate the latest in naval armament. The gun exploded, killing Abel P. Upshur, Secretary of State, Thomas W. Gilmer, Secretary of the Navy, David Gardiner, of Gardiners Island, NY, and several others. Many were injured. The President of the U.S., John Tyler, was on board and narrowly escaped death.

UNIVERSAL, STANDARD AND DAYLIGHT TIMES

Universal Time (UT) is also known as Greenwich Mean Time (GMT) and is the standard time of the Greenwich meridian (0° of longitude). A time given in UT may be converted to local mean time by the addition of east longitude (or the subtraction of west longitude), where the longitude of the place is expressed in time-measure at the rate of one hour for every 15°. Local clock times may differ from standard times, especially in summer when clocks are often advanced by one hour ("daylight saving" or "summer" time).

The time used in this book is Eastern Standard Time. The following table provides conversion between Universal Time and all Time Zones in the United States. An asterisk denotes that the time is on the preceding day.

Universal Time	Eastern Daylight Time	Eastern Standard Time and Central Daylight Time	Central Standard Time and Mountain Daylight Time	Mountain Standard Time and Pacific Daylight Time	Pacific Standard Time
0^h	* 8 P. M.	* 7 P. M.	* 6 P. M.	* 5 P. M.	* 4 P. M.
1	* 9	* 8	* 7	* 6	* 5
2	*10	* 9	* 8	* 7	* 6
3	*11 P. M.	*10	* 9	* 8	* 7
4	0 Midnight	*11 P. M.	*10	* 9	* 8
5	1 A. M.	0 Midnight	*11 P. M.	*10	* 9
6	2	1 A. M.	0 Midnight	*11 P. M.	*10
7	3	2	1 A. M.	0 Midnight	*11 P. M.
8	4	3	2	1 A. M.	0 Midnight
9	5	4	3	2	1 A. M.
10	6	5	4	3	2
11	7	6	5	4	3
12	8	7	6	5	4
13	9	8	7	6	5
14	10	9	8	7	6
15	11 A. M.	10	9	8	7
16	12 Noon	11 A. M.	10	9	8
17	1 P. M.	12 Noon	11 A. M.	10	9
18	2	1 P. M.	12 Noon	11 A. M.	10
19	3	2	1 P. M.	12 Noon	11 A. M.
20	4	3	2	1 P. M.	12 Noon
21	5	4	3	2	1 P. M.
22	6	5	4	3	2
23	7 P. M.	6 P. M.	5 P. M.	4 P. M.	3 P. M.

The longitudes of the standard meridians for the standard time zones are:

Eastern	75° West	Mountain	105° West
Central	90° West	Pacific	120° West

COPYRIGHT © 1985 BY WILLIAM D. CHASE and HELEN M. CHASE

March.

MARCH 1 — SATURDAY
60th Day — Remaining, 305

ARTICLES OF CONFEDERATION: RATIFICATION ANNIVERSARY. Mar 1. This compact made between the original thirteen states had been adopted by the Congress Nov 15, 1777, and submitted to the states for ratification on Nov 17, 1777. Maryland was the last state to approve, on Feb 27, 1781, but Congress named Mar 1, 1781, as the day of formal ratification. The Articles of Confederation remained the supreme law of the nation until Mar 4, 1789.

BERMUDA HIGH SOARING SCHOOL WAVE CAMP. Mar 1-15. Marion, NC. Purpose: "Wave" or air turbulence from Mt. Mitchell makes area one of better "lifts" in Eastern U.S. (Heights over 29,000 ft). Sponsor: Bermuda High Soaring School, Wayne Hatcher, Drawer 809, Chester, SC 29706.

BREAUX, JOHN B: BIRTHDAY. Mar 1. U.S. Representative of Louisiana's 7th district, Democrat, of Crowley, LA, born in Crowley on Mar 1, 1944.

CHALANDRA MARZ. Mar 1. Switzerland (Engadine). Springtime traditional event when costumed young people, ringing bells and cracking whips, drive away the demons of winter.

COMMEMORATION OF THE ARRIVAL OF MARTIN PINZON. Mar 1. Bayona, Spain. Martin Alonzo Pinzon (1440-1493). Spanish ship-builder and navigator (and co-owner of the *Nina* and the *Pinta*), accompanied Christopher Columbus on his first voyage, as commander of the *Pinta*. Storms separated the ships on their return voyage and the *Pinta* first touched land at Bayona, Spain, where Pinzon gave Europe its first news of the discovery of the New World (before Columbus' landing and announcement at Palos). Pinzon's brother, Vicente Yanez Pinzon, was commander of the third caravel of the expedition, the *Nina*. Another brother, Francisco, was pilot of the *Pinta*.

DOLLHOUSE AND MINIATURE SHOW. Mar 1-2. Rhodes Center, Ohio State Fairgrounds, Columbus, OH. Purpose: To raise money for Children's Hospital. Info from: Sue Fenwick, 1700 Essex Rd, Columbus, OH 43221.

HELP SOMEONE SEE WEEK. Mar 1-8. Purpose: Save and donate your discarded eyeglasses for distribution in Third World countries by Medical Group Mission of the Christian Medical Society. Info from: Dr. and Mrs. Fleming Barbour, 2015 Lincoln Dr, Flint, MI 48503.

HUMORISTS ARE ARTISTS MONTH (HAAM). Mar 1-31. Purpose: To recognize the important contributions made by various types of humorists to the high art of living. Info from: Lone Star Publications of Humor, PO Box 29000, Suite 103, San Antonio, TX 78229.

March 1986	S	M	T	W	T	F	S
							1
	2	3	4	5	6	7	8
	9	10	11	12	13	14	15
	16	17	18	19	20	21	22
	23	24	25	26	27	28	29
	30	31					

KOREA: SAMILJOL OR INDEPENDENCE DAY. Mar 1. Koreans observe the anniversary of March 1, 1919 independence movement against Japanese colonial rule.

MENTAL RETARDATION MONTH. Mar 1-31. Purpose: To educate the public about the needs of this nation's 6 million retarded citizens and about ways to prevent retardation. Sponsor: Association for Retarded Citizens, Liz Moore, 2501 Avenue J, Arlington, TX 76011.

MINNESOTA FINLANDIA SKI MARATHON. Mar 1. Buena Vista Ski Area, Bemidji, MN. Cross-country ski race. Sponsor: Buena Vista Ski Area, Mary Lou Norbie, Box 771, Bemidji, MN 56601.

NATIONAL NUTRITION MONTH. Mar 1-31. Purpose: To provide the general public with the latest information about fitness, nutrition and food selection for health. Sponsor: The American Dietetic Assn, 430 N Michigan Ave, Chicago, IL 60611.

NATIONAL PEANUT MONTH. Mar 1-31. Purpose: To promote consumption of peanuts throughout the U.S. Sponsor: Natl Peanut Council and State Grower Associations, Dir of Industry Services, 101 S. Peyton St, Suite 301, Alexandria, VA 22314.

NATIONAL PEANUT MONTH. Mar 1-31. Purpose: To celebrate America's favorite nut and sandwich (peanut butter). Sponsor: Peanut Advisory Board, 1133 Avenue of the Americas, New York, NY 10036.

NATIONAL PIG DAY. Mar 1. Purpose: To accord to the pig its rightful, though generally unrecognized place as one of man's most intelligent and useful domesticated animals. Sponsor: Ellen Stanley, 7006 Miami, Lubbock, TX 79413.

NEBRASKA: ADMISSION DAY. Mar 1. Became 37th State on this day in 1867.

OHIO: ADMISSION DAY. Mar 1. Became 17th State on this day in 1803.

PHILATELIC LITERATURE MONTH. Mar 1-31. Purpose: To draw attention to the importance of philatelic literature for stamp enthusiasts. Sponsor: The Philatelic Journalist, Gustav Detjen, Jr, Editor, 154 Laguna Ct, St. Augustine Shores, FL 32086.

RAILROAD APPRECIATION WEEKEND. Mar 1-2. Greenbo Lake State Resort Park, Greenup, KY. Guest speakers, movies and model train displays. Info from: Carolyn Wallace, Kentucky Dept of Parks, Capital Plaza Tower, Frankfort, KY 40601.

RED CROSS MONTH. Mar 1-31. Presidential Proclamation. ☆ "Always issued each year for March since 1943."

RETURN THE BORROWED BOOK WEEK. Mar 1-7. Purpose: To remind you to make room for those precious old volumes that will be returned to you, by cleaning out all that worthless trash your friends are waiting for. Annually, Mar 1-7. Sponsor: Inter-Global Society for the Prevention of Cruelty to Cartoonists, Al Kaelin, Secy, 3119 Chadwick Dr, Los Angeles, CA 90032.

ROBOT EXPO. Mar 1-31. Buhl Science Center, Pittsburgh, PA. Purpose: To show the general public what real, live robots look like and what they actually do. Sponsor: Buhl Science Ctr, Allegheny Sq, Pittsburgh, PA 15212.

ST. DAVID'S DAY. Mar 1. Wales. Celebrates patron saint of Wales.

SANDHILL CRANE MIGRATION. Mar 1-Apr 15. Purpose: To view the resting grounds of the sandhill and whooping cranes, ducks, geese, eagles and other forms of wildlife from an underground blind. Info from: Platte River Maintenance Trust, 2550 N Diers Ave, Suite H, Grand Island, NE 68801.

WATER-DRAWING FESTIVAL. Mar 1-14. Nara, Japan. "Omizutori" Festival Todaiji, Nara. At midnight, a solemn rite is performed in the flickering light of pine torches. The pious rush for fire-flakes from torches, which are believed to have magic power against evil. Most spectacular on the night of Mar 12. The ceremony of drawing water is observed at 2 o'clock on Mar 13, to accompaniment of ancient Japanese music.

COPYRIGHT © 1985 BY WILLIAM D. CHASE and HELEN M. CHASE

WHA/WOOD ENERGY '86. Mar 1-4. Reno/Sparks Conv Ctr, Reno, NV. Purpose: To show latest wood-heating and solid fuel products including woodstoves and fireplaces and offer continuing education seminars to industry professionals. Info from: Wood Heating Alliance, Judy Walker, 1101 Connecticut Ave, Washington, DC 20036.

YOUTH ART MONTH. Mar 1-31. Purpose: To emphasize the value and importance of participating art in the development of all children and youth. Sponsor: The Art & Craft Materials Institute, Inc., 715 Boylston St, Boston, MA 02116.

MARCH 2 — SUNDAY
61st Day — Remaining, 304

AMERICAN CAMPING WEEK. Mar 2-9. Purpose: To dramatically share with parents and others the quality experience that awaits a child at summer camp. Sponsor: American Camping Assn, Inc. Armand Ball, Exec VP, Bradford Woods, Martinsville, IN 46151.

COWTOWN MARATHON. Mar 2. The stockyards, Fort Worth. Info from: Jim Gilliland, Box 1532, Fort Worth, TX 76101.

DR SEUSS BIRTHDAY PARADE. Mar 2. Purpose: A tribute to Dr. Seuss for the happiness he gives through his books. Children write short notes of cheer and friendship to sick children, forwarded by Mail For Tots. Teachers and librarians promote birthday parties. Info from: Dorita A. Lindahl, The Dr. Seuss Birthday Parade, Box 766, Hibbing, MN 55746.

DONNELLY, BRIAN J: BIRTHDAY. Mar 2. U.S. Representative of Massachusetts' 11th district, Democrat, of Dorchester, MA, born in Dorchester on Mar 2, 1946.

IDITAROD TRAIL INTERNATIONAL SLED DOG RACE. Mar 2-17. Race starts at Anchorage, Alaska and finishes at Nome, Alaska. Each team of 12 to 18 dogs and their musher cover 1,049 miles of the roughest, most beautiful terrain Mother Nature has to offer. Sponsor: Iditarod Trail Committee, Greg Bill, Exec Dir, Pouch X, Wasilla, AK 99687.

MARIAN COLLEGE PEACE WEEK. Mar 2-7. Purpose: To raise the consciousness of Marian's students and the surrounding community concerning the importance of global cooperation and peace. Sponsor: Marian College of Fond du Lac, 45 S National Ave, Fond du Lac, WI 54935.

MICHEL, ROBERT H: BIRTHDAY. Mar 2. U.S. Representative of Illinois' 18th district, Republican, of Peoria, IL, born in Peoria on Mar 2, 1923.

NATIONAL VOLUNTEERS OF AMERICA WEEK. Mar 2-9. Purpose: To celebrate founder's day of Volunteers of America. Sponsor: The Volunteers of America, Jill T. Anding, 3813 N Causeway Blvd, Metairie, LA 70002.

NATIONAL WOMEN'S HISTORY WEEK. Mar 2-8. Purpose: A time for re-examining and celebrating the wide range of women's contributions and achievements, too often overlooked in the telling of U.S. history. Sponsor: Natl Women's History Project, Box 3716, Santa Rosa, CA 95402.

POPE PIUS XII: BIRTHDAY. Mar 2. Eugenio Maria Giovanni Pacelli, 260th Pope of the Roman Catholic Church, born Mar 2, 1876 at Rome, Italy. Elected Pope Mar 2, 1939. Died at Castel Gandolfo, near Rome, Oct 9, 1958.

PORTUGAL: PROCESSION OF SENHOR DOS PASSOS. Mar 2. Celebrated in Lisbon, Portugal.

☆ **SAVE YOUR VISION WEEK.** Mar 2-8. Presidential Proclamation issued most years for the first week of March since 1964, except 1971 and 1972 when issued for the second week of March. Proclamation 5304 of February 21, 1985 is most recent.

SAVE YOUR VISION WEEK. Mar 2-8. Purpose: The presidentially proclaimed observance reminds Americans that vision is one of the most vital of all human needs and its protection is of great significance to the health and welfare of every individual. Sponsor: American Optometric Assn, 243 N Lindbergh Blvd, St Louis, MO 63141.

SCHURZ, CARL: BIRTHDAY. Mar 2. American journalist, political reformer, and Brigadier General in Civil War, born near Cologne, Germany, on Mar 2, 1829. Died, New York City, May 14, 1906. Observance sponsored by: The Philatelic Journalist, 154 Laguna Ct, St. Augustine Shores, FL 32086.

SPACE MILESTONE: PIONEER 10 (US). Mar 2. On Mar 2, 1972, probe begins journey on which it is scheduled to pass and photograph Jupiter, 620 million miles from Earth, in December 1973, cross the orbit of Pluto in 1987, and then become the first known Earth object to leave our solar system.

SPACE MILESTONE: SOYUZ 28 (USSR). Mar 2. Cosmonauts Alexei Gubarev and Vladimir Remek link with Salyut 6 space station Mar 3, visiting crew of Soyuz 26. Returned to Earth Mar 10. Remek, from Czechoslovakia, was first person in space from country other than US or USSR. Launched Mar 2, 1978.

TEXAS INDEPENDENCE DAY. Mar 2. Texas adopted Declaration of Independence from Mexico on this day, 1836.

TEXAS INDEPENDENCE WEEK. Mar 2-9. San Antonio, TX. Historical reenactments of events which took place in San Antonio in 1836. The Texas Sesquicentennial Wagon Train will pass by the Alamo on March 2 and the defenders of the Alamo will be honored on March 6, the day the Alamo fell to Santa Anna's troops. Info from: Convention & Visitors Bureau, Box 2277, San Antonio, TX 78298.

WOMEN'S NATIONAL EXHIBITION. Mar 2-Apr 26. Washington, DC. Purpose: To select and exhibit the best works by women artists from across the nation. Sponsor: Galerie Triangle, 3701 14th St, NW, Washington, DC 20010.

MARCH 3 — MONDAY
62nd Day — Remaining, 303

AGRI-MATION 2. Mar 3-6. Chicago Hilton, Chicago, IL. The International Conference and Exposition on Agricultural Automation for 1986 and beyond. Info from: ASAE, 2950 Niles Rd, St. Joseph, MI 49085.

BETHUNE, NORMAN: BIRTHDAY. Mar 3. Canadian physician who worked in front lines during World War I, Spanish Civil War and the Chinese Revolution. Born, Gravenhurst, Ontario, Mar 3, 1890. Died in China while treating soldiers of Mao's Eighth Route Army, Nov 11, 1939. Said to be the only western man recognized as a hero of Chinese Revolution.

BULGARIA: LIBERATION DAY. Mar 3. Grateful tribute to the Russian, Romanian and Finnish soldiers, and Bulgarian volunteers, who, in the Russo-Turkish War, 1877-1878, liberated Bulgaria from Ottoman rule and five centuries of oppression.

CORPORATE SKI CHALLENGE. Mar 3-8. Alpine Meadows Ski Resort, Tahoe City, CA. Purpose: Corporate employees participate in world-class winter sports competition. Sponsor: Sierra Marketing Corp, Albert G. Guiteras, 1123 Clarenden Crescent, Oakland, CA 94610.

CYCLE WEEK. Mar 3-9. Daytona International Speedway, Daytona Beach, FL. Info from: Daytona International Speedway, Larry Balewski, PR, Daytona Beach, FL 32015.

ENGLAND: DAILY MAIL IDEAL HOME EXHIBITION. Mar 3-31. Earls Court, London. Large annual consumer show of products for the home.

FLORIDA: ADMISSION DAY. Mar 3. Became 27th State on this day in 1845.

JAPAN: DOLL FESTIVAL (HINAMATSURI). Mar 3. Special festival for girls, observed throughout Japan, on third day of third month each year.

MALAWI: MARTYR'S DAY. Mar 3. Public holiday in Malawi.

MOON PHASE: LAST QUARTER. Mar 3. Moon enters Last Quarter phase at 7:17 a.m., E.S.T.

MOROCCO: NATIONAL HOLIDAY. Mar 3. Anniversary of the throne.

COPYRIGHT © 1985 BY WILLIAM D. CHASE and HELEN M. CHASE

NATIONAL ANTHEM DAY. Mar 3. On Mar 3, 1931, the Bill making the Star-Spangled Banner the national anthem was adopted by the Senate and went to President Herbert Hoover for signature. The President signed it the same day and, with his signing of the Bill, the Star-Spangled Banner became the U.S. national anthem by law.

NATIONAL PROCRASTINATION WEEK. Mar 3-9. Purpose: To promote the benefits of relaxing through putting off till tomorrow everything that needn't be done today. Sponsor: Procrastinators' Club of America Inc, Les Waas, Pres, 1111 Broad-Locust Bldg, Philadelphia, PA 19102.

NEWSPAPER IN EDUCATION WEEK. Mar 3-7. Purpose: To highlight work of educators and publishers and to bring newspapers into the classroom. Info from: American Newspaper Publishers Assn Foundation, Dulles Internatl Airport, Box 17401, Washington, DC 20041.

PRESIDENT'S COMMITTEE ON EMPLOYMENT OF THE HANDICAPPED: NATONAL JOURNALISM CONTEST DEADLINE. Mar 3. Purpose: To sensitize young people to the problems and abilities of disabled people through personal contact with disabled people. Sponsor: The President's Committee on Employment of the Handicapped, 1111 20th St, NW, Washington, DC 20036.

PULLMAN, GEORGE MORTIMER: BIRTHDAY. Mar 3. American inventor and cabinetmaker, originator of the railway sleeping car. The first to be called a "Pullman" was the *Pioneer*. Later he was president of the Pullman Palace Car Company. Born Mar 3, 1831 at Brocton, NY, Pullman died at Chicago on Oct 19, 1897.

SURFSIDE SALUTES CANADA WEEK. Mar 3-10. Surfside, FL. Purpose: A salute to Canada in appreciation for decades of patronage each winter season. Sports competitions and entertainment. Sponsor: Surfside Tourist Board, 9301 Collins Ave, Surfside, FL 33154.

MARCH 4 — TUESDAY
63rd Day — Remaining, 302

CONGRESS: ANNIVERSARY OF FIRST MEETING UNDER CONSTITUTION. Mar 4. In 1789 the first Congress met in New York on Mar 4, obtained a quorum (House on Apr 2, Senate on Apr 5), organized on Apr 6, counted electoral votes and that day declared George Washington President (69 votes) and John Adams Vice-President (34 votes).

OLD INAUGURATION DAY. Mar 4. Anniversary of the date set for beginning the U.S. presidential term of office, 1789-1933. Although the Continental Congress had set the first Wednesday in March, 1789, as the date for the new government to convene, a quorum was not present to count the electoral votes until Apr 6. Though George Washington's term of office began on Mar 4, he did not take the oath of office until Apr 30, 1789. All subsequent presidential terms (excepting successions following the death of an incumbent) until Franklin D. Roosevelt's second term began on Mar 4. The 20th Amendment (ratified Jan 23, 1933) provided that "the terms of the President and Vice President shall end at noon on the 20th day of January. . .and the terms of their successors shall then begin." See also entry for Inauguration Day, Jan 20.

PENNSYLVANIA DEEDED TO WILLIAM PENN: ANNIVERSARY. Mar 4. To satisfy a debt of £16,000, King Charles II of England granted a royal charter, deed and governorship to Pennsylvania to William Penn on Mar 4, 1681.

March 1986	S	M	T	W	T	F	S
							1
	2	3	4	5	6	7	8
	9	10	11	12	13	14	15
	16	17	18	19	20	21	22
	23	24	25	26	27	28	29
	30	31					

PULASKI, CASIMIR: BIRTHDAY. Mar 4. American revolutionary hero, General (and chief of cavalry) Kazimierz (Casimir) Pulaski, born in Poland Mar 4, 1747. Died aboard the *Wasp* following wound received at Savannah, Oct 11, 1779.

SMITH, CHRISTOPHER H: BIRTHDAY. Mar 4. U.S. Representative of New Jersey's 4th district, Republican, of Hamilton, NJ, was born in Rahway, NJ, on Mar 4, 1953.

SPACE MILESTONE: OGO 5 (US). Mar 4. Orbiting geophysical laboratory collected data on sun's influence on Earth. Launched Mar 4, 1968.

TOWN MEETING DAY. Mar 4. Vermont. The first Tuesday in March is an official state legal holiday in Vermont. "Nearly every town elects officers, approves budget items and deals with a multitude of other items in a day-long public meeting of the voters. This is a very significant day for Vermonters."

VERMONT: ADMISSION DAY. Mar 4. Became 14th State on this day in 1791.

MARCH 5 — WEDNESDAY
64th Day — Remaining, 301

ATTUCKS, CRISPUS: DAY. Mar 5. New Jersey. Honors Crispus Attucks, likely a runaway slave, a leader of the Boston Massacre, and first to die there, on Mar 5, 1770.

BANK HOLIDAY ANNIVERSARY. Mar 5. President Franklin Delano Roosevelt, in his first inaugural address, on Saturday, Mar 4, 1933, said "This is pre-eminently the time to speak the truth, the whole truth, frankly and boldly. Nor need we shrink from honestly facing conditions in our country today. This great nation will endure as it has endured, will revive and prosper. So first of all let me assert my firm belief that the only thing we have to fear is fear itself." On his first full day in office (Sunday, Mar 5, 1933) he proclaimed a national "Bank Holiday," to help save the nation's faltering banking system. Most banks were able to reopen after the 10-day "holiday" (Mar 4-14), but in the meantime, "scrip" had temporarily replaced money in many American households.

BEDELL, BERKLEY WARREN: BIRTHDAY. Mar 5. U.S. Representative of Iowa's 6th district, Democrat, of Spirit Lake, IA, born there Mar 5, 1921.

BOSTON MASSACRE ANNIVERSARY. Mar 5. Massachusetts. Five men killed and six more injured by British troops commanded by Capt. Thomas Preston.

DELIUS FESTIVAL. Mar 5-7. Purpose. To preserve the music and memory of Frederick Delius. English composer who lived in Florida 1884-85. Lectures, concerts, recitals and national composition competition. Info from: The Dulius Assn of Florida, Inc, Robert F. Sandlin, Pres, Box 5621, Jacksonville, FL 32247.

EIGHT HOUR DAY or LABOR DAY. Mar 5. Western Australia and Tasmania. Parades and celebrations commemorate trade union efforts during the 19th Century to limit working hours. Their slogan: "Eight hours labor, eight hours recreation, eight hours rest!" In New South Wales it is called "Six Hour Day."

"IRON CURTAIN" ANNIVERSARY. Mar 5. Winston Churchill, speaking at Westminster College, Fulton, MO, on Mar 5, 1946, established the cold war boundary with these words: "From Stettin in the Baltic to Trieste in the Adriatic an iron curtain has descended across the continent." Though Churchill was not the first to use the phrase "iron curtain" his speech gave it a new currency and its usage has persisted.

LATTA, DELBERT L: BIRTHDAY. Mar 5. U.S. Representative of Ohio's 5th district, Republican, of Bowling Green, OH, born in Weston, Wood County, OH, Mar 5, 1920.

NATIONAL COLLEGIATE MEN'S AND WOMEN'S SKIING CHAMPIONSHIPS. Mar 5-8. Info from: Natl Collegiate Athletic Assn, Box 1906, Mission, KS 66201.

OKAR, MARY ROSE: BIRTHDAY. Mar 5. U.S. Representative of Ohio's 20th district, Democrat, of Cleveland, OH, born in Cleveland, Cuyahoga County, OH, on Mar 5, 1940.

COPYRIGHT © 1985 BY WILLIAM D. CHASE and HELEN M. CHASE

MARCH 6 — THURSDAY

65th Day — Remaining, 300

BROWN, GEORGE E JR: BIRTHDAY. Mar 6. U.S. Representative of California's 36th district, Democrat, of Riverside, CA, was born at Holtville, CA, on Mar 6, 1920.

BROWNING, ELIZABETH BARRETT: BIRTHDAY. Mar 6. English poet, author of "Sonnets from the Portuguese," wife of poet Robert Browning, and subject of the play, "The Barretts of Wimpole Street," was born near Durham, England, Mar 6, 1806. She died at Florence, Italy, June 29, 1861.

FALL OF THE ALAMO ANNIVERSARY. Mar 6. Anniversary of the fall of the Texan fort, the Alamo, on Mar 6, 1836. The seige, led by Mexican General Santa Anna, began on Feb 23, and reached its climax on Mar 6, when the last of the defenders was slain. Texans, under Gen. Sam Houston, rallied with the war-cry "Remember the Alamo" and, at the Battle of San Jacinto, on Apr 21, defeated and captured Santa Anna who signed a treaty recognizing Texas' Independence.

FOLEY, THOMAS STEPHEN: BIRTHDAY. Mar 6. U.S. Representative of Washington's 5th district, Democrat, of Spokane, WA, born in Spokane on Mar 6, 1929.

FORT LAUDERDALE SPRING HOME SHOW. Mar 6-9. War Memorial Auditorium, Ft Lauderdale, FL. Info from: Perl Exposition Corp, 6915 Red Rd, Suite 228, Coral Gables, FL 33143.

GHANA: NATIONAL HOLIDAY. Mar 6. Independence Day. Received independence from Great Britain on this day, 1957.

GUAM: DISCOVERY DAY or MAGELLAN DAY. Mar 6. Commemorates discovery of Guam on this day, 1521.

HILLIS, ELWOOD HAYNES: BIRTHDAY. Mar 6. U.S. Representative of Indiana's 5th district, Republican, of Kokomo, IN, born there Mar 6, 1926.

MICHELANGELO'S BIRTHDAY. Mar 6. Anniversary of the birth, Mar 6, 1475, at Caprese, Tuscany, of Michelagniolo di Lodovico Buonarroti-Simoni. Died, Feb 18, 1564.

PEALE, ANNA CLAYPOOLE, BIRTHDAY. Mar 6. American painter of miniatures, born Philadelphia, Mar 6, 1791. Died on Dec 25, 1878.

ROCKHOUND ROUNDUP: DEMING GEM AND MINERAL SOCIETY. Mar 6-9. SW New Mexico State Fairgrounds, Deming, NM. Guided rock trips, over 80 dealers and tailgaters, gem and mineral displays and auctions. Info from: Deming Gem & Mineral Society, Box 1459, Deming, NM 88031.

SANIBEL ISLAND SHELL FAIR. Mar 6-9. Sanibel, FL. Juried exhibits only, no commercial sales. Amateur and professional collectors display some of the finest and rarest shells gathered from local areas and around the world. Info from: Sanibel Community Assn, Box 76, Sanibel, FL 33957.

STONEWARE POTTERY APPRECIATION DAY. Mar 6. Purpose: To take the time to observe, critique and appreciate all forms of stoneware pottery. Participate through pottery courses. Sponsor: Nancy Byder, 11315 Grand Oak Dr #1, Grand Blanc, MI 48439.

SWIMMING AND DIVING: NAIA MEN'S DIVISION CHAMPIONSHIP. Mar 6-8. Info from: Natl Assn of Intercollegiate Athletics, 1221 Baltimore, Kansas City, MO 64105.

SWIMMING AND DIVING: NAIA WOMEN'S DIVISION CHAMPIONSHIP. Mar 6-8. Info from: Natl Assn of Intercollegiate Athletics, 1221 Baltimore, Kansas City, MO 64105.

WRESTLING: NAIA MEN'S DIVISION CHAMPIONSHIP. Mar 6-8. Minot, ND. Info from: Natl Assn of Intercollegiate Athletics, 1221 Baltimore, Kansas City, MO 64105.

MARCH 7 — FRIDAY

66th Day — Remaining, 299

BONKER, DON L: BIRTHDAY. Mar 7. U.S. Representative of Washington's 3rd district, Democrat, of Olympia, WA, was born in Denver, CO, on Mar 7, 1937.

BURBANK, LUTHER: BIRTHDAY. Mar 7. Anniversary of birth of American naturalist and author, creator and developer of many new varieties of flowers, fruits, vegetables and trees. Luther Burbank's birthday is observed by some as Bird and Arbor Day. He was born at Lancaster, MA, Mar 7, 1849. Died at Santa Rosa, CA, Apr 11, 1926.

CHALO NITKA. Mar 7-9. Purpose: To promote Lake Okeechobee bass fishing and to bring the Seminoles and the community together for this celebration. Chalo Nitka means "Big Bass" in the Seminole language. Always first three-day weekend in March. Info from: Glades County Chamber of Commerce, Box 490, Moore Haven, FL 33471.

FAIRBANKS ICE FESTIVAL. Mar 7-16. Purpose: A community celebration surrounding the Open North American Sled Dog Races—the "Grandaddy" of sprint racing. Sponsor: Fairbanks Chamber of Commerce, Box 74446, Fairbanks, AK 99707.

FARRIS, VICTOR W: DEATH ANNIVERSARY. Mar 7. American inventor, industrialist and multi-millionaire Victor W. Farris was the holder of more than 200 patents. Among the best known of his inventions is the paper milk carton. Farris died, at age 75, at West Palm Beach, FL, on Mar 7, 1985.

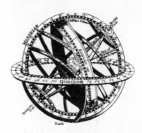

GYMNASTICS: NAIA WOMEN'S DIVISION CHAMPIONSHIP. Mar 7-8. Site to be determined. Info from: Natl Assn of Intercollegiate Athletics, 1221 Baltimore, Kansas City, MO 64105.

HOPKINS, STEPHEN: BIRTHDAY. Mar 7. Colonial governor (Rhode Island) and signer of the Declaration of Independence, born Providence, RI, Mar 7, 1707. Died July 13, 1785.

LEADVILLE CRYSTAL CARNIVAL. Mar 7-9. Winter sports activities for the whole family. Sponsor: Leadville Lions Club, Box 526, Leadville, CO 80461.

MOUNTAIN MEMORIES WEEKEND. Mar 7-8. Purpose: To preserve the rich cultural heritage of Kentucky's mountain people. Folk musicians and tellers of tales featured, plus craft demonstrations. Info from: KY Dept of Parks, John Tierney, Carter Caves State Resort Pk, Olive Hill, KY 41164.

REMAGEN BRIDGE ANNIVERSARY. Mar 7. On this date in 1945, a small advance force of the U.S. 1st Army captured the Ludendorff railway bridge across the Rhine River at Remagen (between Bonn and Coblenz)—the only bridge across the Rhine which had not been blown up by the German defenders—thus acquiring the first bridgehead onto the East bank and the beginning of the Allied advance into Germany—a turning point in World War II.

ROBINSON, TOMMY F: BIRTHDAY. Mar 7. U.S. Representative of Arkansas' 2nd district, Democrat, of Jacksonville, AR, born in Little Rock, AR, on Mar 7, 1942.

SOUTHWEST FARM SHOW AND TRACTOR PULL CHAMPS. Mar 7-9. Tarrant County Conv Ctr, 1111 Houston St, Fort Worth, TX 76102.

STAMFORD MARRIOTT CROSSWORD PUZZLE TOURNAMENT. Mar 7-9. Stamford Marriott Hotel, Stamford, CT. Info from: Bill Stacy, Dir of Marketing, Stamford Marriott, 2 Stamford Forum, Stamford, CT 06901.

TALLAHASSEE JUNIOR MUSEUM GUILD ANTIQUES SHOW AND SALE. Mar 7-9. Fund-raisers event for the Jr Museum. Dealers specializing in a variety of antiques. Info from: Tallahassee Jr Museum, 3945 Museum Dr, Tallahassee, FL 32304.

COPYRIGHT © 1985 BY WILLIAM D. CHASE and HELEN M. CHASE

WORLD DAY OF PRAYER. Mar 7. Theme: "Choose Life." Worldwide expression of prayer and Christian unity. First Friday in March. Sponsor: Church Women United, 475 Riverside Dr, Rm 812, New York, NY 10115.

YUMA SQUARE AND ROUND DANCE FESTIVAL. Mar 7-9. Info from: Chamber of Commerce, Box 230, Yuma, AZ 85364.

MARCH 8 — SATURDAY

67th Day — Remaining, 298

ARTS 'N CRAFTS SHOW AT THE CROSSROADS. Mar 8. National Guard Armory, Perry, GA. Sponsor: The Idaka Club, Box 1128, Perry, GA 31069.

AZALEA TRAIL AND FESTIVAL. Mar 8-May 31. Mobile, AL. Info from: Alabama Tourism and Travel, 532 S. Perry St., Montgomery, AL 36130.

BICYCLE TWIN CENTURY TOUR OF SOUTHERN CALIFORNIA COAST. Mar 8-9. Purpose: 200 mile bicycle tour from La Jolla in San Diego to Lakewood in Long Beach with overnight stop in Lakewood. 100 miles each way along beautiful California coast. Annually, second weekend in March. Sponsor: San Diego Council American Youth Hostels, Inc, 1031 India St, San Diego, CA 92101.

BRICK CITY DAYS. Mar 8. Ocala, FL. Purpose: To celebrate the re-building of downtown Ocala after the fire in the 1890's. Info from: Chamber of Commerce, Box 1210, Ocala, FL 32678.

CANADIAN-AMERICAN DAYS FESTIVAL. Mar 8-16. Concerts, square dances, beach games and sports events. Sponsor: Myrtle Beach Area Chamber of Commerce, 1301 N Kings Highway, Myrtle Beach, SC 29578.

CAROLE KAI BEDRACE AND PARADE. Mar 8. Kapiolani Park, Honolulu, HI. Info from: Hawaii Visitors Bureau, Honolulu, HI 96815.

CAXTON'S "MIRROR OF THE WORLD"—ANNIVERSARY. Mar 8. William Caxton, England's first printer, completed the translation from French into English of *The Mirror of the World*, a popular account of astronomy and other sciences, on Mar 8, 1481. In print soon afterwards, *Mirror of the World* became the first illustrated book printed in England.

DAYTONA SUPERCROSS BY HONDA. Mar 8. Daytona International Speedway, Daytona Beach, FL. Info from: Daytona Internatl Speedway, Larry Balewski, PR, Daytona Beach, FL 32015.

INTERNATIONAL WOMEN'S DAY. Mar 8. An international day observed by the organizations of the United Nations system. Info from: United Nations Dept of Public Information, United Nations, NY 10017.

INTERNATIONAL (WORKING) WOMEN'S DAY. Mar 8. A day to honor women, especially working women. Said to commemorate an 1857 march and demonstration in New York City, by female garment and textile workers. Believed to have been first proclaimed for this date at an international conference of women held in Helsinki, Finland in 1910, "that henceforth March 8 should be declared International Women's Day." The 50th Anniversary observance, at Peking in March 1960, cited Clara Zetkin (1857-1933) as "initiator of Women's Day on March 8." This is perhaps the most widely observed holiday of recent origin, and unusual among holidays originating in the U.S. to have been widely adopted and observed in other nations, including socialist countries. In the U.S.S.R. and the People's Republic of China it is a national holiday and flowers or gifts are presented to women workers.

	S	M	T	W	T	F	S
March							1
1986	2	3	4	5	6	7	8
	9	10	11	12	13	14	15
	16	17	18	19	20	21	22
	23	24	25	26	27	28	29
	30	31					

LOWRY, MIKE: BIRTHDAY. Mar 8. U.S. Representative of Washington's 7th district, Democrat, of Seattle, WA, born in St. John, WA, on Mar 8, 1939.

NATCHEZ PILGRIMAGE. Mar 8-Apr 6. Natchez, Mississippi. More than 30 antebellum homes opened to the public for tours. Info from: Dept of Economic Dev, Box 849, Jackson, MS 39205.

NATIONAL EASTER SEAL TELETHON. Mar 8-9. Purpose: To raise funds for the Easter Seal Society's rehabilitation services for children and adults with disabilities. Sponsor: Natl Easter Seal Society, Keith Roberts, PR Dir, 2023 W Ogden Ave, Chicago, IL 60612.

OCEAN BEACH KITE FESTIVAL. Mar 8. Purpose: Contest judging of homemade kites, parade and kite flying spectacular at beach. Sponsor: Ocean Beach Kiwanis Club and San Diego Parks and Recreation Dept. Info from: Dianne Hoover, 4726 Santa Monica Ave, San Diego, CA 92107.

SYRIAN ARAB REPUBLIC REVOLUTION DAY. Mar 8. Official public holiday commemorating assumption of power by Revolutionary National Council, Mar 8, 1963.

U.S.S.R.: INTERNATIONAL WOMEN'S DAY. Mar 8. Public holiday in U.S.S.R. Women's meetings, concerts, parties and gifts.

VAN BUREN, HANNAH HOES: BIRTHDAY. Mar 8. Wife of Martin Van Buren, 8th President of the U.S., born at Kinderhook, NY, Mar 8, 1783. Died Feb 5, 1819.

MARCH 9 — SUNDAY

68th Day — Remaining, 297

ASSOCIATION OF OPERATING ROOM NURSES CONGRESS. Mar 9-14. Anaheim, CA. Info from: Assn of Operating Room Nurses, Inc, 10170 E Mississippi Ave, Denver, CO 80231.

BATTLE OF HAMPTON ROADS. Mar 9. First engagement between armored vessels—*Monitor* and *Merrimac*—took place on this day, 1862.

BELIZE: PUBLIC HOLIDAY. Mar 9. Baron Bliss Day is observed as official holiday in Belize.

DAYTONA 200 MOTORCYCLE ROAD RACE. Mar 9. Daytona International Speedway, Daytona Beach, FL. Info from: Daytona Internatl Speedway, Larry Balewski, PR, Daytona Beach, FL 32015.

FASCELL, DANTE B: BIRTHDAY. Mar 9. U.S. Representative of Florida's 19th district, Democrat, of Miami, FL, was born in Bridgehampton, Long Island, NY, on Mar 9, 1917.

FUN MAIL WEEK. Mar 9-15. Purpose: To share letter enthusiasm and encourage letter fun. Sponsor: Letter Enjoyers Association, Jerry Lee Hill, Pres, Box 29830, Brooklyn Center, MN 55429.

GIRL SCOUT WEEK. Mar 9-15. Purpose: To mark observance of the anniversary of the founding of Girl Scouts of the USA, the largest voluntary organization for girls and women in the world, which began on March 12, 1912. Sponsor: Girl Scouts of the USA, Bonnie McEwan, Dir, Media Services, 830 Third Ave, New York, NY 10022.

HAWAIIAN SONG FESTIVAL AND SONG COMPOSING CONTEST. Mar 9. Kapiolani Park Bandstand in Waikiki. Info from: Hawaii Visitors Bureau, Honolulu, HI 96815.

LUXEMBOURG: BRETZELSONNDEG. (PRETZEL SUNDAY). Mar 9. Fourth Sunday in Lent is occassion for boys to give pretzel-shaped cakes to sweethearts who may respond, on Easter Sunday, with gift of decorated egg or sweet.

MOTHERING SUNDAY. Mar 9. England. Fourth Sunday in Lent, formerly occasion for attending services at Mother Church, a time for family gatherings and visits to parents. Now popularly known as Mother's Day, and a time for visiting and taking gifts to mothers.

COPYRIGHT © 1985 BY WILLIAM D. CHASE and HELEN M. CHASE

PHILADELPHIA FLOWER SHOW. Mar 9-16. Philadelphia Civic Ctr, Philadelphia, PA. Theme: "Hometown U.S.A." Info from: Pennsylvania Horticultural Society, 325 Walnut St, Philadelphia, PA 19106.

ST. FRANCES OF ROME: FEAST DAY. Mar 9. Patron of motorists and model for housewives and widows. After 40 years of marriage she was widowed in 1436, and later joined the community of Benedictine Oblates. Canonized in 1608. (1384-1440).

SPACE MILESTONE: SPUTNIK 9 (USSR). Mar 9. Dog, Chernushka (Blackie), is passenger. Mar 9, 1961.

VESPUCCI, AMERIGO: BIRTHDAY. Mar 9. Italian navigator for whom the Americas were named, born this day, 1451.

MARCH 10 — MONDAY
69th Day — Remaining, 296

AMERICAN BOWLING CONGRESS CONVENTION. Mar 10-14. Cashman Field Ctr, Las Vegas, NV. Approximately 1,300 delegates from the U.S. and Canada meet to discuss proposed rules changes for 1986-87 season. Info from: American Bowling Congress, 5301 S 76th St, Greendale, WI 53129.

CANADA: COMMONWEALTH DAY. Mar 10. Second Monday in March is observed as Commonwealth Day, but is not a public holiday.

HAWAII: MAUI MARATHON. Mar 10. From Maui Mall, Kahului to Kaanapali Whaler's Village, Kahului, Maui. Info from: Hawaii Visitors Bureau, Honolulu, HI 96815.

"JUPITER EFFECT" ANNIVERSARY. Mar 10. The much talked-about and sometimes-feared planetary configuration of March 10, 1982 (a semi-alignment of the planets on the same side of the sun) occurred on that date without causing any of the disasters or unusual natural phenomena which some had predicted. See the 1982 edition of *Chase's Calendar of Annual Events* for diagram and detailed description.

MOON PHASE: NEW MOON. Mar 10. Moon enters New Moon phase at 9:52 a.m., E.S.T.

TELEPHONE ANNIVERSARY. Mar 10. Alexander Graham Bell transmitted the first telephone message—to his assistant in the next room—"Mr. Watson, come here, I want you," on Mar 10, 1876, at Cambridge, MA.

TRIUMPH OF AGRICULTURE EXPOSITION FARM AND RANCH MACHINERY SHOW. Mar 10-12. Civic Auditorium, Omaha, NE. Info from: Mid-America Expositions, Inc, 666 Farnam Bldg, Omaha, NE 68102.

TUBMAN, HARRIET: DAY. Mar 10. American abolitionist, Underground Railroad leader, born a slave, at Bucktown, Dorchester County, MD, about 1820 or 1821. Died, Auburn, NY, Mar 10, 1913. She escaped from Maryland plantation in 1849, later helped more than 300 slaves reach freedom.

UNITED KINGDOM: COMMONWEALTH DAY. Mar 10. Replaces Empire Day observance recognized until 1958. Observed on second Monday in March.

VIRGINA SLIMS OF DALLAS TENNIS CHAMPIONSHIP. Mar 10-16. Moody Coliseum, Dallas, TX. Info from: Maureen Connolly Brinker Tennis Foundation, Box 7065, Dallas, TX 75209.

WALD, LILLIAN D: BIRTHDAY. Mar 10. American sociologist, founder of the Henry Street Settlement in New York City, and founder of first non-sectarian public health nursing service, born at Cincinnati, OH, Mar 10, 1867. Died at Westport, CT, Sept 1, 1940.

MARCH 11 — TUESDAY
70th Day — Remaining, 295

CAMPBELL, MALCOLM: BIRTH ANNIVERSARY. Mar 11. Record making British auto racer, the first man to travel five miles a minute in an automobile, Sir Malcolm Campbell was born at Chislehurst, Kent, England, on Mar 11, 1885. Campbell died at his home in Surrey, Dec 31, 1948.

INTERNATIONAL ALPINE SKIING COMPETITIONS. Mar 11-12. Borovets, Bulgaria. Men's slalom and giant slalom for the European Cup. Info from: Bulgarian Tourist Office, 161 E 86th St, New York, NY 10028.

JAMES REEB: MURDER ANNIVERSARY. Mar 11. Anniversary of the murder of James Reeb in Selma, AL on March 11, 1965. Info from: Unitarian Universalist Assn, 25 Beacon St, Boston, MA 02108.

JOHNNY APPLESEED DAY. Mar 11. John Chapman, better known as Johnny Appleseed, believed to have been born at Leominster, MA, Sept 26, 1774. Died, Allen County, IN. Mar 11, 1847. Planter of orchards, friend of wild animals and regarded as a great medicine man by the Indians. See also entry for Sept 26.

MAQUINAS HERRAMIENTAS '86. Mar 11-14. Mexico City, Mexico. Solo Exhibition. Metalworking equipment. Info from: Franc Manzolillo, Trade Development, Room 3832, Internatl Trade Admin, U.S. Dept of Commerce, Washington, DC 20230.

PAINE, ROBERT TREAT: BIRTHDAY. Mar 11. Jurist and signer of the Declaration of Independence, born, Boston, MA, Mar 11, 1731. Died there May 11, 1814.

TASSO, TORQUATO: BIRTH ANNIVERSARY. Mar 11. Italian poet of the late Renaissance, born at Sorrento on Mar 11, 1544. Tasso died at Rome, Apr 25, 1595. His violent outbursts and acute sensitivity to criticism led to his imprisonment for 7 years during which the "misunderstood genius" continued his literary creativity.

WILSON, HAROLD: BIRTHDAY. Mar 11. British statesman and twice Prime Minister (1964-1970 and 1974-1976), leader of the Labor Party. Born at Huddersfield, Yorkshire, on Mar 11, 1916.

MARCH 12 — WEDNESDAY
71st Day — Remaining, 294

ARIYOSHI, GEORGE R: BIRTHDAY. Mar 12. George R. Ariyoshi, Governor of Hawaii, Democrat, was born at Honolulu, HI, on Mar 12, 1926.

BASKETBALL: NAIA MEN'S DIVISION CHAMPIONSHIP. Mar 12-15. (Also Mar 17-18). Kansas City, MO. Info from: Natl Assn of Intercollegiate Athletics, 1221 Baltimore, Kansas City, MO 64105.

BASKETBALL: NAIA WOMEN'S DIVISION CHAMPIONSHIP. Mar 12-15. Site to be determined. Info from: Natl Assn of Intercollegiate Athletics, 1221 Baltimore, Kansas City, MO 64105.

COPYRIGHT © 1985 BY WILLIAM D. CHASE and HELEN M. CHASE

BOYCOTT, CHARLES CUNNINGHAM: BIRTHDAY. Mar 12. Charles Cunningham Boycott, born at Norfolk, England, Mar 12, 1832, has been immortalized by having his name become part of the English language. In County Mayo, Ireland, the Tenants' "Land League" in 1880, asked Boycott, an estate agent, to reduce rents (because of poor harvest and dire economic conditions). Boycott responded by serving eviction notices on the tenants who retaliated by refusing to have any dealings with Boycott.

FIRESIDE CHAT DAY. Mar 12. On this date, in 1933, President Franklin Delano Roosevelt made the first of his Sunday evening "fireside chats" to the American people. Speaking by radio from the White House, he reported rather informally on the economic problems of the nation and on his actions to deal with them.

GABON: NATIONAL HOLIDAY. Mar 12.

GREAT BLIZZARD OF '88 ANNIVERSARY. Mar 12. One of the most devastating blizzards to hit northeastern United States, began in the early hours of Monday, Mar 12, 1888. A snowfall of 40-50 inches, accompanied by gale force winds left drifts as high as 30-40 feet. Over 400 persons died in the storm (200 in New York City alone). Some survivors of the storm, "The Blizzard Men of 1888," held annual meetings in New York City as late as 1941 to recount personal recollections of the event.

HELLO PHOENIX, Mar 12-13. Civic Plaza, Phoenix, AZ. Event focuses on one world, and sharing among the diverse cultural and ethnic groups. Dance, drama and sounds of different lands. Info from: City of Phoenix, Parks, Recreation & Library Dept, 125 E Washington, Phoenix, AZ 85004.

LAKE HAVASU INVITATIONAL CRUISING SAILBOAT REGATTA. Mar 12-13. Sponsor: Chamber of Commerce, 65 N Lake Havasu Ave, Suite 2-B, Lake Havasu City, AZ 86403.

MAURITIUS: NATIONAL HOLIDAY. Mar 12. Commemorates attainment of independent nationhood (within British Commonwealth) on Mar 12, 1968.

PIERCE, JANE MEANS APPLETON: BIRTHDAY. Mar 12. Wife of Franklin Pierce, 14th President of the U.S., born at Hampton, NH, Mar 12, 1806. Died Dec 2, 1863.

RIO GRANDE VALLEY LIVESTOCK SHOW AND RODEO. Mar 12-16. Horse shows, carnival, auctions, exhibits, rodeo and dances. Info from: Manager, Box 867, Mercedes, TX 78570.

SPACE MILESTONE: SOYUZ T-4 (USSR). Two cosmonauts (V. Kovalyonok and V. Savinykh) docked at Salyut 6 space station (in orbit since Sept 29, 1977) on Mar 13. Returned to Earth May 26, after 75 days in space. Launch date was Mar 12, 1981.

SUN YAT-SEN: DEATH ANNIVERSARY. Mar 12. The heroic leader of China's 1911 revolution is remembered on anniversary of his death, at Peking, Mar 12, 1925. Observed as Arbor Day on Taiwan.

WHITEHURST, G. WILLIAM: BIRTHDAY. Mar 12. U.S. Representative of Virginia's 2nd district, Republican, of Norfolk, VA, born in Norfolk Mar 12, 1925.

MARCH 13 — THURSDAY
72nd Day — Remaining, 293

BOGGS, CORRINE C. (LINDY): BIRTHDAY. Mar 13. U.S. Representative of Louisiana's 2nd district, Democrat, of New Orleans, LA, born at Brunswick Plantation, LA, Mar 13, 1916.

	S	M	T	W	T	F	S
March							1
1986	2	3	4	5	6	7	8
	9	10	11	12	13	14	15
	16	17	18	19	20	21	22
	23	24	25	26	27	28	29
	30	31					

DELMONICO, LORENZO: BIRTHDAY. Mar 13. Famed restaurateur and gastronomic authority, born at Marengo, Switzerland, operated a number of restaurants in New York City. He died there, Sept 13, 1881.

FILLMORE, ABIGAIL POWERS: BIRTHDAY. Mar 13. First wife of Millard Fillmore, 13th President of the U.S., born at Stillwater, NY, Mar 13, 1798. Died Mar 30, 1853. It is said that the White House was without any books until Abigail Fillmore, formerly a teacher, made a room on the second floor into a library. Within a year, Congress appropriated $250 for the president to spend on library books for the White House.

GOOD SAMARITAN INVOLVEMENT DAY. Mar 13. Purpose: A day to emphasize the importance of unselfish aid to those who need it. Recognized on the anniversary of the killing of Catherine Genovese, Mar 13, 1964, in the Kew Gardens Community, Queens, NY. Reportedly no less than 38 of her neighbors, not wanting "to get involved," witnessed and watched for nearly 30 minutes as the fleeing girl was pursued and repeatedly stabbed by her 29-year-old attacker.

GRENADA: NATIONAL HOLIDAY. Mar 13.

HUBBARD, L. RON: BIRTHDAY. Mar 13. Lafayette Ronald Hubbard, science fiction writer and founder of the Church of Scientology, was born at Tilden, NE, Mar 13, 1911.

LOWELL, PERCIVAL: BIRTHDAY. Mar 13. American astronomer, founder of the Lowell Observatory at Flagstaff, AZ, born at Boston, MA, Mar 13, 1855, and died at Flagstaff on Nov 12, 1916. Lowell was initiator of the search that resulted (25 years after the search began and 14 years after his death) in discovery of the planet Pluto. The discovery was announced on Lowell's birthday, Mar 13, 1930, by the Lowell Observatory.

PLANET URANUS DISCOVERY: ANNIVERSARY. Mar 13. German-born English astronomer, Sir William Herschel, discovered the seventh planet from the sun, Uranus, on Mar 13, 1781.

PRIESTLY, JOSEPH: BIRTHDAY. Mar 13. English clergyman and scientist, discoverer of Oxygen, born at Fieldhead, England, Mar 13, 1733. He and his family narrowly escaped an angry mob attacking their home because of his religious and political views. They moved to the U.S. in 1794, and Priestly died at Northumberland, PA, Feb 6, 1804.

ST. PATRICK'S DAY CELEBRATION. Mar 13-16. University of Missouri, Rolla, MO. Students and community celebrate St. Pat's Day. Parade, games, coronation ceremonies and dance. Info from: St. Pat's Board, H. D. Meriwether, 905 Black St, Rolla, MO 65401.

ST. PATRICK'S DAY: CEREAL CITY DART TOURNAMENT. Mar 13-17. Battle Creek, MI. Purpose: To celebrate and encourage support for the fast growing interest of darting. Info from: Joseph "Bill" Buckner, Springbrook Golf Course, Inc, 1600 Avenue A, Battle Creek, MI 49015.

SUNIA, FOFO I.F.: BIRTHDAY. Mar 13. American Samoa Delegate to 99th Congress, Democrat, of Pago Pago, American Samoa, was born in Fagasa, Pago Pago, Mar 13, 1937.

WRESTLING: NATIONAL COLLEGIATE DIVISION I CHAMPIONSHIP FINALS. Mar 13-15. Univ of Iowa, Iowa City, IA. Info from: NCAA, Box 1906, Mission, KS 66201.

MARCH 14 — FRIDAY
73rd Day — Remaining, 292

ARCADIA ALL-FLORIDA CHAMPIONSHIP RODEO. Mar 14-16. (Also July 4-6.) Arcadia, FL. Info from: All-Florida Championship Rodeo Assn, Box 1266, Arcadia, FL 33821.

AUDUBON PILGRIMAGE. Mar 14-16. A tour of homes and gardens. Sponsor: West Feliciana Historical Society, Box 336, St. Francisville, LA 70775.

CANADIAN NATIONAL SPORTSMAN'S SHOW. Mar 14-23. Info from: Government of Canada, Ottawa, Canada K1A 0H5.

COPYRIGHT © 1985 BY WILLIAM D. CHASE and HELEN M. CHASE

CASEY JONES: BIRTHDAY. Mar 14. Railroad engineer and hero of ballad, whose real name was John Luther Jones, was born near Cayce, KY, Mar 14, 1864 and died bravely in railroad wreck Apr 30, 1900.

EINSTEIN, ALBERT: BIRTHDAY. Mar 14. Theoretical physicist best known for his Theory of Relativity. Born at Ulm, Germany, Mar 14, 1879. Nobel Prize, 1921. Died at Princeton, NJ, Apr 18, 1955.

LUCY HOBBS TAYLOR: BIRTHDAY. Mar 14. Lucy Beaman Hobbs, first woman in America to receive a degree in dentistry (Ohio College of Dental Surgery, 1866) or to be admitted to membership in a state dental association, was born in New York State, Mar 14, 1833. In 1867 she married James M. Taylor, a painter for a railroad, who also became a dentist (after she instructed him in the essentials). She was an active woman's rights advocate. She died at Lawrence, KS, Oct 3, 1910.

MARSHALL, THOMAS RILEY: BIRTHDAY. Mar 14. Twenty-eighth Vice President of the U.S. (1913-1921) born, North Manchester, IN, Mar 14, 1854. Died, Washington, DC, June 1, 1925.

MARX, KARL: DEATH ANNIVERSARY. Mar 14. The German socialist, founder and father of modern communism, author of *Das Kapital* and (with Friedrich Engels) the *Communist Manifesto*, was born at Treves, Germany, May 5, 1818, and died at London, England, Mar 14, 1883.

MILWAUKEE SENTINEL SPORTS, TRAVEL AND BOAT SHOW. Mar 14-23. Milwaukee Exhibition Convention Center, Milwaukee, WI. Travel and resort exhibits, boating and marine sporting goods. Sponsor: Milwaukee Sentinel, Box 371, Milwaukee, WI 53201.

MOTHERS DAY. Mar 14. Purpose: A day set aside to honor moth collectors and specialists, celebrated in museums or libraries having moth collections. Sponsor: Puns Corps, c/o Bob Birch, Grand Punscorpion, Box 2364, Falls Church, VA 22042.

NATIONAL COLLEGIATE MEN'S AND WOMEN'S RIFLE CHAMPIONSHIPS. Mar 14-15. U.S. Naval Academy, Annapolis, MD. Info from: Natl Collegiate Athletic Assn, Box 1906, Mission, KS 66201.

OKLAHOMA 4-H AND FFA LIVESTOCK SHOW. Mar 14-18. Purpose: Over 5,000 cattle, sheep and hogs shown by over 3,000 youngsters representing all 77 Oklahoma counties. Info from: Steve Collier, 1 Santa Fe Plaza, Oklahoma City, OK 73102.

STORYTELLING WEEKEND. Mar 14-15. Greenbo Lake State Resort Park, Greenup, KY. Lee Pennington and other Kentucky storytellers offer entertainment and guidance in trading and telling tales. Info from: Kentucky Dept of Parks, Capital Plaza Tower, Frankfort, KY 40601.

MARCH 15 — SATURDAY
74th Day — Remaining, 291

BUZZARDS DAY. Mar 15. Hinckley, Ohio. Tradition says that on this day the buzzards (also known as turkey vultures or carrion crows) return to Hinckley, Ohio from their winter quarters in the Great Smoky Mountains, to rear their young. Local celebration usually held on following Sunday.

CENTRAL FLORIDA ANTIQUE MARKET SHOW AND SALE. Mar 15-16. Volusia County Fairgrounds, DeLand, FL. Info from: Chamber of Commerce, Box 629, DeLand, FL 32721.

EGGSIBIT '86. Mar 15-16. Purpose: To show and encourage the art of decorating egg shells. Annually, the weekend prior to Palm Sunday. Sponsor: Firth Youth Center, Phillipsburg, NJ. Info from: Kit Stansbury, Dir, 71 Bennett St, Phillipsburg, NJ 08865.

ELK MOUNTAIN SPRING CARNIVAL. Mar 15-16. Info from: Elk Mountain Ski Center, Inc, RD 1, Box 258, Union Dale, PA 18470.

IDES OF MARCH. Mar 15. Julius Caesar assassinated this day in 44 B.C.

JACKSON, ANDREW: BIRTHDAY. Mar 15. Seventh President of the U.S. (Mar 4, 1829-Mar 3, 1837), was born in a log cabin at Waxhaw, SC, Mar 15, 1767. Had reputation as a brawler, reportedly participant in countless duels (in at least one of which his opponent was mortally wounded). Married the same woman (Rachel Robards) twice (1791 and 1794)—once before and once after her divorce. Public reception for his first inaugural, attended by 20,000 persons, was a rowdy affair which left ruined rugs and furnishings and damage in the thousands of dollars at the White House. Jackson was the first president since George Washington who had not attended college. He died at Nashville, TN, June 8, 1845.

MAINE: ADMISSION DAY. Mar 15. Became 23rd State on this day in 1820.

MAPLE FESTIVAL OF NOVA SCOTIA. Mar 15-Apr 14. Northern and Central Nova Scotia. Promotion of the maple industry in Nova Scotia. Info from: Dept of Tourism, Box 456, Halifax, NS Canada B3J 2R5.

NATIONAL ASSOCIATION OF INTERCOLLEGIATE ATHLETICS NATIONAL CONVENTION. Mar 15-18. Kansas City, MO. Info from: Natl Assn of Intercollegiate Athletics, 1221 Baltimore, Kansas City, MO 64105.

NEW YORK FLOWER SHOW. Mar 15-23. Info from: The Horticultural Society of New York, 128 W 58th St, New York, NY 10019.

SPRING AUTO TOUR FOR VIEWING MIGRATORY WATERFOWL MIGRATION. Mar 15-23. DeSoto National Wildlife Refuge, Missouri Valley, IA. Info from: U.S. Fish & Wildlife Service, K.L. Drews, Rt 1, Box 114, Missouri Valley, IA 51555.

SUNDQUIST, DONALD KENNETH: BIRTHDAY. Mar 15. U.S. Representative of Tennessee's 7th district, Republican, of Memphis, TN, was born in Moline, IL, on Mar 15, 1936.

VALENTINE, TIM: BIRTHDAY. Mar 15. U.S. Representative of North Carolina's 2nd district, Democrat, of Nashville, NC, born there, Mar 15, 1926.

WASHINGTON'S ADDRESS TO CONTINENTAL ARMY OFFICERS: ANNIVERSARY. Mar 15. George Washington addressed a meeting (at first forbidden by him) of Continental Army officers who were dissatisfied and rebellious for want of back pay, food, clothing and pensions. The meeting took place at Newburgh, NY, and Gen. Washington called for patience, opening his speech with the words: "I have grown grey in your service. . . ." Congress later acted to satisfy most of the demands.

MARCH 16 — SUNDAY
75th Day — Remaining, 290

ARMSTRONG, WILLIAM L: BIRTHDAY. Mar 16. U.S. Senator from Colorado, Republican, of Aurora, CO, born at Fremont, NE, Mar 16, 1937.

BATTLE OF GUILFORD COURTHOUSE ANNIVERSARY. Mar 16-17. Guilford Courthouse National Military Park, Greensboro, NC 27408.

BLACK PRESS DAY. Mar 16. Anniversary of the founding of first Black newspaper in the U.S., *Freedom's Journal,* on Varick Street in New York City, on March 16, 1827. Observed as "Black Press Day in New York City," by mayoral proclamation in 1977.

CAMP FIRE BIRTHDAY SUNDAY. Mar 16. Purpose: A day when Camp Fire members worship together and participate in the services in their churches or temples. Sponsor: Camp Fire Inc, 4601 Madison Ave, Kansas City, MO 64112.

CAMP FIRE BIRTHDAY WEEK. Mar 16-22. Purpose: To celebrate the anniversary of Camp Fire, founded in 1910 as Camp Fire Girls. Sponsor: Camp Fire, Inc, 4601 Madison Ave, Kansas City, MO 64112.

CARE SUNDAY. Mar 16. England. The fifth Sunday in Lent, also known as Carling Sunday and Passion Sunday. First day of Passiontide, remembering the sorrow and passion of Christ.

CENTRAL AMERICA WEEK. Mar 16-24. Purpose: In commemoration of Salvadoran Archbishop Oscar Romero's assassination (on Mar 24, 1980) local religious and community groups plan events to focus attention on the deepening crisis in Central America. Sponsor: National Council of Churches of Christ in the U.S.A., Attn: Gary Gamer, 475 Riverside Dr, New York, NY 10115.

CLYMER, GEORGE: BIRTHDAY. Mar 16. Signer of the Declaration of Independence and of the U.S. Constitution, born Mar 16, 1739. Died, Philadelphia, PA, Jan 24, 1813.

CURLEW DAY. Mar 16. Traditional arrival date for the long-billed curlew at the Umatilla (Oregon) National Wildlife Refuge. More than 500 of the long-billed curlews have been reported at this location during their nesting season.

DUMB WEEK. Mar 16-22. Greece. "The week preceding Holy Week is known as Dumb Week as no service is held in churches throughout this period except on Friday, eve of the Saturday of Lazarus."

GODDARD DAY. Mar 16. Commemorates first liquid-fuel-powered rocket flight on this day, 1926, devised by Robert Hutchings Goddard (1882-1945) at Auburn, MA.

MACON CHERRY BLOSSOM FESTIVAL. Mar 16-23. Parade, international food festival, home and garden tours, arts festival, exhibits, sporting events, gala street party and fireworks. Sponsor: Macon-Bibb Clean Community Commission, Mrs Carolyn Crayton, Dir, Box 4968, Macon, GA 31213.

MADISON, JAMES: BIRTHDAY. Mar 16. Fourth President of the U.S. (Mar 4, 1809-Mar 3, 1817), born at Port Conway, VA, Mar 16, 1751. He was president when British forces invaded Washington, requiring Madison and other high officials to flee, while the British burned the Capitol, the president's residence, and most other public buildings (Aug 24-25, 1814). Madison died at Montpelier, VA, June 28, 1836.

MOYNIHAN, DANIEL PATRICK: BIRTHDAY. Mar 16. U.S. Senator from New York, Democrat, of Pindars Corners, Delaware County, NY, born in Tulsa, OK, Mar 16, 1927.

MY LAI MASSACRE: ANNIVERSARY. Mar 16. Most publicized atrocity of Vietnam War. On Mar 16, 1968, according to findings of U.S. Army's Peers investigating team, approximately 300 non-combatant Vietnamese villagers (at My Lai and Mykhe, near the South China Sea) were killed by infantrymen of the Americal Division.

NATIONAL POISON PREVENTION WEEK. Mar 16-22. Presidential Proclamation. "Always issued each year for 3rd week of March since 1962." (PL87-319 of Sept 26, 1961).
☆

NATIONAL POISON PREVENTION WEEK. Mar 16-22. Purpose: To encourage the American people to learn the dangers of childhood accidental poisoning and to take preventive measures. Always the third full week in March. Sponsor: Poison Prevention Week Council, Ken Giles, Secy, Box 1543, Washington, DC 20013.

NATIONAL WILDLIFE WEEK. Mar 16-22. Theme: "Discover Wildlife In Your World." Purpose: To call attention to wildlife around us, whether we live in an urban, suburban, rural or wilderness setting. To identify the needs of wildlife and our responsibilities to ensure its survival. Sponsor: Natl Wildlife Federation, 1412 16th St, NW, Washington, DC 20036.

NIXON, THELMA CATHERINE PATRICIA RYAN: BIRTHDAY. Mar 16. Wife of Richard Milhous Nixon, 37th President of the U.S., born at Ely, NV, Mar 16, 1912.

PASSION WEEK. Mar 16-22. The week beginning on the Fifth Sunday in Lent; the week before Holy Week.

PASSIONTIDE. Mar 16-29. The last two weeks of Lent (Passion Week and Holy Week), beginning with the Fifth Sunday in Lent (Passion Sunday) and continuing through the day before Easter (Holy Saturday or Easter Even).

ST. URHO'S DAY. Mar 16. Purpose: To commemorate the saving of the grape crop in Finland by driving the grasshoppers out of that country by the patron saint of the Finnish people, St. Urho. Sponsor: Sauna Society of America, V.S. Choslowsky, Exec Dir. 1001 Connecticut Ave, Washington, DC 20036.

SPACE MILESTONE: GEMINI 8 (US). Mar 16. Executed (with Agena) first docking of orbiting spacecraft. Safe emergency landing after malfunction. Launched Mar 16, 1966.

MARCH 17 — MONDAY
76th Day — Remaining, 289

ADDABBO, JOSEPH PATRICK: BIRTHDAY. Mar 17. U.S. Representative of New York's 6th district, Democrat, of Ozone Park, NY, born in Queens, NY, Mar 17, 1925.

CAMP FIRE FOUNDERS DAY. Mar 17. Purpose: To commemorate the anniversary of the founding of Camp Fire, formerly known as Camp Fire Girls, and the service given to children and youth across the nation. Sponsor: Camp Fire, Inc, 4601 Madison Ave, Kansas City, MO 64112.

EVACUATION DAY. Mar 17. Suffolk County, MA.

IRELAND: NATIONAL DAY. Mar 17. National holiday, St. Patrick's Day, is observed in Ireland.

JONES, BOBBY: BIRTH ANNIVERSARY. Mar 17. Golfing great Robert Tyre Jones, Jr., first golfer to win the grand slam (the four major British and American tournaments in one year), was born at Atlanta, GA, on Mar 17, 1902, and died there Dec 18, 1971.

NATIONAL BAKE WEEK. Mar 17-23. Purpose: To promote American cuisine. National Bake Week encourages families and friends to "Bake American" and enjoy American-style dishes, such as deep dish pizza, sourdough bread, Boston baked beans, brownies, soft pretzels, peach cobbler and meatloaf. Sponsor: Chicago Metallic Products, Inc. Info from: Jasculca/Terman & Associates, Michelle Katzin, 730 N Franklin St, Suite 510, Chicago, IL 60610.

ORTHODOX LENT. Mar 17-May 3. Observed by the Orthodox Church in America and other Orthodox churches during this period.

ST. PATRICK'S DAY. Mar 17. Commemorates the patron saint of Ireland, Bishop Patrick (A.D. 389-461) who, about AD 432 left his home in the Severn Valley, England, and introduced Christianity into Ireland. Feast Day in the Roman Catholic Church. A national holiday in Ireland and Northern Ireland, the highlight of a week of festivity there.

ST. PATRICK'S DAY PARADE. Mar 17. Fifth Ave, New York. Info from: NY Conv & Visitors Bureau, Inc, 2 Columbus Circle, New York, NY 10019.

March 1986

S	M	T	W	T	F	S
						1
2	3	4	5	6	7	8
9	10	11	12	13	14	15
16	17	18	19	20	21	22
23	24	25	26	27	28	29
30	31					

COPYRIGHT © 1985 BY WILLIAM D. CHASE and HELEN M. CHASE

SPACE MILESTONE: VANGUARD 1 (US). Mar 17. Established 'pear-shape' of Earth. 3 lbs. First solar-powered satellite. Mar 17, 1958.

WHITE, MARK W. JR: BIRTHDAY. Mar 17. Mark W. White, Jr, Governor of Texas, Democrat, was born at Henderson, TX, on Mar 17, 1940.

WORLD MARITIME DAY. Mar 17. An international day observed by the organizations of the United Nations system. Info from: United Nations Dept of Public Information, United Nations, NY 10017.

MARCH 18 — TUESDAY
77th Day — Remaining, 288

ARUBA: FLAG DAY. Mar 18. Aruba national holiday. Display of Flags, national music and folkloric events. Info from: Aruba Tourist Bureau, 1270 Avenue of the Americas, Suite 2212, New York, NY 10020.

CALHOUN, JOHN CALDWELL: BIRTHDAY. Mar 18. American statesman born at Abbeville District, SC, Mar 18, 1782. He was the first vice president of the U.S. to resign that office (Dec 28, 1832). Died at Washington, DC, Mar 31, 1850.

CLEVELAND, GROVER: BIRTHDAY. Mar 18. Twenty-second and twenty-fourth President of the U.S., born at Caldwell, NJ, Mar 18, 1837 (given name was Stephen Grover Cleveland). Terms of office as president: Mar 4, 1885-Mar 3, 1889, and Mar 4, 1893-Mar 3, 1897. He ran for president for the intervening term and received a plurality of votes cast, but failed to win Electoral College victory for that term. Only president to serve two non-consecutive terms. Also the only president to be married in the White House. He married 21-year-old Frances Folsom, his ward. Their daughter, Esther, was first child of a president to be born in The White House. Grover Cleveland died at Princeton, NJ, June 24, 1908.

COBLE, HOWARD: BIRTHDAY. Mar 18. U.S. Representative of North Carolina's 6th district, Republican, of Greensboro, NC, born there Mar 18, 1931.

CONFEDERATE STATES CONGRESS ADJOURNMENT. Mar 18. The Congress of the Confederate States adjourned for the last time on Mar 18, 1865.

DIESEL, RUDOLPH: BIRTHDAY. Mar 18. German inventor born Mar 18, 1853. Died Sept 30, 1913.

EXPOCOMER '86. Mar 18-26. Panama City, Panama. Trade fair of general industrial equipment. Info from: EPS, Trade Development, Room 3832, Internatl Trade Admin, U.S. Dept of Commerce, Washington, DC 20230.

MOON PHASE: FIRST QUARTER. Mar 18. Moon enters First Quarter phase at 11:39 a.m., E.S.T.

SPACE MILESTONE: VOSKHOD 2 (USSR). Mar 18. Lt. Colonel Leonov steps out of capsule for 20 minutes in special space suit. Launched Mar 18, 1965.

TURISMO USA: TRAVEL SERVICES. Mar 18-21. Sao Paulo, Brazil. Solo Exhibition. Info from: Richard Sousane, Trade Development, Room 3832, Internatl Trade Admin, U.S. Dept of Commerce, Washington, DC 20230.

MARCH 19 — WEDNESDAY
78th Day — Remaining, 287

BRADFORD, WILLIAM: BIRTH ANNIVERSARY. Mar 19. Pilgrim Father, Governor of Plymouth Colony, born at Yorkshire, England and baptized on Mar 19, 1589. Sailed from Southampton, England on the *Mayflower* in 1620. Bradford died at Plymouth, MA on May 9, 1657.

BRYAN, WILLIAM JENNINGS: BIRTHDAY. Mar 19. American political leader, member of Congress, Democratic presidential nominee (1896), "free silver" advocate, assisted in prosecution of Scopes Trial, known as "the Silver-Tongued Orator," born at Salem, IL, Mar 19, 1860. Died at Dayton, TN, July 26, 1925.

CANBERRA DAY. Mar 19. Australian Capital Territory. Public holiday.

LIVINGSTONE, DAVID: BIRTHDAY. Mar 19. Scottish physician, missionary and explorer born at Blantyre, Scotland, Mar 19, 1813. He was the subject of a famous search, by Henry M. Stanley, who found him, at Ujiji, near Lake Tanganyika, on Nov 10, 1871. Dr. Livingstone died in Africa, May 1, 1873. See also entry for Sir Henry M. Stanley, Jan 28.

ST. JOSEPH'S DAY and FEAST OF ST. JOSEPH. Mar 19. Holy day in Catholic Church, recognizing spouse of the Virgin Mary, foster father of Jesus, patriarch, patron of Catholic Church.

SWALLOWS RETURN TO SAN JUAN CAPISTRANO. Mar 19. Traditional date (St. Joseph's Day) for swallows to return to old mission of San Juan Capistrano, CA, since 1776. See also Oct 23.

U.S. STANDARD TIME ACT: ANNIVERSARY. Mar 19. Anniversary of passage by the Congress of the Standard Time Act, Mar 19, 1918, which authorized the Interstate Commerce Commission to establish standard time zones for the U.S. The Act also established "Daylight-Saving Time," to save fuel and to promote other economies in a country at war. Daylight-saving time first went into operation on Easter Sunday, Mar 31, 1918. The Uniform Time Act of 1966 (see entry for Daylight Saving Time) now governs standard time in the U.S. Info from: National Bureau of Standards Monograph 155.

WARREN, EARL: BIRTHDAY. Mar 19. American jurist, 14th Chief Justice of the U.S., born, Los Angeles, CA, Mar 19, 1891. Died, Washington, DC, July 9, 1974.

MARCH 20 — THURSDAY
79th Day — Remaining, 286

BARNARD, DOUG JR.: BIRTHDAY. Mar 20. U.S. Representative of Georgia's 10th district, Democrat, of Augusta, GA, born there on Mar 20, 1922.

COMBEST, LARRY ED: BIRTHDAY. Mar 20. U.S. Representative of Texas' 19th district, Republican, of Lubbock, TX, was born in Memphis, TX, on Mar 20, 1945.

EARTH DAY. Mar 20. Day of the Vernal Equinox. In 1979, children rang the UN peace bell in New York at the exact moment of the equinox—when the sun crosses the equator. This is the beginning of spring in the Northern Hemisphere and of autumn in the Southern. Participation also in Paris, Tokyo, and other cities. In 1986, the vernal equinox occurs at 5:03 p.m., E.S.T.

ENGLAND: SHAKESPEARE THEATRE SEASON. Mar 20—Jan 1987. Royal Shakespeare Theatre, Stratford-upon-Avon. Season of plays performed by the world renowned company (March-January). Info from: Box Office, Royal Shakespeare Theatre, Stratford-upon-Avon, Warwickshire, CV37 6BB England.

IBSEN, HENRIK: BIRTHDAY. Mar 20. Norwegian playwright, Henrik Johan Ibsen, was born at Skien, Norway, Mar 20, 1828. Among the best remembered plays written by this influential dramatist: *Peer Gynt, The Pillars of Society, The Wild Duck, An Enemy of the People,* and *Hedda Gabler.* Ibsen died at Oslo, May 23, 1906.

COPYRIGHT © 1985 BY WILLIAM D. CHASE and HELEN M. CHASE

LEUKEMIA SOCIETY OF AMERICAN NATIONAL MEDICAL SYMPOSIUM. Mar 20-22. Saddlebrook Resort Hotel, Tampa, FL. Purpose: Information on treatment of leukemia and related diseases to medical professionals. Sponsor: Leukemia Society of America, Martin A. Siederer, 733 Third Ave, New York, NY 10017.

MULRONEY, BRIAN: BIRTHDAY. Mar 20. Born at Baie Comeau, Quebec, on Mar 20, 1939, M. Brian Mulroney, a business executive, lawyer and leader of Canada's Progressive Conservative Party, was sworn in as Canada's 18th prime minister on Sept 17, 1984.

NATIONAL COLLEGIATE WOMEN'S FENCING CHAMPIONSHIPS. Mar 20-22. Princeton University, Princeton, NJ. Info from: Natl Collegiate Athletic Assn, Box 1906, Mission, KS 66201.

NATIONAL CONGRESS ON AVIATION AND SPACE EDUCATION. Mar 20-22. New Orleans, LA. Purpose: To promote aerospace education as an important part of the curriculum in schools and develop grassroots aerospace leaders in local communities. Sponsors: Civil Air Patrol, Natl Aeronautics and Space Admin, Natl Air and Space Museum and Federal Aviation Admin. Info from: Civil Air Patrol, Donald F. Giglio, Lt Col, USAF, Public Affairs Dir, HQ CAP-USAF (AU), Maxwell AFB, AL 36112.

NATIONAL MUSIC THEATER AWARDS. Mar 20. John F. Kennedy Center for the Performing Arts, Washington, DC. Purpose: To honor the winners of the George London Grants for Singers; Medalist Competition; to honor individuals and organizations who made outstanding contributions to the field of Music Theater in America. Sponsor: Natl Institute for Music Theater, Pamela DeSanto, Public Information Officer, Kennedy Center, Washington, DC 20566.

NCAA DIV II BASKETBALL CHAMPIONSHIP. Mar 20-22. Men and Women, Springfield Civic Ctr. Info from: Basketball Hall of Fame, Box 179, 1150 W Columbus Ave, Springfield, MA 01101.

SNOWMAN BURNING. Mar 20. Purpose: Reading of poetry heralding the end of winter and the arrival of spring. Followed by ceremonial burning in effigy, toasts and cheers—(Ole!) Always the first day of spring. Sponsor: Unicorn Hunters of Lake Superior State College, W.T. Rabe, archivist, Poet Peter Thomas, Senior Herald, Sault Ste. Marie, MI 49783.

SPRING. Mar 20-June 21. In the Northern Hemisphere Spring begins today with the Vernal Equinox, at 5:03 p.m., E.S.T. Note that in the Southern Hemisphere today is the beginning of autumn and the occasion of the Autumnal Equinox. The point on Earth from which sun is overhead crosses the equator moving north, this year at longitude 150° W (in the Pacific Ocean, near Christmas Island). Sun rises due east and sets due west everywhere on Earth (except near poles) and the daylight length (interval between sunrise and sunset) is virtually the same everywhere: 12 hours, 8 minutes.

TEXAS LEGISLATIVE CONFERENCE. Mar 20-21. New Braunfels, TX. Purpose: To honor Texan of the year and present views on state and national legislative issues by panels of elected and appointed state and federal officials. Sponsors: TX State Chamber of Commerce and New Braunfels Chamber of Commerce. Info from: Chamber of Commerce, Box 180, New Braunfels, TX 78130.

TUNISIA: INDEPENDENCE DAY. Mar 20. Commemorates treaty of Mar 20, 1956, by which France recognized Tunisian autonomy.

March 1986

S	M	T	W	T	F	S
						1
2	3	4	5	6	7	8
9	10	11	12	13	14	15
16	17	18	19	20	21	22
23	24	25	26	27	28	29
30	31					

MARCH 21 — FRIDAY
80th Day — Remaining, 285

ARIES, THE RAM. Mar 21-Apr 19. In the astronomical/astrological Zodiac, which divides the sun's apparent orbit into twelve segments, the period Mar 21-Apr 19 is identified, traditionally, as the sun-sign of Aries, the Ram. The ruling planet is Mars.

BACH, JOHANN SEBASTIAN: BIRTHDAY. Mar 21. German organist and composer, one of the most influential in musical history, was born on Mar 21, 1685 at Eisenach, Germany. Bach died at Leipzig on July 28, 1750.

BIRD DAY. Mar 21. Iowa.

BROWN TROUT DERBY. Mar 21-June 20. Purpose: Fishermen on their own, fishing within boundaries and weighing their fish for prizes in various categories. Sponsor: Tawas Area Chamber of Commerce, Box 608, Tawas City, MI 48763.

CALIFORNIA STRAWBERRY DAY. Mar 21. Marks the official beginning of California's fresh strawberry season, and honors the irresistible strawberry as the true harbinger of spring. Sponsor: California Strawberry Advisory Board. Info from: Ketchum Public Relations, Julie Morse, 55 Union St, San Francisco, CA 94111.

FRAGRANCE DAY. Mar 21. Purpose: To alert everyone to the fragrances about them—to make people aware of the perfumes and bouquets of the world around us. Sponsor: Richard R. Falk Associates, 147 W 42nd St, New York, NY 10036.

GREAT WESTERN JUNIOR LIVESTOCK AND DAIRY SHOW. Mar 21-26. Pomona, CA. Purpose: A spring show where junior exhibitors with their livestock can compete. Info from: 48th District Agriculture Assn, Bill Arballo, Media Info Dir, Box 2250, Pomona, CA 91769.

INTERNATIONAL DAY FOR THE ELIMINATION OF RACIAL DISCRIMINATION. Mar 21. Observed annually on Mar 21, anniversary of killing of 69 African demonstrators at Sharpeville, South Africa, in 1960. A day to remember "the victims of Sharpeville and those countless others in different parts of the world who have fallen victim to racial injustice." Initiated by United Nations General Assembly in 1966. Info from: United Nations, Dept of Public Information, United Nations, NY 10017.

ITALIAN RENAISSANCE FESTIVAL AT VIZCAYA. Mar 21-23. Madrigal singers, jugglers and jesters, brass ensembles, artisans and craftsmen, in the spirit of the Renaissance. Sbandieratori d'Asti (flag throwers from Asti, Italy) and a living chess tournament recreates a Grand Masters' winning chess game. Info from: Renaissance Festival at Vizcaya, 1122 NE 91st St, Miami Shores, FL 33138.

LEWIS, FRANCIS: BIRTHDAY. Mar 21. Signer, Declaration of Independence, born in Wales, Mar 21, 1713. Died Dec 31, 1802.

MEMORY DAY. Mar 21. Purpose: To encourage awareness of traditional memory system using pattern t,d=1; n=2; m=3; r=4; l=5; j,ch=6; k,q,g-hard=7; f,v=8; b,p=9. Study historic examples of the use of the memory system in the writings of Milton, Thomas Gray, Longfellow, Lincoln, etc. Sponsor: Puns Corps, Robert L. Birch, Coord, 3108 Dashiell Rd, Falls Church, VA 22042.

MEXICO: JUAREZ' BIRTHDAY. Mar 21. Anniversary of the birth of Benito Pablo Juarez (1806-1872), born to Zapotec Indian parents, and orphaned at an early age. Learned Spanish at age 12, became symbol of liberalism and of Mexican resistance to foreign intervention.

NATIONAL AGRICULTURE DAY. Mar 21. The people of the U.S. are called upon to observe this day with appropriate ceremonies and activities in recognition of the nation's "most basic industry." Observed on this date by presidential proclamation since 1981.

NATIONAL TEEN-AGERS DAY. Mar 21. Purpose: To foster better relations between the teen-ager and adult. Sponsor: M.J. Mamakos, Exec Dir, Natl Teen-agers Day, 4348 Van Nuys Blvd, Suite 207, Sherman Oaks, CA 91403.

NAW-RUZ. Mar 21. Baha'i New Year's Day. Astronomically fixed to commence the year. Info from: Baha'i Office of Public Affairs, Baha'i Natl Center, Wilmette, IL 60091.

STRANG, JAMES JESSE (KING STRANG): BIRTHDAY. Mar 21. Perhaps America's only crowned king, born at Scipio, NY, Mar 21, 1813, christened Jesse James Strang (which he later changed to James Jesse Strang), was crowned king of Mormons on Beaver Island, MI, July 8, 1850. He continued to rule kingdom until his death. Elected to Michigan Legislature in 1852 and 1854. Fatally wounded by assassins on June 16, 1856, on Beaver Island. Died at Voree, WI, July 9, 1856.

UNITED NATIONS: WEEK OF SOLIDARITY WITH THE PEOPLES STRUGGLING AGAINST RACISM AND RACIAL DISCRIMINATION. Mar 21-27. Annual observance initiated by UN General Assembly as part of its program of the Decade for Action to Combat Racism and Racial Discrimination. Info from: UN Dept of Public Information, United Nations, NY 10017.

WINTER PARK SIDEWALK ART FESTIVAL. Mar 21-23. Central Park, Winter Park, FL. Info from: Art Festival Commission, Box 597, Winter Park, FL 32790.

MARCH 22 — SATURDAY
81st Day — Remaining, 284

ARCHER, BILL: BIRTHDAY. Mar 22. U.S. Representative of Texas' 7th district, Republican, of Houston, TX, born in Houston on Mar 22, 1928.

BONHEUR, ROSA: BIRTHDAY. Mar 22. French landscape painter born Mar 22, 1822. Died May 25, 1899.

FINGER LAKES CRAFTSMEN SPRING EASTER SHOW. Mar 22-23. Monroe County Fairgrounds Dome Arena, Shortsville, NY. All media and categories including photography and prints. Info from: Finger Lakes Craftsmen Shows, Ronald L. Johnson, 25 Seneca St, Shortsville, NY 14548.

HATCH, ORRIN GRANT: BIRTHDAY. Mar 22. U.S. Senator from Utah, Republican, of Salt Lake City, UT, born in Pittsburgh, PA, Mar 22, 1934.

JORDAN: ARAB LEAGUE DAY. Mar 22. National holiday, The Hashemite Kingdom of Jordan.

MacKAY, KENNETH HOOD (BUDDY): BIRTHDAY. Mar 22. U.S. Representative of Florida's 6th district, Democrat, of Ocala, FL, born there on Mar 22, 1933.

NATIONAL GOOF-OFF DAY. Mar 22. Purpose: A day of relaxation and a time to be just one's self; a day for some good-humored fun and some good-natured silliness. Everyone needs one special day each year to goof off. Sponsor: Monica A. Moeller, Chairperson, Natl Goof-off Day Committee, Box 71, Clio, MI 48420.

SPACE MILESTONE: SOYUZ 39 (USSR). Mar 22. Launched on Mar 22, 1981, two cosmonauts (V. Dzhanibekov and, from Mongolia, J. Gurragcha) docked at Salyut 6 space station Mar 23, where they were greeted by previous team of cosmonauts. Returned to Earth Mar 30. Mar 22, 1981.

SPACE MILESTONE: STS-3 (US). Mar 22. Shuttle *Columbia* launched Mar 22, 1982 on third test flight from Kennedy Space Center, FL, with astronauts Jack Lousma and Gordon Fullerton. Landed at White Sands Missile Range, NM, Mar 30.

TUCSON FESTIVAL '86. Mar 22-Apr 20. Purpose: Celebration of Tucson's multicultural heritage combines Mexican fiestas with Indian dancers, a pageant, dashing frontier cavalry and a heartwarming children's parade. Sponsor: Tucson Festival Society, Jarvis Harriman, Exec Dir, 8 W Paseo Redondo, Tucson, AZ 85705.

WEIRD BEARD CONTEST. Mar 22-23. Popular contest at the Italian Renaissance Festival at Vizcaya. A separate, but equal contest for bearded women. Info from: Renaissance Historical Society, 1122 NE 91st St, Miami Shores, FL 33138.

YOUNG PEOPLE'S PIANO CONCERTO COMPETITION. Mar 22. Memphis State University, Memphis, TN. Competition open to junior and senior high school students. Awards. Info from Young People's Piano Concerto Competition, Inc., Dorothy Cox, Pres, 3891 N Watkins, Memphis, TN 38127.

MARCH 23 — SUNDAY
82nd Day — Remaining, 283

ART WEEK. Mar 23-29. Purpose: To focus attention on art and the artists and their achievements in society. Last full week of March. Sponsor: Richard R. Falk Associates, 147 W 42nd St, New York, NY 10036

CAMP FIRE BIRTHDAY SABBATH. Mar 23. Purpose: A day when Camp Fire members worship together and participate in the services in their churches or temples. Sponsor: Camp Fire Inc, 4601 Madison Ave, Kansas City, MO 64112.

CHILDREN AND HOSPITALS WEEK. Mar 23-29. Purpose: Public education campaign to raise awareness of psychological, social and developmental issues when children are hospitalized. Sponsor: Association For Care of Children's Health, 3615 Wisconsin Ave, NW, Washington, DC 20016.

COLFAX, SCHUYLER: BIRTHDAY. Mar 23. Seventeenth Vice President of the U.S. (1869-1873) born, New York City, Mar 23, 1823. Died, Mankato, MN, Jan 13, 1885.

ENGLAND: SUMMER TIME. Mar 23-Oct 26. In England and much of Europe, "Summer Time" (one hour in advance of Standard Time), similar to "Daylight Saving Time," is observed from 01 hours on the day after the fourth Saturday in March until 01 hours on the day after the fourth Saturday in October.

GROTBERG, JOHN E: BIRTHDAY. Mar 23. U.S. Representative of Illinois' 14th district, Republican, of St. Charles, IL, born at Winnebago, MN, on Mar 23, 1925.

HAWAIIAN HIGHLAND GATHERING. Mar 23. Pearl Harbor, Honolulu, Oahu. Gathering of the clans. Scottish foods, highland dancing, games and pipe bands. Info from: Hawaii Visitors Bureau, Honolulu, HI 96815.

HOLY WEEK. Mar 23-29. Christian observance dating from the Fourth Century, known also as Great Week. The seven days beginning on the sixth and final Sunday in Lent (Palm Sunday), consisting of: Palm Sunday; Monday of Holy Week; Tuesday of Holy Week; Spy Wednesday (or Wednesday of Holy Week); Maundy Thursday; Good Friday; Holy Saturday (or Great Sabbath or Easter Even). A time of solemn devotion to and memorializing the suffering (passion), death and burial of Christ. Formerly a time of strict fasting.

LENT, NORMAN FREDERICK: BIRTHDAY. Mar 23. U.S. Representative of New York's 4th district, Republican, of East Rockaway, NY, born in Oceanside, Nassau County, NY, Mar 23, 1931.

LIBERTY DAY. Mar 23. Anniversary of Patrick Henry's speech for arming the Virginia militia—at St. Johns Church, Richmond, VA, on Mar 23, 1775. "I know not what course others may take, but as for me, give me liberty or give me death."

COPYRIGHT © 1985 BY WILLIAM D. CHASE and HELEN M. CHASE

MERRIE MONARCH FESTIVAL. Mar 23-30. Hilo, HI. Sports events, pageantry and special activities commemorate the gala days of King Kalakaua. Info from: Hawaii Visitors Bureau, Honolulu, HI 96815.

OTAGO AND SOUTHLAND PROVINCIAL ANNIVERSARY. Mar 23. New Zealand. In addition to the statutory public holidays of New Zealand, there is in each provincial district a holiday for the provincial anniversary. This is observed in Otago and Southland on Mar 23.

PALM SUNDAY. Mar 23. Commemorates Christ's last entry into Jerusalem, when his way was covered with palms by the multitude.

PAKISTAN: NATIONAL HOLIDAY. Mar 23. Republic Day. On this day in 1940 the All-India-Muslim league adopted resolution calling for a Muslim Homeland. On this same day in 1956 Pakistan declared itself a republic.

PHILIPPINES: HOLY WEEK. Mar 23-29. National Observance. Flagellants in the streets, cenaculos (passion plays) and other colorful and solemn rituals mark country's observance of Holy Week.

PRINCE KUHIO FESTIVAL. Mar 23-30. Kauai Island, HI. Pageantry with songs and dances of the era of Hawaii's first delegate to Congress. Info from: Hawaii Visitors Bureau, Special Events Dept, Honolulu, HI 96815.

SMITH, NEAL: BIRTHDAY. Mar 23. U.S. Representative of Iowa's 4th district, Democrat, of Altoona, IA, was born at Hedrick, IA, on Mar 23, 1920.

WORLD METEOROLOGICAL DAY. Mar 23. An international day observed by the organizations of the United Nations system. Info from: United Nations Dept of Public Information, United Nations, NY 10017.

MARCH 24 — MONDAY
83rd Day — Remaining, 282

DUNCAN, JOHN JAMES: BIRTHDAY. Mar 24. U.S. Representative of Tennessee's 2nd district, Republican, of Knoxville, TN, born in Scott County, TN, on Mar 24, 1919.

FAST OF ESTHER. Mar 24. Hebrew calendar date: Adar 13, 5746. Commemorates Queen Esther's fast, in the 6th Century BC, to save the Jewish people of ancient Persia.

HOUDINI, HARRY: BIRTHDAY. Mar 24. Magician and escape artist, born at Budapest, Hungary, on Mar 24, 1874. Died at Detroit, MI, on Oct 31, 1926. Lecturer, athlete, author, expert on history of magic, exposer of fraudulent mediums, and motion picture actor. Was best known for his ability to escape from locked restraints (handcuffs, straitjackets, coffins, boxes, and milk cans). Anniversary of his death (Halloween) has been occasion for meetings of magicians and attempts at communication by mediums.

MELLON, ANDREW W: BIRTHDAY. Mar 24. American financier, industrialist, government official (Secy of Treasury), art and book collector, born Mar 24, 1855. Died Aug 27, 1937.

MORRIS, WILLIAM: BIRTHDAY. Mar 24. English poet and artist, born Mar 24, 1834. Died Hammersmith, London, Oct 3, 1896.

NATIONAL BUBBLE GUM WEEK. Mar 24-28. Purpose: Bubble gum is advertised "1¢ each, or 2 for nothing" to encourage distribution of free bubble-blowing, tension-breaking gum to

	S	M	T	W	T	F	S
March 1986	2	3	4	5	6	7	1 8
	9	10	11	12	13	14	15
	16	17	18	19	20	21	22
	23	24	25	26	27	28	29
	30	31					

Northern Michigan University students preparing for final exams. Info from: Northern Michigan Univ, Attn: Richard Harbick, Univ Ctr, Marquette, MI 49855.

POWELL, JOHN WESLEY: BIRTHDAY. Mar 24. American geologist, explorer, ethnologist, born at Mt. Morris, NY, Mar 24, 1834. Died Haven, ME, Sept 23, 1902.

ST. GABRIEL: FEAST DAY. Mar 24. St Gabriel the Archangel, patron saint of postmen, telephone and telegraph workers.

MARCH 25 — TUESDAY
84th Day — Remaining, 281

BARTOK, BELA: BIRTHDAY. Mar 25. Hungarian composer born Mar 25, 1881, at Nagyszentmiklos (now in Yugoslavia). Died at New York City, Sept 26, 1945.

BRUCE, TERRY L: BIRTHDAY. Mar 25. U.S. Representative of Illinois' 19th district, Democrat, of Olney, IL, born at Olney on Mar 25, 1944.

COXEY'S ARMY ANNIVERSARY. Mar 25. Anniversary of a march on the nation's capitol, started Mar 25, 1894. Jacob S. Coxey, businessman, economic reformer, advocate of interest-free government bonds, left Massillon, OH on foot with "army" of about 100 followers. Arrived Washington, DC, May 1st. His hope to influence Congress was thwarted when he, and part of army, arrested for trespassing on government property. Fifty years later he spoke from the capitol steps, reiterating belief in non-interest bearing government bonds.

FAWELL, HARRIS W: BIRTHDAY. Mar 25. U.S. Representative of Illinois' 13th district, Republican. of Naperville, IL, born in West Chicago, IL, on Mar 25, 1929.

FEAST OF ANNUNCIATION. Mar 25. Celebrated in the Roman Catholic Church in commemoration of the message of the Angel Gabriel to Mary that she was to be the Mother of Christ.

GLOBAL UNDERSTANDING DAY. Mar 25. Purpose: To draw attention to the need for, and feasibility of, understanding among peoples of the world. Since they are ultimately responsible for the preservation and sound functioning of their planet, such understanding is crucial. Sponsor: People for Global Understanding, Paul H. Jordan, MD, Pres. Info from: Virginia H. Jordan, 1125 Jordan Lane, Grand Blanc, MI 48439.

GREECE: NATIONAL HOLIDAY. Mar 25. Independence Day. Celebrates independence from Turkey, 1821.

HAWAIIAN FESTIVAL OF MUSIC. Mar 25-Apr 8. Waikiki Shell, Honolulu. Music groups from Hawaii and mainland U.S. compete. Info: Hawaii Visitors Bureau, Honolulu, HI 96815.

MARYLAND DAY. Mar 25. Commemorates arrival of Lord Baltimore's first settlers in Maryland in 1634.

MOON PHASE: FULL MOON. Mar 25. Moon enters Full Moon phase at 10:02 p.m., E.S.T.

OMAHA HOME SHOW. Mar 25-30. Civic Auditorium, Omaha, NE. Info from: Mid-America Expositions, Inc. 666 Farnam Bldg, Omaha, NE 68102.

PURIM. Mar 25. Hebrew calendar date: Adar II 14, 5746. Feasts, gifts and charity mark this joyous commemoration of Queen Esther's intervention, in the 6th Century BC, to save the Jews of ancient Persia. Haman's plot to exterminate the Jews was thwarted and he was hanged on the very day he had set for execution of the Jews.

SCHNEIDER, CLAUDINE: BIRTHDAY. Mar 25. U.S. Representative of Rhode Island's 2nd district, Republican, of Narragansett, RI, born in Clairton, PA, Mar 25, 1947.

MARCH 26 — WEDNESDAY
85th Day — Remaining, 280

BANGLADESH: INDEPENDENCE DAY. Mar 26. Celebrated with parades, youth festivals and symposia.

BELLAMY, EDWARD: BIRTH ANNIVERSARY. Mar 26. American author best remembered for his novel *Looking Backward* (1888) was born at Chicopee Falls, MA, on Mar 26, 1850 and died there on May 28, 1898.

COPYRIGHT © 1985 BY WILLIAM D. CHASE and HELEN M. CHASE

BOWDITCH, NATHANIEL: BIRTHDAY. Mar 26. American mathematician and astronomer, author of the *New American Practical Navigator*, born Salem, MA, Mar 26, 1773. Died, Boston, Mar 16, 1838.

DELANO, JANE: BIRTHDAY. Mar 26. Jane Arminda Delano, dedicated American nurse and teacher, superintendent of the U.S. Army Nurse Corps, Chairman of the American Red Cross Nursing Service, and recipient (posthumously) of the Distinguished Service Medal of the U.S., was long believed to have been born Mar 12, 1862. Recently uncovered records in Miss Delano's handwriting reveal that she was born Mar 26, 1858, near Townsend, NY. While on an official visit to review Red Cross activities she died Apr 15, 1919, in an army hospital at Savenay, France. Her last words: "What about my work? I must get back to my work." Buried first at Loire, France, her remains were re-interred at Arlington National Cemetery, in 1920. Revised birthdate info from: American Red Cross, Natl Hq, Washington, DC 20006.

ENGLAND: HARROGATE INTERNATIONAL YOUTH MUSIC FESTIVAL. Mar 26-Apr 2. Harrogate, North Yorkshire, England. Over a thousand musicians, singers and dancers.

FROST, ROBERT LEE: BIRTHDAY. Mar 26. American poet who tried his hand at farming, teaching, shoemaking and editing, before winning acclaim as a poet. Pulitzer Prize winner. Born at San Francisco, CA, Mar 26, 1874. Died at Boston, MA, Jan 29, 1963.

KUHIO DAY. Mar 26. Hawaii. Also known as Prince Jonah Kuhio Kalanianaole Day, honoring birthday of Hawaii's second delegate to Congress.

O'CONNOR, SANDRA DAY: BIRTHDAY. Mar 26. Associate Justice of the Supreme Court of the United States, nominated by Pres Reagan on July 7, 1981. Took Oath of Office on Sept 25, 1981. Justice O'Connor was born at El Paso, TX, on Mar 26, 1930. She was the first woman nominated and the first appointed to the U.S. Supreme Court.

MARCH 27 — THURSDAY
86th Day — Remaining, 279

ALASKA EARTHQUAKE ANNIVERSARY. Mar 27. Severe earthquake Mar 27, 1964.

APPLEGATE, DOUGLAS: BIRTHDAY. Mar 27. U.S. Representative of Ohio's 18th district, Democrat, of Steubenville, OH, born there on Mar 27, 1928.

BEVILL, TOM: BIRTHDAY. Mar 27. U.S. Representative of Alabama's 4th district, Democrat, of Jasper, AL, born in Townley, AL, on Mar 27, 1921.

CARR, BOB: BIRTHDAY. Mar 27. U.S. Representative of Michigan's 6th district, Democrat, of Okemos, MI, was born in Janesville, WI, Mar 27, 1943.

ICE HOCKEY: NATIONAL COLLEGIATE DIVISION I MEN'S CHAMPIONSHIP FINALS. Mar 27-29. Providence Civic Ctr, Providence, RI. Info from: NCAA, Box 1906, Mission, KS 66201.

McGRATH, RAYMOND J: BIRTHDAY. Mar 27. U.S. Representative of New York's 5th district, Republican, of Valley Stream, NY, born in Valley Stream on Mar 27, 1942.

MAUNDY THURSDAY or HOLY THURSDAY. Mar 27. The Thursday before Easter, originally "dies mandate," celebrates Christ's injunction to love one another, "Mandatus novum do vobis . . ." ("A new commandment I give to You . . .").

MAYOR SCHAEFER'S EASTER PARTY. Mar 27. War Memorial Plaza, Baltimore, MD. Musical entertainment and performances given in celebration of Easter. A best decorated Easter egg contest and the Easter Bunny also featured. Info from: Virginia Baker, Mayor's Office of Adventures in Fun, 100 Holiday St, Rm 355, Baltimore, MD 21202.

MORIONE'S FESTIVAL. Mar 27-30. Marinduque Island, Philippine Islands. Province-wide masquerade, Lenten plays and celebrations. (Holy Thursday through Easter Sunday.)

NATIONAL EXCHANGE CLUB BIRTHDAY. Mar 27. Anniversary of the day in 1911, when the first Exchange Club was founded in Detroit, MI. Celebrated annually by nearly fifty thousand Exchangites in the U.S. and Puerto Rico. Sponsor: The Natl Exchange Club, 3050 Central Ave, Toledo, OH 43606.

NORTH SEA OIL RIG DISASTER: ANNIVERSARY. Mar 27. The Alexander L. Keilland Oil Rig capsized, Mar 27, 1980, during a heavy storm in the Norwegian sector of the North Sea. The pentagon-type, French-built oil rig had about 200 persons aboard, and 123 lives were lost.

PASHAYAN, CHARLES JR.: BIRTHDAY. Mar 27. U.S. Representative of California's 17th district, Republican, of Fresno, CA, born there Mar 27, 1941.

ROENTGEN, WILHELM KONRAD: BIRTHDAY. Mar 27. German scientist who discovered X-rays (1895), and won Nobel Prize in 1901. Born at Lennep, Prussia, Mar 27, 1845. Died at Munich, Feb 10, 1923.

SCRATCH ANKLE FESTIVAL. Mar 27. Festival features a parade and fair, a 10,000 meter run and the Little Mr. and Miss Scratch Ankle pageant. Info from: Milton City Youth Council, 903 Robin Ave, Milton, FL 32570.

SPACE MILESTONE: VENERA 8 (USSR). Mar 27. Soft landing on Venus July 22, with radio transmission of surface data. Launched Mar 27, 1972.

STEICHEN, EDWARD: BIRTHDAY. Mar 27. Celebrated American photographer born Mar 27, 1879. Died Mar 25, 1973.

SWANSON, GLORIA: BIRTHDAY. Mar 27. American film actress and businesswoman was born Gloria May Josephine Svensson in Chicago, Mar 27, 1899. Author of an autobiography, *Swanson on Swanson*, published in 1980, she died at New York City, Apr 4, 1983.

VIRGIN ISLANDS: HOLY THURSDAY. Mar 27. Celebrated with evening church services and Holy Communion.

MARCH 28 — FRIDAY
87th Day — Remaining, 278

BATTLE OF GLORIETTA: ANNIVERSARY. Mar 28. On Mar 28, 1862, at Pigeon's Ranch, a stagecoach stop on the Santa Fe Trail (about 19 miles southeast of Santa Fe, NM), Confederate forces briefly prevailed over Union troops in what some have called the most important battle of the Civil War in the Southwest. It was feared that if Union troops failed to hold here the Confederate forces would proceed to Fort Union and on to control of the rich gold fields of Colorado and California. A re-enactment of the battle in 1985 drew attention to the battlefield and the adobe remains of Pigeon's Ranch.

CHAPPIE, (EUGENE A.) GENE: BIRTHDAY. Mar 28. U.S. Representative of California's 2nd district, Republican, of Chico, CA, born in Sacramento, CA, Mar 28, 1920.

GOOD FRIDAY. Mar 28. Observed in commemoration of the crucifixion. Oldest Christian celebration. Possible corruption of "God's Friday." Observed in some manner by most Christian sects everywhere, and as public holiday or part holiday in many places.

COPYRIGHT © 1985 BY WILLIAM D. CHASE and HELEN M. CHASE

GREAT ESCAPE WEEKEND. Mar 28-30. Petit Jean State Park, Morrilton, AR. A weekend of outdoor activities dedicated to spring. Sponsor: Petit Jean State Park, Rt 3 Box 340, Morrilton, AR 72110.

MURKOWSKI, FRANK HUGHES: BIRTHDAY. Mar 28. U.S. Senator from Alaska, Republican, of Fairbanks, AK, was born in Seattle, WA, on Mar 28, 1933.

NORTHERN IRELAND: CIRCUIT OF IRELAND MOTOR RALLY. Mar 28-Apr 1. International motor race covering 1,500 mile course around Ireland, starting and finishing at Belfast.

PERTINAX' ASSASSINATION ANNIVERSARY. Mar 28. Roman emperor Pertinax, on Mar 28, A.D. 193, according to Edward Gibbon, "disdaining either flight or concealment, advanced to meet his assassins and recalled to their minds his own innocence, and the sanctity of their recent oath. For a few moments they stood in silent suspense, ashamed of their own atrocious design, and awed by the venerable aspect and majestic firmness of their sovereign . . . His head separated from his body and placed on a lance, was carried in triumph to Praetorian camp, in the sight of a mournful and indignant people, who lamented the unworthy fate of that excellent prince, and the transient blessings of a reign the memory of which could only serve to aggravate their approaching misfortunes."

RECREATIONAL VEHICLE, BOAT AND MOBILE HOME SHOW. Mar 28-30. Billings, MT. Info from: Dixie Green Promotions, Inc. 3141 W Christy Dr, Phoenix, AZ 85029.

ST. JOHN NEPOMUCENE NEUMANN: BIRTHDAY. Mar 28. First male Saint of the U.S., was born at Prachatice, Bohemia, on Mar 28, 1811, and came to the U.S. in 1836. As Bishop of Philadelphia he was affectionately known as the "Little Bishop." Died at Philadelphia, Jan 5, 1860. Beatified Oct 13, 1963. Canonized June 19, 1977. Pope Paul VI, in proclaiming Sainthood, said: "For the honor of the most Holy Trinity, for the exaltation of the Catholic faith and the increase of the Christian life, by the authority of our Lord Jesus Christ, of the Holy Apostles Peter and Paul and by our own authority, after having reflected for a long time and invoked the counsel of many of our brother bishops, we inscribe his name in the Calendar of Saints and establish that he should be devoutly honored among the saints of the Universal church."

SCOTLAND: EDINBURGH FOLK FESTIVAL. Mar 28-Apr 6. Edinburgh, Lothian. Concerts, ceilidhs, lectures, exhibitions. Presents some of the best folk music in the world.

SPACE MILESTONE: NOAA 8 (US). Mar 28. Search and Rescue Satellite (SARSAT) launched from Vandenburg Air Force Base, CA to aid in locating ships and aircraft in distress. Kosmos 1383, launched on July 1, 1982, by the USSR, in cooperative rescue effort, is credited with saving more than 20 lives. Mar 28, 1983.

TAIWAN: BIRTHDAY OF KUAN YIN, GODDESS OF MERCY. Mar 28. Nineteenth day of Second Moon of the Lunar calendar, celebrated at Taipei's Lungshan (Dragon Mountain) and other temples.

TEACHERS' DAY. Mar 28. Czechoslovakia. Celebrates birth on this day of Jan Amos Komensky (Comenius), Moravian educational reformer (1592-1671).

THREE MILE ISLAND NUCLEAR POWER PLANT ACCIDENT ANNIVERSARY. Mar 28. A series of accidents beginning at 4 a.m., E.S.T., Mar 28, 1979, at Three Mile Island on the Susquehanna River about 10 miles southeast of Harrisburg, PA (equipment and other failures which reportedly brought TMI close to a meltdown of the uranium core, threatening extensive radiation contamination) were responsible for extensive re-evaluation of the safety of existing nuclear power generating operations.

WHIM CONFERENCE. Mar 28-Apr 1. Arizona State University, Tempe, AZ. Theme: "American Humor." WHIM (Western Humor and Irony Membership) scholars in the fields of anthropology, psychology, American and British literature, philosophy, religion and popular culture will present papers. Info from: Don L.F. Nilsen, WHIM, English Dept, Arizona State Univ, Tempe, AZ 85287.

MARCH 29 — SATURDAY

88th Day — Remaining, 277

BASKETBALL: NATIONAL COLLEGIATE DIVISION I MEN'S CHAMPIONSHIP FINALS. Mar 29-31. Reunion Arena, Dallas, TX. Info from: NCAA, Box 1906, Mission, KS 66201.

BLESSING OF THE ANIMALS. Mar 29. Recognition of the animal kingdom for the many benefits provided to mankind. All domestic animals and pets welcome. El Pueblo de Los Angeles State Historic Park, 845 N Alameda St, Los Angeles, CA 90012.

CAROLINA CUP: STEEPLECHASE. Mar 29. Camden, South Carolina. Thoroughbred steeplechase and flat racing. Info from: Patricia D. Cooper, Box 280, Camden, SC 29020.

CHINCOTEAGUE EASTER DECOY FESTIVAL. Mar 29-30. Wildfowl carving and wildlife art exhibits. (Easter weekend). Sponsor: Chincoteague Chamber of Commerce, Box 258, Chincoteague Island, VA 23336.

CYPRUS: THE PROCESSION OF ICON OF ST. LAZARUS. Mar 29. Larnaca, Cyprus. The day before Easter Sunday.

EASTER EVEN. Mar 29. The Saturday before Easter. Last day of Holy Week and of Lent.

HOOVER, LOU HENRY: BIRTHDAY. Mar 29. Wife of Herbert Clark Hoover, 31st President of the U.S., born at Waterloo, IA, Mar 29, 1875. Died Jan 7, 1944.

JOHN PARTRIDGE "DEATH" HOAX ANNIVERSARY. Mar 29. English astrologer John Partridge (real name: John Hewson) so offended readers by his foolish predictions that he became the target of parodies and jokes, most serious of which was that of the satirist, Jonathan Swift. Under the pseudonym, Isaac Bickerstaff, Swift published his own Almanac, for the year 1708, in which he predicted that Partridge would die at 11 p.m., Mar 29, 1708, "of a raging fever." Poor Partridge made the mistake of trying to prove he was still alive, only to find writers, citizens, and even the court more amused by continuing the fiction of his death.

MADAGASCAR: COMMEMORATION DAY. Mar 29. Commemoration Day for the victims of the rebellion in 1947 against the French colonization.

PENN STATE BLACK ARTS FESTIVAL. Mar 29-Apr 14. Purpose: A celebration of the past, present and future of African-American culture reflected in art, music, theatre, literature, food, philosophy and dance. Sponsor: Paul Robeson Cultural Center, Penn State Univ, University Park, PA 16802.

PRESSLER, LARRY: BIRTHDAY. Mar 29. U.S. Senator from South Dakota, Republican, of Humboldt, SD, born in Humboldt on Mar 29, 1942.

QUINLAN, KAREN ANN: BIRTH ANNIVERSARY. Mar 29. Born at Scranton, PA, on Mar 29, 1954, Karen Ann Quinlan became the center of an international legal, medical and ethical controversy over the right to die. Reportedly she became irreversibly comatose on Apr 14, 1975. A petition filed by her adoptive parents in New Jersey's Superior Court, Sept 12, 1975, sought permission to discontinue use of a respirator, allowing her to die "with grace and dignity." Eventually (in 1976) the petition was upheld (by New Jersey's Supreme Court). Miss Quinlan lived nearly a decade without the

	S	M	T	W	T	F	S
March							1
	2	3	4	5	6	7	8
1986	9	10	11	12	13	14	15
	16	17	18	19	20	21	22
	23	24	25	26	27	28	29
	30	31					

COPYRIGHT © 1985 BY WILLIAM D. CHASE and HELEN M. CHASE

respirator—until June 11, 1985. Described by some as unconsiously one of the world's great teachers, her life and tragic plight brought into focus the ethical dilemmas of advancing medical technology—the need for new understanding of life and death, the right to die, the role of judges, doctors and hospital committees in deciding when to prolong or when *not* to prolong life.

TAIWAN: YOUTH DAY. Mar 29. Public holiday observed annually on Mar 29.

TYLER COUNTY DOGWOOD FESTIVAL. Mar 29. (Also Apr 5) "Western Weekend" and "Queen's Weekend," held during height of dogwood blooming season. Parades, rodeo, arts, crafts, historical pageant and dances. Last Saturday in March, first Saturday in April. Info from: Chamber of Commerce, 507 N Pine St, Woodville, TX 75979.

TYLER, JOHN: BIRTHDAY. Mar 29. Tenth President of the U.S. (Apr 6, 1841-Mar 3, 1845), was born at Charles City County, VA, Mar 29, 1790. Tyler succeeded to the presidency upon the death of William Henry Harrison. Tyler's first wife died while he was president and he remarried before the end of his term of office, becoming the first president to marry while in office. Fifteen children were born of the two marriages. In 1861 he was elected to the Congress of the Confederate States, but died, at Richmond, VA, Jan 18, 1862, before being seated. His death received no official tribute from the U.S. government.

MARCH 30 — SUNDAY
89th Day — Remaining, 276

DOCTORS' DAY. Mar 30. Traditional annual observance since 1933, to honor America's physicians on anniversary of occasion when Dr. Crawford W. Long became the first acclaimed physician to use ether as an anaesthetic agent in a surgical technique, on Mar 30, 1842. Red carnation has been designated official flower of Doctors' Day.

EASTER PARADE. Mar 30. Fifth Ave, New York. Info from: NY Conv & Visitors Bureau, Inc, 2 Columbus Circle, New York, NY 10019.

EASTER SUNDAY. Mar 30. Commemorates the Resurrection of Christ. Most joyous festival of the Christian year. The date of Easter, a movable feast, is derived from the lunar calendar (as prescribed by the Council of Nice, A.D. 325): the first Sunday following the first full moon on or after the Vernal Equinox (March 20)—always between March 22 and April 25. Many other dates in the Christian year are derived from the date of Easter.

EASTER SUNDAYS TO THE YEAR 2000.

1987, April 19	1994, April 3
1988, April 3	1995, April 16
1989, March 26	1996, April 7
1990, April 15	1997, March 30
1991, March 31	1998, April 12
1992, April 10	1999, April 4
1993, April 11	2000, April 23

GOYA, FRANCISCO JOSE DE: BIRTHDAY. Mar 30. Spanish painter and etcher, born at Aragon, Spain, Mar 30, 1746. It is estimated that he executed more than 1,800 paintings, drawings and lithographs during his lifetime. Died at Bordeaux, France, Apr 16, 1828.

"I AM IN CONTROL" DAY. Mar 30. Anniversary of former Secretary of State Alexander Haig's televised announcement on Mar 30, 1981 (while Pres Ronald Reagan was undergoing surgery after being shot by a would-be assassin): "As of now, I am in control here in the White House . . ." Haig continued to say: "Constitutionally, gentlemen, you have the president, the vice president and the secretary of state in that order . . ."

McCURDY, DAVE: BIRTHDAY. Mar 30. U.S. Representative of Oklahoma's 4th district, Democrat, of Norman, OK, born in Canadian, TX, Mar 30, 1950.

MARKSVILLE EASTER EGG KNOCKING CONTEST. Mar 30. Purpose: Competition among owners of chicken, goose, turkey, guinea eggs after they have been dyed and boiled. Sponsor: Chamber of Commerce, Box 365, Marksville, LA 71351.

MATHEMATICS EDUCATION WEEK. Mar 30-Apr 5. Purpose: One week during the year dedicated to the observance and recognition of the importance of mathematics. A national focus for local schools and community activities at all grade levels. Sponsor: Natl Council of Teachers of Mathematics, Jan R. Goldenberg, 1906 Association Dr, Reston, VA 22091.

MORAVIAN EASTER SUNRISE SERVICE. Mar 30. Outdoor religious service featuring Moravian bands playing in streets to awaken sleepers. Service begins in square in Old Salem and ends in Moravian graveyard at daybreak. Info from: Salem Congregation, 500 S Church St, Winston-Salem, NC 27101.

O'CASEY, SEAN: BIRTHDAY. Mar 30. Irish playwright born at Dublin, Mar 30, 1880. Died at Torquay, England, on Sept 18, 1964.

PETERS HOLLOW EASTER EGG FIGHT. Mar 30. Purpose: To see whose hen lays the hardest egg. Tradition on Easter Sunday since 1823. Sponsor: Uncle Tom Peters, Ole Mayor (Unofficial) of Peters Hollow, Rt 10, Box 1360, Elizabethton, TN 37643.

RONALD REAGAN ASSASSINATION ATTEMPT: ANNIVERSARY. Mar 30. President Ronald Reagan was shot in the chest by a 25-year-old gunman, about 2:30 p.m., Mar 30, 1981, in Washington, DC. Three other persons were wounded. John W. Hinckley, Jr, the accused attacker, was arrested at the scene. On June 21, 1982, a federal jury in the District of Columbia found Hinckley not guilty by reason of insanity and he was committed to St. Elizabeth's Hospital, at Washington, for an indefinite time.

SMITH, ROBERT C: BIRTHDAY. Mar 30. U.S. Representative of New Hampshire's 1st district, Republican, of Tuftonboro, NH, born in Trenton, NJ, on Mar 30, 1941.

SUMMER TIME (DAYLIGHT SAVING TIME-EUROPE). Mar 30-Sept 28. Many European countries observe daylight saving (summer) time from 2 a.m. on the last Sunday in March until 3 a.m. on the last Sunday in September.

VAN GOGH, VINCENT: BIRTHDAY. Mar 30. Dutch post-impressionist painter, especially known for his bold and powerful use of color, born at Groot Zundert, Holland, Mar 30, 1853. Died at Auvers-sur-Oise, France, July 29, 1890.

MARCH 31 — MONDAY
90th Day — Remaining, 275

BUNSEN BURNER DAY. Mar 31. A day to honor the inventor of the Bunsen Burner, Robert Wilhelm Eberhard von Bunsen, who provided chemists and chemistry students with one of their most indispensable instruments. The Bunsen Burner allowed the user to regulate the proportions of flammable gas and air to create the most efficient flame. Bunsen was born at Gottingen, Germany, on Mar 31, 1811, and was a professor of chemistry at the universities at Kassel, Marburg, Breslau and Heidelberg. He died at Heidelberg, Aug 16, 1899.

COPYRIGHT © 1985 BY WILLIAM D. CHASE and HELEN M. CHASE

CATHOLIC LIBRARY ASSOCIATION ANNUAL CONVENTION. Mar 31-Apr 3. Anaheim, CA. Info from: Catholic Library Assn, 461 W Lancaster Ave, Haverford, PA 19041.

DESCARTES, RENE: BIRTHDAY. Mar 31. French philosopher and mathematician, known as the "father of modern philosophy," was born at La Haye, Touraine, France, on Mar 31, 1596. Cartesian philosophical precepts are often remembered because of his famous proposition, "I think, therefore I am," (Cogito ergo sum . . .). Descartes died, of pneumonia, at Stockholm, Sweden, on Feb 11, 1650.

EASTER MONDAY. Mar 31. North Carolina.

EASTER MONDAY. Mar 31. Holiday or bank holiday in many places, including England, Northern Ireland, Wales and Canada.

EGG SALAD WEEK. Mar 31-Apr 6. Purpose: Dedicated to the many delicious uses for all of the Easter eggs that have been cooked, colored, hidden and found. (The full week after Easter.) Sponsor: American Egg Board, 1460 Renaissance Dr, Park Ridge, IL 60068.

EMAISHEN. Mar 31. Luxembourg (city). Popular traditional market and festival on the "Marche-aux-Poissons." Young lovers present each other with earthenware articles, sold only on this day. Easter Monday each year.

ENGLAND; HALLATON BOTTLE KICKING. Mar 31. Ancient annual custom (dates back at least 600 years). Always on Easter Monday. Hallaton, Leicestershire.

FITZGERALD, EDWARD: BIRTHDAY. Mar 31. English author, born Mar 31, 1809. Perhaps best known for his translation of Omar Khayyam's *Rubaiyat*. Died June 14, 1883.

FRANK, BARNEY: BIRTHDAY. Mar 31. U.S. Representative of Massachusetts' 4th district, Democrat, of Newton, MA, born in Bayonne, NJ, on Mar 31, 1940.

GOGOL, NIKOLAI VASILEVICH: BIRTHDAY. Mar 31. Russian author of plays, novels and short stories, born at Sorochinsk on Mar 31, 1809. He died at Moscow, Mar 4, 1852. Gogol's most famous work was the novel, *Dead Souls.*

GORE, ALBERT, JR: BIRTHDAY. Mar 31. U.S. Senator from Tennessee, Democrat, of Carthage, TN was born on Mar 31, 1948.

HAYDN, FRANZ JOSEPH: BIRTHDAY. Mar 31. Franz Joseph Haydn, "father of the symphony," was born at Rohrau, Austria-Hungary, on Mar 31, 1732. He composed about 120 symphonies, more than a hundred works for chamber groups, a dozen operas, and hundreds of other musical works. Hadyn died at Vienna, on May 31, 1809.

March 1986	S	M	T	W	T	F	S
							1
	2	3	4	5	6	7	8
	9	10	11	12	13	14	15
	16	17	18	19	20	21	22
	23	24	25	26	27	28	29
	30	31					

INTERNATIONAL LARRY WILDE JOKE TELLING CONTEST. Mar 31. Arizona State University, Tempe, AZ. Purpose: Contestants vie for cash prizes. Judges vote on delivery, timing, presentation and originality of material. Culminating event of WHIM Humor Conference. Info from: Don L.F. Nilsen, Chairman, English Dept, ASU, Tempe, AZ 85287.

LEAHY, PATRICK J: BIRTHDAY. Mar 31. U.S. Senator from Vermont, Democrat, of Burlington, VT, born in Montpelier, VT, on Mar 31, 1940.

MALTA: NATIONAL DAY. Mar 31. Republic Day. Festive activities.

MARVELL, ANDREW: BIRTHDAY. Mar 31. English poet born at Winestead, Yorkshire, England, Mar 31, 1621. Died at London, Aug 18, 1678.

RICHARD PEARSE FLIGHT ANNIVERSARY. Mar 31. Near Temuka, New Zealand, Richard Pearse, farmer-inventor, flew, according to claim, in monoplane he designed and built, including steerable tricycle undercarriage and internal combustion engine. Pearse flew several hundred yards along a road, landing on a 12-foot-high hedge, on Mar 31, 1903. Pearse commemorative medal was issued on Sept 19, 1971, by Museum of Transport and Technology, Auckland, New Zealand.

ROYAL MANITOBA WINTER FAIR. Mar 31-Apr 5. Brandon, Manitoba Canada. Features the Manitoba classic horse show and all breed bull sale. Farm and home exposition. Info from: Travel Manitoba, Dept 5058, Winnipeg, Manitoba, R3C 3H8 Canada.

ST. PETERSBURG FESTIVAL OF STATES. Mar 31-Apr 12. Purpose: To salute civic endeavor and highlight the 50 states. National band championships, art shows, parades, antique cars and golf tournament. Sponsor: St. Petersburg Festival of States, Box 1731, St. Petersburg, FL 33731.

SEWARD'S DAY. Mar 31. Alaska. Observed near anniversary of the acquisition of Alaska from Russia in 1867, (Last Monday in March.)

SWITZERLAND: EGG RACES. Mar 31. Rural northwest Swiss Easter Monday custom. Race between competitors carrying large number of eggs while running to neighboring village.

VANCOUVER, BRITISH COLUMBIA: BIRTHDAY WEEK. Mar 31-Apr 6. Celebration of Vancouver's 100th Birthday. Official birthday is Apr 6. Info from: The Centennial Commission, Box 49386, Suite 3374, Bentall 4, 1055 Dunsmuir St, Vancouver, BC V7X 1L5 Canada.

VIRGIN ISLANDS: TRANSFER DAY. Mar 31. Commemorates transfer resulting from purchase of the Virgin Islands by the U.S. from Denmark, Mar 31, 1917, for $25 million.

WHITE HOUSE EASTER EGG ROLL. Mar 31. Traditionally held at executive mansion's south lawn on Easter Monday. Custom said to have started at Capitol grounds about 1810. Transferred to White House lawn in 1870s.

COPYRIGHT © 1985 BY WILLIAM D. CHASE and HELEN M. CHASE

Aprill.

APRIL 1 — TUESDAY
91st Day — Remaining, 274

APRIL FOOLS' or ALL FOOLS' DAY. Apr 1. "The joke of the day is to deceive persons by sending them upon frivolous and nonsensical errands; to pretend they are wanted when they are not, or, in fact, any way to betray them into some supposed ludicrous situation, so as to enable you to call them 'An April Fool.' "—Brady's *Clavis Calendaria*, 1812. "The first of April, some do say, Is set apart for All Fools' Day, But why the people call it so, Nor I nor they themselves do know." - *Poor Robin's Almanack* for 1760.

BURTON, SALA GALANT: BIRTHDAY. Apr 1. U.S. Representative of California's 5th district, Democrat, from San Francisco, CA, was born in Bialystok, Poland, Apr 1, 1925.

CANCER CONTROL MONTH. Apr 1-30. Presidential Proclamation. "Always issued for April since 1938." (Pub Res No. 82 of Mar 28, 1938).

CANCER CONTROL MONTH. Apr 1-30. In support of the nation's fight against cancer. During this month the American Cancer Society conducts its annual fund raising and educational Cancer Crusade. Sponsor: American Cancer Society, JoAnn Schellenbach, Dir Press Relations, 4 W 35th St, New York, NY 10001.

EXCHANGE CLUB CHILD ABUSE PREVENTION MONTH. Apr 1-30. Purpose: Nationwide effort to raise awareness for Exchange Club Sponsored Child Abuse Prevention Effort. Sponsor: The Natl Exchange Club, 3050 Central Ave, Toledo, OH 43606.

FREEDOM SHRINE MONTH. Apr 1-30. Purpose: To bring America's heritage of freedom to public attention through presentations or rededications of Freedom Shrines by Exchange Clubs. Sponsor: The Natl Exchange Club, James A. Schnoering, Exec VP, 3050 Central Ave, Toledo, OH 43606.

GRAND STRAND FISHING RODEO. Apr 1-Oct 31. Myrtle Beach, SC. Awards for pier, surf, small boat, deep sea fish catches. Info from: Chamber of Commerce, Box 2115, Myrtle Beach, SC 29578.

GREAT SPRING HARDWARE SALE. Apr 1-30. Purpose: Industry-wide campaign of independent, locally owned retail hardware stores and home centers to concentrate on best seasonal values in name-brand merchandise. Sponsor: Natl Retail Hardware Assn, Neal Suppiger, Promotion Dir, 770 N High School Rd, Indianapolis, IN 46224.

HOME IMPROVEMENT TIME. Apr 1-Sept 30. Purpose: To explain the investment advantages of spending disposable income for home improvement to create family better living and improved community environment. (May is a promotion focal point.) Info from: Home Improvement Time, J.A. Stewart, Program Admn, Old Steubenville Pike, Oakdale, PA 15071.

INTERNATIONAL TWIT AWARD MONTH. Apr 1-30. Purpose: Any famous name (celebrity with the worst sense of humor) is eligible for most Tiresome Wit (TWIT) of 1986. Info from: Lone Star Publications of Humor, Box 29000, Suite #103, San Antonio, TX 78229.

MOON PHASE: LAST QUARTER. Apr 1. Moon enters Last Quarter phase at 2:30 p.m., E.S.T.

NATIONAL HOME IMPROVEMENT MONTH. Apr 1-30. Purpose: To increase the pleasures and comforts of domestic living through improvements to the American home. Sponsor: Natl Home Improvement League, Harry F. Klemfuss; Dir, 61 Cupsaw Lake, Ringwood, NJ 07456.

NATIONAL HUMOR MONTH. Apr 1-30. Purpose: To recognize and celebrate the importance of laughter and how it can improve our health and enrich our lives. Begins on April Fools Day with joke-telling contest at Arizona State University WHIM Humor Conference. Info from: Larry Wilde, Founder, Box 86, The Sea Ranch, CA 95497.

OCEANS MIAMI. Apr 1-30. Purpose: To celebrate the scientific, academic and entertainment facets of our ocean world. Films and exhibits. Info from: Oceans Miami, Internatl Oceanographic Foundation, 3979 Rickenbacker Causeway, Miami, FL 33149.

PARKINSON'S AWARENESS MONTH. Apr 1-30. Purpose: To raise public awareness of the problems faced by Parkinson patients and their families and the need for continued research. Sponsors: Parkinson's Disease Foundation and Parkinson's Educational Program/USA. Info from: Parkinson's Disease Foundation, 650 W 168th St, New York, NY 10032.

PETS ARE WONDERFUL MONTH. Apr 1-30. Purpose: PAW Month is a national salute to the joys and rewards of responsible pet ownership. Sponsor: Pets Are Wonderful Council, Jeanne Neylon, 500 N Michigan Ave, Chicago, IL 60611.

PHILATELIC SOCIETIES MONTH. Apr 1-30. Purpose: Recognition to efforts of stamp collecting societies for promotion of hobby for all ages—for recreation, education, therapy and financial advantage. Sponsor: Society of Philaticians, 154 Laguna Ct, St. Augustine Shores, FL 32086.

PUBLICITY STUNT WEEK. Apr 1-7. Purpose: To alert everyone to the value of publicity stunts in bringing worthy causes to the attention of the public and honor the famed stunt men behind them. Sponsor: Richard R. Falk Associates, 147 W 42nd St, New York, NY 10036.

ST. LASARUS' DAY. Apr 1. Bulgaria. Ancient Slav holiday of young girls, in honor of the goddess of spring and love.

VD AWARENESS MONTH. Apr 1-30. California. Purpose: To inform the public that VD is still with us and becoming a bigger problem each year because of public apathy. Info from: California Dept of Health Services, Attn: Charles J. Dobbins, Box 2230, Sacramento, CA 95810.

ZOO FLING '86. Apr 1-30. Purpose: A celebration of animals, April and the arts. Sponsor: North Carolina Zoological Park, Rt 4, Box 83, Asheboro, NC 27203.

APRIL 2 — WEDNESDAY
92nd Day — Remaining, 273

ANDERSEN, HANS CHRISTIAN: BIRTH ANNIVERSARY. Apr 2. Danish author chiefly remembered for his more than 150 fairy tales, many of which are regarded as classics of children's literature. Anderson was born at Odense, Denmark on Apr 2, 1805 and died at Copenhagen on Aug 4, 1875.

ARGENTINA: NATIONAL HOLIDAY. Apr 2. "Commemoration of the intent of recovery of the Malvinas Islands."

BERTHOLDI, FREDERIC AUGUSTE: BIRTHDAY. Apr 2. French sculptor who created "Liberty Enlightening the World" which stands in New York harbor. Also remembered for the "Lion of Belfort" in Belfort, France. Bertholdi was born at Colman, in Alsace, on Apr 2, 1834 and died at Paris on Oct 4, 1904.

COPYRIGHT © 1985 BY WILLIAM D. CHASE and HELEN M. CHASE

CASANOVA, GIACOMO GIROLAMO: BIRTHDAY. Apr 2. Celebrated Italian writer-librarian and, by his own account, philanderer, adventurer, rogue, seminarian, soldier and spy, born at Venice, Apr 2, 1725. As the Chevalier de Seingalt, he died at Dux, Bohemia, June 4, 1798, while serving as librarian and working on his lively and frank *History of My Life*, a brilliant picture of 18th century life.

INTERNATIONAL CHILDREN'S BOOK DAY. Apr 2. Info from: Internatl Children's Book Day, Leonhardsgraben 38a, CH-4051 Basle, Switzerland.

INTERNATIONAL CHILDREN'S BOOK DAY. Apr 2. Purpose: To commemorate the international aspects of children's literature and to observe Hans Christian Andersen's birthday. Sponsor: Internatl Board on Books for Young People, Alida Cutts, USBBY Secretariat, Internatl Reading Assn, Box 8139, Newark, DE 19714.

KANJORSKI, PAUL EDMUND: BIRTHDAY. Apr 2. U.S. Representative of Pennsylvania's 11th district, Democrat, of Nanticoke, PA, was born in Nanticoke on Apr 2, 1937.

TAMPA/ST PETERSBURG SPRING HOME SHOW. Apr 2-6. Florida State Fair Grounds. Info from: Perl Exposition Corp, 6915 Red Rd, Suite 228, Coral Gables, FL 33143.

UNITED STATES MINT: BIRTHDAY. Apr 2. The first U.S. Mint was established at Philadelphia as authorized by Act of Congress dated Apr 2, 1792.

YUMA COUNTY FAIR. Apr 2-6. Yuma County Fairgrounds. Info from: Chamber of Commerce, Box 230, Yuma, AZ 85364.

ZOLA, EMILE: BIRTHDAY. Apr 2. Prolific French novelist of the Naturalist School, remembered especially for his role in the Dreyfus case (resulting in retrial and vindication of Alfred Dreyfus). Emile Edouard Charles Antoine Zola was born at Paris, Apr 2, 1840. Defective venting of a stove flue in his bedroom (which some believed to be the work of political enemies) resulted in his death from carbon monoxide poisoning, at Paris, Sept 28, 1902.

APRIL 3 — THURSDAY
93rd Day — Remaining, 272

ARMENIAN APPRECIATION DAY. Apr 3. "Lighthearted research on the contribution of legendary Armenians such as Palboonian (Paul Bunyan) and Torontonian to American folklore, with special emphasis on studies of the relationship of the Smithsonian Institusian Collecsian to the history of Armenian-American folklore." Sponsor: Puns Corps, c/o Robert L. Birch, Box 2364, Falls Church, VA 22042.

ART EXPO NEW YORK. Apr 3-7. Jacob Javits Convention Ctr, New York, NY. Purpose: International fine art trade fair designed for entertainment of the public and art business professionals discovering new talents and new art opportunities. Sponsor: Internatl Art Expo, Inc, 509 Madison Ave, New York, NY 10022.

AUSTIN-TRAVIS COUNTY LIVESTOCK SHOW AND RODEO. Apr 3-13. Texas Expo and Heritage Ctr. Parade, quarter horse show, cutting horse competition, Country Western entertainers, cross-country horse race, barbecue, carnival, rodeos, and commercial and livestock exhibits. Info from: Austin-Travis Co Livestock Show, Box 15703, Austin, TX 78761.

BURROUGHS, JOHN: BIRTHDAY. Apr 3. American naturalist and author born at Roxbury, NY, Apr 3, 1837. "Time does not become sacred to us until we have lived it" he wrote in 1877. Died Mar 29, 1921.

April 1986	S	M	T	W	T	F	S
			1	2	3	4	5
	6	7	8	9	10	11	12
	13	14	15	16	17	18	19
	20	21	22	23	24	25	26
	27	28	29	30			

CHILES, LAWTON, JR: BIRTHDAY. Apr 3. U.S. Senator from Florida, Democrat, of Lakeland, FL, born there Apr 3, 1930.

DORNAN, ROBERT K: BIRTHDAY. Apr 3. U.S. Representative of California's 38th district, Republican, of Garden Grove, CA, born in New York City, Apr 3, 1933.

ENGLAND: HORSERACING: GRAND NATIONAL MEETING. Apr 3-5. Aintree Racecourse, Liverpool. "The Grand National is Britian's premier and most famous steeplechase run over four miles on this famous course."

HONG KONG: BIRTHDAY OF PAK TAI. Apr 3. Pak Tai Temple, Cheung Chau, Hong Kong. Info from: Cheung Chau Rural Comm, 2 Church Rd, Cheung Chau.

HOUSTON FESTIVAL. Apr 3-13. Houston, TX. Purpose: Musicians and artists from around the country join celebration of the arts and of Houston—in the parks and plazas, towers and tunnels, arenas and bayous of downtown Houston. Sponsor: Houston Festival Foundation, Inc, 1964 W Gray, Suite 227, Houston, TX 77019.

INTERNATIONAL FASHION AND BOUTIQUE TRADE SHOW. Apr 3-6. Convention Ctr, Miami Beach, FL. Trade Show for beauty manufacturers to meet buyers of their choice. Info from: Southline Promotions, Inc, Box 735, Rockville Centre, Long Island, NY 11571.

IRVING, WASHINGTON: BIRTHDAY. Apr 3. Birth anniversary of Washington Irving, American author, attorney and one-time U.S. minister to Spain, born at New York City, Apr 3, 1783. Creator of *Rip Van Winkle* and *The Legend of Sleepy Hollow*. Also author of many historical and biographical works, including *A History of the Life and Voyages of Christopher Columbus*, and the *Life of Washington*. Irving died at Tarrytown, NY, Nov 28, 1859.

NAFELS PILGRIMAGE. Apr 3. Switzerland (Canton Glarus). Commemoration of the Battle of Nafels, fought on Apr 9, 1388. Observed annually on first Thursday in Apr, with processions, prayers, sermon and a reading out of the names of those killed in the battle.

RAND, SALLY: BIRTHDAY. Apr 3. American actress, ecdysiast, and inventor of the fan dance (which gained fame in 1933 at the Chicago World's Fair), was born Helen Gould Beck, at Hickory County, MO, on Apr 3, 1904. She died at Glendora, CA, Aug 31, 1979.

SWIMMING: NATIONAL COLLEGIATE DIVISION I MEN'S CHAMPIONSHIP FINALS. Apr 3-5. Indianapolis, IN. Info from: NCAA, Box 1906, Mission, KS 66201.

TWEED DAY. Apr 3. Purpose: Day to consider the cost of political corruption. Birthday of William Marcy Tweed, New York City political boss, whose "Tweed Ring" is said to have stolen 30 to 200 million dollars from the city. Tweed was born at New York City, Apr 3, 1823, and died in his cell in New York's Ludlow Street Jail, Apr 12, 1878. Cartoonist Thomas Nast deserves much credit for Tweed's arrests and convictions.

WOMEN'S INTERNATIONAL BOWLING CONGRESS CHAMPIONSHIP TOURNAMENT. Apr 3-June 15. Orange County, CA. Purpose: To determine champions of Women's International Bowling Congress and provide competition on a national basis. Info from: WIBC, Mr. Augie Karcher, PR Mgr, 5301 S 76th St, Greendale, WI 53129.

APRIL 4 — FRIDAY
94th Day — Remaining, 271

AMERICAN HUMANIST ASSOCIATION NATIONAL CONFERENCE. Apr 4-6. Capital Plaza Holiday Inn, Sacramento, CA. Theme: "Humanism in a New Age." Info from: American Humanist Assn, 7 Harwood Dr, Box 146, Amherst, NY 14226.

ARBOR DAY (ARIZONA). Apr 4. In the counties of Apache, Navajo, Coconino, Mohave and Yavapai, the Friday following Apr 1, and in all other counties the Friday following Feb 1, in each year, shall be known as Arbor Day. See also entry for Feb 7.

COPYRIGHT © 1985 BY WILLIAM D. CHASE and HELEN M. CHASE

CLINGER, WILLIAM F JR: BIRTHDAY. Apr 4. U.S. Representative of Pennsylvania's 23rd district, Republican, of Warren, PA, born there on Apr 4, 1929.

DIX, DOROTHEA LYNDE; BIRTH ANNIVERSARY. Apr 4. American social reformer and author was born at Hampden, Maine, on Apr 4, 1802. She left home at ten, was teaching at 14, and founded a home for girls in Boston while still in her teens. In spite of frail health she was a vigorous crusader for humane conditions in insane asylums, jails and almshouses, and for the establishment of state supported institutions to serve those needs. She was named superintendent of women nurses during the Civil War. Dix died at Trenton, NJ on July 17, 1887.

HATE WEEK. Apr 4-10. Recognizes the day on which the fictional character Winston Smith started his secret diary, and wrote the words "DOWN WITH BIG BROTHER," Wednesday, Apr 4, 1984. From George Orwell's anti-Utopian novel, *Nineteen Eighty-Four,* portraying the end of human privacy and the destruction of the individual in a totalitarian state (first published in 1949). "Hates" varied from the daily two-minute concentrated hate to the grand culmination observed during Hate Week.

HUNGARY: NATIONAL HOLIDAY. Apr 4. Anniversary of the liberation of Hungary.

KING, MARTIN LUTHER, JR: ASSASSINATION ANNIVERSARY. Apr 4. The Rev. Martin Luther King, Jr, was shot at Memphis, TN, 1968. James Earl Ray serving 99-year sentence for the crime. See also entry for Jan 15.

LUGAR, RICHARD G: BIRTHDAY. Apr 4. U.S. Senator from Indiana, Republican, of Indianapolis, IN, born there on Apr 4, 1932.

LYNCHBURG, VIRGINIA: FESTIVAL OF THE ARTS. Apr 4-13. Purpose: A ten-day celebration of visual and performing arts with local and national artists to honor the city's bicentennial. Info from: Bicentennial Commission of Lynchburg, Box 1132, Lynchburg, VA 24505.

MULE DAY. Apr 4-6. Purpose: To look at our heritage and the history of this area when the mule made Columbia famous as the "Mule Capital of the World". Info from: Mule Day, Box 66, Columbia, TN 38402.

NATO ANNIVERSARY. Apr 4. Delegates from twelve nations met in Washington, DC, to sign the North Atlantic Treaty, Apr 4, 1949.

SENEGAL: NATIONAL HOLIDAY. Apr 4. Independence Day.

SOUTHWEST KANSAS SQUARE DANCE FESTIVAL. Apr 4-5. Civic Ctr, Dodge City, KS. Square and round dancing, workshops and special entertainment. Sponsor: Square and Round Dance Clubs, Dodge City Recreation Committee and SW Kansas Square Dance Callers Assn. Info from: Les Houser, 2211 3rd Ave, Dodge City, KS 67801.

SPACE MILESTONE: STS-6 (US). Apr 4. Shuttle Challenger launched from Kennedy Space Center, FL Apr 4, 1983, with four astronauts (Paul Weitz, Karol Bobko, Story Musgrave and Donald Peterson). Four-hour spacewalk by Musgrave and Peterson. Landed Edwards Air Force Base, CA, Apr 9.

STUDENT GOVERNMENT DAY. Apr 4. Massachusetts. (First Friday of April.)

STUMP, BOB: BIRTHDAY. Apr 4. U.S. Representative of Arizona's 3rd district, Republican, of Tolleson, AZ, born in Phoenix, AZ, Apr 4, 1927.

VOLKMER, HAROLD LEE: BIRTHDAY. Apr 4. U.S. Representative of Missouri's 9th district, Democrat, of Hannibal, MO, born in Jefferson City, MO, Apr 4, 1931.

YALE, LINUS: BIRTHDAY. Apr 4. American portrait painter and inventor of the lock which is named for him, was born at Salisbury, NY, Apr 4, 1821. He was creator of the "Yale Infallible Bank Lock," and developer of the cylinder lock. Yale died at New York City, Dec 25, 1868.

APRIL 5 — SATURDAY
95th Day — Remaining, 270

ANN ARBOR SPRING ART FAIR. Apr 5-6. Ann Arbor, MI. Over 250 artists and craftsmen, who have achieved national reputations, will display and sell their work. Info from: Audree Levy, 10629 Park Preston, Dallas, TX 75230.

DAYTONA SKYFEST '86. Apr 5-6. Daytona Beach Airport, Daytona, FL. A festival in the sky, with major military jet teams. (First weekend in April.) Info from: Chamber of Commerce, Box 2775, Daytona Beach, FL 32015.

DOGWOOD FESTIVAL. Apr 5-13. Atlanta, GA. Info from: Atlanta Dogwood Festival, 1776 Peachtree St, NW, 634 South Tower, Atlanta, GA 30309.

HIGHLAND LAKES BLUEBONNET TRAIL. Apr 5-6. (Also Apr 12-13.) Texas Hill Country communities of Buchanan Dam, Burnet, Kingsland, Llano, Marble Falls, Austin, Lampasas and Lago Vista each sponsor an arts and crafts fair while the bluebonnets are in full bloom. Info from: Highland Lakes Tourist Assn, Carol Stuewe, Dir, Box 1967, Austin, TX 78767.

INDIAN DANCE FESTIVAL AND PIONEER FAIR. Apr 5-6. DeSoto Caverns, Childersburg, AL. Purpose: To show America's Indian heritage and expert craftsmanship of regional artists and craftspeople. Indian games and dancing. Country and bluegrass music. Info from: Caryl Lynn Mathis, 93 Ivy Trail NE, Atlanta, GA 30342.

LISTER, JOSEPH: BIRTHDAY. Apr 5. English physician who was the founder of asceptic surgery, was born Apr 5, 1827 at Upton, Essex. Lister died at Walmer, England, on Feb 10, 1912.

PENNSYLVANIA MAPLE FESTIVAL. Apr 5-6. (Also Apr 9-12) Purpose: To celebrate the miracle of the maple. Sponsor: Pennsylvania Maple Festival, Box 222, Meyersdale, PA 15552.

PRAIRIE DOG CHILI COOK-OFF AND WORLD CHAMPIONSHIP OF PICKLED QUAIL-EGG EATING. Apr 5-6. Traders Village, Grand Prairie, TX. Tongue-in-cheek salute to the official state dish of Texas, chili con carne, or "Texas Red." World championship of pickled quail-egg eating featuring contestants devouring as many of these gourmet delights as possible in the 30-second time limit. Info from: Traders Village, Doug Beich, 2602 Mayfield Rd, Grand Prairie, TX 75051.

ST. JOHN'S RIVER CATFISH FESTIVAL. Apr 5. Purpose: To promote fisheries products of St. John's River. Catfish, alligator, blue crabs, catfish chowder and smoked mullet. Annually, the first Saturday in April. Sponsor: Crescent City Rotary Club, Ronnie Hughes, 330 N Summit, Crescent City, FL 32012.

SATURDAY MARKET. Apr 5-Dec 20. Downtown, Eugene, OR. A gathering place for artisans, performers, crafts people, chefs and farmers to show and sell work uniquely their own. (First Saturday in April through last Saturday before Christmas each year.) Info from: Saturday Market, Box 427, Eugene, OR 97440.

SPRING ARTS FESTIVAL. Apr 5-6. Northeast First Street, Gainesville, FL. Artists and craftsmen from all areas of the United States. Sponsor: Spring Arts Festival, Box 1530, Gainesville, FL 32602.

COPYRIGHT © 1985 BY WILLIAM D. CHASE and HELEN M. CHASE

SPRING "LIVING HISTORY" WEEK. Apr 5-11. Purpose: To acquaint visitors with planting time on a mid-nineteenth century farm. Info from: Duke Homestead State Historic Site, 2828 Duke Homestead Rd, Durham, NC 27705.

TAIWAN: NATIONAL TOMB-SWEEPING DAY. Apr 5. National holiday since 1972. According to Chinese custom, the tombs of ancestors are swept "clear and bright" on this day and rites honoring ancestors are held. Tomb-Sweeping Day is observed on Apr 5, except in Leap Years, when it falls on Apr 4.

TEXAS TREK. Apr 5-6. Anderson, Grimes County, TX. Celebration, historic home tour and special events with proceeds for restoration and preservation. Sponsor: Historic Anderson, Inc, Trevia W. Beverly, Publicity Chrmn, Box 268, Anderson, TX 77830.

WASHINGTON, BOOKER TALIAFERRO: BIRTHDAY. Apr 5. Black educator and leader born, Franklin County, VA, Apr 5, 1856. "No race can prosper," he wrote in *Up from Slavery*, "till it learns that there is as much dignity in tilling a field as in writing a poem." Died Nov 14, 1915.

WORLD CATFISH FESTIVAL. Apr 5. Belzoni, Mississippi. Catfish eating, fiddling contest and canoe race. Tours of fish ponds. Info from: Chamber of Commerce, Box 268, Belzoni, MS 39038.

APRIL 6 — SUNDAY
96th Day — Remaining, 269

BRIGHAM YOUNG'S LAST MARRIAGE: ANNIVERSARY. Apr 6. Brigham Young, Mormon Church leader, married his 27th, and last, wife on Apr 6, 1868. Observed in Utah.

CHAKRI DAY. Apr 6. Thailand. Commemorates foundation of present dynasty by King Rama I (1782-1809) who also established Bangkok as capital of Thailand.

CHING MING FESTIVAL. Apr 6. Widely observed Chinese festival (literally: "Pure and Bright"), Ching Ming is now regarded as an All Souls' Day. Families gather at graves of ancestors, leaving flowers and food after tidying the graves. A picnic spirit prevails, rather than solemnity. Set for the 106th day after the winter solstice, the Gregorian calendar date may vary slightly.

ECKART, DENNIS EDWARD: BIRTHDAY. Apr 6. U.S. Representative of Ohio's 11th district, Democrat, of Concord Township, OH, born in Cleveland, OH, on Apr 6, 1950.

FOUNDING OF THE MORMON CHURCH. Apr 6. On this day in 1830 Joseph C. Smith and Oliver Cowdery organized the Church of Jesus Christ of Latter Day Saints.

HARMONY WEEK. Apr 6-12. Purpose: To celebrate the founding of the Society for the Preservation and Encouragement of Barber Shop Quartet Singing in America. Sponsor: SPEBSQSA Internatl Office, Robb Ollett, Communications Dir, 6315 3rd Ave, Kenosha, WI 53140.

HAWAII: BUDDHA DAY. Apr 6. Flower festival pageant at island temples to celebrate the birth of Buddha. Info from: Hawaii Visitors Bureau, Honolulu, HI 96815.

NATIONAL BIRTHPARENTS WEEK. Apr 6-12. Purpose: A time to recognize and honor the five million mothers and fathers who, at great personal sacrifice, have been separated from their children by adoption and to focus attention on the rights of all family members to know each other. Sponsor: Concerned United Birthparents, Inc (CUB), 595 Central Ave, Dover, NH 03820.

NATIONAL CHERRY BLOSSOM FESTIVAL. Apr. 6-13. Washington, DC. Purpose: To recognize springtime in the nation's capital and the blossoming of famous cherry trees. Sponsor: National Conference of State Societies. Info from: Washington Convention & Visitors Assn, 1575 Eye St NW, Washington, DC 20005.

NATIONAL LIBRARY WEEK. Apr. 6-12. Purpose: To promote use and support of all types of libraries: public, school, academic and special, and to make the public aware of the many services available at their local library. Sponsor: American Library Assn, Linda Wallace, Dir, Public Info Office, 50 E Huron St, Chicago IL 60611.

PASSAGE OF FIRST U.S. CREDIT UNION LAW. Apr. 6. Purpose: To charter the Ste. Marie credit union of Manchester, NH, with the help of Alphonse Desjardins, Canadian credit union pioneer on Apr 6, 1909. Info from: Credit Union Natl Assn, Lucy Harr Schultz, VP, PR, Box 431, Madison, WI 53701.

RAPHAEL: BIRTHDAY. Apr. 6. Raffaello Santi (Sanzio), Italian painter and architect was born, probably on Apr. 6, 1483, at Urbino. Raphael died on his 37th birthday, at Rome, Apr. 6, 1520.

SACRED HARP CONVENTION. Apr. 6. Traditional choral music sung by reading shape notes. Info from: Westville, Box 1850, Lumpkin, GA 31815.

SPACE MILESTONE: STS-11 (US). Apr. 6. Shuttle Challenger launched Apr 6, 1984, with five astronauts (Robert Crippen, Francis Scobee, George Nelson, Terry Hart and James Van Hoften) had mission requiring recovery and repair of damaged satellite. Landed at Edwards Air Force Base, CA, Apr.13.

THOMAS, LOWELL: BIRTHDAY. Apr. 6. World-traveller, reporter, editor and radio newscaster, whose broadcasts spanned more than half a century, 1925-1976, was born at Woodington, OH, on Apr. 6, 1892 and died at Pawling, NY, on Aug. 29, 1981. His radio sign-off, "So long until tomorrow," was known to millions of listeners, and he is said to have been the first to broadcast from a ship, airplane, submarine and from a coal mine.

VAN RIEBEECK DAY. Apr. 6. Republic of South Africa. Jan van Riebeeck was the first commander of the Dutch East India Co that established a halfway station at the Cape of Good Hope. This day is regarded in South Africa as the day on which Western civilization was established on the southern tip of the continent.

WEEK OF THE YOUNG CHILD. Apr. 6-12. Purpose: To bring to the attention of the nation the needs of all young children, and to inform the public of the services available for children. Sponsor: Natl Assn for the Education of Young Children, Dr. Marilyn M. Smith, Exec Dir, 1834 Connecticut Ave, NW, Washington, DC 20009.

APRIL 7 — MONDAY
97th Day — Remaining, 268

AMERICAN INSTITUTE FOR DESIGN AND DRAFTING: CONVENTION. Apr 7-10. Diplomat Hotel, Hollywood, Fl. Info from: AIDD, Phil Nowers, Conv Mgr, 966 Hungerford Dr, Suite 10-B, Rockville, MD 20850.

FAIRCHILD, DAVID GRANDISON: BIRTHDAY. Apr 7. American botanist, government official and explorer, born at E Lansing, MI, Apr 7, 1869. Noted for scientific studies on importation of tropical plant species such as avocados and mangoes. Died at Miami, FL, Aug 6, 1954.

INTERNATIONAL GROSS DAY. Apr 7. Purpose: To restore dignity to people with the surname of Gross. "Ongoing event, every year." Sponsor: Terry Gross, Box 2720, Casper, WY 82602.

KING, WILLIAM RUFUS DeVANE: BIRTHDAY. Apr 7. Thirteenth Vice President of the U.S., died on the 46th day after taking the oath of office, of tuberculosis, at Cahawba, AL, on Apr 18, 1853. The oath of office had been administered to

	S	M	T	W	T	F	S
April			1	2	3	4	5
1986	6	7	8	9	10	11	12
	13	14	15	16	17	18	19
	20	21	22	23	24	25	26
	27	28	29	30			

COPYRIGHT © 1985 BY WILLIAM D. CHASE and HELEN M. CHASE

King at Havana, Cuba, as authorized by a special act of Congress (the only presidential or vice presidential oath to be administered outside the U.S.). Born in Sampson County, NC on Apr 7, 1786, King was the only vice president of the U.S. who had served in both the House of Representatives and the Senate. Never married, King's term of office as vice president was Mar 4-Apr 18, 1853.

MUSLIM FESTIVAL; LAILAT al MIRAJ. Apr 7. Commemorates ascent of the Prophet Muhammed into Heaven. Muslim calendar date: Rajab 27, 1406. Date of observance on Gregorian calendar may vary by one day.

NATIONAL DESIGN/DRAFTING WEEK. Apr 7-12. Purpose: To bring focal attention to the services provided by those in the profession of design and drafting. Sponsor: American Institute for Design and Drafting, 966 Hungerford Dr, Suite 10B, Rockville, MD 20850.

TATER DAY. Apr 7. Salute to the tasty sweet potato. Parade, arts and crafts, mule-pulling contest and carnival. Info from: Marshall County Chamber of Commerce, Route 7, Benton, KY 42025.

WORDSWORTH, WILLIAM: BIRTHDAY. Apr 7. English lake poet and philosopher born on this day, 1770. "Poetry," he said, "is the spontaneous overflow of powerful feelings: it takes its origin from emotion recollected in tranquility." Wordsworth died Apr 23, 1850.

WORLD HEALTH DAY. Apr 7. Commemorates establishment on Apr 7, 1948 of World Health Organization. A special observance of the United Nations. Info from: UN Dept of Public Information. United Nations, NY 10017.

APRIL 8 — TUESDAY
98th Day — Remaining, 267

BUSTAMANTE, ALBERT GARZA: BIRTHDAY. Apr 8. U.S. Representative of Texas' 23rd district, Democrat, of San Antonio, TX, born in Asherton, TX, Apr 8, 1935.

DELAY, THOMAS D: BIRTHDAY. Apr 8. U.S. Representative of Texas' 22nd district, Republican, of Sugar Land, TX, born in Laredo, TX, on Apr 8, 1947.

ECLIPSE: PARTIAL ECLIPSE OF THE SUN. Apr 8-9. Not visible in North America. Visible: part of Indonesia, Australia, New Guinea, S. of New Zealand, part of Antarctica. Begins at 11:09 p.m. E.S.T. on Apr 8 and ends at 3:31 a.m., E.S.T. on Apr 9.

FISCUS, KATHY: DEATH ANNIVERSARY. Apr 8. Three-year-old Kathy Fiscus of San Marino, CA, fell while playing into an abandoned well pipe 14 inches wide and 120 feet deep. Rescue workers toiled ceaselessly for two days while thousands watched and while national attention was focussed on the tragedy. Her body was recovered Apr 10, 1949. An alarmed nation suddenly became attentive to other abandoned wells and similar hazards and "Kathy Fiscus laws" were enacted in a number of places requiring new safety measures to prevent recurrence of such a tragic accident.

FLOWER FESTIVAL (HANA MATSURI). Apr 8. Japan. Commemorates Buddha's birthday. Ceremonies in all temples.

FORD, ELIZABETH (BETTY) BLOOMER WARREN: BIRTHDAY. Apr 8. Wife of Gerald Rudolph Ford, 38th President of the U.S., born at Chicago, IL, Apr 8, 1918.

MORRIS, LEWIS: BIRTHDAY. Apr 8. Signer of the Declaration of Independence, born, Westchester County, NY, Apr 8, 1726. Died Jan 22, 1798.

SPRING SENIOR AMERICAN SPECIAL. Apr 8-10. Petit Jean State Park, Morrilton, AR. Celebration of the coming of spring. Fellowship, learning and entertainment. Sponsor: Petit Jean State Park, Jennifer Danley, Rt 3 Box 340, Morrilton, AR 72110.

WILLIAMS, WILLIAM: BIRTHDAY. Apr 8. Signer of the Declaration of Independence, born, Lebanon, CT, Apr 8, 1731. Died there Aug 2, 1811.

APRIL 9 — WEDNESDAY
99th Day — Remaining, 266

CIVIL WAR ENDING: ANNIVERSARY. Apr 9. At 1:30 p.m., on Sunday, Apr 9, 1865, General Robert E. Lee, commander of the Army of Northern Virginia, surrendered to General Ulysses S. Grant, commander-in-chief of the Union Army, ending four years of civil war. Meeting took place in the house of Wilmer McLean at the village of Appomattox Court House, Virginia. Confederate soldiers were permitted to keep their horses and go free to their homes, while Confederate officers were allowed to retain their swords and side arms as well. Death toll during Civil War is estimated at more than 500,000 men.

ENGLAND: LONDON BOOK FAIR. Apr 9-11. Barbican Centre, London. "The only British book/publishing trade fair." Info from: London Book Fair, 16 Pembridge Rd, London W11 3HL, England.

Geoffrey Chaucer

FIELDS, W.C.: BIRTHDAY. Apr 9. Claude William Dukenfield (W.C. Fields), stage and motion picture actor and expert juggler, born at Philadelphia, PA, Apr 9, 1879. He died on Christmas morning, Dec 25, 1946, at Pasadena, CA. He wrote his own epitaph: "On the whole, I'd rather be in Philadelphia."

GRIFTON SHAD FESTIVAL. Apr 9-13. Purpose: To provide family-oriented fun for all ages. Sponsor: Grifton Shad Festival, Inc., Mrs Ruthanne Rhem, Box 928, Grifton, NC 28530.

JENKINS'S EAR DAY. Apr 9. Anniversary of the day in 1731 when English master mariner Robert Jenkins lost an ear (for which a war was named). Spanish guardacosta boarded and plundered the British ship *Rebecca* off Jamaica on Apr 9, 1731, and, among other outrages, cut off Jenkins's ear. Little notice was taken until seven years later when Jenkins exhibited the detached ear and described the atrocity to a committee of the House of Commons. In consequence, Britain declared war on Spain in Oct 1739, a war which lasted until 1743 and which is still known as the "War of Jenkins's Ear." Nothing else is known of Robert Jenkins.

MARIAN ANDERSON EASTER CONCERT ANNIVERSARY. Apr 9. On Easter Sunday, Apr 9, 1939, Black American contralto Marian Anderson sang in open air concert from the steps of the Lincoln Memorial in Washington, DC, to an audience of 75,000, after having been denied use of the Daughters of the American Revolution (DAR) Constitution Hall. The event became an American anti-discrimination cause celebre and led Eleanor Roosevelt, wife of the U.S. president, to resign from the DAR.

MARTYRS' DAY. Apr 9. Tunisia.

MOON PHASE: NEW MOON. Apr 9. Moon enters New Moon phase at 1:08 a.m., E.S.T.

MUYBRIDGE, EADWEARD: BIRTHDAY. Apr 9. English photographer famed for his photographic studies of animals in motion, born Edward James Muggeridge, at Kingston-on-Thames, England, Apr 9, 1830. Died there May 8, 1904.

COPYRIGHT © 1985 BY WILLIAM D. CHASE and HELEN M. CHASE

PHILIPPINES: BATAAN DAY. Apr 9. National observance. To commemorate the "fall" of Bataan in 1942. The infamous "Death March" is re-enacted at the Mt Samat Shrine, the Dambana ng Kagitingan.

SPACE MILESTONE: SOYUZ 35 (USSR). Apr 9. Two cosmonauts (Valery Ryumin and Leonid Popov) launched Apr 9, 1980 from Baikonur space center in Kazakhstan. Docked at Salyut 6 on Apr 10. Ryumin and Popov returned to Earth Oct 11, 1980, after setting a new space endurance record of 185 days.

SPENCE, FLOYD DAVIDSON: BIRTHDAY. Apr 9. U.S. Representative of South Carolina's 2nd district, Republican, of Lexington, SC, born in Columbia, SC, Apr 9, 1928.

TAKING CHARGE, TAKING CARE. Apr 9-12. Purpose: To offer vital ideas and information for sharpening professional skills and increasing knowledge in the field of aging. Sponsor: The Natl Council on the Aging, Inc, Ruth Crary Blank, Dir, 600 Maryland Ave, SW, W Wing 100, Washington, DC 20024.

UNIVERSITY HOSPITAL ANTIQUES SHOW. Apr 9-13. 103rd Engineers Armory, Philadelphia, PA. Museum-quality antiques, symposiums, appraisals and guided tours by Philadelphia Museum of Art. Sponsor: University Hospital, 34th and Spruce Sts, Philadelphia, PA 19104.

WINSTON CHURCHILL DAY. Apr 9. Anniversary of enactment of legislation in 1963, which made the late British statesman an honorary citizen of the U.S.

APRIL 10 — THURSDAY
100th Day — Remaining, 265

BULGARELLI SPRING OR REAL SPRING IN THE GREAT NORTHEAST. Apr 10. (5:03 p.m. E.S.T.) Purpose: To recognize that authentic spring weather often does not exist in the Northeast until three weeks after calendar spring. Sponsor: George Bulgarelli, Meteorologist, Berkshire Eagle, Pittsfield, MA 01201. Info from: Bob Cudmore, Talk Show Host, WGY, Box 1410, Schenectady, NY 12301.

COMMODORE PERRY DAY. Apr 10. Matthew Calbraith Perry, Commodore in the U.S. Navy, negotiator of first treaty between U.S. and Japan (Mar 31, 1854), born Apr 10, 1794. Died Mar 4, 1858.

GROTIUS, HUGO: BIRTHDAY. Apr 10. Anniversary of the birth of Hugo Grotius, the Dutch Theologian, attorney, scholar and statesman whose beliefs profoundly influenced American thinking, especially with regard to the conscience of humanity. Born at Delft, Apr 10, 1583, Grotius was long an exile from his own country. He died at Rostock, Germany, Aug 28, 1645.

HAYWOOD MALL ARTS AND CRAFTS SHOW. Apr 10-13. Greenville, SC. Info from: Carole Sirmans, 400 Browns Crossing Rd, NW, Milledgeville, GA 31061.

PERKINS, FRANCES: BIRTHDAY. Apr 10. First woman member of a U.S. presidential cabinet, Frances Perkins was born at Boston, MA, Apr 10, 1880. She was appointed Secretary of Labor by President Franklin D. Roosevelt in 1933, a post in which she served until 1945. She was married, in 1915, to Paul Caldwell Wilson, but used her maiden name in public life. She died at New York City, May 14, 1965.

PULITZER, JOSEPH: BIRTHDAY. Apr 10. American journalist, founder of the Pulitzer Prizes, born at Budapest, Hungary, on Apr 10, 1847. Died at Charleston, SC, Oct 29, 1911. Pulitzer Prizes awarded annually since 1917. Info from: Pulitzer Prize Board, 702 Journalism, Columbia University, New York, NY 10027.

	S	M	T	W	T	F	S
April			1	2	3	4	5
1986	6	7	8	9	10	11	12
	13	14	15	16	17	18	19
	20	21	22	23	24	25	26
	27	28	29	30			

SALVATION ARMY FOUNDER'S DAY. Apr 10. On this day in 1829 William Booth, founder of the Salvation Army, was born in Nottingham, England.

SPRING SOUTHERN FURNITURE MARKET. Apr 10-18. Wholesale furniture tradeshow. Sponsor: Furniture Factories' Marketing Assn of the South, Box 5687, High Point, NC 27262.

TAMPA/ST. PETERSBURG SPRING HOME SHOW. Apr 10-13. Florida State Fairgrounds, Tampa, FL. Info from: Perl Exposition Corp, 6915 Red Road, Suite 228, Coral Gables, FL 33143.

WOODWARD, ROBERT BURNS: BIRTHDAY. Apr 10. Nobel Prize (1965) winning Harvard University science professor whose special field of study was molecular structure of complex organic compounds, was called "one of the most outstanding scientific minds of the century." Born at Boston, MA, Apr 10, 1917. Died July 8, 1979.

APRIL 11— FRIDAY
101st Day — Remaining, 264

BARBERSHOP QUARTET DAY. Apr 11. Commemorates the gathering of some 26 persons in Tulsa, OK, on Apr 11, 1938, and the founding there of the Society for the Preservation and Encouragement of Barber Shop Quartet Singing in America.

CIVIL RIGHTS ACT OF 1968: ANNIVERSARY. Apr 11. On Apr 11, 1968, exactly one week after the assassination of Martin Luther King, Jr, the Civil Rights Act of 1968 (protecting civil rights workers, expanding the rights of Native Americans, and providing anti-discrimination measures in housing) was signed into law by Pres Lyndon B. Johnson, who said: " . . . the proudest moments of my presidency have been times such as this when I have signed into law the promises of a century."

COUGHLIN, LAWRENCE: BIRTHDAY. Apr 11. U.S. Representative of Pennsylvania's 13th district, Republican, of Villanova, PA, was born in Wilkes-Barre, PA, on Apr 11, 1929.

EVERETT, EDWARD: BIRTHDAY. Apr 11. American statesman and orator, born at Dorcester, MA, on Apr 11, 1794. It was Edward Everett who delivered the main address at the dedication of Gettysburg National Cemetery, Nov 19, 1863. President Abraham Lincoln also spoke at the dedication and his brief speech (less than two minutes), has been called one of the most eloquent in the English language. Once a candidate for vice president of the U.S. (1860), Everett died at Boston, MA on Jan 15, 1865.

FORT PULASKI: ANNIVERSARY. Apr 11. Fort Pulaski National Monument, Tybee Island, GA. Commemorates the siege and reduction of the fort in 1862. On that date, the age of masonry fortification ended and the era of rifled artillery began, with the surrender of the Confederate garrison after a thirty-hour siege.

FRENCH QUARTER FESTIVAL. Apr 11-13. New Orleans, LA. Theme: "The French Quarter is for Everyone." Hours of free musical entertainment, contests and the "World's Largest Jazz Brunch." Info from: French Quarter Festival, John Frazier, Box 53362, New Orleans, LA 70153.

HALLEY'S COMET CLOSEST TO EARTH. Apr 11. On Apr 11, 1986, Halley's Comet will reach a point nearest Earth, about 39,060,000 miles. The predicted most favorable period for observing Halley's Comet with naked eye is Mar 2-Apr 21, with best view Mar 21-Apr 20. The next apparition is expected to be about mid-year, 2062.

HEFNER, W.G. (BILL): BIRTHDAY. Apr 11. U.S. Representative of North Carolina's 8th district, Democrat, of Concord, NC, was born in Elora, TN, on Apr 11, 1930.

HOLIDAY IN DIXIE. Apr 11-20. A spring festival with parades, Cajun festival, arts, crafts, regattas and sporting events. Info from: Holiday In Dixie, Judy O. Williams, Exec Dir, 800 American Tower, Shreveport, LA 71101.

COPYRIGHT © 1985 BY WILLIAM D. CHASE and HELEN M. CHASE

HUGHES, CHARLES EVANS: BIRTHDAY. Apr 11. Eleventh Chief Justice of U.S. Supreme Court, born at Glens Falls, NY, Apr 11, 1862, Died at Osterville, MA, Aug 27, 1948.

INTERNATIONAL RESISTANCE MOVEMENT DAY. Apr 11. Czechoslovakia. Anniversary of the liberation of Buchenwald.

NORTH CAROLINA WILD FOODS WEEKEND. Apr 11-13. Purpose: Learn to collect and prepare foods found in the spring. Enjoy fellowship and wild feast. Info from: Ken Perkins, Box 396, Elon College, NC 27244.

RETAIL BAKERS OF AMERICA SUPERMARKET BAKERY CONFERENCE. Apr 11-12. Hyatt Regency Hotel, Milwaukee, WI. Info from: RBA, Richard C. Gohla, Exec VP, Presidential Bldg, Suite 250, 6525 Belcrest Rd, Hyattsville, MD 20782.

SPACE MILESTONE: APOLLO 13 (US). Apr 11. Astronauts Lovell, Haise and Swigert endangered when oxygen tank ruptured. Planned moon landing cancelled. Details of accident made public and world shared concern for crew who splashed down successfully in Pacific Apr 17. Launched Apr 11, 1970.

UGANDA: LIBERATION DAY. Apr 11. Republic of Uganda celebrates anniversary of "overthrow of Idi Amin's dictatorship," on Apr 11, 1979.

WHITE WATER WEEKEND. Apr 11-13. Cumberland Falls State Resort Park, Corbin, KY. A White Water Rafting Trip on the Cumberland River. Info from: Kentucky Dept of Parks, Capital Plaza Tower, Frankfort, KY 40601.

APRIL 12 — SATURDAY
102nd Day — Remaining, 263

ANNIVERSARY OF THE BIG WIND. Apr 12. Mount Washington, NH. The highest velocity natural wind ever recorded occurred on the morning of Apr 12, 1934, at the Mount Washington, NH Observatory. Three weather observers, Wendell Stephenson, Alexander McKenzie and Salvatore Pagliuca observed and recorded the phenomenon in which gusts reached 231 miles per hour—"the strongest natural wind ever recorded on the earth's surface." The 50th anniversary was observed at the site in 1984, with the three original observers participating in the ceremony.

BILLINGS, JOHN SHAW: BIRTHDAY. Apr 12. American librarian and army physician born Apr 12, 1838. Died Mar 11, 1913.

EARL, ANTHONY S: BIRTHDAY. Apr 12. Anthony S. Earl, Governor of Wisconsin, Democrat, was born at Lansing, MI, on Apr 12, 1936.

HALIFAX INDEPENDENCE DAY. Apr 12. North Carolina. Anniversary of the Resolution adopted by the Provincial Congress of North Carolina at Halifax, April 12, 1776, authorizing the delegates from North Carolina to the Continental Congress to vote for a Declaration of Independence.

HEALTH FAIR OF THE MIDLANDS. Apr 12-20. Purpose: To provide health screenings and education to persons 18 years of age and older so that they can better understand how lifestyle choices affect health. Sponsor: Health Fair of the Midlands, 3838 Dewey Ave, Omaha, NE 68105.

JOHN WILKES BOOTH ESCAPE ROUTE TOUR. Apr 12-Sept 13. Clinton, MD. Purpose: A 12 hour bus tour over the route used by Lincoln's assassin. Sponsor: Surratt House & Tavern, Box 427, Clinton, MD 20735.

LONDON BRIDGE REGATTA. Apr 12-13. Sponsor: Chamber of Commerce, 65 N Lake Havasu Ave, Suite 2-B, Lake Havasu City, AZ 86403.

MAN IN SPACE ANNIVERSARY. Apr 12. Yuri Gagarin became the first man in space on Apr 12, 1961, when he made a 108-minute voyage, orbiting Earth in a 10,395 lb vehicle, *Vostok I*, launched by the U.S.S.R.

RETAIL BAKERS OF AMERICA CONVENTION-EXHIBITION. Apr 12-15. Hyatt Regency Hotel, Milwaukee, WI. Info from: RBA, Richard C. Gohla, Exec VP, Presidential Bldg, Suite 250, 6525 Belcrest Rd, Hyattsville, MD 20782.

SALK VACCINE: ANNIVERSARY. Apr 12. Anniverary of announcement in 1955 that the Salk Vaccine (developed by American physician, Dr. Jonas E. Salk) was declared "safe, potent and effective. Incidence of the dreaded Infantile Paralysis or Poliomyelitis almost miraculously declined following introduction of preventive vaccines.

SOUTH MOUNTAIN VILLAGE FAIR. Apr 12. South Mountain Activity Complex. Phoenix, AZ. Festivities include games, foot races, hikes and horseback riding. Displays center around outdoor recreation and awareness. Info from: City of Phoenix, Parks, Recreation & Library Dept, 125 E Washington, Phoenix, AZ 85004.

SPACE MILESTONE: *DISCOVERY* (US). Apr 12. On its 16th mission (from Kennedy Space Center, FL) *Discovery* carried a U.S. Senator (Jake Garn) as a member of its crew of seven. Apr 12, 1985.

SPACE MILESTONE: STS 1 (US). Apr 12. First flight Apr 12, 1981, of Shuttle Columbia. Two astronauts (John Young and Robert Crippen), first manned U.S. space mission since Apollo-Soyuz in July 1976, spent 54 hours in space (36 orbits of Earth) before gliding to landing at Edwards Air Force Base, CA, Apr 14.

SPACE MILESTONE: VOSTOK 1 (USSR). Apr 12. First man in space, Yuri Gagarin orbited Earth in 10,417 pound vehicle (108-minute voyage). Launched April 12, 1961.

WILD TURKEY DAYS AND TRI STATE TURKEY CALLING CONTEST. Apr 12-13. Purpose: To show areawide appreciation for restoration of wild turkey in North Missouri. Sponsor: El Kadir Shrine Club, Everett Farr, 1709 E McPherson, Kirksville, MO 63501.

APRIL 13 — SUNDAY
103rd Day — Remaining, 262

AUSTIN, TEXAS: TRADITIONAL MUSICAL FESTIVAL. Apr. 13. Pioneer Farm, Austin, TX. Festival features Central Texas musicians. Gospel, country, conjunto and czech polka music. Info from: City of Austin, Sesquicentennial Commission, 610 E Eleventh St, Austin, TX 78701.

JEFFERSON, THOMAS: BIRTHDAY. Apr 13. Presidential ☆ Proclamation 2276, of Mar 21, 1938, "covers all succeeding years." (Pub. Res. No 60 of Aug 16, 1937.)

JEFFERSON, THOMAS: BIRTHDAY. Apr 13. Third President of the U.S. (Mar 4, 1801 - Mar 3, 1809), was born at Albermarle County, VA, Apr 13, 1743. Jefferson, who died at Charlottesville, VA on July 4, 1826, wrote his own epitaph: "Here was buried Thomas Jefferson, author of the Declaration of American Independence, of the statute of Virginia for religious freedom, and father of the University of Virginia."

MUSIC-VIDEO WEEK. Apr 13-19. Purpose: To honor achievements of artists in the music-video profession for contributions to the music, video, broadcasting and entertainment industries. Info from: C. B. Hart, NPAR, Box 1606, Beltsville, MD 20705.

NATIONAL BUILDING SAFETY WEEK. Apr 13-19. Purpose: To make all Americans aware of the important health and life safety services available to them from their state and local

COPYRIGHT © 1985 BY WILLIAM D. CHASE and HELEN M. CHASE

professional building departments. Sponsor: Natl Conference of States on Building Codes and Standards, Inc and Council of American Building Officials. Info from: Marla Bethel, NCSBCS, 481 Carlisle Dr, Herndon, VA 22070.

PAN AMERICAN WEEK. Apr 13-19. Presidential Proclamation. ☆ "Always issued for the week including Apr 14, except in 1965, from 1946 thru 1948, 1955 thru 1977, and 1979."

SINGAPORE: SONGKRAN FESTIVAL. Apr 13-15. Public holiday. Thai water festival. To welcome the new year the image of Buddha is bathed with holy or fragrant water, and lustral water is sprinkled on celebrants. Joyous event, especially observed at Thai Buddhist temples. (Dates of observance subject to alteration.)

SUNKIST WOMEN'S TENNIS ASSOCIATION CHAMPION-SHIPS. Apr 13-20. Amelia Island Plantation, Amelia Island, FL. The official championships of the Women's Tennis Assn. Info from: Chamber of Commerce, Box 472, Fernandina Beach, FL 32034.

UNIVERSITY OF VIRGINIA: FOUNDER'S DAY. Apr 13. Charlottesville, VA. Celebration marks the 243rd anniversary of the birth of the University's founder, Thomas Jefferson. Info from: University of Virginia, Information Services, Monroe Hill House, Charlottesville, VA 22903.

APRIL 14 — MONDAY
104th Day — Remaining, 261

ATKINS, CHESTER G: BIRTHDAY. Apr 14. U.S. Representative of Massachusett's 5th district, Democrat, of Concord, MA, was born in Geneva, Switzerland, on Apr 14, 1948.

GEKAS, GEORGE WILLIAM: BIRTHDAY. Apr 14. U.S. Representative of Pennsylvania's 17th district, Republican, of Harrisburg, PA, born in Harrisburg on Apr 14, 1930.

HAITI: PAN AMERICAN DAY. Apr 14. Bank and public holiday. Info from: Haiti Government Tourist Bureau, 1270 Avenue of the Americas, New York, NY 10020.

HERITAGE GOLF CLASSIC. Apr 14-20. Hilton Head Island, South Carolina. Top pros play the Harbour Town Golf Links. Info from: Carol Fetter, 11 Lighthouse Lane, Hilton Head Island, SC 29928.

HONDURAS: DIA DE LAS AMERICAS. Apr 14. Honduras. Pan American Day, a national holiday.

LINCOLN, ABRAHAM: ASSASSINATION ANNIVERSARY. Apr 14. President Abraham Lincoln was shot while watching a performance of *Our American Cousin* at Ford's Theatre, Washington, DC, Apr 14, 1865. He died the following day. Assassin was John Wilkes Booth, a young actor.

PAN AMERICAN DAY. Apr 14. Presidential Proclamation 1912, ☆ of May 28, 1930, "had effect of covering every Apr 14 (req'd by Governing Board of Pan American Union). Proc 2386, Feb 12, 1940, observes Union's 50th Anniversary. Proc issued each year since 1948."

TOYNBEE, ARNOLD JOSEPH: BIRTHDAY. Apr 14. English historian, author of monumental *Study of History*, was born at London, Apr 14, 1889. Died at York, England, Oct 22, 1975.

APRIL 15 — TUESDAY
105th Day — Remaining, 260

BERMAN, HOWARD L: BIRTHDAY. Apr 15. U.S. Representative of California's 26th district, Democrat, of Panorama City (including the San Fernando Valley and parts of Los Angeles), was born in Los Angeles, CA on Apr 15, 1941.

April 1986	S	M	T	W	T	F	S
			1	2	3	4	5
	6	7	8	9	10	11	12
	13	14	15	16	17	18	19
	20	21	22	23	24	25	26
	27	28	29	30			

CIVITAN INTERNATIONAL ANNIVERSARY. Apr 15. Purpose: To commemorate the founding of Civitan International on Apr 15, 1920 in Birmingham, AL. Sponsor: Civitan Internatl, Wendell Andrews, Exec Admn, Box 2102, Birmingham, AL 35201.

INCOME TAX PAY-DAY. Apr 15. A day all Americans need to know—the day by which taxpayers are supposed to make their accounting of the previous year and pay their share of the cost of government. The U.S. Internal Revenue Service provides free forms.

LONGYEAR, JOHN MUNROE: BIRTHDAY. Apr 15. American capitalist, president of a bank and a button factory, land owner, philanthropist, one-time mayor of Marquette, MI. Disapproving of a railway route through Marquette, he caused his home, a stone castle-like showplace, to be torn down in 1903, and moved, stone by stone and stick by stick (in more than 190 freight cars), a distance, he said, of more than 1,300 miles, by rail, and re-erected at Brookline, MA. Longyear was born in Lansing, MI, Apr 15, 1850, and died May 28, 1922.

NATIONAL GRIPER'S DAY. Apr 15. Purpose: To provide a forum for those who want to complain when no one will listen. Info from: Jack Gilbert, The Amicus Group, 303 Fallis Rd, Columbus, OH 43214.

PEALE, CHARLES WILSON: BIRTHDAY. Apr 15. American portrait painter (best known for his many portraits of colonial and American Revolutionary War figures) was born in Queen Anne County, MD, Apr 15, 1741. Died at Philadelphia on Feb 22, 1827.

QUARTERLY ESTIMATED FEDERAL INCOME TAX PAYERS' DUE DATE. Apr 15. For those individuals whose fiscal year is the calendar year and who make quarterly estimated federal income tax payments, today is one of the due dates. (Jan 15, Apr 15, June 16, and Sept 15, 1986.)

SINKING OF THE *TITANIC*: ANNIVERSARY. Apr 15. The "unsinkable" luxury liner, *Titanic*, on its maiden voyage (from England to New York), struck an iceberg just before midnight on Apr 14, 1912, and sank at 2:27 a.m., Apr 15. The *Titanic* had 2,224 persons aboard. Of these, 1,513 lives were lost. The surviving passengers were rescued from the icy waters off Newfoundland by the liner *Carpathia*, which reached the scene about twenty minutes after the *Titanic* went down.

APRIL 16 — WEDNESDAY
106th Day — Remaining, 259

CHAPLIN, CHARLES SPENCER: BIRTHDAY. Apr 16. Celebrated film comedian born at London, England, Apr 16, 1889. Film debut in 1914. Knighted in 1975. Died at Vevey, Switzerland, Dec 25, 1977. In his autobiography Chaplin wrote: "There are more valid facts and details in works of art than there are in history books."

DENMARK: QUEEN MARGRETHE'S BIRTHDAY. Apr 16. Thousands of children gather to cheer the Queen at Amalienborg Palace, and the Royal Guard wears scarlet gala uniforms. A national holiday.

DIEGO, JOSE DE: BIRTHDAY. Apr 16. Puerto Rico. Celebrates birth on this day, 1867, of Puerto Rican patriot and political leader Jose de Diego.

MOORE, ARCH A JR: BIRTHDAY. Apr 16. Arch A Moore, Jr., Governor of West Virginia, Republican, was born at Moundsville, WV, on Apr 16, 1923.

NATURAL BRIDGES NATIONAL MONUMENT ANNIVERSARY. Apr 16. Utah. Natural Bridges National Monument was established Apr 16, 1908.

SLAVERY ABOLISHED IN DISTRICT OF COLUMBIA: ANNIVERSARY. Apr 16. Congress abolished slavery in the District of Columbia on Apr 16, 1862. One million dollars was appropriated to compensate owners of freed slaves and $100,000 was set aside to pay district slaves who wished to emigrate to Haiti, Liberia or any other country outside the U.S.

COPYRIGHT © 1985 BY WILLIAM D. CHASE and HELEN M. CHASE

SLOANE, HANS: BIRTH ANNIVERSARY. Apr 16. Sir Hans Sloane, British medical doctor and naturalist whose personal collections became the nucleus of the British Museum, was born at County Down, Ireland, on Apr 16, 1660. Upon his death at Chelsea, on Jan 11, 1753, his collections of books, manuscripts, coins, medals and antiquities were bequeathed to Britain, and accepted by an Act of Parliament which incorporated the British Museum. It was opened to the public at London on Jan 15, 1759. It is the national depository, museum and library of the United Kingdom.

SPACE MILESTONE: APOLLO 16 (US). Apr 16. On Apr 16, 1972, Astronauts John W. Young, Charles M. Duke, Jr., and Thomas K. Mattingly II (command module pilot), began 11-day mission which included 71-hour exploration of moon (Apr 20-23). Landing Module (LM) named "Orion." Splashdown in Pacific Ocean within a mile of target, Apr 27.

SUE BENNETT FOLK FESTIVAL. Apr 16-19. London, KY. Appalachian region celebration, arts and crafts, music, dancing and singing performances and lectures. Info from: KY Dept of Travel, Capital Plaza Office Tower, Frankfort, KY 40601.

SYNGE, JOHN MILLINGTON: BIRTHDAY. Apr 16. Irish dramatist and poet, most of whose plays were written in the brief span of six years before his death at age 37, of lymphatic sarcoma. His best known work was *The Playboy of the Western World*, (1907) which caused protests and rioting at early performances. Synge (pronounced "Sing") was born near Dublin on Apr 16, 1871, and died in that city on Mar 24, 1909.

WRIGHT, WILBUR: BIRTHDAY. Apr 16. Aviation pioneer born Apr 16, 1867, Millville, IN; died at Dayton, OH, May 30, 1912.

APRIL 17 — THURSDAY
107th Day — Remaining, 258

AMERICAN SAMOA: FLAG DAY. Apr 17. Commemorates first raising of American flag in what was formerly Eastern Samoa, on Apr 17, 1900. Public holiday with singing, dancing, costumes and parades.

BANDARANAIKE, SIRIMAVO: BIRTHDAY. Apr 17. World's first woman prime minister (Sri Lanka). Born at Ratnapura, Sri Lanka (formerly called Ceylon) on Apr 17, 1916.

CHASE, SAMUEL: BIRTHDAY. Apr 17. American Revolutionary leader, signer of the Declaration of Independence, and justice of the U.S. Supreme Court, born in Somerset County, MD, Apr 17, 1741. Died, June 19, 1811.

ENGLAND: BADMINTON HORSE TRIALS. Apr 17-20. Badminton, Avon. Dressage, cross-country and showjumping, Badminton House is the home of the Duke of Beaufort. Info from: Box Office, Badminton Horse Trials, Badminton, Avon GL9 1DF England.

INTERNATIONAL AZALEA FESTIVAL. Apr 17-20. Purpose: To recognize and salute NATO, to honor the large military population and provide entertainment for citizens of Norfolk. Sponsor: Chamber of Commerce and City of Norfolk, 420 Bank St, Norfolk, VA 23510.

KAMPUCHEA: NATIONAL DAY. Apr 17. National holiday is observed in Kampuchea.

MOON PHASE: FIRST QUARTER. Apr 17. Moon enters First Quarter phase at 5:35 a.m., E.S.T.

MORGAN, JOHN PIERPONT: BIRTHDAY. Apr 17. American financier and corporation director. Born at Hartford, CT, on Apr 17, 1837. Morgan died on Mar 31, 1913, leaving an estate valued at more than $70 million.

SPACE MILESTONE: SURVEYOR 3 (US). Apr 17. Lunar probe vehicle made soft landing on moon on Apr 20 and with its digging apparatus established surface qualities. Launched Apr 17, 1967.

SYRIAN ARAB REPUBLIC. Independence Day. Apr 17. Official holiday.

VERRAZANO DAY. Apr 17. Celebrates discovery of New York Harbor, 1524, by Giovanni Verrazano, Florentine navigator, 1480 (?)-1527.

WEST IS BEST. Apr 17-20. El Oso Park, Phoenix, AZ. Activities include a parade, carnival and variety show all focusing on the Fair Days theme of the year. Info from: City of Phoenix, Parks, Recreation & Library Dept, 125 E Washington, Phoenix, AZ 85004.

WEST IS BEST FAIR DAYS. Apr 17-20. Purpose: To unite the many organizations in the community in a festive entertaining event with the goal of upgrading the image of the community. Sponsor: Chamber of Commerce, 4355 W Indian School Rd, Suite C-2, Phoenix, AZ 85031.

WILDER, THORNTON: BIRTHDAY. Apr 17. Pulitzer Prize winning American playwright and novelist, born at Madison, WI, Apr 17, 1897. Died at Hamden, CT, Dec 7, 1975.

APRIL 18 — FRIDAY
108th Day — Remaining, 257

ABRAHAM BALDWIN AGRICULTURAL COLLEGE HOMECOMING CELEBRATION. Apr. 18-19. Reunions, banquets, beauty revue, music and dance. Info from: ABAC, Michael D. Chason, PR Dir, ABAC Station, Tifton, GA 31793.

ARKANSAS FOLK FESTIVAL. Apr 18-20. (Also Apr 25-27.) Music and crafts of the Ozarks. Blacksmithing, pottery, quilting, basketry, primitive furniture making, musical instrument making, candle dipping, soap making, spinning, weaving. Info from: Ozark Folk Ctr, Mountain View, AR 72560.

CANADA: CONSTITUTION ACT OF 1982: ANNIVERSARY. Apr 18. Replacing the British North America Act of 1867, the Canadian Constitution Act of 1982 provides Canada with a new set of fundamental laws and civil rights. Signed by Queen Elizabeth II, at Parliament Hill, Ottawa, Saturday, Apr 17, 1982, it went into effect at 12:01 a.m., Sunday, Apr 18, 1982.

DARROW, CLARENCE SEWARD: BIRTHDAY. Apr 18. American attorney often associated with unpopular causes, from the Pullman strike in 1894 to the Scottsboro case in 1932, born at Kinsman, OH, Apr 18, 1857. At the Scopes trial, July 13, 1925, Darrow said: "I do not consider it an insult, but rather a compliment to be called an agnostic. I do not pretend to know where many ignorant men are sure—that is all that agnosticism means. Darrow died at Chicago, Mar 13, 1938.

FIESTA '86. Apr 18-27. San Antonio, TX. Parades, including the unique "Fiesta River Parade," plus 150 other entertaining events. Full blown Mexican rodeo. Info from: Fiesta San Antonio Commission, Inc, 1145 E Commerce, San Antonio, TX 78205.

FOND du LAC JAZZ FESTIVAL. Apr 18-19. Marian College, Fond du Lac, WI. Jazz headliners and jam sessions. Info from: Convention & Visitors Bureau, 207 N Main St, Fond du Lac, WI 54935.

FT WALTON BEACH SEAFOOD FESTIVAL. Apr 18-20. Fort Walton Beach, FL. Seafood booths, arts & crafts. Info from: Ft. Walton Beach Art Museum Assn., Box 4081, Ft. Walton Beach, FL 32549.

COPYRIGHT © 1985 BY WILLIAM D. CHASE and HELEN M. CHASE

GEM AND MINERAL SHOW AND SWAP. Apr 18-20. Display of minerals, crystals, fossils, shells, handmade jewelry and gems. Exhibitors from clubs and universities as well as individual collectors. Sponsor: Science Museum of Virginia, Mary Randolph Spencer, 2500 W Broad St, Richmond, VA 23220.

HYDE, HENRY J: BIRTHDAY. Apr 18. U.S. Representative of Illinois' 6th district, Republican, of Bensenville, IL, was born in Chicago, IL, on Apr 18, 1924.

NATIONAL YOUTH LEADERSHIP CONFERENCE OF THE AMERICAN DIABETES ASSOCIATION. Apr 18-21. Key Bridge Marriott Hotel, Arlington, VA. Purpose: To offer leadership skills and training to the future leaders of the association and the USA. Sponsor: American Diabetes Assn, 2 Park Ave, New York, NY 10016.

PACKER, ALFERD E: DAY. Apr 18. University Memorial Center. Annual observance since 1968. Purpose: Joyous celebration in honor of Colorado's and the U.S.'s only convicted cannibal. Sponsor: Program Council and University Food Service. Contact: Food Service Dir, Campus Box 202, Univ of Colorado, Boulder, CO 80309.

PAUL REVERE'S RIDE ANNIVERSARY. Apr 18. The "Midnight Ride" of Paul Revere and William Dawes started at about 10 p.m. on Apr 18, 1775, to warn American patriots between Boston and Concord of the approaching British.

RIVER CITIES FESTIVAL. Apr 18-20. Hialeah and Miami Springs, FL. Purpose: To focus attention on the beauty of the Miami River and the need to keep it clean. Festival includes a 10-K race, "Anything That Floats" competition and paddle boat rides on the river. Info from: Chamber of Commerce, 59 W 5th St, Hialeah, FL 33010.

SAN FRANCISCO EARTHQUAKE ANNIVERSARY. Apr 18. Business section of San Francisco, some 10,000 acres, destroyed by earthquake, Apr 18, 1906. First quake at 5:13 a.m., followed by fire. Nearly 4,000 lives lost.

STAMP EXPO '86/SOUTH. Apr 18-20. Sheraton Hotel, Anaheim, CA. Purpose: International postage stamp exposition honoring U.S. space achievements. Sponsor: Internatl Stamp Collectors Society, Box 854, Van Nuys, CA 91408.

SUGARLOAF'S SPRING ARTS AND CRAFTS FAIR. Apr 18-20. Gaithersburg, MD. Over 300 professional artists and craftspeople, demonstrations, live music, marionette shows and a petting zoo. Sponsor: Sugarloaf Mt Works, Inc, Ijamsville, MD 21754.

"THIRD WORLD" DAY. Apr 18. Anniversary of the first use of the phrase, "third world," in the opening speech, by Indonesia's President Sukarno, at the Bandung Conference, Apr 18, 1955. Representatives of nearly 30 African and Asian countries (2,000 attendees) heard Sukarno praise the American war of independence, "the first successful anti-colonial war in history." More than half the world's population, he said, was represented at this "first intercontinental conference of the so-called colored peoples in the history of mankind." The phrase and the idea of a "third world" rapidly gained currency, generally signifying the aggregate of non-aligned peoples and nations—generally the non-white and underdeveloped portion of the world.

WHITTEN, JAMIE L: BIRTHDAY. Apr 18. U.S. Representative of Mississippi's 1st district, Democrat, of Charleston, MS, born at Cascilla, MS, on Apr 18, 1910.

ZIMBABWE: INDEPENDENCE DAY. Apr 18. National holiday.

	S	M	T	W	T	F	S
April			1	2	3	4	5
1986	6	7	8	9	10	11	12
	13	14	15	16	17	18	19
	20	21	22	23	24	25	26
	27	28	29	30			

APRIL 19 — SATURDAY
109th Day — Remaining, 256

CONCORD-YORKTOWN DAY. Apr 19. Yorktown, VA. Activities at the Yorktown Victory Center recognize the link between the towns at which the Revolutionary War began and ended. Re-enactment groups in the Center's outdoor encampment, depict the life of the revolutionary soldier. Info from: Box 1976, Yorktown, VA 23690.

GARFIELD, LUCRETIA RUDOLPH: BIRTHDAY. Apr 19. Wife of James Abram Garfield, 20th President of the U.S., born at Hiram, OH, Apr 19, 1832. Died Mar 14, 1918.

GREAT LAKES INVITATIONAL BARBERSHOP SHOW. Apr 19. Grand Rapids, MI. Presented by Grand Rapids Chapter of Society for the Preservation and Encouragement of Barber Shop Quartet Singing in America. Info from: J. Schneider, 1311 Northlawn, NE, Grand Rapids, MI 49505.

HISTORIC GARDEN WEEK IN VIRGINIA. Apr 19-27. Statewide celebration. Info from: Historic Garden Week Hq, 12 E Franklin St, Richmond, VA 23219.

INTERNATIONAL FAIR. Apr 19-20. Providence, RI. Info from: RI Dept of Economic Dev, Tourism Div, 7 Jackson Walkway, Providence, RI 02903.

MEET ME DOWNTOWN FESTIVAL. Apr 19-20. Boca Raton, FL. Purpose: To attract both local citizens and tourists to downtown Boca Raton. Continuous entertainment, food and artists and craftsmen. Info from: Boca Raton Redevelopment Agency, 201 W Palmetto Park Rd, Boca Raton, FL 33432.

MONTE CARLO FUN NIGHT. Apr 19. Purpose: Fund-raiser for Cleveland State University Engineering Student Enrichment Fund. Info from: Jeffrey W Compton, Chrmn, Monte Carlo Fun Night, 9505 Midwest Ave, Cleveland, OH 44125.

NETHERLANDS-UNITED STATES: DIPLOMATIC ANNIVERSARY. Apr 19. Anniversary of establishment of America's oldest continuously peaceful diplomatic relations. On Apr 19, 1782, the States General of the Netherlands United Provinces admitted John Adams (later to become 2nd President of the U.S.) as Minister Plenipotentiary of the young American republic. This was the second diplomatic recognition of the U.S. as an independent nation. Adams succeeded in bringing about, on Oct 8, 1782, the signing at The Hague of the first Treaty of Amity and Commerce between the two countries.

PARKER, JOHN: DAY. Apr 19. Remembering John Parker's order, at Lexington Green, Apr 19, 1775; "Stand your ground. Don't fire unless fired upon; but if they mean to have a war, let it begin here." John Parker, revolutionary soldier, captain of minutemen, born Lexington, MA, July 13, 1729. Died, Sept 17, 1775.

PEACE FESTIVAL. Apr 19-27. Vancouver, British Columbia. A peace festival which includes a large symposium that will be attended by a number of important figures from around the world. Info from: The Centennial Commission, Box 49386, Suite 3374, Bentall 4, 1055 Dunsmuir St, Vancouver, BC V7X 1L5 Canada.

PROFITABLE MARKETING STRATEGIES FOR INDEPENDENT PUBLISHERS: SEMINAR-WORKSHOP. Apr 19. San Diego, CA. Info from: American Bookdealers Exchange, Al Galasso, Box 2525, La Mesa, CA 92041.

RIVER CITY BLUES FESTIVAL. Apr 19-20. Purpose: To increase public appreciation of the fine musicians instrumental in the development of Baton Rouge blues and to promote the study and appreciation of blues in general. Sponsor: River City Festivals Assn, Richard Sabino, 427 Laurel St, Baton Rouge, LA 70801.

ST. OLAF COLLEGE: INTERNATIONAL FAIR. Apr 19-20. Purpose: To celebrate the ethnic and diverse backgrounds of St. Olaf College and highlight them in song, dance, dress and food in a grand festival. Info from: Dan Jorgensen, News Services Dir, St. Olaf College, Northfield, MN 55057.

COPYRIGHT © 1985 BY WILLIAM D. CHASE and HELEN M. CHASE

SHAW, E. CLAY, JR: BIRTHDAY. Apr 19. U.S. Representative of Florida's 15th district, Republican, of Fort Lauderdale, FL, born in Miami, FL, Apr 19, 1939.

SHERMAN, ROGER: BIRTHDAY. Apr 19. American statesman, member of the Continental Congress (1774-1781 and 1783-1784), signer of the Declaration of Independence and of the Constitution, was born at Newton, MA, Apr 19, 1721 (Old Style). He also calculated astronomical and calendar information for an almanac. Sherman died at New Haven, CT, July 23, 1793.

SIERRA LEONE: NATIONAL HOLIDAY. Apr 19. Sierra Leone became a republic on Apr 19, 1971.

SPACE MILESTONE: SALYUT 7 (USSR). Apr 19. New space station launched from Tyuratam to replace the aging Salyut 6. Apr 19, 1982.

TARPON SPRINGS ARTS AND CRAFTS FESTIVAL. Apr 19-20. Tarpon Springs, FL. Info from: Chamber of Commerce, 115 S. Ring Ave, Tarpon Springs, FL 33589.

APRIL 20 — SUNDAY
110th Day — Remaining, 255

APPLE CHILL STREET FAIR. Apr 20. Purpose: A day for local crafts-people and entertainers to display their talents. Sponsor: Chapel Hill Parks and Recreation, 306 N Columbia St, Chapel Hill, NC 27514.

BIKE SAFETY WEEK. Apr 20-26. Purpose: To increase youngsters' knowledge about how to drive a bike properly and safely. Info from: Natl Safety Council, Community Safety Programs Area, 444 N Michigan Ave, Chicago, IL 60611.

BLOCK HOUSE STEEPLECHASE RACES. Apr 20. Block House Course, Tryon, NC. Races are run in two states (North and South Carolina) and three counties (Greenville, Spartanburg and Polk) on the National Historic Block House grounds. Sponsor: Tryon Riding & Hunt Club, Box 1095, Tryon, NC 28782.

CANADA-UNITED STATES GOODWILL WEEK. Apr 20-26. Purpose: To bring about a better understanding of the American and Canadian ways of life. Sponsor: Program Development Dept, Kiwanis Internatl, 3636 Woodview Trace, Indianapolis, IN 46268.

CONSUMER PROTECTION WEEK. Apr 20-26. Purpose: To make Americans aware of fraud operators who use the mails to misrepresent a variety of products and services sold by mail. Sponsor: U.S. Postal Service, Director, Media Relations, U.S. Postal Service Hqs, Washington, DC 20260.

FRENCH, DANIEL CHESTER: BIRTHDAY. Apr 20. American sculptor born Apr 20, 1850. Died Oct 7, 1931.

GRANGE WEEK. Apr 20-26. Purpose: To create public awareness of the Grange influence on community, state and nation and to increase public awareness of local benefits and services. Info from: Kermit W. Richardson, Program Dir, National Grange, RFD 2, Barre, VT 05641.

HAMILTON, LEE HERBERT: BIRTHDAY. Apr 20. U.S. Representative of Indiana' 9th district, Democrat, of Nashville, IN, was born in Daytona Beach, FL, Apr 20, 1931.

HITLER, ADOLPH: BIRTH ANNIVERSARY. Apr 20. German dictator, frustrated artist, son of Alois (Schicklgruber) Hitler, obsessed with superiority of the "Aryan race" and the evil of Marxism (which he saw as a Jewish plot), was born at Braunau am Inn, Austria, on Apr 20, 1889. Turning to politics, despite a 5-year prison sentence (of which he served only nine months during which he wrote *Mein Kampf)* his rise was predictable and, on Aug 19, 1934, a German plebiscite vested sole executive power in Führer, Adolph Hitler. Facing certain defeat by the Allied Forces, on Apr 30, 1945, he shot himself while his mistress, Eva Braun, took poison, in a Berlin bunker where they had been hiding for over three months.

JONES, ED: BIRTHDAY. Apr 20, U.S. Representative of Tennessee's 8th district, Democrat, of Yorkville, TN, born in Yorkville on Apr 20, 1912.

KEEP AMERICA BEAUTIFUL WEEK. Apr 20-26. Purpose: To educate Americans about their personal responsibility for environmental improvement and how to make communities better places to live. Sponsor: Keep America Beautiful, Inc, Communications Dept, 99 Park Ave, New York, NY 10016.

NATIONAL YWCA WEEK. Apr 20-26. Purpose: to alert the public and bring awareness of what the YWCA stands for in its 127th year. Its purpose/accomplishments/benefits for girls and women 12 years of age and up. Sponsor: Natl Bd, YWCA of the USA, Jane Pinkerton, Dir of Communications/PR Div, 726 Broadway, New York, NY 10003.

PROFESSIONAL SECRETARIES WEEK. Apr 20-26. Purpose: Acknowledgement of the contributions of all secretaries to the vital roles of business, industry, education, government, and the professions. Sponsor: Professional Secretaries Internatl, 301 E Armour Blvd, Kansas City, MO 64111.

ROBERTS, CHARLES PATRICK (PAT): BIRTHDAY. Apr 20. U.S. Representative of Kansas' 1st district, Republican of Dodge City, KS, was born in Topeka, KS, Apr 20, 1936.

STEVENS, JOHN PAUL: BIRTHDAY. Apr 20. Associate Justice of the Supreme Court of the United States, nominated by Pres. Ford on Dec 1, 1975. (Sworn in, Dec 19, 1975). Justice Stevens was born in Chicago, IL, on Apr 20, 1920.

TAURUS, THE BULL. Apr 20-May 20. In the astronomical/astrological Zodiac which divides the sun's apparent orbit into twelve segments, the period Apr 20-May 20 is identified, traditionally, as the sun-sign of Taurus, the Bull. The ruling planet is Venus.

WORLD WEEK FOR LABORATORY ANIMALS. Apr 20-27. Purpose: To call attention to needless and painful experiments done on animals, educate the public and the media and create pressure for change. Sponsor: Mobilization for Animals, Box 1679, Columbus, OH 43216.

APRIL 21 — MONDAY
111th Day — Remaining, 254

AMERICAN NEWSPAPER PUBLISHERS ASSOCIATION: CONVENTION. Apr 21-23. San Francisco, CA. Purpose: To review through a three day program of speakers, panels and discussion sessions those matters which bear upon present and future operations of newspaper publishing. Info from: ANPA William Schabacker, Mgr, Public Affairs, The Newspaper Ctr, Box 17407, Dulles Internatl Airport, Washington, DC 20041.

BIRTHDAY OF ROME. Apr 21. Italy. National celebration of the founding of Rome. Traditionally in 753 BC.

BOREN, DAVID LYLE: BIRTHDAY. Apr 21. U.S. Senator from Oklahoma, Democrat, of Seminole, OK, born in Washington, DC, on Apr 21, 1941.

BRAZIL: TIRADENTES DAY. Apr 21. National holiday commemorating execution of national hero, dentist Jose de Silva Xavier, nicknamed Tiradentes (tooth-puller), a conspirator in revolt against Portuguese in 1789.

COPYRIGHT © 1985 BY WILLIAM D. CHASE and HELEN M. CHASE

BRONTE, CHARLOTTE: BIRTHDAY. Apr 21. English novelist born Apr 21, 1816, at Hartshead, Yorkshire, England. "Conventionality," she wrote in the preface to *Jane Eyre*, "is not morality. Self-righteousness is not religion. To attack the first is not to assail the last." She died on Mar 31, 1855.

CIMARRON TERRITORY CELEBRATION. Apr 21-26. Purpose: A homesteader festival highlighted by the World Champion Cow Chip Throwing Contest. Rodeos, parade and artisans demonstrating homesteading techniques and crafts. Antiques, coins, guns and crafts show. Info from: Beaver Chamber of Commerce, Box 878, Beaver, OK 73932.

DRAKE BULLDOG BEAUTY CONTEST. Apr 21. Nollen Plaza, Des Moines, IA. Purpose: To pick the "most beautiful Bulldog" from a world-class field of 50 hairy hopefuls. Winner reigns as mascot of the Drake Relays. Sponsor: Midland Financial Savings & Loan, 606 Walnut/Financial Ctr, Des Moines, IA 50309.

FESTIVAL OF RIDVAN. Apr 21-May 2. Annual Baha'i festival commemorating the twelve days (Apr 21-May 2, 1863) when Baha'u'llah, the prophet-founder of the Baha'i faith, resided in the Garden of Ridvan (Paradise) in Baghdad, at which time he publicly proclaimed his mission as God's messenger for this age. Info from: Baha'i Office of Public Affairs, Baha'i Natl Center, Wilmette, IL 60091.

KARTINI DAY. Apr 21. Honors Raden Adjeng Kartini, pioneer in the emancipation of the women of Indonesia. Republic of Indonesia.

KEAN, THOMAS H: BIRTHDAY. Apr 21. Thomas H. Kean, Governor of New Jersey, Republican, was born at Livingston, NJ, on Apr 21, 1935.

MUIR, JOHN: BIRTHDAY. Apr 21. American naturalist, explorer, conservationist and author from whom the 550-acre Muir Woods National Monument (near San Francisco, CA) is named. Muir, born at Dunbar, Scotland on Apr 21, 1838, emigrated to the U.S. in 1849, where he urged establishment of national parks and profoundly influenced U.S. forest conservation. Died at Los Angeles, CA on Dec 24, 1914.

NEWFOUNDLAND: ST. GEORGE'S DAY. Apr 21. Holiday observed in Newfoundland on Monday nearest Feast Day (Apr 23) of St. George.

PATRIOT'S DAY. Apr 21. Massachusetts and Maine. Commemorates Battle of Lexington and Concord, 1775. (Third Monday in April.)

SAN JACINTO DAY. Apr 21. Texas. Commemorates Battle of San Jacinto, Apr 21, 1836, in which Texas won independence from Mexico. A 570-foot monument, dedicated on the 101st anniversary of the battle marks the site on the banks of the San Jacinto River, about 20 miles from the present city of Houston, where General Sam Houston's Texans decisively defeated the Mexican forces led by Santa Anna in the final battle between Texas and Mexico.

SPACE MILESTONE: COPERNICUS, OAO 4 (US). Apr 21. Orbiting Astronomical Observer, named in honor of Polish astronomer. Launched Apr 21, 1972.

APRIL 22 — TUESDAY
112th Day — Remaining, 253

ARBOR DAY. Apr 22. Nebraska. First observance of Arbor Day was in this state, Apr 10, 1872. Now observed on many different dates in different states and countries.

BRAZIL: DISCOVERY OF BRAZIL DAY. Apr 22. Commemorates discovery by Pedro Alvarez Cabral, 1500.

April 1986

S	M	T	W	T	F	S
		1	2	3	4	5
6	7	8	9	10	11	12
13	14	15	16	17	18	19
20	21	22	23	24	25	26
27	28	29	30			

EARTH DAY: ANNIVERSARY. Apr 22. First observed Apr 22, 1970, with message "Give Earth a Chance," and attention to reclaiming the purity of the air, water and living environment. Special tenth anniversary observance on Apr 22, 1980, with assistance from U.S. Environmental Protection Agency. Although there is, reportedly, no continuing organization for observance, it is expected that there will be observances in many places on this date each year. Info from: Environmental Protection Agency, Office of Public Awareness, 401 M St, SW, Washington, DC 20460. Note: "Earth" days have been observed by many groups and on various dates. The Vernal Equinox has been chosen by some for this observance.

FIEDLER, BOBBI: BIRTHDAY. Apr 22. U.S. Representative of California's 21st district, Republican, of Northridge, CA, was born in Santa Monica, CA, on Apr 22, 1937.

FREDERICKSBURG DAY. Apr 22. Purpose: To fund (statewide) one historic garden restoration in Virginia per year. Spring tour of historic homes and gardens. Info from: Visitor Center, 706 Caroline St, Fredericksburg, VA 22401.

GIRL SCOUT LEADER'S DAY. Apr 22. Purpose: Opportunity for girls involved in Girl Scouting to honor their troop leaders. Sponsor: Girl Scouts of the USA, Attn: Bonnie McEwan, 830 Third Ave, New York, NY 10022.

ICELAND: "FIRST DAY OF SUMMER." Apr 22. Celebration of the "first day of summer" in Iceland.

LENIN, NIKOLAI: BIRTHDAY. Apr 22. Russian socialist and revolutionary leader (real name: Vladimir Ilyitch Ulyanov), ideological follower of Karl Marx. Born at Simbirsk, on the Volga, Apr 22, 1870 (New Style), (Apr 10, 1870 Old Style). Leader of the Great October Socialist Revolution of 1917. Lenin died at Gorky, near Moscow, on Jan 21, 1924. His embalmed body, in a glass coffin at the Lenin Mausoleum, has been viewed by millions of visitors to Moscow's Red Square.

OKLAHOMA CITY FESITVAL OF THE ARTS. Apr 22-27. Purpose: Oklahoma City's way of celebrating spring, fine art, performing arts and the best of international foods. Info from: Oklahoma City Arts Council, Elizabeth K. Eickman, 400 W California, Oklahoma City, OK 73102.

OKLAHOMA DAY. Apr 22. Oklahoma.

QUEBEC INTERNATIONAL BOOK FAIR. Apr 22-27. Info from: Quebec Internatl Book Fair, 2590 Blvd Laurier, Chambre 860, Sainte-Foy, Quebec G1V 4M6, Canada.

RUN FOR EARTH. Apr 22. Mammoth Cave National Park, KY. Purpose: In celebration of Earth Day. 5 kilometer run, 1 mile fun run on winding, wooded park roadways and cave tours. Sponsor: Mammoth Cave Natl Park, Mammoth Cave, KY 42259.

APRIL 23 — WEDNESDAY
113th Day — Remaining, 252

ACC CRAFTFAIR AT DALLAS. Apr 23-27. Dallas Market Hall, Dallas, TX. Info from: American Craft Enterprises, Inc, Box 10, New Paltz, NY 12561.

BOOK DAY and LOVER'S DAY. Apr 23. Barcelona, Spain. Saint George's Day and the anniversary of the death of Spanish writer Miguel de Cervantes have been observed with special ceremonies in the Palacio de la Disputacion and throughout the city since 1714. Book stands are set up in the plazas and on street corners. The gift of a rose and a book to someone dear is especially appropriate and especially prized on this day.

BUCHANAN, JAMES: BIRTHDAY. Apr 23. The 15th President of the U.S., born at Cove Gap, PA, on Apr 23, 1791, was the only president who never married. He served one term in office, Mar 4, 1857 - Mar 3, 1861, and died at Lancaster, PA, on June 1, 1868.

CERVANTES SAAVEDRA, MIGUEL DE: DEATH ANNIVERSARY. Apr 23. Spanish poet, playwright and novelist died in his 69th year, at Madrid, on Apr 23, 1616 (also the day of William Shakespeare's death). The exact date of

COPYRIGHT © 1985 BY WILLIAM D. CHASE and HELEN M. CHASE

Cervantes's birth at Alcala de Henares is unknown but he was baptized Oct 9, 1547, and some believe he was born on Michaelmas, Sept 29th. As soldier and tax collector, Cervantes travelled widely. He spent more than five years in prisons in Spain, Italy and North Africa. His greatest creation was Don Quixote, the immortal Knight of La Mancha whose profession was chivalry. Riding his nag, Rozinante, and accompanied by Squire Sancho Panza, Don Quixote tilts at windmills of the mind in the world's best known novel. Nearly a thousand editions of *Don Quixote* (a best seller since its first appearance in 1605) have been published and, next to the Bible, it has been translated into more languages than any other book.

DAUB, HAL: BIRTHDAY. Apr 23. U.S. Representative of Nebraska's 2nd district, Republican, of Omaha, NE, born in Fort Bragg, NC, Apr 23, 1941.

GIRLS CLUBS OF AMERICA NATIONAL CONFERENCE. Apr 23-27. Sheraton Palace, San Francisco, CA. Info from: Girls Clubs of America, Inc, Mary Jo Gallo, PR Dir, 205 Lexington, Ave, New York, NY 10016.

PEPPERCORN CEREMONY. Apr 23. St. George, Bermuda. Commemorates the payment of one peppercorn in 1816 to the Governor of Bermuda for rental of Old State House by the Masonic Lodge.

PROFESSIONAL SECRETARIES DAY. Apr 23. Sponsor: Professional Secretaries Internatl, 301 E Armour Blvd, Kansas City, MO 64111.

RUNNING OF THE RODENTS. Apr 23. Spalding University, Louisville, KY. Purpose: A pre-Derby event sponsored by Spalding University Math-Science Dept. Races, pomp, ceremony, and naming of Mr and Ms Rodent. Info from: Spalding Univ, PR Office, Louisville, KY 40203.

ST. GEORGE: FEAST DAY. Apr 23. Martyr and patron saint of England, who died Apr 23, A.D. 303. He was hero of George and the Dragon legend. Story says his faith helped him slay vicious dragon which demanded daily live sacrifice when king's daughter became intended victim.

SHAKESPEARE, WILLIAM: BIRTHDAY. Apr 23. England's most famous, most revered, and perhaps least known, poet and playwright. He was born at Stratford-on-Avon, Apr 23, 1564, baptized three days later, and died there on his birthday, Apr 23, 1616. Author of at least 36 plays and 154 sonnets. Virtually every "fact" about Shakespeare, from the spelling of his name to the authorship of the plays bearing his name, has been the subject of controversy and challenge. His epitaph: "Good frend for Jesus sake forbeare, To digg the dust encloased heare. Blese be ye man that spares thes stones, And curst be he that moves my bones."

SPACE MILESTONE: SOYUZ 10 (USSR). Apr 23. Cosmonauts V.A. Shatalov, A.S. Yeliseyev, N.N. Rukavishnikov docked Apr 24 with Salyut 1 orbital space station. Return Earth landing in Kazakhstan, Apr 24. Launched Apr 23 1971.

SYMMS, STEVE: BIRTHDAY. Apr 23. U.S. Senator from Idaho, Republican, of Caldwell, ID, was born in Nampa, ID, on Apr 23, 1938.

TACOMA BOAT SHOW. Apr 23-27. Tacoma Dome, Tacoma, WA. Info from: Northwest Marine Trade Assn, #233 Mariner's Sq, 1900 N Northlake Way, Seattle WA 98103.

TURKEY: NATIONAL SOVEREIGNTY and CHILDREN'S DAY. Apr 23. Commemorates Grand National Assembly's inauguration, on Apr 23, 1923.

APRIL 24 — THURSDAY

114th Day — Remaining, 251

ARMENIAN MARTYRS DAY. Apr 24. Commemorates the massacre of Armenians under the Ottoman Turks in 1915. Also called Armenian Liberation Day. In 1985 an international controversy concerning this event was revived when it was reported that Adolph Hitler, in a speech at Obersalzberg on Aug 22, 1939, said "Who today remembers the Armenian extermination?" in an apparent justification of genocide.

BIRMINGHAM FESTIVAL OF ARTS. Apr 24-May 4. Birmingham, AL. Info from: Alabama Tourism and Travel, 532 S Perry St, Montgomery, AL 36130.

CARTWRIGHT, EDMUND: BIRTHDAY. Apr 24. English cleric and inventor (developed the power loom and other weaving inventions) was born at Nottinghamshire, England, Apr 24, 1743. He died at Hastings, Sussex, England, Oct 30, 1823.

ECLIPSE: TOTAL ECLIPSE OF THE MOON. Apr 24. Visible: W. of North America, Australasia, Antarctica and E. Asia. Moon enters umbra at 6:02 a.m. and leaves it at 9:22 a.m., E.S.T. Totality lasts from 7:10 a.m. until 8:15 a.m., E.S.T.

FORT LAUDERDALE WEEK OF THE OCEAN CELEBRATION. Apr 24-May 4. Fort Lauderdale area, FL. Billfish tournament, seafood samplings, marine fair, environmental seminars, beachwalk, sea chanties, arts, crafts and sea turtle release. Info from: Cynthia Hancock, Week of the Ocean, Inc., Box 179, Ft Lauderdale, FL 33302.

HILER, JOHN PATRICK: BIRTHDAY. Apr 24. U.S. Representative of Indiana's 3rd district, Republican, of La Porte, IN, born in Chicago, IL, on Apr 24, 1953.

LIBRARY OF CONGRESS BIRTHDAY. Apr 24. Congress approved, on Apr 24, 1800, an act providing "for the purchase of such books as may be necessary for the use of Congress... and for fitting up a suitable apartment for containing them." Thus began one of the world's greatest libraries.

MOON PHASE: FULL MOON. Apr 24. Moon enters full Moon phase at 7:46 a.m., E.S.T.

NEBRASKA CITY, NE: ARBOR DAY CELEBRATION. Apr 24-27. Purpose: To look to the future through the care and planting of trees; and to make our community a more healthful and beautiful place to live. Sponsor: Chamber of Commerce, Box 245, Nebraska City, NE 68410.

PESACH or PASSOVER, FIRST DAY. Apr 24. Hebrew calendar date: Nisan 15, 5746. Begins eight-day celebration of delivery of Jews from slavery in Egypt. Unleavened bread (matzoh) is eaten at this time.

SPACE MILESTONE: CHINA 1 (PEOPLE'S REPUBLIC OF CHINA). Apr 24. China becomes fifth nation to orbit satellite with its own rocket. Broadcast Chinese song "Tang Fang Hung" (The East is Red) and telemetric signals. Apr 24, 1970.

SPRING ANTIQUE SHOW. Apr 24-27. Somerset Mall, Troy, MI. Purpose: Hard to find repair and replacement services offered. Crystal grinding, chair caning, rushing and splint-seat weaving. Haviland china, sterling and silverplate replacement and lamp doctor. Info from: Peg DuBois, 2801 Somerset Mall, Troy, MI 48084.

SPRING WILDFLOWER PILGRIMAGE. Apr 24-26. Gatlinburg, TN. Nature studies, guided photo trips, motor and hiking tours to explore the spring flora of the Great Smoky Mountains National Park. Info from: Chamber of Commerce, Box 527, Gatlinburg, TN 37738.

THOMAS, ROBERT BAILEY: BIRTHDAY. Apr 24. Founder and editor of *The Farmer's Almanac* (first issue for 1793), was born at Grafton, MA, Apr 24, 1766. Thomas died May 19, 1846, while working on the 1847 edition.

COPYRIGHT © 1985 BY WILLIAM D. CHASE and HELEN M. CHASE

TROLLOPE, ANTHONY: BIRTHDAY. Apr 24. English novelist, born London, Apr 24, 1815. Died there Dec 6, 1882. "Of all the needs a book has," he wrote in his autobiography, "the chief need is that it be readable."

WASHINGTON STATE APPLE BLOSSOM FESTIVAL. Apr 24-May 4. Purpose: To celebrate the spring blossoms of one of our most important crops, apples. Parades, arts and crafts, horse show, forklift rodeo, "ridge to river relay," gem and mineral show, theatrical productions and carnival. Sponsor: Washington State Apple Blossom Festival Assn, Box 850, Wenatchee, WA 98801.

WILDFOWL CARVING WORKSHOP. Apr 24. Ocean City Conv Hall, Ocean City, MD. Purpose: Series of wood carving and painting seminars. Always the Thursday before the last weekend in April. Sponsor: The Ward Foundation, 655 S Salisbury Blvd, Salisbury, MD 21801.

APRIL 25 — FRIDAY
115th Day — Remaining, 250

ANZAC DAY. Apr 25. Australia and New Zealand. Memorial day and veterans' observance, especially to mark World War I Anzac landing at Gallipoli, on Apr 25, 1915 (ANZAC: Australia and New Zealand Army Corps).

BOOM TOWN DAYS. Apr 25-27. Dunnellon, FL. Purpose: Celebration of 1890's Dunnellon phosphate mining boom. Contests, music, tournaments and exhibitions. Sponsor: Chamber of Commerce, Box 868, Dunnellon, FL 32630.

BRENNAN, WILLIAM J. JR: BIRTHDAY. Apr 25. Associate Justice of Supreme Court of the United States, appointed by Pres Eisenhower on Oct 15, 1956. (Oath of Office, Oct 16, 1956.) Justice Brennan was born at Newark, NJ, on Apr 25, 1906.

COORS/PIRELLI CHIMNEY ROCK HILLCLIMB. Apr 25-27. Chimney Rock Park, NC. Purpose: Most challenging sports car hillclimb in the country on asphalt. 1.8 mile course includes 19 curves—13 hairpin. Sponsor: Chimney Rock Park, Box 39, Chimney Rock, NC 28720.

CRAWFISH FESTIVAL AND AQUA CULTURE FAIR. Apr 25-26. Purpose: To promote South Carolina crawfish harvest and industry. Sponsor: Anne Barr, Box 69, Pawleys Island, SC 29585.

DENMARK: COMMON PRAYER DAY. Apr 25. Public holiday. The fourth Friday after Easter, known as "Store Bededag," is a day for prayer and festivity.

DRAKE RELAYS. Apr 25-26. Drake University, Des Moines, IA. Purpose: Track and field classic for top collegiate and international talent in the country. Info from: Drake University, Bob MacKenzie, Promotion Dir, Drake Fieldhouse, Des Moines, IA 50311.

FESTIVAL OF NATIONS 1986. Apr 25-27. St. Paul Civic Ctr, St. Paul, MN. Ethnic celebration by more than 55 ethnic groups presenting food specialties, folk dances and folk arts to the public. Info from: International Institute of Minnesota, 1694 Como Ave, St. Paul, MN 55108.

GOLDEN AGE HOBBY SHOW. Apr 25-May 2. Ohio State Fairgrounds, Columbus, OH. Over 1,500 items handmade by adults over sixty are displayed in juried show. Info from: Columbus Recreation & Parks Dept, Linda Schuler, 600 E Eleventh Ave, Columbus, OH 43211.

KENTUCKY DERBY FESTIVAL. Apr 25-May 4. Louisville, KY. A civic celebration involving the entire community which heightens the drama and excitement leading up to the running of "America's greatest horse race." Sponsor: Kentucky Derby Festival, Inc, 224 W Muhammad Ali Blvd, Louisville, KY 40202.

MACAU: ANNIVERSARY OF THE PORTUGUESE REVOLUTION. Apr 25. Macau. Marks the anniversary of the 1974 revolution.

MAD FESTIVAL. Apr 25-26. Music, art, drama, featuring concerts, plays, ballets and chamber music concerts. Info from: Valerie Miller, Fine Arts Ctr of Kershaw County, Inc, 310 York St, Camden, SC 29020.

MANGUM RATTLESNAKE DERBY. Apr 25-27. Mangum, OK. Hunters stalk the wily rattlesnake and attempt to bring in the longest, the shortest and the most pounds. Snake skins and meat are sold. Flea market and carnival. Annually, last weekend in April. Info from: Chamber of Commerce, 222 W. Jefferson, Mangum, OK 73554.

MAPLE SUGAR FESTIVAL. Apr 25-27. Purpose: Regional tribute and festival to honor producers of maple products at St. Johnsbury, maple center of the world. Sponsor: Chamber of Commerce, Terry Hoffer, Exec Dir, 30 Western Ave, St. Johnsbury, VT 05819.

MARCONI, GUGLIELMO: BIRTHDAY. Apr 25. Inventor of wireless telegraphy (1895) born at Bologna, Italy, on this date, 1874. Died, Rome, July 20, 1937.

MOUNTAIN AND HAMMER DULCIMER CONTESTS AND WORKSHOPS. Apr 25-26. Purpose: Brings together contestants for Southern Region Championships and features Appalachian (mountain) dulcimers and hammer (prairie) dulcimers. Info from: Ozark Folk Ctr, Mountain View, AR 72560.

NATIONAL DISC-JOCKEY DAY. Apr 25. Purpose: To recognize, laud and honor the profession of radio personalities in the industry. Observed on the last Friday in April. Sponsor: WGCY Radio, Dan W. Jones, Assistant Gen Mgr, Box 192, Gibson City, IL 60936.

NATURE PHOTOGRAPHY WEEKEND. Apr 25-27. Cumberland Falls State Resort Park, Corbin, KY. Info from: Kentucky Dept of Parks, Capital Plaza Tower, Frankfort, KY 40601.

NEW BEGINNING FESTIVAL. Apr 25-26. Coffeyville, KS. A multi-state arts and crafts festival. Info from: Chamber of Commerce, Box 457, Coffeyville, KS 67337.

NEW ORLEANS JAZZ AND HERITAGE FESTIVAL. Apr 25-May 4. Purpose: To present music (jazz, gospel, blues and rhythm and blues), food and crafts in both fair and concert formats emphasizing New Orleans jazz and heritage. Sponsor: New Orleans Jazz & Heritage Foundation, 1205 N Rampart, New Orleans, LA 70116.

PIONEER FLORIDA OLD TIME MUSIC CHAMPIONSHIP. Apr 25-26. Info from: Ernie Williams, Pioneer Florida Museum, Pioneer Museum Rd, Dade City, FL 33525.

PORTUGAL'S DAY. Apr 25. Portugal. Public Holiday.

PULASKI FESTIVAL. Apr 25-27. Celebration of Polish culture commemorates the life of General Pulaski and promotes an understanding of Polish history, culture and values. Info from: The Pulaski Foundation, Box 1201, Moravian Station, Bethlehem, PA 18018.

SHAWNEE HILLS SPRING POETRY WORKSHOP. Apr 25-27. Greenbo Lake State Resort Park, Greenup, KY. A workshop on how to write and edit work and poetry reading. Info from: Kentucky Dept of Parks, Capital Plaza Tower, Frankfort, KY 40601.

SHOWCASE '86 TRADE AND HOME SHOW. Apr 25-27. Purpose: Homeshow featuring exhibits, food and entertainment. Sponsor: Zion Park District, 2400 Dowie Dr, Zion, IL 60099.

SMITH, LAWRENCE JACK: BIRTHDAY. Apr 25. U.S. Representative of Florida's 16th district, Democrat, of Hollywood, FL, born in Brooklyn, NY on Apr 25, 1941.

April 1986

S	M	T	W	T	F	S
		1	2	3	4	5
6	7	8	9	10	11	12
13	14	15	16	17	18	19
20	21	22	23	24	25	26
27	28	29	30			

COPYRIGHT © 1985 BY WILLIAM D. CHASE and HELEN M. CHASE

TEXAS STATE CHAMPIONSHIP FIDDLERS FROLICS. Apr 25-27. Purpose: Old-time fiddling championship of Texas decided with proceeds going to various charities. Sponsor: Knights of Columbus, Box 46, Hallettsville, TX 77964.

WESTERN SAMOA: ANZAC DAY. Apr 25. ANZAC stands for Autralian and New Zealand Army Corps and the day commemorates their landing at Gallipoli during World War I. The day is celebrated in much the same way as the United States' Memorial Day, including a march of veterans, wreath laying, and a sunrise service at the War Memorial in memory of all who have fallen in battle. Info from: Samoan Mission to the UN, 820 2nd Ave, New York, NY 10017.

WICHITA JAZZ FESTIVAL. Apr 25-27. Purpose: To promote the educational aspects of the art of jazz in the city of Wichita, KS and present top-flight jazz entertainment. Sponsor: Wichita Jazz Festival, Christine Curless, Exec Dir, 243 N Dellrose, Wichita, KS 67208.

WILBUR WRIGHT FLY IN. Apr 25-27. Wright Brothers National Memorial, Kill Devil Hills, NC. Purpose: To celebrate flight. Aircraft from around the country descend on the memorial, including antiques, classics, warbirds, ultralights and home builts. Sponsor: First Flight Society, Gene O'Bleness, Box 475, Nags Head, NC 27959.

WORLD CHAMPIONSHIP WILDFOWL CARVING COMPETITION. Apr 25-27. Conv Ctr, Ocean City, MD. Purpose: Contest for decorative lifesize, miniature and floating carvings, for novice, amateur and professional carvers. Always the last full week-end in April. Info from: Ward Foundation, Knute Bartrug, Chrmn, 707 Eastern Shore Dr, Salisbury, MD 21801.

APRIL 26 — SATURDAY
116th Day — Remaining, 249

ARBOR DAY CELEBRATION. Apr 26-27. Nebraska City, NE. Purpose: To celebrate Arbor Day, the tree planters' holiday. Sponsors: The Natl Arbor Day Foundation and Nebraska City Chamber of Commerce. Info from: The Natl Arbor Day Foundation, 100 Arbor Ave, Nebraska City, NE 68410.

AUDUBON, JOHN JAMES: BIRTHDAY. Apr 26. American artist and naturalist, born Haiti, Apr 26, 1785. Died Jan 27, 1851.

CALLAWAY GARDENS ARTS AND CRAFTS FESTIVAL. Apr 26-27. Arts, crafts and plants festival. Info from: Carole Sirmans, 400 Browns Crossing Rd NW, Milledgeville, GA 31061.

CONFEDERATE MEMORIAL DAY. Apr 26. Florida and Georgia. See also: Confederate Memorial Day entries for May 10, for the last Monday in April and for the last Monday in May.

GAINES EASTERN REGIONAL DOG OBEDIENCE CHAMPIONSHIP. Apr 26-27. Richmond, VA. Purpose: To select the best dog/handler team in standard obedience classes including novice, open and super dog, the top category representing best-trained dog in the region. Sponsor: Gaines Dog Care Center, A.S. Willett, Red Oak Plaza, 70 W Red Oak Lane, White Plains, NY 10604.

GUERNICA MASSACRE: ANNIVERSARY. Apr 26. Late in the afternoon of Monday, Apr 26, 1937, the ancient Basque Town of Guernica, in Northern Spain, was attacked without warning by German-made airplanes. Three hours of intensive bombing left the town in flames. Citizens who fled to the fields and ditches around Guernica were machine-gunned from the air. This atrocity inspired Pablo Picasso's mural *Guernica.* Responsibility for the bombing was never officially established, but the suffering and anger of the victims and their survivors are still evident at anniversary demonstrations.

HAWAII: KONA SPORTS FESTIVAL. Apr 26-May 10. Kailua-Kona, Hawaii. Info from: Hawaii Visitors Bureau, Honolulu, HI 96815.

MARTIN, DAVID O'BRIEN: BIRTHDAY. Apr 26. U.S. Representative of New York's 26th district, Republican, of Canton, NY, born at Ogdensburg, NY, Apr 26, 1944.

NORTH BEND BLENNERHASSETT SPRING NATURE TOUR. Apr 26-27. North Bend State Park, Charleston, WV. Info from: Maxine Scarbro, WV Dept of Natural Resources, Charleston, WV 25305.

OLMSTED, FREDERICK LAW: BIRTHDAY. Apr 26. American landscape architect, who participated in design of Yosemite National Park, New York City's Central Park and parks for Boston, Hartford and Louisville, was born at Hartford, CT, Apr 26, 1822, and died at Waverly, MA, Aug 28, 1903.

POLK COUNTY RAMP TRAMP. Apr 26. Big Frog Mountain, Benton, TN. A tribute to the ramp, a wild onion-like plant which grows only in the Appalachian Mountains, Bluegrass music and feast of the ramps. Info from: Don Ledford, Big Frog Mountain, Benton, TN 37307.

RICHTER SCALE DAY. Apr 26. A day to recognize the importance of Charles Richter's research and development of the earthquake magnitude scale which bears his name. American seismologist, Charles Richter, was born Apr 26, 1900, near Hamilton, OH. Reportedly, an Earthquake Awareness Week has honored him.

SIKORSKI, GERRY: BIRTHDAY. Apr 26. U.S. Representative of Minnesota's 6th district, Democratic-Farmer-Labor, of Stillwater, MN, was born in Breckenridge, MN, on Apr 26, 1948.

SPRING FARM DAYS. Apr 26-27. Tallahassee Jr Museum. Traditional rural craft demonstrations on Museum's Big Bend Farm. Info from: Tallahassee Jr Museum, 3945 Museum Dr, Tallahassee, FL 32304.

SPRING ON THE FARM. Apr 26-27. Purpose: Take part in over 100 different craft demonstrations on 1880's living historical farm. Info from: Dayton-Montgomery County Park District, Carriage Hill Farm, 7860 Shull Rd, Dayton, OH 45424.

TANZANIA: UNION DAY. Apr 26. Celebrates union between mainland Tanzania (formerly Tanganyika) and the islands of Zanzibar and Pemba, in 1964.

TEXAS WILDFLOWER DAY. Apr 26. Purpose: Celebration of efforts to preserve/conserve beautiful Texas wildflowers. Carroll Abbott Memorial Symposium, exhibits and awards. Annually, the fourth Saturday in April. Sponsor: Texas Woman's Univ, Denton, TX. Info from: Dr Robert E Collier, Dean, Box 22675, TWU Station, Denton, TX 76204.

WORLD COW CHIP THROWING CHAMPIONSHIP. Apr 26. Beaver, OK. "A highly specialized athletic event which draws dung flingers from around the world. A special division of this competition is held for politicians, who are known to be highly practiced in this area." Info from: Beaver Chamber of Commerce, Box 878, Beaver, OK 73932.

APRIL 27 — SUNDAY
117th Day — Remaining, 248

AFGHANISTAN: NATIONAL HOLIDAY. Apr 27. Anniversary of the Saur Revolution.

BLOSSOMTIME FESTIVAL OF SOUTHWESTERN MICHIGAN. Apr 27-May 3. Purpose: To promote the abundant fruit industry and tourism in Michigan. Spring comes alive as the blossoms announce the forthcoming arrival of the season's most delectable fruits. Sponsor: Blossomtime, Inc, Carol Weller, Exec Dir, 151 E Napier Ave, Benton Harbor, MI 49022.

DAYLIGHT SAVING TIME. Apr 27-Oct 26. Begins at 2:00 a.m. The Uniform Time Act of 1966, administered by the U.S. Dept of Transportation, provides that standard time in each zone be advanced one hour from 2:00 a.m. on the last Sunday in April until 2:00 a.m. on the last Sunday in October (except where state legislatures provide exemption). Many use the popular rule: "Spring forward, Fall Back," to remember which way to turn their clocks. See Oct 26 for resumption of Standard Time.

GIBBON, EDWARD: BIRTHDAY. Apr 27. English historian and author. His *History of the Decline and Fall of the Roman Empire* remains a model of literature and history. "The various modes of worship, which prevailed in the Roman world," he wrote, "were all considered by the people, as equally true; by the philosopher, as equally false; and by the magistrate, as equally useful." Born on Apr 27, 1737, at Putney, Surrey, he died at London on Jan 6, 1794.

GODWIN, MARY WOLLSTONECRAFT: BIRTHDAY. Apr 27. English writer whose best known book was *Vindication of the Rights of Women*, published in 1792. Born at London, Apr 27, 1759, and died there Sept 10, 1797. Her daughter, Mary, was the wife of poet Percy Bysshe Shelley, but is best remembered as the author of *Frankenstein*, published in 1818.

GRANT, ULYSSES SIMPSON: BIRTHDAY. Apr 27. Eighteenth President of the U.S. (Mar 4, 1869 - Mar 3, 1877), born Hiram Ulysses Grant at Point Pleasant, Ohio, Apr 27, 1822. Graduated from U.S. Military Academy in 1843. Pres Lincoln promoted Grant to Lt General, in command of all the Union armies, Mar 9, 1864. On Apr 9, 1865, Grant received General Robert E. Lee's surrender, at Appomattox, VA, which he announced to the Secretary of War as follows: "General Lee surrendered the Army of Northern Virginia this afternoon on terms proposed by myself. The accompanying additional correspondence will show the conditions fully." Nicknamed "Unconditional Surrender Grant," he died at Mount McGregor, NY, July 23, 1885, just four days after completing his memoirs. He was buried in Riverside Park, New York City, where Grant's Tomb was dedicated in 1897.

HELL HOLE SWAMP FESTIVAL. Apr 27-May 4. Purpose: To highlight early history and customs practiced then and now. Featuring music, arts and crafts, whiskey making during prohibition and the "Hell Hole Swamp Gang." Sponsor: Hell Hole Swamp Festival, Inc, Box 125, Jamestown, SC 29453.

MAGELLAN, FERDINAND: DEATH ANNIVERSARY. Apr 27. Portuguese explorer, Ferdinand Magellan, was probably born near Oporto, about 1480, but neither the place nor the date is certain. Usually thought of as the first man to circumnavigate the earth, he died before completing the voyage; thus his co-leader, Basque navigator Juan Sebastian de Elcano, became the world's first circumnavigator. The westward, round-the-world expedition began on Sept 20, 1519, with five ships and about 250 men. Magellan was killed by natives of the Philippine island of Mactan, Apr 27, 1521.

MATANZAS MULE DAY. Apr 27. In one of the first naval actions of the Spanish-American War, U.S. naval forces, on Apr 27, 1898, bombarded the Cuban village of Matanzas. It was widely reported that the only casualty of the bombardment was one mule. "The Matanzas Mule" became instantly famous and remains a footnote in the history of the Spanish-American War.

MOAKELY, JOHN JOSEPH: BIRTHDAY. Apr 27. U.S. Representative of Massachusetts' 9th district, Democrat, of Boston, MA, was born on Apr 27, 1927.

MORSE, SAMUEL FINLEY BREESE: BIRTHDAY. Apr 27. American artist and inventor, after whom the Morse Code is named, was born at Charlestown, MA, Apr 27, 1791, and died at New York City, Apr 2, 1872. Morse conceived the idea of an electromagnetic telegraph while on shipboard, returning from art instruction in Europe, in 1832, and he proceeded to develop his idea. With financial assistance approved by the Congress, the first telegraph line in the U.S. was constructed, between Washington, DC, and Baltimore, MD. The first message, keyed in at the U.S. Capitol on May 24, 1884, was: "What hath God wrought?"

NATIONAL WEEK OF THE OCEAN '86. Apr 27-May 3. Purpose: To call attention to the influence of the ocean on our lives—its historic, cultural, commercial and recreational significance and its bountiful resources of food, water, and energy. Info from: Cynthia Hancock, Week of the Ocean, Inc, Box 179, Ft Lauderdale, FL 33302.

SULTANA EXPLOSION ANNIVERSARY. Apr 27. Early in the morning of Apr 27, 1865, America's worst steamship disaster occurred. The *Sultana*, heavily overloaded with an estimated 2,300 passengers, exploded in the Mississippi River, just north of Memphis, en route to Cairo, IL. Most of the passengers were Union soldiers who had been prisoners of war and were eagerly returning to their homes. Although there was never an accurate accounting of the dead, estimates range from the Naval History Division's 1,450 to nearly 2,000. Cause of the explosion was not determined, but the little-known event is unparalleled in U.S. history.

TOGO: INDEPENDENCE DAY. Apr 27. National holiday.

APRIL 28 — MONDAY
118th Day — Remaining, 247

BAKER, JAMES ADDISON III: BIRTHDAY. Apr 28. James A. Baker III, U.S. Secretary of the Treasury (confirmed by the Senate on Jan 29, 1985) was born at Houston, TX, Apr 28, 1930.

BARRYMORE, LIONEL: BIRTHDAY. Apr 28. Famed American actor of celebrated acting family, Lionel Barrymore was born Lionel Blythe, at Philadelphia, PA, Apr 28, 1878. He died at Van Nuys, CA, Nov 15, 1954. U.S. Postal Service stamp issued in June 1982 featuring Ethel, John and Lionel Barrymore.

BROOMFIELD, WILLIAM S: BIRTHDAY. Apr 28. U.S. Representative of Michigan's 18th district, Republican, of Birmingham, MI, was born in Royal Oak, MI, on Apr 28, 1922.

CONFEDERATE MEMORIAL DAY. Apr 28. Alabama and Mississippi (Last Monday in April). Observed on other dates in some states; April 26 in Florida and Georgia; May 10 in North Carolina and South Carolina; last Monday in May in Virginia.

FAST DAY. Apr 28. New Hampshire. Dates from the days of "Public humiliation, fasting and prayer" proclaimed by royal governors during the 17th century settlement of New England. (Fourth Monday in April.)

MARYLAND: RATIFICATION DAY. Apr 28. Seventh State to ratify constitution, on this day in 1788.

MONROE, JAMES: BIRTHDAY. Apr 28. The 5th President of the U.S., was born at Westmoreland County, VA, and served two terms in that office (Mar 4, 1817-Mar 3, 1825). The capital city of Liberia, in Africa, is named after him, as is the Monroe Doctrine which he enunciated at Washington on Dec 2, 1823. Last of three presidents to die on the U.S. Independence Day, Monroe died at New York City, July 4, 1831.

WOMEN'S INTERNATIONAL BOWLING CONGRESS ANNUAL MEETING. Apr 28-30. Convention Ctr, Anaheim, CA. Info from: WIBC, Mr Augie Karcher, PR Mgr, 5301 S 76th St, Greendale, WI 53129.

April 1986

S	M	T	W	T	F	S
		1	2	3	4	5
6	7	8	9	10	11	12
13	14	15	16	17	18	19
20	21	22	23	24	25	26
27	28	29	30			

COPYRIGHT © 1985 BY WILLIAM D. CHASE and HELEN M. CHASE

APRIL 29 — TUESDAY

119th Day — Remaining, 246

ANAYA, TONEY: BIRTHDAY. Apr 29. Toney Anaya, Governor of New Mexico, Democrat, was born at Moriarty, NM, on Apr 29, 1941.

ELLSWORTH, OLIVER: BIRTHDAY. Apr 29. Third Chief Justice of the U.S. Supreme Court, born at Windsor, CT, on Apr 29, 1745. Died there, Nov 26, 1807.

HEARST, WILLIAM RANDOLPH: BIRTHDAY. Apr 29. American newspaper editor and publisher, born at San Francisco, CA, Apr 29, 1863. Died at Beverly Hills, CA, Aug 14, 1951.

JAPAN: EMPEROR'S BIRTHDAY. Apr 29. National holiday.

MARRIAGE OF FATHER DIVINE TO HIS SPOTLESS VIRGIN BRIDE. Apr 29. Purpose: To bring about the universal brotherhood of man and the propagation of Virtue, Honesty and Truth. Sponsor: Father Divine's Peace Mission Movement, 1622 Spring Mill Rd., Gladwyne, PA 19035.

MITCHELL, PARREN J: BIRTHDAY. Apr 29. U.S. Representative of Maryland's 7th district, Democrat, of Baltimore, MD, born there Apr 29, 1922.

ST. CATHERINE OF SIENA: FEAST DAY. Apr 29. Youngest of 20 children, Catherine of Siena was born in 1347. Patron saint of Italy. She died Apr 29, 1380, a week after suffering a stroke.

SPACE MILESTONE: CHALLENGER (US). Apr 29. *Challenger* launched from Kennedy Space Center, FL, on Apr 29, 1985, with crew of seven and animal menagerie including monkeys and rats. Landed after 111 orbits of Earth on May 6, 1985, at Edwards AFB, CA.

TAIWAN: CHENG CHENG KUNG LANDING DAY. Apr 29. Commemorates landing in Taiwan on this day in 1661 of Ming Dynasty loyalist, Cheng Cheng Kung (Koxinga), who ousted Dutch colonists who had occupied Taiwan for 37 years. Main ceremonies held at Tainan, in south Taiwan, where Dutch had their headquarters and where Cheng is buried. Cheng's birthday is also joyously celebrated, but according to the lunar calendar—on the 14th day of the seventh moon.

APRIL 30 — WEDNESDAY

120th Day — Remaining, 245

CLAY, WILLIAM L: BIRTHDAY. Apr 30. U.S. Representative of Missouri's 1st district, Democrat, of St. Louis, born in St. Louis on Apr 30, 1931.

GIFTED/TALENTED DAY. Apr 30. Purpose: A day to recognize and focus on the gifted and talented . . . tomorrow's future. Sponsor: Creative Resources, Lillie Petit Gallagher, Box 4053, Baton Rouge, LA 70821.

HARRISON, MARY SCOTT LORD DIMMICK: BIRTHDAY. Apr 30. Second wife of Benjamin Harrison, 23rd President of the U.S., born at Honesdale, PA, Apr 30, 1858. Died Jan 5, 1948.

INTERNATIONAL LAND, PASTURE AND RANGE JUDGING CONTEST. Apr 30-May 1. Purpose: 800 contestants from over 30 states appraise and categorize land and identify range and pasture plants. Info from: Steve Collier, 1 Santa Fe Plaza, Oklahoma City, OK 73102.

LILLY, WILLIAM: BIRTHDAY. Apr 30. English astrologer, author and almanac compiler, born at Diseworth. Leicestershire, on Apr 30, 1602. His almanacs were among the most popular in Britain from 1644 until his death, June 9, 1681, at Hersham, Surrey.

LIVINGSTON, ROBERT L. JR: BIRTHDAY. Apr 30. U.S. Representative of Louisiana' 1st district, Republican, of Metairie, LA, born in Colorado Springs, CO, on Apr 30, 1943.

LOUISIANA: ADMISSION DAY. Apr 30. Became 18th State on this day in 1812.

MOON PHASE: LAST QUARTER. Apr 30. Moon enters Last Quarter phase at 10:22 p.m., E.S.T.

NETHERLANDS: NATIONAL HOLIDAY. Apr 30. Celebration of the Queen's official birthday—the Dutch National Day.

PRESIDENT'S COMMITTEE ON EMPLOYMENT OF THE HANDICAPPED: ANNUAL MEETING. Apr 30-May 2. Purpose: Thousands of disabled and non-disabled people from U.S. and foreign countries meet to deal with problems impeding full opportunities for disabled people, especially job opportunities. Sponsor: The President's Committee on Employment of the Handicapped, 1111 20th St, NW, 6th Fl, Washington, DC 20036.

SEIZURE OF IRANIAN EMBASSY, LONDON: ANNIVERSARY. Apr 30. On Apr 30, 1980, three dissident Arabs from Khuzestan Province of Iran seized the Iranian Embassy in London, England, and took about 20 persons hostage. British commandos of the Special Air Service (SAS) stormed the embassy on May 5, 1980, freeing the 19 remaining hostages and killing or capturing the perpetrators of the seizure.

WALPURGIS NIGHT. Apr 30. Northern Europe. Witches' Sabbath. Eve of May Day. Celebrated particularly by university students.

WORLD YWCA DAY. Apr 30. Purpose: To alert the public and bring awareness of what the YWCA stands for, its purpose/accomplishments/ benefits for girls and women, 12 years of age and up. Sponsor: Natl Bd, YWCA of the USA, Jane Pinkerton, Dir of Communications/PR Div, 726 Broadway, New York, NY 10003.

COPYRIGHT © 1985 BY WILLIAM D. CHASE and HELEN M. CHASE

Maye.

MAY 1 — THURSDAY

121st Day — Remaining, 244

ADDISON, JOSEPH: BIRTHDAY. May 1. English essayist born Milston, Wiltshire, England on May 1, 1672. Died London, June 17, 1719. "We are," he wrote in *The Spectator*, "always doing something for Posterity, but I would fain see Posterity do something for us."

AMERICA'S LOVE RUN. May 1-31. Participants arrange for sponsors to pledge money toward the cumulative total of miles run during regular daily jogging or training. While keeping fit at their own pace, participants are raising money for the fight against muscle disease. Sponsor: Muscular Dystrophy Assn, 810 Seventh Ave, New York, NY 10019.

BELGIUM: PLAY OF ST. EVERMAAR. May 1. Annual performance (for over a thousand years) by the village inhabitants of a "real mystery" play, in its original form.

BETTER SLEEP MONTH. May 1-31. Purpose: To encourage Americans to re-evaluate their bedtime habits and to check bedding for signs of old age. Sponsor: The Better Sleep Council. Info from: Kaufman Public Relations, 2233 Wisconsin Ave NW, Washington, DC 20007.

CHRISTMAS IN MAY. May 1-31. Purpose: To stimulate peoples of the world to visit a handicapped child in their local hospitals or institutions and to take along a gift and some love. Sponsor: Turtles Internatl, 2018 Aldrich Ct, Downers Grove, IL 60516.

CORRECT POSTURE MONTH. May 1-31. Purpose: To help broaden public awareness of the importance of correct posture as an integral part of everyday health care, particularly appropriate in youth health education. Sponsor: American Chiropractic Assn, Communications Dir, 1916 Wilson Blvd, Arlington, VA 22201.

DENMARK: TIVOLI GARDENS SEASON. May 1-Sept 21. Copenhagen, Denmark. World famous for its variety of entertainment, symphony concerts, pantomime and ballet. Beautiful flower arrangements and excellent restaurants. Traditional season: May 1 until the third Sunday in Sept.

ENGLAND: NATIONAL GARDEN FESTIVAL. May 1-Oct 26. Stoke-on-Trent, Staffordshire. 180 acres of gardens, exhibitions and floral displays.

FESTIVAL OF THE HARE. May 1. Celebrates the official opening of the turtle thoroughbred racing season by honoring the trained exercise rabbits on a job well done in conditioning the mock thoroughbreds for the summer races. Sponsor: Turtles Internatl, 2018 Aldrich Ct, Downers Grove, IL 60516.

May
1986

S	M	T	W	T	F	S
				1	2	3
4	5	6	7	8	9	10
11	12	13	14	15	16	17
18	19	20	21	22	23	24
25	26	27	28	29	30	31

"500" FESTIVAL. May 1-26. Indianapolis, IN. Info from: "500" Festival Associates, Inc, Mrs. Josephine Hauck, Exec Dir, Box 817, Indianapolis, IN 46206.

FOOT HEALTH MONTH. May 1-31. Purpose: To educate the public about the importance of foot health and the role of the podiatrist. Sponsor: American Podiatry Assn, Louis G. Buttell, Dir of Public Affairs, 20 Chevy Chase Circle, NW, Washington, DC 20015.

GAZPACHO AFICIANADO TIME. May 1-Oct 31. Purpose: A time to appreciate one of Spain's finest contributions to international cuisine: Gazpacho, a nutritious cold soup made from fresh tomatoes and other vegetables. Observed whenever tomatoes are ripe.

HAWAII: KAUAI MUSEUM LEI-MAKING COMPETITION. May 1. Lihue, Kauai. Kauai Museum. Info from: Hawaii Visitors Bureau, Honolulu, HI 96815.

INTERNATIONAL AIR TRAVEL MONTH. May 1-31. Purpose: To promote the social, cultural and educational pleasures of air travel abroad. Sponsor: Internatl Air Travel Council Inc, H.F. Klemfuss, Dir, 61 Cupsaw Dr, Ringwood, NJ 07456.

ITALY: FESTIVAL OF ST. EFISIO. May 1-4. Cagliari, Italy. Said to be one of the biggest and most colorful processions in the world. Several thousand pilgrims on foot, in carts and on horseback wearing costumes dating from the 17th century accompany the statue of the saint through the streets.

JONES, MARY HARRIS (MOTHER JONES): BIRTHDAY. May 1. Irish-born, American labor leader. After death of her husband and four children (Memphis yellow fever epidemic of 1867) and loss of her belongings in Chicago Fire, 1871, she devoted her energies and her life to organizing and advancing the cause of labor. It seemed she was present wherever there were labor troubles. Gave her last speech on her 100th birthday. Born at Cork, Ireland, May 1, 1830. Died Nov 30, 1930.

KANSAS BARBED WIRE SWAP/SELL. May 1-3. LaCrosse, KS. Barbed Wire Collectors Association show and meeting. Info from: Brad Weaver, Kansas Barbed Wire Collectors Assn, General Office, LaCrosse, KS 67548.

KRAUT/FURTER BARBECUE TIME. May 1. Purpose: To launch the barbecue and outdoor eating season with the popular and tasty team of kraut and frankfurters. Sponsor: Natl Kraut Packers Assn. Info from: Burson-Marsteller, 1 E Wacker Dr, Chicago, IL 60601.

LAW DAY. May 1. Presidential Proclamation. "Issued each year ☆ for May 1 since 1958." (PL87-20 of Apr 7, 1961).

LAW DAY USA. May 1. Purpose: To advance equality and justice under law; to encourage citizen support of law observance and law enforcement; and to foster respect for law and understanding of its essential place in the life of every citizen of the United States. Sponsor: American Bar Assn, Marcia L. Kladder, Assistant Staff Dir, Special Events, 750 N Lake Shore Dr, Chicago, IL 60611.

LEI DAY. May 1. Waikiki Shell, Kapiolani Park, Honolulu, HI. Celebration featuring statewide lei exhibits and competitions. Lei Day Queen Pageant.

LOYALTY DAY. May 1. Presidential Proclamation. "Issued each ☆ year for May 1 since 1959. (PL85-529 of July 18, 1958). Note that an earlier Proclamation was issued in 1955.

MAY DAY. May 1. The first day of May has been observed as a holiday since ancient times. Spring festivals, maypoles and maying still are common, but political content of May Day has grown since the 1880s when it became a workers' day in the U.S. Now widely observed in socialist countries as a workers' holiday. More recently Loyalty Day and Law Day observances have been encouraged in the U.S. (by Presidential and other proclamations) on May 1, contrasting strongly with the workers' demonstrations abroad. In most European countries, when May Day falls on Saturday or Sunday, the Monday following is observed as a holiday, with bank and store closings, parades and other festivities.

COPYRIGHT © 1985 BY WILLIAM D. CHASE and HELEN M. CHASE

MISSOURI VALLEY QUILT SHOW. May 1-3. Purpose: Opportunity for quilters to exhibit their work. Quilts judged on workmanship and design. Sponsor: R.S.V.P., Marilyn Schottel, Box 7, Savannah, MO 64485.

NATIONAL ASPARAGUS MONTH. May 1-31. Purpose: To acquaint the public with the dietetic qualities and ease of preparation of asparagus. Sponsor: Washington Asparagus Growers Assn, Richard L. Martin, Mgr, Box 150, Sunnyside, WA 98944.

NATIONAL BARBECUE MONTH. May 1-31. Purpose: To encourage people to start enjoying barbecuing early in the season when Daylight Saving Time lengthens the day. Sponsor: Barbecue Industry Association. Info from: Mary S. Murphy, Myers ComminiCounsel, Inc., 11 Penn Plaza, Suite 200, New York, NY 10001.

NATIONAL GOOD CAR*KEEPING MONTH. May 1-31. Sponsor: Good Car*Keeping Institute, 230 N Michigan Ave, Suite 1020, Chicago, IL 60601.

NATIONAL HIGH BLOOD PRESSURE MONTH. May 1-31. Purpose: To promote the control and treatment of high blood pressure. Sponsor Natl High Blood Pressure Education Program, Natl Heart, Lung & Blood Institute, High Blood Pressure Information Ctr, 120/80 National Institutes of Health, Bethesda, MD 20205.

NATIONAL HOME DECORATING MONTH. May 1-31. Purpose: To promote home decorating with national contest and distribution of free booklets by retailers. Sponsor: Natl Decorating Products Assn, 1050 N Lindbergh Blvd, St Louis, MO 63132.

NATIONAL MIME MONTH. May 1-31. Purpose: To acknowledge and pay tribute to the mime art form and its performers. Sponsor: General Mills, Inc, Robert Jackson, Dept of Communications/Consumer Foods, Box 1113, Minneapolis, MN 55440.

NATIONAL PAINT MONTH. May 1-31. Purpose: To celebrate paint as a decorative product and to urge consumers everywhere to picture it painted. Sponsor: The Natl Paint & Coating Assn. Info from: Henry J. Kaufman & Associates, Inc, 2233 Wisconsin Ave NW, Washington, DC 20007.

NATIONAL PHYSICAL FITNESS AND SPORTS MONTH. May 1-31. Purpose: To encourage active participation in physical fitness and sports activities and programs. Info from: The President's Council on Physical Fitness and Sports, Dr. Matthew Guidry, PhD, 450 Fifth St, NW, Suite 7103, Washington, DC 20001.

OHIO HISTORIC PRESERVATION MONTH. May 1-31. Purpose: Ohio's history, architecture and archaeology are highlighted by special events at landmarks and historic sites statewide. Sponsor: Ohio Historic Preservation Office, Thomas M. Wolf, 1985 Velma Ave, Columbus, OH 43211.

OLDER AMERICANS MONTH. May 1-31. Presidential Proclamation. "(From 1963 thru 1973 this was called 'Senior Citizens Month.' In May 1974 it became Older Americans Month. In 1980 the title included Senior Citizens Day, which was observed on May 8, 1980.)"

PHILIPPINES: FEAST OF OUR LADY OF PEACE AND GOOD VOYAGE. May 1-31. Pilgrimage to the shrine of Nuestra Sra de la Paz y Buen Viaje in Antipolo, Rizal.

PHILIPPINES: SANTACRUZAN. May 1-31. Nationwide. Lovely girls participate in Maytime pageant-procession that recalls the quest of Queen Helena and Prince Constantine for the Holy Cross.

RESPECT FOR LAW WEEK. May 1-7. Purpose: To generate public participation in the dispensation of justice, combat apathy towards crime and educate the public concerning the responsibilities of law enforcement officials. Sponsor: Optimist Internatl, Hugh H. Cranford, Exec Secy, 4494 Lindell Blvd, St. Louis, MO 63108.

ST. TAMENEND'S DAY. May 1. Colonial American joyous May Day celebration, recently revived. Legendary American Indian sage, Chief Tamenend, canonized by fun-loving young colonists asserting independence from old world patrons. Modern celebrants, tired of over-serious political observances, identify selves by pinning dollar bill to their jackets. Info from: Dr. Nicholas Varga, Loyola College, Baltimore, MD 21210.

SENIOR CITIZENS MONTH. May 1-31. Massachusetts.

SHAW FESTIVAL 1986. May 1-Oct 13. Niagara-on-the-Lake, Ontario, Canada. Purpose: A unique theatre festival devoted to producing the works of Bernard Shaw and his contemporaries. Three theatres: Festival Theatre, Royal George and The Court House. Sponsor: Shaw Festival, Box 774, Niagara-on-the-Lake, Ontario, Canada L0S 1J0.

SHENANDOAH APPLE BLOSSOM FESTIVAL. May 1-4. Purpose: To celebrate the arrival of Spring and the blossoming of the apple trees of the Shenandoah Valley of Virginia, Info from: Shenandoah Apple Blossom Festival, William S. Collins, Box 3099, Winchester, VA 22601.

STEELMARK MONTH. May 1-31. Presidential Proclamation. ☆ "Always May since 1967. Proclamation 3778, Apr 8, 1967, covers all succeeding years." (PL89-703 of Nov 2, 1966).

STORYTELLING FESTIVAL. May 1-4. Jefferson National Expansion Memorial (Arch Grounds). A gathering of storytellers from a variety of disciplines—teachers, librarians, traditional and professional storytellers. Info from: St. Louis Conv & Visitors Bureau, 10 S Broadway, Suite 300, St. Louis, MO 63102.

TEILHARD DE CHARDIN, PIERRE: BIRTHDAY. May 1. French Jesuit author, paleontologist and philosopher, born at Sarcenat, France, May 1, 1881, he died at New York City, Apr 10, 1955.

TOURING THEATRE MONTH. May 1-31. Purpose: To call attention to performers, actors and numerous cultural touring groups that go to every state from September to June. Sponsor: Richard R. Falk Associates, Richard R. Falk, Dir, 147 W 42nd St, New York, NY 10036.

U.S.S.R. INTERNATIONAL LABOR DAY. May 1-2. Public holiday in U.S.S.R. "Official May Day demonstrations of working people."

U-2 INCIDENT: ANNIVERSARY. May 1. On the eve of a summit meeting between U.S. President Dwight D. Eisenhower and Soviet Premier Nikita Khruschev, a U-2 espionage plane flying at about 60,000 feet was shot down over Sverdlovsk, in central U.S.S.R., May 1, 1960. The pilot, CIA agent Francis Gary Powers, survived the crash, as did large parts of the aircraft, a suicide kit and sophisticated surveillance equipment. The sensational event, which U.S. officials described as a weather reconnaisance flight gone astray, resulted in cancellation of the summit meeting. Powers was tried, convicted and sentenced to ten years in prison, in a Moscow court. In 1962 he was returned to the U.S. in exchange for an imprisoned Soviet spy, but found an unfriendly American public which apparently believed he should have used his suicide kit. He died in a helicopter crash in 1977. See also entry for Powers, Aug 17.

MAY 2 — FRIDAY
122nd Day — Remaining, 243

ART INVITATIONAL EXHIBIT AND SALE. May 2-4. Somerset Mall, Troy, MI. Fine arts and three-dimensional works. Mixed media exhibit and sale. Info from: Somerset Mall, Peg DuBois, 2801 W Big Beaver Rd, Troy, MI 48084.

CARTER COUNTY WILDFLOWER TOURS AND BIRD WALKS. May 2-4. Roan Mountain, TN. Guest speakers and naturalist guided hikes. Info from: Roan Mountain State Resort Park, Rt 1, Box 236, Roan Mountain, TN 37687.

CROSBY, HARRY LILLIS (BING): BIRTHDAY. May 2. American singer, composer and actor, born at Tacoma, WA, May 2, 1904. Died while playing golf near Madrid, Spain, Oct 14, 1977.

DOWNTOWN DETROIT ETHNIC FESTIVALS. May 2-Sept 14. Philip A. Hart Plaza on the riverfront, Detroit, MI. Purpose: To preserve and display the rich ethnic heritage of the many diverse nationalities in the Detroit area. Each three-day weekend features a different ethnic group. Info from: Recreation Dept, 735 Randolph St, Detroit, MI 48226.

ENGLAND: EASTBOURNE INTERNATIONAL FOLK FESTIVAL. May 2-5. Various venues, Eastbourne, East Sussex.

EXPO 86: THE 1986 WORLD EXPOSITION. May 2-Oct 13. Vancouver, B.C., Canada. A 5½-month sanctioned World Exposition bringing together the arts and sciences for a unique celebration of the world's transportation and communications achievements. More than 15 million persons are expected to visit the Exposition which will host more than 40 nations on its 165-acre waterfront sites adjacent to downtown Vancouver. Info from: Expo 86, PO Box 1986, Station A, Vancouver, B.C., Canada V6C 2X5.

FESTIVAL OF HISTORIC HOUSES. May 2-4. Providence, RI. Info from: RI Dept of Economic Dev, Tourism Div, 7 Jackson Walkway, Providence, RI 02903.

GERMANY: THEATRE MEETING BERLIN. May 2-20. Info from: Berliner Festspiele, Budapester Strasse 50, 1 Berlin 30.

INTERNATIONAL STRANGE MUSIC WEEKEND. May 2-3. Carter Caves State Resort Park, Olive Hill, KY. Strange music is the rule, not the exception. Music played on everything from vacuum cleaners to instruments dating to antiquity. Workshops, concerts and enjoyment. Info from: John Tierney, Strange Music Weekend, Carter Caves State Park, Olive Hill, KY 41164.

INTERNATIONAL TUBA DAY. May 2. Purpose: To recognize tubists in musical organizations around the world who have to go through the hassle of handling a tuba. Annually, the first Friday in May. Sponsor: Joel Day, Unit 11, 10 Llanfair Rd, Ardmore, PA 19003.

ISLE OF EIGHT FLAGS SHRIMP FESTIVAL. May 2-4. Fernandina Beach, FL. Outdoor art festival along unique Centre Street in historic district. Big bands, aerobatics and blessing of the fleet. Info from: Chamber of Commerce, Box 472, Fernandina Beach, FL 32034.

LEONARDO DA VINCI: DEATH ANNIVERSARY. May 2. Italian artist died May 2, 1519, at age 67.

LOWERY, WILLIAM DAVID: BIRTHDAY. May 2. U.S. Representative of California's 41st district, Republican, of San Diego, CA, born there May 2, 1947.

MAY FELLOWSHIP DAY. May 2. Theme: "Let us speak together, pray together, Sisters." Focuses on building positive relationships in local communities. First Friday in May. Sponsor: Church Women United, 475 Riverside Dr, Rm 812, New York, NY 10115.

MAYFEST '86. May 2-3. State House Grounds and Senate Street, Columbia, SC. Street dance, international food fair, arts, crafts, entertainment and exhibits. Annually, the first weekend in May. Info from: Columbia Action Council, Judith Stringer, Festival Dir, 1527 Senate St, Columbia, SC 29201.

MEMPHIS IN MAY INTERNATIONAL FESTIVAL. May 2-31. Purpose: Five free weekend events, art exhibitions, business and education to celebrate Memphis traditions, while honoring a different country each year. 1986 festival salutes Japan. Sponsor: Memphis in May Internatl Festival, Kathi Olpin, Marketing Dir, 245 Wagner Place, Suite 220, Memphis, TN 38103.

NIXA SUCKER DAY. May 2. Nixa, MO. Purpose: To eat sucker, meet 20,000 new and old friends and have fun. Fish fry, gospel singing, "sucker grabbing," parade and coronation of Miss Sucker Day Queen. (Annually, the 1st Friday in May.) Info from: Jack Crotser, Publicity Chrmn, The Print Shop, Box E, Nixa, MO 65714.

OLD DOVER DAYS. May 2-4. Dover, DE. Info from: Delaware Development Office, Box 1401, Dover, DE 19903.

PHILADELPHIA OPEN HOUSE. May 2-18. Foot, bicycle, boat and bus tours of the Philadelphia area's contemporary homes and gardens. Sponsor: Friends of Independence National Historical Park, 313 Walnut St, Philadelphia, PA 19106.

POPE LEO XIII: BIRTHDAY. May 2. Giocchino Vincenzo Pecci, 256th Pope of the Roman Catholic Church, born at Carpineto, Italy, May 2, 1810. Elected Pope Feb 20, 1878. Died July 20, 1903.

ROBERT'S RULES DAY. May 2. Anniversary of the birth of Henry M. Robert (General, U.S. Army), author of *Robert's Rules of Order*, a standard parliamentary guide. Born May 2, 1837. Died May 11, 1923.

SOUTH CAROLINA FESTIVAL OF ROSES. May 2-4. Princess of roses pageant, canoe race, golf, tennis and softball tournaments, road races, concerts, puppet shows and arts and crafts. Info from: Chamber of Commerce, Box 328, Orangeburg, SC 29116.

SPRING FESTIVAL OF ARTS. May 2-4. Crafts and entertainment on the square. Info from: Marietta Parks & Recreation Dept, Box 609, Marietta GA 30061.

SUGARLOAF'S SPRING CRAFTS FESTIVAL. May 2-4. Maryland State Fairgrounds, Timonium, MD. Over 250 professional artists and craftspeople, demonstrations, live music, children's entertainment and delicious food. Sponsor: Sugarloaf Mt Works, Inc, Ijamsville, MD 21754.

TAD OF SAVANNAH. May 2-4. Savannah, GA. Restaurants serve their specialties in "bite-size portions" on the Plaza. Big bands, cloggers, singing groups and arts and crafts. Info from: Savannah Waterfront Assn, Box 572, Savannah, GA 31402.

TENNESSEE CRAFTS FAIR. May 2-4. Centennial Park, Nashville, TN. Purpose: Craft sales by 150 Tennessee craftspeople. Sponsor: Tennessee Crafts Fair, Inc, Alice C. Merritt, Dir, Box 150704, Nashville, TN 37215.

VALLEY OF FLOWERS FESTIVAL. May 2-4. Florissant Civic Center and Knights of Columbus Park. Tour of historic homes in Florissant, parade, craft show, carnival and bar-be-que. Info from: St. Louis Conv & Visitors Bureau, 10 S Broadway, Suite 300, St. Louis, MO 63102.

WALES: INTERNATIONAL WELSH RALLY. May 2-4. Motor racing throughout Wales.

WILDFLOWER WEEKEND. May 2-4. Natural Bridge State Resort Park, Slade, KY. Field trips and guest lecturers emphasizing the identification and appreciation of native flowers. Info from: Kentucky Dept. of Parks, Capital Plaza Tower, Frankfort, KY 40601.

MAY 3 — SATURDAY
123rd Day — Remaining, 242

APPLE BLOSSOM FESTIVAL. May 3-4. South Mountain Fairgrounds, Arendtsville, PA. Purpose: To promote the fruit industry of Adams County. Sponsor: Gettysburg Adams County Area Chamber of Commerce, 33 York St, Gettysburg, PA 17325.

BLUE RIDGE COMMUNITY COLLEGE FOLK ARTS FESTIVAL. May 3-4. Weyers Cave, VA. Purpose: Annual event in which 150-200 Shenandoah Valley craftsmen and musicians exhibit and demonstrate crafts. Sponsor: Student Govt Assn, Blue Ridge Community College, Mrs. Linda S. Hurt, Student Activities Advisor, Box 80, Weyers Cave, VA 24486.

BUCKS COUNTY KITE DAY. May 3. Core Creek Park, Langhorne, PA. Kite flying demonstrations, tips and techniques, stunting and kite fly—bring your own! Sponsor: Bucks County Dept of Parks & Recreation, 901 E Bridgetown Pike, Langhorne, PA 19047.

CENTRAL FLORIDA ANTIQUE MARKET SHOW AND SALE. May 3-4. Volusia County Fairgrounds, DeLand, FL. Info from: Chamber of Commerce, Box 629, DeLand, FL 32721.

May 1986

S	M	T	W	T	F	S
				1	2	3
4	5	6	7	8	9	10
11	12	13	14	15	16	17
18	19	20	21	22	23	24
25	26	27	28	29	30	31

CINCO de MAYO FIESTA. May 3-4. Traders Village, Grand Prairie, TX. Purpose: Salute to Mexican-American heritage with folklorico dancers, music, food. Info from: Traders Village, 2602 Mayfield Rd, Grand Prairie, TX 75051.

CONSTITUTION DAY or SWIETO TRZECIEGO MAJO. May 3. Poland. Celebrates ratification of Poland's first constitution, 1794.

EUROPEAN BRASS BAND CHAMPIONSHIPS. May 3-4. St. David's Hall, Cardiff, South Glamorgan, Wales.

FIESTA OF FIVE FLAGS: 10,000 METER RUN. May 3. Pensacola, FL. 10,000 meter course dropping from 95 feet above sea level at start to 5 feet above sea level at finish. (First Saturday in May.) Info from: Fiesta of Five Flags, Box 1943, Pensacola, FL 32589.

GILLIKINS OF OZ CONVENTION. May 3. Purpose: To celebrate the birth of L. Frank Baum, Royal Historian of Oz. Sponsor: Internatl Wizard of Oz Club, Inc, Fred M. Meyer, Secy, 220 N 11th St, Escanaba, MI 49829.

GONZALEZ, HENRY B: BIRTHDAY. May 3. U.S. Representative of Texas' 20th district, Democrat, of San Antonio, TX, born there on May 3, 1916.

HALL, RALPH MOODY: BIRTHDAY. May 3. U.S. Representative of Texas' 4th district, Democrat, of Rockwall, TX, born in Fate, TX on May 3, 1923.

JAPAN: CONSTITUTION MEMORIAL DAY. May 3. National holiday.

KENTUCKY DERBY. May 3. Churchill Downs, Louisville, KY. Annual running of "America's premier" thoroughbred horse race, inaugurated in 1875. First jewel in the "Triple Crown," traditionally followed by the Preakness (second Saturday after Derby) and the Belmont Stakes (fifth Saturday after Derby). Info from: Churchill Downs, 700 Central Ave, Louisville, Ky 40208.

MALTA: CARNIVAL. May 3-4. Valletta, Malta. Festival dates from 1535 when Knights of St. John introduced Carnival in Malta. Dancing, bands, decorated trucks and grotesque masks. Celebrated on the first weekend after May 1, each year.

MAYDAY IN METAMORA. May 3-4. Metamora, IN. Info from: Merchants Assn of Metamora, Duck Creek Place Restaurant, Metamora, IN 47030.

MEXICO: DAY OF THE HOLY CROSS. May 3. Celebrated especially by construction workers and miners, a festive day during which anyone who is building must give a party for the workers. A flower-decorated cross is placed on every piece of new construction in the country.

MIDWEST DOLL AND MINIATURE SHOW AND SALE. May 3-4. Purpose: One of midwest's largest displays of antique dolls, miniatures, dollhouses, doll clothes. Sponsor: Zion Park District, 2400 Dowie Dr, Zion, IL 60099.

NATIONAL HOMEBREW DAY. May 3. Purpose: A day for amateur brewers and friends to encourage and celebrate the enjoyment of quality homemade beer. Annually, the first Saturday of May. Sponsor: American Homebrewers Assn/Zymurgy, Box 287, Boulder, CO 80306.

NATIONAL PUBLIC RADIO BIRTHDAY. May 3. National non-commercial radio network, financed by Corporation for Public Broadcasting, began programming on May 3, 1971.

PRAGUE KOLACHE FESTIVAL. May 3. Purpose: To celebrate Czech heritage by the Czech people, named for their homeland city. (Always first Saturday in May.) Sponsor: Prague Kolache Festival, M. Moore, Box 7, Prague, OK 74864.

QUILT SHOW. May 3-4. Purpose: Display of old and new quilts from SE Pennsylvania. Sponsor: Boyertown Area Historical Society, 43 S Chestnut St, Boyertown, PA 19512.

SOHO FESTIVAL. May 3. Prince Street (Between West Broadway and 6th Avenue), New York, NY. Organized by the Soho Center for Arts and Education, a non profit organization serving the downtown New York City community. Sponsor: Soho Center for Arts and Education, Stacy Cohen, Festival Coordinator, 170 Thompson St, New York, NY 10012.

STRAWBERRY FESTIVAL. May 3-4. Village takes on the air of a country fair with feasting on fresh strawberries. Sponsor: Peddler's Village, PR Dept, Lahaska, PA 18931.

WYDEN, RONALD LEE: BIRTHDAY. May 3. U.S. Representative of Oregon's 3rd district, Democrat, of Portland, OR, born in Wichita, KS, May 3, 1949.

MAY 4 — SUNDAY
124th Day — Remaining, 241

ASIAN/PACIFIC AMERICAN HERITAGE WEEK. May 4.
☆ Presidential Proclamation. Dates not set at press time, but has been proclaimed annually for a week beginning during the first week of May since 1979. Pres. Reagan promised to continue it in a letter dated Oct 4, 1980. (May 4 begins the first full week of May, 1986.)

ASSOCIATION OF AMERICAN GEOGRAPHERS ANNUAL MEETING. May 4-7. Detroit, MI. Purpose: National meeting of members, workshops, paper and poster sessions and field trips. Sponsor: Assn of American Geographers, Robert T. Aangeenbrug, Exec Dir, 1710 16th St NW, Washington, DC 20009.

BE KIND TO ANIMALS WEEK. May 4-10. Purpose: To promote kindness and humane care towards animals. Annually, the first full week in May. Sponsor: American Humane Assn, 9725 E Hampden, Denver, CO 80231.

BED RACE FOR CURE. May 4. Rome, Georgia. Purpose: To raise money for Childrens United Research Effort, cancer and leukemia research and for Emory University Hospital in Atlanta, GA. Sponsor: WQTV, Leeta McDougald, Box 1187, Rome, GA 30161.

FRANKENMUTH SKYFEST. May 4. Frankenmuth Middle School, Frankenmuth, MI. Purpose: To encourage participation in a healthy outdoor sport that adapts to all age groups. First Sunday in May. Sponsors: Kite Kraft and Frankenmuth Parks & Recreation Dept. Info from: Audrey Fischer, Kite Kraft/School Haus Sq, Frankenmuth, MI 48734.

GOODWILL INDUSTRIES WEEK. May 4-10. Purpose: To call national attention to Goodwill Industries as a leader in vocational rehabilitation and employment services for disabled people. (Always the 1st full week in May.) Sponsor: Goodwill Industries of America, Inc, Communications Dept, 9200 Wisconsin Ave, Bethesda, MD 20814.

HAMMERSCHMIDT, JOHN PAUL: BIRTHDAY. May 4. U.S. Representative of Arkansas' 3rd district, Republican, of Harrison, AR, born there May 4, 1922.

MANN, HORACE: BIRTHDAY. May 4. American educator, author, public servant, known as the "father of public education in the U.S.," was born at Franklin, MA, on May 4, 1796. Founder of Westfield (MA) State College and editor of the influential *Common School Journal*. Mann died at Yellow Springs, OH, on Aug 2, 1859.

MICHIGAN RECYCLE WEEK. May 4-10. Purpose: To emphasize the need to recycle, how to recycle and where to take material collected. First full week of May. Sponsor: Michigan Recycling Coalition, Box 10240, Lansing, MI 48901.

MT WILSON METRIC CENTURY. May 4. 100 kilometer bicycle ride from Griffith Park, Los Angeles, to top of Mt Wilson and return. One mile climb. First Sunday in May each year. Info from: Palos Verdes Hostel Club, Frances E. Wielin, 16 Seaview Dr S, Rolling Hills Estates, CA 90274.

COPYRIGHT © 1985 BY WILLIAM D. CHASE and HELEN M. CHASE

NATIONAL FAMILY WEEK. May 4-10. Traditionally the first Sunday and the first full week in May are observed as National Family Week in many Christian churches.

NATIONAL INSECTOCUTOR WEEK. May 4-10. Purpose: To promote a wider use of insectocutors for the control of flying insects by means of electricity. Sponsor: Devpro Machine, Inc, Insectocutor Div, 80 Telegraph Rd, Middleport, NY 14105.

NATIONAL MUSIC WEEK. May 4-11. Theme: "Music for Mankind's Important Moments." Sponsor: Natl Fed of Music Clubs, 1336 N Delaware St, Indianapolis, IN 46202.

NATIONAL PET WEEK. May 4-10. Purpose: To promote public awareness of veterinary medical service as it relates to animal health and care. Sponsor: Auxiliary to the American Veterinary Medical Assn, Maxine Caley, Exec Secy, 227 S Wind Place, Manhattan, KS 66502.

NATIONAL POSTCARD WEEK. May 4-10. Purpose: To advertise use of picture postcards for correspondence and collecting. Annually, the first full week of May. Sponsor: Postcard Dealer & Collector, John H. McClintock, Editor, Box 1765, Manassas, VA 22110.

ORTHODOX EASTER SUNDAY. May 4. Observed by the Orthodox Church in America and other Orthodox churches on this date.

PEOPLE'S REPUBLIC OF CHINA: CHINESE YOUTH DAY. May 4.

RHODE ISLAND INDEPENDENCE DAY. May 4. Rhode Island abandoned allegiance to Great Britain on this day, 1776.

ROGATION SUNDAY. May 4. The fifth Sunday after Easter is the beginning of Rogationtide (Rogation Sunday and the three following days before Ascension Day). Rogation Day rituals date from the 5th century.

ROSEY'S GRAND MUTT DERBY. May 4. Michigan State Fair Coliseum, Detroit, MI. Fun for all dogs as they run every which way for ribbons and cash. Sponsor: The *Detroit News*, for the benefit of the Michigan Humane Society's Rosey Rescue League which aids injured animals. Info from: Charley Manos, News Columnist, *The Detroit News*, 615 Lafayette Blvd, Detroit, MI 48231.

SARATOGA ROTARY ART SHOW. May 4. Arts and crafts show, held annually on the first Sunday in May. Sponsor: Saratoga Rotary Club, Box 96, Saratoga, CA 95071.

SHAD FESTIVAL. May 4. Shad dinner and lectures on shad and its historical importance. Info from: Historic Bethlehem, Inc, 501 Main St, Bethlehem, PA 18018.

SPRING OPEN HOUSE. May 4. Durham, NC. Crafts of mid-nineteenth century rural North Carolina. Info from: Duke Homestead State Historic Site, 2828 Duke Homestead Rd, Durham, NC 27705.

STUDENTS' MEMORIAL DAY. May 4. Services in memory of four students (Allison Krause, 19; Sandra Lee Scheuer, 20; Jeffrey Glenn Miller, 20; and William K. Schroeder, 19) killed by National Guards during anti-war demonstrations at Kent (Ohio) State University, on May 4, 1970, and of all other students martyred in the cause of human rights.

TYLER, JULIA GARDINER: BIRTHDAY, May 4. Second wife of John Tyler, 10th president of the U.S., born at Gardiners Island, NY, May 4, 1820. Died July 10, 1889.

WINTERTHUR POINT-TO-POINT. May 4. Winterthur, DE. First Sunday in May. Info from: Winterthur, Rt 52, Winterthur, DE 19735.

May 1986

S	M	T	W	T	F	S
				1	2	3
4	5	6	7	8	9	10
11	12	13	14	15	16	17
18	19	20	21	22	23	24
25	26	27	28	29	30	31

MAY 5 — MONDAY
125th Day — Remaining, 240

AMERICAN BOWLING CONGRESS MASTERS TOURNAMENT. May 5-10. Cashman Field Ctr, Las Vegas, NV. Columbia 300. Top professional and non-professional bowlers compete for $200,000 prize fund. Info from: American Bowling Congress, 5301 S 76th St, Greendale, WI 53129.

AMY JOHNSON FLIGHT ANNIVERSARY. May 5. On May 5, 1930, Yorkshire born Amy Johnson began the first successful solo flight by a woman from England to Australia. Leaving Croydon Airport in a de Havilland D.H. 60 Gypsy Moth named "Jason," she flew 9,960 miles to Port Darwin, Australia, arriving May 28th. Song, "Amy, Wonderful Amy," celebrated fame of this "wonder girl of the air," who became a legend in her own lifetime. Fiftieth anniversary re-enactment at Croydon, on May 5, 1980, attracted more than 50,000 spectators. Amy Johnson, working as an air ferry pilot during World War II, was lost over the Thames Estuary in 1941.

BASKETBALL HALL OF FAME ENSHRINEMENT DAY. May 5. New electees to the Basketball Hall of Fame will be enshrined at the Hall of Fame. Info from: Basketball Hall of Fame, Box 179, 1150 W Columbus Ave, Springfield, MA 01101.

BASKETBALL HALL OF FAME ENSHRINEMENT DINNER. May 5. Chez Joseph, Agawam, MA. Info from: Pioneer Valley Assn, Box 749, Northampton, MA 01061.

CINCO de MAYO. May 5. Mexican national holiday recognizing anniversary of Battle of Puebla, May 5, 1862, in which Mexican troops under General Ignacio Zaragoza, outnumbered three-to-one, defeated invading French forces of Napoleon III. Anniversary is observed by Mexicans everywhere with parades, festivals, dances and speeches.

CINCO de MAYO CELEBRATION. May 5. Celebration of one of Mexico's great holidays with puppet shows, mariachi music and folklorico dancing. Info from: El Pueblo de Los Angeles State Historic Park, 845 N Alameda St, Los Angeles, CA 90012.

CINCO de MAYO FIESTAS. May 5. Phoenix, Tucson, Scottsdale, AZ. Traditional Mexican celebration of Mexico's victory over France. Info from: Arizona Office of Tourism, 1480 E Bethany Home, #180, Phoenix, AZ 85012.

EAST, JOHN PORTER: BIRTHDAY. May 5. U.S. Senator from North Carolina, Republican, of Greenville, NC, born in Springfield, IL, on May 5, 1931.

HALFWAY POINT OF SPRING. May 5. In Northern Hemisphere the midpoint of the spring season occurs on May 5 at 4:13 a.m., E.S.T. Spring, the second longest season of this year, lasts 92 days, 18 hours and 13 minutes.

JAPAN: CHILDREN'S DAY. May 5. National holiday. Observed on the fifth day of the fifth month each year.

JONES, JAMES R: BIRTHDAY. May 5. U.S. Representative of Oklahoma's 1st district, Democrat, of Tulsa, OK, born in Muskogee, OK, on May 5, 1939.

KOREA: CHILDREN'S DAY. May 5. A time for families to take their children on excursions. The various parks and children's centers throughout the country are packed with excited and colorfully dressed children. A national holiday since 1975.

MAY DAY BANK HOLIDAY. May 5. England, Wales, Scotland and Northern Ireland. Bank and public holiday.

NATIONAL GOLDEN GLOVES TOURNAMENT OF CHAMPIONS. May 5-10. Cedar Rapids, IA. Purpose: To determine national amateur boxing champions. Sponsor: Golden Gloves Assn of America, Inc, Stan Gallup, Exec Secy, 9000 Menaul NE, Albuquerque, NM 87112.

NATIONAL PHOTO WEEK. May 5-11. Purpose: A tribute to photography and picture-taking. Celebrated in the United States and Canada by photo hobbyists, members of the photography industry and amateur photographers of all ages—a

COPYRIGHT © 1985 BY WILLIAM D. CHASE and HELEN M. CHASE

time to "Remember with Pictures." (Begins on first Monday in May.) Sponsor: Photo Marketing Assn, 3000 Picture Place, Jackson, MI 49201.

NELLY BLY: BIRTHDAY. May 5. Nelly Bly, American journalist and fighter for women's rights, whose real name was Elizabeth Cochrane Seaman, was born at Armstrong County, PA, May 5, 1867. Her career is said to have started as result of her heated response to newspaper article entitled "What Girls Are Good For." Called "the best reporter in America" she courageously wrote on then dangerous subjects of divorce, insanity, mashers, factory conditions, poverty, capital punishment, etc. Died of pneumonia, at New York City, Jan 27, 1922. Marker placed on her grave 56 years later, June 22, 1978.

NETHERLANDS: LIBERATION DAY. May 5. Marks liberation of the Netherlands from Nazi Germany, May 5, 1945.

NORTHERN IRELAND: BELFAST CITY MARATHON. May 5. Belfast, County Antrim. Info from: Belfast Marathon, City Hall, Belfast BT1 5GS.

SPACE MILESTONE: FREEDOM 7 (US). May 5. First US astronaut, second man in space, Alan Shepard, Jr, projected 115 miles into space in suborbital flight reaching a speed of over 5,000 miles per hour. May 5, 1961.

STAFF APPRECIATION WEEK. May 5-9. Purpose: To create awareness of, and express gratitude for, the dedication of all school staffs. Celebrated during the first week of May in the Flint, MI, Community Schools. Info from: Flint Community Schools, Len Blewett, Public Affairs Div, 923 E Kearsley St, Flint, MI, 48502.

SWITZERLAND: PACING THE BOUNDS. May 5. Liestal, Switzerland. Citizens set off at 8 a.m., and march along boundaries to beat of drums and firing of pistols and muskets. Occasion for fetes (Monday before Ascension Day.)

THAILAND: CORONATION DAY: ANNIVERSARY. May 5. Thailand.

ZAMBIA: LABOR DAY. May 5. Zambia. Dedicated to "Freedom and Labor," the motto of Zambia's only political party, UNIP. A day of mobilization for maximum productivity. First Monday in May.

MAY 6 — TUESDAY

126th Day — Remaining, 239

BIRTHDAY OF THE FIRST ADHESIVE POSTAGE STAMP. May 6. Purpose: To commemorate the birthday of the first adhesive Postage Stamp (Penny Black of Great Britain) and to promote philately. First postage stamp issued May 6, 1840. Sponsor: *The Philatelic Journalist*, Gustav Detjen, Jr, Editor, 154 Laguna Ct, St. Augustine Shores, FL 32086.

ECKERT, FRED J: BIRTHDAY. May 6. U.S. Representative of New York's 30th district, Republican, of Rochester, NY, born there on May 6, 1941.

HINDENBURG DISASTER ANNIVERSARY. May 6. At 7:20 p.m., on May 6, 1937, the dirigible *Hindenburg* exploded as it approached the mooring mast at Lakehurst, NJ, after a trans-Atlantic voyage. Of its 97 passengers and crew, 36 died in the accident, which ended the dream of mass transportation via dirigible.

ISRAEL: YOM HASHOAH (HOLOCAUST DAY). May 6. A day established by Israel's Knesset as a memorial to the Jewish dead of World War II. Anniversary on Jewish calendar of Nisan 27, 5705 (corresponding to Apr 10, 1945 on the Gregorian calendar), the day on which Allied troops liberated the first Nazi concentration camp, one of the most notorious, Buchenwald, north of Weimar, established in 1937, where about 56,000 prisoners, many of them Jewish, perished.

LEATH, JAMES MARVIN: BIRTHDAY. May 6. U.S. Representative of Texas' 11th district, Democrat, of Waco, TX, born at Henderson, TX, on May 6, 1931.

MOORHEAD, CARLOS J: BIRTHDAY. May 6. U.S. Representative of California's 22nd district, Republican, of Glendale, CA, born at Long Beach, CA, on May 6, 1922.

NATIONAL NURSES' DAY. May 6. Purpose: To pay tribute to all those in the nursing profession for their vital contribution to mankind in providing health care services to people of all ages. Info from: Edwin L. Scanlan, Founder & Sponsor, Natl Nurses' Day, Box 95, Red Bank, NJ 07701.

NATIONAL ONLINE MEETING. May 6-8. Sheraton Centre Hotel, New York, NY. Three full days of online activities with three main events—presented papers, an exhibition and product review sessions. Info from: Natl Online Meeting, Martha E. Williams, Program Chrmn, Univ of Illinois, Coordinated Science Laboratory, 1101 W Springfield, Urbana, IL 61801.

PENN, JOHN: BIRTHDAY. May 6. Signer of the Declaration of Independence, born, Caroline County, VA, May 6, 1740. Died Sept. 14, 1788.

SACK OF ROME: ANNIVERSARY. May 6. The Renaissance ends with barbarous Sack of Rome beginning on May 6, 1527. Imperialist troops, unpaid and mutinous, under Charles, Duke of Bourbon (who was killed during first assault on city), killed some 4,000 inhabitants of Rome, looted works of art and libraries. Pope Clement VII surrendered on June 7th and was imprisoned at the Castel St. Angelo. Nearly a year passed before order could be restored in the city.

SHELBY, RICHARD C: BIRTHDAY. May 6. U.S. Representative of Alabama's 7th district, Democrat of Tuscaloosa, AL, born in Birmingham, AL, on May 6, 1934.

TAGORE, RABINDRANATH: BIRTHDAY. May 6. Hindu poet, mystic and musical composer, was born at Calcutta, May 6, 1861. Received Nobel Prize (Literature) in 1913. Died at Calcutta, Aug 7, 1941. His birthday is observed in Bangladesh on the 25th day of the Bengali month of Baishakha (2nd week of May), when the poet laureate is honored with songs, dances and discussions of his works.

VALENTINO, RUDOLPH: BIRTHDAY. May 6, Rodolpho Alfonzo Rafaello Pietro Filiberto Guglieimi Di Valentina D'Antonguolla, whose professional name was Rudolph Valentino, was born on May 6, 1895, at Castellaneta, Italy. Popular cinema actor. Press reports claim that "at least one weeping veiled woman in black has brought flowers to his tomb" (at Hollywood Memorial Park) on the anniversary every year since his death at New York City, Aug 23, 1926.

MAY 7 — WEDNESDAY

127th Day — Remaining, 238

BEAUFORT SCALE DAY. May 7. A day to honor the British naval officer, Sir Francis Beaufort, who devised (1805) a scale of wind force from 0 (calm) to 12 (hurricane) which was based on observation, not requiring any special instruments. The scale was adopted for international use in 1874, and has since been enlarged and refined. Beaufort was born at Flower Hill, Meath, Ireland, on May 7, 1774, and died at Brighton, England on Dec 17, 1857.

BROWNING, ROBERT: BIRTHDAY. May 7. English poet, born May 7, 1812. Died, Venice, Dec 12, 1889.

DOMENICI, PETE V: BIRTHDAY. May 7. U.S. Senator from New Mexico, Republican, of Albuquerque NM, born in Albuquerque on May 7, 1932.

FIRST PRESIDENTIAL INAUGURAL BALL ANNIVERSARY. May 7. Commemorating the inauguration of George Washington, the first Presidential Inaugural Ball was held in New York City, May 7, 1789.

COPYRIGHT © 1985 BY WILLIAM D. CHASE and HELEN M. CHASE

GRAND BLANC'S YOUNG AUTHORS' CONFERENCE. May 7. Grand Blanc, MI. Purpose: To promote continued interest in writing by recognizing the achievements of talented young writers. Sponsor: Grand Blanc Community Schools, Dr. Gary Lipe, Assistant Superintendent, 11920 S Saginaw Rd, Grand Blanc, MI 48439.

HAMBURG: HARBOR BIRTHDAY. May 7. Hamburg, Germany. "Hafengeburtstag" celebrates establishment of Hamburg as a free city, May 7, 1189.

LUSITANIA **SINKING: ANNIVERSARY.** May 7. British passenger liner *Lusitania*, on return trip from New York to Liverpool, carrying nearly 2,000 passengers, was torpedoed by German submarine off the coast of Ireland, sinking within minutes on May 7, 1915. 1,198 lives lost. U.S. President Wilson sent note of protest to Berlin on May 13, but Germany, which had issued warning in advance, pointed to *Lusitania's* cargo of ammunition for Britain. U.S. maintained "neutrality," for the time being.

MacLEISH, ARCHIBALD: BIRTHDAY. May 7. American poet and Librarian of Congress (1939-1944) was born at Glencoe, IL, May 7, 1892. MacLeish, who was also a playwright, Pulitzer Prize winner, editor, lawyer, professor and farmer, died at Boston, MA, on Apr 20, 1982.

UNITED CEREBRAL PALSY ASSOCIATION CONFERENCE. May 7-10. Purpose: To exchange information and ideas on current treatment and services for people with disabilities and to discuss research and legislation benefiting the handicapped. Sponsor: United Cerebral Palsy Assn, Inc, 66 E 34th St, New York, NY 10016.

MAY 8 — THURSDAY
128th Day — Remaining, 237

ASCENSION DAY. May 8. Forty days after Easter Sunday. Commemorates Christ's ascension into Heaven. Observed since A.D. 68.

BELGIUM: PROCESSION OF THE HOLY BLOOD. May 8. Religious historical procession. Recalls heroic, adventurous crusaders, including Count Thierry of Alsace who carried back relic of the Holy Blood. Always on Ascension Day.

DE CONCINI, DENNIS: BIRTHDAY. May 8. U.S. Senator from Arizona, Democrat, of Tucson, AZ, born there May 8, 1937.

DUNANT, JEAN HENRI: BIRTHDAY. May 8. Swiss author and philanthropist, founder of the Red Cross Society, was born at Geneva, May 8, 1828. Nobel Prize winner in 1901. Dunant died at Heiden, Switzerland, Oct 30, 1910.

ENGLAND: BEATING THE BOUNDS or PAROCHIAL PERAMBULATIONS. May 8. Usually observed during Rogationtide, and especially on Ascension Day. Ancient custom of walking around the parish boundaries, to preserve "a correct knowledge of and due respect for, the bounds of parochial and individual property." A triennial ceremony at the Tower of London (1981, 1984, 1987, etc). Also sometimes called Gauge Days. Custom dates from 16th century.

ENGLAND: HELSTON FURRY DANCE. May 8. The world famous Helston Furry Dance is held each year on May 8 (except when the 8th is a Sunday or Monday in which case it is held on the previous Saturday). Dancing around the streets of Helston, Cornwall, begins early in the morning and continues throughout the day. The "Furry" dance leaves Guildhall at the stroke of noon and winds its way in and out of many of the larger buildings. Final dance at 5 p.m.

LAVOISIER, ANTOINE LAURENT: EXECUTION ANNIVERSARY. May 8. French chemist and the "father of modern chemistry." Especially noted for having first explained the real nature of combustion and for showing that matter is not destroyed in chemical reactions. Born at Paris on Aug 26, 1743, Lavoisier was guillotined on May 8, 1794 at the Place de la Revolution for his former position as a tax collector. The Revolutionary Tribunal is reported to have responded to a plea to spare his life with the statement: "We need no more scientists in France."

MINT 400. May 8-11. Las Vegas, NV. Racing buggies, sedans and trucks ballot one of the toughest off-road racing courses in the world. Info from: Nevada Commission on Tourism, Capitol Complex, Carson City, NV 89710.

MOON PHASE: NEW MOON. May 8. Moon enters New Moon phase at 5:10 p.m., E.S.T.

PELLA TULIP TIME FESTIVAL. May 8-10. Purpose: To pay homage to the founders of this predominantly Dutch community. Activities include coronation of queen, parades, Dutch singing and dancing. Sponsor: Pella Historical Society, Box 145, Pella, IA 50219.

PRINCE GEORGE REGIONAL FOREST EXHIBITION. May 8-11. Exhibition Park, Prince George, British Columbia, Canada. Purpose: To alert public awareness to the forests and the importance of the industry to the country. Sponsor: Prince George Regional Forest Exhibition Society, 3851 18th Ave, Prince George, BC, Canada V2N 1B1.

SEATTLE INTERNATIONAL FILM FESTIVAL. May 8-June 8. The Egyptian Theatre, Seattle, WA. Purpose: To promote film awareness and appreciation in the Seattle community. Sponsor: The Seattle Internatl Film Festival, 801 E Pine St, Seattle, WA 98122.

SPOKANE LILAC FESTIVAL. May 8-18. Spokane, WA. A spring festival with lilac show, selection of the lilac festival queen and the Lilac Festival/Armed Forces Torchlight Parade. Info from: Spokane Lilac Festival, Box 802, Spokane, WA 99210.

THOMPSON, JAMES R: BIRTHDAY. May 8. James R. Thompson, Governor of Illinois, Republican, was born at Chicago, IL, on May 8, 1936.

TRAFICANT, JAMES A JR: BIRTHDAY. May 8. U.S. Representative of Ohio's 17th district, Democrat, of Poland, OH, born in Youngstown, OH, May 8, 1941.

TRUMAN, HARRY S: BIRTHDAY. May 8. The 33rd President of the U.S., succeeded to that office upon the death of Franklin D. Roosevelt, Apr 12, 1945 and served until Jan 20, 1953. Born at Lamar, MO, May 8, 1884, Truman was the last of nine U.S. presidents who did not attend college. Affectionately nicknamed "Give 'em Hell Harry" by admirers. The only employment of atomic bombs on populated areas during war occurred during his presidency (Aug 6 and Aug 9, 1945, at Hiroshima and Nagasaki, Japan). Truman died at Kansas City, MO, on Dec 26, 1972.

VE DAY. May 8. Victory in Europe Day commemorates unconditional surrender of Germany to Allied Forces. The surrender document was signed by German representatives at General Dwight D. Eisenhower's headquarters at Rheims, to become effective, and hostilities to end, at one minute past midnight on May 9, 1945. President Harry S Truman on May 8th, declared May 9, 1945 to be "V-E Day." A separate German surrender to the U.S.S.R. was signed at Karlshorst, near Berlin, on May 8th. See May 9 for Victory Day observance in the U.S.S.R.

MAY 9 — FRIDAY
129th Day — Remaining, 236

ASHCROFT, JOHN DAVID: BIRTHDAY. May 9. John D. Ashcroft, Governor of Missouri, Republican, was born at Chicago, IL, on May 9, 1942.

May 1986

S	M	T	W	T	F	S
				1	2	3
4	5	6	7	8	9	10
11	12	13	14	15	16	17
18	19	20	21	22	23	24
25	26	27	28	29	30	31

COPYRIGHT © 1985 BY WILLIAM D. CHASE and HELEN M. CHASE

ASSOCIATION OF COLLEGE UNIONS-INTERNATIONAL CHAMPIONSHIP. May 9. Cashman Field Ctr, Las Vegas, NV. Top regional bowlers vie for titles with the all events champion earning a berth in the World Cup. Info from: American Bowling Congress, 5301 S 76th St, Greendale, WI 53129.

BOYD, BELLE: BIRTHDAY. May 9. Notorious Confederate spy who later became an actress and lecturer, was born at Martinsburg, VA, on May 9, 1843. Author of the book, *Belle Boyd in Camp and Prison*, she died June 11, 1900.

BROWN, JOHN: BIRTHDAY. May 9. Abolitionist leader born, Torrington, CT, May 9, 1800. Hanged, Dec 2, 1859. Leader of attack on Harpers Ferry, Oct 16, 1859, which was intended to give impetus to movement for escape and freedom for slaves. His aim was frustrated, in fact resulting in increased polarization and sectional animosity. Legendary martyr.

CZECHOSLOVAKIA: NATIONAL HOLIDAY. May 9.

EUROPEAN COMMUNITIES: ANNIVERSARY OBSERVANCE. May 9. "Anniversary of the Declaration of Robert Schuman." Info from: European Community Information Service, Delegation of the Commission of the European Communities, 2100 M St, NW, Suite 707, Washington, DC 20037. (EC, the Common Market, commemorates the May 9, 1950, announcement by French statesman, Robert Schuman, of the "Schuman Plan" for establishing a single authority for production of coal, iron and steel in France and Germany.)

HANG GLIDING SPECTACULAR. May 9-11. Purpose: Competitions for novice and advanced pilots from around the U.S. to promote hang gliding for fun. Second weekend in May. Sponsor: Kitty Hawk Kites, Box 340, Nags Head, NC 27959.

LITTLE RIVER DAYS. May 9-10. Little River Park, Hopkinsville, KY. A celebration of spring with street dance, golf tournaments, barbecue, arts, crafts, canoe and road races. Sponsor: WKOA Radio, Edward Owen, Box 951, Hopkinsville, KY 42240.

McMILLAN, J ALEX III: BIRTHDAY. May 9. U.S. Representative of North Carolina's 9th district, Republican, of Charlotte, NC, born in Charlotte on May 9, 1932.

TRIBUTE TO GRANDPA JONES. May 9-10. Ozark Folk Center. "Special ceremonies honoring the 50+ years of show business." Info from: Ozark Folk Ctr, Mountain View, AR 72560.

TULIP FESTIVAL. May 9-12. Albany, NY. Coronation of Queen, parade and displays and flower shows. Info from: Albany County Conv & Visitors Bureau, 600 Broadway, Albany, NY 12207.

U.S.S.R.: VICTORY DAY. May 9. National holiday observed annually to commemorate the defeat of Nazi Germany in World War II, and to honor the 20 million Soviet people who died in that war. Among the traditional rituals of this celebration, veterans renew wartime friendships, reminisce and swap stories, sing again some of the front-line songs and visit national cemeteries. Hostilities ceased and the German surrender became effective at one minute after midnight on May 9, 1945. See May 8 entry for VE Day.

WICHITA RIVER FESTIVAL. May 9-18. Music, sports, food, drama and offbeat events. Info from: Wichita Festivals, 1305 E Waterman, Suite D, Wichita, KS 67211.

WORLD WHIMMY DIDDLE COMPETITION. May 9-10. Purpose: Gee Haw Whimmy Diddle Competitions with awards, demonstrations, storytelling and musical entertainment. Sponsor: Southern Highland Handicraft Guild, Blair H White, Box 9545, Asheville, NC 28815.

MAY 10 — SATURDAY

130th Day — Remaining, 235

AMERICAN ASSOCIATION OF ORTHODONTISTS ANNUAL MEETING. May 10-14. Chicago, IL. Sponsor: American Assn of Orthodontists, 460 North Lindbergh Blvd, St. Louis, MO 63141.

AMERICAN BOWLING CONGRESS NATIONAL SENIORS TOURNAMENT. May 10-11. Cashman Field Ctr, Las Vegas, NV. Age division champions (70 and over, 65-69, 60-64, 55-59) from more than 40 states compete for national titles. Info from: American Bowling Congress, 5301 S 76th St, Greendale, WI 53129.

BLACK HILLS BALLOON INVITATIONAL. May 10-11. Ft Meade Parade Grounds, Sturgis, SD. Family oriented entertainment. Sponsor: McPherson Propane, Box 126, Sturgis, SD 57785.

BRAILLE INSTITUTE TRACK AND FIELD OLYMPICS. May 10. Braille Institute Youth Center, Los Angeles, CA 90068. Purpose: To offer athletic competition to blind and visually handicapped youths. Sponsor: Braille Institute, Doyle Peck, Communications Dir, 741 N Vermont Ave, Los Angeles, CA 90029.

CONFEDERATE MEMORIAL DAY, May 10. North Carolina and South Carolina.

CRAFT FAIR USA: INDOOR SHOW. May 10-11. Wisconsin State Fair Park. Sale of handcrafted items: jewelry, pottery, weaving, leather, wood, glass and sculpture. Info from: Dennis R. Hill, Dir, 3233 S Villa Circle, West Allis, WI 53227.

DIXIE HANDICAP AT PIMLICO RACE COURSE. May 10. One of the oldest and richest thoroughbred races in North America. Conducted on the turf course at one mile and one-half. Open to 3 year olds and upward. Info from: Pimlico Race Course, Baltimore, MD 21215.

FIESTA DE LA RIBA. May 10. St. Petersburg, FL. Purpose: To celebrate Salvador Dali's Birthday. Museum gallery tours, entertainment and a giant birthday card for all to sign. Sponsor: The Salvador Dali Museum, 1000 3rd St, South, St. Petersburg, FL 33701.

GOLDEN SPIKE DAY. May 10. Anniversary of the meeting of Union Pacific and Central Pacific railways, at Promontory Point, UT, May 10, 1869. On that day a golden spike valued at about $400 was driven by Leland Stanford, president of the Central Pacific, to celebrate the linkage. (It is said that he missed the first stroke!) The golden spike was promptly removed for preservation. Long called the final link in the ocean-to-ocean railroad, this event cannot be accurately described as completing the transcontinental railroad, but it did complete continuous rail tracks between Omaha and Sacramento. See Aug 15 entry for final link.

GRAND PRAIRIE WESTERN DAYS. May 10-18. Purpose: Tribute to western heritage featuring Professional Rodeo Cowboys Assn rodeo performances, western art show, Old West gun show, parade and barbecue. Info from: Traders Village, 2602 Mayfield Rd, Grand Prairie, TX 75051.

GUNDERSON, STEVEN CRAIG: BIRTHDAY. May 10. U.S. Representative of Wisconsin's 3rd district, Republican, of Osseo, WI, born at Eau Claire, WI, May 10, 1951.

IROQUOIS STEEPLECHASE. May 10. Nashville, TN. Purpose: To raise money for Vanderbilt Children's Hospital and to provide amateur racing at its very best. Annually, the second Saturday in May. Sponsor: Volunteer State Horsemen's Assn, Box 22711, Nashville, TN 37202.

JAMESTOWN SETTLEMENT CELEBRATION. May 10-11. Jamestown, VA. Celebration at Jamestown Festival Park commemorates Jamestown's founding in 1607. Craft demonstrations, games, music and military drills. Info from: Special Events Coord, Box JF, Williamsburg, VA 23187.

COPYRIGHT © 1985 BY WILLIAM D. CHASE and HELEN M. CHASE

JUBILEE ARTS FESTIVAL. May 10. Bennettsville, SC. Purpose: To promote arts and crafts in the community. Sponsor: Marlboro Area Arts Council, 729 Lakeshore Dr, Bennettsville, SC 29512.

KENTUCKY SCOTTISH WEEKEND. May 10-11. General Butler State Resort Park, Carrollton, KY. A celebration of Scottish heritage with pipe bands, highland and country dancing, athletic competition and border-collie herding demonstration. Info from: Kentucky Scottish Weekend, Inc, Box 5396, Louisville, KY 40205.

LOG DRIVER HALF MARATHON. May 10. Purpose: A TAC-certified marathon between Hayward and the Telemark resort near Cable, WI. Info from: American Classic, Box 31, Hayward, WI 54843.

MUSLIM HOLIDAY: RAMADHAN. May 10. Beginning of month of fasting. Muslim calendar date: Ramadhan 1, 1406. Gregorian calendar date of observance may vary by one day. The month of Ramadhan traditionally begins when Moslem sheiks in Saudi Arabia sight the new moon. During this holy month of Islam, Moslems abstain from food, drink, smoking, gambling and sex from sunrise to sunset.

NATIONAL MUSHROOM HUNTING CHAMPIONSHIP. May 10-11. Boyne City, MI. Info from: Chamber of Commerce, 28 S Lake St, Boyne City, MI 49712.

NATIONAL WINDMILL DAY. May 10. Netherlands. Second Saturday in May each year. About 950 windmills survive and some 300 are still used occasionally and have been designated national monuments by the government. As many windmills as possible are in operation on National Windmill Day for the benefit of tourists.

NATIVE AMERICAN DAY. May 10. Formerly American Indian Day. Traditional observance has been on 2nd Saturday in May or the 4th Friday in September. First proclaimed for the year 1916. Observance dates vary.

"100 TONS OF FUN." May 10. Danville, VA. Purpose: To promote people who weigh over 200 pounds and to build pride in bigness. Mr. and Ms. 100 Tons of Fun Beauty Pageant. Annually, the second Saturday in May. Sponsor: WAKG Radio, Danville, VA. Info from: Tom Miller, Station Mgr. WAKG, Box 1629, Danville, VA 24541.

PRATER'S MILL COUNTRY FAIR. May 10-11. (Also Oct 11-12.) Arts and crafts show in the atmosphere of an old-fashioned country fair. Info from: The Prater's Mill Country Fair, 101 Timberland Dr, Dalton, GA 30720.

PREAKNESS FESTIVAL WEEK. May 10-17. A week of activities celebrating the 111th running of the Preakness Stakes throughout downtown Baltimore. Info from: Baltimore Office of Promotion and Tourism, 34 Market Place, Suite 310, Baltimore, MD 21202.

ROSS, GEORGE: BIRTHDAY. May 10. Lawyer and signer of the Declaration of Independence, born, New Castle, DE, May 10, 1730. Died, Philadelphia, PA July 14, 1779.

STILWELL STRAWBERRY FESTIVAL. May 10. Purpose: To promote the strawberry industry in and around the Stilwell area. Sponsor: Stilwell Kiwanis Club, Stilwell, OK 74960.

TANGLEWOOD STEEPLECHASE. May 10. Tanglewood Park, Winston-Salem, NC. Info from: Tanglewood Park, Box 1040, Clemmons, NC 27012.

VANCOUVER, GEORGE: DEATH ANNIVERSARY. May 10. English navigator, explorer and author for whom Vancouver Island and the cities of Vancouver (British Columbia and Washington) are named, was born in 1758 (exact date unknown) and joined the navy at the age of 13. He surveyed the coasts of Australia, New Zealand and western North America, and sailed with Capt. James Cook to the Arctic in 1780. Vancouver died at Petersham, Surrey on May 10, 1798, just as he was correcting the final pages of his *Journal* which was published in three volumes at London later that year.

MAY 11 — SUNDAY
131st Day — Remaining, 234

BOB MARLEY DAY. May 11. Anniversary of the death, at Miami, FL, on May 11, 1981, of Bob Marley. Marley, with his musical group, The Wailers, was one of the most popular and influential performers of reggae music, an "off-beat-accented Jamaican" music closely associated with the political/religious Rastafarian movement (admirers of the late Ethiopian emperor, Haile Selassie). Marley, who died of cancer, was born Feb 6, 1945 at Rhoden Hall in northern Jamaica. The anniversary of his death has been observed as Bob Marley Day in Jamaica.

FAIRBANKS, CHARLES WARREN: BIRTHDAY. May 11. Twenty-sixth Vice President of the U.S. (1905-1909) born, Unionville Center, OH, May 11, 1852. Died, Indianapolis, IN, June 4, 1918.

FIESTA OF FIVE FLAGS. May 11-18. Purpose: Re-enactment of landing of Don Tristen de Luna and his Spanish colonists in 1559. Parades and Pageants. (Second Sunday in May.) Sponsor: Fiesta of Five Flags Assn, 2121 W Intendencia St, Box 1943, Pensacola, FL 32589.

GIRLS CLUB WEEK. May 11-17. Purpose: To focus national and local attention on the growth of GCA as an advocacy organization for the rights and needs of girls. Sponsor: Girls Clubs of America, Inc, Mary Jo Gallo, Dir PR. 205 Lexington Ave, 2nd Floor, New York, NY 10016.

HART, JOHN: DEATH ANNIVERSARY. May 11. Signer of the Declaration of Independence, farmer and legislator, born about 1711 (exact date unknown), in Stonington, CT. Died May 11, 1779.

JEFFORDS, JAMES M: BIRTHDAY. May 11. U.S. Representative at large from Vermont, Republican of Rutland, VT, born in Rutland on May 11, 1934.

JEWISH HERITAGE WEEK. May 11-18. Purpose: To foster intergroup understanding and greater appreciation of each other's culture, history and heritage. Celebrated by public and private schools, communities and organizations throughout the country. Sponsor: Jewish Community Relations Council of NY, 111 West 40th St, New York, NY 10018.

KIWANIS PRAYER WEEK. May 11-17. Purpose: Encourages Kiwanis clubs to promote religious activities throughout their communities and recognize individuals for their contributions to spiritual welfare. Sponsor: Kiwanis Internatl, Program Development Dept, 3636 Woodview Trace, Indianapolis, IN 46268.

MINNESOTA: ADMISSION DAY. May 11. Became 32nd State on this day in 1858.

MOTHER'S DAY. May 11. Presidential Proclamation. "Always ☆ the 2nd Sunday in May." (Pub Res No 2 of May 8, 1914.)

MOTHER'S DAY. May 11. Observed first in 1907 at the request of Anna Jarvis of Philadelphia who asked her church to hold service in memory of all mothers on anniversary of her mother's death. (Second Sunday in May.)

NATIONAL HISTORIC PRESERVATION WEEK. May 11-17. Purpose: To draw public attention to accomplishments of groups working to preserve neighborhoods, districts, landmark buildings, open space and maritime heritage. Sponsor: Natl Trust for Historic Preservation, Kate Merlino, Public Affairs, Div, 1785 Massachusetts Ave, NW, Washington, DC 20036.

NATIONAL HOSPITAL WEEK. May 11-17. Purpose: To focus attention on the work that hospitals are performing in providing high quality health care. Sponsor: American Hospital Assn, 840 N Lake Shore Dr, Chicago, IL 60611.

NATIONAL NURSING HOME WEEK. May 11-17. Purpose: To acquaint the public with the services nursing homes and other long-term health care facilities provide. Activities are conducted by individual nursing homes on a local basis. Begins

May 1986

S	M	T	W	T	F	S
				1	2	3
4	5	6	7	8	9	10
11	12	13	14	15	16	17
18	19	20	21	22	23	24
25	26	27	28	29	30	31

COPYRIGHT © 1985 BY WILLIAM D. CHASE and HELEN M. CHASE

Mother's Day and ends following Saturday. Sponsor: American Health Care Assn, Dept of Public Affairs, 1200 15th St NW, Washington, DC 20005.

NATIONAL TRANSPORTATION WEEK. May 11-17. Presi-
☆ dential Proclamation. "Issued for week including 3rd Friday in May since 1960." (PL 86-475 of May 20, 1960, first asked; PL 87-449 of May 14, 1962 asks for an annual proclamation.)

NORTHERN IRELAND: SEALINK CLASSIC FISHING FESTIVAL. May 11-17. "Fished on the Erne waters, in and around Enniskillen, County Fermanagh. Considered to be the most densely populated coarse fishing waters in Western Europe. Fished by the world's leading coarse fisherman."

POLICE WEEK. May 11-17. Presidential Proclamation. "Always
☆ week including May 15, since 1962. Proc 3537, May 4, 1963, covers all succeeding years." (PL87-726 of Oct 1, 1962.)

MAY 12 — MONDAY
132nd Day — Remaining, 233

DANIEL, DAN: BIRTHDAY. May 12. U.S. Representative of Virginia's 5th district, Democrat, of Danville, VA, born at Chatham, VA, on May 12, 1914.

DYMALLY, MERVYN M: BIRTHDAY. May 12. U.S. Representative of California's 31st district, Democrat, of Compton, CA, was born in Cedros, Trinidad, West Indies, on May 12, 1926.

HUTTO, EARL: BIRTHDAY. May 12. U.S. Representative of Florida's 1st district, Democrat, of Panama City, FL, born in Midland City, AL, on May 12, 1926.

LEAR, EDWARD: BIRTHDAY. May 12. English artist and author, best remembered for his light verse and limericks. Lear was born at Highgate, England on May 12, 1812, and died at San Remo, Italy, Jan 29, 1888. See also: entry for Limerick Day, below.

LIMERICK DAY. May 12. Observed on the birthday of one of its champions, Edward Lear (q.v.). The limerick, which dates from the early 18th century, has been described as the "only fixed verse form indigenous to the English language." It gained its greatest popularity following the publication of Edward Lear's *Book of Nonsense* (and its sequels). Write a limerick today! Example: There was a young poet named Lear/Who said, it is just as I fear/Five lines are enough/For this kind of stuff/Make a limerick each day of the year.

LUJAN, MANUEL JR: BIRTHDAY. May 12. U.S. Representative of New Mexico's 1st district, Republican of Albuquerque, NM, born in San Ildefonso, NM, on May 12, 1928.

NATIONAL SALVATION ARMY WEEK. May 12-18. Purpose: To extend public knowledge of the religious and social welfare ministry of The Salvation Army. Sponsor: The Salvation Army, Lt. Colonel Leon Ferraez, Dir, Natl Communications Dept, 799 Bloomfield Ave, Verona, NJ 07044.

NIGHTINGALE, FLORENCE: BIRTHDAY. May 12. English nurse and public health activist who, through her unselfish devotion to nursing, contributed more than perhaps any other single person to the development of modern nursing procedures and dignity of nursing as a profession. Founder of the Nightingale training school for nurses. Author of *Notes on Nursing*. Born at Florence, Italy, May 12, 1820. Died Aug 13, 1910.

PILGRIMAGE TO FATIMA. May 12-13. Portugal. Commemorates first appearance of the Virgin of the Rosary to little shepherd children May 13, 1917. Pilgrims come to Cova da Iria, religious center, candle-lit procession, Mass of the sick, for annual observance.

STUDDS, GERRY E: BIRTHDAY. May 12. U.S. Representative of Massachusetts' 10th district, Democrat, of Cohasset, MA, born in Mineola, NY, May 12, 1937.

VIRGIN ISLANDS: NURSE OF THE YEAR AWARD. May 12. Annually, on anniversary of birth of Florence Nightingale (May 12, 1820), the Virgin Islands Nurses' Assn selects two nurses for special recognition. Awards are named in honor of deceased outstanding Virgin Island nurses.

WOODMEN RANGER'S DAY. May 12. Purpose: To celebrate the founding of the National Youth Activities Program of Woodmen Of The World. Info from: Woodmen Of The World, Larry Wegener, Mgr, Youth Activities, 1700 Farnam, Omaha, NE 68102.

MAY 13 — TUESDAY
133rd Day — Remaining, 232

ATTEMPTED ASSASSINATION OF POPE JOHN PAUL II: ANNIVERSARY. May 13. On May 13, 1981, Pope John Paul II was shot twice at close range while riding in an open automobile at St. Peter's Square, in Rome. Two other persons also were wounded. An escaped terrorist, Mehmet Ali Agca, (already under sentence of death for the murder of a Turkish journalist) was immediately arrested, and was convicted, July 22, 1981, of attempted murder of the Pope. After convalescence Pope John Paul II was pronounced recovered by his doctors, on Aug 14, 1981.

COBEY, WILLIAM WILFRED JR: BIRTHDAY. May 13. U.S. Representative of North Carolina's 4th district, Republican, of Chapel Hill, NC, born in Washington, DC, on May 13, 1939.

KASICH, JOHN R: BIRTHDAY. May 13. U.S. Representative of Ohio's 12th district, Republican, of Westerville, OH, born in McKees Rocks, PA, May 13, 1952.

LOUIS, JOE: BIRTHDAY. May 13. World heavyweight boxing champion, 1937-1949, nicknamed the "Brown Bomber," Joseph Louis Barrow was born near Lafayette, AL, May 13, 1914. He died April 12, 1981 at Las Vegas, NV. Burial at Arlington National Cemetery. (Louis' burial there, by presidential waiver, was the 39th exception ever to the eligibility rules for burial in Arlington National Cemetery.)

MACAU: PROCESSION OF OUR LADY OF FATIMA. May 13. To commemorate the miracle of 1917, when the Madonna appeared to residents of Fatima, Portugal, an image of Our Lady is carried in pilgrimage from Sao Domingos Church to Penha Church, generally around 6 p.m.

MORRISON, SID W: BIRTHDAY. May 13. U.S. Representative of Washington's 4th district, Republican, of Zillah, WA, born in Yakima, WA, May 13, 1933.

PHILADELPHIA POLICE BOMBING ANNIVERSARY. May 13. On May 13, 1985, during the siege of a "radical group" in Philadelphia, PA, police in a helicopter reportedly dropped a bomb containing the powerful military plastic explosive, C-4, on the building in which the group was housed. The bomb and the resulting fire left 11 persons dead (including 4 children) and destroyed 61 homes.

ST. LAWRENCE SEAWAY ACT ANNIVERSARY. May 13. President Dwight D. Eisenhower signed legislation authorizing U.S.-Canadian construction of a waterway which would make it possible for ocean-going ships to reach the Great Lakes.

SULLIVAN, ARTHUR: BIRTHDAY. May 13. English composer best known for light operas (with Sir William Gilbert), born May 13, 1842. Died Nov 22, 1900.

U.S.-MEXICO WAR DECLARATION ANNIVERSARY. May 13. Although the war had been in progress since March, when General Zachary Taylor crossed the Rio Grande and established Fort Brown on Mexican territory, the declaration of war by the U.S. did not take place until May 13, 1846.

VIRGINIA POULTRY FESTIVAL. May 13-18. Purpose: To draw attention to impact poultry has on economy and say thanks to consumers and those in industry. Parade, dance and chicken pluckers fun day. Sponsor: Virginia Poultry Federation, Jane Moss, Festival Coord, Box 552, Harrisonburg, VA 22801.

WOMEN'S INTERNATIONAL BOWLING CONGRESS QUEEN'S TOURNAMENT. May 13-17. New Kona Lanes, Costa Mesa, CA. Purpose: To determine champions of the higher average bowlers. Info from: WIBC, Mr. Augie Karcher, PR Mgr, 5301 S 76th St, Greendale, WI 53129.

MAY 14 — WEDNESDAY
134th Day — Remaining, 231

ACC CRAFTFAIR SAN FRANCISCO. May 14-18. The Concourse, San Francisco, CA. Info from: American Craft Enterprises, Inc, Box 10, New Paltz, NY 12561.

BIG EIGHT BASEBALL CHAMPIONSHIPS. May 14-17. All Sports Stadium, Oklahoma City, OK. Info from: Chamber of Commerce, Stanley Draper, Jr, One Santa Fe Plaza, Oklahoma City, OK 73102.

DORGAN, BYRON L: BIRTHDAY. May 14. U.S. Representative at large from North Dakota, Democrat, of Bismarck, ND, was born in Dickinson, ND, May 14, 1942.

FAHRENHEIT, GABRIEL DANIEL: 300TH BIRTH ANNIVERSARY. May 14. German physicist whose name is attached to one of the major temperature measurement scales. He introduced the use of mercury in thermometers and greatly improved their accuracy. Born at Dantzig on May 14, 1686, he died at Amsterdam on Sept 16, 1736.

GAINSBOROUGH, THOMAS: BIRTHDAY. May 14. English landscape and portrait painter. Among his most remembered works: *The Blue Boy, The Watering Place* and *The Market Cart.* Born at Sudbury, Suffolk, on May 14, 1727, he died at London on Aug 2, 1788.

HOLLAND TULIP TIME FESTIVAL. May 14-17. Purpose: To promote the Tulip as a flower and preserve the Dutch cultural heritage for the people of the city of Holland. Sponsor: Holland Tulip Time Festival, Inc, 150 W 8th St, Holland, MI 49423.

ISRAEL INDEPENDENCE DAY (YOM HA'ATZMA'UT). May 14. Hebrew calendar date: Iyar 5, 5746. Commemorates proclamation of independence by Palestinian Jews and establishment of the provisional government of Israel on May 14, 1948 (Hebrew calendar date: Iyar 5, 5708).

JAMESTOWN, VIRGINIA: FOUNDING ANNIVERSARY. May 14. The first permanent English settlement in what is now the United States, took place at Jamestown, VA (named for England's King James I) on May 14, 1607. Captains John Smith and Christopher Newport were among the leaders of the group of royally chartered Virginia Company settlers who had travelled from Plymouth, England, in three small ships: *Susan Constant, Godspeed* and *Discovery.*

MALAWI: KAMUZU DAY. May 14. Public holiday in Malawi.

MOLLOHAN, ALAN B: BIRTHDAY. May 14. U.S. Representative of West Virginia's 1st district, Democrat, of Fairmont, WV, born in Fairmont on May 14, 1943.

NORWAY: MIDNIGHT SUN AT NORTH CAPE. May 14-July 30. North Cape. Norway. First day of the season with around-the-clock sunshine. At North Cape, the sun never dips below the horizon from May 14 to July 30, but the night is bright long before and after these dates.

OWEN, ROBERT: BIRTHDAY. May 14. English progressive owner of spinning works, philanthropist, Utopian socialist, founder of New Harmony, IN, born at Newtown, Wales, May 14, 1771. Died there Nov 17, 1858.

PARAGUAY: NATIONAL HOLIDAY. May 14-15. Two-day celebration begins, commemorating independence from Spain, attained on May 14, 1811.

PHILIPPINES: CARABAO FESTIVAL. May 14-15. Pulilan, Bulacan; Nueva Ecija; Angono, Rizal. Parade of farmers to honor their patron saint, San Isidro, with hundreds of "dressed up" carabaos participating.

PREAKNESS FROG HOP. May 14. War Memorial Plaza, Baltimore, MD. Event determines Baltimore's entry to the Internatl frog jump contest. Info from: Mayor's Office of Adventures in Fun, 100 Holiday St, Baltimore, MD 21202.

SPACE MILESTONE: SOYUZ 40 (USSR). May 14. Two cosmonauts (L. Popov and, from Rumania, D. Prunariu) docked at Salyut 6 space station on May 15. Returned to Earth on May 22. Launched May 14, 1981.

"THE STARS AND STRIPES FOREVER" DAY. May 14. Anniversary of the first public performance of John Philip Sousa's march, "The Stars and Stripes Forever," in Philadelphia on May 14, 1897. The occasion was the unveiling of a statue of George Washington, and Pres. William McKinley was present. A bill was introduced in the Congress in 1985, to make "The Stars and Stripes Forever" the official national march of the U.S.

MAY 15 — THURSDAY
135th Day — Remaining, 230

BAUM, LYMAN FRANK: BIRTHDAY. May 15. American newspaperman who wrote the Wizard of Oz stories was born at Chittenango, NY on May 15, 1856. Although the *Wonderful Wizard of Oz* was the most famous, Baum also wrote many other books for children, including more than a dozen about Oz. He died at Hollywood, CA, May 6, 1919.

BIENNALE OF SYDNEY. May 15-June 6. Sydney, Australia. The Sixth Biennale of Sydney, Australia's largest, most important exhibition of international contemporary art, will take place at the Art Gallery of New South Wales and venues throughout the city of Sydney. The Sixth Biennale "will question originality in a wide range of work." Sponsored by government and semi-government authorities around the world. Info from: Secretariat, Biennale of Sydney, Ltd, 100 George St, Sydney, N.S.W. 2000, Australia.

CALAVERAS COUNTY FAIR AND JUMPING FROG JUBILEE. May 15-18. Calaveras County Fairgrounds, Angels Camp, CA. County fair and the reenactment of Mark Twain's story, *The Celebrated Jumping Frog of Calaveras County.* Info from: Calaveras County Fair & Jumping Frog Jubilee, Box 96, Angels Camp, CA 95222.

CREVE COEUR DAYS. May 15-18. Parade, pet show and civic related events. Info from: St. Louis Conv & Visitors Bureau, 10 S Broadway, Suite 300, St. Louis, MO 63102.

DUBUQUEFEST '86. May 15-18. A celebration of folk and fine arts. Dance, music, mime, art, crafts, poetry theatre and architecture. Info from: Dubuque County Fine Arts Society, Ruth Nash, 422 Loras Blvd, Dubuque, IA 52001.

EASTERN PACIFIC HURRICANE SEASON. May 15-Nov 30. Eastern Pacific defined as: Coast to 140° West Longitude. Info from: U.S. Dept of Commerce, Natl Oceanic and Atmospheric Administration, Rockville, MD 20852.

INTERNATIONAL PICKLE WEEK. May 15-24. Purpose: "To give national recognition to the world's most humorous vegetable." Sponsor: Pickle Packers Internatl, Inc, 108½ E Main St, St. Charles, IL 60174. Info from: Burson-Marsteller, 1 E Wacker Dr, Chicago, IL 60601.

May *1986*	S	M	T	W	T	F	S
					1	2	3
	4	5	6	7	8	9	10
	11	12	13	14	15	16	17
	18	19	20	21	22	23	24
	25	26	27	28	29	30	31

COPYRIGHT © 1985 BY WILLIAM D. CHASE and HELEN M. CHASE

JAPAN: HOLLYHOCK FESTIVAL (AOI MATSURI). May 15. Kyoto, Japan. The festival features pageant reproducing Imperial processions that paid homage to the shrine of Shimogamo and Kamigamo in ancient times.

MEXICO: SAN ISIDRO DAY. May 15. Day of San Isidro Labrador celebrated widely in farming regions to honor St. Isidore, the Plowman. Livestock gaily decorated with flowers. Celebrations usually begin about May 13th and continue for about a week.

OCONALUFTEE INDIAN VILLAGE. May 15-Oct 25. Purpose: To portray an Indian community of the 1750 period. Sponsor: Cherokee Historical Assn, Cherokee, NC 28719.

ORANGE CITY IOWA TULIP FESTIVAL. May 15-17. Purpose: Celebration of Dutch heritage. Parades, street scrubbing, Dutch dancing and a broadway play. Info from: Chamber of Commerce, 125 Central Ave, SE, Orange City, IA 51041.

PEACE OFFICERS MEMORIAL DAY. May 15. Presidential ☆ Proclamation. "Always May 15 each year since 1963; however first issued in 1962 for May 14. Proc 3537, May 4, 1963, covers all succeeding years." (PL87-726 of Oct 1, 1962.)

RECREATIONAL VEHICLE AND ON THE WATER BOAT SHOW. May 15-18. Puddingstone Lake, Pomona, CA. Info from: Dixie Green Promotions, Inc, 3141 W Christy Dr, Phoenix, AZ 85029.

SCHNITZLER, ARTHUR: BIRTH ANNIVERSARY. May 15. Austrian playwright, novelist and medical doctor, Arthur Schnitzler, was born at Vienna on May 15, 1862. Noted for his psycho-analytical examination of Viennese society. Schnitzler died Oct 21, 1931.

SOFTBALL: NAIA WOMEN'S FAST-PITCH CHAMPIONSHIP. May 15-17. Site to be determined. Info from: Natl Assn of Intercollegiate Athletics, 1221 Baltimore, Kansas City, MO 64105.

SPACE MILESTONE: FAITH 7 (US). May 15. Major Gordon Leroy Cooper orbits Earth 22 times. May 15, 1963.

WILSON, ELLEN LOUISE AXSON: BIRTHDAY. May 15. First wife of Woodrow Wilson, 28th president of the U.S., born at Savannah, GA, May 15, 1860. Died Aug 6, 1914.

MAY 16 — FRIDAY

136th Day — Remaining, 229

BACH CHOIR FESTIVAL. May 16-17. (Also May 23-24.) Bethlehem, PA. Info from: Bach Choir of Bethelem, 423 Heckewelder Place, Bethlehem, PA 18018.

BIOGRAPHERS DAY. May 16. Anniversary of the meeting, in London, on May 16, 1763, of James Boswell and Samuel Johnson, beginning history's most famous biographer-biographee relationship. Boswell's *Journal of a Tour to the Hebrides* (1785) and his *Life of Samuel Johnson* (1791) are regarded as models of biographical writing. Thus, this day is recommended as one on which to start reading, or writing, biography.

BLACK-EYED SUSAN STAKES. May 16. Pimlico Race Course, Baltimore, MD. A mile and one-sixteenth $100,000-added race for 3-year-old fillies on the main track. Info from: Pimlico Race Course, Baltimore, MD 21215.

CAJUN COUNTRY OUTDOOR OPRY AND ARTS AND CRAFTS SHOW. May 16-18. (Also Oct 17-19). Purpose: Preservation of Cajun music and crafts and promotion of Louisiana talent. Info from: Cajun Country Opry Assn, Laverna Babin, 1221 Schley St, Houma, LA 70360.

COATS, DANIEL R: BIRTHDAY. May 16. U.S. Representative of Indiana's 4th district, Republican, of Fort Wayne, IN, was born at Jackson, MI, on May 16, 1943.

CONYERS, JOHN JR: BIRTHDAY. May 16. U.S. Representative of Michigan's 1st district, Democrat, of Detroit, MI, born there May 16, 1929.

FAMILY BLUEGRASS MUSIC WEEKEND. May 16-18. Pomme de Terre State Park, Pittsburg, MO. Info from: Missouri Dept of Natural Resources, Box 176, Jefferson City, MO 65102.

FONDA, HENRY: BIRTHDAY. May 16. American stage and screen actor, Motion Picture Academy award winner, born Henry Jaynes Fonda, May 16, 1905, at Grand Island, NE. Began his acting career at the Omaha (NE) Playhouse. Fonda died at Los Angeles, Aug 12, 1982.

FREDERICK CRAFT FAIR. May 16-18. Frederick, MD. Craft items for sale by 350 of the "country's best" craft professionals. Always the weekend before Memorial Day weekend. Info from: Noel Clark, Dir, Natl Crafts Ltd, Gapland, MD 21736.

GREAT SMOKY MOUNTAINS-GATLINBURG HIGHLAND GAMES. May 16-18. Gatlinburg, TN. Celebration of Scotland, its people and traditions. Info from: Chamber of Commerce, Box 527, Gatlinburg, TN 37738.

GWINNETT, BUTTON: DEATH ANNIVERSARY. May 16. Signer of the Declaration of Independence, born, Down Hatherley, Gloucestershire, England, about 1735 (exact date unknown). Died following a duel, May 16, 1777.

HONG KONG: BIRTHDAY OF LORD BUDDHA. May 16. Religious observances are held in Buddhist temples and Buddha's statue is bathed. Po Lin Monastery and the other monasteries on Lantau Island are visted by many worshippers during the festival. Eighth day of fourth lunar month.

HORATIO ALGER AWARDS PROGRAM. May 16. Westin Galleria, Houston, TX. Purpose: To honor Americans who have risen from humble beginnings to positions of leadership, in the Horatio Alger tradition, by taking advantage of the opportunities afforded by America's free enterprise system. Info from: Horatio Alger Assn of Distinguished Americans, Inc, 1 Rockefeller Plaza, Suite 1609, New York, NY 10020.

KENTUCKY GUILD OF ARTISTS AND CRAFTSMEN'S SPRING FAIR. May 16-18. Berea, KY. Displays of close to 100 exhibiting members of the guild juried for excellence. Info from: KY Dept of Travel, Capital Plaza Office Tower, Frankfort, KY 40601.

MEMPHIS IN MAY INTERNATIONAL BARBECUE COOKING CONTEST. May 16-17. Tom Lee Park, Memphis, TN. Info from: Memphis in May Internatl Festival, Inc, Kathi Olpin, PR Dir, 245 Wagner Place, Suite 220, Memphis, TN 38103.

MOON PHASE: FIRST QUARTER. May 16. Moon enters First Quarter phase at 8:00 p.m., E.S.T.

MORTON, LEVI PARSONS: BIRTHDAY. May 16. Twenty-second Vice President of the U.S. (1889-1893) born, Shoreham, VT, May 16, 1824. Died, Rhinebeck, NY, May 16, 1920.

NATIONAL DEFENSE TRANSPORTATION DAY. May 16. ☆ Presidential Proclamation. "Issued each year for 3rd Friday in May since 1957." (PL85-32 of May 16, 1957.)

ROOSTER DAY CELEBRATION. May 16-17. Carnival, parade, crowning of Miss Chick, rodeo and grandstand entertainment. Sponsor: Chamber of Commerce, 123 N Main, Broken Arrow, OK 74012.

SEWARD, WILLIAM HENRY: BIRTHDAY. May 16. American statesman, Secretary of State under Lincoln and Andrew Johnson. Seward negotiated the purchase of Alaska from Russia for $7,200,000. At the time some felt the price was too

COPYRIGHT © 1985 BY WILLIAM D. CHASE and HELEN M. CHASE

high and referred to the purchase as "Seward's Folly." Born on May 16, 1801, at Florida, NY, he died at Auburn, NY, on Oct 10, 1872.

WBAI SPRING CRAFTS FAIR. May 16-18. (Also May 30-June 1.) Ferris Booth Hall, Columbia University, New York, NY. Purpose: "A major crafts event in the largest consumer marketplace in the US with 250 professional artisans participating." Info from: Matthew Alperin, WBAI Crafts Fair, Box 889, Times Sq Station, New York, NY 10108.

WEICKER, LOWELL P JR: BIRTHDAY. May 16. U.S. Senator from Connecticut, Republican, of Greenwich, CT, was born at Paris, France, on May 16, 1931.

MAY 17 — SATURDAY
137th Day — Remaining, 228

A DAY IN OLD NEW CASTLE. May 17. New Castle, DE. Third Saturday in May. Info from: Delaware Development Office, Box 1401, Dover, DE 19903.

ARMED FORCES DAY. May 17. Presidential proclamation.
☆ "Always the third Saturday in May since 1950. Proc 4934, Apr 16, 1982, covers third Saturday of each May. Originally proclaimed as 'Army Day' for Apr 6, beginning in 1936 (S.Con.Res. 30 of Apr 2, 1936). S.Con.Res 5 of Mar 16, 1937, requested annual Apr 6 issuance which was done thru 1949. Traditionally issued by each Administration."

BETHLEHEM SIDEWALK ART SHOW. May 17. Bethlehem, PA. Info from: Miss Janet Popyach, c/o Wilbur Savings & Loan, 231 E Broad St, Bethlehem, PA 18018.

BEVERLY HILLS "AFFAIRE IN THE GARDENS." May 17-18. (Also Oct 18-19.) Santa Monica/Rodeo Gardens. Purpose: To foster appreciation of fine arts and crafts. Sponsor: Beverly Hills Recreation & Parks Dept, 450 N Crescent Dr, Beverly Hills, CA 90210.

BIKE-A-RAMA. May 17. A day of biking routes for the whole family to benefit the Boys Clubs of Richmond, VA. Info from: Bike-A-Rama, 408 N Robinson St, Richmond, VA 23220.

BLOWING ROCK MIGHTY KITE FLIGHT. May 17. Open to everyone. Cash prizes in each category. Grand prize to highest flying kite. Sponsor: Blowing Rock Parks & Recreation, Box 43, Blowing Rock, NC 28605.

DULCIMER DAYS. May 17-18. Old-time dulcimer music, contests and workshops. (Annually the 3rd weekend in May.) Info from: Roscoe Village Foundation, 381 Hill St, Coshocton, OH 43812.

GERMANY: THEATRE MEETING OF THE YOUTH. May 17-25. Info from: Berliner Festspiele, Budapester Strasse 50, 1 Berlin 30.

GETTYSBURG OUTDOOR ANTIQUE SHOW. May 17. Features 180 dealers in antiques with exhibits and displays. Info from: Gettysburg Travel Council, 35 Carlisle St, Gettysburg, PA 17325.

HOUBY (MUSHROOM) DAYS. May 17-18. Czech Village, Cedar Rapids, IA. Focus on heritage of Czech people. Mushroom hunt and mushroom food. Info from: Czech Village Assn, 59-16th Ave, SW, Cedar Rapids, IA 52404.

INTERNATIONAL CHICKEN FLYING MEET. May 17. Purpose: Chicken flying contest to see which chicken can crack the world's chicken flying record of 302′8″. Open to the world. Info from: Bob Evans Farms Inc, Mary Cusick, 3776 S High St, Columbus, OH 43207.

JACKPOT PIGEON RACE. May 17. Bay Cities, CA. Over three thousand pigeons compete in this race from Bay Cities, CA to Jackpot, NV. Info from: Nevada Commission on Tourism, Capitol Complex, Carson City, NV 89710.

LA PUENTE, CALIFORNIA VALLEY AREA SPECIAL OLYMPICS. May 17. Purpose: To provide athletic competition in a variety of sports for over 700 mentally retarded citizens eight years of age through senior years. Info from: Delhaven Community Ctr, Bobbie Seal, Area Dir, 1431 N Hacienda Blvd, La Puente, CA 91747.

LILAC FESTIVAL/ARMED FORCES TORCHLIGHT PARADE. May 17. Spokane, WA. Always the third Saturday of May. Info from: Spokane Lilac Festival, Box 802, Spokane, WA 99210.

MARKET SQUARE FAIR. May 17. Purpose: To create an awareness of Fredericksburg's historic heritage. Arts, crafts, food and entertainment. Info from: Visitor Center, 706 Caroline St, Fredericksburg, VA 22401.

MICHIGAN WEEK. May 17-24. Purpose: To teach Michigan citizens more about Michigan. To tell people of other states and nations about Michigan and to work together to make Michigan even better. A state-wide volunteer effort to "sell" Michigan. Sponsor: Greater Michigan Foundation, 809 Center St, Lansing, MI 48906.

MILLER, GEORGE: BIRTHDAY. May 17. U.S. Representative of California's 7th district, Democrat, of Martinez, CA, was born in Richmond, CA, on May 17, 1945.

NATIONAL PIKE FESTIVAL. May 17-18. Purpose: Festival is historical in nature celebrating the building of the road in 1818, starting at West Alexander, Washington County, PA and extending 87 miles eastward along U.S. Route 40. Info from: Washington County Tourist Promotion Agency, Box 877, Washington, PA 15301.

NEW YORK STOCK EXCHANGE: BIRTHDAY. May 17. On May 17, 1792, some two-dozen merchants and brokers agreed to establish what is now known as the New York Stock Exchange. In fair weather they operated under a buttonwood tree on Wall Street, in New York City. In bad weather they moved to the shelter of a coffee house to conduct their business.

NORWAY: CONSTITUTION DAY: NATIONAL HOLIDAY. May 17. Constitution Day or Independence Day. Constitution signed and Norway separated from Denmark on this day, 1814. Parades and children's festivities.

PHILIPPINES: FERTILITY RITES. May 17-19. Obando, Bulacan. A triple religious fete in honor of San Pascual, Santa Clara and the Virgin of Salambao marked by dancing of childless couples.

PREAKNESS STAKES. May 17. Pimlico Race Course, Baltimore, MD. Running of the Preakness Stakes, middle jewel in the Triple Crown, was inaugurated in 1873. Traditionally, the second Saturday after Kentucky Derby, and followed, three Saturdays later, by the Belmont Stakes. Info from: Maryland Jockey Club, Pimlico Race Course, Baltimore, MD 21215.

SPRING ARTS AND CRAFTS FAIR. May 17-18. Tilles County Park, St. Louis, MO. Info from: Parks & Recreations, Recreation Div, 41 S Central Ave, St. Louis, MO 63105.

TENNIS: NATIONAL COLLEGIATE DIVISION I MEN'S CHAMPIONSHIP. May 17-25. University of Georgia, Athens, GA. Info from: NCAA, Box 1906, Mission, KS 66201.

TWO STATE TWO-STEP. May 17. Harrison Park, Hammond, IN. Combined course—5- and 10-kilometer run through the streets of Hammond, IN, and Calumet City, IL. Purpose: To emphasize the fact that fitness today can lead to a healthier tomorrow. Info from: Marjorie Wenzel, Educ Serv Dept, Saint Margaret Hospital, 5454 Hohman Ave, Hammond, IN 46320.

WORLD TELECOMMUNICATION DAY. May 17. An international day observed by the organizations of the United Nations system. Info from: United Nations Dept of Public Information, United Nations, NY 10017.

May *1986*

S	M	T	W	T	F	S
				1	2	3
4	5	6	7	8	9	10
11	12	13	14	15	16	17
18	19	20	21	22	23	24
25	26	27	28	29	30	31

COPYRIGHT © 1985 BY WILLIAM D. CHASE and HELEN M. CHASE

MAY 18 — SUNDAY
138th Day — Remaining, 227

BIRTHDAY OF MOTHER'S WHISTLER. May 18. Purpose: "On his birthday, the world's mellowest whistler celebrates by honoring birds for the beautiful music they offer so unselfishly. This is done not through mere lip service, but by actually puckering up and joining them in song." Sponsor: Mother's Whistler, Warfield & Twin Silo Lanes, Huntingdon Valley, PA 19006.

ENGLAND: MALVERN FESTIVAL. May 18-June 3. Malvern, Hereford and Worcester. Performances of works by George Bernard Shaw and Sir Edward Elgar.

INTERNATIONAL MUSEUM DAY. May 18. Purpose: To pay tribute to museums of the world. "Museums are an important means of cultural exchange, enrichment of cultures and development of mutual understanding, cooperation and peace among people." Observed annually on May 18th. Sponsor: Internatl Council of Museums, AAM/ICOM Coord, 1055 Thomas Jefferson St, NW, Suite 428, Washington, DC 20007.

MARQUETTE, JACQUES: DEATH ANNIVERSARY. May 18. Father Jacques Marquette (Pere Marquette), Jesuit missionary-explorer of the Great Lakes region, died May 18, 1675 near Ludington or Frankfort, MI.

MT. ST. HELENS ERUPTION ANNIVERSARY. May 18. A major eruption of Mt. St. Helens volcano, in southwestern Washington, on May 18, 1980, blew steam and ash more than 11 miles into sky. First major eruption of Mt. St. Helens since 1857, though, on Mar 26, 1980, there had been a warning eruption of smaller magnitude.

PENTECOST. May 18. The Christian feast of Pentecost commemorates descent of the Holy Spirit unto the Apostles, fifty days after Easter. Observed on the seventh Sunday after Easter. Recognized since the 3rd century. See also: Whitsunday.

POPE JOHN PAUL II: BIRTHDAY. May 18. Karol Wojtyla, 264th Pope of the Roman Catholic Church, born at Wadowice, Poland, May 18, 1920. Elected Pope on Oct 16, 1978. He was the first non-Italian to be elected Pope in 456 years (since the election of Pope Adrian VI, in 1522), and the first Polish Pope.

PUBLIC RELATIONS WEEK. May 18-24. Purpose: To honor public relations, publicity and press agent workers for their service to the good of humanity. Sponsor: Richard R. Falk Associates, Richard Falk, Info Officer, 147 W 42nd St, New York, NY 10036.

RUDMAN, WARREN BRUCE: BIRTHDAY. May 18. U.S. Senator from New Hampshire, Republican, of Nashua, NH, born in Boston, MA, May 18, 1930.

SPACE MILESTONE: APOLLO 10 (US). May 18. Col. Thomas Stafford, Commander Eugene Cernan, brought lunar module (LM) "Snoopy" within 9 miles of moon's surface, May 22. Apollo 10 circled moon 31 times and returned to Earth, May 26. Launched May 18, 1969.

STAMP EXPO '86/EAST. May 18-20. Penta Internatl Hotel, New York, NY. International Postage Stamp Exposition honoring the "Statue of Liberty." Sponsor: Internatl Stamp Collectors Society, Box 854, Van Nuys, CA 91408.

VISIT YOUR RELATIVES DAY. May 18. Purpose: A day to renew family ties and joys by visiting often-thought-of-seldom seen relatives. Sponsor: A.C. Moeller, Box 71, Clio, MI 48420.

WHITSUNDAY. May 18. Whitsunday, the seventh Sunday after Easter, is a popular time for baptism. "White Sunday" is named for the white garments formerly worn by the candidates for baptism, and occurs at the Christian feast of Pentecost (q.v.).

MAY 19 — MONDAY
139th Day — Remaining, 226

ANDREWS, MARK: BIRTHDAY. May 19. U.S. Senator from North Dakota, Republican, of Mapleton, ND, was born on May 19, 1926.

DARK DAY IN NEW ENGLAND: ANNIVERSARY. May 19. At mid-day on May 19, 1780, near total darkness unaccountably descended on much of New England. Candles were lighted, fowls went to roost, and many fearful persons believed that doomsday had arrived. At New Haven, CT, Col Abraham Davenport opposed adjournment of the town council in these words: "I am against adjournment. The day of judgement is either approaching or it is not. If it is not there is no cause for an adjournment. If it is, I choose to be found doing my duty. I wish therefore that candles may be brought." No scientifically verifiable cause for this widespread phenomenon was ever discovered.

HO CHI MINH: BIRTH ANNIVERSARY. May 19. Vietnamese leader and first president of the Democratic Republic of Vietnam, born in central Vietnamese village of Kim Lien (Nghe An Province), probably on May 19, 1890. His original name was Nguyen That Thanh. Died, Hanoi, Sept 3, 1969.

MALCOLM X: BIRTH ANNIVERSARY. May 19. Black nationalist and civil rights activist, Malcolm X, was born Malcolm Little, May 19, 1925, at Omaha, NE. While serving a prison term he resolved to transform his life. On his release in 1952 he changed his name to Malcolm X and worked for the Nation of Islam until he was suspended by Black Muslim leader Elija Muhammad on Dec 4, 1963. Malcolm X later (Mar 12, 1964) delivered a "Declaration of Independence" statement to a press conference in New York City and announced that he was forming the Organization of American Unity. He was assassinated as he spoke to a meeting at the Audubon Ballroom in New York City, on Feb 21, 1965.

MAY RAY DAY. May 19. Purpose: To celebrate the beginning of the warm outside days the sun gives us. Also, a day for people named Ray. Sponsor: Richard Ankli, Broadway Fun Spot, 639 Fifth St, Ann Arbor, MI 48103.

NATIONAL ANTHEM MEMORIZING RESOLUTION ANNIVERSARY. May 19. On May 19, 1932, Congressman Claude A. Fuller, of Arkansas, introduced in the House of Representatives a Resolution: "To promote patriotism by providing that all officers and employes of the United States and the District of Columbia shall know the national anthem." His resolution would have compelled each Civil Service employe to prove his ability to sing, recite or write from memory the words of the Star-Spangled Banner; those who failed to do this would not be eligible for appointment to any Federal position. The Resolution died in the Committee on the Judiciary. (From: *History of the Star-Spangled Banner*, U.S. Dept of Interior.)

PEALE, SARAH MIRIAM: BIRTHDAY. May 19. American portrait painter, member of famous early American family of painters, born at Philadelphia on May 19, 1800. Died there on Feb 4, 1885.

SIMPLON TUNNEL ANNIVERSARY. May 19. Tunnel officially opened on this day in 1906. Construction started in 1898. From Brig, Switzerland to Iselle, Italy.

SPACE MILESTONE: MARS 2 and MARS 3 (USSR). May 19 and 28. Entered Martian orbits on Nov 27 and Dec 2, respectively. Mars 3 sent down a TV-equipped capsule which soft-landed and transmitted pictures for 20 seconds. Launch dates: May 19, 28, 1971.

TENNIS: NAIA MEN'S DIVISION CHAMPIONSHIP. May 19-23. Kansas City, MO. Info from: Natl Assn of Intercollegiate Athletics, 1221 Baltimore, Kansas City, MO 64105.

COPYRIGHT © 1985 BY WILLIAM D. CHASE and HELEN M. CHASE

TENNIS: NAIA WOMEN'S DIVISION CHAMPIONSHIP. May 19-23. Overland Park, KS. Info from: Natl Assn of Intercollegiate Athletics, 1221 Baltimore, Kansas City, MO 64105.

TURKEY: YOUTH AND SPORTS DAY. May 19. Public holiday commemorating beginning of national movement for independence in 1919, led by Mustafa Kemal Ataturk.

VICTORIA DAY. SOVEREIGN'S BIRTHDAY. May 19. Canada. (First Monday preceding May 25, each year.)

WHITMONDAY. May 19. The day after Whitsunday is observed as a public holiday in many countries.

MAY 20 — TUESDAY
140th Day — Remaining, 225

BALZAC, HONORE DE: BIRTHDAY. May 20. French novelist born at Tours, May 20, 1799. "It is easier," Balzac wrote in 1829, "to be a lover than a husband for the simple reason that it is more difficult to be witty every day than to say pretty things from time to time." Died at Paris on Aug 18, 1850.

CAMEROON: NATIONAL HOLIDAY. May 20. Republic of Cameroon. Commemorates declaration of the republic on May 20, 1972.

COUNCIL OF NICAEA I: ANNIVERSARY. May 20-Aug 25. First ecumenical council of Christian church, called by Constantine I, first Christian emperor of Roman Empire. Nearly 300 bishops are said to have attended this first of 21 ecumenical councils (latest, Vatican II, began Sept 11, 1962), which was held at Nicaea, Bithynia, in Asia Minor in the year 325. Dates and attendance are approximate. The council condemned Arianism (which denied divinity of Christ), formulated the Nicene Creed, and fixed the date of Easter).

DOOLITTLE, ELIZA: DAY. May 20, Purpose: To honor Miss Doolittle (heroine of Bernard Shaw's *Pygmalion*) for demonstrating the importance of speaking one's native language properly. Sponsor: Doolittle Day Development Committee, 2460 Devonshire Rd, Ann Arbor, MI 48104.

ENGLAND: CHELSEA FLOWER SHOW. May 20-23. Royal Hospital, Chelsea, London. Britain's major flower show. Twenty-two acres of gardens and garden equipment. Private view on May 20.

FERRARY DAY. May 20. Purpose: To remember the day of the death of the internationally known stamp collector Philipp La Renotiere von Ferrary (1850-1917). Sponsor: The Philatelic Journalist, 154 Laguna Ct, St. Augustine Shores, FL 32086.

FORD, HAROLD: BIRTHDAY. May 20. U.S. Representative of Tennessee's 9th district, Democrat, of Memphis, TN, born there on May 20, 1945.

GEJDENSON, SAMUEL: BIRTHDAY. May 20. U.S. Representative of Connecticut's 2nd district, Democrat, of Bozrah, CT, was born in Eschwege, Germany, on May 20, 1948.

GERMANY, FRANKFURT: WALDCHESTAG. May 20. Since the 19th century Frankfurters have spent the Tuesday after Whitsun in their forest. "Waldchestag in the city forest."

GIGLI, BENIAMINO: BIRTHDAY. May 20. Celebrated Italian tenor born at Recanati, Italy on May 20, 1890. Died in Rome on Nov 30, 1957.

LAFAYETTE DAY. May 20. Massachusetts.

LINDBERGH FLIGHT ANNIVERSARY. May 20-21. Anniversary of the first solo trans-Atlantic flight. Capt Charles Augustus Lindbergh (q.v.), 25-year old aviator, departed from rainy, muddy Roosevelt Field, Long Island, NY, alone at 7:52 a.m., May 20, 1927, in a Ryan monoplane named *Spirit of St. Louis*, and landed at Le Bourget airfield, Paris, at 10:24 p.m. Paris time (5:24 p.m., NY time) on May 21, winning a $25,000 prize

offered by Raymond Orteig for the first non-stop flight between New York City and Paris (3,600 miles). The "flying fool"as he had been dubbed by some doubters became "Lucky Lindy," an instant world hero.

McKERNAN, JOHN R JR: BIRTHDAY. May 20. U.S. Representative of Maine's 1st district, Republican, of Cumberland, ME, born at Bangor, ME, on May 20, 1948.

MADISON, DOLLY (DOROTHEA) DANDRIDGE PAYNE TODD: BIRTHDAY. May 20. Wife of James Madison, 4th President of the U.S., born at Guilford County, NC, May 20, 1768. Died July 12, 1849.

MECKLENBURG DAY. May 20. North Carolina. Commemorates claimed signing of a declaration of independence from England by citizens of Mecklenburg County on this day, 1775.

NORTHERN IRELAND: ROYAL ULSTER AGRICULTURAL SOCIETY SHOW. May 20-23. Showgrounds, Balmoral, Belfast. The 119th annual show and industrial exhibition.

RAHALL, NICK J II: BIRTHDAY. May 20. U.S. Representative of West Virginia's 4th district, Democrat, of Beckley, WV, born there on May 20, 1949.

ROUSSEAU, HENRI JULIEN FELIX: BIRTHDAY. May 20. Henri Rosseau, nicknamed Le Douanier because of his one-time post as customs toll-keeper. Celebrated French painter born at Laval, Mayenne, France, May 20, 1844. Clarinet player in a regimental band, painter of deceptively "primitive" pictures of exotic foliage, flowers and fruit of the jungle, with stilted human and animal figures. Died at Hospital Necker, Paris, Sept 4, 1910.

SLAUGHTER, D FRENCH JR: BIRTHDAY. May 20. U.S. Representative of Virginia's 7th district, Republican, of Culpeper, VA, born there on May 20, 1925.

SPACE MILESTONE: PIONEER VENUS 1 (US). May 20. Became first Venus orbiter on Dec 4. Launched May 20, 1978.

WEIGHTS AND MEASURES DAY. May 20. Anniversary of international treaty, signed May 20, 1875, providing for the establishment of an International Bureau of Weights and Measures. The Bureau was founded on international territory at Sevres, France.

MAY 21 — WEDNESDAY
141st Day — Remaining, 224

CURTISS, GLENN HAMMOND: BIRTH ANNIVERSARY. May 21. American inventor and aviator, born at Hammondsport, NY, on May 21, 1878. The aviation pioneer died at Buffalo on July 23, 1930.

DURER, ALBRECHT: BIRTHDAY. May 21. German painter and engraver, one of the greatest artists of the Renaissance, was born at Nuremberg on May 21, 1471, and died there Apr 6, 1528.

FRY, ELIZABETH GURNEY: BIRTHDAY. May 21. English reformer dedicated her life to improving the condition of the poor and especially of women in prison, born at Earlham, Norfolk, England, May 21, 1780. Died at Ramsgate, England on Oct 12, 1845.

GEMINI, THE TWINS. May 21-June 20. In the astronomical/astrological Zodiac, which divides the sun's apparent orbit into twelve segments, the period May 21-June 20 is identified, traditionally, as the sun-sign period of Gemini, the Twins. The ruling planet is Mercury.

MOONSHINE FESTIVAL. May 21-26. Purpose: To promote our village. During prohibition days, we were known as the "Moonshine Capitol of the World." Sponsor: New Straitsville Betterment Assn, Box 36, New Straitsville, OH 43766.

NEW ZEALAND: NATIONAL CONFERENCE OF TOASTMASTERS. May 21-25. Ashburton, New Zealand. Info from: New Zealand Government Tourist Offices, 630 Fifth Ave, New York, NY 10111.

POLAND: INTERNATIONAL BOOK FAIR. May 21-26. Warsaw, Poland. Info from: Ars Polona, Internatl Book Fair, PO Box 1001, 00-950 Warsaw, Poland.

May *1986*	S	M	T	W	T	F	S
					1	2	3
	4	5	6	7	8	9	10
	11	12	13	14	15	16	17
	18	19	20	21	22	23	24
	25	26	27	28	29	30	31

COPYRIGHT © 1985 BY WILLIAM D. CHASE and HELEN M. CHASE

POPE, ALEXANDER: BIRTHDAY. May 21. English poet born at London, May 21, 1688. "A man," Pope wrote in 1727, "should never be ashamed to own he has been in the wrong, which is but saying, in other words, that he is wiser today than he was yesterday." Died Twickenham, Eng, May 30, 1744.

MAY 22 — THURSDAY
142nd Day — Remaining, 223

ALL AMERICAN BUCKLE-UP. May 22-29. The All American Buckle-Up is a challenge to motorists to buckle their safety belts, for one week, every time they ride in a car. Goal: Development of a life-long, life-saving habit. Sponsor: Natl Highway Safety Administration. Info from: Indiana State Police, Alison Walker, Information Specialist, 100 N Senate Ave, Indianapolis, IN 46204.

AMERIPEX '86. May 22-June 1. O'Hare Expo Center, Chicago, IL. Purpose: International stamp show officially hosted by United States every 10 years. Featuring stamps, postal stationery and postal history, stamp organizations, postal administrations, exhibits and dealers. Sponsor: AMERIPEX Organizing Committee, Les Winick, Exec Dir, 5944 W Montrose Ave, Chicago, IL 60634.

CONAN DOYLE, ARTHUR: BIRTHDAY. May 22. English physician, Sir Arthur Conan Doyle is best remembered as a detective story writer, especially for the creation of Sherlock Holmes and Dr. Watson. Conan Doyle was born at Edinburgh, on May 22, 1859. He was deeply interested in and lectured on the subject of spiritualism. Conan Doyle died at Crowborough, Sussex, on July 7, 1930.

ELK'S MAY DAYS. May 22-25. Purpose: To raise money to help needy, handicapped and less fortunate children. Sponsor: Prince George Elks Club, John Sawers, Chrmn, 1116 6th Ave, Prince George, BC V2L 3M6.

JIM BUTLER DAYS. May 22-26. Tonopah, NV. Celebrates Nevada's mining history with mucking and drilling state championships, beard contests and liar's contest. Info from: Chamber of Commerce, Box 869, Tonopah, NV 89049.

KENTUCKY MOUNTAIN LAUREL FESTIVAL. May 22-25. Pineville, KY. Grand balls, concerts, picnic, golf, tennis and hiking. Info from: KY Dept of Travel, Capital Plaza Office Tower, Frankfort, KY 40601.

LEFT BANK ART FAIR. May 22-23. Vintage Champaign Mall, Champaign, IL. Quality arts and crafts exhibited and sold. Sponsor: Vintage Champaign Council, 115 N Neil, Suite 105, Champaign, IL 61820.

NATIONAL APPAREL TECHNOLOGY SHOW. May 22-24. Place Bonaventure, Montreal, Quebec, Canada. Machinery, tools, equipment, systems, accessories, raw materials, fabrics, trimmings and supplies concerning clothing manufacturing process. Info from: P.R. Charette, Inc, 5890 Monkland, Suite 206, Montreal, Quebec, Canada H4A 1G2.

NATIONAL MARITIME DAY. May 22. Presidential Proclamation. "Always issued for May 22 since 1933." (Pub Res No 7 of May 20, 1933.)

NATIONAL MARITIME DAY. May 22. Anniversary of departure for first steamship crossing of Atlantic from Savannah, Georgia to Liverpool, England, steamship *Savannah*, 1819.

ROGUE RIVER BOATNIK. May 22-26. Grants Pass, OR. White water adventurers compete for prizes over perilous 50-mile course on southern Oregon's Rogue River. Parade and carnival. Info from: Chamber of Commerce, Box 970, Grants Pass, OR 97526.

SHENANDOAH SPRING FESTIVAL. May 22-26. Carnival, parade, canoe races, lamplight dinners, flea and craft markets. Sponsor: Chamber of Commerce, Box 186, Shenandoah, VA 22849.

TENNESSEE WALKING HORSE SPRING FUN SHOW. May 22-24. Celebration Grounds, Shelbyville, TN. Info from: Celebration, Inc, Ron Thomas, Exec Dir, Box 1010, Shelbyville, TN 37160.

TRACK AND FIELD (OUTDOOR): NAIA MEN'S DIVISION CHAMPIONSHIP. May 22-24. Site to be determined. Info from: Natl Assn of Intercollegiate Athletics, 1221 Baltimore, Kansas City, MO 64105.

TRACK AND FIELD (OUTDOOR): NAIA WOMEN'S DIVISION CHAMPIONSHIP. May 22-24. Site to be determined. Info from: Natl Assn of Intercollegiate Athletics, 1221 Baltimore, Kansas City, MO 64105.

WILDFLOWER PILGRIMAGE. May 22-25. Blackwater Falls State Park, Charleston, WV. Info from: Maxine Scarbro, WV Dept of Natural Resources, Charleston, WV 25305.

MAY 23 — FRIDAY
143rd Day — Remaining, 222

ALMA HIGHLAND FESTIVAL AND GAMES. May 23-25. Alma, MI. Info from: Chamber of Commerce, Box 506, Alma, MI 48801.

DECLARATION OF THE BAB. May 23. Baha'i commemoration of May 23, 1844, when the Bab, the herald of Baha'u'llah (prophet-herald of the Baha'i faith) publicly announced his mission, in Shiraz, Persia. Info from: Baha'i Office of Public Affairs, Baha'i National Center, Wilmette, IL 60091.

DEVON HORSE SHOW AND COUNTRY FAIR. May 23-31. Devon Horse Show Grounds, Devon, PA 19333. Info: Devon Horse Show & Country Fair, Inc, Box 865, Devon, PA 19333.

ENGLAND: BATH FESTIVAL. May 23-June 8. Bath, Avon. International festival of music and the arts.

FALLON WILD BUNCH STAMPEDE. May 23-26. Fallon, NV. Unique rodeo that features the stock rather than cowboys. Info from: Nevada Commission on Tourism, Capitol Complex, Carson City, NV 89710.

FESTFORALL '86. May 23-25. Purpose: To show the talents of more than 1,500 local performing artists and the works of some 170 artists and craftsmen. Concerts, demonstrations and international cuisine. Sponsor: River City Festivals Assn, Richard Sabino, 427 Laurel St, Baton Rouge, LA 70801.

FLORIDA FOLK FESTIVAL. May 23-25. Features folk music, dances, songs, tales, traditional crafts and regional foods. Workshops in storytelling, instruments and song swaps. Info from: Florida Folklife Programs, Stephen Foster Center, White Springs, FL 32096.

GENERAL CLINTON CANOE REGATTA. May 23-26. General Clinton Park, Bainbridge, NY. 70 mile world championship flat water endurance race. Sponsor: Chamber of Commerce, Inc, Box 2, Bainbridge, NY 13733.

HODEL, DONALD PAUL: BIRTHDAY. May 23. Donald Paul Hodel, U.S. Secretary of the Interior (confirmed by the Senate on Feb 6, 1985) was born at Portland, OR, on May 23, 1935.

JUBILEE. May 23-25. Montgomery, Alabama. Info from: Alabama Tourism and Travel, 532 S Perry St, Montgomery, AL 36130.

LINNAEUS DAY. May 23. Stenbrohult, Sweden. Commemorates birth, May 23, 1707, of Carolus Linnaeus (Carl von Linne), Swedish naturalist. Died at Uppsala Jan 10, 1778.

MESMER, FRIEDRICH ANTON: BIRTHDAY. May 23. German physician born May 23, 1734, after whom Mesmerism was named. Magnetism and hypnotism used by him in treating disease. Died Mar 5, 1815.

COPYRIGHT © 1985 BY WILLIAM D. CHASE and HELEN M. CHASE

MILLER, JOHN RIPIN: BIRTHDAY. May 23. U.S. Representative of Washington's 1st district, Republican, of Seattle, WA, born in New York City, May 23, 1938.

MOON PHASE: FULL MOON. May 23. Moon enters Full Moon phase at 3:45 p.m., E.S.T.

NORTHWEST FOLKLIFE FESTIVAL. May 23-26. Seattle Center, Seattle, WA. Folk and ethnic celebration with 15 stages, 700 performances, 200 crafts, film festival and workshops. Info from: Northwest Folklife Festival, 305 Harrison St, Seattle, WA 98109.

PERIGEAN SPRING TIDES. May 23. The highest possible tides, which occur when New Moon or Full Moon takes place within 24 hours of the moment the Moon is nearest Earth (perigee) in its monthly orbit. May 23, at 10 p.m., E.S.T.

RIVERSPREE FESTIVAL. May 23-25. Purpose: A celebration of life on the river, featuring the facade of the James Adams Floating Theatre. Fun, food, crafts, entertainment. Info: Chamber of Commerce, Box 426, Elizabeth City, NC 27909.

SOUTH CAROLINA: RATIFICATION DAY. May 23. Eighth State to ratify constitution on this day in 1788.

SPOLETO FESTIVAL. May 23-June 8. Charleston, SC. Opera, ballet, modern dance, theatre, symphonic, choral and chamber music, jazz, visual arts. Info from: Spoleto Festival USA, Box 157, Charleston, SC 29402.

TRYON HORSE SHOW. May 23-25. Harmon Field, Tryon, NC. A hunter/jumper show for all ages. Sponsor: Tryon Riding & Hunt Club, Box 1095, Tryon, NC 28782.

WEBSTER COUNTY WOODCHOPPING FESTIVAL. May 23-26. Purpose: South Eastern United States World Championship Woodchopping Contest. (Memorial Day weekend). Sponsor: Woodchopping Festival Committee, Box 227, Webster Springs, WV 26288.

MAY 24 — SATURDAY
144th Day — Remaining, 221

AMERICAN BOOKSELLERS ASSOCIATION TRADE EXHIBIT AND CONVENTION. May 24-27. New Orleans Convention Ctr, New Orleans, LA. Exhibitor publishers display fall titles for attending booksellers or all interested in reaching the retail bookseller. Book related items also on display. Info from: American Booksellers Assn, Victoria Stanlet, Meetings and Conventions Dir, 122 E 42nd St, New York, NY 10168.

APPALACHIAN TRADE FESTIVAL. May 24-25. Appalachian Fair Grounds, Gray, TN. Arts, crafts, antiques, coins, guns, etc. Annually, Memorial Day Weekend. Sponsor: Kiwanis Club of Kingsport, Box 3506, Kingsport, TN 37664.

BROOKLYN BRIDGE: BIRTHDAY. May 24. Nearly 14 years in construction the $16 million Brooklyn Bridge over the East River opened May 24, 1883. Designed by John A. Roebling, the steel suspension bridge has a span of 1,595 feet.

BULGARIA: ENLIGHTENMENT AND CULTURE DAY. May 24. National holiday festively celebrated by school children, students, people of science and art. Manifestations, concerts, etc. to express love for education and culture.

FINE ARTS FAIR. May 24-25. Arrow Rock State Historic Site, Arrow Rock, MO. Info from: Missouri Dept of Natural Resources, Box 176, Jefferson City, MO 65102.

FOUNDERS DAY FESTIVAL. May 24. An all antique show on the square with over 90 exhibitors, entertainment and games. Info from: Marietta Parks & Recreation Dept, Box 609, Marietta, GA 30061.

GEORGIA FOLK FESTIVAL. May 24-25. Arts, crafts, drama, music and dance. Exhibits, demonstrations, performances and workshops. Info from: Carole Sirmans, 400 Browns Crossing Rd NW, Milledgeville, GA 31061.

GREAT ARCATA TO FERNDALE CROSS COUNTRY KINETIC SCULPTURE RACE. May 24-26. Purpose: To have fun. Sponsor: Hobart Galleries, Hobart R Brown, Box 916, Main and Brown Sts, Ferndale, CA 95536.

GREAT MONTEREY SQUID FESTIVAL. May 24-25. Purpose: In celebration of the historic Monterey fishing industry. Sponsor: Kiwanis Club. Info from: Bostrom Corp, Robert Massaro, Dir, 2600 Garden Rd, #208, Monterey, CA 93940.

LEUTZE, EMANUEL: BIRTHDAY. May 24. Obscure itinerant painter, born in Germany, May 24, 1816, came to U.S. when nine years old, began painting by age fifteen. Painted some of most famous American works, such as: *Washington Crossing the Delaware, Washington Rallying the Troops at Monmouth,* and *Columbus Before the Queen.* Died July 18, 1868.

LOUISIANA KEEPSAKE DAY. May 24. Purpose: A day to celebrate all that is near and dear to Louisianian's hearts...food, fairs, festivals, folklore and French. "Laissez les bons temps rouler!" Sponsor: Creative Resources, Lillie Petit Gallagher, Pres, Box 4053, Baton Rouge, LA 70821.

MIAMI/FT. LAUDERDALE HOME SHOW. May 24-June 1. Miami Beach Conv Hall, Miami Beach, FL. Info from: Perl Exposition Corp, Larry Perl, Pres, 6915 Red Road, Suite 228, Coral Gables, FL 33143.

NEWHOUSE, SAMUEL I: BIRTHDAY. May 24. Mysterious multi-millionaire businessman who built family publishing and communications empire. Born to immigrant parents in a New York City tenement on May 24, 1895, Newhouse became "America's most profitable publisher." He accumulated 31 newspapers, 7 magazines, 6 television stations, 5 radio stations, 20 cable television systems. His success with the "bottom line" in publishing and communications was without parallel. He died at New York City, Aug 29, 1979.

PEALE, JAMES: DEATH ANNIVERSARY. May 24. American portrait and miniature painter (painted portraits of George and Martha Washington, and General Sir Thomas Shirley) was born at Chestertown, MD in 1749 (exact date unknown) and died May 24, 1831.

ROWLAND, JOHN G: BIRTHDAY. May 24. U.S. Representative of Connecticut's 5th district, Republican, of Waterbury, CT, born there on May 24, 1957.

SPACE MILESTONE: AURORA 7 MERCURY SPACE CAPSULE (US). May 24. Scott Carpenter becomes second American to orbit Earth. Three orbits. Launched May 24, 1962.

SPRING MOUNTAIN FREE TRAPPERS' RENDEZVOUS. May 24-26. Black power events and a tepee village depict the fur trading period from 1800 to 1840. Info from: Spring Mountain Free Trappers, Box 85111, Las Vegas, NV 89104.

TEXAS STATE ARTS AND CRAFTS FAIR. May 24-25. (Also May 31-June 1). Kerrville, TX. Top Texas craftsmen and artists. Demonstrations and exhibits. Info from: Texas Arts & Crafts Foundation, Box 1527, Kerrville, TX 78029.

TOLEDO BEND TRASH FESTIVAL. May 24-26. North of Toledo Bend Dam on the lake. Purpose: Scuba divers gather to retrieve more than 2 tons of debris from bottom of lake. Queen coronation, spearfishing tournament, treasure hunt and crawfish boil. Sponsor: J & L Marina and Resort & Dive Club, Emmett Smallwood, Rt 1, Box 390, Anacoco, LA 71403.

UTICA OLD FASHIONED ICE CREAM FESTIVAL. May 24-26. Purpose: Saluting "America's favorite dessert," ice cream, with a weekend of fun and entertainment—parade, queen contest, arts, crafts and ice cream eating contest. Info from: Ray Lewis, Utica Sertoma, Box 303, Utica, OH 43080.

VICTORIA BOAT DISASTER: ANNIVERSARY. May 24. "On May 24, 1881, one of Canada's worst marine disasters occurred on the Thames River (near London, Ontario). The *Victoria,* a small, double-decked stern-wheeler commanded by Captain Donald Rankin was conducting holiday excursion trips between London and Springbank Park. On a return trip to London the boat was dangerously overcrowded with more than

May *1986*	S	M	T	W	T	F	S
					1	2	3
	4	5	6	7	8	9	10
	11	12	13	14	15	16	17
	18	19	20	21	22	23	24
	25	26	27	28	29	30	31

COPYRIGHT © 1985 BY WILLIAM D. CHASE and HELEN M. CHASE

600 passengers. . . .crowd repeatedly shifted from side to side resulting in flooding and a precarious rocking motion of the boat. It finally heeled over and the boiler crashed through the bulwarks, bringing the upper-deck and large awning down upon the struggling crowd. The *Victoria* sank immediately and at least 182 people, the majority from London, lost their lives." Info from: historical marker near the site, erected by the Ontario Heritage Foundation, Ministry of Culture and Recreation.

WYOMING STATE CHAMPIONSHIP FIDDLE CONTEST. May 24-25. Top fiddlers from the state and region participate in this fun event. (Always Memorial Day Weekend). Info from: Chamber of Commerce, Box 324, Shoshoni, WY 82649.

MAY 25 — SUNDAY
145th Day — Remaining, 220

AFRICAN FREEDOM DAY. May 25. Public holiday in Chad, Zambia and some other African states. Members of the Organization for African Unity (formed May 25, 1963) commemorate their independence from colonial rule. Sports contests, political rallies and tribal dances.

AMERICAN BEER WEEK. May 25-31. Purpose: To celebrate and recognize the significance of quality beer and its contribution to life in America. Sponsor: American Homebrewers Assn, Box 287, Boulder, CO 80306.

AMERICAN UNITARIAN ASSOCIATION FOUNDING ANNIVERSARY. May 25. Anniversary of founding May 25, 1825 of the American Unitarian Association. Info from: Unitarian Universalist Assn, 25 Beacon St, Boston, MA 02108.

ANDERSONVILLE NATIONAL HISTORIC SITE MEMORIAL DAY PROGRAM. May 25. Andersonville National Historic Site, Andersonville, GA. Purpose: To honor the military men and women who have died while serving their country and to commemorate the men and women who have served honorably in the armed forces. Sponsor: Superintendent John Tucker, Natl Park Service, Andersonville Natl Historic Site, Andersonville, GA 31711.

ARGENTINA: NATIONAL HOLIDAY. May 25. Anniversary of establishment of independent republic, following revolt of the provinces against Spanish rule, May 25, 1810.

BIG SINGING DAY. May 25. Court House, Benton, KY. Purpose: Old-time Southern harmony singing from original shaped-note songbook of William Walker. (Always fourth Sunday in May). Info from: Society for the Preservation of Southern Harmony Singing, Ray Mofield, Pres, 301 E 14th St, Benton, KY 42025.

DOWIE, JOHN ALEXANDER: BIRTH ANNIVERSARY. May 25. Evangelist and claimant of the title "Elijah the Restorer," was born at Edinburgh, Scotland, on May 25, 1847. He established, near Chicago, the Christian Catholic Church in Zion, where some 5,000 followers created a unique community without pharmacies, physicians, theatres, dance halls, and where smoking, drinking and the eating of pork were prohibited. Dowie's ostentatiously expensive personal life style and his unsuccessful attempt to convert New York City were partially responsible for the falling away of his followers. He was expelled from the church in 1906 and died, at Chicago, Mar 9, 1907.

EMERSON, RALPH WALDO: BIRTHDAY. May 25. American author and philosopher born at Boston, MA, May 25, 1803. Died there Apr 27, 1882. It was Emerson who wrote (in his Essay on self-Reliance, 1841) "A foolish consistency is the hobgoblin of little minds, adored by little statesmen and philosophers and divines. With consistency a great soul has simply nothing to do."

FABULOUS 50'S REVIVAL. May 25-26. Purpose: To feature live music of the 50's, DJ shows with trivia, hula-hoop and dance contests. Sponsor: Mount Hope Estate & Winery, Box 685, Cornwall, PA 17016.

FESTIVAL WEEK '86. May 25-June 1. Roanoke, VA. An eight day celebration of life and the arts. Begins the Sunday before Memorial Day. Info from: Roanoke's Festival in the Park, Box 8276, Roanoke, VA 24014.

INDIANAPOLIS 500 MILE RACE. May 25. Culmination of "500" Festival. First race, 1911. (Annually, the Sunday of Memorial Day weekend.) Info from: Indianapolis Motor Speedway Corp, Box 24152, Indianapolis, IN 46224.

ITALY: PALIO DEI BALESTRIERI. May 25. Gubbio. The last Sunday in May is set aside for a medieval crossbow contest between Gubbio and Sansepolcro; medieval costumes, arms.

JORDAN: NATIONAL HOLIDAY. May 25. Independence Day. Commemorates treaty of May 25, 1946, proclaiming autonomy and establishing monarchy.

MURRAY, PHILIP: BIRTH ANNIVERSARY. May 25. American labor leader and founder of the Congress of Industrial Organizations, also active and a leader of the United Mine Workers, was born near Blantyre, Scotland, on May 25, 1886. Murray died at San Francisco, CA, on Nov 9, 1952.

NATIONAL MISSING CHILDREN'S DAY. May 25. Purpose: To promote awareness of the problem of missing children; to offer a forum for change; and to offer safety programs for children in school and community. Sponsor: Child Find, Inc, Box 277, New Paltz, NY 12561.

SPACE MILESTONE: SKYLAB 2 (US). May 25. Charles (Pete) Conrad, Jr., Joseph P. Kerwin, Paul J. Weitz spend 28 days in space experimentation. Pacific splashdown June 22. Launched May 25, 1973.

TITO'S BIRTHDAY. May 25. Josip Broz, Yugoslavian soldier and political leader, born near Zagreb, May 25, 1892. Died May 4, 1980 and interred in garden of his private residence at Belgrade. Funeral was attended by leaders of most of the world's major nations.

TRINITY SUNDAY. May 25. Christian Holy Day on the Sunday after Pentecost (q.v.) commemorates the Holy Trinity, the three divine persons: Father, Son and Holy Spirit, in one God.

TUNNEY, JAMES JOSEPH (GENE): BIRTHDAY. May 25. Heavyweight boxing champion, business executive. The famous "long-count" occurred in seventh round of Jack Dempsey-Gene Tunney world championship fight, Sept 22, 1927, at Soldier Field, Chicago. Tunney was born at New York City, May 25, 1898. Died at Greenwich, CT, Nov. 7, 1978.

VIVA! VIENNA! '86. May 25. Purpose: Family Fun Festival. Sponsor: Greater Vienna Chamber of Commerce, 110 Maple Ave E, Vienna, VA 22180.

WEEK OF SOLIDARITY WITH THE COLONIAL PEOPLES OF SOUTHERN AFRICA. May 25-June 1. Observed annually beginning on African Liberation Day, May 25. In 1972 the United Nations General Assembly appealed to governments and peoples of the world to observe this week. Info from: United Nations, Dept of Public Information, United Nations, NY 10017.

MAY 26 — MONDAY
146th Day — Remaining, 219

AMERICAN FILM FESTIVAL. May 26-31. Purpose: To show 16mm films and video tapes for use in schools, libraries, universities and other institutions. Sponsor: The Educational Film Library Assn, Sandy Mandelberger, Festival Dir, 45 John St, New York, NY 10038.

CONFEDERATE MEMORIAL DAY. May 26. Virginia. (Last Monday in May.)

ENGLAND: BANK HOLIDAY. May 26. Spring Bank Holiday observed on this date in England, Wales, Scotland and Northern Ireland.

EVANS, COOPER: BIRTHDAY. May 26. U.S. Representative of Iowa's 3rd district, Republican, of Grundy Center, IA, born in Cedar Rapids, IA, on May 26, 1924.

FEAST OF ST. AUGUSTINE OF CANTERBURY. May 26. Pope Gregory sent Augustine to convert the pagan English. Augustine became the first Archbishop of Canterbury. Augustine died May 26, 604.

JOLSON, AL: BIRTHDAY. May 26. Actor, singer (born Asa Yoelson, St. Petersburg, Russia, May 26, 1886). Died San Francisco, CA, Oct 23, 1950.

MEMORIAL DAY. May 26. Presidential Proclamation. "Issued
☆ each year since 1948 per Congressional request. PL81-512 of May 11, 1950, asks President to proclaim annually this day as a day of prayer for permanent peace. PL90-363 of June 28, 1968, requires that beginning in 1971 it will be observed the last Monday in May. Title often contains 'Prayer for Peace' therein as occurred in 1983."

MEMORIAL DAY. May 26. Legal public holiday. (PL90-363 sets Memorial Day on the last Monday in May. Applicable to federal employes and to the District of Columbia.) Also known as Decoration Day. Most countries designate a day each year for decorating graves with flowers and for other memorial tributes to the dead. Often especially an occasion for honoring those who have died in battle. Dates from Civil War years in U.S. (first documented observance at Waterloo, NY, May 5, 1865). See also: Confederate Memorial Day.

MEMORIAL DAY PARADE AND SERVICES. May 26. Gettysburg National Cemetery. 2,000 school children strew flowers over the unknown graves. Memorial services follow parade. Info from: Gettysburg Travel Council, 35 Carlisle St, Gettysburg, PA 17325.

MEMORIAL DAY RIVERBOAT RACE. May 26. St. Louis Riverfront. A St. Louis tradition between the St. Louis County Executive and the Mayor of St. Louis aboard the Huck Finn and Tom Sawyer Riverboats. Info from: St. Louis Conv & Visitors Bureau, 10 S Broadway, Suite 300, St. Louis, MO 63102.

MONTAGU, LADY MARY WORTLEY: DAY. May 26. English author baptized May 26, 1689. Died Aug 21, 1762.

PUSHKIN, ALEXANDER: BIRTHDAY. May 26. Russian author born May 26, 1799. Died Jan 29, 1837.

RIDE, SALLY KRISTEN: BIRTHDAY. May 26. Dr. Sally Ride, one of seven women in the U.S astronaut corps and the first American woman in space, was born at Encino, CA, May 26, 1951. The 32-year-old astronaut was married, in 1982, to another astronaut, Steve Hawley. Her flight aboard the space shuttle, *Challenger*, was launched from Cape Canaveral, FL on June 18, and landed at Edwards Air Force Base, CA, on June 24, 1983. The six-day flight was termed "nearly a perfect mission."

SPACE MILESTONE: SOYUZ 36 (USSR). May 26. Cosmonauts Bertalan Farkas, of Hungary, and Valery Kubasov docked at Salyut 6 on May 27 for week-long visit with Ryumin and Popov before returning to Earth. Launched May 26, 1980.

STRATFORD FESTIVAL. May 26-Oct 13. Stratford, Ontario, Canada. "North America's premier classical repertory theatre company, Stratford offers numerous productions on three stages, featuring the work of renowned actors, directors and designers." Info from: The Stratford Festival, Box 520, Stratford, Ontario, Canada N5A 6V2.

May *1986*	S	M	T	W	T	F	S
					1	2	3
	4	5	6	7	8	9	10
	11	12	13	14	15	16	17
	18	19	20	21	22	23	24
	25	26	27	28	29	30	31

TEN BEST CENSORED STORIES OF 1985. May 26-30. Purpose: To announce the 10 best censored news stories of 1985 as determined by a national panel of jurors. Info from: Carl Jensen, Ph.D, Dir, Project Censored, Sonoma State University, Rohnert Park, CA 94928.

VIRGIN ISLANDS: MEMORIAL DAY. May 26. Parades and ceremonies take place throughout the islands. Yacht races featured on St. Croix. Observed annually on last Monday in May.

WAYNE, JOHN: BIRTHDAY. May 26. American motion picture actor, born Marion Michael Morrison, at Winterset, IA on May 26, 1907. Died at Los Angeles, CA, June 11, 1979. "Talk low, talk slow, and don't say too much" was his advice on acting.

MAY 27 — TUESDAY
147th Day — Remaining, 218

BENNETT, ARNOLD: BIRTH ANNIVERSARY. May 27. English novelist, playwright and critic (Enoch) Arnold Bennett was born at Hanley, in the pottery manufacturing district of North Staffordshire on May 27, 1867. Best known of his novels is *The Old Wives' Tale* (1908), and most harshly criticized (by the literati) of his books was the popular *How to Live on Twenty-Four Hours a Day*. (1908). His *Journals* (from 1896 until near the time of his death in 1931) provide insight into Bennett's life, thought, technique of observation of the world around him and his writing methods. "The price of justice," Arnold wrote, "is eternal publicity." He died at London on Mar 27, 1931.

BLOOMER, AMELIA JENKS: BIRTHDAY. May 27. American social reformer and women's rights advocate, born at Homer, NY, May 27, 1818. Her name is remembered especially because of her work for more sensible dress for women and her recommendation of a costume which had been introduced about 1849 by Elizabeth Smith Miller, but which came to be known as the "Bloomer Costume," or "Bloomers." Amelia Bloomer died at Council Bluffs, IA, Dec 30, 1894.

CARSON, RACHEL (LOUISE): BIRTHDAY. May 27. American scientist and author, born at Springdale, PA, May 27, 1907. Author of *Silent Spring* (1962), a book which provoked widespread controversy over the use of pesticides. Died Apr 14, 1964.

DODD, CHRISTOPHER J: BIRTHDAY. May 27. U.S. Senator from Connecticut, Democrat, of East Haddam, CT, born in Willimantic, CT, on May 27, 1944.

DUNCAN, ISADORA: BIRTHDAY. May 27. American-born interpretive dancer who revolutionized entire concept of the dance. Bare-footed, freedom-loving, liberated woman and rebel against tradition, experienced world-wide professional success and profound personal tragedy (her two children drowned, her marriage failed, and she met a bizarre death when the long scarf she was wearing caught in a wheel of the open car in which she was riding, strangling her). Born at San Francisco, CA, May 27, 1878. Died at Nice, France, Sept 14, 1927.

HOMEBREWERS CONFERENCE. May 27-30. Denver, CO. Purpose: To promote the brewing of quality beer and create an awareness for the American public. Lectures, seminars, exhibits and demonstrations. Sponsor: The American Homebrewers Assn, Box 287, Boulder, CO 80306.

HUMPHREY, HUBERT HORATIO: BIRTHDAY. May 27. Born, Wallace, SD, May 27, 1911. Thirty-eighth Vice-President of the U.S. Died, Waverly, MN, Jan 13, 1978.

LAG B'OMER. May 27. Hebrew calendar date: Iyar 18, 5746. Literally, the 33rd day of the omer (harvest time), the 33rd day after the beginning of Passover. Traditionally a joyous day for weddings, picnics and outdoor activities.

NATIONAL HOMEBREW COMPETITION. May 27-28. Purpose: To evaluate and judge homebrewed beers for the benefit of improving the quality of homebrewed beers and to choose the "Homebrewer of the Year." Sponsor: The American Homebrewers Assn, Box 287, Boulder, CO 80306.

COPYRIGHT © 1985 BY WILLIAM D. CHASE and HELEN M. CHASE

RMS QUEEN MARY ANNIVERSARY. May 27. Anniversary of the maiden voyage from Southampton, England to New York Harbor on May 27, 1936. Info from: Wrather Port Properties, LTD, Kelli M. Fast, PR Coordinator, Box 8, Long Beach, CA 90801.

WALES: NATIONAL YOUTH EISTEDDFOD. May 27-31. Dyffryn Ogwen, near Bethesda, Gwynedd, Wales.

MAY 28 — WEDNESDAY
148th Day — Remaining, 217

AGASSIZ, JEAN LOUIS RODOLPHE: BIRTHDAY. May 28. Swiss geologist, teacher and author, born May 28, 1807. Died at Cambridge, MA, Dec 14, 1873. "The eye of the trilobite," Agassiz wrote in 1870, "tells us that the sun shone on the old beach where he lived; for there is nothing in nature without a purpose, and when so complicated an organ was made to receive the light, there must have been light to enter it."

CELEBRATE FOLK ART '86. May 28. Folk Art Center, Asheville, NC. A celebration of folk art and its makers in the southern Appalachians. A day to honor and recognize some of the Guild's living treasures—the artists. Info from: Southern Highland Handicraft Guild, Box 9545, Asheville, NC 28815.

DIONNE QUINTUPLETS: BIRTHDAY. May 28. Five daughters (Marie, Cecile, Yvonne, Emilie, and Annette) were born to Oliva and Elzire Dionne, near Callander, Ontario, on May 28, 1934.

GOLF: NATIONAL COLLEGIATE DIVISION I MEN'S CHAMPIONSHIP. May 28-31. Wake Forest University, Winston-Salem, NC. Info from: NCAA, Box 1906, Mission, KS 66201.

GUILLOTIN, JOSEPH IGNACE: BIRTHDAY. May 28. French physician and member of the Constituent Assembly who urged use of a machine which was sometimes called the "Maiden" for execution of death sentences—in a less painful, more certain way of dispatching those sentenced to death. The Guillotine was first used on Apr 25, 1792 for the execution of a highwayman, Nicolas Jacques Pelletier. Other machines for decapitation had been in use from time to time in other countries since the middle ages.

MICROBREWERS CONFERENCE. May 28-30. Denver, CO. Purpose: To educate brewers and potential brewers, promoting awareness and appreciation of the quality and variety of beer. Sponsor: The Institute for Fermentation and Brewing Studies, Box 287, Boulder, CO 80306.

NATIONAL COLLEGIATE WOMEN'S GOLF CHAMPIONSHIPS. May 28-31. Ohio State University, Columbus, OH. Info from: Natl Collegiate Athletic Assn, Box 1906, Mission, KS 66201.

PETRI, THOMAS E. BIRTHDAY. May 28. U.S. Representative of Wisconsin's 6th district, Republican, of Fond du Lac, WI, born in Marinette, WI, on May 28, 1940.

PITT, WILLIAM: BIRTHDAY. May 28. British prime minister from 1783 to 1801 and from 1804 to 1806. Influenced by Adam Smith's economic theories he reduced England's large national debt caused by the American Revolution. Born on May 28, 1759 at Hayes, Kent. Died Jan 23, 1806 at Putney. He was the son of William Pitt, First Earl of Chatham, for whom the city of Pittsburg was named.

ST. BERNARD OF MONTJOUX: FEAST DAY. May 28. Patron saint of mountain climbers, founder of Alpine hospices of the Great and Little St. Bernard, died at age 85, probably on May 28, 1081.

STRAWBERRY FESTIVAL. May 28-June 1. Lebanon, OR. Parades, exhibits, country fair, tournaments, carnival, and "world's largest strawberry shortcake." Info from: Chamber of Commerce, 1040 Park St, Lebanon, OR 97355.

THORPE, JAMES FRANCIS: BIRTHDAY. May 28. Jim Thorpe, distinguished American athlete, winner of pentathlon and decathlon events at the 1912 Olympic Games, professional baseball and football player, American Indian, born near Prague, OK, May 28, 1888. Died at Lomita, CA, Mar 28, 1953.

Patrick Henry

MAY 29 — THURSDAY
149th Day — Remaining, 216

ASCENSION OF BAHA'U'LLAH. May 29. Baha'i observance of the anniversary of the death in exile of Baha'u'llah (prophet-founder of the Baha'i faith), May 29, 1892. One of the nine days of the year when Baha'is suspend work. Info from: Baha'i Office of Public Affairs, Baha'i Natl Center, Wilmette, IL 60091.

CHARLES II: RESTORATION ANNIVERSARY. May 29. Restoration of Charles II to English throne, May 29, 1660. Also his birthday (May 29, 1630). English monarchy restored after Commonwealth period under Oliver Cromwell. Observance by *Cavalier Comments*, Mark and Jennie Gist, Editors, 530 E Weber Rd, Columbus, OH 43202.

CHESTERTON, GILBERT KEITH: BIRTHDAY. May 29. English author. May 29, 1874-June 14, 1936.

COLEMAN, E. THOMAS: BIRTHDAY. May 29. U.S. Representative of Missouri's 6th district, Republican, of Kansas City, MO, born there on May 29, 1943.

CORPUS CHRISTI. May 29. Roman Catholic festival celebrated in honor of the Eucharist. A solemnity observed on the Thursday following Trinity Sunday since 1246. In the U.S. Corpus Christi is celebrated on the Sunday following Trinity Sunday.

EDGAR, BOB: BIRTHDAY. May 29. U.S. Representative of Pennsylvania's 7th district, Democrat, of Middletown, PA, born in Philadelphia, PA, on May 29, 1943.

ENGLAND: INTERNATIONAL CONTEMPORARY ART FAIR. May 29-June 1. Olympia, London.

ENGLAND: OAK-APPLE DAY. May 29. Anniversary of Charles II's entry into Whitehall, May 29, 1660. Oak-apple Day actually commemorates the adventures and concealment of Charles in Boscobel's famous oak tree, in 1651. Wearing of an oak twig or leaf or an oak-apple on this day formerly was popular, along with Maypole ceremonies. Oak-apple Day is sometimes called Royal Oak Day or Shick-Shack Day.

FESTIVAL '86. May 29-30. Interlochen, MI, festival of free arts events. Concerts, plays, exhibitions and readings featuring students from each of the academy's fine arts divisions. Info from: Interlochen Arts Academy, Bruce W. Galbraith, Dir, Interlochen, MI 49643.

HENRY, PATRICK: BIRTHDAY. May 29. American revolutionary leader and orator, born, Studley, VA, May 29, 1736. Died near Brookneal, VA, June 6, 1799. Especially remembered for his speech (March 23, 1775) for arming the Virginia militia, at St. Johns Church, Richmond, VA, when he declared: "I know not what course others may take, but as for me, give me liberty or give me death."

INTERNATIONAL SCHOOL SPIRIT SEASON. May 29-Sept 30. Purpose: To recognize everyone who has helped to make school spirit better and to provide time to plan improved spirit ideas for the coming school year. Sponsor: Pepsters, Jim Hawkins, Committee for More School Spirit, Box 2652, San Diego, CA 92112.

KENNEDY, JOHN FITZGERALD: BIRTHDAY. May 29. Thirty-fifth President of the U.S., born at Brookline, MA, May 29, 1917. Assassinated while riding in an open automobile, in Dallas, TX, Nov 22, 1963. (Accused assassin. Lee Harvey Oswald, was killed at the Dallas police station by a gunman, Jack Rubenstein [Ruby], two days later.) Kennedy was the youngest man ever elected to the presidency, the first Roman Catholic, and the first president to have served in the U.S.

COPYRIGHT © 1985 BY WILLIAM D. CHASE and HELEN M. CHASE

Navy. He was the fourth U.S. president to be killed by an assassin, and the second to be buried at Arlington National Cemetery (first was William Howard Taft).

RHODE ISLAND: RATIFICATION DAY. May 29. Thirteenth state to ratify constitution, on this day in 1790.

SINNER, GEORGE A: BIRTHDAY. May 29. George A. Sinner, Governor of North Dakota, Democrat, was born at Casselton, ND, on May 29, 1928.

SPENGLER, OSWALD: BIRTHDAY. May 29. German historian, author of *The Decline of the West*, born at Blankenburg-am-Harz, Germany, on May 29, 1880. Died at Munich, May 8, 1936.

WISCONSIN: ADMISSION DAY. May 29. Became 30th state on this day in 1848.

MAY 30 — FRIDAY
150th Day — Remaining, 215

COLLEGE WORLD SERIES. May 30-June 8. Rosenblatt Stadium, Omaha, NE. NCAA Division I Mens Baseball Championships. Double elimination tournament of eight NCAA regional teams for the Division I college baseball championship. Info from: Charles Ammons, 2561 Whitmore St, Omaha, NE 68112.

GERMANY: MARBURG UNIVERSITY ANNIVERSARY. May 30. University of Marburg was founded May 30, 1527.

GREAT AMERICAN BEER FESTIVAL. May 30-31. Denver, CO. Purpose: To celebrate the depth, variety and distinctive beers brewed by American breweries. Over 100 beers from all of America's breweries. Sponsor: The American Homebrewers Assn, Box 287, Boulder, CO 80306.

HALL OF FAME ANNIVERSARY. May 30. The Hall of Fame for Great Americans at New York University in New York City was dedicated and opened to the public on May 30, 1901.

HELLDORADO DAYS. May 30-June 8. Parade, carnival, arts & crafts, and rodeo. Info from: Nevada Commission on Tourism, Capitol Complex, Carson City, NV 89710.

LINCOLN MEMORIAL DEDICATION ANNIVERSARY. May 30. The Lincoln Memorial, in Washington, DC, was dedicated May 30, 1922.

MOON PHASE: LAST QUARTER. May 30. Moon enters Last Quarter phase at 7:55 a.m., E.S.T.

MUSLIM FESTIVAL: LAILAT al-QADR. May 30. "The Night of Power" is observed on this date. Muslim calendar date: Ramadhan 21, 1406. Gregorian calendar date of observance may vary by one day.

PORTLAND ROSE FESTIVAL. May 30-June 15. Celebration includes more than 50 events featuring grand floral parade, hot air balloons, band festivals, auto and ski races, carnival and Navy ship visits. Sponsor: Portland Rose Festival Assn, Ken Strobeck, 220 NW 2nd Ave, Portland, OR 97209.

May 1986	S	M	T	W	T	F	S
					1	2	3
	4	5	6	7	8	9	10
	11	12	13	14	15	16	17
	18	19	20	21	22	23	24
	25	26	27	28	29	30	31

ROLEX INTERNATIONAL. May 30-June 1. Lexington, KY. Top equestrians from around the world compete in dressage, cross country and stadium jumping. Info from: KY Dept of Travel, Capital Plaza Office Tower, Frankfort, KY 40601.

SPACE MILESTONE: MARINER 9 (US) May 30. Unmanned spacecraft entered Martian orbit Nov 13, studied temperature and gravitational fields and sent back photographs. First spacecraft to orbit another planet. Launched May 30, 1971.

SPACE MILESTONE: NASA ATS-6 (US) May 30. Communications satellite with expected 6-year life. Stationary orbit. Launched May 30, 1974.

ST. JOAN OF ARC: FEAST DAY. May 30. French heroine and martyr, known as The Maid of Orleans, led French against English invading army. Captured, found guilty of heresy, and burned at the stake in 1431 (at age 19). Innocence declared in 1456. Canonized in 1920.

MAY 31 — SATURDAY
151st Day — Remaining, 214

HERRINGTON, JOHN S: BIRTHDAY. May 31. John S. Herrington, U.S. Secretary of Energy, (sworn in Feb 7, 1985) was born at Los Angeles, CA, on May 31, 1939.

HUNTER, DUNCAN LEE: BIRTHDAY. May 31. U.S. Representative of California's 45th district, Republican, of Coronado, CA, was born at Riverside, CA, May 31, 1948.

JOHNSTOWN FLOOD ANNIVERSARY. May 31. More than 2,000 lives lost when heavy rains caused Conemaugh Dam to collapse, flooding Johnstown, PA, May 31, 1889.

MARBLE MEET AT AMANA. May 31-June 1. Holiday Inn, Amana, IA. Seminar, banquet and exhibits. Collectors buy, sell and trade marbles. Sponsor: Marbles Collectors Unlimited, Box 206, Northboro, MA 01532.

MERLE TRAVIS FINGER PICKING GUITAR CONTEST. May 31. Purpose: To bring together finger pickers with an ear for traditional Southern mountain music. Info from: Ozark Folk Ctr, Mountain View, AR 72560.

POPE PIUS XI: BIRTHDAY. May 31. Ambrogio Damiano Achille Ratti, 259th Pope of the Roman Catholic Church, born at Desio, Italy, May 31, 1857. Elected Pope Feb 6, 1922. Died Feb 10, 1939.

SOUTH AFRICA: REPUBLIC DAY. May 31. National holiday. On May 31, 1910, the Union of South Africa was established. On May 31, 1961, it became the Republic of South Africa.

WHITMAN, WALT: BIRTHDAY. May 31. American poet, author of *Leaves of Grass*, born May 31, 1819. Died Mar 26, 1892. "No really great song," Whitman wrote, "can ever attain full purport till long after the death of its singer—till it has accrued and incorporated the many passions, many joys and sorrows, it has itself aroused."

WISCONSIN FOLK FESTIVAL. May 31-June 1. Fond du Lac County Fairgrounds, Fond du Lac, WI. Folk dance groups, cultural displays, ethnic foods, arts and crafts. Info from: Conv & Visitors Bureau, 207 N. Main St, Fond du Lac, WI 54935.

COPYRIGHT © 1985 BY WILLIAM D. CHASE and HELEN M. CHASE

Iune.

JUNE 1 — SUNDAY

152nd Day — Remaining, 213

ATLANTIC, CARIBBEAN AND GULF HURRICANE SEASON. June 1-Nov 30. Info from: U.S. Dept of Commerce, National Oceanic and Atmospheric Administration, Rockville, MD 20852.

CENTRAL PACIFIC HURRICANE SEASON. June 1-Oct 31. Central Pacific defined as: 140° West Longitude to International Date Line (180° West Longitude). Info from: U.S. Dept of Commerce, Natl Oceanic and Atmospheric Administration, Rockville, MD 20852.

CONNECTICUT TEL-MED WEEK. June 1-7. Purpose: To encourage and promote health awareness among Connecticut state residents. Info from: Barbara Mahoney, Connecticut Tel-Med Council, 56 Franklin St, Waterbury, CT 06702.

CORPUS CHRISTI (U.S. OBSERVANCE). June 1. A moveable Roman Catholic celebration commemorating the institution of the Holy Eucharist. The solemnity has been observed on the Thursday following Trinity Sunday, since 1246, except in the U.S. where it is observed on the Sunday following Trinity Sunday.

DAY OF THE RICE GOD. June 1. Chiyoda, Japan. Annual rice-transplanting festival observed on first Sunday of June. Centuries-old rural folk-ritual revived in 1930s and celebrated with colorful costumes, parades, music, dancing and prayers to the Shinto rice god, Sanbai-sama.

EARLY BIRD DAY. June 1. Purpose: Time to plan ahead. Schedule 1987 celebrations and observances and submit them for listing in *Chase's Annual Events*.

ELFRETH'S ALLEY FETE DAYS. June 1. Philadelphia, PA. "Elfreth's Alley, the oldest street in the United States, opens its homes to the public along with Colonial crafts and a bake sale at Museum House, 126 Elfreth's Alley." Info from: Conv & Visitors Bureau, Three Penn Ctr Plaza, Suite 2020, Philadelphia, PA 19102.

ENGLAND: OBSERVER TRANSATLANTIC RACE BEGINS. June 1. Plymouth, Devon. Two hundred yachts race from Plymouth, England to Newport, RI. Info from: Royal Western Yacht Club of England, 9 Grand Parade, Plymouth PL1 3DG.

FIGHT THE FILTHY FLY MONTH. June 1-30. Purpose: To alert the public to the danger of tolerating house flies and the importance of eliminating these disease-carrying insects. Sponsor: Devpro Machine, Inc, Insectocutor Div, 80 Telegraph Rd, Middleport, NY 14105.

INTERNATIONAL MOTHERS' PEACE DAY. June 1. Purpose: To provide an opportunity for mothers worldwide to demonstrate for peace. "Those who nurture life on earth are of one mind in their opposition to those who would destroy it." Founded June 2, 1872 by Julia Ward Howe and observed on first Sunday in June. Sponsor: Internatl Mothers' Peace Day Committee, Jeanne Schramm, Chrmn, Box 102, West Liberty, WV 26074.

ITALY: GIOCO DEL PONTE. June 1. Pisa. The first Sunday in June is set aside for the Battle of the Bridge, a medieval parade and contest for possession of the bridge.

JUNE DAIRY MONTH. June 1-30. Purpose: Since 1937, the dairy industry has set aside June as "a time to salute cows, the dairy industry and its food products." Sponsor: American Dairy Assn, Jane A. Holmes, VP, Dir Publicity, 6300 N River Rd, Rosemont, IL 60618.

KENTUCKY: ADMISSION DAY. June 1. Became 15th State on this day in 1792.

KITCHENEERING WEEK. June 1-7. Purpose: Dedicated to a revival of the homemaking arts. Sponsor: Mme Ginette's Original School For Brides, 3369 Hamilton Way, Los Angeles, CA 90026.

KITTY HAWK TRIATHALON. June 1. Kitty Hawk Kites, Nags Head, NC. Purpose: A triathalon composed of hang gliding, windsurfing and sailing to benefit the Leukemia Society. Sponsor: Kitty Hawk Kites, Box 340, Nags Head, NC 27959.

LA FETE: NATIONAL FESTIVAL OF FOOD AND COOKERY. June 1-Aug 31. New Orleans, LA. Purpose: Celebration of food, wine and music in the food capital of the United States. Emphasis on creole and cajun cuisines. Sponsor: La Fete, Mark Romig, Exec Dir, 580 Oil and Gas Bldg, New Orleans, LA 70112.

MONROE, MARILYN: BIRTHDAY. June 1. American actress (Norma Jean Mortenson) born Los Angeles, June 1, 1926. Died Aug 5, 1962.

NATHANIEL ULYSSES TURTLE DAY. June 1. Purpose: Turtle New Year's day. Festivities start on the eve of this day to ring out the old 9953 year and ring in the 9954 year of the turtle. Sponsor: Turtles Internatl, Box 96, Westchester, IL 60153.

NATIONAL ADOPT-A-CAT MONTH. June 1-30. Purpose: To help promote the adoption of homeless cats and kittens. Sponsor: 9-Lives Cat Food for The American Humane Assn. Info from: Daniel J. Edelman, Inc, 211 E Ontario St, Chicago, IL 60611.

NATIONAL RAGWEED CONTROL MONTH. June 1-30. Purpose: Destroy weeds—Protect health. "Get ragweed before it gets you." Sponsor: Air Pollution Control League, Charles N. Howison, Exec Secy, 18 E 4th St, Cincinnati, OH 45202.

NATIONAL ROSE MONTH. June 1-30. Purpose: To recognize the Rose, America's Favorite Flower, grown in all fifty states. Sponsors: (1) Roses Inc, James C. Krone, Exec Dir, Box 99, Haslett, MI 48840, and (2) The American Rose Society, Harold S. Goldstein, Exec Dir, Box 30,000, Shreveport, LA 71130 and (3) All-America Rose Selections, Inc, Mr. George Rose, Box 218, Shenandoah, IA 51601.

NATIONAL SAFE BOATING WEEK. June 1-7. Purpose: A week when all boating organizations work together to promote safety on our waters. Sponsor: U.S. Coast Guard. Info from: John Bernhartsen, U.S. Coast Guard HQ (G-BBS-4), 2100 2nd St, SW, Washington, DC 20593.

NATIONAL SIMPLE SPEAK DAY. June 1. Purpose: To encourage politicians, educators, executives, bureaucrats, journalists, lawyers and all others to observe this day by using ordinary, understandable language. Sponsor: Bartlett V. Ames, Pres, Fawecettstown University, 303 Fallis Rd, Columbus, OH 43214.

NATIONAL THEATRE WEEK. June 1-7. Purpose: To perpetuate the memory and spirit of those who have fostered theatre in America and raise public consciousness of live theatre. Sponsor: Committee for National Theatre Week, Philip Paskert, Pres, 1807 Market St, San Francisco, CA 94103.

NEW COLLEGE MUSIC FESTIVAL. June 1-21. Purpose: An international celebration of chamber music teaching and performing by world-class guest faculty artists and selected young

COPYRIGHT © 1985 BY WILLIAM D. CHASE and HELEN M. CHASE

talented musicians. Sponsor: New College Music Festival, Millicent Fleming, Admin Dir, 5700 N Tamiami Trail, Sarasota, FL 33580.

PEOPLE'S REPUBLIC OF CHINA; INTERNATIONAL CHILDREN'S DAY. June 1. Shanghai.

PHILATELIC WRITERS MONTH. June 1-30. Purpose: To honor philatelic writers and journalists and to recognize their importance in the world of philately. Sponsor: Society of Philaticians, G. Detjen, Jr, Secy, 154 Laguna Ct, St. Augustine Shores, FL 32086.

PLYMOUTH PLANTATION EARTHQUAKE ANNIVERSARY. June 1. The first earthquake in the U.S. to have been recorded and described in writing occurred at Plymouth, MA, on June 1, 1638, at 2 p.m. Governor William Bradford described the event in his *History*: "... it was very terrible for ye time; and as ye men were set talking in ye house, some women and others were without ye doors, and ye earth shooke with ye violence as they could not stand without catching hold of ye posts... but ye violence lasted not long. And about halfe an hower, or less, came an other noyse & shaking, but neither so loud nor strong as ye former, but quickly passed over, and so it ceased."

PORTER, JOHN EDWARD: BIRTHDAY. June 1. U.S. Representative of Illinois' 10th district, Republican, of Winnetka, IL, was born in Evanston, IL, on June 1, 1935.

SONOMA VALLEY CHAMBER OF COMMERCE OX ROAST. June 1. Historic Sonoma Plaza, Sonoma, CA. All-American typical family bar-b-cue in the park. Navy band and barbershop chorus. Sponsor: Sonoma Valley Chamber, Audrey L. Barnard, 453 First St, East, Sonoma, CA 95476.

SOUTHWEST FESTIVAL OF THE ARTS. June 1. Southwest Washington Waterfront Park, Washington, DC. A festival celebrating the arts and cultural diversity of the community. Info from: Southwest Festival Of Arts, Box 8091, Washington, DC 20024.

SPACE MILESTONE: SOYUZ 9 (USSR). June 1. Cosmonauts Nikolayev and Sevastyanov set space endurance record of 17 days, 16 hours and 59 minutes. Launched June 1, 1970.

TEACHER "THANK YOU" WEEK. June 1-7. Purpose: Write or call teachers and professors who influenced your life. Tell them about it. Send, or better yet take, a big red apple. (Annually, first week in June.) Sponsor: Lake Superior State College Unicorn Hunters, W.T. Rabe, Sault Ste. Marie, MI 49783.

TEACHERS' DAY. June 1. Massachusetts. (First Sunday in June.)

TENNESSEE ADMISSION DAY. June 1. Became 16th State on this day in 1796.

TUNISIA: NATIONAL HOLIDAY. June 1.

WESTERN SAMOA: NATIONAL HOLIDAY. June 1.

WILSON, CHARLES: BIRTHDAY. June 1. U.S. Representative of Texas's 2nd district, Democrat, of Lufkin, TX, born in Trinity, TX, June 1, 1933.

YOUNG, BRIGHAM: BIRTHDAY. June 1. Mormon church leader born at Whittingham, VT, June 1, 1801. He died at Salt Lake City, UT on Aug 29, 1877, and was survived by 17 wives and 47 children. Utah observes, as a State Holiday, the anniversary of his entrance into the Salt Lake Valley, July 24, 1847.

ZOO AND AQUARIUM MONTH. June 1-30. Purpose: To educate the public about zoo animals and their habitats. Sponsor: North Carolina Zoological Park, Rt 4, Box 83, Asheboro, NC 27203.

June *1986*

S	M	T	W	T	F	S
1	2	3	4	5	6	7
8	9	10	11	12	13	14
15	16	17	18	19	20	21
22	23	24	25	26	27	28
29	30					

JUNE 2 — MONDAY
153rd Day — Remaining, 212

BELGIUM: PROCESSION OF THE GOLDEN CHARIOT. June 2. Mons, Belgium. Horse-drawn coach carrying a reliquary of St. Waudru circles the town of Mons. Procession commemorates delivery of Mons from the Plague in 1349. In the town square, in afternoon, St. George fights the dragon. Lumecon symbolizes triumph of good over evil, and when victory is won the spectators sing traditional songs.

GOLF: BRITISH AMATEUR CHAMPIONSHIP. June 2-7. Royal Lytham and St. Annes Golf Course, Lytham St. Annes, Lancashire. The Lancashire Golf Club celebrates its centenary in 1986.

HRISTO BOTEV DAY. June 2. Bulgaria. Poet and national hero, fell fighting Turks, 1876.

ITALY: NATIONAL HOLIDAY. June 2. (Republic Day). Commemorates referendum on June 2, 1946, in which republic status was selected instead of return to monarchy.

MARQUIS DE SADE: BIRTHDAY. June 2. Donatien Alphonse Francois, Comte de Sade, was born at Paris, June 2, 1740. French military man, governor-general and author, who spent much of his life in prison because of his acts of cruelty and violence, outrageous behavior and debauchery. The word "sadism" was created from his name to describe cruelty and gratification in inflicting pain. He died near Paris, at the Charenton lunatic asylum, on Dec. 2, 1814.

NATIONAL SOARING WEEK. June 2-8. Purpose: Introduction to and celebration of motorless flight in sail planes across the country. Sponsor: The Soaring Society of America, Box 66071, Los Angeles, CA 90066.

ST. PIUS X: BIRTHDAY. June 2. Giuseppe Melchiorre Sarto, 257th Pope of the Roman Catholic Church, born June 2, 1835, at Riese, Italy. Elected Pope Aug 4, 1903. Died Aug 20, 1914. Canonized May 29, 1954.

TRACK (OUTDOOR): NATIONAL COLLEGIATE DIVISION I MEN'S & WOMEN'S CHAMPIONSHIPS. June 2-7. Indianapolis, IN. Info from: NCAA, Box 1906, Mission, KS 66201.

WAR MEMORIAL PLAZA GRAND OPENING. June 2. Official summer opening of War Memorial Plaza's daily summer events. Entertainment and performances. Info from: Mayor's Office of Adventures in Fun, 100 Holliday St, Baltimore, MD 21202.

JUNE 3 — TUESDAY
154th Day — Remaining, 211

DAVIS, JEFFERSON: BIRTHDAY. June 3. American statesman, U.S. Senator, only president of the Confederate States of America, imprisoned May 10, 1865-May 13, 1867, but never brought to trial, deprived of rights of citizenship after the Civil War. Davis was born at Todd County, KY, June 3, 1808, and died at New Orleans, LA, Dec 6, 1889. His citizenship was restored, posthumously, on Oct 17, 1978, when Pres. Carter signed an Amnesty Bill. Carter stated: "Our nation needs to clear away the guilts and enmities and recriminations of the past, to finally set at rest the divisions that threatened to destroy our nation and to discredit the great principles on which it was founded." This bill, he said "officially completes the long process of reconciliation that has reunited our people following the tragic conflict between the states." Davis' birthday is observed in some states on the first Monday in June.

DUKE OF WINDSOR MARRIAGE ANNIVERSARY. June 3. The Duke of Windsor who, as King Edward VIII, had abdicated the British throne on Dec 11, 1936, was married to Mrs. Wallis Warfield Simpson of Baltimore, MD. The marriage took place in Monts, France on June 3, 1937.

FISH, HAMILTON, JR: BIRTHDAY. June 3. U.S. Representative of New York's 21st district, Republican, of Millbrook, NY, born in Washington, DC, on June 3, 1926.

COPYRIGHT © 1985 BY WILLIAM D. CHASE and HELEN M. CHASE

GOLF: NAIA MEN'S DIVISION CHAMPIONSHIP. June 3-6. Site to be determined. Info from: Natl Assn of Intercollegiate Athletics, 1221 Baltimore, Kansas City, MO 64105.

HOBART, GARRET AUGUSTUS: BIRTHDAY. June 3. Twenty-fourth vice-president of the U.S. (1897-1899) born, Long Branch, NJ, June 3, 1844. Died, Patterson, NJ, Nov 21, 1899.

HONE, WILLIAM: BIRTHDAY. June 3. English author and bookseller born at Bath, England, June 3, 1780. Died at Tottenham, Nov 6, 1842. Compiler of *The Every-Day Book; or Everlasting Calendar of Popular Amusements* (1826). It was William Hone who said: "A good lather is half the shave."

MISSION SAN CARLOS BORROMEO DE CARMELO ANNIVERSARY. June 3. California Mission to the Indians founded June 3, 1770.

ORTIZ, SOLOMON PORFIRIO: BIRTHDAY. June 3. U.S. Representative of Texas's 27th district, Democrat, of Corpus Christi, TX, born in Robstown, TX, on June 3, 1938.

SPACE MILESTONE: GEMINI 4 (US). June 3. Major McDivitt and Major White make 66 orbits. White takes spacewalk and maneuvers 20 minutes outside capsule. Launched June 3, 1965.

JUNE 4 — WEDNESDAY
155th Day — Remaining, 210

AVIATION: FIRST FREE FLIGHT BY A WOMAN: ANNIVERSARY. June 4. Marie Thible, of Lyons, France, accompanied by a pilot (Monsieur Fleurant), on June 4, 1784, became the first woman in history to fly in a free balloon. According to her pilot, Mme Thible gave voice to her high spirits by "singing like a bird" as she drifted across Lyons in a balloon named *Le Gustave* (for King Gustave III, of Sweden, who was watching the ascent). The balloon reached a height of 8,500 feet in a flight which lasted about 45 minutes. The event occurred less than six months after the first flight in history by a man.

BULGARIA: SOFIA INTERNATIONAL BOOK FAIR. June 4-9. Info from: Internatl Book Fair, 11 Slaveikov Square, Sofia, Bulgaria.

FINLAND: FLAG DAY. June 4. Finland's armed forces honor the birth anniversary of Carl Gustaf Mannerheim, born June 4, 1867.

GEORGE III: BIRTHDAY. June 4. The English King against whom American revolution was directed. June 4, 1738-Jan 29, 1820.

HORSERACING: THE DERBY. June 4. Epsom Racecourse, Epsom, Surrey, England. "The most famous and prestigious horse race in the world, was devised at a noble dinner party in 1779 and named after one of the diners — Lord Derby." Info from: United Racecourses Ltd, Racecourse Paddock, Epsom, Surrey, England KT18 5NJ. Note: The Derby is followed by the Coronation Cup on June 5th, Canada Day on June 6th, and the Oaks Stakes on June 7th, all at Epsom Racecourse.

INTERNATIONAL DAY OF INNOCENT CHILDREN VICTIMS OF AGGRESSION. June 4. The United Nations General Assembly, on Aug 19, 1982, decided to commemorate June 4 of each year as International Day of Innocent Children Victims of Aggression. Info from: United Nations Dept of Public Information, United Nations, NY 10017.

JACK JOUETT'S RIDE ANNIVERSARY. June 4. Jack Jouett, born at Albermarle County, VA, on Dec 7, 1754, made an heroic 45-mile ride on horseback during the night of June 3-4, 1781, to warn Virginia's Governor Thomas Jefferson and the legislature that the British were coming. Jouett rode from a tavern in Louisa County to Charlottesville, VA, in about 6½ hours, arriving at Jefferson's home about dawn on June 4th. Lt. Col. Tarleton's British forces raided Charlottesville, but Jouett's warning gave the Americans time to escape. Jouett died at Bath, KY, in 1822 (exact date unknown). Reportedly,

Jack Jouett Day, commemorating the historic and heroic ride, is observed on the first Saturday in June in the Charlottesville area.

MALAYSIA: BIRTHDAY OF HIS MAJESTY THE KING. June 4. National holiday in Malaysia. Observed on the first Wednesday in June. Info from: Embassy of Malaysia, 2401 Massachusetts Ave NW, Washington, DC 20008.

METZENBAUM, HOWARD M: BIRTHDAY. June 4. U.S. Senator from Ohio, Democrat, of Lyndhurst, OH, was born in Cleveland, OH, on June 4, 1917.

OLD MAID'S DAY. June 4. Purpose: To honor old maids and all never-married women over 35; a time to celebrate with fun and humor. Roses and daisies are symbols of the day. Established by Miss Marian Richards of Norristown, PA, Old Maid's Day has been observed since 1948. Sponsors: Mrs. Judith A. Tomecsek, 224 N Jefferson St, Allentown, PA 18102 & Miss Grace Kercsmar, 639 William St, Bethlehem, PA 18015.

RITTENHOUSE SQUARE ART ANNUAL. June 4-8. Philadelphia, PA. Open air gallery, top professional artists and more than 20,000 works of fine art. Info from: Conv & Visitors Bureau, Three Penn Ctr Plaza, Suite 2020, Philadelphia, PA 19102.

SPINA BIFIDA ASSOCIATION OF AMERICA CONFERENCE. June 4-7. Dearborn, MI. Purpose: To inform individuals born with spina bifida, their parents and professionals about the latest health care, educational opportunities and general information available to them. Info from: SBAA, 1986 Conference, Kent Smith, Exec Dir, 343 S Dearborn, Suite 310, Chicago, IL 60604.

TONGA: NATIONAL DAY. June 4. National holiday observed in Tonga.

JUNE 5 — THURSDAY
156th Day — Remaining, 209

BROOKLYN: ANNIVERSARY DAY. June 5. Brooklyn, NY. Purpose: The day when all churches unite in one grand demonstration of fraternal amity. Parade and "practically a holiday in Brooklyn." Observed on first Thursday in June, unless Memorial Day falls in same week, in which case it is the second Thursday. Sponsor: Brooklyn Sunday School Union, 125 Ft. Green Pl, Brooklyn, NY 11217.

CALHOUN COUNTY WOOD FESTIVAL. June 5-7. Purpose: To emphasize wood crafts and the uses of wood in our area. Carnival and competitive events. Sponsor: Calhoun County Wood Festival, Box 382, Grantsville, WV 26147.

CEREAL CITY FESTIVAL. June 5-7. Downtown Mall, Battle Creek, MI. Purpose: Fun, entertainment and surprises for the whole family including the "World's longest breakfast table." Info from: Visitor & Convention Bureau, 172 W Van Buren, Battle Creek, MI 49017.

CLARK, CHARLES JOSEPH (JOE): BIRTHDAY. June 5. Canadian politician, born at High River, Alberta, June 5, 1939. Clark became Canada's 16th Prime Minister (and the youngest ever) on June 4, 1979 and served in that post until Mar 3, 1980.

DENMARK: CONSTITUTION DAY. June 5. National holiday. Offices and stores close at noon.

DICKINSON, WILLIAM LOUIS: BIRTHDAY. June 5. U.S. Representative of Alabama's 2nd district, Republican, of Montgomery, AL, was born in Opelika, AL on June 5, 1925.

ENGLAND: HORSERACING: CORONATION CUP. June 5. Epsom Racecourse, Epsom, Surrey, England.

FIRST BALLOON FLIGHT: ANNIVERSARY. June 5. The first public demonstration of a hot air balloon flight took place at Annonay, France, on June 5, 1783, where the co-inventor brothers, Joseph and Jacques Montgolfier, succeeded in launching their 33-foot-diameter "globe aerostatique." It rose an estimated 1,500 feet and travelled, windborne, about 7,500 feet before landing after the 10-minute flight—the first sustained flight of any object achieved by man.

KENNEDY, ROBERT F: ASSASSINATION ANNIVERSARY. June 5. Senator Kennedy was shot while campaigning for presidential nomination, in Los Angeles, CA, June 5, 1968; died following day. Sirhan Sirhan convicted of his murder.

NATIONAL INTERCOLLEGIATE ROWING CHAMPIONSHIPS (IRA). June 5-7. Onondaga Lake, Liverpool, NY. Info from: Syracuse Univ, Lawrence Kimball, Sports Info Office, Manley Field House, Syracuse, NY 13210.

PINK TOMATO FESTIVAL. June 5-7. Warren, AR. Purpose: To promote Bradley County tomatoes. Info from: Chamber of Commerce, Municipal Bldg, 206 N Myrtle St, Warren, AR 71671.

SEYCHELLES: LIBERATION DAY. June 5. Republic of Seychelles celebrates National Holiday.

SMITH, ADAM: BIRTHDAY. June 5. Scottish economist and philosopher, author of *An Enquiry into the Nature and Causes of the Wealth of Nations* (published in 1776), born June 5, 1723 at Kirkaldy, Fifeshire, Scotland. Died at Edinburgh, July 17, 1790. "Consumption," he wrote, "is the sole end and purpose of production; and the interest of the producer ought to be attended to only so far as it may be necessary for promoting that of the consumer."

SPACE MILESTONE: SOYUZ T-2 (USSR). June 5. Launched on June 5, 1980, Cosmonauts Yuri Malyshev and Vladimir Aksenov docked at Salyut 6 on June 6, returned to Earth June 9.

WORLD CAMPAIGN FOR THE BIOSPHERE. June 5. (World Environment Day) Purpose: To awaken people to their responsibilities toward the Biosphere as our planetary life-support system of which we constitute an integral part and yet threaten increasingly by our ever-increasing population and profligate activities. Meetings this month of World Council for the Biosphere, International Society for Environmental Education and the sponsoring organization: Foundation for Environmental Conservation, Dr. Nicholas Polunin, Pres, 7 Chemin Taverney, 1218 Grand-Saconnex, Geneva, Switzerland.

WORLD ENVIRONMENT DAY. June 5. Observed annually on June 5, the anniversary of the opening of the UN Conference on the Human Environment held in Stockholm in 1972, which led to establishment of UN Environment Programme, based in Nairobi. The General Assembly has urged marking day with activities reaffirming concern for the preservation and enhancement of the environment. Info from: UN Dept of Public Information, United Nations, NY 10017.

JUNE 6 — FRIDAY
157th Day — Remaining, 208

ANTIQUE AUTOMOBILE CLUB OF AMERICA: SPRING MEET. June 6-8. Kingsport, TN. Info from: Box 417, Hershey, PA 17033.

BAHAMAS: LABOR DAY. June 6. Public holiday. First Friday in June celebrated with parades, displays and picnics.

June	S	M	T	W	T	F	S
1986	1	2	3	4	5	6	7
	8	9	10	11	12	13	14
	15	16	17	18	19	20	21
	22	23	24	25	26	27	28
	29	30					

BEANBLOSSOM BLUEGRASS FESTIVAL. June 6-15. Beanblossom, IN. Info from: James Monroe, Booking Agent, 3819 Dickerson Rd, Nashville, TN 37207.

BONIOR, DAVID EDWARD: BIRTHDAY. June 6. U.S. Representative of Michigan's 12th district, Democrat, of Mount Clemens, MI, born in Detroit, MI, on June 6, 1945.

CURWOOD FESTIVAL. June 6-8. Owosso, MI. Commemorates birthday of James Oliver Curwood, Owosso-born author and conservationist (June 12, 1878-Aug 13, 1927) and other famous sons. Parade, raft races, etc. (First full weekend in June.) Info from: Curwood Festival, Box 461, Owosso, MI 48867.

D-DAY (OPERATION OVERLORD) ANNIVERSARY. June 6. Allied Expeditionary Force landed in Normandy on this day in 1944.

DEUKMEJIAN, GEORGE: BIRTHDAY. June 6. George Deukmejian, Governor of California, Republican, was born at Menands, NY, on June 6, 1928.

DONUT DAY. June 6. Chicago, IL. Founded in 1937 by the Salvation Army for fund raising during the great depression, Donut Day is now an annual tradition. Recalling the donuts served to doughboys by the Salvation Army during World War I, symbolic paper "donuts" are given to contributors. Always observed on first Friday in June. Info from: Robert A. Bonesteel, Dir of Communications, The Salvation Army, Metropolitan Divisional Hq, 875 N Dearborn, Chicago, IL 60610.

ENGLAND: ALDEBURGH FESTIVAL. June 6-22. Aldeburgh, Suffolk. Festival of music and arts founded in 1948 by the English composer, Benjamin Britten.

ENGLAND: HORSERACING: CANADA DAY. June 6. Epsom Racecourse, Epsom, Surrey, England.

FESTIVAL '86. June 6-8. Calder Plaza, Grand Rapids, MI. Purpose: A summer celebration and showcase of the arts representing a full range of artistic activities in West Michigan. Sponsor: Arts Council of Greater Grand Rapids, M. Patricia Rosely, Program Dir, 205-B Waters Bldg, Grand Rapids, MI 49503.

HARBORFEST. June 6-8. Norfolk, VA. Tall ships, sailboat races, music and watershows. Info from: Harborfest, 207 Granby St, Suite 311, Norfolk, VA 23510.

KHACHATURIAN, ARAM (ILICH): BIRTHDAY. June 6. Russian musician and composer, noted for compositions based on folk music and legend, born at Tbilisi, Georgia, U.S.S.R., June 6, 1903. Died May 1, 1978.

KOREA: MEMORIAL DAY. June 6. Nation pays tribute to the war dead and memorial services are held at the National Cemetery in Seoul. Legally recognized Korean holiday.

MIAMI/BAHAMAS GOOMBAY FESTIVAL. June 6-8. Purpose: Celebration of black culture and heritage of Bahamian settlers in Miami's Coconut Grove in 1880's. Sponsor: Miami/Bahamas Goombay Festival, Susan Neuman, 555 NE 15th St, #25-K, Miami, FL 33132.

OLD TIME FIDDLERS CONTEST. June 6-7. Dunseith, North Dakota. Info from: Dean Mortenson, International Peace Garden, Dunseith, ND 58329.

OZARK FOLK CENTER QUILT SHOW. June 6-8. Ozark Folk Center, Mountain View, AR. Purpose: Arkansas quilters display their technique and talent in this traditional art. Info from Ozark Folk Ctr, Mountain View, AR 72560.

PAPILLION DAYS. June 6-8. Halleck Park, Papillion, Nebraska. Purpose: A community celebration with parades, games, flea market, carnival and entertainment. Sponsor: Chamber of Commerce, 122 E Third St, Papillion, NE 68046.

PHILATELIC WRITERS DAY. June 6. Purpose: To honor philatelic writers and publicists. Sponsor: Society of Philaticians, G. Detjen, Jr, Secy, 154 Laguna Ct, St. Augustine Shores, FL 32086.

PORTSMOUTH SEAWALL FESTIVAL. June 6-8. A celebration of art, music and food. Water events and fireworks. Info from: Chamber of Commerce, Box 70, Portsmouth, VA 23705.

COPYRIGHT © 1985 BY WILLIAM D. CHASE and HELEN M. CHASE

PROPOSITION 13: ANNIVERSARY, June 6. California voters (65% of them) supported a primary election ballot initiative, June 6, 1978, to cut property taxes 57%. Regarded as possible omen of things to come across country, a taxpayer's revolt against high taxes and government spending.

SOUND AND LIGHT SPECTACULAR: "THE IMMORTAL SHOWBOAT". June 6-Sept 1. Purpose: An outdoor drama that tells the story of the World War II battleship through spoken word, music, sound effects and lighting. Info from USS North Carolina Battleship Memorial, Box 417, Wilmington, NC 28402.

SPACE MILESTONE: SOYUZ 11 (USSR). June 6. Cosmonauts G.T. Dobrovolsky, V.N. Volkov, V.I. Patsayev died during return landing after 24-day space flight, June 30. Soyuz 11 had docked at Salyut orbital space station June 7-29 where scientific experiments had been conducted. First humans to die in space. Launched on June 6, 1971.

SUN FUN FESTIVAL. June 6-9. Beach games, parades, beauty contests, sports events. Sponsor: Myrtle Beach Area Chamber of Commerce, 1301 N Kings Highway, Myrtle Beach, SC 29577.

SWEDEN: FLAG DAY. June 6. Commemorates the day upon which Gustavus I (Gustavus Vasa) ascended the throne of Sweden in 1523.

THREE RIVERS ARTS FESTIVAL. June 6-22. Downtown Pittsburgh, PA. Purpose: Annual celebration attracts 500,000 to its juried visual arts exhibits, invited exhibitions, artists' market, special events, performing arts and demonstrations. Sponsor: Three Rivers Arts Festival, Exec Dir, 5 Gateway Ctr, Pittsburgh, PA 15222.

U.S. INDUSTRIAL FILM FESTIVAL AWARDS PRESENTATIONS. June 6. Chicago, IL. Selection and recognition of "world's most outstanding" industrial audio visual presentations. Info from: U.S. Industrial Film Festival, J.W. Anderson, Chrmn, 841 N Addison Ave, Elmhurst, IL 60126.

WOODMEN OF THE WORLD FOUNDERS DAY. June 6. Purpose: To celebrate the founding of Woodmen Of The World. Info from: Woodmen Of The World, Larry Wegener, Mgr, Youth Activities, 1700 Farnam, Omaha, NE 68102.

JUNE 7 — SATURDAY
158th Day — Remaining, 207

ARTS AND FLOWERS FESTIVAL. June 7-8. Purpose: The village salutes the season and welcomes summer with grounds full of award winning gardens, brick paths and rare evergreens. Sponsor: Peddler's Village, PR Dept, Lahaska, PA 18931.

BILLY BOWLEGS FESTIVAL. June 7-14. Ft. Walton Beach, FL. Capt. Billy Bowlegs and his krewe, portrayed by local businessmen, storm the city in the pirate ship "Blackhawk" for a week of pageantry and fun. Treasure hunt, international food fair, sailboat regatta and midnight run. Sponsor: Chamber of Commerce, Box 640, Ft. Walton Beach, FL 32549.

BRUMMELL, GEORGE BRYAN (BEAU BRUMMELL): BIRTH ANNIVERSARY. June 7. Born at London on June 7, 1778, Beau Brummell was, early in his life, a popular English men's fashion leader, the "arbiter elegantarium" of taste in dress. From wealth and popularity his extravagance and lack of tact (it was he who reportedly said—indicating the Prince of Wales, later George IV—"Who's your fat friend?") led him to poverty and disrepute. Once imprisoned for debt he became careless of dress and personal appearance. He died in a charitable asylum at Caen, France, on Mar 30, 1840.

CANADIAN INTERNATIONAL AIR SHOW. June 7-8. Info from: Government of Canada, Ottawa, Canada K1A 0H5.

COUNTRYSIDE VILLAGE ART FAIR. June 7-8. 125 artists from 15 states. Info from: Countryside Merchants Assn, Judy Drawbaugh, 3268 S 130th St, Omaha, NE 68144.

CYPRUS: KATAKLYSMOS. June 7. Festivities in all the seaside towns. Celebration of the "flood." Unique and colorful Cypriot celebration associated with the Pentecost, as well as with sea games.

DARE DAY. June 7. Manteo, NC. Arts, crafts, military band, clogging, food festival and gospel groups. Sponsor: Town of Manteo & County of Dare, Box 1000, Manteo, NC 27954.

DENMARK: EEL FESTIVAL. June 7-8. Jyllinge (near Roskilde). Three-day festival since 1968. Every restaurant and pub in town serves delicious fried eel. Other entertainments include theatre, sports, tattoo bands, sailing competitions, flea markets and fireworks. Three days, the first week-end in June.

EGGS-IBIT SOUTHWEST. June 7-8. Dallas, TX. Purpose: Exhibitors and dealers from over 25 states come to exhibit decorated eggshells. Annually, the weekend before Fathers Day weekend. Sponsor: Eggs-Ibit Southwest, Box 38406, Dallas, TX 75238.

ENGLAND: HORSERACING: OAKS STAKES. June 7. Epsom Racecourse, Epsom, Surrey, England.

FORT SISSETON HISTORICAL FESTIVAL. June 7-8. Days of the cavalry are brought to life at the well-preserved frontier army outpost. Authentic army and Indian costumes. Info from: Fort Sisseton State Park, Lake City, SD 57247.

FREDERICKSBURG ART FESTIVAL. June 7-8. Juried exhibit of fine art works by area and east coast artists. Outdoor sidewalk sale of works. Info from: Visitor Center, 706 Caroline St, Fredericksburg, VA 22401.

GAINES WESTERN REGIONAL DOG OBEDIENCE CHAMPIONSHIP. June 7-8. Fresno, CA. Purpose: To select the best dog/handler team in standard obedience classes including novice, open and super dog, the top category representing the best-trained dog in the region. Sponsor: Gaines Dog Care Center, A. S. Willett, Red Oak Plaza, 70 W Red Oak Lane, White Plains, NY 10604.

GASLIGHT FESTIVAL. June 7-8. Anderson, IN. Info from: Rosie Forkner, 1323 8th St, Anderson, IN 46011.

GAUGIN (EUGENE HENRI) PAUL: BIRTHDAY. June 7. French painter born at Paris, June 7, 1848. Died at Atuana, Marquesas Islands, May 8, 1903.

GREAT WISCONSIN DELLS HOT AIR BALLOON RALLY. June 7-8. Wisconsin Dells, WI. Over 80 vividly colored balloons compete in the annual event. Info from: Visitors & Convention Bureau, Box 390, Wisconsin Dells, WI 53965.

KENNER OKRA FESTIVAL. June 7-8. Kenner, LA. Sponsors: City of Kenner and Kenner Cultural Arts Commission, 1801 Williams Blvd, Kenner, LA 70062.

LEVINE, MEL: BIRTHDAY. June 7. U.S. Representative of California's 27th district, Democrat, of Los Angeles, CA, born there June 7, 1943.

MANHEIM HISTORICAL SOCIETY FLEA MARKET. June 7. (Also Sept 6). Purpose: To raise money to help operate the Manheim Historical Society in its railroad station restoration and other projects. Info from: Manheim Historical Society, Charles Hammer, 767 Pearl Ave, Manheim, PA 17545.

MOON PHASE: NEW MOON. June 7. Moon enters New Moon phase at 9:00 a.m., E.S.T.

NATIONAL TROLLEY FESTIVAL. June 7-8. Narrated parades of over 23 antique trolley cars. Demonstrations and rides on cars. Info from: Shore Line Trolley Museum, 17 River St, East Haven, CT 06512.

COPYRIGHT © 1985 BY WILLIAM D. CHASE and HELEN M. CHASE

OPERATION YOUTH. June 7-14. Xavier University, Cincinnati, OH. Purpose: To provide a hands-on exercise in democracy for teen-agers. Students elect, from their ranks, city officials who join their real counterparts in a Cincinnati council meeting. Speakers from education, industry and government. Info from: William Smith, CPA, Professor of Accounting, Dir of Operation Youth, Xavier Univ, Cincinnati, OH 45207.

PATTERNS WORTH REPEATING. June 7-July 6. The Dairy Barn, Southeastern Ohio Cultural Arts Ctr, Athens, OH. An exhibition of traditional quilts from 18 southeastern Ohio counties. Sponsor: The Dairy Barn, Inc, Box 747, Athens, OH 45701.

RODINO, PETER WALLACE, JR.: BIRTHDAY. June 7. U.S. Representative of New Jersey's 10th district, Democrat, of Newark, NJ, born there on June 7, 1909.

SAN ANTONIO FESTIVAL. June 7-28. San Antonio, TX. An international arts festival with performances at theatres and concert halls in downtown San Antonio. Info from: Convention & Visitors Bureau, Box 2277, San Antonio, TX 78298.

SCOTLAND: ROBERT BURNS FESTIVAL. June 7-15. Ayr, Alloway and Largs, Irvine and Kilmarnock, Strathclyde.

SPECIAL LIBRARIES ASSOCIATION: ANNUAL CONFERENCE. June 7-12. Boston, MA. Info from: Special Libraries Assn, 1700 18th St, NW, Washington, DC 20009.

TURNER, JOHN NAPIER: BIRTHDAY. June 7. Canadian politician, sworn in as Canada's 17th prime minister on June 30, 1984, serving until Sept 17, 1984, when he was succeeded by Brian Mulroney (q.v.). Born on June 7, 1929, at Richmond, Surrey, England.

VIVIEN KELLEMS MEMORIAL DAY. June 7. Purpose: Celebrates birth, June 7, 1896, of industrialist Vivien Kellems. She protested what she considered unfair taxation when she refused to withhold taxes from her employes' wages unless the government named her an agent of Internal Revenue Dept, paid her a salary, and reimbursed her expenses in collecting taxes. Sponsor: Albert L. Maguire, PO Box 1848, Santa Maria, CA 93456.

WALLEYE WEEKEND. June 7-8. Lakeside Park on Lake Winnebago. Event is centered around Mercury Marine's National Walleye Tournament. Fish fry, sports olympics, milk carton boat races, band concerts and fishing clinics. Info from: Conv & Visitors Bureau, 207 N Main St, Fond du Lac, WI 54935.

WINNEMUCCA BASQUE FESTIVAL. June 7-8. Colorful cultural festival with dance, handball and weightlifting contests. Info from: Winnemucca Chamber of Commerce, 48 W Winnemucca Blvd, Winnemucca, NV 89445.

JUNE 8 — SUNDAY
159th Day — Remaining, 206

AMERICAN PHYSICAL THERAPY ASSOCIATION CONFERENCE. June 8-12. Hyatt Regency, Chicago, IL. Purpose: To discuss health issues and the latest physical therapy techniques. Sponsor: American Physical Therapy Assn, Mary Gleason, PR Dir, 1111 N Fairfax St, Alexandria, VA 22314.

ASSOCIATION FOR THE CARE OF CHILDREN'S HEALTH CONFERENCE. June 8-11. San Francisco Hilton, San Francisco, CA. Purpose: To focus on the transitions in pediatric health care and the impact of those transitions on the quality and types of psychosocial programming for children and their families. Info from: Assn For The Care of Children's Health, Lee Ann Slayton, Conf Coord, 3615 Wisconsin Ave, NW, Washington, DC 20016.

June **1986**

S	M	T	W	T	F	S
1	2	3	4	5	6	7
8	9	10	11	12	13	14
15	16	17	18	19	20	21
22	23	24	25	26	27	28
29	30					

ATTACK ON THE U.S.S. LIBERTY: ANNIVERSARY. June 8. At 2 p.m. local time on June 8, 1967, the unescorted U.S. intelligence ship, U.S.S. *Liberty*, sailing in international waters off the Egyptian coast, was attacked without warning by Israeli jet planes and three Israeli torpedo boats. She was strafed and hit repeatedly by rockets, cannon, napalm and finally by a torpedo. Casualties: out of a crew of 294 Americans, there were 34 dead and 171 wounded. Israel apologized, claiming mistaken identity, but surviving crew members charged deliberate attack by Israel and cover-up by U.S. authorities.

BLESSING OF THE FLEET. June 8. Bayou La Batre, Mobile, AL. Shrimping fleets from Bayou La Batre, Coden and Dauphin Island parade down the bayou before receiving the blessing of boats as they "go out to sea." Info from: St Margaret's Church, Box 365, Bayou La Batre, AL 36509.

BUSH, BARBARA PIERCE: BIRTHDAY. June 8. Wife of George Herbert Walker Bush, 43rd Vice-President of the U.S., was born at Rye, NY, June 8, 1925. They were married on Jan 6, 1945.

CHILDREN'S DAY. June 8. Massachusetts. (Second Sunday in June).

CHILDREN'S SUNDAY. June 8. Traditionally the second Sunday in June is observed as Children's Sunday in many Christian churches.

FESTIVAL OF THE RED ROSE. June 8. Purpose: To make annual rental payment of one red rose to an heir of Baron Henry William Stiegel, for land deeded to the Zion Lutheran Church in 1772. Observed annually the second Sunday of June. Sponsor: Zion Lutheran Church. Info from: John D. Kendig, Rose Festival Committee, 65 Main St, Manheim, PA 17545.

GRANT WOOD ART FESTIVAL. June 8. Stone City-Anamosa, IA. Purpose: Promotion of the arts in Grant Wood country, in tribute to native-born son, artist Grant Wood. Annual observance on second Sunday in June. Sponsor: Grant Wood Art Festival, Inc, Marguerite Stoll, Publicity Dir, Box 137, Anamosa, IA 52205.

LAKI VOLCANO ERUPTION ANNIVERSARY. June 8. On June 8, 1783, one of the most violent and important volcanic eruptions of recorded history began. Laki, or Skafta, Volcano in southern Iceland continued eruption for eight months, expelling an estimated 4½ cubic miles of lava, ultimately causing a famine and the deaths of nearly 10,000 persons. Acid rain reached western Europe and other climatic and atmospheric changes were worldwide. English naturalist Gilbert White (q.v.) described some of the "horrible phenomena" of the summer of 1783, including the "peculiar haze, or smokey fog...unlike anything known within the memory of man." The effects of this volcanic eruption and its possible long-term consequences are still being studied by scientists.

McKINLEY, IDA SAXTON: BIRTHDAY. June 8. Wife of William McKinley, 25th President of the U.S., born at Canton, OH, June 8, 1847. Died May 26, 1907.

NATIONAL FLAG WEEK. June 8-14. Presidential Proclama-☆ tion. "Issued each year since 1966 for the week including June 14." (PL89-443 of June 9, 1966).

NATIONAL FRATERNAL WEEK. June 8-14. Purpose: To celebrate fraternalism and Flag Day. Sponsor: Natl Fraternal Congress of America, Raymond A. Klee, Exec VP, 230 W Monroe St, Chicago, IL 60606.

NATIONAL PHYSICAL THERAPY WEEK. June 8-14. Purpose: To focus attention on the contributions of physical therapy to the improvement of the health of all Americans. Sponsor: American Physical Therapy Assn, Mary Gleason, PR Dir, 1111 N Fairfax St, Alexandria, VA 22314.

RACE UNITY DAY. June 8. Baha'i sponsored observance to focus attention on the principle of unity in diversity, and the belief that achievement of racial unity will assure world peace. Second Sunday in June annually. Info from: Baha'i Office of Public Affairs, Baha'i Natl Center, Wilmette, IL 60091.

RED CLOUD INDIAN ART SHOW. June 8-Aug 10. Pine Ridge, SD. Purpose: To encourage native American artists and give them a chance for exposure. Sponsor: Red Cloud Indian School, Bro. C. M. Simon, SJ, Pine Ridge, SD 57770.

SPACE MILESTONE: VENERA 9 AND 10 (USSR). June 8 and 14. Launched on June 8 and June 14, 1975. Venus exploration vehicles landed on Venus Oct 22 and 25. Sent first pictures ever transmitted from another planet, atmospheric analysis, temperature (905°F.), and other data.

WHITE, BYRON RAYMOND: BIRTHDAY. June 8. Associate Justice of the Supreme Court of the United States, nominated by Pres Kennedy on Apr 3, 1962. (Oath of Office, Apr 16, 1962.) Justice White was born at Fort Collins, CO, on June 8, 1917.

WRIGHT, FRANK LLOYD: BIRTH ANNIVERSARY. June 8. American architect born at Richland Center, WI, on June 8, 1867. In his autobiography Wright wrote: "No house should ever be *on* any hill or on anything. It should be *of* the hill, belonging to it, so hill and house could live together each the happier for the other." Wright died at Phoenix, AZ, Apr 9, 1959.

WRITER'S WORKSHOP. June 8-13. Carter Caves State Resort Park, Olive Hill, KY. Sessions on writing and relaxing with nature, led by Lee Pennington. Storytelling, concerts, and entertainment. Info from: Kentucky Dept. of Parks, Capital Plaza Tower, Frankfort, KY 40601.

WYTHE, GEORGE: DEATH ANNIVERSARY. June 8. Signer of the Declaration of Independence. Born, Elizabeth County, VA, about 1726 (exact date unknown). Died, Richmond, VA, June 8, 1806.

JUNE 9 — MONDAY
160th Day — Remaining, 205

BADHAM, ROBERT EDWARD: BIRTHDAY. June 9. U.S. Representative of California's 40th district, Republican, of Newport Beach, CA, born in Los Angeles, CA, June 9, 1929.

DONALD DUCK: BIRTHDAY. June 9. Walt Disney's character, Donald Duck, celebrates anniversary of birth: June 9, 1934. Info from: Publicity Dept, Walt Disney Productions, 500 S Buena Vista St, Burbank, CA 91521.

HONG KONG LEASE ANNIVERSARY. June 9. Hong Kong, consisting of about 400 square miles (islands and mainland) with more than 5 million persons, has been administered as a British Crown Colony since a 99-year lease was signed on June 9, 1898. In 1997, Hong Kong's sovereignty will revert to the People's Republic of China.

INTERNATIONAL COUNTRY MUSIC FAN FAIR. June 9-15. Purpose: Celebration of country music with the stars, fans, fan clubs and record companies. Fiddling and dancing championships. Sponsors: Country Music Assn, Mrs. Jo Walker-Meador, Box 22299, Nashville, TN 37202 and Grand Ole Opry, Jerry Strobel, PR Dir, 2804 Opryland Dr, Nashville, TN 37214.

MUSLIM HOLIDAY: ID al-FITR. June 9. Feast marks end of month-long fast of Ramadhan. Muslim calendar date: Shawwal 1, 1406. Feast ordinarily continues for two or three days. Gregorian calendar date of observance may vary by one day.

NATIONAL CARP WEEK. June 9-15. Purpose: A day for recognition and appreciation of one of our largest renewable resources. Info from: Richard Guindon, The Detroit Free Press, 321 W Lafayette, Detroit, MI 48231.

NATIONAL LITTLE LEAGUE BASEBALL WEEK. June 9-15. ☆ Presidential Proclamation. "Always the week beginning the 2nd Monday of June. (H. Con. Res. 17 of June 1, 1959). Procs. 3296, June 4, 1959 and 3407, Apr 18, 1961, cover all succeeding years."

NIELSEN, CARL: BIRTHDAY. June 9. Danish composer born June 9, 1865. Died Oct 3, 1931. Funen Quartet plays birthday concert in the composer's childhood home at Lyndelse, near Odense, Denmark.

NIGH, GEORGE: BIRTHDAY. June 9. George Nigh, Governor of Oklahoma, Democrat, was born at McAlester, OK, on June 9, 1927.

PAYNE, JOHN HOWARD: BIRTHDAY. June 9. American author, actor, diplomat, born, New York City, June 9, 1791. Died at Tunis, Apr 9, 1852. Author of opera libretto (*Clari, or, The Maid of Milan*) which contained the song "Home, Sweet Home."

SENIOR CITIZENS DAY. June 9. Oklahoma.

SISISKY, NORMAN: BIRTHDAY. June 9. U.S. Representative of Virginia's 4th district, Democrat, resident at Cavalier Farms, Petersburg, VA, was born June 9, 1927.

STEPHENSON, GEORGE: BIRTHDAY. June 9. English inventor, developer of the steam locomotive, born near Newcastle, June 9, 1781. Died near Chesterfield, Aug 12, 1848.

YOUNG, DON: BIRTHDAY June 9. U.S. Representative at large from Alaska, Republican, of Fort Yukon, AK, born in Meridian, CA, on June 9, 1933.

JUNE 10 — TUESDAY
161st Day — Remaining, 204

ALCOHOLICS ANONYMOUS: FOUNDING ANNIVERSARY. June 10. Established, at Akron, OH, by William G. Wilson and Dr. Robert Smith on June 10, 1935.

CZECHOSLOVAKIA: RAPE OF LIDICE ANNIVERSARY. June 10. On June 10, 1942, Nazi German troops executed by shooting, all male inhabitants of the Czechoslovakian village of Lidice (total population about 500 persons), burned every house and deported the women and children to Germany for "re-education." One of the most remembered atrocities of World War II.

GARLAND, JUDY: BIRTHDAY. June 10. American actress and singer, born Frances Gumm, at Grand Rapids, MN, June 10, 1922. Died at London, England, June 22, 1969.

JOHNSTON, J. BENNETT: BIRTHDAY, June 10. U.S. Senator from Louisiana, Democrat, of Shreveport, LA, born in Shreveport on June 10, 1932.

JORDAN: GREAT ARAB REVOLT AND ARMY DAY. June 10. Commemorates the beginning of the Great Arab Revolt (June 10, 1916). National holiday in Jordan.

PORTUGAL: DAY OF PORTUGAL. June 10. National holiday. Anniversary of the death of Portugal's national poet, Luis Vas de Camoes (Camoens), born in 1524 (exact date unknown) either at Lisbon or possibly Coimbra. Died at Lisbon, June 10, 1580.

SHAKESPEARE IN THE PARK. June 10-29. Trinity Park, Fort Worth. Info from: Sharon Benge, Box 9376, Fort Worth, TX 76107.

UNITED KINGDOM: BIRTHDAY OF PRINCE PHILIP, DUKE OF EDINBURGH. June 10. Born Philip Mountbatten, on the Greek Island of Corfu, June 10, 1921, he was created Duke of Edinburgh on the eve of his marriage (at Westminster Abbey) to Princess Elizabeth, now Queen Elizabeth II of the United Kingdom of Great Britain and Northern Ireland on Nov. 20, 1947.

JUNE 11 — WEDNESDAY
162nd Day — Remaining, 203

CONSTABLE, JOHN: BIRTHDAY. June 11. English landscape painter. Born at East Bergholt, Suffolk, on June 11, 1776. He died at London on Mar 31, 1837.

DRAGON BOAT FESTIVAL. June 11. An important Chinese observance, the Dragon Boat Festival commemorates a hero of ancient China, poet Qu Yuan, who drowned himself in protest against injustice and corruption. It is said that rice dumplings were cast into the water to lure fish away from the body of the martyr, and this is remembered by the eating of "zhong zi," glutinous rice dumplings filled with meat and wrapped in bamboo leaves. Dragon boat races are held on rivers. The Dragon Boat Festival is observed in most countries by their Chinese population. Always the fifth day of fifth lunar month.

JONSON, BEN: BIRTHDAY ANNIVERSARY. June 11. English playwright and poet, born June 11, 1572. "Talking and eloquence," he wrote, "are not the same: to speak and to speak well, are two things." Jonson died at London on Aug 6, 1637. The epitaph, written on his tombstone in Westminster Abbey: "O rare Ben Jonson."

KING KAMEHAMEHA I DAY. June 11. Designated state holiday in Hawaii honors memory of Hawaiian monarch (1737-1819). Governor appoints State commission to plan annual celebration.

KOREA: TANO DAY. June 11. Fifth day of 5th lunar month. Summer food offered at the household shrine of the ancestors. Also known as Swing Day, since girls dressed in their prettiest clothes often compete in swinging matches. The Tano Festival usually lasts from the 3rd through 8th day of the fifth lunar month.

NATIONAL IMPRESSIONISTS DAY. June 11. Purpose: To gather vocal impressionists and salute the rare and universally enjoyed talent of imitating well-known voices. Sponsor: Michael L. Cabot, III, RD#1, Box 66, Frenchtown, NJ 08825.

RANGEL, CHARLES B: BIRTHDAY. June 11. U.S. Representative of New York's 16th district, Democrat-Liberal-Republican, of New York, NY, born in Harlem, New York, NY, on June 11, 1930.

RANKIN, JEANNETTE: BIRTHDAY. June 11. First woman elected to the U.S. Congress, a reformer, feminist, and pacifist, was born at Missoula, Montana, June 11, 1880. She was the only member of Congress to vote against a declaration of war against Japan in Dec 1941. Died May 18, 1973.

June 1986	S	M	T	W	T	F	S
	1	2	3	4	5	6	7
	8	9	10	11	12	13	14
	15	16	17	18	19	20	21
	22	23	24	25	26	27	28
	29	30					

SILJANDER, MARK DELI: BIRTHDAY. June 11. U.S. Representative of Michigan's 4th district, Republican, of Three Rivers, MI, born in Chicago, IL, on June 11, 1951.

STRAUSS, RICHARD GEORG: BIRTHDAY. June 11. German composer, musician and conductor whose best remembered works are *Till Eulenspiegel* (1895), *Also Sprach Zarathustra* (1896) and *Don Quixote* (1898). Born at Munich on June 11, 1864, he died at Garmisch-Partenkirchen after a heart attack on Sept 8, 1949.

JUNE 12 — THURSDAY
163rd Day — Remaining, 202

BUDWEISER SPRINGNATIONALS. June 12-15. National Trail Raceway, Granville, OH. Purpose: National Hot Rod Association Championship Drag Racing Meet. Sponsor: Natl Trail Raceway, 120 Linden Pl, Granville, OH 43023.

BUSH, GEORGE HERBERT WALKER: BIRTHDAY. June 12. Forty-third Vice-President of the U.S., born at Milton, MA, June 12, 1924. Married to Barbara Pierce, Jan 6, 1945.

EGYPTIAN EVENT. June 12-15. Lexington, KY. Purebred Egyptian Arabian horses, show competition, art exhibit and Saluki dog show. Info from: KY Dept of Travel, Capital Plaza Office Tower, Frankfort, KY 40601.

FESTIVAL OF THE BLUEGRASS. June 12-15. Lexington, KY. Bluegrass music in an outdoor concert setting, more than 30 bands to perform. Info from: KY Dept of Travel, Capital Plaza Office Tower, Frankfort, KY 40601.

FIRST MAN-POWERED FLIGHT ACROSS ENGLISH CHANNEL: ANNIVERSARY. June 12. Bryan Allen, 26-year-old Californian, pedalled the 70 pound *Gossamer Albatross* 22 miles across the English Channel, from Folkestone, England to Cape Gris-Nez, France, in 2 hours, 49 minutes on June 12, 1979, winning (with the crafts' designer, Paul MacCready of Pasadena, CA) the £100,000 prize which had been offered Nov 30, 1977, by British industrialist Henry Kremer, for the first man-powered flight across the English Channel.

GERMANFEST. June 12-15. Fort Wayne, IN. Purpose: A celebration of our German heritage with folk music, folk dancing, beer tent, soccer, volksmarsching, bicycle racing, Mannerchor singing, Gottesdienste, genealogy workshops and classical music. Sponsor: Fort Wayne Germanfest Committee, Jim Sack, 720 Union St, Fort Wayne, IN 46804.

GOLF: U.S. OPEN CHAMPIONSHIP. June 12-15. Shinnecock Hills Golf Club, Southampton, NY. National golf championship in U.S. Sponsor: U.S. Golf Assn, Golf House, Far Hills, NJ 07931.

McCLOSKEY, FRANK: BIRTHDAY. June 12. U.S. Representative of Indiana's 8th district, Democrat, of Bloomington, IN, born in Philadelphia, PA, on June 12, 1939.

NATIONAL ASPARAGUS FESTIVAL. June 12-14. Purpose: To promote Michigan grown asparagus and Oceana County, Michigan. Annually, the second weekend in June. Sponsor: Natl Asparagus Festival, Diane M. Fethke, Box 117, Shelby, MI 49455.

NATIONAL BASEBALL HALL OF FAME: ANNIVERSARY. June 12. The National Baseball Hall of Fame and Museum, Inc. was dedicated at Cooperstown, NY, June 12, 1939. Nearly 200 individuals have been honored for their contributions to the game of baseball by induction into the Baseball Hall of Fame. The first players chosen for membership (1936) were: Ty Cobb, Honus Wagner, Babe Ruth, Christy Mathewson and Walter Johnson. Relics and memorabilia from the history of baseball are housed at this "shrine" of America's national sport.

OK MOZART INTERNATIONAL FESTIVAL. June 12-22. Festival features world-class artists performing with Solisti New York Chamber Orchestra and Ransom Wilson, conductor and artistic director in an atmosphere of Austria. Info from: OK Mozart Internatl Festival, Box 1027, Bartlesville, OK 74005.

COPYRIGHT © 1985 BY WILLIAM D. CHASE and HELEN M. CHASE

ORTHODOX ASCENSION DAY. June 12. Observed by the Orthodox Church in America and other Orthodox churches on this date.

PHILIPPINES: NATIONAL HOLIDAY. June 12. Independence Day. Declared independence from Spain on this day, 1898.

POCONO LAUREL BLOSSOM FESTIVAL. June 12-24. Purpose: To recognize the beauty of Pennsylvania's laurel. Info from: Pocono Mountains Vacation Bureau, 1004 Main St, Box K, Stroudsburg, PA 18360.

PORTUGAL: ALL SAINTS FESTIVAL. June 12-29. Religious festival celebrated in Lisbon and Oporto, Portugal.

PORTUGAL: ST. ANTHONY'S EVE. June 12. Dancing in the streets of Old Lisbon on this holiday dedicated to St. Anthony, the patron saint of young lovers. Colorful lantern processions. Lisbon, Portugal.

SPACE MILESTONE: VENERA 4 (USSR). June 12. Launched on June 12, 1967, this instrumented capsule landed on Venus by parachute on Oct 18, and reported temperature of 536° Fahrenheit.

SPIKE RAIL CHEESE FESTIVAL. June 12-15. Brewster, OH. Purpose: To show history of railroad and cheese industry in Brewster. Homemade food, games, flea market and parade. Info from: Brewster Fire Dept, Jon Witting, 110 E Main St, Brewster, OH 44613.

JUNE 13 — FRIDAY
164th Day — Remaining, 201

ANTIQUE AUTOMOBILE CLUB OF AMERICA: SPRING MEET. June 13-14. Houghton Lake, MI. Info from: Box 417, Hershey, PA 17033.

BLAME SOMEONE ELSE DAY. June 13. Purpose: To share the responsibility and the guilt for the mess we're in. Blame someone else! Observed on the first Friday the 13th of each year. Sponsor: A.C. Moeller, Box 71, Clio, MI 48420.

BOLLES, DON: DEATH ANNIVERSARY. June 13. Don Bolles, investigative reporter for *The Arizona Republic*, died June 13, 1976, as a result of injuries received when bomb exploded in his automobile, June 2, 1976, while he was engaged in journalistic investigation of alleged Mafia story. Bolles was awarded, posthumously, the University of Arizona's John Peter Zenger Award, Dec 9, 1976.

"CHIMES AND CHEERS: SALUTE TO STATEHOOD." June 13-15. Little Rock, AR. Purpose: To celebrate Arkansas' 150 years of statehood, to promote pride in Arkansas and pride in being an Arkansan. Info from: Sesquicentennial Celebration Committee, 1111 S University, Suite 900, Little Rock, AR 72204.

FRIDAY THE THIRTEENTH. June 13. Variously believed to be a lucky or unlucky day. Every year has at least one Friday the thirteenth, but never more than three.

GENERAL SYNOD OF THE ANGLICAN CHURCH OF CANADA. June 13-22. Winnipeg, Manitoba, Canada. Triennial meeting of the chief legislative and policy-setting body for the Anglican Church of Canada. Info from: The Anglican Church of Canada, The General Secy, 600 Jarvis St, Toronto, Ontario, Canada M4Y 2J6.

INTERNATIONAL FAN CLUB ORGANIZATION DINNER AND SHOW. June 13. Tennessee State Fair Grounds, Nashville, TN. Purpose: Participation in the annual Fan Fair. Sponsor: Internatl Fan Club Organization, Loudilla, Loretta & Kay Johnson, Box 177, Wild Horse, CO 80862.

INTERNATIONAL FOLK FESTIVAL. June 13-15. Bettendorf, IA. More than 20 different nationalities display their native costumes, crafts, foods and entertainment. Second weekend in June. Info from: Chamber of Commerce, 1630 State St, Bettendorf, IA 52722.

LAKEFRONT FESTIVAL OF ARTS. June 13-15. Milwaukee's Lakefront. Professional outdoor art show. Paintings, sculpture, ceramics, photography and glass. Sponsor: Friends of Art of the Milwaukee Art Museum. Info from: Milwaukee Art Museum, 750 N Lincoln Memorial Dr, Milwaukee, WI 53202.

MISSION SAN LUIS REY DE FRANCIA ANNIVERSARY. June 13. California mission to the Indians founded June 13, 1798. Abandoned by 1846 and restoration started in 1892.

NORTH CAROLINA BLUE CRAB DERBY AND FESTIVAL. June 13-14. Purpose: to promote crabbing industry. Crab races, games, auctions and family fun. Sponsor: Morehead City Kiwanis Club, Richard Evans, 4028 Arendell St, Morehead City, NC 28557.

POTOMAC RIVER FESTIVAL. June 13-15. Purpose: To promote the attractions of Colonial Beach, VA and historic Westmoreland County. Sponsor: Chamber of Commerce, 2 Boundary St, Colonial Beach, VA 22443.

ST. ANTHONY OF PADUA: FEAST DAY. June 13. Born at Lisbon, Portugal, Aug 15, 1195, St. Anthony is patron of the illiterate and the poor. Died, Padua, June 13, 1231. Public holiday, Lisbon.

SCOTT, WINFIELD: BICENTENNIAL BIRTH ANNIVERSARY. June 13. American army general, negotiator of peace treaties with Indians, and twice nominated for president (1848 and 1852). Leader of brilliant military campaign in Mexico in 1847. Scott died at West Point, NY, on May 29, 1866.

SHAVUOT or FEAST OF WEEKS. June 13. Observed on the following day also. Jewish holy day. Hebrew date, Sivan 6, 5746. Celebrates giving of Torah (The Law) to Moses on Mt. Sinai.

START OF SUMMER CELEBRATION. June 13-15. Arts and crafts fair with parade, canoe races, contests, games, food, flea market and music. Info from: Start of Summer Celebration, Inc, 35 Courtland St, Rockford, MI 49341.

SUGARLOAF'S MANASSAS CRAFTS FESTIVAL. June 13-15. Prince William County Fairgrounds, Manassas, VA. Over 230 professional artists and craftspeople, demonstrations, live music, children's entertainment and delicious food. Sponsor: Sugarloaf Mt Works, Inc, Ijamsville, MD 21754.

TURPENTINE FESTIVAL. June 13-14. Rosinville, SC. Purpose: Funding for the Upper Dorchester County Rescue Squad. Sponsor: Upper Dorchester County Rescue Squad, Charles Kizer, Rt 1, Box 164, St. George, SC 29477.

VANCOUVER DAY. June 13. Vancouver, British Columbia. A three day festival celebrating the arrival of Captain Vancouver in Vancouver Harbour plus the anniversary of the fire that destroyed the city in 1886. Info from: The Centennial Commission, Box 49386, Suite 3374, Bentall 4, 1055 Dunsmuir St, Vancouver, BC V7X 1L5.

WORLD SAUNTERING DAY. June 13. Grand Hotel, Mackinac Island, MI. Purpose: To revive the lost art of Victorian sauntering and discourage jogging. Certificates awarded on basis of elan, panache and compliance with standards of Grand Hotel sauntering (speed not a factor). Nominations accepted for Sauntering Hall of Fame. (Second Friday in June.) Info from: World Sauntering Society of Lake Superior State College Unicorn Hunters, W.T. Rabe (chief stroller), Sault Ste. Marie, MI 49783.

COPYRIGHT © 1985 BY WILLIAM D. CHASE and HELEN M. CHASE

YEATS, WILLIAM BUTLER: BIRTH ANNIVERSARY. June 13. Nobel prize-winning Irish poet and dramatist, born at Dublin on June 13, 1865. He once wrote: "If a poet interprets a poem of his own he limits its suggestibility." Yeats died in France on Jan 28, 1939. After World War II, his body was returned, as he had wished, for re-burial in a churchyard at Drumcliff, Ireland.

JUNE 14 — SATURDAY
165th Day — Remaining, 200

ALZHEIMER, ALOIS: BIRTH ANNIVERSARY. June 14. The German pyschiatrist and pathologist, Alois Alzheimer, was born at Markbreit, a.m., on June 14, 1864. In 1907 an article by Alzheimer appeared in "Allgemeine Zeitschrift fur Psychiatrie," first describing the disease which was named for him. It was thought of as a kind of pre-senile dementia, usually beginning at age 40-60, but whether Alzheimer's Disease is an entity separate from senile dementia remains unanswered. Alzheimer died at Breslau, on Dec 19, 1915.

ANTIQUE AUTO SWAP MEET. June 14-15. Purpose: Over 500 vendors from across the U.S. gather to sell, trade or buy automobiles, parts and accessories. Info from: Traders Village, 2602 Mayfield Rd, Grand Prairie, TX 75051.

ARMY BIRTHDAY. June 14. Anniversary of Congressional Resolution of June 14, 1775, establishing the Army as the first U.S. military service.

BARTLETT, JOHN: BIRTHDAY. June 14. American editor and compiler (Bartlett's *Familiar Quotations* (1855) and other works) was born at Plymouth, MA, on June 14, 1820. Though he had little formal education he created one of the most used reference works of the English language. No quotation of his own is among the more than 22,000 listed today, but in the preface to the first edition he wrote that the object of this work "originally made without any view of publication" was to show "the obligation our language owes to various authors for numerous phrases and familiar quotations which have become 'household words.'" Bartlett died at 85, at his Cambridge, MA home, on Dec 3, 1905.

COUNTRY MUSIC CONVENTION. June 14-15. Purpose: Country and bluegrass competitions and festivals featuring fiddles, flattop guitars, mandolins and banjos. Info from: Bob Evans Farms, Inc, Mary Cusick, 3776 S High St, Columbus, OH 43207.

DAIRY GOAT AWARENESS WEEK. June 14-21. Info from: Kent Leach, Publisher, Dairy Goat Journal, Box 1808, Scottsdale, AZ 85252.

ENGLAND: QUEEN'S OFFICIAL BIRTHDAY and TROOPING THE COLOR. June 14. Horse Guards Parade, London. Occasion for celebrating Queen's "official" birthday and for military pageant dating from 1775. Precision marching and ceremonial carrying of the Color. Christened Elizabeth Alexandra Mary. Queen Elizabeth II was born in Bruton St, London, on Apr 21, 1926, but "official" birthday is celebrated on a Saturday in June.

FESTIVAL OF FOUNTAINS. June 14-Sept 1. Longwood Gardens, Kennett Sq, PA. Illuminated fountain displays and garden concerts. Info from: Longwood Gardens, Kennett Square, PA 19348.

FIRST NON-STOP TRANSATLANTIC FLIGHT ANNIVERSARY. June 14-15. Capt. John Alcock and Lt. Arthur W. Brown flew a Vickers Vimy bomber 1,900 miles non-stop from St. Johns, Newfoundland to Clifden, County Galway, Ireland, June 14-15, 1919. In spite of their crash landing in an Irish peat bog, their flight inspired public interest in aviation and led to many other flights. See also entry (May 20) for Charles A. Lindbergh's solo trans-Atlantic flight eight years later.

FLAG DAY. June 14. Presidential Proclamation. "Issued each ☆ year for June 14. proc. 1335, May 30, 1916, covers all succeeding years. Has been issued annually since 1941." (PL81-203 of Aug 3, 1949). Note: Anniversary of the Stars and Stripes. On June 14, 1777, John Adams introduced the following resolution before the Continental Congress, meeting at Philadelphia: "Resolved, That the flag of the thirteen United States shall be thirteen stripes, alternate red and white; that the union be thirteen stars, white on a blue field, representing a new constellation." Legal holiday in Pennsylvania.

FLAG DAY CEREMONIES. June 14. Betsy Ross House, 239 Arch Street, Philadelphia, PA. 11:00 am program followed by band concert in Atwater Kent Gardens of Betsy Ross House. Info from: Rosen-Coren Agency, Inc, 4138 Benjamin Fox Pavilion, Foxcroft Sq, Jenkintown, PA 19046.

FLAG DAY—PAUSE FOR THE PLEDGE. June 14. Purpose: "Pause and join your fellow Americans at 7 p.m. (EDT) to reaffirm faith in your country by reciting the Pledge of Allegiance to the Flag." National ceremony at Fort McHenry (National Monument and Historic Shrine). Visit Star-Spangled Banner Flag House (National Historic Landmark) where Mary Pickersgill made flag that inspired Francis Scott Key to write the National Anthem. Sponsor: Natl Flag Day Foundation, Inc, 418 S Broadway, Baltimore, MD 21231.

FLINT ART FAIR. June 14-15. Flint Institute of Arts, Flint, MI. More than 100 artists participate in juried art fair. (Always second weekend in June.) Sponsor: Friends of Modern Art. Info from: Flint Institute of Arts, Barbara Gerholz, 1120 E Kearsley, Flint, MI 48503.

FRANKENMUTH BAVARIAN FESTIVAL. June 14-21. Purpose: To celebrate the German heritage of Frankenmuth with good food and great entertainment. Sponsor: Frankenmuth Civic Events Council, Carrie Rowe, Festival Dir, 635 S Main St, Frankenmuth, MI 48734.

GLENN MILLER BIRTHPLACE SOCIETY FESTIVAL. June 14. Clarinda, IA. Purpose: To commemorate Glenn Miller's contribution to big band music through exhibits, music, films and performances by winners of Glenn Miller scholarships. Sponsor: Glenn Miller Birthplace Society, Wilda Martin, 200 A South 15th St, Clarinda, IA 51632.

GOD'S COUNTRY MARATHON XII. June 14. A 26.2 mile marathon from Galeton High School to Coudersport Area Recreation Park, crossing over Denton Hill Mountain, the Eastern Continental Divide of the United States. Info from: Potter County Recreation, Inc, Ralph J. Wentz, Exec Dir, Box 245, Coudersport, PA 16915.

HISTORICAL HERITAGE FESTIVAL. June 14-15. Purpose: To commemorate the 205th anniversary of the siege of Ninety Six at Star Fort by patriot soldiers during the latter part of the Revolutionary War. Sponsor: Ninety Six Natl Historic Site, Box 496, Ninety Six, SC 29666.

HONOR AMERICA: 21 DAY SALUTE. June 14-July 4. Purpose: That there be public gatherings and activities throughout America at which the people can celebrate and honor their country in an appropriate manner. July 4 Honor America program concludes 21-day salute. Sponsor: The American Historic and Cultural Society, Inc, 926 National Press Bldg, Washington, DC 20045.

HOYER, STENY H: BIRTHDAY. June 14. U.S. Representative of Maryland's 5th district, Democrat, of Berkshire, MD, born in New York City, NY, on June 14, 1939.

JAPAN RICE PLANTING FESTIVAL. June 14. Osaka, Japan. Ceremonial transplanting of rice seedlings in paddyfield at Sumiyashi Shrine, Osaka.

JAPANESE FESTIVAL. June 14-22. Missouri Botanical Garden. Celebration of the Japanese culture through dance, music, food and crafts. Info from: St. Louis Conv & Visitors Bureau, 10 S Broadway, Suite 300, St. Louis, MO 63102.

June 1986

S	M	T	W	T	F	S
1	2	3	4	5	6	7
8	9	10	11	12	13	14
15	16	17	18	19	20	21
22	23	24	25	26	27	28
29	30					

COPYRIGHT © 1985 BY WILLIAM D. CHASE and HELEN M. CHASE

KISSIMMEE BOAT-A-CADE. June 14-22. Purpose: To introduce boaters to Florida's beautiful and scenic waterways. Sponsor: Kissimmee Boat-A-Cade, Inc, Box 1855, Kissimmee, FL 32742.

LILYPONS' LOTUS BLOSSOM FESTIVAL. June 14-15. Purpose: To view 85 varieties of water lilies and 11 varieties of lotus. Sponsor: Lilypons Water Gardens, Box 188, Brookshire, TX 77423.

LONGWOOD GARDENS FESTIVAL OF FOUNTAINS. June 14-Aug 31. A magical nighttime mixture of rainbow-hued fountains, alfresco garden concerts and leisurely evenings in the conservatory. Info from: Longwood Gardens, Kennett Square, PA 19348.

MIDDLEFIELD SWISS CHEESE FESTIVAL. June 14-15. Info from: Middlefield Swiss Cheese Festival, Box 734, Middlefield, OH 44062.

NEBRASKALAND DAYS AND BUFFALO BILL RODEO. June 14-22. Purpose: To relive the old West. Parades, contests, shoot-outs, art shows, frontier revue, top stars. Info: Nebraskaland Days, Box 706-CC, North Platte, NE 69103.

PAST 80 PARTY. June 14. Purpose: To honor all citizens who have lived for 80 or more years, with dinner, gifts and entertainment. Second Saturday of June each year. Sponsor: Richwood Jaycees, Gary Johnson, Box 631, Richwood, WV 26261.

PONY EXPRESS-JESSE JAMES FESTIVAL. June 14-15. Festival marks start of Pony Express and end of Jesse James at sites where events occurred. A re-ride to California will be emphasis. Crafts, melodrama and beer garden. Sponsor: Pony Express Historical Assn, Patee House Museum, 12th and Penn Streets, St. Joseph, MO 64502.

SEA MUSIC FESTIVAL. June 14-15. Purpose: Music on the grounds and major vessels. Workshops and demonstrations for Seaport visitors. Info from: Public Affairs Dept, Mystic Seaport, Mystic, CT 06355.

SENSENBRENNER, F. JAMES JR: BIRTHDAY. June 14. U.S. Representative of Wisconsin's 9th district, Republican, of Menomonee Falls, WI, born in Chicago, IL, on June 14, 1943.

SPACE MILESTONE: MARINER 5 (US). June 14. Interplanetary probe of Venus established 72½-87½ percent carbon dioxide content of atmosphere on Oct 18 flyby of planet. Launched June 14, 1967.

SPACE MILESTONE: VOSTOK 5 (USSR). June 14. Lt. Col. Valery Bykovsky orbits Earth 81 times, 2,046,000 miles. Landed June 19. Launched June 14, 1963.

SPANISH NIGHTWATCH CEREMONY. June 14-15. St. Augustine, FL. Reenactment of an 18th century ceremony. Authentically dressed Spanish and Scottish troops commemorate the 1740 seige of the town. Salutes of cannon and musket. Candlelight parade. Info from: Robert Hall, 42 Spanish, St. Augustine, FL 32084.

STOWE, HARRIET BEECHER: BIRTHDAY. June 14. American writer, Harriet Beecher Stowe, daughter of the Rev. Lyman Beecher and sister of Henry Ward Beecher, author of *Uncle Tom's Cabin,* was born at Litchfield, CT, June 14, 1811. She died at Hartford, CT, July 1, 1896.

SUN INN STRAWBERRY FESTIVAL. June 14. Outdoor sale of strawberry desserts commemorates Martha Washington's visit to Sun Inn in June 1779. Info from: Sun Inn Preservation Assn, 564 Main St, Bethlehem, PA 18018.

TAUZIN, WILBERT J. (BILLY): BIRTHDAY. June 14. U.S. Representative of Louisiana's 3rd district, Democrat, of Thibodaux, LA, was born in Chackbay, LA, June 14, 1943.

TUPPER LAKE FLATWATER WEEKEND. June 14-15. Races for canoes, kayaks and guideboats. Info from: Chamber of Commerce, 55 Park St, Tupper Lake, NY 12986.

UNIVAC BIRTHDAY. June 14. Univac 1, the world's first commercial computer, designed for the U.S. Bureau of the Census, was unveiled, demonstrated and dedicated at Philadelphia, June 14, 1951. Though this milestone of the computer age was the first commercial electronic computer, it had been preceded by ENIAC (Electronic Numeric Integrator And Computer) completed under the supervision of J. Presper Eckert, Jr. and John W. Mauchly, at the Moore School of Electrical Engineering, University of Pennsylvania, in 1946.

VINTAGE AUTO ENGINE SHOW. June 14-15. White Pine Village, Ludington, MI. Antique auto exhibit, swap meet and awards. Info from: Mason County Historical Society, Connie Newkirk, 1687 S Lakeshore Dr, Ludington, MI 49431.

JUNE 15 — SUNDAY

166th Day — Remaining, 199

A FRIEND IN NEED IS A FRIEND INDEED DAY. June 15. Purpose: To recognize the ongoing support of new and old friends who have been there through thick and thin. Communicate through letter and phone calls. Sponsor: Nancy Byder, 11315 Grand Oak Dr #1, Grand Blanc, MI 48439.

ARKANSAS: ADMISSION DAY. June 15. Became 25th State on this day in 1836.

COELHO, TONY: BIRTHDAY. June 15. U.S. Representative of California's 15th district, Democrat, of Merced, CA, born at Los Banos, CA, on June 15, 1942.

CUOMO, MARIO M: BIRTHDAY. June 15, 1932. Mario M. Cuomo, Governor of New York, Democrat, was born at Queens, NY, on June 15, 1932.

FATHER'S DAY. June 15. Presidential Proclamation. "Issued ☆ for 3rd Sunday in June in 1966 and each year since 1971." (PL92-278 of Apr 24, 1972).

FATHER'S DAY. June 15. Recognition of the third Sunday in June as Father's Day occurred first at the request of Mrs. John B. Dodd of Spokane, WA, on June 19, 1910. It was proclaimed for that date by the mayor of Spokane and recognized by the governor of Washington. The idea was publicly supported by Pres. Calvin Coolidge in 1924, but not presidentially proclaimed until 1966. It was assured of annual recognition by Public Law 92-278, of Apr 24, 1972.

FIRST FATAL AVIATION ACCIDENT: ANNIVERSARY. June 15. Two French aeronauts, Jean Francois Pilatre de Rozier and P.A. de Romain, attempting to cross the English Channel from France to England in a balloon, were killed June 15, 1785, when their balloon caught fire and crashed to the ground. Pilatre de Rozier, the first man to fly thus became a fatality in the first fatal accident in aviation history.

GRIEG, EDVARD: BIRTHDAY. June 15. Norway. Special celebrations at Lofthus on the Hardanger fjord where Grieg's cabin still stands. (June 15, 1843-Sept 4, 1907.)

HUG HOLIDAY. June 15. Purpose: To honor, recognize and appreciate others through any acceptable form, especially a simple hug. Sponsors: Dr. James and Mrs. Ingeborg Johnston, 821 W Sample Rd, Pompano Beach, FL 33064.

JACKSON, RACHEL DONELSON ROBARDS: BIRTHDAY. June 15. Wife of Andrew Jackson, 7th President of the U.S., born at Halifax County, NC, June 15, 1767. Died Dec 22, 1828.

MAGNA CARTA DAY. June 15. Anniversary of King John's sealing, in 1215, of the Magna Carta "in the meadow called Ronimed between Windsor and Staines on the fifteenth day of June in the seventeenth year of our reign." This document is regarded as the first charter of English liberties and one of the

COPYRIGHT © 1985 BY WILLIAM D. CHASE and HELEN M. CHASE

most important documents in the history of political and human freedom as understood today. Four original copies of the 1215 charter survive.

MANITOBA MARATHON. June 15. Winnipeg, Manitoba, Canada, 42 km, 21 km and relay marathons following the park and river system through the city. Info from: Travel Manitoba, Dept 5058, Winnipeg, Manitoba, Canada R3C 3H8.

MOON PHASE: FIRST QUARTER. June 15. Moon enters First Quarter phase at 7:00 a.m., E.S.T.

NORFOLK CHAMBER MUSIC FESTIVAL. June 15-Aug 9. Chamber music concerts by artist/faculty of Yale Summer School of Music. Info from: Yale Summer School of Music, 96 Wall St, New Haven, CT 06520.

SMILE POWER DAY. June 15. Purpose: Smile Power Day is to remind everyone how important smiling is. A smile creates a happier life and better world around us. Info from: Dr. Robert M. Gibson, Suite 717, 1441 Kapiolani Blvd, Honolulu, HI 96814.

SPACE MILESTONE: SOYUZ 29 (USSR). June 15. Launched on June 15, 1978, Cosmonauts Vladimir Kovalyonok and Alexander Ivanchenkov docked with Salyut 6 space station on June 17. Returned to Earth in Soyuz 31, Nov 2, after 4½ months stay, and visits by two pairs of cosmonauts while there. Return landing in Kazakhstan.

STEVE OWENS MEMORIAL DAY LIAR'S RACE. June 15. Walker Lake, NV. Weird and wacky water parade for anything that floats. Info from: Cliff House Marina, P.O. Box 1874, Hawthorne, NV 89415.

300TH ANNIVERSARY OF KING'S CHAPEL, BOSTON. June 15. Anniversary of King's Chapel, Boston on June 15, 1686. Info from: Unitarian Universalist Assn, 25 Beacon St, Boston, MA 02108.

UDALL, MORRIS K: BIRTHDAY. June 15. U.S. Representative of Arizona's 2nd district, Democrat, of Tucson, AZ, was born in St. Johns, AZ, on June 15, 1922.

UNITED STATES JAYCEES ANNUAL MTG. June 15-20. Milwaukee, WI. Info from: Meetings Mgr, The U.S. Jaycees, Box 7, Tulsa, OK 74121.

JUNE 16 — MONDAY
167th Day — Remaining, 198

BLOOMSDAY. June 16. Anniversary of events in Dublin (June 16, 1904) recorded in James Joyce's *Ulysses*, whose central character is Leopold Bloom.

COUNTRY MUSIC DAYS. June 16-21. Regional amateur talent for bluegrass, country, rock, gospel and clogging. (Third week in June starting on Monday, through Saturday.) Info from: Elizabethton/Carter County Chamber of Commerce, Box 190, Elizabethton, TN 37643.

GRIFFIN, JOHN HOWARD: BIRTHDAY. June 16. American author and photographer deeply concerned about racial problems in U.S. To better understand Blacks in the American South, Griffin blackened his skin by the use of chemicals and ultraviolet light, keeping a journal as he travelled through the South resulting in his best known book *Black Like Me*. Born Dallas, TX, June 16, 1920. Died Fort Worth, TX, Sept 9, 1980.

INTERNATIONAL DAY OF SOLIDARITY WITH THE STRUGGLING PEOPLE OF SOUTH AFRICA. June 16. In November 1976, the United Nations General Assembly proclaimed June 16, the anniversary of the beginning of the 1976 student uprising in Soweto and other areas of South Africa as the International Day of Solidarity with the Struggling

People of South Africa, to be observed annually by Governments and organizations. Info from: United Nations Centre against Apartheid, United Nations, NY 10017.

NATIONAL OLD-TIME FIDDLERS' CONTEST. June 16-21. Purpose: To help perpetuate the old-time fiddling of pioneer America. Sponsor: Chamber of Commerce, 8 E Idaho St, Weiser, ID 83672.

NOVA SCOTIA FORESTRY EXHIBITION. June 16-18. Windsor, Nova Scotia. Promotion of the forestry industry along with displays and entertainment. Info from: Dept of Tourism, Box 456, Halifax, NS B3J 2R5.

QUARTERLY ESTIMATED FEDERAL INCOME TAX PAYERS' DUE DATE. June 16. For those individuals whose fiscal year is the calendar year and who make quarterly estimated federal income tax payments, today is one of the due dates. (Jan 15, Apr 15, June 16, and Sept 15, 1986.)

RHODODENDRON FESTIVAL. June 16-22. Over 600 acres of beautiful flowering rhododendron in full bloom. Arts and crafts at State Park. Sponsor: Roan Mountain Citizens Club. Info from: Elizabethton/Carter County Chamber of Commerce, Box 190, Elizabethton, TN 37643.

SMITH, ROBERT FREEMAN: BIRTHDAY. June 16. U.S. Representative of Oregon's 2nd district, Republican, of Burns, OR, born at Portland, OR, on June 16, 1931.

SOWETO DAY. June 16. International Day of Solidarity with the Struggling People of South Africa, proclaimed by United Nations General Assembly. Anniversary of 1976 uprising of oppressed people in Soweto and other areas. Info from: United Nations, Dept of Public Information, United Nations, NY 10017.

VIRGIN ISLANDS: ORGANIC ACT DAY. June 16. Commemorates the enactment by the U.S. Congress, on July 22, 1954, of the Revised Organic Act, under which the government of the Virgin Islands is organized. Observed annually on the third Monday in June.

SPACE MILESTONE: WOMAN IN SPACE ANNIVERSARY. June 16. Valentina Tereshkova, 26, former cotton mill worker, born on collective farm near Yaroslavl, USSR, became the first woman in space when her 10,300 lb spacecraft, *Vostok-6* took off from the Tyuratam launch site on June 16, 1963. She manually controlled *Vostok-6* during the 70.8 hour flight through 48 orbits of earth, and landed by parachute (separate from her cabin) on June 19, 1963. In November 1963 she married cosmonaut Andrian Nikolayev, who had piloted *Vostok-3* through 64 earth orbits, Aug 11-15, 1962. Their child Yelena (1964) was the first born to space-traveller parents.

JUNE 17 — TUESDAY
168th Day — Remaining, 197

BIG BROTHERS/BIG SISTERS OF AMERICA: NATIONAL CONFERENCE. June 17-21. Clearwater, FL. Purpose: To promote professional growth and provide an exchange of ideas among affiliated agencies, staff and board volunteers. Info from: Big Brothers/Big Sisters of America, 230 N 13th St, Philadelphia, PA 19107.

BUNKER HILL DAY. June 17. Suffolk County, Massachusetts. Battle of this day, 1775.

BURLINGTON STEAMBOAT DAYS. June 17-22. Purpose: The American Music Festival featuring top name entertainment live on the Mississippi River. Arts, crafts, parades and fireworks. Info from: Rita Long, Exec Dir, Burlington Steamboat Days, Inc, Box 271, Brulington, IA 52601.

ENGLAND: HORSERACING ROYAL ASCOT. June 17-20. Ascot Racecourse, Ascot, Berkshire. "Attended by members of the Royal Family, this important event in the racegoer's calendar is almost as popular for its grand show of fashion and outrageous hats as it is for the high standard of racing." For admission to the Royal Enclosure, visitors from overseas should apply to their respective Ambassadors or High Commission in London.

June *1986*	S	M	T	W	T	F	S
	1	2	3	4	5	6	7
	8	9	10	11	12	13	14
	15	16	17	18	19	20	21
	22	23	24	25	26	27	28
	29	30					

COPYRIGHT © 1985 BY WILLIAM D. CHASE and HELEN M. CHASE

GERMANY: DAY OF UNITY. June 17. Public holiday throughout Germany.

GINGRICH, NEWT: BIRTHDAY. June 17. U.S. Representative of Georgia's 6th district, Republican, of Jonesboro, GA, born in Harrisburg, PA, on June 17, 1943.

HAWAIIAN FESTIVAL OF MUSIC. June 17-24. Waikiki Shell, Honolulu. Music groups from mainland U.S. and Hawaii compete. Info from: Hawaii Visitors Bureau, Honolulu, HI 96815.

HOOPER, WILLIAM: BIRTHDAY. June 17. Signer of the Declaration of Independence, born, Boston, MA, June 17, 1742. Died Oct 14, 1790.

ICELAND: INDEPENDENCE DAY. June 17. Anniversary of founding of Republic is major festival, especially in Reykjavik. Parades, competitions, street dancing.

KAPTUR, MARCIA (MARCY) CAROLYN: BIRTHDAY. June 17. U.S. Representative of Ohio's 9th district, Democrat, of Toledo, OH, born in Toledo on June 17, 1946.

MURPHY, AUSTIN J: BIRTHDAY. June 17. U.S. Representative of Pennsylvania's 22nd district, Democrat, of Charleroi, PA, born in North Charleroi, June 17, 1927.

MURTHA, JOHN P: BIRTHDAY. June 17. U.S. Representative of Pennsylvania's 12th district, Democrat, of Johnstown, PA, born at New Martinsville, WV, on June 17, 1932.

NATIONAL ASSOCIATION OF LEFT-HANDED GOLFERS. June 17-20. Disney World, Orlando, FL. Purpose: To establish a National Left-Handed Open and Senior Champion. Info from: Natl Assn of Left-Handed Golfers, 10149 Hammerly, #714, Houston, TX 77080.

O'BRIEN, GEORGE M: BIRTHDAY. June 17. U.S. Representative of Illinois' 4th district, Republican, of Joliet, IL, born in Chicago, IL, on June 17, 1917.

STRANG, MICHAEL LATHROP: BIRTHDAY. June 17. U.S. Representative of Colorado's 3rd district, Republican, of Carbondale, CO, born at Bucks County, PA, on June 17, 1929.

STRAVINSKY, IGOR FEDOROVICH: BIRTHDAY. June 17. Russian composer and author, born at Oranienbaum (near Leningrad) June 17 (new style), 1882. Died at New York City, Apr 6,1971.

WATERGATE DAY. June 17. Anniversary of arrests, at Democratic Party Headquarters (in Watergate complex, Washington, DC) on June 17, 1972, which led to revelations of political espionage, imminent impeachment of the president and on Aug 9, 1974, the resignation of Pres Richard M. Nixon.

JUNE 18 — WEDNESDAY
169th Day — Remaining, 196

BATTLE OF WATERLOO ANNIVERSARY. June 18. Commemorates decisive defeat of Napoleon by Wellington and Blucher, near Waterloo in central Belgium, in 1815.

FIRST AMERICAN WOMAN IN SPACE ANNIVERSARY. June 18. Dr. Sally Ride, 32-year-old physicist and pilot, functioned as a "mission specialist" and became the first American woman in space on June 18, 1983 when she began a six-day mission aboard the space shuttle, *Challenger*. The "near perfect" mission was launched from Cape Canaveral, FL, and landed, June 24, 1983, at Edwards Air Force Base, CA. See also entries for: Sally Ride birthday (May 26) and Woman in Space Anniversary, June 16 (1963).

FOLGER, HENRY CLAY, JR: BIRTHDAY. June 18. American businessman and industrialist who developed one of the finest collections of Shakespeareana in the world and bequeathed it (The Folger Shakespeare Library, Washington, DC) to the American people. Born at New York City on June 18, 1857. Died June 11, 1930.

GOLF: U.S. WOMEN'S AMATEUR PUBLIC LINKS CHAMPIONSHIP. June 18-22. Sentry World Golf Course, Stevens Point, WI. National championship for female amateur golfers who are bona fide, public golf course players. Sponsor: U.S. Golf Assn, Golf House, Far Hills, NJ 07931.

KYSER, KAY: BIRTH ANNIVERSARY. June 18. American band leader whose band, "Kay Kyser's College of Musical Knowledge," enjoyed immense popularity in the swing era. He was born James King Kern Kyser at Rocky Mount, NC, on June 18, 1906. Kyser, a shrewd showman and performer said he never learned to read music or play an instrument. Among his hit recordings were "Three Little Fishes" and "Praise the Lord and Pass the Ammunition," a World War II favorite. Kyser retired from show business in 1951, and died at Chapel Hill, NC, July 23, 1985.

MALLORY, GEORGE LEIGH: BIRTHDAY. June 18. English explorer and mountain climber born at Mobberley, Cheshire, England, June 18, 1886. Last seen climbing through the mists toward the summit of the highest mountain in the world, Mt. Everest, on the morning of June 8, 1924. Best remembered for his answer when asked whey he wanted to climb Mt. Everest: "Because it is there."

ROCKEFELLER, JOHN D (JAY) III: BIRTHDAY. June 18. U.S. Senator from West Virginia, Democrat, of Charleston, WV, born in New York City on June 18, 1937.

SPACE MILESTONE: STS-7 (US). June 18. Shuttle Challenger, launched from Kennedy Space Center, FL June 18, 1983 with crew of five, including Sally K. Ride, first American woman in space, Robert Crippen, Norman Thagard, John Fabian and Frederick Houck. Landed at Edwards Air Force Base, CA on June 24 after near-perfect 6-day mission.

JUNE 19 — THURSDAY
170th Day — Remaining, 195

ANTIQUE AUTO FAIR AND SWAP MEET. June 19-22. Museum of Automobiles, Petit Jean Mountain, Morrilton, AR. Sponsors: Mid-America Old Time Auto Assn and The Museum of Automobiles, Rt 3, Petit Jean Mountain, Morrilton, AR 72110.

BURDICK, QUENTIN N: BIRTHDAY. June 19. U.S. Senator from North Dakota, Democrat, endorsed by Nonpartisan League, of Fargo, ND, born in Munich, ND, on June 19, 1908.

COOPER, JAMES HAYES SHOFNER: BIRTHDAY. June 19. U.S. Representative of Tennessee's 4th district, Democrat, of Shelbyville, TN, born and raised in Shelbyville, TN, on June 19, 1954.

CRANSTON, ALAN: BIRTHDAY. June 19. U.S. Senator from California, Democrat, of Los Angeles, CA, was born in Palo Alto, CA, on June 19, 1914.

EMANCIPATION DAY IN TEXAS. June 19. In honor of the emancipation of the slaves in Texas on June 19, 1865.

GARFIELD: BIRTHDAY. June 19. "America's favorite lasagna-loving cat celebrates his 8th birthday." The "Garfield" comic strip, created by Jim Davis and syndicated by United Feature Syndicate, first appeared on June 19, 1978. Info from: United Feature Syndicate, Nancy Nicolelis, PR Mgr, 200 Park Ave, New York, NY 10166.

© 1978 United Feature Syndicate, Inc

GEHRIG, LOU: BIRTH ANNIVERSARY. June 19. Baseball great Henry Louis Gehrig (lifetime batting average of .341) who played in seven World Series, was born at New York, NY, on June 19, 1903, and died there June 2, 1941.

HEFLIN, HOWELL THOMAS: BIRTHDAY. June 19. U.S. Senator from Alabama, Democrat, of Tuscumbia, AL, born June 19, 1921.

COPYRIGHT © 1985 BY WILLIAM D. CHASE and HELEN M. CHASE

JUNETEENTH. June 19. Celebrated in Texas and other parts of the Deep South in memory of this day in 1865 when Union General Granger proclaimed the slaves of Texas free.

KASTEN, ROBERT W. JR: BIRTHDAY. June 19. U.S. Senator from Wisconsin, Republican, of Milwaukee, WI, born there on June 19, 1942.

NATIONAL MOUNTAIN STYLE SQUARE DANCE & CLOGGING FESTIVAL. June 19-21. Natural Bridge State Resort Park, Slade, KY. Some of the finest clogging teams in the country perform in costume on Hoedown Island. Info from: Kentucky Dept. of Parks, Capital Plaza Tower, Frankfort, KY 40601.

PASCAL, BLAISE: BIRTHDAY. June 19. French philosopher and author, born June 19, 1623. Died, Paris, Aug 19, 1662. It was Pascal who said "Had Cleopatra's nose been shorter, the whole history of the world would have been different." And, in his *Provincial Letters*, he wrote "I have made this letter longer than usual, because I lack the time to make it short."

ROSENBERG EXECUTION: ANNIVERSARY. June 19. Anniversary of the electrocution of the only married couple ever executed together in the U.S. Julius (35) and Ethel (37) Rosenberg were executed, for espionage, at Sing Sing Prison, Ossining, NY, June 19, 1953. Time for the execution was advanced several hours to avoid conflict with the Jewish Sabbath.

SPACE MILESTONE: ARIANE (ESA). June 19. Launched from Kourou, French Guiana, June 19, 1981. Ariane carried two satellites into orbit (Meteostat 2, ESA weather satellite, and Apple, a geostationary communications satellite for India, to be stationed over Sumatra).

TAIWAN: BIRTHDAY OF CHENG HUANG. June 19. Thirteenth day of fifth moon. Procession of actors on stilts. Dragon and lion dances.

VERMILION FESTIVAL OF THE FISH. June 19-22. Antique boats, crazy raft race, carnival and fish dinners. Info from: Herb Feakins, Box 418, Vermilion, OH 44089.

VIOLA GOPHER COUNT. June 19. Viola, MN. Purpose: a celebration of catching pesky gophers. The third Thursday in June is set aside for counting gopher feet, paying cash prizes and celebrating with family picnics and reunions. Info from: Viola Gopher Count Assn, Lee Christensen, Box 7, Viola, MN 55980.

JUNE 20 — FRIDAY
171st Day — Remaining, 194

ANNAPOLIS ARTS FESTIVAL. June 20-22. Annapolis City Dock. Local and nationally famous talent on waterside stage. Artists and craftsmen. Info from: Kathy Greentree, Annapolis fine Arts Foundation, Box 228, Annapolis, MD 21404.

ANTIQUE AUTOMOBILE CLUB OF AMERICA: SPRING MEET. June 20-22. Cherry Hill, NJ. Info from: Box 417, Hershey, PA 17033.

COVERED BRIDGE CELEBRATION. June 20-22. Purpose: To celebrate the birthday of our covered bridge. Handmade craft exhibits, bike race, golf tournament and antique/classic auto show. Sponsor: Elizabethton/Carter County Chamber of Commerce, Box 190, Elizabethton, TN 37643.

DENMARK: VIKING FESTIVAL. June 20-July 6. Frederikssund (about 25 miles northwest of Copenhagen). Famous outdoor plays based on Danish legends. (Annual from next to last Friday in June until first Sunday in July.)

June *1986*	S	M	T	W	T	F	S
	1	2	3	4	5	6	7
	8	9	10	11	12	13	14
	15	16	17	18	19	20	21
	22	23	24	25	26	27	28
	29	30					

DETROIT INTERNATIONAL GRAND PRIX. June 20-22. One in a series of Formula One Grand Prix championship races. A 2.5-mile course along the Detroit River, past the Renaissance Center. Festivities include qualifying and support races. Tentative date info from: Detroit Renaissance, Robert E. McCabe, Pres, 100 Renaissance, Ctr, Suite 1760, Detroit, MI 48243.

FOLK ON THE ROCKS. June 20-22. Features Inuit and Dene performers, throat singers, drum dancers, fiddlers and folk artists from Northwest Territories, Yukon, Southern Canada and the USA. Craft displays include native handicrafts. Celebrated annually the weekend closest to June 21. Info from: Society for Encouragement of Northern Talent, Box 326, Yellowknife, N.W.T. X1A 2N3.

GREAT SEAL OF THE UNITED STATES: ANNIVERSARY. June 20. Charles Thomson, first official record keeper of the US, submitted his report to the congress, recommending a design for the Great Seal, on June 20, 1782. The congress adopted his report on the same day. See also: entries for Jan 28, July 4, and Sept 16.

HILLBILLY DAYS. June 20-22. Bennett Spring State Park, Lebanon, MO. Info from: Missouri Dept of Natural Resources, Box 176, Jefferson City, MO 65102.

INTERNATIONAL FREEDOM FESTIVAL. June 20-July 4. Detroit, MI and Windsor, Ontario. Parades, concerts, special exhibits and super-spectacular fireworks display. Info from: Kathleen McNamara, Detroit Renaissance Foundation, 100 Renaissance Ctr, Suite 1760, Detroit, MI 48243.

INTERNATIONAL WIZARD OF OZ CLUB CONVENTION. June 20-22. Illinois Beach Resort and Conference Center, Zion, IL. Sponsor: Internatl Wizard of Oz Club, Inc, Fred M Meyer, Secy, 220 N 11th St, Escanaba, MI 49829.

MICHIGAN SUGAR BEET FESTIVAL. June 20-22. Purpose: To show the area's appreciation to the sugar industry which has purchased sugar beet crops and processed sugar here since 1902. Sponsor: Sebewaing Actions Council, Gail Kelly, Pres, 930 E Main, Sebewaing, MI 48759.

MIDNIGHT GOLF TOURNAMENT. June 20. Yellowknife, N.W.T. Canada. "Thieving ravens stealing well-placed chip shots off the sand 'greens' are one of the legendary hazards awaiting golfers at this all night event. Join local golf nuts and visiting celebrities in this rolicking social event that starts at 3:00 pm and ends around 6:00 am Saturday." (Always the Friday closest to June 21st.) Info from: Yellowknife Golf Club, Box 388, Yellowknife, N.W.T. Canada X1A 2N3.

MILWAUKEE JOURNAL/WYSA SOCCER CLASSIC. June 20-30. Purpose: State-wide junior soccer tournament in 15 age groups for boys and girls age 6-19. Sponsor: Milwaukee Journal, Greg Sbaraglia, Box 661, Milwaukee, WI 53201.

MONSON, DAVID SMITH: BIRTHDAY. June 20. U.S. Representative of Utah's 2nd district, Republican, of Salt Lake City, UT, born there on June 20, 1945.

PHOENIX JUNETEENTH JUBILEE. June 20-21 East Lake Park, Phoenix, AZ. Emancipation Proclamation celebration includes a citywide youth talent show, parade, festival, food and craft sales and a Black Art Show. Info from: City of Phoenix, Parks, Recreation & Library Dept, 125 E Washington, Phoenix, AZ 85004.

QUECHEE HOT AIR BALLOON FESTIVAL. June 20-22. Village Green, Quechee, VT. Balloon ascensions, craft show, entertainment and barbecue. Info from: Quechee Chamber of Commerce, Box 757, Quechee, VT 05059.

RED RIVER EXHIBITION. June 20-29. Winnipeg, Manitoba. Industrial showcases, midway, stage shows and casino. Info from: Travel Manitoba, Dept 5058, Winnipeg, Manitoba, Canada R3C 3H8.

RENO RODEO. June 20-29. Reno, Nevada. Carnival, parade, contests and western arts and crafts. Info from: Reno Rodeo Office, PO Box 12335, Reno, NV 89510.

"SHAKE-SPEARE" FESTIVAL AND ELIZABETHAN FAIRE. June 20-22. (Also June 27-29). Ojai, CA. Purpose: Royal "Shake-speare" Revels are accompanied by colorfully

COPYRIGHT © 1985 BY WILLIAM D. CHASE and HELEN M. CHASE

costumed performers and vendors with dozens of shows, arts, crafts and musicians. Locally produced volunteer program. Sponsor: Royal "Shake-speare" Revels, Attn: Helen Alexander, Box 575, Ojai, CA 93023.

WEST VIRGINIA: ADMISSION DAY. June 20. Became 35th state on this day in 1863.

JUNE 21 — SATURDAY
172nd Day — Remaining, 193

AMERICAN NEWSPAPER PUBLISHERS ASSOCIATION: OPERATIONS MANAGEMENT CONFERENCE AND EXPOSITION. June 21-25. Georgia World Congress Ctr, Atlanta GA. Purpose: Trade show of newspaper systems and equipment and conference program to help improve newspaper operations. Info from: The Newspaper Ctr, Peter P. Romano, Tech Services Dir, Box 17407, Dulles Internatl Airport, Washington, DC 20041.

AMERICAN SOCIETY OF RADIOLOGIC TECHNOLOGISTS CONFERENCE. June 21-26. San Antonio, TX. Info from: American Society of Radiologic Technologists, 15000 Central Ave, SE, Albuquerque, NM 87123.

BURTON, DANNY LEE: BIRTHDAY. June 21. U.S. Representative of Indiana's 6th district, Republican, of Indianapolis, IN, born in Indianapolis on June 21, 1938.

CANCER, THE CRAB. June 21-July 22. In the astronomical/astrological Zodiac, which divides the sun's apparent orbit into twelve segments, the period June 21-July 22 is identified, traditionally, as the sun-sign of Cancer, the Crab. The ruling planet is the moon.

ENGLAND: BIRTHDAY OF PRINCE WILLIAM OF WALES. June 21. Born June 21, 1982, William Arthur Philip Louis, son of Charles and Diana, the Prince and Princess of Wales.

HECKLER, MARGARET M: BIRTHDAY. June 21. Margaret M. Heckler, U.S. Secretary of Health and Human Services (sworn in on Mar 9, 1983) was born at Flushing, NY, on June 21, 1931.

HILLSBOROUGH, NORTH CAROLINA HOG DAY. June 21. Purpose: To provide Hillsborough community with a good time. Sponsor: Chamber of Commerce, 228 S Churton St, Hillsborough, NC 27278.

MADAM LOU BUNCH DAY. June 21. Central City, CO. Purpose: The "richest square mile on earth" celebrates the Madams and Sporting House Girls of a by-gone era with "The Original Bed Race" and "The Madams and Miners Ball." (Celebrated annually on 3rd Saturday of June.) Info from: Kathryn Hemlock, Central City Hall, Box 249, Central City, CO 80427.

MIDNIGHT SUN BASEBALL GAME. June 21. Fairbanks, AK. Purpose: To celebrate the summer solstice. Game is played without artificial lights at 11:00 p.m. Info from: Alaska Goldpanners, Box 1154, Fairbanks, AK 99707.

MOON PHASE: FULL MOON. June 21. Moon enters Full Moon phase at 10:42 p.m., E.S.T.

NATIONAL HOLLERIN' CONTEST. June 21. Purpose: To revive the almost lost art of hollerin' which was a means of communication in days gone by. Annually, third Saturday in June. Sponsor: Natl Hollerin' Contest, Ermon Godwin, Jr, Box 332, Spivey's Corner, NC 28334.

NEW HAMPSHIRE: RATIFICATION DAY. June 21. Ninth State to ratify constitution, on this day in 1788.

NEW OXFORD FLEA MARKET AND ART AND CRAFT SHOW. June 21. Annual event featuring arts and crafts, antiques and flea market. Held in the streets of New Oxford, PA near Gettysburg. Info from: Gettysburg Travel Council, 35 Carlisle St, Gettysburg, PA 17325.

PERIGEAN SPRING TIDES. June 21. Spring tides, the highest possible tides, occur when New Moon or Full Moon takes place within 24 hours of the moment the moon is nearest Earth (perigee) in its monthly orbit. June 21, at 8 a.m., E.S.T.

QUILT AND NEEDLEWORK SHOW. June 21-29. Mansion House Inn, 214 E Main St, Centerville, IN. Info from: Jane B. Mercier, Dir, 114 N West 28th St, Richmond, IN 47374.

RHODODENDRON FESTIVAL CELEBRATION. June 21-22. Roan Mountain, TN. Celebration of the blooming of the magnificent rhododendron. Music, dancing and crafts. Info from: Roan Mountain State Resort Park, Rt 1, Box 236, Roan Mountain, TN 37687.

ROSCOE VILLAGE ART SHOW AND SALE. June 21-22. Held in conjunction with the Coshocton Art Guild. Info from: Roscoe Village Foundation, 381 Hill St, Coshocton, OH 43812.

SARTRE, JEAN PAUL: BIRTHDAY. June 21. French philosopher, "father of existentialism," born at Paris, June 21, 1905. In 1964, Sartre rejected the Nobel Prize for Literature when it was awarded to him. He died at Paris, Apr 15, 1980. In *Being and Nothingness*, he wrote: "Man can will nothing unless he has first understood that he must count on no one but himself; that he is alone, abandoned on earth in the midst of his infinite responsibilities, without help, with no other aim than the one he sets himself, with no other destiny than the one he forges for himself on this earth."

SHRINE TRAILRIDERS RODEO. June 21-22. Purpose: To show appreciation of the art of handling animals with care and pleasure and to generate funds for Shrine hospitals. Sponsor: El Kadir Shrine Club, Box 235, Kirksville, MO 63501.

SUMMER. June 21-Sept 23. In the Northern Hemisphere summer begins today with the Summer Solstice, at 11:30 a.m., E.S.T. Note that in the Southern Hemisphere today is the beginning of winter, and the occasion of the Winter Solstice. The point on Earth from which sun is overhead reaches its farthest north for the year, on the Tropic of Cancer, latitude 23½° N., this year at longitude 67.5° W (about 400 miles north of Puerto Rico). Anywhere between Equator and Arctic Circle, the sun rises and sets farthest north on the horizon for the year, and length of daylight is maximum (12 hours, 8 minutes at Equator, increasing to 24 hours at Arctic Circle).

SUMMER MUSIC FESTIVAL AND MARKETPLACE. June 21-22. DeSoto Caverns Park, Childersburg, AL. Jazz and country bands, rock n' roll, bluegrass, folk music and dancing. Arts, crafts and antiques. Info from: Caryl Mathis, 93 Ivy Trail NE, Atlanta, GA 30342.

TOMPKINS, DANIEL D. BIRTHDAY. June 21. Sixth vice-president of the U.S. (1817-1825), born, Fox Meadows, NY, June 21, 1774. Died, Staten Island, NY, June 11, 1825.

WARWICK SUMMER FESTIVAL. June 21. Family festival featuring favorite local talent, strolling clowns and magicians. Info from: Chester County Parks & Recreation, 235 W Market St, West Chester, PA 19382.

WASHINGTON, MARTHA DANDRIDGE CUSTIS: BIRTHDAY. June 21. Wife of George Washington, First President of the U.S., born at New Kent County, VA, June 21, 1731. Died May 22, 1802.

WOODCHOPPERS JAMBOREE. June 21-22. Encampment, WY. Wyoming's largest timber carnival with rodeo, barbeque, dancing, all kinds of lumberjack games. Info: Saratoga Chamber of Commerce, Box 1095, Saratoga, WY 82331.

COPYRIGHT © 1985 BY WILLIAM D. CHASE and HELEN M. CHASE

JUNE 22 — SUNDAY

173rd Day — Remaining, 192

CHESAPEAKE-LEOPARD AFFAIR: ANNIVERSARY. June 22. One of the events leading to the War of 1812, occurred June 22, 1807, about 40 miles east of Chesapeake Bay. The U.S. frigate *Chesapeake* was fired upon and boarded by the crew of the British man-of-war *Leopard*. The *Chesapeake's* commander, James Barron, was court-martialled and convicted of not being prepared for action. Later Barron killed one of the judges (Stephen Decatur) in a duel fought at Bladensburg, MD, Mar 22, 1820.

CHURCH AND SYNAGOGUE LIBRARY ASSOCIATION CONFERENCE. June 22-24. Concordia Lutheran College, Austin, TX. Theme: "Congregational Libraries: a Life-giving Service." Sponsor: Church & Synagogue Library Assn, Dorothy Rodda, Exec Secy, Box 1130, Bryn Mawr, PA 19010.

HOOTENANNY. June 22. Fairfield County Museum, Winnsboro, SC, Country, bluegrass, gospel, and folk music. (Always the fourth Sunday in June.) Info from: Kathlyn Fritz, Curator, South Congress St, Winnsboro, SC 29180.

INTERLOCHEN ARTS FESTIVAL. June 22-Aug 18. National Music Camp, Interlochen, MI. Music, dance, threatre and visual arts. Performances by nationally famous groups, artist faculty members and Interlochen students. Info from: Interlochen Center for the Arts, Interlochen, MI 49643.

INTERNATIONAL SCIENTIFIC MEETING ON DIABETES. June 22-24. Anaheim Convention Ctr, Anaheim, CA. Purpose: To provide a major forum for reporting the latest advances in diabetes research and new treatment approaches to scientists and health care professionals from around the world. Sponsor: American Diabetes Assn, Two Park Ave, New York, NY 10016.

JOE LOUIS - BRADDOCK AND SCHMELING FIGHT ANNIVERSARIES. June 22. At Chicago's Comiskey Park, on June 22, 1937, Joe Louis won the World Heavyweight Championship title by knocking out James J. Braddock (8th round). Louis retained the title until his retirement in 1949. Exactly one year after the Braddock fight, on June 22, 1938, Louis met Germany's Max Schmeling, at New York City's Yankee Stadium. Louis knocked out Schmeling in the first round.

JOHNSON COUNTY PEACH FESTIVAL. June 22-29. Purpose: To celebrate peach harvest. Beauty pageants, terrapin race, tobacco and peach seed spitting contests. Sponsor: Johnson County Peach Festival, Box 517, Clarksville, AR 72830.

KIWANIS INTERNATIONAL CONVENTION. June 22-25. Houston, TX. Info from: Kiwanis Internatl, 3636 Woodview Trace, Indianapolis, IN 46268.

LINDBERGH, ANNE MORROW: BIRTHDAY. June 22. American author and aviator, born, June 22, 1907. In *Gift from the Sea*, she wrote: "By and large, mothers and housewives are the only workers who do not have regular time off. They are the great vacationless class."

MALTA: MNARJA. June 22-23. Buskett Gardens, Malta. A folk-cum-harvest festival. An all-night traditional Maltese "festa" with folk music, dancing and impromptu Maltese folk singing (ghana). This festival originated in the Middle Ages and the word "Mnarja" is derived for "luminarja" because the countryside and the bastions around Mdina, Malta's ancient capital, used to be illuminated by "Fjakkoli" (torches made of sand mixed with oil and animal fat) on the eve and on the feast day itself.

June 1986	S	M	T	W	T	F	S
	1	2	3	4	5	6	7
	8	9	10	11	12	13	14
	15	16	17	18	19	20	21
	22	23	24	25	26	27	28
	29	30					

NATIONAL ASSOCIATION OF CONGREGATIONAL CHRISTIAN CHURCHES ANNUAL MEETING. June 22-25. YMCA Camp, Estes Park, CO. Info from: Natl Assn of Congregational Christian Churches, 8473 S Howell Ave, Oak Creek, WI 53154.

NATIONAL FINK WEEK. June 22-28. Purpose: To restore dignity to the honorable surname of Fink by honoring all Finks. Fink Olympics, golf tournament and yacht racing. Info from: Robert L. Fink, Pres, Finks Internatl, 205 Ralston, Converse TX 78109.

NATIONAL TENNIS WEEK. June 22-30. Purpose: To develop tennis at the grassroots level. Players can participate in Lipton Iced Tea Mixed Doubles qualifying tournaments and clinics at over 2,300 tennis facilities nationwide. Sponsor: Thomas J. Lipton. Info from: National Tennis Week, Judy LaMarche, Tennis Promotions, 495 Westport Ave, Norwalk, CT 06856.

ORTHODOX PENTECOST. June 22. Observed by the Orthodox Church in America and other Orthodox churches on this date.

PEARL S. BUCK BIRTHDAY CELEBRATION. June 22. Purpose: To celebrate the 94th anniversary of Pearl Buck's Birth. Sponsor: Pearl S. Buck Birthplace Foundation, Michael Dotson, Exec Dir, Box 126, Hillsboro, WV 24946.

PUNXSUTAWNEY GROUNDHOG FESTIVAL. June 22-28. Punxsutawney, PA. Purpose: To provide residents and visitors a festive week of summer celebration. Music, contests, crafts, food, theater and entertainers. Sponsor: Groundhog Festival Committee, Mrs Judy Freed, Secy, RD 2, Box 127, Punxsutawney, PA 15767.

SEWANEE CONCERTS AND FESTIVAL. June 22-July 27. Sewanee, TN. Intensive training for serious students in orchestra and chamber music with private instruction. Info from: Sewanee Summer Music Ctr, Martha McCrory, Dir, Sewanee, TN 37375.

SINGING ON THE MOUNTAIN. June 22. Linville, NC. Modern and traditional gospel music featuring top groups and nationally known speakers. Annually the fourth Sunday in June. Info from: Grandfather Mountain, Harris Prevost, Box 995, Linville, NC 28646.

SWITZERLAND: MORAT BATTLE COMMEMORATION. June 22. The little walled town of Morat played a decisive part in Swiss history. There, on June 22, 1476, the Confederates were victorious over Charles the Bold of Burgundy, laying the basis for French-speaking areas to become Swiss. Now an annual children's festival.

U.S. DEPARTMENT OF JUSTICE: BIRTHDAY. June 22. Established by Act of June 22, 1870, the Department of Justice is headed by the Attorney General. Prior to 1870, the Attorney General (whose office had been created Sept 24, 1789) had been a member of the President's Cabinet, but had not been the head of a department.

VUCANOVICH, BARBARA FARRELL: BIRTHDAY. June 22. U.S. Representative of Nevada's 2nd district, Republican, of Reno, NV, born in Camp Dix, NJ, on June 22, 1921.

JUNE 23 — MONDAY

174th Day — Remaining, 191

ACC CRAFTFAIR AT WEST SPRINGFIELD. June 23-29. Eastern States Expo Ctr, West Springfield, MA. Info from: American Craft Enterprises, Inc, Box 10, New Paltz, NY 12561.

CN TOWER: BIRTHDAY. June 23. Birthday of the world's tallest free-standing, self-supporting structure, the Canadian National Tower, 1,821 feet high, Toronto, Ontario, Canada, opened on June 23, 1976.

COBB, IRVIN S: BIRTHDAY. June 23. American writer and humorist born June 23, 1876. Died Mar 10, 1944.

DENMARK: MIDSUMMER EVE. June 23. Celebrated all over the country with bonfires and merrymaking.

COPYRIGHT © 1985 BY WILLIAM D. CHASE and HELEN M. CHASE

ENGLAND: LAWN TENNIS CHAMPIONSHIPS. June 23-July 6. All England Lawn Tennis and Croquet Club, Wimbledon, London SW 19.

GAY PRIDE WEEK. June 23-29. Purpose: Commemorates the Stonewall Riot in 1969, when gays first resisted harassment, affirming right to social and legal equality. Sponsor: Natl Gay Task Force, 80 Fifth Ave, New York, NY 10011.

LUXEMBOURG: NATIONAL HOLIDAY. June 23. Official birthday of H.R.H., The Grand Duke.

MAYFLOWER CLASSIC GOLF TOURNAMENT. June 23-29. Indianapolis, IN. Info from: Mayflower Corp, Box 107B, Indianapolis, IN 46206.

MIDSUMMER DAY. June 23. Celebrates the beginning of summer with maypoles, music, dancing and bonfires. Observed mainly in Northern Europe, especially Scandinavian countries. Day of observance is sometimes St. John's Day (June 24), with celebration on St. John's Eve (June 23) as well. Time approximates the Summer Solstice (q.v.).

NEWFOUNDLAND: DISCOVERY DAY. June 23.

SWEDEN: MIDSUMMER. June 23-24. Celebrated throughout Sweden. Maypole dancing, games and folk music.

JUNE 24 — TUESDAY
175th Day — Remaining, 190

BEECHER, HENRY WARD: BIRTHDAY. June 24. Famous American clergyman and orator was born at Litchfield, CT. June 24, 1813. Died, Mar 8, 1887. His dying words were "Now comes the mystery."

DAHLONEGA BLUEGRASS FESTIVAL. June 24-28. Mountain Music Park, Dahlonega, GA. Family entertainment. Info from: Norman Adams, Box 98, Dahlonega, GA 30533.

DEMPSEY, JACK: BIRTHDAY. June 24. William Harrison Dempsey, known as "The Manassa Mauler," was world heavyweight boxing champion, 1919-1926. After his boxing career Dempsey became a successful New York restaurant operator. Born on June 24, 1895, at Manassa, CO, he died on May 31, 1983, at New York City.

FLYING SAUCER ANNIVERSARY. June 24. First reported sighting of "Flying Saucers" reported flying over Mount Rainier, Washington, on June 24, 1947, by Kenneth Arnold of Boise, ID.

ITALY: GIOCO DEL CALCIO. June 24-28. Florence. Revival of a 16th century football match, in medieval costumes. Fireworks also on June 24th.

MACAU DAY. June 24. Macau. Celebrates defeat of the Dutch invasion of 1622, and pays homage to patron saint of Macau, St. John the Baptist.

PERU: COUNTRYMAN'S DAY. June 24. Half day public holiday in Peru.

RENO RODEO. June 24-29. Top professional cowboys ride in one of the west's richest rodeos. Info from: Nevada Commission on Tourism, Capitol Complex, Carson City, NV 89710.

ST. JOHN THE BAPTIST DAY. June 24. Celebrates birth of saint.

SPACE MILESTONE: SOYUZ T-6 (USSR). June 24. Three man crew (V. Dzhanibekov, A. Ivanchenkov and Jean-Loup Chretien) docked at Salyut 7, visiting two other cosmonauts in residence there before returning to Earth on July 2. Launched June 24, 1982.

VENEZUELA: BATTLE OF CARABOBO. June 24th. Public holiday in Venezuela. Info from: Government & Tourist Information Ctr, 7 East 51st St, New York, NY 10022.

JUNE 25 — WEDNESDAY
176th Day — Remaining, 189

ARNOLD, HENRY H. "HAP": BIRTH ANNIVERSARY. June 25. Commanding General of U.S. Army Air Force in World War II, Arnold, who had received flying instruction from Orville Wright in 1911, was born at Gladwyne, PA on June 25, 1886. Arnold retired in 1946 and died near Sonoma, CA, on Jan 15, 1950.

CUSTER'S LAST STAND. June 25. Lt Col George Armstrong Custer, leading military force of more than 200 men, attacked encampment of Sioux Indians led by Chiefs Sitting Bull and Crazy Horse, near Little Big Horn River, Montana. Custer and all men in his immediate command were killed. Brief battle (about two hours) of Little Bighorn occurred on Sunday, June 25, 1876. One horse, named Comanche, said to have been only living survivor among Custer's forces.

FESTIVAL OF AMERICAN FOLKLIFE. June 25-29. (Also July 2-6.) National Mall, Washington, DC. Purpose: To honor and share with visitors the traditional music, crafts and foods of participants from featured areas. Usually a state and country are highlighted. Sponsor: Smithsonian Institution, Office of Folklife Programs, L'Enfant 2600, Washington, DC 20560.

FESTIVAL OF THE STRAIT. June 25-29. Port Hawkesbury, Nova Scotia. Annual seaside festival with giant parade. Info from: Dept of Tourism, Box 456, Halifax, NS B3J 2R5.

KOREAN WAR ANNIVERSARY. June 25. Invasion began June 25, 1950, and U.S. ground forces entered conflict June 30. Armistice signed at Panmunjom, South Korea on July 27, 1953.

LAUBACH LITERACY BIENNIAL CONFERENCE 1986. June 25-29. Rhodes College, Memphis, TN. Purpose: To improve the services; understand the plight of illiterates, to understand public resistance to the problem; to share concerns through public relations; to coordinate with each other and improve our self-image. Info from: Laubach Literacy Internatl, Laubach Literacy Action, New Readers Press, Marie J. Johnson, PR Officer, 1320 Jamesville Ave, Syracuse, NY 13210.

"LEON." June 25. Tampa Bay Area, Florida. Purpose: To bring Christmas excitement and fun to the middle of summer, and to help the children at All Children's Hospital. (Half a year away from Christmas, "LEON" is "NOEL" spelled backwards.) Sponsor: Jack Harris, AM 97/WFLA Radio, 801 Jackson St, Tampa, FL 33602.

MOZAMBIQUE: NATIONAL DAY. June 25. National holiday is observed in Mozambique.

ORWELL, GEORGE: BIRTHDAY. June 25. English satirist, author of *Animal Farm*, *Nineteen Eighty-Four*, and other works was born at Motihari, Bengal, on June 25, 1903. George Orwell was the pseudonym of Eric Arthur Blair. Died at London, Jan 21, 1950.

VIRGINIA RATIFICATION DAY. June 25. Tenth State to ratify constitution, on this day in 1788.

WHITE PINE VILLAGE: SENIOR CITIZEN'S DAY. June 25. Old time silent movies, senior bands, box lunches and quilting bees. Info from: Mason County Historical Society, Connie Newkirk, 1687 S Lakeshore Dr, Ludington, MI 49431.

JUNE 26 — THURSDAY
177th Day — Remaining, 188

BUCK, PEARL SYDENSTRICKER: BIRTHDAY. June 26. American author, noted authority on China, born Hillsboro, WV, June 26, 1892. Died, Mar 6, 1973.

COPYRIGHT © 1985 BY WILLIAM D. CHASE and HELEN M. CHASE

ENGLAND: ALDERSHOT ARMY DISPLAY. June 26-29. Rushmoor Arena, Fleet Road, Aldershot, Hampshire. Static displays by corps and Regiments of the Army and associated civilian organizations.

GOLF: U.S. SENIOR OPEN CHAMPIONSHIP. June 26-29. Scioto Country Club, Columbus, OH. National championship for golfers age 50 and older. Sponsor: U.S. Golf Assn, Golf House, Far Hills, NJ 07931.

MADAGASCAR: INDEPENDENCE DAY. June 26. National holiday.

MIDDLETON, ARTHUR: BIRTHDAY. June 26. American Revolutionary leader and signer of the Declaration of Independence, born, near Charleston, SC, June 26, 1742. Died, Goose Creek, SC, Jan 1, 1787.

MONTGOLFIER, JOSEPH MICHEL: DEATH ANNIVERSARY. June 26. French merchant and inventor, born at Vidalonlez-Annonay, in 1740 (exact date unknown) who, with his brother Jacques Etienne (q.v.) in November 1782 conducted experiments with paper and fabric bags filled with smoke and hot air, which led to invention of the hot air balloon and man's first flight. Died at Balaruc-les-Bains, June 26, 1810. See also entries for June 5 and Nov 1.

NATIONAL SQUARE DANCE CONVENTION. June 26-29. Indianapolis, IN. Info from: Ed Hayworth, 6020 Wind Penny Lane, Indianapolis, IN 46220.

NORTHERN IRELAND GAME AND COUNTRY FAIR. June 26-28. Clandeboye Estate, near Bangor, County Down. Ireland's premier field sports event covering all aspects of outdoor sports and country life.

NOVA SCOTIA TATTOO. June 26-30. Halifax, Nova Scotia. The Tattoo combines military and civilian performers in singing, dancing and marching. Highlight is the thrilling Naval Gun Run competition. Info from: Dept of Tourism, Box 456, Halifax, NS B3J 2R5.

ROBB, CHARLES S: BIRTHDAY. June 26. Charles S. Robb, Governor of Virgina, Democrat, was born at Phoenix, AZ, on June 26, 1939.

ST. LAWRENCE SEAWAY DEDICATION ANNIVERSARY. June 26. President Dwight D. Eisenhower and Queen Elizabeth II jointly dedicated the St. Lawrence Seaway in formal ceremonies at St. Lambert, Quebec, June 26, 1959. A project undertaken jointly by Canada and the U.S., the waterway (which provides access between the Atlantic Ocean and the Great Lakes) had been opened to traffic on Apr 25, 1959.

SHEFFIELD, WILLIAM: BIRTHDAY. June 26. William Sheffield, Governor of Alaska, Democrat, was born at Spokane, WA, on June 26, 1928.

SIGNING OF THE FEDERAL CREDIT UNION ACT ANNIVERSARY. June 26. Purpose: Commemorates signing by President Franklin Delano Roosevelt of the Federal Credit Union Act, on June 26, 1934, thus enabling the formation of credit unions anywhere in the U.S. Info from: Credit Union Natl Assn, Inc, Lucy Harr Schultz, VP, PR, Box 431, Madison, WI 53701.

SUMMERFEST. June 26-July 6. Milwaukee, WI. Bluegrass, dixieland, blues, rock, pop, polka, classical, folk and swing. Professional artists and craftsmakers and ethnic and American cuisine. Info from: Summerfest, Mary Farley, PR Dir, 200 N Harbor Dr, Milwaukee, WI 53202.

WATERMELON THUMP. June 26-28. Features watermelon judging, eating and seed-spitting. Street carnival, auto rally, fiddler's contest and tournaments. Info from: Mrs Ann Manford, Box 710, Luling, TX 78648.

June 1986

S	M	T	W	T	F	S
1	2	3	4	5	6	7
8	9	10	11	12	13	14
15	16	17	18	19	20	21
22	23	24	25	26	27	28
29	30					

WORLD-WIDE AUTOMOBILE LICENSE PLATE COLLECTORS CONVENTION. June 26-28. Springfield, IL. Purpose: To trade, buy, sell, display and talk license plates. Info from: Jeff Szymonski, 110 Racine St, #2, Rapid City, SD 57701.

JUNE 27 — FRIDAY

178th Day — Remaining, 187

ANTIQUE AUTO SHOW AND COLLECTOR CAR FESTIVAL. June 27-28. St. Ignace, MI. Parade, two "fifties night" programs, model car contest, auto world celebrities. Entries from fourteen states and Canada. Info from: Ed and Mary Ellen Reavie, 268 Hillcrest Blvd, St. Ignace, MI 49781.

ANTIQUE AUTOMOBILE CLUB OF AMERICA: SPRING MEET. June 27-28. Sheridan, WY. Info from: Box 417, Hershey, PA 17033.

ASPEN MUSIC FESTIVAL. June 27-Aug 24. Aspen, CO. Nine weeks of concerts performed by highly acclaimed artists. Sponsor: Music Associates of Aspen, Inc, Debra L. Ayers, Box AA, Aspen, CO 81612.

BABBITT, BRUCE E: BIRTHDAY. June 27. Bruce E. Babbitt, Governor of Arizona, Democrat, was born at Flagstaff, AZ, on June 27, 1938.

DJIBOUTI: NATIONAL HOLIDAY. June 27.

"DOWN MEMORY LANE" PARADE. June 27. St. Ignace, MI. Kick off for the Straits Area Antique Auto Show weekend. Info from: Merv Wyse, 98 Joseph St, St. Ignace, MI 49781.

FRONTIER WEEK RODEO. June 27-29. Purpose: A rodeo with proceeds going to the improvement of town roads and camp areas. Sponsor: Town of Love Valley, Ellenora S. Barker, Box 607, Love Valley, NC 28677.

"GOLDEN AGE OF RADIO" REUNION FESTIVAL. June 27-29. Purpose: To perpetuate and preserve the days of live radio broadcasting. Sponsor: National Radio Heritage Association, Nadine Dreager, Pres, 8 Gayland Dr, Council Bluffs, IA 51501.

GRANTSVILLE DAYS. June 27-29. Grantsville, MD. Crafts, parade, dance, fiddle contest and chicken barbecue. Sponsor: Grantsville Lion's Club. Info from: Gerry Beachy, Beachy's Pharmacy, Box 188, Grantsville, MD 21536.

HAWAII: STATE FARM FAIR. June 27-July 6, McKinley High School grounds, Honolulu. Info from: Hawaii Visitors Bureau, Honolulu, HI 96815.

HEARN, LAFCADIO: BIRTHDAY. June 27. American author, born at Leukas, Greece, June 27, 1850, best remembered for writings about the Far East. Died at Tokyo, Sept 26, 1904.

KELLER, HELEN: BIRTHDAY. June 27. American writer, worldwide advocate of help for the blind and prevention of blindness. Born at Tuscumbia, AL, June 27, 1880. Blind and deaf from 19 months. Died at Easton, CT, June 1, 1968. Yearly observances promoted by organization she helped found in 1915. Special aim is conquest of world blindness by year 2000. Info from: Helen Keller Internatl, Mrs. Lila Rosenblum, 15 West 16th St, New York, NY 10011.

"MICAJAH", June 27-July 5. Autryville, NC. Purpose: To promote patriotism and local history and heritage. "Micajah" is an outdoor drama about Micajah Autry, local hero of the Battle of the Alamo. Sponsor: Autryville Area Fire Dept, Donna N. Cashwell, Secy, Box 126, Autryville, NC 28318.

MICHIGAN STORYTELLER'S FESTIVAL '86. June 27-28. Historical Crossroads Village, Flint, MI. Purpose: Dedicated to the preservation and promotion of storytelling, an ageless form of homespun entertainment. Outstanding performers from around the country, workshops for adults and activities for children. Info from: Children's Community Service Dept, Flint Public Library, 1026 E Kearsley St, Flint, MI 48502.

NEW MEXICO ARTS AND CRAFTS FAIR. June 27-29. New Mexico State Fairgrounds, Albuquerque, NM. Over 200 artists, and craftsmen. Demonstrations and entertainment. Info from: New Mexico Arts & Crafts Fair, 2745 San Mateo NE, Suite G Albuquerque, NM 87110.

COPYRIGHT © 1985 BY WILLIAM D. CHASE and HELEN M. CHASE

PARNELL, CHARLES STEWART: BIRTHDAY. June 27, Irish nationalist leader and Home Rule advocate born at Avondale, County Wicklow, on June 27, 1846. Died at Brighton, Oct 6, 1891.

PERPICH, RUDY: BIRTHDAY. June 27. Rudy Perpich, Governor of Minnesota, Democrat, was born at Carson Lake, MN, on June 27, 1928.

PUGWASH GATHERING OF THE CLANS AND FISHERMAN'S REGATTA. June 27-July 1. Pugwash, Nova Scotia. Kirkin of the tartan, massed pipe band march, street parade, piping, drumming and Highland dancing competitions. Info from: Dept of Tourism, Box 456, Halifax, NS B3J 2R5.

RICHMOND AREA ROSE FESTIVAL. June 27-July 6. Info from: Richmond Area Rose Festival, Box 1332, Richmond, IN 47375.

SMITHSON, JAMES: DEATH ANNIVERSARY. June 27, Scientist and founder of the Smithsonian Institution, James Smithson, illegitimate son of Hugh Smithson, Duke of Northumberland, and Elizabeth Hungerford Keats, was born in France in 1765 (exact date unknown). His will, dated Oct 23, 1826, expressed his feeling about the circumstances of his birth by bequeathing his great wealth to a nation he had never visited, to found "at Washington under the name of the Smithsonian Institution, an establishment for the increase and diffusion of knowledge among men." In spite of opposition, the Congress approved, on Aug 10, 1846, an Act to establish the Smithsonian Institution. Most of Smithson's personal documents, books and collections were destroyed by fire in 1865. Smithson died at Genoa, Italy, June 27, 1829. His remains were removed from there to Washington in 1904.

SPACE MILESTONE: SOYUZ 30 (USSR). June 27. Launched on June 27, 1978, Cosmonauts Pyotr Klimuk and Miroslav Hernaszewski (from Poland) linked with Salyut 6 on June 28, greeting crew of Soyuz 29. Returned to Earth July 5.

SPACE MILESTONE: SOYUZ T-9 (USSR). June 27. Launched from Tyuratam June 27, 1983 with two cosmonauts (V. Lyakhov and A. Aleksandrov). The 40-ton Soyuz T-9 docked at Salyut 7 the next day and returned to Earth nearly five months later, Nov 23.

SPACE MILESTONE: STS-4 (US). June 27. Shuttle Columbia launched from Kennedy Space Center, FL on June 27, 1982 with astronauts K. Mattingly and Henry Hartsfield along with 22,000 lbs of cargo, landed at Edwards Air Force Base, CA on July 4.

JUNE 28 — SATURDAY
179th Day — Remaining, 186

AMERICAN RADIO RELAY LEAGUE: FIELD DAY. June 28-29. Purpose: To test emergency preparedness of nation's Amateur Radio operators under simulated disaster conditions. (Fourth full weekend in June.) Sponsor: American Radio Relay League, Inc, 225 Main St, Newington, CT 06111.

ANN ARBOR SUMMER FESTIVAL. June 28-July 22. Purpose: To present a season of special summer entertainment, including music, dance, and theatre as well as film festivals and art exhibitions. Info from: Ann Arbor Summer Festival, Inc, Robert H. Alexander, Exec Dir, Box 4070, Ann Arbor, MI 48106.

CIVIL WAR HERITAGE DAYS. June 28-July 6. An annual observance held first week in July. Info from: Gettysburg Travel Council, 35 Carlisle St, Gettysburg, PA 17325.

CROSBY GARDENS FESTIVAL OF THE ARTS. June 28-29. Crosby Gardens, Toledo, OH. Info from: Toledo Area Conv & Visitors Bureau, 218 Huron St, Toledo, OH 43604.

CYPRUS: ST. PAUL'S FEAST. June 28-29. Kato Paphos, Cyprus. Religious festivities at Kato Paphos at which the Archbishop officiates. Procession of the Icon of St. Paul through the streets.

DUBLIN KIWANIS FROG JUMP. June 28-29. Middle School, Dublin, OH. Purpose: To raise money for community projects. Info from: Robert F. Schnetzer, 3270 Polley Rd, Columbus, OH 43220.

FLOWER AND CAMERA DAY. June 28. Decorated with colorful flowers, Olvera Street becomes a photographer's paradise. People in costumes gladly pose for pictures for our annual photo contest. Info from: El Pueblo de Los Angeles State Historic Park, 845 N Alameda St, Los Angeles, CA 90012.

FRANCE: FESTIVAL OF THE TARASQUE. June 28. Tarascon (Bouches du Rhone), France. Re-enactment of legendary monstrous beast that lurked near banks of the Rhone, capsizing boats and devouring flocks and men. St. Martha is credited with having tamed the monster.

FREEDOM FESTIVAL. June 28-July 4. Philadelphia, PA. Hot air balloon race, Olde City Restaurant Festival, Summer Mummers Parade and free concerts. Special ceremonies on July 4. Info from: Philadelphia Conv & Visitors Bureau, Three Penn Ctr Plaza, Suite 2020, Philadelphia, PA 19102.

THE GREAT LUMBERTOWN MUSIC FESTIVAL. June 28-July 7. Muskegon, MI. Art fair, polkafest, village market, parade, live music and fireworks. Info from: Lumbertown Music Festival, 561 W Western Ave, Muskegon, MI 49440.

GREAT MERAMEC RIVER RAFT RACE AND FESTIVAL. June 28. Hundreds of homemade rafts ranging from floating autos to double level structures participate in this 4½ hour float on the Meramec River. Info from: St. Louis Conv & Visitors Bureau, 10 S Broadway, Suite 300, St. Louis, MO 63102.

HEIDI FESTIVAL. June 28-29. New Glarus, WI. Last full weekend in June. To celebrate Johanna Spyri's great classic. Info from: Heidi Festival, Box 713, New Glarus, WI 53574.

INTERNATIONAL SAUSAGE FESTIVAL. June 28. Purpose: Feasting and entertainment. Taste the various types of sausages while you listen to a combination of bluegrass and country music. Info from: Visitor & Convention Bureau, 172 W Van Buren, Battle Creek, MI 49017.

KOLBE, JIM: BIRTHDAY. June 28. U.S. Representative of Arizona's 5th district, Republican, of Tucson, AZ, born at Evanston, IL. June 28, 1942.

KUTZTOWN PENNSYLVANIA DUTCH FOLK FESTIVAL. June 28-July 6. Purpose: To perpetuate the life and customs of the Pennsylvania Dutch people. Crafts, food and pageantry. 1500 handmade quilts. Sponsor: PA Folklife Society and Ursinus College, PR Dir, 461 Vine Lane, Kutztown, PA 19530.

LANCASTER COUNTY BIER FEST. June 28-Aug 31. Adamstown, PA. German-style celebration. Info from: Ed Stoudt's Black Angus, Route 272, Adamstown, PA 19501.

LEVIN, CARL: BIRTHDAY. June 28. U.S. Senator from Michigan, Democrat, of Detroit, MI, born in Detroit on June 28, 1934.

McQUADE DISTRIBUTING COMPANY SOFTBALL TOURNAMENT. June 28-29. Bismarck-Mandan Softball Diamonds. "World's largest slowpitch softball tournament." Info from: Sam W. McQuade, Sr, Bismarck, ND 58501.

MICAJAH AUTRY DAY. June 28. Autryville, NC. Purpose: To provide entertainment and raise funds for equipment for Autryville Area Fire Dept. Sponsor: Autryville Area Fire Dept, Box 126, Autryville, NC 28318.

MIDWEST ANTIQUE AND CLASSIC BOAT CLUB SHOW. June 28-29. Fond du Lac Lakeside Park Yacht Club. A parade of collector's and classic boats on the waters of Lake Winnebago. Info from: Conv & Visitors Bureau, 207 N Main St, Fond du Lac, WI 54935.

MOON PHASE: LAST QUARTER. June 28. Moon enters Last Quarter phase at 7:53 p.m., E.S.T.

COPYRIGHT © 1985 BY WILLIAM D. CHASE and HELEN M. CHASE

NATIONAL FINK DAY. June 28. Purpose: Finks from all over the world gather in Fink, Texas for reunion of Finks. Fink Invitational Golf Tournament, Fink Hall of Fame and naming of Fink of the Year. Sponsor: Robert L. Fink, Pres, Finks Internatl, 205 Ralston, Converse TX 78109 and Dovie Halliburton, Mayor, Fink, TX, Rt 2, Box 240, Pottsboro, TX 75076.

NATIONAL TOBACCO SPITTING CONTEST. June 28. Raleigh, Mississippi. World's contest is held at Billy John Crumpton farm. Also political speaking, live entertainment and good food. Info from: Crumpton Farm, Box 158, Raleigh, MS 39153.

OWENS, MAJOR ROBERT ODELL: BIRTHDAY. June 28. U.S. Representative of New York's 12th district, Democrat, of Brooklyn, NY, born in Memphis, TN, June 28, 1936.

PANETTA, LEON EDWARD: BIRTHDAY. June 28. U.S. Representative of California's 16th district, Democrat, of Carmel Valley, CA, born in Monterey, CA June 28, 1938.

ROUSSEAU, JEAN JACQUES: BIRTHDAY. June 28. Philosopher, born in Geneva, Switzerland, June 28, 1712. Died July 2, 1778. "Man is born free," he wrote in *The Social Contract*, "and everywhere he is in chains."

RUBENS, PETER PAUL: BIRTHDAY. June 28. Flemish painter and diplomat born June 28, 1577, at Siegen, Westphalia. Died, of gout, at Antwerp, May 30, 1640.

WORLD WAR I: BEGINNING AND ENDING ANNIVERSARY. June 28. Archduke Francis Ferdinand and his wife assassinated at Sarajevo, Bosnia, on June 28, 1914, touching off the conflict that became World War I. Also, the anniversary of signing of the Treaty of Versailles, on June 28, 1919, formally ending the war.

JUNE 29 — SUNDAY
180th Day — Remaining, 185

ANTIQUE CAR SHOW. June 29. Lakeside Park, Lake Winnebago, Fond du Lac, WI. Features over 500 antique vehicles. Info from: Conv & Visitors Bureau, 207 N Main St, Fond du Lac, WI 54935.

GOETHALS, GEORGE WASHINGTON: BIRTHDAY. June 29. American engineer and army officer, chief engineer of the Panama Canal, and first civil governor of the Canal Zone, born at Brooklyn, NY, June 29, 1858. Died at New York City, Jan 21, 1928.

INDEPENDENCE SUNDAY. June 29. Iowa. (Sunday preceding July 4, proclamation of the governor.)

KEY CLUB INTERNATIONAL CONVENTION. June 29-July 2. Phoenix, AZ. Info from: Key Club Internatl, 3636 Woodview Trace, Indianapolis, IN 46268.

LEXINGTON'S FOURTH OF JULY FESTIVAL. June 29-July 4. Lexington, KY. Arts, crafts, 10,000 meter race, international foods, parade and fireworks. Info from: Lexington Festival Commission, Mary Wathen, Office of the Mayor, 200 E Main St, Lexington, KY 40507.

MANCHESTER MUSIC FESTIVAL. June 29-Aug 10. Chamber music and orchestral concerts. Info from: Manchester Music Festival, Michael Rudiakov, 93 Franklin Ave, Yonkers, NY 10705.

MAYO, WILLIAM JAMES: BIRTHDAY. June 29. American surgeon, one of the Mayo brothers, establishers of the Mayo Foundation, born at LeSueur, MN, June 29, 1861. Died July 28, 1939.

June 1986	S	M	T	W	T	F	S
	1	2	3	4	5	6	7
	8	9	10	11	12	13	14
	15	16	17	18	19	20	21
	22	23	24	25	26	27	28
	29	30					

P E N INTERNATIONAL CONGRESS. June 29-July 4. Hamburg, Germany. Info from: International PEN, 38 King St, London WC2 E8JT, England.

PETER AND PAUL DAY. June 29. Feast day for St. Peter and St. Paul. Commemorates dual martyrdom of Christian Apostles Peter (by crucifixion) and Paul (by beheading) during persecution by Roman Emperor Nero. Observed since third century.

PINEKNOTTER DAYS. June 29-July 5. Purpose: Live entertainment and large fireworks display to show others the community spirit. Sponsor: Pineknotter Assn, Jeff Kimball, Pres, Box 252, Northumberland, PA 17857.

S.P.E.B.S.Q.S.A. INTERNATIONAL CONVENTION AND CONTESTS. June 29-July 6. Salt Lake City, UT. Purpose: To choose our international quartet and chorus champions. Info from: SPEBSQSA, Internatl Office, Robb Ollett, Communications Dir, 6315 3rd Ave, Kenosha, WI 53140.

ST. PETER'S DAY. June 29. Antakya, Turkey. First preached Christianity at this place. Ceremonies at St. Peter's Grotto, early Christian cave near Antakya.

JUNE 30 — MONDAY
181st Day — Remaining, 184

CHARLES BLONDIN'S CONQUEST OF NIAGARA FALLS: ANNIVERSARY. June 30. Charles Blondin, a French acrobat and aerialist (whose real name was Jean Francois Gravelet), on June 30, 1859, in view of a crowd estimated at more than 25,000 persons, walked across Niagara Falls on a tightrope. The walk required only about five minutes. He later crossed blind-folded, pushing a wheelbarrow, carrying a man on his back, and even on stilts. (Blondin was born Feb 28, 1824, at St. Omer, France, and died at London, Feb 19, 1897.)

ENGLAND: ROYAL INTERNATIONAL AGRICULTURAL SHOW. June 30-July 3. National Agricultural Centre, Stoneleigh, Kenilworth, Warwickshire. Premier agricultural show in Britain; an international meeting point for agricultural specialists from around the world.

LEAP SECOND ADJUSTMENT TIME. June 30. June 30 is one of the times which has been favored for the addition or subtraction of a second from man's clock time (to coordinate atomic and astronomical time). The determination to adjust is made by the Bureau International de l'Heure, in Paris. See also note about Leap Seconds on page 219.

MONROE, ELIZABETH KORTRIGHT: BIRTHDAY. June 30. Wife of James Monroe, 5th President of the U.S., born at New York, NY, June 30, 1768. Died Sept 23, 1830.

SIBERIAN EXPLOSION ANNIVERSARY. June 30. Early on the morning of June 30, 1908, a spectacular explosion occurred over central Siberia. The seismic shock, fire storm, ensuing "black rain," and the illumination which was reportedly visible for hundreds of miles, led to speculation about whether a meteorite or an extra-terrestrial visitor was the most probable cause. Said to have been the most powerful explosion in history.

SKEEN, JOSEPH RICHARD (JOE): BIRTHDAY. June 30. U.S. Representative of New Mexico's 2nd district, Republican, of Picacho, NM, born at Roswell, NM, on June 30, 1927.

SMITH, VIRGINIA (MRS. HAVEN): BIRTHDAY. June 30. U.S. Representative of Nebraska's 3rd district, Republican, of Chappell, NE, born in Randolph, IA, June 30, 1911.

WHEELER, WILLIAM ALMON: BIRTHDAY. June 30. Nineteenth Vice-President of the U.S. (1877-1881), born, Malone, NY, June 30, 1819. Died there June 4, 1887.

Iulye.

JULY 1 — TUESDAY

182nd Day — Remaining, 183

BIRTHDAY OF THE FIRST U.S. POSTAGE STAMPS. July 1. Purpose: To observe the birthday (July 1, 1847) of U.S. postage stamps and draw attention to stamp collecting as a hobby. Sponsor: Gustav Detjen, Jr, Editor, The Philatelic Journalist, 154 Laguna Ct, St. Augustine Shores, FL 32086.

BLERIOT, LOUIS: BIRTHDAY. July 1. Louis Bleriot, aviation pioneer and first man to fly an airplane across the English Channel (July 25, 1909), was born at Cambrai, France, July 1, 1872. He died at Paris, Aug 2, 1936.

BURUNDI: NATIONAL HOLIDAY. July 1. Independence Day. Anniversary of establishment of independence, July 1, 1962.

CANADA: CANADA DAY. July 1. National Holiday. Canada's National Day, formerly known as Dominion Day. Observed on following day when July 1 is a Sunday. Commemorates the confederation of Upper and Lower Canada and some of the Maritime Provinces into the Dominion of Canada on this day in 1867.

CARNEY, WILLIAM: BIRTHDAY. July 1. U.S. Representative of New York's 1st district, Conservative-Republican, of Hauppauge, NY, born in Brooklyn, NY, on July 1, 1942.

CLEMSON, THOMAS GREEN: BIRTHDAY. July 1. The man for whom Clemson University was named, was born at Philadelphia on July 1, 1807. The mining engineer and agriculturist married John C. Calhoun's daughter, Anna. Clemson bequeathed the old Calhoun plantation to South Carolina, and Clemson Agricultural College (now Clemson University) was founded there in 1889. Clemson died at Clemson, SC, Apr 6, 1888.

FLAGSTAFF FESTIVAL OF THE ARTS. July 1-Aug 4. Flagstaff, AZ. Celebration of the arts featuring artists and musicians from all over the country. Info from: Chamber of Commerce, 101 W Santa Fe Ave, Flagstaff, AZ 86001.

FOLK FESTIVAL. July 1. Fort George Park, Prince George, British Columbia. Purpose: To celebrate Canada's birthday. Ethnic performances featuring dances, music and songs. Sponsor: Prince George Folkfest-Multicultural Heritage Society, Box 2469, Prince George, BC, Canada V2N 2S6.

GHANA: REPUBLIC DAY. July 1. National Holiday.

HATCHER, CHARLES FLOYD: BIRTHDAY. July 1. U.S. Representative of Georgia's 2nd district, Democrat, of Albany, GA, was born at Doerun, GA, on July 1, 1939.

HERITAGE FESTIVAL. July 1-26. Vancouver, British Columbia. Festival features major groups from each of Canada's ten provinces. Info from: The Centennial Commission, Box 49386, Suite 3374, Bentall 4, 1055 Dunsmuir St, Vancouver, BC, V7X 1L5.

HITCH HIKING MONTH. July 1-31. Purpose: To call attention to the pleasures and health of hitch hiking, a great American pastime. Sponsor: Richard R. Falk, Associates, Richard Falk, Dir, 147 W 42nd St, New York, NY 10036.

INTERNATIONAL FESTIVAL. July 1-4. Main Street, Akron, OH. Ethnic foods and entertainment. Sponsor: Downtown Akron Association, Judy Heller, Exec Dir, 1 Cascade Plaza, Akron, OH 44308.

LA FIESTA DE BURRO (DONKEYFEST). July 1. Purpose: to upgrade the status of the donkey. To point out the good qualities and to preserve the diminishing wild ass herds of the world. Info from: Turtles Internatl, 2018 Aldrich Ct, Downers Grove, IL 60516.

"LIFE: BE IN IT." WEEK. July 1-6. Purpose: To promote recreation activities that are wholesome, inexpensive and fun! Sponsor: Jonesborough Parks & Recreation, 215 W Main St, Jonesborough, TN 37659.

MALTA: INTERNATIONAL FAIR. July 1-15. Info from: Embassy of Malta, 2017 Connecticut Ave NW, Washington, DC 20008.

MANDAN JAYCEE RODEO DAYS. July 1-4. Mandan, ND. Info from: Chamber of Commerce, Box 546, Mandan, ND 58554.

MEADOW BROOK HALL: SUMMER TOURS. July 1-Aug 31. The former home of Alfred and Matilda Wilson open for tours. Guests are invited to visit three floors of this 100-room architectural masterpiece, complete with original furnishings, art and family collectibles. Info from: Meadow Brook Hall, Oakland Univ, Rochester, MI 48063.

NATIONAL ANTI-BOREDOM DAY. July 1. Purpose: If the first half of your year was boring, get busy to make the rest of it exciting! Dedicated to the memory of mythical Lionel K. Boring, founder of the Boring Institute. Sponsor: The Boring Institute, Alan Caruba, Box 40, Maplewood, NJ 04040.

NATIONAL BAKED BEAN MONTH. July 1-31. Purpose: To pay tribute to one of America's favorite and most healthful and nutritious foods, baked beans, made with dry or canned beans. Sponsor: Michigan Bean Commission, James Byrum, Exec Secy, Box 22037, Lansing, MI 48909.

NATIONAL EDUCATION ASSOCIATION: ANNUAL MEETING. July 1-6. Info from: National Education Assn, Peter Ridenour/Patricia Epps, 1201 16th St, NW, Washington, DC 20036.

NATIONAL HOT DOG MONTH. July 1-31. Purpose: To inform public of new and varied ways to prepare hot dogs and call attention to versatility and nutritious content of product. Sponsor: Natl Hot Dog & Sausage Council, 1211 W 22nd St, Suite 1100, Oak Brook, IL 60521.

NATIONAL ICE CREAM MONTH. July 1-31. Purpose: To call attention to a "nutritious and wholesome food enjoyed by over ninety percent of the people in the United States." Info from: Internatl Assn of Ice Cream Manufacturers, 888 Sixteenth St, NW, Washington, DC 20006.

NATIONAL JULY BELONGS TO BLUEBERRIES MONTH. July 1-31. Purpose: To make the public conscious of the fact that this is the peak month for fresh blueberries. Sponsor: North American Blueberry Council, Secy/Mgr, Box 166, Marmora, NJ 08223.

NATIONAL PEACH MONTH. July 1-31. Purpose: To promote fresh peaches and their nutritional values during the peach season. Sponsor: Natl Peach Council, Box 1085, Martinsburg, WV 25401.

NORTHWOOD INSTITUTE: FESTIVAL OF THE LAKES. July 1-Aug 10. Midland, MI. Concerts featuring the Northwood Orchestra and guest artists. Sponsor: Northwood Institute, Midland, MI 48640.

PEOPLE'S REPUBLIC OF CHINA: ANNIVERSARY OF FOUNDING OF CHINESE COMMUNIST PARTY. July 1. Shanghai. Info from: Shanghai Travel & Tourist Administration, 14 Zhongshan Road (e.1), Shanghai.

COPYRIGHT © 1985 BY WILLIAM D. CHASE and HELEN M. CHASE

PEPSICO SUMMERFARE 1986. July 1-31. Performing Arts Center, SUNY Purchase, NY. International festival of the arts. Sponsors: PepsiCo, Inc and SUNY Purchase. Info from: Performing Arts Center, Rosalind Ashford, SUNY Purchase, NY 10577.

PLEASURE WEEK. July 1-7. Times Square, 42nd and Broadway, New York, NY. Purpose: To alert the world to the "Pleasure Dome," the 200 acre entertainment complex surrounding Times Square that is open 24 hours every day of the year for the purpose of entertaining. Sponsor: Times Square Authority, Richard R. Falk, Pres, 147 W 42nd St, New York, NY 10036.

RHODES, CECIL JOHN: BIRTHDAY. July 1. English-born, South African millionaire politician. Said to have controlled at one time 90% of the world's diamond production. His will founded the Rhodes Scholarships at Oxford University (for unmarried men, aged 19-25). Rhodesia was named for him. Born July 1, 1853 at Bishop's Stortford, Hertfordshire, England, Rhodes died Mar 26, 1902 at Cape Town, South Africa.

RWANDA: NATIONAL HOLIDAY. July 1. Independence Day. Commemorates attainment of independence, July 1, 1962.

SAND, GEORGE: BIRTHDAY. July 1. French novelist, author of more than 100 volumes, whose real name was Amandine Aurore Lucile (Dupin) Dudevant, was born at Paris on July 1, 1804. Died at Nohant, France, on June 8, 1876. She is better remembered for having been a liberated woman during a Romantic epoch than for her literary works.

SPACE MILESTONE: KOSMOS 1383 (USSR). July 1. First search and rescue satellite—equipped to hear distress calls from aircraft and ships—launched in co-operative project with the U.S. and France. July 1, 1982.

SPIRIT OF VICTORY: SUMMER AT YORKTOWN VICTORY CENTER. July 1-Aug 31. Daily lifestyle of Revolutionary War participants depicted. Info from: Yorktown Victory Center, Box 1976, Yorktown, VA 23690.

WILD ASS HUNTERS ASSOCIATION CONFERENCE OF INSPECTOR GENERALS. July 1. Purpose: Award ceremonies honoring inspector generals with highest scores for previous year, and to determine better ways of preserving the wild ass herds of the world. Lifetime memberships available. Info from: T.I.A. Group, 2018 Aldrich Ct, Downers Grove, IL 60516.

ZAMBIA: UNITY DAY. July 1. First Tuesday in July. Memorial day for Zambians who died in the struggle for independence. Political rallies stressing solidarity throughout country.

JULY 2 — WEDNESDAY
183rd Day — Remaining, 182

ADIRONDACK GUIDEBOAT SHOW. July 2-7. Display of handcrafted Adirondack guideboats by old masters and new builders. Info from: Chamber of Commerce, 30 Main St, Saranac Lake, NY 12983.

CASTLE, MICHAEL N: BIRTHDAY. July 2. Michael N. Castle, Governor of Delaware, Republican, was born at Wilmington, DE, on July 2, 1939.

CRANMER, THOMAS: BIRTHDAY. July 2. English clergyman, reformer, and martyr, born at Aslacton, Nottinghamshire, England, July 2, 1489. One of the principal authors of *The English Book of Common Prayer*. Archbishop of Canterbury. Tried for treason and burned at the stake, Oxford, England, Mar 21, 1556.

DECLARATION OF INDEPENDENCE RESOLUTION ANNIVERSARY. July 2. Anniversary of adoption by the Continental Congress, Philadelphia, July 2, 1776, of a Resolution introduced on June 7, 1776, by Richard Henry Lee, of Virginia: "Resolved, That these United Colonies are, and of right ought to be, free and independent States, that they are absolved from all allegiance to the British Crown, and that all political connection between them and the State of Great Britain is, and ought to be, totally dissolved. That it is expedient forthwith to take the most effectual measures for forming foreign Alliances. That a plan of confederation be prepared and transmitted to the respective Colonies for their consideration and approbation." This resolution prepared the way for adoption, on July 4, 1776, of the Declaration of Independence. (See entry for July 4.)

GARFIELD, JAMES ABRAM: ASSASSINATION ANNIVERSARY. July 2. President James A. Garfield, was shot as he entered the railway station at Washington, DC, July 2, 1881. He died Sept 19, 1881, never having recovered from the wound. The assassin, Charles J. Guiteau, was hanged June 30, 1882.

HALFWAY POINT OF 1986. July 2. The year 1986 is half over at noon, standard time in every time zone.

MANDAN JAYCEE ANNIVERSARY RODEO. July 2-4. Mandan Rodeo Grounds, Mandan, ND. Purpose: Rodeos, parades, bucking horses, bull riding, street dance and fun, fun, fun. Info from: Darrell Nitschke, 1814 LaForest Ave East, Bismarck, ND 58501.

MARSHALL, THURGOOD: BIRTHDAY. July 2. Associate Justice of the Supreme Court of the United States, nominated by Pres. Johnson on June 13, 1967 (took Judicial Oath and was seated on Oct 2, 1967). Justice Marshall was born at Baltimore, MD, July 2, 1908. He was the first Black to serve in that office.

MIDDLE CHILDREN'S DAY. July 2. Purpose: To salute the middle-born children whose youthful activities were limited due to their always being "too young or too old." Today, they are JUST RIGHT! Sponsor: Mid-Kid Company, 402 Oak Ave, Sebring, FL 33870.

NATIONAL TOM SAWYER DAYS. July 2-6. Hannibal, MO. Raft racing, frog jumping and fireworks launched from barge moored in the Mississippi River. Highlight is the Tom Sawyer Fence Painting Contest. Sponsor: Hannibal Jaycees. Info from: Hannibal Visitors Bureau, Box 624, Hannibal, MO 63401.

SHILOH PARK: FOURTH OF JULY FESTIVAL. July 2-6. Shiloh Park, Zion, IL. Info from: Zion Park District, 2400 Dowie Memorial Dr, Zion, IL 60099.

SITTING BULL STAMPEDE. July 2-4. Mobridge, SD. Rodeo, named after famed Sioux leader Sitting Bull, draws top cowboys from across the nation. Western show, carnival and fireworks. Info from: SD Tourism, Box 6000, Pierre, SD 57501.

SUNUNU, JOHN H: BIRTHDAY. July 2. John H. Sununu, Governor of New Hampshire, Republican, was born at Havana, Cuba, on July 2, 1939.

JULY 3 — THURSDAY
184th Day — Remaining, 181

ALEXANDER, LAMAR: BIRTHDAY. July 3. Lamar Alexander, Governor of Tennessee, Republican, was born at Maryville, TN, on July 3, 1940.

AMERICAN MENSA ANNUAL GATHERING. July 3-6. Grand Hyatt Hotel, New York, NY. Purpose: Gathering of members from high IQ society for annual convention. Info from: Mensa, Sheila Skolnik, Office Mgr, 2626 E 14th St, Brooklyn, NY 11235.

BELGIUM: OMMEGANG PAGEANT. July 3. Splendid historic festival of medieval pageantry at the illuminated Grand-Place in Brussels. The annual event (first Thursday in July) recreates an entertainment given in honor of Charles the Fifth and his court.

	S	M	T	W	T	F	S
July 1986			1	2	3	4	5
	6	7	8	9	10	11	12
	13	14	15	16	17	18	19
	20	21	22	23	24	25	26
	27	28	29	30	31		

COPYRIGHT © 1985 BY WILLIAM D. CHASE and HELEN M. CHASE

COMPLIMENT-YOUR-MIRROR DAY. July 3. Participation consists in complimenting your mirror on having such a wonderful owner and keeping track of whether other mirrors you meet during the day smile at you. Sponsor: Puns Corps, c/o: Bob Birch, Grand Punscorpion, Box 2364, Falls Church, VA 22042.

CRESTON'S HERITAGE DAYS. July 3-4. Purpose: Parade, gandy dancers contest and model railroad display celebrating Creston's railroad heritage. Info from: Chamber of Commerce, Box 471, Creston, IA 50801.

DIXON PETUNIA FESTIVAL. July 3-6. Carnival, raft race, beer garden, parade and fireworks. Sponsor: Petunia Festival Corp, 74 Galena Ave, Dixon, IL 61021.

DOG DAYS. July 3-Aug 15. Hottest days of the year in Northern Hemisphere. Usually about 40 days, but variously reckoned at 30-54 days. Popularly believed to be an evil time "when the sea boiled, wine turned sour, dogs grew mad, and all creatures became languid, causing to man burning fevers, hysterics and phrensies" (from Brady's *Clavis Calendarium*, 1813). Originally the days when Sirius, the Dog Star, rose just before or at about the same time as sunrise (no longer true owing to precession of the equinoxes). Ancients sacrificed a brown dog at beginning of Dog Days to appease the rage of Sirius, believing that star was the cause of hot, sultry weather.

ENGLAND: HENLEY ROYAL REGATTA. July 3-6. Henley-on-Thames, Oxfordshire. An international rowing event which is one of the important social occasions of the year.

FIRST WISCONSIN LAKEFRONT FIREWORKS. July 3. Milwaukee, WI. Purpose: "One of the nation's largest fireworks displays." Band concert precedes fireworks. Sponsor: First Wisconsin Banks. Info from: Barkin, Herman, Solochek & Paulsen, Inc, 777 E Wisconsin Ave, Milwaukee, WI 53202.

FREEDOM FESTIVAL. July 3-13. Evansville, IN. Info from: Thuerbach Associates, 314 SE Riverside Dr, Evansville, IN 47713.

FREEDOM WEEKEND ALOFT. July 3-6. Greenville, South Carolina. Hot-air balloon races, entertainment and fireworks. Info from: Chamber of Commerce, Box 10048, Greenville, SC 29603.

GAYDOS, JOSEPH M: BIRTHDAY. July 3. U.S. Representative of Pennsylvania's 20th district, Democrat, of McKeesport, PA, born in Braddock, PA, July 3, 1926.

GREENVILLE RINGER CLASSIC. July 3-6. Competitive horseshoe pitching in four divisions—men's, women's, junior boys and girls. Top pitchers from throughout U.S. and Canada. Info from: Darke County Horseshoe Club, Fritz Worner, 150 Ridgeview Dr, Greenville, OH 45331.

HUNTINGTON, SAMUEL: BIRTHDAY. July 3. President of Continental Congress. Governor of Connecticut, Signer of the Declaration of Independence, born Windham, CT, July 3, 1731. Died, Norwich, CT, Jan 5, 1796.

IDAHO: ADMISSION DAY. July 3. Became 43rd State on this day in 1890.

NATIONAL HUCKLEBERRY FESTIVAL. July 3-5. Jay, Oklahoma. Purpose: Jay, OK, called the "huckleberry capitol of the world," holds festival to celebrate the picking of wild huckleberries. Sponsor: Chamber of Commerce, Box 806, Jay, OK 74346.

PAUL REVERE 250 ROAD RACE. July 3. Daytona International Speedway, Daytona Beach, FL. Info from: Daytona Internatl Speedway, Larry Balewski, PR, Daytona Beach, FL 32015.

ST. PAUL RODEO. July 3-5. Info from: St. Paul Rodeo Assn, 3318 Blanchet Ave, St. Paul, OR 97137.

SPACE MILESTONE: SOYUZ 14 (USSR). July 3. Launched July 3, 1974, Cosmonauts P. Popovich and Y. Artyukhin linked with Salyut 3 Space Station during 15-day mission.

VIRGIN ISLANDS: DANISH WEST INDIES EMANCIPATION DAY. July 3. Commemorates freeing of slaves in the Danish West Indies in 1848. Ceremony in Frederiksted, St. Croix, where actual proclamation was first read by governor-General Peter Von Scholten.

JULY 4 — FRIDAY
185th Day — Remaining, 180

ARMSTRONG, LOUIS: BIRTH ANNIVERSARY. July 4. Jazz musician born this day in New Orleans, LA, 1900. Died, New York, NY, July 6, 1971. Asked to define jazz, Armstrong reportedly replied "Man, if you gotta ask you'll never know."

BARK PEELERS' CONVENTION. July 4-5. Purpose: In commemoration of the glory days of logging. Demonstrations of bark peeling, sawing, timber hewing, chopping, blacksmithing and horse drawn log skidding. Info from: PA Lumber Museum, Box K, Galeton, PA 16922.

BLACK HILLS ROUND-UP. July 4-6. Belle Fourche, SD. Professional rodeo. Info from: Bill Schuft, Box 39, Belle Fourche, SD 57717.

BOYNE RIVER RAFT RACE. July 4. Info from: Chamber of Commerce, 28 S Lake St, Boyne City, MI 49712.

BRATTLEBORO FAMILY DAY. July 4. Brattleboro, VT. Parade, bingo, fireworks and day-long activities for the whole family. Info from: Chamber of Commerce, 180 Main Street, Brattleboro, VT 05301.

CALGARY EXHIBITION AND STAMPEDE. July 4-13. Stampede Park, Calgary Alberta, Canada. Purpose: An annual exhibition and stampede featuring rodeo, chuckwagon races, outdoor stage show, agriculture exhibits, Indian village, western town, crafts, midway, casino and downtown street celebrations. Sponsor: Calgary Exhibition & Stampede, Mike Whittle, Box 1060, Calgary, Alberta, T2P 2K8, Canada.

CHURCH POINT BUGGY FESTIVAL. July 4-6. Church Point, LA. Purpose: To celebrate Church Point's proud title as "Buggy Capital of the World." Sponsor: Acadia-St. Landry Medical Foundation, 810 S Broadway, Church Point, LA 70525.

CIVIL WAR TROOP ENCAMPMENT RE-ENACTMENT. July 4. Mystic Seaport Museum, Mystic, CT. Demonstrations of campsite cookery, military drills, musters, artillery drills. Parade of costumed staff lead visiting children through the village. Info from: Mystic Seaport, Public Affairs Office, Mystic, CT 06355.

COOLIDGE, CALVIN: BIRTHDAY. July 4. The 30th President of the U.S. was born John Calvin Coolidge, at Plymouth, VT, July 4, 1872. He succeeded to the presidency Aug 3, 1923, following the death of Warren G. Harding. Coolidge was elected president once, in 1924, but did "not choose to run for president in 1928." Nicknamed Silent Cal, he is reported to have said, "If you don't say anything you won't be called on to repeat it." Coolidge died at Northampton, MA, Jan 5, 1933.

DECLARATION OF INDEPENDENCE ANNIVERSARY. July 4. On July 4, 1776 the Declaration of Independence was signed, at Philadelphia: "Signed by Order and in Behalf of the Congress, John Hancock, President, Attest, Charles Thomson, Secretary." The remaining signatures were probably affixed on

Aug 2, 1776. The manuscript Journals of Congress for that date state: "The declaration of independence being engrossed and compared at the table was signed by the members."

DENMARK: REBILD FESTIVAL. July 4. This celebration of the American Independence Day, at the Rebild National Park, Aalborg, Denmark, is described as "the largest single gathering for this occasion in the world." Guest speakers and Danish/American entertainments.

FIDDLERS JAMBOREE AND CRAFTS FESTIVAL. July 4-5. Smithville, TN. Home of Joe L. Evins Appalachian Regional Crafts Ctr and Edgar Evins State Park. Info from: Chamber of Commerce, Box 64, Smithville, TN 37166.

FOSTER, STEPHEN: BIRTHDAY. July 4. Stephen Collins Foster, one of America's most famous and best loved song writers, was born at Lawrenceville, PA, on July 4, 1826. Among his nearly 200 songs: "Oh! Susanna," "Camptown Races," "Old Folks at Home" ("Swanee River"), "Jeanie With the Light Brown Hair," "Old Black Joe," "Beautiful Dreamer." Foster died in poverty at Bellevue Hospital in New York City on Jan 13, 1864. The anniversary of his death has been observed as "Stephen Foster Memorial Day" by Presidential Proclamation since 1952.

FREDERICKSBURG HERITAGE FESTIVAL. July 4-6. Purpose: To create an awareness of Fredericksburg's historic heritage. Parade, raft race, hayrides, country music, fireworks and Civil War battle reenactment. Info from: Visitor Center, 706 Caroline St, Fredericksburg, VA 22401.

GETTYSBURG CIVIL WAR RELIC AND COLLECTOR'S SHOW. July 4-6. Accouterments, weapons, uniforms and personal effects from American military history, 1865 and earlier. Leading collectors and dealers of Civil War material. Info from: Gettysburg Travel Council, 35 Carlisle St, Gettysburg, PA 17325.

GREAT SEAL OF THE UNITED STATES: ANNIVERSARY. July 4. The Continental Congress, meeting at Philadelphia, after voting on July 4, 1776, to adopt the Declaration of Independence, went on to approve the following: "Resolved, that Dr. Franklin, Mr. J. Adams and Mr. Jefferson, be a committee, to bring in a device for a seal for the United States of America," thus beginning the history of the Great Seal of the United States on the first day of independence.

INDEPENDENCE DAY or FOURTH OF JULY. July 4. The United States of America commemorates adoption by the Continental Congress, of the Declaration of Independence from Great Britain, July 4, 1776. The Nation's birthday. Legal holiday in all States and Territories.

INDEPENDENCE DAY CHALLENGE RUN. July 4. Eight-mile course includes 1¼ mile uphill grade and several other hills on paved and gravel roads overlooking Lake Charlevoix. Info from: Chamber of Commerce, 28 S Lake St, Boyne City, MI 49712.

INTERNATIONAL BB GUN CHAMPIONSHIPS. July 4-7. Bowling Green, KY. Purpose: Competition of state champion teams from across the nation composed of shooters age 8 through 14. Sponsor: Daisy Manufacturing Co. Info from: U.S. Jaycees, Box 7, Tulsa, OK 74121.

LANDERS, ANN: BIRTHDAY. July 4. Advice columnist Ann Landers (Mrs. Ester P. Lederer) was born Ester Pauline Friedman at Sioux City, IA, July 4, 1918. Twin sister of Abigail Van Buren, also an advice columnist.

LYNCHBURG, VIRGINIA: BICENTENNIAL STADIUM SPECTACULAR. July 4. Hot-air balloons, music, sky divers, baseball and fireworks. Info from: Bicentennial Commission of Lynchburg, Box 1132, Lynchburg, VA 24505.

July 1986

S	M	T	W	T	F	S
		1	2	3	4	5
6	7	8	9	10	11	12
13	14	15	16	17	18	19
20	21	22	23	24	25	26
27	28	29	30	31		

MUSIC FOR AMERICANS. July 4. Victory Stadium, Roanoke, VA. Purpose: Outstanding music and spectacular fireworks to celebrate the birth of our nation. Info from: Roanoke Times & World-News, Betsy Russo, Corp Services, Box 2491, Roanoke, VA 24010.

OLD FASHIONED AMERICAN MUSIC CELEBRATION. July 4. Stephen Foster State Folk Culture Center, White Springs, FL. Features music dating back to turn of the century. Games and contests, patriotic bell concerts and popular American foods. Info from: Dept of State's Florida Folklife Programs, Box 265, White Springs, FL 32096.

PEPSI FIRECRACKER 400 NASCAR WINSTON CUP. (Grand National Stock Car Race). July 4. Daytona International Speedway, Daytona Beach, FL. Info from: Daytona Internatl Speedway, Larry Balewski, PR, Daytona Beach, FL 32015.

PHILIPPINES: FIL-AMERICAN FRIENDSHIP DAY. July 4. National. Formerly the National Independence Day, now celebrated as Fil-American Friendship Day.

ROARING CAMP JUMPIN' FROG CONTEST AND GREAT TRAIN ROBBERY. July 4-6. Purpose: Bring a frog or rent one. History re-enactors portray California lawmen and bandits in train robberies. Info from: Roaring Camp & Big Trees Narrow-gauge Railroad, Felton, Santa Cruz County, CA 95018.

STATUE OF LIBERTY TORCH RELIGHTING CEREMONY. July 4. Liberty Island, New York, NY. Purpose: To celebrate the completion of the Statue of Liberty restoration. Major fireworks display. Sponsor: The Statue of Liberty Ellis Island Foundation, Inc, Hank Nielsen, Dir of Public Affairs, 101 Park Ave, New York, NY 10178.

STONE SKIPPING OPEN TOURNAMENT. July 4. Iroquois Hotel Beach, Mackinac Island, MI. Purpose: To preserve and perfect kingly sport of stone skipping, and to challenge previous world record (24 skips). Sponsor: Lake Superior State College, Stone Skipping & Ge-Plunking Club, Attn: W.T. Rabe, Sault Ste. Marie, MI 49783.

STRASBURG'S OLD-TIME INDEPENDENCE DAY CELEBRATION. July 4. Purpose: A colorful, theatrical pageant built around the theme of God, Man, and Country. Sponsor: Historic Strasburg Inn, Terri Brown, Rte 896/Historic Dr, Strasburg, PA 17579.

THOMPSON NICKEL DAYS. July 4-6. Thompson, Manitoba, Canada. National King Miner contest, Indian days and powwow dancing. Info from: Travel Manitoba, Dept 5058, Winnipeg, Manitoba, Canada R3C 3H8.

VAN BUREN, ABIGAIL: BIRTHDAY. July 4. Advice columnist Abigail Van Buren, twin sister of advice columnist Ann Landers, was born at Sioux City, IA, July 4, 1918.

WASHINGTON, DC: INDEPENDENCE DAY CELEBRATION. July 4. The nation's capital celebrates the Fourth of July with parade past many historic monuments on the Mall. National Symphony Orchestra concert in evening followed by spectacular fireworks display over the Washington Monument. Info from: Conv & Visitors Assn, 1575 Eye St NW, Washington, DC 20005.

YORKTOWN'S OLD FASHIONED FOURTH. July 4. Yorktown, VA. Celebrates anniversary of adoption of Declaration of Independence at the place where Washington's decisive victory assured American independence. Parade, patriotic and military displays, music and fireworks. Info from: Publicity Chrmn, Fourth of July Committee, Box 4444, Yorktown, VA 23690.

JULY 5 — SATURDAY
186th Day — Remaining, 179

"BIGGEST ALL NIGHT SINGING IN THE WORLD." July 5. Bonifay, FL. Gospel singing quartets from all over the nation. Sponsor: Kiwanis Club, J. Harvey Etheridge, Box 655, Bonifay, FL 32425.

COPYRIGHT © 1985 BY WILLIAM D. CHASE and HELEN M. CHASE

CAPE VERDE: INDEPENDENCE DAY. July 5. National holiday.

CIVIL WAR LIVING HISTORY ENCAMPMENT. July 5-6. Stones River National Battlefield, Murfreesboro, TN 37130.

DRIER, DAVID: BIRTHDAY. July 5. U.S. Representative of California's 33rd district, Republican, of La Verne, CA, born at Kansas City, MO, on July 5, 1952.

EARTH AT APHELION. July 5. At approximately 5 a.m., E.S.T., planet Earth will reach Aphelion, that point in its orbit when it is farthest from the Sun (about 94,510,000 miles). The Earth's mean distance from the Sun (mean radius of its orbit) is reached early in the months of April and October. Note that Earth is farthest from the Sun during Northern Hemisphere summer. See also: entry for Earth at Perihelion, Jan 2.

ELKO NATIONAL BASQUE FESTIVAL. July 5-6. Elko, NV. Colorful cultural festival with traditional contests of strength as well as dance and handball competition. Info from: Elko Chamber of Commerce, P.O. Box 470, Elko, NV 89801.

ENGLAND: CHELTENHAM INTERNATIONAL FESTIVAL OF MUSIC. July 5-20. Cheltenham, Gloucestershire. Modern British composers along with the classics, jazz and folk singing.

ENGLAND: TYNWALD DAY. July 5. Tynwald Hill at St. John's, Isle of Man. Traditionally, the island's parliament of Tynwald assembles at the meeting place of the Vikings, to promulgate new laws.

GREAT GATSBY DAYS. July 5-6. Cornwall, PA. Purpose: Antique cars, flapper fashions and American Jazz and Dixieland. Sponsor: Mount Hope Estate & Winery, Box 685, Cornwall, PA 17016.

GREAT HOUSEBOAT/CRUISER RACE AND PARADE. July 5. Rough River State Resort Park, Falls of Rough, KY. Decorated boats, cruiser race, fire works and parade. Info from: KY Dept of Parks, Capital Plaza Tower, Frankfort, KY 40601.

INTERNATIONAL CHERRY PIT SPITTING CONTEST. July 5. Tree-Mendus Fruit Farm, Eau Claire, MI. Purpose: To encourage folks to visit a producing fruit farm where they can gain firsthand knowledge of how the cherry is produced and to promote the use of the Red Tart Cherry. An entrant eats a cherry; then spits his pit as far as he can on blacktop surface. The pit that goes the farthest including the roll is the "Champ." (Annually, first Saturday in July.) Sponsor: Tree-Mendus Fruit Farm, Herb Teichman, owner, East Eureka Rd, Eau Claire, MI 49111.

MUSKELLUNGE SWIM. July 5. Purpose: A 5-kilometer endurance swim in Lake Hayward. Info from: American Classic, Box 31, Hayward, WI 54843.

MUZZLELOADING RIFLE SHOOT. July 5. Purpose: To promote the sport of black powder shooting with muzzleloading rifles in the upper East Tennessee area. Costumes are encouraged. Sponsor: Jonesborough Parks & Recreation, Anne Baer, Dir, 215 W. Main St, Jonesborough, TN 37659.

PORTUGAL: COLETE ENCARNADO. July 5-6. Vila Franca de Xira, near Lisbon. "Highlight of festival is the running of the bulls. Bulls are turned loose while making their way to the bullring. Young would-be toureiros try their hand at some fancy capework. Portugese cowboys, folk dances, fireworks and fiesta."

RAFFLES, STAMFORD: BIRTHDAY. July 5. Sir Stamford Raffles, English colonial official, founder of Singapore, where he is supposed to have landed on Jan 29, 1819, was born at sea, off Jamaica, on July 5, 1781. Discoverer, with Joseph Arnold, of an East Indian fungus which is named after them (Rafflesia Arnoldi). Raffles died near London, England, on his birthday, July 5, 1826.

350th ANNIVERSARY OF FIRST PARISH, CONCORD, MASSACHUSETTS. July 5. Anniversary of First Parish on July 5, 1636 in Concord, MA. Info from: Unitarian Universalist Assn, 25 Beacon St, Boston MA 02108.

VENEZUELA: NATIONAL HOLIDAY. July 5. Independence Day. Commemorates Proclamation of Independence from Spain on this date in 1811.

ZETKIN, CLARA: BIRTHDAY. July 5. German women's rights advocate, born at Wiederau, Germany, July 5, 1857. Zetkin has been credited with being the initiator of International Women's Day (q.v.) which has been observed on March 8 at least since 1910. She died at Arkhangelskoe, U.S.S.R., June 20, 1933.

JULY 6 — SUNDAY
187th Day — Remaining, 178

BE NICE TO NEW JERSEY WEEK. July 6-12. Purpose: A time to recognize the assets of the state most maligned by American comedians. (Always the second week in July.) Info from: Lone Star Publications of Humor, Box 29000, Suite 103, San Antonio, TX 78229.

CLAM FESTIVAL. July 6. Parrsboro, Nova Scotia, Canada. Info from: Chamber of Commerce, Box 122, Parrsboro, NS, Canada BOM 1SO.

COMMEMORATION DAY OF BURNING OF JOHN HUS. July 6. Czechoslovakia.

COMOROS: NATIONAL HOLIDAY. July 6. Federal and Islamic Republic of Comoros commemorates Declaration of Independence on July 6, 1975.

ENGLAND: CITY OF LONDON FESTIVAL. July 6-19. Various venues in the City of London. Arts festival taking place in many of the city's most interesting historical buildings.

ETTELBRUCK, LUXEMBOURG: REMEMBRANCE DAY. July 6. In honor of U.S. General George Patton, Jr, liberator of the Grand-Duchy in 1945, who is buried at the American Military Cemetery in Hamm, among 5,100 soldiers of his famous Third Army.

HERITAGE DAY. July 6. Purpose: "Easton's unique Independence Day celebrating the re-reading of The Declaration of Independence as done in 1776." Annually, on the Sunday closest to July 8th. Info from: Heritage Day, Inc, 157 S Fourth St, Easton, PA 18042.

JONES, JOHN PAUL: BIRTHDAY. July 6. American naval officer born at Kirkbean, Scotland, July 6, 1747. Best remembered for his victory in the battle of his ship, the *Bonhomme Richard* with the British frigate, *Serapis*, Sept 23, 1779. When Jones was queried: "Do you ask for quarter?" he made his famous reply: "I have not yet begun to fight!" Jones was victorious, but the *Bonhomme Richard*, badly damaged, sank two days later. Jones died at Paris, July 18, 1792.

MALAWI: NATIONAL HOLIDAY. July 6. Independence Day. Commemorates attainment of independence from Britain on July 6, 1964. Malawi became a republic on July 6, 1966.

MAN WATCHERS' COMPLIMENT WEEK. July 6-12. Purpose: Since men aren't used to receiving compliments, make it a point to find something nice to say to a man. P.S.: Women like compliments too. Sponsor: Man Watchers, Inc, Suzy Mallery, Pres, 8033 Sunset, #363, Los Angeles, CA 90046.

MOON PHASE: NEW MOON. July 6. Moon enters New Moon phase at 11:55 p.m., E.S.T.

COPYRIGHT © 1985 BY WILLIAM D. CHASE and HELEN M. CHASE

NATIONAL CHERRY FESTIVAL. July 6-12. Purpose: Civic celebration featuring parades and band competitions. Family fun, food and entertainment. Sponsor: National Cherry Festival, Doyle Heffron, Exec Mgr, Box 141, Traverse City, MI 49685.

PARRSBORO CLAM FESTIVAL. July 6. Parrsboro, Nova Scotia. Clam eating, clam-shucking contests and games. Info from: Dept of Tourism, Box 456, Halifax, NS B3J 2R5.

POTTER, (HELEN) BEATRIX: BIRTHDAY. July 6. Creator of the Peter Rabbit stories for children, born at London, July 6, 1866. Died, Sawrey, Lancashire, England, Dec 22, 1943.

REAGAN, NANCY DAVIS: BIRTHDAY. July 6. Second wife of Ronald Wilson Reagan, 40th President of the U.S., was born Anne Francis Robbins, in New York City, July 6, 1923. Adopted by her stepfather, Dr. Loyal Davis, a Chicago neurosurgeon, in 1935, she graduated from Smith College in June 1943, and performed in motion pictures. She married Ronald Reagan, Mar 4, 1952.

SPACE MILESTONE: SOYUZ 21 (USSR) July 6. Two cosmonauts, Col. B. Volynov and Lt. Col. V. Zholobov, travel to Salyut 5 Space Station (launched Jun 22, 1976) to study Earth's surface and conduct zoological-botanical experiments. Forty-eight day stay on space station. Return landing on Aug 24. Launch date was July 6, 1976.

SPECIAL RECREATION WEEK. July 6-12. Purpose: To focus attention on the recreation rights, needs, aspirations and abilities of people who are disabled. Sponsor: Special Recreation, Inc, John A. Nesbitt, Pres, 362 Koser Ave, Iowa City, IA 52240.

TURTLE WATCH OPERATION. July 6-Aug 15. Jensen Beach, FL. Purpose: To watch Green Sea turtles lay their eggs. Info from: Chamber of Commerce, 1910 NE Commerical St, Jensen Beach, FL 33457.

WILLARD HANMER GUIDEBOAT AND CANOE RACE. July 6. Lake and downriver course for canoe, kayak and guideboat. Info from: Chamber of Commerce, 30 Main St, Saranac Lake, NY 12983.

JULY 7 — MONDAY
188th Day — Remaining, 177

ARMEY, RICHARD KEITH: BIRTHDAY. July 7. U.S. Representative of Texas' 26th district, Republican, of Denton, TX, born in Cando, ND, July 7, 1940.

CARIBBEAN DAY. July 7. Public holiday observed on the first Monday in July each year by nations participating in the Caribbean Common Market, including Barbados and the Republic of Guyana.

CARICOM DAY. July 7. The anniversary of the Treaty establishing the Caribbean Community (also called the Treaty of Chaguaramas), signed by the Prime Ministers of Barbados, Guyana, Jamaica and Trinidad and Tobago on July 4, 1973, is commemorated annually on the first Monday in July.

DIXON ALAN J: BIRTHDAY. July 7. U.S. Senator from Illinois, Democrat, of Belleville, IL, was born on July 7, 1927.

FUTURE HOMEMAKERS OF AMERICA LEADERSHIP MEETING. July 7-10. Orlando, FL. Purpose: To provide leadership training for student members of future Homemakers of America. Sponsor: Future Homemakers of America, Carolyn Waymack, 1910 Association Dr, Reston, VA 22091.

HUBBARD, CARROLL JR: BIRTHDAY. July 7. U.S. Representative of Kentucky's 1st district, Democrat, of Mayfield, KY, was born in Murray, Calloway County, KY on July 7, 1937.

	S	M	T	W	T	F	S
July			1	2	3	4	5
1986	6	7	8	9	10	11	12
	13	14	15	16	17	18	19
	20	21	22	23	24	25	26
	27	28	29	30	31		

JAPAN: STAR FESTIVAL (TANABATA). July 7. As an offering to the stars, children set up bamboo branches to which colorful strips of paper bearing poems are tied.

JUNIOR LEAGUE HORSE SHOW. July 7-12. Lexington, KY. "Largest outdoor show in the country for the American Saddlebred." Info from: KY Dept of Travel, Capital Plaza Office Tower, Frankfort, KY 40601.

LINCOLN ASSASSINATION CONSPIRATORS: HANGING ANNIVERSARY. July 7. Four persons convicted of complicity with John Wilkes Booth in the assassination of President Abraham Lincoln (Apr 14, 1865) were hanged at Washington, DC, on July 7, 1865. The four: Mary E. Surratt, Lewis Payne, David E. Harold and George A. Atzerodt.

SOLOMON ISLANDS: NATIONAL HOLIDAY. July 7.

SWITZERLAND: SEMPACH BATTLE COMMEMORATION. July 7. On the morning of the first Monday after July 4, the Lucerne Government, military and student delegations and historical groups make their way in solemn procession to the battlefield of 1386. Commemorative address, battle report and solemn service in the chapel. Also an evening procession.

TANZANIA: SABA SABA DAY. July 7. Marks the day in 1954 when Tanzania mainland's ruling party, TANU, was formed.

ZAMBIA: HEROES DAY. July 7. First Monday in July is Zambian National holiday—memorial day for Zambians who died in the struggle for independence. Political rallies stress solidarity.

JULY 8 — TUESDAY
189th Day — Remaining, 176

DECLARATION OF INDEPENDENCE: FIRST PUBLIC READING. July 8. Col. John Nixon reads the Declaration of Independence to the assembled residents at Philadelphia's Independence Square, July 8, 1776.

DINGELL, JOHN D: BIRTHDAY. July 8. U.S. Representative of Michigan's 16th district, Democrat, of Trenton, MI, born at Colorado Springs, CO July 8, 1926.

DIPRETE, EDWARD DANIEL: BIRTHDAY. July 8. Edward D. Diprete, Governor of Rhode Island, Republican, was born at Cranston, RI on July 8, 1934.

ENGLAND: GREAT YORKSHIRE SHOW. July 8-10. Great Yorkshire Showground, Hookstone Oval, Harrogate, North Yorkshire. Extensive show of livestock and machinery, with overseas pavilion and export bureau.

GRAMM, WILLIAM PHILIP (PHIL): BIRTHDAY. July 8. U.S. Senator from Texas, Republican, of College Station, TX, born at Fort Benning, GA, on July 8, 1942.

LLANGOLLEN INTERNATIONAL MUSICAL EISTEDDFOD. July 8-13. Llangollen, North Wales. Thousands of singers and folk dancers from more than 30 countries take part in this international annual music festival. Friendly rivalry of amateur groups performing in a giant marquee pavilion set in the Dee Valley, amidst the Welsh rivers and mountains. Info from: Llangollen Internatl Eisteddfod Office, Llangollen, North Wales LL20 8NG.

OLIVE BRANCH PETITION ANNIVERSARY. July 8. Representatives of New Hampshire, Massachusetts Bay, Rhode Island and Providence, Connecticut, New York, New Jersey, Pennsylvania, Delaware, Maryland, Virginia, North Carolina and South Carolina signed, on July 8, 1775, a Petition from the Congress to the King (George III), a final attempt by moderates in the Second Continental Congress to avoid a complete break with England.

ROCKEFELLER, NELSON ALDRICH: BIRTHDAY. July 8. Born at Bar Harbor, Maine, July 8, 1908. Governor of New York State, (1958-1973). Nominated as Vice President by President Ford on Aug 20, 1974, under provisions of the Twenty-fifth Amendment. Sworn in on Dec 19, 1974, after confirmation by the Senate, and served until Jan 20, 1977.

COPYRIGHT © 1985 BY WILLIAM D. CHASE and HELEN M. CHASE

Died at New York City, Jan 26, 1979. Rockefeller was the second person to become Vice President without having been elected (Gerald R. Ford was the first).

JULY 9 — WEDNESDAY
190th Day — Remaining, 175

CHESAPEAKE TURTLE DERBY. July 9. War Memorial Plaza, Baltimore, MD. Ten races with winner of each race competing in special grand sweepstakes race to determine the grand champ. Info from: Mayor's Office of Adventures in Fun, 100 Holliday St, Baltimore, MD 21202.

ENGLAND: ROYAL TOURNAMENT. July 9-26. Earls Court, Warwick Rd, London SW5. "Military spectacular with displays of skill and pageantry by members of the Royal Navy, the Royal Marines, the Army and the Air Force."

HENRY, PAUL B: BIRTHDAY. July 9. U.S. Representative of Michigan's 5th district, Republican, of Grand Rapids, MI, born in Chicago, IL, July 9, 1942.

HOWE, ELIAS: BIRTHDAY. July 9. American inventor of sewing machine. Born on July 9, 1819 at Spencer, MA. He died on Oct 3, 1867 at Brooklyn, NY.

LUKEN, THOMAS A: BIRTHDAY. July 9. U.S. Representative of Ohio's 1st district, Democrat, of Cincinnati, OH, born there on July 9, 1925.

MARTYRDOM OF THE BAB. July 9. Baha'i observance of the anniversary of the execution by a firing squad, July 9, 1850, in Tabriz, Iran, of 30-year-old Mirza Ali Muhammed, the Bab (prophet of the Baha'i faith). Info from: Baha'i Office of Public Affairs, Baha'i Natl Center, Wilmette, IL 60091.

RADCLIFFE, ANN WARD: BIRTHDAY. July 9. English novelist famous for her Gothic novels (fiction works especially popular in the late 18th and early 19th centuries). Among her works were *The Romance of the Forest*, *The Mysteries of Udolpho*, and *The Italian*. She was born on July 9, 1764 at London and died there on Feb 7, 1823.

RESPIGHI, OTTORINO: BIRTHDAY. July 9. Italian composer born at Bologna on July 9, 1879. He died at Rome on Apr 18, 1936.

JULY 10 — THURSDAY
191st Day — Remaining, 174

ANTIQUE AUTOMOBILE CLUB OF AMERICA: GRAND NATIONAL MEET: July 10-12. Asheville, NC. Info from: Box 417, Hershey, PA 17033.

BAHAMAS: INDEPENDENCE DAY. July 10. Public holiday. At 12:01 a.m., on July 10, 1973, The Bahamas gained its independence after 250 years as a British Crown Colony.

CENTRAL PENNSYLVANIA FESTIVAL OF THE ARTS. July 10-13. Purpose: To celebrate all the arts by featuring 350 sidewalk artists, performing arts stages and 10 indoor exhibitions. Info from: Central Pennsylvania Festival of the Arts, Lurene Frantz, Box 1023, State College, PA 16804.

CHILE: DIA DEL BIBLIOTECARIO. July 10. "Day of the Librarian," commemorates the government decree of July 10, 1969, creating the Colegio de Bibliotecarios de Chile (Chilean Association of Librarians).

DALLAS, GEORGE MIFFLIN: BIRTHDAY. July 10. Eleventh vice-president of the U.S. (1845-1849), born, Philadelphia, PA, July 10, 1792. Died there Dec 31, 1864.

GERMAN ALPS FESTIVAL. July 10-27. Hunter Mountain, NY. Purpose: Features German entertainment and products display. Info from: Don Conover, Bridge St, Hunter, NY 12442.

GOLF: U.S. WOMEN'S OPEN CHAMPIONSHIP. July 10-13. NCR Club, Dayton, OH. National championship for female golfers. Sponsor: U.S. Golf Assn, Golf House, Far Hills, NJ 07931.

KENNELLY, BARBARA B: BIRTHDAY. July 10. U.S. Representative of Connecticut's 1st district, Democrat, of Hartford, CT, born there July 10, 1936.

LA KERMESSE DE LA BASTILLE (BASTILLE DAYS). July 10-13. Milwaukee, WI. A French festival in the American tradition . . . celebrating French concept of "Liberte," Franco-American friendship and Milwaukee's "French connection." French market-place, street musicians and performers. Go-Kart Grand Prix and "Storm the Bastille" midnight run. Info from: Gene C. Harrison, AdMAX, Box 616, Cedarburg, WI 53012.

NORTH AMERICAN INDIAN DAYS. July 10-13. Browning, Montana. Celebration includes games, chanting, dancing and parades. Info from: Travel Montana, 1424 9th Ave, Helena, MT 59620.

PICTOU LOBSTER CARNIVAL. July 10-13. Pictou, Nova Scotia. Lobster suppers, street parade and fireworks. Info from: Dept of Tourism, Box 456, Halifax, NS B3J 2R5.

PROUST, MARCEL: BIRTHDAY. July 10. Anniversary of birth of famed French author (July 10, 1871-Nov 19, 1922). "Happiness," he wrote in *The Past Recaptured*, "is beneficial for the body but it is grief that develops the powers of the mind."

RAINBOW WARRIOR SINKING ANNIVERSARY. July 10. The 160-foot ship, the *Rainbow Warrior*, operated by Greenpeace, an environmentalist organization, was sunk and a photographer aboard was killed while the ship was at Marsden Wharf, Auckland, New Zealand, on July 10, 1985. Reportedly it was caused by a bomb attached to the underside of the ship by saboteurs. The ship had been scheduled for use in a protest against nuclear tests in the South Pacific Ocean by the French government.

ROUND BARN FESTIVAL. July 10-12. Rochester, IN. Guided tours of round barns and restored one-room schools and museums. Info from: Round Barn Festival, Inc, Box 512, Rochester, IN 46975.

SPACE MILESTONE: TELSTAR (US). July 10. First privately owned satellite (American Telephone and Telegraph Company), and first satellite to relay live TV pictures across the Atlantic. Launched on July 10, 1962.

TESLA, NIKOLA: BIRTHDAY. July 10. Famous electric pioneer, originator of the alternating current system. Born in Smiljan, Lika, Yugoslavia, 1856. Died Jan 7, 1943 in New York City. Info from: The Philatelic Journalist, 154 Laguna Ct, St. Augustine Shores, FL 32086.

WHISTLER, JAMES ABBOTT McNEILL: BIRTHDAY. July 10. American painter (especially known for painting of his mother), born, Lowell, MA, July 10, 1834. Died, London, July 17, 1903. When a lady declared that a landscape reminded her of Whistler's paintings, he reportedly said "Yes madam, Nature is creeping up."

WHITE PINE VILLAGE: CHILDREN'S DAY. July 10. Children's games and theatre, puppets, clowns and spelling bees. Info from: Mason County Historical Society, Connie Newkirk, 1687 S Lakeshore Dr, Ludington, MI 49431.

WINNIPEG FOLK FESTIVAL. July 10-13. Winnipeg, Manitoba, Canada. Blues, country, old-time, Cajun, French and traditional and contemporary folk music workshops. Info from: Travel Manitoba, Dept 5058, Winnipeg, Manitoba, Canada R3C 3H8.

WYOMING: ADMISSION DAY. July 10. Became 44th State on this day in 1890.

COPYRIGHT © 1985 BY WILLIAM D. CHASE and HELEN M. CHASE

JULY 11 — FRIDAY
192nd Day — Remaining, 173

ADAMS, JOHN QUINCY: BIRTHDAY. July 11. Sixth president of the U.S., and the son of the second president, John Quincy Adams was born at Braintree, MA, July 11, 1767. After his single term as president, he served 17 years as a member of Congress, from Plymouth, MA. He died Feb 23, 1848, at the House of Representatives (in the same room in which he had taken the presidential oath of office on Mar 4, 1825). John Quincy Adams was the only president whose father had also been president of the U.S.

ANTHONY WAYNE DAY. July 11. Purpose: To recognize the contributions of American Revolutionary War general, Anthony Wayne (Jan 1, 1745-Dec 15, 1796). Observed in Michigan since governor's proclamation of 1971. Sponsor: Wayne State University, Bob MacDonald, PR Info Officer, Detroit, MI 48202.

ANTIGONISH HIGHLAND GAMES. July 11-13. Antigonish, Nova Scotia. Major Scottish festival with pipe bands, highland dancing and traditional Scottish athletic events. Info from: Dept. of Tourism, Box 456, Halifax, NS B3J 2R5.

BLISS MUSIC FESTIVAL. July 11-13. Bliss, MI. Family event with workshops for kids and adults. Music styles from Irish to Bluegrass. Info from: The Grain Train, 421 Howard St, Petoskey, MI 49770.

BOWDLER'S DAY. July 11. A day to remember the prudish medical doctor, Thomas Bowdler, born near Bath, England, on July 11, 1754. He gave up the practice of medicine and undertook the cleansing of the works of Shakespeare by removing all the words and expressions which he considered to be indecent or impious. His *Family Shakespeare*, in ten volumes, omitted all those words "which cannot with propriety be read aloud in a family." He also "purified" Edward Gibbon's *History of the Decline and Fall of the Roman Empire* and selections from the *Old Testament*. So offensive was his censorship that his name became synonymous with self-righteous expurgation and the word "bowdlerize" has become part of the English language. Bowdler died at Rhyddings, in South Wales, Feb 24, 1825.

GREAT BALLOON RACE AND FLY DAYS. July 11-13. Wadsworth Municipal Airport, Wadsworth, OH. Purpose: A fun-filled weekend of activities for the entire family. Sponsors: Chamber of Commerce & Wadsworth Airmen's Assn, Box 324, Wadsworth, OH 44281.

JOLIET SUMMERFEST. July 11-13. Joliet, IL. Info from: Downtown Development Council, 19 E Van Buren, Joliet, IL 60431.

LA FESTA ITALIANA. July 11-13. Omaha Civic Auditorium, Omaha, NE. Info from: American Italian Heritage Society, Mary Jo Petersen, PR Dir, 2941 S 115th Ave, Omaha, NE 68144.

MARKEY, EDWARD J: BIRTHDAY. July 11. U.S. Representative of Massachusetts' 7th district, Democrat, of Malden, MA, born there July 11, 1946.

MID-AMERICA FESTIVAL OF THE ARTS. July 11-20. Classical and popular music, theatre, exhibits, dance and literary events highlighting our varied American heritage. Sponsor: Mid-America Festival of the Arts, Sidney Reger, 202 E 6th St, Bloomington, IN 47401.

MILLER HIGH LIFE SLOW PITCH SOFTBALL TOURNAMENT. July 11-13. Elm Park, Williamsport, PA. Charitable tournament for MS Society with 52 teams. Special Slam (home run) and Hit-n-run contests. Info from: Williamsport Beverage Co, Inc, Don Phillips, 532 Sylvan Dr, South Williamsport, PA 17701.

MONGOLIAN PEOPLE'S REPUBLIC: NATIONAL HOLIDAY. July 11. Commemorates establishment of Mongolian Communist government, on July 11, 1921.

NATIONAL CHEER UP THE LONELY DAY. July 11. Purpose: To help stamp out loneliness by being a "cheerer upper" and visit the lonely shut-ins and the lonely in hospitals and nursing homes. Info from: the C.U. Club, 66 Maryland Dr, Battle Creek, MI 49017.

SMITH, JAMES: DEATH ANNIVERSARY. July 11. Signer of the Declaration of Independence, born in Ireland about 1719 (exact date unknown). Died, July 11, 1806.

SOUTH CAROLINA FESTIVAL OF FLOWERS. July 11-13. Purpose: Summer flower trial gardens, flower shows, arts and crafts, beauty pageant, garden tours. Sponsor: Chamber of Commerce, Al Parker, Exec VP, Box 980, Greenwood, SC 29648.

SOUTH CAROLINA PEACH FESTIVAL. July 11-20. Tractor pull, country and pop artists, state beauty pageant, gigantic parade and fireworks. Info from: South Carolina Peach Festival, Box 549, Gaffney, SC 29342.

SPACE MILESTONE: SKYLAB (US). July 11. Eighty-two-ton spacecraft which was launched May 14, 1973, re-entered Earth's atmosphere on July 11, 1979. Expectation was that 20-25 tons probably would survive to hit Earth, including one piece of about 5,000 pounds. Intense international public interest in where it would fall. Chance that some person would be hit by a piece of Skylab was calculated at one in 152. Targets were drawn, Skylab parties held, and there was broad media coverage of the largest man-made object to fall to Earth from orbit. Skylab broke up and fell to Earth in a shower of pieces over the Indian Ocean and Australia, with no known or reported casualties. July 11, 1979.

SPECIAL RECREATION DAY. July 11. Purpose: To focus attention on the recreation rights, needs, aspirations and abilities of people who are disabled. Sponsor: Special Recreation, Inc, John A. Nesbitt, Pres, 362 Koser Ave, Iowa City, IA 52240.

WATERVILLE VALLEY FESTIVAL OF THE ARTS. July 11-20. Top names in jazz, folk, pop and classical music. Sponsor: Waterville Valley Center for the Arts, Debbie Moore, News Bureau, Waterville Valley, NH 03223.

WILD HORSE STAMPEDE. July 11-13. Wolf Point, Montana. The "Granddaddy" of all Montana rodeos features a wild horse race, 3 rodeos and 3 parades. Info from: Travel Montana, 1424 9th Ave, Helena, MT 59620.

WINKIES OF OZ CONVENTION. July 11-13. Purpose: To celebrate Dorothy's melting of the Wicked Witch of the West. Sponsor: The Internatl Wizard of Oz Club, Inc, Fred M. Meyer, Secy, 220 N. 11th St, Escanaba, MI 49829.

JULY 12 — SATURDAY
193rd Day — Remaining, 172

ART FAIR ON THE SQUARE. July 12-13. Madison, WI. Over 400 artists representing 25 states and Canada exhibit their work. Info from: Madison Art Center, 211 State St, Madison, WI 53703.

CHILI COOK-OFF. July 12. Holiday Inn West, Fort Pierce, FL. Purpose: Money raised goes to the Exchange Center for the Prevention of Child Abuse. Goal of the center is to detect and rehabilitate abused children and their parents. Info from: Fort Pierce Exchange Club, Box 2083, Fort Pierce, FL 33454.

COMEDY CELEBRATION DAY. July 12. Golden Gate Park, San Francisco, CA. Purpose: A comedy extravaganza from local and nationally known comics to say thank you to the city

	S	M	T	W	T	F	S
July 1986			1	2	3	4	5
	6	7	8	9	10	11	12
	13	14	15	16	17	18	19
	20	21	22	23	24	25	26
	27	28	29	30	31		

COPYRIGHT © 1985 BY WILLIAM D. CHASE and HELEN M. CHASE

that's nurtured so many comedic artists. Sponsors: The San Francisco Chronicle and local comedy clubs. Info from: Jose Simon, Dir, 2114 28th Ave, San Francisco, CA 94116.

DETROIT CITY AIR SHOW. July 12-13. Detroit City Airport, Detroit, MI. Purpose: To foster interest in and preserve the heritage of aviation. Features World War II bombers and fighters, classic aircraft, gliders, parachute and free fall teams, ultralight aircraft, aerobatics, fly-bys of military formations, wingwalkers, police aviation demonstrations and international barnstorming champions. Info from: Lillian Snyder, Detroit City Airport, 11499 Conner Ave, Detroit, MI 48213.

DIFFERENT COLORED EYES DAY. July 12. Purpose: To become aware of the individuality of people and especially recognize the uniqueness of people with two different colored eyes. Sponsor: Jeanne Fetch, 1708 Hawkins Dr, Southampton, PA 18966.

EASTER IN JULY LILY FESTIVAL. July 12-13. Featured are sunrise church services, food and crafts, booths constructed of Easter lilies and lily float competitions. Sponsor: Smith River Kiwanis Club. Info from: Chamber of Commerce, Box 246, Crescent City, CA 95531.

ENGLAND: YORK EARLY MUSIC FESTIVAL. July 12-21. Various venues, York, North Yorkshire. Festival of medieval, Renaissance, baroque and classical music in period halls and churches.

EDWARDS, MARVIN H. MICKEY: BIRTHDAY. July 12. U.S. Representative of Oklahoma's 5th District, Republican, of Oklahoma City, OK, was born July 12, 1937.

GRANDFATHER MOUNTAIN HIGHLAND GAMES. July 12-13. Scottish sports, highland dancing, piping, drumming, ceremonies and pageantry. Info from: Grandfather Mountain, Harris Prevost, Box 995, Linville, NC 28646.

HATFIELD, MARK O: BIRTHDAY. July 12. U.S. Senator from Oregon, Republican, of Tigard, OR, born in Dallas, OR, July 12, 1922.

HOMESTEADING DAYS. July 12-13. Purpose: Homesteading skills which depict early American farm life are demonstrated on 1100-acre Bob Evans Farm. Info from: Bob Evans Farms, Inc, Mary Cusick, 3776 S High St, Columbus, OH 43207.

KIRIBATI: NATIONAL HOLIDAY. July 12. Republic of Kiribati attained independence July 12, 1979.

McCOLLUM, BILL JR: BIRTHDAY. July 12. U.S. Representative of Florida's 5th district, Republican, of Altamonte Springs, FL, born in Brooksville, FL, on July 12, 1944.

NATIONAL NUDE DAYS. July 12-13. Purpose: "To promote understanding of the clothes-optional recreation movement as a natural solution to many problems of modern living." Sponsor: The Naturist Society, Box 132, Oshkosh, WI 54902.

NATIONAL THERAPEUTIC RECREATION WEEK. July 12-18. Purpose: Therapeutic Recreation activity seeks "to improve quality of life" through promotion of "physical, mental and emotional well-being, without addictions." Info from: Marion Somers, Chairperson, Natl Therapeutic Recreation Week, 601 7th St, Brooklyn, NY 11215.

NORTHERN IRELAND: BATTLE OF BOYNE NATIONAL HOLIDAY. July 12. Commemorates Battle of Boyne, July 1 (Old Style), 1690.

NORTHWEST WATER CARNIVAL. July 12-20. Detroit Lakes, MN. Miss Northwest Pageant, sailboat regatta and air show. Sponsor: Detroit Lakes Jaycees, Box 456, Detroit Lakes, MN 56501.

ORANGEMEN'S DAY. July 12. Annual observance on July 12 commemorates Battle of Boyne, July 1, (Old Style) 1690, in which the forces of King William III of England, Prince of Orange, defeated those of James II, at Boyne River in Ireland.

OSLER, SIR WILLIAM: BIRTHDAY. July 12. Anniversary of birth at Tecumseh, Ontario, on July 12, 1849, of William Osler, physician, teacher and author of *Principles and Practice of Medicine*. Osler died at Oxford, England, Dec 29, 1919.

SAO TOME and PRINCIPE: NATIONAL DAY. July 12. National holiday observed.

SEAFAIR. July 12-Aug 3. Seattle, WA. Seafair hosts 55 events including the Torchlight Parade. Unlimited hydroplane race on Lake Washington. Info from: Seafair, 901 Occidental South, Seattle, WA 98134.

SUMMER SWAMP STOMP. July 12. Tallahassee Jr Museum. State and local bluegrass and folk performers. Info from: Tallahassee Jr Museum, 3945 Museum Dr, Tallahassee, FL 32304.

THOREAU, HENRY DAVID: BIRTHDAY. July 12. American author and philosopher, born Concord, MA, July 12, 1817. Died there May 6, 1862. In *Walden*, he wrote "I frequently tramped eight or ten miles through the deepest snow to keep an appointment with a beechtree, or a yellow birch, or an old acquaintance among the pines."

THREE RIVERS FESTIVAL. July 12-20. Purpose: A festival of fun and civic pride. Arts, crafts, raft race, ethnic heritage activities, sports, music, food and entertainment. Sponsor: Three Rivers Festival, 2301 Fairfield Ave, Suite 107, Fort Wayne, IN 46807.

TUPPER LAKE WOODSMEN'S DAYS. July 12-13. Competitions for woodsmen and lumberjacks. Info from: Tupper Lake Woodsmen's Committee, Box JJ, Tupper Lake, NY 12986.

WEDGEWOOD, JOSIAH: BIRTHDAY. July 12. Famed English pottery designer and manufacturer, born at Burslem, Staffordshire, July 12, 1730. Died at Etruria, Staffordshire, Jan 3, 1795.

JULY 13 — SUNDAY

194th Day — Remaining, 171

BIDE-A-WEE WESTHAMPTON CHILDREN'S PET FAIR. July 13. Westhampton, L.I. New York. Purpose: To increase awareness of Bide-A-Wee and teach youngsters about the importance of humane treatment of animals. Anything that walks, crawls, swims or flies is eligible. Info from: Susan Brooks, Bide-A-Wee, 410 E 38th St, New York, NY 10016.

CHANDLER, ROD: BIRTHDAY. July 13. U.S. Representative of Washington's 8th district, Republican, of Redmond, WA, born at La Grande, OR, July 13, 1942.

FORREST, NATHAN BEDFORD: BIRTHDAY. July 13. Confederate cavalry commander whose birthday is observed as a holiday in Tennessee. Forrest was born July 13, 1821, Bedford County, TN, and died Oct 29, 1877, at Memphis, TN.

GREEN RIVER RENDEZVOUS PAGEANT. July 13. Rendezvous Grounds, Pinedale, WY. Purpose: The reenactment of the rendezvous held on the same site during the Rocky Mountain fur trade era. Sponsor: Sublette County Historical Society, Alice Harrower, 208 S Fremont, Pinedale, WY 82941.

JAPAN: FEAST OF LANTERNS (BON FESTIVAL). July 13-15. Religious rites throughout Japan in memory of the dead who, according to Buddhist belief, revisit earth during this period. Lanterns are lighted for the souls. Spectacular bonfires in the shape of the character 'dai' are burned on hillsides on last day of the Bon or O-Bon Festival, bidding farewell to the spirits of the dead.

COPYRIGHT © 1985 BY WILLIAM D. CHASE and HELEN M. CHASE

KEMP, JACK: BIRTHDAY. July 13. U.S. Representative of New York's 31st district, Republican (endorsed by Conservative Party,) of Hamburg, NY, born at Los Angeles, CA, July 13, 1935.

"LIVE AID" CONCERTS ANNIVERSARY. July 13. Concerts at Philadelphia and London (Kennedy and Wembley Stadiums) were seen by 162,000 attendees and an estimated 1.5 billion television viewers. Organized to raise funds for African famine relief, the musicians performed without fee and nearly $100 million was pledged toward aid to the hungry.

NATIONAL ICE CREAM DAY. July 13. Purpose: To establish the second Sunday in July as "National Ice Cream Day" and the week in which it falls each as "National Ice Cream Week," on behalf of all the dairy farmers who produce the milk and cream, the people in the ice cream plants who produce the ice cream, those who keep the coolers in the grocery stores stocked and most of all those who consume ice cream. Info from: Internatl Assn of Ice Cream Manufacturers, 888 Sixteenth St, NW, Washington, DC 20006.

NATIONAL ICE CREAM WEEK. July 13-19. Week beginning with second Sunday in July. (See also entries for National Ice Cream Month, July 1 and national Ice Cream Day, July 13.) Info from: Internatl Assn of Ice Cream Manufacturers, 888 Sixteenth St, NW, Washington, DC 20006.

NEWPORT MUSIC FESTIVAL. July 13. Newport, RI. "America's primo Festivale" held in Newport's fabled mansions. Chamber music, world renowned artists and North American debuts. Info from: The Newport Music Festival, 50 Washington Sq, Newport, RI 02840.

NIGHT WATCH or LA RETRAITE AUX FLAMBEAUX. July 13. France. Celebrates Eve of the Bastille's fall.

OLD CRAFTS DAY. July 13. Galloway House and Village, Fond du Lac, WI. Purpose: To demonstrate old crafts of late 1800's—as many as 30 different craftsmen. Sponsor: Fond du Lac County Historical Society, 332 14th St, Fond du Lac, WI 54935.

JULY 14 — MONDAY
195th Day — Remaining, 170

ALPENFEST. July 14-19. Gaylord, MI. Commemorates the rejuvenation of town to an Alpine village. Sponsor: Alpenfest, Inc, Chamber of Commerce, Box 513, Gaylord, MI 49735.

BASTILLE DAY or FETE NATIONAL. July 14. France. Public holiday commemorating the fall of the Bastille at the beginning of the French Revolution, on July 14, 1789. Also celebrated or observed in many other countries.

ENGLAND: BIRMINGHAM RIOT ANNIVERSARY. July 14. Following a dinner on July 14, 1791, celebrating the second anniversary of the fall of the Bastille, an angry mob rioted in Birmingham, England. The main target of their wrath was the home of scientist (discoverer of Oxygen) Joseph Priestley (q.v.) who was unpopular because of his religious views and his approval of the American and French revolutionary causes. The mob ruled Birmingham for three days, burning Priestley's home and laboratory as well as the homes of his friends. Priestley, in disguise, and his family narrowly escaped with their lives. They lived for a time in London before moving, in 1794, to America.

FORD, GERALD RUDOLPH: BIRTHDAY. July 14. 38th President of the U.S. Born Leslie King, at Omaha, Nebraska, July 14, 1913. (Ford became 41st Vice-President of the U.S. Dec 6, 1973, by appointment following resignation of Spiro T. Agnew from that office on Oct 10, 1973. Ford became President on Aug 9, 1974, following the resignation from that office on that day of Richard M. Nixon.) He was the first non-elected Vice-President and President of the U.S.

GOLF: U.S. AMATEUR PUBLIC LINKS CHAMPIONSHIP. July 14-19. Tanglewood Park, Clemmons, NC. National championship for amateur golfers who are bona fide public links players. Sponsor: U.S. Golf Assn, Golf House, Far Hills, NJ 07931.

GUTHRIE, WOODROW WILSON "WOODIE": BIRTHDAY. July 14. American folk-singer, composer, July 14, 1912-Oct 3, 1967.

INTERNATIONAL CONFERENCE OF WORLD FUTURE SOCIETY. July 14-17. Penta Hotel, New York, NY. Purpose: Together with business and U.N. officials, examine alternative options and futures for humanity and all human spheres of activity. Sponsor: World Future Society, Ralph E. Hamil, Co-Representative to U.N., 4916 St Elmo Ave, Bethesda, MD 20814.

MISSION SAN ANTONIO DE PADUA ANNIVERSARY. July 14. California. Mission to the Indians founded July 14, 1771.

MOON PHASE: FIRST QUARTER. July 14. Moon enters First Quarter phase at 3:10 p.m., E.S.T.

NORTHERN IRELAND: ULSTER HARP DERBY. July 14. Horse racing at the Down Royal Racecourse, Maze, County Down. "The most important flat race in the Northern Ireland calendar."

SARTO, ANDREA DEL: 500th BIRTH ANNIVERSARY. July 14. Celebrated Italian painter was born near Florence on July 14, 1486. "Sarto," a nickname referring to his father's trade as a tailor, was the name he chose during his lifetime, though the real surname was probably either Vanucchi or di Francesco. One of the most renowned artists of his time, his paintings hang in the great galleries of the world. He died at Florence, Jan 22, 1531.

JULY 15 — TUESDAY
196th Day — Remaining, 169

DENTON, JEREMIAH A, JR: BIRTHDAY. July 15. U.S. Senator, Republican, Mobile, Al, born at Mobile on July 15, 1924.

ENGLAND: CUTTY SARK TALL SHIPS RACE. July 15-Aug 14. From Newcastle upon Tyne to Gothenburg, Sweden. Prior to departure on July 19th, ships can be viewed at Newcastle. Race goes to Bremerhaven, West Germany (July 24-27) before arriving in Gothenburg (from Aug 10). Info from: Sail Training Assn, 5 Mumby Rd, Gosport, Hampshire PO12 1AA, England.

HEMINGWAY DAYS FESTIVAL. July 15-21. Key West, FL. Purpose: To pay tribute to Ernest Hemingway, Key West's most famus adopted son. Sponsor: Sloppy Joe's Bar, Michael Whalton, Co-Dir., 201 Duval St, Key West, FL 33040.

JONES, INIGO: BIRTHDAY. July 15. English architect, born London, July 15, 1573. Died there June 21, 1652.

MOORE, CLEMENT CLARKE: BIRTHDAY. July 15. American author and teacher, best remembered for his popular verses: "A visit from Saint Nicholas," ('Twas the Night Before Christmas) which were first published anonymously and without Moore's knowledge in a newspaper on Dec 23, 1823. Moore was born at New York City, July 15, 1779, and died at Newport, RI, on July 10, 1873.

RUDD, ELDON: BIRTHDAY. July 15. U.S. Representative of Arizona's 4th district, Republican, of Scottsdale, AZ, born in Camp Verde, AZ, on July 15, 1920.

ST. FRANCES XAVIER CABRINI: BIRTHDAY. July 15. First American Saint, last of thirteen children, founder of schools, orphanages, convents and hospitals, born in Lombardy, Italy, July 15, 1850. Died of Malaria, at Chicago, Dec 22, 1917. Canonized July 7, 1946.

July 1986

S	M	T	W	T	F	S
		1	2	3	4	5
6	7	8	9	10	11	12
13	14	15	16	17	18	19
20	21	22	23	24	25	26
27	28	29	30	31		

COPYRIGHT © 1985 BY WILLIAM D. CHASE and HELEN M. CHASE

ST. SWITHIN'S DAY. July 15. Swithun (Swithin), bishop of Winchester (A.D. 852-862), died July 2, 862. Little is known of his life, but his relics were translated into Winchester Cathedral on July 15, 971, a day on which there was heavy rainfall. According to old English belief, rain for forty days hereafter when it falls on this day. "St. Swithin's Day, if thou dost rain, for forty days it will remain; St. Swithin's Day, if thou be fair, for forty days, 'twill rain nae mair."

ST. SWITHUN'S SOCIETY ANNUAL CELEBRATION. July 15. Toronto, Ontario, Purpose: To promote feelings of goodwill. Encourages spontaneous celebration throughout the year and "creates annual honourary members." Sponsor: St. Swithun's Society, Norman A. McMullen, Pres, 547 Steeles Ave, W, Townhouse 58, Willowdale, Ontario M2M 3Y1.

SHARP, PHILIP R: BIRTHDAY. July 15. U.S. Representative of Indiana's 2nd district, Democrat, of Muncie, IN, born in Baltimore, MD, on July 15, 1942.

SPACE MILESTONE: APOLLO-SOYUZ TEST PROJECT (US, USSR). July 15. After three years of planning, negotiation and preparation the first US-USSR joint space project reached fruition with the link-up in space of Apollo 18 (crew: T. Stafford, V. Brand, D. Slayton; landed in Pacific Ocean July 24, during 136th orbit) and Soyuz 19 (crew: A.A. Leonov, V.N. Kubasov; landed July 21, after 96 orbits). Apollo 18 and Soyuz 19 were linked 47 hours (July 17-19) while joint experiments and transfer of personnel and materials back and forth between craft took place. Launch date was July 15, 1975.

JULY 16 — WEDNESDAY
197th Day — Remaining, 168

AMUNDSEN, ROALD: BIRTHDAY. July 16. Norwegian explorer and author, Roald Amundsen was the first man to sail from Atlantic to Pacific Oceans via the Northwest Passage (1903-1905). He discovered the South Pole (Dec 14, 1911) and flew over the North Pole in a dirigible in 1926. Born near Oslo, Norway, July 16, 1872. He flew, with five companions, from Norway, June 18, 1928, in a daring effort to rescue survivors of an Italian Arctic expedition. No trace of the rescue party or the airplane was ever located.

ATOMIC BOMB DAY. July 16. Anniversary of the first atomic bomb explosion. At 5:30 a.m., on July 16, 1945, the first atomic bomb was detonated on top of a steel tower at Trinity Site, Alamagordo Air Base, 120 miles south of Albuquerque, NM. Light visible 400 miles away, fireball one mile in diameter, mushroom cloud 40,000 feet high, quarter-mile crater, and desert surface fused to glass for 800 yards around blast site. Birth of the nuclear bomb age.

BILIRAKIS, MICHAEL: BIRTHDAY. July 16. U.S. Representative of Florida's 9th district, Republican, of Palm Harbor, FL, born at Tarpon Springs, FL on July 16, 1930.

BRYAN, RICHARD H: BIRTHDAY. July 16. Richard H. Bryan, Governor of Nevada, Democrat, was born at Washington, DC, on July 16, 1937.

EDDY, MARY BAKER: BIRTHDAY. July 16. Founder of Christian Science, born near Concord, NH, July 16, 1821. Died at Chestnut Hill, MA, Dec 3, 1910.

ENGLAND: SHREWSBURY INTERNATIONAL MUSIC FESTIVAL. July 16-23. Shrewsbury, Shropshire. Music and dance groups of every type are invited to attend this non-competitive festival.

HOG CALLING CONTEST. July 16. War Memorial Plaza, Baltimore, MD. Amateur hog callers compete for prizes. Country music entertainment. Info from: Mayor's Office of Adventures in Fun, 100 Holliday St, Baltimore, MD 21202.

LA PAZ DAY. July 16. Foundation of city, now capitol of Bolivia, on this day, 1548.

MISS CRUSTACEAN USA BEAUTY PAGEANT AND OCEAN CITY CREEP. July 16. 12th St Beach, Ocean City, NJ. Participants are Hermit Tree Crabs. Purpose: "To determine most beautiful tree crab and fastest tree crab on earth." Info from: City of Ocean City, Mark Soifer, PR Dir, City Hall, Ocean City, NJ 08226.

MISSION SAN DIEGO DE ALCALA FOUNDING ANNIVERSARY. July 16. First of 21 California missions to the Indians, founded July 16, 1769.

REYNOLDS, JOSHUA: BIRTHDAY. July 16. English portrait painter whose paintings of 18th century English notables are among the best of the time. Born at Plympton, Devon on July 16, 1723. Sir Joshua died at London on Feb. 23, 1792. "He who resolves never to ransack any mind but his own," Reynolds told students of the Royal Academy, in 1774, "will be soon reduced, from mere barrenness, to the poorest of all imitations; he will be obliged to imitate himself, and to repeat what he has before often repeated."

SPACE MILESTONE: APOLLO 11 (US). July 16. Launched on July 16, 1969 and resulted in man's first moon landing. Lunar module "Eagle" lands on moon, 4:17 p.m. EDT, July 20. Commander Neil Armstrong descends from Eagle to moon's surface, followed shortly by Col. Edwin Aldrin, Jr. After rejoining spaceship "Columbia," piloted by Lt. Col. Michael Collins, astronauts returned to Earth, July 24, bringing first-hand reports of lunar surface, photographs and rock samples. Man's first landing on extraterrestrial body. July 16, 1969.

THORNBURGH, RICHARD L: BIRTHDAY. July 16. Richard L. Thornburgh, Governor of Pennsylvania, Republican, was born at Pittsburgh, PA, on July 16, 1932.

JULY 17 — THURSDAY
198th Day — Remaining, 167

DISNEYLAND: BIRTHDAY. July 17. Disneyland celebrates anniversary of opening: July 17, 1955. Info from: Publicity Dept, Disneyland, 1313 Harbor Blvd, Anaheim, CA 92803.

GARDNER, ERLE STANLEY: BIRTHDAY. July 17. American author of detective fiction, born at Malden, MA, July 17, 1889. Best remembered for his Perry Mason detective story series about lawyer-detective, Gardner also wrote novels under the pen name, A.A. Fair. Gardner died at Temecula, CA, Mar 11, 1970.

GERRY, ELBRIDGE: BIRTHDAY. July 17. Fifth vice-president of the U.S. (1813-1814) born, Marblehead, MA, July 17, 1744. Died, Washington, DC Nov 23, 1814. His name became part of the language (Gerrymander) after he signed a redistricting bill, while governor of Massachusetts, in 1812.

GOLF: BRITISH OPEN CHAMPIONSHIP. July 17-20. The 115th staging of this top golfing event is being held at Turnberry, Ayrshire. Regional and Final Qualifying Competitions on July 7 and July 13-14, respectively, at various venues. Info from: The Royal and Ancient Golf Club of St. Andrews, Fife, Scotland.

IRAQ: NATIONAL DAY. July 17. National holiday observed in Iraq.

KANSAS CITY HOTEL DISASTER. July 17. Anniversary of the collapse of aerial walkways at the Hyatt Regency Hotel in Kansas City, MO about 7 p.m., on July 17, 1981. About 1,500 people were attending the popular weekly "tea dance," when

COPYRIGHT © 1985 BY WILLIAM D. CHASE and HELEN M. CHASE

two concrete and steel walkways broke loose and fell on guests in the hotel's crowded lobby, killing more than a hundred persons.

KOREA: CONSTITUTION DAY. July 17. Legal national holiday. Commemorates the proclamation of the Constitution of the Republic Korea on July 17, 1948. Ceremonies at Seoul's capitol plaza and all major cities.

RED RIVER STREET FAIR. July 17-19. Fargo, ND. Artists and craftspeople exhibit paintings, sculpture, graphics, fibers, photography, jewelry, wood, metal, textiles, glass, candles, clay and leatherwork. Sponsor: Downtown Business Assn, Kenneth S. Umbehocker, Exec Dir, Box 962, Fargo, ND 58107.

RIVERA, MUNOZ: BIRTHDAY. July 17. Puerto Rico. Celebrates birth on this day, 1859, of Puerto Rican patriot and journalist, Luis Munoz Rivera.

SCOTLAND: COMMONWEALTH ARTS FESTIVAL. July 17-Aug 2. Edinburgh, Lothian. Major arts festival running in conjunction with the Commonwealth Games (q.v.) with music and dance from most of the competing countries.

SOUTHERN HIGHLAND HANDICRAFT GUILD FAIR '86. July 17-20. Civic Center, Asheville, NC. Handmade crafts from the southern Appalachian region, demonstrations and special exhibits. Info from: Southern Highland Handicraft Guild, Box 9545, Asheville, NC 28815.

SPACE MILESTONE: SOYUZ T-12 (USSR). July 17. Launched on July 17, 1984 Cosmonaut Svetlana Savitskaya became the first woman to walk in space (July 25) and the first woman to make more than one space voyage. With cosmonauts V. Dzhanibekov and I. Volk. Docked at Salyut 7 on July 18 and returned to Earth July 29. July 17, 1984.

"WRONG WAY" CORRIGAN DAY. July 17. On July 17, 1938, Douglas Groce Corrigan, an unemployed airplane mechanic, left Brooklyn, NY's Floyd Bennett field, ostensibly headed for Los Angeles, California, in a 1929 Curtiss Robin monoplane. He landed 28 hours, 13 minutes later at Dublin, Ireland's Baldonnell airport, after 3150 mile non-stop flight without radio or special navigation equipment, and in violation of American and Irish flight regulations. Born at Galveston, Texas, on Jan 22, 1907, Corrigan received hero's welcome home, was nicknamed "Wrong Way" Corrigan because he claimed he accidentally followed wrong end of his compass needle. The 31-year-old bachelor commented, on return, "I can't get over the number of girls who seem to think because I flew the Atlantic I would make a perfect husband."

JULY 18 — FRIDAY
199th Day — Remaining, 166

ANTIQUE AUTOMOBILE CLUB OF AMERICA: FALL MEET. July 18-19. Stone Mountain, GA. Info from: Box 417, Hershey, PA 17033.

BAY DAYS FESTIVAL. July 18-20. Ashland, WI. Sailboat regatta, bike and foot races, cow chip toss, power weight lifting, canoe races and arts and crafts fair. Info from: Chamber of Commerce, Box 746, Ashland, WI 54806.

BLACK-EYED PEA JAMBOREE. July 18-20. Purpose: Pea cooks gather from all over the country to compete for prizes. Parade, 10 kilometer run, arts and crafts, carnival and country and western show with top entertainers. Info from: Chamber of Commerce, Box 608, Athens, TX 75751.

July 1986

S	M	T	W	T	F	S
		1	2	3	4	5
6	7	8	9	10	11	12
13	14	15	16	17	18	19
20	21	22	23	24	25	26
27	28	29	30	31		

CHEYENNE FRONTIER DAYS. July 18-27. Purpose: "The world's biggest outdoor rodeo celebration." Rodeo, western parades, top country entertainment and U.S. Championship Chuckwagon races. Info from: Cheyenne Frontier Days Committee, Box 2666, Cheyenne, WY 82003.

CHRISTMAS CITY FAIR. July 18-20. Bethlehem, PA. Purpose: Bethlehem's Birthday celebration featuring ethnic foods, arts, crafts and hot air balloons. Info from: Fine Arts Commission, Richard Szulborski, Chrmn, 437 Main St, Suite 304, Bethlehem, PA 18018.

DELAWARE STATE FAIR. July 18-26. Harrington, DE.

GLENN, JOHN HERSCHEL, JR: BIRTHDAY. July 18. U.S. Senator from Ohio, Democrat, of Columbus, OH, born in Cambridge, OH, on July 18, 1921.

GRAYSON COUNTY FIDDLIN' FESTIVAL. July 18-20. Leitchfield, KY. Official state championship old-timers fiddlers contest. Arts, crafts, hobby and collectors fair. Info from: KY Dept of Travel, Capital Plaza Office Tower, Frankfort, KY 40601.

LIVING HISTORY DAYS. July 18-20. A look at the activities and daily crafts of 18th and 19th century Bethlehem residents. Info from: Historic Bethlehem, Inc, 501 Main St, Bethlehem, PA 18018.

MARINERFEST. July 18-20. Tawas Bay, MI. Fishing contests, lighted boat parade, antiques and auto and boat show. Info from: Chamber of Commerce, 402 Lake St, Tawas City, MI 48763.

MINNEAPOLIS AQUATENNIAL. July 18-27. Purpose: To provide a summer break for the residents of Minneapolis as they take out ten days to enjoy the city of lakes and show it off to visitors from near and far. Info from: Program Dir, 702 Wayzata Blvd, Commodore Ct, Minneapolis, MN 55403.

NORTH DAKOTA STATE FAIR. July 18-26. Minot, ND. Exhibits, carnival, entertainment, rodeos and races. Info from: ND State Fair Assn, Jerry Iverson, Box 1796, Minot, ND 58701.

SALEM ART FAIR AND FESTIVAL. July 18-20. Bush's Pasture Park, Salem, OR. Over 200 artists and craftspersons. Entertainment, demonstrations, fun run, food booths, children's parade and art area, folk arts, Oregon wine and cheese tasting and tours of historic Bush House. Info from: Salem Art Assn, 600 Mission St, SE, Salem OR 97302.

SPACE MILESTONE: ROHINI 1 (INDIA). July 18. First successful launch from India, orbited 77 lb satellite. July 18, 1980.

THACKERAY, WILLIAM MAKEPEACE: BIRTHDAY. July 18. English author, best remembered for his novels, especially *Pendennis* and *Vanity Fair*, was born at Calcutta, India on July 18, 1811. Thackeray died at London, Dec 23, 1863.

WHITE, GILBERT: BIRTHDAY. July 18. Born at Selborne, Hampshire, England on July 18, 1720, Gilbert White has been called the "father of British naturalists." His book, *The Natural History of Selborne*, published in 1788 enjoyed immediate success and is said to have never been out of print. White died near his birthplace, June 26, 1793. His home survives as a museum.

JULY 19 — SATURDAY
200th Day — Remaining, 165

ALL AMERICAN TEDDY BEAR'S PICNIC. July 19-20 Peddler's Village, Lahaska, PA. Bring your teddy bear to Peddler's Village for a day of excitement and festivities. Teddy bear competitions and teddy bear craftspersons. Info from: Peddler's Village, Rt 202 & 263, Lahaska, PA 18931.

AMERICANA FESTIVAL. July 19-20. Purpose: A nostalgia weekend, with antique auto show, old-time entertainment and demonstrations, antique and collectibles flea market. Info from: Roscoe Village Foundation, 381 Hill St, Coshocton, OH 43812.

COPYRIGHT © 1985 BY WILLIAM D. CHASE and HELEN M. CHASE

CHARITON RAFT RACE AND FLOAT. July 19. Kirksville, MO. Purpose: To provide entertainment for the Kirksville and area residents. Sponsors: Pepsi Cola, Busch Beer and Pizza Hut. Info from: KRXL Radio, Box 130, Kirksville, MO 63501.

CRAFT FAIR USA: INDOOR SUMMER SHOW. July 19-20. Wisconsin State Fair Park. Sale of handcrafted items: Jewelry, pottery, weaving, leather, wood, glass, yulecraft and sculpture. Info from: Dennis R. Hill, Dir, 3233 S. Villa Circle, West Allis, WI 53227.

CRICKET: BENSON AND HEDGES CUP FINAL. July 19. Lord's Cricket Ground, St. John's Wood, London.

ENGLAND: CLEVELAND INTER-TIE. July 19-26. Middlesbrough, Cleveland. Cleveland's 11th biennial international eisteddfod.

FAIRBANKS GOLDEN DAYS. July 19-27. A celebration of the first discovery of gold, on July 22, 1902. Info from: Chamber of Commerce, Box 74446, Fairbanks, AK 99707.

FIRST WOMEN'S RIGHTS CONVENTION ANNIVERSARY. July 19. First such convention in U.S., met at Seneca Falls, NY in 1848.

FRIENDSVILLE FIDDLER'S CONTEST. July 19. Fiddlers from Garrett County and surrounding region participate in event. Old-time bluegrass entertainment. Info from: Deep Creek Lake-Garrett County Promotion Council, Court House, Oakland, MD 21550.

GREAT TAN-OFF. July 19. Santa Cruz Beach Boardwalk, Santa Cruz, CA. Bronzed competitors parade on the beach bandstand to decide who has the best overall tan. Info from: Glenn LaFrank, Santa Cruz Beach Boardwalk, 400 Beach St, Santa Cruz, CA 95060.

HONG KONG: BIRTHDAY OF LU PAN. July 19. The birthday of Lu Pan, the Master Builder, is a holiday for everybody connected with the building trades. Ceremonies sponsored by the Builders' Guilds are held at Lu Pan Temple in Kennedy Town. Festive dinner parties. Thirteenth day of 6th lunar month.

HUCKABY, THOMAS J (JERRY): BIRTHDAY. July 19. U.S. Representative of Louisiana's 5th district, Democrat, of Ringgold, LA, was born in Hodge, Jackson Parish, LA, July 19, 1941.

INTERNATIONAL BRICK AND ROLLING PIN THROWING COMPETITION. July 19. Hurlers in Stroud, Oklahoma compete against teams in Stroud, England, Stroud, Canada and Stroud, Australia to see who can throw a five-pound brick and a two-pound rolling pin the greatest distance. International performance reports tabulated via telephone. Always the third weekend in July. Info from: Stroud Chamber of Commerce, 219 W Main St, Stroud, OK 74079.

JAMBOREE IN THE HILLS. July 19-20. St. Clairsville, OH. Outdoor country music festival with live country music and major country stars. Info from: Wheeling Broadcasting Company, 1015 Main St, Wheeling, WV 26003.

JULY JOYGERM JUBILEE. July 19. Purpose: "A tribute to Joygerms unfurled all over the world who believe the bright side is the right side, there's no time like the pleasant and antibody that's antibody is a Joygerm." Happy day parade in downtown Syracuse, NY. Info from: Joygerm Joan E. White, Joygerms Unltd, Box 219, Eastwood Sta, Syracuse, NY 13206.

LINCOLN, ABRAHAM: BIRTHPLACE: FOUNDERS DAY WEEKEND. July 19-20. Held annually on the weekend nearest to July 17, the anniversary of the park's founding date. Weekend activities include pioneer demonstrations, drama and musical programs, museum exhibits and the traditional Lincoln Birthplace Cabin. Picnicking and hiking trails. Info from: U.S. Dept of the Interior, Natl Park Service, Abraham Lincoln Birthplace Natl Historic Site, Rt 1, Hodgenville, KY 42748.

MAYO, CHARLES HORACE: BIRTHDAY. July 19. American surgeon, one of the Mayo Brothers, founders of the Mayo Clinic and Mayo Foundation, born at Rochester, MN, July 19, 1865. Died at Chicago, IL, May 26, 1939.

NICARAGUA: NATIONAL LIBERATION DAY. July 19. Following the National Day of Joy (July 17—anniversary of date in 1979 when dictator Anastasio Somoza Debayle fled Nicaragua) is annual July 19 observance of National Liberation Day, anniversary of day the National Liberation Army claimed victory over the Somoza dictatorship.

OLD TIME FIDDLERS CONTEST. July 19-20. Rough River Dam State Resort Park, Falls of Rough, KY. Governor's Cup Trophy will be awarded to the state championship fiddler. Info from: Kentucky Dept. of Parks, Capital Plaza Tower, Frankfort, KY 40601.

PENFIELD CIVIL WAR MUSTER. July 19-20. White Pine Village, Ludington, MI. Civil War re-enactments, camps, band and workshops. Info from: Mason County Historical Society, Connie Newkirk, 1687 S Lakeshore Dr, Ludington, MI 49431.

PRINCE LOT HULA FESTIVAL. July 19. Celebration in honor of Prince Lot, later King Kamehameha V, who sought to revive the Hawaiian culture in mid-1800's. Exhibition of ancient and modern hula, Hawaiian arts and crafts. (Third Saturday in July.) Info from: Moanalua Gardens Foundation, 1352 Pineapple Pl, Honolulu, HI 96819.

SASKATCHEWAN HANDCRAFT FESTIVAL. July 19-21. Battleford, Saskatchewan, Canada. Info from: Saskatchewan Craft Council, Box 7408, Saskatoon, Saskatchewan, Canada S7K 4J3.

SHENANDOAH VALLEY FARM CRAFT DAYS. July 19-20. Historic craft demonstrations, live bluegrass music and country food. Info from: Belle Grove, Inc, Box 137, Middletown, VA 22645.

TUPPER LAKE TIN MAN TRIATHLON. July 19. An ultimate test of endurance. 1.2 mile swim, 56 mile bike, and 13.1 mile run. Info from: Chamber of Commerce, 55 Park St, Tupper Lake, NY 12986.

WALES: FISHGUARD MUSIC FESTIVAL. July 19-26. Fishguard, Dyfed. International music festival including orchestral and choral concerts, poetry readings and visual arts.

JULY 20 — SUNDAY
201st Day — Remaining, 164

CAPTIVE NATIONS WEEK. July 20-26. Presidential Proclamation. "Issued each year since 1959 for the 3rd week of July." (PL 86-90 of July 17, 1959.) Note: In 1985, Presidential Proclamation 5357 designated Captive Nations Week as the week beginning July 21, 1985.

CIVITAN INTERNATIONAL CONVENTION. July 20-23. Oslo, Norway. Info from: Wendall Andrews, Exec Admn, Box 2102, Birmingham, AL 35201.

COLOMBIA: NATIONAL HOLIDAY. July 20. Independence Day. Gained independence from Spain, 1819.

CRAIG, LARRY E: BIRTHDAY. July 20. U.S. Representative of Idaho's 1st district, Republican, of Midvale, ID, was born at Council, ID, on July 20, 1945.

ENGLAND: BRITISH GRAND PRIX. July 20. Brands Hatch Circuit, Fawkham, Kent. Premier event in British motor racing. World's top drivers in action.

GENEVA ACCORDS. July 20. An agreement covering cessation of hostilities in Vietnam, signed at Geneva, July 20, 1954 on behalf of the commanders-in-chief of French forces in Vietnam and the People's Army of Vietnam. A further declaration of the

COPYRIGHT © 1985 BY WILLIAM D. CHASE and HELEN M. CHASE

Geneva Conference was released July 21, 1954. Partition, foreign troop withdrawal, and elections for a unified government, within 2 years, were among provisions.

HILLARY, SIR EDMUND PERCIVAL: BIRTHDAY. July 20. Explorer, mountaineer born at Auckland, New Zealand on July 20, 1919. With Tenzing Norgay, a Sherpa guide, became first to ascend summit of highest mountain in the world, Mt. Everest (29,028 ft), at 11:30 a.m. on May 29, 1953. "We climbed because nobody climbed it before," he said.

ITALY: FEAST OF THE REDEEMER. July 20. Venice, Italy. Procession of gondolas and other craft commemorating the end of the epidemic of 1575. Third Sunday in July.

LEHMAN, RICHARD HENRY: BIRTHDAY. July 20. U.S. Representative of California's 18th district, Democrat, of Sanger, CA, born there July 20, 1948.

MEYERS, JAN: BIRTHDAY. July 20. U.S. Representative of Kansas' 3rd district, Republican, of Overland Park, KS, born in Lincoln, NE, on July 20, 1928.

MIKULSKI, BARBARA ANN: BIRTHDAY. July 20. U.S. Representative of Maryland's 3rd district, Democrat, of Baltimore, MD, born there July 20, 1936.

SPACE MILESTONE: MOON DAY. July 20. Anniversary of man's first landing on moon. Two U.S. astronauts (Neil Alden Armstrong and Edwin Eugene Aldrin Jr.) landed lunar module *Eagle* at 4:17 p.m. EDT, July 20, 1969, and remained on lunar surface 21 hours, 36 minutes and 16 seconds. The landing was made from the Apollo XI's orbiting command and service module, code named *Columbia*, whose pilot, Michael Collins remained aboard. Armstrong was first to set foot on moon. Armstrong and Aldrin were outside spacecraft, walking on moon's surface, approximately 2¼ hours.

NATIONAL EXTENSION HOMEMAKERS COUNCIL, INC: ANNUAL CONFERENCE. July 20-24. Virginia Tech, Blacksburg, VA. Golden Anniversary celebration with special programs and speakers. Info from: Eleanor Whittemore, Box 389, Hollis, NH 03049.

NATIONAL EXTENSION HOMEMAKERS WEEK. July 20-24. Purpose: To give recognition to homemakers across the nation. Special events in 44 member states, Puerto Rico and U.S. Virgin Islands. Sponsor: Natl Extension Homemakers Council, Inc, Box 389, Hollis, NH 03049.

NEW ENGLAND MORGAN HORSE SHOW. July 20-26. "Largest one-breed show east of the Mississippi." Three County Fairgrounds, Northampton, MA. Info from: Pioneer Valley Conv & Visitors Bureau, Box 749, Northampton, MA 01061.

SPACE WEEK. July 20-26. The calendar week containing July 20 has been observed in a number of communities and states as Space Week, commemorating the July 20, 1969 landing on the moon by two U.S. astronauts, Neil Alden Armstrong and Edwin Eugene Aldrin, Jr. See Also: entry for July 20.

SWITZERLAND: DORNACH BATTLE COMMEMORATION. July 20. The victory at Dornach in 1499 is remembered on the battlefield and in the city of Solothurn on the Sunday nearest to July 22. Dornach observes commemorative festival every five years.

TUPPER LAKE ART SHOW. July 20-26. Juried art show from around the region. Info from: Chamber of Commerce, 55 Park St, Tupper Lake, NY 12986.

July
1986

S	M	T	W	T	F	S
		1	2	3	4	5
6	7	8	9	10	11	12
13	14	15	16	17	18	19
20	21	22	23	24	25	26
27	28	29	30	31		

JULY 21 — MONDAY
202nd Day — Remaining, 163

ASPIN, LES: BIRTHDAY. July 21. U.S. Representative of Wisconsin's 1st district, Democrat, of East Troy, WI, born in Milwaukee, WI, on July 21, 1938.

BATES, JIM: BIRTHDAY. July 21. U.S. Representative of California's 44th district, Democrat, of San Diego, CA, born in Denver, CO, on July 21, 1941.

BELGIUM: NATIONAL HOLIDAY. July 21. Marks accession of first Belgian king, Leopold I, at independence from Netherlands on this day, 1831.

CLEVELAND, FRANCES FOLSOM: BIRTHDAY. July 21. Wife of Grover Cleveland, 22nd President of the U.S., born at Buffalo, NY, July 21, 1864. Died Oct 29, 1947.

FIRST ROBOT-HOMICIDE: ANNIVERSARY. July 21. The first reported killing of a human by a robot occurred at Jackson, MI. On July 21, 1984, a robot turned and caught a 34-year-old worker between it and a safety bar, crushing him. He died of the injuries on July 26. According to the National Institute for Occupational Health and Safety, it was "the first documented case of a robot-related fatality in the U.S."

GUAM: LIBERATION DAY. July 21. Guam ceded to U.S. by Spain, 1898. U.S. forces returned to Guam on this day, 1944.

HEMINGWAY, ERNEST: BIRTHDAY. July 21. American novelist born at Oak Park, IL, July 21, 1899. Died, Ketchum, ID, July 2, 1961.

INTERNATIONAL PINTO CHAMPIONSHIP SHOW. July 21-25. State Fair Arena, Oklahoma City, OK. Over 500 horses from the U.S. and Canada compete in this showcase of the Pinto breed. Info from: Steve Collier, 1 Santa Fe Plaza, Oklahoma City, OK 73102.

McLUHAN, MARSHALL: BIRTHDAY. July 21. (Herbert) Marshall McLuhan, university professor and author, called "the Canadian sage of the electronic age," was born at Edmonton, Alberta, July 21, 1911. *Understanding Media* and *The Medium is the Massage* (not to be confused with his widely quoted aphorism: "The medium is the message"), among other books, were widely acclaimed for their fresh view of communication. McLuhan is reported as saying: "Most people are alive in an earlier time, but you must be alive in our own time." He died at Toronto, Ontario, Dec 31, 1980.

MOON PHASE: FULL MOON. July 21. Moon enters Full Moon phase at 5:40 a.m., E.S.T.

NATIONAL WOMEN'S HALL OF FAME: DEDICATION ANNIVERSARY. July 21. Seneca Falls, NY. Founded to honor American women whose contributions "have been of the greatest value in the development of their country." Located in community known as "birthplace of women's rights," where first Women's Suffrage Movement convention was held, in 1848. Dedicated with 23 inductees, on July 21, 1979. Earlier National Women's Hall of Fame, honoring "Twenty outstanding women of the Twentieth Century," was dedicated at New York World's Fair, on May 27, 1965.

TENNIS: OPEN CLAY COURTS CHAMPIONSHIP. July 21-28. Info from: Indianapolis Sports Center, Dale Neuberger, 725 W New York St, Indianapolis, IN 46202.

TOWNS, EDOLPHUS: BIRTHDAY. July 21. U.S. Representative of New York's 11th district, Democrat, of Brooklyn, NY, born at Chadbourn, NC, on July 21, 1934.

TRAXLER, BOB: BIRTHDAY. July 21. U.S. Representative of Michigan's 8th district, Democrat, of Bay City, MI, born in Kawkawlin, MI, on July 21, 1931.

WALES: ROYAL WELSH SHOW. July 21-24. Royal Welsh Showground. Builth Wells, Powys. National agricultural show with exhibitions of livestock, agricultural machinery, forestry and horticulture.

COPYRIGHT © 1985 BY WILLIAM D. CHASE and HELEN M. CHASE

JULY 22 — TUESDAY

203rd Day — Remaining, 162

DOLE, ROBERT J: BIRTHDAY. July 22. U.S. Senator from Kansas, Republican, of Russell, KS, born there July 22, 1923.

GOLF: U.S. JUNIOR AMATEUR CHAMPIONSHIP. July 22-26. Muirfield Village Golf Club, Dublin, OH. National championship for amateur golfers age 18 and under. Sponsor: U.S. Golf Assn, Golf House, Far Hills, NJ 07931.

LUCAS COUNTY FAIR. July 22-27. Lucas County Recreation Center, Maumee, OH. Info from: Toledo Area Conv & Visitors Bureau, 218 Huron St, Toledo, OH 43604.

PIED PIPER OF HAMELIN ANNIVERSARY. July 22. According to legend, the German town of Hamelin, plagued with rats, bargained with a piper who promised to, and did, pipe the rats out of town and into the Weser River. Refused payment for his work, the piper then piped the children out of town and into a hole in a hill, never to be seen again. All on July 22, 1376, according to sixteenth century accounts. More recent historians suggest that the event occurred in 1284 when young men of Hamelin left the city on colonizing adventures.

POLAND: NATIONAL HOLIDAY. July 22. National Liberation Day commemorates enactment of Constitution in 1952 and end of war in 1944.

RAT-CATCHERS DAY. July 22. A day to recognize the rat-catchers who labor to exterminate members of the genus, Rattus, disease carrying rodents which infest most of the "civilized" world. Observed on anniversary of the extraordinary fete of the Pied Piper of Hamelin on July 22, 1376 (according to the sixteenth century chronicler, Richard Rowland Verstegen).

ROTH, WILLIAM V, JR: BIRTHDAY. July 22. U.S. Senator from Delaware, Republican, of Wilmington, DE, was born in Great Falls, MT, on July 22, 1921.

SCOTTVILLE CLOWN BAND/ICE CREAM SOCIAL. July 22. White Pine Village, Ludington, MI. Outdoor clown band performance, ice cream social, corn and hot dog roast. Info from: Mason County Historical Society, Connie Newkirk, 1687 S Lakeshore Dr, Ludington, MI 49431.

SPOONER'S DAY. July 22. A day named for the Rev. William Archibald Spooner (born at London, July 22, 1844, Warden of New College, Oxford, 1903-1924, died at Oxford, Aug 29, 1930), whose frequent slips of the tongue led to coinage of the term "spoonerism" to describe them. A day to remember and emulate the scholarly and gentle man whose accidental transpositions gave us: Blushing crow (for crushing blow), tons of soil (for sons of toil), queer old dean (for dear old queen), swell foop (for fell swoop), and half-warmed fish (for half-formed wish).

JULY 23 — WEDNESDAY

204th Day — Remaining, 161

AMERICA'S YOUTH ON PARADE. July 23-27. Notre Dame Univ, South Bend, IN. Thirty-eight national and world championship contests and events in baton twirling and pageantry. Info from: AYOP, Box 266, Janesville, WI 53545.

EGYPT, ARAB REPUBLIC OF: NATIONAL DAY. July 23. Anniversary of the Revolution of July 23, 1952.

FARMER'S FESTIVAL. July 23-27. Farm tours, quilt show, parade, contests and M-46 state champion horseshow tournament. Info from: Chamber of Commerce, John Walsh, 24 S Main St, Pigeon, MI 48755.

JAPAN: WILD HORSE CHASING (SOMA NO UMAOI). July 23-25. Hibarigahara, Haramachi, Fukushima Prefecture, Japan. A thousand horsemen clad in ancient armor compete for possession of three shrine flags shot aloft on Hibarigahara Plain and men in white costumes attempt to catch wild horses coralled by the horsemen.

LEO, THE LION. July 23-Aug 22. In the astronomical/astrological Zodiac, which divides the sun's apparent orbit into twelve segments, the period July 23-Aug 22 is identified, traditionally, as the sun-sign of Leo, the Lion. The ruling planet is the sun.

McCANDLESS, ALFRED A (AL): BIRTHDAY. July 23. U.S. Representative of California's 37th district, Republican, of Bermuda Dunes, CA, born in Brawley, CA on July 23, 1927.

NATIONAL ORGANIZATION OF MOTHERS OF TWINS CLUBS, INC, CONVENTION. July 23-26. Albuquerque, NM. Speakers and workshops on all aspects of the well-being of the entire family unit. Sponsor: Natl Organization of Mothers of Twins Clubs, Inc, 5402 Amberwood Lane, Rockville, MD 20853.

PERSEID METEOR SHOWERS. July 23-Aug 20. Among the best known and most spectacular meteor showers are the Perseids, peaking on Aug 12-13. As many as 50-100 may be seen in a single night. Wish upon a "falling star!"

ST. APOLLINARIS: FEAST DAY. July 23. First bishop of Ravenna, and a martyr, of unknown date. Feast day observed July 23.

SPACE MILESTONE: SOYUZ 37 (USSR). July 23. Launched on July 23, 1980 Cosmonauts Viktor Gorbatko, and the first non-Caucasian in space, Lt. Col. Pham Tuan (Vietnam), docked at Salyut 6 on July 24. Returned to Earth July 31.

JULY 24 — THURSDAY

205th Day — Remaining, 160

BANGOR STATE FAIR. July 24-Aug 2. Info from: Joseph V. Pate, 100 Dutton St, Bangor, ME, 04401.

BOLIVAR, SIMON: BIRTHDAY. July 24. "The Liberator," born July 24, 1783, at Caracas, Venezuela. Commemorated in Venezuela and other Latin American countries. Died Dec 17, 1830, at Santa Marta, Colombia.

BRIGHAM YOUNG ENTERS SALT LAKE VALLEY: ANNIVERSARY. July 24. Utah State Holiday commemorating event on this date in 1847.

CAMPBELL, CARROLL ASHMORE, JR: BIRTHDAY. July 24. U.S. Representative of South Carolina's 4th district, Republican, of Greenville, SC, born at Greenville on July 24, 1940.

COMMONWEALTH GAMES (XIII). July 24-Aug 2. Edinburgh, Scotland. Thirteenth in a series of quadrennial amateur athletic events which began with British Empire Games of 1930, at Hamilton, Ontario. For amateurs from British Commonwealth member countries. Sports include: athletics, badminton, bowling, boxing, cycling, rowing, shooting, swimming and diving, weightlifting and wrestling. Program will also feature canoeing and judo. Info from: Commonwealth Games (Scotland 1986) Ltd, Canning House, 19 Canning St, Edinburgh EH3 8TH.

COPYRIGHT © 1985 BY WILLIAM D. CHASE and HELEN M. CHASE

DAYTON INTERNATIONAL AIRSHOW AND TRADE EXPOSITION. July 24-27. Dayton International Airport, Dayton, OH. The latest in aerospace technology and spectacular demonstration of precision flying. Sponsor: Dayton Chamber of Commerce. Info from: George J Wedekind, Jr., Exec Dir, Room 214, Dayton Internatl Airport, Vandalia, OH 45377.

DETROIT'S BIRTHDAY. July 24. Anniversary of the landing, on July 24, 1701, at the site of Detroit, by Antoine de la Mothe Cadillac, in the service of Louis XIV of France. Fort Pontchartrain du Detroit was first settlement on site.

DUMAS, ALEXANDRE: BIRTHDAY. July 24. French playwright and novelist, born at Villers-Cotterets, July 24, 1802. He is said to have managed the production of more than 1,200 volumes, including *The Count of Monte Cristo* and *The Three Musketeers*. Father of Alexandre Dumas (Dumas Fils), also a novelist and playwright (1824-1895). Dumas died near Dieppe, Dec 5, 1870.

EARHART, AMELIA: BIRTHDAY. July 24. American aviatrix lost on flight from New Guinea to Howland Island, in the Pacific Ocean, July 3, 1937. Born, Atchison, KS July 24, 1898.

FAST OF TAMMUZ. July 24. Jewish holiday. Hebrew calendar date: Tammuz 17, 5746. Shiva Asar B'Tammuz begins at first light of day and commemorates the First Century Roman siege which breached the walls of Jerusalem. Begins a 3-week time of mourning.

HOWARD, JAMES J: BIRTHDAY. July 24. U.S. Representative of New Jersey's 3rd district, Democrat, of Spring Lake Heights, NJ, born in Irvington, NJ, July 24, 1927.

MATHIAS, CHARLES McC., Jr: BIRTHDAY. July 24. U.S. Senator from Maryland, Republican, of Frederick, MD, born in Frederick on July 24, 1922.

MISCELLANEOUS SUN TANNING TOURNAMENT. July 24. Ocean City Boardwalk, Ocean City, NJ. Purpose: "Sun tanning tournament for those who don't normally have an opportunity to compete in sun tanning tournaments i.e. best left arm tan for salesmen and drivers, palest ring finger, best T-shirt tan . . ." Sponsor: City of Ocean City, Mark Soifer, PR Dir, PR Dept, City Hall, Ocean City, NJ 08226.

PIONEER DAY. July 24. Utah. Commemorates first settlement on this day, 1847, by Brigham Young.

RIVERBOAT DAYS AND STATE CATFISH COOKING CONTEST. July 24-26. Newport, AR. Info from: Chamber of Commerce, Box 518, Newport, AR 72112.

WEBER, VIN: BIRTHDAY. July 24. U.S. Representative of Minnesota's 2nd district, Republican, of North Mankato, MN, was born in Slayton, MN, July 24, 1952.

JULY 25 — FRIDAY
206th Day — Remaining, 159

ANTIQUE AUTOMOBILE CLUB OF AMERICA: FALL MEET. July 25-27. Cedar Rapids, IA. Info from: Box 417, Hershey, PA 17033.

BAVARIAN FUN FEST. July 25-27. (Also July 31-Aug 3.) Purpose: The sights, sounds and aromas of the great European Oktoberfest are recreated with plenty of beer, food, dance and song. Sponsor: Bavarian Fun Fest, Jim Guerino, Chrmn, 110 Connelly Blvd, Sharon, PA 16146.

BRICKFEST V. July 25-26. Purpose: To have fun and celebrate Malvern's being the "Brick Capital of the World." Sponsor: Chamber of Commerce, 213 W Third, Malvern, AR 72104.

July 1986	S	M	T	W	T	F	S
			1	2	3	4	5
	6	7	8	9	10	11	12
	13	14	15	16	17	18	19
	20	21	22	23	24	25	26
	27	28	29	30	31		

DING DONG DAYS FESTIVAL. July 25-28. Purpose: Civic promotion and entertainment. Name is derived from 1930's song "I'm a Ding Dong Daddy from Dumas." Info from: Chamber of Commerce, Dumas, AR 71639.

DODGE CITY DAYS. July 25-Aug 2. Western celebration with parades, P.R.C.A. rodeo, street dance, cookouts and 4-H fair. Info from: Chamber of Commerce, Box 939, Dodge City, KS 67801.

FAMILY BLUEGRASS MUSIC WEEKEND. July 25-27. Sam A. Baker State Park, Patterson, MO. Info from: Missouri Dept of Natural Resources, Box 176, Jefferson City, MO 65102.

FIRST AIRPLANE CROSSING OF ENGLISH CHANNEL: ANNIVERSARY. July 25. On Sunday, July 25, 1909, Louis Bleriot (q.v.), after asking from the cockpit "Where is England?" took off from Les Baraques (near Calais) France, and landed on English soil at Northfall Meadow, near Dover, where he was greeted first by English police and customs officers. This, the world's first international overseas airplane flight, was accomplished in a 28-horsepower monoplane with wing span of 23 feet. Bleriot was born at Cambrai, France, July 1, 1872.

GILROY GARLIC FESTIVAL. July 25-27. Midsummer harvest celebration in the "Garlic Capital of the World." Great garlic recipe contest/cook-off. 100 food booths with every ethnic background represented. Continuous entertainment on four stages, arts, crafts and garlic queen pageant. Sponsor: Gilroy Garlic Festival Assn, Inc, Box 2311, Gilroy, CA 95021.

HARRISON, ANNA SYMMES: BIRTHDAY. July 25. Wife of William Henry Harrison, 9th President of the U.S., born at Morristown, NJ, July 25, 1775. Died Feb 25, 1864.

HOLLAND FESTIVAL. July 25-26. Cedar Grove, WI. Purpose: Celebration of Dutch heritage with street scrubbing, Dutch costumes, parade and pageant. Last Friday and Saturday of July. Sponsor: Holland Guild Gezelschap, Erwin Claussen, Pres, Cedar Grove, WI 53013.

LEWIS AND CLARK EXPEDITION FESTIVAL. July 25-27. Cut Bank, Montana. Outdoor pageant depicting the experiences of the famed explorers. Parade, horse shows, art auction and barbeque. Info from: Travel Montana, 1424 9th Ave, Helena, MT 59620.

LOIZA ALDEA FIESTA. July 25-28. Best known of Puerto Rico's patron saint festivities. Villagers of Loiza Aldea, 20 miles east of San Juan, don devil masks and colorful costumes to participate in variety of traditional activities.

NORTHERN IRELAND: INTERNATIONAL ULSTER MOTOR RALLY. July 25-26. Start and finish at Belfast, County Antrim. The qualifying round of the British Open International Championship starts at 6 p.m., Friday and finishes at 5:30 p.m., Saturday.

PACIFIC NORTHWEST ARTS AND CRAFTS FAIR. July 25-27. Bellevue Square, Bellevue, WA. Juried show representing over 400 artisans plus performing arts. Sponsor: Pacific Northwest Arts & Crafts Assn, 301 Bellevue Sq, Bellevue, WA 98004.

PUERTO RICO: CONSTITUTION DAY. July 25. Also called Commonwealth Day or Occupation Day. Commemorates proclamation of constitution on July 25, 1952.

ST. JOHN LOYALIST DAYS. July 25-31. St. John, New Brunswick, Canada. Costume parades, music, entertainment and the re-enactment of the landing of the Loyalists.

ST. LOUIS STRASSENFEST. July 25-27. Features bratwurst, pretzels, German food and drink, Oom-pa-pa bands, dancing and cultural events. Info from: St. Louis Conv & Visitors Bureau, 10 S Broadway, Suite 300, St. Louis, MO 63102.

STAMP EXPO '86/CALIFORNIA. July 25-27. Sheraton Anaheim Hotel, Anaheim, CA. Sponsor: Internatl Stamp Collectors Society, Box 854, Van Nuys, CA 91408.

TEST-TUBE BABY ANNIVERSARY. July 25. Anniversary of the birth of Louise Brown, on this date in 1978, at Oldham, England. First documented birth of a baby conceived outside

COPYRIGHT © 1985 BY WILLIAM D. CHASE and HELEN M. CHASE

the body of a woman. Parents: Gilbert John and Lesley Brown, of Bristol, England. Physicians: Patrick Christopher Steptoe and Robert Geoffrey Edwards.

WORLD'S LARGEST GARAGE SALE. July 25-27. Purpose: To attract consumers to the Washington Road Business Area of Mt. Lebanon, PA. (Always last full weekend in July.). Info from: World's Largest Garage Sale, Box 11631, Mt. Lebanon, PA 15228.

JULY 26 — SATURDAY
207th Day — Remaining, 158

ANNIE OAKLEY DAYS. July 26-27. Greenville, OH. Purpose: To keep alive the memory of Annie Oakley. Sponsor: Annie Oakley Days Committee, Inc, Mrs Toni Seiler, Dir, Garst Museum, 205 N Broadway, Greenville, OH 45331.

ANTIQUE AND CLASSIC BOAT RENDEZVOUS. July 26. Purpose: Pre-1940 power and sailing yachts on view for Seaport visitors. Mystic River parade. Info from: Public Affairs Office, Mystic Seaport, Mystic, CT 06355.

BANJO PICKIN' CONTEST. July 26. Amphitheatre, Raystown Lake, Hesston, PA. Purpose: Amateur Banjo Pickin' competition open to all. Info from: Huntingdon County Tourist Promotion Agency, 508 Penn St, Huntingdon, PA 16652.

CLINTON, GEORGE: BIRTHDAY. July 26. Fourth vice-president of the U.S. (1805-1812) born, Little Britain, NY, July 26, 1739. Died, Washington, DC, Apr 20, 1812.

CUBA: NATIONAL HOLIDAY. July 26. Anniversary of 1953 beginning of Fidel Castro's revolutionary "26th of July Movement."

ESPERANTO: ANNIVERSARY OF PUBLICATION OF FIRST ESPERANTO BOOK. July 26. Purpose: To commemorate the anniversary of the publication of Dr. Zamenhof's first textbook about the International Language, Esperanto, July 26, 1887. Sponsor: Meadpenn Esperanto Library, RFD 6, Box 198, Meadville, PA 16335.

HUXLEY, ALDOUS: BIRTH ANNIVERSARY. July 26. English author, satirist, mystic and philosopher, Aldous Leonard Huxley, was born at Godalming, Surrey, on July 26, 1894. Best known of his works are: *Brave New World, Crome Yellow* and *Point Counter Point.* Huxley died at Los Angeles, CA, on Nov 22, 1963.

LIBERIA: NATIONAL HOLIDAY. July 26. Independence Day. Became republic on this day, 1847, under aegis of the U.S. societies for repatriating Negroes in Africa.

MALDIVES: NATIONAL DAY. July 26. National holiday is observed in Maldives.

MONTANA STATE FIDDLERS CHAMPIONSHIPS. July 26-27. Polson, Montana. Annual competition for fiddlers of all ages. Info from: Travel Montana, 1424 9th Ave, Helena, MT 59620.

NEW YORK RATIFICATION DAY. July 26. Eleventh State to ratify constitution, on this day in 1788.

NORTH DAKOTA PRISON RODEO. July 26-27. North Dakota State Penitentiary Bismarck, ND. A rodeo in which all contestants are inmates at the prison. Unique events, talented clowns, country music bands and much more excitement. Info from: Winston Satran, ND State Penitentiary, Box 1497, Bismarck, ND 58502.

QUADLINGS OF OZ CONVENTION. July 26. Fort Worth, TX. Purpose: To celebrate Dorothy's meeting with Glinda who told her how the magic shoes would take her home to Kansas. Sponsor: The Internatl Wizard of Oz Club, Inc, Fred M. Meyer, Secy, 220 N 11th St, Escanaba, MI 49829.

SAWDUST FESTIVAL AND STATEWIDE LOGGERS CONTEST. July 26-27. Payson, AZ. A contest between men and women of the logging industry throughout the U.S. Info from: Payson Chamber, Drawer A, Payson, AZ 85541.

SHAW, GEORGE BERNARD: BIRTHDAY. July 26. Irish playwright, essayist, vegetarian, socialist, antivivisectionist and, he said, ". . . one of the hundred best playwrights in the world." Born at Dublin on July 26, 1856. Died at Ayot St. Lawrence, England, Nov 2, 1950.

SPACE MILESTONE: APOLLO 15 (US). July 26. Launched on July 26, 1971, Astronauts David R. Scott and James B. Irwin landed on moon (Lunar Module "Falcon") while Alfred M. Worden piloted Command Module "Endeavor." Rover 1, a 4-wheel vehicle, was used for further exploration. Departed Moon Aug 2, after nearly 3 days. Pacific landing Aug. 7. July 26, 1971.

VIRGINIA SCOTTISH GAMES. July 26-27. Bagpipes, highland dance, drumming, fiddling, celtic harp competition, animal trials and Scottish athletic games competition. Scottish food and gifts are sold. Info from: Alexandria Tourist Council, 221 King St, Alexandria, VA 22314.

WORLD CONGRESS OF ESPERANTO (Universala Kongreso DeEsperanto). July 26-Aug 2. Beijing, Peoples Republic of China. Purpose: Congress of speakers of the international language Esperanto from all countries of the world. Lectures, seminars, entertainment. Sponsor: Universala Esperanto-Assoc, c/o ELNA, Box 1129, El Cerrito, CA 94530.

JULY 27 — SUNDAY
208th Day — Remaining, 157

ATLANTIC TELEGRAPH CABLE ANNIVERSARY. July 27. Cable-laying successfully completed on this day, 1866.

BARBOSA, JOSE: BIRTHDAY. July 27. Puerto Rico. Celebrates birth on this day, 1857, of Puerto Rican physician and patriot, Jose Celso Barbosa.

BYRON, BEVERLY BARTON BUTCHER: BIRTHDAY. July 27. U.S. Representative of Maryland's 6th district, Democrat, of Frederick, MD, was born in Baltimore, MD, on July 27, 1932.

CURING BARN PARTY. July 27. A recreation of the nineteenth century activity of "barning tobacco" during the harvest season. Info from: Duke Homestead State Historic Site, 2828 Duke Homestead Rd, Durham, NC 27705.

DOWDY, WAYNE: BIRTHDAY. July 27. U.S. Representative of Mississippi's 4th district, Democrat, of Summit, MS, born in Fitzgerald, GA, on July 27, 1943.

DUMAS, ALEXANDRE (DUMAS FILS): BIRTHDAY. July 27. French novelist and playwright, as was his father. Author of *La Dame aux camelias.* Dumas Fils was born at Paris, July 27, 1824 and died at Marly-le-Roi on Nov 27, 1895.

HANNA'S TOWN FOLK-FESTIVAL. July 27. Greensburg, PA. Pioneer crafts, outdoor antique show, music, dancers, fiddlers and frontier games. Info from: Westmoreland County Historical Society, Greensburg, PA 15601.

KOREAN WAR ARMISTICE. July 27. Armistice agreement ending war which had lasted three years and 32 days, was signed at Panmunjom, Korea, July 27, 1953 (July 26, U.S. time), by U.S. and North Korean delegates. Both sides claimed victory at conclusion of 2 years, 17 days of truce negotiations.

COPYRIGHT © 1985 BY WILLIAM D. CHASE and HELEN M. CHASE

MIDSUMMER: A CELEBRATION OF THE ARTS. July 27. Hillandale Park. Purpose: To provide a showcase of talent in Western Virginia to highlight the uniqueness of the history, nature and arts of the Shenandoah Valley. Arts and crafts, drama, dance and music. Info from: Dept of Parks and Recreation, Harrisonburg, VA 22801.

PROFESSIONAL SECRETARIES INTERNATIONAL: ANNUAL CONVENTION. July 27-Aug 1. Wyndham Franklin Plaza, Philadelphia, PA. Info from: Professional Secretaries Internatl, Audrey Forman CPS, Conv Mgr, 301 E Armour Blvd, Kansas City, MO 64111.

JULY 28 — MONDAY

209th Day — Remaining, 156

BOSCO, DOUGLAS H: BIRTHDAY. July 28. U.S. Representative of California's 1st district, Democrat, of Occidental, CA, was born in New York on July 28, 1946.

BRADLEY, BILL: BIRTHDAY. July 28. U.S. Senator from New Jersey, Democrat, of Denville, NJ, born in Crystal City, MO, on July 28, 1943.

HEYWARD, THOMAS: BIRTHDAY. July 28. American Revolutionary soldier, signer of the Declaration of Independence, born July 28, 1746. Died Mar 6, 1809.

HURRICANE SUPPLICATION DAY. July 28. Virgin Islands. Fourth Monday of July. Legal holiday. Population attends churches to pray for protection from hurricanes.

KOOLA KOALA BIRTHDAY ANNIVERSARY. July 28. Purpose: To celebrate first magical Koala and all cuddly Koalas worldwide. "Legend says make a wish and place it in Koalas magic pouch and it will come true." Info from: Martha Rutty, Box 687, Chesterland, OH 44026.

MOON PHASE: LAST QUARTER. July 28. Moon enters Last Quarter phase at 10:34 a.m., E.S.T.

ONASSIS, JACQUELINE LEE BOUVIER KENNEDY: BIRTHDAY. July 28. Widow of John Fitzgerald Kennedy, 35th President of the U.S., born at Southampton, NY, July 28, 1929. Later married (Oct 20, 1968) Aristotle Socrates Onassis who died Mar 15, 1975.

PERU; NATIONAL INDEPENDENCE DAYS. July 28-30. At defeat of Spain by Simon Bolivar, Peru became independent, 1824.

SHUMWAY, NORMAN D: BIRTHDAY. July 28. U.S. Representative of California's 14th district, Republican of Stockton, CA, born in Phoenix, AZ on July 28, 1934.

SINGING TELEGRAM BIRTHDAY. July 28. Anniversary of the first singing telegram, said to have been delivered to singer Rudy Vallee on his 32nd birthday, July 28, 1933. Early singing telegrams often were delivered in person by uniformed messengers on bicycle. Later they were usually sung by telephone.

SPACE MILESTONE: RANGER 7 (US). July 28. Televised back to Earth 4,308 close-up photographs of moon. Launched July 28, 1964.

SPACE MILESTONE: SKYLAB 3 (US). July 28. Launched on July 28, 1973, Alan L. Bean, Owen K. Garriott, Jack R. Lousma started record 59-day mission to test man's space flight endurance. Pacific splashdown Sept 25.

TERRY FOX DAY. July 28. Birthday of Terrence Stanley Fox, Canadian youth who captured the hearts and admiration of millions during his brief life. Stricken with cancer, requiring amputation of the athlete's right leg at age 18, Fox determined to devote his life to a fight against the disease. His "Marathon of Hope," a planned 5,200 mile run westward across Canada, started Apr 12, 1980 at St. John's, Newfoundland, and continued 3,328 miles to Thunder Bay, Ontario, Sept 1, 1980 when he was forced by spread of the disease to stop. During the run (on an artificial leg) he raised $24 million for cancer research and inspired millions with his courage. Terry Fox was born at Winnipeg, Manitoba, July 28, 1958, and died at New Westminster (near Vancouver), British Columbia, June 28, 1981.

VETERANS BONUS ARMY EVICTION: ANNIVERSARY. July 28. Some 15,000 unemployed veterans of World War I marched on Washington, DC, in the summer of 1932, demanding payment of a war bonus. After two months' encampment in Washington's Anacostia Flats, eviction of the bonus marchers by the U.S. Army was ordered by President Herbert Hoover. Under the leadership of General Douglas MacArthur, Major Dwight D. Eisenhower and Major George S. Patton, Jr. (among others), cavalry, tanks and infantry attacked. Fixed bayonets, tear gas and the burning of the veterans' tents hastened the end of the confrontation. One death was reported.

JULY 29th — TUESDAY

210th Day — Remaining, 155

DOLE, ELIZABETH HANFORD: BIRTHDAY. July 29. Elizabeth Hanford Dole, U.S. Secretary of Transportation (sworn in on Feb 7, 1983) was born at Salisbury, NC, on July 29, 1936.

KASSEBAUM, NANCY LANDON: BIRTHDAY. July 29. U.S. Senator from Kansas, Republican, of Wichita, KS, born in Topeka, KS, on July 29, 1932.

MUSSOLINI, BENITO: BIRTH ANNIVERSARY. July 29. The anniversary of birth of Italian Fascist leader, at Dovia Italy, July 29, 1883. Self-styled "Il Duce" (the leader), Mussolini governed Italy, first as prime minister and later as absolute dictator, 1922-1943. Reportedly, under his regime "the trains ran on time." It was Mussolini who said: "War alone . . . puts the stamp of nobility upon the peoples who have the courage to face it." But military defeat of Italy in World War II was Mussolini's downfall. Repudiated and arrested by the Italian government, he was temporarily rescued by German paratroops in 1943. Later, as they attempted to flee in disguise to Switzerland, he and his mistress, Clara Petacci, were shot and killed by Italian partisans near Lake Como, Apr 28, 1945.

NORWAY: OLSOK EVE. July 29. Norway. Commemorates Norway's Viking King St. Olav, who fell in battle at Stiklestad near Trondheim, July 29, 1030. Bonfires, historical pageants.

PERU: NATIONAL HOLIDAY. July 29. Public holiday in Peru celebrated with a military parade and a gala horse race in Monterrico Race Track.

RAIN DAY IN WAYNESBURG, PENNSYLVANIA. July 29. Legend has it that rain will fall in Waynesburg, PA, on July 29th as it has most years for the last century, according to local records in this community which was laid out in 1796 and incorporated in 1816.

ROOSEVELT, ALICE HATHAWAY LEE: BIRTHDAY. July 29. First wife of Theodore Roosevelt, 26th President of the U.S., born at Chestnut Hill, MA, July 29, 1861. Died Feb 14, 1884.

SARANAC LAKE ANTIQUE SHOW AND SALE. July 29-31. Info from: Nancy Depuy, Auxiliary of the General Hospital of Saranac Lake, Lake Colby Dr, Saranac Lake, NY 12983.

TARKINGTON, BOOTH: BIRTHDAY. July 29. American novelist, born Indianapolis July 29, 1869. Died there, May 19, 1946.

ZAMBIA: MUTOMBOKO CEREMONY. July 29. Ancient annual ceremony to honor Senior Chief, the traditional leader of the Luunda peoples of the Luapula Province in north-central Zambia. Joyous communal party and cultural get-together.

July 1986

S	M	T	W	T	F	S
		1	2	3	4	5
6	7	8	9	10	11	12
13	14	15	16	17	18	19
20	21	22	23	24	25	26
27	28	29	30	31		

COPYRIGHT © 1985 BY WILLIAM D. CHASE and HELEN M. CHASE

JULY 30 — WEDNESDAY
211th Day — Remaining, 154

BRONTE, EMILY: BIRTHDAY. July 30. English novelist, born July 30, 1818. Died Dec 19, 1848.

CHINCOTEAGUE PONY PENNING. July 30-31. Chincoteague Island, VA. Purpose: To round up the 150 wild ponies living on Assateague Island and swim them across the inlet to Chincoteague where about 40 of them are sold. Info from: Chamber of Commerce, Ms Nicki West, Box 258, Chincoteague, VA 23336.

FORD, HENRY: BIRTHDAY. July 30. Automotive pioneer, born in Dearborn Twp, MI, July 30, 1863, remembered especially for developing an assembly line production system, introducing a $5.00-a-day wage for automotive workers, and for his statement: "History is bunk." Ford died at Dearborn, Apr 7, 1947.

HOFFA, JIMMIE: DISAPPEARANCE ANNIVERSARY. July 30. Former Teamsters Union leader, 62-year-old James Riddle Hoffa, was last seen July 30, 1975, outside a restaurant in Bloomfield Twp, near Detroit, MI. His 13-year federal prison sentence had been commuted by former President Richard M. Nixon, in 1971. On Dec 8, 1982, seven years and 131 days after his disappearance, an Oakland County judge declared Hoffa officially dead, as of July 30, 1982.

SCHROEDER, PATRICIA: BIRTHDAY. July 30. U.S. Representative of Colorado's 1st district, Democrat, of Denver, CO, was born at Portland, OR, July 30, 1940.

SCOTLAND: ABERDEEN INTERNATIONAL YOUTH FESTIVAL. July 30-Aug 9. University of Aberdeen, Elphinstone Rd, Aberdeen, Grampian. Annual festival of youth orchestras, choirs, bands and dance groups.

VANUATU: NATIONAL DAY. July 30. Vanuatu became an independent republic on July 30, 1980, and observes its national holiday today.

VEBLEN, THORSTEIN: BIRTHDAY. July 30. American economist, born Valders, WI, July 30, 1857. Died, Menlo Park, CA, Aug 3, 1929. "Conspicuous consumption," he wrote in *The Theory of the Leisure Class*, "of valuable goods is a means of reputability to the gentleman of leisure."

JULY 31 — THURSDAY
212th Day — Remaining, 153

BENNETT, WILLIAM J: BIRTHDAY. July 31. William J. Bennett, U.S. Secretary of Education (confirmed by Senate on Feb 6, 1985) was born at Brooklyn, NY, on July 31, 1943.

CANADA NATIONAL UKRAINIAN FESTIVAL. July 31-Aug 3. Purpose: To further enrich the Canadian mosaic by promoting the art and culture of the Ukrainian people who settled in Canada by carrying on without pecuniary gain. Info from: Canada's National Ukrainian Festival, 119 Main St S, Dauphin, Manitoba, Canada R7N 1K4.

DAVIS, ROBERT W: BIRTHDAY. July 31. U.S. Representative of Michigan's 11th district, Republican, of Gaylord, MI, was born in Marquette, MI, on July 31, 1932.

FEAST OF ST. IGNATIUS OF LOYOLA. July 31. 1491-1556. Founder of the Society of Jesus and Jesuits. Canonized in 1622.

FESTIVAL OF THE TARTANS. July 31-Aug 3. New Glasgow, Nova Scotia. Major Scottish event featuring Highland dancing, piping, drumming, sports and Scottish concert. Info from: Dept of Tourism, Box 456, Halifax, NS B3J 2R5.

FIRST U.S. PATENT ANNIVERSARY. July 31. Samuel Hopkins of Vermont received the first U.S. government patent, issued July 31, 1790, and signed by George Washington and Thomas Jefferson. Patent was for a process for manufacturing potash.

FRENZEL, BILL: BIRTHDAY. July 31. U.S. Representative of Minnesota's 3rd district, Republican, of Golden Valley, MN, born in St. Paul, MN, July 31, 1928.

HUNTER COUNTRY MUSIC FESTIVAL. July 31-Aug 3. Four straight days with the "country's top" country stars. Info from: Don Conover, Bridge St, Hunter, NY 12442.

KENNEDY INTERNATIONAL AIRPORT ANNIVERSARY. July 31. New York's International Airport at Idlewild Field was dedicated by President Harry S Truman on July 31, 1948. It was later renamed John F. Kennedy International Airport.

PENNSYLVANIA DESIGNER CRAFTSMEN STATE FAIR. July 31-Aug 3. Franklin and Marshall College, Lancaster, PA. Info from: Pennsylvania Designer-Craftsmen, Box 206, Bedford, PA 15522.

TEXAS FOLKLIFE FESTIVAL. July 31-Aug 3. Purpose: To provide historic understanding of the crafts, art, food, music and cultures representing the heritages of more than 30 different cultural and ethnic groups who helped settle and develop the state of Texas. Sponsor: Institute of Texan Cultures, Box 1226, San Antonio, TX 78294.

WISCONSIN STATE FAIR. July 31-Aug 10. State Fair Park, Milwaukee, WI. Info from: Wisconsin State Fair Park, Visitor Info, West Allis, WI 53214.

COPYRIGHT © 1985 BY WILLIAM D. CHASE and HELEN M. CHASE

August.

AUGUST 1 — FRIDAY

213th Day — Remaining, 152

AUSTIN AQUA FESTIVAL. Aug 1-10. Parades, pageants and water-related activities. Lighted night water parade and fireworks. Info from: Austin Aqua Festival, Box 1967, Austin, TX 78767.

BEAUTY QUEEN WEEK. Aug 1-7. Purpose: To call local and national attention to promotion of beauty queens and their value to the economy. (First week in August.) Sponsor: Richard R. Falk Associates, Richard R. Falk, Chief Judge, 147 W 42nd St, New York, NY 10036.

BOOM DAYS CELEBRATION. Aug 1-3. Purpose: Celebration of the mining of the early years in Leadville. Held in connection with Leadville's International Championship Burro Race. Info from: Chamber of Commerce, Elaine Kochevar, Exec Dir, Box 861, Leadville, CO 80461.

BOUCHER, FREDERICK C. (RICK): BIRTHDAY. Aug 1. U.S. Representative of Virginia's 9th district, Democrat, of Abingdon, VA, was born in Washington County, VA, Aug 1, 1946.

D'AMATO, ALFONSE M: BIRTHDAY. Aug 1. U.S. Senator from New York, Republican, of Island Park, NY, born in Brooklyn, NY, Aug 1, 1937.

ENGLAND: SIDMOUTH INTERNATIONAL FOLKLORE FESTIVAL. Aug 1-8. Sidmouth, Devon. The 32nd Sidmouth International Folklore Festival features singing, dancing, workshops and events for children.

EXPERIMENTAL AIRCRAFT ASSOCIATION INTERNATIONAL FLY-IN. Aug 1-8. "The world's most spectacular and significant aviation event." Thousands of aircraft on display, including warbirds, antiques, homebuilts and ultralights. Info from: EAA, Wittman Airfield, Oshkosh, WI 54903.

GOLF: CURTIS CUP MATCH. Aug 1-2. Prairie Dunes Country Club, Hutchinson, KS. International match between ten women amateur golfers from U.S. against ten women amateur golfers from Great Britain and Ireland. Sponsors: Royal & Ancient Golf Club of St. Andrews, Scotland; and U.S. Golf Assn, Golf House, Far Hills, NJ 07931.

KEY, FRANCIS SCOTT: BIRTHDAY. Aug 1. American attorney, social worker, poet and author of the U.S. National Anthem. While on a legal mission, Key was detained on shipboard off Baltimore, during the British bombardment of Fort McHenry on the night of Sept 13-14, 1814. Thrilled to see the American flag still flying over the fort at daybreak, Key wrote the poem, "The Star Spangled Banner." Printed in the *Baltimore American* Sept 21, 1814, it was soon popularly sung to the music of an old English tune, "Anacreon in Heaven." It did not become the official U.S. National Anthem until 117 years later when, on Mar 3, 1931, Pres. Herbert Hoover signed into law an Act for that purpose. Key was born at Frederick County, MD, Aug 1, 1779, and died at Baltimore on Jan 11, 1843.

LOEFFLER, TOM: BIRTHDAY. Aug 1. U.S. Representative of Texas' 21st district, Republican, of Hunt, TX, born at Fredericksburg, TX, Aug 1, 1946.

MELVILLE, HERMAN: BIRTHDAY. Aug 1. American author, best known for his novel *Moby Dick*, born at New York City, Aug 1, 1819. Died Sept 28, 1891.

MUNCHKINS OF OZ CONVENTION. Aug 1-3. Wilmington, DE. Purpose: To celebrate Dorothy's arrival over the rainbow in Oz. Sponsor: The International Wizard of Oz Club, Inc, Fred M. Meyer, Secy, 220 N 11th St, Escanaba, MI 49829.

NATIONAL CLOWN WEEK. Aug 1-7. Purpose: To call public attention to the charitable activities of clowns and the wholesome entertainment they provide. Sponsor: Clowns of America, Inc, Bill Bailey, Natl Chrmn, 200 Powelton Ave, Woodlynne, NJ 08107.

NATIONAL ROLLER SKATING CHAMPIONSHIPS. Aug 1-14. Indianapolis, IN. Purpose: To name age and ability division champions in artistic and speed roller sports events. 2,500 amateur skaters on national level with top placements advancing to world competition. Sponsor: U.S. Amateur Confederation of Roller Skating, Box 83067, Lincoln, NE 68501.

OLD LINCOLN COUNTY DAYS. Aug 1-3. Lincoln, NM. Purpose: To celebrate the last escape of Billy The Kid from the Old Lincoln County Courthouse and the cultural heritage of Lincoln County. Info from: Lincoln Pageant & Festivals Corp, Box 92, Lincoln, NM 88338.

PARAPROFESSIONAL'S DAY OF RECOGNITION. Aug 1. Purpose: To recognize all those professionals who are not secretaries, clerks or executives, but fill an important slot in business. Info from: Susan Tobias, Rt 2 Box 133, Plattsburgh, NY 12901.

PEOPLE'S REPUBLIC OF CHINA: ARMY DAY. Aug 1. Shanghai. Anniversary of founding of Chinese People's Liberation Army. Info from: Shanghai Travel & Tourism Administration, 14 Zhongshan Road (E.1), Shanghai.

PRO FOOTBALL HALL OF FAME FESTIVAL. Aug 1-2. Canton, OH. Purpose: To honor NFL professional football greats. Sponsor: Greater Canton Chamber of Commerce, Janice C Meyer, Festival Mgr, Box 1044, Canton, OH 44701.

SOURWOOD FESTIVAL. Aug 1-2. Black Mountain, NC. Purpose: A time to relax and appreciate the beauty of our valley and our way of life in the mountains. Sponsor: Chamber of Commerce, 201 E State St, Black Mountain, NC 28711.

SQUARE FAIR. Aug 1-3. Town Square Park, Lima, OH. Multi-arts festival featuring traditional and ethnic performing arts, ethnic foods, demonstrating and exhibiting artists. Sponsor: Council for Arts of Greater Lima, Sandra Klaver, Box 1124, Lima, OH 45802.

SWEET PEA FESTIVAL. Aug 1-3. Bozeman, Montana. Juried art show, flower show and workshops. Info from: Travel Montana, 1424 9th Ave, Helena, MT 59620.

SWITZERLAND: NATIONAL DAY. Aug 1. Anniversary of founding of Swiss Confederation. Commemorates pact made in 1291. Parades, patriotic gatherings, bonfires and fireworks. Young citizens' coming-of-age ceremonies. Observed since 600th anniversary of Swiss Confederation was celebrated in 1891.

TOMATO FESTIVAL. Aug 1-3. Purpose: A festival with special historic flavor, including dancing, cooking, music, historic reenactments, exhibits and picnics in an atmosphere of the 1800's. Sponsor: Bicentennial Commission of Lynchburg, Box 1132, Lynchburg, VA 24505.

August 1986

S	M	T	W	T	F	S
					1	2
3	4	5	6	7	8	9
10	11	12	13	14	15	16
17	18	19	20	21	22	23
24	25	26	27	28	29	30
31						

COPYRIGHT © 1985 BY WILLIAM D. CHASE and HELEN M. CHASE

UNITED STATES CUSTOMS ANNIVERSARY. Aug 1. "The first U.S. customs officers began to collect the revenue and enforce the Tariff Act of July 4, 1789 on Aug 1, 1789. Since then, the customhouse and the customs officer have stood as symbols of national pride and sovereignty at ports of entry along the land and sea borders of our country." (From Presidential Proclamation 4306.)

U.S. NATIONAL HOT AIR BALLOON CHAMPIONSHIP. Aug 1-9. Purpose: To host the U.S. National Hot Air Balloon Championship and determine the National Champion to fly at world event. Info from: Natl Balloon Champ, Ltd, Box 346, Indianola, IA 50125.

WHITE RIVER PARK STATE GAMES. Aug 1-3. Indianapolis, IN. "Largest multi-sport event in Indiana for amateur athletes." Info from: Susan Polakoff, PR Dir, Indiana Sports Corp, 251 N Illinois, Suite 910, Indianapolis, IN 46204.

WOODMEN'S SHOW. Aug 1-2. Purpose: Display of lumbering and logging equipment with contests in cross cut sawing, log rolling, log chopping, tree felling and chain sawing. Sponsor: Penn-York Lumber's Assn, 12 West Street, Galeton, PA 16922.

AUGUST 2 — SATURDAY
214th Day — Remaining, 151

ALBERT EINSTEIN'S ATOMIC BOMB LETTER: ANNIVERSARY. Aug 2. Albert Einstein, world famous scientist, a refugee from Nazi Germany, wrote a letter to U.S. President Franklin D. Roosevelt, Aug 2, 1939, first mentioning a possible "new phenomenon . . . chain reactions . . . vast amounts of power" and "the construction of bombs." "A single bomb of this type," he wrote, "carried by boat and exploded in a port, might very well destroy the whole port together with some of the surrounding territory." An historic letter which marked the beginning of atomic weaponry. Six years and four days later, Aug 6, 1945, the Japanese port of Hiroshima was destroyed by the first atomic bombing of a populated place.

DE LUGO, RON: BIRTHDAY. Aug 2. Virgin Islands Delegate to 99th Congress, born on Aug 2, 1930.

DECLARATION OF INDEPENDENCE: SIGNING ANNIVERSARY. Aug 2. Philadelphia. "Contrary to widespread misconception, the 56 signers did not sign as a group and did not do so on July 4, 1776. The official event occurred on August 2, 1776, when 50 men probably took part. Later that year, five more apparently signed separately and one added his name in a subsequent year." (From "Signers of the Declaration . . .," U.S. Dept of the Interior, 1975.)

EGG SHOW AND SALE. Aug 2-3. Marriott Hotel, Gaithersburg, MD. Purpose: To further public awareness of egg art and to provide a medium for artisans to share their talents. Sponsor: Maryland Eggery Artists, Alice Doll, Dir, 4588 Montgomery Rd, Ellicott City, MD 21043.

EUSTIS AMATEUR SLALOM SKI CHAMPIONSHIP. Aug 2. Eustis, FL. Info from: Chamber of Commerce, Box 1210, Eustis, FL 32726.

FOLK ARTS FESTIVAL. Aug 2-3. Princess Anne Park, Virginia Beach, VA. Info from: City of Virginia Beach, Office of Public Info, Municipal Ctr, Virginia Beach, VA 23456.

GAINES CENTRAL REGIONAL DOG OBEDIENCE CHAMPIONSHIP. Aug 2-3. Birmingham, AL. Purpose: To select the best dog/handler team in standard obedience classes including novice, open and super dog, the top category representing the best-trained dog in the region. Sponsor: Gaines Dog Care Center, A. S. Willett, Red Oak Plaza, 70 W Red Oak Lane, White Plains, NY 10604.

INTERNATIONAL FOOD FESTIVAL. Aug 2-4. George Street, Prince George, British Columbia. Purpose: To introduce and encourage enjoyment of the special foods of various ethnic groups. Sponsor: Prince George Folkfest-Multicultural Heritage Society, Box 2469, Prince George, BC, Canada V2N 2S6.

LAXALT, PAUL: BIRTHDAY. Aug 2. U.S. Senator from Nevada, Republican, of Carson City, NV, born in Reno, NV on Aug 2, 1922.

L'ENFANT, PIERRE CHARLES: BIRTHDAY. Aug 2. The architect, engineer and revolutionary war officer who designed the plan for the city of Washington, DC, Pierre Charles L'Enfant was born at Paris on Aug 2, 1754. He died in Prince Georges County, MD, on June 14, 1825.

NATIONAL HOBO CONVENTION. Aug 2. Britt, Iowa. Parade and Mulligan Stew. Coronation of King and Queen of Hoboes. Annually, the first Saturday of August. Info from: Britt Chamber of Commerce, Britt, IA 50423.

NORTHERN MAINE FAIR. Aug 2-10. Info from: Robert H. Flewelling, Box 804, Presque Isle, ME 04769.

NOTTINGHAM COUNTRY FAIR. Aug 2-3. Purpose: Crafts, contests, agricultural exhibits and demonstrations. Info from: Chester County Parks & Recreation, 235 W Market St, West Chester, PA 19382.

OLD BEDFORD VILLAGE BLUEGRASS FESTIVAL. Aug 2-3. Info from: Old Bedford Village, Patricia J. Mauk, PR Dir, Bedford, PA 15522.

SAILING: COWES WEEK. Aug 2-10. Cowes, Isle of Wight. Yachting festival covering all classes of yacht racing.

ST. ELIAS DAY (ILLINDEN). Aug 2. Most sacred, honored and celebrated day of the Macedonian people. Anniversary of the uprising, on Aug 2, 1903, of Macedonians against Turkey. Turkish reprisals against the insurgents were ruthless, including the destruction of 105 villages and the execution of more than 1,700 noncombatants.

SHAKER FESTIVAL AND FLEA MARKET. Aug 2. Shaker Museum complex, Old Chatham, NY. Info from: Shaker Festival & Flea Market, Old Chatham, NY 12136.

TAWAS BAY WATERFRONT ART SHOW. Aug 2-3. Amateur and professional artists and craftsmen exhibit. Info from: Tawas Bay Art Council, 1115 Bay Dr, Tawas City, MI 48763.

TWINS DAY FESTIVAL. Aug 2-3. Glenn Chamberlin Park, Twinsburg, OH. Purpose: A festival for twins, held "in the only city in the world named to honor twins." Twinsburg, OH, was named in honor of Moses and Aaron Wilcox, early settlers (identical twins) in 1817. Parade, games, flea market, twins contests, musicians, exhibitions and dancers. Info from: The Twins Days Committee, 10075 Ravenna Rd, Twinsburg, OH 44087.

WALES: ROYAL NATIONAL EISTEDDFOD. Aug 2-9. Fishguard, Dyfed, Wales. Cultural event with competitive festival of music, drama, literature, arts and crafts. Chief glory is its choir singing. Venue changes each year. Info from: Royal Natl Eisteddfod, 10 Park Grove, Cardiff, South Glamorgan.

WILBER NEBRASKA CZECH FESTIVAL. Aug 2-3. Purpose: Preservation and continuation of Czechoslovakian culture, music, dance, history, costumes, foods, art, tongue pageant. Sponsor: Nebraska Czechs of Wilber, Irma Ourecky, Secy, Box 652, Wilber, NE 68465.

YUGOSLAVIA; SINJSKA ALKA. Aug 2. Near Split, Yugoslavia, Sinj spear-throwing chivalric contest, a game on horses, founded in 1715 to commemorate victory over Turkish army. Weapons and colorful costumes from the 18th century.

AUGUST 3 — SUNDAY
215th Day — Remaining, 150

AMERICAN FAMILY DAY. Aug 3. Observed on the first Sunday in August. The observance date is designated by statute in Arizona and Michigan.

ARMY NURSES PAY RAISE ANNIVERSARY. Aug 3. Although it had been known from the time the Second Continental Congress authorized the Continental Army (June 14, 1775) that ". . . the sick suffered much for want of good female nurses . . . ." (General Washington had asked the Congress to authorize a matron and nurses), progress was slow. The pay of a nurse, originally $2.00 per month and one ration per day, was increased to $8.00 per month and one ration per day, on Apr 7, 1777. On Aug 3, 1861, the Congress authorized the Surgeon General to employ women as nurses for Army hospitals at a salary of $12.00 per month plus one ration.

ARRIVAL OF FIRST SHAKERS IN AMERICA. Aug 3. Purpose: To commemorate the arrival in America of Mother Ann Lee and eight of her followers in New York City on August 6, 1774. Voyage begun at Liverpool, England on May 19. Info from: Shaker Village, Inc, Canterbury, NH 03224.

BAY PORT FISH SANDWICH DAY. Aug 3. Purpose: To recall commerical fishing industry, when Bay Port was "the biggest fresh-water fishing port in the world." Sponsor: Chamber of Commerce, Forrest Williams, Pres, Bay Port, MI 48720.

BOURGUIBA, HABIB: BIRTHDAY. Aug 3. Public holiday in Tunisia commemorating birth, Aug 3, 1902, of Tunisia's first president.

BURRO RACE. Aug 3. Leadville, CO. Info from: Chamber of Commerce, Box 861, Leadville, CO 80461.

CARLIN, JOHN W: BIRTHDAY. Aug 3. John W. Carlin, Governor of Kansas, Democrat, was born at Salina, KS, on Aug 3, 1940.

CELEBRATION OF PEACE. Aug 3. Purpose: To bring people of all opinions together in unity to reflect on peace and justice and to celebrate life. Sponsor: Natl Peace Day Campaign, Marie M. Strain, Dir, 93 Pilgrim Rd, Concord, MA 01742.

COLUMBUS' SAILING ANNIVERSARY. Aug 3. Christopher Columbus, "Admiral of the Ocean Sea," set sail half an hour before sunrise from Palos, Spain, on Friday, Aug 3, 1492. With three ships, *Nina*, *Pinta*, and *Santa Maria*, and a crew of ninety, he sailed "for Cathay," but found instead a New World of the Americas, first landing at Guanahani (San Salvador Island in the Bahamas) on October 12. (q.v.).

CONCOURS d' ELEGANCE. Aug 3. Meadow Brook Hall, Rochester, MI. A prestigious showing of approximately 150 of the world's most beautiful antique and classic cars. Info from: Meadow Brook Hall, Oakland University, Rochester, MI 48063.

GUINEA-BISSAU: NATIONAL HOLIDAY. Aug 3. Colonization Martyr's Day is observed.

HARMONY COLLEGE. Aug 3-9. Western State University, St. Joseph, MO. Purpose: A school to intensify performance aspects of the barbershop style of singing. Sponsor: Robb Ollett, S.P.E.B.S.Q.S.A., Inc, 6315 Third Ave, Kenosha, WI 53140.

INTERNATIONAL AEROBATIC CHAMPIONSHIPS. Aug 3-9. Fond du Lac, WI. Pilots demonstrate their skills and courage as they compete for championship trophies. Info from: Conv & Visitor's Bureau, 207 N Main St, Fond du Lac, WI 54935.

INTERNATIONAL TURTLE CREEPSTAKES. Aug 3. Info from: Turtles Internatl, Ltd, 2018 Aldrich Ct, Downers Grove, IL 60516.

ITALY: JOUST OF THE QUINTANA. Aug 3. Ascoli/Piceno. The first Sunday in August is set aside for the Torneo della Quintana, an historical pageant with 15th century costumes.

KLAMATH SALMON FESTIVAL. Aug 3. A salmon barbeque, logging show, parade and a day of excitement on the Klamath River. Info from: Chamber of Commerce, Box 246, Crescent City, CA 95531.

LAMM, RICHARD D: BIRTHDAY. Aug 3. Richard D. Lamm, Governor of Colorado, Democrat, was born at Madison, WI, on Aug 3, 1935.

PSYCHIC WEEK. Aug 3-9. Purpose: To utilize the power of the psyche to bring peace, find lost individuals and concentrate 'psychic power' on beneficial causes. Sponsor: Richard R. Falk, Associates, 1472 Broadway, New York, NY 10036.

SCOPES, JOHN T: BIRTHDAY. Aug 3. Central figure in a cause célèbre (the "Scopes Trial" or the "Monkey Trial"), John Thomas Scopes was born Aug 3, 1900, at Paducah, KY. An obscure 24-year-old schoolteacher at the Dayton, TN, high school in 1925, he became the focus of world attention. Scopes never uttered a word at his trial which was a contest between two of America's best known lawyers (William Jennings Bryan and Clarence Darrow). The trial, July 10-21, 1925, resulted in Scopes' conviction. He was fined $100 "for teaching evolution" in Tennessee. The verdict was upset on a technicality and the statute he was accused of breaching was repealed in 1967. Scopes died at Shreveport, LA, Oct 21, 1970.

STENNIS, JOHN CORNELIUS: BIRTHDAY. Aug 3. U.S. Senator from Mississippi, Democrat, of De Kalb, MS, was born in Kemper County, MS, on Aug 3, 1901.

TURTLES INTERNATIONAL AWARENESS WEEK. Aug 3-10. Theme: "The United Resistance To Life's Everyday Setbacks." Purpose: A world-wide concentrated effort by millions of Turtle members to spread humor, promote friendship, initiate new members and thereby aid in the effort of Turtles International, Ltd, to help needy children. Sponsor: Turtles International, Ltd, 2018 Aldrich Ct, Downers Grove, IL 60516.

U.S. OPEN CHESS CHAMPIONSHIP. Aug 3-15. McAfee, NJ. Annual tournament since 1900, to select U.S. Open Champion and winners in other categories. Info from: U.S. Chess Federation, 186 Route 9W, New Windsor, NY 12550.

UMPIRE APPRECIATION WEEK. Aug 3-9. Purpose: To thank the men and women who contribute to baseball (softball), as umpires—from sandlot to professional ball. Sponsor: Guy Patrick Garraghan, 16th Fairway, Windham, NY 12496.

VOLKSFEST. Aug 3. New Glarus, WI. Celebration of Swiss Independence Day. Info from: Volksfest, Box 713, New Glarus, WI 53574.

W.C. HANDY FESTIVAL. Aug 3-9. Florence, AL. Purpose: A week-long street-strutting, toe-tapping and hand-clapping celebration of the musical heritage of Florence native W.C. Handy—the father of the blues—culminating in a spectacular Saturday evening concert. Info from: W.C. Handy Festival, Nancy C. Gonce, Publicity Dir, 118 E Mobile, Florence, AL 35630.

AUGUST 4 — MONDAY
216th Day — Remaining, 149

ALL-AMERICAN SOAP BOX DERBY. Aug 4-9. Purpose: A week-long festival culminating in world championship race by regional champs from USA, Canada, Germany, Venezuela, New Zealand, Australia and Philippines. Sponsor: Internatl Soap Box Derby, Inc, Wayne Alley, Gen Mgr, Box 7233, Akron, OH 44306.

ANTIGUA AND BARBUDA: AUGUST MONDAY. Aug 4-5. The first Monday in August and the day following form the August Monday Public Holiday in Antigua and Barbuda.

BAHAMAS: EMANCIPATION DAY. Aug 4. Public holiday in Bahamas. First Monday in August.

BORDEN, LIZZIE: LIBERATION DAY. Aug 4. Purpose: To free name of Lizzie Borden from unproven charge ("L.B. took an axe . . .") of matri-cum-patricide. (Annually, August fourth.) Sponsor: Friends of Lizzie Borden of Lake Superior State College Unicorn Hunters, W.T. Rabe, Court Reporter, Lake Superior State College, Sault Ste Marie, MI 49783.

BLACKHILLS MOTORCYCLE CLASSIC. Aug 4-10. Sturgis, SD. A.M.A. sanctioned motorcycle races. Info from: Chamber of Commerce, Box 504, Sturgis, SD 57785.

August
1986

S	M	T	W	T	F	S
					1	2
3	4	5	6	7	8	9
10	11	12	13	14	15	16
17	18	19	20	21	22	23
24	25	26	27	28	29	30
31						

COPYRIGHT © 1985 BY WILLIAM D. CHASE and HELEN M. CHASE

BOURKINA FASSO: NATIONAL DAY. Aug 4. Anniversary of the day (Aug 4, 1984) on which the Republic of Upper Volta changed its name to Bourkina Fasso (or Burkina Faso). The Republic of Upper Volta formerly commemorated attainment of autonomy, Dec 11, 1958, as its National Day.

CIVIC HOLIDAY. Aug 4. Canada. The first Monday in August is observed as a holiday in seven of Canada's ten provinces: Civic Holiday in Manitoba, New Brunswick, Northwest Territories, Ontario and Saskatchewan; British Columbia Day in B.C; and Heritage Day in Alberta.

COAST GUARD DAY. Aug 4. Celebrates anniversary of founding of the U.S. Coast Guard, Aug 4, 1790.

COLORADO DAY. Aug 4. Colorado. (First Monday in August.) Commemorates Admission Day, Aug 1, 1876, when Colorado became 38th State.

EVANS, LANE: BIRTHDAY. Aug 4. U.S. Representative of Illinois' 17th district, Democrat, of Rock Island, IL, born there Aug 4, 1951.

GOLF: U.S. GIRLS' JUNIOR AMATEUR CHAMPIONSHIP. Aug 4-9. Peach Tree Country Club, Marysville, CA. National championship for female amateur golfers age 18 and under. Sponsor: U.S. Golf Assn, Golf House, Far Hills, NJ 07931.

GOLF: U.S. WOMEN'S AMATEUR CHAMPIONSHIP. Aug 4-9. Pasatiempo Golf Club, Santa Cruz, CA. National championship for female amateur golfers. Sponsor: U.S. Golf Assn, Golf House, Far Hills, NJ 07931.

JAMAICA: INDEPENDENCE DAY. Aug 4. National holiday observing achievement of Jamaican independence on Aug 6, 1962. Always observed on first Monday in August.

KID'S SWAP SHOP. Aug 4. War Memorial Plaza, Baltimore, MD. Purpose: For children to trade any used item (games, puzzles, toys, books) they no longer wish to keep. Youngsters 14 years of age and under permitted to participate. Info from: Virginia Baker, Mayor's Office of Adventures in Fun, 100 Holliday St, Rm 355, Baltimore, MD 21202.

NATIONAL SMILE WEEK. Aug 4-10. Purpose: "Share a smile and it will come back to you, bringing happiness to you and the giver." Always the week beginning with first Monday in August. Sponsor: Heloise, Box 32000, San Antonio, TX 78232.

NOVA SCOTIA GAELIC MOD. Aug 4-9. St. Ann's, Cape Breton, Nova Scotia. Competitions in Highland dancing, bagpipe music and Gaelic singing. Info from: Dept of Tourism, Box 456, Halifax, NS B3J 2R5.

PICNIC DAY. Aug 4. Australia. Monday, Aug 4, 1986, is a bank holiday in New South Wales, and Picnic Day in Northern Territory.

SCALIGER, JOSEPH JUSTUS: BIRTHDAY. Aug 4. French scholar who has been called the founder of scientific chronology. Born at Agen, France, Aug 4, 1540, the 10th son of classical scholar Julius Caesar Scaliger. In 1582 he suggested a new system for measuring time and numbering years. His "Julian Period" (named for his father) consisted of 7,980 consecutive years, (beginning Jan 1, 4713 B.C.), the relationship of which was relatively easily understood. His Julian Period is still in use. He died at Leyden, France, Jan 21, 1609.

SCOTLAND: BANK HOLIDAY. Aug 4. Observed throughout Scotland on this date. Bank and public holiday.

SLATTERY, JAMES CHARLES: BIRTHDAY. Aug 4. U.S. Representative of Kansas' 2nd district, Democrat, of Topeka, KS, was born in community of Good Intent, Atchison County, KS, on Aug 4, 1948.

VIRGIN ISLANDS: NICOLE ROBIN DAY. Aug 4. Commemorates the safe return of *Nicole Robin* and her crew on Aug 4, 1973, after harrowing 23-day experience. "Nicole Robin Day" shall be celebrated by appropriate ceremonies and festivities throughout the Virgin Islands.

ZAMBIA YOUTH DAY. Aug 4. First Monday in August. National holiday. Youth activities are order of the day. Focal point is Lusaka's Independence Stadium.

AUGUST 5 — TUESDAY
217th Day — Remaining, 148

AIKEN, CONRAD: BIRTH ANNIVERSARY. Aug 5. American poet, short story writer, critic and Pulitzer Prize winner (poetry, 1916), was born at Savannah, GA on Aug 5, 1899, and died there Aug 17, 1973.

BEARD, MARY R: BIRTH ANNIVERSARY. Aug 5. American historian Mary Ritter Beard was born at Indianapolis, IN, on Aug 5, 1876. Many of her books were written in collaboration with her husband, Charles A. Beard. She died at Phoenix, AZ, on Aug 14, 1958.

ELIOT, JOHN: BIRTH ANNIVERSARY. Aug 5. John Eliot, American "Apostle to the Indians," translator of the Bible into an Indian tongue (the first Bible to be printed in America), was born in Hertfordshire, England, on Aug 5, 1604. He died at Roxbury, MA, on May 21, 1690.

FEDERAL INCOME TAX: BIRTHDAY. Aug 5. On Aug 5, 1861, Abraham Lincoln signed into law the first federal income tax, to become effective Jan 1, 1862. It was a 3% tax levied on incomes over $800, as an emergency wartime measure only. It was rescinded in 1872.

FIRST ENGLISH COLONY IN NORTH AMERICA: FOUNDING ANNIVERSARY. Aug 5. Sir Humphrey Gilbert, English navigator and explorer, aboard his sailing ship, the *Squirrel*, sighted the Newfoundland coast and took possession of the area around St. Johns harbor in the name of the Queen, Aug 5, 1583, thus establishing the first English colony in North America. Gilbert was lost at sea, in a storm off the Azores, on his return trip to England.

HI-TECH USA. Aug 5. Guadalajara, Mexico. Solo exhibition. Computers and peripheral devices. Info from: Terry Rettig, Trade Development, Room 3832, Internatl Trade Admin, U.S. Dept of Commerce, Washington, DC 20230.

LYNCH, THOMAS: BIRTHDAY. Aug 5. Signer, Declaration of Independence, born Prince George's Parish, SC, Aug 5, 1749. Died 1779 (lost at sea, exact date of death unknown).

MONTGOMERY, GILLESPIE V: BIRTHDAY. Aug 5. U.S. Representative of Mississippi's 3rd district, Democrat, of Meridian, MS, born in Meridian on Aug 5, 1920.

MOON PHASE: NEW MOON. Aug 5. Moon enters New Moon phase at 1:36 p.m., E.S.T.

AUGUST 6 — WEDNESDAY
218th Day — Remaining, 147

ABBOTT'S MAGIC GET-TOGETHER. Aug 6-9. Colon, MI. Magic convention. Sponsor: Abbott's Magic Company, Greg Bordner, Colon, MI 49040.

ANNIVERSARY OF FIRST ATOMIC BOMB DROPPED ON INHABITED AREA. Aug 6. Hiroshima, Japan. At 8:15 a.m., local time, an American B-29 bomber, the *Enola Gay*, dropped an atomic bomb named "Little Boy" over the center of the city of Hiroshima, Japan. The bomb exploded about 1,800 feet above the ground, killing more than 105,000 civilians and destroying the city. It is estimated that another 100,000 persons were injured and died subsequently as a direct result of the bomb and the radiation it produced. This was the first time in history that such a devastating weapon had been used by any nation.

COPYRIGHT © 1985 BY WILLIAM D. CHASE and HELEN M. CHASE

BOLIVIA: NATIONAL HOLIDAY. Aug 6. Independence Day. Gained freedom from Spain, 1825.

DOLL SHOW. Aug 6. War Memorial Plaza, Baltimore, MD. Open to girls and boys 14 years of age and under. Nine different categories of dolls. Trophies and prizes for winners. Info from: Mayor's Office of Adventures in Fun, 100 Holliday St, Baltimore, MD 21202.

FESTIVAL OF HUNGRY GHOSTS. Aug 6-Sept 3. Important Chinese festival, also known as Ghosts Month. According to Chinese legend, during the seventh lunar month, the souls of the dead are released from purgatory to roam the earth. Joss sticks are burnt in homes; prayers, food and "ghost money" are offered to appease the ghosts. Market stallholders combine to hold celebrations to ensure that their businesses will prosper in coming year. Wayang (Chinese street opera) and puppet shows are performed, and fruit and Chinese delicacies are offered to the spirits of the dead. Chung Yuan (All Souls' Day) is observed on the 15th day of the seventh lunar month: Aug 20, in 1986.

FLEMING, ALEXANDER: BIRTHDAY. Aug 6. Sir Alexander Fleming, Scottish bacteriologist, discoverer of penicillin and 1954 Nobel Prize recipient, was born at Lochfield, Scotland, Aug 6, 1881. He died at London, Mar 11, 1955.

FORD, WILLIAM DAVID: BIRTHDAY. Aug 6. U.S. Representative of Michigan's 15th district, Democrat, of Taylor, MI, born in Detroit, MI, on Aug 6, 1927.

GEORGIA MOUNTAIN FAIR. Aug. 6-17. Georgia Mountain Fairgrounds, Hiawassee, GA. Purpose: To better the community and country. Sponsor: Lions Club and Georgia Mountain Fair, Box 444, Hiawassee, GA 30546.

HARLEM WEEK. Aug 6-17. Info from: NY Conv & Visitors Bureau, 2 Columbus Circle, New York, NY 10019.

HIROSHIMA DAY. Aug 6. Memorial observances in many places for victims of first atomic bombing of populated place, at Hiroshima, Japan, Aug 6, 1945.

JUDGE CRATER DAY. Aug 6. Anniversary of mysterious disappearance at age 41, on Aug 6, 1930, of Joseph Force Crater, Justice of the New York State Supreme Court. Never seen or heard from after disappearance on this date. Although he was declared legally dead in 1939, *Time* Magazine reported (Sept 17, 1979) that police still receive 300 or so reports yearly about Judge Crater's whereabouts.

NEARING, SCOTT: BIRTHDAY. Aug 6. American sociologist, anti-war crusader, back-to-the-land advocate, and author, with his wife Helen, of *Living the Good Life* (1954), was born at Morris Run, PA, Aug 6, 1883. He died a century later at his farm, Harborside, ME, on Aug 24, 1983.

OAHE DAYS. Aug 6-10. Purpose: People of all ages participate in activities, including raft, boat and bicycle races. North American Buffalo chip flip finals. Info from: Chamber of Commerce, Box 548, Pierre, SD 57501.

PEACE FESTIVAL. Aug 6. Hiroshima, Japan. The festival held annually at Peace Memorial Park is observed in memory of the victims of the Aug 6, 1945 atomic bomb explosion there.

PERKINS, CARL C: BIRTHDAY. Aug 6. U.S. Representative of Kentucky's 7th district, Democrat, of Leburn, KY, born in Washington, DC, on Aug 6, 1954.

ROOSEVELT, EDITH KERMIT CAROW: BIRTHDAY. Aug 6. Second wife of Theodore Roosevelt, 26th President of the U.S., born at Norwich, CT, Aug 6, 1861. Died Sept 30, 1948.

SINGAPORE: MARKET FESTIVAL. Aug 6-Sept 3. Month-long festival on lavish scale. Tropical fruit and Chinese delicacies offered to spirits of dead by stallholders in the markets.

August 1986

S	M	T	W	T	F	S
					1	2
3	4	5	6	7	8	9
10	11	12	13	14	15	16
17	18	19	20	21	22	23
24	25	26	27	28	29	30
31						

SPACE MILESTONE: VOSTOK 2 (USSR). Aug 6. Launched on Aug 6, 1961, Gherman Titov orbited Earth 17 times over period of 25 hours, 18 minutes. Titov broadcast messages in passage over countries, controlled spaceship manually for two hours.

TENNYSON, ALFRED: BIRTHDAY. Aug 6. English poet born at Somersby, Lincolnshire, England, Aug 6, 1809. Died at Aldworth, Oct 6, 1892.

AUGUST 7 — THURSDAY
219th Day — Remaining, 146

BATEMAN, HERBERT H: BIRTHDAY. Aug 7. U.S. Representative of Virginia's 1st district, Republican, of Newport News, VA, born in Elizabeth City, NC, on Aug 7, 1928.

BLUEBERRY HARVEST FESTIVAL. Aug 7-10. Amherst, Nova Scotia. Blueberry suppers, teas and breakfasts. Info from: Dept of Tourism, Box 456, Halifax, NS B3J 2R5.

BOOTHEEL RODEO. Aug 7-10. Sikeston, MO. Nationally known riders and country music stars. Info from: Chamber of Commerce, Box 99, #1 Industrial Dr, Sikeston, MO 63801.

BUNCHE, RALPH JOHNSON: BIRTHDAY. Aug 7. American statesman, United Nations official, Nobel Peace Prize recipient, born at Detroit, MI, Aug 7, 1904. Died Dec 9, 1971.

EDWARDS, EDWIN W: BIRTHDAY. Aug 7. Edwin W. Edwards, Governor of Louisiana, Democrat, was born at Marksville, LA, on Aug 7, 1927.

GOLF: PGA CHAMPIONSHIP. Aug 7-10. Inverness Country Club, Toledo, OH. Final Grand Slam golf championship of the year. Crowns champion of competition conducted by the Professional Golfers' Association of America. Info from: Professional Golfers' Assn of America, Jim Warters, Dir, News & Public Awareness, Box 12458, Palm Beach Gardens, FL 33410.

GREAT OHIO RIVER FLAT BOAT RACE. Aug 7-9. Race starts in Owensboro, ends in Henderson. Info: KY Dept of Travel, Capital Plaza Office Tower, Frankfort, KY 40601.

GREENE, NATHANIEL: BIRTHDAY. Aug 7. Born at Patowomut, RI, American Revolutionary War General Nathaniel Greene was described as the "ablest military officer of the Revolution under Washington." Greene died at Savannah, GA, June 19, 1786.

GULF OF TONKIN RESOLUTION ANNIVERSARY. Aug 7. Congress, on Aug 7, 1964, approved the "Gulf of Tonkin Resolution" which gave President Lyndon Johnson authority "to take all necessary measures to repel any armed attack against the forces of the United States and to prevent further aggression."

HALFWAY POINT OF SUMMER. Aug 7. In Northern Hemisphere the midpoint of the summer season occurs on Aug 7 at 2:44 a.m., E.S.T. Summer, the longest season of this year (lasting 94 days, 15 hours and 29 minutes), is half over!

HARTNETT, THOMAS FORBES: BIRTHDAY. Aug 7. U.S. Representative of South Carolina's 1st district, Republican, of Charleston, SC, born at Charleston on Aug 7, 1941.

ILLINOIS STATE FAIR. Aug 7-17. State Fairgrounds, Springfield, Illinois. Info from: Dept of Commerce & Community Affairs, 620 E Adams St, Springfield, IL 62701.

IOWA CHAMPIONSHIP RODEO. Aug 7-10. Sidney, IA. America's top cowboys compete. Big name entertainment. First Thursday through Sunday of August. Info from: Iowa Championship Rodeo Office, Sidney, IA 51652.

KLAMATH COUNTY FAIR. Aug 7-11. Klamath County Fairgrounds, Klamath Falls, OR. Exhibits, music, arts and crafts. Info from: Visitors & Conv Bureau, 125 N Eighth St, Klamath Falls, OR 97601.

MARITIME DAYS ON THE LAKESHORE. Aug 7-10. Manitowoc and Two Rivers, WI. Purpose: To celebrate the rich and unique maritime heritage of the Manitowoc-Two Rivers area. Sponsor: Manitowoc Maritime Museum, 809 S 8th St, Manitowoc, WI 54220.

MOUNTAIN DANCE AND FOLK FESTIVAL. Aug 7-9. Purpose: To help preserve the cultural heritage of the Southern Appalachian Mountains in the forms of music and dance. Sponsor: Folk Heritage Committee, Chamber of Commerce, Box 1011, Asheville, NC 28802.

NATIONAL POLKA FESTIVAL. Aug 7-10. Hunter Mountain, NY. Purpose: Features top polka bands and artisans from Europe demonstrating work. Info from: Don Conover, Bridge St, Hunter, NY 12442.

PAINT AND PALETTE FESTIVAL ART SHOW AND SALE. Aug 7-10. Info from: Millie Wagner, Paint & Palette Assn, 132 Lake St, Saranac Lake, NY 12983.

PALOMINO LEAGUE BASEBALL WORLD SERIES. Aug 7-14. Cincinnati, OH. International young adult baseball World Series for players of league age 17 and 18. Sponsor: Pony Baseball, Inc, Box 225, Washington, PA 15301.

PENNSYLVANIA STATE SINGING CONVENTION. Aug 7-10. Morrisons Cove Memorial Park, Martinsburg, PA. 50 gospel groups. Sponsor: Vicksburg Quartet, Duncansville, PA 16635.

PURPLE HEART: ANNIVERSARY. Aug 7. At Newburgh, NY, on Aug 7, 1782, General George Washington ordered the creation of a Badge of Military Merit. The Badge consisted of a purple cloth heart with silver braided edge. Only three are known to have been awarded during the Revolutionary War. The award was reinstituted on the Bicentennial of Washington's birth, Feb 22, 1932, and recognizes those wounded in action.

SCHULZE, RICHARD T: BIRTHDAY. Aug 7. U.S. Representative of Pennsylvania's 5th district, Republican, of Berwyn, PA, born in Philadelphia, PA, on Aug 7, 1929.

SKANEATELES FESTIVAL. Aug 7-9. (Also Aug 14-16, Aug 21-23, Aug 28-30.) Live performances of classical music by professional musicians for the benefit of the central New York audience. Info from: Skaneateles Festival, Box 385, Skaneateles, NY 13152.

SPACE MILESTONE: FIRST PICTURE OF EARTH FROM SPACE ANNIVERSARY. Aug 7. U.S. satellite Explorer VI transmitted the first picture of Earth from space Aug 7, 1959, and for the first time man had a likeness of his planet based on more than Earth measurements, projections and conjectures.

AUGUST 8 — FRIDAY
220th Day — Remaining, 145

BLANCHARD, JAMES J: BIRTHDAY. Aug 8. James J. Blanchard, Governor of Michigan, Democrat, was born at Detroit, MI, on Aug 8, 1942.

DIXON, JULIAN CAREY: BIRTHDAY. Aug 8. U.S. Representative of California's 28th district, Democrat, of Los Angeles, CA, born in Washington, DC, on Aug 8, 1934.

INDIAN KEY FESTIVAL. Aug 8-10. Purpose: Community activity and involvement. Sponsor: Chamber of Commerce, Pat Hall, Dir, Islamorada Bank, Box 2808, Key Largo, FL 33037.

McLAIN FAMILY BAND FESTIVAL. Aug 8-10. Big Hill Farm, Berea, KY. Purpose: To provide an international outdoor bluegrass music festival of family bands. Sponsor: McLain Family Band, Inc, Box 1322, Berea, KY 40404.

MARLENEE, RONALD CHARLES: BIRTHDAY. Aug 8. U.S. Representative of Montana's 2nd district, Republican, of Scobey, MT, born there on Aug 8, 1935.

MONDALE, JOAN ADAMS: BIRTHDAY. Aug 8. Wife of 42nd Vice-President of the U.S., Walter F. Mondale, born at Eugene, OR, on Aug 8, 1930. Married Dec 27, 1955.

NATIONAL CORVETTE HOMECOMING. Aug 8-10. Bowling Green, KY. Tours of GM Corvette assembly plant, car show and drag racing. Info from: KY Dept of Travel, Capital Plaza Office Tower, Frankfort, KY 40601.

OMAK STAMPEDE AND SUICIDE RACE. Aug 8-10. Omak, Washington. Professional rodeo.

ROCKHOUND ROUND-UP. Aug 8-10. Parrsboro, Nova Scotia. Craftspeople and rock collectors workshops and demonstrations. Info from: Dept of Tourism, Box 456, Halifax, NS B3J 2R5.

SALT FORK ARTS AND CRAFTS FESTIVAL. Aug 8-10. City Park, Cambridge, OH. Over 200 exhibitors. (Always 2nd full weekend in August.) Info from: Ohio Arts and Crafts Foundation, Box 488, Cambridge, OH 43725.

SCOTLAND: EDINBURGH FESTIVAL FRINGE. Aug 8-30. Edinburgh, Lothian.

SCOTLAND: EDINBURGH MILITARY TATTOO. Aug 8-30. A display of military color and pageantry, evenings, on the Esplanade of Edinburgh Castle.

SOUTH CAROLINA PEANUT PARTY. Aug 8-9. Pelion, SC. Parade, cooking contest, square dance, crafts and Peanut Princess pageant. Info from: Tommy Long, Chrmn, Box 7, Pelion, SC 29123.

SPACE MILESTONE: PIONEER VENUS MULTIPROBE (US). Aug 8. Second craft in Pioneer Venus program. Split into five and probed Venus atmosphere Dec 9. Launched on Aug 8, 1978.

STAFFORD, ROBERT THEODORE: BIRTHDAY. Aug 8. U.S. Senator from Vermont, Republican, of Rutland, VT, born there on Aug 8, 1913.

TALLON, ROBERT M, JR (ROBIN): BIRTHDAY. Aug 8. U.S. Representative of South Carolina's 6th district, Democrat, of Florence, SC, born in Hemingway, SC, Aug 8, 1946.

WEAVER, JIM: BIRTHDAY. Aug 8. U.S. Representative of Oregon's 4th district, Democrat, of Eugene, OR, born at Brookings, SD, on Aug 8, 1927.

AUGUST 9 — SATURDAY
221st Day — Remaining, 144

ANNIVERSARY OF SECOND ATOMIC BOMB DROPPED ON INHABITED AREA. Aug 9. Nagasaki, Japan. On Aug 9, 1945, three days after the atomic bombing of Hiroshima, an American B-29 bomber named Bock's Car left its base on Tinian Island carrying a plutonium bomb nicknamed "Fat Man." Its target was the Japanese city of Kokura, but because of clouds and poor visibility the bomber headed for a secondary target, Nagasaki, where at 11:02 a.m., local time, it dropped the bomb, killing an estimated 70,000 persons and destroying about half the city. In 1985, it was said that the bombardier who pushed the button releasing the bomb would like to apologize to the survivors (called hibakusha), but the mayor of Nagasaki declined, saying he could not find it in his heart to meet him. Memorial services are held annually at Nagasaki, and also at Kokura where those who were spared because of weather also grieve for those at Nagasaki who suffered in their stead.

ANTIQUE AUTO SHOW AND FLEA MARKET. Aug 9-10. Info from: Chamber of Commerce, 28 S Lake St, Boyne City, MI 49712.

COPYRIGHT © 1985 BY WILLIAM D. CHASE and HELEN M. CHASE

EXON, J JAMES JR: BIRTHDAY. Aug 9. U.S. Senator from Nebraska, Democrat of Lincoln, NE, born Geddes, Charles Mix County, SD, on Aug 9, 1921.

FINGER LAKES CRAFTSMEN SUMMER INDOOR ARTS AND CRAFTS SHOW. Aug 9-10. Monroe County Fairgrounds Dome Arena. All media and categories. Info from: Finger Lakes Craftsmen Shows, Ronald L. Johnson, 25 Seneca St, Shortsville, NY 14548.

GADSBY'S TAVERN DAYS. Aug 9-10. Gadsby's Tavern Museum, Alexandria, VA. Purpose: To recreate the diverse kinds of activities found in the 18th century tavern. Colonial food and drink. Sponsor: Gadsby's Tavern Museum, 134 N Royal St, Alexandria, VA 22314.

HALLMARK NATIONAL JIGSAW PUZZLE DESIGN CONTEST. Aug 9-17. Purpose: Puzzlers and puzzle artists compete for prize money in this annual fun event. Sponsor: The Dairy Barn, Inc, Box 747, Athens, OH 45701.

INTERNATIONAL DAY OF SOLIDARITY WITH THE STRUGGLE OF WOMEN OF SOUTH AFRICA AND NAMIBIA. Aug 9. The United Nations General Assembly in December 1981 invited all governments and organizations to observe this day annually, on the anniversary of demonstration of South African women against racist pass laws, Aug 9, 1956. Info from: Centre Against Apartheid, Officer-in-Charge, United Nations, New York, NY 10017.

IZAAC WALTON DAY. Aug 9. English author of classic treatise on fishing, *The Compleat Angler*, published in 1653, was born at Stafford, England, Aug 9, 1593. Died at Winchester, Dec 15, 1683. "Angling," Walton wrote, "may be said to be so like the mathematics, that it can never be fully learnt."

McLAIN FAMILY BAND FESTIVAL. Aug 9-10. Berea, KY. Bluegrass music featuring 17 bands. Info from: KY Dept of Travel, Capital Plaza Office Tower, Frankfort, KY 40601.

MOMENT OF SILENCE. Aug 9. Nagasaki, Japan. Memorial observance for victims of second atomic bombing (Nagasaki, Japan, Aug 9, 1945) held at Peace Memorial Park.

MYSTIC OUTDOOR ART FESTIVAL. Aug 9-10. A major exhibition by 400 artists from the Eastern seaboard. Fine arts only. Info from: Chamber of Commerce, Mystic, CT 06355.

NATIONAL FESTIVAL OF FOLK DANCES AND SONGS. Aug 9-12. Koprivshtitsa, Bulgaria. More than 10,000 best performers of Bulgarian folk art, on 9 stages demonstrate the most valuable from the enormous folk heritage. Info from: Bulgarian Tourist Office, 161 E 86th St, New York, NY 10028.

NATIONAL NURSE ANESTHETIST WEEK. Aug 9-13. Purpose: To honor the 23,000 certified registered nurse anesthetists who adminster more than half of all the approximately 20 million anesthetics provided annually, their commitment to excellence, and their compassion, communication and one-on-one patient care. Sponsor: American Assn of Nurse Anesthetists, c/o Public Relations Board, Inc, 150 E Huron, Chicago, IL 60601.

NISEI WEEK JAPANESE FESTIVAL. Aug 9-17. Little Tokyo, Los Angeles, CA. Purpose: To celebrate the Japanese American cultural heritage. Info from: Nisei Week Japanese Festival, Inc, 244 S San Pedro St, Room 501, Los Angeles, CA 90012.

OJAI SUMMER CRAFTS FESTIVAL. Aug 9-10. Ojai Art Center, Ventura County, CA. Handcrafted work of craftspeople from all over California. Info from: Ojai Art Center, Cary Sterling, Box 331, Ojai, CA 93023.

OLD FIDDLER'S PICNIC. Aug 9. Hibernia Park, Coatesville, PA. Old time musicians gather to make their traditional music. Info from: Parks & Recreation Dept, 235 W Market St, West Chester, PA 19382.

PRESIDENTIAL RESIGNATION ANNIVERSARY. Aug 9. Effective at noon, Aug 9, 1974, the resignation from the presidency of the U.S. by Richard Milhouse Nixon had been announced in a speech to the American people on Thursday evening, Aug 8th. Nixon, under threat of impeachment as a result of the Watergate scandal, became the first person to resign the presidency. He was succeeded by his nominee, Gerald Rudolph Ford, first person to serve as Vice-President and President without having been elected to either office. Ford granted Nixon a "full, free and absolute pardon" on Sept 8, 1974. Although Nixon was the first U.S. president to resign, two vice-presidents had resigned: John C. Calhoun, Dec 28, 1832, and Spiro T. Agnew, Oct 10, 1973.

SCOTLAND: EDINBURGH INTERNATIONAL FILM FESTIVAL. Aug 9-24. Filmhouse, 88 Lothian Rd, Edinburgh. "The best of new international cinema," seminars and discussions.

SINGAPORE: NATIONAL DAY. Aug 9. Most festivals in Singapore are Chinese, Indian or Malay, but celebration of National Day is shared by all to commemorate achievement of Independence in 1965. Music, parades, dancing.

TEDDY BEAR RALLY. Aug 9. Amherst, MA. Purpose: A congregation, at the Amherst Town Common, of Teddy Bear lovers from all over the country. Benefits to Hampshire County Assn for Retarded Citizens. Info from: Chamber of Commerce, Attn Ann Campney, 11 Spring St, Amherst, MA 01002.

UMPIRE APPRECIATION DAY. Aug 9. Purpose: To thank the men and women who contribute to baseball (softball), as umpires—from sandlot to professional ball. Sponsor: Guy Patrick Garraghan, 16th Fairway, Windham, NY 12496.

WINTER HARBOR LOBSTER FESTIVAL. Aug 9. Purpose: Lobster festival featuring lobster dinner cooked on shore. Lobster boat races, craft fair, marine trade show, and parade. Info from: Chamber of Commerce, Winter Harbor, ME 04693.

AUGUST 10 — SUNDAY
222nd Day — Remaining, 143

CAMPBELL, ANGUS: BIRTHDAY. Aug 10. Professor of psychology and sociology, author, and director of the Institute for Social Research at the University of Michigan, called a "man with a scientist's mind and a humanist's heart," was born Aug 10, 1910, at Leiters, IN. He was one of the principal researchers in studies of social and racial problems and attitudes. Campbell died Dec 15, 1980, at Ann Arbor, MI.

CARNATION CITY FESTIVAL. Aug 10-17. Purpose: To celebrate Alliance, OH, the home of the scarlet carnation, the state flower of Ohio. Sponsor: Carnation City Festival, Inc, 210 E Main St, Alliance, OH 44601.

CHESTER RACE WEEK. Aug 10-16. Chester, Nova Scotia. The largest yachting regatta in Atlantic Canada, open to many classes of boats. Info from: Dept of Tourism, Box 456, Halifax, NS B3J 2R5 Canada.

CROCKETT, GEORGE WILLIAM JR: BIRTHDAY. Aug 10. U.S. Representative of Michigan's 13th district, Democrat, of Detroit, MI, was born at Jacksonville, FL, Aug 10, 1909.

ECUADOR: NATIONAL HOLIDAY. Aug 10. Independence Day. Celebrates attainment of independence Aug 10, 1809.

FAMILY DAY. Aug 10. Purpose: To focus attention on family solidarity and its potential as the best teacher of basic beliefs and values. Sponsor: Program Development Dept, Kiwanis Internatl, 3636 Woodview Trace, Indianapolis, IN 46268.

FOLKLORAMA. Aug 10-17. Winnipeg, Manitoba. Multicultural festival with more than 50 ethnic groups. Forty pavilions. Info from: Travel Manitoba, Dept 5058, Winnipeg, Manitoba, Canada R3C 3H8.

August 1986

S	M	T	W	T	F	S
					1	2
3	4	5	6	7	8	9
10	11	12	13	14	15	16
17	18	19	20	21	22	23
24	25	26	27	28	29	30
31						

COPYRIGHT © 1985 BY WILLIAM D. CHASE and HELEN M. CHASE

HOOVER, HERBERT CLARK: BIRTHDAY. Aug 10. The 31st President of the U.S. was born at West Branch, IA, Aug 10, 1874. Hoover was the first president born west of the Mississippi River, and the first to have a telephone on his desk (installed Mar 27, 1929). "Older men declare war. But it is youth that must fight and die," he said in Chicago at the Republican National Convention, June 27, 1944. Hoover died at New York City, Oct 20, 1964. The Sunday nearest Aug 10 is observed in Iowa as Herbert Hoover Day.

HOOVER, HERBERT: DAY. Aug 10, Iowa. (Sunday nearest Aug 10.)

HUNTINGDON COUNTY FAIR. Aug 10-16. Fairground, Huntingdon, PA. Home town country fair with livestock, crafts and home made food. Info from: George Fitzgerald, Box 235, Huntingdon, PA 16652.

ITALY: PALIO DEL GOLFO. Aug 10. La Spezia. A rowing contest over a 2000-meter course is held on the second Sunday of August.

MISSOURI: ADMISSION DAY. Aug 10. Became 24th state on this day in 1821.

ROASTING EARS OF CORN FOOD FEST. Aug 10. The Museum, Allentown, PA. Traditional American Indian event with activities for the whole family. Info from: Lenni Lenape Historical Society, Rt 2, Fish Hatchery Rd, Allentown, PA 18103.

ROSE, CHARLIE: BIRTHDAY. Aug 10. U.S. Representative of North Carolina's 7th district, Democrat, of Fayetteville, NC, born in Fayetteville, Cumberland County, NC, Aug 10, 1939.

SCOTLAND: EDINBURGH FESTIVAL. Aug 10-30. International. "World's greatest arts festival." Info from: Edinburgh Festival Society, 21 Market St, Edinburgh, Scotland, EH1 1BW.

SPACE MILESTONE: DISCOVERER 13 (US). Aug 10. Ejected space capsule, First object recovered after orbiting. Launched Aug 10, 1960.

AUGUST 11 — MONDAY
223rd Day — Remaining, 142

CHAD: NATIONAL HOLIDAY. Aug 11. Independence Day.

INGERSOL, ROBERT GREEN: BIRTHDAY. Aug 11. American author, orator, lawyer, politician and agnostic, was born at Dresden, NY, Aug 11, 1833, and died at Dobb's Ferry, NY, July 21, 1899. "An honest God," he wrote, "is the noblest work of man."

INTER-STATE FAIR AND RODEO. Aug 11-17. Coffeyville, KS. "Largest outdoor fair and rodeo event in SE Kansas and NE Oklahoma." Sponsor: Montgomery County Fair Assn, Box 457, Coffeyville, KS 67337.

NATIONAL SCUBA DIVING WEEK. Aug 11-17. Purpose: To recognize the recreation of scuba diving and the people responsible for its creation—the schools and students. Celebration includes scallop and other seafood feasts, underwater film festivals, seminars, contests and awards. Info from: Harry Truitt, c/o Lighthouse Diving Ctr, 8215 Lake City Way NE, Seattle, WA 98115.

O'NEILL, WILLIAM A: BIRTHDAY. Aug 11. William A. O'Neill, Governor of Connecticut, Democrat, was born at Hartford, CT, on Aug 11, 1930.

PINE TO PALM GOLF TOURNAMENT. Aug 11-17. Detroit Lakes Country Club, Detroit Lakes, MN. Men's amateur tournament with players from over 20 states and Canada. Info from: Chuck Merry, 1054 West Lake Drive, Detroit Lakes, MN 56501.

PRESIDENTIAL JOKE DAY. Aug 11. A day to recall presidential jokes. Anniversary of President Ronald Reagan's voice test joke of Aug 11, 1984. In preparation for a radio broadcast, during a thought-to-be off-the-record voice level test, instead of counting "one, two, three...," the president said: "My fellow Americans, I am pleased to tell you I just signed legislation which outlaws Russia forever. The bombing begins in five minutes." The statement was picked up by live television cameras and microphones and was seen and heard by millions worldwide. The incident provoked national and international reactions, including a news network proposal of new ground rules concerning the use of "off-the-record" remarks.

PRINTING HOUSE CRAFTSMEN: INTERNATIONAL CONVENTION. Aug 11-14. Chicago, IL. Sponsor: International Assn of Printing House Craftsmen, Inc, John A. Davies, Exec VP, 7599 Kenwood Rd, Cincinnati, OH 45236.

SPACE MILESTONE: VOSTOK 3 (USSR). Aug 11. Launched Aug 11, 1962, Andrian Nikolayev orbits Earth 64 times over a period of 94 hours, 25 minutes, covering distance of 1,242,500 miles. Achieved radio communication with Vostok 4 and telecast from spacecraft.

AUGUST 12 — TUESDAY
224th Day — Remaining, 141

BEWICK, THOMAS: BIRTHDAY. Aug 12. English artist, woodengraver and author, remembered especially for his book illustrations in *History of Quadrapeds*, *British Birds*, and *Fables of Aesop*. Born at Cherryburn, Northumberland, Aug 12, 1753. Died at Gateshead, Durham, on Nov 8, 1828.

BUMPERS, DALE: BIRTHDAY. Aug 12. U.S. Senator from Arkansas, Democrat, of Charleston, AR, born in Charleston on Aug 12, 1925.

COLT LEAGUE BASEBALL WORLD SERIES. Aug 12-18. Lafayette, IN. International youth baseball World Series for players of league age 15 and 16. Sponsor: Pony Baseball, Inc, Box 225, Washington, PA 15301.

DeMILLE, CECIL BLOUNT: BIRTHDAY. Aug 12. Motion picture producer and director, born at Ashfield, MA, Aug 12, 1881. Died at Hollywood, CA, Jan 21, 1959.

FOX HILL DAY. Aug 12. Nassau, Bahamas. Second Tuesday in August.

INDIAN DAY. Aug 12. Massachusetts.

KING PHILIP ASSASSINATION ANNIVERSARY. Aug 12. Native American, Philip, son of Massasoit, chief of the Wampanog tribe, was killed Aug 12, 1676, near Mt. Hope, RI, by a renegade Indian of his own tribe, bringing to an end the first and bloodiest war between American Indians and white settlers of New England, a war which had raged for nearly two years and which was known as King Philip's War.

MATHEWSON, CHRISTY: BIRTHDAY. Aug 12. Famed American baseball player, Christopher (Christy) Mathewson, one of the first players named to Baseball's Hall of Fame, was born at Factoryville, PA, Aug 12, 1880. Died at Saranac Lake, NY, Oct 7, 1925. He pitched three complete games during the 1905 World Series without allowing opponents to score a run. In 17 years he won 372 games while losing 188, and striking out 2,499 players.

MOON PHASE: FIRST QUARTER. Aug 12. Moon enters First Quarter phase at 9:21 p.m., E.S.T.

SPACE MILESTONE: ECHO 1 (US). Aug 12. First successful communications balloon. Launched Aug 12, 1960.

COPYRIGHT © 1985 BY WILLIAM D. CHASE and HELEN M. CHASE

SPACE MILESTONE: ENTERPRISE (US). Aug 12. Reusable orbiting vehicle (space shuttle) makes 1st successful flight on its own within Earth's atmosphere. Launched from Boeing 747 on Aug 12, 1977.

THAILAND: BIRTHDAY OF THE QUEEN. Aug 12. The entire Kingdom of Thailand celebrates the birthday of Queen Sirikit.

AUGUST 13 — WEDNESDAY
225th Day — Remaining, 140

BERLIN WALL ANNIVERSARY. Aug 13. Early in the morning of Sunday, Aug 13, 1961, the East German government closed the border between East and West sectors of Berlin with barbed wire fence to discourage further population movement to the West. Telephone and postal services were interrupted and, later in the week, a concrete wall was built to strengthen the barrier between official crossing points.

CANADIAN NATIONAL EXHIBITION. Aug 13-Sept 1. Exhibition Place, Toronto, Ontario, Canada. Purpose: Competitions, buildings and exhibits covering entertainment, sports, agriculture and young fun, on 350 acres of land. Info from: Exhibition Place, Information Services, Toronto, Ontario, Canada M6K 3C3.

CAXTON, WILLIAM: BIRTHDAY. Aug 13. First English printer, born Aug 13, 1422. Died, London 1491. Caxton produced the first book printed in English (while he was still at Bruges), the *Recuyell of the Histories of Troy*, in 1476, and in the autumn of 1476 set up a print shop in Westminster, becoming the first printer in England.

CENTRAL AFRICAN REPUBLIC: NATIONAL DAY. Aug 13. Commemorates Proclamation of Independence of the Central African Republic, on Aug 13, 1960.

HALIFAX COUNTY EXHIBITION. Aug 13-16. Middle Musquodoboit, Nova Scotia. Agricultural exhibition with street parade, displays of handicrafts and ox and horse pulling. Info from: Dept of Tourism, Box 456, Halifax, NS B3J 2R5.

HITCHCOCK, ALFRED (JOSEPH): BIRTHDAY. Aug 13. English film director, master of suspense, was born at London, Aug 13, 1899. Died Apr 29, 1980.

INDIANA STATE FAIR. Aug 13-24. Indianapolis, IN. Info from: Sid Hutchcraft, 1202 E 38th St, Indianapolis, IN 46205.

INTERNATIONAL LEFTHANDERS DAY. Aug 13. Purpose: To recognize the needs and frustrations of lefthanders by special attention to actions and tasks done with the left hand. Info from: Exec Dir, Lefthanders Internatl, Box 8249, Topeka, KS 66608.

KIDS' DAY Aug 13. War Memorial Plaza, Baltimore, MD. All kids under twelve enjoy an hour of free fun and games. Puppet and magic show plus refreshments. Info from: Mayor's Office of Adventures in Fun, 100 Holliday St, Rm 355, Baltimore, MD 21202.

NUDIST CONVENTION. Aug 13-17. Treehouse Fun Ranch, Devore, CA. Purpose: Business and social event. Annually, second Wednesday in August through following Sunday. Sponsor: American Sunbathing Assn, Inc, 1703 North Main St, Kissimmee, FL 32743.

TUNISIA: WOMEN'S DAY. Aug 13. General Holiday. Celebration of independence of women.

VISCLOSKY, PETER JOHN: BIRTHDAY. Aug 13. U.S. Representative of Indiana's 1st district, Democrat, of Merrillville, IN, born in Gary, IN, on Aug 13, 1949.

August 1986

S	M	T	W	T	F	S
					1	2
3	4	5	6	7	8	9
10	11	12	13	14	15	16
17	18	19	20	21	22	23
24	25	26	27	28	29	30
31						

AUGUST 14 — THURSDAY
226th Day — Remaining, 139

ATLANTIC CHARTER DAY. Aug 14. Anniversary of an eight-point agreement, The Atlantic Charter, signed on Aug 14, 1941, by U.S. President Franklin D. Roosevelt and British Prime Minister Winston S. Churchill. The Charter grew out of a three-day conference aboard ship in the Atlantic Ocean, off the Newfoundland coast, and stated policies and hopes for the future agreed to by the two nations.

BABY PARADE. Aug 14. (Annually, second Thursday in August.) Info from: PR Dept, City Hall, Ocean City, NJ 08226.

BRATWURST FESTIVAL. Aug 14-16. Bratwurst eating and frolicking. Parades, bier gardens and midway. Art and craft shows, outdoor entertainment. Info from: Bratwurst Festival, Inc, Box 175, Bucyrus, OH 44820.

BRONCO LEAGUE BASEBALL WORLD SERIES. Aug 14-21. St. Joseph, MO. International youth baseball World Series for players of league age 11-12. Sponsor: Pony Baseball, Inc, Box 225, Washington, PA 15301.

COLOGNE CATHEDRAL ANNIVERSARY. Aug 14. Cologne, Germany. The Cologne Cathedral, largest Gothic church in northern Europe, was completed Aug 14, 1880, just 632 years after rebuilding began on Aug 14, 1248. In fact, there had been a church on its site since 873, but a fire in 1248 made rebuilding necessary. The Cathedral was again damaged, by bombing, during World War II.

ENGLAND: BATTLE OF FLOWERS. Aug 14. Jersey, Channel Islands. "First held in 1902 to mark the coronation of Edward VII and Queen Alexandra, this event is not so much a battle as a parade of floats displaying thousands of flowers."

HANSEN, JAMES V: BIRTHDAY. Aug 14. U.S. Representative of Utah's 1st district, Republican, of Farmington, UT, was born in Salt Lake City, UT, on Aug 14, 1932.

HOPE WATERMELON FESTIVAL. Aug 14-17. Hope, AR. Purpose: An event the entire family can participate in inexpensively while promoting the city of Hope and having fun. Sponsor: Hope-Hempstead County Chamber of Commerce, Box 250, Hope, AR 71801.

INTERTRIBAL INDIAN CEREMONIAL. Aug 14-17. Gallup, NM. A major Indian festival with over 50 tribes from the U.S. and Mexico. Parades, Indian dances, rodeos, arts and crafts and foods. Info from: Intertribal Indian Ceremonial, Box 1, Church Rock, NM 87311.

IOWA STATE FAIR. Aug 14-24. Fairgrounds, Des Moines, IA. Info from: Iowa Development Commission, 600 E Court Ave, Des Moines, IA 50309.

KENTUCKY STATE FAIR AND WORLD'S CHAMPIONSHIP HORSE SHOW. Aug 14-23. Kentucky State Fair and Expo Ctr. Exhibits, midway, music and world champion saddle bred horses. Info from: Kentucky State Fair, Box 37130, Louisville, KY 40233.

LIBERTY TREE DAY. Aug 14. Massachusetts.

LITTLESTOWN GOOD OLD DAYS CELEBRATION. Aug 14-16. Antique show, arts and crafts, flea market, music and entertainment. Info from: Gettysburg Travel Council, 35 Carlisle St, Gettysburg, PA 17325.

MISSOURI STATE FAIR. Aug 14-23. Sedalia, MO. Info from: Missouri State Fair, Box 111, Sedalia, MO 65301.

PONY LEAGUE BASEBALL WORLD SERIES. Aug 14-21. Washington, PA. National youth baseball World Series for players of league age 13 and 14. Sponsor: Pony Baseball, Inc, Box 225, Washington, PA 15301.

POPCORN FESTIVAL. Aug 14-16. Van Buren, IN. Info from: Bob Hemmick, Hemmick Hardware, 109 E Main St, Van Buren, IN 46991.

SCANDINAVIAN FESTIVAL. Aug 14-17. Junction City, OR. Info from: Scandinavian Festival Assn, Box 5, Junction City, OR 97448.

SOCIAL SECURITY ACT: BIRTHDAY. Aug 14. The Congress approved, on Aug 14, 1935, the Social Security Act, which contained provisions for the establishment of a Social Security Board to administer federal old-age and survivors insurance . . . in the U.S.

SOLOMON, GERALD B: BIRTHDAY. Aug 14. U.S. Representative of New York's 24th district, Republican, of Glens Falls, NY, born in Okeechobee, FL, Aug 14, 1930.

TISHA B'AV or FAST OF AV. Aug 14. Hebrew calendar date: Av 9,5746. Commemorates and mourns the destruction of the first and second Temples in Jerusalem (586 BC and AD 70).

TONTITOWN GRAPE FESTIVAL. Aug 14-16. Tontitown, AR. Info from: Tontitown Grape Festival, Tontitown, AR 72770.

VICTORY DAY or VJ DAY. Aug 14. Anniversary of President Truman's announcement, on Aug 14, 1945, that Japan had surrendered to the Allies, setting off celebrations across the nation. Official ratification of surrender occurred aboard the USS *Missouri* in Tokyo Bay, on Sept 2 (Far Eastern Time).

AUGUST 15 — FRIDAY

227th Day — Remaining, 138

ASSUMPTION OF THE VIRGIN MARY. Aug 15. Greek and Roman Catholic churches celebrate Mary's ascent to Heaven.

BARRYMORE, ETHEL: BIRTHDAY. Aug 15. Celebrated award-winning actress of stage, screen and television, born Ethel Blythe, at Philadelphia, PA, Aug 15, 1879. Died at Beverly Hills, CA, June 18, 1959. U.S. Postal Service stamp was issued in 1982 featuring Ethel, John and Lionel Barrymore.

BLACK HILLS STEAM AND GAS THRESHING BEE. Aug 15-17. Sturgis, SD. Purpose: Antique farming equipment demonstrated. Parade, exhibitions and antique automobiles. Info from: Chamber of Commerce, Box 504, Sturgis, SD 57785.

CHAUVIN DAY. Aug 15. A day named for Nicholas Chauvin, French soldier from Rochefort who idolized Napoleon and who eventually became a subject of ridicule because of his blind loyalty and dedication to anything French. Originally referring to bellicose patriotism, chauvinism has come to mean blind or absurdly intense attachment to any cause. Observed on Napoleon's birth anniversary because Chauvin's birth date is unknown.

CONGO: NATIONAL HOLIDAY. Aug 15. Congolese National Day.

COSHOCTON CANAL FESTIVAL. Aug 15-17. Purpose: Celebrates the arrival of first canal boat in Roscoe. Crafts, parades and old-time entertainment. (Annually the 3rd weekend in August.) Info from: Roscoe Village Foundation, 381 Hill St, Coshocton, OH 43812.

DORMITION OF THEOTOKOS. Aug 15. Orthodox Church observance of Assumption of the Virgin Mary, depends on use of Old or New Calendar. According to New Calendar the Dormition Fast is observed Aug 1-14, followed by Dormition of Theotokos on Aug 15.

ELVIS PRESLEY SALUTE. Aug 15. War Memorial Plaza, Baltimore, MD. Purpose: Salutes rock and roll singer Elvis Presley. Elvis look alike and sing alike contest. Info from: Virginia Baker, Mayor's Office of Adventures in Fun, 100 Holliday St, Rm 355, Baltimore, MD 21202.

FLIPPO, RONNIE G: BIRTHDAY. Aug 15. U.S. Representative of Alabama's 5th district, Democrat, of Florence, AL, born in Florence on Aug 15, 1937.

HARDING, FLORENCE KLING DeWOLFE: BIRTHDAY. Aug 15. Wife of Warren Gamaliel Harding, 29th President of the U.S., born at Marion, OH, Aug 15, 1860. Died Nov 21, 1924.

HAWAII ADMISSION DAY HOLIDAY. Aug 15. The third Friday in August is observed as a State holiday each year, recognizing the anniversary of Hawaii's statehood. Hawaii became the 50th state on Aug 21, 1959.

INDIA: INDEPENDENCE DAY. Aug 15. Anniversary of Indian independence (1947).

INTERNATIONAL CELTIC FESTIVAL. Aug 15-17. Hunter Mountain, NY. Purpose: Features Irish, Scottish and Welsh entertainment. Exposition of products from Wales, Scotland and Ireland. Info from: Don Conover, Bridge St, Hunter, NY 12442.

KOREA: LIBERATION DAY. Aug 15. National holiday commemorates acceptance by Japan of Allied terms of surrender in 1945, thereby freeing Korea from thirty-six years of Japanese domination. Also marks formal proclamation of the Republic of Korea in 1948. Military parades and ceremonies throughout the country.

MONTROSE BLUEBERRY FESTIVAL. Aug 15-17. Purpose: To develop recreation in the city and township of Montrose. Always the third weekend in August. Sponsor: Montrose Blueberry Festival, Box 316, Montrose, MI 48457.

NAPOLEON'S DAY. Aug 15. Anniversary of birth of French emperor, Napoleon Bonaparte, on island of Corsica, Aug 15, 1769. He died in exile, at 5:49 p.m., May 5, 1821, on island of St. Helena. Napoleon's Day is public holiday in Corsica.

NATIONAL CANOE AND KAYAK MARATHON CHAMPIONSHIP. Aug 15-17. Barren River, Bowling Green, KY. Purpose: To determine a national champion in 19 different classes of canoes and kayaks. Also National Canoe Triathlon Championships. Info from: U.S. Canoe Assn, 617 S 94th St, Milwaukee, WI 53214.

NATIONAL FAILURE'S DAY. Aug 15. Purpose: To honor all persons who have experienced failure in pursuit of a noble dream, unconventional idea or impossible goal. Sponsor: The Amicus Group, Jack Gilbert, 303 Fallis Rd, Columbus, OH 43214.

NATIONAL RELAXATION DAY. Aug 15. Purpose: Everyone should have a special day during the year for total relaxation. Today is a time to think about and encourage new ideas for enjoyment of a relaxation day. Sponsor: Sean Moeller, 12079 Belann Court, Clio, MI 48420.

OWEN SOUND SUMMERFOLK FESTIVAL. Aug 15-17. Kelso Beach Park, Owen Sound, Ontario, Canada. Purpose: A celebration of traditional and contemporary folk music, dance, crafts, workshops and concerts. Canadian and International artists. Info from: Georgian Bay Folk Society, Box 521, Owen Sound, Ont, Canada N4K 5R1.

PACIFIC NATIONAL EXHIBITION. Aug 15-Sept 1. Vancouver, British Columbia. Exhibition includes three major areas in salute to the city's centennial. Major historical ride on site, various street scapes of early Vancouver and examples of 1936 floats in the parade. Info from: The Centennial Commission, Box 49386, Suite 3374, Bentall 4, 1055 Dunsmuir St, Vancouver, BC V7X 1L5.

SCOTT, SIR WALTER: BIRTHDAY. Aug 15. Anniversary of birth in Edinburgh of famed Scottish poet and novelist (Aug 15, 1771-Sept 21, 1832). "But no one shall find me rowing against the stream," he wrote in the introduction to *The Fortunes of Nigel*," I care not who knows it—I write for the general amusement."

SOUTHEAST ALASKA STATE FAIR. Aug 15-17. Haines, AK. Agriculture Fair. Info from: SE Alaska State Fair, Box 385, Haines, AK 99827.

SUMMER MUSIC-FEST. Aug 15-24. Heritage Park, Frankenmuth, MI. Purpose: "A family affair." Continuous polka music on wooden dance floors. Country and western music, ethnic foods, dance lessons and contest. Sponsor: Mitas Music, Inc, Box 8, Frankenmuth, MI 48734.

TRANSCONTINENTAL U.S. RAILWAY COMPLETION: ANNIVERSARY. Aug 15. The Golden Spike ceremony at Promontory Point, Utah, May 10, 1869 (q.v.) was long regarded as the final link in a transcontinental railroad track reaching from an Atlantic port to a Pacific port. In fact, that link occurred unceremoniously on another date in another state. Diaries of engineers working at the site establish "the completion of a transcontinental track at a point 928 feet east of today's milepost 602, or 3,812 feet east of the present Union Pacific depot building at Strasburg (formerly Comanche)," Colorado. The final link was made at 2:53 p.m., on Aug 15, 1870. (See: Robert A. LeMassena's ". . . The True Transcontinental Hook-up" in *Kansas* Quarterly, Vol. III, No 2.) Annual celebration at Strasburg, on 3rd weekend of August.

WALLACE, GEORGE C: BIRTHDAY. Aug 15. George C. Wallace, Governor of Alabama, Democrat, was born at Clio, AL, on Aug 15, 1919.

WORLD'S OLDEST CONTINUOUS RCA RODEO. Aug 15-17. Payson, AZ. "The world's first rodeo of record, the Payson Rodeo has been held continuously since 1884." Info from: Payson Chamber, Drawer A, Payson, AZ 85541.

AUGUST 16 — SATURDAY
228th Day — Remaining, 137

ART AT MEADOW BROOK. Aug 16-17. Meadow Brook Hall, Oakland University, Rochester, MI. Invitational fine arts and crafts exhibit and sale. Info from: Meadow Brook Hall, Oakland University, Rochester, MI 48063.

AUGUST COURT DAYS. Aug 16-17. Purpose: To promote and assist with restoration of historic buildings and sites in Loudoun County, VA. Sponsor: Loudoun Restoration & Preservation Society, Box 351, Leesburgh, VA 22075.

BATTLE OF BLUE LICKS CELEBRATION. Aug 16-17. Blue Licks Battlefield State Park, Mount Olivet, KY. Commemorates the anniversary of Battle of Bluelicks, which involved such men as Daniel Boone. Living history demonstrations, arts, crafts, games, competitions and battle re-enactment. Info from: KY Dept of Parks, Capital Plaza Tower, Frankfort, KY 40601.

BATTLE OF CAMDEN: ANNIVERSARY. Aug 16. Revolutionary War battle fought near Camden, SC, on Aug 16, 1780. American troops led by Gen. Horatio Gates suffered disastrous losses. Nearly 1,000 Americans killed and another 1,000 captured by the British. British losses about 325. One of America's worst defeats in the war.

BENNINGTON BATTLE DAY. Aug 16. Anniversary of battle fought Aug 16, 1777, is legal holiday in Vermont.

CATALINA WATER SKI RACE. Aug 16-24. Purpose: Water ski racing teams race 52 miles across open seas, roundtrip from Long Beach to Catalina Island and back. Info from: Long Beach Boat & Ski Club, Box 7784, Newport Beach, CA 92658.

CIRCLE K INTERNATIONAL CONVENTION. Aug 16-20. Boston, MA. Info from: Circle K Dept, Kiwanis Internatl, 3636 Woodview Trace, Indianapolis, IN 46268.

August *1986*	S	M	T	W	T	F	S
						1	2
	3	4	5	6	7	8	9
	10	11	12	13	14	15	16
	17	18	19	20	21	22	23
	24	25	26	27	28	29	30
	31						

CRICKET: GOLDEN OLDIES CRICKET FESTIVAL. Aug 16-24. Brighton, East Sussex, England. Teams from all over the world compete in 40 and over matches. All players must be over 40.

DANISH FESTIVAL. Aug 16-17. Greenville, MI. Purpose: To honor the Danish heritage of the area. Sponsor: Danish Festival Inc, 327 S Lafayette St, Greenville, MI 48838.

ELY'S PONY EXPRESS DAYS. Aug 16-17. (Also Aug 23-24.) Ely, NV. Info from: Chamber of Commerce, Box 239, Ely, NV 89301.

FOOTHILLS FESTIVAL. Aug 16-17. Juried arts and crafts, entertainment and international food. Sponsor: Easley Arts Council, Margo Eubanks, 204 Echo Circle, Easley, SC 29640.

HALLMARK NATIONAL JIGSAW PUZZLE CHAMPIONSHIPS. Aug 16-17. Purpose: Puzzlers and puzzle artists compete for prize money in this annual fun event. Sponsor: The Dairy Barn, Inc, Box 747, Athens, OH 45701.

HOLZFEST. Aug 16-17. Purpose: Woodcrafters of all types display and sell products. Fellowship, entertainment and demonstrations. Sponsor: Personalized Wood Products, RC Eichacker, Box 193, Amana, IA 52203.

HOME TOWN DAYS. Aug 16-17. Strasburg, CO. Purpose: "To remind people of the first truly continuous chain of railways from an Atlantic to a Pacific port which were joined Aug 15, 1870 at Comanche, renamed Strasburg," Info from: Emma Michell, Box 485, Strasburg, CO 80136.

INTERNATIONAL FESTIVAL WEEK. Aug 16-23. Purpose: Ethnic entetainment and food. Info from: Visitor & Convention Bureau, 172 W VanBuren, Battle Creek, MI 49017.

MACFADDEN, BERNARR: BIRTHDAY. Aug 16. Physical culture enthusiast and publisher, born at Mill Springs, MO, Aug 16, 1868. He was once publisher of *Physical Culture Magazine, True Story Magazine, True Romances, True Detective Mysteries Magazine* and many others. MacFadden made parachute jumps on his 81st, 83rd and 84th birthdays. He died at Jersey City, NJ of jaundice, following a 3-day fast, on Oct 12, 1955.

MANCHESTER MASSACRE or BATTLE OF PETERLOO. Aug 16. Anniversary of demonstration by more than 50,000 persons protesting unemployment, starvation wages, overcrowding, high costs and British government policies. The mass meeting, Aug 16, 1819, was held in St. Peter's Fields, Manchester, England. Police and cavalry charged the unarmed crowd with sabres. Casualty estimates for the 10-minute battle varied widely, but several deaths and up to 500 injuries were claimed.

MASTERS OF HANG GLIDING CHAMPIONSHIP. Aug 16-24. From the peaks of Grandfather Mountain, top pilots in the world compete in invitational event. Excellent flying and viewing. Info from: Grandfather Mountain, Harris Prevost, Box 995, Linville, NC 28646.

MICHIGAN RENAISSANCE FESTIVAL. Aug 16-Sept 28. Holly, MI. An outdoor 16th century themed educational and cultural event with artists and craftspeople. Sponsor: Michigan Renaissance Festival, 700 E Maple, Birmingham, MI 48011.

MINNESOTA RENAISSANCE FESTIVAL. Aug 16-Sept 28. A celebration of Renaissance Europe with entertainment, food, arts, crafts, games and equestrian events. Info from: Minnesota Renaissance Festival, 3525 W 145th St, Shakopee, MN 55379.

MITCHELL, MARGARET: DEATH ANNIVERSARY. Aug 16. American novelist, author of the best-selling novel in U.S. history: *Gone With the Wind*, published in 1936, for which she received the Pulitzer Prize for fiction in 1937. Born at Atlanta, GA, in 1900 (exact date unknown), she died there, after being struck by an automobile, on Aug 16, 1949. *Gone With the Wind* was her first and only novel.

MUSIKFEST '86. Aug 16-24. Purpose: To feature Bethlehem's extensive musical heritage and historic district. Emphasis on German and Moravian music but includes folk, classical, jazz and popular. Sponsor: Bethlehem Musikfest Assn, Roland Kushner, Coord, 556 Main St, Bethlehem, PA 18018.

COPYRIGHT © 1985 BY WILLIAM D. CHASE and HELEN M. CHASE

MUSLIM FESTIVAL: ID al-HAJJ. Aug 16. Muslim calendar date: Dhu al-Hijja 10, 1406. Festival ordinarily continues for several days. Gregorian calendar date of observance may vary by one day.

OSSAWALD CRUMB FOLK MUSIC FESTIVAL. Aug 16. White Pine Village, Ludington, MI. Folk and bluegrass music. Info from: Mason County Historical Society, 1687 S Lakeshore Dr, Ludington, MI 49431.

PETOSKEY ART AND CRAFT SHOW. Aug 16. Pennsylvania Park, Petoskey, MI. Display of arts and crafts. Info from: Chamber of Commerce, Box 306, Petoskey, MI 49770.

ROWING: WORLD ROWING CHAMPIONSHIPS. Aug 16-24. National Watersports Centre, Holme Pierrepont, Nottingham, England. 40 nations are expected to take part in the 1986 championships.

SUN PRAIRIE'S SWEET CORN FESTIVAL. Aug 16-17. Family oriented fun. Carnival, midget auto races, parade, beer, brats, food, exhibits and all the hot buttered sweet corn you can eat. Sponsor: Chamber of Commerce, 133 W Main, Sun Prairie, WI 53590.

AUGUST 17 — SUNDAY
229th Day — Remaining, 136

AMERICAN THEATRE ASSOCIATION: ANNUAL CONVENTION. Aug 17-20. New York, NY. 50th Anniversary. Sessions and workshops on all aspects of non-commercial professional and amateur theatre. Sponsor: American Theatre Assn, Jerry Beatty, 1010 Wisconsin Ave, NW, Washington, DC 20007.

BALLOON CROSSING OF ATLANTIC OCEAN: ANNIVERSARY. Aug 17. Three Americans, Max Anderson, 44, Ben Abruzzo, 48, and Larry Newman, 31, all of Albuquerque, NM, became first to complete trans-Atlantic trip in a balloon. Starting from Presque Isle, ME, Aug 11, they traveled some 3,200 miles in 137 hours, 18 minutes, landing at Miserey, France (about 60 miles west of Paris), in their craft, named the *Double Eagle II*, on Aug 17, 1978.

CROCKETT, DAVID: BIRTHDAY. Aug 17. American frontiersman, adventurer, and soldier, born Aug 17, 1786, in Hawkins County, TN. Died during final heroic defense of the Alamo, Mar 6, 1836. In his *Autobiography* (1834), Crockett wrote "I leave this rule for others when I'm dead, Be always sure you're right—then go ahead."

GOLDWYN, SAMUEL: BIRTHDAY. Aug 17. Motion picture producer and industry pioneer, born Samuel Goldfish, at Warsaw, Poland, Aug 17, 1882. Goldwyn died at Los Angeles, CA, Jan 31, 1974. Attributed to Goldwyn is the observation: "Anybody who goes to see a psychiatrist ought to have his head examined."

INDONESIA: NATIONAL HOLIDAY. Aug 17. Independence Day. Republic proclaimed on this day, 1945, upon withdrawal of Japanese.

KLONDIKE GOLD DISCOVERY: ANNIVERSARY. Aug 17. In the Klondike region of the Yukon, at Bonanza Creek (formerly known as Rabbit Creek), George Washington Carmack discovered gold on Aug 17, 1896. During the following year more than 30,000 people joined the gold rush to the area. Anniversary is celebrated as a holiday (Discovery Day) in the Yukon, on nearest Monday.

MAE DAY. Aug 17. Purpose: A day for remembering Mae West—an innovative, liberated lady who was way ahead of her time. Man Watchers, Inc, will give the Mae West award, annually, in her memory. Sponsor: Man Watchers, Inc, Suzy Mallery, Pres, 8033 Sunset, Suite 363, Los Angeles, CA 90046.

NATIONAL WHITE HOUSE CONFERENCE ON SMALL BUSINESS. Aug 17-21. Authorized by Public Law 98-276, approved by the President on May 8, 1984.

O-BON FESTIVAL. Aug 17. Purpose: Traditional Japanese summer festival welcomes the ancestral spirits back to earth with folk dancing, folk music, games and amusements. Sponsor: The Morikami Museum, Larry Rosensweig, Dir, 4000 Morikami Park Rd, Delray Beach, FL 33446.

OUR LADY OF GIRSTERKLAUS PROCESSION. Aug 17. Rosport, Luxembourg. Tradition since 1328. Always the Sunday after Aug 15.

POWERS, FRANCIS GARY: BIRTHDAY. Aug 17. One of America's most famous spies, Francis Gary Powers was born at Jenkins, KY, Aug 17, 1929. The CIA agent, pilot of a U-2 overflight across the Soviet Union, was shot down May 1, 1960, near Sverdlovsk. He was tried, convicted and sentenced to ten years imprisonment, at Moscow, in Aug 1960. Returned to the U.S. in 1962, in exchange for an imprisoned Soviet spy (Col. Rudolf Abel), he found an unwelcoming homeland. Powers died in a helicopter crash near Los Angeles, CA, Aug 2, 1977.

AUGUST 18 — MONDAY
230th Day — Remaining, 135

AMERICAN NEUTRALITY APPEAL ANNIVERSARY. Aug 18. President Woodrow Wilson, on Aug 18, 1914, followed his Aug 4 Proclamation of Neutrality with an appeal to the American people to remain impartial in thought and deed with respect to the war that was raging in Europe (World War I).

CANADIAN LAWN BOWLING CHAMPIONSHIPS. Aug 18. Vancouver, BC, Canada. Info from: Vancouver Centennial Commission, Box 49386, Bentall 4, 1055 Dunsmuir St, Vancouver, BC V7X 1L5.

CARTER (ELEANOR) ROSALYNN SMITH: BIRTHDAY. Aug 18. Wife of James Earl (Jimmy) Carter, 39th President of the U.S., born at Plains, GA, Aug 18, 1927. Married July 7, 1946.

DARE, VIRGINIA: BIRTHDAY. Aug 18. Virginia Dare, the first child of English parents to be born in the New World, was born to Ellinor and Ananias Dare, at Roanoke Island, Aug 18, 1587. When ship arrived to replenish supplies in 1591, the settlers (including Virginia Dare) had vanished, without leaving a trace of the settlement.

FIELD, MARSHALL: BIRTHDAY. Aug 18. American businessman and philanthropist, founder of department stores, born at Conway, MA, Aug 18, 1835. Died at New York City, Jan 16, 1906.

LEWIS, MERIWETHER: BIRTHDAY. Aug 18. American explorer (of Lewis and Clark expedition), born Aug 18, 1774. Died Oct 11, 1809.

PLANT OPERATION AND SAFETY EQUIPMENT. Aug 18-23. Taipei, Taiwan. Solo Exhibition. Metalworking equipment. Info from: William McClure, Trade Development, Room 3832, Internatl Trade Admin, U.S. Dept of Commerce, Washington, DC 20230.

WEINBERGER, CASPAR WILLARD: BIRTHDAY. Aug 18. U.S. Secretary of Defense (took oath of office on Jan 21, 1981) was born at San Francisco, CA, on Aug 18, 1917.

WYOMING STATE FAIR. Aug 18-24. Douglas, WY. Features state fair parade, rodeos, horse shows and open class and youth exhibits in livestock, arts, crafts and photography. Info from: Bill Ogg, Drawer 10, Douglas, WY 82633.

COPYRIGHT © 1985 BY WILLIAM D. CHASE and HELEN M. CHASE

AUGUST 19 — TUESDAY

231st Day — Remaining, 134

BROYHILL, JAMES THOMAS: BIRTHDAY. Aug 19. U.S. Representative of North Carolina's 10th district, Republican, of Lenoir, NC, born there on Aug 19, 1927.

CLINTON, BILL: BIRTHDAY. Aug 19. Bill Clinton, Governor of Arkansas, Democrat, was born at Hope, AR, on Aug 19, 1946.

DURENBERGER, DAVID F: BIRTHDAY. Aug 19. U.S. Senator from Minnesota, Republican, of Minneapolis, MN, was born in St. Cloud, MN, on Aug 19, 1934.

GERMAN PLEBISCITE ANNIVERSARY. Aug 19. In a plebiscite, Aug 19, 1934, 89.9% of German voters approved giving Chancellor Adolf Hitler the additional office of President, placing the Fuhrer in uncontestable and supreme command of that country's destiny.

INTERLOCHEN CHAMBER MUSIC CONFERENCE. Aug 19-26. Master classes in piano, violin, viola, cello and chamber music. Ensemble and repertory classes. Concerts every evening. Info from: Chamber Music Conf, Interlochen Ctr for the Arts, Interlochen, MI 49643.

JONES, WALTER B: BIRTHDAY. Aug 19. U.S. Representative of North Carolina's 1st district, Democrat, of Farmville, NC, was born at Fayetteville, NC, on Aug 19, 1913.

LITTLE LEAGUE BASEBALL WORLD SERIES. Aug 19-23. Williamsport, PA. Purpose: To determine the world champions of Little League Baseball. Sponsor: Little League Baseball, Inc, Steven Keener, PR, Box 3485, Williamsport, PA 17701.

MOON PHASE: FULL MOON. Aug 19. Moon enters Full Moon phase at 1:54 p.m., E.S.T.

NASH, OGDEN: BIRTHDAY. Aug 19. American writer, best remembered for his humorous verse, born at Rye, NY, Aug 19, 1902. Died May 19, 1971. Undeniably brash/Was young Ogden Nash,/Whose notable verse/Was admirably terse/And written with panache.

NATIONAL AVIATION DAY. Aug 19. Presidential Proclamation. "Always August 19 of each year since 1939. Proc. 2343 of 1939 covers all succeeding years.".

NATIONAL AVIATION DAY. Aug 19. Observed annually on anniversary of birth of Orville Wright who piloted "first self-powered flight in history," Dec 17, 1903. First proclaimed by Pres. Franklin D. Roosevelt in 1939.

PENN STATE'S AG PROGRESS DAYS. Aug 19-21. Rock Springs, PA. The past, present and future in agriculture. Exhibits, demonstrations and agriculture in operation. Info from: Joseph D. Harrington, Gen Mgr, Pennsylvania State Univ, 432 Agricultural Admin Bldg, University Park, PA 16802.

SPACE MILESTONE: SOYUZ T-7 (USSR). Aug 19. Launched from Tyuratam on Aug 19, 1982 with second woman in space, test pilot Svetlana Savitskaya and two other cosmonauts. Docked at Salyut 7 and visited the cosmonauts in residence there for the three previous months before returning to Earth on Aug 27 in the Soyuz T-5 vehicle which had been docked there. The Soyuz T-7 returned to Earth Dec 10 with the remaining two cosmonauts.

SPACE MILESTONE: SPUTNIK 5 (USSR). Aug 19. Space menagerie satellite launched on Aug 19, 1960. Recovered. Dogs, Belka and Strelka, become first living organisms recovered from orbit. Aug 19, 1960.

August 1986

S	M	T	W	T	F	S
					1	2
3	4	5	6	7	8	9
10	11	12	13	14	15	16
17	18	19	20	21	22	23
24	25	26	27	28	29	30
31						

TAIWAN: CHENG CHENG KUNG BIRTHDAY. Aug 19. Joyous celebration of birth of Cheng Cheng Kung (Koxinga), the Ming Dynasty loyalist who ousted the Dutch colonists from Taiwan in 1661. Landing is commemorated annually on Apr 29, but Cheng's birthday is honored on 14th day of seventh moon according to the Chinese lunar calendar.

WRIGHT, ORVILLE: BIRTHDAY. Aug 19. Aviation pioneer born at Dayton, OH. (Aug 19, 1871-Jan 30, 1948.)

AUGUST 20 — WEDNESDAY

232nd Day — Remaining, 133

FUQUA, DON: BIRTHDAY. Aug 20. U.S. Representative of Florida's 2nd district, Democrat, of Altha, FL, was born at Jacksonville, FL, Aug 20, 1933.

GRAY, WILLIAM H. III: BIRTHDAY. Aug 20. U.S. Representative of Pennsylvania's 2nd district, Democrat, of Philadelphia, PA, was born at Baton Rouge, LA, on Aug 20, 1941.

GUARINI, FRANK J: BIRTHDAY. Aug 20. U.S. Representative of New Jersey's 14th district, Democrat, of Jersey City, NJ, born there Aug 20, 1924.

GUEST, EDGAR ALBERT: BIRTHDAY. Aug 20. Newspaperman and author of folksy, homespun verse which enjoyed great popularity and was syndicated in more than 100 newspapers, born at Birmingham, England, Aug 20, 1881. Died at Detroit, MI, Aug 5, 1959. "Eddie Guest Day" usually proclaimed on birth anniversary in Detroit.

HARRISON, BENJAMIN: BIRTHDAY. Aug 20. The 23rd President of the U.S., born at North Bend, OH, Aug 20, 1833, was the grandson of William Henry Harrison, ninth President of the U.S. His term of office, Mar 4, 1889-Mar 3, 1893, was preceded and followed by the presidential terms of Grover Cleveland (who thus became the 22nd and the 24th President of the U.S.). Harrison died at Indianapolis, Mar 13, 1901.

MITCHELL, GEORGE JOHN: BIRTHDAY. Aug 20. U.S. Senator from Maine, Democrat, of Portland, ME, was born in Waterville, ME, on Aug 20, 1933.

O'HIGGINS, BERNARDO: BIRTHDAY. Aug 20. First ruler of Chile after its declaration of independence, called the "Liberator of Chile," born at Chillan, Chile, Aug 20, 1778. Died at Lima, Peru, Oct 24, 1842.

OLD THRESHERMEN'S REUNION. Aug 20-23. Kinzers, Lancaster County, PA. Purpose: Celebration of the era of steam, and a reunion of collectors of steam and gasoline equipment. Info from: Rough and Tumble Engineers' Historical Assn, Inc, Box 9, Kinzers, PA 17535.

PRECANEX 1986. Aug 20-24. Recreation Center, Wildwood, NJ. Purpose: Postage stamp exhibit held in conjunction with annual convention of the National Association. Sponsor: Natl Assn of Precancel Collectors, Inc, Glen W. Dye, Secy, 5121 Park Blvd, Wildwood, NJ 08260.

SAARINEN, (GOTTLIEB) ELIEL: BIRTHDAY. Aug 20. Famed architect born at Helsinki, Finland, Aug 20, 1873. Died, Bloomfield Hills, MI, July 1, 1950.

SPACE MILESTONE: VIKING 1 and 2 (US). Aug 20-Sept 9. Sister ships launched toward Mars from Cape Canaveral, Florida on Aug 20 and Sept 9, 1975. Viking 1's lander touched down on Mars July 20, 1976, and Viking 2's lander on Sept 3, 1976. Sent back to Earth high quality photographs, analysis of atmosphere, weather information, and results of sophisticated experiments intended to determine whether life may be present on Mars.

SPACE MILESTONE: VOYAGER 2 (US). Aug 20. Launched Aug 20, 1977, unmanned spacecraft starts trip to Jupiter (1979), Saturn (1981), Uranus (1986) and Neptune (1989).

TURKEY: VICTORY DAY. Aug 20. Nationwide. Military parades, performing of the Mehtar band, the world's oldest military band, fireworks.

XEROX 914 ANNIVERSARY. Aug 20. On Aug 20, 1985, the original Xerox 914 copying machine (which had been introduced to the public 25 years earlier—in March 1960) was formally presented to the Smithsonian Institution's National Museum of American History, in Washington, DC. Invented by Chester Carlson, a patent lawyer, the quick and easy copying of documents by machine revolutionized the world's offices.

AUGUST 21 — THURSDAY
233rd Day — Remaining, 132

ACTON FAIR. Aug 21-24. A typical country fair with shows of beef and dairy cattle, sheep and goats. Exhibits of home canned food and fancy work. Info from: Lista C Staples, Box 75, Shapleigh, ME 04076.

AMERICAN BAR ASSOCIATION ANNIVERSARY. Aug 21. Organized at Sarasota, NY, Aug 21, 1878.

ANTIQUE ENGINE AND TRACTOR SHOW. Aug 21-24. Jay County Fairgrounds, Portland, IN. Purpose: A working exhibition of antique gasoline engines, tractors, threshing, saw milling and apple butter making. Sponsor: Tri-State Gas Engine and Tractor Assn, Inc, Rt 4, Box 421, Muncie, IN 47302.

AQUINO ASSASSINATION ANNIVERSARY. Aug 21. Filipino opposition leader Begnigno S. Aquino, Jr. was shot down at the Manila airport on his return to the Philippines on Aug 21, 1983. The killing precipitated further unrest and anti Marcos-government feeling. The anniversary of the assassination was marked by demonstrations in which hundreds of thousands of persons participated.

BEARDSLEY, AUBREY VINCENT: BIRTHDAY. Aug 21. English artist and illustrator born at Brighton, England, Aug 21, 1872. Died at Menton, France, March 16, 1898.

DEL NORTE COUNTY FAIR. Aug 21-24. Featured are the Miss Del Norte contest, rodeo, carnival, art show, agriculture and homecrafts. Info from: Chamber of Commerce, Box 246, Crescent City, CA 95531.

MINNESOTA STATE FAIR. Aug 21-Sept 1. St. Paul, MN. Info from: Communications Group, Minnesota State Fair, St. Paul, MN 55108.

OZMA'S BIRTHDAY. Aug 21. Purpose: Celebration of the birth of the Queen of Oz. Sponsor: Internatl Wizard of Oz Club, Inc, Fred M. Meyer, Secy, 220 North 11th St, Escanaba, MI 49829.

PIONEER DAYS. Aug 21-24. Harrodsburg, KY. Commemoration of Kentucky's first settlement. Pioneer attire, arts, crafts and bean soup cook-off. Info from: KY Dept of Travel, Capital Plaza Office Tower, Frankfort, KY 40601.

SALON NAUTIQUE DU VIEUX-PORT DE QUEBEC. Aug 21-24. Old Harbor, Quebec City, Quebec. Sailboats, cruisers, marine motors and accessories. Info from: P.R. Charette, Inc, 5890 Monkland, Suite 206, Montreal, Quebec, Canada H4A 1G2.

SOLDIERS' REUNION CELEBRATION. Aug 21. Newton, NC. Parade climaxes 95th annual soldiers' reunion celebration—"oldest patriotic event of its kind in the US, honoring all veterans." Concerts, arts, crafts and games. Info from: Soldiers' Reunion Committee, Box 267, Newton, NC 28658.

SPACE MILESTONE: GEMINI 5 (US). Aug 21. Launched on Aug 21, 1965, Lt. Colonel Cooper and Lt. Commander Conrad orbit Earth 128 times for new international record of 8 days. First launch of a satellite from a manned spacecraft.

TENNESSEE WALKING HORSE NATIONAL CELEBRATION. Aug 21-30. Shelbyville, TN. This show determines which of the thousand or more entries is crowned World Champion. Ten days and nights of pageantry and excitement. Info from: Celebration, Inc, Box 1010, Shelbyville, TN 37160.

AUGUST 22 — FRIDAY
234th Day — Remaining, 131

ALASKA STATE FAIR. Aug 22-Sept 1. Purpose: "State's largest horse show." Sporting events, rodeo, high-caliber entertainment and exhibits of all phases of agriculture and homemaking. Sponsor: Alaska State Fair, Inc, Box 1128, Palmer, AK 99645.

APPALACHIAN ARTS AND CRAFTS FESTIVAL. Aug 22-24. Raleigh County Armory, Civic Ctr, Beckley, WV. Info from: Chamber of Commerce, Box 1798, Beckley, WV 25802.

CHARLOTTE NEWS CAROLINA MOON RIDE. Aug 22. Purpose: Midnight bicycle ride (12 miles) starting and ending in mid-town, riding to suburbs and back. Bike races prior to ride. Info from: The Charlotte News, Box 32188, Charlotte, NC 28232.

DEBUSSY, CLAUDE: BIRTHDAY. Aug 22. (Achille) Claude Debussy, French musician and composer, especially remembered for his impressionistic "tone poems," was born at San Germain-en-Laye, on Aug 22, 1862. He died at Paris, Mar 25, 1918.

HAMAMBEE FESTIVAL. Aug 22-24. Springfield, MA. Live local and national entertainment. Golf, tennis and basketball tournaments, children's games, food and crafts. Sponsor: Harambee Holiday, Inc, Box 3551, Springfield, MA 01101.

INTERNATIONAL YACHT RACE ANNIVERSARY. Aug 22. A silver trophy (then known as the "Hundred Guinea Cup," and offered by the Royal Yacht Squadron) was won in a race around the Isle of Wight, Aug 22, 1851, by the U.S. yacht *America*. The trophy, later turned over to the New York Yacht Club, became known as the America's Cup.

KENTUCKY HEARTLAND FESTIVAL. Aug 22-24. Elizabethtown, KY. Kentucky heartland run, arts and crafts, parade and antique auto show. Info from: KY Dept of Travel, Capital Plaza Office Tower, Frankfort, KY 40601.

KING RICHARD III'S DEATH. Aug 22. Last of Plantagenets slain at Bosworth Field, this day 1485. Memorial by: Richard III Society Inc, William Hogarth, Chrmn, Box 217, Sea Cliff, NY 11579.

MICHIGAN STATE FAIR. Aug 22-Sept 1. State Fairgrounds, Detroit, MI. Info from: Marketing Office, Dept of Natural Resources, 1120 W State Fair Ave, Detroit, MI 48203.

NEW YORK STATE FAIR. Aug 22-Sept 1. State Fairgrounds, Syracuse, NY. Exhibits, demonstrations, grandstand shows and top entertainment. Info from: NY State Fairgrounds, Syracuse, NY 13209.

OHIO TOBACCO FESTIVAL. Aug 22-24. Ripley, OH. Purpose: A celebration in honor of southern Ohio's cash crop of white burley tobacco. Parade, bluegrass, country and western music, arts, crafts, tobacco hornworm race, quilt show and antique car show. Info from: Ohio Tobacco Festival, Box 91, Ripley, OH 45167.

OREGON STATE FAIR. Aug 22-Sept 1. Salem, OR. Thoroughbred racing, carnival, big name entertainment, exhibits, and horse show. Info from: Oregon State Fair, Salem, OR 97310.

OZARK FOLK CENTER AUTOHARP CONTEST. Aug 22-23. Ozark Folk Center, Mountain View, AR. Purpose: To promote and preserve traditional music played on the autoharp. Info from: Ozark Folk Ctr, Mountain View, AR 72560.

COPYRIGHT © 1985 BY WILLIAM D. CHASE and HELEN M. CHASE

PHILADELPHIA FOLK FESTIVAL. Aug 22-24. Old Poole Farm, Schwenksville, PA. International performers and groups from the folk music world perform in concerts and workshops. Sponsor: Philadelphia Folksong Society. Info from: Conv & Visitors Bureau, Three Penn Ctr Plaza, Suite 2020, Philadelphia, PA 19102.

WILLARD, ARCHIBALD M: BIRTHDAY. Aug 22. American artist, best known for his painting, *The Spirit of '76*, was born at Bedford, Ohio on Aug 22 or 26, 1836. Willard died at Cleveland, Ohio, Oct 11, 1918.

AUGUST 23 — SATURDAY
235th Day — Remaining, 130

BOBBY JONES OPEN. Aug 23-24. Ann Arbor, MI. Purpose: A golf tournament for people named Bobby Jones. Bobs and Bobbies from the U.S. and abroad gather for comaraderie and raising funds to research Syringomyelia. Sponsor: Robert A. Jones, Bobby Jones Open Committee, 29792 Telegraph Rd, Southfield, MI 48034.

CIVILIAN CONSERVATION CORPS: REUNION. Aug 23. Woodbine Picnic Area, Richwood, WV. Purpose: A get together for Civilian Conservation Corps Alumni. Info from: V. B. Vance, CCC Alumni Chapter #1, 216 Johnstown, Richwood, WV 26261.

DANKFEST. Aug 23-24. Harmony Museum, Harmony, PA. Old crafts, German food and music. Info from: Harmonist Historic & Memorial Assn, John Ruch, Pres, Harmony, PA 16037.

FIRST MAN-POWERED FLIGHT ANNIVERSARY. Aug 23. At Schafter, California, on Aug 23, 1977, Bryan Allen pedalled the 70-lb *Gossamer Condor* for a mile at a "minimal altitude of two pylons," in a flight certified by the Royal Aeronautical Society of Britain, winning a £50,000 prize offered by British industrialist Henry Kremer. See also entry for June 12.

GREAT AMERICAN DUCK RACE. Aug 23-24. Deming, NM. "World's richest duck race" features Duck Queen and Darling Duckling contest, parade and other festivities. Info from: The Great American Duck Race, 800 E Pine St, Deming, NM 88030.

INTERNATIONAL ZUCCHINI FESTIVAL. Aug 23. Harrisville, NH. Purpose: A day for exploring and exploiting the zucchini, with Agricultural Hall contests indoors and zucchini food, fun and games outdoors. Sponsor: The Zucchini Central Committee, Box 128, Harrisville, NH 03450.

IRELAND, ANDY: BIRTHDAY. Aug 23. U.S. Representative of Florida's 10th district, Republican of Winter Haven, FL, born in Cincinnati, OH, Aug 23, 1930.

LEADVILLE 100-MILE ULTRA RUN. Aug 23-24. 100-mile course through the Rocky Mountains with aid stations. Info from: Chamber of Commerce, Box 861, Leadville, CO 80461.

MASTERS, EDGAR LEE: BIRTHDAY. Aug 23. American poet, author of the *Spoon River Anthology*, was born at Garnett, KS, Aug 23, 1869. He died at Melrose Park, PA, Mar 5, 1950.

NICOLA SACCO and BARTOLOMEO VANZETTI MEMORIAL DAY. Aug 23. Sacco, a shoemaker, and Vanzetti, a fish peddler, were electrocuted at the Charlestown, MA Prison on Aug 23, 1927. Six years of appeals had marked this American cause célèbre, Sacco and Vanzetti having maintained their innocence to the end. Massachusetts governor Michael S. Dukakis proclaimed the fiftieth anniversary, Aug 23, 1977, a memorial day, noting that the 1921 trial had been "permeated by prejudice."

PERRY, OLIVER HAZARD: BIRTHDAY. Aug 23. American naval hero (Battle of Lake Erie in 1813), born Aug 23, 1785. Died Aug 23, 1819. Best remembered is his announcement of victory at the Battle of Lake Erie, on Sept 10, 1813: "We have met the enemy, and they are ours."

ROMANIA: NATIONAL HOLIDAY. Aug 23. Liberation Day.

SPACE MILESTONE: INTELSAT-4 F-7 (US). Aug 23. International Communications Satellite Consortium—Intelsat—to relay communications from North and South America to Europe and Africa. Launched Aug 23, 1973.

VIRGO, THE VIRGIN. Aug 23-Sept 22. In the astronomical/astrological Zodiac, which divides the sun's apparent orbit into twelve segments, the period Aug 23-Sept 22 is identified, traditionally, as the sun-sign of Virgo, the Virgin. The ruling planet is Mercury.

WILSON, PETE: BIRTHDAY. Aug 23. U.S. Senator from California, Republican, of San Diego, CA, born in Lake Forest, IL, on Aug 23, 1933.

AUGUST 24 — SUNDAY
236th Day — Remaining, 129

BELGIUM: BEGONIA FESTIVAL. Aug 24-26. Lochristi, Belgium. Belgium's famed begonias displayed in huge flower carpets and floats during this floral festival.

COYNE, WILLIAM J: BIRTHDAY. Aug 24. U.S. Representative of Pennsylvania's 14th district, Democrat, of Pittsburgh, PA, born there on Aug 24, 1936.

DU QUOIN STATE FAIR. Aug 24-Sept 2. DuQuoin, IL. Info from: DuQuoin State Fair, Info Office, Box 191, DuQuoin, IL 62832.

FREEDOM OF ENTERPRISE WEEK. Aug 24-30. Purpose: To focus attention upon the contributions made to our way of life by the free enterprise system. Sponsor: Program Development Dept, Kiwanis Internatl, 3636 Woodview Trace, Indianapolis, IN 46268.

ST. BARTHOLOMEW'S DAY MASSACRE. Aug 24. Anniversary of the massacre in Paris and throughout France of thousands of Huguenots, as ordered by King Charles IX (and approved by his mother, the regent, Catherine de Medicis). The massacre began when the church bells tolled at dawn on St. Bartholomew's Day, Aug 24, 1572, and continued for several days. Pope Gregory XIII ordered a medal struck to commemorate the event, but Protestant countries abhorred the killings, estimated at 2,000 to 70,000.

SCHUEBERMESS/SHEPHERD'S FAIR. Aug 24-Sept 6. Luxembourg. Fair dates from 1340. (Two weeks beginning on the last but one Sunday of August).

VESUVIUS DAY. Aug 24. Anniversary of the eruption of Vesuvius, an active volcano in southern Italy, on Aug 24, 79 A.D., which destroyed the cities of Pompeii, Stabiae, and Herculaneum.

WASHINGTON, DC: INVASION ANNIVERSARY. Aug 24-25. British forces briefly invaded and raided Washington, DC, burning the capitol, the President's House, and most other public buildings, Aug 24-25, 1814. President James Madison and other high U.S. Government officials fled to safety until British troops (not knowing the strength of their position) departed the city two days later.

AUGUST 25 — MONDAY
237th Day — Remaining, 128

ENGLAND: BANK HOLIDAY. Aug 25. Summer Bank Holiday observed on this date in England, Wales and Northern Ireland.

HARTE, BRET: BIRTHDAY. Aug 25. Francis Bret(t) Harte, journalist, poet, printer, teacher and novelist, especially remembered for his early stories of California ("The Luck of

August 1986

S	M	T	W	T	F	S
					1	2
3	4	5	6	7	8	9
10	11	12	13	14	15	16
17	18	19	20	21	22	23
24	25	26	27	28	29	30
31						

COPYRIGHT © 1985 BY WILLIAM D. CHASE and HELEN M. CHASE

Roaring Camp," "The Outcasts of Poker Flat," and "How Santa Claus Came to Simpson's Bar") was born at Albany, NY, Aug 25, 1836. He died at London, England, May 5, 1902.

HONG KONG LIBERATION DAY. Aug 25. Last Monday in August. Public holiday.

ITALY: STRESA MUSICAL WEEKS. Aug 25-Sept 20. Stresa. The 25th international festival will include 19 concerts by symphonic orchestras, chamber music, recitals, and a series by young winners of international musical contests. Info from: Associazione Settimane Musicali di Stresa, Via R. Bonghi 4, 28049 Stresa (Lago Maggiore), Italy.

KELLY, WALT: BIRTHDAY. Aug 25. Anniversary of birth of Walter Crawford Kelly, cartoonist, creator of the comic strip "Pogo," at Philadelphia, PA, on Aug 25, 1913. A day to remember Pogo. Kelly died at Hollywood, CA, Oct 18, 1973.

NORTHERN IRELAND: OULD LAMMAS FAIR. Aug 25-26. Ballycastle,County Antrim. Traditional Irish fair, chartered in 1606, but probably dating from much earlier time. Always on the last consecutive Monday and Tuesday in August.

PINKERTON, ALLAN: BIRTHDAY. Aug 25. Scottish-born, American detective, founder of detective agency in Chicago, 1850, first chief of U.S. Army's secret service, remembered now because of his strike-breaking employments and his lack of sympathy for working people. Pinkerton was born at Glasgow, Scotland, Aug 25, 1819, and died at Chicago, IL, July 1, 1884.

URUGUAY: NATIONAL HOLIDAY. Aug 25. Independence Day. Declared independence from Brazil on this day, 1825.

AUGUST 26 — TUESDAY
238th Day — Remaining, 127

ANTHONY, SUSAN B: DAY. Aug 26. Massachusetts.

CUMBERLAND COUNTY EXHIBITION. Aug 26-30. Oxford, Nova Scotia. Beef, dairy cattle, steer sale. Home cooked meals, midway and street parade. Info from: Dept of Tourism, Box 456, Halifax, NS B3J 2R5.

DE FOREST, LEE: BIRTHDAY. Aug 26. American inventor and pioneer developer of wireless telegraphy, radio, television and talking pictures, was born at Council Bluffs, IA, on Aug 26, 1873. In 1950 his autobiography, *Father of Radio*, was published. DeForest died at Hollywood, CA on June 30, 1961.

FERRARO, GERALDINE ANNE: BIRTHDAY. Aug 26. Geraldine A. Ferraro, of Queens, NY, the first woman to be nominated as candidate of a major political party for the office of U.S. vice-president, was born Aug 26, 1935 at Newburgh, NY. Married to New York businessman John A. Zaccaro in 1960, she continued to use her maiden name. The former schoolteacher and attorney was first elected to the Congress in 1978, and was nominated for the vice-presidency at the Democratic National Convention, San Francisco, July 1984.

GOLF: U.S. AMATEUR CHAMPIONSHIP. Aug 26-31. Shoal Creek, Shoal Creek, AL. National championship for amateur golfers in the U.S. Sponsor: U.S. Golf Assn, Golf House, Far Hills, NJ 07931.

KINDNESS, THOMAS N: BIRTHDAY. Aug 26. U.S. Representative of Ohio's 8th district, Republican, of Hamilton, OH, born at Knoxville, TN, on Aug 26, 1929.

KRAKATOA ERUPTION ANNIVERSARY. Aug 26. Anniversary of the biggest explosion in historic times. The eruption of the Indonesian volcanic island, Krakatoa (Krakatau), on Aug 26, 1883, was heard 3,000 miles away, created tidal waves 120 feet high (killing 36,000 persons), hurled five cubic miles of earth fragments into the air (some to a height of 50 miles), and affected the oceans and the atmosphere for years.

NAMIBIA DAY. Aug 26. Namibia (formerly named South West Africa) came under direct United Nations responsibility in 1966. U.N. General Assembly initiated annual observance of this day in 1973. Info from: United Nations Dept of Public Information, United Nations, NY 10017.

RIDGE, THOMAS JOSEPH: BIRTHDAY. Aug 26. U.S. Representative of Pennsylvania's 21st district, Republican, of Erie, PA, was born in Munhall, PA, on Aug 26, 1945.

SOUTH DAKOTA STATE FAIR. Aug 26-Sept 1. Huron, SD.

SPACE MILESTONE: SOYUZ 15 (USSR). Aug 26. Launched on Aug 26, 1974, Cosmonauts G. Sarafanov and L. Demin returned to Earth Aug 28, making emergency night landing.

SPACE MILESTONE: SOYUZ 31 (USSR). Aug 26. Launched on Aug 26, 1978, Valery Bykovsky and Sigmund Jaehn docked at Salyut 6 on Aug 27, stayed for a week, then returned to Earth in Soyuz 29 vehicle, leaving their Soyuz 31 docked at space station. Earth landing on Sept 3.

TORRICELLI, ROBERT G: BIRTHDAY. Aug 26. U.S. Representative of New Jersey's 9th district, Democrat, of Hackensack, NJ, born in Paterson, NJ, on Aug 26, 1951.

U.S. OPEN TENNIS CHAMPIONSHIPS. Aug 26-Sept 7. Purpose: America's premier tennis event—singles, doubles, and mixed doubles, and competition for junior and senior players. Sponsor: U.S. Tennis Assn, 51 E 42nd St, New York, NY 10017.

VANDER JAGT, GUY: BIRTHDAY. Aug 26. U.S. Representative of Michigan's 9th district, Republican, of Luther, MI, born at Cadillac, MI, on Aug 26, 1931.

WOMEN'S EQUALITY DAY. Aug 26. Presidential Proclamation 5364 of Aug 23, 1985. Issued in 1973 and 1974 at request and from 1975 through 1985 without request.

WOMEN'S EQUALITY DAY. Aug 26. Anniversary of certification as part of U.S. Constitution, in 1920, of the Nineteenth Amendment, prohibiting discrimination on the basis of sex with regard to voting. Congresswoman Bella Abzug's bill to designate Aug 26 of each year as "Women's Equality Day" in August 1974, became Public Law 93-392.

WORLD CYCLING CHAMPIONSHIPS. Aug 26-Sept 4. Purpose: To select 1986 world champions, men and women, for road and track. Sponsor: U.S. Cycling Federation, Dianne Fritschner, 1750 E Boulder St, Colorado Springs, CO 80909.

AUGUST 27 — WEDNESDAY
239th Day — Remaining, 126

BALTIMORE PLANT WORKSHOP. Aug 27. War Memorial Plaza, Baltimore, MD. Purpose: Demonstrations on potting and transplanting plants, info on potting soils, water, light, nutrition. Info: Virginia Baker, Mayor's Office of Adventures in Fun, 100 Holiday St, Rm 355, Baltimore, MD 21202.

DAWES, CHARLES GATES: BIRTHDAY. Aug 27. Thirtieth Vice President of the U.S. (1925-1929), born, Marietta, OH, Aug 27, 1865. Died, Evanston, IL, Apr 23, 1951.

DREISER, THEODORE: BIRTHDAY. Aug 27. Anniversary of birth, in Terre Haute, IN, of American novelist (Aug 27, 1871-Dec 28, 1945).

HAMLIN, HANNIBAL: BIRTHDAY. Aug 27. Fifteenth Vice President of the U.S. (1861-1865) born, Paris, ME, Aug 27, 1809. Died, Bangor, ME, July 4, 1891.

JOHNSON, LYNDON BAINES: BIRTHDAY. Aug 27. The 36th President of U.S. succeeded to the presidency following the assassination of John F. Kennedy. Johnson's term of office: Nov 22, 1963-Jan 20, 1969. In 1964, he said: "The challenge of the next half-century is whether we have the wisdom to use [our] wealth to enrich and elevate our national life—and to advance the quality of American civilization." Johnson was born near Stonewall, TX, and died at San Antonio, TX, Jan 22, 1973.

KERREY, ROBERT: BIRTHDAY. Aug 27. Robert Kerrey, Governor of Nebraska, Democrat, was born at Lincoln, NE, on Aug 27, 1943.

MONTREUX-DETROIT JAZZ FESTIVAL. Aug 27-Sept 1. Detroit, MI. Purpose: Celebration for music lovers and festival fans. Features Detroit groups as well as international stars and reflects Detroit's roots in the development of American jazz. Info from: Kathleen McNamara, Detroit Renaissance, 100 Renaissance Ctr, Suite 1760, Detroit, MI 48243.

MOON PHASE: LAST QUARTER. Aug 27. Moon enters Last Quarter phase at 3:38 a.m., E.S.T.

MOUNTBATTEN, LOUIS: ASSASSINATION ANNIVERSARY. Aug 27. Lord Mountbatten (Louis Francis Albert Victor Nicholas Mountbatten), celebrated British war hero, cousin of Queen Elizabeth II, last Viceroy of India, son of Prince Louis of Battenberg (Battenberg family changed name to Mountbatten, and renounced German titles during World War I), was killed by bomb, along with his 14-year-old grandson and two others, while on his yacht in Donegal Bay, on Aug 27, 1979. Provisional Irish Republican Army claimed responsibility for the explosion and for the killing of 18 British soldiers later the same day, deepening the crisis and conflict between Protestants and Catholics and between England and Ireland. Lord Mountbatten was born at Windsor, England, June 25, 1900.

YATES, SIDNEY R: BIRTHDAY. Aug 27. U.S. Representative of Illinois' 9th district, Democrat, of Chicago, IL, born there on Aug 27, 1909.

AUGUST 28 — THURSDAY
240th Day — Remaining, 125

BOYER, CHARLES: BIRTHDAY. Aug 28. American film star born at Figeac, France, Aug 28, 1889. Died at Scottsdale, AZ, Aug 26, 1978.

COHEN, WILLIAM S: BIRTHDAY. Aug 28. U.S. Senator from Maine, Republican, of Bangor, ME, born there on Aug 28, 1940.

FEAST OF ST. AUGUSTINE. Aug 28. Bishop of Hippo, author of *Confessions* and *The City of God*, died Aug 28, 430.

GOETHE, JOHANN WOLFGANG: BIRTH ANNIVERSARY. Aug 28. German author-philosopher born Aug 28, 1749. Died Mar 22, 1832.

HAYES, LUCY WARE WEBB: BIRTHDAY. Aug 28. Wife of Rutherford Birchard Hayes, 19th President of the U.S., born at Chilicothe, OH, Aug 28, 1831. Died June 25, 1889. She was nicknamed "Lemonade Lucy" because she and the president, both abstainers, served no alcoholic beverages at White House receptions.

MIDWEST OLD SETTLERS AND THRESHERS REUNION. Aug 28-Sept 1. Purpose: To preserve agriculture's past for tomorrow's generations through a living history presentation where memories of early days are harvested during five-day steam festival. Sponsor: Midwest Old Threshers, Rt 1, Mt Pleasant, IA 52641.

NATIONAL HOT ROD ASSOCIATION U.S. NATIONALS. Aug 28-Sept 1. Info from: Indianapolis Raceway Park, Bob Daniels, Gen Mgr, Box 34377, Indianapolis, IN 46234.

August 1986	S	M	T	W	T	F	S
						1	2
	3	4	5	6	7	8	9
	10	11	12	13	14	15	16
	17	18	19	20	21	22	23
	24	25	26	27	28	29	30
	31						

POLISH FEST. Aug 28-31. Purpose: A four day spree of Polish music, polka music, dancing, food, folk dancing and cultural demonstrations. Sunday outdoor Polish mass. Held annually from Thursday through Sunday of Labor Day weekend. Sponsor: Polish Festivals, Inc, Richard Gralinski, 3741 W National Ave, Milwaukee, WI 53215.

SETON, ELIZABETH ANN BAYLEY: BIRTHDAY. Aug 28. First American-born saint born on this day in 1774. See her Feast Day, Jan 4, for further information.

SOUTH MOUNTAIN FAIR. Aug 28-Sept 1. Display of agricultural products, arts, crafts and industrial and agricultural exhibits. Info from: Gettysburg Travel Council, 35 Carlisle St, Gettysburg, PA 17325.

THRESHERMAN'S REUNION AND HORSE SHOW. Aug 28-Sept 1. Purpose: To preserve the memories of steam threshing. Includes tractor pull, flea market. Sponsor: Central States Threshermen's Reunion Assn, Carl Ogle, Pontiac Natl Bank, 223 N Mill, Pontiac, Il 61764.

UNITED PARCEL SERVICE: BIRTHDAY. Aug 28. The American Messenger Company, forerunner of United Parcel Service, commenced a small local messenger service, in Seattle, WA, Aug 28, 1907. Two teenagers, Jim Casey and Claude Ryan, were the organizers. Info from: "RoundUPS," United Parcel Service, Greenwich Office Park 5, Greenwich, CT 06830.

WESTERN SQUARE DANCE FESTIVAL. Aug 28-31. Natural Bridge State Resort Park, Slade, KY. Western-style square dancers in colorful costumes gather from all over the country to "swing their partners." Info from: Kentucky Dept. of Parks, Capital Plaza Tower, Frankfort, KY 40601.

AUGUST 29 — FRIDAY
241st Day — Remaining, 124

"ACCORDING TO HOYLE" DAY. Aug 29. A day to remember Edmond Hoyle, and a day for fun and games *according to the rules*. Little is known about Edmond Hoyle. Even his birthplace and birthday are unknown. He is believed to have been born about 1672 and to have studied law. For many years he lived in London and gave instructions in the playing of games. His "Short Treatise" on the game of Whist (published in 1742) became a model guide to the rules of the game. Hoyle's name became synonymous with the idea of correct play according to the rules, and the phrase "according to Hoyle" became a part of the English language. Hoyle died in London on Aug 29, 1769.

BEHEADING OF ST. JOHN THE BAPTIST. Aug 29. Commemorates the martyrdom of Saint John the Baptist, beheaded upon order from King Herod, about A.D. 29.

BERGMAN, INGRID: BIRTHDAY. Aug 29. "One of cinema's greatest actresses," Bergman was born at Stockholm, Sweden, Aug 29, 1915, and died at London, England on her 67th birthday, Aug 29, 1982. Three times a winner of Motion Picture Academy Awards, controversy over her personal life made her and her films unpopular to American audiences during an interval of several years between periods of awards and adulation.

BRATTLEBORO HOME, INDUSTRIAL AND CRAFT SHOW. Aug 29-31. Gibson-Aiken Ctr, Brattleboro, VT. Info from: Chamber of Commerce, Samiha N. Northup, Exec VP, 180 Main St, Brattleboro, VT 05301.

CARROLL, ANNA ELLA: BIRTHDAY. Aug 29. American writer and publicist for the Union cause during the Civil War, was born in Somerset County, MD on Aug 29, 1815. Her actions in the Civil War were the subject of several books. She died at Washington, DC, Feb 18, 1894.

FLORIO, JAMES J: BIRTHDAY. Aug 29. U.S. Representative of New Jersey's 1st district, Democrat, of Pine Hill, NJ, was born in Brooklyn, NY, on Aug 29, 1937.

COPYRIGHT © 1985 BY WILLIAM D. CHASE and HELEN M. CHASE

GOVERNOR'S RODEO. Aug 29-31. Purpose: A rodeo with proceeds going to the improvement of town roads and camp areas. Sponsor: Town of Love Valley, Ellenora S. Barker, Box 607, Love Valley NC 28677.

HOLMES, OLIVER WENDELL: BIRTHDAY. Aug 29. American physician and author, born Cambridge, MA, Aug 29, 1809. Died, Boston, MA, Oct 7, 1894. "A moment's insight," he wrote, "is sometimes worth a life's experience."

JUBILEE DAYS FESTIVAL. Aug 29-Sept 1. Parade, steer roasts, arts and crafts and ice cream social. Info from: Jubilee Days Festival, Inc, Box 23, Zion, IL 60099.

LARBAUD, VALERY NICOLAS: BIRTHDAY. Aug 29. French novelist, essayist and translator of English literature, born at Vichy, Aug 29, 1881. Died there Feb 2, 1957.

LITTLE ITALY FESTIVAL. Aug 29-Sept 1. Parade, grape stomping, polka dancing, cooking demonstrations, bocce tournaments, art, music and wine garden. Spaghetti and pizza eating contest. Info: Little Italy Festival, Box 6, Clinton, IN 47842.

LOUISIANA SHRIMP AND PETROLEUM FESTIVAL AND FAIR. Aug 29-Sept 1. Purpose: To recognize and celebrate importance of the shrimp and oil industry to the area. Street fair and dance, arts, crafts, parade and blessing of the fleet. Sponsor: Louisiana Shrimp & Petroleum Festival & Fair Assn, Box 103, Morgan City, LA 70381.

McCAIN, JOHN SIDNEY III: BIRTHDAY. Aug 29. U.S. Representative of Arizona's 1st district, Republican, of Tempe, AZ, born in CoCo Solo, Panama Canal Zone on Aug 29, 1936.

MARYLAND STATE CHAMPIONSHIP CHILI JAMBOREE AND COOK-OFF. Aug 29-31. Ali Ghan Shrine Temple Picnic Grounds, Cumberland, MD. Purpose: To select Maryland chili champion, raise funds for Shrine charities. Sponsor: Ali Ghan Shrine Temple, Box 1416, Cumberland, MD 21502.

NATIONAL HOOVERCRAFT RALLY. Aug 29-Sept 1. Indianapolis, IN. Info from: Chris Fitzgerald, Fort Harrison Industrial Park, Terre Haute, IN 47904.

PRYOR, DAVID H: BIRTHDAY. Aug 29. U.S. Senator from Arkansas, Democrat, of Little Rock, AR, born at Camden, AR, Aug 29, 1934.

ROANOKE BEACH PARTY. Aug 29. Roanoke Market Square. Annual beach party featuring tons of sand covering market square, shells, live music, etc. Sponsor: Roanoke Special Events Committee, 210 Reserve Ave, SW, Roanoke, VA 24016.

SHAYS REBELLION. Aug 29. Daniel Shays, veteran of Lexington, Bunker Hill, Ticonderoga, Saratoga and Stony Point, after whom rebellion was named, was one of the leaders of over 1,000 rebelling discontents who sought redress of grievances during depression days of 1786-1787. On Aug 29, 1786 they prevented the general court sessions and Sept 26 Supreme Court sessions at Springfield, MA. On Jan 25, 1787 they attacked the Federal Arsenal at Springfield, and on Feb 2, Shays's troops were routed and fled. Shays sentenced to death, but pardoned June 13, 1788. Later received small pension for services in American Revolution.

TEXAS SESQUICENTENNIAL CELEBRATION. Aug 29-Oct 26. Dallas, TX. Musicals, gridiron rivalry, livestock and horse shows, exhibits and entertainment. Info from: State Fair of Texas, Box 26010, Dallas, TX 75226.

THREE COUNTY FAIR. Aug 29-Sept 6. Three County Fairgrounds, Northhampton. Info from: Pioneer Valley Conv & Visitors Bureau, Box 749, Northampton, MA 01061.

TOLEDO FESTIVAL: A CELEBRATION OF THE ARTS. Aug 29-Sept 1. A celebration of the visual and performing arts. Info from: Arts Commission of Greater Toledo, Diana Thomure, 618 N Michigan St, Toledo, OH 43624.

TROIS-RIVIERES GRAND PRIX. Aug 29-31. Speed car racing through city streets. Info from: Trois-Rivieres, Box 124, Trois-Rivieres, Quebec, Canada G9A 5E3.

WEST VIRGINIA ITALIAN HERITAGE FESTIVAL. Aug 29-31. Info from: Italian Heritage Festival Office, Box 1632, Clarksburg, WV 26301.

AUGUST 30 — SATURDAY
242nd Day — Remaining, 123

ARTHUR, ELLEN LEWIS HERNDON: BIRTHDAY. Aug 30. Wife of Chester Alan Arthur, 21st President of the U.S., born at Fredericksburg, VA, Aug 30, 1837. Died Jan 12, 1880.

CALVERT COUNTY JOUSTING TOURNAMENT. Aug 30. "Maryland's official state sport performed in state's oldest tournament with colorful pageantry." Annually, the last Saturday in August. Info from: The Rev John E. Howanstine, Christ Church, Port Republic, MD 20676.

CAPITAL DAY. Aug 30. Purpose: The Saturday before Labor Day is designated to honor the American savers and investors who directly or indirectly provide the funds for our capitalistic economy to grow and to progress. Sponsor: Albert L. Maguire, 1094 Maple St, Arroyo Grande, CA 93420.

CLASSIC YACHT REGATTA. Aug 30. Newport, RI. Info from: RI Dept of Economic Dev, Tourism Div, 7 Jackson Walkway, Providence, RI 02903.

CLEVELAND NATIONAL AIR SHOW. Aug 30-Sept 1. Burke Lakefront Airport, Cleveland, OH. Purpose: "To present the finest aviation exposition in the country, from the Blue Angels to historic aircraft; midget air racers to the Concorde. Hundreds of displays." Sponsor: Cleveland Natl Air Show, Jim Foster, Burke Lakefront Airport, Cleveland, OH 44114.

DENMARK: HO SHEEP MARKET. Aug. 30. The village of Ho, near Esbjerg, holds its annual sheep market on the last Saturday of August, when some 50,000 people visit the fair.

KANSAS CITY RENAISSANCE FESTIVAL. Aug 30-Oct 5. Purpose: 16th century harvest festival featuring over 2,500 costumed craftsmen, etc. Info: The Renaissance of Kansas City, 207 Westport Rd, #206, Kansas City, MO 64111.

LABOR DAY SOCCER TOURNAMENT. Aug 30-31. Ft Wayne, IN. Features teams from Chicago, Milwaukee, Toledo, St. Louis and Detroit areas challenging the Fort Wayne Sport Club. Info from: Fort Wayne Sport Club, Jim Sack, 3102 Ardmore Ave, Fort Wayne, IN 46804.

LONG, HUEY PIERCE: BIRTHDAY. Aug 30. Louisiana politician, known as the "Kingfish," elected governor 1928 and U.S. Senator 1930, born at Winnfield, LA, Aug 30, 1893. Dictatorial and flamboyant, Long became nationally famous and a potential contender for the U.S. presidency with his "Share Our Wealth: Every Man a King" plan (which would have guaranteed every family $5,000 a year and confiscated personal annual income over $1,000,000 and inheritances over $5,000,000). Long was shot (allegedly by Dr. Carl Austin Weiss, Jr.) at the Louisiana State Capital, Baton Rouge, on Sept 8, 1935, and died two days later. Huey P. Long Day is observed as a Louisiana state holiday annually on his birthday, Aug 30.

LONG, HUEY P: DAY. Aug 30. Louisiana.

MACTAQUAC FESTIVAL. Aug 30-31. Mactaquac Provincial Park, Fredericton, NB, Canada. Major craft and music event of the New Brunswick year. Info from: Anne Marie Picot, NB Craft Council, Box 1231, Fredericton, NB, Canada E3B 5C8.

COPYRIGHT © 1985 BY WILLIAM D. CHASE and HELEN M. CHASE

MOUNTAIN EAGLE INDIAN FESTIVAL. Aug 30-Sept 1. Hunter Mt, NY. Native American Indian participation with crafts, dancing competitions and storytelling. Info from: Indian Festival Committee, Bridge St, Hunter, NY 12442.

OZARK MUZZLELOADERS SHOOT. Aug 30-31. Ozark Folk Center, Mountain View, AR. Purpose: A blackpowder shooting match and "hawk" throwing competition. Info from: Ozark Folk Ctr, Mountain View, AR 72560.

PERU: SAINT ROSE OF LIMA'S DAY. Aug 30. Saint Rose of Lima is the first saint canonized during the Colony in the 16th century. Public holiday in Peru.

PIQUA HERITAGE FESTIVAL. Aug 30-Sept 1. Johnston Farm, Piqua, OH. Purpose: To promote the culture and heritage of frontier Ohio. Mountain man encampment, weaving and pioneer crafts. Sponsor: Piqua Heritage Festival, Inc, Box 1418, Piqua, OH 45356.

POWERS' CROSSROADS COUNTRY FAIR AND ART FESTIVAL. Aug 30-Sept 1. Purpose: A community event to obtain proceeds for community projects and to promote arts and crafts in the area. Sponsor: Coweta Festivals, Inc, Box 899, Newnan, GA 30264.

ROARING CAMP STEAM FESTIVAL. Aug 30-Sept 1. Antique steam and gas engines operated and displayed. Info from: Roaring Camp & Big Trees Narrow-gauge Railroad, Felton, Santa Cruz County, CA 95018.

ST. LUCIA: LA ROSE FESTIVAL. Aug 30. Flower society festival. Info from: St. Lucia Tourist Board, 41 E 42nd St, New York NY 10017.

SHARP CORN FESTIVAL. Aug 30-31. Purpose: To promote awareness of downtown architecture and one of the area's #1 agricultural products. Crafts, music, farm displays and special corn foods. Info from: Shippensburg Historic & Recreational Planning Society, Rose Dillner, Shippensburg, PA 17257.

SPACE MILESTONE: *DISCOVERY*. Aug 30. Space shuttle *Discovery* makes maiden flight with 6-member crew. Launched from Kennedy Space Center, FL, on Aug 30, 1984, deployed 3 satellites and used robot arm before landing, Sept 5, 1984 at Edwards AFB, CA.

SPACE MILESTONE: STS-8 (US). Aug 30. Shuttle Challenger with five astronauts (Richard Truly, Daniel Brandenstein, Guion Bluford Jr, Dale Gardner and William Thornton) was launched from Kennedy Space Center, FL Aug 30, 1983. Landed at Edwards Air Force Base, CA on Sept 5.

STEAM HARVEST DAYS. Aug 30-Sept 1. Rockville, IN. Info from: Kay Hinds, Billie Creek Village, RR 2, Box 27, Rockville, IN 47872.

TOLEDO FESTIVAL. Aug 30-Sept 2. Riverfront, Maumee River Downtown, Toledo, OH. Labor Day weekend is celebrated along Toledo's riverfront. Visual and performing arts. Info from: Arts Commission of Greater Toledo, 618 N Michigan St, Toledo, OH 43624.

VERMONT STATE FAIR. Aug 30-Sept 7. Fairgrounds, Rutland, Vermont. Info from: Dept of Economic Dev, Montpelier, VT 05602.

WILHELM TELL FESTIVAL. Aug 30-Sept 1. Tell Grounds, New Glarus, WI. Info from: Wilhelm Tell Festival, Box 875, New Glarus, WI 53574.

WILKINS, ROY: BIRTHDAY. Aug 30. Roy Wilkins, grandson of a Mississippi slave, civil rights leader, active in the Natl Assn for the Advancement of Colored People (NAACP), retiring as its executive director in 1977, was born at St. Louis, MO, Aug 30, 1901. He died at New York City, Sept 8, 1981.

August 1986

	S	M	T	W	T	F	S
						1	2
	3	4	5	6	7	8	9
	10	11	12	13	14	15	16
	17	18	19	20	21	22	23
	24	25	26	27	28	29	30
	31						

WORLD CHAMPIONSHIP BARBEQUE GOAT COOK-OFF. Aug 30. Richards Park. Purpose: To promote Brady and the sheep and goat industry. Arts and crafts fair featuring local and statewide artists. Sponsor: Chamber of Commerce, 101 E 1st St, Brady TX 76825.

AUGUST 31 — SUNDAY
243rd Day — Remaining, 122

CHARLESTON EARTHQUAKE CENTENNIAL. Aug 31. Charleston, SC. The first major earthquake in the recorded history of the eastern US occurred Aug 31, 1886. It is believed that about 100 persons perished in the quake centered near Charleston but felt up to 800 miles away. The first shock was at 9:51 p.m., EST, and is described in the US Commerce Dept's *Earthquake History of the United States* as follows: "The earthquake started with a barely perceptible tremor, then a sound like a heavy body rolling along; the sound became a roar, all movable objects began to shake and rattle, and the tremor became a rude, rapid quiver. There was no break in the increasingly heavy jar. Everyone feared instant death. Finally, the earth became quiet, the roar stopped, and human cries of pain and fear, wailing and excited shouts became audible." Though a number of smaller Eastern US quakes had been described and recorded, beginning in 1638, this was the most terrible and affected persons living in an area of some two million square miles.

GREAT MISSOURI RIVER RAFT REGATTA. Aug 31. Purpose: Teams of 2 in 4-man inflatable rafts race down Missouri River 26.5 miles vying for prize money. Sponsor: The Great Missouri River Raft Regatta, 2725 Iowa St, Omaha, NE 68112.

HAWKINS, AUGUSTUS F: BIRTHDAY. Aug 31. U.S. Representative of California's 29th district, Democrat, of Los Angeles, CA, born in Shreveport, LA, Aug 31, 1907.

HERB TASTING PARTY. Aug 31. Purpose: To educate visitors on the importance of herbs in the life of the nineteenth century rural inhabitants. Sponsor: Duke Homestead State Historic Site, 2828 Duke Homestead Rd, Durham, NC 27705.

INDIA: JANMASHTAMI. Aug 31. Birth anniversary of Lord Krishna, believed to be the reincarnation of Vishnu and the author of the Bhagvad Gita. Observed throughout India.

JERRY LEWIS LABOR DAY TELETHON FOR MUSCULAR DYSTROPHY. Aug 31-Sept 1. Info from: Muscular Dystrophy Assn, 810 7th Ave, New York, NY 10019.

MALAYSIA: NATIONAL HOLIDAY. Aug 31. Commemorates attainment of independent membership in British Commonwealth on Aug 31, 1957.

NATIONAL FRISBEE FESTIVAL. Aug 31. Purpose: "Frisbee for the Family." Exhibitions of throwing and catching skills, frisbee catching dogs and clinics for the audience. Sponsor: Natl Frisbee Festival, Box 220, White Plains, MD 20695.

NATIONAL NEIGHBORHOOD DAY. Aug 31. Purpose: To recognize the neighborhood as a vital national asset and to celebrate the accomplishments of neighborhood organizations. (The Saturday before Labor Day.) Sponsor: Crescent Hill Community Council, Inc, Stephen P. Imhoff, Chrmn, Suite 406, 310 W Liberty St, Louisville, KY 40202.

NEBRASKA STATE FAIR. Aug 31-Sept 9. Lincoln, NE.

SAROYAN, WILLIAM: BIRTHDAY. Aug 31. American writer, of Armenian descent, author of *The Human Comedy*, and of Pulitzer Prize-winning play, *The Time of Your Life*, was born at Fresno, CA, Aug 31, 1908, and died there on May 18, 1981. In April, 1981, he gave reporters a final statement for publication after his death: "Everybody has got to die, but I have always believed an exception would be made in my case. Now what?"

SCHWINDEN, TED: BIRTHDAY. Aug 31. Ted Schwinden, Governor of Montana, Democrat, was born at Wolf Point, MT, on Aug 31, 1925.

TRINIDAD AND TOBAGO: INDEPENDENCE DAY. Aug 31. National holiday. Became Commonwealth nation Aug 31, 1962.

COPYRIGHT © 1985 BY WILLIAM D. CHASE and HELEN M. CHASE

September.

SEPTEMBER 1 — MONDAY

244th Day — Remaining, 121

BE KIND TO EDITORS AND WRITERS MONTH. Sept 1-30. Purpose: A time for editors and writers to show uncommon courtesy toward each other. Info from: Lone Star Publications of Humor, Box 29000, Suite 103, San Antonio, TX 78229.

BRAZIL: INDEPENDENCE WEEK. Sept 1-7. The independence of Brazil is commemorated with civic and cultural ceremonies promoted by federal, state and municipal authorities. On Sept 7, a grand military parade takes place and the National Defense League organizes the Running Race in Honor of the Symbolic Torch of the Brazilian Nation.

CABLE TV MONTH. Sept 1-30. Purpose: To celebrate the many cable TV artists and broadcasters who bring information and entertainment to millions of viewers. Sponsor: Richard R. Falk Associates, Richard R. Falk, Pres, 147 W 42nd St, New York, NY 10036.

CARTIER, JACQUES: DEATH ANNIVERSARY. Sept 1. French navigator and explorer who sailed from St. Malo, Apr 20, 1534, in search of a northwest passage to the Orient. Instead, he discovered the St. Lawrence River, explored Canada's coastal regions, and took possession of the country for France. Cartier was born at St. Malo, France, about 1491 (exact date unknown) and died there on Sept 1, 1557.

CHILE: NATIONAL MONTH. Sept 1-30. A month of special significance in Chile: arrival of spring, Anniversary of the Independence of Chile (proclaimed Sept 18, 1810), Anniversary of the armed forces rising of Sept 11, 1973 to overthrow the government, and celebration of the 1980 Constitution, and Army Day, Sept 19th.

EMERGENCY CARE MONTH. Sept 1-30. Purpose: To educate and instruct the public in the performance of emergency medical techniques, to enable individuals to administer immediate life saving care before medical help arrives, and to pay tribute to those practiced in the medical skills required in the care of people in emergency situations. Sponsor: Natl Emergency Care Organization, Steven L. Arnold MD, Chrmn, 2080 Century Park East, Suite 1206, Century City, Los Angeles, CA 90067.

EMERGENCY CARE WEEK. Sept 1-7. Purpose: To educate and instruct the public in the performance of emergency medical techniques, to enable individuals to administer immediate life saving care before medical help arrives, and to pay tribute to those practiced in the medical skills required in the care of people in emergency situations. Sponsor: Natl Emergency Care Organization, Steven L. Arnold MD, Chrmn, 2080 Century Park East, Suite 1206, Century City, Los Angeles, CA 90067.

EMMA M. NUTT DAY. Sept 1. A day to honor the first woman telephone operator, Emma M. Nutt, who reportedly began that professional career at Boston, MA, on Sept 1, 1878, and continued working as a telephone operator for some 33 years.

ENGLAND: FARNBOROUGH INTERNATIONAL—AEROSPACE EXHIBITION AND FLYING DISPLAY. Sept 1-7. Royal Aircraft Establishment Airfield, Farnborough, Hampshire. "World's largest international presentation of aerospace products."

FULL EMPLOYMENT WEEK. Sept 1-7. An extension of Labor Day to include the full week beginning with that holiday. Meetings, rallies, etc, were held during 1977 Full Employment Week to demonstrate that "Americans want work, and there is plenty of work to do."

GERMANY: BERLIN FESTIVAL WEEKS. Sept 1-Oct 4. Info from: Berliner Festspiele, Budapester Strasse 50, 1 Berlin 30.

JAPAN: KANTO EARTHQUAKE MEMORIAL DAY. Sept 1. Day to remember the 57,000 people who died during Japan's greatest earthquake which took place on Sept 1, 1923.

KOREAN AIR LINES FLIGHT 007 DISASTER ANNIVERSARY. Sept 1. Korean Air Lines Flight 007, en route from New York City to Seoul, Korea, reportedly strayed more than 100 miles off course, flying over secret Soviet military installations on the Kamchatka Peninsula and Sakhalin Island. Two and one half hours after it was said to have entered Soviet airspace, at 3:26 a.m., Korean time (Aug 31 at 1:26 p.m., E.S.T.) a Soviet interceptor plane destroyed the Boeing 747 with 269 persons on board (240 passengers and 29 crew members) which then crashed in the Sea of Japan. There were no survivors. Pres. Reagan, in Proclamation 5093, appointed Sunday, Sept 11, 1983, as a National Day of Mourning, and recommended "homage to the memory of those who died."

LA MERIENDA WEEK. Sept 1-6. Purpose: Early California Spanish barbecuing festival for picknickers or patio parties. Sponsor: Cordon Bleu Ouest College of Barbecuing, 3369 Hamilton Way, Los Angeles, CA 90026.

LABOR DAY. Sept 1. Legal public holiday. (Public Law 90-363 sets Labor Day on the first Monday in September.) Observed on this day in all states and in Canada. First observance believed to have been a parade at 10 a.m., Tuesday, Sept 5, 1882, in New York City, probably organized by Peter J. McGuire, a carpenters and joiners union secretary. In 1883, a union resolution declared "the first Monday in September of each year a Labor Day." By 1893 more than half of the states were observing Labor Day on one or another day, and a bill to establish Labor Day as a federal holiday was introduced in Congress. On June 28, 1894, President Grover Cleveland signed into law an act making the first Monday in September a legal holiday for federal employes and the District of Columbia.

LIBYAN ARAB REPUBLIC: REVOLUTION DAY. Sept 1. Commemorates the revolution of Sept 1, 1969. National holiday.

MACKINAC BRIDGE WALK. Sept 1. By tradition Labor Day is the only day of the year pedestrians are permitted to walk across the five-mile-long span, one of the world's longest suspension bridges, connecting Michigan's two peninsulas, Mackinaw City to St. Ignace.

MISSION SAN LUIS OBISPO DE TOLOSA ANNIVERSARY. Sept 1. California mission to the Indians founded Sept 1, 1772.

NATIONAL SIGHT-SAVING MONTH. Sept 1-30. Purpose: Alerting the public to the value of early detection of eye problems, of proper eye care, and the need for eye safety. Sponsor: Natl Society to Prevent Blindness, Lydia Maguire, PR Dir, 79 Madison Ave, New York, NY 10016.

PASSENGER PIGEON-WATCHERS ANNUAL COUNT. Sept 1. Purpose: To watch for, count and report all sightings of passenger pigeons. Date commemorates death, Sept 1, 1914, of Martha, the last known passenger pigeon in captivity, at

COPYRIGHT © 1985 BY WILLIAM D. CHASE and HELEN M. CHASE

Cincinnati Zoo. Sponsor: Passenger Pigeon Count Hq, Unicorn Hunters, Lake Superior State College, Sault Ste. Marie, MI 49783.

PHILATELIC PUBLICATIONS MONTH. Sept 1-30. Purpose: To honor philatelic publications which are devoted to the promotion of stamp collecting and to gain greater recognition for their important part in philately. Sponsor: The Philatelic Journalist, 154 Laguna Ct, St. Augustine Shores, FL 32086.

PIONEER FLORIDA DAY. Sept 1. Dade City, FL. Info from: Pioneer Florida Museum, Box 335, Dade City, FL 34297.

REUTHER, WALTER PHILIP: BIRTHDAY. Sept 1. American labor leader who began work in a steel factory at 16 and later became president of the United Automobile Workers (U.A.W.) and the Congress of Industrial Organizations (C.I.O.). Born at Wheeling, WV, on Sept 1, 1907, Reuther spent several years in his twenties in world travel and worked for two years in a Russian automobile factory. Often at the center of controversy, he was the target of an assassin in 1948. Reuther and his wife died in an airplane crash on May 9, 1970, near the U.A.W. Family Education Center at Black Lake, MI. The Family Education Center, a project which he had cherished, was later named for Walter and May Reuther.

RINALDO, MATTHEW J: BIRTHDAY. Sept 1. U.S. Representative of New Jersey's 7th district, Republican, of Union, NJ, born in Elizabeth, Union County, NJ, Sept 1, 1931.

RIVERFEST. Sept 1. On the banks of the Ohio River, Cincinnati, OH. An end of summer celebration with music, continuous entertainment and spectacular fireworks. Info from: William R Barrett, Cincinnati Recreation Commission, 222 E Central Parkway, Cincinnati, OH 45202.

SETTLER'S DAY. Sept 1. Republic of South Africa. First Monday in September.

SIGOURNEY, LYDIA: BIRTHDAY. Sept 1. Prolific American author, Lydia Howard Huntley Sigourney, was born Sept 1, 1791, at Norwich, CT. Her writings, mainly moral and religious works, included such titles as *How to Be Happy*, *Letters to Young Ladies*, and *Pleasant Memories of Pleasant Lands*. More than 65 books came from her pen before her death on June 10, 1865, at Hartford, CT.

WOOD ENERGY MONTH. Sept 1-30. Purpose: To provide consumer information on the use of fireplaces, stoves and woodburning equipment. Sponsor: Wood Heating Alliance, Judith Walker, Communications Dir, 1101 Connecticut Ave, NW, Washington, DC 20036.

SEPTEMBER 2 — TUESDAY
245th Day — Remaining, 120

BISON-TEN-YELL DAY. Sept 2. Sponsor: Puns Corps, c/o: Bob Birch, Grand Punscorpion, Box 2364, Falls Church, VA 22042.

CALENDAR ADJUSTMENT DAY ANNIVERSARY. Sept 2. Pursuant to the British Calendar Act of 1751, Britain (and the American colonies) made the "Gregorian Correction" on Sept 2, 1752. The Act proclaimed that the day following Wednesday, Sept 2nd, should become Thursday, Sept 14, 1752. There was rioting in the streets by those who felt cheated and who demanded the eleven days back. The Act also provided that New Year's Day (and the change of year number) should fall on Jan 1st (instead of Mar 25th) in 1752 and every year thereafter. See also entries for Feb 24 and Oct 4.

DAYS OF MARATHON: ANNIVERSARY. Sept 2-9. Anniversary of the events in 490 B.C. from which the marathon race is derived: Phidippides, "an Athenian and by profession and

September 1986

S	M	T	W	T	F	S
	1	2	3	4	5	6
7	8	9	10	11	12	13
14	15	16	17	18	19	20
21	22	23	24	25	26	27
28	29	30				

practice a trained runner," according to Herodotus, was dispatched from Marathon to Sparta (26 miles), Sept 2nd (Metageitnion 28) to seek help in repelling the invading Persian army. Help being unavailable by religious law until after the next full moon, Phidippides ran the 26 miles back to Marathon on Sept 4. Under the leadership of Miltiades, and without Spartan aid, the Athenians defeated the Persians at the Battle of Marathon (q.v.) on Sept 9. According to legend Phidippides carried the news of the battle to Athens and died as he spoke the words "Rejoice, we are victorious." The marathon race was revived at the 1896 Olympic Games in Athens, to commemorate Phidippides' heroism. The standard course distance, since 1924, is 26 miles, 385 yards. Oldest in the U.S. is the Boston Marathon, an annual event since 1897.

GREAT FIRE OF LONDON ANNIVERSARY. Sept 2-5. The fire generally credited with bringing about our system of fire insurance started Sept 2, 1666 in the wooden house of a baker named Farryner, in London's Pudding Lane, near the Tower. During the ensuing three days more than 13,000 houses were destroyed, though it is believed that only six lives were lost in the fire. London had experienced three disastrous fires previously, in 798, 982 and 1212.

MOODY, JIM: BIRTHDAY. Sept 2. U.S. Representative of Wisconsin's 5th district, Democrat, of Milwaukee, WI, was born in Richlands, VA, on Sept 2, 1935.

PROSPERITY DAY. Sept 2. Observed on birthday of Henry George (1839-1897), widely read American author. Birthday parties at Henry George Schools. Sponsor: Common Ground, 206 Pearlcroft Rd, Cherry Hill, NJ 08034.

SIMPSON, ALAN K: BIRTHDAY. Sept 2. U.S. Senator from Wyoming, Republican, of Cody, WY, born in Denver, CO, on Sept 2, 1931.

VIETNAM: INDEPENDENCE DAY. Sept 2. On Sept 2, 1945, Ho Chi Minh formally proclaimed the independence of Vietnam and the establishment of the Democratic Republic of Vietnam.

SEPTEMBER 3 — WEDNESDAY
246th Day — Remaining, 119

AMATI, NICOLO: BIRTHDAY. Sept 3. Celebrated Italian violin maker. Sept 3, 1596-Aug 12, 1684.

BARNES, MICHAEL DARR: BIRTHDAY. Sept 3. U.S. Representative of Maryland's 8th district, Democrat, of Kensington, MD, born in Washington, DC, Sept 3, 1943.

CRANDALL, PRUDENCE: BIRTHDAY. Sept 3. American schoolteacher who sparked controversy in the 1830s with her efforts to educate Black girls. Born on Sept 3, 1803 to a Quaker family at Hopkinton, RI. When her private academy for girls was boycotted because she admitted a Black girl, she started a school for "young ladies and misses of colour." She died on Jan 28, 1890.

FILENE, EDWARD ALBERT: BIRTHDAY. Sept 3. American merchant, philanthropist who established U.S. credit union movement 1921, born Salem, MA, Sept 3, 1860. Died Paris, France, Sept 26, 1937. Info from: Credit Union Natl Assn, Inc, Lucy Harr Schultz, VP, PR, Box 431, Madison, WI 53701.

KOLTER, JOSEPH PAUL: BIRTHDAY. Sept 3. U.S. Representative of Pennsylvania's 4th district, Democrat, of New Brighton, PA, born in McDonald, OH, Sept 3, 1926.

MISS INDIAN AMERICA PAGEANT. Sept 3-7. Purpose: Indian pageant with talent, costume, dancing and singing contests. Info from: Jack Booth, Box 81, Bismarck, ND 58502.

NEVADA STATE FAIR. Sept 3-7. Reno, NV. Carnival, exhibits and music. Info from: Nevada State Fair, 1350 N.Wells, Reno, NV 89520.

QATAR: INDEPENDENCE DAY. Sept 3. National holiday.

TREATY OF PARIS ANNIVERSARY. Sept 3. Treaty between Britain and the United States, ending the Revolutionary War, signed in Paris, Sept 3, 1783. American signatories: John Adams, Benjamin Franklin and John Jay.

COPYRIGHT © 1985 BY WILLIAM D. CHASE and HELEN M. CHASE

WARREN COUNTY PRIME BEEF FESTIVAL. Sept 3-6. Calf show and auction, market hog show and auction, parade, entertainment, arts and crafts. Info from: Chamber of Commerce, Box 245, Monmouth, IL 61462.

WORLD WAR II DECLARATION ANNIVERSARY. Sept 3. British ultimatum to Germany, demanding halt to invasion of Poland (which had started at dawn on Sept 1), expired at 11 a.m., G.M.T. Sept 3, 1939. At 11:15 a.m., in a radio broadcast, Prime Minister Neville Chamberlain announced the declaration of war against Germany. France, Canada, Australia, New Zealand and South Africa quickly issued separate declarations of war. Winston Churchill was named First Lord of the Admiralty. See also entry for VE Day, May 8.

SEPTEMBER 4 — THURSDAY
247th Day — Remaining, 118

BRUCKNER, ANTON: BIRTHDAY. Sept 4. Austrian composer born at Ansfelden, Sept 4, 1824. Died at Vienna, Oct 11, 1896.

BUHL DAY. Sept 4. Buhl Farm, Sharon, PA. Purpose: To honor the laboring man. Info from: Nancy Emmett, Box 709, Sharon, PA 16146.

BURNHAM, DANIEL: BIRTHDAY. Sept 4. American architect, Daniel Hudson Burnham, born Sept 4, 1846, at Henderson, NY. Burnham was an advocate of the tall, fireproof buildings, probably the first to be called "sky-scrapers." Burnham died June 1, 1912, at Heidelberg, Germany.

CHATEAUBRIAND, FRANCOIS RENE de: BIRTHDAY. Sept 4. French poet, novelist, historian, explorer and statesman, witness to the French Revolution and traveller in the United States, was born at St. Malo, France, Sept 4, 1768. Chateaubriand died at Paris, July 4, 1848.

DEFEAT OF JESSE JAMES DAYS. Sept 4-7. Northfield, MN. Bank raid re-enactment, drum and bugle corps competition, 5 and 15 km runs, arts, crafts, bike race, steam locomotive rides and professional rodeo. Info from: Chamber of Commerce, Box 198, Northfield, MN 55057.

EAGLETON, THOMAS FRANCIS: BIRTHDAY. Sept 4. U.S. Senator from Missouri, Democrat, of St. Louis, MO, born in St. Louis on Sept 4, 1929.

FESTIVAL OF FESTIVALS. Sept 4-13. Toronto, Ontario, Canada. Purpose: A world class film festival presenting an exciting cross-section of Canadian and international cinema. Sponsor: World Film Festival of Toronto, Inc, 69 Yorkville Ave, Suite 205, Toronto, Ontario, Canada M5S 1B7.

FORT LAUDERDALE FALL HOME SHOW. Sept 4-7. War Memorial Auditorium, Ft Lauderdale, FL. Info from: Perl Exposition Corp, 6915 Red Rd, Suite 228, Coral Gables, FL 33143.

GENERAL CONVENTION OF UNIVERSALISTS FOUNDING. Sept 4. Anniversary of the founding on Sept 4, 1793 of the General Convention of Universalists. Info from: Unitarian Universalist Assn, 25 Beacon St, Boston, MA 02108.

KIELBASA FESTIVAL. Sept 4-7. Chicopee, MA. "The Kielbasa capital of the world." Info from: Pioneer Valley Conv & Visitors Bureau, Box 749, Northampton, MA 01061.

LAGOMARSINO, ROBERT J: BIRTHDAY. Sept 4. U.S. Representative of California's 19th district, Republican, of Ventura, CA, born in Ventura, Ventura County, CA, on Sept 4, 1926.

LOS ANGELES, CALIFORNIA: BIRTHDAY. Sept 4. Los Angeles founded, by decree, on Sept 4, 1781, and called "El Pueblo de Nuestra Senora La Reina de Los Angeles de Porciuncula."

LOS ANGELES CITY'S BIRTHDAY CELEBRATION. Sept 4. Civic ceremony, music and dancing to celebrate the founding of Los Angeles which took place Sept 4, 1781. Info from: El Pueblo de Los Angeles State Historic Park, 845 N Alameda St, Los Angeles, CA 90012.

MOON PHASE: NEW MOON. Sept 4. Moon enters New Moon phase at 2:10 a.m., E.S.T.

NAVAJO NATION FAIR AND RODEO. Sept 4-8. Window Rock, AZ. Traditional Navajo tribal fair featuring the "world's largest" Indian rodeo and native dances, foods and exhibits. Info from: The Navajo Tribe, Window Rock, AZ 86515.

NEVADA STATE FAIR. Sept 4-8. Reno Fairgrounds, Reno, NV.

NEWSPAPER CARRIER DAY. Sept 4. Anniversary of the hiring of the first "newsboy" in the U.S., 10-year-old Barney Flaherty, who is said to have answered the following classified advertisement which appeared in *The New York Sun*, Sept 4, 1833: "To the Unemployed—A number of steady men can find employment by vending this paper. A liberal discount is allowed to those who buy to sell again."

POLK, SARAH CHILDRESS: BIRTHDAY. Sept 4. Wife of James Knox Polk, 11th President of the U.S., born at Murfreesboro, TN, Sept 4, 1803. Died Aug 14, 1891.

POWER DAY, (NEW YORK CITY). Sept 4. New York, NY. Purpose: To acknowledge Thomas Edison's company giving light to New York City on Sept 4, 1882. Sponsor: WPLJ RADIO (POWER 95), Lisa Tonacci, 1330 Ave of Americas, New York, NY 10019.

SEPTEMBER 5 — FRIDAY
248th Day — Remaining, 117

ALL OHIO BALLOON RALLY AND AIR SHOW. Sept 5-7. Union County Airport, Marysville, OH. Purpose: "Fun and excitement for all ages. A chance to turn strangers into friends you've yet to meet." (Weekend after Labor Day.) Sponsor: Marysville Area Chamber of Commerce, Box 135, Marysville, OH 43040.

ANNIVERSARY OF FIRST CONTINENTAL CONGRESS ASSEMBLY. Sept 5. Philadelphia, PA (Sept 5, 1774. Peyton Randolph, delegate from Virginia, elected president).

ARTFEST '86. Sept 5-Oct 4. Knoxville, TN. Info from: The Arts Council, Box 2506, Knoxville, TN 37901.

BE LATE FOR SOMETHING DAY. Sept 5. Purpose: To create a release from the stresses and strains resulting from a consistent need to be on time. Sponsor: Procrastinators' Club of America Inc, Les Waas, Pres, Broad Locust Bldg, Philadelphia, PA 19102.

DANFORTH, JOHN CLAGGETT: BIRTHDAY. Sept 5. U.S. Senator from Missouri, Republican, of Newburg, MO, born at St. Louis MO, Sept 5, 1936.

GLENDI '86. Sept 5-7. Greek Cultural Ctr, Springfield, MA. Purpose: Greek celebration with arts, music, dance, cultural events and foods. Info from: Pioneer Valley Conv & Visitors Bureau, Box 749, Northampton, MA 01061.

KENTUCKY FRIED CHICKEN BLUEGRASS MUSIC FESTIVAL. Sept 5-7. Riverfront Plaza/Belvedere, Louisville, KY. Purpose: To show bands playing the full range of bluegrass music. Sponsor: Kentucky Fried Chicken, Clara Kinner, KFC Corp, Box 32070, Louisville, KY 40232.

MICHIGAN'S GREAT FIRE OF 1881 ANNIVERSARY. Sept 5. According to Michigan Historical Commission "Small fires were burning in the forests of the 'Thumb area of Michigan,' tinder-dry after a long, hot summer, when a gale swept in from the southwest on Sept 5, 1881. Fanned into an inferno, the fire raged for three days. A million acres were devastated in Sanilac and Huron counties alone. At least 125 persons died, and thousands more were left destitute. The new American Red Cross won support for its prompt aid to the fire victims. This was the first disaster relief furnished by this great organization."

NATIONAL CHAMPIONSHIP INDIAN POWWOW. Sept 5-7. Traders Village, Grand Prairie, TX. Hundreds of Indians gather for colorful traditional dance contests, Indian arts and crafts show, home-made tepee competition and Indian food. Info from: Dallas-Fort Worth Inter-Tribal Assn, Traders Village, 2602 Mayfield Rd, Grand Prairie, TX 75051.

NIELSEN, ARTHUR CHARLES: BIRTHDAY. Sept 5. Marketing research engineer, founder of A.C. Nielsen Co., in 1923, known for radio and TV audience surveys, was born Sept 5, 1897, and died, at Chicago, June 1, 1980.

OHIO RIVER STERNWHEEL FESTIVAL. Sept 5-7. Riverfront Park, Downtown Marietta, OH. Purpose: To celebrate a significant era of Marietta's history by providing an event for the enjoyment of our citizens and tourists. Sponsor: Ohio River Sternwheel Festival Committee, 316 Third St, Marietta, OH 45750.

PEKIN MARIGOLD FESTIVAL. Sept 5-7. Purpose: Participation and pride in the community. Marigold parade, art show, musicians, paddle boat riders on a sunny lagoon and "Best Ball" golf tournament. Info from: Chamber of Commerce, 116 S Capitol St, Pekin, IL 61554.

PUFFERBILLY DAYS. Sept 5-7. Boone, Iowa celebrates its railroad heritage. Info from: Chamber of Commerce, Box 306, Boone, IA 50036.

ST. GOTTHARD AUTOMOBILE TUNNEL ANNIVERSARY. Sept 5. Switzerland. The longest underground motorway in the world, the St. Gotthard Auto Tunnel in Switzerland, was opened to traffic on Sept 5, 1980. More than ten miles long, requiring $417,000,000 and ten years for construction, it became the most direct route from Switzerland to the southern regions of the continent. The St. Gotthard Pass, the main passage since the Middle Ages, was closed much of every year by massive snow drifts.

SPACE MILESTONE: VOYAGER 1 (US). Sept 5. Launched on Sept 5, 1977, twin of Voyager 2 which was launched Aug 20.

TULELAKE BUTTE VALLEY FAIR. Sept 5-8. Tulelake Fairgrounds, Tulelake, CA 96134.

UNITED TRIBES POWWOW. Sept 5-7. Bismarck, ND. Indian singing and dancing competition in colorful costumes. Info from: United Tribes Educational Technical Center, 3315 South Airport Rd., Bismarck, ND 58501.

UTAH STATE FAIR. Sept 5-15. Salt Lake City, UT. Info from: Utah State Fair, 155 N 1000 W, Salt Lake City, UT 84116.

SEPTEMBER 6 — SATURDAY
249th Day — Remaining, 116

ADDAMS, JANE: BIRTHDAY. Sept 6. American worker for peace, social welfare, rights of women, founder of Hull House (Chicago), co-winner of Nobel Prize, 1931, born at Cedarville, IL, Sept 6, 1860. Died May 21, 1935, at Chicago.

"BIRDS IN ART" EXHIBITION. Sept 6-Nov 2. Leigh Yawkey Woodson Art Museum, Wausau, WI. "Internationally famous exhibition of bird paintings and sculptures." Info from: Leigh Yawkey Woodson Art Museum, Franklin & 12th St, Wausau, WI 54401.

CANTERBURY SHAKER ANTIQUE FAIR AND SALE. Sept 6. Info from: Shaker Village, Inc, Canterbury, NH 03224.

September *1986*	S	M	T	W	T	F	S
		1	2	3	4	5	6
	7	8	9	10	11	12	13
	14	15	16	17	18	19	20
	21	22	23	24	25	26	27
	28	29	30				

CARRY NATION FESTIVAL. Sept 6-8. Holly, MI. Purpose: Recreates the historical visit of Carry Nation, the Kansas City saloon smasher. Pageant, parade, international grape stomp, pig wrestling and crafts. (Always weekend after Labor Day.) Info from: Ardath Regan, 701 E Maple, Holly, MI 48442.

DENMARK: AARHUS FESTIVAL WEEK. Sept 6-15. Observed from the first Saturday in Sept and for nine days after, since 1965, with theater, ballet, opera, sports, exhibitions and special programs for children.

FESTIVAL '86. Sept 6-7. Paris Landing State Park, TN. Purpose: To promote the work of artists and craftsmen. Sponsor: Tri-County Arts & Craft Guild, Box 3004, Paris TN 38242.

GERMANTOWN PRETZEL FESTIVAL. Sept 6-7. Crafts, food and entertainment. Info from: Germantown Pretzel Festival, Box 42, Germantown, OH 45327.

GOLDEN HARVEST FESTIVAL. Sept 6-7. Purpose: An old-fashioned fair with over 100 artists and craftsmen demonstrating and selling their work. Bluegrass and old-time music. Sponsor: Beaver Lake Nature Ctr, 8477 E Mud Lake Rd, Baldwinsville, NY 13027.

GREAT RENO BALLOON RACE. Sept 6-7. Reno, NV. Info from: Candi Pearce, Harrah's, Reno, NV 89502.

HIGHLAND FOLK FESTIVAL. Sept 6-7. Jenny Wiley State Resort Park, Prestonsburg, KY. Music, crafts, and stories of the mountains of eastern Kentucky. Info from: Kentucky Dept. of Parks, Capital Plaza Tower, Frankfort, KY 40601.

LAFAYESTA. Sept 6-7. Indiana Veterans Home. Purpose: Juried art fair—major fund raiser for Museum of Art. Sponsor: Greater Lafayette Museum of Art, Sue Paschke, Promotions Coord, 101 S 9th, Lafayette, IN 47901.

LEVIN, SANDER MARTIN: BIRTHDAY. Sept 6. U.S. Representative of Michigan's 17th district, Democrat, of Southfield, MI, born in Detroit, MI, on Sept 6, 1931.

LIGONIER HIGHLAND GAMES. Sept 6. Idlewild Park, Ligonier, PA. Purpose: Competitions in piping, drumming, highland dancing, fiddling. Pipe bands, athletic events, sheepdogs, weaving demonstrations and Scottish fair. (First Saturday after Labor Day.) Sponsor: Clan Donald. Info from: David Peet, 1208 24th Ave, Altoona, PA 16601.

LILYPONS' KOI FESTIVAL. Sept 6-7. Purpose: To view thousands of Japanese Koi, water lilies and aquatic plants. Sponsor: Lilypons Water Gardens, Box 188, Brookshire, TX 77423.

LONGS PEAK SCOTTISH HIGHLAND FESTIVAL. Sept 6-7. Scottish-Irish celebration day with pipe bands, highland and Irish dancing, athletic championships and gathering of the clans. Info from: Longs Peak Scottish Highland Festival, Inc, Box 1820, Estes Park, CO 80517.

McKINLEY, WILLIAM: ASSASSINATION ANNIVERSARY. Sept 6. President William McKinley shot at Buffalo, NY, Sept 6, 1901. He died Sept 14, 1901. Assassin Leon Czolgosz was executed Oct 29, 1901.

MATTOON ARTS FESTIVAL. Sept 6-7. Mattoon St, Springfield, MA. Arts and crafts fair. Info from: Pioneer Valley Conv & Visitors Bureau, Box 749, Northampton, MA 01061.

MELCHER, JOHN: BIRTHDAY. Sept 6. U.S Senator from Montana, Democrat, of Forsyth, MT, born in Sioux City, IA, Sept 6, 1924.

MUSLIM NEW YEAR. Sept 6. Year 1407 of the Muslim or Islamic era, or the Era of the Hegira, begins at sunset on this day. Muslim calendar date: Muharram 1, 1407.

MYSTIC SEAPORT PHOTO DAY. Sept 6. Mystic, CT. Purpose: An entire day designated with photographers in mind. Costumed models, scenic ships and grounds. Sponsor: Mystic Seaport, Public Affairs Dept, Mystic, CT 06355.

NATIONAL ART EXHIBITION. Sept 6-Oct 25. Washington, DC. Purpose: To select and exhibit the best works by artists from across the nation. Info from: Galerie Triangle, 3701 14th St, NW, Washington, DC 20010.

COPYRIGHT © 1985 BY WILLIAM D. CHASE and HELEN M. CHASE

PAULDING MEADOWS ARTS AND CRAFTS FESTIVAL. Sept 6-7. Dallas, GA. Local artists and craftsmen. Antiques and related items. Info from: Paulding Festivals, Inc, Box 654, Dallas, Ga 30132.

POLISH FESTIVAL. Sept 6-7. Music, games, dancing and ethnic foods. Info from: St Louis Conv & Visitors Bureau, 10 S Broadway, Suite 300, St Louis, MO 63102.

SCOTLAND: BRAEMAR ROYAL HIGHLAND GATHER-ING. Sept 6. Braemar, Grampian. "Kilted clansmen from all over Scotland tossing cabers, dancing, playing bagpipes and games."

SWAZILAND; NATIONAL HOLIDAY. Sept 6. Commemorates attainment of national independence on Sept 6, 1968.

TOUR DE RADISSON. Sept 6-7. Purpose: A two-day, 350-kilometer bicycle endurance race in northwestern Wisconsin. Info from: American Classic, Box 31, Hayward, WI 54843.

VIRGINIA CITY CAMEL RACES. Sept 6-7. Virginia City, NV. Info from: Virginia City Chamber of Commerce, P.O. Box 464, Virginia City, NV 89440.

SEPTEMBER 7 — SUNDAY

250th Day — Remaining, 115

AUTOFEST '86. Sept 7. Antique cars, vans and customized vehicles. Info from: Big Tupper Ski Area, Box 820, Tupper Lake, NY 12986.

BRAZIL: NATIONAL HOLIDAY. Sept 7. Independence Day. Declared independence from Portugal on this day, 1822.

CELEBRATE HEALTH FESTIVAL. Sept 7-13. Purpose: To promote physical, mental and spiritual health with a week-long showcase of sports and games. Sponsor: Bergan Mercy Hospital, Donna F. Jarmusz, PR Dir, 7500 Mercy Rd, Omaha, NE 68124.

CORBETT-SULLIVAN PRIZE FIGHT ANNIVERSARY. Sept 7. John L. Sullivan was knocked out by James J. Corbett in the 21st round of a prize fight at New Orleans, LA, Sept 7, 1892. It was the first major fight under the Marquess of Queensberry Rules.

GRANDMA MOSES DAY. Sept 7. Anna Mary (Robertson) Moses, modern primitive American painter born at Greenwich, NY, Sept 7, 1860. Started painting at the age of 78. Her hundredth birthday was proclaimed Grandma Moses Day in New York State. Died at Hoosick Falls, NY, Dec 13, 1961.

GUNSTON HALL CAR SHOW. Sept 7. Purpose: Trophies awarded for oldest car; best car in class; most popular; and best in show. Info from: Gunston Hall Plantation, Lorton, VA 22079.

HOLLY, BUDDY: BIRTHDAY. Sept 7. American popular music performer, composer and band leader. Called one of the most innovative and influential musicians of his time, he was a pioneer of Rock 'n Roll. His hits included "That'll Be the Day" and "Peggy Sue." Born Charles Harden Holley, at Lubbock, TX, Buddy Holly died at age 22, in an airplane crash near Mason City, IA, on Feb 3, 1959.

INOUYE, DANIEL KEN: BIRTHDAY. Sept 7. U.S. Senator from Hawaii, Democrat, of Honolulu, HI, born there on Sept 7, 1924.

ITALY: HISTORICAL REGATTA. Sept 7. Venice. Traditional competition between two-oar racing gondolas, preceded by a procession of Venetian ceremonial boats of the epoch of the Venetian Republic. First Sunday in Sept.

ITALY: JOUST OF THE SARACEN. Sept 7. Arezzo. The first Sunday in September is set aside for the Giostra del Saracino, a tilting contest of the 13th century, with knights in armor.

NATIONAL FINANCIAL SERVICES WEEK. Sept 7-13. Purpose: A pat on the back for those employees who work to keep our businesses financially healthy. Sponsor: Tuality Community Hospital, Joyce Curran, Personnel Mgr, Box 309, Hillsboro, OR 97123.

NATIONAL GRANDPARENTS DAY. Sept 7. Presidential
☆ Proclamation. "First Sunday in September following Labor Day. (PL96-62 of Sept 6, 1979) Proc. 4679, Sept 6, 1979, covers all succeeding years. First issued in 1978 (Proc. 4580, Aug 3, 1978, req'd by PL 95-325 of July 28, 1978)."

NEITHER SNOW NOR RAIN DAY. Sept 7. Anniversary of the opening to the public, on Labor Day, 1914, of the New York Post Office Building at Eighth Avenue between 31st and 33rd Streets. On the front of this building was an inscription supplied by William M. Kendall, of the architectural firm which planned the building. The inscription, a free translation from Herodotus: "Neither snow nor rain nor heat nor gloom of night stays these couriers from the swift completion of their appointed rounds." Long believed to be the motto of the U.S. Post Office and Postal Service, they have, in fact, no motto... but the legend remains. Info from: New York Post Office Public Information Office, and U.S. Postal Service.

QUEEN ELIZABETH I: BIRTHDAY. Sept 7. Queen of England, daughter of Henry VIII and Anne Boleyn, after whom the "Elizabethan Era" was named, born Sept 7, 1533. Died Mar 24, 1603.

SEPTEMBER 8 — MONDAY

251st Day — Remaining, 114

FORD, WENDELL HAMPTON: BIRTHDAY. Sept 8. U.S. Senator from Kentucky, Democrat, of Owensboro, KY, born in Daviess County, KY on Sept 8, 1924.

INTERNATIONAL LITERACY DAY. Sept 8. An international day observed by the organizations of the United Nations system. Info from: United Nations Dept of Public Information, United Nations, NY 10017.

LONG, HUEY P: ASSASSINATION ANNIVERSARY. Sept 8. Louisiana senator Huey P. Long was shot at Baton Rouge, LA, Sept 8, 1935. The assassin, Dr. Carl A. Weiss, was killed by Long's bodyguards.

MALTA: SIEGE ANNIVERSARY. Sept 8. "Two Sieges and Regatta Day" festivities now commemorate victory over the Turks, Sept 8, 1565, when the siege which began in May 1565 was broken by the Maltese and the Knights of St. John after a loss of nearly 10,000 lives. Also commemorated is survival of the 1943 siege by the Axis Powers. Parades, fireworks, boat races, etc, especially at the capital, Valleta, and the Grand Harbour.

MISSION SAN GABRIEL ARCHANGEL ANNIVERSARY. Sept 8. California mission to the Indians founded Sept 8, 1771.

NATIONAL BOSS/EMPLOYEE EXCHANGE DAY. Sept 8. Purpose: to help bosses and employees appreciate each other by sharing each other's point of view for a day. Observed annually on the first Monday after Labor Day. Sponsor: A.C. Moeller, Box 71, Clio, MI 48420.

NUNN, SAM: BIRTHDAY. Sept 8. U.S. Senator from Georgia, Democrat, of Perry, GA, born there Sept 8, 1938.

PARDON DAY. Sept 8. Anniversary of the "full, free, and absolute pardon unto Richard Nixon, for all offenses against the United States which he, Richard Nixon, has committed or may have committed or taken part in during the period from January 20, 1969, through August 9, 1974." (Presidential Proclamation 4311, Sept 8, 1974, by Gerald R. Ford.)

COPYRIGHT © 1985 BY WILLIAM D. CHASE and HELEN M. CHASE

PEPPER, CLAUDE DENSON: BIRTHDAY. Sept 8. U.S. Representative of Florida's 18th district, Democrat, of Miami, FL, born near Dudleyville, Chambers County, AL, on Sept 8, 1900.

PIERCE, SAMUEL RILEY, JR: BIRTHDAY. Sept 8. Samuel Riley Pierce, Jr., U.S. Secretary of Housing and Urban Development (sworn in on Jan 23, 1981) was born at Glen Cove, L.I., NY, on Sept 8, 1922.

SIEBERLING, JOHN F: BIRTHDAY. Sept 8. U.S. Representative of Ohio's 14th district, Democrat, of Akron, OH, born in Akron on Sept 8, 1918.

SELLERS, PETER (RICHARD HENRY): BIRTHDAY. Sept 8. Award-winning British comedian and film star, especially remembered for his role as the bumbling character, Inspector Clouseau, was born Sept 8, 1925. Died at London, July 24, 1980.

SEPTEMBER 9 — TUESDAY
252nd Day — Remaining, 113

ADVANCE MEDICO '86. Sept 9-11. Mexico City, Mexico. Solo exhibition. Medical instruments, equipment and supplies. Info from: Howard Fleming, Trade Development, Room 3832, Internatl Trade Admin, U.S. Dept of Commerce, Washington, DC 20230.

BATTLE OF MARATHON: ANNIVERSARY. Sept 9. On the day of the ninth month's full moon (Boedromion 6) in the year 490 B.C., the numerically superior invading army of Persia was met and defeated on the Plain of Marathon by the Athenian army, led by Miltiades. More than 6,000 men died in the day's battle which drove the Persians to the sea, and the mound of earth covering the dead is still visible at the site. See also: Days of Marathon, Sept 2-4, for the legendary running of Phidippides and the origin of the marathon race. Info from: Greswell's *Origines Kalendariae Hellenicae.*

BULGARIA: NATIONAL HOLIDAY. Sept 9. Anniversary of the Socialist Revolution in Bulgaria.

CALIFORNIA: ADMISSION DAY. Sept 9. Became 31st State on this day in 1850.

KOREA: NATIONAL DAY. Sept 9. National holiday is observed in Korea.

LUXEMBOURG: LIBERATION CEREMONY. Sept 9. Petange, Luxembourg. Commemoration of liberation of Grand-Duchy by the Allied Forces in 1944. Ceremony at monument of the American soldier.

MAO TSE-TUNG DEATH ANNIVERSARY. Sept 9. People's Republic of China pays tribute to memory of late Chinese leader, who died on Sept 9, 1976. Memorial Hall, where his flag-draped body lies encased in crystal, was opened at Tienanmen Square in Peking on the first anniversary of his death.

PARRIS, STAN: BIRTHDAY. Sept 9. U.S. Representative of Virginia's 8th district, Republican, of Fairfax County, VA, born in Champaign, IL, on Sept 9, 1929.

SEPTEMBER 10 — WEDNESDAY
253rd Day — Remaining, 112

BELIZE: ST. GEORGE'S CAYE DAY. Sept 10. A public holiday in the Caribbean country of Belize.

BRAXTON, CARTER: BIRTHDAY. Sept 10. American revolutionary statesman and signer of the Declaration of Independence. Born on Sept 10, 1736 at Newington, VA. Died on Oct 10, 1797 at Richmond, VA.

September 1986

S	M	T	W	T	F	S
	1	2	3	4	5	6
7	8	9	10	11	12	13
14	15	16	17	18	19	20
21	22	23	24	25	26	27
28	29	30				

EASTERN STATES EXPOSITION. Sept 10-21. Big E Grounds, West Springfield, MA. "New England's Great State Fair." Entertainment, crafts, contests, agricultural shows—fun for all ages. Info from: Eastern States Expo, Betsi Sheehan Taylor, Mktg Dir, 1305 Memorial Ave, W Springfield, MA 01089.

FUNK, ISAAC KAUFFMAN: BIRTHDAY. Sept 10. American publisher born at Clifton, OH, Sept 10, 1839. Partner in Funk and Wagnalls. Died at Montclair, NJ, Apr 4, 1912.

MORTON PUMPKIN FESTIVAL. Sept 10-13. Carnival, parade, entertainment and fantastic food. Info from: Chamber of Commerce, 415 W Jefferson St, Morton, IL 61550.

NATIONAL POPCORN FARMERS DAY FESTIVAL. Sept 10-13. Purpose: To provide enjoyment for all ages. Stage entertainment, Nashville stars and one ton of freshly popped popcorn given away on Popcorn Day (Second Saturday in September). Info from: Natl Popcorn Farmers Day, Inc, Box 231, Ridgway, IL 62979.

OBERSTAR, JAMES L: BIRTHDAY. Sept 10. U.S. Representative of Minnesota's 8th district, Democrat-Farmer-Labor, of Chisholm, MN, was born in Chisholm, Sept 10, 1934.

PENDLETON ROUND-UP. Sept 10-13. Purpose: One of nation's "most famous" rodeos. Features Indian pow-wow and other activities during Happy Canyon Pageant, Info from: Pendleton Round-Up Assn, Box 609, Pendleton, OR 97801.

SWAP IDEAS DAY. Sept 10. Purpose: To encourage people to explore ways in which their ideas can be put to work for benefit of humanity, and to encourage development of incentives and prods that will encourage use of creative imagination. Sponsor: Puns Corps, c/o: Robert L. Birch, Publicity Chrmn, Box 2364, Falls Church, VA 22042.

WERFEL, FRANZ: BIRTHDAY. Sept 10. Austrian author, born at Prague, Sept 10, 1890. Died at Hollywood, CA, Aug 26, 1945.

WOODMONT CONSECRATION & DEDICATION. Sept 10-12. Purpose: To universalize Woodmont Estate as a symbol of the highest spiritual state of consciousness. Sponsor: Father Divine's Peace Mission Movement, 1622 Spring Mill Rd, Gladwyne, PA 19035.

SEPTEMBER 11 — THURSDAY
254th Day — Remaining, 111

AKAKA, DANIEL KAHIKINA: BIRTHDAY. Sept 11. U.S. Representative of Hawaii's 2nd district, Democrat, of Honolulu, HI, born there Sept 11, 1924.

AMERICAN MUSIC THEATER FESTIVAL. Sept 11-Oct 12. Philadelphia, PA. Opera, musical comedy, music drama experimental work and performance art. Sponsor: American Music Theater Festival, Lisa Blumberg, PR Dir, 1617 JFK Blvd, Suite 905, Philadelphia, PA 19103.

BLACK GOLD FESTIVAL. Sept 11-14. Hazard, KY. Arts and crafts, parade, auto show, marathons, music and square dancing. Info from: KY Dept. of Travel, Capital Plaza Office Tower, Frankfort, KY 40601.

CALLAHAN, HERBERT (SONNY) LEON: BIRTHDAY. Sept 11. U.S. Representative of Alabama's 1st district, Republican, of Mobile, AL, born there Sept 11, 1932.

LAWRENCE, DAVID HERBERT: BIRTHDAY. Sept 11. English novelist, author of *Lady Chatterley's Lover*, born at Eastwood, Nottinghamshire, England, Sept 11, 1885. Died Mar 2, 1930.

LOS ANGELES COUNTY FAIR. Sept 11-28. Pomona, CA. Purpose: Features livestock, horse racing, flower and garden show, home arts, fine arts, commercial exhibits and international exhibition of photography. Sponsor: Los Angeles County Fair Assn, Bill Arballo, Media Info Dir, Box 2250, Pomona, CA 91769.

MOON PHASE: FIRST QUARTER. Sept 11. Moon enters First Quarter phase at 2:41 a.m., E.S.T.

NATCHER, WILLIAM H: BIRTHDAY. Sept 11. U.S. Representative of Kentucky's 2nd district, Democrat, of Bowling Green, Warren County, KY, born in Bowling Green on Sept 11, 1909.

NATIONAL CHAMPIONSHIP AIR RACES. Sept 11-14. Reno, NV. Eight races held each day in four classes of aircraft ranging from home-made airplanes to World War II fighters. Info from: Reno Air Races, Box 1429, Reno, NV 89505.

O HENRY BIRTHDAY. Sept 11. William Sydney Porter, American author, best known for his short stories, who wrote under the pen-name O Henry, born Greensboro, NC, Sept 11, 1862. Died June 5, 1910 at New York City.

PACKWOOD, BOB: BIRTHDAY. Sept 11. U.S. Senator from Oregon, Republican, of Portland, OR, was born in Portland on Sept 11, 1932.

PAKISTAN: PUBLIC HOLIDAY. Sept 11. Pakistan recognizes observance of the death anniversary in 1948 of Quaid-i-Azam Mohammed Ali Jinnah (founder of Pakistan) with public holiday.

SENIOR CITIZENS OLYMPICS. Sept 11. Nursing home residents compete in wheelchair and walking races, bubble gum blowing, frisbee and softball toss at Convoy Care Center, Convoy, OH. Olympics style flag raising ceremony. Info from: Shane Hill Nursing Home, Dorothy Trisel, Activities Dir, 10731 SR118, Rockford, OH 45882.

SNACK-A-PICKLE TIME. Sept 11-20. Purpose: To dramatize role of pickles as a snack food. Sponsor: Pickle Packers Internatl, Inc, 108½ E Main St, St. Charles, IL 60174. Info from: Burson-Marsteller, 1 E Wacker Dr, Chicago, IL 60601.

SEPTEMBER 12 — FRIDAY
255th Day — Remaining, 110

BALD IS BEAUTIFUL CONVENTION AND CONTESTS. Sept 12-14. "Bald Room," Mrs Willis Restaurant, Morehead City, NC. Purpose: Recognition of the bald head through humor, fellowship and fun. Mayor of Morehead proclaims, "Bald Is Beautiful Week in Morehead, less hair!" Sponsor: Bald Headed Men of America Club, John T. Capps III, Founder, PO Drawer 1466, Morehead City, NC 28557.

CHARLES LEROUX'S LAST JUMP: ANNIVERSARY. Sept 12. American aeronaut of French extraction, born in New York City about 1857, claimed by *Soviet Life* to have been a nephew of President Abraham Lincoln, achieved world fame as a parachutist. After his first public performance (Philadelphia, 1887) he toured European cities where his parachute jumps attracted wide attention. Credited with 238 successful jumps. On Sept 12, 1889, he jumped from a balloon over Tallinn, Estonia, and perished in the Bay of Reval. A monument to his memory was erected at Tallinn five years after his death.

DEFENDERS DAY. Sept 12. Maryland. Annual re-enactment of bombardment of Ft. McHenry in 1814 which inspired Francis Scott Key to write the "Star Spangled Banner."

ENGLAND: SOUTHHAMPTON INTERNATIONAL BOAT SHOW. Sept 12-20. Mayflower Park, Southhampton, Hampshire. "Largest show of its kind in the United Kingdom."

ETHIOPIA: NATIONAL HOLIDAY. Sept 12. Observed as National Revolution Day.

GUINEA-BISSAU: NATIONAL HOLIDAY. Sept 12. Amilcar Cabral's birthday, Sept 12, is observed as national holiday.

INTERNATIONAL FESTIVAL '86. Sept 12-14. Richmond Coliseum. Food and entertainment from many lands. Sponsor: Boys' Clubs of Richmond & Internatl Community of Richmond. Info from: W.R. Hutchinson, 408 N Robinson St, Richmond, VA 23220.

MENCKEN, HENRY LOUIS: BIRTHDAY. Sept 12. American newspaperman, lexicographer, and critic, "the Sage of Baltimore," was born at Baltimore, MD, Sept 12, 1880 and died

there Jan 29, 1956. "If, after I depart this vale," he wrote in 1921 (Epitaph, *Smart Set*), "you ever remember me and have thought to please my ghost, forgive some sinner and wink your eye at some homely girl."

MOUNT PLEASANT NATIONALITY DAYS. Sept 12-13. Purpose: Celebrates the ethnic heritage of residents of the Mount Pleasant area. Sponsor: Chamber of Commerce, Municipal Bldg, Mount Pleasant, PA 15666.

NIELSON, HOWARD CURTIS: BIRTHDAY. Sept 12. U.S. Representative of Utah's 3rd district, Republican, of Provo, UT, born at Richfield, UT, Sept 12, 1924.

OWENS, JESSE: BIRTHDAY. Sept 12. James Cleveland (Jesse) Owens, American athlete, winner of four gold medals at the 1936 Olympic Games in Berlin, was born at Oakville, AL, Sept 12, 1913. Died at Tucson, AZ, Mar 31, 1980. Owens set eleven world records in track and field. During one track meet, at Ann Arbor, MI, Owens, representing Ohio State University, broke five world records and tied a sixth in the space of 45 minutes, on May 25, 1935.

SOLARZ, STEPHEN J: BIRTHDAY. Sept 12. U.S. Representative of New York's 13th district, Democrat, of Brooklyn, NY, born in New York City, Sept 12, 1940.

SPACE MILESTONE: LUNA 2 (USSR). Sept 12. First spacecraft to land on moon. Launched on Sept 12, 1959.

SPACE MILESTONE: LUNA 16 (USSR). Sept 12. First unmanned spacecraft to land on moon (Sea of Fertility), collect samples, and return to Earth. Launched on Sept 12, 1970.

SWIFT, AL: BIRTHDAY. Sept 12. U.S. Representative of Washington's 2nd district, Democrat, of Bellingham, WA, born at Tacoma, WA, on Sept 12, 1935.

TENNESSEE STATE FAIR. Sept 12-21. Tennessee State Fairgrounds, Nashville, TN. Info from: Tennessee State Fair, Box 40208, Nashville, TN 37204.

WARNER, CHARLES DUDLEY: BIRTHDAY. Sept 12. American newspaperman, born at Plainfield, MA, Sept 12, 1829. Author of many works, perhaps best remembered for a single sentence (in an editorial, *Hartford Courant*, Aug 24, 1897): "Everybody talks about the weather, but nobody does anything about it." The quotation is often mistakenly attributed to his friend, Mark Twain. Died at Hartford, CT, Oct 20, 1900.

WAXMAN, HENRY A: BIRTHDAY. Sept 12. U.S. Representative of California's 24th district, Democrat, of Los Angeles, CA, born there Sept 12, 1939.

SEPTEMBER 13 — SATURDAY
256th Day — Remaining 109

ANDERSON, SHERWOOD: BIRTHDAY. Sept 13. American author and newspaper publisher, born at Camden, OH, Sept 13, 1876. His best remembered book is *Winesburg, Ohio*. Anderson died at Colon, Panama, Mar 8, 1941.

AUTUMN AUTO SHOW. Sept 13. Petoskey, MI. Display of antique classic and hot rod cars. Info from: Chamber of Commerce, Box 306, Petoskey, MI 49770.

BARRY DAY. Sept 13. Commemorates day in 1803, on which Commodore John Barry died. Fought in Revolutionary War. First American commodore.

CHEROKEE STRIP CELEBRATION. Sept 13. Purpose: To commemorate the opening of the Cherokee Strip to settlement on Sept 16, 1893. (The Saturday nearest Sept 16.) Sponsor: Chamber of Commerce, Gene C. Wood, Mgr, Box 426, Perry, OK 73077.

CLOVERDALE GRAPE FESTIVAL. Sept 13-15. Exhibits, concerts, art show, grape stomping and winery olympiads. Info from: Cloverdale Citrus Fair Assn, Box 445, Cloverdale, CA 95425.

COOL ART FESTIVAL. Sept 13. Elmwood Park. Roanoke, VA. Festival goers paint a canvas 100 yards long and 15 yards wide while listening to live jazz music. Canvas hung in city for two weeks. Sponsor: Roanoke Special Events Committee, 210 Reserve Ave, SW, Roanoke, VA 24016.

FESTIVAL ON THE RIVER. Sept 13. James River, Lynchburg, VA. Musical shows, dancing, historic reenactments, hot-air balloons and fireworks to celebrate Lynchburg's bicentennial. Info from: Bicentennial Commission of Lynchburg, Box 1132, Lynchburg, VA 24505.

GREAT FOREST PARK BALLOON RACE. Sept 13. Forest Park, St Louis, MO. Hot air balloon race beginning at Forest Park and ending where the wind carries them. Info from: St Louis Conv & Visitors Bureau, 10 S Broadway, Suite 300, St Louis, MO 63102.

HEALTHY AMERICAN FITNESS LEADERS AWARDS CONGRESS. Sept 13. Washington, DC. Purpose: To honor ten American men and women who have contributed to the promotion of physical fitness and health in the U.S. Sponsor: Allstate Life Insurance. Info from: U.S. Jaycees PR Dept, Box 7, Tulsa, OK 74121.

INTERNATIONAL TOWN CRIERS' CHAMPIONSHIP. Sept 13. Halifax, Nova Scotia. At Historic Properties, at 1:30 p.m. Town Criers are judged in 3 categories—best dress, best cry and best scroll. Participants from cities and towns in U.S.A., Great Britain, Germany, Bermuda and Canada. Info from: Dept of Tourism, Box 456 Halifax, NS B3J 2R5.

JANKLOW, WILLIAM J: BIRTHDAY: Sept 13. William J. Janklow, Governor of South Dakota, Republican, was born at Chicago, IL, on Sept 13, 1939.

JOSEPH HOWE FESTIVAL. Sept 13-20. Halifax, Nova Scotia. Schooner races, sailing regatta, whaler-pulling competition, crafts and displays. Info from: Dept of Tourism, Box 456, Halifax, NS B3J 2R5.

NATIONAL JAYCEES LEGISLATIVE WEEK. Sept 13-18. Washington, DC. Purpose: Seventy-member Jaycees executive board meets with several senators, congressmen and White House officials to discuss ways the Jaycees organization can help better America. Info from: U.S. Jaycees, Box 7, Tulsa, OK 74121.

PERSHING, JOHN J: BIRTHDAY. Sept 13. American General and commander of U.S. forces in World War I, born Linn County, MO, Sept 13, 1860. Died July 15, 1948.

POPCORN DAY. Sept 13. The last day of the Natl Popcorn Farmers Day Festival (second Saturday in Sept) is Popcorn Day. "One ton of freshly popped popcorn given away." Info from: Natl Popcorn Farmers Day, Inc, Box 231, Ridgway, IL 62979.

REED, WALTER: BIRTHDAY. Sept 13. American army physician (especially known for his Yellow Fever research), born Sept 13, 1851. Died Nov 22, 1902. The U.S. Army's general hospital in Washington, DC, is named in his honor.

SUWANNEE RIVER JAMBOREE. Sept 13-14. Stephen Foster State·Folk Culture Center, White Springs, FL. Features string-band musicians from all parts of Florida. Sponsor: Dept of State's Florida Folklife Programs, Box 265, White Springs, FL 32096.

TRADITIONAL IRISH MUSIC AND DANCE FESTIVAL. Sept 13. Fischer's Pool, Lansdale, PA. Purpose: Outdoor festival of traditional Irish music and dance with workshops, concerts and craft demonstrations. Sponsor: Philadelphia Ceili Group, 6815 Emlen St, Rm 2, Philadelphia, PA 19119.

SEPTEMBER 14 — SUNDAY
257th Day — Remaining 108

AMERICAN TINNITUS ASSOCIATION ADVISORS MEETING. Sept 14-18. San Antonio, TX. Info from: American Tinnitus Assn, Gloria Reich, Exec Dir, Box 5, Portland, OR 97207.

BATTLE OF BRITAIN WEEK. Sept 14-20. United Kingdom. (Third week of Sept—the week containing Battle of Britain Day, Sept 15.)

DANTE ALIGHIERI: DEATH ANNIVERSARY. Sept 14. Italian poet, author of the *Divine Comedy*, died Sept 14, 1321. He was born in May 1265.

ITALY: GIOSTRA DELLA QUINTANA. Sept 14. Foligno. A revival of a 17th century joust of the Quintana, with 600 knights in costume. Celebrated on the second Sunday of Sept.

LEBANON: BASHIR GEMAYEL ASSASSINATION ANNIVERSARY. Sept 14. Although first government reports described his rescue and quoted him as saying "Thank God I survived this one," later news dispatches indicated that Bashir Gemayel, 34-year-old president-elect of Lebanon, died along with at least eight other persons when a bomb exploded at his Phalange party headquarters in Beirut on Sept 14, 1982. On Sept 21, the Lebanese parliament elected his 39-year-old brother, Amin Gemayel, to succeed him.

MAZOLA CORN OIL: YMCA SHAPE-UP RUN. Sept 14. Central Park, New York, NY. A fun and fitness run open to everyone. Sponsor: Mazola Corn Oil, Best Foods, Box 8000, Englewood Cliffs, NJ 07632.

NATIONAL ALLIANCE OF BUSINESS CONFERENCE. Sept 14-17. Chicago, IL. National forum for discussion of job training, employment and vocational issues. Info from: Natl Alliance of Business, Albert Mark, Communications, 1015 15th St NW, Washington, DC 20005.

NATIONAL ANTHEM DAY. Sept 14. Maryland.

NATIONAL HISPANIC HERITAGE WEEK. Sept 14-20. Presidential proclamation. Issued each year for the week including September 15 and 16 since 1968 (PL90-498 of Sept 17, 1968).

NATIONAL OSTEOPATHIC MEDICINE WEEK. Sept 14-20. Purpose: To salute osteopathic physicians, osteopathic medical students and the people who work in osteopathic hospitals, providing health care to Americans. Sponsors: American Osteopathic Assn and American Osteopathic Hospital Assn. Info from: American Osteopathic Hospital Assn, Frank Engler, Jr, Dir, Communications, 55 W Seegers Rd, Arlington Heights, IL 60005.

SANGER, MARGARET (HIGGINS): BIRTHDAY. Sept 14. Feminist, nurse, and founder of the birth control movement in the U.S., born at Corning, NY, Sept 14, 1879. (Note: birth year not entirely certain because, apparently, Sanger often used a later date when obliged to divulge her birthday. Best evidence now points to Sept 14, 1879, rather than the frequently used 1883 date.) She died at Tucson, AZ, Sept 6, 1966.

SOLO TRANS-ATLANTIC BALLOON CROSSING ANNIVERSARY. Sept 14-18. Joe W. Kittinger, 56-year-old balloonist left Caribou, Maine in a ten-story-tall helium-filled balloon named *Rosie O'Grady's Balloon of Peace* on Sept 14, 1984, crossed the Atlantic Ocean and reached the French coast, above the town of Capbreton, in bad weather on Sept 17 at 4:29 p.m., E.D.T. He crash landed amid wind and rain near Savone, Italy at 8:08 a.m., E.D.T., Sept 18. Kittinger suffered a

September 1986

S	M	T	W	T	F	S
	1	2	3	4	5	6
7	8	9	10	11	12	13
14	15	16	17	18	19	20
21	22	23	24	25	26	27
28	29	30				

COPYRIGHT © 1985 BY WILLIAM D. CHASE and HELEN M. CHASE

broken ankle when he was thrown from the balloon's gondola during the landing. His nearly-84-hour flight, covering about 3,535 miles, was the first solo balloon crossing of the Atlantic Ocean and a record distance for a solo balloon flight.

SEPTEMBER 15 — MONDAY
258th Day — Remaining 107

ASHURA. Sept 15. Iran and Iraq. Muslim holiday commemorates death of Muhammad's grandson. Processions, drama and special costumes. Muslim calendar date: Muharram 10, 1407. Gregorian calendar date of observance may vary by one day.

BARTON, JOE LINUS: BIRTHDAY. Sept 15. U.S. Representative of Texas' 6th district, Republican, of Ennis, TX, born in Waco, TX, on Sept 15, 1949.

BATTLE OF BRITAIN DAY. Sept 15. England. Commemorates end of biggest daylight bombing raid of Britain by German Luftwaffe, on Sunday, Sept 15, 1940. Said to have been the turning point against Hitler's siege of Britain in World War II.

CHRISTIE, AGATHA: BIRTHDAY. Sept 15. English author of nearly a hundred books (mysteries, drama, poetry and nonfiction), born at Torquay, England, Sept 15, 1890. Died at Wallingford, England, Jan 12, 1976. "Every murderer," she wrote, in *The Mysterious Affair at Styles*, "is probably somebody's old friend."

COSTA RICA: NATIONAL HOLIDAY. Sept 15. Independence Day. Gained independence from Spain on this day, 1821.

EL SALVADOR: NATIONAL HOLIDAY. Sept 15. Independence Day. Gained independence from Spain on this day, 1821.

ENGLAND: BIRTHDAY OF PRINCE HENRY CHARLES ALBERT DAVID. Sept 15. Third in line for the British crown, the Prince was born at 4:20 p.m. at St. Mary's Hospital, Paddington, in London on Sept 15, 1984. Second son of Charles and Diana, Prince and Princess of Wales.

FLAMING FALL FOLIAGE IN THE POCONOS. Sept 15-Oct 15. Country fairs, arts, crafts, road tours and chair lift rides at ski areas to see the foliage. Info from: Pocono Mountains Vacation Bureau, 1004 Main St, Box K, Stroudsburg, PA 18360.

GOLF: U.S. SENIOR AMATEUR CHAMPIONSHIP. Sept 15-20. Interlachen Country Club, Edina, MN. National championship for golfers age 55 and older. Sponsor: U.S. Golf Assn, Golf House, Far Hills, NJ 07931.

GUATEMALA: NATIONAL HOLIDAY. Sept 15. Independence Day. Gained independence from Spain on this day in 1821.

HONDURAS: NATIONAL HOLIDAY. Sept 15. Independence Day. Gained independence from Spain on this day, 1821.

MEXICO: INDEPENDENCE DAYS. Sept 15-16. National holiday. At 11 p.m., on the night of Sept 15, all Mexico gives the historic "Grito" for independence. This yell has been a tradition since 1810, when Father Miguel Hidalgo, in the village of Dolores Guanejuato, gave the signal that launched a successful revolution against Spanish colonial government.

NICARAGUA: NATIONAL HOLIDAY. Sept 15. Independence Day. Gained independence from Spain on this day, 1821.

OLD PEOPLE'S DAY or RESPECT FOR THE AGED DAY. Sept 15. Japan. National holiday.

QUARTERLY ESTIMATED FEDERAL INCOME TAX PAYER'S DUE DATE. Sept 15. For those individuals whose fiscal year is the calendar year and who make quarterly estimated federal income tax payments, today is one of the due dates. (Jan 15, Apr 15, June 16, and Sept 15, 1986.)

SPACE MILESTONE: SOYUZ 22 (USSR). Sept 15. Launched on Sept 15, 1976, Cosmonauts V. Bykovsky and V. Asenov enter Earth orbit to study "geological and geographical characteristics on Earth's surface in the interests of the national economy." Returned to Earth on Sept 23.

SWEENY, DAVID McCANN: BIRTHDAY. Sept 15. U.S. Representative of Texas' 14th district, Republican, of Wharton, TX, born there on Sept 15, 1955.

TAFT, WILLIAM HOWARD: BIRTHDAY. Sept 15. The 27th President of the U.S. was born at Cincinnati, OH, Sept 15, 1857. His term of office: Mar 4, 1909-Mar 3, 1913. Following his presidency he became a law professor at Yale University until his appointment as Chief Justice of the U.S. Supreme Court, in 1921. Believed to have been the heaviest U.S. president (weighed 225 pounds at age 20), Taft died at Washington, DC, Mar 8, 1930, and was buried at Arlington National Cemetery.

"WORLD'S LARGEST" WEATHER VANE ANNIVERSARY. Sept 15. At the edge of White Lake in Montague, MI, on Sept 15, 1984, the "world's largest" weather vane was dedicated. Forty-eight feet high with a 26-foot wind arrow, the weather vane weighing 3,500 lbs is adorned with a 14-foot replica of a 19th century Great Lakes schooner.

SEPTEMBER 16 — TUESDAY
259th Day — Remaining, 106

CHEROKEE STRIP DAY. Sept 16. Optional holiday, Oklahoma. Greatest "run" for Oklahoma land in 1893.

GENERAL MOTORS FOUNDING ANNIVERSARY. Sept 16. The giant automobile manufacturing company was founded Sept 16, 1908, by William Crapo "Billy" Durant, a Flint, MI, entrepreneur.

GREAT SEAL OF THE UNITED STATES: ANNIVERSARY. Sept 16. On Sept 16, 1782, the Great Seal of the United States was, for the first time, impressed upon an official document. That document authorized George Washington to negotiate a prisoner of war agreement with the British. See also: entries for Jan 28, June 20, and July 4.

HUSKER HARVEST DAYS. Sept 16-18. Cornhusker Army Ammunition Plant. "Nation's largest irrigated agricultural show on a permanent 970 acre site." 77 acres of exhibits and working demonstrations of tillage, irrigation and harvesting. Info from: Jim Kanter, NE Farmer Magazine, Box 81208, Lincoln NE 68501.

INTERNATIONAL DAY OF PEACE. Sept 16. The United Nations General Assembly, on Nov 30, 1981, declared "that the third Tuesday of September, the opening day of the regular sessions of the General Assembly, shall be officially proclaimed and observed as International Day of Peace and shall be devoted to commemorating and strengthening the ideals of peace both within and among all nations and peoples." An International Year of Peace was proclaimed for 1986. A Peace Month, and a University for Peace have also been proposed and are under consideration.

KILDEE, DALE E: BIRTHDAY. Sept 16. U.S. Representative of Michigan's 7th district, Democrat, of Flint, MI, born in Flint on Sept 16, 1929.

MAYFLOWER DAY. Sept 16. Anniversary of the departure of the *Mayflower* from Plymouth, England, Sept 16, 1620, with 102 passengers and a small crew. Vicious storms were encountered enroute which caused serious doubt about the wisdom of continuing, but she reached Provincetown, MA, on Nov 21, and discharged the Pilgrims at Plymouth, MA, on Dec 26, 1620.

MEXICAN INDEPENDENCE DAY CELEBRATION. Sept 16. A full day of fiesta. Info from: El Pueblo de Los Angeles State Historic Park, 845 N Alameda St, Los Angeles, CA 90012.

COPYRIGHT © 1985 BY WILLIAM D. CHASE and HELEN M. CHASE

NETHERLANDS: PRINSJESDAG. Sept 16. Official opening of parliament at The Hague. On the third Tuesday of September, the Queen of the Netherlands by tradition rides in a golden coach to the hall of knights for the annual opening of parliament.

PALESTINIAN REFUGEE MASSACRE: ANNIVERSARY. Sept 16-17. One of history's most brutal atrocities occurred, Sept 16-17, 1982, at the Chatila and Sabra refugee camps in West Beirut, Lebanon. For 36 hours the killing continued, sparing neither children nor the elderly until, according to contemporary reports, more than 1,000 lay dead. "Christian Phalangist" militia were blamed for the killings but it was reported that little was done by the Lebanese or by the Israeli troops which surrounded the camps to prevent or stop the carnage.

PANIZZI, ANTHONY: BIRTHDAY. Sept 16. Sir Anthony Panizzi, the only librarian ever hanged in effigy, was born Antonio Genesio Maria Panizzi at Brescello, Italy on Sept 16, 1797. As a young man he joined a forbidden Italian patriotic society which advocated the overthrow of the oppressive Austrians who then controlled most of northern Italy. Tried in absentia by an Austrian court in 1820, he was sentenced to death, hanged in effigy, and all his property was confiscated. He fled to England in 1823, learned the language and by 1831 was employed in the British Museum. In spite of his continuing outspoken and unpopular enthusiasm for Italian politics, the naturalized Englishman was, in 1856, named Principal Librarian of the British Museum. Later described as the "prince of librarians," Panizzi died at London on Apr 8, 1879.

PAPUA NEW GUINEA: INDEPENDENCE DAY. Sept 16. National holiday.

PARKMAN, FRANCIS: BIRTHDAY. Sept 16. American historian, author of *The Oregon Trail*, was born at Boston, MA, on Sept 16, 1823, and died there on Nov 8, 1893.

TORQUEMADA, TOMAS de: DEATH ANNIVERSARY. Sept 16. One of history's most malevolent persons, feared and hated by millions. As Inquisitor-General of Spain, he ordered burning at the stake for more than 10,000 persons, and burning in effigy for another 7,000 (according to 18th Century estimates). Torquemada persuaded Ferdinand and Isabella to rid Spain of the Jews. More than a million families were driven from the country and Spain suffered a commercial decline from which it never recovered. Torquemada was born at Valladolide, Spain, in 1420 (exact date unknown) and died at Avila, Sept 16, 1498.

WALES: WELSH INTERNATIONAL FOUR DAY WALKS. Sept 16-19. Llanwrytd Wells, Powys.

SEPTEMBER 17 — WEDNESDAY
260th Day — Remaining, 105

ATLANTA BRANCH OF AMERICAN ASSOCIATION OF UNIVERSITY WOMEN: BOOKFAIR. Sept 17-21. Lenox Square Mall, Atlanta, GA. Books donated and funds support fellowships, scholarships, community projects and educational information and referral service. Info from: AAUW, Mrs. A. B. Tansill, 1410 Moores Mill Rd, NW, Atlanta, GA 30327.

AMERICAN SOYA FESTIVAL. Sept 17-20. Amanda, OH. Features foods prepared with or containing soybean products. Info from: Amanda-Clearcreek Athletic Booster, Don Sharp, 9860 Thomas Hill Rd, Stoutsville, OH 43154.

BATTLE OF ANTIETAM: ANNIVERSARY. Sept 17. Civil War battle, Sept 17, 1862, between Gen. Robert E. Lee's Confederate forces and General George McClellan's Union army, which has been called America's bloodiest day. Estimates vary, but more than 25,000 Union and Confederate soldiers were killed or wounded in this battle on the banks of the Potomac River, in Maryland.

BURGER, WARREN EARL: BIRTHDAY. Sept 17. Chief Justice of the United States, nominated by Pres. Nixon on May 22, 1969. (Qualified, June 23, 1969.) Chief Justice Burger was born at St Paul, MN, on Sept 17, 1907.

CITIZENSHIP DAY. Sept 17. Presidential Proclamation. ☆ "Always issued for September 17." (PL82-261 of Feb 29, 1952).

CONSTITUTION WEEK. Sept 17-23. Presidential Proclamation. ☆ "Always issued for period September 17-23 each year since 1955." (PL84-915 of Aug 2, 1956.)

FOLKFEST. Sept 17-21. Purpose: Bavarian street fair, crafts, parades, dances and folk-loroma. Sponsor: Chamber of Commerce, 425 S 7th St, Bismarck, ND 58501.

GRASSLEY, CHARLES ERNEST: BIRTHDAY. Sept 17. U.S. Senator from Iowa, Republican, of New Hartford, IA, born in New Hartford on Sept 17, 1933.

HENDRICKS, THOMAS ANDREWS: BIRTHDAY. Sept 17. Twenty-first Vice President of the U.S. (1885) born Muskingum County, OH, Sept 17, 1819. Died, Indianapolis, IN, Nov 25, 1885.

HOLT, MARJORIE S: BIRTHDAY. Sept 17. U.S. Representative of Maryland's 4th district, Republican, of Severna Park, MD, was born on Sept 17, 1920.

MATSUI, ROBERT T: BIRTHDAY. Sept 17. U.S. Representative of California's 3rd district, Democrat, of Sacramento, CA, born there Sept 17, 1941.

NATIONAL ASSOCIATION OF FIRE INVESTIGATORS SEMINAR. Sept 17-19. Bismarck Hotel, Chicago, IL. Purpose: Seminar on determining the cause and origin of fires, arson and explosions. Sponsor: Natl Assn of Fire Investigators, 53 W Jackson Blvd, Chicago, IL 60604.

SELFRIDGE, THOMAS E: DEATH ANNIVERSARY. Sept 17. Lt. Thomas E. Selfridge, 26-year-old passenger in 740 lb. biplane piloted by Orville Wright, was killed when, after four minutes in the air, the plane fell from a height of 75 feet. Nearly 2,000 spectators witnessed the crash at Fort Myer, VA, on Sept 17, 1908. The plane was being tested for possible military use by the Army Signal Corps. Orville Wright was seriously injured in the crash. Selfridge Field, MI, was named after the young lieutenant, a West Point graduate, who was the first fatality of powered airplane travel.

SPACE MILESTONE: PEGASUS 1 (US). Sept 17. 23,000-pound research satellite, launched Feb 16, 1965, broke up over Africa and fell to Earth. Major pieces believed to have fallen into Atlantic Ocean off the coast of Angola on Sept 17, 1978.

WEISS, TED: BIRTHDAY. Sept 17. U.S. Representative of New York's 17th district, Democrat-Liberal, of New York, NY, born in Hungary, on Sept 17, 1927.

SEPTEMBER 18 — THURSDAY
261st Day — Remaining, 104

CHILE: NATIONAL HOLIDAY. Sept 18. Independence Day. Gained independence from Spain, 1818.

DIEFENBAKER, JOHN: BIRTHDAY. Sept 18. Canadian lawyer, statesman and Conservative prime minister (1957-1963), born in Ontario on Sept 18, 1895. Died at Ottawa, Aug 16, 1979. Diefenbaker was a member of the Canadian Parliament from 1940 until his death.

FALL ANTIQUE SHOW. Sept 18-21. Somerset Mall, Troy, MI. Forty of the finest dealers from 8 states. Crystal grinding, chair caning, rushing, splint seat weaving, Haviland china, sterling and silverplate replacement, mirror resilvering and lamp doctor. Info from: Peg DuBois, 2801 Somerset Mall, Troy, MI 48084.

September 1986

S	M	T	W	T	F	S
	1	2	3	4	5	6
7	8	9	10	11	12	13
14	15	16	17	18	19	20
21	22	23	24	25	26	27
28	29	30				

COPYRIGHT © 1985 BY WILLIAM D. CHASE and HELEN M. CHASE

HARVEST MOON. Sept 18. The full moon nearest the autumnal equinox extends the hours of light into the evening and helps the harvester with his long day's work.

HAYWOOD MALL ARTS AND CRAFTS SHOW. Sept 18-21. Greenville, SC. Info from: Carole Sirmans, 400 Browns Crossing Rd, NW, Milledgeville, GA 31061.

JOHNSON, SAMUEL: BIRTH ANNIVERSARY. Sept 18. English lexicographer and literary lion, creator of the first great dictionary of the English language (1755) and author of poems and essays. Less well known is his novel *Rasselas: Prince of Abyssinia* (1759) written to pay for his mother's funeral. It begins with what has been called "the most beautiful sentence ever written:" "Ye who listen with credulity to the whispers of fancy, and pursue with eagerness the phantoms of hope; who expect that age will perform the promises of youth, and that the deficiencies of the present day will be supplied by the morrow; attend to the history of Rasselas, Prince of Abyssinia." Johnson was born at Lichfield, in Staffordshire, Sept 18, 1709, and died at London on Dec 13, 1784.

KOREA: CHUSOK. Sept 18. Gala celebration by Koreans everywhere. Autumn harvest thanksgiving moon festival. Observed on 15th day of 8th lunar month (8th full moon of lunar calendar) each year. Koreans pay homage to ancestors and express gratitude to guarding spirits for another year of rich crops. A time to visit tombs, leave food, and prepare for coming winter season. Traditional food is "moon cake," made on eve of Chusok, with rice, chestnuts and jujube fruits. Games, dancing and gift exchanges. Observed since Silla Dynasty (beginning of First Millennium).

LODI GRAPE FESTIVAL. Sept 18-21. Festival Grounds, Lodi, CA. Purpose: Harvest time exhibition of 110 varieties of grapes and professional entertainment. Wine tasting, art and floriculture exhibitions, carnival. Info from: Graeme A. Stewart, Festival Mgr. Box 848, Lodi, CA 95241.

MOON FESTIVAL or MID-AUTUMN FESTIVAL. Sept 18. This festival, observed on the fifteenth day of the eighth moon of the lunar calendar year, is called by different names in different places, but is widely recognized throughout the Far East, including People's Republic of China, Taiwan, Korea, Singapore and Hong Kong. An important harvest festival at the time the moon is brightest, it is also a time for homage to ancestors. Special harvest foods are eaten, especially "moon cakes."

MOON PHASE: FULL MOON. Sept 18. Moon enters Full Moon phase at 12:34 a.m., E.S.T.

READ, GEORGE: BIRTHDAY. Sept 18. Lawyer and signer of the Declaration of Independence, born, Cecil County, MD, Sept 18, 1733. Died Sept 21, 1798.

SPACE MILESTONE: SOYUZ 38 (USSR). Sept 18. Launched on Sept 18, 1980, Cosmonauts Arnaldo Tamayo Mendes (Cuba) and Yuri Romanenko docked at Salyut 6 for week-long mission, returning to Earth Sept 26.

STORY, JOSEPH: BIRTH ANNIVERSARY. Sept 18. Associate justice of the U.S. Supreme Court (1811-1845) was born at Marblehead, MA, on Sept 18, 1779. "It is astonishing" he wrote a few months before his death, "how easily men satisfy themselves that the Constitution is exactly what they wish it to be." Story died on Sept 10, 1845, having served 33 years on the Supreme Court bench.

U.S. AIR FORCE BIRTHDAY. Sept 18. The U.S. Air Force became a separate military service on Sept 18, 1947. Responsible for providing an Air Force that is capable, in conjunction with the other armed forces, of preserving the peace and security of the United States, the department is separately organized under the Secretary of the Air Force and operates under the authority, direction, and control of the Secretary of Defense.

VIRGINIA STATE FAIR. Sept 18-28. Info from: State Fair of Virginia. C. L. Teachworth, Exec VP, Box 26805, Richmond, VA 23261.

VITUPERATION WEEK. Sept 18-24. Purpose: Announce awards given for most vituperative remarks. Sponsor: Society for Revival and Promulgation of Vituperative Speech, Lake Superior State College, W. T. Rabe, Archivist, Sault Ste. Marie, MI 49783.

WHITTAKER, BOB: BIRTHDAY. Sept 18. U.S. Representative of Kansas' 5th district, Republican, of Augusta, KS, born in Eureka, KS, on Sept 18, 1939.

SEPTEMBER 19 — FRIDAY
262nd Day — Remaining, 103

ANTIQUE AUTOMOBILE CLUB OF AMERICA: SPECIAL MEET. Sept 19-21. Lake Placid, NY. Info from: Box 417, Hershey, PA 17033.

BARTLETT, STEVE: BIRTHDAY. Sept 19. U.S. Representative of Texas' 3rd district, Republican, of Dallas, TX, was born on Sept 19, 1947.

BATTLE OF CHICKAMAUGA ANNIVERSARY. Sept 19. Battle fought Sept 19-20. 1863, Chickamauga, GA.

BROUGHAM, HENRY PETER: BIRTHDAY. Sept 19. Scotch jurist and orator born at Edinburgh, Scotland, Sept 19, 1778. Died at Cannes, France, May 7, 1868. Brougham carriage named after him. "Education," he said, "makes a people easy to lead, but difficult to drive; easy to govern, but impossible to enslave."

CARROLL, CHARLES: BIRTHDAY. Sept 19. American Revolutionary leader and signer of the Declaration of Independence, born, Annapolis, MD, Sept 19, 1737. Died (the last surviving signer of the Declaration) Nov 14, 1832.

CHEESE DAYS. Sept 19-21. Purpose: To promote foreign-type cheeses made in 25 small area factories with a festival that attracts people to the "Swiss Cheese Capital of the U.S.A." Info from: Cheese Days, Inc, The Lindgren Agency, Box 516, Monroe, WI 53566.

COMMON GROUND COUNTRY FAIR. Sept 19-21. Info from: Bettina Blanchard, Maine Organic Farmers and Gardeners Assn, Box 2176, Augusta, ME 04330.

CORN ISLAND STORYTELLING FESTIVAL. Sept 19-20. Louisville, KY. "Largest storytelling festival in America." International, national and local yarnspinners in concert at historic sites throughout the city. Info from: KY Dept of Travel, Capital Plaza Office Tower, Frankfort, KY 40601.

LUYTS, JAN: BIRTHDAY. Sept 19. Dutch scholar, physicist, mathematician and astronomer, Jan Luyts was born at Hoorn in western Netherlands on Sept 19, 1655. Little remembered except for his books: *Astronomica Institutio* . . . (1689), and *Introductio ad Geographiam* . . . (1690). Note: The front cover and title-page illustrations of this edition of *Chase's Annual Events* are adapted from the frontispiece of *Astronomica Institutio* . . . .

MID-SOUTH FAIR. Sept 19-28. Memphis, TN. Fair features livestock, live entertainment, educational and commercial exhibits. Info from: Mid-South Fair, 940 Early Maxwell Blvd, Fairgrounds, Memphis, TN 38104.

POWELL, LEWIS F. JR: BIRTHDAY. Sept 19. Associate Justice of the Supreme Court of the United States, nominated by Pres Nixon on Oct 21, 1971. (Took office on Jan 7, 1972.) Justice Powell was born at Suffolk, VA, on Sept 19, 1907.

COPYRIGHT © 1985 BY WILLIAM D. CHASE and HELEN M. CHASE

RAYNE FROG FESTIVAL. Sept 19-21. A celebration having frogs as the "stars of the show." Frog racing, jumping and eating contests. Sponsor: Chamber of Commerce, Hilda Haure, Box 383, Rayne, LA 70578.

ROUKEMA, MARGARET S: BIRTHDAY. Sept 19. U.S. Representative of New Jersey's 5th district, Republican, of Ridgwood, NJ, was born on Sept 19, 1929.

ST. CHRISTOPHER (ST. KITTS) and NEVIS: NATIONAL DAY. Sept. 19. National holiday is observed today.

ST. JANUARIUS (GENNARO): FEAST DAY. Sept 19. Fourth Century bishop of Benevento, martyred near Naples, Italy, whose relics, in the Naples Cathedral are particularly famous because on his feast days the blood in glass vial is said to liquefy in response to prayers of the faithful. In September 1979, the Associated Press reported that some 5,000 persons gathered at the cathedral at dawn, and that "the blood liquefied after 63 minutes of prayers." This phenomenon is said to occur also on the first Saturday in May.

SCOTTDALE COAL AND COKE HERITAGE FESTIVAL. Sept 19-21. Sponsor: Scottdale Coal & Coke Heritage Festival, Box 276, Scottdale, PA 15683.

SHEARWATER INTERNATIONAL AIRSHOW. Sept 19-21. Shearwater, Nove Scotia. Atlantic Canada's major air show featuring air display of world class military and civilian aerobatic performers, aircraft and ground displays. Info from: Dept of Tourism, Box 456, Halifax, NS B2J 2R5.

SOUTHWEST IOWA PROFESSIONAL HOT AIR BALLOON RACES. Sept 19-21. Creston, IA. Hare and hound races held at sunrise and sunset, art and book fairs, parade and marching band contest. Third weekend in Sept. Info from: Chamber of Commerce, Box 471, Creston, IA 50801.

STATE FAIR OF OKLAHOMA. Sept 19-28. International exhibitors, horse and cattle shows, PRCA rodeo, ice capades, FFA, 4-H, car racing, tractor and truckpulls, automobile show, flower and garden exhibits. Info from: State Fair of Oklahoma, Box 74943, Oklahoma City, OK 73147.

SUGARLOAF'S VIRGINIA CRAFTS FESTIVAL. Sept 19-21. Prince William County Fairgrounds, Manassas, VA. Over 230 professional artists and craftspeople, demonstrations, live music and children's entertainment. Sponsor: Sugarloaf Mt Works, Inc, Ijamsville, MD 21754.

TITAN II MISSILE EXPLOSION: ANNIVERSARY. Sept 19. The third major accident involving America's most powerful single weapon occurred near Damascus AR, Sept 19, 1980. The explosion, at 3 a.m., came nearly eleven hours after fire had started in the missile silo. The multi-megaton nuclear warhead (a hydrogen bomb) reportedly was briefly airborne, but came to rest a few hundred feet away. One dead, 21 injured in accident. Previous major Titan Missile accidents: Aug 9, 1965, near Searcy, AR (53 dead); and Aug 24, 1978, near Rock, KS (2 dead, 29 injured).

SEPTEMBER 20 — SATURDAY

263rd Day — Remaining, 102

ANNIVERSARY OF FOUNDING OF EQUAL RIGHTS PARTY. Sept 20. San Francisco, CA. (On Sept 20, 1884, Equal Rights Party formed. Their candidate for president, nominated in convention, was Mrs. Belva Lockwood. Vice presidential candidate, Marietta Stow.)

APPLEJACK FESTIVAL. Sept 20-21. Purpose: To promote our local orchards and their abundant apple harvest. Sponsor: Nebraska City Chamber of Commerce, Box 245, Nebraska City, NE 68410.

September 1986

S	M	T	W	T	F	S
	1	2	3	4	5	6
7	8	9	10	11	12	13
14	15	16	17	18	19	20
21	22	23	24	25	26	27
28	29	30				

ARIZONA OLD TIME FIDDLER'S CONTEST AND FESTIVAL. Sept 20-21 Payson, AZ. Entertainment and competition to determine the state fiddling champion. Info from: Payson Chamber, Drawer A, Payson, AZ 85541.

BANNED BOOKS WEEK—CELEBRATING THE FREEDOM TO READ. Sept 20-27. Purpose: To bring to the attention of the general public the importance of the freedom to read and the harm censorship causes to our society. Sponsors: American Library Assn, American Booksellers Assn, American Society of Journalists and Authors, Assn of American Publishers, Natl Assn of College Stores. Info from: American Library Assn, Judith F. Krug, Office for Intellectual Freedom, 50 E Huron St, Chicago, IL 60611.

BLUE-GRAY AFFAIR. Sept 20-21. Golden Pond, KY. Civil War enthusiasts re-creating life in the Union and Confederate armies, tactical demonstration. Info from: KY Dept of Travel, Capital Plaza Office Tower, Frankfort, KY 40601.

COCA COLA/CHIMNEY ROCK HILLFALL. Sept 20. Chimney Rock Park, NC. Purpose: Gravity-powered tub race with cars that incorporate a No. 2 washtub in seat or chassis. Run on curvy road down the mountain. Sponsor: Chimney Rock Park, Box 39, Chimney Rock, NC 28720.

COVERED BRIDGE FESTIVAL. Sept 20-21. Purpose: To attract tourists to the area to see the 35 covered bridges in the two county area. Sponsor: Washington County Tourist Promotion Agency, Box 877, Washington, PA 15301.

DANISH DAYS. Sept 20-21. Purpose: Renew ties with Denmark by sharing old world customs with visitors—aebleskive breakfasts, folk dancing, music, entertainment and parade. (3rd full weekend in Sept.) Sponsor: Solvang Business Assn & Chamber of Commerce, Box 465, Solvang, CA 93463.

DioGUARDI, JOSEPH J: BIRTHDAY. Sept 20. Representative of New York's 20th district, Republican, of Scarsdale, NY, born in New York City on Sept 20, 1940.

FESTIVALS ACADIENS. Sept 20-21. Girard Park area, Lafayette, LA. Purpose: To celebrate the Cajun lifestyle. Festival includes Festivals De Musique Acadienne, Bayou Food Festival, Acadian Village and University Art Museum events, The Deep South Writers' Conference, The RSVP Senior Fair and Craft Show, Louisiana Native Crafts Festival and Lafayette Jaycees Fair and Trade Show. Info from: Lafayette Conv & Visitors Commission, Box 52066, Lafayette, LA 70505.

FINANCIAL PANIC OF 1873: ANNIVERSARY. Sept 20. For the first time in its history the New York Stock Exchange was forced to close, Sept 20, 1873, because of a banking crisis. Although the worst of the panic and crisis were over within a week, the psychological effect on businessmen, investors and the nation at large were more lasting.

FLORIDA NATIVE AMERICAN HERITAGE FESTIVAL. Sept 20-21. Tallahassee Jr Museum. Southeastern tribes, particularly Seminole, Miccosukee and Creek demonstrate traditional crafts. Native foods, dancing and alligator wrestling. Info from: Tallahassee Jr Museum, 3945 Museum Dr, Tallahassee, FL 32304.

GAY '90s FESTIVAL. Sept 20-21. Purpose: Outdoor open stage banjo and barbershop quartet music, jam sessions. (Annually the 3rd weekend in September.) Sponsor: Roscoe Village Foundation, 381 Hill St, Coshocton, OH 43812.

GETTYSBURG OUTDOOR ANTIQUE SHOW. Sept 20. Features 180 dealers in antiques with exhibits and displays. Info from: Gettysburg Travel Council, 35 Carlisle St, Gettysburg, PA 17325.

HIGHLAND FLING. Sept 20-21. Purpose: To focus attention on, and raise funds for, the historical Old Southwest neighborhood of the City of Roanoke and Highland Park. Sponsor: Old Southwest, Inc, Mr. Jan Wilkins, Pres, 641 Walnut Ave SW, Roanoke, VA 24016.

INDIAN DAY. Sept 20. Oklahoma. (Observed on the first Saturday after the Full Moon in September.)

COPYRIGHT © 1985 BY WILLIAM D. CHASE and HELEN M. CHASE

JOHNNY APPLESEED FESTIVAL. Sept 20-21. Purpose: A return to the pioneer spirit of the early 1800s, at the gravesite of John Chapman, known as the "Johnny Appleseed" who planted hundreds of apple orchards along the early Indiana frontier. Crafts, music, food and storytelling. (3rd weekend of Sept.) Info from: Parks & Recreation Dept, 705 E State Blvd, Fort Wayne, IN 46805.

MORTON, FERDINAND (JELLY ROLL): BIRTHDAY. Sept 20. American jazz pianist, composer, singer and orchestra leader, was born at New Orleans, LA, Sept 20, 1885. Ferdinand Joseph (Jelly Roll) Morton, subject of a biography entitled *Mr. Jelly Roll* (by Alan Lomax), died July 10, 1941, at Los Angeles, CA.

NATIONAL RESEARCH COUNCIL ANNIVERSARY. Sept 20. Anniversary of first meeting of National Research Council, in New York City, Sept 20, 1916. Formed at request of President Woodrow Wilson for the purpose of ". . . encouraging the investigation of natural phenomena . . ." for American business and national security. Sept 20 also marks the anniversary of the first meeting of the American Association for the Advancement of Science, at Philadelphia in 1848.

NIKE KLONDIKE TRAIL OF '98 ROAD RELAY. Sept 20. Skagway-Whitehorse, Yukon, Canada. Mixed mens and ladies teams, 176 km (110 mi) from tidewater, Skagway to Whitehorse. Info from: Yukon Visitor's Assn, 302 Steele St, Whitehorse, Yukon Y1A 2C5.

OKTUPPERFEST. Sept 20-21. A celebration of German heritage. Info from: Chamber of Commerce, 55 Park St, Tupper Lake, NY 12986.

OLD DEERFIELD FALL CRAFT FAIR. Sept 20-21. Memorial Hall Museum, Deerfield, MA. Info from: Pioneer Valley Conv & Visitors Bureau, Box 749, Northampton, MA 01061.

PENNSYLVANIA DUTCH HOT AIR BALLOON CHAMPIONSHIP AND COUNTRY FAIR. Sept 20-21. Purpose: Competition for balloonists and colorful representation of American life in the mid-1800s, when ballooning emerged as an exciting transportation mode in America. Sponsor: Historic Strasburg Inn, Terri Brown, Rte 896, Historic Dr, Strasburg, PA 17579.

PREBLE COUNTY PORK FESTIVAL. Sept 20-21. Preble County Fairgrounds, Eaton, OH. Info from: Tim H. Miller, Box 208, Eaton, OH 45320.

PROFITABLE MARKETING STRATEGIES FOR INDEPENDENT PUBLISHERS: SEMINAR-WORKSHOP. Sept 20. San Diego, CA. Info from: American Bookdealers Exchange, Al Galasso, Box 2525, La Mesa, CA 92041.

RURAL MUSIC REUNION. Sept 20. Hopeville, IA. Ghost town comes alive as old-time and modern country musicians get together to play some old songs just for the fun of it. Annually, third Saturday in Sept. Info from: Clarke County Conservation Board Office, Court House, Osceola, IA 50213.

SCOTTISH GAMES AND HIGHLAND GATHERING. Sept 20. Contestants from U.S. and Canada compete in medieval games of strength and agility. Bagpipers, dancing and fair booths. A "wee bit o'Scotland." Info from: Middleton Place, Rt 4, Charleston, SC 29407.

SEPTEMBER FEST ARTS AND CRAFT FAIR. Sept 20-21. DeSoto Caverns, Childersburg, AL. Regional artists and craftpeople's work. Bluegrass and country music. Info from: Caryl Lynn Mathis, 93 Ivy Trail NE, Atlanta, GA 30342.

SHAKER MUSEUM HARVEST FESTIVAL AND CRAFTS FAIR. Sept 20. Shaker Museum, Old Chatham, NY. Old-time country fair atmosphere with crafts and demonstrations. Info from: The Shaker Museum, Shaker Museum Rd, Old Chatham, NY 12136.

SINCLAIR, UPTON (BEALL): BIRTHDAY. Sept 20. American novelist and politician born at Baltimore, MD, Sept 20, 1878. Died at Bound Brook, NJ, Nov 25, 1968.

SORGHUM AND CIDER FAIR. Sept 20-21. Rockville, IN. Info from: Kay Hinds, Billie Creek Village, RR 2, Box 27, Rockville, IN 47872.

SOUTHWEST IOWA PROFESSIONAL HOT AIR BALLOON RACES. Sept 20-21. Info from: Chamber of Commerce, Box 471, Creston, IA 50801.

SPENCER MOUNTAIN WHISTLE TOOT. Sept 20. Spencer Mountain Farm, Fenwick Mountain, Fenwick, WV. Purpose: To show steam engines that are antique. Info from: Spencer Family, Glenn Spencer, Fenwick, WV 26202.

SUN/HERALD SAND SCULPTURE CONTEST. Sept 20. Biloxi, MS. Purpose: To conduct the "nation's largest" sand sculpture contest and promote the art of sand sculpturing. (3rd Saturday in Sept.) Info from: Gulf Publishing Co, Inc, Nancy White, Dir Mktg Services, Box 4567, Biloxi, MS 39531.

TRAIL OF COURAGE RENDEZVOUS. Sept 20-21. Purpose: Commemorates courage of the Potawatomi Indians on Trail of Death removal from Indiana to Kansas in 1838. Indian and pioneer dances, pioneer foods and crafts, muzzleloading and tomahawk contests. Sponsor: Fulton County Historical Society, 7th & Pontiac, Rochester, IN 46975.

SEPTEMBER 21 — SUNDAY
264th Day — Remaining, 101

AMERICAN NEWSPAPER WEEK. Sept 21-27. Always the full week in which Sept 25 falls (anniversary of the First American Newpaper [q.v.], *Publick Occurrences Both Foreign and Domestick,* published at Boston, Sept 25, 1690). Week-long observance with special days honoring those who make the American newspaper a reality: Sun: American Newspaper Editors' and Publishers' Day; Mon: American Newspaper Reporters' Day; Tues: American Newspaper Carriers' Day; Wed: American Newspaper Advertisers' Day; Thurs: American Newspaper Printers' Day; Fri: American Newspaper Readers' Day; Sat: American Freedom of the Press Day. Sponsor: Comm. for the Observance of American Newspaper Week, Box 68, Montague, MI 49437.

BELIZE: INDEPENDENCE DAY. Sept 21. National holiday.

BICYCLE TOUR OF CENTRAL MARYLAND. Sept 21. 100 mile bicycle tour through Maryland, near Annapolis. Shorter rides also offered. Sponsor: Potomac Pedalers Touring Club, Box 23601, Washington, DC 20026.

CABBAGE PATCH SCARECROW CONTEST. Sept 21-Oct 26. Purpose: Peddler's Village is filled with scarecrows in competition. Sponsor: Peddler's Village, PR Dept, Lahaska, PA 18931.

CUMBERLAND FAIR. Sept 21-27. Horse and ox pulling contests and showing of cattle, sheep, goats, pigs and poultry. Info from: L. Robert Morrill, Nash Rd, South Windham, ME 04082.

DRIED FIG WEEK. Sept 21-27. Purpose: To celebrate the fig harvest in California where nearly all United States figs are grown and dried. Sponsor: The California Dried Fig Advisory Bd, Rowena M. Hubbard, 846 California St, San Francisco, CA 94108.

EMERGENCY MEDICAL SERVICES WEEK. Sept 21-27. Purpose: To enhance public awareness of the specialty of emergency medicine, of advances in emergency medical care and to recognize emergency medical care providers. Sponsor: American College of Emergency Physicians, Kay Barkin, APR, PR Dir, Box 619911, Dallas, TX 75261.

COPYRIGHT © 1985 BY WILLIAM D. CHASE and HELEN M. CHASE

MUSLIM FESTIVAL: IMAMAT DAY. Sept 21. Imamat Day is observed by Ismaili (Shiite) Muslims. Muslim calendar date: Muharram 16, 1407. Gregorian calendar date of observance may vary by one day.

NATIONAL FARM SAFETY WEEK. Sept 21-27. Presidential ☆ Proclamation issued each year since 1944. First observed during July, it has been the third week in Sept since 1982.

NATIONAL FARM SAFETY WEEK. Sept 21-27. Purpose: To inform the agricultural community about farm accident problems and to encourage use of effective, appropriate safety measures. (3rd full week in Sept.) Sponsors: U.S. Dept of Agriculture & Natl Safety Council. Info from: Natl Safety Council, Jack Burke, 444 N Michigan Ave, Chicago, IL 60611.

NATIONAL FOOD SERVICE WORKERS WEEK. Sept 21-27. Purpose: To promote public awareness of the contributions and importance of food service workers to life in America (always the fourth week in September) Sponsor: Women & Infants Hospital of Rhode Island, Dietary Dept, 50 Maude St, Providence, RI 02908.

NATIONAL RETAIL MERCHANTS ASSOCIATION RETAIL SYSTEMS/TECHNOLOGY AND COMMUNICATIONS CONFERENCE. Sept 21-24. Anaheim, CA. Info from: J. Chay, NRMA, 100 W 31st St, New York, NY 10001.

NATIONAL SINGLES WEEK. Sept 21-27. Purpose: To promote a positive image of being single and to help nonprofit singles groups publicize their activities and recruit members. (Begins third Sunday in Sept.) Sponsor: Buckeye Singles Council, M. Bucher, 100 Glenmont Ave, Columbus, OH 43214.

PHILIPPINES: THANKSGIVING DAY. Sept 21. National holiday celebrates the beginning of the New Society as decreed by President Ferdinand Marcos in 1972.

TAYLOR, MARGARET SMITH: BIRTHDAY. Sept 21. Wife of Zachary Taylor, 12th President of the U.S., born at Calvert County, MD, Sept 21, 1788. Died Aug 18, 1852.

TOLKIEN WEEK. Sept 21-27. Purpose: To promote appreciation and enjoyment of the works of J.R.R. Tolkien. Sponsor; American Tolkien Society, Attn: Phil Helms, Box 277, Union Lake MI 48085.

WATTICISM DAY. Sept 21. Anniversary of speech by then U.S. Interior Secretary James Watt to trade association executives at the U.S. Chamber of Commerce, Sept 21, 1983. Referring to his advisory committee, Watt said: "We have every kind of mixture you can have. I have a black, I have a woman, two Jews and a cripple. And we have talent." He later apologized for an "unfortunate choice of words."

WELLS, HERBERT GEORGE: BIRTHDAY. Sept 21. English novelist and historian, born at Bromley, in Kent, on Sept 21, 1866. Among his books: *The Time Machine, The Invisible Man, The War of the Worlds* and *The Outline of History.* Wells died at London, Aug 13, 1946. "Human history," he wrote, "becomes more and more a race between education and catastrophe."

WORLD GRATITUDE DAY. Sept 21. Purpose: To unite all people in a positive emotion, creating a world community. Gratitude Gatherings, any assemblage aware of the spirit of gratitude are encouraged. (Annually, Sept 21.) Sponsor: Edna Fuerth Lemle, World Gratitude Day Foundation, Exec Office, Penthouse, 132 W 31st St, New York, NY 10001.

WORLD PEACE DAY. Sept 21. Purpose: To promote international peace. Observed on third Sunday in Sept. Sponsor. Franklin D. Roosevelt Philatelic Society, 154 Laguna Ct. St. Augustine Shores, FL 32086.

September 1986

S	M	T	W	T	F	S
	1	2	3	4	5	6
7	8	9	10	11	12	13
14	15	16	17	18	19	20
21	22	23	24	25	26	27
28	29	30				

SEPTEMBER 22 — MONDAY
265th Day — Remaining, 100

DANNEMEYER, WILLIAM E: BIRTHDAY. Sept 22. U.S. Representative of California's 39th district, Republican, of Fullerton, CA, was born at Los Angeles, CA Sept 22, 1929.

DE LA GARZA, E. (KIKA): BIRTHDAY. Sept 22. U.S. Representative of Texas' 15th district, Democrat, of Mission, TX, was born in Mercedes, TX, on Sept 22, 1927.

FARADAY, MICHAEL: BIRTHDAY. Sept 22. English scientist and early experimenter with electricity born Sept 22, 1791. Died Aug 25, 1867.

HOBBIT DAY. Sept 22. Purpose: To commemorate the birthdays of Frodo and Bilbo Baggins and their creator J.R.R. Tolkien. Sponsor: American Tolkien Society, Box 277, Union Lake, MI 48085.

ICE CREAM CONE: BIRTHDAY. Sept 22. Italo Marchiony emigrated from Italy in the late 1800s and soon thereafter went into the portable restaurant business in New York City, with a pushcart dispensing lemon ice. Success soon led to a small fleet of pushcarts, and the inventive Marchiony was inspired to develop a cone, first made of paper, later of pastry, to hold the tasty delicacy. On Sept 22, 1903, his application for a patent for his new mold was filed, and U.S. Patent No. 746971 was issued to him on Dec 15, 1903.

LUNGREN, DANIEL E. (DAN): BIRTHDAY. Sept 22. U.S. Representative of California's 42nd district, Republican of Long Beach, CA, born in Long Beach on Sept 22, 1946.

MALI: NATIONAL HOLIDAY. Sept 22. Anniversary of the Proclamation of the Republic, Sept 22, 1960.

NATIONAL WATER WELL EXPOSITION. Sept 22-24. H. Roe Bartle Hall, Kansas City, MO. Purpose: Continuing education, conferences, trade fair of products for the ground water industry. Info from: Natl Water Well Assn, Ms Kathy Butcher, 500 W Wilson Bridge Rd, Worthington, OH 43085.

PENNSYLVANIA BED MAKING CHAMPIONSHIPS. Sept 22. Philadelphia, PA. Purpose: Heralds the coming of Fall. Info from: Stu Coren, Rosen-Coren Agency, Inc, Suite 413B, Benjamin Fox Pavilion, Jenkintown, PA 19046.

RAOUL WALLENBERG DAY. Sept 22. Little known Swedish "diplomat" was voted honorary American citizenship by the U.S. House of Representatives, Sept 22, 1981, by a final vote of 396-2. He was the second foreigner in history to be so honored (first was Winston Churchill, whose mother was born in the U.S.). Wallenberg is claimed to have saved 100,000 lives during World War II. His present whereabouts is unknown.

TACY RICHARDSON'S RIDE: ANNIVERSARY. Sept 22. Remembers early morning ride, Sept 22, 1777, of 23-year-old Tacy Richardson (Jan 1, 1754-June 18, 1807) who rode her favorite horse, "Fearnaught," several perilous miles from the family farm (near the meeting of the Perkiomen and the Schuylkill, Montgomery County, PA) to the James Vaux mansion to warn General George Washington of the approach of British troops led by General William Howe. In reality the British crossing of the Schuylkill at Gordon's Ford was a feint to deceive Washington who indeed hastily withdrew to Pottstown. Gen Howe spent that night in the same quarters Washington had occupied only a few hours earlier. Poems and family tradition memorialize the bravery of Tacy's ride.

WIRTH, TIMOTHY E: BIRTHDAY. Sept 22. U.S. Representative of Colorado's 2nd district, Democrat, of Boulder, CO, born in Santa Fe, NM, Sept 22, 1939.

SEPTEMBER 23 — TUESDAY
266th Day — Remaining, 99

AUTUMN. Sept 23-Dec 21. In the Northern Hemisphere, autumn begins today with the Autumnal Equinox, at 2:59 a.m., E.S.T. Note that in the Southern Hemisphere today is the beginning of spring, and the occasion of the Vernal Equinox. The point on

COPYRIGHT © 1985 BY WILLIAM D. CHASE and HELEN M. CHASE

Earth from which the sun is overhead crosses Equator moving south, this year at longitude 60° E (Indian Ocean, northeast of Seychelles Islands). Everywhere on Earth (except near the poles) the sun rises due east and sets due west, and daylight length is nearly identical—about 12 hours, 8 minutes.

CHECKERS DAY. Sept 23. Purpose: A day to recognize the important role of dogs in American politics. Anniversary of the nationally televised "Checkers Speech" by then Vice-presidential candidate Richard M. Nixon, on Sept 23, 1952. Nixon was found "clean as a hound's tooth" in connection with private fund for political expenses. Nixon declared he would never give back the cocker spaniel dog, Checkers, which had been a gift to his daughters. Other prominent dogs in American politics: Abraham Lincoln's dog, Fido, Lyndon Johnson's beagles, Him and Her, Franklin D. Roosevelt's much travelled terrier, Fala, and Ronald Reagan's dog Lucky.

CORN PALACE FESTIVAL. Sept 23-28. Mitchell, SD. Celebration of the harvest. Info from: Tourism Dev, Box 6000, Pierre, SD 57501.

FERDINAND VI OF SPAIN: BIRTHDAY. Sept 23. King of Spain from 1746 to 1759, his greatest claim to fame was keeping Spain at peace. Born at Madrid on Sept 23, 1713, he died at Villaviciosa de Odon on Aug 10, 1759.

JACKSON COUNTY APPLE FESTIVAL. Sept 23-27. Mountains of apples and barrels of cider. Homemade apple butter, apple pies and candy apples. Info from: Jackson County Apple Festival, Box 8, Jackson, OH 45640.

LIBRA, THE BALANCE. Sept 23-Oct 22. In the astronomical/astrological zodiac, which divides the sun's apparent orbit into twelve segments, the period Sept 23-Oct 22 is identified, traditionally, as the sun-sign of Libra, the Balance. The ruling planet is Venus.

LIPPMANN, WALTER: BIRTH ANNIVERSARY. Sept 23. American journalist, political philosopher and author. Born at New York City on Sept 23, 1889, he died there on Dec 14, 1974. As a syndicated newspaper columnist he was the foremost and perhaps the most influential commentator in the nation. "Without criticism," he said in an address to the International Press Institute in 1965, "and reliable and intelligent reporting, the government cannot govern."

McGUFFEY, WILLIAM HOLMES: BIRTHDAY. Sept 23. American educator and author of the famous *McGuffey Readers*, born at Washington County, PA, Sept 23, 1800. Died at Charlottesville, VA, May 4, 1873.

PLANET NEPTUNE DISCOVERY: ANNIVERSARY. Sept 23. First observed on Sept 23, 1846. Neptune is 2,796,700,000 miles from the sun (about 30 times as far from the sun as Earth). Eighth planet from the sun, Neptune takes 164.8 years to revolve around the sun. Diameter is about 31,000 miles compared to Earth at 7,927 miles.

SAUDI ARABIA: NATIONAL HOLIDAY. Sept 23. Commemorates unification of the Kingdom, on Sept 23, 1932.

WOODHULL, VICTORIA CHAFLIN: BIRTHDAY. Sept 23. American feminist, reformer and first female candidate for the presidency of the U.S. Born at Homer, Ohio on Sept 23, 1838 and died at Norton Park, Bremmons, Worcestershire, England on June 10, 1927.

SEPTEMBER 24 — WEDNESDAY
267th Day — Remaining, 98

COLLINS, CARDISS: BIRTHDAY. Sept 24. U.S. Representative of Illinois' 7th district, Democrat, of Chicago, IL, born in St. Louis, MO, on Sept 24, 1931.

FITZGERALD, F. SCOTT: BIRTHDAY. Sept 24. American short story writer and novelist, author of *This Side of Paradise, The Great Gatsby,* and *Tender Is the Night,* was born Francis Scott Key Fitzgerald, at St. Paul, MN, on Sept 24, 1896. He died at Hollywood, CA, Dec 21, 1940.

GOLF: U.S. SENIOR WOMEN'S AMATEUR CHAMPIONSHIP. Sept 24-26. Lakewood Golf Club, Point Clear, AL. National championship for female amateur golfers aged 50 and older. Sponsor: U.S. Golf Assn, Golf House, Far Hills, NJ 07931.

GUINEA-BISSAU: NATIONAL HOLIDAY. Sept 24. Independence Day is observed.

INTERNATIONAL BANANA FESTIVAL. Sept 24-27. Fulton, KY. "A festival with a real South American flavor, featuring a 1-ton banana pudding that serves 10,000." Arts, crafts, parades and sporting events. Info from: Mrs. Jeff Barclay, Box 428, Fulton, KY 42041.

NATIONAL FOOD SERVICE WORKERS DAY. Sept 24. Purpose: To promote public awareness of the contributions and importance of food service workers to life in America. Sponsor: Women & Infants Hospital of Rhode Island, Dietary Dept, 50 Maude St, Providence, RI 02908.

NEPTUNE FESTIVAL. Sept 24-28. Info: City of Virginia Beach, Office of Public Info, Municipal Ctr, Virginia Beach, VA 23456.

SCHWENKFELDER THANKSGIVING. Sept 24. On this day in 1734 members of the Schwenkfelder Society gave thanks for their deliverance from Old World persecution as they prepared to take up new lives in the Pennsylvania Dutch counties of Pennsylvania. Still celebrated.

SEPTEMBER 25 — THURSDAY
268th Day — Remaining, 97

ALBEMARLE CRAFTSMAN'S FAIR. Sept 25-28. Knobbs Creek Recreation Ctr, Elizabeth City, NC. Craftsmen demonstrate and produce crafts of 'yester year'. Info from: Chamber of Commerce, Box 426, Elizabeth City, NC 27909.

DISCOVERY OF PACIFIC OCEAN DAY. Sept 25. Vasco Nunez de Balboa, Spanish conquistador, became first European to look upon the Pacific Ocean, Sept 25, 1513, and took possession of it in the name of Spain.

ENGLAND: WINCHESTER CATHEDRAL FLOWER FESTIVAL: THE CATHEDRAL AND THE CROWN. Sept 25-28. Winchester, Hampshire.

FIRST AMERICAN NEWSPAPER ANNIVERSARY. Sept 25. The first (and only) edition of *Publick Occurrences Both Foreign and Domestick* was published on Sept 25, 1690, by Benjamin Harris, at the London-Coffee-House, Boston, MA. Authorities considered this first newspaper published in the U.S. offensive and ordered immediate suppression.

GRAPE EXPECTATIONS, A CHAMPAIGNFEST. Sept 25-27. Purpose: To involve the entire community in a fun festival. National Grape Stomping Contest, and continuous entertainment. Sponsor: Vintage Champaign Council, 115 N Neil, Suite 105, Champaign, IL 61820.

MOON PHASE: LAST QUARTER. Sept 25. Moon enters Last Quarter phase at 10:17 p.m., E.S.T.

NATIONAL PICKLED PEPPER WEEK. Sept 25-Oct 4. Purpose: To recognize the zest added to the American menu by the bell, banana, cherry, chili, peperoncini and other members of the hot, mild and sweet pickled pepper family. Sponsor: Pickle

COPYRIGHT © 1985 BY WILLIAM D. CHASE and HELEN M. CHASE

Packers Internatl, Inc, 108½ E Main St, St. Charles, IL 60174. Info from: Burson-Marsteller, 1 E Wacker Dr, Chicago, IL 60601.

PRESTON COUNTY BUCKWHEAT FESTIVAL. Sept 25-28. Purpose: Celebrating the harvest of the grain with the special feature "Buckwheat Cakes and Sausage" dinners. Sponsor: Kingwood Volunteer Fire Dept, Lucille H. Crogan, Festival Secy, Kingwood, WV 26537.

RAMEAU, JEAN PHILLIPPE: BIRTHDAY. Sept 25. Birthday of French composer Jean Phillippe Rameau, baptised at Dijon, Sept 25, 1683. Called by some the greatest French composer and musical theorist of the eighteenth century, Rameau died at Paris, Sept 12, 1764.

RED SMITH: BIRTHDAY. Sept 25. Pulitzer Prize winning sports columnist and newspaperman for 54 years, Walter Wesley (Red) Smith was born at Green Bay, WI, on Sept 25, 1905. Called the "nation's most respected sports writer," Smith's columns appeared in some 500 newspapers. He died at Stamford, CT, Jan 15, 1982.

SHOSTAKOVICH, DMITRI: BIRTHDAY. Sept 25. Russian composer born, St. Petersburg (now Leningrad), Sept 25, 1906. Died, Moscow, Aug 9, 1975.

VALLEY VINEYARDS WINE FESTIVAL. Sept 25-27. Purpose: To celebrate the end of grape harvest season. Sponsor: American Wine Society, Valley Vineyards, Morrow, OH 45152.

SEPTEMBER 26 — FRIDAY
269th Day — Remaining, 96

ARKANSAS STATE FAIR AND LIVESTOCK SHOW: Sept 26-Oct 5. Barton Coliseum, Little Rock, AR. Info from: Arkansas State Fair, Box 907, Little Rock, AR 72203.

ELIOT, THOMAS STEARNS: BIRTHDAY. Sept 26. Poet and critic, born, St Louis, MO, Sept 26, 1888. Died Jan 4, 1965.

FESTIVAL OF THE HORSE. Sept 26-28. Georgetown, KY. Parade, arts and crafts, horse breed exhibits, Civil War re-enactment of Morgan's raid on Georgetown. Info from: KY Dept of Travel, Capital Plaza Office Tower, Frankfort, KY 40601.

GERSHWIN, GEORGE: BIRTHDAY. Sept 26. American composer remembered for his many enduring songs and melodies, including: "The Man I Love," "Strike Up the Band," "Funny Face," "I Got Rhythm," and the opera *Porgy and Bess*. Many of his works were in collaboration with his brother, Ira (q.v.). Born at Brooklyn, NY, on Sept 26, 1898, he died, of a brain tumor, at Beverly Hills, CA, July 11, 1937.

GREAT AMERICAN DULCIMER CONVENTION. Sept 26-27. Purpose: To bring together the best oldtime and modern lap and hammered dulcimer players in concerts, jam sessions, workshops and lessons to foster dulcimer playing and building. Mountain crafts featured with emphasis on dulcimer building and builders. Info from: KY Dept of Parks, Barry Howard, Pine Mt State Park, Box 610, Pineville, KY 40977.

HARVEST MOON BALL. Sept 26. Roanoke Market Square, Roanoke, VA. Outdoor dancing to live music by the light of the harvest moon. Sponsor: Roanoke Special Events Committee, 210 Reserve Ave, SW, Roanoke, VA 24016.

JESSE STUART FESTIVAL. Sept 26-27. Greenbo Lake State Resort Park, Greenup, KY. The works and life of Jesse Stuart will be featured. Info from: Kentucky Dept. of Parks, Capital Plaza Tower, Frankfort, KY 40601.

September 1986

S	M	T	W	T	F	S
	1	2	3	4	5	6
7	8	9	10	11	12	13
14	15	16	17	18	19	20
21	22	23	24	25	26	27
28	29	30				

JOHNNY APPLESEED: BIRTHDAY. Sept 26. John Chapman, better known as Johnny Appleseed, believed to have been born at Leominster, MA, on Sept 26, 1774. Died, Allen County, IN, Mar 11, 1847. Planter of orchards, friend of wild animals, regarded as a great medicine man by the Indians.

MORGAN COUNTY SORGHUM FESTIVAL. Sept 26-28. West Liberty, KY. Sorghum in every form known to man. Parade, crafts, football and music. Info from: KY Dept of Travel, Capital Plaza Office Tower, Frankfort, KY 40601.

NATIVE AMERICAN DAY. Sept 26. Formerly American Indian Day. Traditional observance has been on the 4th Friday in September or on the 2nd Saturday in May. First proclaimed for the year 1916.

OHIO SWISS FESTIVAL. Sept 26-27. Purpose: To promote the swiss cheese industry in Ohio and the village of Sugarcreek. Sponsor: Ohio Swiss Cheese Festival, Inc, Box 361, Sugarcreek, OH 44681.

PEASE, DONALD J. BIRTHDAY. Sept 26. U.S. Representative of Ohio's 13th district, Democrat, of Oberlin, OH, was born in Toledo, OH, Sept 26, 1931.

PENNSYLVANIA STATE CRAFT FESTIVAL. Sept 26-28. Tyler State Park, Richboro, PA. State-wide juried craft festival. Info from: Pennsylvania Designer Craftsmen, Box 206, Bedford, PA 15522.

PIONEER DAYS. Sept 26-28. The stockyards, Fort Worth. Info from: North Fort Worth Business Assn, 131 East Exchange Ave, Fort Worth, TX, 76106.

POPE PAUL VI: BIRTHDAY. Sept 26. Giovanni Battista Montini, 262nd Pope of the Roman Catholic Church, born at Concesio, Italy, on Sept 26, 1897. Elected Pope June 21, 1963. Died at Castel Gandolfo, near Rome, Aug 6, 1978.

TULSA STATE FAIR. Sept 26-Oct 4. Livestock showing and judging, ice capades, tractor pull and giant midway. Info from: Tulsa State Fair, Box 4735, Tulsa, OK 74159.

WALES: SWANSEA MUSICAL FESTIVAL. Sept 26-Oct 18. Swansea, West Glamorgan. A series of musical recitals.

WORLD WIDE ANTIQUES SHOW. Sept 26-28. Tarrant County Conv Ctr, 1111 Houston St, Fort Worth, TX 76102.

YEMEN ARAB REPUBLIC: NATIONAL HOLIDAY. Sept 26. Commemorates proclamation of the republic on Sept 26, 1962.

SEPTEMBER 27 — SATURDAY
270th Day — Remaining, 95

ANCESTOR APPRECIATION DAY. Sept 27. Purpose: A day to express gratitude for one's personal existence, a time to pause for solemn reflection and for joyous, anecdotal review and appreciation of personal ancestral history. Sponsor: A.A.D. Assn, Box 68, Montague, MI 49437.

ARKANSAS STATE FIDDLERS ASSOCIATION CHAMPIONSHIP. Sept 27-28. Ozark Folk Center, Mountain View, AR. Info from: Ozark Folk Ctr, Mountain View, AR 72560.

CABRILLO FESTIVAL. Sept 27-28. Colorful pageant reenacts the historic landing of Portuguese explorer Juan Rodriguez Cabrillo who sailed into San Diego Bay Sept 28, 1542, to discover California. Historical events, Portuguese, Spanish, Native American and Mexican dances. Info from: Cabrillo Natl Monument, Box 6670, San Diego, CA 92106.

CHAUTAUQUA OF THE ARTS. Sept 27-28. Madison, IN. Info from: Dixie McDonough, 1119 W Main St, Madison, IN 47250.

CRAFT FAIR USA. Sept 27-28. Wisconsin State Fair Park, Milwaukee, WI. Sale of handcrafted items: Jewelry, pottery, weaving, leather, wood, glass, yulecraft and sculpture. Info from: Dennis R. Hill, Dir, Craft Fair USA, 3233 S Villa Circle, West Allis, WI 53227.

CRUIKSHANK, GEORGE: BIRTHDAY. Sept 27. English illustrator, especially known for caricatures and for illustration of Charles Dickens' books, born Sept 27, 1792. Died Feb 1, 1878.

COPYRIGHT © 1985 BY WILLIAM D. CHASE and HELEN M. CHASE

FALL SQUARE DANCE ROUNDUP. Sept 27. Civic Center, Dodge City, KS. Square and round dancing. Sponsor: Square and Round Dance Clubs and SW Kansas Square Dance Callers Assn. Info from: Les Houser, 2211 3rd Ave, Dodge City, KS 67801.

FESTIVAL '86. Sept 27-28. Festival features the works of over 200 artists and craftspersons. Entertainment and a variety of regional and ethnic foods. Info from: Creative Arts Guild, Box 375, Dalton, GA 30722.

GARDENA JAPANESE CULTURAL SHOW. Sept 27-28. Gardena Nakaoka Memorial Community Center. Demonstrations and stage presentations of the Japanese arts. Info from: Gardena Valley Gardeners Assn, Loyce Holt, 1700 W 162nd St, Gardena, CA 90247.

HARVEST SHOW. Sept 27-28. Fairmount Park, Philadelphia, PA. Info from: The Pennsylvania Horticultural Society, 325 Walnut St, Philadelphia, PA 19106.

INTERNATIONAL WHISTLE-OFF CONTEST. Sept 27-28. Open to any individual or duet who can whistle a tune with some degree of skill without aid of a musical contrivance in the jowls or under the tongue. Okay if you use hands or fingers. Info from: Chamber of Commerce, 1191 S Carson, Carson City, NV 89701.

KIWANIS KIDS' DAY. Sept 27. Purpose: To honor and assist youth—our greatest resource. Sponsor: Program Development Dept, Kiwanis Internatl, 3636 Woodview Trace, Indianapolis, IN 46268.

KOSTMAYER, PETER HOUSTON: BIRTHDAY. Sept 27. U.S. Representative of Pennsylvania's 8th district, Democrat, of Solebury, PA, was born in New York City on Sept 27, 1946.

LIGHTFOOT, JAMES ROSS: BIRTHDAY. Sept 27. U.S. Representative of Iowa's 5th district, Republican, of Shenandoah, IA, born in Sioux City, IA, on Sept 27, 1938.

MIFFLIN COUNTY GOOSE DAY CELEBRATION. Sept 27-29. Lewiston, PA. "A day set aside for eating goose for luck! Legend has it that if you eat goose on Goose Day, you will increase your fortune." Info from: Juniata Valley Chamber of Commerce, 3 Monument Sq, Suite 104, Lewiston, PA 17044.

MILWAUKEE JOURNAL/AL'S RUN. Sept 27. Purpose: A 5 mile run or 3 mile walk through downtown Milwaukee. Named after Al McGuire, NBC basketball announcer. Always the last Saturday in September. Sponsor: The Milwaukee Journal, Box 661, Milwaukee, WI 53201.

NAST, THOMAS: BIRTHDAY. Sept 27. American political cartoonist born Sept 27, 1840. Died Dec 7, 1902.

NATIONAL HUNTING AND FISHING DAY. Sept 27. Presidential Proclamation. "Proc. 4682, Sept 11, 1979, establishes the 4th Saturday of September 1979 as this day and covers all succeeding years."

NATIONAL HUNTING AND FISHING DAY. Sept 27. Purpose: To recognize sportsmen's contributions to conservation. Approximately 2,500 activities nationwide. (Fourth Saturday of Sept.) Sponsor: Natl Hunting & Fishing Day, Box 1075, Riverside, CT 06878.

NEVADA DAY CELEBRATION. Sept 27-28. Carson City, NV. Nevada Admissions Day commemorated with a parade, beard contests, bed races, rock drilling and weight carrying contests, firefighting competitions and parties. Info from: Chamber of Commerce, 1191 S. Carson, Carson City, NV 89701.

OLD-TIME FIDDLERS' CONTEST. Sept 27-28. Carson City, NV. Info from: Carson City Tourism Authority, Box 1416, Carson City, NV 89701.

PANCAKE DAY. Sept 27. Purpose: Pancakes and all the trimmings are served to all who attend Pancake Day. Entertainment, parade and beauty pageant are highlights of the event. Sponsor: Chamber of Commerce, 128 N 12th, Centerville, IA 52544.

ST. VINCENT DE PAUL: FEAST DAY. Sept 27. French priest, patron of charitable organizations, co-founder of the Sisters of Charity. Canonized 1737. (1581?-1660).

SPACE MILESTONE: SOYUZ 12 (USSR). Sept 27. Two Soviet cosmonauts (V.G. Lazarev and O.G. Makarov) made 2-day flight. Launched Sept 27, 1973.

STRATTON, SAMUEL S: BIRTHDAY. Sept 27. U.S. Representative of New York's 23rd district, Democrat, of Schenectady, NY, was born in Yonkers, NY, on Sept 27, 1916.

SEPTEMBER 28 — SUNDAY
271st Day — Remaining, 94

BOEHLERT, SHERWOOD, L: BIRTHDAY. Sept 28. U.S. Representative of New York's 25th district, Republican, of Utica, NY, born there on Sept 28, 1936.

CABRILLO DAY. Sept 28. California. Commemorates discovery of California on Sept 28, 1542, by Portuguese navigator Juan Rodriguez Cabrillo who reached San Diego Bay on that date. Cabrillo died at San Miguel Island, CA, Jan 3, 1543. His birth date is unknown. The Cabrillo National Monument marks his landfall and Cabrillo Day is still observed in California (in some areas on the Saturday nearest Sept 28).

CAPP, AL: BIRTHDAY. Sept 28. American satirical cartoonist, Al Capp (born Alfred Gerald Caplin), creator of "Li'l Abner," and originator of Sadie Hawkins Day, was born at New Haven, CT, Sept 28, 1909. He died at Cambridge, MA, Nov 5, 1979.

COLONIAL COURT DAYS AT HANNA'S TOWN. Sept 28. Greensburg, PA. Living history portrayed at a colonial fair and market. Info from: Westmoreland County Historical Society, Greensburg, PA 15601.

CONFUCIUS' BIRTHDAY and TEACHERS' DAY. Sept 28. Taiwan. National holiday, designated as Teachers' Day. Confucius is the Latinized name of Kung-futzu, born in Shantung province on the 27th day of the tenth moon (lunar calendar) in the 22nd year of Kuke Hsiang of Lu (551 B.C.). He died at age 72, having spent some 40 years as a teacher. Teachers' Day is observed annually on Sept 28.

GOLD STAR MOTHER'S DAY. Sept 28. Presidential Proclamation. "Always last Sunday of each September since 1936. Proc. 2424 of 1940 covers all succeeding years." (Pub. Res. No. 123 of June 23, 1936.)

KRAKOW FESTIVAL. Sept 28. Purpose: "A family oriented celebration of the cultural heritage brought from Poland by their ancestors." Sponsor: Alliance College, Fullerton Ave, Cambridge Springs, PA 16403.

KUNIN, MADELEINE M: BIRTHDAY. Sept 28. Madeleine M. Kunin, Governor of Vermont, Democrat, was born at Zurich, Switzerland, on Sept 28, 1933.

NATIONAL DEFENSE TRANSPORTATION ASSOCIATION: TRANSPORTATION AND LOGISTICS FORUM AND EXPO. Sept 28-Oct 1. Hyatt Regency, Tampa, FL. Purpose: Major intermodal transportation event of the year with over 500 executives from industry and the government in attendance. Info from: BGEN Malcolm P. Hooker, USAF (Ret), Natl Defense Transportation Assn, 727 N Washington St, Ste 200, Alexandria, VA 22314.

NATIONAL GOOD NEIGHBOR DAY. Sept 28. Purpose: To build a nation and world that cares. To increase appreciation and understanding of our fellow man beginning next door. (Annually, the fourth Sunday in September.) Sponsor: Good Neighbor Day Foundation, Dr. Richard C. Mattson, Drawer R, Lakeside, MT 59922.

WILLARD, FRANCES ELIZABETH CAROLINE: BIRTHDAY. Sept 28. American educator and reformer, president of the Woman's Christian Temperance Union, 1879-1898, and women's suffrage leader, born at Churchville, NY, Sept 28, 1839. Died, New York City, Feb 18, 1898.

SEPTEMBER 29 — MONDAY
272nd Day — Remaining, 93

AMERICAN INDIAN CEREMONIAL DANCING. Sept 29-30. Taos, NM. Sundown dance is performed at dusk each Sept 29th, followed the next day (San Geronimo's Day) with foot races, high pole climb, clowning, feasting and dancing.

FOUR-STATES FAIR AND RODEO. Sept 29-Oct 4. Livestock, agriculture, arts and crafts of area. Sponsor. Four States Fair Assn, Inc, Mrs. Marion Reed, Exec Dir, Box 1915, Four States Fair Grounds, Texarkana, AR-TX 75504.

HAPPY FISCAL NEW YEAR FESTIVAL. Sept 29-Oct 1. Purpose: Celebrate the beginning of a new federal fiscal year and honor distinguished bureaucrats who have professionally interdigitated sound fiscal harmonics. Sponsor: Internatl Assn of Professional Bureaucrats (INATAPROBU), Dr. James H. Boren, Pres, Natl Press Bldg. Washington, DC 20045.

McDADE, JOSEPH MICHAEL: BIRTHDAY. Sept 29. U.S. Representative of Pennsylvania's 10th district, Republican, of Scranton, PA, born there on Sept 29, 1931.

MICHAELMAS. Sept 29. The feast of St. Michael and All Angels in the Greek and Roman Catholic Churches.

NELSON, BILL: BIRTHDAY. Sept 29. U.S. Representative of Florida's 11th district, Democrat, of Melbourne, FL, was born in Miami, FL, on Sept 29, 1942.

NELSON, HORATIO: BIRTHDAY. Sept 29. English naval hero of the Battle of Trafalgar born Sept 29, 1758. Died Oct 21, 1805.

SCOTLAND YARD: BIRTHDAY. Sept 29. The first public appearance of Greater London's Metropolitan Police occurred on Sept 29, 1829, amid jeering and abuse from disapproving political opponents. Public sentiment turned to confidence and respect in the ensuing years. The Metropolitan Police had been established by act of Parliament in June 1829, at the request of Home Secretary Sir Robert Peel, after whom the London police officers became more affectionately known as "bobbies." Scotland Yard, the site of their first headquarters near Charing Cross, soon became the official name of the force.

SPACE MILESTONE: SALYUT 6 (USSR). Sept 29. Soviet space station launched on Sept 29, 1977. Burned up, when it re-entered Earth's atmosphere after nearly five years, July 29, 1982.

XENOPHOBE UNDERSTANDING DAY. Sept 29. Purpose: A day to further the understanding of xenophobes (persons who have an unusual fear of strangers, especially foreigners), and to encourage research toward discovery of a cure for xenophobia. Introduce yourself to a xenophobe on this day. Sponsor: Xenophobe Understanding Day Committee, Box 68, Montague, MI 49437.

SEPTEMBER 30 — TUESDAY
273rd Day — Remaining, 92

ASK A "STUPID" QUESTION DAY. Sept 30. Purpose: To encourage curious people to overcome their timidity and ask that "stupid" question. Call your local library, radio station, university, newspaper, barber shop, or other fount of knowledge. Sponsor: David Larzelere, c/o: *Flint Journal*, 200 E First St, Flint, MI 48502.

BOTSWANA INDEPENDENCE DAY. Sept 30. Botswana. National holiday. The former Bechuanaland Protectorate (British Colony) became the independent Republic of Botswana on Sept 30, 1966.

CAPOTE, TRUMAN: BIRTHDAY. Sept 30. American novelist and literary celebrity, was born Truman Streckfus Persons, at New Orleans, LA, on Sept 30, 1924. He later took the name of his step-father and became Truman Capote. Among his best remembered books: *Other Voices, Other Rooms*; *Breakfast at Tiffany's* and *In Cold Blood*. He was working on a new novel, *Answered Prayers*, at the time of his death in Los Angeles on Aug 25, 1984.

DERRICK, BUTLER CARSON, JR: BIRTHDAY. Sept 30. U.S. Representative of South Carolina's 3rd district, Democrat, of Edgefield, SC, was born Sept 30, 1936.

FEAST OF ST. JEROME. Sept 30. Patron saint of scholars and librarians.

FIRST ANNUAL FAIR IN AMERICA: ANNIVERSARY. Sept 30. According to the Laws and Ordinances of New Netherlands (now New York and New Jersey), on Sept 30, 1641, authorities declared that "henceforth there shall be held annually at Fort Amsterdam" a Cattle Fair (Oct 15) and a Hog Fair (Nov 1), and that "whosoever hath any things to sell or buy can regulate himself accordingly."

HEFTEL, CECIL "CEC": BIRTHDAY. Sept 30. U.S. Representative of Hawaii's 1st district, Democrat, of Honolulu, HI, born in Cook County, IL, on Sept 30, 1924.

HONG KONG: BIRTHDAY OF CONFUCIUS. Sept 30. Religious observances are held by the Confucian Society at Confucius Temple in Causeway Bay. Observed on 27th day of eighth lunar month.

NECKER, JACQUES: BIRTHDAY. Sept 30. French banker and statesman, born at Geneva, Switzerland, Sept 30, 1732. His dismissal from his post as head of France's Department of Finance was the immediate cause of the storming of the Bastille, July 14, 1789. Necker died near Geneva, Apr 9, 1804.

SASSER, JAMES RALPH: BIRTHDAY. Sept 30. U.S. Senator from Tennessee, Democrat, of Nashville, TN, was born in Memphis, TN, Sept 30, 1936.

September *1986*	S	M	T	W	T	F	S
		1	2	3	4	5	6
	7	8	9	10	11	12	13
	14	15	16	17	18	19	20
	21	22	23	24	25	26	27
	28	29	30				

COPYRIGHT © 1985 BY WILLIAM D. CHASE and HELEN M. CHASE

October.

OCTOBER 1 — WEDNESDAY

274th Day — Remaining, 91

BOLAND, EDWARD P: BIRTHDAY. Oct 1. U.S. Representative of Massachusetts' 2nd district, Democrat, of Springfield, MA, born at Springfield, on Oct 1, 1911.

BRAZIL: FESTIVAL OF PENHA. Oct 1-31. Rio de Janeiro, Brazil. Pilgrimages, especially on Saturdays during October, to Church of Our Lady of Penha, which is built on top of a rock, requires climb of 365 steps (representing days of the year), or ride in car on inclined plane (for children, invalids and aged), for those troubled and sick who seek hope or cure.

CARTER, JIMMY: BIRTHDAY. Oct 1. James Earl Carter, Jr., 39th President of the U.S., was born at Plains, GA, Oct 1, 1924. His term of office: Jan 20, 1977-Jan 20, 1981. In a 1976 speech, Carter said: "The first step in providing economic equality for women is to ensure a stable economy in which every person who wants to work can work."

CYPRUS: NATIONAL HOLIDAY. Oct 1. Independence Day.

ENERGY MANAGEMENT IS A FAMILY AFFAIR - IMPROVE YOUR HOME. Oct 1-Mar 31, 1987. Purpose: Replace energy-consuming units with new efficient home conveniences and remodel to prevent heating and cooling loss. Info from: Home Improvement Time, J.A. Stewart, Program Admn, Old Steubenville Pike, Oakdale, PA 15071.

FALL FOLIAGE CELEBRATION. Oct 1-31. Purpose: Celebration of Fayette County Fall Foliage Spectacular. Sponsor: Fayette County Tourism, Box 63, Hopwood, PA 15445.

FRANKFURT BOOK FAIR. Oct 1-6. Frankfurt, Germany. Info from: Ausstellungs-und Messe-GmbH des Borsenvereins des Deutschen Buchhandels, Postfach 2404, D-6000, Frankfurt am Main 1, Federal Republic of Germany.

GINKGO FESTIVAL. Oct 1-7. Monroe, MI. Purpose: To guess when the leaves will fall from the historic Dorsch ginkgo tree. Related events include Ginkgo Prediction Run, Ginkgo Dinner and leaf drop date-guessing contest (usually within 2 hours). Sponsor: Friends of Dorsch Library, Mary Jo Garmire, Head Librarian, 18 E First St, Monroe, MI 48161.

GOURMET ADVENTURES MONTH. Oct 1-31. Purpose: To share dining fun with everyone. To be imaginative and creative, an explorer in the kitchen or with a restaurant menu. Sponsor: Mme. Ginette's Cordon Bleu Ouest French Cooking School, 3369 Hamilton Way, Los Angeles, CA 90026.

GREAT FALL HARDWARE SALE. Oct 1-31. Purpose: Seasonal selling event featuring special values in name-brand merchandise in independent, locally owned retail hardware stores and home centers. Sponsor: Natl Retail Hardware Assn, Neal Suppiger, Promotion Dir, 770 N High School Rd, Indianapolis, IN 46224.

HARRISON, CAROLINE LAVINIA SCOTT: BIRTHDAY. Oct 1. First wife of Benjamin Harrison, 23rd President of the U.S., born at Oxford, OH, Oct 1, 1832. Died Oct 25, 1892.

INTERNATIONAL DOLL COLLECTORS MONTH. Oct 1-31. Purpose: A time to share the joys of collecting dolls with those around you. Sponsor: Marjorie Spangler Creations, Box 3296, Walnut Creek, CA 94598.

INTERNATIONAL MARINE TRAVEL MONTH. Oct 1-31. Purpose: To promote the unique pleasures of sea voyaging — the comforts and gracious living of leisurely travel on board ship. Sponsor: Internatl Marine Travel Council Inc, Harry F. Klemfuss, Dir, 61 Cupsaw Dr, Ringwood, NJ 07456.

JAPAN: NEWSPAPER WEEK. Oct 1-7. Japan. Every year. Oct 1-7 is observed as Newspaper Week. During this time newspapers make an extensive effort to acquaint the general public with their functions and attempts to carry out the role of a newspaper in a free society.

KOREA: ARMED FORCES DAY. Oct 1. National holiday marked by many colorful military parades, aerial acrobatics and honor guard ceremonies, held around the reviewing plaza at Yoido, an island in the Han River.

LAWRENCE, JAMES: BIRTHDAY. Oct 1. Brilliant American naval officer, whose last battle was a defeat, but whose dying words became a most honored naval motto. Lawrence, born at Burlington, NJ, on Oct 1, 1781, was commander of the U.S.S. *Hornet*, and later Captain of the *Chesapeake* when she engaged in a naval duel with H.M.S. *Shannon*, off Boston, on June 1, 1813. The *Chesapeake* was captured and towed to Halifax as a British prize. Lawrence was mortally wounded by a musket ball during the engagement and uttered his famous last words, "Don't give up the ship," as he was being carried off the ship's deck.

LONDON BRIDGE DAYS. Oct 1-12. Sponsor: Chamber of Commerce, 65 N Lake Havasu Ave, Suite 2-B, Lake Havasu City, AZ 86403.

MISSISSIPPI STATE FAIR. Oct 1-12. Mississippi State Fair Grounds, Jackson, MS.

MOUNTAINEER HERITAGE MONTH. Oct 1-31. Purpose: A celebration of West Virginia's heritage. Sponsor: Mountaineer Mall, Kathy Gerritsen, Marketing Dir, 5000 Greenbag Rd, Morgantown, WV 26505.

NATIONAL ADOPT-A-DOG MONTH. Oct 1-31. Purpose: To help promote the adoption of homeless puppies and dogs. Sponsors: Meaty Bone, Jerky Treats and Tuffy's for The American Humane Assn. Info from: Daniel J Edelman, Inc, 211 E Ontario St, Chicago, IL 60611.

NATIONAL APPLE JACK MONTH. Oct 1-31. Purpose: "A month during which Apple Jack will be honored as America's oldest native distilled spirit, established in the early 1700's." Sponsor: Laird's Apple Jack. Info from: Ted Worner, LMP Communications, Warner Lane, Tarrytown, NY 10591.

NATIONAL CAR CARE MONTH. Oct 1-31. United States and Canada. Purpose: To educate motorists about the importance of maintaining their cars in an effort to improve air quality, highway safety and fuel conservation. Sponsor: Natl Car Care Month, Car Care Council, 600 Renaissance Ctr, Detroit, MI 48243.

NATIONAL FAMILY SEXUALITY EDUCATION MONTH. Oct 1-31. Purpose: To support parents as the first and primary sexuality educators of their children by providing information for parents. Sponsor: Planned Parenthood Federation of America, Susan F. Newcomer, Dir of Education, 810 Seventh Ave, New York, NY 10019.

NATIONAL KIDS' FITNESS MONTH. Oct 1-31. Purpose: To encourage kids, parents and teachers to concentrate on kids fitness and to make exercise, health and fitness a regular part of every day. Sponsor: North American Bear. Info from: Jasculca/Terman & Associates, Michelle Katzin, 730 N Franklin St, Suite 510, Chicago, IL 60610.

COPYRIGHT © 1985 BY WILLIAM D. CHASE and HELEN M. CHASE

NATIONAL POPCORN POPPIN' MONTH. Oct 1-31. Purpose: To celebrate the wholesome, economical, natural food value of popcorn, America's native fun snack. Sponsor: The Popcorn Institute, 111 E Wacker Dr, Suite 600, Chicago, IL 60601.

NATIONAL PRETZEL MONTH. Oct 1-31. Purpose: "A celebration in honor of the world's oldest snack food! The pretzel dates back to 610 A.D. and today is enjoyed as one of our healthiest snacks—no sugar or cholesterol, low cal!" Sponsor: Natl Pretzel Bakers Institute, 800 New Holland Ave, Box 1433, Lancaster, PA 17603.

NATIONAL ROLLER SKATING WEEK. Oct 1-7. Purpose: To call attention to the recreational pleasure and health benefits derived from such a popular and characteristically North American sport. Sponsor: Roller Skating Rink Operators Assn, George Pickard, Exec Dir, Box 81846, Lincoln, NE 68501.

NATIONAL SUDDEN INFANT DEATH SYNDROME AWARENESS MONTH. Oct 1-31. Purpose: To create awareness of Sudden Infant Death Syndrome (also called crib death) which is the number one killer of babies under the age of one year. Sponsor: Natl Sudden Infant Death Syndrome Foundation, Exec Dir. 8240 Professional Pl, Suite 205, Landover, MD 20785.

NIGERIA: NATIONAL HOLIDAY. Oct 1. Independence Day. Became independent on this day, 1960, and a republic on this day, 1963.

NORWAY: PAGEANTRY IN OSLO. Oct 1. The Storting (Norway's Parliament) convenes on first weekday in October, when it decides date for the ceremonial opening of the Storting—usually the following weekday—and the parliamentary session is then opened by King Olav V in the presence of Corps Diplomatique, preceded and followed by a military procession between the Royal Palace and the Storting.

PEOPLE'S REPUBLIC OF CHINA: NATIONAL DAY. Oct 1-2. Commemorates the founding of Communist China Oct 1, 1949.

PIZZA FESTIVAL TIME MONTH. Oct 1-31. Purpose: To call attention to the health benefits of pizza and inform the public of its history. Sponsor: Richard R. Falk Associates, Richard Falk, Chief Taster, 147 W 42nd St, New York, NY 10036.

REHNQUIST, WILLIAM HUBBS: BIRTHDAY. Oct 1. Associate Justice of the Supreme Court of the United States, nominated by Pres. Nixon on Oct 21, 1971. (Sworn in, Jan 7, 1972.) Justice Rehnquist was born at Milwaukee, WI, on Oct 1, 1924.

RISING OF THE PALOLO. Oct 1-Nov 30. Western Samoa. Each year at this time, when the moon and tide are just right, a sea annalid known as "palolo" emerges from the reef to begin its annual reproductive cycle. Samoans, who consider the palolo a great delicacy, turn out in force with nets, cheese cloth and gas lanterns, wading out in the dark to scoop up the "caviar of the Pacific." A great carnival-like atmosphere sweeps the islands from midnight to dawn as thousands of Samoans and visitors take to the reefs. Info from: Samoan Mission to the UN, 820 2nd Ave, New York, NY 10017.

SPECTACLE OF THE GEESE. Oct 1-31. Horicon Marsh, 12 miles south of Fond du Lac, WI. The fabulous fall flyway of the Canada Geese brings over one hundred thousand to Horicon Marsh on their trip from Canada to winter grounds. Info from: Conv & Visitors Bureau, 207 N Main St, Fond du Lac, WI 54935.

October
1986

S	M	T	W	T	F	S
			1	2	3	4
5	6	7	8	9	10	11
12	13	14	15	16	17	18
19	20	21	22	23	24	25
26	27	28	29	30	31	

SPINA BIFIDA MONTH. Oct 1-31. Purpose: To inform the general public about spina bifida and the potential of those born with the birth defect; to inform families of services in their area. Sponsor: SBAA, Kent Smith, Exec Dir, 343 S Dearborn, Suite 310, Chicago, IL 60604.

STOCKTON, RICHARD: BIRTHDAY. Oct 1. Lawyer and signer of the Declaration of Independence, born Princeton, NJ, Oct 1, 1730. Died there, Feb 8, 1781.

TUVALU: NATIONAL HOLIDAY. Oct 1.

UNITED STATES 1987 FEDERAL FISCAL YEAR begins. Oct 1, 1986-Sept 30, 1987.

WALT DISNEY WORLD: ANNIVERSARY. Oct 1. Walt Disney World celebrates anniversary of opening: Oct 1, 1971. Info from: Publicity Dept, Walt Disney World, Box 40, Lake Buena Vista, FL 32830.

WORLD DAIRY EXPO. Oct 1-5. Madison, WI. Dairy trade show with over 400 commercial exhibits and 1700 head of "North America's finest purebred dairy cattle." Judging contests for youth, educational programs, crafts, food demonstrations and dairy snacks. Info from: World Dairy Expo, 2135 Rimrock Rd, Madison, WI 53713.

WORLD VEGETARIAN DAY. Oct 1. Purpose: A celebration of solidarity amongst vegetarians worldwide to bring attention to the general public regarding the immeasurable value of this lifestyle. Sponsor: North American Vegetarian Society, Box 72, Dolgeville, NY 13329.

ZOOFEST '86. Oct 1-31. Purpose: A celebration of animals, autumn and the arts. Sponsor: North Carolina Zoological Park, Rt 4, Box 83, Asheboro, NC 27203.

OCTOBER 2 — THURSDAY
275th Day — Remaining, 90

APPLEFEST IV. Oct 2-4. Purpose: To celebrate the apple harvest. Info from: Chamber of Commerce, 1282 Liberty St, Suite 2, Franklin, PA 16323.

CHARLIE BROWN and SNOOPY: BIRTHDAY. Oct 2. The "Peanuts" gang, created by Charles M. Schulz, celebrates 36 years of American humor. Syndicated by United Feature Syndicate, the first "Peanuts" comic strip was published on Oct 2, 1950. It now appears in 2,000 newspapers and is translated into 26 languages in 68 countries. Charlie Brown, the "well-meaning loser who, despite continuing defeats, nurtures an eternal hope to overcome adversity," along with Snoopy, Linus, Lucy and friends celebrate their 36th birthday in print. Info from: United Feature Syndicate, Nancy Nicolelis, PR Mgr, 200 Park Ave, New York, NY 10166.

ENGLAND: NOTTINGHAM GOOSE FAIR. Oct 2. Forest Recreation Ground, Nottingham. Held annually since 1284 (except during the Great Plague in 1665 and the two World Wars), the fair formerly lasted three weeks and boasted as many as 20,000 geese on display. Always the first Thursday of October. Now a traditional fair with modern fun fair style amusements.

FRANKFORT'S 200TH BIRTHDAY HOMECOMING. Oct 2-5. Frankfort, KY. Arts and crafts, big-name entertainment, concerts and family oriented fun. Info from: KY Dept of Travel, Capital Plaza Office Tower, Frankfort, KY 40601.

GANDHI, MAHATMA: BIRTHDAY. Oct 2. Mohandas Karamchand Gandhi, Indian leader born Oct 2, 1869. Assassinated Jan 30, 1948. On this anniversary thousands of Indians gather at the park on the Jumna River in Delhi where Gandhi's body was cremated. Hymns sung and cotton thread spun on small spinning wheels (one of Gandhi's favorite activities).

GUINEA: NATIONAL HOLIDAY. Oct 2. Independence Day. Commemorates proclamation of the republic on Oct 2, 1958.

HULL, CORDELL: BIRTHDAY. Oct 2. American statesman who served in both houses of the Congress and as Secretary of State, was born Oct 2, 1871, at Pickett County, TN. Noted for his contributions to the "Good Neighbor" policies of the U.S.

COPYRIGHT © 1985 BY WILLIAM D. CHASE and HELEN M. CHASE

with regard to countries of the Americas, and to the establishment of the United Nations, Hull died at Bethesda, MD, July 23, 1955.

PHILEAS FOGG'S WAGER DAY. Oct 2. Anniversary, from Jules Verne's *Around the World in Eighty Days*, of the famous wager of Oct 2, 1872, upon which the book is based: "I will bet twenty thousand pounds against any one who wishes, that I will make the tour of the world in eighty days or less." Then, consulting a pocket almanac, Phileas Fogg said: "As today is Wednesday, the second of October, I shall be due in London, in this very room of the Reform Club, on Saturday, the twenty-first of December, at a quarter before nine p.m.; or else the twenty thousand pounds . . . will belong to you." See also entry for Dec 21.

SPACE MILESTONE: RECORD TIME IN SPACE. Oct 2. On Oct 2, 1984, three Soviet cosmonauts returned to Earth after setting record of 237 days in space—at Salyut 7 space station, since Feb 9.

OCTOBER 3 — FRIDAY
276th Day — Remaining, 89

BANCROFT, GEORGE: BIRTHDAY. Oct 3. American historian, born at Worcester, MA, Oct 3, 1800. Died at Washington, DC, Jan 17, 1891.

BINGAMAN, JEFF: BIRTHDAY. Oct 3. U.S. Senator from New Mexico, Democrat, of Santa Fe, NM, born at El Paso, TX, on Oct 3, 1943.

ECLIPSE: ANNULAR-TOTAL ECLIPSE OF THE SUN. Oct 3. Visible: Extreme N.E. Asia, North America except extreme S.W., Arctic regions, Greenland, Iceland, and N. of South America. Begins at 11:57 a.m. and ends at 4:13 p.m., E.S.T.

HONDURAS: PUBLIC HOLIDAY. Oct 3. Honduras honors the birth anniversary (1799) of Francisco Morazan, a national hero.

IRMO OKRA STRUT FESTIVAL. Oct 3-4. Purpose: To promote the town of Irmo and raise money for a local park. Info from: Town of Irmo, Okra Strut Commission, Sharon R. Cribb, Box 406, Irmo, SC.

JEANIE AUDITIONS AND BALL. Oct 3-4. Stephen Foster State Folk Culture Center, White Springs, FL. Purpose: To select an outstanding Florida female vocalist as "Jeanie." Sponsor: Florida Federation of Music Clubs, Barbara Beauchamp, Jeanie Coord, Box 265, White Springs, FL 32096.

KENTUCKY APPLE FESTIVAL OF JOHNSON COUNTY. Oct 3-4. Paintsville, KY. Parade, arts and crafts, flea market, antique cars, band festival and apple delicacies. Info from: KY Dept of Travel, Capital Plaza Office Tower, Frankfort, KY 40601.

KOREA: NATIONAL FOUNDATION DAY. Oct 3. National holiday also called Tangun Day as it commemorates day when legendary founder of the Korean nation, Tangun, established his kingdom of Chosun in 2333 BC.

MANSON, PATRICK: BIRTHDAY. Oct 3. British parasitologist and surgeon sometimes called the "father of tropical medicine." Sir Patrick's research into insects as carriers of parasites was instrumental in later understanding of mosquitoes as transmitters of malaria. Born in Scotland on Oct 3, 1844, Manson died Apr 9, 1922.

MARIETTA COTTON DAYS FESTIVAL. Oct 3-5. Arts and crafts, entertainment and concessions on the square. Info from: Marietta Parks & Recreation Dept, Box 609, Marietta, GA 30061.

MOON PHASE: NEW MOON. Oct 3. Moon enters New Moon phase at 1:55 p.m., E.S.T.

NATIONAL STORYTELLING FESTIVAL. Oct 3-5. Purpose: Master storytellers from across the country gather to swap tales and share storytelling techniques. Highlight is ghost storytelling in the old cemetery. Sponsor: Natl Assn for the Preservation and Perpetuation of Storytelling, Box 112, Jonesborough, TN 37659.

© 1950, 1952, 1958, 1960, 1965, 1966 United Feature Syndicate, Inc.

NETHERLANDS: RELIEF OF LEIDEN DAY. Oct 3. Celebration of the liberation of Leiden in 1574.

NORTHWEST FLORIDA CHAMPIONSHIP RODEO. Oct 3-5. Bonifay, FL. Sponsor: Kiwanis Club, J. Harvey Etheridge, Box 655, Bonifay, FL 32425.

OBEY, DAVID R: BIRTHDAY. Oct 3. U.S. Representative of Wisconsin's 7th district, Democrat, of Wausau, WI, born at Okmulgee, OK, Oct 3, 1938.

OKTOBERFEST. Oct 3-5. Savannah, GA. Restaurants serving German food, continuous entertainment, arts and crafts. Info from: Savannah Waterfront Assn, Box 572, Savannah, GA 31402.

PERRYVILLE BATTLEFIELD CELEBRATION. Oct 3-5. Perryville, KY. Reenactment of one of the most desperate battles of the Civil War, features authentic campsites, drills and demonstrations. Info from: KY Dept of Travel, Capital Plaza Office Tower, Frankfort, KY 40601.

WHOLE ENCHILADA FIESTA. Oct 3-5. Purpose: To bring the citizens of Las Cruces together in a mutual effort to promote community spirit. (First full weekend in October.) Info from: Chamber of Commerce, Beverly Kraenzel, Box 519, Las Cruces, NM 88004.

OCTOBER 4 — SATURDAY
277th Day — Remaining, 88

ALBUQUERQUE INTERNATIONAL BALLOON FIESTA. Oct 4-12. "Over 500 balloons in the greatest spectacle of its kind in the world." Sunrise mass ascensions, Gas Balloon Championships, Jim Franklin's Wild Waco Air Show, U.S. Navy "Blue Angels," and "Leapfrogs," U.S. Army "Golden Knights." Rides, awards banquet and grand ball. Info from: Albuquerque Internatl Balloon Fiesta, Inc, 4804 Hawkins NE, Albuquerque, NM 87109.

ANDERSONVILLE HISTORIC FAIR. Oct 4-5. Civil War Village of Andersonville, GA. Purpose: Beautifying and restoring Andersonville to a Civil War village. Mock Civil War battle, Confederate and Yankee encampments, parade, dancing, arts and crafts. Info from: Peggy Sheppard, Fair Coord, The Andersonville Guild, Andersonville, GA 31711.

APPLE HARVEST FESTIVAL. Oct 4-5. (Also Oct 11-12.) South Mountain Fairgrounds near Gettysburg, PA. Celebration includes Natl Apple Queen Contest, tours of orchards, apple butter boiling and antique cider press. Info from: Gettysburg Travel Council, 35 Carlisle St, Gettysburg, PA 17325.

AUTUMN ON THE FARM. Oct 4-5. Over 100 crafts of the 1800s demonstrated at living historical farm. Info from: Dayton-Montgomery County Park District, Carriage Hill Farm, 7860 Shull Rd, Dayton, OH 45424.

BACCHANALIAN FEAST AND ALBEMARLE HARVEST WINE FESTIVAL. Oct 4-5. Purpose: To promote Virginia wines and the Virginia wine industry. Sponsor: Jeffersonian Wine Grape Growers Society, #2 Boar's Head Lane, Charlottesville, VA 22901.

BALDRIDGE, MALCOLM: BIRTHDAY. Oct 4. Malcolm Baldridge, U.S. Secretary of Commerce (sworn in on Jan 23, 1981) was born at Omaha, NE, on Oct 4, 1922.

BURLINGTON OLD FASHIONED APPLE HARVEST FESTIVAL. Oct 4-5. Purpose: To celebrate the apple harvest in the beautiful Potomac Highlands of West Virginia. Sponsor: Burlington United Methodist Home, Box 96, Burlington, WV 26710.

ENGLAND: NATIONAL BRASS BAND CHAMPIONSHIPS OF GREAT BRITAIN. Oct 4-5. Royal Albert Hall, Kensington Gore, London.

GOPHER HILL FESTIVAL. Oct 4. Ridgeland, SC. Parade, Nashville country music, clogging, turtle race, foot race, tennis and golf tournaments, low country food, arts and crafts. Info from: Jasper County Chamber of Commerce, Daphne Floyd, Box 1267, Ridgeland, SC 29936.

GREGORIAN CALENDAR ADJUSTMENT ANNIVERSARY. Oct 4. Pope Gregory XIII, on Feb 24, 1582, issued a Bull which decreed that the day following Tuesday, Oct 4, 1582, should be Friday, Oct 15, 1582, thus correcting the previously used Julian Calendar, then ten days out of date. This reform was effective in most Catholic countries, though the Julian Calendar continued in use in Britain and the American colonies until 1752. See also entries for Feb 24 and Sept 2.

HAYES, RUTHERFORD B: BIRTHDAY. Oct 4. Rutherford Birchard Hayes, 19th President of the U.S. (Mar 4, 1877-Mar 3, 1881), was born at Delaware, OH, Oct 4, 1822. In his inaugural address, Hayes said: "He serves his party best who serves the country best." He died at Fremont, OH, Jan 17, 1893.

JOHNSON, ELIZA McCARDLE: BIRTHDAY. Oct 4. Wife of Andrew Johnson, 17th President of the U.S., born at Leesburg, TN, Oct 4, 1810. Died Jan 15, 1876.

LEIF ERICSON ROLLER SKI MARATHON. Oct 4. Purpose: "The largest roller ski marathon in the United States", run from the Telemark resort near Cable, WI. Info from: American Classic, Box 31, Hayward, WI 54843.

LESOTHO: NATIONAL HOLIDAY. Oct 4. Independence Day. Attained sovereignty within British Commonwealth on Oct 4, 1966.

LOGAN COUNTY TOBACCO FESTIVAL. Oct 4-12. Russellville, KY. Tobacco judging, pipe smoking contest, arts and crafts, parade, Jesse James robbery re-enactment. Info from: KY Dept of Travel, Capital Plaza Office Tower, Frankfort, KY 40601.

MAKOTI THRESHING SHOW. Oct 4-5. Purpose: To acquire, rebuild and maintain antique farm machinery and motor vehicles. Threshing and other demonstrations. Sponsor: Makoti Threshers, Inc, Loren Quandt, Makoti, ND 58756.

MOORE, W HENSON: BIRTHDAY. Oct 4. U.S. Representative of Louisiana's 6th district, Republican, of Baton Rouge, LA, born in Lake Charles, LA, on Oct 4, 1939.

"1986 AIR AFFAIR AN ULTRALIGHT EXPERIENCE." Oct 4-5. Knight's Action Park, Springfield, IL. Purpose: An organized event for the sport of flying ultralights and an array of ultralights for interested spectators. Contests and prizes. Info from: Air Affair Fly/Drive In, RR 4, Box 204, Springfield, IL 62707.

OCTOBERFEST. Oct 4-5. Tarrant County Conv Ctr, 1111 Houston St, Fort Worth, TX 76102.

PORK BOWL. Oct. 4. Worthington, MN. Purpose: Junior college football game. Bands, pork feed, pig races, county and state pork queens and "Miss Piggy." Info from: Worthington Community College, Worthington, MN 56187.

RECREATIONAL VEHICLE, NEW CAR AND TRUCK SHOW. Oct 4-5. El Paso Civic Ctr, El Paso, TX. Info from: Dixie Green Promotions, Inc, 3141 W Christy Dr, Phoenix, AZ 85029.

RED FLANNEL FESTIVAL. Oct 4. Cedar Springs, MI. Purpose: To promote Cedar Springs. Info from: Red Flannel Festival, Carolyn Zank, Dir, Box 43, Cedar Springs, MI 49319.

RICHARD III SOCIETY: ANNUAL MEETING. Oct 4. New York and London. Purpose: To consider further irrefutable evidence of the innocence of Richard III and the mystery of the "Princes in the Tower." Info from: Richard III Society, Inc, William Hogarth, Chrmn, Box 217, Sea Cliff, NY 11579.

ROEMER, CHARLES ELSON III: BIRTHDAY. Oct 4. U.S. Representative of Louisiana's 4th district, Democrat, born in Shreveport, LA, on Oct 4, 1943.

ROSH HASHANAH or JEWISH NEW YEAR. Oct 4. Jewish holy day; observed on following day also. Hebrew calendar date: Tishri 1, 5747. Rosh Hashanah is beginning of ten days of repentance and spiritual renewal. (Began at sundown of previous day.)

RUNYAN, DAMON: BIRTHDAY. Oct 4. American newspaperman and author, born at Manhattan, KS, Oct 4, 1884. Died at New York City, Dec 10, 1946. "...always try to rub up against money," he wrote, "for if you rub up against money long enough, some of it may rub off on you."

ST. FRANCIS OF ASSISI: FEAST DAY. Oct 4. Giovanni Francesco Bernardone, religious leader, founder of the Friars Minor (Franciscan Order), born at Assisi, Umbria, Italy, in 1181. Died there on Oct 3, 1226. One of the "most attractive and best-loved saints of all time." Feast Day: Oct 4.

SINGAPORE: KUSU ISLAND PILGRIMAGE. Oct 4-Nov 1. During month-long festival about 100,000 Taoists pay respects to Tua Pek, the God of Prosperity, on Kusu Island. Pilgrims take food and flower offerings, joss sticks and candles, and pray for prosperity. Observed throughout the entire ninth lunar month.

SPACE MILESTONE: LUNA 3 (USSR). Oct 4. First satellite to photograph moon's distant side. Launched Oct 4, 1959.

SPACE MILESTONE: SPUTNIK ANNIVERSARY. Oct 4. Anniversary of launching of first successful man-made earth satellite. *Sputnik I* ("fellow traveller of earth") weighing 184 lbs was fired into orbit from the U.S.S.R.'s Tyuratam launch site on Oct 4, 1957. Transmitted radio signal for 21 days, decayed Jan 4, 1958. Beginning of Space Age and man's exploration beyond Earth.

TEN-FOUR DAY. Oct 4. The fourth day of the tenth month is a day of recognition for radio operators, whose code words, "Ten-Four," signal an affirmative reply.

TOLEDO FALL FOLK FESTIVAL. Oct 4-5. Crosby Gardens, Toledo, OH. Info from: Toledo Area Conv & Visitors Bureau, 218 Huron St, Toledo, OH 43604.

WINTER PARK AUTUMN ART FESTIVAL. Oct 4-5. Campus of Rollins College. Info from: Chamber of Commerce, Box 280, Winter Park, FL 32790.

WORLD CHAMPIONSHIP CHICKEN PLUCKIN' CONTEST. Oct 4. Info from: Chamber of Commerce, Box 3083, Spring Hill, FL 33526.

WORLD'S LARGEST GOURD SHOW. Oct 4-5. Displays of fresh gourds, demonstrations of gourdcrafting, gourd theatre and gourds for sale. Info from: Ohio Gourd Show, John Stevens, Secy, Box 274, Mt Gilead, OH 43338.

OCTOBER 5 — SUNDAY
278th Day — Remaining, 87

ANGOLA PRISON RODEO. Oct 5. (Also Oct 12, 19 and 26). Purpose: A joint endeavor between inmates and employees of the Louisiana State Penitentiary and the Department of Corrections with proceeds going to the inmate welfare fund. Sponsor: Louisiana State Penitentiary, Warden's Office, Angola, LA 70712.

ANY AND ALL DOG SHOW. Oct 5. Harmon Field, Tryon, NC. Purpose: Entries for "The Dog Who'd Really Rather Be at Home" and "The Dog with the Most Doubtful Ancestry." Sponsor: Tryon Riding & Hunt Club, Box 1095, Tryon, NC 28782.

October 1986

S	M	T	W	T	F	S
			1	2	3	4
5	6	7	8	9	10	11
12	13	14	15	16	17	18
19	20	21	22	23	24	25
26	27	28	29	30	31	

COPYRIGHT © 1985 BY WILLIAM D. CHASE and HELEN M. CHASE

ARTHUR, CHESTER ALAN: BIRTHDAY. Oct 5. The 21st President of the U.S., Chester Alan Arthur, was born at Fairfield, VT, Oct 5, 1830, and succeeded to the presidency following the death of James A. Garfield. Term of office: Sept 20, 1881-Mar 3, 1885. Arthur was not successful in obtaining his party's (Republican) nomination for the following term. He died at New York City, Nov 18, 1886.

BLESSING OF THE FISHING FLEET. Oct 5. Church of Saints Peter and Paul and Fisherman's Wharf. San Francisco, CA (First Sunday in October each year.)

DALTON RAID DAY. Oct 5. Coffeyville, KS. Anniversary date (1892) of famous Dalton Gang holdup of two banks simultaneously and resultant death of four bandits and four citizens. Info from: Chamber of Commerce, Box 457, Coffeyville, KS 67337.

ENRICO FERMI ATOMIC POWER PLANT ACCIDENT ANNIVERSARY. Oct 5. A radiation alarm and Class I alert at 3:09 p.m., E.S.T., on Oct 5, 1966, signalled a problem at the Enrico Fermi Atomic Power Plant, Lagoona Beach, near Monroe, MI. The accident was contained, but nearly a decade was required to complete the safe decommissioning and disassembly of the plant.

FESTIFALL STREET FAIR. Oct 5. Purpose: A day for local craftspersons, and entertainers to display their talents. Sponsor: Chapel Hill Parks and Recreation, 306 N Columbia St, Chapel Hill, NC 27514.

FIRE PREVENTION WEEK. Oct 5-11. Presidential Proclamation has been issued annually for a week early in October since 1925. For many years prior to 1925, National Fire Prevention Day was observed in October.

FIRE PREVENTION WEEK. Oct 5-11. Purpose: To advocate the need for fire prevention throughout the year. Always the full week that includes Oct 9 (anniversary of the Great Chicago Fire). Also recognized by presidential proclamation since 1922. Sponsor: National Fire Protection Assn, Batterymarch Park, Quincy, MA 02269.

GERMANY: ERNTEDANKFEST. Oct 5. A harvest thanksgiving festival, or potato harvest festival, Erntedankfest or Erntedanktag, is generally observed on the first Sunday in October.

GODDARD, ROBERT HUTCHINGS: BIRTHDAY. Oct 5. The "father of Space Age," Robert H. Goddard, was born at Worcester, MA, on Oct 5, 1882. Largely ignored or ridiculed during his lifetime because of his dreams of rocket travel, including travel to other planets, launched a liquid-fuel-powered rocket on Mar 16, 1926, at Auburn, MA. This American pioneer of rocket propulsion died Aug 10, 1945. See also entries for Mar 16 and Oct 19.

GOLF: U.S. MID-AMATEUR CHAMPIONSHIP. Oct 5-9. Annandale, Madison, MS. Purpose: To determine national champion among amateur golfers age 25 and older who have handicaps of five or less. Sponsor: U.S. Golf Assn, Golf House, Far Hills, NJ 07931.

GRANDPARENTS' DAY. Oct 5. Massachusetts. (First Sunday in October.)

INTERNATIONAL LETTER WRITING WEEK. Oct 5-11. Purpose: To promote letter writing with people throughout the world in order to further friendships and international peace. Sponsor: The Franklin D. Roosevelt Philatelic Society, Gustav Detjen, Jr, Pres, 154 Laguna Ct, St. Augustine Shores, FL 32086.

LEHMAN, WILLIAM: BIRTHDAY. Oct 5. U.S. Representative of Florida's 17th district, Democrat, of Biscayne Park, FL, born in Selma, AL, on Oct 5, 1913.

MINORITY ENTERPRISE DEVELOPMENT WEEK. Oct 5-11. Presidential Proclamation. Dates not established at press time, but has been issued for first full week of October since 1983. President Reagan announced that he would continue to issue this proclamation annually. The 1985 observance (Oct 6-12) was established by Proclamation No. 5347 of May 28, 1985.

MOCK TOBACCO AUCTION. Oct 5. Purpose: To simulate a tobacco warehouse sale with auctioneers, buyers and farmers. Tobacco spitting contest, tobacco harvest crafts and entertainment. Sponsor: Duke Homestead State Historic Site, 2828 Duke Homestead Rd, Durham, NC 27705.

NATIONAL EMPLOY THE HANDICAPPED WEEK. Oct 5-11. Presidential Proclamation issued for a week beginning during first week of October since 1945. Title was changed by PL 91-442 of Oct 8, 1970.

NATIONAL EMPLOY THE HANDICAPPED WEEK. Oct 5-11. Purpose: A time for intensive promotional efforts to remind America of disabled people's abilities. Sponsor: Presidents' Committee on Employment of the Handicapped, 1111 20th St, NW, 6th Fl, Washington, DC 20036.

NATIONAL METRIC WEEK. Oct 5-11. Purpose: To maintain an awareness of the importance of the metric system as the primary system of measurement for the United States. Sponsor: Natl Council of Teachers of Mathematics, Jan R. Goldenberg, 1906 Association Dr, Reston, VA 22091.

NATIONAL NEWSPAPER WEEK. Oct 5-11. Purpose: To highlight newspapers' role in our daily lives. Sponsor: Internatl Circulation Managers Assn, Joseph Forsee, Gen Mgr. Box 17420, Dulles Internatl Airport, Washington, DC 20041. Info from: Terry L. DeVassie, Asst Circulation Dir, Columbus Dispatch, 34 S Third St, Columbus, OH 43216.

PORTUGAL: NATIONAL DAY. Oct 5. Portugal. Establishment of the Republic (in 1910).

SPACE MILESTONE: CHALLENGER. Oct 5. Space shuttle *Challenger* makes sixth mission with crew of 7, including 2 women. Launched and landed at Kennedy Space Center, FL (Oct 5-13, 1984). Kathryn D. Sullivan became the first American woman to walk in space (for 3½ hours).

STONE, THOMAS: DEATH ANNIVERSARY. Oct 5. Signer of the Declaration of Independence, born 1743 (exact date unknown) in Charles County, MD. Died, Alexandria, VA, Oct 5, 1787.

TEENS ON THE TOWN GOURMET CLUB WEEK. Oct 5-11. Purpose: Parents are urged to invite a teenager to dine out and acquire an appreciation and knowledge of good food, or prepare a home cooked gourmet dinner. Sponsor: Mme. Ginette's Cordon Bleu Ouest School of French Cooking, 3369 Hamilton Way, Los Angeles, CA 90026.

TEXAS PRISON RODEO. Oct 5. (Also Oct 12, 19, 26.) Huntsville, TX. Inmates participate in rough-and-tumble traditional rodeo events. (Every Sunday in Oct.) Info from: Texas Prison Rodeo, Box 99, Huntsville, TX 77340.

TWIN CITIES MARATHON. Oct 5. A 26.2 mile run from downtown Minneapolis to downtown Saint Paul. The first Sunday in October. Sponsors: Pillsbury, WCCO Radio, and First Banks. Info from: Twin Cities Marathon, Box 24193, Minneapolis, MN 55424.

UNICORN QUESTING SEASON. Oct 5-31. Purpose: "Every man must seek his own unicorn in his own way. It is the quest, not the capture which is vital."—Peter Thomas, Poet. Season concludes with Quest Masque Ball and Unicorn Banquet at Grand Hotel, Mackinac Island. Info from: Registrar, W. T. Rabe, Unicorn Hunters, Lake Superior State College, Sault Ste Marie, MI 49783.

COPYRIGHT © 1985 BY WILLIAM D. CHASE and HELEN M. CHASE

OCTOBER 6 — MONDAY

279th Day — Remaining, 86

AMERICAN COUNCIL ON EDUCATION ANNUAL MEETING. Oct 6-8. San Francisco, CA. Info from: American Council on Education, Daryl Ferguson, Annual Mtg Mgr, One Dupont Circle, Washington, DC 20036.

AMERICAN LIBRARY ASSOCIATION: BIRTHDAY. Oct 6. Founded at Philadelphia, PA, Oct 6, 1876.

ANWAR EL-SADAT ASSASSINATION ANNIVERSARY. Oct 6. Egyptian president and Nobel Peace Prize recipient, Anwar el-Sadat, was killed by assassins at Cairo on Oct 6, 1981, while he was reviewing a military parade commemorating the 1973 Egyptian-Israeli War. At least eight other persons were reported killed in the attack on Sadat. Anwar el-Sadat was born Dec 25, 1918, at Mit Abu Al-Kom, a village near the Nile River delta.

BEREUTER, DOUG: BIRTHDAY. Oct 6. U.S. Representative of Nebraska's 1st district, Republican, of Utica, NE, born in York, NE, on Oct 6, 1939.

CHILD HEALTH DAY. Oct 6. Presidential Proclamation. ☆ "Always 1st Monday of October. Proc. has been issued since 1928. In 1959 Congress changed celebration day from May 1 to the 1st Monday in October (Pub.Res.No. 46 of May 18, 1928, and PL86-352 of Sept 22, 1959)."

DANIEL BOONE FESTIVAL. Oct 6-11. Barbourville, KY. Citizens dressed in pioneer costumes, parade, carnival, arts and crafts, Indian feast and longrifle shoot out. Info from: KY Dept of Travel, Capital Plaza Office Tower, Frankfort, KY 40601.

ENGLAND: HORSE OF THE YEAR SHOW. Oct 6-11. Wembley Arena, Wembley, London, "...the world's top showjumpers in action over tough courses in the indoor arena."

FAST OF GEDALYA. Oct 6. Jewish holiday. Hebrew calendar date Tishri 3, 5747. Tzom Gedalya begins at first light of day and commemorates the Sixth Century B.C. assassination of Gedalya Ben Achikam.

FOWLER, WYCHE JR: BIRTHDAY. Oct 6. U.S. Representative of Georgia's 5th district, Democrat, of Atlanta, GA, born there Oct 6, 1940.

GRAND NATIONAL AND WORLD CHAMPIONSHIP MORGAN HORSE SHOW. Oct 6-12. Purpose: Over 800 Morgan horses compete. Horses from 35 states exhibited at halter, harness and other classes. Info from: Steve Collier, 1 Santa Fe Plaza, Oklahoma City, OK 73102.

LaFALCE, JOHN J: BIRTHDAY. Oct 6. U.S. Representative of New York's 32nd district, Democrat, of Tonawanda, NY, born in Buffalo, NY, Oct 6, 1939.

LIND, JENNY: BIRTHDAY. Oct 6. Swedish opera singer born at Stockholm, Oct 6, 1820. She died at Malvern, England, Nov 2, 1887.

NATIONAL ASSOCIATION GENERAL MERCHANDISE REPRESENTATIVES CONVENTION. Oct 6-11. MGM Grand Hotel, Las Vegas, NV. NAGMR, J Springer, Exec Dir, 111 E Wacker Dr, Chicago, IL 60601.

NATIONAL BOOKKEEPER'S WEEK. Oct 6-10. Purpose: To acknowledge the importance of bookkeepers in every organization. Always the five day period, Monday through the second Friday in October. Sponsor: Cynthia Ann Pericht, CP Business Accounting Agency, 1464 N Grove Ave, Upland, CA 91786.

October 1986

S	M	T	W	T	F	S
			1	2	3	4
5	6	7	8	9	10	11
12	13	14	15	16	17	18
19	20	21	22	23	24	25
26	27	28	29	30	31	

NATIONAL POSSUM WEEK. Oct 6-11. Purpose: To improve the image of the lowly possum and remind people they should "always have as much fun as Possum-able!". Sponsor: Poor Ol' George, Editor, Possum County News, Box 2572, Owensboro, KY 42302.

SZYMANOWSKI, KAROL: BIRTHDAY. Oct 6. "Birthday of Poland's outstanding composer, whose art has played an essential role in the Polish 20th century music, our greatest composer after Chopin and Moniuszko, and creator of the modern Polish national style." Szymanowski was born at Timoshovka, Ukraine, on Oct 6, 1882, and died Mar 28, 1937.

UNIVERSAL CHILDREN'S DAY. Oct 6. First Monday in October is designated by United Nations General Assembly as Universal Children's Day. First observance was in 1953. A time to honor children with special ceremonies and festivals and to make children's needs known to governments. Also observed on different days and in different ways in more than 120 nations.

WESTINGHOUSE, GEORGE: BIRTHDAY. Oct 6. American inventor born Oct 6, 1846. Died Mar 12, 1914.

OCTOBER 7 — TUESDAY

280th Day — Remaining, 85

GERMAN DEMOCRATIC REPUBLIC: NATIONAL HOLIDAY. Oct 7. Commemorates founding of German Democratic Republic on Oct 7, 1949.

RILEY, JAMES WHITCOMB: BIRTH ANNIVERSARY. Oct 7. American "Hoosier" poet, born at Greenfield, IN, on Oct 7th probably in 1853, but possibly several years earlier. Riley died at Indianapolis on July 22, 1916.

ST. LUCIA: EMANCIPATION DAY. Oct 7. Info from: St. Lucia Tourist Board, 41 E 42nd St, New York, NY 10017.

STALLINGS, RICHARD HOWARD: BIRTHDAY. Oct 7. U.S. Representative of Idaho's 2nd district, Democrat, of Rexburg, ID, born at Ogden, UT, on Oct 7, 1940.

U.S.S.R.: CONSTITUTION DAY. Oct 7. Public holiday with concerts and special programs of multinational Soviet art.

VENTO, BRUCE FRANK: BIRTHDAY. Oct 7. U.S. Representative of Minnesota's 4th district, Democrat-Farmer-Labor, of St. Paul, MN, born there Oct 7, 1940.

WALLACE, HENRY AGARD: BIRTHDAY. Oct 7. Thirty-third Vice President of the U.S. (1941-1945) born, Adair County, IA, Oct 7, 1888. Died Danbury, CT, Nov 18, 1965.

WISE, THOMAS JAMES: BIRTHDAY. Oct 7. English bibliophile and literary forger, born at Gravesend, Oct 7, 1859. One of England's most distinguished bibliographic experts, he was revealed, in 1934, to have forged dozens of "first editions" and "unique" publications over a period of more than 20 years. Many of them had been sold at high prices to collectors and libraries. The forgeries in some cases purported to predate the real first editions. Wise, whose health was broken when the exposure came, died at Hampstead, May 13, 1937.

OCTOBER 8 — WEDNESDAY

281st Day — Remaining, 84

ALVIN C. YORK DAY. Oct 8. On this day in 1918, Sergeant Alvin C. York (in the Argonne Forest, France and separated from his patrol) killed 20 enemy soldiers, and captured a hill, 132 enemy soldiers and 35 machine guns. He was awarded the U.S. Medal of Honor and French Croix de Guerre.

CHICAGO FIRE ANNIVERSARY. Oct 8. Great fire of Chicago began, according to legend, when Mrs. O'Leary's cow kicked over lantern in barn on DeKoven St, on this day, 1871. Large part of city was destroyed, leaving estimated 250 dead and $200 million loss.

MATSUNAGA, SPARK MASAYUKI: BIRTHDAY. Oct 8. U.S. Senator from Hawaii, Democrat, of Honolulu, HI, was born at Kukuiula, Kauai, HI on Oct 8, 1916.

COPYRIGHT © 1985 BY WILLIAM D. CHASE and HELEN M. CHASE

MORRISON, BRUCE A: BIRTHDAY. Oct 8. U.S. Representative of Connecticut's 3rd district, Democrat, of Hamden, CT, born at New York, NY, on Oct 8, 1944.

NATIONAL SPORTING GOODS ASSOCIATION INTERNATIONAL CONVENTION AND SHOW. Oct 8-11. McCormick Place, Chicago, IL. International trade show for the sporting goods industry. Sponsor: Natl Sporting Goods Assn, 1699 Wall St, Mt Prospect, IL 60056.

PERU: DAY OF THE NAVY. Oct 8. Public holiday in Peru.

PESHTIGO FIRE ANNIVERSARY. Oct 8. One of the most disastrous forest fires in history began at Peshtigo, WI, on this day, 1871. Burned across six counties killing more than 1,100 persons.

RICKENBACKER, EDWARD V: BIRTHDAY. Oct 8. American aviator, auto racer, war hero, "Captain Eddie," born Oct 8, 1890. Died July 23, 1973.

SCHUTZ, HEINRICH: BIRTH ANNIVERSARY. Oct 8. German musician and composer sometimes called the "father of German music," born at Kostritz, Saxony, on Oct 8, 1585. Schutz died at Dresden on Nov 6, 1672. His works enjoyed renewed attention on the occasions of the bicentennials (1885) and tricentennials (1985) of two of his most devoted followers: George Frederick Handel and Johann Sebastian Bach, both born in 1685, just a century after Schutz.

OCTOBER 9 — THURSDAY
282nd Day — Remaining, 83

ANTIQUE AUTOMOBILE CLUB OF AMERICA: FALL MEET. Oct 9-11. Hershey, PA. Info from: Box 417, Hershey, PA 17033.

AUTUMN GLORY FESTIVAL. Oct 9-12. Purpose: Foliage celebration with state banjo and fiddle contests, parade, arts, crafts and antique show. Sponsor: Deep Creek Lake-Garrett Co Promotion Council, Festival Hdqs, Court House, Oakland, MD 21550.

BANNEKER, BENJAMIN: DEATH ANNIVERSARY. Oct 9. American astronomer, mathematician, clockmaker, surveyor and almanac author. Called "first Black man of Science." Took part in original survey of City of Washington. Benjamin Banneker's *Almanac* was published in 1792-1797. Born near Baltimore, MD, in 1736. Died in Baltimore County, MD, Oct 9, 1806. A fire which started during his funeral destroyed his home, library, notebooks, almanac calculations, clocks, and virtually all belongings and documents related to his life.

HUMPHREY, GORDON J: BIRTHDAY. Oct 9. U.S. Senator from New Hampshire, Republican, of Chichester, NH, born at Bristol, CT, Oct 9, 1940.

KOREAN ALPHABET DAY (HANGUL). Oct 9. Korea. Celebrates anniversary of promulgation of Hangul (24 letter phonetic alphabet) by King Sejong of the Yi Dynasty, in 1446.

LEIF ERIKSON DAY. Oct 9. Presidential Proclamation. ☆ "Always October 9 since 1964 (PL88-566 of Sept 2, 1964)."

LEIF ERIKSON DAY. Oct 9. Iceland. Celebrates discovery of North America in the year 1000 by Norse explorer.

LENNON, JOHN: BIRTHDAY. Oct 9. John Winston Lennon, English composer, musician, member of "The Beatles," a sensationally popular group of musical performers who captivated audiences first in England and Germany, and later throughout the world, born Liverpool, England, Oct 9, 1940. Assassinated in New York City, Dec 8, 1980.

LOTT, TRENT: BIRTHDAY. Oct 9. U.S. Representative of Mississippi's 5th district, Republican, of Pascagoula, MS, born in Grenada, MS, Oct 9, 1941.

MISSION DELORES FOUNDING ANNIVERSARY. Oct 9. The oldest building in San Francisco, CA. Formerly known as Mission San Francisco de Asis, the mission survived the great earthquake and fire of 1906. Founded, October 9, 1776.

NATIONAL KRAUT SANDWICH WEEK. Oct 9-18. Purpose: To encourage one and all to try kraut not only as a garnish with many sandwiches, but as an integral ingredient with meats, cheeses and other sandwich items. Sponsor: Natl Kraut Packers Assn. Info from: Burson-Marsteller, 1 E Wacker Dr, Chicago, IL 60601.

SPACE MILESTONE: SOYUZ 25 (USSR). Oct 9. Cosmonauts Vladimir Kovalyonok and Valery Ryumin launched on Oct 9, 1977. Intended link with Salyut 6 unsuccessful. Craft returned to Earth Oct 11.

UGANDA: NATIONAL HOLIDAY. Oct 9. Independence Day, commemorating achievement of autonomy on Oct 9, 1962.

WEST VIRGINIA BLACK WALNUT FESTIVAL. Oct 9-12. Purpose: To promote the black walnut and its many uses. Sponsor: WV Black Walnut Commission, City of Spencer, Spencer, WV 25276.

OCTOBER 10 — FRIDAY
283rd Day — Remaining, 82

AUTUMN LEAVES FESTIVAL. Oct 10-12. Purpose: To celebrate the seasonal beauty of autumn and to recognize the culture and traditions of the mountain people. Craft demonstrations. Info from: Chamber of Commerce, James C. Grimes, Exec VP, Box 913, Mount Airy, NC 27030.

BOB EVANS FARM FESTIVAL. Oct 10-12. Purpose: An old-fashioned festival featuring 125 craftspersons, field exhibits and live country entertainment. Info from: Bob Evans Farms Inc, Mary Cusick, 3776 S High St, Columbus, OH 43207.

DOUBLE TENTH DAY. Oct 10. Tenth day of tenth month, Double Tenth Day, is observed by many Chinese as anniversary of the outbreak of the revolution against the imperial Manchu dynasty, Oct 10, 1911. Sun Yat-sen and Huan Hsing were among the revolutionary leaders.

FESTA D'ITALIA. Oct 10-12. Purpose: To preserve Italian heritage and culture with samples of crafts, cooking and entertainment along with viewing Italian museum and library. Info from: American Italian Federation of the SE, 1608 S Salcedo St, New Orleans, LA 70125.

FIJI: INDEPENDENCE DAY. Oct. 10. National holiday.

GUMBO FESTIVAL. Oct 10-12. Purpose: By promoting gumbo, we promote our Cajun-French culture and provide the opportunity for people from everywhere to enjoy real Cajun entertainment and cuisine. Sponsor: Holy Guardian Angels Church, Rev. J. Anthony Luminais, Pastor, Box 9069, Bridge City, LA 70094.

HEALTH-SPORTS DAY. Oct 10. Japan (National Holiday).

KRUGER, PAUL: BIRTHDAY. Oct 10. Stephanus Johannes Paulus Kruger, former president of the South African Republic and a leader of the Boers, was born Oct 10, 1825. His birthday is commemorated in South Africa. Kruger died in Switzerland, July 14, 1904.

LAGNIAPPE ON THE BAYOU. Oct 10-12. Purpose: For support of St. Joseph Catholic Church. Sponsor: St. Joseph Catholic Church, Box 218, Chauvin, LA 70344.

LEE COUNTY COTTON PICKIN' FESTIVAL. Oct 10-12. Bishopville, SC. Arts, crafts, games, cotton picking contest and beauty pageant. Info from: Tracey Bedenbaugh, Lee Co Chamber of Commerce, Box 187, Bishopville, SC 29010.

LINCOLN DAYS CELEBRATION. Oct 10-12. Hodgenville, KY. Art show, pioneer games, costumes, crafts, rail splitting and Lincoln look-alike contest. Info from: KY Dept of Travel, Capital Plaza Office Tower, Frankfort, KY 40601.

MOON PHASE: FIRST QUARTER. Oct 10. Moon enters First Quarter phase at 8:28 a.m., E.S.T.

NATIONAL BOOKKEEPER'S DAY. Oct 10. Purpose: To acknowledge the importance of bookkeepers in every organization. Always the second Friday in October and the last day of Natl Bookkeeper's Week. Sponsor: Cynthia Ann Pericht, CP Business Accounting Agency, 1464 N Grove Ave, Upland, CA 91786.

OKLAHOMA HISTORICAL DAY. Oct 10. Oklahoma.

ROTH, TOBY: BIRTHDAY. Oct 10. U.S. Representative of Wisconsin's 8th district, Republican, of Appleton, WI, was born in Strasburg, ND, on Oct 10 1938.

SCOTLAND: NATIONAL GAELIC MOD. Oct 10-17. Edinburgh, Lothian, Scotland. Festival of Gaelic languages, literature, history, music and art.

OCTOBER 11 — SATURDAY
284th Day — Remaining, 81

APPLE BUTTER FESTIVAL. Oct 11-12. Purpose: Celebration of fall season with apple butter making, concerts, arts & crafts, street theatre and parade. Sponsor: Berkeley Springs-Morgan County Chamber of Commerce, 204 N Washington St, Berkeley Springs, WV 25411.

BRUSSELS SPROUT FESTIVAL. Oct 11-12. The Santa Cruz Central Coast celebrates its status as the brussels sprout capital of the nation. Cooking demonstrations, sprout and recipe giveaways, deep-fried sprouts, chocolate-covered sprouts, sprout-water taffy and a sprout toss competition. Info from: Glenn LaFrank, Santa Cruz Beach Boardwalk, 400 Beach St, Santa Cruz, CA 95060.

CALLAWAY GARDENS ARTS AND CRAFTS FESTIVAL. Oct 11-12. Arts and crafts. Info from: Carole Sirmans, 400 Browns Crossing Rd NW, Milledgeville, GA 31061.

CHOWDER WEEKEND. Oct 11-12. Purpose: Cups of chowder offered for sale on Seaport grounds. Info from: Public Affairs Office, Mystic Seaport, Mystic, CT 06355.

DAY OF SOLIDARITY WITH SOUTH AFRICAN POLITICAL PRISONERS. Oct 11. The United Nations observes a Day of Solidarity with South African Political Prisoners, proclaimed by General Assembly Resolution 31/6C (XXXI) of Nov 9, 1976, which demanded the immediate and unconditional release of all persons imprisoned or restricted for their involvement in the struggle for liberation in South Africa. Info from: Centre against Apartheid, Political Affairs Officer, and from United Nations Dept of Public Information, United Nations, NY 10017.

ELK MOUNTAIN OCTOBER FESTIVAL. Oct 11-12. Info from: Elk Mountain Ski Center, Inc, RD 1, Box 258, Union Dale, PA 18470.

FAMILY HARVEST FESTIVAL. Oct 11-26. Demonstrations of sorghum making, apple and peach butter making and other mountain crafts. Info from: Ozark Folk Ctr, Mountain View, AR 72560.

October 1986

S	M	T	W	T	F	S
			1	2	3	4
5	6	7	8	9	10	11
12	13	14	15	16	17	18
19	20	21	22	23	24	25
26	27	28	29	30	31	

FAZIO, VIC: BIRTHDAY. Oct 11. U.S. Representative of California's 4th district, Democrat, of Sacramento, CA, was born in Winchester, MA, Oct 11, 1942.

FEAST OF THE HUNTERS' MOON. Oct 11-12. Purpose: Celebration at French Fort Ouiatenon, where two hundred years ago Canadian traders, Indians and backwoodsmen converged to feast. Info from: Tippecanoe County Historical Assn, 909 South St, Lafayette, IN 47901.

FOUR COUNTIES DAY. Oct 11. Mammoth Cave National Park, KY. Purpose: In recognition of the patronage of nearby counties. Historic cave tours, crafts, a petting zoo and helicopter display. Sponsor: Mammoth Cave Natl Park, Mammoth Cave, KY 42259.

GENERAL PULASKI MEMORIAL DAY. Oct 11. Presidential ☆ Proclamation. "Always issued for October 11 since 1929. Requested by Congressional Resolution each year beginning in 1929 and thru 1946. (Since 1947 has been issued by custom.) Note: Proc. 4869, October 5, 1981, covers all succeeding years, but Proc. was issued again in 1982 and 1983."

GOLDEN ISLES ARTS AND CRAFTS FESTIVAL. Oct 11-12. Oceanside Neptune Park, St. Simons Island, GA. Purpose: To bring artists, craftsmen and the public together in a quality and fun atmosphere. Sponsor: Coastal Alliance for the Arts, Box 673, St. Simons Island, GA 31522.

GREAT LORIS BOG-OFF. Oct 11. Chicken bog cooking contest, clogging, arts, crafts, run and race and chicken chuckle contest. (Second Saturday in October each year.) Sponsor: Loris Chamber of Commerce. Info from: Singleton Bailey, Box 95, Loris, SC 29569.

HARVEST FESTIVAL DAYS. Oct 11-12. Jamestown, VA. Music, games and festivities at Jamestown Festival Park celebrate the fall harvest events in the Jamestown colony. Info from: Special Events Coord, Box JF, Williamsburg, VA 23187.

INTERNATIONAL NEWSPAPER CARRIER DAY. Oct 11. Purpose: To honor over one million youngsters and adults who deliver daily newspapers to the homes of subscribers. Special programs, selection of outstanding carriers, scholarships, etc. Sponsor: Internatl Circulation Managers Assn, Joseph Forsee, Gen Mgr, Box 17420, Dulles Internatl Airport, Washington, DC 20041. Info from: Terry L. DeVassie, Asst Circulation Dir, Columbus Dispatch, 34 S Third St, Columbus, OH 43216.

KENTUCKY GUILD OF ARTISTS AND CRAFTSMEN'S FALL FAIR. Oct 11-13. Berea, KY. Displays of close to 100 exhibiting members of the guild juried for excellence. Info from: KY Dept of Travel, Capital Plaza Office Tower, Frankfort, KY 40601.

MOUNTAIN GLORY FESTIVAL. Oct 11. Purpose: A celebration of mountain heritage in western North Carolina. Arts, crafts and tours into autumn countryside. Info from: Chamber of Commerce, John R. Birdsong, Exec Dir, 17 N Garden St, Marion, NC 28752.

NATIONAL PEANUT FESTIVAL. Oct 11-25. Dothan AL. Purpose: A festival and fair to honor the peanut agri-business. Sponsor: Natl Peanut Festival Assn, Inc, 1691 Ross Clark Circle SE, Dothan, AL 36301.

NINETEENTH CENTURY CRAFT FESTIVAL. Oct 11-12. Arrow Rock State Historic Site, Arrow Rock, MO. Info from: Missouri Dept of Natural Resources, Box 176, Jefferson City, MO 65102.

OAK HILL SEAFOOD FESTIVAL. Oct 11-12. Purpose: To promote area seafood industry and community organization-associations. Sponsor: Oak Hill Seafood Festival, Box 13, Oak Hill, FL 32759.

OYSTER FESTIVAL. Oct 11. Oysters fixed every way—all you can eat. (Saturday of Columbus Day weekend.) Sponsor: Chincoteague Chamber of Commerce, Box 258, Chincoteague Island, VA 23336.

PARKE COUNTY COVERED BRIDGE FESTIVAL. Oct 11-20. Purpose: To promote the historical covered bridges and the Parke County area. Sponsor: Parke County, Inc, Box 165, Rockville, IN 47872.

COPYRIGHT © 1985 BY WILLIAM D. CHASE and HELEN M. CHASE

PARSON WEEMS' BIRTHDAY. Oct 11. Mason Locke Weems, 19th child of David Weems, and father of ten, was born in Anne Arundel County, Maryland, on Oct 11, 1759. An Episcopal clergyman and travelling bookseller, Weems is remembered for the fictitious stories he presented as historical fact. Best known of his "fables" is the story describing George Washington cutting down his father's cherry tree with a hatchet. Weems' fictionalized histories however delighted many readers who accepted them as true. They became immensely popular and were best sellers for many years. Weems died May 23, 1825, at Beaufort, SC.

PICKLE, JJ (JAKE): BIRTHDAY. Oct 11. U.S. Representative of Texas' 10th district, Democrat, of Austin, TX, born in Roscow, Nolan County, TX, on Oct 11, 1913.

ROOSEVELT, ANNA ELEANOR: BIRTHDAY. Oct 11. Wife of Franklin Delano Roosevelt, 32nd President of the U.S., was born at New York City, Oct 11, 1884. She led an active and independent life, and was the first wife of a president to give her own news conference in the White House (1933). Widely known throughout the world, she was affectionately called "the first lady of the world." She served as U.S. delegate to the United Nations General Assembly for a number of years before her death, at New York City, Nov 7, 1962. A prolific writer, she wrote in *This Is My Story*, "No one can make you feel inferior without your consent."

ROOSEVELT, ELEANOR: BIRTHDAY. Oct 11. Purpose: To commemorate the birthday of Anna Eleanor Roosevelt, devoted wife of Franklin D. Roosevelt and First Lady of the World. (1884-1962.) Sponsor: The Franklin D. Roosevelt Philatelic Society, 154 Laguna Ct, St. Augustine Shores, FL 32086.

TAUKE, THOMAS J: BIRTHDAY. Oct 11. U.S. Representative of Iowa's 2nd district, Republican, of Dubuque, IA, born there Oct 11, 1950.

WHITE PINE VILLAGE: AUTUMN FESTIVAL. Oct 11-12. Hayrides, cider-pressing, Amish baked goods, crafts and fur trapping exhibits. Info from: Mason County Historical Society, Connie Newkirk, 1687 S Lakeshore Dr, Ludington, MI 49431.

WORLD TOBACCO AUCTIONEERING CHAMPIONSHIP. Oct 11. Competition highlighting heritage of the fastest form of sale in the world—the tobacco auction. Competitors speak 500 words-per-minute. Info from: R.J. Reynolds Tobacco Company, Ellen W. Merritt, 401 N Main St, Winston-Salem, NC 27102.

OCTOBER 12 — SUNDAY

285th Day — Remaining, 80

AMERICAN SAMOA: WHITE SUNDAY. Oct 12. Second Sunday in October is a "children's day" on the island. Children lead church services. Everyone is dressed in white.

BRAZIL: CIRIO DE NAZARE. Oct 12-25. Greatest festival of northern Brazil, the Feast of Cirio, starts on second Sunday of October, in city of Belem (Saint Mary of Bethlehem), capital of the state of Para. Festival lasts two weeks.

COLUMBUS DAY (Traditional). Oct 12. Public holiday in most countries in the Americas and in most Spanish-speaking countries. Observed under different names and on different dates (most often, as in U.S., on the 2nd Monday in October). Anniversary of Christopher Columbus' arrival, Oct 12, 1492, after a dangerous voyage across "shoreless Seas," at the Bahamian Island of Guanahani, which he renamed El Salvador and claimed in the name of the Spanish crown. In his *Journal*, he wrote: "As I saw that they (the natives) were friendly to us, and perceived that they could be much more easily converted to our holy faith by gentle means than by force, I presented them with some red caps, and strings of beads to wear upon the neck, and many other trifles of small value, wherewith they were much delighted, and became wonderfully attached to us. . . ."

CREDIT UNION WEEK. Oct 12-18. Purpose: Worldwide observance to recognize the contribution of credit unions to self-help development and practice of democracy. Info from: Credit Union Natl Assn, Inc, Lucy Harr Schultz, VP, PR, Box 431, Madison, WI 53701.

DETROIT FREE PRESS INTERNATIONAL MARATHON. Oct 12. Windsor, Ontario, Canada to Detroit, Michigan, USA. Purpose: A roadrace with some 4,000 runners; the race is 26 miles long, goes across the U.S./Canadian border and features the "underwater mile" through the Detroit-Windsor Tunnel. (Second Sunday in Oct.) Sponsor: Detroit Free Press, Pam Weinstein, Race Coord, 321 W Lafayette, Detroit, MI 48231.

DRAFT HORSE AND MULE DAY. Oct 12. Representative animals of all breeds of heavy horse are exhibited and demonstrate their strength and skill. Mule jump, obstacle courses and pull. Info from: Belle Grove, Inc, Box 137, Middletown, VA.

EQUATORIAL GUINEA: INDEPENDENCE DAY. Oct 12. National holiday.

GARN, EDWIN JACOB (JAKE): BIRTHDAY. Oct 12. U.S. Senator from Utah, Republican, of Salt Lake City, UT, born in Richfield, UT, on Oct 12, 1932.

HERITAGE HOLIDAYS. Oct 12-19. Purpose: To promote tourism in Rome, Georgia. Museums, arts, crafts and wagon train. Sponsor: Heritage Holidays, Inc, Drawer H, Rome, GA 30161.

HONG KONG: CHUNG YEUNG FESTIVAL. Oct 12. This festival relates to the old story of the Han Dynasty, when a soothsayer advised a man to take his family to a high place on the ninth day of the ninth moon for 24 hours in order to avoid disaster. The man obeyed and found, on returning home, that all living things had died a sudden death in his absence. Part of the festival, now, is to climb to high places.

INTERPLANETARY CONFEDERATION DAY. Oct 12. Purpose: A celebration to promote worldwide recognition of our brother planets in the Milky Way Galaxy—32 worlds waiting to join ours in an Interplanetary Confederation. Sponsor: Unarius Educational Foundation, 145 S. Magnolia Ave, El Cajon, CA 92020.

MEXICO: DIA DE LA RAZA. Oct 12. Columbus Day is observed as the "Day of the Race," a fiesta time to commemorate the discovery of America as well as the common interests and cultural heritage of the Spanish and Indian peoples and the Hispanic nations.

NATIONAL PASTA WEEK. Oct 12-18. Purpose: To pay tribute to elbow macaroni, spaghetti, egg noodles and other pasta shapes and sizes that add fun, variety and good taste to so many American meals. Celebrated the week Columbus Day is observed. Sponsor: National Pasta Association. Info from: Kaufman Public Relations, 2233 Wisconsin Ave, NW, Washington, DC 20007.

NATIONAL SCHOOL LUNCH WEEK. Oct 12-18. Presidential ☆ Proclamation. "Issued for the week beginning with the 2nd Sunday of October since 1962 (PL87-780 of Oct 9, 1962)." Note: Not issued in 1981.

NATIONAL SCHOOL LUNCH WEEK. Oct 12-18. Purpose: To celebrate good nutrition and good school lunch. Sponsor: American School Food Service Assn, Ramona I.T. Chun, Editor, School Food Service Journal, 4101 E Iliff Ave, Denver, CO 80222.

NATIONAL YWCA TEEN WEEK. Oct 12-18. Purpose: To alert the public and bring awareness of what the YWCA stands for, its purpose/accomplishments/benefits for girls and women, 12 years of age and up, and their communities. Sponsor: Natl Bd, YWCA of the USA, Jane Pinkerton, Dir of Communications/PR Div, 726 Broadway, New York, NY 10003.

SPAIN: NATIONAL HOLIDAY. Oct 12.

TRUMBULL, JONATHAN: BIRTHDAY. Oct 12. American patriot, counselor and friend of George Washington, governor of Connecticut Colony, born Oct 12, 1710. Died Aug 17, 1785.

THE WHITE HOUSE: BIRTHDAY. Oct 12. The presidential residence at 1600 Pennsylvania Avenue, Northwest, in Washington, D.C., designed by James Hoban (q.v.) observes its birthday on Oct 12. The cornerstone was laid Oct 12, 1792, and the first presidential family to occupy it was that of John Adams, in Nov, 1800. With three stories and more than 100 rooms The White House is the oldest building in Washington, D.C. First described as the "presidential palace" it acquired the name "White House" about ten years after construction was completed. Burned by British troops in 1814, it was reconstructed, refurnished and reoccupied by 1817.

WESTERN SAMOA: WHITE SUNDAY. Oct 12. The second Sunday in October (Lotu-a-Tamaita). For the children of Samoa, this is the biggest day of the year. On this day, traditional roles are reversed, as children lead church services, are served special foods and receive gifts of new church clothes and other special items. All the children dress in white. The following Monday is an official holiday. Info from: Samoan Mission to the UN, 820 2nd Ave, New York, NY 10017.

OCTOBER 13 — MONDAY
286th Day — Remaining, 79

CANADA: THANKSGIVING DAY. Oct 13. Observed on second Monday in October each year.

COLUMBUS DAY. Oct 13. Presidential Proclamation. "Always ☆ October 12 from 1934 thru 1970 (Pub. Res. No. 21 of Apr 30, 1934)." PL90-363 of June 28, 1968, required that beginning in 1971 it would be observed the 2nd Monday in October.

COLUMBUS DAY OBSERVANCE. Oct 13. Public Law 90-363 sets observance of Columbus Day on the second Monday in October—applicable to federal employees and to the District of Columbia, but observed also in most states on this day. Commemorates the landfall of Columbus in the New World, Oct 12, 1492. See also entry for Oct 12 for anniversary information.

DISCOVERERS' DAY. Oct 13. Hawaii. Honors all discoverers, including Pacific and Polynesian navigators. (Second Monday in October.)

MODERN MYTHOLOGY DAY. Oct 13. Purpose: To commemorate the founding of Museum of Modern Mythology, and to promote public recognition of American advertising characters as artifacts of our cultural heritage. Sponsor: Museum of Modern Mythology, Ellen Weis, Exec Dir, 275 Capp St, San Francisco, CA 94110.

NATIONAL CELLULAR TELEPHONE SERVICE DAY. Oct 13. Purpose: To mark the introduction of a revolutionary telecommunications system, introduced in Chicago by Ameritech Mobile Communications on October 13, 1983. Since the Chicago introduction, cellular technology has spread to more than 20 cities nationwide. Sponsor: Ameritech Mobile Communications, Inc. Info from: Golin/Harris Communications, Ellen Ryan, Account Exec, 500 N Michigan Ave, Chicago, IL 60611.

October **1986**

S	M	T	W	T	F	S
			1	2	3	4
5	6	7	8	9	10	11
12	13	14	15	16	17	18
19	20	21	22	23	24	25
26	27	28	29	30	31	

NAVY BIRTHDAY. Oct 13. Commemorates legislation passed by Second Continental Congress Oct 13, 1775, authorizing the acquisition of ships and establishment of a navy.

PITCHER, MOLLY: BIRTHDAY. Oct 13. "Molly Pitcher," heroine of the American Revolution, was a water carrier at the Battle of Monmouth (Sunday, June 28, 1778) where she distinguished herself by loading and firing cannon after her husband, John Hays, was wounded. Affectionately known as "Sergeant Molly" after General Washington issued her a warrant as a non-commissioned officer. Her real name was Mary Hays McCauley (née Ludwig). Born near Trenton, NJ, Oct 13, 1754. Died at Carlisle, PA, on Jan 22, 1832.

ST. EDWARD, THE CONFESSOR: FEAST DAY. Oct 13. King of England, 1042-1066, Edward was the son of King Ethelred the Unready. Born in 1003, he died on Jan 5, 1066. On Oct 13, 1163, his remains were translated in a ceremony which was of national interest. Since then Oct 13 has been observed as his principal feast day.

SCHUETTE, BILL: BIRTHDAY. Oct 13. U.S. Representative of Michigan's 10th district, Republican, of Sanford, MI, born in Midland, MI, Oct 13, 1953.

SPACE MILESTONE: U.S. NATIONAL COMMISSION ON SPACE. Oct 13. Pres. Reagan signed executive order creating a Natl Commission on Space to prepare 20-year agenda for civilian space program. Oct 13, 1984.

THATCHER, MARGARET HILDA ROBERTS: BIRTHDAY. Oct 13. First woman prime minister in 700 years of English parliamentary history. Election of May 3, 1979, gave Conservative Party victory, and Mrs. Thatcher accepted Queen Elizabeth's appointment as prime minister, May 4th. Mrs. Thatcher was born at Grantham, Lincolnshire, Oct 13, 1925.

VIRCHOW, RUDOLF: BIRTHDAY. Oct 13. German political leader and scientist, called "the founder of cellular pathology," was born at Schivelbein, Prussia, on Oct 13, 1821. Teacher and author of many works, Virchow died at Berlin, Sept 5, 1902.

VIRGIN ISLANDS—PUERTO RICO FRIENDSHIP DAY. Oct 13. Virgin Islands. Columbus Day (2nd Monday in October) also celebrates historical friendship between peoples of Virgin Islands and Puerto Rico.

YOM KIPPUR or DAY OF ATONEMENT. Oct 13. Holiest Jewish observance. A day for fasting, repentance and seeking forgiveness. Hebrew calendar date: Tishri 10, 5747.

OCTOBER 14 — TUESDAY
287th Day — Remaining, 78

ALMA COLLEGE: CENTENNIAL ANNIVERSARY. Oct 14. Formal establishment of Alma College, at Alma, MI, was achieved by a Presbyterian Synod resolution on Oct 14, 1886.

COURTER, JIM: BIRTHDAY. Oct 14. U.S. Representative of New Jersey's 12th district, Republican, born in Hackettstown, NJ, on Oct 14, 1941.

EISENHOWER, DWIGHT DAVID: BIRTH ANNIVERSARY. Oct 14. The 34th President of the U.S., Dwight David Eisenhower, was born at Denison, TX, Oct 14, 1890. Serving two terms as president, Jan 20, 1953-Jan 20, 1961, Eisenhower was the first president to be baptized after taking office (Sunday, Feb 1, 1953). Nicknamed "Ike," he held the rank of 5-star General of the Army (resigned in 1952, and restored by act of Congress in 1961). In his Farewell Address (Jan 17, 1961), speaking about the "conjunction of an immense military establishment and a large arms industry," he warned: "In the councils of government, we must guard against the acquisition of unwarranted influence, whether sought or unsought, by the military-industrial complex. The potential for the disastrous rise of misplaced power exists and will persist." Eisenhower died at Washington, DC, Mar 28, 1969.

JAPAN: QUARREL FESTIVAL. Oct 14-15. Himeji, Japan, Palanquin bearers jostle one another to demonstrate their skill and balance in handling their burdens.

COPYRIGHT © 1985 BY WILLIAM D. CHASE and HELEN M. CHASE

PEACE CORPS BIRTHDAY. Oct 14. At the improbable hour of 2:00 a.m., on Oct 14, 1960, then presidential candidate John F. Kennedy spoke impromptu to several thousand university students from the steps of the University of Michigan Union building. He asked: "How many of you who are going to be doctors are willing to spend your days in Ghana? How many of you (technicians and engineers) are willing to work in the Foreign Service . . . ?" The response was quick and favorable, and 19 days later, in San Francisco, Kennedy formally proposed the Peace Corps, which was to draw some 80,000 volunteers into service during the next two decades.

PENN, WILLIAM: BIRTHDAY. Oct 14. Founder of Pennsylvania, born in London on Oct 14, 1644. Died July 30, 1718. "Men are generally more careful," Penn wrote, "of the breed of their horses and dogs than of their children."

SPACE MILESTONE: SOYUZ 23 (USSR). Oct 14. Launched Oct 14, 1976. Cosmonauts V. Zudov and V. Rozhdestvensky unable to dock at Salyut 5 space station as planned. Return landing on Earth Oct 16.

SUNBELT AGRICULTURAL EXPOSITION. Oct 14-16. Spence Field, Moultrie, GA. Info from: Sunbelt Agricultural Expo, Box 1209, Tifton, GA 31794.

OCTOBER 15 — WEDNESDAY
288th Day — Remaining, 77

CIRCLEVILLE PUMPKIN SHOW. Oct 15-18. Purpose: "Over 100,000 pounds of pumpkins, squash and gourds await the more than 100,000 visitors to Circleville, OH." Sponsor: Pumpkin Show Inc, Ned Dresbach, Secy, Box 127, Circleville, OH 43113.

GREENWICH VILLAGE POET LAUREATE CONTEST DAY. Oct 15. Purpose: To call attention to the value of the poets in our society and acknowledge poetic achievement. Sponsor: Richard R. Falk Associates, 147 W 42nd St, New York, NY 10036.

LEACH, JIM: BIRTHDAY. Oct 15. U.S. Representative of Iowa's 1st district, Republican, of Davenport, IA, born in Davenport on Oct 15, 1942.

MANN, MARTY: BIRTHDAY. Oct 15. American social activist and author was born at Chicago on Oct 15, 1904. She was founder, in 1944, of the National Committee for Education on Alcoholism and author of a *New Primer on Alcoholism*. She died at Bridgeport, CT on July 22, 1980.

MISSOURI DAY. Oct 15. The third Wednesday of October each year. Observed by teachers and pupils of schools with appropriate exercises throughout state of Missouri.

NATIONAL GROUCH DAY. Oct 15. Purpose: Honor a grouch; all grouches deserve a day to be recognized. Sponsor: Alan R. Miller, 12281 Alexander St, Clio, MI 48420.

NIETZSCHE, FRIEDRICH WILHELM: BIRTH ANNIVERSARY. Oct 15. Influential German philosopher born at Rocken on Oct 15, 1844. Especially remembered among his philosophical beliefs are contempt for the weak and expected ultimate triumph of a superman. Nietzsche died at Weimar on Aug 25, 1900, a decade after becoming insane.

WHITE CANE SAFETY DAY. Oct 15. Presidential Proclama-
☆ tion. "Always issued for October 15 since 1964 (PL88-628 of Oct 6, 1964)."

WILSON, EDITH BOLLING GALT: BIRTHDAY. Oct 15. Second wife of Woodrow Wilson, 28th President of the U.S., born at Wytheville, VA, Oct 15, 1872. Died Dec 28, 1961.

WODEHOUSE, PELHAM GRENVILLE: BIRTHDAY. Oct 15. English author, humorist, creator of Jeeves, born at Guildford, Surrey, England, Oct 15, 1881. Died, Southampton, Long Island, NY, Feb 14, 1975.

OCTOBER 16 — THURSDAY
289th Day — Remaining, 76

BEN-GURION, DAVID: BIRTH ANNIVERSARY. Oct 16. First prime minister of the State of Israel was born at Plonsk, Poland, on Oct 16, 1886. He died at Tel Aviv on Dec 1, 1973.

DICTIONARY DAY. Oct 16. The birthday of Noah Webster, American teacher and lexicographer, is occasion to encourage every person to acquire at least one dictionary—and to use it regularly.

DOUGLAS, WILLIAM ORVILLE: BIRTHDAY. Oct 16. American jurist, served longer as justice of the U.S. Supreme Court than any other (36 years), world traveler, conservationist, outdoorsman, and author, was born at Maine, MN, Oct 16, 1898, and died at Washington, DC, Jan 19, 1980.

EVANS, DANIEL JACKSON: BIRTHDAY. Oct 16. U.S. Senator from Washington, Republican, of Seattle, WA, born in Seattle on Oct 16, 1925.

FALL SOUTHERN FURNITURE MARKET. Oct 16-24. Wholesale furniture trade show. Info from: Furniture Factories' Marketing Assn of the South, Box 5687, High Point, NC 27262.

GREEN, BILL: BIRTHDAY. Oct 16. U.S. Representative of New York's 15th district, Republican, of New York, NY born in New York City, Oct 16, 1929.

INTERNATIONAL CREDIT UNION DAY. Oct 16. Purpose: To reflect upon contributions of credit union founders worldwide and honor those working today, cooperatively, to bring credit unions to all who wish to receive benefits of membership. Sponsor: World Council of Credit Unions, Hayward Allen, Communications Dir, Box 391, Madison, WI 53705.

JOHN BROWN'S RAID: ANNIVERSARY. Oct 16. On Oct 16, 1859, fanatical abolitionist John Brown, with a band of about 20 men, seized the U.S. Arsenal at Harpers Ferry, WV. Brown was captured and the insurrection put down by Oct 19th. Brown was hanged at Charles Town, WV, Dec 2, 1859.

NATIONAL BOSS DAY. Oct 16. Purpose: For blue and white collar gals and guys to honor their bosses. Info from: Mrs. Patricia Bays Haroski, Originator, The Bridges A6, 3411 Old Vineyard Rd, Winston-Salem, NC 27103.

NICHOLS, WILLIAM: BIRTHDAY. Oct 16. U.S. Representative of Alabama's 3rd district, Democrat, of Sylacauga, AL, was born near Becker, MS on Oct 16, 1918.

O'NEILL, EUGENE GLADSTONE: BIRTHDAY. Oct 16. American playwright, recipient of Pulitzer and Nobel Prizes, born at New York City, Oct 16, 1888. Died at Boston, MA, Nov 27, 1953.

PEACE WITH JUSTICE WEEK. Oct 16-24. Purpose: A week to witness for Peace and Justice, sponsored by more than 20 national religious organizations. Info from: National Council of Churches of Christ in the U.S.A., Attn: Gary Gamer, 475 Riverside Dr, New York, NY 10115.

TAMPA/ST. PETERSBURG FALL HOME SHOW. Oct 16-19. Florida State Fairgrounds, Tampa, FL. Info from: Perl Exposition Corp, 6915 Red Road, Suite 228, Coral Gables, FL 33143.

WAR CRIMINALS (GERMAN) EXECUTION: ANNIVERSARY. Oct 16. The War Crimes Trials (q.v.) of Berlin and Nuremberg had sentenced twelve of the 22 defendants to death by hanging. They were: Hermann Goering, Joachim von

Ribbentrop, Wilhelm Keitel, Ernst Kaltenbrunner, Alfred Rosenberg, Hans Frank, Wilhelm Frick, Julius Streicher, Fritz Sauckel, Alfred Jodl, Martin Bormann and Arthur von Seyss-Inquart. Goering committed suicide a few hours before his scheduled execution, and Martin Bormann had not been found (he was tried in absentia). The remaining ten were hanged at Nuremberg Prison on Oct 16, 1946.

WEBSTER, NOAH: BIRTHDAY. Oct 16. American teacher and journalist whose name became synonymous with the word "dictionary," after his compilations of the earliest American dictionaries of the English language. Born at West Hartford, CT, on Oct 16, 1758. Died at New Haven, CT, on May 28, 1843.

WHEAT, ALAN D: BIRTHDAY. Oct 16. U.S. Representative of Missouri's 5th district, Democrat, of Kansas City, MO, born in San Antonio, TX, Oct 16, 1951.

WILDE, OSCAR: BIRTH ANNIVERSARY. Oct 16. Irish poet and playwright, Oscar (Fingal O'Flahertie Wills) Wilde, was born at Dublin on Oct 16, 1854. At the height of his career he was imprisoned for two years on a morals offense, during which time he wrote "A Ballad of Reading Gaol." Best known of his plays is *The Importance of Being Earnest*. "There is only one thing in the world worse than being talked about," he wrote in his *Picture of Dorian Gray*, "and that is not being talked about." Wilde died, self-exiled, at Paris on Nov 30, 1900. His dying words are said to have been: "This wallpaper is killing me; one of us has got to go."

WORLD FOOD DAY. Oct 16. Annual observance. Purpose: To heighten public awareness of the world food problem and strengthen solidarity in the struggle against hunger, malnutrition and poverty. Date of observance is anniversary of founding of Food and Agriculture Organization (FAO) by 42 countries, Oct 16, 1945, at Quebec. Info from: UN Food & Agriculture Organization, 1001 22nd St, NW, Washington, DC 20437 and from: Natl Committee for World Food Day, Patricia Young, Natl Coord, 1001 22nd St, NW, Washington, DC 20437.

YATRON, GUS: BIRTHDAY. Oct 16. U.S. Representative of Pennsylvania's 6th district, Democrat, of Reading, PA, born there on Oct 16, 1927.

OCTOBER 17 — FRIDAY
290th Day — Remaining, 75

AURORA COUNTRY FESTIVAL. Oct 17-19. Arts, crafts, molasses making, country and gospel music and strut dance. Info from: Marshall County Chamber of Commerce, Rt 7, Benton, KY 42025.

BLACK POETRY DAY. Oct 17. Purpose: "To recognize the contribution of Black poets to American life and culture and honor Jupiter Hammon, first Black in America to publish his own verse. Jupiter Hammon of Huntington, L.I., NY, was born Oct 17, 1711." Sponsor: Black Poetry Day Committee, Clinton-Essex-Franklin Library System, Box 570, Plattsburgh, NY 12901.

DAYTONA PRO-AM MOTORCYCLE RACES. Oct 17-19. Info from: Daytona Internatl Speedway, Larry Balewski, PR, Daytona Beach, FL 32015.

ECLIPSE: TOTAL ECLIPSE OF THE MOON. Oct 17. Not visible in North America. Visible: Australasia, Asia, Africa, Europe, Iceland, E. of Greenland and Arctic regions. Moon enters umbra at 12:29 p.m. and leaves it at 4:06 p.m., E.S.T. Totality lasts from 1:40 p.m. until 2:55 p.m., E.S.T.

October 1986

S	M	T	W	T	F	S
			1	2	3	4
5	6	7	8	9	10	11
12	13	14	15	16	17	18
19	20	21	22	23	24	25
26	27	28	29	30	31	

FALL FESTIVAL OF LEAVES. Oct 17-19. Purpose: Celebration of beauty of the season and region. Folk arts, crafts, music, kiddie tractor pull, flea markets and parades. Sponsor: Fall Festival of Leaves Box 571, Bainbridge, Ross County, OH 45612.

HELLDORADO DAYS. Oct 17-19. Purpose: To relive the historic events of Tombstone. Reenactments of early day gunfights, 1880 fashion show, melodrama, carnival and parade. Sponsor: Helldorado, Inc, Box 297, Tombstone, AZ 85638.

HUGHES, WILLIAM JOHN: BIRTHDAY. Oct 17. U.S. Representative of New Jersey's 2nd district, Democrat, of Ocean City, NJ, born at Salem, NJ, Oct 17, 1932.

HUNTER'S MOON. Oct 17. The full moon following Harvest Moon. Moon's light in evening extends day's length for hunters.

JOHNSON, RICHARD MENTOR: BIRTHDAY. Oct 17. Ninth Vice President of the U.S. (1837-1841) born, Floyd's Station, KY, Oct 17, 1780. Died, Frankfort, KY, Nov 19, 1850.

LOUISIANA STATE FAIR. Oct 17-26. Shreveport, LA, Fairgrounds. Info from: Mr. Ed Nelson, LA State Fairgrounds, PO Box 9100, Shreveport, LA 71139.

LUMBERJACK BLUEGRASS JAMBOREE. Oct 17-19. Twin Falls State Park, Mullens, WV. Info from: Twin Falls State Park, Box 1023, Mullens, WV 25882.

MOON PHASE: FULL MOON. Oct 17. Moon enters Full Moon phase at 2:22 p.m., E.S.T.

NATIONAL CRAFT FAIR. Oct. 17-19. Montgomery County Fairgrounds, Gaithersburg, MD. 400 top professional designer/craftsmen. Info from: Noel Clark, Dir. Natl Crafts Ltd, Gapland, MD 21736.

NORTH CAROLINA STATE FAIR. Oct 17-25. Raleigh, NC.

POPE JOHN PAUL I: BIRTHDAY. Oct 17. Albino Luciani, 263rd Pope of the Roman Catholic Church, born at Forno di Canale, Italy, Oct 17, 1912. Elected Pope Aug 26, 1978. Died at Rome, 34 days after his election, on Sept 28, 1978. Shortest papacy since Pope Leo XI (Apr 1-27, 1605).

ST. LUCIA: LA MARGUERITE. Oct 17. Flower society festival. Info from: St. Lucia Tourist Board, 41 E 42nd St, New York, NY 10017.

SOUTH CAROLINA STATE FAIR. Oct 17-26. Columbia, SC. Purpose: To develop and promote the entire material and industrial interests of the state. Info from: SC State Fair, Gary L. Goodman, Mgr, Box 393, Columbia, SC 29202.

SOUTHERN HIGHLAND HANDICRAFT GUILD FAIR '86. Oct 17-19. Civic Center, Asheville, NC. Handmade crafts from the southern Appalachian region, demonstrations and folk and contemporary entertainment. Info from: Southern Highland Handicraft Guild, Box 9545, Asheville, NC 28815.

SUGARLOAF'S MARYLAND CRAFTS FESTIVAL. Oct 17-19. Maryland State Fairgrounds, Timonium, MD. Professional artists and craftspeople, demonstrations, and live music. Sponsor: Sugarloaf Mt Works, Inc, Ijamsville, MD 21754.

SYNAR, MIKE: BIRTHDAY. Oct 17. U.S. Representative of Oklahoma's 2nd district, Democrat, of Muskogee, OK, born in Vinta, OK, Oct 17, 1950.

OCTOBER 18 — SATURDAY
291st Day — Remaining, 74

ALASKA DAY. Oct 18. Alaska. Anniversary of transfer of Alaska from Russia to the U.S., which became official on Sitka's Castle Hill, Oct 18, 1867.

ANDREE, SALOMON AUGUSTE; BIRTH ANNIVERSARY. Oct 18, Swedish explorer and balloonist was born at Grenna, Sweden, on Oct 18, 1854. His North Pole expedition of 1897 attracted world attention but ended tragically. With two companions, Nils Strindberg and Knut Frankel, Andree left Spitzbergen on July 11, 1897 in a balloon, hoping to place the Swedish flag at the North Pole. The last message from Andree, borne by carrier pigeons, was dated at noon, July 13, 1897.

COPYRIGHT © 1985 BY WILLIAM D. CHASE and HELEN M. CHASE

The frozen bodies of the explorers were found 33 years later, by another polar expedition in the summer of 1930. Taken back to Stockholm they were cremated on Oct 10, 1930. Diaries, maps and exposed photographic negatives also were found. The photos were developed successfully, providing a pictorial record of the ill-fated expedition.

APPLE BUTTER STIRRIN' FESTIVAL. Oct 18-19. Purpose: A real old-time celebration. Watch apple butter being cooked over open fires. Nineteenth century crafts and entertainment. (Annually the 3rd weekend in October.) Info from: Roscoe Village Foundation, 381 Hill St, Coshocton, OH 43812.

BANYAN FESTIVAL. Oct 18-19. Coconut Grove, FL. A weekend of arts, crafts and plants on the sidewalks of picturesque Coconut Grove. Info from: Chamber of Commerce, 3437 Main Hwy, Coconut Grove, FL 33133.

BATON ROUGE FALL CRAFTS FESTIVAL. Oct 18-19. Purpose: To exhibit the talents of high quality craftsmen and increase public appreciation of fine craftsmanship. Demonstrating craftsmen, performing arts and international cuisine. Info from: River City Festivals Assn, Richard Sabino, 427 Laurel St, Baton Rouge, LA 70801.

BERGSON, HENRI: BIRTHDAY. Oct 18. French philosopher, Nobel Prize winner and author of *Creative Evolution*, born Oct 18, 1859. Died Jan 4, 1941.

BROWNS CROSSING CRAFTSMEN FAIR. Oct 18-19. Purpose: To promote public awareness of the value of original handmade arts and crafts. Info from: Carole Sirmans, 400 Browns Crossing Rd, NW, Milledgeville, GA 31061.

FALL AUTO TOUR FOR VIEWING MIGRATORY WATERFOWL MIGRATION. Oct 18-Nov 9. DeSoto National Wildlife Refuge, Missouri Valley, IA. Info from: U.S. Fish & Wildlife Service, K.L. Drews, Rt 1, Box 114, Missouri Valley, IA 51555.

FALL FIESTA OF THE ARTS. Oct 18-19. Swan Lake Gardens, Sumter, SC. Features visual and performing arts, concerts and choral groups. Info from: Sumter Cultural Commission, County Courthouse, Sumter, SC 29150.

FIDDLERS JAMBOREE. Oct 18. Purpose: Southern mountain fiddlers gather from all sections of the country. Info from: Ozark Folk Ctr, Mountain View, AR 72560.

HELMS, JESSE: BIRTHDAY. Oct 18. U.S. Senator from North Carolina, Republican, of Raleigh, NC, born in Monroe, NC, Oct 18, 1921.

MERRILL POTATO FESTIVAL. Oct 18-19. A celebration for a good harvest. Parade, booths, concessions and bar-b-que. (3rd weekend in Oct.) Info from: Visitors & Convention Bureau, 125 N 8th St, Klamath Falls, OR 97601.

OKTOBERFEST. Oct 18-19. Traders Village, Grand Prairie, TX. Purpose: Bavarian biergarten setting featuring polka bands, German, Polish and Czech folk dancing and plenty of German food and beer. Info from: Traders Village, 2602 Mayfield Rd, Grand Prairie, TX 75051.

RATTLESNAKE FESTIVAL AND INTERNATIONAL CHAMPIONSHIP GOPHER RACES. Oct 18. San Antonio City Park, San Antonio, FL. Info from: RAGE, Box 127, San Antonio, FL 33576.

ST. LUKE: FEAST DAY. Oct 18. Patron saint of doctors and artists, himself a physician and painter, author of the third Gospel and Acts of the Apostles. Died about A.D. 68. Legend says that he painted portraits of Mary and Jesus.

SHRINE OYSTER BOWL GAME. Oct 18. Foreman Field, Norfolk, VA. Virginia Tech vs Temple University. Info from: Oyster Bowl Office, Box 11063, Norfolk, VA 23517.

SUKKOT, SUCCOTH, or FEAST OF TABERNACLES, FIRST DAY. Oct 18. Hebrew calendar date: Tishri 15, 5747. Begins nine-day festival in commemoration of Jewish people's 40 years of wandering in the desert, and thanksgiving for the fall harvest. This high holiday season closes with Shemini Atzeret, Oct 25 (q.v.) and Simchat Torah, Oct 26 (q.v.).

SWEETEST DAY. Oct 18. Observed always on the third Saturday in October. Info from: Detroit Sweetest Day Committee, John M. Sanders, Chrmn, 100 Oakman Blvd, Detroit, MI 48203.

SWINDALL, PATRICK LYNN: BIRTHDAY. Oct 18. U.S. Representative of Georgia's 4th district, Republican, of Dunwoody, GA, born in Gadsden, AL, on Oct 18, 1950.

TRUDEAU, PIERRE ELLIOTT: BIRTHDAY. Oct 18. Canadian politician, born at Montreal, Que, Oct 18, 1919. Prime Minister of Canada, Apr 20, 1968-June 4, 1979, and March 3, 1980-June 30, 1984.

WAR CRIMES TRIAL (GERMANY): ANNIVERSARY. Oct 18. The first session of the German war crimes trials started at Berlin on Oct 18, 1945, with indictments against 24 former Nazi leaders. Later sessions were held at Nuremberg, starting Nov 20, 1945. One defendant committed suicide during the trial and another was excused because of his physical and mental condition. The trial lasted more than 10 months and delivery of the judgment was completed on Oct 1, 1946. Twelve were sentenced to death by hanging, three to life imprisonment, four to lesser prison terms, and three were acquitted. It was hoped that the war crimes trials would serve as a deterrent to future world leaders who might consider crimes against humanity.

WORLD CHAMPIONSHIP PAINT HORSE SHOW. Oct 18-22. Purpose: Over 500 Paint horses from throughout the country compete. Horses will be exhibited in halter and performance classes. Info from: Steve Collier, 1 Santa Fe Plaza, Oklahoma City, OK 73102.

WORLD WEEK FOR WILDLIFE. Oct 18-25. Purpose: To call attention to and protest the subjugation and slaughter of wild animals. Sponsor: Mobilization for Animals, Box 1679, Columbus, OH 43216.

OCTOBER 19 — SUNDAY
292nd Day — Remaining, 73

ANNIVERSARY DAY. Oct 19. So named and observed by Robert Hutchings Goddard, rocket pioneer, as anniversary of day (Oct 19, 1899) when he first began to speculate about a space ship that could travel to Mars.

BROWNE, THOMAS: BIRTHDAY. Oct 19. Anniversary of the birth at London on Oct 19, 1605, of physician, scholar and author, Thomas Browne. He wrote: "I could never divide myself from any man upon the difference of an opinion, or be angry with his judgment for not agreeing with me in that from which perhaps within a few days I should dissent myself." At age 55, he wrote: "The long habit of living indisposeth us for dying." His most famous work, *Religio Medici*, was published in 1642. Browne died at Norwich, England, on his 77th birthday, Oct 19, 1682.

JEFFERSON, MARTHA WAYLES SKELTON: BIRTHDAY. Oct 19. Wife of Thomas Jefferson, 3rd President of the U.S. Born Charles City County, VA, Oct 19, 1748. Died Sept 6, 1782.

LANCING TOURNAMENT. Oct 19. Daring horsemen in Colonial costume charge down course spearing a series of two-inch rings in less than six seconds. Foods, music and musical chairs on horseback. Info from: Middleton Place, Route 4, Hwy 61, Charleston, SC 29407.

COPYRIGHT © 1985 BY WILLIAM D. CHASE and HELEN M. CHASE

NATIONAL CLEANER AIR WEEK. Oct 19-25. Purpose: To advance the knowledge and practice of air pollution control at the community level. (Last full week of Oct.) Sponsor: Air Pollution Control League, Charles N. Howison, Exec Secy, 18 E Fourth St, Cincinnati, OH 45202.

NATIONAL FOREST PRODUCTS WEEK. Oct 19-25. Presidential Proclamation. "Always issued for the week beginning with 3rd Sunday of October since 1960 (PL86-753 of Sept 13, 1960)." ☆

WEIGHT WATCHERS PEPSTEP (TM) WALKUP. Oct 19. Special 144 step, 144 yard course on steps of the Philadelphia Museum of Art for benefit of the American Heart Assn. Purpose: To promote the importance of proper exercise and good nutritional practices in maintaining health. Sponsor: Weight Watchers of Philadelphia, 245 New York Dr, Box 2300, Ft Washington, PA 19034.

WORLD'S CHAMPIONSHIP CHILI COOK-OFF. Oct 19. Tropico Goldmine, Rosamond, CA. Purpose: Contestants from all over the United States, Canada, Mexico, Australia, Guam and England compete for the best bowl of "red" chili. Sponsor: Internatl Chili Society, Jim West, Exec Dir, Box 2966, Newport Beach, CA 92663.

YORKTOWN DAY. Oct 19. More than 7,000 English and Hessian troops, led by British General Lord Cornwallis, surrendered to General George Washington at Yorktown, VA, on Oct 19, 1781. The event effectively ended the war between Britain and her American colonies. There were no more major battles, but the provisional treaty of peace was not signed until Nov 30, 1782, and the final Treaty of Paris, on Sept 3, 1783.

YORKTOWN DAY: "AMERICA'S REAL INDEPENDENCE DAY." Oct 19. Yorktown, VA. Representatives of U.S., France and other nations involved in American Revolution gather to celebrate anniversary of the victory which assured American independence. Parade, food and commemorative ceremonies. Info from: The Yorktown Day Assn, Box 210, Yorktown, VA 23690.

OCTOBER 20 — MONDAY
293rd Day — Remaining, 72

BIRTH OF THE BAB. Oct 20. Baha'i observance of anniversary of the birth, Oct 20, 1819, in Shiraz, Persia, of Siyyid Ali Muhammad, who later took the title of "the Bab," and was a prophet of the Baha'i faith. Info from: Baha'i Office of Public Affairs, Baha'i Natl Center, Wilmette, IL 60091.

BORSKI, ROBERT ANTHONY, JR: BIRTHDAY. Oct 20. U.S. Representative of Pennsylvania's 3rd district, Democrat, of Philadelphia, PA, was born at Philadelphia on Oct 20, 1948.

DEWEY, JOHN: BIRTHDAY. Oct 20. American psychologist, philosopher and educational reformer was born at Burlington, VT, on Oct 20, 1859. His philosophical views of education have been termed pragmatism, instrumentalism and experimentalism. Dewey died at New York City on June 1, 1952.

HURRICANE THANKSGIVING DAY. Oct 20. Virgin Islands. Third Monday of October is legal holiday celebrating end of hurricane season.

JAMAICA: NATIONAL HEROES DAY. Oct 20. National holiday established in 1969. Always observed on third Monday in October.

MANN, JAMES ROBERT: BIRTHDAY. Oct 20. American lawyer and legislator, born near Bloomington, IL, Oct 20, 1856. Republican member of Congress from Illinois, from 1896 until his death, Nov 30, 1922. Mann was the author and sponsor of the "White Slave Traffic Act," also known as the "Mann Act," passed by the Congress June 25, 1910. The Act prohibited, under heavy penalties, the interstate transportation of women for immoral purposes.

NATIONAL SAFETY CONGRESS AND EXPOSITION. Oct 20-23. Chicago, IL. Features more than 150 programs and more than 350 exhibitors, involving a variety of safety and health topics, including occupational, traffic, consumer and farm safety. Sponsor: Natl Safety Council, 444 N Michigan Ave, Chicago, IL 60611.

SATURDAY NIGHT MASSACRE. Oct 20. Anniversary of dramatic turning point in the Watergate Affair. The swiftly moving events of Oct 20, 1973: White House announcement (8:24 p.m., E.D.T.) that President Richard M. Nixon had discharged Archibald Cox (Special Watergate Prosecutor) and William B. Ruckelshaus (Deputy Attorney General). The Attorney General, Elliot L. Richardson, resigned. Immediate and widespread demands for impeachment of the President ensued and were not stilled until President Nixon resigned, on Aug 9, 1974.

WREN, CHRISTOPHER: BIRTHDAY. Oct 20. Sir Christopher Wren, English architect, astronomer and mathematician, born Oct 20, 1632. Died Feb 25, 1723. His epitaph, written by his son, is inscribed over the interior of the north door in St. Paul's Cathedral, London: "Si monumentum requiris, circumspice." (If you would see his monument, look about you.)

OCTOBER 21 — TUESDAY
294th Day — Remaining, 71

AUCOIN, LES: BIRTHDAY. Oct 21. U.S. Representative of Oregon's 1st district, Democrat, of Portland, OR, born in Redmond, OR, on Oct 21, 1942.

BATTLE OF TRAFALGAR: ANNIVERSARY. Oct 21. "This famous naval action, on Oct 21, 1805, between the Royal Navy and the combined French and Spanish fleets, removed forever the threat of Napoleon's invasion of England. The British victory, off Trafalgar, set the seal of eternal fame on Viscount Horatio Nelson who died in the moment of victory." Inscription under copy of painting in Main Post Office, near Charing Cross, London.

CARLETON, WILL: DAY. Oct 21. Anniversary of the birth of poet Will Carleton, Oct 21, 1845, observed (by 1919 statute) in Michigan schools where poems of Carleton must be read on this day. Best known of his poems: "Over the Hill to the Poorhouse." Carleton died in 1912.

COLERIDGE, SAMUEL TAYLOR: BIRTHDAY. Oct 21. English poet and essayist born Oct 21, 1772. Died July 25, 1834. In *Table Talk*, he wrote: "I wish our clever young poets would remember my homely definitions of prose and poetry; that is, prose = words in their best order; - poetry = the *best* words in the best order."

ELECTRIC INCANDESCENT LAMP ANNIVERSARY. Oct 21. Anniversary of the invention, Oct 21, 1879, by Thomas Alva Edison, at his Menlo Park, NJ, laboratory, of a practical incandescent electric lamp.

FILLMORE, CAROLINE CARMICHAEL McINTOSH: BIRTHDAY. Oct 21. Second wife of Millard Fillmore, 13th President of the U.S., born at Morristown, NJ, Oct 21, 1813. Died Aug 11, 1881.

LEWIS, JERRY: BIRTHDAY. Oct 21. U.S. Representative of California's 35th district, Republican, of Redlands, CA, born Oct 21, 1934.

RITTER, DONALD LAWRENCE: BIRTHDAY. Oct 21. U.S. Representative of Pennsylvania's 15th district, Republican, of Coopersburg, PA, born in New York, NY, Oct 21, 1940.

SOMALIA: NATIONAL DAY. Oct 21. National holiday observed in Somalia.

October 1986

S	M	T	W	T	F	S
			1	2	3	4
5	6	7	8	9	10	11
12	13	14	15	16	17	18
19	20	21	22	23	24	25
26	27	28	29	30	31	

COPYRIGHT © 1985 BY WILLIAM D. CHASE and HELEN M. CHASE

TAIWAN: OVERSEAS CHINESE DAY. Oct 21. Thousands of overseas Chinese come to Taiwan for this and other occasions that make October a particularly memorable month.

OCTOBER 22 — WEDNESDAY
295th Day — Remaining, 70

CHAFFEE, JOHN HUBBARD: BIRTHDAY. Oct 22. U.S. Senator from Rhode Island, Republican, of Warwick, RI, was born in Providence, RI, on Oct 22, 1922.

CUBAN MISSILE CRISIS ANNIVERSARY. Oct 22. President John F. Kennedy, in a nationwide television address on Oct 22, 1962, demanded the removal from Cuba of Soviet missiles, launching equipment and bombers, and imposed "quarantine" to prevent further weaponry reaching Cuba. On October 28th, the U.S.S.R. announced it would remove the weapons in question.

FANTASY FEST '86. Oct 22-26. Key West, FL. Purpose: Halloween festival with five days of costume parties, masked balls and night-time grand parade. Sponsor: Fantasy Fest '86, Michael Whalton, Co-Dir, 201 Duval St, Key West, FL 33040.

FEIGHAN, EDWARD FARRELL: BIRTHDAY. Oct 22. U.S. Representative of Ohio's 19th district, Democrat, of Lakewood, OH, born in Lakewood, on Oct 22, 1947.

GROLIER, JEAN: DEATH ANNIVERSARY. Oct 22. The celebrated French bibliophile, Jean Grolier de Servieres, whose exact birthday at Lyon in 1479 is unknown, died at Paris, Oct 22, 1565. A government official, Grolier's consuming interest was books and he assembled one of the world's finest collections—a library of more than 3,000 elegantly bound volumes. The Grolier Club, of New York City, is named for him.

HOLY SEE: NATIONAL HOLIDAY. Oct. 22. The State of Vatican City and the Holy See observe Oct 22 as a National Holiday.

LISZT, FRANZ: BIRTHDAY. Oct 22. Hungarian composer. Oct 22, 1811-July 31, 1886.

LOUISIANA YAMBILEE. Oct 22-26. Sweet potato and corn, rice and soybean shows. Grand Louisyam Parade, arts, crafts and an auction of yams. Info from: Louisiana Yambilee, Inc, Box 444, Opelousas, LA 70570.

METROPOLITAN OPERA HOUSE: BIRTHDAY. Oct 22. Grand opening of the original New York Metropolitan Opera House, on Oct 22, 1883, was celebrated with a performance of Gounod's *Faust*.

RANDOLPH, PEYTON: DEATH ANNIVERSARY. Oct 22. First president Continental Congress died Oct 22, 1775. Born about 1721 (exact unknown) probably at Williamsburg, VA.

WORLD'S END DAY. Oct 22. Anniversary of the day, Oct 22, 1844, set as the day on which the world would end, by followers of William Miller, religious leader and creator of a movement known as Millerism. Stories about followers disposing of all earthly possessions and climbing to high places on that date are believed to be apocryphal. (Miller was born at Pittsfield, MA, Feb 15, 1782. Died, Low Hampton, NY, Dec 20, 1849.)

OCTOBER 23 — THURSDAY
296th Day — Remaining, 69

APPERT, NICOLAS: BIRTHDAY. Oct 23. Also known as "Canning Day," this is the anniversary of the birth of French chef, chemist, confectioner, inventor and author, Nicolas Appert, at Chalons-Sur Marne, Oct 23, 1752. Appert, who also invented the bouillion tablet, is best remembered for devising a system of heating foods and sealing them in air-tight containers. Known as the "father of canning," Appert won a prize of 12,000 francs from the French government in 1809, and the title "Benefactor of Humanity" in 1812, for his work and inventions which revolutionized man's previously seasonal diet. Appert died at Massy, June 3, 1841, but the methods he developed for preserving food continue in ever-greater use.

BEIRUT TERRORIST ATTACK ANNIVERSARY. Oct 23. A suicidal terrorist attack on American forces in Beirut, Lebanon, killed 240 U.S. personnel on Oct 23, 1983, when a truck loaded with TNT was driven into and exploded at U.S. Headquarters there. At the same time a similar attack on French forces killed scores more.

HEINZ, JOHN: BIRTHDAY. Oct 23. U.S. Senator from Pennsylvania, Republican, of Pittsburgh, PA, was born in Pittsburgh on Oct 23, 1938.

ST. JOHN OF CAPISTRANO: DEATH ANNIVERSARY. Oct 23. Giovanni da Capistrano, Franciscan lawyer, educator and preacher, was born at Capistrano, Italy, in 1386. He died, of plague, on Oct 23, 1456. Feast Day is March 28.

SCORPIO, THE SCORPION. Oct 23-Nov 22. In the astronomical/astrological zodiac, which divides the sun's apparent orbit into twelve segments, the period Oct 23-Nov 21 is identified, traditionally, as the sun-sign of Scorpio, the Scorpion. The ruling planet is Pluto or Mars.

STEVENSON, ADLAI EWING: BIRTHDAY. Oct 23. Twenty-third Vice President of the U.S. (1893-1897) born, Christian County, KY, Oct 23, 1835. Died, Chicago, IL, June 14, 1914. He was grandfather of Adlai E. Stevenson, Democratic candidate for president in 1952 and 1956. See also entry for Feb 5.

SWALLOWS DEPART FROM SAN JUAN CAPISTRANO. Oct 23. Traditional date for swallows to depart, for the winter, from old mission of San Juan Capistrano, CA. See also Mar 19.

TAMPA/ST PETERSBURG FALL HOME SHOW. Oct 23-26. Florida State Fair Grounds. Info: Perl Exposition Corp, S. Coppola, PR Dir, 6915 Red Rd, Ste 228, Coral Gables, FL 33143.

THAILAND: CHULALONGKORN DAY. Oct 23. Annual commemoration of the death of King Chulalongkorn the Great who died Oct 23, 1910, after a 42-year reign. Special ceremonies with floral tributes and incense at the foot of his equestrian statue in front of Bangkok's National Assembly Hall. It was King Chulalongkorn who abolished slavery in Thailand.

TV TALK SHOW HOST DAY. Oct 23. Purpose: To celebrate the many TV talk show hosts whose personalities and intellects enable them to bring out the best in their guests. Sponsor: Glenn R. Rothenberger, Host, Glenn Rothenberger Show, Rothenberger Productions, Box 303, Allentown, PA 18105.

OCTOBER 24 — FRIDAY
297th Day — Remaining, 68

COWBOY ARTISTS OF AMERICA SALE AND EXHIBITION. Oct 24-Nov 23. Phoenix Art Museum, Phoenix, AZ. Exhibition and sale of new works by 30 members of the Cowboy Artists of America. Info from: Diane Lane, E.B. Lane & Associates, Inc, 733 W McDowell Rd, Phoenix, AZ 85007.

DISARMAMENT WEEK. Oct 24-30. Annual observance begins on anniversary of founding of United Nations. In Dec 1978, the UN General Assembly invited all States during this observance to carry out effective measures to expose the danger of the arms race, propagate the need for its cessation and increase public understanding of the urgent tasks of disarmament. As requested by the Assembly, the Secretary-General drew up in

1979 the elements of a model program for the Week, which might assist States in developing their own observances. Info from: UN Dept of Public Information, United Nations, NY 10017.

FALL "LIVING HISTORY" WEEKEND. Oct 24-26. Purpose: A celebration of harvest time on a mid-nineteenth century farm. Info from: Duke Homestead State Historic Site, 2828 Duke Homestead Rd, Durham, NC 27705.

NATIONAL SPORTING GOODS ASSOCIATION FALL MARKET. Oct 24-26. Anaheim Convention Center, Anaheim, CA. Info from: NSGA, Paul M. Prince, Senior Mgr, Trade Shows, 1699 Wall St, Mt Prospect, IL 60056.

NORTH LAS VEGAS FAIRSHOW. Oct 24-26. Clark County Community College, North Las Vegas, NV. Nevada national championship hot air balloon races. Info from: Betty McCreless, Fairshow Mgr, Chamber of Commerce, 1023 E Lake Mead Blvd, North Las Vegas, NV 89030.

SHERMAN, JAMES SCHOOLCRAFT; BIRTHDAY. Oct 24. Twenty-seventh Vice President of the U.S. (1909-1912) born, Utica, NY, Oct 24, 1855. Died there Oct 30, 1912.

STOCK MARKET PANIC ANNIVERSARY. Oct 24. After several weeks of downward trend in stock prices, investors began panic selling on Black Thursday, Oct 24, 1929. More than 13 million shares dumped. Desperate attempts to support the market brought brief rally. See also entry for Oct 29.

UNITED NATIONS DAY. Oct 24. Presidential Proclamation. ☆ "Always issued for October 24 since 1948. (By unanimous request of the UN General Assembly.)"

UNITED NATIONS DAY. Oct 24. Official United Nations holiday commemorates founding of the United Nations and effective date of the United Nations Charter, Oct 24, 1945. Info from: United Nations, New York, NY 10017.

WORLD DEVELOPMENT INFORMATION DAY. Oct 24. Anniversary of adoption by UN General Assembly, in 1970, of the International Development Strategy for the Second United Nations Development Decade. Object is "drawing the attention of the world public opinion each year to development problems and the necessity of strengthening international cooperation to solve them." Info from: UN Dept of Public Information, United Nations, NY 10017.

ZAMBIA: INDEPENDENCE DAY. Oct 24. Zambia. National holiday, commemorates the Instruments of Independence signed on this day in 1964. Celebrations in all cities, but main parades of military, labor and youth organizations are at capital, Lusaka.

OCTOBER 25 — SATURDAY
298th Day — Remaining, 67

BEAN FEST AND GREAT OUTHOUSE RACE. Oct 25. "Racers vie to see who has the fastest 'privy' in these hills." Music, beans and cornbread. Info from: Chamber of Commerce, Box 133, Mountain View, AR 72560.

CHAMPIONSHIP CAT SHOW. Oct 25-26. Indiana State Fairgrounds, Indianapolis, IN. Exhibition and judging of longhair and shorthair purebred cats and kittens and mixed breed household pets. Sponsor: Indy Cat Club, Cat Fanciers Assn, Maribeth Echard, 8507 N Illinois, Indianapolis, IN 46260.

COMMUNITY LEAGUE FALL FESTIVAL "COUNTRY AFFAIR". Oct 25-26. Country art, craft and antique show. Info from: Community League, Peg Schaus, Box 101, Menominee Falls, WI 53051.

	S	M	T	W	T	F	S
October				1	2	3	4
1986	5	6	7	8	9	10	11
	12	13	14	15	16	17	18
	19	20	21	22	23	24	25
	26	27	28	29	30	31	

CRAFT FAIR USA. Oct 25-26. Wisconsin State Fair Park, Milwaukee, WI. Info from: Dennis R. Hill, Dir, Craft Fair USA, 3233 S Villa Circle, West Allis, WI 53227.

FINGER LAKES CRAFTSMEN CHRISTMAS IN OCTOBER ARTS AND CRAFTS SHOW. Oct 25-26. Monroe County Fairgrounds Dome Arena, Rochester, NY. All media, all categories. Info from: Finger Lakes Craftsmen Shows, 25 Seneca St, Shortsville, NY 14548.

GREAT PUMPKIN FESTIVAL. Oct 25-26. Purpose: Judging of record-breaking pumpkins. Carve or paint a Jack-O-Lantern and see a totem pole of pumpkins. Sponsor: Old Bedford Village, Box 1976, Bedford, PA 15522.

GRENADA INVASION ANNIVERSARY. Oct 25. Some 2,000 U.S. Marines and Army Rangers invaded the Caribbean island of Grenada, taking control after a political coup the previous week had made the island a "Soviet-Cuban colony" according to President Reagan.

HOPKINS, LARRY JONES: BIRTHDAY. Oct 25. U.S. Representative of Kentucky's 6th district, Republican, of Lexington, KY, born in Detroit, MI, on Oct 25, 1933.

KISSIMMEE BOATING JAMBOREE. Oct 25-26. Purpose: A family-oriented pleasure cruise for power boat owners, to introduce boaters to Florida's beautiful and scenic waterways. Sponsor: Kissimmee Boating Jamboree, Box 1855, Kissimmee, FL 32742.

MACAULAY, THOMAS BABINGTON: BIRTHDAY. Oct 25. English essayist and historian, born Oct 25, 1800. Died, Dec 28, 1859. "Nothing," he wrote, "is so useless as a general maxim."

MOON PHASE: LAST QUARTER. Oct 25. Moon enters Last Quarter phase at 5:26 p.m., E.S.T.

NATIONAL HIGHER EDUCATION WEEK. Oct 25-31. Purpose: To focus on contributions of college-educated people to society and to recognize the contributions of higher education to our life and culture. Sponsor: Council for Advancement and Support of Education, Charles M. Helmken, VP, 11 Dupont Circle, NW, Suite 400, Washington, DC 20036.

PEACE, FRIENDSHIP AND GOOD WILL WEEK. Oct 25-31. Purpose: To encourage and foster international understanding, good human relations, friendship, good will and peace throughout the world. Sponsor: Internatl Society of Friendship & Good Will, Dr. Stanley Drake, Pres, Box 756, Shelby, NC 28151.

PICASSO, PABLO RUIZ: BIRTHDAY. Oct 25. Called by many the greatest artist of the 20th century, Pablo Picasso excelled as a painter, sculptor and engraver. He is said to have commented once: "I am only a public entertainer who has understood his time." Born at Malaga, Spain, Oct 25, 1881, Picasso died Apr 8, 1973.

PUMPKIN DAY. Oct 25. Purpose: To enjoy the Arboretum's fall color display. Hayride, haunted barn and pumpkin patch. Sponsor: The Tyler Aboretum, 515 Painter Rd, Lima, PA 19037.

SHEMINI ATZERET. Oct 25. Hebrew calendar date: Tishri 22, 5747. The eighth day of Solemn Assembly, part of the Sukkot Festival (q.v.), with memorial services and cycle of Biblical readings in the synagogue.

SOUREST DAY. Oct 25. Purpose: To emphasize the balance of things in nature. A day for sour (Sauer) people. Sponsor: Richard Ankli, Broadway Fun Spot, 639 Fifth St, Ann Arbor, MI 48103.

TAIWAN: RETROCESSION DAY. Oct 25. Commemorates restoration of Taiwan to Chinese rule, on Oct 25, 1945, after half a century of Japanese occupation.

OCTOBER 26 — SUNDAY
299th Day — Remaining, 66

AUSTRIA: NATIONAL DAY. Oct 26. National holiday observed.

COPYRIGHT © 1985 BY WILLIAM D. CHASE and HELEN M. CHASE

BEILENSON, ANTHONY CHARLES: BIRTHDAY. Oct 26. U.S. Representative of California's 23rd district, Democrat, of Los Angeles, CA, was born in New Rochelle, NY, on Oct 26, 1932.

BIAGGI, MARIO: BIRTHDAY. Oct 26. U.S. Representative of New York's 19th district, Democrat, of Bronx, NY, was born in New York City, Oct 26, 1917.

DR. BLOOD'S PHANTASMAGORIUM OF WAX. Oct 26-31. Wax Museum of the Southwest, Grand Prairie, TX. Purpose: Haunted house of wax. 6 nights of celebration in honor of Halloween. Sponsor: Wax Museum of the Southwest, 601 E Safari Parkway, Grand Prairie, TX 75050.

ERIE CANAL ANNIVERSARY. Oct 26. The Erie Canal, first U.S. man-made major waterway, was opened on Oct 26, 1825, providing a water route from Lake Erie to the Hudson River. Started on July 4, 1817, the canal cost $7,602,000. Cannons fired and celebrations all along the route for the opening.

HANSOM, JOSEPH: BIRTHDAY. Oct 26. English architect and inventor Joseph Aloysius Hansom registered his "Patent Safety Cab" in 1834. The two-wheeled, one-horse, enclosed cab, with driver seated above and behind the passengers, quickly became a familiar and favorite vehicle for public transportation. Hansom was born at York, England, Oct 26, 1803, and died at London, on June 29, 1882.

HORSELESS CARRIAGE DAY. Oct 26. From James Boswell's *Life of Samuel Johnson:* Oct 26, 1769 " . . . we dined together at the Mitre tavern. . . . We went home to his house to tea. . . . There was a pretty large circle this evening. Dr. Johnson was in very good humour, lively, and ready to talk upon all subjects. Mr. Ferguson, the self-taught philosopher, told him of a new-invented machine which went without horses: a man who sat in it turned a handle, which worked a spring that drove it forward. 'Then, Sir (said Johnson), what is gained is, the man has his choice whether he will move himself alone, or himself and the machine too.' "

LAKESIDE HISTORICAL SOCIETY: HOMETOWN REUNION. Oct 26. Info from: Lakeside Historical Society, Shirley Anderson, Box 1886, Lakeside, CA 92040.

LEWIS, TOM: BIRTHDAY. Oct 26. U.S. Representative of Florida's 12th district, Republican, of North Palm Beach, FL, born in Philadelphia, PA, Oct 26, 1924.

MOTHER-IN-LAW'S DAY. Oct 26. Purpose: To honor mothers-in-law for their endless contribution to the success of families and for the good humor they display in suffering all those bad jokes. (Fourth Sunday in October). Sponsor: Florists' Transworld Delivery, Box 2227, Southfield, MI 48037.

MULE DAY. Oct 26. Anniversary of the first importation of Spanish jacks to the U.S., a gift from King Charles III of Spain. Mules are said to have been first bred in this country by George Washington from a pair delivered in Boston on Oct 26, 1785.

NATIONAL MAGIC WEEK. Oct 26-Nov 1. Purpose: To promote brotherly love thorugh magic. Free Magic performances at hospitals and nursing homes. Sponsor: Society of American Magicians, Inc, Anthony D. Murphy, Esq, 11 Angel Rd, North Reading, MA 01864.

OKTOBERFEST. Oct 26. Jensen Beach, FL. Info from: Chamber of Commerce, 1910 NE Commercial St, Jensen Beach, FL 33457.

REFORMATION SUNDAY. Oct 26. Many Protestant churches commemorate Reformation Day (Oct 31—anniversary of the day on which Martin Luther nailed his 95 theses to the door of Wittenberg's Palace church, protesting the sale of papal indulgences, in 1517), on the Sunday preceding Oct 31, each year.

SCARLATTI, DOMENICO: BIRTHDAY. Oct 26. Italian composer, born Oct 26, 1685. Died, July 23, 1757.

SIMCHAT TORAH. Oct 26. Hebrew calendar date: Tishri 23, 5747. Rejoicing in the Torah concludes the nine-day Sukkot Festival (q.v.). Public reading of the Pentateuch is completed and begun again, symbolizing the need for ever-continuing study.

SPACE MILESTONE: SOYUZ 3 (USSR). Oct 26. Launched on Oct 26, 1968. Col. Georgi Beregovoy orbits Earth 64 times, rendezvousing with unmanned Soyuz 2, launched Oct 25, 1968. Both vehicles returned to Earth under ground control.

STANDARD TIME. Oct 26-Apr 26, 1987. Resumes at 2:00 a.m., on the last Sunday in October in each time zone, as provided by Uniform Time Act of 1966. Many use the popular rule, "Spring forward, Fall back," to remember which way to set their clocks. See Apr 27 entry, Daylight Saving Time, for further details.

STENHOLM CHARLES W: BIRTHDAY. Oct 26. U.S. Representative of Texas' 17th district, Democrat, of Avoca, TX, born in Stamford, TX, Oct 26, 1938.

OCTOBER 27 — MONDAY
300th Day — Remaining, 65

GRENADINES: NATIONAL DAY. Oct 27. National holiday observed in Grenadines.

HERSCHLER: ED: BIRTHDAY. Oct 27. Ed Herschler, Governor of Wyoming, Democrat, was born in Lincoln County, WY, on Oct 27, 1918.

NAVY DAY. Oct 27. Observed on this date since 1922.

PAGANINI, NICOLO: BIRTHDAY. Oct 27. Hailed as the greatest violin virtuoso of all time, Paganini was born at Genoa, Italy, Oct 27, 1782. Unusually long arms contributed to his legendary Mephisthophelian appearance—and probably to his unique skills as a performer. His immensely popular concerts brought him great wealth, but his compulsive gambling repeatedly humbled the genius. Paganini died at Nice, France, May 27, 1840.

ROOSEVELT, THEODORE: BIRTHDAY. Oct 27. Theodore Roosevelt, 26th President of the U.S., succeeded to the presidency on the death of William McKinley. His term of office: Sept 14, 1901-Mar 3, 1909. Roosevelt was the first president to ride in an automobile (1902), to submerge in a submarine (1905) and to fly in an airplane (1910). Although his best remembered words quoted "a homely adage which runs, 'Speak softly and carry a big stick,' " he also said: "The first requisite of a good citizen in this Republic of ours is that he shall be able and willing to pull his weight." Born at New York City, Oct 27, 1858, Roosevelt died at Oyster Bay, NY, Jan 6, 1919. His last words: "Put out the light."

SERVETUS, MICHAEL: EXECUTION ANNIVERSARY. Oct 27. Spanish theologian and physician. Servetus was condemned to death on Oct 26, 1553, for blasphemy and burned at the stake at Geneva, Switzerland on Oct 27, 1553. Servetus was born at Tudela, Navarre, Spain in 1511 (exact date unknown).

THOMAS, DYLAN MARLAIS: BIRTHDAY. Oct 27. Welsh poet and playwright, born at Swansea, Oct 27, 1914. Died at New York City, Nov 9, 1953.

WEEK OF SOLIDARITY WITH THE PEOPLE OF NAMIBIA AND ITS LIBERATION MOVEMENT. Oct 27-Nov 3. Proclaimed by the General Assembly of the United Nations in 1976, at the suggestion of the President of Senegal. Info from: United Nations, Dept of Public Information, United Nations, NY 10017.

COPYRIGHT © 1985 BY WILLIAM D. CHASE and HELEN M. CHASE

OCTOBER 28 — TUESDAY

301st Day — Remaining, 64

COOK, JAMES: BIRTHDAY. Oct 28. English sea captain and explorer born Oct 28, 1728. Died Feb 14, 1779.

DICKINSON, ANNA ELIZABETH: BIRTH ANNIVERSARY. Oct 28. Influential American orator and author of the Civil War era was born at Philadelphia, PA, on Oct 28, 1842. As an advocate of abstinence, abolition and woman suffrage, she earned the nickname "American Joan of Arc." She died Oct 22, 1932.

HARVARD UNIVERSITY FOUNDING ANNIVERSARY. Oct 28. Harvard University founded at Cambridge, MA, when, on Oct 28, 1636, the Massachusetts General Court voted to provide 400 pounds for a "schoale or colledge."

NBA DAY IN BASKETBALL CITY, USA. Oct 28. Springfield Civic Center, Springfield, MA. Defending NBA champion will meet another NBA team. Info from: Basketball Hall of Fame, Box 179, 1150 W Columbus Ave, Springfield, MA 01101.

SALK, JONAS: BIRTHDAY. Oct 28. Dr. Jonas Salk, developer of the Salk Polio Vaccine, born at New York City, Oct 28, 1914.

SPACE MILESTONE: INTERNATIONAL SPACE RESCUE AGREEMENT. Oct 28. U.S. and U.S.S.R. officials agreed upon space rescue cooperation. Oct 28, 1970.

STATUE OF LIBERTY: BIRTHDAY. Oct 28. Frederic Auguste Bartholdi's famous sculpture, the statue of "Liberty Enlightening the World," on Bedloe's Island in New York Harbor, was dedicated on Oct 28, 1886. Ground-breaking for the structure was in April, 1883. A sonnet by Emma Lazarus, inside the pedestal of the statue, contains the words: "Give me your tired, your poor, your huddled masses...."

STATUE OF LIBERTY REDEDICATION CEREMONY. Oct 28. Liberty Island, New York, NY. Purpose: To celebrate the Statue of Liberty's 100th birthday. Info from: The Statue of Liberty Ellis Island Foundation, Inc, Hank Nielsen, Dir of Public Affairs, 101 Park Ave, New York, NY 10178.

OCTOBER 29 — WEDNESDAY

302nd Day — Remaining, 63

BOSWELL, JAMES: BIRTHDAY. Oct 29. Scottish biographer, born Edinburgh, Oct 29, 1740. Died, London, May 19, 1795. "I think," he wrote in his monumental biography, the *Life of Samuel Johnson*, "no innocent species of wit or pleasantry should be suppressed; and that a good pun may be admitted among the smaller excellencies of lively conversation."

THE DEADLY SAGA OF THE MAD MINER. Oct 29-31. Tours through the underground mine in a "haunted" fashion. Info from: Reed Gold Mine, Rt 2, Box 101, Stanfield, NC 28163.

EMMETT, DANIEL DECATUR: BIRTHDAY. Oct 29. Creator of words and music for the song "Dixie" which became a fighting song for Confederate troops and unofficial "national anthem" of the South. Emmett was born on Oct 29, 1815 at Mount Vernon, OH where he died on June 28, 1904.

GOEBBELS, PAUL JOSEF: BIRTHDAY. Oct 29. German Nazi leader who became Hitler's minister of propaganda. Originally rejected from the military because of a limp caused by infantile paralysis. Born Oct 29, 1897. Killed himself and his family on May 1, 1945.

HAUNTED HOUSE. Oct 29-31. Klamath Falls, OR. A haunted house for children of all ages. (Always Oct 29-31). Sponsor: Klamath Falls Jaycees. Info from: Visitors & Conv Bureau, 125 N Eighth St, Klamath Falls, OR 97601.

October 1986

S	M	T	W	T	F	S
			1	2	3	4
5	6	7	8	9	10	11
12	13	14	15	16	17	18
19	20	21	22	23	24	25
26	27	28	29	30	31	

MACK, CONNIE 3d: BIRTHDAY. Oct 29. U.S. Representative of Florida's 13th district, Republican, of Cape Coral, FL born in Philadelphia, PA, on Oct 29, 1940.

ORIGINAL OZARK FOLK FESTIVAL. Oct 29-Nov 1. Eureka Springs, AR. Info from: Ozark Folk Festival Board, Box 88, Eureka Springs, AR 72632.

STOCK MARKET COLLAPSE ANNIVERSARY. Oct 29. New York. Prices on the Stock Exchange plummet and virtually collapse, four days after President Herbert Hoover had declared "The fundamental business of the country . . . is on a sound and prosperous basis." More than 16 million shares dumped and billions of dollars lost on Oct 29, 1929. The boom was over and the nation faced nearly a decade of Depression.

TURKEY: NATIONAL HOLIDAY. Oct 29. Anniversary of founding of Republic in 1923.

OCTOBER 30 — THURSDAY

303rd Day — Remaining, 62

ADAMS, JOHN: BIRTHDAY. Oct 30. Second President of the U.S. (term of office: Mar 4, 1797-Mar 3, 1801), had been George Washington's Vice President, and was the father of John Quincy Adams (6th President of the U.S.). Born at Braintree, MA, Oct 30, 1735, once wrote in a letter to Thomas Jefferson: "You and I ought not to die before we have explained ourselves to each other," John Adams and Thomas Jefferson died on the same day, July 4, 1826, the 50th anniversary of adoption of the Declaration of Independence. Adams's last words: "Thomas Jefferson still survives." Jefferson's last words: "Is it the Fourth?"

DARK IN THE PARK. Oct 30-Nov 1. Hibernia, Nottingham and Warwick Parks. Purpose: Ghosts and goblins await visitors on the haunted trails. Refreshments and hayrides. Info from: Chester County Parks & Recreation, 235 W Market St, West Chester, PA 19382.

GERMANY: JAZZFEST BERLIN. Oct 30-Nov 2. Info from: Berliner Festspiele, Budapester Strasse 50, 1 Berlin 30.

HALLOWEEN IN THE VILLAGE. Oct 30. White Pine Village, Ludington, MI. Trick or treat at historic homes in the village and receive traditional treats from the friendly ghosts of those homes. Info from: Mason County Historical Society, Connie Newkirk, 1687 S Lakeshore Dr, Ludington, MI 49431.

LOUISIANA SWINE FESTIVAL. Oct 30-Nov 2. Purpose: To promote the sale and production of pigs. Sponsor: Louisiana Swine Assn, Box 457, Basile, LA 70515.

MONTREAL SKI SHOW. Oct 30-Nov 2. Place Bonaventure, Montreal, Quebec, Canada. Ski equipment, fashions, resorts and travel, films, demonstrations on cross-country and alpine skiing. Info from: Canadian Natl Sportsmen's Shows, 1155 Metcalfe St, Montreal, Quebec, Canada H3B 2V6.

POUND, EZRA LOOMIS: BIRTHDAY. Oct 30. American poet born at Hailey, ID, Oct 30, 1885. As result of his pro-Fascist radio broadcasts from Italy, Pound was indicted for treason July 26, 1943, arrested near Genoa, May 5, 1945, by U.S. Army, confined to St. Elizabeth's Hospital, Washington, DC, 1946-1958 as being mentally unable to stand trial. Never tried for treason. Died in Italy, Nov 1, 1972.

RECREATIONAL VEHICLE, BOAT AND MOBILE HOME SHOW. Oct 30-Nov 2. Cashman Field Ctr, Las Vegas, NV. Info from: Dixie Green Promotions, Inc, 3141 W Christy Dr, Phoenix, AZ 85029.

SAVAGE, GUS: BIRTHDAY. Oct 30. U.S. Representative of Illinois' 2nd district, Democrat, of Chicago, IL, born at Detroit, MI, on Oct 30, 1925.

SHERIDAN, RICHARD BRINSLEY: BIRTHDAY. Oct 30. Dramatist, born Dublin, Ireland, Oct 30, 1751. Died, London, July 7, 1816. Sheridan is said to have extended the following invitation to a young lady: "Won't you come into the garden? I would like my roses to see you."

SISLEY, ALFRED: BIRTHDAY. Oct 30. French impressionist painter, born at Paris, Oct 30, 1839. One of the most influential artists of his time, he died near Fontainbleau, Jan 29, 1899.

COPYRIGHT © 1985 BY WILLIAM D. CHASE and HELEN M. CHASE

VOLUSIA COUNTY FAIR AND YOUTH SHOW. Oct 30-Nov 9. Fairgrounds, Deland, FL. Info from: Chamber of Commerce, Box 629, DeLand, FL 32721.

"WAR OF THE WORLDS" BROADCAST ANNIVERSARY. Oct 30. On Oct 30, 1938, as part of a series of radio dramas based on famous novels, Orson Welles (born Kenosha, WI, May 6, 1915) with the Mercury Players produced H.G. Wells's *War of the Worlds*. Near panic resulted when listeners believed the simulated news bulletins, which described a Martian invasion of New Jersey, to be real.

WILLIAMS, PATRICK: BIRTHDAY. Oct 30. U.S. Representative of Montana's 1st district, Democrat, of Helena, MT, born in Helena, on Oct 30, 1937.

WILLIAMS, TED: BIRTHDAY. Oct 30. American baseball player was born at San Diego, CA, on Oct 30, 1918. Named the American League's Most Valuable Player in 1946 and 1949. Playing for the Boston Red Sox, Williams led the entire American League in batting average, home runs and runs batted in, in 1942 and 1947. Inducted into the Baseball Hall of Fame in 1966.

OCTOBER 31 — FRIDAY
304th Day — Remaining, 61

CHIANG KAI-SHEK: BIRTH ANNIVERSARY. Oct 31. Chinese soldier and statesman, was born at Chekiang, on Oct 31, 1887. He died at Taipei, Taiwan, on Apr 5, 1975.

GREAT GULFCOAST ARTS FESTIVAL. Oct 31-Nov 2. Pensacola, FL. (First full weekend in November.) Info from: Dian Magie, Exec Dir, Arts Council of Northwest Florida, Box 731, Pensacola, FL 32594.

HALLOWEEN or ALL HALLOW'S EVE. Oct 31. Ancient celebration combining Druid autumn festival and Christian customs. Christian feast dates from the seventh century.

HERITAGE EXHIBIT. Oct 31-Nov 9. New Braunfels, TX. Purpose: To illustrate life, activities and events of local community around turn of the century with museum-like exhibits. Sponsor: Chamber of Commerce, Box 180, New Braunfels, TX 78130.

HOUDINI, HARRY: DEATH ANNIVERSARY. Oct 31. Harry Houdini (whose real name was Ehrich Weisz), magician, illusionist and escape artist, died of peritonitis following a blow to the abdomen, at 10:30 p.m., 1926, at Grace Hospital, Detroit, MI. Last words reported to have been "Robert Ingersoll," name of famed agnostic. Houdini's death anniversary, on Halloween, is occasion for meetings of magicians. See also birthday entry, Mar 24.

INCREASE YOUR PSYCHIC POWERS DAY. Oct 31. Purpose: Halloween is selected as a day to enhance the psychic ability and E.S.P. that is latent in all of us. Sponsor: Barbara Donchess, Astrologer, 5 South St, Canton, MA 02021.

KEATS, JOHN: BIRTH ANNIVERSARY. Oct 31. One of England's greatest poets, born at London on Oct 31, 1795 and died (of consumption) at the age of 25, at Rome, on Feb 23, 1821. Keats wrote, to Fanny Brawne (in 1820): "If I should die . . . I have left no immortal work behind me—nothing to make my friends proud of my memory—but I have loved the principle of beauty in all things, and if I had had time I would have made myself remembered."

LOUISIANA PECAN FESTIVAL. Oct 31-Nov 1. Purpose: To promote the pecan industry in Grant Parish and Louisiana. Sponsor: Louisiana Pecan Festival, Inc, Box 78, Colfax, LA 71417.

LOW, JULIETTE GORDON: BIRTHDAY. Oct 31. Founded Girl Scouts of the USA March 12, 1912, in Savannah, GA. Oct 31, 1860-Jan 17, 1927.

NATIONAL MAGIC DAY. Oct 31. Traditionally observed on anniversary of death of Harry Houdini in 1926.

NATIONAL UNICEF DAY. Oct 31. Presidential Proclamation. ☆ "Proc. 3817, Oct 27, 1967, covers all succeeding years."

NEVADA: ADMISSION DAY. Oct 31. Became 36th State on this day in 1864.

REFORMATION DAY. Oct 31. Anniversary of the day on which Martin Luther nailed his 95 theses to the door of Wittenberg's Palace church, denouncing the selling of papal indulgences, on Oct 31, 1517—the beginning of the Reformation in Germany. Observed by many Protestant churches on Reformation Sunday, the Sunday before Oct 31, each year.

SLEIDANUS, JOHANNES: DEATH ANNIVERSARY. Oct 31. German historian, born at Schleiden in 1506, died at Strasbourg, Oct 31, 1556. His *Famous Chronicle of Oure Time*, called *Sleidanes Comentaries*, was first translated into English in 1560. The translator spoke thus to the book: "Go forth my painful Boke, Thou art no longer mine. Eche man may on the loke, The Shame or praise is thine."

SWAN, JOSEPH WILSON: BIRTHDAY. Oct 31. English scientist and inventor born at Sunderland, Durham, England, Oct 31, 1828. Pioneer in photographic chemistry, incandescent electric lamp, and man-made fibres. Died at Warlingham, Surrey, England, May 27, 1914.

TAIWAN: CHIANG KAI-SHEK BIRTHDAY. Oct 31. National holiday to honor memory of Generalissimo Chiang Kai-Shek, born Oct 31, 1887, the first constitutional president of the Republic of China.

TENNESSEE FALL CRAFTS FAIR. Oct 31-Nov 2. State Fairgrounds, Nashville, TN. Craft sales by 120 selected craftspeople representing the highest quality of American crafts. Sponsor: Tennessee Artist-Craftsmen's Assn, Box 120066, Nashville, TN 37212.

TRICK OR TREAT or BEGGAR'S NIGHT. Oct 31.

WESTVILLE FAIR OF 1850. Oct 31-Nov 9. Demonstrations of early Georgia crafts. Special fall activities include cane grinding and cotton ginned by mule power. Info from: Westville, Box 1850, Lumpkin, GA 31815.

WILL ROGERS DAYS. Oct 31-Nov 4. Purpose: A birthday celebration to commemorate Will Rogers' birth. Birthday party, parade, auction and country fare. Info from: Will Rogers Memorial, Dr. Reba Collins, Box 157, Claremore, OK 74018.

WURSTFEST. Oct 31-Nov 9. New Braunfels, TX. Purpose: Celebration of local German heritage through festival featuring sausage. Sponsor: Wurstfest Assn of New Braunfels, Publicity and Promotion, Box 180, New Braunfels, TX 78130.

YOUTH HONOR DAY. Oct 31. Iowa and Massachusetts.

Nouember.

NOVEMBER 1 — SATURDAY
305th Day — Remaining, 60

ALGERIA: NATIONAL HOLIDAY. Nov 1. Anniversary of the Revolution.

ALL-HALLOMAS or ALL HALLOWS or ALL SAINTS DAY. Nov 1. Roman Catholic holy day of obligation. Commemorates the blessed especially those who have no special feast days. Observed on Nov 1st since Pope Gregory IV set the date of recognition in 835.

ANTIGUA AND BARBUDA: NATIONAL HOLIDAY. Nov 1.

AUTUMN HISTORIC FOLKLIFE FESTIVAL. Nov 1-2. Mark Twain Historic District, Hannibal, MO. Purpose: A showcase of authentic crafts, foods, music, performing arts and culture pertaining to Missouri's heritage. Info from: Hannibal Visitors Bureau, Box 624, Hannibal, MO 63401.

AVIATION HISTORY MONTH. Nov 1-30. Anniversary of aeronautical experiments in Nov, 1782 (exact dates unknown), by Joseph Michel Montgolfier and Jacques Etienne Montgolfier, brothers living at Annonay, France. Inspired by Joseph Priestly's book, *Experiments Relating to the Different Kinds of Air,* the brothers experimented with filling paper and fabric bags with smoke and hot air, leading to the invention of the hot air balloon, man's first flight, and the entire science of aviation and flight.

DIA DE LOS MUERTOS CELEBRATION. Nov 1. A day set aside to celebrate the memory of the dead and remind everyone that our spirits will always live through joyous memories. Info from: El Pueblo de Los Angeles State Historic Park, 845 N Alameda St, Los Angeles, CA 90012.

DRAYTON HALL ARTS AND CRAFTS FAIR. Nov 1-2. Charleston, SC. Juried fine arts and crafts show and entertainment. Info from: William Fudge, Rt 4, Hwy 61, Charleston, SC 29407.

GOOD NUTRITION MONTH (A VOTRE SANTE). Nov 1-30. Purpose: To make America conscious of the wonderful foods available in the USA and how to use them wisely and well. Sponsor: Gourmet Adventures Club and Mme Ginette's Cordon Bleu Ouest French Cooking School, 3369 Hamilton Way, Los Angeles, CA 90026.

GREENBO CHALLENGE 5K ROAD RACE. Nov 1. Greenbo Lake State Resort Park, Greenup, KY. Info from: Kentucky Dept of Parks, Capital Plaza Tower, Frankfort, KY 40601.

November 1986

S	M	T	W	T	F	S
						1
2	3	4	5	6	7	8
9	10	11	12	13	14	15
16	17	18	19	20	21	22
23	24	25	26	27	28	29
30						

HALIFAX ART FESTIVAL. Nov 1-2. The Ormond Hotel, Ormond Beach, FL. Sponsor: Museum of Arts & Sciences Guild, Box 504, Ormond Beach, FL 32074.

INTERNATIONAL CREATIVE CHILD AND ADULT MONTH. Nov 1-30. Purpose: To help the public create an environment which will cherish and positively reinforce creative contributions of the gifted and talented in music, art, writing, science and business and to help all individuals realize creative problem solving in everyday situations improves the quality of life. Sponsor: The Natl Assn for Creative Children & Adults, Ann F. Isaacs, 8080 Springvalley Dr, Cincinnati, OH 45236.

LIBERTY DAY. Nov 1. Virgin Islands. Officially "D. Hamilton Jackson Memorial Day," commemorating establishment of the first press in Virgin Islands, in 1915.

LONGWOOD GARDENS CHRYSANTHEMUM FESTIVAL. Nov 1-23. Fifteen thousand mums indoors in the conservatories, musical programs, arts and crafts. Info from: Longwood Gardens, Kennett Square, PA 19348.

MAVROULES, NICHOLAS: BIRTHDAY. Nov 1. U.S. Representative of Massachusetts' 6th district, Democrat, of Peabody, MA, born in Peabody on Nov 1, 1929.

MEXICO: DAY OF THE DEAD. Nov 1-2. Observance begins during last days of October when "Dead Men's Bread" is sold in bakeries—round loaves, decorated with sugar skulls. Departed souls are remembered not with mourning but with spirit of friendliness and good humor. Cemeteries are visited and graves decorated.

MILLER, CLARENCE E: BIRTHDAY. Nov 1. U.S. Representative of Ohio's 10th district, Republican, of Lancaster, OH, born in Lancaster on Nov 1, 1917.

MISSION SAN JUAN CAPISTRANO FOUNDING ANNIVERSARY. Nov 1. California mission founded Nov 1, 1776, collapsed during 1812 earthquake. The swallows of Capistrano nest in ruins of the old mission church, departing each year on Oct 23, and returning the following year on or near St. Joseph's Day (Mar 19).

NATIONAL ASSOCIATION FOR GIFTED CHILDREN: ANNUAL CONVENTION. Nov 1-6. Denver, CO. Purpose: To share the variety of ways of nurturing giftedness and learn about new approaches. Sponsor: Natl Assn for Gifted Children, 5100 N Edgewood Dr, St Paul, MN 55112.

NATIONAL AUTHORS' DAY. Nov 1. Purpose: To show patriotism, loyalty and appreciation of the men and women who have made American literature possible and encourage and inspire others to give of themselves in making a better America. Founder: Nellie Verne Burt McPherson. Info from: Mrs Sue Cole, 191 W Cole St, Macon, IL 62544.

NATIONAL DIABETES MONTH. Nov 1-30. Purpose: To increase public concern for diabetes and its serious complications, which kill more Americans than all other diseases except cancer and cardiovascular problems. Special activities aimed at prevention and control of diabetes. Sponsor: American Diabetes Assn, Two Park Ave, New York, NY 10016.

NATIONAL EPILEPSY MONTH. Nov 1-30. Purpose: To increase understanding of epilepsy and public awareness of the fact that most people with the disorder can lead normal healthy lives. Sponsor: Epilepsy Foundation of America, Ann Scherer, Dir, Public Health Ed & Info, 4351 Garden City Dr, Landover, MD 20785.

NATIONAL STAMP COLLECTING MONTH. Nov 1-30. Purpose: To promote stamp collecting as a hobby, for recreation, education, therapy and financial advantage. Sponsor: The Philatelic Journalist, 154 Laguna Ct, St. Augustine Shores, FL 32086.

NORTHERN ILLINOIS EGG SHOW. Nov 1-2. Rochelle, IL. Purpose: "Eggers" from many states get together to show and share ideas and sell decorated eggs. Info from: Ruth Burhenn, Reynolds Rd, Box 52, Ashton, IL 61006.

COPYRIGHT © 1985 BY WILLIAM D. CHASE and HELEN M. CHASE

ONE NATION UNDER GOD MONTH. Nov 1-30. Purpose: To encourage the American people to protect and strengthen the concepts of individual moral responsibility and dependence on God. Sponsor: The Natl Exchange Club, James A. Schnoering, Exec VP, 3050 Central Ave, Toledo, OH 43606.

SADIE HAWKINS DAY. Nov 1. (First Saturday, or other day in November). Tradition established in "Li'l Abner" comic strip in 1930s by cartoonist Al Capp. Widely observed in U.S., usually on a Saturday in November. Popularly an occasion when women and girls are encouraged to take the initiative in inviting the man of their choice for a date.

SOUTH MIAMI ART SHOW. Nov 1-2. Purpose: To give artists an opportunity to show and sell their work and give the public an awareness of current trends in visual arts. Sponsor: Chamber of Commerce, Box 430585, South Miami, FL 33243.

SPRATT, JOHN M, JR: BIRTHDAY. Nov 1. U.S. Representative of South Carolina's 5th district, Democrat, of York, SC, born in Charlotte, NC, on Nov 1, 1942.

WASHINGTON'S REVIEW OF THE TROOPS. Nov 1. Colonial regiments reenact George Washington's 1798 military review at Gadsby's Tavern. Info from: Alexandria Tourist Council, 221 King St, Alexandria, VA 22314.

NOVEMBER 2 — SUNDAY
306th Day — Remaining, 59

ALL-SOULS DAY. Nov 2. Commemorates the faithful departed. Catholic observance.

BOONE, DANIEL: BIRTHDAY. Nov 2. American frontiersman, explorer and militia officer, born in Berks County, near Reading, PA, on Nov 2, 1734 (New Style). In Feb, 1778, he was captured at Blue Licks, KY, by Shawnee Indians, under Chief Blackfish, whose adopted son he became when inducted into the tribe as "Big Turtle." Boone escaped after five months, and in 1781 was captured briefly by the British. He experienced a series of personal and financial disasters during his life, but continued a rugged existence, hunting until in his eighties. Boone died at St. Charles County, MO, Sept 26, 1820. The bodies of Daniel Boone and his wife, Rebecca, were moved to Frankfort, KY, in 1845.

BRENNAN, JOSEPH E: BIRTHDAY. Nov 2. Joseph E. Brennan, Governor of Maine, Democrat, was born in Portland, ME, on Nov 2, 1934.

ENGLAND: RAC LONDON TO BRIGHTON VETERAN CAR RUN. Nov 2. Purpose: A run for maximum of 330 veteran cars, along the A23 road from Serpentine Row, Hyde Park, London, to Madiera Drive, Brighton, England. Celebrates emancipation —the abolition of a man walking in front of motor vehicles, in the UK, carrying a red flag. Always the first Sunday in November. Organizers: RAC Motor Sports Assn. Ltd, Martin Whitaker, 31 Belgrave Square, London, SW1X 8QH, England.

FRENCH CONVERSATION WEEK. Nov 2-8. Purpose: For L'Amitie Universelle (Universal Friendship). To encourage the learning or use of French—the language of our neighbor Quebec province, Canada and much of Louisiana. Sponsor: French Conversation Club of Hollywood and la Ville de St. Affrique, Tarn, France. Celebrate LeReveillon! Info from: Mme Marguerite Ginette, 3369 Hamilton Way, Los Angeles, CA 90026.

HARDING, WARREN GAMALIEL: BIRTHDAY. Nov 2. The 29th President of the U.S., and the first to have a radio, was born at Corsica, OH, Nov 2, 1865. His term of office: Mar 4, 1921-Aug 2, 1923 (died in office). His undistinguished administration was tainted by the "Teapot Dome Scandal," and his sudden death, while on a western speaking tour (San Francisco, CA, Aug 2, 1923) prompted many dark rumors. In 1927, a book, *The President's Daughter*, by Nan Britton, and dedicated "to all unwedded mothers, and to their innocent children whose fathers are usually not known to the world," added doubts about morality in high political places.

KEY CLUB INTERNATIONAL WEEK. Nov 2-8. Purpose: To recognize service projects of over 110,000 school members to their homes, schools and communities. Sponsor: Key Club Internatl, 3636 Woodview Trace, Indianapolis, IN 46268.

MAZZOLI, ROMANO L: BIRTHDAY. Nov 2. U.S. Representative of Kentucky's 3rd district, Democrat, of Louisville, KY, born in Louisville, Jefferson County, KY, on Nov 2, 1932.

MOON PHASE: NEW MOON. Nov 2. Moon enters New Moon phase at 1:02 a.m., E.S.T.

NATIONAL CARD AND LETTER WRITING WEEK. Nov 2-8. Purpose: National Card and Letter Writing Week reminds Americans everywhere of the crucial role letters and letter-writing play in binding our great nation together. Sponsor: U.S. Postal Service, Director, Media Relations, U.S. Postal Service Hqs, Washington, DC 20260.

NATIONAL MICROWAVE COOKING WEEK. Nov 2-8. Purpose: To salute America's new way of cooking and celebrate easy living, made possible because of the speed and convenience of microwave cooking. Sponsor: Nordic Ware Microwave Products. Info from: S. J. Thoms, Marketing/Communications Consultant, 3329 St. Paul Ave, Minneapolis, MN 55416.

NATIONAL NOTARY PUBLIC WEEK. Nov 2-8. Purpose: To recognize the fundamental contributions made by notaries to the law and the people of the U.S. (The week that contains Nov 7.) Sponsor: American Society of Notaries, Eugene E. Hines, Exec Dir, 918 16th St, NW, Washington, DC 20006.

NORTH DAKOTA: ADMISSION DAY. Nov 2. Became 39th State on this day in 1889.

POLK, JAMES KNOX: BIRTHDAY. Nov 2. The eleventh President of the U.S. was born at Mecklenburg County, NC, Nov 2, 1795. His term of office: Mar 4, 1845-Mar 3, 1849. A compromise candidate at the 1844 Democratic Party convention, Polk was awarded the nomination on the ninth ballot. He declined to be a candidate for a second term, and declared himself to be "exceedingly relieved" at the completion of his presidency. He died shortly after at Nashville, TN, June 15, 1849.

SOUTH DAKOTA: ADMISSION DAY. Nov 2. Became 40th State on this day in 1889.

SPRUCE GOOSE FLIGHT: ANNIVERSARY. Nov 2. "Howard Hughes' mammoth flying boat, fondly called the Spruce Goose, made its only flight on Nov 2, 1947 when Howard Hughes brought the airplane 70 feet above the choppy waters of Long Beach Harbor for approximately one mile. The 200-ton Spruce Goose is currently berthed in the world's largest clear-span aluminum dome in Long Beach." Info from: Wrather Port Properties, LTD, Kelli M. Fast, PR Coordinator, Box 8, Long Beach, CA 90801.

WOLPE, HOWARD E: BIRTHDAY. Nov 2. U.S. Representative of Michigan's 3rd district, Democrat, of Lansing, MI, was born in Los Angeles, CA, on Nov 2, 1939.

NOVEMBER 3 — MONDAY
307th Day — Remaining, 58

AMERICAN MUSIC WEEK. Nov 3-9. Purpose: Celebration of all kinds of American music—blues, jazz, experimental, traditional and classical presented through symphonic, chamber and staged events. Sponsor: American Music Center, Robin Kirck, 250 W 54th St, Suite 300, New York, NY 10019.

BRYANT, WILLIAM CULLEN: BIRTHDAY. Nov 3. American poet born Cummington, MA, Nov 3, 1794. Died, New York City, June 12, 1878.

CRANE, PHILIP M: BIRTHDAY. Nov 3. U.S. Representative of Illinois' 12th district, Republican, of Mount Prospect, IL, was born at Chicago, IL, Nov 3, 1930.

CULTURE DAY. Nov 3. Japan. (National holiday.)

DOMINICA: NATIONAL HOLIDAY. Nov 3.

COPYRIGHT © 1985 BY WILLIAM D. CHASE and HELEN M. CHASE

DUKAKIS, MICHAEL S: BIRTHDAY. Nov 3. Michael S. Dukakis, Governor of Massachusetts, Democrat, was born at Brookline, MA, on Nov 3, 1933.

LONG, RUSSELL B: BIRTHDAY. Nov 3. U.S. Senator from Louisiana, Democrat, of Baton Rouge, LA, born in Shreveport, LA, Nov 3, 1918.

MANTON, THOMAS JOSEPH: BIRTHDAY. Nov 3. U.S. Representative of New York's 9th district, Democrat, of Queens, NY, born in Manhattan, New York City on Nov 3, 1932.

NATIONAL MEDICAL ASSISTANTS WEEK. Nov 3-7. Purpose: To call attention to the contribution made by the nation's medical assistants. Sponsor: American Assn of Medical Assistants, Inc, 20 N Wacker Dr, Chicago, IL 60606.

NATIONAL RADIOLOGIC TECHNOLOGY WEEK. Nov 3-9. Purpose: To increase public awareness of the health professionals who utilize medical radiation and diagnostic imaging techniques to aid in the diagnosis and treatment of disease. Sponsor: American Society of Radiologic Technologists, 15000 Central Ave SE, Albuquerque, NM 87123.

PANAMA: NATIONAL HOLIDAY. Nov 3. Independence Day. Panama declared itself independent of Colombia on this day, 1903.

RECREATION DAY. Nov 3. Australia. Monday, Nov 3, 1986, is observed as Recreation Day in Northern Tasmania.

SANDWICH DAY. Nov 3. A day to recognize the inventor of the sandwich, John Montague, Fourth Earl of Sandwich, who was born Nov 3, 1718. England's First Lord of the Admiralty, Secretary of State for the northern Department, Postmaster General, the man after whom Capt Cook named the Sandwich Islands in 1778. A rake and a gambler, he is said to have invented the sandwich as a time-saving nourishment while he was engaged in a 24-hour-long gambling session in 1762. He died at London, Apr 30, 1792.

SPACE MILESTONE: SPUTNIK 2 (USSR). Nov 3. Dog, Laika, first animal projected by man into space. Radiation measurements. 1,121 lbs. Nov 3, 1957.

WORLD CHAMPIONSHIP APPALOOSA HORSE SHOW. Nov 3-9. Purpose: To show a thousand of "world's finest" Appaloosa horses from U.S. and Canada. Horses exhibited in fifty different classes of competition. Info from: Steve Collier, 1 Santa Fe Plaza, Oklahoma City, OK 73102.

NOVEMBER 4 — TUESDAY
308th Day — Remaining, 57

GENERAL ELECTION DAY: U.S. Nov 4. Always the first Tuesday after the first Monday in November. Observed in years of presidential and general elections.

MELBOURNE CUP DAY: MELBOURNE, AUSTRALIA. Nov 4. Info from: Australian Information Service, 1601 Massachusetts Ave NW, Washington, DC 20036.

MISCHIEF NIGHT. Nov 4. Observed in England, Australia and New Zealand. Nov 4, the eve of Guy Fawkes Day (q.v.) is occasion for bonfires and firecrackers to commemorate failure of the plot to blow up the House of Parliament, Nov 5, 1605.

PANAMA: FLAG DAY. Nov 4. Public holiday in Panama.

PHILLPOTTS, EDEN: BIRTH ANNIVERSARY. Nov 4. English novelist, poet and playwright, born in India on Nov 4, 1862. A friend of Arnold Bennett, Phillpotts wrote more than a hundred novels. He died near Exeter, England, on Dec 29, 1960.

November
1986

S	M	T	W	T	F	S
						1
2	3	4	5	6	7	8
9	10	11	12	13	14	15
16	17	18	19	20	21	22
23	24	25	26	27	28	29
30						

ROGERS, WILL: BIRTHDAY. Nov 4. William Penn Adair Rogers, American writer, actor, humorist and grass-roots philosopher, born at Oologah, Indian Territory (now Oklahoma), Nov 4, 1879. With aviator Wiley Post, he was killed in an airplane crash near Point Barrow, AK; Aug 15, 1935. "My forefathers," he said, "didn't come over on the *Mayflower*, but they met the boat."

ROGERS, WILL: DAY. Nov 4. Oklahoma.

SEIZURE OF U.S. EMBASSY, TEHERAN: ANNIVERSARY. Nov 4. On Nov 4, 1979, about 500 Iranian "students" seized the U.S. Embassy in Teheran, taking about 90 hostages, of whom about 60 were Americans. They vowed to hold the hostages until the former Shah, Mohammed Riza Pahlevi (in the U.S. for medical treatments) was returned to Iran for trial. The Shah died July 27, 1980, in an Egyptian military hospital near Cairo. The remaining 52 American hostages were released and left Teheran on Jan 20, 1981, after 444 days of captivity. The release occurred on America's Presidential Inauguration Day, and during the hour in which the American Presidency was transferred from Jimmy Carter to Ronald Reagan.

NOVEMBER 5 — WEDNESDAY
309th Day — Remaining, 56

DEBS, EUGENE VICTOR: BIRTHDAY. Nov 5. American politician, first president of the American Railway Union, founder of the Social Democratic Party of America, and Socialist Party candidate for President of the U.S. in 1904, 1908, 1912 and 1920, sentenced to 10-year prison term in 1918 (for sedition) and pardoned by Pres. Harding in 1921. Debs was born at Terre Haute, IN, Nov 5, 1855, and died at Elmhurst, IL, Oct 20, 1926.

DURANT, WILL: BIRTHDAY. Nov 5. American author and popularizer of history and philosophy. Among his books: *The Story of Philosophy* and *The Story of Civilization* (a 10-volume series of which the last four were co-authored by his wife, Ariel). Born at North Adams, MA, on Nov 5, 1885.

GUY FAWKES DAY. Nov 5. United Kingdom. Anniversary of the "Gunpowder Plot." Conspirators planned to blow up the Houses of Parliament and King James I, on Nov 5, 1605. Twenty barrels of gunpowder which they had secreted in a cellar under parliament were discovered on the night of Nov 4-5, the very eve of the intended explosion, and the conspirators were arrested. They were tried and convicted, and on Jan 31, 1606, eight survivors (including Guy Fawkes) were beheaded and their heads displayed on pikes at London Bridge. Though there were at least eleven conspirators, Guy Fawkes is most remembered. In 1606, the parliament which was to have been annihilated enacted a law establishing Nov 5 as a day of public thanksgiving. It is still observed, and on the night of Nov 5, "the whole country lights up with bonfires and celebration." "Guys" are burned in effigy; and the old verses repeated: "Remember, remember the fifth of November,/Gunpowder treason and plot;/I see no reason why Gunpowder Treason/Should ever be forgot."

KUWAIT: ARABIC BOOK EXHIBITION. Nov 5-14. Kuwait. Info from: Kuwait Internatl Fair, PO Box 656, Safat Kuwait.

NEW YORK WEEKLY JOURNAL: FIRST ISSUE ANNIVERSARY. Nov 5. John Peter Zenger, colonial American printer and journalist, published the first issue of the *New York Weekly Journal* newspaper on Nov 5, 1733. He was arrested and imprisoned on Nov 17, 1734 (q.v.) for libel. The trial remains an important landmark in the history of the struggle for freedom of the press.

NORTHERN IRELAND: INTERNATIONAL PLOUGHING CHAMPIONSHIPS. Nov 5-6. Info from Northern Ireland Ploughing Assn, 475 Antrim Road, Belfast BT15 3DA.

TARBELL, IDA M: BIRTHDAY. Nov 5. American writer, editor and historian, born Nov 5, 1857. Died Jan 6, 1944.

COPYRIGHT © 1985 BY WILLIAM D. CHASE and HELEN M. CHASE

VOLLEYBALL: HIGH SCHOOL GIRLS PROVINCIAL CHAMPIONSHIPS. Nov 5. Vancouver, BC, Canada. Girls AA volleyball championships. Info from: Vancouver Centennial Commission, Box 49386, Bentall 4, 1055 Dunsmuir St, Vancouver, BC V7X 1L5.

NOVEMBER 6 — THURSDAY
310th Day — Remaining, 55

BRAWLEY CATTLE CALL. Nov 6-9. Purpose: A celebration saluting the cattle industry. Bluegrass, pit barbeques, parade and rodeo performances. Sponsor: Chamber of Commerce, Box 218, Brawley, CA 92227.

GUSTAVAS ADOLPHUS DAY. Nov 6. Honors Sweden's military leader killed in 1632.

HALFWAY POINT OF AUTUMN. Nov 6. In northern hemisphere the midpoint of the Autumn season occurs on Nov 6 at 8:58 p.m., E.S.T. Autumn lasts 90 days and 3 hours and 57 minutes this year.

MRAZEK, ROBERT J: BIRTHDAY. Nov 6. U.S. Representative of New York's 3rd district, Democrat, of Huntington, NY, born at Newport, RI, on Nov 6, 1945.

NAISMITH, JAMES: BIRTHDAY. Nov 6. Inventor of the game of basketball was born at Almonte, Ontario, Nov 6, 1861. Died, Lawrence, KS, Nov 28, 1939. Basketball became an Olympic sport in 1936.

PADEREWSKI, IGNACE JAN: BIRTHDAY. Nov 6. Polish composer, pianist, patriot born at Kurylowka, Podolia, Nov 6, 1860. He died at New York City, June 29, 1941.

RETURN DAY. Nov 6. Georgetown, DE. The day when officially tabulated election returns are read from the balcony of Georgetown's red brick, Greek Revival courthouse to the throngs of voters assembled below. Always the second day after a general election. An official "half-holiday" in Sussex County. Reportedly Return Day has become so popular "that it is for all intents and purposes a state holiday as well."

RICHARD NIXON'S "LAST" PRESS CONFERENCE: ANNIVERSARY. Nov 6. After defeat in his campaign for election as Governor of California, Richard M. Nixon (later a President of the U.S., and the first to resign that office) told the press (on Nov 6, 1962): "You won't have Dick Nixon to kick around any more."

SAMPSON COUNTY EXPO. Nov 6. Purpose: To promote products and services in Sampson County and provide entertainment, good food and information. Sponsor: Chamber of Commerce, Box 467, Clinton, NC 28328.

SAXOPHONE DAY. Nov 6. A day to recognize the birth anniversary of Adolphe Sax, Belgian musician and inventor of the saxophone and the saxotromba. Born at Dinant, Belgium on Nov 6, 1814, Antoine Joseph Sax, later known as Adolphe, was the eldest of eleven children of a musical instrument builder. Sax contributed an entire family of brass wind instruments to band and orchestra use. He was accorded fame and great wealth but business misfortunes led to bankruptcy. Sax died in poverty at Paris on Feb 7, 1894.

SOUSA, JOHN PHILIP: BIRTHDAY. Nov 6. American composer and band conductor, remembered for many stirring marches such as "Stars and Stripes Forever," "Semper Fidelis," "El Capitan," etc, born at Washington, DC, Nov 6, 1854. Died at Reading, PA, Mar 6, 1932. See also: May 14.

NOVEMBER 7 — FRIDAY
311th Day — Remaining, 54

BOSCHWITZ, RUDY: BIRTHDAY. Nov 7. U.S. Senator from Minnesota, Independent-Republican, of Plymouth, MN, born in Berlin, Germany, Nov 7, 1930.

CAMUS, ALBERT: BIRTHDAY. Nov 7. French writer and philosopher, winner of the Nobel Prize for Literature in 1957, was born at Mondavi, Algeria, Nov 7, 1913. "The struggle to reach the top is itself enough to fulfill the heart of man. One must believe that Sisyphus is happy," he wrote, in *Le Mythe de Sisyphe.* Camus was killed in an automobile accident in France, Jan 4, 1960.

CURIE, MARIE SKLODOWSKA: BIRTHDAY. Nov 7. Polish chemist and physicist, born Warsaw, Nov 7, 1867. Died, July 4, 1934.

FESTIVAL OF THE MASTERS. Nov 7-9. Walt Disney World Village, Lake Buena Vista, FL. Purpose: Juried show involving more than 200 award-winning artists and craftsmen from throughout the U.S. Sponsor: Walt Disney World, Village Special Events, Box 35, Lake Buena Vista, FL 32830.

FOUR CORNER STATES BLUEGRASS FESTIVAL IN WICKENBURG. Nov 7-9. Purpose: Old time fiddle, banjo, mandolin, flat-pick guitar championships. Square dancing, clogging, gospel music, arts and crafts. Sponsor: Chamber of Commerce, Drawer CC, Wickenburg, AZ 85358.

MISTLETOE SHOW. Nov 7-9. Knobbs Creek Recreation Ctr, Elizabeth City, NC. Christmas crafts galore for the tree and home, created by coastal craftsmen. Info from: Elizabeth City Jr Woman's Club, Box 1521, Elizabeth City, NC 27909.

NATIONAL FARM TOY COLLECTOR'S SHOW. Nov 7-9. Beckman High School, Dyersville, IA. Purpose: To display and sell farm toy replicas. Sponsor: The Toy Farmer, Mr. Claire Scheibe, LaMoure, ND 58458.

NATIONAL NOTARY PUBLIC DAY. Nov 7. Purpose: To recognize the fundamental contributions made by notaries to the law and the people of the U.S. (Annually, November 7th.) Sponsor: American Society of Notaries, Eugene E. Hines, Exec Dir, 810 18th St, NW, Washington, DC 20006.

NEAL, STEPHEN L: BIRTHDAY. Nov 7, 1934. U.S. Representative of North Carolina's 5th district, Democrat, of Winston-Salem, NC, born in Winston-Salem, on Nov 7, 1934.

OLD STOUGHTON MUSICAL SOCIETY: 200TH ANNIVERSARY. Nov 7-8. Purpose: To commemorate the anniversary of the "oldest choral society in the United States." Organized on November 7, 1786. Focus on music by New England Composers. Sponsor: Old Stoughton Musical Society, Box 794, Stoughton, MA 02072.

PIEDMONT CRAFTS FAIR. Nov 7-9. Memorial Coliseum, Winston-Salem, NC. Craft fair showing only juried work of exhibiting members of Piedmont Craftsmen, Inc, a 22-year-old guild based in Winston-Salem. Info from: Piedmont Craftsmen, Inc, Jan Detter, Dir, 300 S Main St, Winston-Salem, NC 27101.

SCOTTISH INTERNATIONAL HIGHLAND GAMES. Nov 7-16. Austin, TX. Annual games of the Scots International. Info from: City of Austin, Sesquicentennial Commission, 610 E Eleventh St, Austin, TX 78701.

U.S.S.R.: ANNIVERSARY OF THE GREAT OCTOBER SOCIALIST REVOLUTION: Nov 7-8. The main holiday in the Soviet Union, observed for two days. According to old Russian calendar, the revolution took place on Oct 25, 1917. Soviet calendar reform causes observance to fall on Nov 7th.

WALSH INVITATIONAL RIFLE TOURNAMENT. Nov 7-9. (Also Nov 14-16 and Nov 21-23.) Xavier University, Cincinnati, OH. Purpose: To promote marksmanship and sportsmanship in the competitive spirit of collegiate athletics. International smallbore rifle and air rifle match open to all competitors. Recognized as "the largest indoor international rifle match in

COPYRIGHT © 1985 BY WILLIAM D. CHASE and HELEN M. CHASE

the nation." Sponsor: Xavier Univ Athletic Dept. Info from: Alan Joseph, Dept of Athletics, O'Conner Sports Ctr, Xavier Univ, Cincinnati, OH 45207.

WESTERN SAMOA: ARBOR DAY. Nov 7. The first Friday in November is observed as Arbor Day in Western Samoa.

WORLD COMMUNITY DAY. Nov 7. Theme: "Look to the Mountains." Focuses on prayer for the establishment of just and durable peace. (First Friday in November.) Sponsor: Church Women United, 475 Riverside Dr, Rm 812, New York, NY 10115.

NOVEMBER 8 — SATURDAY
312th Day — Remaining, 53

ABET AND AID PUNSTERS DAY. Nov 8. Purpose: Laugh at instead of groaning at incredibly dreadful puns. "All-time greatest pun: Though he's not very humble, there's no police like Holmes." Register worst puns with Punsters Unlimited of Lake Superior State College Unicorn Hunters, W. T. Rabe, Sault Ste. Marie, MI 49783.

ANN ARBOR WINTER ART FAIR. Nov 8-9. Ann Arbor, MI. Over 275 artists and craftsmen, who have achieved national reputations, will display and sell their work. Info from: Audree Levy, 10629 Park Preston, Dallas, TX 75230.

BARNARD, CHRISTIAAN NEETHLING: BIRTHDAY. Nov 8. South African surgeon and medical pioneer who performed the first known human heart transplant, was born at Beaufort West, South Africa, on Nov 8, 1922. The first human heart transplant operation took place at a Cape Town hospital in 1967. The organ donor had been killed in an automobile accident and the recipient lived less than a month after the surgery. In the following year more than a hundred such transplants were performed, but the number declined in succeeding years. In his book, *Good Life, Good Death: A Doctor's Case for Euthanasia and Suicide,* Dr. Barnard wrote: "I have learned from my life in medicine that death is not always an enemy . . . it achieves what medicine cannot achieve—it stops suffering."

CAROLINA CRAFTSMEN JURIED CRAFTS SHOW. Nov 8-10. South Carolina State Fairgrounds, Columbia, SC. Info from: Carolina Craftsmen, Clyde Gilmore, III, Exec Dir, Box 13224, Greensboro, NC 27405.

ENGLAND: LONDON LORD MAYOR'S PROCESSION AND SHOW. Nov 8. London. When the Lord Mayor is inaugurated for his year in office, a procession takes place from the Guildhall to the Royal Courts of Justice. Each year there is a parade based on the profession or interests of the new Lord Mayor. Crowds gather along the route to watch this traditional event which has been observed on the second Saturday of November for nearly 600 years.

HALLEY, EDMUND: BIRTHDAY. Nov 8. English astronomer and mathematician born at London, Nov 8, 1656. Astronomer Royal, 1721-1742. Died at Greenwich, Jan 14, 1742. He observed the great comet of 1682 (now named for him), first conceived its periodicity and wrote in his *Synopsis of Comet Astronomy:* ". . . I may venture to foretell that this Comet will return again in the year 1758." It did, and Edmund Halley's memory is kept alive by the once-every-generation appearance of Comet Halley. There have been 28 recorded appearances of this comet since 240 B.C. Average time between appearances is 76 years. Often regarded a harbinger of disaster, Halley's Comet is next expected to be visible in 1985-1986.

November 1986

S	M	T	W	T	F	S
						1
2	3	4	5	6	7	8
9	10	11	12	13	14	15
16	17	18	19	20	21	22
23	24	25	26	27	28	29
30						

MERCHANT SAILING SHIP PRESERVATION DAY. Nov. 8. Purpose: On this day in 1941 the whaler Charles W. Morgan arrived in Mystic, CT, to be restored. This was the first of numerous such restorations. Info from: Library, Natl Maritime Museum, Bldg E, 3rd Fl, Fort Mason, San Francisco, CA 94123.

MONTANA: ADMISSION DAY. Nov 8. Became 41st State on this day in 1889.

MOON PHASE: FIRST QUARTER. Nov 8. Moon enters First Quarter phase at 4:11 p.m., E.S.T.

NATIONAL SPLIT PEA SOUP WEEK. Nov 8-15. Purpose: To promote the use of split peas in split pea soup. Sponsor: American Dry Pea & Lentil Assn, Harold Blain, Box 8566, Moscow, ID 83843.

X-RAY DISCOVERY DAY: ANNIVERSARY. Nov 8. Physicist Wilhelm Conrad Roentgen (q.v.) discovered X-rays on Nov 8, 1895, beginning a new era in physics and medicine. Although X-rays had been observed previously, it was Roentgen, a professor at the University of Wurzburg (Germany) who successfully repeated X-ray experimentation, and is credited with the discovery.

NOVEMBER 9 — SUNDAY
313th Day — Remaining, 52

AGNEW, SPIRO THEODORE: BIRTHDAY. Nov 9. Thirty-ninth Vice-President of the U.S. born at Baltimore, MD, Nov 9, 1918. Twice elected vice-president (1968 and 1972) Agnew, on Oct 10, 1973, became the second person to resign that office (see entry for John C. Calhoun). Agnew entered a plea of no contest to a charge of income tax evasion (on contract kickbacks received while he was Governor of Maryland and after he became vice-president), and was sentenced to pay a $10,000 fine and serve three years probation. On Apr 27, 1981, following a class-action suit, a Maryland circuit court ruled that Agnew must pay the state $248,735 ($147,500 in kickbacks plus $101,235 in interest) for violating the public trust. Agnew did not testify at the trial.

BAHAMAS: REMEMBRANCE DAY. Nov 9. The Governor general, Prime Minister, members of the Diplomatic Corps and civic leaders lay wreaths in memory of the war dead at service in the Garden of Remembrance, downtown Nassau.

CONTE, SILVIO O: BIRTHDAY. Nov 9. U.S. Representative of Massachusett's 1st district, Republican, of Pittsfield, MA, born in Pittsfield, on Nov 9, 1921.

EAST COAST BLACKOUT ANNIVERSARY. Nov 9. Massive electric power failure starting in western New York State at 5:16 p.m., Nov 9, 1965, cut electric power to much of northeastern U.S. and Ontario and Quebec in Canada. More than 30 million persons in an area of 80,000 square miles were affected. The experience provoked studies of the vulnerability of 20th century societal technology and some thought about what people do in the dark.

GRAHAM, ROBERT: BIRTHDAY. Nov 9. Robert Graham, Governor of Florida, Democrat, was born at Miami, FL, on Nov 9, 1936.

HENDON, BILL: BIRTHDAY. Nov 9. U.S. Representative of North Carolina's 11th district, Republican, of Asheville, NC, born in Asheville on Nov 9, 1944.

LOVEJOY, ELIJAH P: BIRTHDAY. Nov 9. American newspaper publisher and abolitionist born Nov 9, 1802. Died Nov 7, 1837.

PASTAVILLE USA. Nov 9-15. Purpose: To educate people on the use of durum and to promote pasta products. Info from: Convention and Visitors Bureau, 200 S Broadway, Minot, ND 58701.

TUNISIA: TREE FESTIVAL. Nov 9. Tunisia. National Agricultural Festival. Always on second Sunday in November.

COPYRIGHT © 1985 BY WILLIAM D. CHASE and HELEN M. CHASE

WORLD MUTUAL SERVICE WEEK. Nov 9-15. Purpose: To alert the public and bring awareness of what the YWCA stands for, its purpose/accomplishments/benefits for girls and women 12 years of age and up. Sponsor: Natl Bd, YWCA of the USA, Jane Pinkerton, Dir of Communications/PR Div, 726 Broadway, New York, NY 10003.

YOUTH APPRECIATION WEEK. Nov 9-15. Purpose: To recognize the positive achievements of youth in today's society. Sponsor: Optimist Internatl, Hugh H. Cranford, Exec Secy, 4494 Lindell Blvd, St. Louis, MO 63108.

NOVEMBER 10 — MONDAY
314th Day — Remaining, 51

BURTON, RICHARD: BIRTHDAY. Nov 10. Welsh-born stage and film actor. Richard Burton was never knighted and never an Oscar-winner, but he was generally regarded as the possessor of one of the great acting talents of his time. Born Richard Jenkins at Pontrhydyfen, South Wales, on Nov 10, 1925, the son of a coal miner later took the name of his guardian, schoolmaster Philip Burton. An intense and tempestuous personal life and career suggested a self-destructive bent. Burton died at Geneva, Switzerland, of a cerebral hemorrhage, at age 58, on Aug 5, 1984.

EDMUND FITZGERALD SINKING: ANNIVERSARY. Nov 10. The ore carrier *Edmund Fitzgerald* broke in two during a heavy storm in Lake Superior (near Whitefish Point) Nov 10, 1975. There were no survivors of this, the worst Great Lakes ship disaster of the decade, which took the lives of 29 crew members.

GOLDSMITH, OLIVER: BIRTHDAY. Nov 10. Irish writer. Nov 10, 1728-Apr 4, 1774. "A book may be amusing with numerous errors," he wrote (Advertisement to *The Vicar of Wakefield*), "or it may be very dull without a single absurdity."

HOGARTH, WILLIAM: BIRTHDAY. Nov 10. English painter and engraver, famed for his satiric series of engravings (A Harlot's Progress, A Rake's Progress, Four Stages of Cruelty, etc.), born at London, Nov 10, 1697, and died there on Oct 26, 1764.

KIRTLAND, JARED: BIRTH ANNIVERSARY. Nov 10. American physician and naturalist, Dr. Jared Potter Kirtland (for whom Kirtland's Warbler is named) was born at Wallingford, CT, on Nov 10, 1793. The first of the now rare Kirtland's Warblers to be identified and studied was found on his farm near Cleveland, OH, in 1851. Dr. Kirtland died at Rockport, near Cleveland, on Dec 10, 1877.

LUTHER, MARTIN: BIRTHDAY. Nov 10. Birthday of Martin Luther, the Augustinian monk who was a founder and leader of the Reformation and of Protestantism. Born at Eisleben, Saxony, Nov 10, 1483, Luther tacked his 95 Theses "On the Power of Indulgences" on the door of Wittenburg's castle church, on Oct 31, 1517, the eve of All Saints' Day. Luther asserted that the Bible was the sole authority of the church, called for reformation of abuses by the Roman Catholic Church, and denied the supremacy of the Pope. Tried for heresy by the Roman church, threatened with excommunication and finally banned by A Papal Bull (Jan 2, 1521), he responded by burning the Bull. Leaving his monastic order, he married, in 1525, a former nun. Six children were born of the marriage. Luther died near his birthplace, at Eisleben, Feb 18, 1546.

MARINE CORPS BIRTHDAY. Nov 10. Commemorates Corps' establishment in 1775.

SPACE MILESTONE: LUNA 17 (USSR). Nov 10. Launched on Nov 10, 1970, this unmanned spacecraft landed and released Lunakhod 1 (8-wheel, radio controlled vehicle) on moon's Sea of Rains, Nov 17, explored lunar surface, sending data back to Earth.

UNITED NATIONS CONFERENCE. Nov 10-28. Geneva, Switzerland. United Nations Conference for the Promotion of International Cooperation in the Peaceful Uses of Nuclear Energy.

NOVEMBER 11 — TUESDAY
315th Day — Remaining, 50

ADAMS, ABIGAIL SMITH: BIRTHDAY. Nov 11. Wife of John Adams, 2nd President of the U.S., born at Weymouth, MA, Nov 11, 1744. Died Oct 28, 1818.

ALDRICH, THOMAS BAILEY: 150th BIRTH ANNIVERSARY. Nov 11. American author and editor. Best known of his books: *The Story of a Bad Boy* (1870), an autobiographical work. Aldrich was born at Portsmouth, NH, on Nov 11, 1836, and died at Boston, MA, on Mar 19, 1907.

ANGOLA: NATIONAL DAY. Nov 11. National holiday observed.

ARMISTICE DAY. Nov 11. Anniversary of Armistice between Allied and Central Powers, signed at 5 a.m., Nov 11, 1918, in Marshal Foch's railway car in the Forest of Compiegne, France. Hostilities ceased at 11 a.m. Also recognized in some places as Remembrance Day, Veterans Day, Victory Day and World War I Memorial Day. Many places observe silent memorial at the eleventh hour of the eleventh day of the eleventh month each year. See also entries for Veterans Day.

BOXER, BARBARA: BIRTHDAY. Nov 11. U.S. Representative of California's 6th district, Democrat, of Greenbrae, CA, born in Brooklyn, NY, Nov 11, 1940.

CELESTE, RICHARD F: BIRTHDAY. Nov 11. Richard F. Celeste, Governor of Ohio, Democrat, was born at Lakewood, OH, on Nov 11, 1937.

CONCORDIA DAY. Nov 11. St Maarten Leeward Islands. Ceremonies take place at the border to observe the amicable agreement reached in 1648, when the island was divided between the Dutch and the French.

DOSTOYEVSKY, FYODOR MIKHAILOVICH: BIRTHDAY. Nov 11. Russian novelist, author of *The Brothers Karamazov*, *Crime and Punishment*, and *The Idiot*, was born at Moscow, Nov 11, 1821 (New Style) and died at St. Petersburg, Feb 9, 1881 (New Style). A political revolutionary, he was tried, convicted and sentenced to death, but instead of execution he served a sentence in a Siberian prison and later served in the army there.

MARTINMAS. Nov 11. The Feast Day of St. Martin of Tours, who lived about 316-397. A bishop, who became one of the most popular saints of the Middle Ages. The period of warm weather often occurring about the time of his feast day is sometimes called St. Martin's Summer (especially in England).

PROXMIRE, WILLIAM: BIRTHDAY. Nov 11. U.S. Senator, Democrat, of Wisconsin, born Nov 11, 1915 at Lake Forest, IL.

REMEMBRANCE DAY. Nov 11. Canada (Public holiday).

SPACE MILESTONE: GEMINI 12 (US). Nov 11. Last Project Gemini manned Earth orbit. Nov 11, 1966.

SPACE MILESTONE: STS-5 (US). Nov 11. Shuttle Columbia launched from Kennedy Space Center, FL Nov 11, 1982 with four astronauts: Vance Brand, Robert Overmyer, William Lenoir and Joseph Allen. "First operational mission" delivered two satellites into orbit for commercial customers. Columbia landed at Edwards Air Force Base, CA, Nov 16.

STARK, FORTNEY H JR (PETE): BIRTHDAY. Nov 11. U.S. Representative of California's 9th district, Democrat, of Oakland, CA, was born in Milwaukee, WI, Nov 11, 1931.

COPYRIGHT © 1985 BY WILLIAM D. CHASE and HELEN M. CHASE

SWITZERLAND: MARTINMAS GOOSE (MARTINIGIANS). Nov 11. Sursee, Canton Lucerne. At 3 p.m., on Martinmas (the day on which interest is due), the "Gansabhauet" is staged in front of Town Hall. Blindfolded participants try to bring down, with a single sword stroke, a dead goose suspended on a wire.

VETERANS DAY. Nov 11. Presidential Proclamation.
☆ "Formerly called 'Armistice Day' and proclaimed each year since 1926 for November 11. PL83-380 of June 1, 1954, changed the name to 'Veterans Day.' PL90-363 required that beginning in 1971 it would be observed the 4th Monday in October. PL 94-97 of Sept 18, 1975, required that effective Jan 1, 1978, the observance would revert to November 11."

VETERANS DAY. Nov 11. Veterans Day was observed on Nov 11th from 1919 through 1970. Public Law 90-363, the "Monday Holiday Law," provided that, beginning in 1971, Veterans Day would be observed on "the fourth Monday in October." This movable observance date, which separated Veterans Day from the Nov 11 anniversary of World War I Armistice, proved unpopular. State after state moved observance back to the traditional Nov 11 date, and finally, Public Law 94-97 of Sept 18, 1975, required that, effective Jan 1, 1978, the observance of Veterans Day revert to Nov 11. See also entry for Armistice Day, this date.

VONNEGUT, KURT: BIRTHDAY. Nov 11. American novelist born on this day in 1922.

WASHINGTON: ADMISSION DAY. Nov 11. Became 42nd State on this day in 1889.

ZORINSKY, EDWARD: BIRTHDAY. Nov 11. U.S. Senator from Nebraska, Democrat, of Omaha, NE, born in Omaha Nov 11, 1928.

NOVEMBER 12 — WEDNESDAY
316th Day — Remaining, 49

BIRTH OF BAHA'U'LLAH. Nov 12. Baha'i observance of anniversary of the birth of Baha'u'llah (born Mirza Husayn Ali) on Nov 12, 1817, in Nur, Persia. Baha'u'llah was prophet-founder of the Baha'i faith. Info from: Baha'i Office of Public Affairs, Baha'i Natl Center, Wilmette, IL 60091.

BLACKMUN, HARRY A: BIRTHDAY. Nov 12. Associate Justice of the Supreme Court of the United States, nominated by Pres. Nixon on Apr 14, 1970. (Qualified, June 9, 1970.) Justice Blackmun was born at Nashville, IL, on Nov 12, 1908.

KELLY, GRACE PATRICIA: BIRTHDAY. Nov 12. American award-winning actress who became Princess Grace of Monaco when she married that country's ruler, Prince Rainier III, in 1956, was born in Philadelphia, Nov 12, 1929. She died of injuries sustained in an automobile accident, Sept 14, 1982.

MINETA, NORMAN YOSHIO: BIRTHDAY. Nov 12. U.S. Representative of California's 13th district, Democrat, of San Jose, CA, born there Nov 12, 1931.

NORTHERN IRELAND: BELFAST FESTIVAL OF ARTS AT QUEEN'S. Nov 12-29. Queen's University, Belfast, County Antrim. International festival of music: classical, jazz and folk.

RODIN, AUGUSTE: BIRTHDAY. Nov 12. French sculptor born at Paris, Nov 12, 1840. Died Nov 17, 1917.

SPACE MILESTONE: STS-2 (US). Nov 12. Shuttle Columbia launched from Kennedy Space Center, FL, Nov 12, 1981 with Joe Engle and Richard Truly, became first spacecraft launched from Earth for second orbiting mission. Landed at Edwards Air Force Base, CA, Nov 14.

November 1986	S	M	T	W	T	F	S
							1
	2	3	4	5	6	7	8
	9	10	11	12	13	14	15
	16	17	18	19	20	21	22
	23	24	25	26	27	28	29
	30						

STANTON, ELIZABETH CADY: BIRTH ANNIVERSARY. Nov 12. American woman suffragist and reformer, Elizabeth Cady Stanton, was born at Johnstown, NY, on Nov 12, 1815. "We hold these truths to be self-evident," she said at the first Woman's Rights Convention, in 1848, "that all men and women are created equal." She died at New York City on Oct 26, 1902.

SUN YAT-SEN: TRADITIONAL BIRTHDAY. Nov 12. Although his actual birth date (in 1866) is not known, Dr. Sun Yat-Sen's traditional birthday commemoration is held on Nov 12. Heroic leader of China's 1911 revolution, he died at Peking, on Mar 12, 1925. The death anniversary is also widely observed. See also: entry for Mar 12.

TRANSIT OF MERCURY. Nov 12-13. Mercury transits the Sun's disk on Nov 12-13. Exterior contact begins at 8:43 p.m., E.S.T. on Nov 12 and ends 1:31 a.m., E.S.T. on Nov 13. Not visible in North America. The event is visible from the Pacific Ocean except the eastern part, Australasia, Asia, the Indian Ocean, part of Antarctica, Africa except the northwestern part and eastern Europe.

TYLER, LETITIA CHRISTIAN: BIRTHDAY. Nov 12. First wife of John Tyler, 10th President of the U.S., born at New Kent County, VA, Nov 12, 1790. Died Sept 10, 1842.

VOLLEYBALL: HIGH SCHOOL BOYS PROVINCIAL CHAMPIONSHIPS. Nov 12. Vancouver, BC, Canada. Boys AA volleyball championships. Info from: Vancouver Centennial Commission, Box 49386, Bentall 4, 1055 Dunsmuir St, Vancouver, BC V7X 1L5.

NOVEMBER 13 — THURSDAY
317th Day — Remaining, 48

BOOTH, EDWIN (THOMAS): BIRTHDAY. Nov 13. Famed American actor and founder of the Players Club, born near Bel Air, MD, Nov 13, 1833. Died, New York City, June 7, 1893.

BRANDEIS, LOUIS DEMBITZ: BIRTHDAY. Nov 13. American jurist, associate justice of U.S. Supreme Court (1916-1939), born at Louisville, KY, Nov 13, 1856. Died at Washington, DC, Oct 5, 1941.

CANDLELIGHT TOURS OF NEMACOLIN CASTLE. Nov 13-16. Brownsville, PA. Castle is decorated for the holiday. All rooms are candle lit. Sponsor: Fayette County Tourism, Box 63, Hopwood, PA 15445.

CHRISTMAS SEAL CAMPAIGN 1986. Nov 13-Dec 31. Purpose: Campaign to support the American Lung Association program dedicated to the prevention and control of lung diseases and their causes. Sponsor: The American Lung Association, Kathleen M. Davis, Dir of Communications, 1740 Broadway, New York, NY 10019.

HOLLAND TUNNEL ANNIVERSARY. Nov 13. On Nov 13, 1927, the Holland Tunnel, running under the Hudson River between New York City and Jersey City, NJ, was opened to traffic. The tunnel was built and operated by the New York-New Jersey Bridge and Tunnel Commission.

HUGHES, HARRY R: BIRTHDAY. Nov 13. Harry R. Hughes, Governor of Maryland, Democrat, was born at Easton, MD, on Nov 13, 1926.

MAXWELL, JAMES CLERK: BIRTHDAY. Nov 13. British physicist noted for his work in the field of electricity and magnetism. Born at Edinburgh on Nov 13, 1831, he died of cancer on Nov 5, 1879, at Cambridge, England.

STEVENSON, ROBERT LOUIS: BIRTHDAY. Nov 13. Scottish author, born Edinburgh, Nov 13, 1850. Died, Samoa, Dec 3, 1894.

TRELAWNEY, EDWARD JOHN: BIRTHDAY. Nov 13. English traveller and author, friend of Shelley and Byron, was born at London, Nov 13, 1792. He died at Sompting, Sussex, Aug 13, 1881, and was buried at Rome, next to Shelley.

NOVEMBER 14 — FRIDAY
318th Day — Remaining, 47

BLOOD TRANSFUSION ANNIVERSARY. Nov 14. Samuel Pepys, diarist and Fellow of the Royal Society, wrote in his diary for Nov 14, 1666: "Dr. Croone told me . . . there was a pretty experiment of the blood of one dog let out, till he died, into the body of another on one side, while all his own run out on the other side. The first died upon the place, and the other very well and likely to do well. This did give occasion to many pretty wishes, as of the blood of a Quaker to be let into an Archbishop, and such like; but, as Dr. Croone says, may, if it takes, be of mighty use to man's health, for the amending of bad blood by borrowing from a better body." Two days later, Nov 16th, Pepys noted: "This noon I met with Mr. Hooke, and he tells me the dog which was filled with another dog's blood, at the College the other day, is very well, and like to be so as ever, and doubts not its being found of great use to men . . ."

EISENHOWER, MAMIE DOUD: BIRTHDAY. Nov 14. Wife of Dwight David Eisenhower, 34th President of the U.S., born at Boone, IA, Nov 14, 1896. Died Nov 1, 1979, at Washington, DC.

FULTON, ROBERT: BIRTH ANNIVERSARY. Nov 14. Inventor of the steamboat, born Nov 14, 1765. Died Feb 24, 1815.

GRAY, KENNETH J: BIRTHDAY. Nov 14. U.S. Representative of Illinois' 22nd district, Democrat, of West Frankfort, IL, born there on Nov 14, 1924.

GUINEA-BISSAU: NATIONAL HOLIDAY. Nov 14. Re-Adjustment Movement's Day is observed.

INDIA: CHILDREN'S DAY. Nov 14. Holiday observed throughout India.

JOHN GILPIN'S RIDE: PUBLICATION ANNIVERSARY. Nov 14. William Cowper's popular and memorable ballad: "The diverting History of John Gilpin, Showing How He Went Farther Than He Intended, and Came Safe Home Again," was first published, anonymously, in *The Public Advertiser*, London, Nov 14, 1782.

JORDAN: NATIONAL HOLIDAY. Nov 14. H.M. King Hussein's birthday is nationally honored each year on the anniversary of his birth, on Nov 14, 1935.

MONET, CLAUDE: BIRTHDAY. Nov 14. French painter born Nov 14, 1840. Died Dec 5, 1926.

NEHRU, JAWAHARLAL: BIRTHDAY. Nov 14. Indian leader and first prime minister after independence. Born Nov 14, 1889. Died May 27, 1964.

NOVEMBER HOME SHOW. Nov 14-19. Coconut Grove Exhibition Ctr, Miami, FL. Info from: Perl Exposition Corp, 6915 Red Rd, Suite 228, Coral Gables, FL 33143.

SOUTHWEST ARTS AND CRAFTS FESTIVAL. Nov 14-16. Emphasis on Southwest art. Info from: Southwest Arts & Crafts Festival, Jackie Fallis, 2717 San Mateo NE, Albuquerque, NM 87110.

SPACE MILESTONE: APOLLO 12 (US). Nov 14. Launched on Nov 14, 1969, this was the second manned lunar landing—in Ocean of Storms. Astronauts Conrad, Bean and Gordon. First pinpoint landing. Astronauts visited Surveyor 3 and took samples. Earth splashdown Nov 24.

YMCA ARTS AND CRAFTS FAIR. Nov 14-16. Virginia Tech Campus, Blacksburg, VA. Purpose: Display and sale of traditional and modern crafts by craftspeople from 10 states. Local musicians and dancers. Sponsor: YMCA at VPI, Betty Williams, 304 Squires Student Ctr, Blacksburg, VA 24060.

NOVEMBER 15 — SATURDAY
319th Day — Remaining, 46

AMERICAN ENTERPRISE DAY. Nov 15. Purpose: To celebrate the American free enterprise system through activities designed to increase appreciation of its contribution to

America's economy. Annually Nov 15. Sponsor: Future Business Leaders of America, Phi Beta Lambda, Inc, Yvonne Easter, 1908 Association Dr, Reston, VA 22091.

AMERICAN FEDERATION OF LABOR: BIRTHDAY. Nov 15. Anniversary of the founding, at Pittsburgh, PA, on Nov 15, 1881, of the Federation of Organized Trades and Labor Unions of the United States and Canada which, reorganized in 1886, became the American Federation of Labor.

BELGIUM: DYNASTY DAY. Nov 15. National holiday in honor of Belgian monarchy.

BRAZIL: REPUBLIC DAY. Nov 15. Commemorates the Proclamation of the Republic on Nov 15, 1889.

CHILDREN'S SHRINE VISITING DAY (SHICHI-GO-SAN). Nov 15. Japan. "All children aged three, five, seven, scrubbed and spotless, are taken to shrines by their parents to offer thanks for good health and to pray for continued good fortune." Observed throughout Japan.

CLARK AIR BASE CHILI COOK-OFF. Nov 15. Clark Air Base, Republic of the Philippines. Purpose: Base selects best team of chili cooks, team with best showmanship, a Miss Local Chili Pepper and a Miss Imported Chili Pepper. Info from: Mary C. Rike, Club Dir, Silver Wing Recreation Ctr, 3 CSG/SSRR, APO San Francisco, CA 96274.

DYSON, ROY P: BIRTHDAY. Nov 15. U.S. Representative of Maryland's 1st district, Democrat, of Dyson Farm, Great Mills, MD, was born on Nov 15, 1948.

GAINES DOG OBEDIENCE CLASSIC. Nov 15-16. Houston, TX. Purpose: To select the best dog/handler team in standard obedience classes including novice, open and super dog, the top category representing the best-trained dog in the nation. Sponsor: Gaines Dog Care Center, A.S. Willett, Red Oak Plaza, 70 W Red Oak Lane, White Plains, NY 10604.

HOLIDAYS ARE PICKLE DAYS. Nov 15-Jan 1, 1987. Purpose: To promote the contribution of pickles to holiday entertaining—Thanksgiving, Christmas and New Year's. Sponsor: Pickle Packers Internatl, Inc, 108½ E Main St, St Charles, IL 60174, Info from: Burson-Marsteller, 1 E Wacker Dr, Chicago, IL 60601.

MUSLIM FESTIVAL: BIRTH OF PROPHET MUHAMMAD. Nov 15. Mulid al-Nabi (Birth of the Prophet Muhammad) is observed on Muslim calendar date, Rabi al-Awal 12, 1407. Gregorian calendar date of observance may vary by one day.

PLANTATION DAYS. Nov 15-16. Charleston, SC. Harvest time activities, sugar cane milling, wood dyeing, cider making and cornshucking at Middleton Place. Info from: Middleton Place, Rt 4, SC 61, Charleston, SC 29407.

RICHARDSON, WILLIAM BLAINE: BIRTHDAY. Nov 15. U.S. Representative of New Mexico's 3rd district, Democrat, of Santa Fe, NM, was born in Pasadena, CA, on Nov 15, 1947.

SPELVIN, GEORGE: DAY. Nov 15. Believed to be the anniversary of George Spelvin's theatrical birth—in Charles A. Gardiner's play, *Karl the Peddler*, New York, Nov 15, 1886. Spelvin, a fictitious creation, is said to have appeared in more than 10,000 Broadway performances. The name (or equivalent Georgina, Georgetta, etc.) is used in play programs to conceal the fact that an actor is performing in more than one role. For British equivalent see Walter Plinge Day.

COPYRIGHT © 1985 BY WILLIAM D. CHASE and HELEN M. CHASE

THAILAND: ELEPHANT ROUND-UP AT SURIN. Nov 15. Elephant demonstrations in morning, elephant races, tug-of-war between 100 men and one elephant, etc. Observed since 1961 on third Saturday in November. Special trains from Bangkok on previous day.

WHITAKER ASSOCIATION: YEAR OF THE ANIMALS. Nov 15-Nov 14, 1987. Purpose: To view man's tenancy of Earth from the standpoint of other animals and to assure safe space for all animal life through the preservation and protection of adequate areas of undisturbed wilderness. Sponsor: The Whitaker Assn, Attn: Merritt W. Johnston, 1232 Clayton St, Denver, CO 80206.

WORLD CHAMPIONSHIP QUARTER HORSE SHOW. Nov 15-22. Purpose: Over 1200 Quarter horses from 50 states and Canada compete in 62 classes. Exhibition and trade show, collegiate judging contest, horse sale and Super Horse competition. Info from: Stanley Draper, Jr, Chamber of Commerce, 1 Santa Fe Plaza, Oklahoma City, OK 73102.

NOVEMBER 16 — SUNDAY
320th Day — Remaining, 45

ALASCATTALO DAY. Nov 16. Anchorage, AK. Purpose: To honor humor in general and Alaskan humor in particular. Event is named after "alascattalo," said to be the genetic cross between a moose and a walrus. Sponsor: Parsnackle Press, Steven C. Levi, Editor, 8512 E. 4th Ave., Anchorage, AK 99504.

AMERICAN EDUCATION WEEK. Nov 16-22. Presidential ☆ Proclamation. Issued many years since 1921. Proclamation 4967, of Sept 13, 1982 covers all succeeding years.

AMERICAN EDUCATION WEEK. Nov 16-22. Purpose: To build public support for American schools. Sponsors: Natl Congress of Parents and Teachers (PTA), Natl Education Assn, Natl School Boards Assn, American Legion and U.S. Dept of Education. Info from: American Education Week, Box 509, West Haven, CT 06516.

COLONIAL CUP: STEEPLECHASE. Nov 16. Camden, SC. Info from: Patricia D. Cooper, Box 280, Camden, SC 29020.

GERMANY: VOLKSTRAUERTAG (MEMORIAL DAY). Nov 16.

HANDY, WILLIAM CHRISTOPHER: BIRTHDAY. Nov 16. American composer, bandleader, "Father of the Blues," W.C. Handy was born at Florence, AL, Nov 16, 1873. He died at New York City, Mar 28, 1958.

HINDEMITH, PAUL: BIRTHDAY. Nov 16. Prolific composer and teacher, born at Hanau, Germany, Nov 16, 1895. Became a resident and citizen of the U.S. during World War II. Died at Frankfurt, Germany, Dec 28, 1963.

MOON PHASE: FULL MOON. Nov 16. Moon enters Full Moon phase at 7:12 a.m., E.S.T.

OKLAHOMA, ADMISSION DAY. Nov 16. Became 46th State on this day in 1907.

SPACE MILESTONE: SKYLAB 4 (US). Nov 16. Thirtieth manned US space flight was launched on Nov 16, 1973. Three astronauts (G. P. Carr, W. R. Page and E. G. Gibson). Space walks. Returned to Earth after 84 days, on Feb 8, 1974.

SPACE MILESTONE: VENERA 3 (USSR). Nov 16. Launched Nov 16, 1965, it crashed into Venus, Mar 1, 1966. First man-made object on another planet. Nov 16, 1965.

November 1986

S	M	T	W	T	F	S
						1
2	3	4	5	6	7	8
9	10	11	12	13	14	15
16	17	18	19	20	21	22
23	24	25	26	27	28	29
30						

STATIA AND AMERICA DAY. Nov 16. St. Eustatius, Leeward Islands. To commemorate the first salute to an American flag by a foreign government from Fort Oranje in 1776. Festivities include sports events and dancing. During the American Revolution St. Eustatius was an important trading center and a supply base for the colonies

WORLDWIDE WHIST TOURNAMENT. Nov 16-17. Glasgow, Montana. Features card players from throughout Montana and Canada. Info from: Travel Montana, 1424 9th Ave, Helena, MT 59620.

NOVEMBER 17 — MONDAY
321st Day — Remaining, 44

BRANSTAD, TERRY E: BIRTHDAY. Nov 17. Terry E. Branstad, Governor of Iowa, Republican, was born at Leland, IA, on Nov 17, 1947.

HOME MADE BREAD DAY. Nov 17. Purpose: A day for the family to remember and enjoy the making, baking and eating of nutritious home made bread. Sponsor: Home Made Bread Day Committee, Box 68, Montague, MI 49437.

NATIONAL CHILDREN'S BOOK WEEK. Nov 17-23. Purpose: To encourage the enjoyment of reading for children. Sponsor: The Children's Book Council, Inc, John Donovan, Exec Dir, 67 Irving Pl, New York, NY 10003.

NATIONAL EATING DISORDERS WEEK. Nov 17-21. Purpose: An intensive effort to educate people to the physical and mental ravages of anorexia and bulimia eating disorders and what can be done via proper inpatient treatment and self help therapy. Info from: Anorexia/Bulimia Treatment & Education Ctr, Felix Larocca, MD, Dir, 1027 Bellevue Ave, St Louis, MO 63117.

ORR, ROBERT D: BIRTHDAY. Nov 17. Robert D. Orr, Governor of Indiana, Republican, was born at Ann Arbor, MI, on Nov 17, 1917.

PEALE, TITIAN RAMSEY: BIRTHDAY. Nov 17. American artist, naturalist, son of Charles Willson Peale, born at Philadelphia on Nov 17, 1799. Died there on Mar 13, 1885.

QUEEN ELIZABETH DAY. Nov 17. Anniversary of accession of Elizabeth I to English throne, Nov 17, 1558; celebrated as a holiday in England for over a century after her death in 1603. Observance by *Cavalier Comments*, Mark and Jennie Gist, Editors, 530 E Weber Rd, Columbus, OH 43202.

SUEZ CANAL ANNIVERSARY. Nov 17. Formal opening of the Suez Canal, Nov 17, 1869.

ZENGER, JOHN PETER: ARREST ANNIVERSARY. Nov 17. Colonial printer and journalist who established the *New York Weekly Journal* (first issue on Nov 5, 1733). Zenger was arrested on Nov 17, 1734, for libels against the colonial governor, but continued to edit his newspaper from jail. Trial was held during August, 1735. Zenger's acquittal was important early step toward freedom of the press in America.

NOVEMBER 18 — TUESDAY
322nd Day — Remaining, 43

DAGUERRE, LOUIS: BIRTHDAY. Nov 18. French artist and scientist, inventor of photographic Daguerrotype, born Nov 18, 1789. Died July 12, 1851.

GALLI—CURCI, AMELITA: BIRTHDAY. Nov 18. Italian born operatic soprano, made U.S. debut November 18, 1916, in Chicago. Born at Milan Nov 18, 1889. She died at LaJolla, CA, November 26, 1963.

GILBERT, SIR WILLIAM SCHWENCK: BIRTHDAY. Nov 18. English author of librettos for the famed Gilbert and Sullivan comic operas, born at London, Nov 18, 1836. Died May 29, 1911, as a result of a heart attack experienced while saving a woman from drowning.

COPYRIGHT © 1985 BY WILLIAM D. CHASE and HELEN M. CHASE

HAITI: ARMY DAY. Nov 18. Commemorates the Battle of Vertieres, Nov 18, 1803, at which Haitians defeated the French.

LATVIA: INDEPENDENCE DAY. Nov 18. National holiday.

LOMBROSO, CESARE: 150th BIRTH ANNIVERSARY. Nov 18. Italian founder of criminology, born at Verona, Nov 18, 1836. A professor of psychiatry, Lombroso believed that criminality could be identified with certain physical types of people. He died at Turin on Oct 19, 1909.

MICKEY MOUSE: BIRTHDAY. Nov 18. The comical activities of squeaky voiced Mickey Mouse first appeared Nov 18, 1928, on the screen of the Colony Theatre in New York City. The film, Walt Disney's "Steamboat Willie," was the first animated cartoon talking picture. Info from: Publicity Dept, Walt Disney Productions, 500 S Buena Vista St, Burbank, CA 91521.

OMAN: NATIONAL HOLIDAY. Nov 18. Sultanate of Oman celebrates its National Day.

PINCHBECK, CHRISTOPHER: DEATH ANNIVERSARY. Nov 18. English inventor, jeweler and clockmaker. Inventor of the copper and zinc alloy which looked like gold, but became synonymous with cheapness. Noted manufacturer of automated musical clocks and instruments. Born at Clerkenwell, London, about 1670 (exact date unknown). Died at London, Nov 18, 1732.

STEVENS, TED: BIRTHDAY. Nov 18. U.S. Senator from Alaska, Republican, of Anchorage, AK, was born at Indianapolis, IN, on Nov 18, 1923.

U.S. UNIFORM TIME ZONE PLAN ANNIVERSARY. Nov 18. Charles Ferdinand Dowd, a Connecticut school teacher and one of the early advocates of uniform time, proposed a time zone plan of the U.S. (four zones of 15 degrees), which he and others persuaded the railroads to adopt and place in operation, on Nov 18, 1883. Info from: National Bureau of Standards Monograph 155. See also entry for U.S. Standard Time Act: Anniversary, Mar 19.

NOVEMBER 19 — WEDNESDAY
323rd Day — Remaining, 42

ACKERMAN, GARY L: BIRTHDAY. Nov 19. U.S. Representative of New York's 7th district, Democrat, of Queens, NY, born in Brooklyn, NY on Nov 19, 1942.

ANNIVERSARY OF LINCOLN'S GETTYSBURG ADDRESS: Nov 19. Celebrated with brief memorial services at the Soldiers' National Monument in Gettysburg National Cemetery. Info from: Gettysburg Travel Council, 35 Carlisle St, Gettysburg, PA 17325.

BELIZE: PUBLIC HOLIDAY. Nov 19. Garifuna Day is observed as a public holiday in Belize.

CLARK, GEORGE ROGERS: BIRTHDAY. Nov 19. American soldier and frontiersman, born in Albermarle County, Virginia, on Nov 19, 1752. Died, Louisville, KY, on Feb 13, 1818.

FIRST PRESIDENTIAL LIBRARY ANNIVERSARY. Nov 19. On Nov 19, 1939, President Franklin D. Roosevelt laid the cornerstone for his presidential library at Hyde Park, NY. He donated the land but public donations provided funds for the building which was dedicated on June 30, 1941.

GARFIELD, JAMES ABRAM: BIRTHDAY. Nov 19. The 20th President of the U.S. (and the first left-handed president) was born at Orange, OH, Nov 19, 1831. While walking into the Washington, DC railway station on the morning of July 2, 1881, Garfield was shot by a disappointed office seeker. He survived, in very weak condition, until Sept 19, 1881, when he succumbed to blood poisoning at Elberon, NJ (where he had been taken for recuperation). The assassin, Charles J. Guiteau, was tried, convicted and, on June 30, 1882, hanged at the jail in Washington.

GERMANY: BUSS AND BETTAG. Nov 19. (Prayer and repentance.)

HARKIN, THOMAS R: BIRTHDAY. Nov 19. U.S. Senator from Iowa, Democrat, of Cumming, IA, born there Nov 19, 1939.

JONESTOWN MASSACRE ANNIVERSARY. Nov 19. Jonestown, Guyana. On Nov 19, 1978, Indiana born, 47 year-old Reverend Jim Jones, leader of the "Peoples Temple," was reported to have directed the killing of more than 900 persons. U.S. Rep. Leo J. Ryan, of California, and 4 members of his party were killed in ambush at Port Kaituma airstrip on Nov 18, 1978, when they attempted to leave after investigative visit to remote jungle location of religious cult. On following day, Jones and his mistress killed themselves after watching administration of Kool-Aid laced with deadly poison cyanide to members of cult. At least 911 persons died in biggest murder-suicide in history.

LINCOLN'S GETTYSBURG ADDRESS ANNIVERSARY. Nov 19. On this day in 1863, seventeen acres of the battlefield at Gettysburg, PA, were dedicated as a national cemetery. Noted orator Edward Everett's two-hour speech preceded that of President Lincoln. The address that Lincoln delivered in less than two minutes was quickly recognized as one of the most eloquent of the English language. Five manuscript copies in Lincoln's hand survive, including the rough draft commenced in ink at the Executive Mansion in Washington and concluded in pencil at Gettysburg on the morning of the dedication. That copy resides at the Library of Congress.

MONACO: NATIONAL HOLIDAY. Nov 19.

PENNY, TIMOTHY J: BIRTHDAY. Nov 19. U.S. Representative of Minnesota's 1st district, Democrat, of New Richland, MN, born in Freeborn County, MN, Nov 19, 1951.

PUERTO RICO: DISCOVERY DAY. Nov 19. Public Holiday. Columbus discovered Puerto Rico on his second voyage to the New World, in 1493.

NOVEMBER 20 — THURSDAY
324th Day — Remaining, 41

BELLO, ANDRES: BIRTHDAY. Nov 20. Venezuelan diplomat, author and humanist, was born at Caracas, Venezuela, Nov 20, 1781. Bello died at Santiago, Chile, Oct 15, 1865.

BIDEN, JOSEPH ROBINETTE JR: BIRTHDAY. Nov 20. U.S. Senator from Delaware, Democrat, of Wilmington, DE, born in Scranton, PA, on Nov 20, 1942.

BYRD, ROBERT C: BIRTHDAY. Nov 20. U.S. Senator from West Virginia, Democrat, of Sophia, Raleigh County, WV, was born in North Wilkesboro, NC, on Nov 20, 1917.

GOULD, CHESTER: BIRTH ANNIVERSARY. Nov 20. Creator of the comic strip, "Dick Tracy," was born at Pawnee, OK, on Nov 20, 1900. Gould's "Dick Tracy," which first appeared Oct 4, 1931 in *The Detroit Daily Mirror*, later was syndicated in nearly 1,000 newspapers worldwide and it was said that Dick Tracy's name was more widely known than that of the president of the U.S. Among the villains over whom Dick Tracy triumphed were: Pruneface, Flattop, Flyface, Mole, and 88 Keys. Notable among the innovations appearing in the comic strip before they were used in real life were the two-way wrist radio and televison and the use of closed-circuit TV line-ups. Gould drew and wrote the comic strip himself from 1931 until his retirement in 1977. He died at Woodstock, IL, May 11, 1985.

COPYRIGHT © 1985 BY WILLIAM D. CHASE and HELEN M. CHASE

KENNEDY, ROBERT FRANCIS: BIRTHDAY. Nov 20. U.S. Senator and brother of John F. Kennedy (35th president), was born at Brookline, MA, Nov 20, 1925. An assassin shot him in Los Angeles, CA, June 5, 1968, while he was campaigning for the presidential nomination. He died on June 6, 1968. Sirhan Sirhan was convicted of his murder.

LAGERLOF, SELMA: BIRTHDAY. Nov 20. Swedish author, member of the Swedish Academy and the first woman to receive the Nobel Prize for Literature (1909) was born in Sweden's Varmland Province on Nov 20, 1858. She died there Mar 16, 1940.

LAURIER, SIR WILFRED: BIRTHDAY. Nov 20. Canadian statesman (premier, 1896-1911) born Nov 20, 1841. Died Feb 17, 1919.

MEXICO: REVOLUTION ANNIVERSARY. Nov 20. Anniversary of the social revolution launched by Francisco I Madero in 1910. National holiday.

THOMAS, ROBERT LINDSAY: BIRTHDAY. Nov 20. U.S. Representative of Georgia's 1st district, Democrat, of Statesboro, GA, born at Patterson, GA on Nov 20, 1943.

WOLCOTT, OLIVER: BIRTHDAY. Nov 20. Signer of the Declaration of Independence. Governor of Connecticut, born, Windsor, CT, Nov 20, 1726. Died Dec 1, 1797.

NOVEMBER 21 — FRIDAY
325th Day — Remaining, 40

AMERICAN SPEECH-LANGUAGE-HEARING ASSOCIATION CONVENTION: Nov 21-24. Cobo Hall, Detroit, MI. Scientific sessions on language, speech disorders, hearing science and hearing disorders and matters of professional interest to speech-language pathologists and audiologists. Info from: American Speech-Language-Hearing Assn, Frances J. Johnston, Conv Dir, 10801 Rockville Pike, Rockville, MD 20852.

BEAUMONT, WILLIAM: BIRTHDAY. Nov 21. U.S. Army surgeon whose contribution to classic medical literature and world fame resulted from another man's shotgun wound. When the Canadian fur trapper, Alexis St. Martin, received an apparently mortal wound on June 6, 1822—a nearly point blank blast to the abdomen—Dr. Beaumont began observing his stomach and digestive processes through an opening in the abdominal wall. His findings were published in 1833 in *Experiments and Observations on the Gastric Juice and the Physiology of Digestion.* St. Martin returned to Canada in 1834 and resisted Beaumont's efforts to return him for further study. He outlived his doctor by twenty years and was buried at a depth of eight feet to discourage any attempt at posthumous examination. Beaumont, born at Lebanon, CT, on Nov 21, 1785, died Apr 25, 1853 at St. Louis, MO.

DURBIN, RICHARD: BIRTHDAY. Nov 21. U.S. Representative of Illinois' 20th district, Democrat, of Springfield, IL, was born in East St. Louis, IL, Nov 21, 1944.

GREEN, HETTY: BIRTHDAY. Nov 21. Henrietta Howland Robinson Green, better known as Hetty Green, reported to have been the richest woman in America, was born at New Bedford, MA, Nov 21, 1835. She was an able financier who managed her own wealth, which was estimated to have been in excess of 100 million dollars. Died at New York City, July 3, 1916.

HOLIDAY FOLK FAIR. Nov 21-23. Milwaukee Expo and Conv Ctr, Milwaukee, WI. Purpose: to appreciate ethnic richness of 50 participating groups. Cultural exhibits, ethnic foods, folk dancing and world mart craftsmanship treasures. Weekend prior to Thanksgiving each year. Info from: Holiday Folk Fair, 2810 W Highland Blvd, Milwaukee, WI 53208.

MAN'S FIRST FREE FLIGHT (BALLOON): ANNIVERSARY. Nov 21. Jean Francois Pilatre de Rozier and the Marquis Francois Laurent d'Arlandes became the first men to fly when they ascended in a Montgolfier hot air balloon, at Paris, on Nov 21, 1783, less than six months after the first public balloon flight demonstration (June 5, 1783), and only a year after the first experiments with small paper and fabric balloons by the Montgolfier brothers, Joseph and Jacques, at Annonay, France, in November 1782. The first manned free flight lasted about 25 minutes and carried the passengers nearly six miles at a height of about 300 feet, over the city of Paris. Benjamin Franklin was one of the spectators at this flight.

NATIONAL FARM-CITY WEEK. Nov 21-27. Presidential ☆ Proclamation. Has been issued for a week in November since 1956.

NATIONAL FARM-CITY WEEK. Nov 21-27. Theme: "Partners in Progress." Purpose: To promote and encourage the rural and urban segments of society, agriculture and business in working together on the basis of a mutual understanding. Sponsor: The Natl Farm-City Council, W. Thomas Nelson, Secy, Kiwanis Internatl, 3636 Woodview Trace, Indianapolis, IN 46268.

NORTH CAROLINA: RATIFICATION DAY. Nov 21. Twelfth State to ratify constitution, on this day in 1789.

POPE BENEDICT XV: BIRTHDAY. Nov 21. Giacomo dela Chiesa, 258th Pope of the Roman Catholic Church, born at Pegli, Italy, Nov 21, 1854, Elected Pope Sept 3, 1914. Died Jan 22, 1922.

RECREATIONAL VEHICLE, BOAT AND MOBILE HOME SHOW. Nov 21-23. Phoenix Coliseum, Phoenix, AZ. Info from: Dixie Green Promotions, Inc, 3141 W Christy Dr, Phoenix, AZ 85029.

SUGARLOAF'S AUTUMN CRAFTS FESTIVAL. Nov 21-23. Montgomery County Fairgounds, Gaithersburg, MD. Over 300 professional artists and craftspeople, demonstrations, children's entertainment. Sponsor: Sugarloaf Mt Works, Inc, Ijamsville, MD 21754.

VOLTAIRE, JEAN FRANCOIS MARIE: BIRTHDAY. Nov 21. French author and philosopher to whom is attributed (perhaps erroneously) the statement: "I disapprove of what you say, but I will defend to the death your right to say it." Born Nov 21, 1694. Died May 30, 1778.

WORLD HELLO DAY. Nov 21. Purpose: "Everyone who chooses to participate says 'Hello' to ten people. Heads of state of 85 countries have expressed their approval of this global activity for promoting world peace." Sponsor: Hello Day Internatl, Box 993, Omaha, NE 68101.

NOVEMBER 22 — SATURDAY
326th Day — Remaining, 39

BRITTEN, (EDWARD) BENJAMIN: BIRTHDAY. Nov 22. English composer born, Lowestoft, Suffolk, Nov 22, 1913. Lord Britten, Baron Britten of Aldeburgh, died at Aldeburgh, Dec 4, 1976.

CARMICHAEL, HOAGIE: BIRTHDAY. Nov 22. Hoagland Howard Carmichael, attorney who gave up the practice of law to become an actor and songwriter, was born at Bloomington, IN, Nov 22, 1899. Among his many popular songs: "Stardust," "Lazybones," "Two Sleepy People," and "Skylark." Carmichael died at Rancho Mirage, CA, Dec 27, 1981.

DARDEN, GEORGE BUDDY: BIRTHDAY. Nov 22. U.S. Representative of Georgia's 7th district, Democrat, of Marietta, GA, born at Hancock County, GA, on Nov 22, 1943.

	S	M	T	W	T	F	S
November							1
1986	2	3	4	5	6	7	8
	9	10	11	12	13	14	15
	16	17	18	19	20	21	22
	23	24	25	26	27	28	29
	30						

ELIOT, GEORGE: BIRTH ANNIVERSARY. Nov 22. English novelist George Eliot, whose real name was Mary Anne Evans, was born at Chilvers Coton, Warwickshire, on Nov 22, 1819. She died at Chelsea, Dec 22, 1880.

GARNER, JOHN NANCE: BIRTHDAY. Nov 22. Thirty-second Vice-President of U.S. (1933-1941) born Red River County, TX, Nov 22, 1868. Died, Uvalde, TX, Nov 7, 1967.

KENNEDY, JOHN F: ASSASSINATION ANNIVERSARY. Nov 22. President John F. Kennedy was slain by sniper while riding in open automobile at Dallas, TX, Nov 22, 1963. Accused Lee Harvey Oswald was killed while in police custody awaiting trial as assassin.

LEBANON: NATIONAL HOLIDAY. Nov 22. Independence Day.

PELL, CLAIBORNE: BIRTHDAY. Nov 22. U.S. Senator from Rhode Island, Democrat, of Newport, RI, born in New York City, on Nov 22, 1918.

POST, WILEY: BIRTHDAY. Nov 22. Barnstorming aviator, stunt parachutist and adventurer, Wiley Post, was born at Grand Plain, TX, on Nov 22, 1898. Post, who taught himself to fly, and his plane, the *Winnie Mae*, were the center of world attention in the 1930s. He was coauthor (with his navigator, Harold Gatty) of *Around the World in Eight Days*. In 1935, Post and friend Will Rogers started on flight to the Orient. Plane crashed near Point Barrow, AK on Aug 15, 1935; both were killed.

ST. CECILIA: FEAST DAY. Nov 22. Roman virgin, Christian martyr and patron of music and musicians lived during third century. Survived sentences of burning and beheading. Subject of poetry and musical compositions, her feast day is still occasion for musical events.

WALES: CARDIFF FESTIVAL OF MUSIC. Nov 22-Dec 6. Cardiff, South Glamorgan. A series of concerts presenting music of the 20th century along with music from earlier periods.

NOVEMBER 23 — SUNDAY
327th Day — Remaining, 38

ADOPTION WEEK. Nov 23-29. Purpose: A time to celebrate with thankfulness the strength and uniqueness of adoptive families and focus attention on over 200,000 U.S. children without permanent parents. Sponsor: North American Council on Adoptable Children, 413 Duke St, Suite 203, Alexandria, VA 22314.

BILLY THE KID: BIRTH ANNIVERSARY. Nov 23. Legendary outlaw of western U.S. Probably named Henry McCarty at birth, in New York City, Nov 23, 1859, he was better known as William H. Bonney. Ruthless killer, a failure at everything legal, at age 21, he escaped from jail while under sentence of hanging. Recaptured at Stinking Springs, NM, and returned to jail, he again escaped, only to be shot through heart by pursuing Lincoln County sheriff Pat Garrett, at Fort Sumner, NM, during night of July 14, 1881. His last words, answered by two shots, reportedly were "Who is there?" Few reliably documented facts known about him.

BROCK, WILLIAM EMERSON: BIRTHDAY. Nov 23. William E. Brock, U.S. Secretary of Labor, (confirmed by Senate on Apr 26, 1985), born Chattanooga, TN on Nov 23, 1930.

CHRISTKINDLESMARKT. Nov 23-Dec 21. Adamstown, PA. A German-themed holiday market fair and Christmas fantasyland. Info from: Ed Stoudt's Black Angus, Route 272, Adamstown, PA 19501.

GALLO, DEAN A: BIRTHDAY. Nov 23. U.S. Representative of New Jersey's 11th district, Republican, of Parsippany, NJ, born in Hackensack, NJ, on Nov 23, 1935.

LABOR THANKSGIVING DAY. Nov 23. Japan (National holiday).

LATIN AMERICA WEEK. Nov 23-29. Purpose: To promote closer cultural and economic ties with all Latin Republics and USA on a community level. (Last full week in Nov.) Sponsor: Richard R. Falk Associates, Richard Falk, Dir, 147 W 42nd St, New York, NY 10036.

MOLINARI, GUY V: BIRTHDAY. Nov 23. U.S. Representative of New York's 14th district, Republican, of Staten Island, NY, born in New York City, Nov 23, 1928.

MOTHER GOOSE PARADE. Nov 23. Purpose: "A gift to the children." Floats depict Mother Goose rhymes and fairy tales. Bands, equestrians and clowns. Traditionally, the Sunday before Thanksgiving. Info from: Mother Goose Parade Assn, Box 1155, El Cajon, CA 92022.

MYRTLE BEACH HOLIDAY FIESTA. Nov 23-Dec 31. Turkey shoots, golf tournaments, caroling, concerts and church services. Info from: Chamber of Commerce, Box 2115, Myrtle Beach, SC 29578.

NATIONAL ADOPTION WEEK. Nov 23-29. Purpose: To commemorate success of 3 kinds of adoption—infant, special needs, and intercountry—through a variety of special events. (Annually, week of Thanksgiving.) Sponsor: Natl Committee for Adoption, Jeffrey Rosenberg, MSW, Dir of Public Policy, 1346 Connecticut Ave NW, Suite 326, Washington, DC 20036.

NATIONAL BIBLE WEEK. Nov 23-30. Purpose: An interfaith campaign to promote reading and study of the Bible. Observed annually, from the Sunday preceding Thanksgiving to the Sunday after. Sponsor: Layman's Natl Bible Committee, Inc, 815 Second Ave, New York, NY 10017.

NATIONAL FAMILY WEEK. Nov 23-29. Presidential Proclama-
☆ tion. "Issued in 1972 and 1976 through 1982 at Congressional request for the week including Thanksgiving." Note: Although issued as indicated above, there is no assurance for issuance in future years.

NATIONAL FAMILY WEEK. Nov 23-29. Purpose: To highlight the fundamental role of strong families in strengthening the nation. Always the week which includes Thanksgiving. Info from: American Family Society, Washington, DC 20088.

PIERCE, FRANKLIN: BIRTHDAY. Nov 23. The 14th President of the U.S. (Term of office: Mar 4, 1853-Mar 3, 1857), was born at Hillsboro, NH, Nov 23, 1804. Not nominated until the 49th ballot at the Democratic party convention in 1852, he was refused his party's nomination, in 1856, for a second term. Pierce died at Concord, NH, Oct 8, 1869.

REPUDIATION DAY. Nov. 23. Maryland. Half-holiday ordinarily, Frederick County.

RUTLEDGE, EDWARD: BIRTHDAY. Nov 23. Signer of the Declaration of Independence, governor of South Carolina, born, Charleston, SC, Nov 23, 1749. Died there Jan 23, 1800.

SAGITTARIUS, THE ARCHER. Nov 23-Dec 21. In the astronomical/astrological zodiac, which divides the sun's apparent orbit into twelve segments, the period Nov 22-Dec 21 is identified, traditionally, as the sun-sign of Sagittarius, the Archer. The ruling planet is Jupiter.

SCHUMER, CHARLES ELLIS: BIRTHDAY. Nov 23. U.S. Representative of New York's 10th district, Democrat, of Brooklyn, NY, born there Nov 23, 1950.

WYLIE, CHALMERS P: BIRTHDAY. Nov 23. U.S. Representative of Ohio's 15th district, Republican, of Worthington, OH, was born in Norwich, OH, on Nov 23, 1920.

COPYRIGHT © 1985 BY WILLIAM D. CHASE and HELEN M. CHASE

NOVEMBER 24 — MONDAY

328th Day — Remaining, 37

BARKLEY, ALBEN WILLIAM: BIRTHDAY. Nov 24. Thirty-fifth Vice-President of the U.S. (1949-1953) born, Graves County, KY, Nov 24, 1877. Died, Lexington, VA, Apr 30, 1956.

CARNEGIE, DALE: BIRTHDAY. Nov 24. American inspirational lecturer and author, Dale Carnegie was born at Maryville, MO, Nov 24, 1888. His best known book, *How to Win Friends and Influence People*, published in 1936, sold nearly five million copies and was translated into 29 languages. Carnegie died in New York City, Nov 1, 1955.

"D.B. COOPER" HIJACKING ANNIVERSARY. Nov 24-25. A middle-aged man whose plane ticket was made out to "D.B. Cooper" parachuted from a Northwest Airlines 727 jet liner on Nov 25, 1971, carrying $200,000 which he had collected from the airline as ransom for the plane and passengers as a result of threats he made during his Nov 24th flight from Portland, OR, to Seattle, WA. He jumped from the plane over an area of wilderness south of Seattle, and was never apprehended. Several thousand dollars of the marked ransom money turned up in Feb 1980, along the Columbia River, near Vancouver, WA.

DELLUMS, RONALD V: BIRTHDAY. Nov 24. U.S. Representative of California's 8th district, Democrat, of Oakland, CA, born there Nov 24, 1935.

GLICKMAN, DAN: BIRTHDAY. Nov 24. U.S. Representative of Kansas' 4th district, Democrat, of Wichita, KS, born in Wichita on Nov 24, 1944.

JOPLIN, SCOTT: BIRTHDAY. Nov 24. American musician and composer famed for his piano rags, born Texarkana, TX, Nov 24, 1868. Died, New York City, Apr 1, 1917.

MOON PHASE: LAST QUARTER. Nov 24. Moon enters Last Quarter phase at 11:50 a.m., E.S.T.

ONION MARKET (ZIBELEMARIT). Nov 24. Berne, Switzerland. Best known and most popular of Switzerland's many autumn markets. Great heaps of onions in front of federal Palace. Fourth Monday in November commemorates granting of market right to people after great fire of Berne in 1405.

SPINOZA, BARUCH: BIRTHDAY. Nov 24. Dutch philosopher, born Amsterdam, Nov 24, 1632. Died Feb 21, 1677. "Peace is not an absence of war," wrote Spinoza, in 1670, "it is a virtue, a state of mind, a disposition for benevolence, confidence, justice."

STERNE, LAURENCE: BIRTHDAY. Nov 24. Novelist, author, born Nov 24, 1713. Died, London, Mar 18, 1768. In his Dedication to *Tristram Shandy*, Sterne wrote: "I live in a constant endeavour to fence against the infirmities of ill health, and other evils of life, by mirth; being firmly persuaded that every time a man smiles,—but much more so, when he laughs, that it adds something to this Fragment of Life."

TAYLOR, ZACHARY: BIRTHDAY. Nov 24. The soldier who became 12th President of the U.S. (Term of office: Mar 4, 1849-July 9, 1850) was born at Orange County, VA, Nov 24, 1784. Nominated at the Whig party convention in 1848, but the story is told that he did not accept the letter notifying him of his nomination because it had postage due. He cast his first vote in 1846, when he was 62 years old. Becoming ill on July 4, 1850, he died at The White House, July 9th. His last words: "I am sorry that I am about to leave my friends."

	S	M	T	W	T	F	S
November							1
	2	3	4	5	6	7	8
1986	9	10	11	12	13	14	15
	16	17	18	19	20	21	22
	23	24	25	26	27	28	29
	30						

WORLD'S CHAMPIONSHIP DUCK CALLING CONTEST. Nov 24-29. Purpose: World's championship in duck calling. Queen Mallard contest, arts and crafts and duck gumbo cook-off. Sponsor: Chamber of Commerce, Box 932, Stuttgart, AR 72160.

ZAIRE: NATIONAL HOLIDAY. Nov 24.

NOVEMBER 25 — TUESDAY

329th Day — Remaining, 36

AUTOMOBILE SPEED REDUCTION ANNIVERSARY. Nov 25. Anniversary of the presidential order, Nov 25, 1973, requiring a cutback from 70 mile-per-hour speed limit. The 55 mile-per-hour National Maximum Speed Limit (NMSL) was established by the Congress in Jan 1974, made permanent by Public Law 93-643. The National Highway Traffic Administration reports that "Analyses of available data show that the 55 mph NMSL forestalled 48,310 fatalities through 1980. There were also reductions in crash related injuries and property damage. Motor fuel savings have been estimated at 2.4 billion gallons per year since the 55 mph NMSL was established."

CARNEGIE, ANDREW: BIRTHDAY. Nov 25. American financier, philanthropist and benefactor of more than 2,500 libraries, was born at Dunfermline, Scotland, Nov 25, 1835. Carnegie Hall, Carnegie Foundation, and the Carnegie Endowment for International Peace are among his gifts. Carnegie wrote, in 1889, "Surplus wealth is a sacred trust which its possessor is bound to administer in his lifetime for the good of the community . . . The man who dies . . . rich dies disgraced." Carnegie died at his summer estate, "Shadowbrook," MA, on Aug 11, 1919.

GERMANY: FRANKFURT: CHRISTMAS MARKET. Nov 25-Dec 23. "Weinachtsmarkt auf dem Romerberg," the Christmas market in Frankfurt, is one of Germany's best. Bells are rung simultaneously from nine downtown churches. Glockenspiel by hand and trumpets are blown from the old St. Nicolas Church.

NATION, CARRY AMELIA MOORE: BIRTHDAY. Nov 25. American temperance leader, famed as hatchet-wielding smasher of saloons, born at Garrard County, KY, Nov 25, 1846. Died at Leavenworth, KS, June 9, 1911.

POPE JOHN XXIII: BIRTHDAY. Nov 25. Angelo Roncalli, 261st Pope of the Roman Catholic Church, born at Sotte il Monte, Italy, on Nov 25, 1881. Elected Pope, Oct 28, 1958. Died, June 3, 1963.

ST. CATHERINE'S DAY. Nov 25. Patron saint of maidens, mechanics and philosophers, as well as of all who work with wheels.

SURINAME: NATIONAL HOLIDAY. Nov 25. Independence Day.

WORLD CONGRESS ON EATING DISORDERS. Nov 25-29. St. Louis, MO. Medical authorities will talk symptoms, diagnosis and treatment of anorexia and bulimia affecting almost 60 percent of college-age students. Info from: Bulimia, Anorexia Self Help (B.A.S.H.), 1027 Bellevue Ave, St Louis, MO 63117.

NOVEMBER 26 — WEDNESDAY

330th Day — Remaining, 35

ANNIVERSARY OF FIRST U.S. HOLIDAY BY PRESIDENTIAL PROCLAMATION. Nov 26. Pres George Washington proclaimed Nov 26, 1789, to be Thanksgiving Day. Both Houses of Congress, by their joint committee, requested him to recommend a day of public thanksgiving and prayer, to be observed by acknowledging with grateful hearts the many and signal favors of Almighty God, especially by affording them an opportunity peaceably to establish a form of government for their safety and happiness. Proclamation issued Oct 3, 1789.

COPYRIGHT © 1985 BY WILLIAM D. CHASE and HELEN M. CHASE

GRIMKÉ, SARAH MOORE: BIRTHDAY. Nov 26. American antislavery and women's rights advocate along with her sister Angelina. Born on Nov 26, 1792 at Charleston, SC, and died on Dec 23, 1873 at Hyde Park, MA.

HARVARD, JOHN: DAY. Nov 26. English clergyman and scholar, founder of Harvard College. Nov 26, 1607-Sept 14, 1638.

KLECZKA, GERALD DANIEL: BIRTHDAY. Nov 26. U.S. Representative of Wisconsin's 4th district, Democrat, of Milwaukee, WI, born there on Nov 26, 1943.

MAYOR SCHAEFER'S THANKSGIVING PARTY. Nov 26. War Memorial Plaza, Baltimore, MD. City of Baltimore presents its annual Thanksgiving party. Everyone is invited to stop by to sample cider. Free turkey raffle and turkey costume contest. Info from: Virginia Baker, Mayor's Office of Adventures in Fun, 100 Holliday St, Rm 355, Baltimore, MD 21202.

SHOPPING REMINDER DAY. Nov 26. A reminder to shoppers that there are only 24 more shopping days after today until Christmas, and that one month from today a new countdown will begin for Christmas, 1987.

SOJOURNER TRUTH DAY. Nov 26. American abolitionist, civil rights leader, lecturer. Born a slave, in Ulster County, NY, about 1790. Died, Battle Creek, MI, Nov 26, 1883. Changed her name to Sojourner Truth about 1843 when she began crusading travels for abolition movement.

WALKER, MARY EDWARDS: BIRTHDAY. Nov 26. American physician and women's rights leader, born at Oswego, NY, Nov 26, 1832. First female surgeon in U.S. Army (Civil War). Spent four months in Confederate prison. First and only woman ever to receive Medal of Honor (Nov 11, 1865). Two years before her death, on June 3, 1916, a government review board asked that her award be revoked. She continued to wear it, in spite of official revocation, until her death, Feb 21, 1919. On June 11, 1977, the Secretary of the Army restored the Medal of Honor to Dr. Walker, posthumously. Special commemorative U.S. postage stamp was issued in 1982, marking 150th anniversary of her birth.

NOVEMBER 27 — THURSDAY

331st Day — Remaining, 34

BEARD, CHARLES A: BIRTH ANNIVERSARY. Nov 27. American historian Charles Austin Beard who wrote many books in collaboration with his wife, Mary R. Beard, was born near Knightstown, IN, on Nov 27, 1874. He died at New Haven, CT, Sept 1, 1948.

BENEDICT, JULIUS: BIRTHDAY. Nov 27. The German-born musician and composer Sir Julius Benedict was born at Stuttgart, on Nov 27, 1804. Knighted in 1871, Benedict died at London, June 5, 1885.

GIMBELS THANKSGIVING DAY PARADE. Nov 27. Philadelphia, PA. Parade starts at Benjamin Franklin Parkway and officially opens the holiday season in Philadelphia. Info from: Ann Stuart, Dir, Special Events, Gimbels, 10th and Market Sts, Philadelphia, PA 19107.

JEWISH BOOK MONTH. Nov 27-Dec 27. Purpose: To promote interest in books of Jewish interest. Sponsor: JWB Jewish Book Council, 15 E 26th St, New York, NY 10010.

KEMBLE, FANNY: BIRTH ANNIVERSARY. Nov 27. Frances Anne Kemble, English actress, born, London, England, Nov 27, 1809. Died, Jan 15, 1893.

LELAND, MICKEY: BIRTHDAY. Nov 27. U.S. Representative of Texas' 18th district, Democrat, of Houston, TX, was born on Nov 27, 1944.

LIVINGSTON, ROBERT R: BIRTHDAY. Nov 27. Member of the Continental Congress, farmer, diplomat and jurist, was born at New York City, Nov 27, 1746. It was Livingston who administered the oath of office to President George Washington in 1789. He died at Clermont, NY, Feb 26, 1813.

MACY'S THANKSGIVING DAY PARADE. Nov 27. New York. Info from: NY Conv & Visitors Bureau, 2 Columbus Circle, New York, NY 10019.

REV. FRANCIS GASTRELL'S EJECTMENT: ANNIVERSARY. Nov 27. On Nov 27, 1759, the Stratford-Upon-Avon town corporation gave orders to bring an "action of Ejectment" against the Rev. Francis Gastrell, Vicar of Frodsham, who lived in William Shakespeare's home. Gastrell, it is said, had cut down the 150-year-old mulberry tree which had been planted by William Shakespeare. Gastrell maliciously felled the tree because he was annoyed by the many Shakespeare enthusiasts who came to look at it. He sold the tree for firewood, but it was recovered by a jeweller-woodcarver, Thomas Sharp, who fashioned hundreds of relics from it. Gastrell was ejected from Stratford "amid the ragings and cursings of its people, a citizen well lost"—for one of "the meanest petty infamies in our annals." The Rev Gastrell's wife, Jane, is said to have been an accomplice in this celebrated arboricide.

SOUTH CAROLINA STATE BLUEGRASS FESTIVAL. Nov 27-29. Convention Ctr, Myrtle Beach, SC. Family entertainment. Info from: Norman Adams, Box 98, Dahlonega, GA 30533.

SPACE MILESTONE: SOYUZ T-3 (USSR). Nov 27. Launched on Nov 27, 1980, three cosmonauts, O. Makarov, L. Kizim and G. Strekalov, docked at Salyut 6 space station on Nov 28. Returned to Earth Dec 10, 1980.

THANKSGIVING DAY. Nov 27. Presidential Proclamation. ☆ "Always issued for the 4th Thursday in November."

THANKSGIVING DAY. Nov 27. Legal public holiday, (Public Law 90-363 sets Thanksgiving Day on the fourth Thursday in November). Observed on this day in all states.

WEIZMANN, CHAIM: BIRTHDAY. Nov 27. Israeli statesman born near Pinsk, U.S.S.R., Nov 27, 1874. Important role bringing about British government's Balfour Declaration, calling for establishment of a national home for Jews in Palestine. Died at Tel Aviv, Israel, Nov 9, 1952.

YOUNG, ROBERT A: BIRTHDAY. Nov 27. U.S. Representative of Missouri's 2nd district, Democrat, of Maryland Heights, MO, born in St. Louis, MO, on Nov 27, 1923.

NOVEMBER 28 — FRIDAY

332nd Day — Remaining, 33

AMATEUR RADIO COMMUNICATION FROM SPACE: ANNIVERSARY. Nov 28. US Mission STS-9, Shuttle Columbia, launched Nov 28, 1983, carried Owen Garriott, W5LFL, first person to use amateur radio to contact hams on Earth from space. Info from: American Radio Relay League, Attn E. Karpiej, KA1DTU, 225 Main St, Newington, CT 06111.

BENTLEY, HELEN DELICH: BIRTHDAY. Nov 28. U.S. Representative of Maryland's 2nd district, Republican, of Lutherville, MD, was born in Ruth, NV, on Nov 28, 1923.

BLAKE, WILLIAM: BIRTHDAY. Nov 28. English poet and artist, born London, Nov 28, 1757. Died there Aug 12, 1827.

BUNYAN, JOHN: BIRTHDAY. Nov 28. English cleric and author, born Nov 28, 1628. Died London, Aug 31, 1688.

COPYRIGHT © 1985 BY WILLIAM D. CHASE and HELEN M. CHASE

CHRISTMAS WITH THE GUILD. Nov 28-Dec 31. Holiday celebration includes theme trees, exhibits and special musical programs. Info from: Southern Highland Handicraft Guild, Box 9545, Asheville, NC 28815.

CINCINNATI CRAFTS AFFAIR. Nov 28-30. Cincinnati Convention Ctr, Cincinnati, OH. Craft fair featuring the best work of 150 professional American craftsmen. Sponsor: Ohio Designer Craftsmen Enterprises, 2164 Riverside Dr, Columbus, OH 43221.

FINGER LAKES CRAFTSMEN THANKSGIVING WEEK-END-CHRISTMAS ARTS AND CRAFTS SHOW. Nov 28-30. Monroe County Fairgrounds Dome Arena, Rochester, NY. All media, all categories. Info from: Finger Lakes Craftsmen Shows, 25 Seneca St, Shortsville, NY 14548.

GATLINBURG'S TWELVE DAYS OF CHRISTMAS FESTIVAL. Nov 28-Dec 21. Contemporary and traditional events. Yule log burnings, electrical parade of ornaments, living Christmas tree and festival of trees. Info from: Chamber of Commerce, Box 527, Gatlinburg, TN 37738.

HART, GARY: BIRTHDAY. Nov 28. U.S. Senator from Colorado, Democrat, of Denver, CO, was born in Ottawa, KS, Nov 28, 1936.

HOLIDAY CRAFT AND GIFT SHOW. Nov 28-30. Wisconsin State Fair Park, West Allis, WI. Combined show with 200 commercial gift exhibitors and 400 craftsmen. Info from: Dennis R. Hill, Dir, 3233 S Villa Circle, West Allis, WI 53227.

IMSA EASTERN AIRLINES NATIONAL CHAMPIONSHIP FINALE. Nov 28-30. Daytona International Speedway, Daytona Beach, FL. Info from: Daytona Internatl Speedway, Larry Balewski, PR, Daytona Beach, FL 32015.

LULLY, JEAN BAPTISTE: BIRTHDAY. Nov 28. Versatile musician and composer, born at Florence, Italy, on Nov 28, 1632, who chose France for his homeland. Noted for his quick temper, it is said that he struck his own foot with a baton while in a rage. The resulting wound led to blood poisoning, from which he died, at Paris, Mar 22, 1687.

MAURITANIA: NATIONAL HOLIDAY. Nov 28. Independence Day. Attained sovereignty Nov 28, 1960.

PACE MANAGEMENT TRUCK AND TRACTOR PULL. Nov 28-30. Info from: Tarrant County Conv Ctr, 1111 Houston St, Fort Worth, TX 76102.

PANAMA: INDEPENDENCE FROM SPAIN. Nov 28. Public holiday in Panama.

ROARING CAMP'S MOUNTAIN MAN RENDEZVOUS. Nov 28-30. Purpose: Trappers and mountain men reenact the life and times of the 1830s to 1860s American West. Info from: Roaring Camp & Big Trees Narrow-gauge Railroad, Felton, Santa Cruz County, CA 95018.

SPACE MILESTONE: MARINER 4 (US). Nov 28. Launched Nov 28, 1964 toward Mars. On July 14, 1965, after 228 days, approached within 6,118 miles of Mars. Took photographs.

SPACE MILESTONE: STS-9 (US). Nov 28. Shuttle Columbia launched from Kennedy Space Center, FL Nov 28, 1983 with five astronauts (John Young, Brewster Shaw Jr, Owen Garriott, Robert Parker, Byron Lichtenberg and German physicist Ulf Merbold). Landed at Edwards Air Force Base, CA on Dec 8.

STAMP EXPO '86/PACIFIC. Nov 28-30. Anaheim Hotel, Anaheim, CA. Purpose: International postage stamp exposition honoring "Thanksgiving." Sponsor: Internatl Stamp Collectors Society, Box 854, Van Nuys, CA 91408.

November
1986

S	M	T	W	T	F	S
2	3	4	5	6	7	1 8
9	10	11	12	13	14	15
16	17	18	19	20	21	22
23	24	25	26	27	28	29
30						

TEHERAN CONFERENCE ANNIVERSARY. Nov 28-Dec 1. President Franklin D. Roosevelt, British Prime Minister Winston Churchill, and Soviet Premier Joseph Stalin met at Teheran, Iran, Nov 28-Dec 1, 1943, to discuss and determine a plan for an Allied assault, a second front, in western Europe. The resulting plan was "Operation Overlord," which commenced the landing on Normandy's beaches June 6, 1944 ("D-day").

WBAI HOLIDAY CRAFTS FAIR. Nov 28-30. (Also Dec 12-14 and Dec 19-21.) Ferris Booth Hall, Columbia Univ, New York, NY. Winter crafts marketplace, with 375 professional artisans from over 30 states participating. Info from: Matthew Alperin, WBAI Crafts Fair, Box 889, Times Sq Station, New York, NY 10108.

YOU'RE WELCOMEGIVING DAY. Nov 28. Purpose: to create a four-day weekend. Sponsor: Richard Ankli, Broadway Fun Spot, 639 Fifth St., Ann Arbor, MI 48103.

NOVEMBER 29 — SATURDAY
333rd Day — Remaining, 32

ALBANIA: NATIONAL DAY. Nov 29. National holiday observed.

ALCOTT, LOUISA MAY: BIRTHDAY. Nov 29. American author, born Philadelphia, Nov 29, 1832. Died, Boston, Mar 6, 1888.

ARMY-NAVY FOOTBALL GAME. Nov 29. Veterans Stadium, Philadelphia, PA. West Point and the Naval Academy.

BAPTIST HOSPITAL OF MIAMI ARTISTS' SHOWCASE. Nov 29-30. Miami, FL. Purpose: Over 100 artists exhibit and sell their works at annual juried show to raise money for hospital's foundation. Sponsor: Baptist Hospital Foundation, Dorothy Stein, Publications Coord, 8900 N Kendall Dr, Miami, FL 33176.

BASKETBALL HALL OF FAME TIP-OFF CLASSIC. Nov 29. Civic Center, Springfield, MA. Official opening game of collegiate basketball season. Info from: Tip-Off Classic, Box 1660, Springfield, MA 01101.

CHILDREN'S FIELD DAY. Nov 29. Purpose: Hoop rolling, running races and other games for children aged 4-12 on Mystic Seaport's village green. Info from: Mystic Seaport, Public Affairs Office, Mystic, CT 06355.

COLEMAN, RONALD D: BIRTHDAY. Nov 29. U.S. Representative of Texas' 16th district, Democrat, of El Paso, TX, born there on Nov 29, 1941.

FOOTBALL: GREY CUP. Nov 29. Vancouver, British Columbia. Canada's annual football classic. Info from: The Centennial Commission, Box 49386, Suite 3374, Bentall 4, 1055 Dunsmuir St, Vancouver, BC V7X 1L5.

GIANT TINKERTOY EXTRAVAGANZA. Nov 29-Dec 1. The Franklin Institute, Philadelphia, PA. "Do your building thing under the gaze of one of the country's leading innovators. Unfettering imaginations, a high tolerance for disorder and comfortable shoes are recommended for all would-be tinkerers." Info from: Franklin Institute, Benjamin Franklin Pkwy, Philadelphia, PA 19103.

HALL OF FAME ARABIAN HORSE SHOW. Nov 29-30. Ocala Arabian Show Grounds, Ocala, FL. All Arabian horse show. Weekend after Thanksgiving. Info from: Ocala Arabian Breeders Society, Box 4647, Ocala, FL 32678.

INTERNATIONAL DAY OF SOLIDARITY WITH THE PALESTINIAN PEOPLE. Nov 29. Observance proclaimed by UN General Assembly in 1977. At request of Assembly, observance is organized by Secretary-General in consultation with Committee on the Exercise of the Inalienable Rights of the Palestinian People. Recommendations include a plan for return of the Palestinians to their homes and the establishment of an "independent Palestinian entity." Info from: UN Dept of Public Information, United Nations, NY 10017.

COPYRIGHT © 1985 BY WILLIAM D. CHASE and HELEN M. CHASE

PENNSYLVANIA GINGERBREAD HOUSE INN-VITA-TIONAL. Nov 29. Strasburg, PA. Individuals participate in making gingerbread creations. Info from: The Historic Strasburg Inn, Route 896, Historic Dr, Strasburg, PA 17579.

PHILLIPS, WENDELL: BIRTHDAY. Nov 29. American women's suffrage, anti-slavery, prison reform leader, born Nov 29, 1811. Died Feb 2, 1884.

SIMON, PAUL: BIRTHDAY. Nov 29. U.S. Senator from Illinois, Democrat, of Makanda, IL, born in Eugene, OR, Nov 29, 1928.

TARHEEL TRIANGLE CAT FANCIERS' CAT SHOW. Nov 29. State Fairgrounds, Raleigh, NC. CFA championship cat show, held every Thanksgiving Saturday. Sponsor: Tarheel Triangle Cat Fanciers, Diane Clarke, Secy, Box 30004, Raleigh, NC 27622.

THOMSON, CHARLES: BIRTHDAY. Nov 29. America's first official record keeper. Chosen secretary of the First Continental Congress on Sept 5, 1774, he recorded proceedings for 15 years and delivered his journals together with tens of thousands of records to the federal government in 1789. Born in Ireland, Nov 29, 1729. Died Aug 16, 1824. It was Thomson who notified George Washington of his election as president.

YUGOSLAVIA: NATIONAL HOLIDAY. Nov 29-30. Commemorates Proclamation of the Republic in 1945.

NOVEMBER 30 — SUNDAY
334th Day — Remaining, 31

ADVENT, FIRST SUNDAY. Nov 30. Advent includes the four Sundays before Christmas.

ARTICLES OF PEACE BETWEEN GREAT BRITAIN AND THE UNITED STATES: ANNIVERSARY. Nov 30. These provisional articles of peace, which were to end America's War of Independence, were signed at Paris, Nov 30, 1782. The refined and definitive treaty of peace between Great Britain and the U.S. was signed at Paris, on Sept 3, 1783. In it "His Britannic Majesty acknowledges the said United States . . . to be free, sovereign and independent states; that he treats them as such; and for himself, his heirs and successors, relinquishes all claims to the government, propriety and territorial rights of the same, and every part thereof . . ."

BARBADOS: INDEPENDENCE DAY. Nov 30. National holiday.

BENIN, PEOPLE'S REPUBLIC OF: NATIONAL DAY. Nov 30. Public holiday.

BULGARELLI WINTER OR REAL WINTER IN THE GREAT NORTHEAST. Nov 30. (11:02 p.m. E.S.T.) Purpose: To recognize that winter weather often exists in the Northeast three weeks before calendar winter. Sponsors: George Bulgarelli, Meteorologist, Berkshire Eagle, Pittsfield, MA 01201 and Bob Cudmore, Talk show host, WGY, Box 1410, Schenectady, NY 12301.

CHURCHILL, WINSTON: BIRTHDAY. Nov 30. Winston Leonard Spencer Churchill, British statesman and the first man to be made an honorary citizen of the U.S. (by act of Congress, Apr 9, 1963), born (prematurely), Nov 30, 1874, at Blenheim Palace, Oxfordshire, England. Died, Jan 24, 1965, London, England.

CLEMENS, SAMUEL LANGHORNE (MARK TWAIN): BIRTH ANNIVERSARY. Nov 30. Celebrated American author, whose books included: *The Adventures of Tom Sawyer*,

The Adventures of Huckleberry Finn, and *The Prince and the Pauper*. Born at Florida, MO, Nov 30, 1835, Twain is quoted as saying "I came in with Halley's Comet in 1835. It is coming again next year, and I expect to go out with it." He did. Twain died at Redding, CT, on Apr 21, 1910 (just one day after Comet Halley's perihelion.)

ENGLISH, GLENN: BIRTHDAY. Nov 30. U.S. Representative of Oklahoma's 6th district, Democrat, of Cordell, OK, born in Cordell, on Nov 30, 1940.

HECHT, CHIC: BIRTHDAY. Nov 30. U.S. Senator from Nevada, Republican, of Las Vegas, NV born at Cape Girardeau, MO, on Nov 30, 1928.

KENNEDY, JOHN F: DAY. Nov 30. Massachusetts. (Last Sunday in Nov).

MORAVIAN CHRISTMAS PUTZ. Nov 30-Dec 31. Purpose: A presentation of the Christmas story using lights, sound and carved figures in an indoor setting. Sponsor: Central Moravian Church, Putz Committee, Main & Church Sts, Bethlehem, PA 18018.

PASADENA DOO DAH PARADE. Nov 30. Purpose: A parade with no theme, no judging, no prizes, no parade order and no motorized vehicles. Always the Sunday following Thanksgiving Day. Sponsor: Pasadena Doo Dah Parade, Peter Apanel, Dir, 539 E Villa St, Suite 20, Pasadena, CA 91101.

PHILIPPINES: BONIFACIO DAY. Nov 30. Also known as National heroes' day. Commemorates birth of Andres Bonifacio, leader of the 1896 revolt against Spain, Bonifacio was born Nov 30, 1863.

ST. ANDREW'S DAY. Nov 30. Feast day of the apostle and martyr, Andrew, who died about A.D. 60. Patron saint of Scotland.

SIDNEY, PHILIP: BIRTH ANNIVERSARY. Nov 30. English poet, statesman and soldier was born at Penshurst, Kent, on Nov 30, 1554. Best known of his poems is "Arcadia" (1580). Mortally wounded as he led an English detachment aiding the Dutch near Zutphen, on Sept 22, 1586, Sidney gave his water bottle to another dying soldier with the words "Thy necessity is yet greater than mine." He died at Arnheim on Oct 17, 1586, and all of England mourned the death of this man who had given new meaning to English patriotism.

SWIFT, JONATHAN: BIRTHDAY. Nov 30. Clergyman and satirist, born Dublin, Nov 30, 1667. Died there Oct 19, 1745. "I never saw, heard, nor read," Swift wrote in *Thoughts on Religion*, "that the clergy were beloved in any nation where Christianity was the religion of the country. Nothing can render them popular but some degree of persecution."

December.

DECEMBER 1 — MONDAY
335th Day — Remaining, 30

BINGO'S BIRTHDAY MONTH. Dec 1-31. Purpose: To celebrate the innovation and manufacture of the game of Bingo in 1929 by Edwin S. Lowe, which today has grown to a four billion dollar a year charitable fund raiser. Sponsor: Bingo Bugle, Inc, Roger Snowden, Pres, Box 527, Vashon, WA 98070.

CENTRAL AFRICAN REPUBLIC: NATIONAL DAY. Dec 1. Commemorates Proclamation of the Republic on Dec 1, 1958. Usually observed on first Monday of December.

CHRISTMAS AT BILTMORE. Dec 1-31. Biltmore Estate, Asheville, NC. Christmas is celebrated in much the same fashion as it was in 1895. Concert series and candlelight tours. Info from: The Biltmore Company, Marketing Dept, One Biltmore Plaza, Asheville, NC 28803.

CHRISTMAS CITY NIGHT LIGHT TOURS. Dec 1-30. Bethlehem, PA. Guides in Moravian dress lead tours to see the 85,000 white Christmas lights. Info from: Chamber of Commerce, 459 Old York Rd, Bethlehem, PA 18018.

CHRISTMAS IN OLDE JONESBOROUGH. Dec 1-25. Purpose: Old-fashioned celebration in Tennessee's "oldest town." Tour of homes and other activities. Info from: Christmas in Olde Jonesborough, Box 375, Jonesborough, TN 37659.

CHRISTMAS WALK. Dec 1-31. Pella Historical Village, Pella, IA. Purpose: To celebrate an old-fashioned Christmas. Info from: Pella Historical Society, Pella, IA 50219.

ENGLAND: ROYAL SMITHFIELD SHOW AND AGRICULTURAL MACHINERY EXHIBITION. Dec 1-4. Earls Court, Warwick Road, London SW5. "Outstanding event in the farming calendar with a wide range of livestock and exhibitions."

HI NABOR MONTH. Dec 1-31. Purpose: Spread good cheer for the New Year by sending holiday greeting card to Senior Citizens, or those confined to institutions. Sponsor: Hi Nabor! Club, Marguerite Ginnette, Dir, 3369 Hamilton Way, Los Angeles, CA 90026.

ICELAND: UNIVERSITY STUDENTS' CELEBRATION. Dec 1. Marks the day in 1918 when Iceland became an independent state from Denmark but under the King of Denmark.

MOON PHASE: NEW MOON. Dec 1. Moon enters New Moon phase at 11:43 a.m., E.S.T.

December	S	M	T	W	T	F	S
1986		1	2	3	4	5	6
	7	8	9	10	11	12	13
	14	15	16	17	18	19	20
	21	22	23	24	25	26	27
	28	29	30	31			

NETHERLANDS: MIDWINTER HORN BLOWING. Dec 1. 1986-Jan 6, 1987. Twente, and several other areas in the Netherlands. Midwinter horn blowing, folklore custom of announcing the birth of Christ, begins with Advent and continues to Jan 6 each year.

PORTUGAL: INDEPENDENCE DAY. Dec 1. Public holiday.

READ A NEW BOOK MONTH. Dec 1-31. Purpose: Get acquainted with the classics in French, German, Italian, Spanish. Begin new year by reading a new book. Sponsor: Book Parties Guild, 3369 Hamilton Way, Los Angeles, CA 90026.

RESTORATION OF INDEPENDENCE DAY. Dec 1. Macau.

ROCKEFELLER CENTER CHRISTMAS TREE LIGHTING. Dec 1. Info from: NY Conv & Visitors Bureau, Inc, John P. MacBean, VP, Public Relations, Two Columbus Circle, New York, NY 10019.

ROSA PARKS DAY. Dec 1. Anniversary of the arrest of Mrs. Rosa Parks, Dec 1, 1955, in Montgomery, AL for refusing to give up her seat and move to the back of a municipal bus. Her arrest triggered a year-long boycott of the city bus system and led to legal actions which ended racial segregation on municipal buses throughout southern U.S. The event has been called the birth of the modern civil rights movement. Rosa McCauley Parks was born at Tuskegee, AL, on Feb 4, 1913.

TREES AT SUNRISE. Dec 1-31. Sunrise Museum, Charleston, WV. An exhibition of sparkling historic and international holiday trees with handcrafted ornaments. Sponsor: Sunrise Museums, 746 Myrtle Rd, Charleston, WV 25314.

UNIVERSAL HUMAN RIGHTS MONTH. Dec 1-31. Purpose: To disseminate throughout the world information about human rights and distribute copies of the Universal Declaration of Human Rights in English and other languages. Sponsor: Internatl Society of Friendship & Good Will, Box 756, Shelby, NC 28151.

DECEMBER 2 — TUESDAY
336th Day — Remaining, 29

BENNETT, CHARLES E: BIRTHDAY. Dec 2. U.S. Representative of Florida's 3rd district, Democrat, of Jacksonville, FL, born Dec 2, 1910.

BROWN, JOHN: EXECUTION ANNIVERSARY. Dec 2. Abolitionist leader who is remembered for his raid on the U.S. Arsenal at Harper's Ferry, was hanged for treason, at Charles Town, WV, Dec 2, 1859.

CALLAS, MARIA: BIRTHDAY. Dec 2. American opera singer born at New York City, Dec 2, 1923. Died at Paris, Sept 16, 1977.

LAOS: NATIONAL HOLIDAY. Dec 2.

MEESE, EDWIN III: BIRTHDAY. Dec 2. Edwin Meese III, U.S. Attorney General (confirmed by the Senate on Feb 23, 1985) was born at Oakland, CA, on Dec 2, 1931.

MEMORIES OF CHRISTMAS HOUSE TOUR. Dec 2-5. Columbia, SC. Holiday tours of house museums, Info from: Historic Columbia Foundation, 1616 Blanding St, Columbia, SC 29201.

MONROE DOCTRINE: ANNIVERSARY. Dec 2. President James Monroe, in his annual message to the Congress, Dec 2, 1823, enunciated the doctrine which bears his name and which was long hailed as a statement of U.S. policy. ". . . In the wars of the European powers in matters relating to themselves we have never taken any part . . . we should consider any attempt on their part to extend their system to any portion of this hemisphere as dangerous to our peace and safety. . . ."

PAN AMERICAN HEALTH DAY. Dec 2. Presidential Proclamation. "Proc. 2447, Nov 23, 1940, covers all succeeding years."

PERIGEAN SPRING TIDES. Dec 2. Spring tides, the highest possible tides, occur when New Moon or Full Moon takes place within 24 hours of the moment the moon is nearest Earth (perigee) in its monthly orbit. Dec 2, at 6 a.m., E.S.T.

COPYRIGHT © 1985 BY WILLIAM D. CHASE and HELEN M. CHASE

PLINGE, WALTER: DAY. Dec 2. A day to recognize Walter Plinge, said to have been a London pub-landlord in 1900. His generosity to actors led to the use of his name as an actor, in play programs, usually to conceal the fact that several roles were being played by one actor. See George Spelvin Day for U.S. equivalent.

REID, HARRY: BIRTHDAY. Dec 2. U.S. Representative of Nevada's 1st district, Democrat, of Las Vegas, NV, born in Searchlight, NV, Dec 2, 1939.

SEURAT, GEORGES PIERRE: BIRTHDAY. Dec 2. French painter born Paris, Dec 2, 1859. Died there Mar 29, 1891.

SPACE MILESTONE: SOYUZ 16 (USSR). Dec 2. Six-day mission began Dec 2, 1974, with cosmonauts A.V. Filipchenko and N.N. Rukavishnikov. Rehearsal for US–USSR link-up in July 1975.

UNITED ARAB EMIRATES: NATIONAL DAY. Dec 2.

DECEMBER 3 — WEDNESDAY
337th Day — Remaining, 28

CHRISTMAS AT MEADOW BROOK HALL. Dec 3-14. Oakland University, Rochester, MI. Extravaganza of holiday decorations/displays created by major metro-Detroit floral artists and designers. Info from: Meadow Brook Hall, Oakland University, Rochester, MI 48063.

CONRAD, JOSEPH: BIRTHDAY. Dec 3. Polish novelist born Dec 3, 1857. Died Aug 3, 1924.

FIRST HEART TRANSPLANT ANNIVERSARY. Dec 3. Dr. Christiaan Barnard, a South African surgeon, performed the world's first heart transplantation on Dec 3, 1967 at Cape Town, South Africa. See also: Nov. 8.

FIRST NIGHT. Dec 3. Purpose: Celebration of beginning of Christmas season with tree lighting and caroling, steeped in tradition and folklore. Sponsor: City of Lewisburg, P.L. Gainer, Mayor, Box 548, Lewisburg, WV 24901.

FOGLIETTA, THOMAS M: BIRTHDAY. Dec 3. U.S. Representative of Pennsylvania's 1st district, Democrat, of Philadelphia, PA, born there on Dec 3, 1928.

HILL, SIR ROWLAND: BIRTHDAY. Dec 3. Purpose: To observe the birthday of Sir Rowland Hill (Dec 3, 1795-Aug 27, 1879) who introduced the first adhesive postage stamp (Penny Black of Great Britain). Sponsor: The Philatelic Journalist, 154 Laguna Ct, St. Augustine Shores, FL 32086.

ILLINOIS: ADMISSION DAY. Dec 3. Became 21st State on this day in 1818.

MORAVIAN CANDLE TEA. Dec 3-13. Single Brothers' House, Old Salem, Winston-Salem, NC. Purpose: To share traditions of the Moravian Church and prepare the visitors for the coming of the Christmas season. Sponsor: Womens' Fellowship of Home Moravian Church, Beth Baldwin, 1001 Englewood Dr, Winston-Salem, NC 27106.

REGULA, RALPH: BIRTHDAY. Dec 3. U.S. Representative of Ohio's 16th district, Republican, of Navarre, OH, born in Beach City, Stark County, OH, on Dec 3, 1924.

STUART, GILBERT CHARLES: BIRTHDAY. Dec 3. American portrait painter whose most famous painting is that of George Washington. He also painted portraits of Madison, Monroe, Jefferson and other important Americans. Stuart was born near Narragansett, RI on Dec 3, 1755 and died July 9, 1828 at Boston.

DECEMBER 4 — THURSDAY
338th Day — Remaining, 27

BUTLER, SAMUEL: BIRTHDAY. Dec 4. English author, born, Dec 4, 1835. Died, London, June 18, 1902.

CARLYLE, THOMAS: BIRTHDAY. Dec 4. Scottish essayist and historian, born Dec 4, 1795. Died, London, Feb 4, 1881. "A well-written Life is almost as rare as a well-spent one," Carlyle wrote in his *Critical and Miscellaneous Essays*.

CHASE'S ANNUAL EVENTS 29TH BIRTHDAY. Dec 4. First copies of first edition of *Chase's Calendar of Annual Events* (for the year 1958) were delivered by the printer at Flint, MI, Dec 4, 1957. Two thousand copies, consisting of 32 pages and listing 364 events, were printed.

CHRISTMAS TOUR OF HOMES. Dec 4. Pella, IA. Five homes decorated for holidays by Pella Garden Club members. Open to public. Christmas tea at Pella Historical Village. Info from: Pella Historical Society, Box 145, Pella, IA 50219.

COLUMBUS WINTERFAIR. Dec 4-7. Ohio State Fairgrounds, Columbus, OH. Craft fair featuring the best work of 325 professional American craftsmen. Sponsor: Ohio Designer Craftsmen Enterprises, 2164 Riverside Dr, Columbus, OH 43221.

DAY OF THE ARTISANS. Dec 4. Mexico. Honors the nation's workers.

FESTIVAL OF TREES. Dec. 4-8. Gatlinburg, TN. Trees decorated in historical, regional and international themes. Info from: Chamber of Commerce, Box 527, Gatlinburg, TN 37738.

LONGWOOD GARDENS CHRISTMAS DISPLAY. Dec 4-Jan 1, 1987. Christmas features 2,300 poinsettias indoors, organ and choral concerts and outdoors, 30,000 lights on 80 trees. Info from: Longwood Gardens, Kennett Square, PA 19348.

MISSION SANTA BARBARA ANNIVERSARY. Dec 4. Santa Barbara, California. Franciscan Mission to the Indians founded Dec 4, 1786. Present structure is the fourth to stand on same site. Last one destroyed by 1812 earthquake.

MITTEN TREE. Dec 4. Municipal Bldg Lobby, Baltimore, MD. Mittens donated by citizens for the mitten tree are sent to Salvation Army for distribution. Info from: Mayor's Office of Adventures in Fun, 100 Holliday St, Baltimore, MD 21202.

NIGHTWATCH ILLUMINATION CEREMONY. Dec 4-5. St. Augustine, FL. Reenactment of 18th century British garrison town custom of securing the town. Authentically dressed British soldiers, fife and drum corps, candlelight parade. Info from: Robert Hall, 42 Spanish St, St. Augustine, FL 32084.

RUSSELL, LILLIAN: BIRTHDAY. Dec 4. American singer and actress who in 1881 gained fame in the comic opera *The Great Mogul*. Born Helen Louise Leonard on Dec 4, 1861 at Clinton, IA. Married four times, and died on June 6, 1922 at Pittsburgh, PA.

ST. OLAF COLLEGE: CHRISTMAS FESTIVAL. Dec 4-6. Purpose: To celebrate the simplicity and the grandeur of Christmas through a worship service in and of sacred music. 75th anniversary of the festival. Info from: St. Olaf College, Dan Jorgensen, News Service Dir, Northfield, MN 55057.

DECEMBER 5 — FRIDAY
339th Day — Remaining, 26

BIZARRE BAZAAR. Dec 5-7. Richmond Arena, Richmond, VA. Christmas gift show with many handcrafts. Info from: Virginia Div of Tourism, 202 N. 9th St, Suite 500, Richmond, VA 23219.

CHRISTMAS SHOWCASE OF THE OZARK FOOTHILLS CRAFT GUILD. Dec 5-7. Statehouse Convention Center, Little Rock, AR. Info from: Ozark Foothills Craft Guild, Box 800, Mountain View, AR 72560.

CHRISTMAS TREE TRIMMING CONTEST: TREE LIGHTING CEREMONY. Dec 5. Memorial Plaza, Baltimore, MD. City departments decorate trees that best represent the service each provides. Mayor Schaefer lights official city Christmas tree. Info from: Mayor's Office of Adventures in Fun, 100 Holliday St, Baltimore, MD 21202.

ELGIN CATFISH STOMP. Dec. 5-7. Elgin, SC. Parade, catfish stew, carnival, arts, crafts and entertainment. (First weekend in December.) Info from: Margie C. Howard, Box 277, Elgin, SC 29045.

COPYRIGHT © 1985 BY WILLIAM D. CHASE and HELEN M. CHASE

FLORIDA TOURNAMENT OF BANDS. Dec 5-6. St. Petersburg, FL. Purpose: Award winning Florida high school bands compete in stage, parade, concert and field show presentations. (First weekend in December.) Sponsor: St. Petersburg Festival of States, Albert J. Castronovo, Box 1731, St. Petersburg, FL 33731.

GOODLING, WILLIAM F: BIRTHDAY. Dec 5. U.S. Representative of Pennsylvania's 19th district, Republican, of Jacobus, PA, was born in Loganville, PA, on Dec 5, 1927.

HAITI: DISCOVERY DAY. Dec 5. Commemorates the discovery of Haiti by Christopher Columbus in 1492. Public holiday.

LANTERN LIGHT TOURS. Dec 5-21. Purpose: Costumed guides with lanterns lead groups to exhibits where glimpses of Christmases past are portrayed. Evening walking tours. Info from: Public Affairs Office, Mystic Seaport, Mystic, CT 06355.

OLD TYME CHRISTMAS. Dec 5-7. Purpose: To celebrate Christmas as it was in the nineteenth century. Sponsor: Harpers Ferry Merchants Assn, Box 262, Harpers Ferry, WV 25425.

PROHIBITION REPEAL: ANNIVERSARY. Dec 5. Congress proposed repeal of Amendment XVIII ("... the manufacture, sale, or transportation of intoxicating liquors, within, the importation thereof into, or the exportation thereof from the United States and all territory subject to the jurisdiction thereof, for beverage purposes is hereby prohibited ...") on Feb 20, 1933. By Dec 5, 1933, the repeal amendment had been ratified by the required 36 states and went into effect immediately as Amendment XXI to the U.S. Constitution.

SINGING CHRISTMAS TREE. Dec 5-7. Ovens Auditorium, Charlotte, NC. The 100 voice chorus of the Charlotte Choral Society presents a festive Christmas show featuring the chorus on a 27-foot decorated tree. Info from: Charlotte Choral Society, 110 E 7th St, Charlotte, NC 28202.

SNOWBALL DERBY. Dec 5-7. Five Flags Speedway, Pensacola, FL. Short track stock car race. Info from: David Pavlock, 7340 Mimosa Dr, Pensacola, FL 32506.

THAILAND: KING'S BIRTHDAY AND NATIONAL DAY. Dec 5. Celebrated throughout the kingdom with colorful pageantry. Stores and houses decorated with spectacular illuminations at night. Public holiday.

THURMOND, STROM: BIRTHDAY. Dec 5. U.S. Senator from South Carolina, Republican, of Aiken, SC, was born in Edgefield, SC, on Dec 5, 1902.

VAN BUREN, MARTIN: BIRTHDAY. Dec 5. The eighth President of the U.S. (Term of office: Mar 4, 1837-Mar 3, 1841) was the first to have been born a citizen of the U.S. A widower for nearly two decades before he entered the White House, his daughter-in-law, Angelica, served as White House hostess during an administration troubled by bank and business failures, depression and unemployment. Van Buren was born at Kinderhook, NY, Dec 5, 1782, and died there July 24, 1862, leaving an estate of about $250,000.

WONDERFUL WINTER WEEKEND. Dec 5-7. Lake Barkley State Resort Park, Cadiz, KY. Info from: Kentucky Dept of Parks, Capital Plaza Tower, Frankfort, KY 40601.

DECEMBER 6 — SATURDAY

340th Day — Remaining, 25

BLUE ANGEL MARATHON. Dec 6. Naval Air Station, Pensacola, FL. Purpose: To generate physical fitness among military/civilian via marathon. Info from: Naval Air Station, James W. Currie, Athletic Dir, Recreation Dept, Pensacola, FL 32508.

December 1986

S	M	T	W	T	F	S
	1	2	3	4	5	6
7	8	9	10	11	12	13
14	15	16	17	18	19	20
21	22	23	24	25	26	27
28	29	30	31			

CHRISTMAS CANDLELIGHTING. Dec 6. An 1800's Christmas celebration. Lighting of village tree, informal caroling, old-time holiday decorations. (Annually the 1st Saturday in December.) Info from: Roscoe Village Foundation, 381 Hill St, Coshocton, OH 43812.

CRAFT FESTIVAL. Dec 6-7. Ojai Art Center, Ventura County, CA. Purpose: Sale of quality handcrafted work of craftspeople from all of California. Info from: Ojai Art Center, Box 331, Ojai, CA 93023.

ECUADOR: DAY OF QUITO. Dec 6. Commemorates founding of city of Quito by Spaniards in 1534.

FINLAND: NATIONAL HOLIDAY. Dec 6. Independence Day. Declaration of Independence from Russia on this day, 1917.

FORT NECESSITY CANDLELIGHT TOURS. Dec 6-7. (Also Dec 13-14.) Fort Necessity National Park, Farmington, PA. Sponsor: Fort Necessity Natl Park, Farmington, PA 15437.

GERSHWIN, IRA: BIRTHDAY. Dec 6. Pulitzer Prize-winning American lyricist and author who collaborated with his brother, George, and with many other composers. Among his Broadway successes: "Lady Be Good," "Funny Face," "Strike Up the Band," and such songs as: "The Man I Love," "Someone to Watch Over Me," "I Got Rhythm," and hundreds of others. Born at New York City, Dec 6, 1896, died at Beverly Hills, CA Aug 17, 1983.

GILMAN, BENJAMIN A: BIRTHDAY. Dec 6. U.S. Representative of New York's 22nd district, Republican, of Middletown, NY, born at Poughkeepsie, NY, on Dec 6, 1922.

GINGERBREAD HOUSE COMPETITION. Dec 6-31. Peddler's Village, Lahaska, PA. Design, bake and decorate a Christmas gingerbread house and compete for prizes. Three categories: Traditional Gingerbread House, Incredibly Unusual Gingerbread Dwelling, or Victorian Christmas in Gingerbread. Info from: Peddler's Village, Rt 202 & 263, Lahaska, PA 18931.

KILMER, JOYCE (ALFRED): BIRTH ANNIVERSARY. Dec 6. American poet most famous for the poem "Trees," which was published in 1913. Kilmer was killed in action in France in World War I, on July 30, 1918. Camp Kilmer was named for him.

McHUGH, MATTHEW FRANCIS: BIRTHDAY. Dec 6. U.S. Representative of New York's 28th district, Democrat, of Ithaca, NY, born at Philadelphia, PA, Dec 6, 1938.

NICKLES, DONALD LEE: BIRTHDAY. Dec 6. U.S. Senator from Oklahoma, Republican, of Ponca City, OK, born in Ponca City on Dec 6, 1948.

ST. NICHOLAS' DAY. Dec 6. One of the most venerated saints, of both eastern and western Christian churches, of whose life little is known, except that he was Bishop of Myra in the fourth century, and that from early times he has been one of the most often pictured saints, especially noted for his charity. Santa Claus and the presentation of gifts said to derive from St. Nicholas.

SANTA ANA'S TOYS ON PARADE. Dec 6. A 1.9 mile parade route through historic Santa Ana. Giant helium filled balloons, custom-designed floats, high school and youth bands, equestrians, Disneyland characters, and the arrival of Santa Ana and Mrs. Claus. Info from: Visitor & Cultural Events Ctr, Box 1988-M-86, Santa Ana, CA 92702.

SANTA BY STAGE COACH PARADE. Dec 6. El Centro, CA. (First Saturday in December.) Sponsor: El Centro Chamber of Commerce, W.G. Duflock, Exec VP, Box 3006, El Centro, CA 92244.

SCOTTISH CHRISTMAS WALK. Dec 6. Purpose: Alexandria's annual salute to its 18th century Scottish founders. Parade of kilted pipers, highland dancers. Festivities include sales, crafts and children's events. Info from: Alexandria Tourist Council, 221 King St, Alexandria, VA 22314.

THOMAS, WILLIAM M: BIRTHDAY. Dec 6. U.S. Representative of California's 20th district, Republican, of Bakersfield, CA, was born at Wallace, ID, on Dec 6, 1941.

DECEMBER 7 — SUNDAY
341st Day — Remaining, 24

CATHER, WILLA: BIRTHDAY. Dec 7. American author born Winchester, VA, Dec 7, 1873. Died New York City, Apr 24, 1947.

CHRISTMAS CANDLELIGHT TOUR. Dec 7. Fredericksburg, VA. Purpose: To instill the spirit of Christmases past by opening historic homes to the public. 18th century music played throughout the tour. Info from: Visitor Ctr, 706 Caroline St, Fredericksburg, VA 22401.

COCHRAN, THAD: BIRTHDAY. Dec 7. U.S. Senator from Mississippi, Republican, of Jackson, MS, born at Pontotoc, MS, Dec 7, 1937.

COLLINS, MARTHA LAYNE: BIRTHDAY. Dec 7. Martha Layne Collins, Governor of Kentucky, Democrat, was born in Shelby County, KY, Dec 7, 1936.

DELAWARE: RATIFICATION DAY. Dec 7. First State to ratify constitution, on this day in 1787.

HERTEL, DENNIS MARK: BIRTHDAY. Dec 7. U.S. Representative of Michigan's 14th district, Democrat, of Harper Woods, MI, born in Detroit, MI, on Dec 7, 1948.

IVORY COAST: INDEPENDENCE DAY. Dec 7. National holiday. Attained full independence, 1960.

LIGHT OF THE WORLD NATIVITY PAGEANT. Dec 7. (Also Dec 14.) A nativity pageant with more than 10,000 lights. Info from: Chamber of Commerce, Box 375, Minden, NE 68959.

NATIONAL RODEO FINALS. Dec 7-15. Las Vegas, NV. Rodeo's best athletes competing in the Professional Rodeo Cowboys Association's premier event. Info from: Las Vegas Events, Inc., 1900 E. Flamingo, Suite 159, Las Vegas, NV 89109.

PALM HARBOR ART, CRAFT AND MUSIC FESTIVAL. Dec 7-8. Palm Harbor, FL. Exhibitors from all over the U.S. Juried art and craft show. Info from: Palm Harbor Art Gallery, Box 685, Palm Harbor, FL 33563.

PEARL HARBOR DAY. Dec 7. At 7:55 a.m. (local time) on Dec 7, 1941, "a date that will live in infamy," nearly 200 Japanese aircraft attacked Pearl Harbor, Hawaii, long considered the U.S. "Gibraltar of the Pacific." The raid, which lasted little more than one hour, left nearly 3,000 dead. Nearly the entire U.S. Pacific Fleet was at anchor there and few ships escaped damage and several were sunk or disabled, while 200 U.S. aircraft on the ground were destroyed. The attack on Pearl Harbor brought about immediate U.S. entry into World War II, a Declaration of War being requested by President Franklin D. Roosevelt, and voted for by the Congress on Dec 8, 1941.

SPACE MILESTONE: APOLLO 17 (US). Dec 7. Launched on Dec 7, 1972, three-man crew: Eugene A. Cernan, Harrison H. Schmidt, Ronald E. Evans, explored moon, Dec 11-14. Lunar landing module named "Challenger." Pacific splashdown, Dec 19.

TUSSAUD, MARIE GROSHOLTZ: BIRTHDAY. Dec 7. Creator of Madame Tussaud's waxwork museum born at Strasbourg, France, Dec 7, 1761. Many of the wax figures she created are still on view at Madame Tussaud's in London. She died, London, Apr 15, 1850.

DECEMBER 8 — MONDAY
342nd Day — Remaining, 23

CIVIL RIGHTS WEEK. Dec 8-14. Massachusetts.

DURANT, WILLIAM CRAPO: BIRTHDAY. Dec 8. "Billy" Durant, a leading producer of carriages in Flint, MI, promoter of the Buick car, co-founder of Chevrolet, was founder, in 1908, of General Motors. He lost, regained, and again lost control of GM, after which he founded Durant Motors, went bankrupt in the Depression, and operated a Flint bowling alley in his last working years. Durant was born at Boston, MA, on Dec 8, 1861, and died at New York City, Mar 18, 1947.

FEAST OF THE IMMACULATE CONCEPTION. Dec 8. Roman Catholic Holy Day of Obligation.

HOBAN, JAMES: DEATH ANNIVERSARY. Dec 8. Irish-born architect who designed the U.S. President's Executive Mansion, later known as The White House. He was born in 1762 (exact date unknown) and died Dec 8, 1831. The cornerstone for the White House, Washington's oldest public building, was laid in 1792.

JOHN LENNON REMEMBRANCE DAY. Dec 8. Purpose: To observe, on his death anniversary, the musical and humanitarian contributions the former Beatle made to the world. Sponsor: Nancy J. Byder, 11315 Grand Oak Dr # 1, Grand Blanc, MI 48439.

LADY OF CAMARIN DAY. Dec 8. Guam. Declared a legal holiday by Guam legislature on Mar 2, 1971.

MOON PHASE: FIRST QUARTER. Dec 8. Moon enters First Quarter phase at 3:01 a.m., E.S.T.

MORAVIAN LOVE FEAST. Dec 8. Hensdale Chapel, Methodist College, Fayetteville, NC. A service of fellowship, communion and singing. Info from: Dr. Kenneth Collins, Chaplain, Box M-1, Methodist College, Fayetteville, NC 28301.

RIVERA, DIEGO: BIRTHDAY. Dec 8. Mexican painter whose murals became center of political controversy and demands for banishment, born at Guanajuato, Mexico, Dec 8, 1886. Died in his studio at San Angel, near Mexico City, Nov 25, 1957.

THURBER, JAMES: BIRTHDAY. Dec 8. James Grover Thurber, American humorist and artist, born at Columbus, OH, Dec 8, 1894. Died, New York City, Nov 2, 1961.

WORLD CHAMPIONSHIP BARRELL RACING FUTURITY. Dec 8-14. State Fair Arena, Oklahoma City, OK. Purpose: 700 horses compete for prize money during 6 exciting days of competition. Info from: Stanley Draper, Jr, 1 Santa Fe Plaza, Oklahoma City, OK 73102.

WORTLEY, GEORGE CORNELIUS: BIRTHDAY. Dec 8. U.S. Representative of New York's 27th district, Republican, of Fayetteville, NY, born in Syracuse, NY, Dec 8, 1926.

DECEMBER 9 — TUESDAY
343rd Day — Remaining, 22

AMERICA'S FIRST FORMAL CREMATION: ANNIVERSARY. Dec 9. The first formal cremation of a human body in America took place near Charleston, NC, on Dec 9, 1792. Henry Laurens, colonial statesman and signer of the Treaty of Paris, ending the Revolutionary War, in his Will, provided: "I do solemnly enjoin it on my son, as an indispensable duty, that as soon as he conveniently can, after my decease, he cause my body to be wrapped in twelve yards of tow cloth and burned until it be entirely consumed, and then, collecting my bones, deposit them wherever he may think proper." Laurens died Dec 8, 1792, at his plantation, and was cremated there.

BIRDSEYE, CLARENCE: BIRTHDAY. Dec 9. American industrialist who developed a way of deep-freezing foods. He was marketing frozen fish by 1925 and was one of the founders of General Foods Corp. Born on Dec 9, 1886 at Brooklyn, NY. Died in 1956.

DASCHLE, THOMAS ANDREW: BIRTHDAY. Dec 9. U.S. Representative at large from South Dakota, Democrat, of Aberdeen, SD, born in Aberdeen on Dec 9, 1947.

ERDREICH, BEN: BIRTHDAY. Dec 9. U.S. Representative of Alabama's 6th district, Democrat, of Birmingham, AL, born there Dec 9, 1938.

GENOCIDE CONVENTION ANNIVERSARY. Dec 9. The United Nations General Assembly unanimously approved the Convention on Prevention and Punishment of the Crime of Genocide on Dec 9, 1948. It took effect Jan 12, 1951 when ratification by 20 nations had been completed. President Truman sent it to the U.S. Senate for approval on June 16, 1949. Presidents Kennedy, Johnson, Nixon, Ford, Carter and Reagan have asked for approval of the Convention which has been ratified by more than 90 nations.

HARRIS, JOEL CHANDLER: BIRTHDAY. Dec 9. American author, creator of the "Uncle Remus" stories, born Dec 9, 1848. Died July 3, 1908.

MILTON, JOHN: BIRTHDAY. Dec. 9. English poet and defender of freedom of the press born in Bread Street, Cheapside, London, on Dec 9, 1608. Died from gout, Nov 8, 1674. "No man who knows aught," he wrote, "can be so stupid to deny that all men naturally were born free."

O'NEILL, THOMAS P Jr: BIRTHDAY. Dec 9. U.S. Representative of Massachusett 8th district, Democrat, of Cambridge, MA, was born Dec 9, 1912.

SANDYS, EDWIN; BIRTHDAY. Dec 9. Sir Edwin Sandys, English statesman and one of the founders of the Virginia Colony (treasurer, the Virginia Company, 1619-1620), born at Worcestershire, Dec 9, 1561. Died in October 1629 (exact date unknown).

TANZANIA: INDEPENDENCE AND REPUBLIC DAY. Dec 9. On Dec 9, 1961 Tanganyika became independent of Britain and on Dec 9, 1962 it became a republic within the Commonwealth. The republics of Tanganyika and Zanzibar joined to become one state (Apr 27, 1964) renamed (Oct 29, 1964) the United Republic of Tanzania.

DECEMBER 10 — WEDNESDAY
344th Day — Remaining, 21

DEWEY, MELVIL: BIRTHDAY. Dec 10. American librarian and inventor of the Dewey Decimal book classification system, was born at Adams Center, NY, on Dec 10, 1851. Born Melville Louis Kossuth Dewey, he was an advocate of spelling reform, urged use of the metric system and was interested in many other educational reforms. Dewey died at Highlands County, FL, on December 26, 1931.

DICKINSON, EMILY: BIRTHDAY. Dec 10. American poet born at Amherst, MA, Dec 10, 1830. Died there, May 15, 1886, leaving hundreds of unpublished poems.

HUMAN RIGHTS DAY. Dec 10. Presidential Proclamation.
☆ "Proc. 2866, Dec. 6, 1949, covers all succeeding years, however Presidents often include this Proc. when issuing Human Rights Week."

HUMAN RIGHTS DAY. Dec 10. Official United Nations observance day. General Assembly invited all States and interested organizations to observe Dec 10 each year as Human Rights Day. Date is anniversary of adoption of the "Universal Declaration of Human Rights" in 1948. The Declaration sets forth basic rights and fundamental freedoms to which all men and women everywhere in the world are entitled. Info from: UN Dept of Public Information, United Nations, NY 10017.

HUMAN RIGHTS WEEK. Dec 10-16. Presidential Proclama-
☆ tion. "Issued since 1958 for week of December 10-16."

MISSISSIPPI: ADMISSION DAY. Dec 10. Became 20th State on this day in 1817.

December 1986	S	M	T	W	T	F	S
		1	2	3	4	5	6
	7	8	9	10	11	12	13
	14	15	16	17	18	19	20
	21	22	23	24	25	26	27
	28	29	30	31			

NOBEL, ALFRED BERNHARD: DEATH ANNIVERSARY. Dec 10. Swedish chemist and engineer who invented dynamite born in Stockholm, Oct 21, 1833 and died at San Remo, Italy, Dec 10, 1896. His will established the Nobel Prize.

NOEL NIGHT. Dec 10. Detroit Cultural Center, Detroit, MI. Info from: Sandra Kaeding, David MacKenzie House, UCCA, 4735 Cass, Detroit, MI 48202.

SPACE MILESTONE: SOYUZ 26 (USSR). Dec 10. Launched on Dec 10, 1977, Cosmonauts Yuri Romanenko and Georgi Grechko link up with Salyut 6 space station on Dec 11. Returned to Earth in Soyuz 27, Mar 16, 1978, after record-setting 96 days in space.

SRI LANKA: COLOMBO CHILDREN'S BOOK FAIR. Dec 10-24. Columbo, Sri Lanka. Info from: Colombo Children's Book Fair, 415 Galle Rd, Colombo 4, Sri Lanka.

SWEDEN: NOBEL PRIZE CEREMONY. Dec 10. City Hall, Stockholm. Traditionally on anniversary of death of Alfred Nobel (q.v.).

THAILAND: CONSTITUTION DAY. Dec 10. A public holiday throughout Thailand.

DECEMBER 11 — THURSDAY
345th Day — Remaining, 20

ALASKA'S FIRST BROADCAST TELEVISION STATION: BIRTHDAY. Dec 11. At 6:00 p.m., on Dec 11, 1953, KTVA, Channel 11, at Anchorage, Alaska, signed on the air, becoming Alaska's first broadcast television station.

BAUCUS, MAX: BIRTHDAY. Dec 11. U.S. Senator from Montana, Democrat, of Missoula, MT, was born in Helena, MT, Dec 11, 1941.

CANNON, ANNIE JUMP: BIRTHDAY. Dec 11. American astronomer and discoverer of five stars, was born at Dover, DE on Dec 11, 1863. Author and winner of the National Academy of Science Draper Medal. She died at Cambridge, MA, Apr 13, 1941.

EDWARD VIII: ABDICATION ANNIVERSARY. Dec 11. Christened Edward Albert Christian George Andrew Patrick David, King Edward VIII was born at Richmond Park, on June 23, 1894, and became Prince of Wales in July 1911. He succeeded to the English throne upon the death of his father, George V, on Jan 20, 1936, but coronation never took place. He abdicated on Dec 11, 1936, in order to marry "the woman I love," twice divorced American, Wallis Warfield Simpson. They were married in France, June 3, 1937. Edward was created Duke of Windsor by his brother-successor, George VI. The Duke died at Paris, May 28, 1972, but was buried in England, near Windsor Castle.

ENGLAND: OLYMPIA INTERNATIONAL SHOWJUMPING CHAMPIONSHIPS. Dec 11-15. Olympia, London. Annual international equestrian competition.

INDIANA: ADMISSION DAY. Dec 11. Became 19th State on this day in 1816.

KERRY, JOHN F: BIRTHDAY. Dec 11. U.S. Senator from Massachusetts, Democrat, of Boston, MA, born in Denver, CO, on Dec 11, 1943.

LA GUARDIA, FIORELLO HENRY: BIRTHDAY. Dec 11. Popularly known as the "Little Flower," Fiorello H. LaGuardia was not too busy as Mayor of New York City to read the "funnies" to radio listeners during the New York newspaper strike. He said of himself: "When I make a mistake it's a beaut!" LaGuardia was born in New York City, Dec 11, 1882, and died there on Sept 20, 1947.

MARTIN, JAMES G: BIRTHDAY. Dec 11. James G. Martin, Governor of North Carolina, Republican, was born at Savanah, GA, on Dec 11, 1935.

UNICEF ANNIVERSARY. Dec 11. Anniversary of the establishment by the UN General Assembly, Dec 11, 1946, of the UN International Children's Emergency Fund (UNICEF). An international day observed by the organizations of the United Nations system. Info from: United Nations Dept of Public Information, United Nations, NY 10017.

DECEMBER 12 — FRIDAY
346th Day — Remaining, 19

FLAMINGO FANDANGO. Dec 12-14. Flamingo Park, Miami Beach, FL. Info from: Miami Beach Recreation Dept, City Hall, 1700 Convention Ctr Dr, Miami Beach, FL 33139.

GUNSTON HALL CAROLS BY CANDLELIGHT. Dec 12-14. The candlelit hall will be decorated for Christmas in the Eighteenth century manner. Eighteenth century music and caroling in the reception center. Info from: Gunston Hall, Lorton, VA 22079.

HORTON, FRANK: BIRTHDAY. Dec 12. U.S. Representative of New York's 29th district, Republican, of Rochester, NY, born in Cuero, TX, on Dec 12, 1919.

KENYA: NATIONAL HOLIDAY. Dec 12. (Independence Day.) Commemorates proclamation of sovereignty on Dec 12, 1963.

MEXICO: GUADALUPE DAY. Dec 12. One of Mexico's major celebrations. Honors the "Dark Virgin of Guadalupe," the republic's patron saint. Parties and pilgrimages, with special ceremonies at the Shrine of Our Lady of Guadalupe, in Mexico City.

NATIONAL DING-A-LING DAY. Dec 12. Purpose: To promote the idea that a Ding-A-Ling is a wonderful, friendly, intelligent, loving, responsible and desirable person . . . A Real Bell-Ringer! Sponsor: Natl Ding-A-Ling Club, Franky Hyle, Pres, 3930-D Montclair Rd, Birmingham, AL 35213.

OZARK CHRISTMAS. Dec 12-14. Purpose: To relive a traditional Christmas in the Ozarks. Music programs and craft demonstrations. Info from: Ozark Folk Ctr, Mountain View, AR 72560.

PENNSYLVANIA: RATIFICATION DAY. Dec 12. Second State to ratify constitution, on this day in 1787.

POINSETTIA DAY. Dec 12. A day to enjoy poinsettias and to honor Dr. Joel Roberts Poinsett, the American diplomat who introduced the Central American plant which is named for him, into the U.S. Poinsett was born at Charleston, SC, Mar 2, 1779. He served as a member of Congress and as a Secretary of War, in addition to his diplomatic positions. He died near Statesburg, SC, Dec 12, 1851. The poinsettia has become a favorite Christmas season plant.

SINATRA, FRANK: BIRTHDAY. Dec 12. American popular singer and motion picture actor, born Francis Albert Sinatra, at Hoboken, NJ, on Dec 12, 1915.

SUGARLOAF'S WINTER CRAFTS FESTIVAL. Dec 12-14. Montgomery County Fairgrounds, Gaithersburg, MD. Professional artists and craftspeople, demonstrations, prize drawings and delicious food. Sponsor: Sugarloaf Mt Works, Inc., Ijamsville, MD 21754.

DECEMBER 13 — SATURDAY
347th Day — Remaining, 18

ARMY AND NAVY UNION DAY. Dec 13, Massachusetts. (Second Saturday in December.)

BATTLE OF FREDERICKSBURG, VIRGINIA: ANNIVERSARY. Dec 13. Confederate forces were victorious at the Battle of Fredericksburg, VA, on Dec 13, 1862. Total casualties on both sides estimated at over 16,000 killed, injured or missing. General Ambrose E. Burnside led Union troops; General Robert E. Lee led the Confederates.

BROOKS, PHILLIPS: BIRTHDAY. Dec 13. American clergyman and composer born at Boston, MA, Dec 13, 1835. Perhaps best remembered for his lyrics for the Christmas carol "O Little Town of Bethlehem." Brooks died at Boston, Jan 23, 1893.

DECEMBER ON THE FARM. Dec 13. Tallahassee Jr. Museum. Purpose: Demonstrations of rural crafts including spinning, weaving, basket making, blacksmithing and pottery making. Info from: Tallahassee Jr. Museum, 3945 Museum Dr, Tallahassee, FL 32304.

FINGER LAKES CRAFTSMEN CHRISTMAS "2" ARTS AND CRAFTS SHOW. Dec 13-14. Monroe County Fairgrounds Dome Arena, Rochester, NY. All media, all categories. Info from: Finger Lakes Craftsmen Shows, 25 Seneca St, Shortsville, NY 14548.

FRANKLIN, WILLIAM WEBSTER: BIRTHDAY. Dec 13. U.S. Representative of Mississippi's 2nd district, Republican, of Greenwood, MS, born there on Dec 13, 1941.

HEINE, HEINRICH: BIRTHDAY. Dec 13. German author, born, Dusseldorf, Dec 13, 1797. Died, Paris, Feb 17, 1856.

LINCOLN, MARY TODD: BIRTHDAY. Dec 13. Wife of Abraham Lincoln, 16th President of the U.S., born at Lexington, KY, Dec 13, 1818. Died July 16, 1882.

MALTA: REPUBLIC DAY. Dec 13. National holiday. Malta became a republic on Dec 13, 1974.

OZCANABANS OF OZ CONVENTION. Dec 13. Escanaba, MI. Purpose: To celebrate Christmas in OZ. Sponsor: The Internatl Wizard of Oz Club, Inc, Fred M. Meyer, Secy, 220 N 11th St, Escanaba, MI 49829.

ST. LUCIA: NATIONAL HOLIDAY. Dec 13.

SHULTZ, GEORGE PRATT: BIRTHDAY. Dec 13. U.S. Secretary of State (sworn in July 16, 1982) George P. Shultz was born at New York, NY, on Dec 13, 1920.

SWEDEN: SANTA LUCIA DAY. Dec 13. Nationwide celebration of return of light after darkest time of year. Many hotels have their own Lucia, a young blonde girl attired in long flowing white gown who serves guests coffee and lussekatter (saffron buns) in the early morning.

DECEMBER 14 — SUNDAY
348th Day — Remaining, 17

ALABAMA: ADMISSION DAY. Dec 14. Became 22nd State on this day in 1819.

DOOLITTLE, JAMES HAROLD: BIRTHDAY. Dec 14. American aviator and World War II hero, General James Doolittle, was born at Alameda, CA, Dec 14, 1896. He led the first U.S. aerial raid on Japan in World War II. The 16 B-25 medium bombers dropped bombs on Tokyo, Yokohama, Osaka, Kobe and Nagoya, Apr 18, 1942.

HALCYON DAYS. Dec 14-28. Traditionally, the seven days before and the seven days after the winter solstice. To the ancients a time when fabled bird (called the halcyon) calmed the wind and waves—a time of calm and tranquility.

NOSTRADAMUS: BIRTHDAY. Dec 14. French physician, best remembered for his astrological predictions (written in rhymed quatrains) was born Michel de Notredame, at St. Remy, Provence, France, Dec 14, 1503. Many believed that his book of prophecies foretold the future. Nostradamus died at Salon, France, July 2, 1566.

RE-ENACTMENT OF THE BOSTON TEA PARTY. Dec 14. Congress Street Bridge, Boston, MA. Purpose: Reenactment of "Boston's most notorious protest, the single most important

COPYRIGHT © 1985 BY WILLIAM D. CHASE and HELEN M. CHASE

event leading to the American revolution." Info from: Boston Tea Party Ship, Barbara J. Attianese, Dir, Congress St Bridge, Boston, MA 02210.

SMITH, MARGARET CHASE: BIRTHDAY. Dec 14. First woman to be elected to both houses of the U.S. Congress, born at Skowhegan, ME, Dec 14, 1897.

SOUTH POLE: DISCOVERY ANNIVERSARY. Dec 14. The elusive object of many expeditions dating from the seventh century, the South Pole was located and visited Dec 14, 1911, by Roald Amundsen (q.v.) with four companions and 52 sled dogs. All five men and 12 of the dogs returned to base camp safely. Next to visit the South Pole, on Jan 17, 1912, was a party of five led by Capt. Robert F. Scott, all of whom perished during the return trip. A search party found their frozen bodies eleven months later.

TELL SOMEONE THEY'RE DOING A GOOD JOB WEEK. Dec 14-20. Purpose: Every day this week tell someone "you're doing a good job." Sponsor: Joe Hoppel, Radio Station WCMS, 900 Commonwealth Place, Virginia Beach, VA 23464.

WASHINGTON, GEORGE: DEATH ANNIVERSARY. Dec 14. The first president died at Mount Vernon, VA, on Dec 14, 1799.

DECEMBER 15 — MONDAY
349th Day — Remaining, 16

BILL OF RIGHTS DAY. Dec 15. Presidential Proclamation.
☆ "Has been proclaimed each year since 1962, but was omitted in 1967 & 1968. (Issued in 1941 & 1946 at Congressional request and in 1947 without request.) Since 1968 has been included in Human Rights Week Proclamations." Editor's note: On Dec 15, 1791, the Bill of Rights became part of the U.S. Constitution, and on Dec 10, 1948, the UN General Assembly adopted the Universal Declaration of Human Rights.

BILL OF RIGHTS DAY. Dec 15. The first ten Amendments to the U.S. Constitution, known as the Bill of Rights, became effective following ratification by Virginia on Dec 15, 1791. Often a Presidential Proclamation.

CHRISTMAS AT THE ZOO. Dec 15-Jan 1. Purpose: Caroling to the animals, Christmas tree for the birds, activities for children. Sponsor: North Carolina Zoological Park, Rt 4, Box 83, Asheboro, NC 27203.

LIBBY, WILLARD FRANK: BIRTHDAY. Dec 15. American educator, chemist, atomic scientist, and Nobel Prize winner was born at Grand Valley, CO, Dec 17, 1908. He was the inventor of the Carbon-14 "atomic clock" method for dating ancient and prehistoric plant and animal remains and minerals. Died at Los Angeles, CA, Sept 8, 1980.

MAD ANTHONY WAYNE: DEATH ANNIVERSARY. Dec 15. American Revolutionary War general whose daring, sometimes reckless, conduct earned him the nickname "Mad Anthony" Wayne. His courage and shrewdness as a soldier made him a key figure in the capture of Stony Point, NY (1779), in preventing Benedict Arnold's "delivery" of West Point to the British (1780), and in subduing hostile Indians of the Northwest Territory (1794). He was born at Waynesboro, PA, Jan 1, 1745, and died at Presque Isle, PA, Dec 15, 1796. Wayne was buried at Erie, PA, but in 1809 his body was exhumed. A portion of his remains was re-buried at Erie and another portion at Radnor, PA; thus he has two separate gravesites.

December **1986**

S	M	T	W	T	F	S
	1	2	3	4	5	6
7	8	9	10	11	12	13
14	15	16	17	18	19	20
21	22	23	24	25	26	27
28	29	30	31			

MORAVIAN ACADEMY PUTZ TOUR. Dec 15. Bethlehem, PA. Purpose: A day for visiting area homes to view traditional family Putz followed by Christmas music and Moravian sugar cake at Moravian Academy. Sponsor: Moravian Academy Alumni Assn, 4313 Green Pond Rd, Bethlehem, PA 18017.

PALM BEACH POLO. Dec 15-May 1, 1987. West Palm Beach, FL. Purpose: As the recognized winter headquarters for the sport of polo, Palm Beach Polo and Country Club hosts the Piaget World Cup of Polo and major international polo games. Info from: Palm Beach Polo & Country Club, 13198 Forest Hill Blvd, West Palm Beach, FL 33414.

PUERTO RICO: NAVIDADES. Dec 15-Jan 6, 1987. Traditional Christmas season begins mid-December and ends on Three Kings Day. Elaborate nativity scenes, carolers, special Christmas foods. Trees from Canada and U.S. Gifts on Christmas Day and on Three Kings Day.

REELFOOT EAGLE TOURS. Dec 15-Mar 15, 1987. Reelfoot Lake State Resort Park, Tiptonville, TN. A prime winter nesting area for the American bald eagle, Reelfoot Lake annually hosts 150 to 200 eagles. Info from: Tennessee Tourist Dev, Box 23170, Nashville, TN 37202.

SPACE MILESTONE: VEGA 1 (USSR) Dec 15. Craft launched Dec 15, 1984 to rendezvous with Halley's Comet in Mar 1986. Vega 2, launched Dec 21 is part of same mission which, in cooperation with the U.S. carries U.S.-built "comet-dust" detection equipment. Dec 15 and 21, 1984.

WATKINS, WESLEY WADE (WES): BIRTHDAY. Dec 15. U.S. Representative of Oklahoma's 3rd district, Democrat, of Ada, OK, was born in DeQueen, AR, on Dec 15, 1938.

ZAMENHOF, DR. LL: BIRTHDAY ANNIVERSARY. Dec 15. Purpose: To honor the founder of the International Language, Esperanto. Sponsor: Meadpenn Esperanto Library, RFD 6, Box 198, Meadville, PA 16335.

DECEMBER 16 — TUESDAY
350th Day — Remaining, 15

AUSTEN, JANE: BIRTHDAY. Dec 16. English novelist born Dec 16, 1775. Died July 18, 1817.

BAHRAIN: NATIONAL HOLIDAY. Dec 16. Independence Day.

BANGLADESH: VICTORY DAY. Dec 16. National holiday in the People's Republic of Bangladesh.

BEETHOVEN DAY IN MICHIGAN. Dec 16. Michigan Legislature, House Concurrent Resolution 113: ". . . Whereas, We do indeed owe a debt of gratitude to the memory of this amazing man for the priceless pleasure which his music has given us all; now, therefore, be it Resolved . . . that the sixteenth of December be hereby designated and commemorated as Beethoven Day in Michigan in celebration of the musical genius of Ludwig van Beethoven."

BEETHOVEN, LUDWIG van: BIRTHDAY. Dec 16. Regarded by some as the greatest orchestral composer of all time, Ludwig van Beethoven was born at Bonn, Germany, Dec 16, 1770. Impairment of his hearing began before he was 30, but even total deafness did not halt his composing and conducting. His last appearance on the concert stage was to conduct the premiere of his Ninth Symphony, at Vienna, May 7, 1824. He was unable to hear either the orchestra or the applause. Often in love, he never married. Of a stormy temperament, he is said to have died during a violent thunderstorm on Mar 26, 1827, at Vienna.

BOSTON TEA PARTY: ANNIVERSARY. Dec 16. Anniversary of Dec 16, 1773, Boston patriots' boarding of British vessel at anchor in Boston Harbor. Contents of nearly 350 chests of tea dumped into the harbor.

DICKS, NORMAN DEVALOIS: BIRTHDAY. Dec 16. U.S. Representative of Washington's 6th district, Democrat, of Bremerton, WA, born there on Dec 16, 1940.

COPYRIGHT © 1985 BY WILLIAM D. CHASE and HELEN M. CHASE

LAS POSADAS. Dec 16-24. El Pueblo De Los Angeles State Historic Park, Los Angeles, CA. Candlelight procession depicting the journey of Mary and Joseph into Bethlehem seeking shelter. Info from: El Pueblo De Los Angeles State Historic Park, 845 N Alameda St, Los Angeles, CA 90012.

MAN WILL NEVER FLY SOCIETY MEETING. Dec 16. Kitty Hawk, NC. Purpose: Group meets to prove that man will never fly. Society motto: "Birds fly, men drink." Info from: Ed North, Nags Head, NC 27959.

MARTIN, LYNN: BIRTHDAY. Dec 16. U.S. Representative of Illinois' 16th district, Republican, of Rockford, IL, born in Chicago, IL, on Dec 16, 1939.

MEAD, MARGARET: BIRTHDAY. Dec 16. American anthropologist and author, especially known for her studies of primitive peoples of southwest Pacific Ocean area, and for her forthright manner in speaking and writing. Born at Philadelphia, Dec 16, 1901. Died at New York City, Nov 15, 1978.

MEXICO: POSADAS. Dec 16-24. A nine-day annual celebration throughout Mexico. Processions of "pilgrims" knock at doors asking for posada (shelter), commemorating the search by Joseph and Mary for a shelter in which the infant Jesus might be born. Invited inside, fun and merrymaking ensue with blindfolded guests trying to break a "piñata" (papier mache decorated earthenware utensil filled with gifts and goodies) suspended from the ceiling. Once broken the gifts are distributed and celebration continues.

MOON PHASE: FULL MOON. Dec 16. Moon enters Full Moon phase at 2:04 a.m., E.S.T.

PHILIPPINES: PHILIPPINE CHRISTMAS. Dec 16-Jan 6, 1987. Philippine Islands. Said to be world's longest Christmas celebration.

PHILIPPINES: SIMBANG GABI. Dec 16-25. Nationwide. A nine-day novena of pre-dawn masses, also called "Misa de Gallo." One of the traditional Filipino celebrations of the holiday season.

YOUNG, C.W. BILL: BIRTHDAY. Dec 16. U.S. Representative of Florida's 8th district, Republican, of St. Petersburg, FL, was born in Harmarville, PA, on Dec 16, 1930.

DECEMBER 17 — WEDNESDAY
351st Day — Remaining, 14

AZTEC CALENDAR STONE DISCOVERY: ANNIVERSARY. Dec. 17. Mexico City. On Dec 17, 1790, one of the wonders of the western hemisphere—the Aztec Calendar or Solar Stone—was found beneath the ground by workmen repairing Mexico City's Central Plaza. The centuries-old, intricately carved stone, 11 ft, 8 in. in diameter and weighing nearly 25 tons, proved to be a highly developed calendar monument to the sun. Believed to have been carved in the year 1479, this extraordinary time-counting basalt tablet stood originally in the Great Temple of the Aztecs. Buried, along with other Aztec idols, soon after the Spanish conquest in 1521, it remained hidden until 1790. Its 52-year cycle had regulated many Aztec ceremonies, including grisly human sacrifices to save the world from destruction by the gods.

BHUTAN: NATIONAL DAY. Dec 17. National holiday observed.

BOLIVAR, SIMON: DEATH ANNIVERSARY. Dec 17. Commemorated in Venezuela and other Latin American countries. Bolivar, called "The Liberator," was born July 24, 1783, at Caracas, Venezuela, and died on Dec 17, 1830, at Santa Marta, Colombia.

FIRST FLIGHT CELEBRATION. Dec 17. Each year since 1928, on anniversary of the Wright Brothers' first successful heavier-than-air flight at Kitty Hawk, NC, Dec 17, 1903, a celebration has been sponsored cooperatively by the National Park Service and aviation associations. Begins at 9:30 a.m., at Wright Brothers National Memorial, Kill Devil Hills, NC, (regardless of weather!). Memorial wreaths and flyover and other celebrative observances. Info from: First Flight Society, Box 1903, Kitty Hawk, NC 27949.

FLOYD, WILLIAM: BIRTHDAY. Dec 17. Signer of the Declaration of Independence, member of Congress, born, Brookhaven, Long Island, Dec 17, 1734. Died Westernville, NY, Aug 4, 1821.

PAN AMERICAN AVIATION DAY. Dec 17. Presidential ☆ Proclamation. "Proc. 2446, Nov 18, 1940, covers all succeeding years (Pub. Res No. 105 of Oct 10, 1940)."

SALEM CHRISTMAS. Dec 17-18. Old Salem, Winston-Salem, NC. Re-creation of the sights, sounds and smells of the Moravian town of Salem at Christmas. Info from: Old Salem Inc, Drawer F, Salem Station, Winston-Salem, NC 27108.

SATURNALIA. Dec 17-23. Anniversary of ancient Roman festival honoring Saturn, the planter god. Approximates the winter solstice. Most festive and abandoned period of the year in Rome, and immensely popular. Gifts, lights and the closing of businesses marked the period. Some say that the date for observance of the nativity of Jesus was selected by the early Christian church leaders to fall on Dec 25th partly to counteract the popular but disapproved pre-Christian Roman festival of Saturnalia.

WHITTIER, JOHN GREENLEAF: BIRTHDAY. Dec 17. American author born at Haverhill, MA, Dec 17, 1807. Died Sept 7, 1892.

WRIGHT BROTHERS DAY. Dec 17. Presidential Proclamation. ☆ "Always issued for December 17 since 1963 (PL88-209 of Dec 17, 1963). Issued twice earlier at Congressional request in 1959 and 1961."

WRIGHT BROTHERS FIRST POWERED FLIGHT: ANNIVERSARY. Dec 17. Kitty Hawk, NC. On Dec 17, 1903, Orville and Wilbur Wright, brothers, bicycle shop operators, inventors and aviation pioneers, after three years of experimentation with kites and gliders, achieved the first documented successful powered and controlled flights of an airplane. The flights, near Kitty Hawk, NC, piloted first by Orville then by Wilbur Wright, were sustained for less than one minute; nevertheless they represented man's first powered airplane flight, and the beginning of a new form of transportation. Orville Wright was born at Dayton, OH, Aug 19, 1871, and died there Jan 30, 1948. Wilbur Wright was born at Millville, IN, Apr 16, 1867, and died at Dayton, OH, May 30, 1912.

DECEMBER 18 — THURSDAY
352nd Day — Remaining, 13

AUDUBON CHRISTMAS BIRD COUNT. Dec 18-Jan 5, 1987. Purpose: Census of winter bird life of the continent by 1,477 groups (more than 35,000 bird-watchers). Annual event since 1900. North and Central America. Sponsor: Natl Audubon Society, Susan Roney Drennan, Ed, American Birds, 950 Third Ave, New York, NY 10022.

BROOKS, JACK: BIRTHDAY. Dec 18. U.S. Representative of Texas' 9th district, Democrat, of Beaumont, TX, was born on Dec 18, 1922.

COBB, TYRUS RAYMOND (TY): BIRTHDAY. Dec 18. Famed American baseball player born Narrows, GA, Dec 18, 1886. Died at Atlanta, GA, July 17, 1961. Lifetime batting average of .367 compiled over 24 years during which he played in more than 3,000 games.

GRIMALDI, JOSEPH: BIRTHDAY. Dec 18. Known as the "greatest clown in history" and the "king of pantomime," Joseph Grimaldi began his stage career at two years of age. He was an accomplished singer, dancer and acrobat. Born at London on Dec 18, 1778, he is best remembered as the original "Joey the Clown," and for the innovative humor he brought to the clown's role in theater. Illness forced his retirement in 1823, and he died at London on May 31, 1837.

MEXICO: FEAST OF OUR LADY OF SOLITUDE. Dec 18. Oaxaca. Pilgrims venerate the patron of the lonely.

NEW JERSEY: RATIFICATION DAY. Dec 18. Third State to ratify constitution, on this day in 1787.

NIGER: REPUBLIC DAY. Dec 18. National holiday.

SPACE MILESTONE: SOYUZ 13 (USSR). Dec 18. Two Soviet cosmonauts (P.I. Klimuk and V.V. Lebedev) begin, Dec 18, 1973, 8-day orbit of Earth. Returned to Earth on Dec 26, 1973.

STRADIVARI, ANTONIO: DEATH ANNIVERSARY. Dec 18. Celebrated Italian violin maker was born probably in the year 1644, and died at Cremona, Dec 18, 1737.

THIRTEENTH AMENDMENT: ANNIVERSARY. Dec 18. On Dec 18, 1865, ratification of the Thirteenth Amendment to the U.S. Constitution was proclaimed, abolishing slavery in the nation. "Neither slavery nor involuntary servitude, save as a punishment for crime whereof the party shall have been duly convicted, shall exist within the United States, or any place subject to their jurisdiction." See also: "Emancipation Proclamation Anniversary," (Jan 1) for Abraham Lincoln's proclamation freeing slaves in the rebelling states.

WEBER, CARL MARIA von: BICENTENNIAL BIRTH ANNIVERSARY. Dec 18. German composer "founder of German romantic school," was born at Eutin, on Dec 18, 1786. Member of a musical family, he is remembered mainly for his operas, especially the immensely popular *Der Freischutz* (1821). He died at London on June 5, 1826

DECEMBER 19 — FRIDAY
353rd Day — Remaining, 12

CHRISTMAS GREETINGS FROM SPACE: ANNIVERSARY. Dec 19. At 3:15 p.m., E.S.T., Dec 19, 1958, the U.S. Earth satellite *Atlas* began first radio voice broadcast from space, a 58-word recorded Christmas greeting from President Dwight D. Eisenhower: "to all mankind America's wish for peace on earth and good will toward men everywhere." Satellite had been launched from Cape Canaveral on previous day.

CHRISTMAS SING IN THE CAVE. Dec 19. Mammoth Cave National Park, KY. Purpose: Christmas caroling by barbershop chorus and children's groups in a large cave passageway lit by lantern light. Hot apple cider and cookies afterwards. Sponsor: Mammoth Cave Natl Park, Mammoth Cave, KY 42259.

FISKE, MINNIE MADDERN: BIRTHDAY. Dec 19. American theatre actress with a long, distinguished career. First stage appearance at the age of three as "Little Minnie Maddern." Born on Dec 19, 1865 at New Orleans, LA, and died on Feb 15, 1932.

LIVERMORE, MARY ASHTON: BIRTHDAY. Dec 19. American reformer and woman's suffrage leader, born Dec 19, 1821. Died May 23, 1905.

December 1986	S	M	T	W	T	F	S
		1	2	3	4	5	6
	7	8	9	10	11	12	13
	14	15	16	17	18	19	20
	21	22	23	24	25	26	27
	28	29	30	31			

PAGEANT OF CHRIST'S BIRTH. Dec 19-23. Worth (Alsip), IL. Outdoor re-enactment of events of Christ's birth with live animals and costumed people moving to Biblical narration. Info from: Lutheran Church of the Apostles, 5100 W 115th St, Worth (Alsip), IL 60482.

PARRY, WILLIAM: BIRTHDAY. Dec 19. British explorer, Sir William Edward Parry, was born at Bath, England, on Dec 19, 1790. Remembered for his Arctic expeditions and for his search for a Northwest Passage, Parry died at Ems, Germany, July 8, 1855.

PURSELL, CARL DUANE: BIRTHDAY. Dec 19. U.S. Representative of Michigan's 2nd district, Republican, of Plymouth, MI, was born at Imlay City, MI on Dec 19, 1932.

SPACE MILESTONE: COSMOS 1614. Dec 19. Unmanned space shuttle made one orbit before splash-down in Black Sea. Dec 19, 1984.

SPACE MILESTONE: INTELSAT 4 F-3 (US). Dec 19. Communications satellite launched by NASA on contract with COMSAT. Mission was intercontinental relay of phone and TV communications. Dec 19, 1971.

UNDERDOG DAY. Dec 19. Always the third Friday in December. Purpose: To salute, before the year's end, all of the underdogs and unsung heroes—the Number Two people who contribute so much to the Number One people we read about. (Sherlock Holmes' Dr. Watson and Robinson Crusoe's Friday are examples.) Sponsor: P. Moeller, Chief Underdog, Box 71, Clio, MI 48420.

DECEMBER 20 — SATURDAY
354th Day — Remaining, 11

FIRESTONE, HARVEY S: BIRTHDAY. Dec 20. American industrialist, businessman and founder of the Firestone Tire and Rubber Co., Harvey Samuel Firestone was born at Columbiana County, OH, Dec 20, 1868. A close friend of Henry Ford, Thomas Edison and John Burroughs, Firestone was also author of two books about rubber. He died at Miami Beach, FL, Feb 7, 1938.

LANGER, SUSANNE K: BIRTH ANNIVERSARY. Dec 20. Susanne Langer, a leading American philosopher, author of *Philosophy in a New Key; A Study in the Symbolism of Reason, Rite, and Art*, was born at New York City on Dec 20, 1895. Her studies of esthetics and art exerted a profound influence on thinking in the fields of psychology, philosophy and the social sciences. She died at Old Lyme, CT, on July 17, 1985.

LIVE BETHLEHEM CHRISTMAS PAGEANT. Dec 20-21. Bethlehem, PA. Volunteers garbed in costumes of ancient times and live animals join together for the re-enactment of the Christmas story. Info from: Mr. John Cornish, 711 W Goepp St, Bethlehem, PA 18018.

LOUISIANA PURCHASE DAY. Dec 20. One of the greatest real estate deals in history was completed on Dec 20, 1803, when more than a million square miles of the Louisiana Territory were turned over to the U.S. by France, for a price of about $20 per square mile.

LUDENDORFF, ERICK: DEATH ANNIVERSARY. Dec 20. German general who, during the last years of World War I, was chiefly responsible for military policy and strategy. Born on Apr 9, 1865 near Pozen, Prussia. Died on Dec 20, 1937 at Tutzing.

MENZIES, ROBERT GORDON: BIRTHDAY. Dec 20. Australian statesman and conservative leader, born Dec 20, 1894, at Jeparit, Victoria. Sir Robert died at Melbourne, May 14, 1978.

MUDD DAY. Dec 20. A day to remember Dr. Samuel A. Mudd (born near Bryantown, MD, Dec 20, 1833), sentenced to life imprisonment for giving medical aid to disguised John Wilkes Booth, fleeing assassin of Abraham Lincoln. Imprisoned four years before being pardoned by Pres. Andrew Johnson. Died on Jan 10, 1883.

COPYRIGHT © 1985 BY WILLIAM D. CHASE and HELEN M. CHASE

SACAGAWEA: DEATH ANNIVERSARY. Dec 20. As a young Shoshone Indian woman, Sacagawea in 1805 (with her 2-month old boy strapped to her back) travelled with the Lewis and Clark Expedition, serving as an interpreter. It is said that the expedition could not have succeeded without her aid. She was born about 1787, and died at Fort Manuel on the Missouri River, Dec 20, 1812. Few women have been so often honored. There are statues, fountains and memorials of her and her name has been given to a mountain peak. Few facts about her life are firmly established and some legends have her living to nearly a hundred years of age.

SKELTON, IKE: BIRTHDAY. Dec 20. U.S. Representative of Missouri's 4th district, Democrat, of Lexington, MO, born in Lexington on Dec 20, 1931.

SOUTH CAROLINA: SECESSION ANNIVERSARY. Dec 20. South Carolina's legislature voted, Dec 20, 1860, to secede from the United States of America. The first state to do so.

TWELVE DAYS OF CHRISTMAS. Dec 20-31. Special holiday activities include caroling, concerts, games and other festivities. Info from: Special Events Coord, Jamestown Festival Park, Box JF, Williamsburg, VA 23187.

VIRGINIA COMPANY EXPEDITION TO AMERICA: ANNIVERSARY. Dec 20. Three small ships, the *Susan Constant*, the *Godspeed* and the *Discovery*, commanded by Capt. Christopher Newport, departed London, England, on Dec 20, 1606, bound for America, where the royally chartered Virginia Company's approximately 120 persons established the first permanent English settlement in what is now the United States at Jamestown, VA, on May 14, 1607.

DECEMBER 21 — SUNDAY
355th Day — Remaining, 10

BOLL, HEINRICH: BIRTH ANNIVERSARY: Dec 21. German novelist, winner of the 1972 Nobel Prize for Literature, author of some twenty books including *Billiards at Half-Past Nine*, *The Clown* and *Group Portrait With Lady*, was born Dec 21, 1917 at Cologne. He died near Bonn on July 16, 1985.

DISRAELI, BENJAMIN: BIRTHDAY. Dec 21. British novelist and statesman, born Dec 21, 1804. Died, Apr 19, 1881. "No government," he wrote, "can be long secure without a formidable Opposition."

FOREFATHER'S DAY. Dec 21. Observed mainly in New England in commemoration of landing at Plymouth Rock on this day, 1620.

LOOK AT THE BRIGHT SIDE DAY. Dec 21. Purpose: To remind us that when the gloom of winter is upon us in the Northern Hemisphere, summertime is being enjoyed by all those "down under." Moral: There's always a bright side; find it, and remember the admonition of the sun dial: "Count only the sunny hours." Sponsor: Sunny Dials Timely Instruments, Box 147, Whitehall, MI 49461.

NATIONAL FLASHLIGHT DAY. Dec 21. Purpose: To promote awareness of how various flashlights play a vital role in one's everyday life. Sponsor: Bright Star Industries, Constance M. Mikolajczyk, 600 Getty Ave, Clifton, NJ 07015.

PARKINSON, JAMES: DEATH ANNIVERSARY. Dec 21. The remarkable English physician and paleontologist who first described the "shaking palsy" later had it named for him— Parkinson's Disease. He was the author of numerous books and articles on a variety of subjects. His *Organic Remains of a Former World* is called the first attempt to give a scientific account of fossils—"a memorable event in the history of British paleontology." Under oath, Parkinson declared that he was a member of the group that hatched the "Pop-gun Plot" to assassinate King George III in a theatre, using a poisoned dart for the deed. His birthplace and date (about 1755) are unknown, but Dr. Parkinson died at London on Dec 21, 1824.

PHILEAS FOGG WINS A WAGER DAY. Dec 21. Anniversary, from Jules Verne's *Around the World in Eighty Days*, of the winning of Phileas Fogg's wager, on Dec 21, 1872, when Fogg walked into the saloon of the Reform Club in London, announcing "Here I am gentlemen!" exactly 79 days, 23 hours, 59 minutes and 59 seconds after starting his trip "around the world in 80 days," to win his £20,000 wager. See also Oct 2.

SHORTS DAY. Dec. 21. Purpose: In honor of the first day of winter, the "shortest" day of the year, employees wear crazy shorts to bring laughter to the residents. Sponsor: Township Manor Nursing Ctr, Jeanne Fetch, Recreation Dir, 265 E Township Line Rd, Elkins Park, PA 19117.

SPACE MILESTONE: APOLLO 8 (US). Dec 21. First Moon voyage launched on Dec 21, 1968, and manned by Col. Frank Borman, Capt. James A. Lovell, Jr., Major William A. Anders, orbited Moon on Dec 24, returned to Earth on Dec 27. First men to see the side of the Moon away from Earth. Dec 21, 1968.

STALIN, JOSEPH VISSARIONOVICH: BIRTH ANNIVERSARY. Dec 21. Russian dictator whose family name was Dzhugashvili, was born at Gori, Georgia, U.S.S.R., Dec 21, 1879. One of the most powerful and most feared men of the 20th century, Stalin died (of a stroke) at the Kremlin, in Moscow, Mar 5, 1953.

WINTER. Dec 21-Mar 20 (1987). In the Northern Hemisphere winter begins today with the Winter Solstice, at 11:02 p.m., E.S.T. Note that in the Southern Hemisphere today is the beginning of summer, and the occasion of the Summer Solstice. The point on Earth from which the sun is overhead reaches its farthest south for the year, on the Tropic of Capricorn, latitude 23½° S, this year at longitude 120° E (near Mt. Newman in Western Australia). Between Equator and Arctic Circle, the sunrise and sunset points on the horizon are farthest south for the year, and daylight length is minimum (ranging from 12 hours, 8 minutes at the equator to zero at the Arctic Circle).

DECEMBER 22 — MONDAY
356th Day — Remaining, 9

CAPRICORN, THE GOAT. Dec 22-Jan 19. In the astronomical and astrological Zodiac, which divides the sun's apparent orbit into twelve segments, the period Dec 22-Jan 19, is identified, traditionally, as the sun-sign of Capricorn, the Goat. The ruling planet is Saturn.

ELLERY, WILLIAM: BIRTHDAY. Dec 22. Signer of the Declaration of Independence, born, Dec 22, 1727. Died, Feb 15, 1820.

INTERNATIONAL ARBOR DAY. Dec 22. Purpose: Plant trees at a time favorable in most nations and climates and abolish hunting sports on public lands. Sponsor: I.A.D. Committee, 2920 Woodrich Dr, Tallahassee, FL 32301.

JOHNSON, CLAUDIA ALTA (LADY BIRD) TAYLOR: BIRTHDAY. Dec 22. Wife of Lyndon Baines Johnson, 36th President of the U.S., born at Karnack, TX, Dec 22, 1912.

LIPINSKI, WILLIAM OLIVER: BIRTHDAY. Dec 22. U.S. Representative of Illinois' 5th district, Democrat, of Chicago, IL, born there Dec 22, 1937.

OGLETHORPE, JAMES EDWARD: BIRTH ANNIVERSARY. Dec 22. English general, author and colonizer of Georgia. Founder of the city of Savannah. Oglethorpe was born at London on Dec 22, 1696. He died June 30, 1785.

COPYRIGHT © 1985 BY WILLIAM D. CHASE and HELEN M. CHASE

PUCCINI, GIACOMO: BIRTHDAY. Dec 22. Italian composer, born Dec 22, 1858. Died, Nov 29, 1924.

WRIGHT, JAMES C JR: BIRTHDAY. Dec 22. U.S. Representative of Texas' 12th district, Democrat, of Fort Worth, TX, born in Fort Worth on Dec 22, 1922.

DECEMBER 23 — TUESDAY
357th Day — Remaining, 8

EGYPT: PUBLIC HOLIDAY. Dec 23. Victory Day is observed on Dec 23. Info from: Egyptian Tourist Authority, 630 Fifth Ave, New York, NY 10111.

FEDERAL RESERVE SYSTEM: BIRTHDAY. Dec 23. Established pursuant to authority contained in the Federal Reserve Act of Dec 23, 1913, the system serves as the nation's central bank, has responsibility for execution of monetary policy. It is called on to contribute to the strength and vitality of the U.S. economy, in part by influencing the lending and investing activities of commercial banks and the cost and availability of money and credit.

METRIC CONVERSION ACT: ANNIVERSARY. Dec 23. The Congress of the United States, on Dec 23, 1975, passed Public Law 94-168, known as the Metric Conversion Act of 1975. This act declares that the SI (International System of Units) will be this country's basic system of measurement and establishes the United States Metric Board which is responsible for the planning, coordination and implementation of the Nation's voluntary conversion to SI. (Congress had authorized the metric system as a legal system of measurement in the U.S., by an act passed on July 28, 1866. In 1875, the U.S. became one of the original signers of the Treaty of the Metre, which established an international metric system.)

MEXICO: FEAST OF THE RADISHES. Dec 23. Oaxaca, Mexico. Figurines of people and animals cleverly carved out of radishes are sold during festivities.

MONROE, HARRIET: BIRTHDAY. Dec 23. American poet, editor and founder of *Poetry* magazine. Born Dec 23, 1860 at Chicago, IL. Miss Monroe died on Sept 26, 1936.

SMILES, SAMUEL: BIRTHDAY. Dec 23. Scottish writer, born Dec 23, 1812. Died, London, Apr 17, 1904. "A place for everything," he wrote in *Thrift*, "and everything in its place."

SMITH, JOSEPH: BIRTHDAY. Dec 23. Mormon prophet born at Sharon, VT, Dec 23, 1805. Killed by a mob while in Carthage, IL, jail, June 27, 1844.

TOJO HIDEKI: EXECUTION ANNIVERSARY. Dec 23. Tojo Hideki, prime minister of Japan from Oct 16, 1941 until his resignation on July 19, 1944. After Japan's surrender in Aug, 1945, Tojo was arrested as a war criminal, tried by a military tribunal, and sentenced to death on Nov 12, 1948. He was hanged (with six other Japenese wartime military leaders) at Sugamo Prison in Tokyo on Dec 23, 1948, the sentence being carried out by the U.S. Eighth Army.

WALKER, ROBERT SMITH: BIRTHDAY. Dec 23. U.S. Representative of Pennsylvania's 16th district, Republican, of East Petersburg, PA, was born in Bradford, PA, on Dec 23, 1942.

DECEMBER 24 — WEDNESDAY
358th Day — Remaining, 7

ARNOLD, MATTHEW: BIRTHDAY. Dec 24. English poet, born Dec 24, 1822. Died, Apr 15, 1888. "One has often wondered," he wrote in *Culture and Anarchy*, "whether upon the whole earth there is anything so unintelligent, so unapt to perceive how the world is really going, as an ordinary young Englishman of our upper class."

AUSTRIA: "SILENT NIGHT, HOLY NIGHT" CELEBRATIONS. Dec 24. Oberndorf, Hallein and Wagrain, Salzburg, Austria. Commemorating the creation of the Christmas carol here in 1818.

CARSON, CHRISTOPHER: BIRTHDAY. Dec 24. American frontiersman, soldier, trapper, guide and Indian agent best known as Kit Carson. Born on Dec 24, 1809 in Madison County, KY, he died at Fort Lyon, CO on May 23, 1868.

CHRISTMAS EVE. Dec 24. Family gift-giving occasion in many Christian countries.

HUGHES, HOWARD ROBARD: BIRTHDAY. Dec 24. Wealthy American recluse born Dec 24, 1905. Died in airplane en route from Acapulco, Mexico, to Houston, TX, on Apr 5, 1976.

JOULE, JAMES PRESCOTT: BIRTH ANNIVERSARY. Dec 24. English physicist and inventor after whom Joule's Law was named, was born at Salford, Lancashire, England, on Dec 24, 1818. Joule died at Cheshire on Oct 11, 1889.

MOON PHASE: LAST QUARTER. Dec 24. Moon enters Last Quarter phase at 4:17 a.m., E.S.T.

RUSH, BENJAMIN: BIRTHDAY. Dec 24. Physician, patriot and humanitarian of the American Revolution, born on a plantation at Byberry, PA, Dec 24, 1745. Died Philadelphia, PA, Apr 19, 1813.

DECEMBER 25 — THURSDAY
359th Day— Remaining, 6

BARTON, CLARA: BIRTHDAY. Dec 25. Clarissa Harlowe Barton, American nurse and philanthropist, founder of the American Red Cross, was born at Oxford, MA, Dec 25, 1821. In 1881, she became first president of the American Red Cross (founded May 21, 1881). She died at Glen Echo, MD, Apr 12, 1912.

BOOTH, EVANGELINE CORY: BIRTH ANNIVERSARY. Dec 25. Salvation Army general, active in England, Canada and the U.S. Author and composer of songs, Booth was born at London, England on Dec 25, 1865. She died at Hartsdale, NY, on July 17, 1950.

BOGART, HUMPHREY: BIRTHDAY. Dec 25. American stage and screen actor, Humphrey DeForest Bogart was born at New York City on Dec 25, 1899. Among his best remembered films were: *The African Queen*, *Maltese Falcon*, *Casablanca* and *To Have and Have Not*. Bogart died Jan 14, 1957.

CHRISTMAS. Dec 25. Christian festival commemorating the birth of Jesus of Nazareth. Most popular of Christian observances, Christmas as a Feast of the Nativity dates from the fourth century. Although Jesus' birth date is not known, the Western church selected Dec 25 for the feast, possibly to counteract the non-Christian festivals of that approximate date. Many customs from non-Christian festivals (Roman Saturnalia, Mithraic sun's birthday, Teutonic yule, Druidic and other winter solstice rites) have been adopted as part of the Christmas celebration (lights, mistletoe, holly and ivy, holiday tree, wassailing and gift-giving, for example). Theophany (recognition of the divinity of Jesus) is observed on this date and also on Jan 6, especially by the Eastern church.

JINNAH, MOHAMMED ALI: BIRTHDAY. Dec 25. The founder of the Islamic Republic of Pakistan, Mohammed Ali Jinnah, was born at Karachi, Dec 25, 1876. When Pakistan came into independent political being (Aug 15, 1947), Jinnah became its first governor general. He died at Karachi, Sept 11, 1948.

NEWTON, ISAAC: BIRTH ANNIVERSARY. Dec 25. Sir Isaac Newton, mathematician, scientist and author, was born near Grantham (Lincolnshire), England on Dec 25, 1642. Best known of his works is the *Philosophiae Naturalis Principia*

December 1986	S	M	T	W	T	F	S
		1	2	3	4	5	6
	7	8	9	10	11	12	13
	14	15	16	17	18	19	20
	21	22	23	24	25	26	27
	28	29	30	31			

COPYRIGHT © 1985 BY WILLIAM D. CHASE and HELEN M. CHASE

Mathematica (1687) in which he enunciated the famed three laws of motion. Newton died at London on Mar 20, 1727, and was buried in Westminster Abbey.

WASHINGTON CROSSING THE DELAWARE RE-ENACTMENT. Dec 25. Washington Crossing, PA. Purpose: Re-enactment pageant of George Washington's crossing of the Delaware, December 25, 1776, which led to the victory at Trenton, turning point of the American Revolution. Sponsor: Washington Crossing Foundation, Ann Hawkes Hutton, Washington Crossing, PA 18977.

WEST, REBECCA: BIRTHDAY. Dec 25. English author, literary critic, prize-winning journalist and noted feminist, Dame Rebecca West was born Cicely Isabel Fairfield at London, on Dec 25, 1892. She died there Mar 15, 1983.

DECEMBER 26 — FRIDAY
360th Day — Remaining, 5

ALL COLLEGE BASKETBALL TOURNAMENT. Dec 26-27. Purpose: "Oldest and best basketball tournament in country." Always held between Christmas and New Year's. Info from: Stanley Draper, Jr, Oklahoma City All Sports Assn, 1 Santa Fe Plaza, Oklahoma City, OK 73102.

AMERICAN YOUTH HOSTELS: CHRISTMAS TRIP. Dec 26-31. Purpose: A six day bicycling adventure through the mountains, deserts and coastal areas of southern California. Begins and ends in San Diego. Sponsor: San Diego Council, American Youth Hostels, Inc, 1031 India St, San Diego, CA 92101.

BAHAMAS: JUNKANOO. Dec 26. Kaleidoscope of sound and spectacle combining a bit of Mardi Gras, Mummer's parade and ancient African tribal rituals. Revelers in colorful costumes parade through the streets to sounds of cowbells, goat skin drums, and many other homemade instruments. Always on Boxing Day.

BOXING DAY. Dec 26. Ordinarily observed on the first regular "working day" after Christmas. Now a legal holiday in Canada, the United Kingdom (except Scotland) and many other countries. Formerly (according to Robert Chambers) a day when Christmas gift boxes were "regularly expected by a postman, the lamplighter, the dustman, and generally by all those functionaries who render services to the public at large, without receiving payment therfore from any individual." When Boxing Day falls on a Saturday or Sunday, the Monday or Tuesday immediately following may be proclaimed or observed as a bank or public holiday.

DAY OF THE WREN. Dec 26. Dingle Peninsula, Ireland. Masked revelers and musicians go from door to door asking for money. Traditional day and night of public merrymaking.

KWANZA. Dec 26-Jan 1, 1987. American black family observance (since 1966) in recognition of traditional African harvest festivals. Stresses unity of the black family, with community-wide harvest feast (karamu) on seventh day. Kwanza, "first-fruit" in Swahili. An optional observance to avoid commercialization of Christmas traditions.

LOVERA, JUAN: BIRTHDAY. Dec 26. Venezuelan "Artist of Independence," whose best known canvases commemorate the independence dates of Apr 19, 1810, and July 5, 1811, known as the founder of historical painting in Venezuela, was born Dec 26, 1778. Died in 1841 (exact date unknown).

MAO TSE-TUNG BIRTHDAY. Dec 26. Chinese librarian, teacher, communist-revolutionist, and "founding father" of the People's Republic of China, born in Hunan Province, China, on Dec 26, 1893. Died at Peking, Sept 9, 1976.

MILLER, HENRY (VALENTINE): BIRTHDAY. Dec 26. Controversial American novelist born at New York City, Dec 26, 1891. Died at Pacific Palisades, CA, June 7, 1980.

NATIONAL WHINER'S DAY. Dec 26. Purpose: A day dedicated to whiners, especially those who return Christmas gifts and need lots of attention on this day. Sponsor: Kevin C. Zaborney, 10434 Ataberry Dr, Clio, MI 48420.

NELSON, THOMAS: BIRTHDAY. Dec 26. Merchant and signer of the Declaration of Independence, born Yorktown, VA, Dec 26, 1738. Died, Hanover County, VA, Jan 4, 1789.

ST. STEPHEN'S DAY. Dec 26. One of the seven deacons, named by the apostles to distribute alms, died during first century. Feast Day is Dec 26, and is observed as a public holiday in Austria.

SECOND CHRISTMAS. Dec 26. Observed as holiday in many places.

WORLD ENDURO CHAMPIONSHIP KART RACES. Dec 26-30. Daytona International Speedway, Daytona Beach, FL. Info from: Daytona Internatl Speedway, Larry Balewski, PR, Daytona Beach, FL 32015.

DECEMBER 27 — SATURDAY
361st Day — Remaining, 4

AMERICAN HISTORICAL ASSOCIATION: ANNUAL MEETING. Dec 27-30. Hyatt Regency, Chicago, IL. Approximately 100 sessions covering a wide range of scholarly, professional and pedagogical topics dealing with world history. Sponsor: American Historical Assn, 400 A St, SE, Washington, DC 20003.

CAYLEY, GEORGE: BIRTHDAY. Dec 27. Aviation pioneer Sir George Cayley, English scientist and inventor, credited as the father of aerodynamics, and theoretician who designed airplanes, helicopters, gliders, and was pilot of the world's first manned glider flight. Born at Scarborough, Yorkshire, England, Dec 27, 1773. Died at Brompton Hall, Yorkshire, Dec 15, 1857.

CHANUKAH. Dec 27-Jan 3, 1987. Feast of Lights or Feast of Dedication. Festival lasting 8 days, beginning on Kislev 25. Commemorates victory of Maccabees over Syrians (165 BC) and rededication of Temple at Jerusalem. Begins on Hebrew calendar date Kislev 25, 5747.

CRUCIAN CHRISTMAS FIESTA. Dec 27-Jan 6 1987. St. Croix, Virgin Islands. An annual celebration featuring native food and beverages, entertainment, and a parade on Three Kings Day.

KEPLER, JOHANNES: BIRTHDAY. Dec 27. One of the world's greatest astronomers, called "the father of modern astronomy," German mathematician Johannes Kepler was born at Wurttemberg on Dec 27, 1571. Died at Regensburg, Nov 15, 1630.

McCLURE, JAMES A: BIRTHDAY. Dec 27. U.S. Senator from Idaho, Republican, of McCall, ID, born at Payette, ID, Dec 27, 1924.

PASTEUR, LOUIS: BIRTHDAY. Dec 27. French chemist-bacteriologist born at Dole, Jura, France, Dec 27, 1822. Died at Villeneuve l'Etang, France, Sept 28, 1895. Discoverer of prophylactic inoculation against rabies. Pasteurization process named for him.

RADIO CITY MUSIC HALL: ANNIVERSARY. Dec 27. Radio City Music Hall, in New York City, opened Dec 27, 1932.

ST. JOHN, APOSTLE-EVANGELIST: FEAST DAY. Dec 27. Son of Zebedee, Galilean fisherman, and Salome. Died about A.D. 100. Roman Rite Feast Day is Dec 27. (Observed on May 8 by Byzantine Rite.)

COPYRIGHT © 1985 BY WILLIAM D. CHASE and HELEN M. CHASE

DECEMBER 28 — SUNDAY
362nd Day — Remaining, 3

AUSTRALIA: PROCLAMATION DAY. Dec 28. Observed in South Australia.

GRADISON, WILLIS D. JR: BIRTHDAY. Dec 28. U.S. Representative of Ohio's 2nd district, Republican, of Cincinnati, OH, born in Cincinnati on Dec 28, 1928.

HOLY INNOCENTS DAY (CHILDERMAS). Dec 28. Commemoration of the massacre of children in Bethlehem, ordered by King Herod, with a view of destroying, among them, the infant Savior. Early and Medieval accounts claimed as many as 144,000 victims, but more recent writers, noting that Bethlehem was a very small town, have revised the estimates of the number of children killed to between six and twenty.

IOWA: ADMISSION DAY. Dec 28. Became 29th State on this day in 1846.

MESSINA EARTHQUAKE: ANNIVERSARY. Dec 28. Messina, Sicily. The ancient town of Messina was struck by an earthquake on Dec 28, 1908. Nearly 80,000 persons died in the disaster and half of the town's buildings were destroyed.

MOLSON, JOHN: BIRTHDAY. Dec 28. John Molson, an orphan, left his home at Lincolnshire, England, to settle in Montreal, in 1782. He soon acquired a brewery and became patriarch of the Molson brewery family. Born at Lincolnshire, Dec 28, 1763. Died at Montreal, Quebec, Jan 11, 1836.

NEPAL: NATIONAL HOLIDAY. Dec 28. The birthday of His Majesty the King is a public holiday.

POOR RICHARD'S ALMANACK: ANNIVERSARY. Dec 28. The *Pennsylvania Gazette*, on Dec 28, 1732, carried the first known advertisement for the first issue of *Poor Richard's Almanack*, by Richard Saunders (Benjamin Franklin) for the year 1733. The advertisement promised "many pleasant and witty verses, jests and sayings . . . new fashions, games for kisses . . . men and melons . . . breakfast in bed, &c." America's most famous almanac, *Poor Richard* was published through the year 1758, and has been imitated many times since.

VICE-PRESIDENTIAL RESIGNATION: ANNIVERSARY. Dec 28. John C. Calhoun, who had served as Vice-President of the U.S. under two presidents (John Quincy Adams and Andrew Jackson) Mar 4, 1825-Dec 28, 1832, finding himself in growing disagreement with President Jackson, resigned the office of vice-president on Dec 28, 1832. He was the first to resign from that office. Calhoun subsequently served as a U.S. Senator from South Carolina, and as Secretary of State.

WALGREN, DOUG: BIRTHDAY. Dec 28. U.S. Representative of Pennsylvania's 18th district, Democrat, of Pittsburgh, PA, was born in Rochester, NY, on Dec 28, 1940.

WILSON, WOODROW: BIRTHDAY. Dec 28. The 28th president of the U.S. was born Thomas Woodrow Wilson at Staunton, VA, Dec 28, 1856. Twice elected president (1912 and 1916), it was Wilson who said "The world must be made safe for democracy," as he asked the Congress to declare war on Germany, Apr 2, 1917. His first wife, Ellen, died Aug 6, 1914, and he married Edith Bolling Galt on Dec 18, 1915. He suffered a paralytic stroke Sept 26, 1919, never regaining his health. There were many dark speculations about who (possibly Mrs. Wilson?) was running the government during his illness. His second term of office ended Mar 3, 1921, and he died at Washington, DC, Feb 3, 1924.

December 1986

S	M	T	W	T	F	S
	1	2	3	4	5	6
7	8	9	10	11	12	13
14	15	16	17	18	19	20
21	22	23	24	25	26	27
28	29	30	31			

DECEMBER 29 — MONDAY
363rd Day — Remaining, 2

CASALS, PABLO: BIRTHDAY. Dec 29. Famed cellist, Pablo Carlos Salvador Defillio de Casals, born Venrell, Spain, Dec 29, 1876. Died, Rio Pedros, Puerto Rico, Oct 22, 1973.

GLADSTONE, WILLIAM EWART: BIRTHDAY. Dec 29. English statesman and author for whom the Gladstone (luggage) bag was named. Inspiring orator, eccentric individual, intensely loved or hated by those who knew him (cheered from the streets and jeered from the balconies), Gladstone is said to have left more writings (letters, diaries, journals, books) than any other major English politician. However, his preoccupation with the charitable rehabilitation of prostitutes was perhaps easily misunderstood. Born at Liverpool on Dec 29, 1809, he was four times Britain's prime minister. Gladstone died at Hawarden, Wales, on May 19, 1898.

JOHNSON, ANDREW: BIRTHDAY. Dec 29. Seventeenth president of the U.S. Andrew Johnson, proprietor of a tailor shop in Laurens, SC, before he entered politics, was born Dec 29, 1808, at Raleigh, NC. Upon Abraham Lincoln's assassination Johnson became president. He was the only U.S. president to be impeached, and he was acquitted Mar 26, 1868. After his term of office as president (Apr 15, 1865-Mar 3, 1869) he made several unsuccessful attempts to find public office. Finally he was elected to the U.S. Senate from Tennessee, and served in the Senate from Mar 4, 1875, until his death, at Carter's Station, TN, on July 31, 1875.

NEPAL: BIRTHDAY OF HIS MAJESTY THE KING. Dec 29. National holiday of Nepal. Three day celebration with huge public rally at Tundikkel, gay pageantry, musical bands and illumination in the towns at night.

ST. THOMAS OF CANTERBURY: FEAST DAY. Dec 29. Thomas Becket, Archbishop of Canterbury, was born at London, in 1118, and was murdered in the Canterbury Cathedral, Dec 29, 1170.

SPELLMAN, JOHN: BIRTHDAY. Dec 29. John Spellman, Governor of Washington, Democrat, was born at Bellevue, WA, on Dec 29, 1926.

TEXAS: ADMISSION DAY. Dec 29. Became 28th State on this day in 1845.

TRIBLE, PAUL S. JR: BIRTHDAY. Dec 29. U.S. Senator from Virginia, Republican, of Kilmarnock, VA, was born in Baltimore, MD, on Dec 29, 1946.

WAR MEMORIAL HIGH SCHOOL BASKETBALL TOURNAMENT. Dec 29-30. War memorial Arena, Johnstown, PA. Purpose: See the best in high school boys basketball from the U.S. Top ranked teams in nation. Sponsor: Cambria County War Memorial, 326 Napoleon St, Johnstown, PA 15901.

WOUNDED KNEE MASSACRE: ANNIVERSARY. Dec 29. Anniversary of the massacre of more than 200 American Indian men, women and children by the U.S. Seventh Cavalry on Dec 29, 1890, at Wounded Knee Creek, SD. Government efforts to suppress a ceremonial religious practice, the Ghost Dance (which called for a messiah who would restore the bison to the plains, make the white men disappear and bring back the old Indian way of life), had resulted in the death of Sitting Bull on Dec 15, 1890, which further inflamed the unhappy Indians and culminated in slaughter at Wounded Knee on Dec 29.

DECEMBER 30 — TUESDAY
364th Day — Remaining, 1

GUGGENHEIM, SIMON: BIRTHDAY. Dec 30. American capitalist and philanthropist, born at Philadelphia, PA, Dec 30, 1867. He established, in memory of his son, the John Simon Guggenheim Memorial Foundation, in 1925. Died, Nov 2, 1941.

COPYRIGHT © 1985 BY WILLIAM D. CHASE and HELEN M. CHASE

KIPLING, RUDYARD: BIRTHDAY. Dec 30. English poet and novelist, born Bombay, India, Dec 30, 1865. Died, London, Jan 18, 1936.

LEACOCK, STEPHEN: BIRTHDAY. Dec 30. Canadian economist and humorist, born Dec 30, 1869. Died, Mar 28, 1944. "Lord Ronald. . ," he wrote in *Nonsense Novels*, "flung himself upon his horse and rode madly off in all directions."

MADAGASCAR: ANNIVERSARY OF THE DEMOCRATIC REPUBLIC OF MADAGASCAR. Dec 30.

MONITOR SINKS: ANNIVERSARY. Dec 30. The Union iron-clad ship the *Monitor* (which achieved fame after the Battle of the Monitor and the Merrimack) sank on Dec 30, 1862 off Cape Hatteras during a storm.

MOON PHASE: NEW MOON. Dec 30. Moon enters New Moon phase at 10:10 p.m., E.S.T.

PERIGEAN SPRING TIDES. Dec 30. Spring tides, the highest possible tides, occur when New Moon or Full Moon takes place within 24 hours of the moment the moon is nearest Earth (perigee) in its monthly orbit. Dec 30, at 6 p.m., E.S.T.

PHILIPPINES: RIZAL DAY. Dec 30. The Philippines. Commemorates martyrdom of Dr. Jose Rizal on this day in 1896.

TOJO HIDEKI: BIRTHDAY. Dec 30. Japanese prime minister during World War II. Born on Dec 30, 1884 at Tokyo. Arrested in Aug 1945 as a war criminal and hanged on Dec 23, 1948.

DECEMBER 31 — WEDNESDAY

365th Day — Remaining, 0

FIESTA BOWL PARADE. Dec 31. Phoenix, AZ. Floats, horse units and bands. Info from: Fiesta Bowl Office, 4631 E Thomas Rd, Phoenix, AZ 85018.

FIRST NIGHT '87. Dec 31. Purpose: Public celebration of New Year through the arts. Performances at historic indoor sites, procession of giant puppets, artists and musicians, civic plazas as wonderlands of ice, steam, sound and light. Performances include dance, music, mime, theater, film and poetry. Info from: First Night, Inc, Box 573, Back Bay Annex, Boston, MA 02117.

GHANA: REVOLUTION DAY. Dec 31. National Holiday.

HOGMANAY. Dec 31. Scottish celebration of New Year's Eve.

JAPAN: NAMAHAGE. Dec 31. In evening, groups of "Namahage" men disguised as devils make door-to-door visits, growling "Any good-for-nothing fellow hereabout?" The object of this annual event is to give sluggards an opportunity to change their minds and become diligent. Otherwise, according to legend, they will be punished by devils. Oga Peninsula, Akita Prefecture, Japan.

KING ORANGE JAMBOREE PARADE. Dec 31. Miami, FL. Gala annual parade of bands and floats ushers in the New Year on downtown Biscayne Blvd. Info from: Al Wolfe Associates, Inc, 5225 NW 87th Ave, Miami, FL 33166.

LEAP SECOND ADJUSTMENT TIME. Dec 31. December 31 is one of the times which has been favored for the addition or subtraction of a second from man's clock time (to coordinate atomic and astronomical time). The determination to adjust is made by the Bureau International de l'Heure, in Paris. See also the Note about Leap Seconds below.

MARSHALL, GEORGE CATLETT: BIRTHDAY. Dec 31. American soldier and statesman, author of the "Marshall Plan," Nobel Peace Prize recipient, born at Uniontown, PA, Dec 31, 1880. General Marshall died at Walter Reed Army Hospital, Washington, DC, Oct 16, 1959.

NEW YEAR'S EVE. Dec 31.

NEW YEAR'S EVE CELEBRATION. Dec 31. Purpose: Features fireworks, celebrities, and music on the "brightest-lit street in the world." Sponsor: Downtown Progress Assn of Las Vegas, Ira David Sternberg, Marketing Dir, 302 E Carson Ave, Suite 808, Las Vegas, NV 89101.

NIXON, JOHN: DEATH ANNIVERSARY. Dec 31. Commander of the Philadelphia City Guard, born 1733 (exact date unknown). Died, Philadelphia, PA, Dec 31, 1808. Appointed to conduct the first public reading of the Declaration of Independence, July 8, 1776. Nixon, a revolutionary patriot and businessman, was the son of Richard and Sarah Nixon.

NOON YEAR'S EVE PARTY. Dec 31. Classic Hotel, Albuquerque, NM. Purpose: A New Year's Eve party for early risers who have difficulty staying awake until midnight. Celebration includes countdown to 12 (noon) and "Happy Noon Year!" greeting. Sponsor: KOB Radio, Larry Ahrens, Morning show host, 77 Broadcast Plaza SW, Albuquerque, NM 87103.

ROGERS, HAROLD DALLAS: BIRTHDAY. Dec 31. U.S. Representative of Kentucky's 5th district, Republican, of Somerset, KY, was born in Barrier, KY, on Dec 31, 1937.

ST. SYLVESTER'S DAY. Dec 31. Observed in Belgium, Germany, France, Switzerland. Commemorates death of Pope Sylvester I in 1335. Feasting, particularly upon "St. Sylvester's Carp."

WESTERN SAMOA: SAMOAN FIRE DANCE. Dec 31. New Year's Eve is occasion for Samoan bamboo fireworks, singing, and traditional performances such as the Samoan Fire Dance.

LEAP SECONDS

Because of Earth's slightly erratic rotation, it has become necessary to add a "leap second" from time to time to man's clocks to co-ordinate them with astronomical time. Rotation of the Earth has been slowing since 1900, making an astronomical second longer than an atomic second. Since 1972, by international agreement, adjustments must be made to keep astronomical and atomic clocks within 0.9 seconds of each other. The determination to add (or subtract) seconds is made by the Bureau International de l'Heure, in Paris. Preferred times for adjustment are December 31 and June 30, but any time may be designated by the Bureau International de l'Heure. The additions have been made at 23:59:60 Co-ordinated Universal Time (6:59:60 E.S.T.) on the dates selected for adjustments. Thirteen seconds have been added since 1972. One "leap" second has been added on each of the following dates: June 30, 1972; Dec. 31, 1972; Dec. 31, 1973; Dec. 31, 1974; Dec. 31, 1975; Dec. 31, 1976; Dec. 31, 1977; Dec. 31, 1978; Dec. 31, 1979; June 30, 1981; June 30, 1982; June 30, 1983; June 30, 1985;

COPYRIGHT © 1985 BY WILLIAM D. CHASE and HELEN M. CHASE

PRESIDENTIAL PROCLAMATIONS
ISSUED, JANUARY 1, 1984 - AUGUST 31, 1985
(See Index and Chronological Text for Expected 1986 Presidential Proclamations.)

No. Title, Observance Dates, (Date of Signing).

5143 Alaska Statehood Day: Jan 3, 1984. (Jan 3, 1984).
5144 National Consumers Week: Week beginning Apr 23, 1984. (Jan 3, 1984).
5145 Small Business Week: Week beginning May 6, 1984. (Jan 3, 1984).
5146 National Fetal Alcohol Syndrome Awareness Week: Jan 15 through Jan 21, 1984. (Jan 12, 1984).
5147 National Sanctity of Human Life Day: Jan 22, 1984. (Jan 13, 1984).
5148 Centennial of the Birth of Harry S Truman: May 8, 1984. (Jan 25, 1984).
5149 National Tourism Week: Week beginning May 27, 1984. (Feb 1, 1984).
5150 Save Your Vision Week: Week beginning Mar 4, 1984. (Feb 13, 1984).
5151 National Surveyors Week: Week beginning Mar 11, 1984. (Feb 13, 1984).
5152 National Agriculture Day: Mar 20, 1984. (Feb 13, 1984).
5153 Municipal Clerk's Week: Week beginning May 13, 1984. (Feb 13, 1984).
5154 Cancer Control Month: Month of April 1984. (Feb 27, 1984).
5155 Women's History Week: Week beginning Mar 4, 1984. (Mar 2, 1984).
5156 National Beta Club Week: Week beginning Mar 4, 1984. (Mar 5, 1984).
5157 Frozen Food Day: Mar 6, 1984. (Mar 6, 1984).
5158 35th Anniversary of NATO: . . . throughout this anniversary year . . . (Mar 6, 1984).
5159 Red Cross Month: Month of March. (Mar 8, 1984).
5160 World Trade Week: Week beginning May 20, 1984. (Mar 15, 1984).
5161 National Employ the Older Worker Week: Week beginning Mar 11, 1984. (Mar 16, 1984).
5162 National Energy Education Day: Mar 23, 1984. (Mar 17, 1984).
5163 National Organ Donation Awareness Week: Apr 22 through Apr 28, 1984. (Mar 17, 1984).
5164 Import Fees on Certain Sugars, Sirups and Molasses. (Mar 19, 1984).
5165 Afghanistan Day: Mar 21, 1984. (Mar 20, 1984).
5166 National Single Parent Day: Mar 21, 1984. (Mar 21, 1984).
5167 National Social Work Month: Month of March 1984. (Mar 22, 1984).
5168 National Safe Boating Week: Week beginning Jun 3, 1984. (Mar 22, 1984).
5169 Loyalty Day: May 1, 1984. (Mar 22, 1984).
5170 National Eye Donor Month: Month of March, 1984. (Mar 31, 1984).
5171 Pan American Day and Pan American Week: Pan American Day—Apr 14, 1984, Pan American Week—Week beginning Apr 8, 1984. (Apr 2, 1984).
5172 National Child Abuse Prevention Month: Month of April, 1984. (Apr 3, 1984).
5173 Mother's Day: May 13, 1984. (Apr 3, 1984).
5174 National Mental Health Counselors Week: Week beginning April 8, 1984. (Apr 8, 1984).
5175 Law Day U.S.A.: May 1, 1984. (Apr 9, 1984).
5176 Parkinson's Disease Awareness Week: April 8-14, 1984. (Apr 9, 1984).
5177 National Hearing Impaired Awareness Week: Week beginning April 8, 1984. (Apr 13, 1984).
5178 Asian/Pacific American Heritage Week: Week beginning May 5, 1984. (Apr 13, 1984).
5179 National Maritime Day: May 22, 1984. (Apr 13, 1984).
5180 Prayer for Peace Memorial Day: May 28, 1984. (Apr 13, 1984).
5181 Education Day, U.S.A.: April 13, 1984. (Apr 13, 1984).
5182 Crime Victims Week: Week beginning Apr 15, 1984. (Apr 13, 1984).
5183 Older Americans Month: Month of May, 1984. (Apr 16, 1984).
5184 Military Spouse Day: May 23, 1984. (Apr 17, 1984).
5185 Father's Day: Jun 17, 1984. (Apr 18, 1984).
5186 Student Awareness of Drunk Driving Month: Month of June, 1984. (May 3, 1984).
5187 National Correctional Officers Week: Week beginning May 6, 1984. (May 5, 1984).
5188 National Photo Week: May 7 through May 13, 1984. (May 5, 1984).
5189 National Defense Transportation Day and National Transportation Week: National Defense Transportation Day—May 18, 1984; National Transportation Week—Week beginning May 13, 1984. (May 5, 1984).
5190 Jewish Heritage Week: May 6 through May 13, 1984. (May 7, 1984).
5191 National Tuberous Sclerosis Week: May 6 through May 13, 1984. (May 9, 1984).
5192 National P.O.W./M.I.A. Recognition Day: July 20, 1984. (May 9, 1984).
5193 National Asthma and Allergy Awareness Week: Week beginning May 6, 1984. (May 11, 1984).

5194 Missing Children Day: May 25, 1984. (May 15, 1984).
5195 Return and Final Interment of Unknown American Killed in Vietnam: . . . flag at half staff . . . May 25, 26, 27 and 28, 1984. (May 20, 1984).
5196 National Arts With the Handicapped Week: May 20 through May 26, 1984. (May 20, 1984).
5197 Year of Excellence in Education: The period commencing April 1, 1984 and ending March 31, 1985. (May 22, 1984).
5198 Galway's Quincentennial Year, 1984: The year 1984. (May 23, 1984).
5199 National Farm Safety Week: Sept 16 through Sept 22, 1984. (May 24, 1984).
5200 National Digestive Diseases Awareness Week: May 20, 1984 through May 26, 1984. (May 25, 1984).
5201 National Physical Fitness and Sports Month: Month of May, 1984. (May 31, 1984).
5202 National Animal Health Week: Week beginning May 27, 1984. (May 31, 1984).
5203 National Theatre Week: June 3 through June 9, 1984. (May 31, 1984).
5204 Flag Day and National Flag Week: Flag Day—June 14, 1984; National Flag Week—Week beginning June 10, 1984. (May 31, 1984).
5205 Citizenship Day and Constitution Week: Citizenship Day—Sept 17, 1984; Constitution Week—Week beginning Sept 17 and ending Sept 23, 1984. (May 31, 1984).
5206 D-Day National Remembrance: June 6, 1984. (May 31, 1984).
5207 Application of Certain Laws of the United States to Citizens of the Northern Mariana Islands. (Jun 7, 1984).
5208 Family Reunion Month: The period between May 13 and Jun 17, 1984. (Jun 14, 1984).
5209 Baltic Freedom Day: Jun 14, 1984. (Jun 14, 1984).
5210 National Child Passenger Safety Awareness Day: Jun 18, 1984. (Jun 18, 1984).
5211 Federal Credit Union Week: Week beginning Jun 24, 1984. (Jun 18, 1984).
5212 Harmon Killebrew Day: Jun 13, 1984. (Jun 18, 1984).
5213 Minority Enterprise Development Week: Oct 7 through Oct 13, 1984. (Jun 19, 1984).
5214 Helen Keller Deaf-Blind Awareness Week: Week beginning Jun 24, 1984. (Jun 22, 1984).
5215 1992 Chicago-Seville International Exposition. (Jun 27, 1984).
5216 National Duck Stamp Week; Golden Anniversary Year of the Duck Stamp: National Duck Stamp Week—Jul 1 through July 8, 1984; Golden Anniversary Year of the Duck Stamp—1984. (Jul 3, 1984).
5217 Veterans' Preference Month: Month of June 1984. (Jul 5, 1984).
5218 African Refugees Relief Day: Jul 9, 1984. (Jul 9, 1984).
5219 National Ice Cream Month and National Ice Cream Day: National Ice Cream Month—Jul 1984; National Ice Cream Day—Jul 15, 1984. (Jul 9, 1984).
5220 Food for Peace Day: Jul 10, 1984. (Jul 10, 1984).
5221 Year of the St. Lawrence Seaway and St. Lawrence Seaway Day: Year of the St. Lawrence Seaway—1984; St. Lawrence Seaway Day—Jun 27, 1984. (Jul 11, 1984).
5222 Year of the Ocean: Jul 1, 1984 to Jul 1, 1985. (Jul 13, 1984).
5223 Captive Nations Week: Week beginning July 15, 1984. (Jul 16, 1984).
5224 Space Exploration Day: Jul 20, 1984. (Jul 20, 1984).
5225 Coast Guard Day: Aug 4, 1984. (Jul 27, 1984).
5226 National Volunteer Firefighters Recognition Day: Aug 18, 1984. (Jul 27, 1984).
5227 Women's Equality Day: Aug 26, 1984. (Aug 16, 1984).
5228 Fortieth Anniversary of the Warsaw Uprising: Aug 1, 1984. (Aug 17, 1984).
5229 Polish American Heritage Month: August 1984. (Aug 17, 1984).
5230 Hawaii Statehood Silver Jubilee Day: Aug 21, 1984. (Aug 21, 1984).
5231 Ostomy Awareness Month: August 1984. (Aug 28, 1984).
5232 National Hispanic Heritage Week: Week beginning Sept 10, 1984. (Sept 10, 1984).
5233 National Sewing Month: September 1984. (Sept 21, 1984).
5234 Youth of America Week: Sept 2 through Sept 8, 1984. (Sept 21, 1984).
5235 National School-Age Child Care Awareness Week: Sept 2 through Sept 8, 1984. (Sept 21, 1984).
5236 National Drug Abuse Education and Prevention Week: Week beginning Sept 23, 1984. (Sept 21, 1984).
5237 Columbus Day: Oct 8, 1984. (Sept 21, 1984).
5238 Leif Erikson Day: Oct 9, 1984. (Sept 21, 1984).

COPYRIGHT © 1985 BY WILLIAM D. CHASE and HELEN M. CHASE

PRESIDENTIAL PROCLAMATIONS (con't)
ISSUED, JANUARY 1, 1984 - AUGUST 31, 1985.
(See Index and Chronological Text for Expected 1986 Presidential Proclamations.)

No. Title, Observance Dates, (Date of Signing).

5239 National Historically Black Colleges Week: Week beginning Sept 23, 1984. (Sept 24, 1984).

5240 National Community Leadership Week: Week beginning Sept 9, 1984. (Oct 3, 1984).

5241 Emergency Medicine Week: Sept 16 through Sept 22, 1984. (Oct 3, 1984).

5242 World War I Aces and Aviators Day: Sept 21, 1984. (Oct 3, 1984).

5243 National Adult Day Care Center Week: Week beginning Sept 23, 1984. (Oct 3, 1984).

5244 Child Health Day: Oct 1, 1984. (Oct 3, 1984).

5245 National Birds of Prey Conservation Week: Oct 7 through Oct 13, 1984. (Oct 3, 1984).

5246 National Neighborhood Housing Services Week: Week beginning Oct 7, 1984. (Oct 3, 1984).

5247 National Employ the Handicapped Week: Week beginning Oct 7, 1984. (Oct 4, 1984).

5248 National Children's Week: Oct 7 through Oct 13, 1984. (Oct 4, 1984).

5249 National Quality Month: Month of October 1984. (Oct 4, 1984).

5250 National Hi-Tech Week: Sept 30 through Oct 6, 1984. (Oct 5, 1984).

5251 National Spina Bifida Month: Month of October 1984. (Oct 5, 1984).

5252 National Down's Syndrome Month: Month of October 1984. (Oct 9, 1984).

5253 Fire Prevention Week: Oct 7 through Oct 13, 1984. (Oct 9, 1984).

5254 Mental Illness Awareness Week: Week beginning Oct 7, 1984. (Oct 9, 1984).

5255 Smokey Bear Week: Oct 7 through Oct 13, 1984. (Oct 11, 1984).

5256 General Pulaski Memorial Day: Oct 11, 1984. (Oct 11, 1984).

5257 National School Lunch Week: Week beginning Oct 14, 1984. (Oct 12, 1984).

5258 National Housing Week: Week beginning Oct 14, 1984. (Oct 12, 1984).

5259 White Cane Safety Day: Oct 15, 1984. (Oct 12, 1984).

5260 World Food Day: Oct 16, 1984. (Oct 16, 1984).

5261 Myasthenia Gravis Awareness Week: Week beginning Oct 14, 1984. (Oct 15, 1984).

5262 National Head Injury Awareness Month: Month of October 1984. (Oct 18, 1984).

5263 National Forest Products Week: Week beginning Oct 21, 1984. (Oct 18, 1984).

5264 Lupus Awareness Week: Oct 21 through Oct 27, 1984. (Oct 18, 1984).

5265 National Women Veterans Recognition Week: Week beginning Nov 11, 1984. (Oct 18, 1984).

5266 A Time of Remembrance for All Victims of Terrorism Throughout the World: Oct 23, 1984. (Oct 19, 1984).

5267 United Nations Day: Oct 24, 1984. (Oct 19, 1984).

5268 Veterans Day: Nov 11, 1984. (Oct 19, 1984).

5269 Thanksgiving Day: Nov 22, 1984. (Oct 19, 1984).

5270 National Christmas Seal Month: Month of November 1984. (Oct 30, 1984).

5271 National Diabetes Month: Month of November 1984. (Oct 30, 1984).

5272 National Hospice Month: November 1984. (Oct 30, 1984).

5273 Commemoration of the Great Famine in the Ukraine: Nov 4, 1984. (Oct 30, 1984).

5274 National Drunk and Drugged Driving Awareness Week: Dec 9 through Dec 15, 1984. (Oct 30, 1984).

5275 National Alzheimer's Disease Month: Month of November 1984. (Nov 1, 1984).

5276 National Blood Pressure Awareness Week: Week beginning Nov 11, 1984. (Nov 1, 1984).

5277 National Reye's Syndrome Week: Nov 12 through Nov 18, 1984. (Nov 1, 1984).

5278 Women in Agriculture Week: Nov 11 through Nov 17, 1984. (Nov 13, 1984).

5279 National Farm-City Week: The period Nov 16 through Nov 22, 1984. (Nov 13, 1984).

5280 National Adoption Week: Nov 19 through Nov 25, 1984. (Nov 13, 1984).

5281 National Family Week: Nov 18 through Nov 24, 1984. (Nov 15, 1984).

5282 National Home Care Week: Nov 25 through Dec 1, 1984. (Nov 26, 1984).

5283 National Epidermolysis Bullosa Awareness Week: Nov 25 through Dec 1, 1984. (Nov 26, 1984).

5284 Conferral of Honorary Citizenship of the United States Upon William Penn and Hannah Callowhill Penn. (Nov 28, 1984).

5285 National Care and Share Day: Dec 15, 1984. (Dec 3, 1984).

5286 National Pearl Harbor Remembrance Day: Dec 7, 1984. (Dec 4, 1984).

5287 Bill of Rights Day: Human Rights Day and Week: Bill of Rights Day—Dec 15, 1984; Human Rights Day—Dec 10, 1984; and Human Rights Week—Week beginning Dec 10, 1984. (Dec 10, 1984).

5288 Wright Brothers Day: Dec 17, 1984. (Dec 12, 1984).

5289 National Cerebral Palsy Month: Month of January 1985. (Dec 27, 1984).

5290 National Poison Prevention Week: Week beginning Mar 17, 1985. (Dec 27, 1984).

5291 To Modify Duties on Certain Articles Used in Civil Aircraft and on Globes. (Dec 28, 1984).

1985

5292 National Sanctity of Human Life Day: Jan 20, 1985. (Jan 14, 1985).

5293 National Jerome Kern Day: Jan 27, 1985. (Jan 23, 1985).

5294 Import Quotas on Certain Sugar Containing Articles. (Jan 28, 1985).

5295 American Heart Month: Month of February 1985. (Jan 29, 1985).

5296 National Day of Prayer: May 2, 1985. (Jan 29, 1985).

5297 Modification of Tariffs on Certain Sugars, Sirups, and Molasses. (Jan 31, 1985).

5298 Red Cross Month: Mar 1985. (Feb 2, 1985).

5299 International Youth Year: 1985. (Feb 6, 1985).

5300 National Big Brothers and Big Sisters Week: The period from Feb 17 through Feb 23, 1985. (Feb 11, 1985).

5301 National DECA Week: Week beginning Feb 10 through Feb 16, 1985. (Feb 12, 1985).

5302 Lithuanian Independence Day: Feb 16, 1985. (Feb 16, 1985).

5303 National Safe Boating Week: Week beginning June 2, 1985. (Feb 20, 1985).

5304 Save Your Vision Week: Week beginning Mar 3, 1985. (Feb 21, 1985).

5305 Duty Reductions on High Technology Products: (Feb 21, 1985).

5306 National Consumers Week: Week beginning Apr 21, 1985. (Mar 4, 1985).

5307 Women's History Week: Week beginning Mar 3, 1985. (Mar 9, 1985).

5308 To Amend Proclamation 5133 Implementing the Caribbean Basin Economic Recovery Act: (Mar 14, 1985).

5309 Afghanistan Day: Mar 21, 1985. (Mar 21, 1985).

5310 National Skin Cancer Prevention and Detection Week: Mar 24 through Mar 30, 1985. (Mar 22, 1985).

5311 Cancer Control Month: Month of April 1985. (Mar 22, 1985).

5312 Small Business Week: May 5 through May 11, 1985. (Mar 27, 1985).

5313 Suspension and Modification of Import Fees on Certain Sugars, Sirups and Molasses: (Mar 29, 1985).

5314 National Weather Satellite Week: Week beginning Mar 31 through Apr 6, 1985. (Apr 4, 1985).

5315 National Child Abuse Prevention Month: Month of April 1985. (Apr 4, 1985).

5316 World Health Week and World Health Day: World Health Week—Week beginning Apr 1 through Apr 7, 1985; and World Health Day—Apr 7, 1985. (Apr 4, 1985).

5317 Education Day, U.S.A.: Apr 2, 1985. (Apr 4, 1985).

5318 Pan American Day and Pan American Week: Pan American Day—Apr 14, 1985; and Pan American Week—Week beginning Apr 14 through Apr 20, 1985. (Apr 15, 1985).

5319 Loyalty Day: May 1, 1985 (Apr 15, 1985).

5320 Law Day, U.S.A.: May 1, 1985. (Apr 15, 1985).

5321 Jewish Heritage Week: Apr 21 through Apr 28, 1985. (Apr 19, 1985).

5322 Victims of Crime Week: Week beginning Apr 14, 1985. (Apr 19, 1985).

5323 World Trade Week: Week beginning May 19, 1985. (Apr 22, 1985).

5324 National Organ Donation Awareness Week: Apr 21 through Apr 27, 1985. (Apr 22, 1985).

5325 Asian/Pacific American Heritage Week: Week beginning May 5, 1985. (Apr 22, 1985).

5326 National Defense Transportation Day and National Transportation Week: National Defense Transportation Day—May 17, 1985; and National Transportation Week—Week beginning May 12 through May 18, 1985. (Apr 23, 1985).

5327 National DES Awareness Week: Apr 21 through Apr 27, 1985. (Apr 25, 1985).

5328 Older Americans Month: Month of May 1985. (Apr 25, 1985).

5329 Fair Housing Month: Month of April 1985. (Apr 25, 1985).

5330 Prayer for Peace Memorial Day: May 27, 1985. (Apr 26, 1985).

COPYRIGHT © 1985 BY WILLIAM D. CHASE and HELEN M. CHASE

PRESIDENTIAL PROCLAMATIONS (con't)
ISSUED, JANUARY 1, 1984 - AUGUST 31, 1985.

(See Index and Chronological Text for Expected 1986 Presidential Proclamations.)

No.   Title, Observance Dates, (Date of Signing).

5331 National Child Safety Awareness Month: May 1985. (Apr 29, 1985).

5332 Mother's Day: May 12, 1985. (Apr 29, 1985).

5333 National Tourism Week: Week beginning May 19, 1985. (Apr 29, 1985).

5334 Helsinki Human Rights Day: May 7, 1985. (Apr 30, 1985).

5335 Dr. Jonas E. Salk Day: May 6, 1985. (May 6, 1985).

5336 Vietnam Veterans Recognition Day: May 7, 1985. (May 7, 1985).

5337 National Correctional Officers Week: Week beginning May 5, 1985. (May 10, 1985).

5338 National Asthma and Allergy Awareness Week: Week beginning May 5 through May 11, 1985. (May 10, 1985).

5339 National Science Week: May 12 through May 18, 1985. (May 14, 1985).

5340 Modification of Import Quotas on Certain Sugar Containing Articles. (May 17, 1985).

5341 Senior Center Week: Week of May 12, 1985. (May 17, 1985).

5342 National Digestive Diseases Awareness Week: Week of May 12, 1985. (May 17, 1985).

5343 National Maritime Day: May 22, 1985. (May 21, 1985).

5344 National Osteoporosis Awareness Week: May 20 through May 26, 1985. (May 21, 1985).

5345 National Medical Transcriptionist Week: May 20 through May 26, 1985. (May 21, 1985).

5346 National Farm Safety Week: Week of Sept 15 through Sept 21, 1985. (May 23, 1985).

5347 Minority Enterprise Development Week: Week of Oct 6 through Oct 12, 1985. (May 28, 1985).

5348 Very Special Arts U.S.A. Month: Month of May 1985. (May 29, 1985).

5349 Youth Suicide Prevention Month: Month of June 1985. (June 4, 1985).

No.   Title, Observance Dates, (Date of Signing).

5350 Father's Day: June 16, 1985. (June 13, 1985).

5351 Family Reunion Month: The period between May 12 and June 16, 1985. (June 14, 1985).

5352 Baltic Freedom Day: June 14, 1985. (June 14, 1985).

5353 Flag Day and National Flag Week: Flag Day—June 14, 1985; and National Flag Week—Week beginning June 9, 1985. (June 14, 1985).

5354 Increase in the Rates of Duty for Certain Pasta Articles From the European Economic Community. (June 21, 1985).

5355 Helen Keller Deaf-Blind Awareness Week: Week of June 23 through June 29, 1985. (June 26, 1985).

5356 National P.O.W./M.I.A. Recognition Day: July 19, 1985. (June 27, 1985).

5357 Captive Nations Week: Week beginning July 21, 1985. (July 19, 1985).

5358 Space Exploration Day: July 20, 1985. (July 20, 1985).

5359 National Disability in Entertainment Week: July 25-31, 1985. (July 30, 1985).

5360 Freedom of the Press Day: Aug 4, 1985. (Aug 2, 1985).

5361 Polish American Heritage Month: August 1985. (Aug 13, 1985).

5362 National Neighborhood Crime Watch Day: Aug 13, 1985. (Aug 13, 1985).

5363 Modification of the Effective Date for Increased Rates of Duty for Certain Pasta Articles From the European Economic Community. (Aug 15, 1985).

5364 Women's Equality Day: Aug 26, 1985. (Aug 23, 1985).

5365 To Implement Reductions in U.S. Rates of Duty Pursuant to the United States-Israel Free Trade Area Agreement, and for Other Purposes. (Aug 30, 1985).

THE CONGRESSIONAL PROCESS
FOR DECLARING SPECIAL OBSERVANCES
By The Hon. Dale E. Kildee, Member of Congress, 7th District, Michigan

From the first proclamation of a public holiday (George Washington's proclamation of Nov. 26, 1789, as Thanksgiving Day) to the present, the federal government has been active in seeing that special observances be set aside to commemorate people, events, ideas and activities worthy of national recognition. These have ranged from the proclamation of official holidays to the recognition or commemoration of subjects through special days, weeks, months or years.

The first usual step in having something so commemorated is the introduction of a bill in the House of Representatives or in the Senate calling for a day, week, month or year to be set aside for special recognition.

Because of the large number of such resolutions introduced, there are much more restrictive rules applied to these resolutions than are applied to other legislative measures. In the House, such a resolution needs at least 218 co-sponsors (a majority of the members) before it will be considered by the Post Office and Civil Service Committee. Once the resolution has its 218 co-sponsors, it is taken up by the Subcommittee on Census and Population, and usually routinely referred to the whole Committee, which then reports the resolution to the floor of the full House. It is voted upon at that point, but from the time the resolution has its 218 co-sponsors there is little question about its eventual success. After House passage, the resolution also must be voted upon by the Senate. If it passes there, it goes to the President for signing.

On the Senate side, commemorative legislation goes directly to the Senate Judiciary Committee. It will not be considered by the Committee, however, unless it has at least 25 co-sponsors with at least 10 of them being from each party. After being passed by the full Committee, the process then is the same as for House resolutions, with passage required by the House and signing by the President.

Under unusual circumstances, this process can be circumvented by the chairpersons of the House and Senate committees. However, in nearly every case, this procedure is followed.

Both committees also have policies on what types of commemorative legislation they will consider. Neither committee, for example, will report for floor consideration commemorative legislation concerning a commercial enterprise, specific product or political organization. Neither committee also will report any proposal, other than official holidays, to be a recurring annual commemoration, which explains why the same commemorative day or week may fall on different dates in different years, as each year they must be re-introduced. In addition, the House specifically will not consider commemorative legislation regarding living persons or governmental units.

The President also has the authority to declare by presidential proclamation any commemorative event, but as a matter of fact this is rarely done and virtually all commemorative celebrations come about by going through the congressional legislative process, after which they are issued as presidential proclamations.

COPYRIGHT © 1985 BY WILLIAM D. CHASE and HELEN M. CHASE

PRESIDENTIAL PROCLAMATION 5351

Facsimile of Presidential Proclamation 5351 as reproduced from *Federal Register*, Vol. 50, No. 117, Tuesday, June 18, 1985.

Proclamation 5351 of June 14, 1985

Family Reunion Month, 1985

By the President of the United States of America

A Proclamation

Family reunions are occasions that renew the feelings of love, pride, and support that nurture our lives. There is no more joyous and poignant family reunion than the return to the family of a child who has run away from home.

The number of young people between the ages of 10 and 17 who ran away from home last year is estimated at more than one million. The heartache of such a breakdown in family relationships is incalculable. But for many thousands of families, the joy of reunion was realized with the return of a son or daughter and a resolution of the conditions that precipitated the flight of the child.

In all likelihood, the return was aided by one of the professionals and volunteers who staff runaway shelters throughout the country. Last year alone, some 200,000 young Americans and their families received counseling aimed at resolving family conflicts and pressures. Almost half the young people who sought help were returned safely to their homes.

Much remains to be done, and all of us can play a role. Volunteers are needed to help staff crisis intervention programs. Parents themselves must recognize the importance of keeping open lines of communications with their children and strive to strengthen family relationships.

Families are the cornerstone of America. All of America's families should be encouraged to continue strengthening their ties through gatherings and activities such as family reunions that involve as many members as possible.

The Congress, by House Joint Resolution 64, has designated the period between Mother's Day, May 12, and Father's Day, June 16, 1985, as "Family Reunion Month" and authorized and requested the President to issue a proclamation in observance of this period.

NOW, THEREFORE, I, RONALD REAGAN, President of the United States of America, do hereby proclaim the period between May 12 and June 16, 1985, as Family Reunion Month. I call upon all Americans to celebrate this period with appropriate ceremonies and activities and recognition of the resources available to help strengthen families.

IN WITNESS WHEREOF, I have hereunto set my hand this fourteenth day of June, in the year of our Lord nineteen hundred and eighty-five, and of the Independence of the United States of America the two hundred and ninth.

Ronald Reagan

Presidential Proclamation 5351 of June 18, 1985, designating the period between Mother's Day and Father's Day as Family Reunion Month and encouraging activities to emphasize the importance of the family and to recognize the resources available to help strengthen families.

COPYRIGHT © 1985 BY WILLIAM D. CHASE and HELEN M. CHASE

CALENDAR INFORMATION FOR THE YEAR 1986

Time shown is Eastern Standard Time. All dates are given in terms of the Gregorian calendar.

(Based in part on information prepared by The Nautical Almanac Office, United States Naval Observatory.)

ERA	YEAR	BEGINS
Byzantine	7495	Sept 14
Jewish (A.M.)*	5747	Oct 3
Chinese	4623	Feb 9
Roman (A.U.G.)	2739	Jan 14
Nabonassar	2735	Apr 27
Japanese	2646	Jan 1
Grecian	2298	Sept 14 (or Oct 14)
Indian (Saka)	1908	Mar 22
Diocletian	1703	Sept 11
Islamic (Hegira)*	1407	Sept 5

*Year begins at sunset

RELIGIOUS CALENDARS

Epiphany	Jan 6
Ash Wednesday	Feb 12
Palm Sunday	Mar 23
Good Friday	Mar 28
Easter Day	Mar 30
Ascension Day	May 8
Whit Sunday—Pentecost	May 18
Trinity Sunday	May 25
First Sunday in Advent	Nov 30
Christmas Day	Dec 25

First Day of Passover (Pesach)	Apr 24
Feast of Weeks (Shebuoth)	June 13
Jewish New Year (tabular) (Rosh Hashanah)	Oct 4
Day of Atonement (Yom Kippur)	Oct 13
First Day of Tabernacles (Succoth)	Oct 18

Islamic New Year (tabular)	Sept 6
First Day of Ramadan (tabular)	May 10

(Jewish and Islamic holidays begin at sunset on the day before the dates given above.)

CIVIL CALENDAR—USA—1986

New Year's Day	Jan 1
Martin Luther King's Birthday	Jan 20
Lincoln's Birthday	Feb 12
Washington's Birthday	Feb 17
Memorial Day	May 26
Independence Day	July 4
Labor Day	Sept 1
Columbus Day	Oct 13
Election Day	Nov 4
Veterans Day	Nov 11
Thanksgiving Day	Nov 27

CIVIL CALENDAR—CANADA—1986

New Year's Day	Jan 1
Commonwealth Day	Mar 10
Victoria Day	May 19
Canada Day	July 1
Labor Day	Sept 1
Thanksgiving	Oct 13
Remembrance Day	Nov 11
Boxing Day	Dec 26

CIVIL CALENDAR—MEXICO—1986

New Year's Day	Jan 1
Constitution Day	Feb 5
Benito Juarez Birthday	Mar 21
Labor Day	May 1
Battle of Puebla Day	May 5
Independence Day	Sept 16
Dia de La Raza	Oct 12
Mexican Revolution Day	Nov 20
Guadalupe Day	Dec 12

CIVIL CALENDAR—UNITED KINGDOM—1986

Accession of Queen Elizabeth II	Feb 6
St. David (Wales)	Mar 1
Commonwealth Day	Mar 10
St. Patrick (Ireland)	Mar 17
Birthday of Queen Elizabeth II	Apr 21
St. George (England)	Apr 23
Coronation Day	June 2
Birthday of Prince Philip, Duke of Edinburgh	June 10
The Queen's Official Birthday	June 14
Remembrance Sunday	Nov 9
Birthday of the Prince of Wales	Nov 14
St. Andrew (Scotland)	Nov 30

BANK AND PUBLIC HOLIDAYS—UNITED KINGDOM

Observed during 1986 in England and Wales, Scotland and Northern Ireland unless otherwise indicated.

New Year	Jan 1
Bank Holiday (Scotland)	Jan 2
St. Patrick's Day (Northern Ireland)	Mar 17
Good Friday	Mar 28
Easter Monday (England & Wales, Northern Ireland)	Mar 31
May Day and Bank Holiday	May 5
Spring Bank Holiday	May 26
Battle of the Boyne Holiday (Northern Ireland)	July 14
Bank Holiday (Scotland)	Aug 4
Summer Bank Holiday (England & Wales, Northern Ireland)	Aug 25
Christmas Day	Dec 25
Boxing Day	Dec 26

COPYRIGHT © 1985 BY WILLIAM D. CHASE and HELEN M. CHASE

ASTRONOMICAL PHENOMENA FOR THE YEAR 1986

Time shown is Eastern Standard Time. All dates are given in terms of the Gregorian calendar.

(Based in part on information prepared by The Nautical Almanac Office, United States Naval Observatory.)

PRINCIPAL PHENOMENA, 1986
EARTH

Perihelion .... Jan 2
Aphelion.. July 5
Equinoxes............................... Mar 20, Sept 23
Solstices .... June 21, Dec 21

ECLIPSES and TRANSIT OF MERCURY

Partial eclipse of the Sun .... Apr 8-9
Total eclipse of the Moon .... Apr 24
Annular-total eclipse of the Sun .... Oct 3
Total eclipse of the Moon .... Oct 17
Transit of Mercury .... Nov 12-13

For further details of eclipses see chronological section under dates shown above.

PHASES OF THE MOON

New Moon	First Quarter	Full Moon	Last Quarter
			Jan 3
Jan 10	Jan 17	Jan 25	Feb 1
Feb 8	Feb 16	Feb 24	Mar 3
Mar 10	Mar 18	Mar 25	Apr 1
Apr 9	Apr 17	Apr 24	Apr 30
May 8	May 16	May 23	May 30
June 7	June 15	June 21	June 28
July 6	July 14	July 21	July 28
Aug 5	Aug 12	Aug 19	Aug 27
Sept 4	Sept 11	Sept 18	Sept 25
Oct 3	Oct 10	Oct 17	Oct 25
Nov 2	Nov 8	Nov 16	Nov 24
Dec 1	Dec 8	Dec 16	Dec 24
Dec 30			

VISIBILITY OF PLANETS
IN MORNING AND EVENING TWILIGHT

	Morning	Evening
VENUS	Nov 12-Dec 31	Mar 2-Oct 31
MARS	Jan 1-July 10	July 10-Dec 31
JUPITER	Mar 4-Sept 10	Jan 1-Feb 5
		Sept 10-Dec 31
SATURN	Jan 1-May 28	May 28-Nov 17
	Dec 22-Dec 31	

CHRONOLOGICAL CYCLES

Dominical Letter .... E
Epact 19
Golden Number (Lunar Cycle) XI
Julian Period (year of)............................. 6699
Roman Indiction...................................... 9
Solar Cycle 7

THE NAMING OF HURRICANES

(Compiled from information issued by the U.S. Department of Commerce, National Oceanic and Atmospheric Administration.)

ATLANTIC HURRICANE NAMES

1986	1987	1988	1989	1990	1991
ALLEN	ARLENE	ALBERTO	ALLISON	ARTHUR	ANA
BONNIE	BRET	BERYL	BARRY	BERTHA	BOB
CHARLEY	CINDY	CHRIS	CHANTAL	CESAR	CLAUDETTE
DANIELLE	DENNIS	DEBBY	DEAN	DIANA	DANNY
EARL	EMILY	ERNESTO	ERIN	EDOUARD	ELENA
FRANCES	FLOYD	FLORENCE	FELIX	FRAN	FABIAN
GEORGES	GERT	GILBERT	GABRIELLE	GUSTAV	GLORIA
HERMINE	HARVEY	HELENE	HUGO	HORTENSE	HENRI
IVAN	IRENE	ISAAC	IRIS	ISIDORE	ISABEL
JEANNE	JOSE	JOAN	JERRY	JOSEPHINE	JUAN
KARL	KATRINA	KEITH	KAREN	KLAUS	KATE
LISA	LENNY	LESLIE	LUIS	LILI	LARRY
MITCH	MARIA	MICHAEL	MARILYN	MARCO	MINDY
NICOLE	NATE	NADINE	NOEL	NANA	NICHOLAS
OTTO	OPHELIA	OSCAR	OPAL	OMAR	ODETTE
PAULA	PHILIPPE	PATTY	PABLO	PALOMA	PETER
RICHARD	RITA	RAFAEL	ROXANNE	RENE	ROSE
SHARY	STAN	SANDY	SEBASTIEN	SALLY	SAM
TOMAS	TAMMY	TONY	TANYA	TEDDY	TERESA
VIRGINIE	VINCE	VALERIE	VAN	VICKY	VICTOR
WALTER	WILMA	WILLIAM	WENDY	WILFRED	WANDA

EASTERN PACIFIC HURRICANE NAMES

1986	1987	1988	1989	1990	1991
AGATHA	ADRIAN	ALETTA	ADOLPH	ALMA	ANDRES
BLAS	BEATRIZ	BUD	BARBARA	BORIS	BLANCA
CELIA	CALVIN	CARLOTTA	COSME	CRISTINA	CARLOS
DARBY	DORA	DANIEL	DALILIA	DOUGLAS	DOLORES
ESTELLE	EUGENE	EMILIA	ERICK	ELIDA	ENRIQUE
FRANK	FERNANDA	FABIO	FLOSSIE	FAUSTO	FEFA
GEORGETTE	GREG	GILMA	GIL	GENEVIEVE	GUILLERMO
HOWARD	HILARY	HECTOR	HENRIETTE	HERNAN	HILDA
ISIS	IRWIN	IVA	ISMAEL	ISELLE	IGNACIO
JAVIER	JOVA	JOHN	JULIETTE	JULIO	JIMENA
KAY	KNUT	KRISTY	KIKO	KENNA	KEVIN
LESTER	LIDIA	LANE	LORENA	LOWELL	LINDA
MADELINE	MAX	MIRIAM	MANUEL	MARIE	MARTY
NEWTON	NORMA	NORMAN	NARDA	NORBERT	NORA
ORLENE	OTIS	OLIVIA	OCTAVE	ODILE	OLAF
PAINE	PILAR	PAUL	PRISCILLA	POLO	PAULINE
ROSLYN	RAMON	ROSA	RAYMOND	RACHEL	RICK
SEYMOUR	SELMA	SERGIO	SONIA	SIMON	SANDRA
TINA	TODD	TARA	TICO	TRUDY	TERRY
VIRGIL	VERONICA	VICENTE	VELMA	VANCE	VIVIAN
WINIFRED	WILEY	WILLA	WINNIE	WALLIS	WALDO

COPYRIGHT © 1985 BY WILLIAM D. CHASE and HELEN M. CHASE

WORLD'S FAIRS AND INTERNATIONAL EXHIBITIONS

(The following is selected and quoted, with kind permission of the Secretary General of the Bureau International Des Expositions, Paris, from the publication "The International Bureau of Exhibitions and Regulations Respecting International Exhibitions," and from the list of Expositions registered with the Bureau since its creation. Readers seeking detailed information should, of course, consult the original document, as well as the "Protocol signed at Paris on 30 November 1972." For U.S. participation in international exhibitions see Public Law 91-269 of May 27, 1970: "An Act To provide for Federal Government recognition of and participation in international expositions proposed to be held in the United States . . ." and Title 15—Commerce and Foreign Trade, Chapter XII—United States Travel Service, Department of Commerce, Part 1202—Official U.S. Government Recognition of and Participation in International Expositions held in the United States. Dated: July 20, 1975.)

HISTORICAL BACKGROUND

Exhibitions are not a recent invention. They date back to the times when large-scale markets were regularly held in cities which, because they were located at major route intersections, attracted visitors and brought prosperity. Crowds of people, some of whom had travelled great distances, would visit these markets, stay at the site, and exchange a wide variety of articles. These events thus provided a forum for expressing and evaluating ideas and for demonstrating and comparing skills.

Through these gatherings a highly beneficial atmosphere of mutual understanding and fellowship developed between people of different nations and often conflicting cultures. Buyers and sellers would flock to the cities of Lyons, Frankfurt and Leipzig in particular from all over medieval Europe.

The commercial transactions of long ago thus paved the way for the international exhibitions of today, which play an educational role and are instrumental in promoting understanding in the world.

The first "universal and international" exhibition in the modern sense of the term took place in 1851 in London, capital of England, the world's leading industrial power, which with its vast empire had profited handsomely from free trade and the prosperity of the Victorian era. The exhibition was an overwhelming success.

Every nation was invited to contribute to the exhibition, which constituted an inventory of all branches of human endeavour. Paris took over and organized brilliant exhibitions in 1867, 1878, 1889 and 1900. Soon other large centers were also eager to welcome craftsmen and manufacturers from all over the world, and among the most successful international exhibitions were those held in Vienna, Amsterdam, Brussels, Barcelona, St. Louis, Turin and Philadelphia.

These events inevitably gave rise to numerous conflicts of interest and were often characterized by very poor organization. This state of confusion caused the participating governments serious problems, and, as a result, they felt the need to establish regulations to prevent the proliferation of exhibitions and provide participants with certain guarantees. As interest and experience in exhibitions grew it became apparent that the various parties had to be brought together and their differences aired in an attempt to solve common problems.

An international agreement seemed necessary. Paris had been calling for one since 1907. In 1912 the German government took the initiative and called interested governments together in order to work out the basis for an agreement.

The governments were quick to respond, and they expressed the desire to establish regulations to improve relations between organizers and participants and between inviting governments and official or private exhibitors.

It was the Berlin Diplomatic Conference that established the basis for an international convention governing international exhibitions. However, the diplomatic decision that resulted could not be ratified because of the War of 1914.

The governments took up the matter again in 1920, but it was not until Nov 22, 1928, at another conference in Paris, that delegates of thirty-one countries signed the first convention governing, in a constructive manner, the organization of international exhibitions.

The International Convention of 1928 brought order to the world exhibitions situation by regulating their frequency and outlining the rights and obligations of the exhibitors and organizers. At the same time the International Bureau of Exhibitions was created in order to ensure compliance with the provisions of the Convention.

Subsequently two protocols—one concluded in 1948 and the other in 1966—amended the Convention on the key issue of exhibition frequency.

In view of the precedents that have been set during the International Bureau of Exhibition's fifty years of existence and also in view of new economic data (faster rate of progress, decreased travel time, and the appearance of new countries on the world scene), a thorough revision of the 1928 Convention was necessary.

This revision was undertaken in 1965 and resulted in the signing of the Protocol of November 30, 1972, which has since governed the organization of international exhibitions.

DEFINITION

Article 1 of the Convention defines these exhibitions (those governed by the 1928 Convention amended by the Protocol of November 30, 1972) as follows:

> An exhibition is a display which, whatever its title, has as its principal purpose the education of the public; it may exhibit the means at man's disposal for meeting the needs of civilization, or demonstrate the progress achieved in one or more branches of human endeavour, or show prospects for the future. An exhibition is international when more than one State is invited to take part in it.

The definition indicates that an exhibition is above all a vehicle for informing and educating people—a fact which distinguishes it from a (trade) fair, with which it is all too often confused . . .

In limiting its jurisdiction to exhibitions which meet precise criteria, the Convention exempted from its authority certain events of a specific nature such as:

—exhibitions lasting less than three weeks;

—fine arts exhibitions;

—exhibitions of an essentially commercial nature.

CATEGORIES: UNIVERSAL EXHIBITIONS AND SPECIALIZED EXHIBITIONS

Having defined international exhibitions, the Convention distinguishes between two main categories: universal exhibitions and specialized exhibitions.

Universal exhibitions illustrate progress achieved in all branches of human endeavour. They usually have very general, often philosophically inspired themes, as exemplified by the following: "Evaluation of Mankind for a More Human World," Brussels, 1958; "Man and His World," Montreal, 1967; and "Progress and Harmony for Mankind," Osaka, 1970.

The participating governments must construct their pavilions at their own expense and no rent may be charged by the organizer for the sites alloted for these pavilions.

Specialized exhibitions, on the other hand, are devoted to a single branch of human endeavour such as transportation, Munich, 1965; hunting, Budapest, 1971; the environment, Spokane, 1974; and the sea, Okinawa, 1975.

In the case of specialized exhibitions the cost of constructing pavilions and display booths is borne by the organizer, who is thus justified in charging rent. . . .

OFFICIAL EXHIBITIONS AND OFFICIALLY RECOGNIZED EXHIBITIONS

Whether universal or specialized, exhibitions may, according to the Convention, be official or officially recognized.

An official exhibition is an exhibition organized by the government itself.

An officially recognized exhibition is an exhibition organized by a legal entity that has been officially recognized by the government, which guarantees the fulfillment of that legal entity's obligations.

In both cases the government of the state on whose territory the exhibition is held appoints a commissioner general, who is responsible for representing the state and guaranteeing the fulfillment of commitments made with respect to the International Bureau of Exhibitions and the other countries.

WORLD'S FAIRS AND INTERNATIONAL EXHIBITIONS (con't)

DURATION OF EXHIBITIONS

In order that the effort required of the exhibitors not be unduly prolonged, the Convention decided to limit the duration of international exhibitions to a maximum of six months . . .

FREQUENCY OF EXHIBITIONS

Of all the regulations laid down by the Convention the one concerning the frequency of exhibitions is undoubtedly the most important; the need to solve the problem of frequency was, in fact, one of the main reasons for the international agreement.

The frequency of exhibitions is determined according to the scope that the organizers wish to give them. It is logical that an exhibition presenting the full range of production techniques should be held less often than a display that involves a limited category of exhibitors.

It is also important to realize that the success of an exhibition would be compromised if displays of the same nature were held too frequently—a burden that the governments would not be willing to shoulder.

In view of these considerations, the Convention set minimum required intervals between exhibitions, as follows:

Type of Exhibition	Interval Which Must Elapse	
	In The Same Country	In Different Countries
Universal exhibitions	20 years	10 years
Specialized exhibitions of the same nature	10 years	5 years
Specialized exhibitions of different nature	5 years	2 years
Universal and specialized exhibitions	5 years	—

The International Bureau of Exhibitions is empowered to shorten the intervals specified above for specialized exhibitions and to shorten to not less than seven years the interval between universal exhibitions organized in different countries.

Historical considerations, the special interest presented by an exhibition of the fact that it is to take place in a part of the world in which no major exhibition has been staged for a long time may be cited as reasons for shortening intervals.

EXPOSITIONS REGISTERED BY THE INTERNATIONAL BUREAU OF EXPOSITIONS SINCE ITS CREATION

Year	Place	Category	Theme or Subject
1933	Milan	3	V Triennale: Decorative Arts, Modern Industry and Architecture
1935	Brussels	1	
1936	Stockholm	3	Aviation
1936	Milan	3	VI Triennale
1937	Paris	2	Art and Technology in Modern Life
1938	Helsinki	3	Aviation
1939	New York	2	The World of Tomorrow
1939	Liege	3	Technology of Water
1940	Bergen	4	Polar Exposition
1940	Cologne	4	Transportation and Communication
1940	Milan	3	VII Triennale
1942	Rome	4	
1947	Milan	3	VIII Triennale
1947	Paris	3	Urban Planning and Housing
1949	Port-au-Prince	2	
1949	Stockholm	3	Sports
1949	Lyon	3	Rural Environment
1951	Milan	3	IX Triennale
1951	Lille	3	Textiles

Year	Place	Category	Theme or Subject
1953	Jerusalem	3	Conquest of the Desert
1953	Rome	3	Agriculture
1954	Naples	3	Navigation
1954	Strasbourg	4	Productivity
1954	Milan	3	X Triennale
1955	Turin	3	Sports
1955	Helsingborg	3	Applied Arts: Modern Man and his Milieu
1956	Beit Dagon	3	Fruit
1957	Milan	3	XI Triennale
1957	Berlin	3	Building
1958	Brussels	1	Global Humanism Evaluation
1960	Milan	3	XII Triennale
1960	Rotterdam	3	Horticulture
1961	Turin	3	Labor
1962	Seattle	2	Century 21
1963	Hamburg	3	Horticulture
1964	Vienna	3	Horticulture
1964	Milan	3	XIII Triennale
1965	Munich	3	Transportation
1967	Moscow	4	
1967	Montreal	1	Man and his World
1968	San Antonio	3	HemisFair
1968	Milan	3	XIV Triennale
1969	Paris	3	Horticulture
1970	Osaka	1	Human Progress toward Harmony
1971	Budapest	3	Hunting
1972	Amsterdam	3	Horticulture
1972	Rio de Janeiro	4	Progress through Knowledge
1973	Hamburg	3	Horticulture
1974	Vienna	3	Horticulture
1974	Spokane	3	Progress without Pollution
1975	Okinawa	3	The Sea
1976	Philadelphia	4	The Promise of People
1976	Quebec	4	Horticulture
1980	Montreal	3	Horticulture
1981	Los Angeles	4	People to People: Routes to Understanding
1981	Plovdiv	3	Hunting
1982	Amsterdam	3	Horticulture
1982	Knoxville	3	Energy
1983	Munich	3	Horticulture
1984	Liverpool	3	Horticulture
1984	New Orleans	3	The World of Rivers
1985	Tsukuba	3	Dwellings and Surroundings
1985	Plovdiv	3	Achievement of the Young Inventors
1986	Vancouver	3	Transportation Expo 86
1988	Brisbane	3	Leisure in the Age of Technology
1989	Paris	4	Paths to Liberty: Project for the Third Millennium.
1992	Chicago/Seville	1	Age of Discovery

Classification of Exhibition Categories:

1. General Expositions of 1st Category

2. General Expositions of 2nd Category

3. Special Expositions

4. Expositions registered with the B.I.E., but not held.

Note: Following the application of the 1972 Protocol, only two types of international exhibitions are recognized:

1. **Universal Exhibitions** replace the General Expositions of the 1st Category.

2. **Special Exhibitions** replace the General Expositions of the 2nd Category and the Special Expositions.

LOOKING FORWARD

1987 - Bicentennial of Constitution of the United States, approved at Philadelphia, Sept 17, 1787.
- International Year of Shelter for the Homeless (United Nations).

1988 - Games of the 24th Olympiad: Summer at Seoul, Korea (Sept 17-Oct 2); Winter at Calgary, Alberta, Canada.
- Special Exposition: "Leisure in the Age of Technology" at Brisbane, Australia.
- United States Presidential Election, Nov 8, 1988.

1989 - Bicentennial of inauguration of George Washington as first President of the United States, Apr 30, 1789, at New York City.
- French Revolution Bicentennial.
- Universal Exposition: "Les Chemins de la Liberté—Projet pour un IIIe Millenaire" at Paris, France.

1990 - The 21st Decennial Census of the United States, as required by the Constitution.

1991 - United States Bill of Rights: Bicentennial of Adoption, Dec 15, 1791.

1992 - Christopher Columbus Quincentennial. Celebrates 500th anniversary of Columbus's discovery of America.
- Universal Exposition commemorating 500 years since Columbus's first visit to North America. Chicago, IL, and Seville, Spain.
- United States Presidential Election, Nov 3, 1992.

1996 - United States Presidential Election, Nov 5, 1996.

1997 - British lease of Hong Kong expires.

1999 - Bicentennial of death of George Washington, at Mount Vernon, VA, Dec 14, 1799.

2000 - United States Presidential Election, Nov 7, 2000.
- Holy Year. Traditionally observed by Roman Catholic Church at 25-year intervals since 1450, in addition to extraordinary Holy Years.

2050 - World population predicted to reach 10 billion, according to 1984 World Bank estimate.

SELECTED SPECIAL YEARS: 1957-1987

Intl. Geophysical Year: July 1, 1957-Dec 31, 1958

World Refugee Year: July 1, 1959-June 30, 1960

Intl. Cooperation Year: 1965

Intl. Book Year: 1972

World Population Year: 1974

Intl. Women's Year: 1975

Intl. Year of the Child: 1979

Intl. Year for Disabled Persons: 1981

World Communications Year: 1983

Intl. Youth Year: 1985

Intl. Year of Peace: 1986

Intl. Year of Shelter for the Homeless: 1987

SATELLITE BOX SCORE
(as of August 28, 1985)

The Satellite Box Score, furnished by the North American Aerospace Defense Command (NORAD), "reflects under current catalog status, the numbers of objects now in space by type—payload or debris—and by owning nation or organization. The debris includes pieces launched into space along with the functioning payloads, as well as fragments produced by in-space breakups. The historical catalog status section shows the numbers that have decayed—that is, that either impacted or that have landed on other planets and the moon."

The nerve center of NORAD's Spacetrack mission is the Space Defense Operations Center (SPADOC), located deep inside Cheyenne Mountain in the Colorado Rockies. There, computers keep a constant record of the movements of thousands of man-made space objects circling the earth. These computers receive a steady flow of data from a network of radars and other satellite-watching devices located around the world. The Satellite Box Score is one of the unclassified statistical products of this mission.

CURRENT CATALOG STATUS

COUNTRY	ESV P/L	SP P/L	ESV DEB	SP DEB	TOTAL
USA	475	30	2291	44	2840
USSR	847	33	1675	9	2564
UK	9	0	1	0	10
ITALY	1	0	0	0	1
CANADA	14	0	0	0	14
ESRO/ESA	0	0	0	0	0
FRANCE	13	0	21	0	34
AUSTRALIA	1	0	0	0	1
JAPAN	25	2	35	2	64
FRG	3	2	0	1	6
NATO	6	0	0	0	6
PRC	3	0	2	0	5
NETHERLANDS	0	0	0	0	0
INDIA	7	0	4	0	11
SPAIN	1	0	0	0	1
ESA	15	1	17	0	33
FRANCE/FRG	2	0	0	0	2
CZECH	0	0	0	0	0
INDONESIA	3	0	0	0	3
ITSO	34	0	0	0	34
BRAZIL	1	0	0	0	1
SAUDI ARABIA	2	0	0	0	2
MEXICO	1	0	0	0	1
TOTAL	1463	68	4046	56	5633

HISTORICAL CATALOG STATUS

COUNTRY	P/L DECAYED	DEBRIS DECAYED	TOTAL
USA	541	1974	2515
USSR	1222	6447	7669
UK	6	4	10
ITALY	4	0	4
CANADA	0	0	0
ESRO	7	3	10
FRANCE	7	49	56
AUSTRALIA	1	0	1
JAPAN	5	23	28
FRG	3	5	8
NATO	0	0	0
PRC	13	33	46
NETHERLANDS	1	3	4
INDIA	2	3	5
SPAIN	0	0	0
ESA	0	1	1
FRANCE/FRG	0	0	0
CZECH	1	0	1
INDONESIA	1	0	1
ITSO	0	0	0
BRAZIL	0	0	0
SAUDI ARABIA	0	0	0
MEXICO	0	0	0
TOTAL	1814	8545	10359

ESV P/L: Earth Satellite Vehicle Payload, which are those in Earth orbit.
SP P/L: Space Probe Payload.
DEB: Debris.
ESRO/ESA: European Space Research Organization/European Space Agency.
FRG: Federal Republic of Germany.
PRC: People's Republic of China.
ITSO: International Telecommunications Satellite Organization.
UK: United Kingdom.

COPYRIGHT © 1985 BY WILLIAM D. CHASE and HELEN M. CHASE

ALPHABETICAL INDEX

Index indicates only initial date for each event.

See chronology for inclusive dates of events lasting more than one day.

COPYRIGHT © 1985 BY WILLIAM D. CHASE and HELEN M. CHASE

COPYRIGHT © 1985 BY WILLIAM D. CHASE and HELEN M. CHASE

COPYRIGHT © 1985 BY WILLIAM D. CHASE and HELEN M. CHASE

ORDER FORM

To order additional copies of CHASE'S ANNUAL EVENTS, 1986, use this form and mail to:

Best Publications, Dept. C
180 N. Michigan
Chicago, IL   60601

Ship to:_____

Address_____

_____

City_____ State_____ Zip_____

Please send me _____ copies of the 1986 Edition of
CHASE'S ANNUAL EVENTS at $14.95 each $_____
Illinois residents add 7% sales tax.
California residents add 6% sales tax. $_____
Plus $2.50 for shipping/handling for first book
Plus $.75 for shipping/handling for each additional book $_____

Total $_____

☐ Check enclosed $_____

   Payable to: Best Publications

Charge my   ☐ VISA   ☐ MasterCard

Acct #_____ Exp. Date_____ / _____

X_____
Signature (required only if charging to bankcard)

GUARANTEE: Any book you order is unconditionally guaranteed and may be returned within 10 days of receipt for full cash refund.   BB86

CHASE'S ANNUAL EVENTS, 1986 is available at quantity discounts when used to promote products or services. For information please write to Premium Marketing Director, Contemporary Books, 180 N. Michigan, Chicago, IL   60601.

COPYRIGHT © 1985 BY WILLIAM D. CHASE and HELEN M. CHASE

HOW TO SUBMIT INFORMATION TO *CHASE'S ANNUAL EVENTS*

It's easy to submit your own suggestions for new entries for forthcoming editions of *Chase's Annual Events*. New events and additional information about established events are welcome.

For 29 years the editors of '*Chase's*' have maintained an International Clearing House File of forthcoming events. Each year hundreds of new entries are accepted for inclusion in the new edition of *Chase's Annual Events*. Readers are encouraged to send their nominations of events or other information to the editors. The address and full instructions for submitting information are provided below.

1. Fill in the Questionnaire form below or furnish on a separate sheet the information requested, by June 1, 1986.

2. Confirm and circle the exact inclusive dates for your event on the 1987 calendar below. Please be sure that your dates are correct for 1987!

3. If the date(s) of the event are set by formula (for example: always the first Monday in June) or if dates of observance for future years are known, please supply that information.

4. Additional background information about the history and observance of each event will be appreciated for our reference files.

5. Please use a separate sheet for each event submitted.

6. Information selected by the editors may be used and publicized through their books, syndicated services and/or other related products and services. The editors reserve the right to select and edit information received.

7. If acknowledgement is requested please enclose a self-addressed, stamped envelope.

Please mail all information to: Chase's Calendar Editor
Box 7335—Liberty Station
Ann Arbor, MI 48107

---

1. Exact name of event:

2. Place of observance (if local or regional):

3. Exact INCLUSIVE DATES: for 1987:

4. Purpose of event (25 words or less):

5. Sponsor, with name & address of person or agency
   from whom further information may be obtained:

6. Signature & title of person furnishing above information: (no information accepted unless this form is signed):

Name, title, and phone no.

1987

	S	M	T	W	T	F	S
JAN.					1	2	3
	4	5	6	7	8	9	10
	11	12	13	14	15	16	17
	18	19	20	21	22	23	24
	25	26	27	28	29	30	31
FEB.	1	2	3	4	5	6	7
	8	9	10	11	12	13	14
	15	16	17	18	19	20	21
	22	23	24	25	26	27	28
MAR.	1	2	3	4	5	6	7
	8	9	10	11	12	13	14
	15	16	17	18	19	20	21
	22	23	24	25	26	27	28
	29	30	31				

	S	M	T	W	T	F	S
APR.				1	2	3	4
	5	6	7	8	9	10	11
	12	13	14	15	16	17	18
	19	20	21	22	23	24	25
	26	27	28	29	30		
MAY						1	2
	3	4	5	6	7	8	9
	10	11	12	13	14	15	16
	17	18	19	20	21	22	23
	24	25	26	27	28	29	30
	31						
JUNE		1	2	3	4	5	6
	7	8	9	10	11	12	13
	14	15	16	17	18	19	20
	21	22	23	24	25	26	27
	28	29	30				

	S	M	T	W	T	F	S
JULY				1	2	3	4
	5	6	7	8	9	10	11
	12	13	14	15	16	17	18
	19	20	21	22	23	24	25
	26	27	28	29	30	31	
AUG.							1
	2	3	4	5	6	7	8
	9	10	11	12	13	14	15
	16	17	18	19	20	21	22
	23	24	25	26	27	28	29
	30	31					
SEPT.			1	2	3	4	5
	6	7	8	9	10	11	12
	13	14	15	16	17	18	19
	20	21	22	23	24	25	26
	27	28	29	30			

	S	M	T	W	T	F	S
OCT.					1	2	3
	4	5	6	7	8	9	10
	11	12	13	14	15	16	17
	18	19	20	21	22	23	24
	25	26	27	28	29	30	31
NOV.	1	2	3	4	5	6	7
	8	9	10	11	12	13	14
	15	16	17	18	19	20	21
	22	23	24	25	26	27	28
	29	30					
DEC.			1	2	3	4	5
	6	7	8	9	10	11	12
	13	14	15	16	17	18	19
	20	21	22	23	24	25	26
	27	28	29	30	31		

Note: This page may be photo-copied in order to submit additional event entries to *Chase's Annual Events*.